AMERICAN DECADES
PRIMARY SOURCES

1930–1939

AMERICAN DECADES
PRIMARY SOURCES

1930–1939

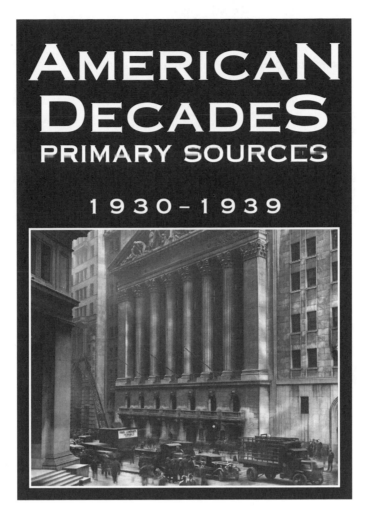

CYNTHIA ROSE, PROJECT EDITOR

GALE
CENGAGE Learning

Detroit • New York • San Francisco • New Haven, Conn • Waterville, Maine • London

GALE
CENGAGE Learning

American Decades Primary Sources, 1930–1939

Project Editor
Cynthia Rose

Editorial
Jason M. Everett, Rachel J. Kain, Pamela A. Dear, Andrew C. Claps, Thomas Carson, Kathleen Droste, Christy Justice, Lynn U. Koch, Michael D. Lesniak, Nancy Matuszak, John F. McCoy, Michael Reade, Rebecca Parks, Mark Mikula, Polly A. Rapp, Mark Springer

Data Capture
Civie A. Green, Beverly Jendrowski, Gwendolyn S. Tucker

Permissions
Margaret Abendroth, Margaret A. Chamberlain, Lori Hines, Jacqueline Key, Mari Masalin-Cooper, William Sampson, Shalice Shah-Caldwell, Kim Smilay, Sheila Spencer, Ann Taylor

Indexing Services
Lynne Maday

Imaging and Multimedia
Dean Dauphinais, Leitha Etheridge-Sims, Mary K. Grimes, Lezlie Light, Daniel W. Newell, David G. Oblender, Christine O'Bryan, Kelly A. Quin, Luke A. Rademacher, Denay Wilding, Robyn V. Young

Product Design
Michelle DiMercurio

Composition and Electronic Prepress
Evi Seoud

Manufacturing
Rita Wimberley

For more information, contact
Gale
27500 Drake Rd.
Farmington Hills, MI 48331-3535
Or you can visit our Internet site at
gale.cengage.com

Cover photographs reproduced by permission of AP/Wide World Photos (Franklin D. Roosevelt, spine; Igor Sikorsky, center), Bettmann/Corbis (Angelo Herndon, left), Hulton-Deutsch Collection/Corbis (New York Stock Exchange building, background), and The Library of Congress (Eleanor Roosevelt, right).

LIBRARY OF CONGRESS CATALOGING-IN-PUBLICATION DATA

American decades primary sources / edited by Cynthia Rose.
v. cm.
Includes bibliographical references and index.
Contents: [1] 1900-1909 — [2] 1910-1919 — [3] 1920-1929 — [4] 1930-1939 — [5] 1940-1949 — [6] 1950-1959 — [7] 1960-1969 — [8] 1970-1979 — [9] 1980-1989 — [10] 1990-1999.
ISBN 0-7876-6587-8 (set : hardcover : alk. paper) — ISBN 0-7876-6588-6 (v. 1 : hardcover : alk. paper) — ISBN 0-7876-6589-4 (v. 2 : hardcover : alk. paper) — ISBN 0-7876-6590-8 (v. 3 : hardcover : alk. paper) — ISBN 0-7876-6591-6 (v. 4 : hardcover : alk. paper) — ISBN 0-7876-6592-4 (v. 5 : hardcover : alk. paper) — ISBN 0-7876-6593-2 (v. 6 : hardcover : alk. paper) — ISBN 0-7876-6594-0 (v. 7 : hardcover : alk. paper) — ISBN 0-7876-6595-9 (v. 8 : hardcover : alk. paper) — ISBN 0-7876-6596-7 (v. 9 : hardcover : alk. paper) — ISBN 0-7876-6597-5 (v. 10 : hardcover : alk. paper)
1. United States—Civilization—20th century—Sources. I. Rose, Cynthia.
E169.1.A471977 2004
973.91—dc21 2002008155

Printed in the United States of America
4 5 6 7 8 9 14 13 12 11 10 09

CONTENTS

Entries are arranged in chronological order by date of primary source. For entries with one primary source, the entry title is the primary source title. Entries with more than one primary source have an overall entry title, followed by the titles of the primary sources.

Business and the Economy

Education

Fashion and Design

Government and Politics

Law and Justice

Lifestyles and Social Trends

The Media

Medicine and Health

Religion

Science and Technology

Sports

Advisors and Contributors

Advisors

CARL A. ANTONUCCI, JR. has spent the past ten years as a reference librarian at various colleges and universities. Currently director of library services at Capital Community College, he holds two master's degrees and is a doctoral candidate at Providence College. He particularly enjoys researching Rhode Island political history during the 1960s and 1970s.

KATHY ARSENAULT is the dean of library at the University of South Florida, St. Petersburg's Poynter Library. She holds a master's degree in Library Science. She has written numerous book reviews for *Library Journal*, and has published articles in such publications as the *Journal of the Florida Medical Association*, and *Collection Management*.

JAMES RETTIG holds two master's degrees. He has written numerous articles and has edited *Distinguished Classics of Reference Publishing* (1992). University librarian at the University of Richmond, he is the recipient of three American Library Association awards: the Isadore Gibert Mudge Citation (1988), the G.K. Hall Award for Library Literature (1993), and the Louis Shores-Oryx Press Award (1995).

HILDA K. WEISBURG is the head library media specialist at Morristown High School Library and specializes in building school library media programs. She has several publications to her credit, including: *The School Librarians Workshop*, *Puzzles, Patterns, and Problem Solving: Creative Connections to Critical Thinking*, and *Learning, Linking & Critical Thinking: Information Strategies for the K-12 Library Media Curriculum.*

Contributors

GLEN BESSEMER holds a B.A. in Peace and Conflict Studies from Northland College. In addition, he earned his M.A, Ph.D., and A.B.D., all in history, from Wayne State University. Currently employed at the National Lawyers Guild of Michigan, his research interests include urban history, crime in twentieth century America, and Detroit history.

Chapter: Law and Justice.

STEPHEN BRAUER is an assistant professor of English at St. John Fisher College in Rochester, NY. His research focuses on twentieth century American literature and culture, with an emphasis on crime culture and sports culture. He holds a Ph.D. in English and American Literature from New York University. His article, "The Aesthetics of Crime" can be found in the September of 2001 issue of *American Quarterly*.

Chapter: Sports.

PETER J. CAPRIOGLIO is a professor emeritus at Middlesex Community College, where he taught social sciences for thirty years prior to his retirement. He has a master's degree in sociology, and he is currently at work on a book entitled, *The Glory of God's Religions:*

A Beginner's Guide to Exploring the Beauty of the World's Faiths.

Chapter: Religion.

JAMES N. CRAFT has been the president and owner of Southill, LLC in Royal Oak, Michigan, since 1999. He is also a senior consultant for Lee Hecht Harrision. He has previously worked as a history teacher and as a curriculum consultant for the Detroit Historical Museum and the Detroit 300 Committee. His research interests include the nineteenth century (particularly the 1840s), the Progressive Era, and primary source-based curriculum material.

Chapter: The Arts, Business and Economy, Government and Politics, Lifestyles and Social Trends.

PAUL G. CONNORS earned a doctorate in American History from Loyola University in Chicago. He has a strong interest in Great Lakes maritime history, and has contributed the article "Beaver Island Ice Walkers" to *Michigan History*. He has worked for the Michigan Legislative Service Bureau as a research analyst since 1996.

Essay: Using Primary Sources. ***Chronologies:*** Selected Events Outside the United States; Government and Politics, Sports Chapters. ***General Resources:*** General, Government and Politics, Sports.

CHRISTOPHER CUMO is a staff writer for *The Adjunct Advocate Magazine*. Formerly an adjunct professor of history at Walsh University, he has written two books, *A History of the Ohio Agricultural Experiment Station, 1882-1997* and *Seeds of Change*, and has contributed to numerous scholarly journals. He holds a doctorate in history from the University of Akron.

Chapter: Science and Technology. ***Chapter Chronology and General Resources:*** Business and the Economy, Education, Medicine and Health, Science and Technology.

LORI HALL currently serves as human resources consultant for Clark, Schaefer, Hacket & Co. in Columbus, Ohio. She has over ten years experience in human resource management and her writing has been published in the *Career Journal*. Her personal interests include the study of World War II and family history.

Chapter: The Arts.

JENNIFER HELLER holds bachelor's degrees in Religious Studies and English Education, as well as a master's degree in Curriculum and Instruction, all from the University of Kansas. She has been an adjunct associate professor at Johnson County Community College in Kansas since 1998. She is currently at work on a dissertation on contemporary women's religious literature.

Chapter Chronology, General Resources: Religion.

DAVID M. HOLFORD has worked as an adjunct instructor at Ohio University, Park College, and Columbus State Community College; education curator for the Ohio Historical Society; and held editorial positions at Glencoe/McGraw Hill and Holt, Rinehart, and Winston. He also holds a doctorate degree in History from Ohio State University. A freelance writer/editor since 1996, he has published *Herbert Hoover* (1999) and *Abraham Lincoln and the Emancipation Proclamation* (2002).

Chapter Chronology, General Resources: Lifestyles and Social Trends, The Media.

LISA R. LAWSON earned her bachelor's degree in History from Texas A&M University at Commerce. A freelance writer and editor, she lives in Trenton, TX. Her interests include history, philosophy, and politics.

Chapter: Fashion and Design.

NADINE FRANCE MARTINE PINÈDE serves as program coordinator for Grantmakers Without Borders. She holds a doctorate in History, Philosophy, and Policy Studies in Education and an M.A. in Philanthropic Studies from Indiana University, as well as an M.A. in English and Modern Languages from St. John's College and a B.A. in Literature and Social Criticism from Harvard University. She has contributed articles to such publications as *The New York Times* and *Radcliffe Quarterly*.

Chapter: Education.

DAN PROSTERMAN is an adjunct professor of history at St. Francis College, as well as an adjunct lecturer at Pace University. He holds an M.A. in History at New York University and is working on his doctoral dissertation on the subject of anti-Communism in New York City during the Great Depression and World War II.

Chapter: The Media.

LORNA BIDDLE RINEAR is the editor and co-author of *The Complete Idiot's Guide to Women's History*. A Ph.D. candidate at Rutger's University, she holds a B.A. from Wellesley College and a master's degree from Boston College. She resides in Bellingham, MA.

Chapter Chronology, General Resources: The Arts, Fashion and Design.

MARY HERTZ SCARBROUGH earned both her B.A. in English and German and her J.D. from the University of South Dakota. Prior to becoming a freelance writer in 1996, she worked as a law clerk in the Federal District Court for the District of South Dakota and as legal counsel for the Immigration and Naturalization Service. She lives in Storm Lake, IA.

Chapter Chronology, General Resources: Law and Justice.

SUSAN P. WALTON is a librarian, freelance writer, editor, and researcher. Her primary interest is the history of science and medicine. Her writings have appeared in *The New York Times*, *International Wildlife*, *Health*, and others.

Chapter: Medicine and Health.

Acknowledgments

Following is a list of the copyright holders who have granted us permission to reproduce material in this volume of American Decades Primary Sources. *Every effort has been made to trace copyright, but if omissions have been made, please let us know.*

Copyrighted material in *American Decades Primary Sources, 1930–1939*, was reproduced from the following periodicals: *Bulletin of the American Library Association*, v. 27, December, 1933. Reproduced by permission. — *Esquire Magazine*, June, 1939. Reproduced by permission. —"First Lecture of Marriage Course," in a lecture delivered June, 1939 by Alfred Kinsey. Copyright (c) The Kinsey Institute for Research in Sex, Gender, and Reproduction, Inc. 1939. Reproduced by permission of The Kinsey Institute for Research in Sex, Gender, and Reproduction, Inc. —From "The Guiding Principles of Reform Judaism—1937," delivered, on 1999 at the Central Conference of American Rabbis in Columbus. Copyright(c) 1999. Reprinted with permission. —General Motors Agreement, February 11, 1937. Reproduced by permission of Walter P. Reuther Library, Wayne State University. —Guthrie, Woody, words and music for "Dust Bowl Blues." TRO - (c) Copyright 1964, renewed, 1977 Ludlow Music, Inc. New York, NY. Reprinted with permission. —Guthrie, Woody, words and music for "I Ain't Got No Home." TRO - (c) Copyright 1961, renewed, 1964, renewed, Ludlow Music, Inc., New York, NY. Reproduced by permission. —Guthrie, Woody, words and music for "(If You Ain't Got The) Do Re Mi." TRO - (c) Copyright 1961, renewed, 1963, renewed, Ludlow Music, Inc., New York, NY. Reproduced by permission. — *Journal of the National Education Association*, v. XXIV, January–December, 1935. Reproduced by permission. —Lawrence, Ernest O. From "The Evolution of the Cyclotron," in Nobel Lecture, December 11, 1951. (c) The Nobel Foundation. Reproduced by permission. —Metze, Gertrude. From "Radio in a Modern School Program," delivered on March 20, 1939, on a radio address by Gertrude Metze. UW Oshkosh Series 15. Copyright (c) The Board of Regents of the University of Wisconsin System, 1939. Reproduced with permission of the University of Wisconsin, Oshkosh Archives and Area Research Center. —Motion Picture Association of America, Inc. From "The Production Code of the Motion Picture Producers and Directors of America, Inc. — 1930–1934." Reproduced by permission. — *The Nation*, v. 142, January 15, 1936; v. 145, August 7, 1937; December 17, 1938. Reproduced by permission. — *The New York Times*, August 4, 1931; May 22, 1935; August 1, 1936; June 7, 1937; June 16, 1938; October 31, 1938; November 1, 1938. Copyright (c) 1931, 1935, 1936, 1937, 1938 by The New York Times Company. Reproduced by permission. — *Opportunity, Journal of Negro Life*, September 1933; October 1933. Reproduced by permission. — *The New Republic*, December 27, 1933; April 27, 1938. Reproduced by permission. — *The Saturday Evening Post*, May 7, 1938. Reproduced by permission. — *Time*, v. XXIV, December 24, 1934; v. XXX, December 27, 1937. Copyright 1934, 1937, Time Inc. Reproduced by permission.

Copyrighted material in *American Decades Primary Sources, 1930–1939*, was reproduced from the following books: Anderson, Marian. From "Easter Sunday," in *My Lord, What a Morning*. The Viking Press, 1956. Copyright (c) 1956 by The Viking Press, renewed 1984 by

Marion Anderson. All rights reserved. Reproduced by permission of Viking Penguin, a division of Penguin Putnam. —Benedict, Ruth. From *Patterns of Culture*. Houghton Mifflin Company, Boston, 1934. Copyright 1934 by Ruth Benedict, copyright (c) renewed 1961 by Ruth Valentine. Reproduced by permission of Houghton Mifflin Co. All rights reserved. —Counts, George S. From *Dare the School Build a New Social Order*. Southern Illinois University Press, 1932. Copyright (c) 1959 by George S. Counts. All rights reserved. Reproduced by permission. —Einstein, Albert. From "Some Notes on My American Impressions" in *The World As I See It*. Covici, Friede, Inc., 1934. Copyright (c) 1934 by Covici Friede, Inc, renewed 1962 by Crown Publishers. All rights reserved. Reproduced by permission of Crown Publishers, a division of Random House, Inc. —Faulkner, Howard J. and Virginia D. Pruitt. From "Depression and Anxiety," in *Dear Dr. Menninger: Women's Voices from the Thirties*. University of Missouri Press, 1997. Copyright (c) 1997 by The Curators of the University of Missouri Press. All rights reserved. Reproduced by permission. —Fischer, Ernst Peter and Carol Lipson. From "Light and Life-The Great Challenge," in *Thinking About Science: Max Delbruck and the Origins of Molecular Biology*. W. W. Norton & Company, 1988. Copyright (c) 1988 by Ernst Peter Fischer and Carol Lipson. All rights reserved. Reproduced by permission of W. W. Norton & Company, Inc. —Fuess, Claude M. and Emory S. Basford. From "The School Readers," in *Unseen Harvests: A Treasury of Teaching*. The Macmillan Company, 1947. Copyright (c) 1947 by The Macmillan Company; copyright renewed (c) 1975 by Emory S. Bradford and Cora Frances Fuess. All rights reserved. Reproduced by permission of Scribner, an imprint of Simon & Schuster & Schuster Adult Publishing Group. —Fosdick, Harry Emerson. From "Chapter 1: The Idea of God," in *A Guide to Understanding the Bible*. Harper & Brothers, 1938. Reproduced by permission of the author's estate. —Guiterman, Arthur. From "Education," in *Death and General Putnam and 101 Other Poems*. E.P. Dutton & Co., Inc., 1935. Copyright (c) 1935 by E.P. Dutton & Co., Inc; renewed 1963 by Vida Lindo Guiterman. All rights reserved. Reproduced by permission. —Henie, Sonja. In *Wings on My Feet*. Prentice-Hall, Inc., 1940. Copyright (c) 1940 by Prentice-Hall, Inc. —Hitchcock, Jr., Henry-Russell and Philip Johnson. From *The International Style: Architecture Since 1922*. W.W. Norton & Company, Inc., 1932. Copyright (c) 1932 by W.W. Norton & Company, Inc, copyright renewal 1960 by Henry Russell Hitchcock and Philip Johnson. All rights reserved. Reproduced by permission of W.W. Norton & Company, Inc. —Jones, Robert Tyre (Bobby), Jr. From *Golf is My Game*. Doubleday and Co., Inc., 1959. Copyright (c) 1959, 1960 by Robert Tyre Jones, Jr. All rights reserved. Reproduced by permission of Doubleday, a division of Random House, Inc. —Kennedy, Rose Fitzgerald. From "Golden Girls," in *Times to Remember*. Doubleday, 1974. Copyright (c) 1974 by Joseph P. Kennedy, Jr. Foundation. All rights reserved. Reproduced by permission. —Lamb, Ruth DeForest. From "It's a Racket!," in *American Chamber of Horrors: The Truth About Food and Drugs*. Farrar & Rinehart, Inc., 1936. Copyright (c) 1936, renewed 1963 by Ruth DeForest Lamb. —Lewis, Sinclair. From chapter 8, in *It Can't Happen Here, A Novel*. Doubleday, Doran & Company, Inc., 1936. Copyright (c) 1935 by Sinclair Lewis, renewed 1962 by Michael Lewis. All rights reserved. Reproduced by permission. —Lynd, Robert S. and Helen Lynd. From "Training the Young," in *Middletown in Transition, A Study in Cultural Conflicts*. Harcourt, Brace and Company, 1937. Copyright (c) 1937 by Harcourt, Inc, renewed 1965 by Robert S. Lynd and Helen M. Lynd. All rights reserved. Reproduced by publisher. —Madenwald, Abbie Morgan. From *Arctic Schoolteacher, Kulukak, Alaska, 1931–33*. University of Oklahoma Press, 1992. Copyright (c) 1992 by Mary Madenwald McKeown. All rights reserved. Reproduced by permission. —Millikan, Robert A. From *Science and the New Civilization*. Charles Scribner's Sons, 1930. Copyright 1930, Charles Scribner's Sons. —Mollenhoff, Clark R. From Appendix A in *Atanasoff*. Iowa State University Press, 1988. Copyright (c) 1988 by Iowa State University Press. All rights reserved. Reproduced by permission. —Paige, LeRoy (Satchel) as told to David Lipman. From *Maybe I'll Pitch Forever: A Great Baseball Player Tells the Hilarious Story Behind the Legend*. University of Nebraska Press, 1962. Copyright (c) 1962 by University of Nebraska Press. All rights reserved. Reproduced by permission. —Parran, Thomas. From "Syphilis, the White Man's Burden," in *Shadow on the Land*. Waverly Press, 1937. Copyright (c) 1937 by Waverly Press. All rights reserved. Reproduced by permission. —Pauling, Linus. From preface to the First Edition, in *The Nature of the Chemical Bond and the Structure of Molecules and Crystals: An Introduction to Modern Structural Chemistry*, 3rd edition. The Cornell University Press, 1940. Copyright (c) 1940, renewed 1960, by Cornell University Press, Inc., All rights reserved. Reproduced by permission of the publisher, Cornell University Press. —Rampersad, Arnold and David Roessel. From "Ballad of Roosevelt," in *The Collected Poems of Langston Hughes*. Alfred A. Knopf. Copyright (c) 1994 by the Estate of Langston Hughes. All rights reserved. Reproduced by permission of Harold Ober Associates Incorporated and Alfred A. Knopf, a division of Random House, Inc. —Rampersad, Arnold and David Roessel. From "Let America Be America Again," in *The Collected Poems of Langston Hughes*. Alfred A. Knopf. Copyright (c) 1994 by the Estate of Langston Hughes. All rights reserved. Reproduced by permission of Harold Ober Associates Incorporated and Alfred A. Knopf, a division of Random House, Inc. —Rampersad, Arnold and David Roessel. From "Scottsboro," in *The Collected Poems of Langston Hughes*. Alfred A. Knopf. Copyright (c) 1994 by the Estate of Langston Hughes. All rights reserved. Reproduced by permission of Harold Ober Associates Incorporated and Alfred A. Knopf, a division of Random House, Inc. —Ruth, Babe as told to Bob Considine. From *The Babe Ruth Story*. E.P. Dutton, 1948. Copyright (c) 1948 by George Herman Ruth, renewed (c) 1976 by Mildred Considine. All rights reserved. Reproduced by permission of Dutton, a division of Penguin Putnam Inc. —Sloan, Alfred P. From "Evolution of the Automobile," in *My Years With General Motors*. Doubleday & Company, 1964. Copyright (c) 1963 by Alfred P. Sloan. All rights reserved. Reproduced by permission of the Harold Matson Co., Inc. —Sloan, Alfred P. From introduction, in *My Years With General Motors*. Doubleday & Company, 1964. Copyright (c) 1964 by Doubleday & Company. All rights reserved. Reproduced by permission. —Sloan, Alfred P. From "Policy Creation," in *My Years With General Motors*. Doubleday & Company, 1964. Copyright (c) 1964 by Doubleday & Company. All rights reserved. Reproduced by permission. —Sloan, Alfred P. From "The Great Opportunity—II," in *My Years With General Motors*. Doubleday & Company, 1964. Copyright (c) 1964 by Doubleday & Company. All rights reserved. Reproduced by permission. —Sloan, Alfred P. From "Transformation of the Automobile Market," in *My Years With General Motors*. Doubleday & Company, 1964. Copyright (c) 1964 by Doubleday & Company. All rights reserved. Reproduced by permission. —Solomon, Arthur K. From "Atom Smashers 3—The Cyclotron," in *Why Smash Atoms?* Cambridge, Mass.: Harvard University Press, 1940. Copyright (c) 1940, 1946 by the President and Fellows of Harvard College, renewed 1968 by Arthur Kaskel Solomon. All rights reserved. Reproduced by permission of the publisher. —Standing Bear, Luther. From *Land of the Spotted Eagle*. University of Nebraska Press, 1933. Copyright (c) 1933 by Luther Standing Bear. Copyright renewed 1960 by May Jones. All rights reserved. Reproduced by permission. —Steinbeck, John. From chapter 1, in *The Grapes of Wrath*. Penguin Books, 1939. Copyright (c) 1939, renewed 1967 by John Steinbeck. All rights reserved. Reproduced by permission of Viking Penguin, a division of Penguin Putnam, Inc. —Steinbeck, John. From "Chapter 18," in *The Grapes of Wrath*. Penguin Books, 1939. Copyright 1939, renewed (c) 1967 by John Steinbeck. All rights reserved. Reproduced by permission of Viking Penguin, a division of Penguin Group (USA) Inc. and Penguin Books, Ltd. —Zaharias, Babe Didrikson. From *This Life I've Led: My Autobiography*. A.S. Barnes and Co., 1955. Copyright (c) 1955 by A.S. Barnes and Co. All rights reserved. Reproduced by permission.

Copyrighted material in *American Decades Primary Sources, 1930–1939,* was reproduced from the following web sites:

Father and Mother Divine. "Civilizations Have Perished." Father and Mother Divine's International Peace Mission Movement. Online at: http://www.libertynet.org/fdipmm/word1/38060113.html (February 9, 2002). Reprinted with permission of The Palace Mission, Inc. —"Flash Gordon in Episode Two." Online at: http://www.gernericradio.com/library.htm (May 4, 1935).

About the Set

American Decades Primary Sources is a ten-volume collection of more than two thousand primary sources on twentieth-century American history and culture. Each volume comprises about two hundred primary sources in 160–170 entries. Primary sources are enhanced by informative context, with illustrative images and sidebars—many of which are primary sources in their own right—adding perspective and a deeper understanding of both the primary sources and the milieu from which they originated.

Designed for students and teachers at the high school and undergraduate levels, as well as researchers and history buffs, *American Decades Primary Sources* meets the growing demand for primary source material.

Conceived as both a stand-alone reference and a companion to the popular *American Decades* set, *American Decades Primary Sources* is organized in the same subject-specific chapters for compatibility and ease of use.

Primary Sources

To provide fresh insights into the key events and figures of the century, thirty historians and four advisors selected unique primary sources far beyond the typical speeches, government documents, and literary works. Screenplays, scrapbooks, sports box scores, patent applications, college course outlines, military codes of conduct, environmental sculptures, and CD liner notes are but a sampling of the more than seventy-five types of primary sources included.

Diversity is shown not only in the wide range of primary source types, but in the range of subjects and opinions, and the frequent combination of primary sources in entries. Multiple perspectives in religious, political, artistic, and scientific thought demonstrate the commitment of *American Decades Primary Sources* to diversity, in addition to the inclusion of considerable content displaying ethnic, racial, and gender diversity. *American Decades Primary Sources* presents a variety of perspectives on issues and events, encouraging the reader to consider subjects more fully and critically.

American Decades Primary Sources' innovative approach often presents related primary sources in an entry. The primary sources act as contextual material for each other—creating a unique opportunity to understand each and its place in history, as well as their relation to one another. These may be point-counterpoint arguments, a variety of diverse opinions, or direct responses to another primary source. One example is President Franklin Delano Roosevelt's letter to clergy at the height of the Great Depression, with responses by a diverse group of religious leaders from across the country.

Multiple primary sources created by particularly significant individuals—Dr. Martin Luther King, Jr., for example—reside in *American Decades Primary Sources.* Multiple primary sources on particularly significant subjects are often presented in more than one chapter of a volume, or in more than one decade, providing opportunities to see the significance and impact of an event or figure from many angles and historical perspectives. For example, seven primary sources on the controversial Scopes "monkey" trial are found in five chapters of the

1920s volume. Primary sources on evolutionary theory may be found in earlier and later volumes, allowing the reader to see and analyze the development of thought across time.

Entry Organization

Contextual material uses standardized rubrics that will soon become familiar to the reader, making the entries more accessible and allowing for easy comparison. Introduction and Significance essays—brief and focused—cover the historical background, contributing factors, importance, and impact of the primary source, encouraging the reader to think critically—not only about the primary source, but also about the way history is constructed. Key Facts and a Synopsis provide quick access and recognition of the primary sources, and the Further Resources are a stepping-stone to additional study.

Additional Features

Subject chronologies and thorough tables of contents (listing titles, authors, and dates) begin each chapter. The main table of contents assembles this information conveniently at the front of the book. An essay on using primary sources, a chronology of selected events outside the United States during the twentieth century, substantial general and subject resources, and primary source-type and general indexes enrich *American Decades Primary Sources.*

The ten volumes of *American Decades Primary Sources* provide a vast array of primary sources integrated with supporting content and user-friendly features. This value-laden set gives the reader an unparalleled opportunity to travel into the past, to relive important events, to encounter key figures, and to gain a deep and full understanding of America in the twentieth century.

Acknowledgments

A number of people contributed to the successful completion of this project. The editor wishes to acknowledge them with thanks: Eugenia Bradley, Luann Brennan, Neva Carter, Katrina Coach, Pamela S. Dear, Nikita L. Greene, Madeline Harris, Alesia James, Cynthia Jones, Pamela M. Kalte, Arlene Ann Kevonian, Frances L. Monroe, Charles B. Montney, Katherine H. Nemeh, James E. Person, Tyra Y. Phillips, Elizabeth Pilette, Noah Schusterbauer, Andrew Specht, Susan Strickland, Karissa Walker, Tracey Watson, and Jennifer M. York.

Contact Us

The editors of *American Decades Primary Sources* welcome your comments, suggestions, and questions. Please direct all correspondence to:

Editor, *American Decades Primary Sources*
Gale
27500 Drake Road
Farmington Hills, MI 48331–3535
(800) 877–4253

For email inquiries, please visit the Gale website at gale.cengage.com, and click on the Contact Us tab.

About the Volume

The United States in the 1930s was dominated by the economic difficulties of the Great Depression, which impacted life on all levels for much of the population. The Depression spurred federal programs in business and industry and investment in the arts and humanities, generating a heretofore unparalleled support for and public interest in literature, architecture, photography, and other ventures. At the same time, the country's economic woes did not discourage crime or social debate. The 1930s was a decade rich in new cultural and social programs, as well as political debate and legal challenge. The following documents are just a sampling of the offerings available in this volume.

Highlights of Primary Sources, 1930–1939

- "Notes on a Cowboy Ballet," Aaron Copland's notes for "Billy the Kid"
- "Progress in Michigan," newsletter of the Works Progress Administration
- *Land of the Spotted Eagle,* by Luther Standing Bear
- *A Century of Progress Exposition: Official Pictures in Color,* exposition booklet
- "What's the Matter with Congress?" by Senator Lester J. Dickinson
- Text facsimile of Al Capone's indictment
- Eleanor Roosevelt's letter of resignation from the Daughters of the American Revolution
- "Will the New Deal Be a Square Deal for the Negro?" by Jesse O. Thomas
- *Saga of the CCC,* by John D. Guthrie
- "Are We Going Communist? A Debate," by Everett Dean Martin and Earl Browder
- Photography of the Great Depression: Dorothea Lange, Arthur Rothstein, Walker Evans
- Cover and pages from "Action Comics No. 1," by Jerome Siegel and Joe Shuster
- "Children Hurt at Work," by Gertrude Folks Zimand
- Letter from Albert Einstein to President Franklin D. Roosevelt
- Box score of the Cincinnati Reds–Brooklyn Dodgers game on June 15, 1938

Volume Structure and Content

Front matter

- Table of Contents—lists primary sources, authors, and dates of origin, by chapter and chronologically within chapters.
- About the Set, About the Volume, About the Entry essays—guide the reader through the set and promote ease of use.
- Highlights of Primary Sources—a quick look at a dozen or so primary sources gives the reader a feel for the decade and the volume's contents.

- Using Primary Sources—provides a crash course in reading and interpreting primary sources.
- Chronology of Selected World Events Outside the United States—lends additional context in which to place the decade's primary sources.

Chapters:

- The Arts
- Business and the Economy
- Education
- Fashion and Design
- Government and Politics
- Law and Justice
- Lifestyles and Social Trends
- The Media
- Medicine and Health
- Religion
- Science and Technology
- Sports

Chapter structure

- Chapter table of contents—lists primary sources, authors, and dates of origin chronologically, showing each source's place in the decade.
- Chapter chronology—highlights the decade's important events in the chapter's subject.
- Primary sources—displays sources surrounded by contextual material.

Back of the Book

- General Resources—promotes further inquiry with books, periodicals, websites, and audio and visual media, all organized into general and subject-specific sections.
- General Index—provides comprehensive access to primary sources, people, events, and subjects, and cross-referencing to enhance comparison and analysis.
- Primary Source Type Index—locates primary sources by category, giving readers an opportunity to easily analyze sources across genres.

About the Entry

The primary source is the centerpiece and main focus of each entry in *American Decades Primary Sources.* In keeping with the philosophy that much of the benefit from using primary sources derives from the reader's own process of inquiry, the contextual material surrounding each entry provides access and ease of use, as well as giving the reader a springboard for delving into the primary source. Rubrics identify each section and enable the reader to navigate entries with ease.

Entry structure

- Key Facts—essential information pertaining to the primary source, including full title, author, source type, source citation, and notes about the author.
- Introduction—historical background and contributing factors for the primary source.
- Significance—importance and impact of the primary source, at the time and since.
- Primary Source—in text, text facsimile, or image format; full or excerpted.
- Synopsis—encapsulated introduction to the primary source.
- Further Resources—books, periodicals, websites, and audio and visual material.

Navigating an Entry

Entry elements are numbered and reproduced here, with an explanation of the data contained in these elements explained immediately thereafter according to the corresponding numeral.

Entry Title, Primary Source Type

•1• "Ego"

•2• **Magazine article**

•1• ENTRY TITLE The entry title is the primary source title for entries with one primary source. Entry titles appear as catchwords at the top outer margin of each page.

•2• PRIMARY SOURCE TYPE The type of primary source is listed just below the title. When assigning source types, great weight was given to how the author of the primary source categorized it. If a primary source comprised more than one type—for example, an article about art in the United States that included paintings, or a scientific essay that included graphs and photographs—each primary source type included in the entry appears below the title.

Composite Entry Title

•3• Debate Over *The Birth of a Nation*

•1• **"Capitalizing Race Hatred"**

•2• **Editorial**

•1• "Reply to the *New York Globe*"

•2• Letter

•3• **COMPOSITE ENTRY TITLE** An overarching entry title is used for entries with more than one primary source, with the primary source titles and types below.

Key Facts

•4• **By:** Norman Mailer

•5• **Date:** March 19, 1971

•6• **Source:** Mailer, Norman. "Ego." *Life* 70, March 19, 1971, 30, 32–36.

•7• **About the Author:** Norman Mailer (1923–) was born in Long Branch, New Jersey. After graduating from Harvard and military service in World War II (1939–1945), Mailer began writing, publishing his first book, the best-selling novel *The Naked and the Dead,* in 1948. Mailer has written over thirty books, including novels, plays, political commentary, and essay collections, as well as numerous magazine articles. He won the Pulitzer Prize in 1969 and 1979. ■

•4• **AUTHOR OR ORIGINATOR** The name of the author or originator of the primary source begins the Key Facts section.

•5• **DATE OF ORIGIN** The date of origin of the primary source appears in this field, and may differ from the date of publication in the source citation below it; for example, speeches are often given before they are published.

•6• **SOURCE CITATION** The source citation is a full bibliographic citation, giving original publication data as well as reprint and/or online availability (usually both the deep-link and home-page URLs).

•7• **ABOUT THE AUTHOR** A brief bio of the author or originator of the primary source gives birth and death dates and a quick overview of the person's life. This rubric has been customized in some cases. If the primary source is the autobiography of an artist, the term "author" appears; however, if the primary source is a work of art, the term "artist" is used, showing the person's direct relationship to the primary source. Terms like "inventor" and "designer" are used similarly. For primary sources created by a group, "organization" may have been used instead of "author." If an author is anonymous or unknown, a brief "About the Publication" sketch may appear.

Introduction and Significance Essays

•8• Introduction

. . . As images from the Vietnam War (1964–1975) flashed onto television screens across the United States in the late 1960s, however, some reporters took a more active role in questioning the pronouncements of public officials. The broad cultural changes of the 1960s, including a sweeping suspicion of authority figures by younger people, also encouraged a more restive spirit in the reporting corps. By the end of the decade, the phrase "Gonzo Journalism" was coined to describe the new breed of reporter: young, rebellious, and unafraid to get personally involved in the story at hand. . . .

•8• **INTRODUCTION** The introduction is a brief essay on the contributing factors and historical context of the primary source. Intended to promote understanding and jump-start the reader's curiosity, this section may also describe an artist's approach, the nature of a scientific problem, or the struggles of a sports figure. If more than one primary source is included in the entry, the introduction and significance address each one, and often the relationship between them.

•9• Significance

Critics of the new style of journalism maintained that the emphasis on personalities and celebrity did not necessarily lead to better reporting. As political reporting seemed to focus more on personalities and images and less on substantive issues, some observers feared that the American public was ill-served by the new style of journalism. Others argued that the media had also encouraged political apathy among the public by superficial reporting. . . .

•9• **SIGNIFICANCE** The significance discusses the importance and impact of the primary source. This section may touch on how it was regarded at the time and since, its place in history, any awards given, related developments, and so on.

Primary Source Header, Synopsis, Primary Source

•10• Primary Source

The Boys on the Bus [excerpt]

•11• **SYNOPSIS:** A boisterous account of Senator George McGovern's ultimately unsuccessful 1972 presidential bid, Crouse's work popularized the term "pack journalism," describing the herd mentality that gripped reporters focusing endlessly on the same topic. In later years, political advisors would become more adept at "spinning" news stories to their candidates' advantage, but the essential dynamics of pack journalism remain in place.

•12• The feverish atmosphere was halfway between a high school bus trip to Washington and a gambler's jet junket to Las Vegas, where small-time Mafiosi were lured into betting away their restaurants. There was giddy camaraderie mixed with fear and low-grade hysteria. To file a story late, or to make one glaring factual error, was to chance losing everything—one's job, one's expense account, one's drinking buddies, one's mad-dash existence, and the methedrine buzz that comes from knowing stories that the public would not know for hours and secrets that the public would never know. Therefore reporters channeled their gambling instincts into late-night poker games and private bets on the outcome of the elections. When it came to writing a story, they were as cautious as diamond-cutters. . . .

•10• **PRIMARY SOURCE HEADER** The primary source header signals the beginning of the primary source, and "[excerpt]" is attached if the source does not appear in full.

•11• **SYNOPSIS** The synopsis gives a brief overview of the primary source.

•12• **PRIMARY SOURCE** The primary source may appear excerpted or in full, and may appear as text, text facsimile (photographic reproduction of the original text), image, or graphic display (such as a table, chart, or graph).

Text Primary Sources

The majority of primary sources are reproduced as plain text. The font and leading of the primary sources are distinct from that of the context—to provide a visual clue to the change, as well as to facilitate ease of reading. Often, the original formatting of the text was preserved in order to more accurately represent the original (screenplays, for example). In order to respect the integrity of the primary sources, content some readers may consider sensitive was retained where it was deemed to be integral to the source. Text facsimile formatting was used sparingly and where the original provided additional value (for example, Aaron Copland's typing and handwritten notes on "Notes for a Cowboy Ballet").

Narrative Break

•13• I told him I'd rest and then fix him something to eat when he got home. I could hear someone enter his office then, and Medgar laughed at something that was said. "I've got to go, honey. See you tonight. I love you." "All right," I said. "Take care." Those were our last words to each other.

■ ■ ■

Medgar had told me that President Kennedy was speaking on civil rights that night, and I made a mental note of the time. We ate alone, the children and I. It had become a habit now to set only four places for supper. Medgar's chair stared at us, and the children, who had heard about the President's address to the nation, planned to watch it with me. There was something on later that they all wanted to see, and they begged to be allowed to wait up for Medgar to return home. School was out, and I knew that Van would fall asleep anyway, so I agreed.

•13• **NARRATIVE BREAK** A narrative break appears where there is a significant amount of elided material, beyond what ellipses would indicate (for example, excerpts from a nonfiction work's introduction and second chapter, or sections of dialogue from two acts of a play).

Image Primary Sources

Primary source images (whether photographs, text facsimiles, or graphic displays) are bordered with a distinctive double rule. The Primary Source header and Synopsis appear under the image, with the image reduced in size to accommodate the synopsis. For multipart images, the synopsis appears only under the first part of the image; subsequent parts have brief captions.

•14• "Art: U.S. Scene": *The Tornado* by John Steuart Curry (2 OF 4)

•14• **PRIMARY SOURCE IMAGE HEADER** The primary source image header assists the reader in tracking the images in a series. Also, the primary source header listed here indicates a primary source with both text and image components. The text of the *Time* magazine article "Art: U.S. Scene," appears with four of the paintings from the article. Under each painting, the title of the article appears first, followed by a colon, then the title of the painting. The header for the text component has a similar structure, with the term "magazine article" after the colon. Inclusion of images or graphic elements from primary sources, and their designation in the entry as main primary sources, is discretionary.

Further Resources

•15• **Further Resources**

BOOKS

Dixon, Phil. *The Negro Baseball Leagues, 1867–1955: A Photographic History.* Mattituck, N.Y.: Amereon House, 1992.

PERIODICALS

"Steven Spielberg: The Director Says It's Good-Bye to Spaceships and Hello to Relationships." *American Film* 13, no. 8, June 1988, 12–16.

WEBSITES

Architecture and Interior Design for 20th Century America, 1935–1955. American Memory digital primary source collection, Library of Congress. Available online at http://memory.loc.gov/ammem/gschtml/gotthome

.html; website home page: http://memory.loc.gov/ammem/ammemhome.html (accessed March 27, 2003).

AUDIO AND VISUAL MEDIA

E.T.: The Extra-Terrestrial. Original release, 1982, Universal. Directed by Steven Spielberg. Widescreen Collector's Edition DVD, 2002, Universal Studios.

•15• FURTHER RESOURCES A brief list of resources provides a stepping stone to further study. If it's known that a resource contains additional primary source material specifically related to the entry, a brief note in italics appears at the end of the citation. For websites, both the deep link and home page usually appear.

Using Primary Sources

The philosopher R.G. Collingwood once said, "Every new generation must rewrite history in its own way." What Collingwood meant is that new events alter our perceptions of the past and necessitate that each generation interpret the past in a different light. For example, since September 11, 2001, and the "War on Terrorism," the collapse of the Soviet Union seemingly is no longer as historically important as the rise of Islamic fundamentalism, which was once only a minor concern. Seen from this viewpoint, history is not a rigid set of boring facts, but a fascinating, ever-changing field of study. Much of this fascination rests on the fact that historical interpretation is based on the reading of primary sources. To historians and students alike, primary sources are ambiguous objects because their underlying meanings are often not crystal clear. To learn a primary document's meaning(s), students must identify its main subject and recreate the historical context in which the document was created. In addition, students must compare the document with other primary sources from the same historical time and place. Further, students must cross-examine the primary source by asking of it a series of probing investigative questions.

To properly analyze a primary source, it is important that students become "active" rather than "casual" readers. As in reading a chemistry or algebra textbook, historical documents require students to analyze them carefully and extract specific information. In other words, history requires students to read "beyond the text" and focus on what the primary source tells us about the person or group and the era in which they lived. Unlike chemistry and algebra, however, historical primary sources have the additional benefit of being part of a larger, interesting story full of drama, suspense, and hidden agendas. In order to detect and identify key historical themes, students need to keep in mind a set of questions. For example, Who created the primary source? Why did the person create it? What is the subject? What problem is being addressed? Who was the intended audience? How was the primary source received and how was it used? What are the most important characteristics of this person or group for understanding the primary source? For example, what were the authors' biases? What was their social class? Their race? Their gender? Their occupation? Once these questions have been answered reasonably, the primary source can be used as a piece of historical evidence to interpret history.

In each *American Decades Primary Sources* volume, students will study examples of the following categories of primary sources:

- Firsthand accounts of historic events by witnesses and participants. This category includes diary entries, letters, newspaper articles, oral-history interviews, memoirs, and legal testimony.
- Documents representing the official views of the nation's leaders or of their political opponents. These include court decisions, policy statements, political speeches, party platforms, petitions, legislative debates, press releases, and federal and state laws.

- Government statistics and reports on such topics as birth, employment, marriage, death, and taxation.
- Advertisers' images and jingles. Although designed to persuade consumers to purchase commodities or to adopt specific attitudes, advertisements can also be valuable sources of information about popular beliefs and concerns.
- Works of art, including paintings, symphonies, play scripts, photographs, murals, novels, and poems.
- The products of mass culture: cartoons, comic books, movies, radio scripts, and popular songs.
- Material artifacts. These are everyday objects that survived from the period in question. Examples include household appliances and furnishings, recipes, and clothing.
- Secondary sources. In some cases, secondary sources may be treated as primary sources. For example, from 1836 to 1920, public schools across America purchased 122 million copies of a series of textbooks called the McGuffey Reader. Although current textbooks have more instructional value, the Reader is an invaluable primary source. It provides important insights into the unifying morals and cultural values that shaped the worldview of several generations of Americans, who differed in ethnicity, race, class, and religion.

Each of the above-mentioned categories of primary sources reveals different types of historical information. A politician's diary, memoirs, or collection of letters, for example, often provide students with the politicians' unguarded, private thoughts and emotions concerning daily life and public events. Though these documents may be a truer reflection of the person's character and aspirations, students must keep in mind that when people write about themselves, they tend to put themselves at the center of the historical event or cast themselves in the best possible light. On the other hand, the politician's public speeches may be more cautious, less controversial, and limited to advancing his or her political party's goals or platform.

Like personal diaries, advertisements reveal other types of historical information. What information does the WAVES poster on this page reveal?

John Phillip Faller, a prolific commercial artist known for his *Saturday Evening Post* covers, designed this recruitment poster in 1944. It was one of over three hundred posters he produced for the U.S. Navy while enrolled in that service during World War II. The purpose of the poster was to encourage women to enlist in the WAVES (Women Accepted for Volunteer Emergency Service), a women's auxiliary to the Navy established in

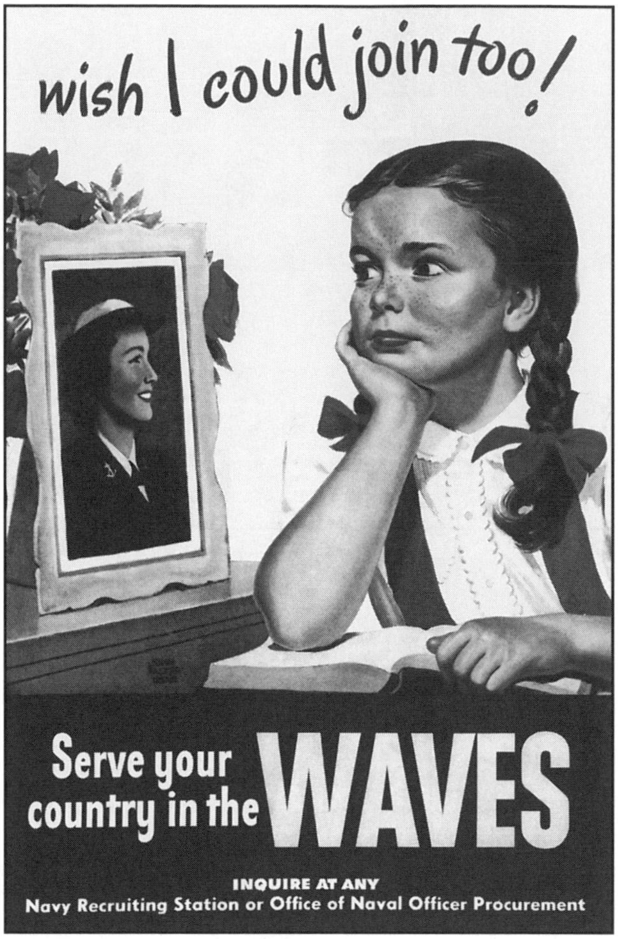

COURTESY OF THE NAVAL HISTORICAL FOUNDATION. REPRODUCED BY PERMISSION.

1942. It depicts a schoolgirl gazing admiringly at a photograph of a proud, happy WAVE (perhaps an older sister), thus portraying the military service as an appropriate and admirable aspiration for women during wartime. However, what type of military service? Does the poster encourage women to enlist in military combat like World War II male recruitment posters? Does it reflect gender bias? What does this poster reveal about how the military and society in general feel about women in the military? Does the poster reflect current military and societal attitudes toward women in the military? How many women joined the WAVES? What type of duties did they perform?

Like personal diaries, photographs reveal other types of historical information. What information does the next photograph reveal?

Today, we take electricity for granted. However, in 1935, although 90 percent of city dwellers in America had electricity, only 10 percent of rural Americans did. Private utility companies refused to string electric lines

THE LIBRARY OF CONGRESS.

to isolated farms, arguing that the endeavor was too expensive and that most farmers were too poor to afford it anyway. As part of the Second New Deal, President Franklin Delano Roosevelt issued an executive order creating the Rural Electrification Administration (REA). The REA lent money at low interest rates to utility companies to bring electricity to rural America. By 1950, 90 percent of rural America had electricity. This photograph depicts a 1930s tenant farmer's house in Greene County, Georgia. Specifically, it shows a brand-new electric meter on the wall. The picture presents a host of questions: What was rural life like without electricity? How did electricity impact the lives of rural Americans, particularly rural Georgians? How many rural Georgians did not have electricity in the 1930s? Did Georgia have more electricity-connected farms than other Southern states? What was the poverty rate in rural Georgia, particularly among rural African Americans? Did rural electricity help lift farmers out of poverty?

Like personal diaries, official documents reveal other types of historical information. What information does the next document, a memo, reveal?

From the perspective of the early twenty-first century, in a democratic society, integration of the armed services seems to have been inevitable. For much of American history, however, African Americans were prevented from joining the military, and when they did enlist they were segregated into black units. In 1940, of the nearly 170,000-man Navy, only 4,007, or 2.3 percent, were African American personnel. The vast majority of these men worked in the mess halls as stewards—or, as labeled by the black press, "seagoing bellhops." In this official document, the chairman of the General Board refers to compliance with a directive that would enlist African Americans into positions of "unlimited general service." Who issued the directive? What was the motivation behind the new directive? Who were the members of the General Board? How much authority did they wield? Why did the Navy restrict African Americans to the "messman branch"? Notice the use of the term "colored race." Why was this term used and what did it imply? What did the board conclude? When did the Navy become integrated? Who was primarily responsible for integrating the Navy?

~~CONFIDENTIAL~~

DOD DIR. 5200.10, June 29, 1960
NND by RB date Oct. 5, 1961

DOWNGRADED AT 3 YEAR INTERVALS;
DECLASSIFIED AFTER 12 YEARS
DOD DIR 5200.10 NARS-NT

~~SECRET~~

G.B. No. 421
(Serial No. 201)
SECRET

Feb 3, 1942

From: Chairman General Board.
To: Secretary of the Navy.

Subject: Enlistment of men of colored race to other than Messman branch.

Ref: (a) SecNav let. (SC)P14-4/MM (03200A)/Gen of Jan 16, 1942.

1. The General Board, complying with the directive contained in reference (a), has given careful attention to the problem of enlisting in the Navy, men of the colored race in other than the messman branch.

2. The General Board has endeavored to examine the problem placed before it in a realistic manner.

A. Should negroes be enlisted for unlimited general service?

(a) Enlistment for general service implies that the individual may be sent anywhere, - to any ship or station where he is needed. Men on board ship live in particularly close association; in their messes, one man sits beside another; their hammocks or bunks are close together; in their common tasks they work side by side; and in particular tasks such as those of a gun's crew, they form a closely knit, highly coordinated team. How many white men would choose, of their own accord, that their closest associates in sleeping quarters, at mess, and in a gun's crew should be of another race? How many would accept such conditions, if required to do so, without resentment and just as a matter of course? The General Board believes that the answer is "Few, if any," and further believes that if the issue were forced, there would be a lowering of contentment, teamwork and discipline in the service.

(b) One of the tennets of the recruiting service is that each recruit for general service is potentially a leading petty officer. It is true that some men never do become petty officers, and that when recruiting white men, it is not possible to establish which will be found worthy of and secure promotion and which will not. If negroes are recruited for general service, it can be said at once that few will obtain advancement to petty officers. With every desire to be fair, officers and leading petty officers in general will not recommend negroes for promotion to positions of authority over white men.

DOWNGRADED AND DECLASSIFIED

~~SECRET~~

- 1 -

~~CONFIDENTIAL~~

CONFIDENTIAL

The General Board is convinced that the enlistment of negroes for unlimited general service is unadvisable.

B. Should negroes be enlisted in general service but detailed in special ratings or for special ships or units?

(a) The ratings now in use in the naval service cover every phase of naval activity, and no new ratings are deemed necessary merely to promote the enlistment of negroes.

(b) At first thought, it might appear that assignment of negroes to certain vessels, and in particular to small vessels of the patrol type, would be feasible. In this connection, the following table is of interest:

Type of Ship	Total Crew	Men in Pay Grades 1 to 4	Men in Pay Grades 5 to 7 (Non-rated)
Battleship	1892	666	1226
Light Cruiser (10,000 ton)	988	365	623
Destroyer (1630 ton)	206	109	97
Submarine	54	47	7
Patrol Boat (180 foot)	55	36	19
Patrol Boat (110 foot)	20	15	5

NOTE: Pay grades 1 to 4 include Chief Petty Officers and Petty Officers, 1st, 2nd and 3rd Class; also Firemen, 1st Class and a few other ratings requiring length of service and experience equal to that required for qualification of Petty Officers, 3rd class. Pay grades 5 to 7 include all other non-rated men and recruits.

There are no negro officers and so few negro petty officers in the Navy at present that any vessels to which negroes might be assigned must have white officers and white petty officers. Examination of the table shows the small number of men in other than petty officer ratings that might be assigned to patrol vessels and indicates to the General Board that such assignments would not be happy ones. The assignment of negroes to the larger ships, where well over one-half of the crews are non-rated men, with mixture of whites and negroes, would inevitably lead to discontent on the part of one or the other, resulting in clashes and lowering of the efficiency of the vessels and of the Navy.

- 2 -

CONFIDENTIAL

COURTESY OF THE HARRY S. TRUMAN LIBRARY. REPRODUCED BY PERMISSION.

The material collected in these volumes of *American Decades Primary Sources* are significant because they will introduce students to a wide variety of historical sources that were created by those who participated in or witnessed the historical event. These primary sources not only vividly describe historical events, but also reveal the subjective perceptions and biases of their authors. Students should read these documents "actively," and with the contextual assistance of the introductory material, history will become relevant and entertaining.

—Paul G. Connors

Chronology of Selected World Events Outside the United States, 1930–1939

1930

- Max Beckmann paints *Self-Portrait With Saxophone.*
- Luis Buñuel's movie *L'Age d'or* (The Golden Age) is released.
- Agatha Christie's mystery novel *The Murder at the Vicarage* is published.
- Sigmund Freud's *Das Unbehagen in der Kultur* (Civilization and Its Discontents), a study of the political consequences of neurosis, is published.
- Alfred Hitchcock's movie *Murder* is released.
- Wyndham Lewis's novel *The Apes of God* is published.
- The Villa Savoye, designed by Le Corbusier, is completed in Poissy-sur-Seine, France.
- José Ortega y Gasset's *La Rebelión de Las Masas* (The Revolt of the Masses), a study of political authoritarianism, is published.
- Ezra Pound's *A Draft of XXX Cantos,* the first collected edition of Cantos 1–30 in his ongoing epic poem *The Cantos,* is published.
- Diego Rivera's murals *Fall of Cuernavaca* and *Cortez and His Mercenaries* are unveiled at the Palacio de Cortez in Mexico City.
- Stephen Spender's *Twenty Poems* is published.
- Tristan Tzara's *L'Homme approximatif* (Approximate Man), a Dadaist prose poem, is published.
- Uruguay wins the first World Cup soccer championship.
- British Arctic explorer H.G. Watkins continues to explore Greenland.
- Dr. Alfred Wegener leads a German scientific expedition to Greenland.
- Sir Douglas Mawson, of Great Britain, and Hjalmar Riiser-Larsen continue independent investigations of Antarctica.
- On January 1, the Indian National Congress, meeting at Lahore, votes for India's complete independence from Great Britain.
- On January 15, four hundred thousand Dubliners pour into the streets to welcome Archbishop Pasquale Robinson, an Irish-born prelate. He is the first papal nuncio to Ireland in more than three hundred years.
- From January 21 to April 22, the world's major naval powers meet in London to discuss limiting the tonnage and armaments of their navies. The conference concludes with the signing of a treaty by Great Britain, Italy, France, Japan, and the United States.
- On January 28, Spanish strongman Miguel Primo de Rivera resigns as prime minister because of ill health. He dies on March 16.
- On February 3, France passes a national workman's compensation law.
- On February 12, the Church of England, following the example of Roman Catholic Pope Pius XI, protests against the Soviet Union's antireligion campaign.
- On March 11, authorized by the All-India Trade Congress, Mohandas Gandhi begins a civil disobedience campaign against British rule by leading a 165-mile march to extract salt from the sea.
- On May 5, Gandhi is arrested by British authorities.
- On May 19, South Africa gives white women the right to vote. Black Africans of both sexes remain unable to vote.
- On June 30, in accordance with the Treaty of Versailles, Allied troops leave the Rhineland.

- On July 30, the fascist National Union Party is formed in Portugal.
- On September 2, French aviators Dieudonné Coste and Maurice Bellonte make the first nonstop flight from Paris to New York.
- On September 8, a joint United States–League of Nations commission reports that slavery is still practiced in Liberia.
- On September 14, in German national elections, Adolf Hitler's National Socialist (Nazi) Party wins 107 seats in the Reichstag, on the promise of a dictatorial government.
- On September 24, Noël Coward's play *Private Lives* premieres at the Phoenix Theatre in London.
- On October 13, newly elected Nazi delegates arrive at the Reichstag in uniform, a violation of parliamentary rules.
- On October 20, the British government issues the Passfield White Paper, which recommends that the immigration of Jews to Palestine be halted until the problem of unemployment among Palestinian Arabs can be addressed.
- On October 26, the ballet *Zoloty vek* (The Age of Gold), with music by Dmitry Shostakovich, premieres in Leningrad.
- On October 30, Greece and Turkey sign an agreement accepting the status quo in the eastern Mediterranean.
- On November 2, thirty-nine-year-old Ras (Prince) Tafari takes the name Haile Selassie and is crowned emperor of Ethiopia. He reigns until 1974.
- On November 5, Chinese Nationalist troops begin an offensive against communist forces in Hunan, Hupeh, and Kiangsi provinces.
- On November 14, Japanese prime minister Hamaguchi Osachi is shot by a right-wing militant. He dies several months later.
- On December 12, in accordance with the Treaty of Versailles, Allied troops leave the Saarland.
- On December 15, in response to increased Republican activity, martial law is declared in Spain.
- On December 24, Federico García Lorca's play *La zapatera prodigiosa* (The Shoemaker's Prodigious Wife) premieres at the Teatro Español in Madrid.

1931

- Salvador Dalí paints *The Persistence of Memory.*
- Frida Kahlo paints *Portrait of Frida and Diego,* a self-portrait of the artist with her husband, muralist Diego Rivera.
- Paul Klee paints *The Ghost Vanishes.*
- Fritz Lang's movie *M* is released.
- The planned capital of New Delhi, India, designed by British architects Edwin L. Lutyens and Herbert Baker, is formally opened.
- Paul Maximilian Landowski's statue *Christ the Redeemer* is dedicated atop a mountain overlooking Rio de Janeiro, Brazil.
- Anthony Powell's novel *Afternoon Men* is published.
- Jean Renoir's movie *La Chienne* (The Bitch) is released.
- George Seferis's *Strophe,* a volume of poetry, is published.
- Virginia Woolf's novel *The Waves* is published.
- Professor Auguste Picard becomes the first human to venture into the stratosphere, ascending to a height of fifty-two thousand feet in a balloon.
- On January 8, Pope Pius XI condemns birth control and common-law marriages. He also denounces divorce as contrary to the "laws and nature of God."
- On January 26, British authorities release Mohandas Gandhi from prison.
- On January 29, Winston Churchill resigns from the conservative government of Stanley Baldwin because of differing opinions on the India question.
- On February 8, the Spanish monarchy restores the country's constitution and sets March as the date for parliamentary elections.
- On March 1, the Soviet government purges 138,000 government employees.
- On March 4, Indian nationalists agree to end civil disobedience in India in return for the release of political prisoners.
- On March 24, President Mustapha Kemal restructures Turkey's government along fascist lines.
- On April 12, municipal elections in Spain result in victory for those favoring the establishment of a republic. Republican leader Niceta Alcalá Zamora will become president of a new provisional government.
- On April 14, King Alfonso XIII leaves Spain after a forty-five-year reign, paving the way for the creation of a republic.
- On April 26, Frederick Ashton's ballet *Façade* premieres at Cambridge Theatre in London.
- On April 27, Pope Pius XI states that "fascistic practices" inspire hate in youths, rendering almost impossible the practice of religious faith.
- On April 30, troops led by rebel general Chen Jitang seize control of the Chinese city of Canton from forces loyal to Chiang Kai-shek.
- On May 11, the failure of the Austrian bank Kreditanstalt precipitates a financial panic in Germany and eastern Europe.
- On June 17, Vietnamese nationalist leader Ho Chi Minh is arrested by British authorities in China.
- On July 1, the Benguela-Katanga Railway, the last link in the Trans-African Railway, is finished.
- On August 3, a dam bursts on the Yangtze River in China, flooding forty thousand square miles, killing hundreds, and precipitating widespread famine.
- On August 24, amid disputes over the nation's financial crisis, Great Britain's Labour government collapses, but Prime Minister Ramsay MacDonald is able to assemble a new coalition, which governs until 1935.
- On September 10, economic austerity measures provoke riots in London, Liverpool, and Glasgow.
- On September 18, Japanese officers bomb a section of the South Manchurian Railway. Attributing the explosion to

Chinese terrorists, Japan uses the blast as a pretext for attacking all of Manchuria.

- On November 4, Jean Giraudoux's play *Judith* premieres at the Comédie des Champs-Elysées in Paris.
- On November 12, the republican government of Spain finds King Alfonso XIII guilty of treason in absentia, preventing his return from exile.
- On December 9, Spain adopts a republican constitution. Alcalá Zamora becomes the country's first president.

1932

- Jean de Brunhoff's *L'Histoire de Babar* (The Story of Babar), the first of a popular series of children's books featuring Babar the Elephant, is published.
- Aldous Huxley's novel *Brave New World* is published.
- Henri Matisse completes his mural of *La Danse.*
- François Mauriac's novel *Le Nœud de vipères* (Vipers' Tangle) is published.
- Pablo Picasso paints *Girl Before a Mirror.*
- Joseph Roth's novel *Radetzkymarsch: Roman* (Radetzky March) is published.
- Georges Rouault paints *Christ Mocked by Soldiers.*
- Chemists at Imperial Chemical Industries in Great Britain synthesize the first plastic.
- German biochemist Gerhard Domagk discovers sulfa drugs, revolutionizing the treatment of infectious diseases.
- Civil war rages in El Salvador, where communist insurgents attack the military oligarchy.
- Labour Party M.P. (member of Parliament) Oswald Mosley establishes the British Union of Fascists.
- Severe famine sweeps through Russia, owing in part to outdated Soviet agricultural policy.
- On January 4, Mohandas Gandhi is arrested again for civil disobedience to protest British rule. The Indian National Congress is outlawed, but after a six-day fast Gandhi succeeds in changing the law that governs the treatment of the "untouchables," the lowest of the rigidly defined castes in India.
- On January 4, the Japanese occupation of Shanhaikwan, Manchuria, effectively solidifies Japan's control over southern Manchuria.
- On January 7, the United States formally protests the Japanese occupation of Manchuria.
- On January 22, American and British warships are summoned to quell a communist uprising in the republic of El Salvador.
- From January 28 to March 4, Japanese forces attack the Chinese city of Shanghai.
- On February 5, Germany's minister of defense permits Nazis to join the army.
- On February 18, acting for Japanese authorities, Chinese officials in Manchuria proclaim that province the independent nation of Manchukuo.
- On February 21, Arnold Schoenberg's *Four Orchestral Songs* premieres at Frankfurt-am-Main.
- On March 9, the Dail Eireann (parliament) of the Irish Free State elects American-born Eamonn de Valera as president. He takes the oath of allegiance to the king of England.
- On March 18, the Harbor Bridge, the largest arch bridge in the world, opens in Sydney, Australia.
- On April 4, the Ballets Russes de Monte Carlo stages *Cotillon* at the Théâtre de Monte Carlo.
- On April 13, German president Paul Hindenburg dissolves Hitler's 500,000-man "Brownshirt" army.
- On May 6, French president Paul Doumer is assassinated by a deranged Russian émigré. He is succeeded by Albert Lebrun.
- On May 15, Japanese prime minister Inukai Tsuyoshi is assassinated by military reactionaries.
- On May 20, Austrian minister of agriculture Engelbert Dollfuss forms a new government.
- On May 28, the Dutch complete nine years of work on a dike that reclaims millions of acres of farmland from the Zuider Zee.
- On May 30, Heinrich Brüning resigns as head of the German government. A political crisis arises after no German party polls a majority of votes. Franz von Papen forms a government responsible to German president Paul Hindenburg alone.
- On July 4, 150,000 communists and socialists demonstrate in Berlin against the suppression of a radical newspaper.
- On July 5, António de Oliveira Salazar becomes premier of Portugal. He is dictator of the country for nearly thirty-eight years.
- On July 31, German elections reveal that the Nazis have 230 seats in the Reichstag; socialists, 33; centrists, 97; and communists, 89. No party secures a majority, and no coalition forms.
- On August 10, military leaders in Seville launch a revolt against Spain's republican government. Troops loyal to the government suppress the revolt.
- On August 13, Hitler refuses German president Hindenburg's request to serve as vice chancellor under Franz von Papen.
- On August 30, Nazi leader Hermann Göring is elected president of the German Reichstag.
- On September 12, the German Reichstag is dissolved, and new elections are called.
- On September 16, Germany leaves an international conference on land armaments in Geneva, Switzerland because the French refuse to disarm before the signing of security arrangements.
- On October 3, Iraq is admitted to the League of Nations.
- On November 6, although the Nazis lose seats and the communists gain seats in the German national election, no party is able to break the Reichstag political deadlock.
- On November 12, the Soviet government transfers 25,000 Moscow government office workers to work on farms and factories.
- On November 17, Franz von Papen resigns as chancellor of Germany. Adolf Hitler rejects the position after President Hindenburg refuses to increase the powers of the office.

- On December 2, General Kurt von Schleicher forms a new German cabinet.

1933

- Colette's novel *La Chatte* (The Cat) is published.
- Dazai Osamu's novel *Gyofukuki* is published.
- Alberto Giacometti sculpts *The Palace at Four A.M.*
- Henri Matisse completes his painting *Danse* II.
- George Orwell's first book, the autobiographical *Down and Out in Paris and London,* is published.
- Diego Rivera's controversial mural *Man at the Crossroads,* at Rockefeller Center in New York, is destroyed for including a portrait of Russian leader Vladimir Lenin.
- Ignazio Silone's antifascist novel, *Fontamara,* is published.
- Gertrude Stein's memoir, *The Autobiography of Alice B. Toklas,* is published.
- Franz Werfel's novel *Die Vierzig Tage des Musa Dagh* (The Forty Days of Musa Dagh) is published.
- The Soviet Union completes two massive public works projects: the Dnieper River Dam (overseen by Hugh Lincoln Cooper) and the Baltic–White Sea Stalin Ship Canal.
- On January 8, anarchists and syndicalists in Barcelona foment a rebellion against the Spanish government. The uprising is suppressed.
- On January 28, Kurt von Schleicher's government in Germany collapses.
- On January 30, Nazi leader Adolf Hitler becomes German chancellor. In the absence of a political majority, elections are set for March 5.
- On February 3, Hitler issues a memorandum informing German naval officers that he intends to commit Germany to a massive rearmament campaign.
- On February 24, the League of Nations Assembly formally adopts a policy of not recognizing the Japanese protectorate of Manchukuo.
- On February 27, the Reichstag is destroyed by a fire likely set by the Nazis. Hitler denounces the fire as a communist plot and secures an emergency decree from President Hindenburg, allowing Nazi storm troopers to attack political enemies with impunity.
- On March 4, responding to growing political confusion in Austria, Chancellor Engelbert Dollfuss suspends parliament and constitutional rights. "Austria's Parliament has destroyed itself," he explains, "and nobody can say when it will be allowed to take up its dubious activities again."
- On March 5, the Nazis win 44 percent of the vote in the German elections.
- On March 7, German leader Hermann Wilhelm Göring orders the suspension of the nudist movement, claiming that it constitutes "one of the greatest dangers to German culture and morals."
- On March 20, in Dachau, Germany, near Munich, the Nazis establish their first concentration camp for party enemies.
- On March 23, the Reichstag passes the Enabling Act, giving the Nazi government dictatorial powers until April 1, 1937.
- On March 24, the Berlin Central Union of German Citizens of the Jewish Faith denounces foreign press reports of atrocities committed by Nazis against German Jews as "pure inventions."
- On April 1, the Nazis inaugurate a national boycott of all Jewish-owned businesses and professions in Germany. As a result, ten thousand Jews leave for Poland, France, and Belgium.
- On April 8, France dispatches a military envoy to Moscow for the first time since World War I.
- On May 17, the Spanish government nationalizes church property and abolishes religious education.
- On May 26, Australia assumes control of almost one-third of Antarctica.
- On May 27, Japan announces its withdrawal from the League of Nations, effective in two years.
- On June 19, the Austrian government dissolves the Austrian Nazi Party.
- On July 1, despite Nazi opposition to the performance of works by Jews, Richard Strauss's opera *Arabella,* with a libretto by part-Jewish Austrian writer Hugo von Hofmannsthal, is performed at the Staatsoper in Dresden.
- On July 14, the Nazi Party is declared the sole political party in Germany.
- On July 20, the Vatican signs a concordat with the Nazi government of Germany, stating that the Nazis will tolerate Catholic religion and education in return for political neutrality from Catholic officials in Germany.
- On August 1, Mohandas Gandhi is arrested again in India, but he is released after a few days because his health is deteriorating from a hunger strike.
- On September 12, Fulgencio Batista y Zalívar leads a successful military coup against the government of Cuba.
- On October 15, Dmitry Shostakovich's Concerto for Piano, Trumpet, and String Orchestra premieres in Leningrad.
- On November 12, Chancellor Adolf Hitler wins a 90 percent vote of confidence from German voters in a plebiscite on Nazi policy. No electoral opposition is permitted.
- On November 16, the United States and Soviet Union establish diplomatic relations.
- On November 19, Spanish elections result in gains for right-wing groups, who occupy 44 percent of the seats in the Córtes.
- On December 29, Romanian premier Ion Duca is assassinated by members of the fascist Iron Guard. Gheorghe Tatarescu assumes the premiership.

1934

- Morley Callaghan's novel *Such Is My Beloved* is published.
- Isak Dinesen's *Seven Gothic Tales* is published.
- German geographer Karl Haushoker's *Macht und Erde* (Power and Earth) is published. The Nazis use this geopolitical study to justify their policy of seeking lebensraum (living space).
- René Magritte's painting *Homage to Mack Sennett* is unveiled.

- Pablo Picasso paints *The Bullfight.*
- Christina Stead's *The Salzburg Tales,* a collection of short stories, is published.
- P. Pamela Travers's children's book *Mary Poppins* is published.
- T'sao Yu's play *Thunderstorm,* an attack on Chinese traditionalism, premieres in Peking.
- Jean Vigo's movie *L'Atalante* is released.
- Evelyn Waugh's *A Handful of Dust* is published.
- The British conduct two Arctic expeditions to Greenland, Baffin Island, and outlying islands.
- Australian John Rymill leads a two-year exploratory expedition to the Antarctic.
- American aviator Adm. Richard Byrd begins his second large Antarctic expedition.
- On January 22, Dmitry Shostakovich's opera *Lady Macbeth of the Mtsensk District* premieres at the Maly Opera House in Leningrad with popular success, but government and critic sources express opposition.
- On January 26, Germany and Poland sign a ten-year nonaggression pact.
- From February 6 to February 9, street riots erupt in France following revelations of government corruption and cover-ups of the illegal activities of Serge-Alexandre Stavisky, a Russian-born con man who committed suicide on January 8.
- On February 9, Turkey, Greece, Romania, and Yugoslavia sign the Balkan Pact, designed to protect their territorial integrity against invasion by Bulgaria.
- From February 11 to February 15, Austrian Chancellor Engelbert Dollfuss ruthlessly suppresses the Socialist Party. Fighting breaks out in the streets of Vienna as police raid the party headquarters and bombard a Socialist housing unit.
- On February 21, Nicaraguan strongman Gen. Anastasio Somoza García invites guerrilla leader Gen. Augusto César Sandino to a peace conference and then has him murdered.
- On March 1, the Nanking National Relief Commission reports that sixty-five million Chinese in fourteen provinces are refugees due to civil wars, famine, banditry, droughts, and floods.
- On March 12, the Estonian military establishes Konstantin Päts as dictator.
- On March 20, the world's first practical radar tests are conducted by German naval scientist Rudolf Kuhnold in Kiel.
- On March 25, the Italian Fascist Grand Council proposes a slate of four hundred fascist candidates for parliament. The electorate approves of the slate by a vote of 10,045,477 to 15,201.
- On April 19, a prominent Belgium communist is assassinated and twenty other are injured. The violence signals the rise of the *Blue Shirt* movement.
- On April 30, a new Austrian constitution grants Chancellor Dollfuss near-dictatorial powers.
- On May 8, the Soviet Union establishes Biro-Bidgan, a Jewish state located in Siberia. It is half the size of Great Britain and has 50,000 inhabitants, 12,000 of whom are Jews.
- On May 15, following a military coup in Latvia, Karlis Ulmanis becomes dictator.
- On May 19, with the aid of Bulgarian ruler Boris III, fascists in that nation overthrow the constitutional government. Boris becomes dictator. On June 12, all political parties are abolished.
- On May 24, Tomás Masaryk is re-elected president of Czechoslovakia.
- On May 29, the United States accedes to the removal from the Cuban constitution of the Platt Amendment of 1902, which gave the United States the right to intervene in the internal affairs of the island.
- On June 30, prominent Nazis attempt to assassinate Chancellor Hitler. In response, in what becomes known as the Night of Long Knives, Hitler loyalists conduct a political purge of their own membership, executing seventy-seven people.
- On July 2, Gen. Lárzaro Cárdenas is elected president of Mexico. Mexican muralists Diego Rivera, José Clemente Orozco, and David Alfaro Siqueiros subsequently return to that country as Cárdenas begins a program of land reform and socialization of industry.
- On July 13, Nazi leader Heinrich Himmler is appointed head of German concentration camps.
- On July 25, Nazi leaders in Austria assassinate Chancellor Dollfuss in an attempt to overthrow the government.
- On July 30, following the collapse of the Nazi coup in Austria, Dollfuss's associate Kurt von Schuschnigg forms a new cabinet in Austria.
- On August 19, following the death of German president Paul Hindenburg on August 2, Hitler becomes president, preferring the title Führer (leader).
- On September 18, the Soviet Union joins the League of Nations.
- On September 27, effectively sabotaging French efforts to promote eastern European security arrangements, Poland announces that it will not allow Soviet troops to cross Poland to fulfill treaty obligations.
- In October, Mao Tse-tung's Chinese Communist troops begin their famous Long March, with Nationalist Chinese forces in pursuit. Mao leads his troops six thousand miles, over eighteen mountain ranges and six major rivers, saving the majority of his army.
- On October 6, Catalonia declares independence from Spain. The Spanish government will successfully suppress the independence movement.
- On October 9, King Alexander of Yugoslavia and French foreign minister Louis Barthou are assassinated in Marsailles by a Macedonian terrorist.
- On December 1, Sergey M. Kirov, one of Joseph Stalin's most trusted aides, is assassinated in Leningrad. Stalin uses the assassination as justification for a major purge of the Soviet Communist Party.
- On December 5, Italian and Ethiopian troops clash on the border between Ethiopia and Italian Somaliland.

- On December 14, Turkish women secure the right to vote and to sit in the national assembly.
- On December 29, Federico García Lorca's play *Yerma* premieres at the Teatro Español in Madrid.

1935

- Alfred Hitchcock's movie *The 39 Steps* is released.
- Afrikaans poet N. P. van Wyk Louw's *Alleenspraak* (Monologue) is published.
- Nazi propagandist Leni Riefenstahl's *Triumph of the Will,* a documentary of her party's Nuremberg rallies, is released.
- German radio bans jazz music of African American or Jewish origin.
- American Lincoln Ellsworth successfully flies twenty-three hundred miles across the Antarctic.
- On January 7, France and Italy announce diplomatic agreements regarding conflicting interests in Africa.
- On January 13, a plebiscite in the Saarland results in the return of that territory to Germany, effective March 1. Afterward, Jews, French and other anti-Nazis flee to neighboring France.
- On January 14, the Lower Zambezi railroad bridge is completed and is the world's longest until the completion of the Huey P. Long Bridge in Metairie, Louisiana, on December 10.
- From January 15 to January 17, Soviet Communists Grigory Zinovyev, Lev Kamenev, and others are tried for treason in connection with their alleged complicity in the murder of Sergey Kirov and are sent to prison for terms of five to ten years.
- On March 8, Hitler reveals the existence of a German air force and announces plans to expand the size and strength of German armed forces.
- On March 16, Germany formally denounces the disarmament clauses of the Treaty of Versailles. Hitler announces the reintroduction of universal military conscription.
- On March 19, the Soviet Union arrests and exiles 1,074 former members of the aristocracy and bourgeoisie.
- On March 24, Persia officially changes its name to Iran.
- From April 11 to April 14, French, British, and Italian representatives meet in the Italian resort city of Stresa to negotiate common responses to German rearmament.
- On April 17, the League of Nations formally condemns Germany's repudiation of the Treaty of Versailles.
- On April 23, Poland adopts a new, authoritarian constitution.
- On May 2, France and the Soviet Union conclude a pact of mutual military assistance.
- On May 16, the Soviet Union and Czechoslovakia conclude a pact of mutual military assistance.
- On May 18, Ethiopian Emperor Haile Selassie abolishes selfdom.
- On May 31, Emlyn Williams's play *Night Must Fall* premieres at the Duchess Theatre in London.
- On June 7, Stanley Baldwin replaces Ramsay MacDonald as British Prime Mnister.
- On June 12, Bolivia and Paraguay end a three-year war over the disputed Chaco region but do not sign a peace treaty until 1938.
- On June 15, T.S. Eliot's play *Murder in the Cathedral* premieres at the Canterbury Festival; on November 1 it opens at the Mercury Theatre in London.
- On June 18, an Anglo-German naval agreement is announced, allowing Germany to exceed limits on naval tonnage placed on it by the Treaty of Versailles, so long as German tonnage does not exceed 35 percent of the combined fleets of the British Commonwealth.
- From July 25 to August 20, at the meeting of the Third International in the Soviet Union, the Communist Party announces the strategy of creating Popular Front coalitions of liberals, communists, and other leftists to combat fascism.
- On August 2, the British Parliament approves the Government of India Act, radically restructuring the administration of British possessions in Asia.
- On August 30, Soviet coal miner Aleksey Grigorievich Stakhanov and his crew bring in a record tonnage of coal mined in a single night, becoming the symbol of Stalin's Stakhanov movement to increase industrial productivity.
- On September 15, the Nuremberg Laws, which deprive Jews of the rights of citizenship and forbids intermarriage between Gentiles and Jews, are decreed in Germany. Further, these laws authorize the Swastika as the national flag.
- On September 25, the Nazi government places the German Protestant churches under state control.
- On October 3, Italian troops invade Ethiopia.
- On November 3, radical, socialist, and communist parties in France unite to form an antifascist Popular Front coalition.
- On November 18, the League of Nations votes to impose economic sanctions on Italy because of its invasion of Ethiopia.
- On November 21, Jean Giraudoux's play *La Guerre de Troie n'aura pas lieu* (The Trojan War Will Not Take Place) premieres at the Théâtre de l'Athénée in Paris.
- On December 13, Tómas Masaryk resigns as president of Czechoslovakia and is succeeded by foreign minister Edvard Benes.

1936

- T.S. Eliot's *Collected Poems 1909–1935* is published.
- Max Ernst paints *La Ville Entière.*
- Aldous Huxley's novel *Eyeless in Gaza* is published.
- Robin Hyde's novel *Passport to Hell* is published.
- Piet Mondrian paints *Composition in Yellow and Black.*
- Meret Oppenheim produces her *Fur Breakfast,* a fur-covered teacup, saucer and spoon.
- Leni Riefenstahl's documentary movie *Olympia* is released.
- Georges Rouault paints *The Old King.*
- Simon Vestdijk's novel *Meer Visser's hellevaarb* (Mr. Visser's Descent Into Hell) is published.
- The Soviet Communist Party begins its Great Purge. By 1938, an estimated ten million people will have died.

- On January 9, Noël Coward's plays *The Astonished Heart* and *Red Peppers* are staged at the Phoenix Theatre in London.
- On January 30, President Franklin D. Roosevelt proposes an Inter-American Conference on Western Hemispheric Security.
- On February 4, Switzerland forbids National Socialists from politically organizing.
- On February 6, Lithuania abolishes all political parties except the fascist Nationalist Union.
- On February 14, Ramón María del Valle-Inclán's play *Los cuernos de don Friolera* (The Horns of Don Friolera) is staged at the Teatro de la Zarzuela in Madrid.
- On February 15, Hitler opens the annual auto show with the announcement that Germany has solved the problem of manufacturing synthetic rubber and gasoline.
- On February 16, a left-liberal Popular Front coalition wins a decisive victory over right-wing parties in Spanish elections.
- On February 26, prominent Japanese officials, including Keeper of the Privy Seal Saito Makoto and Finance Minister Takahashi Korekiyo, are assassinated in an uprising of young army officers.
- On February 27, the French Chamber of Deputies ratifies the Franco-Soviet Pact, a mutual-defense agreement.
- On March 7, battalions of German infantry move into the demilitarized zone of the Rhineland in violation of the Versailles and Locarno Treaties.
- On March 12, Great Britain, France, Belgium, and Italy denounce German militarization of the Rhineland.
- On April 1, Austria resumes military conscription.
- On April 30, Great Britain announces the construction of thirty-eight new warships.
- On May 5, Italian troops occupy Addis Ababa, completing their invasion of Ethiopia. In a June 30 address to the League of Nations, Ethiopian emperor Haile Selassie warns, "It is us today. It will be you tomorrow."
- On May 10, Manuel Azaña y Díaz is elected the new president of Spain.
- On May 24, in Belgian parliamentary elections, the Rexists, a fascist party led by Léon Degrelle, win twenty-one seats.
- On June 2, the government of Nicaragua is overthrown by Gen. Anastasio Somoza García, head of the National Guard, who installs himself as dictator.
- On June 5, in France, the first Popular Front government is formed by Socialist Party leader Léon Blum.
- On June 12, France establishes the forty-hour workweek.
- On July 11, Rome and Berlin conclude a secret agreement wherein Italy acquiesces to German ambitions in Austria.
- On July 18, Spanish military officers in Morocco rise up against the republican government of Spain, beginning the Spanish Civil War.
- On August 4, Greek premier Ioannis Metaxas declares himself dictator, proclaims martial law, and dissolves the parliament.
- From August 19 to August 23, in the Soviet Union, Grigory Zinovyev, Lev Kamenev, and sixteen others, who had plotted to assassinate Stalin, are once again put on trial by Stalinists, found guilty of treason, and executed.
- On September 10, Joseph Goebbels, German minister of propaganda, accuses Czechoslovakia of harboring Soviet air forces.
- On October 1, General Francisco Franco assumes command of the fascist rebels in Spain.
- On October 12, British fascist leader Oswald Mosley leads an anti-Jewish march in London.
- On October 19, the German government announces the beginning of the Four-Year Plan, a program to develop economic self-sufficiency in strategic materials.
- On October 25, Germany and Italy form the Rome-Berlin Axis.
- On October 27, Mrs. Wallis Warfield Simpson is granted a divorce from her husband on the grounds of infidelity.
- On November 18, Germany and Italy recognize Francisco Franco's new fascist government in Spain.
- On November 25, Germany and Japan sign the Anti-Comintern Pact, a security accord aimed at mutual protection from the Soviet Union.
- On December 10, King Edward VIII of Great Britain voluntarily abdicates the throne to marry an American-born divorcée, Wallis Warfield Simpson. The first British king to give up the crown of his own accord, Edward VIII is succeeded by his brother, George VI.

1937

- André Breton's Surrealist novel *L'Amour fou* (Mad Love) is published.
- Kawabata Yasunari's novel *Yukiguni* (The Snow Country) is published.
- Paul Klee paints *Revolutions of the Viaducts.*
- Arthur Koestler's *Spanish Testament,* a pro-Republican account of the Spanish Civil War, is published.
- René Magritte paints *The Pleasure Principle.*
- Joan Miró paints *Still Life With Old Shoe.*
- George Orwell's *The Road to Wigan Pier,* a study of the British unemployed is published.
- J.R.R. Tolkien's novel *The Hobbit* is published.
- Leon Trotsky's *The Revolution Betrayed,* an indictment of Stalinism, is published.
- The Nazis open their first exhibition of "degenerate art," mostly abstract works that they consider decadent.
- The Soviet Union establishes a research station near the North Pole.
- The Soviet Union opens the Moscow-Volga ship canal.
- Frozen foods are introduced in Great Britain.
- From January 23 to January 30, public show trials of communist leaders charged with treason in Moscow result in long prison terms or death sentences.

- On January 24, Bulgaria and Yugoslavia conclude a nonaggression pact.
- On January 28, the communists and nationalists in the Chinese civil war declare a truce to join in opposition to Japanese military and political pressure.
- On January 30, Hitler, while celebrating the fourth anniversary of Nazi rule, forbids Germans from accepting future Nobel Peace Prizes.
- On February 26, Christopher Isherwood and W.H. Auden's play *The Ascent of F6* opens at the Mercury Theatre in London.
- On March 25, Italy and Yugoslavia conclude a nonaggression pact.
- On April 26, German warplanes destroy the defenseless Basque town of Guernica. Pablo Picasso's 1937 painting *Guernica* is his outraged protest against this bombing and war in general.
- On May 28, following the retirement of Stanley Baldwin, Chancellor of the Exchequer Neville Chamberlain becomes British prime minister.
- On May 31, German warships bombard Almería, Spain.
- On June 12, Stalin's government executes Soviet military leaders who allegedly conspired with Germany and Japan.
- On June 17, Soviet fliers Valeri P. Chkalov, Georgi P. Baidukov, and Alexander V. Beliakov fly nonstop over the North Pole from Moscow to Vancouver.
- On June 19, the French Popular Front government of Léon Blum falls after failing to gain emergency fiscal powers. Radical socialist leader Camille Chautemps forms a new government.
- On July 7, the Japanese launch full-scale military operations against China.
- On July 8, the Peel Report, recommending the division of Palestine into Arab and Jewish states, is published in London. Parliament rejects the proposal.
- On July 9, Turkey signs a nonaggression pact with Iraq, Iran, and Afghanistan.
- On July 14, Russian aviator Mikhail Gromov and two companions fly nonstop over the North Pole from Moscow to Riverside, California, setting a new nonstop distance record.
- On July 16, the Nazis open a concentration camp for political prisoners at Buchenwald, near Weimar.
- On July 28, Peking falls to the Japanese.
- From August 8 to November 8, fierce fighting between Japanese and Chinese troops results in the Japanese occupation of Shanghai. Japan earns worldwide condemnation for its bombing of Chinese cities.
- On August 25, the Japanese navy begins a blockade of all but European possessions on the South China Sea coast.
- On August 27, Pope Pius XI recognizes the fascist government of Spain.
- On August 29, China and the Soviet Union conclude a nonaggression pact, allowing military aircraft sales to China.
- On September 8, a Pan-Arab Congress meeting at Bludan, Syria, rejects the Peel plan for the division of Palestine.
- On September 27, Italian Premier Mussolini arrives in Munich in a special bulletproof train to meet with Hitler. The next day, both dictators pledge world peace.
- From October 5 to October 6, the League of Nations and the United States formally condemn Japanese actions in China.
- On October 13, the German government promises not to violate Belgian sovereignty so long as Belgium abstains from military action against Germany.
- On November 6, Italy signs the Anti-Comintern Pact.
- On November 7, Mexico's National Revolutionary Party prepares a report of the number of Jews in Mexico, their citizenship status, and an estimate of their capital worth.
- On November 10, Brazilian president Getúlio Vargas proclaims a new constitution and assumes dictatorial powers, which he will exercise for the next fifteen years.
- On November 20, the Chinese capital is moved from Nanking to Chungking.
- On November 21, Dmitry Shostakovich's *Symphony No. 5* premieres to acclaim in Leningrad.
- On November 26, Robert Schumann's *Concerto for Violin and Orchestra in D minor,* written in 1853, is performed for the first time, at the Deutsches Opernhaus in Berlin.
- On November 28, naval forces loyal to Francisco Franco blockade Spain.
- On December 11, Italy withdraws from the League of Nations.
- On December 12, Japanese bombers attack American and British ships near Nanking, provoking a serious diplomatic confrontation.
- On December 13, after serious fighting, Nanking falls to the Japanese.
- On December 28, King Carol of Romania appoints fascist leader Octavian Goga prime minister. Goga immediately embarks on a program of anti-Semitic legislation.

1938

- Isak Dinesen's novel *Out of Africa* is published.
- Sergey Eisenstein's movie *Aleksandr Nevsky* is released.
- Daniel O. Fagunwa's novel *Ogboju Ode Iinn Igbo Irummale* (The Forest of Thousand Demons) is published.
- Alfred Hitchcock's movie *The Lady Vanishes* is released.
- George Orwell's *Homage to Catalonia,* about his experiences fighting the fascists in the Spanish Civil War, is published.
- Marcel Pagnol's movie *La Femme du boulanger* (The Baker's Wife) is released.
- Jean-Paul Sartre's novel *La Nausée* (Nausea) is published.
- Violence escalates between Jews and Arabs in British-controlled Palestine.
- Hitler declares that he will protect ethnic Germans living outside the Reich by military force if necessary.
- On January 18, the Soviet Union announces the end of the purges from the Communist Party.

- On February 4, British engineer John L. Baird demonstrates mechanically based high-definition color television in London.
- On February 10, King Carol of Romania dismisses Prime Minister Octavian Goga, suspends the constitution, and abolishes all political parties.
- On February 12, at Berchtesgaden, Adolf Hitler demands that Austrian Chancellor Kurt Schuschnigg accede to increased participation of Austrian Nazis in the Austrian government or face German military occupation.
- On February 14, Hitler shakes up his diplomatic corps and army with the announcement of numerous resignations *for reasons of health.*
- On February 20, British foreign secretary Anthony Eden resigns his post in protest over Britain's negotiations with Italy over spheres of influence in the Mediterranean. He is succeeded by Edward F.L. Wood, Baron Irwin (later Earl of Halifax).
- From March 2 to March 15, Soviet authorities try, convict, and execute Bolshevik leaders Nikolay Bukharin, Aleksey Rykov, and other enemies of Stalin.
- On March 9, responding to increasing political turmoil, Chancellor Kurt Schuschnigg announces a plebiscite on Austrian independence to be held the following Sunday; only "Yes" ballots are to be provided.
- On March 10, Camille Chautemp's government in France collapses; Edouard Daladier reorganizes the French cabinet.
- On March 11, Germany demands postponement of the Austrian independence plebiscite and the resignation of Chancellor Schuschnigg.
- On March 12, German troops cross the Austrian border to enforce the German *Anschluss* of Austria. Austrian Nazi Arthur Seyss-Inquart becomes chancellor.
- On March 14, Hitler arrives in Vienna to take formal possession of Austria.
- On March 18, the Mexican government nationalizes $450 million worth of American and British oil properties.
- On March 28, the Japanese install a puppet government in occupied areas of China.
- On April 10, a rigged plebiscite in Austria results in overwhelming approval of the German *Anschluss.*
- On April 24, Sudeten German leader Konrad Henlein issues his Karlsbad program, demanding complete autonomy for German Czechs.
- From May 3 to May 9, Hitler pays a state visit to Rome.
- On May 26, the Volkswagen (people's car) factory is dedicated in Wolfsburg, Germany. The low-cost "Beetle" automobile is designed by engineer Ferdinand Porsche on commission from Hitler. Despite the dedication of the car plant, mass production of the Volkswagen will not occur for ten years.
- From July 11 to August 10, Soviet and Japanese troops clash along the border between Siberia and China.
- On July 21, the ballet *St. Francis,* with choreography by Léonide Massine and music by Paul Hindemith, is performed at Drury Lane Theatre in London.
- On August 3, Italy passes laws governing the conduct of the Italian Jews.
- On August 10, William Butler Yeats's play *Purgatory* premieres at the Abbey Theatre in Dublin.
- On September 7, France calls up its military reservists.
- On September 15, British Prime Minister Neville Chamberlain flies to Berchtesgaden to negotiate a resolution of the Czech crisis with Hitler.
- On September 22, Prime Minister Chamberlain flies to the German city of Godesberg for further negotiations with Hitler over the Czech crisis.
- On September 24, as British and French peace negotiations with the Germans deadlock, Czechoslovakia mobilizes its armed forces for war with Germany.
- On September 27, in response to the Czech crisis, Britain and France mobilize their armed forces.
- On September 29, representatives of Great Britain, France, Italy, and Germany meet in Munich in a last-ditch effort to avert war over Czechoslovakia.
- On October 1, the Munich Conference ends with an agreement that cedes the Sudetenland to Germany, leaving the rest of Czechoslovakia outside the German Reich.
- On October 4, following socialist and communist objections to the Munich Pact, the French Popular Front collapses. The Daladier government turns right in search of political support.
- On October 5, Edvard Benes resigns as president of Czechoslovakia.
- From October 6 to October 8, Slovakia and Ruthenia are separated from Czechoslovakia as autonomous states.
- On October 18, British troops retake the old city of Jerusalem, which is occupied by Arab extremists.
- On October 21, following a ruthless bombing campaign, Japanese troops occupy Canton.
- On November 1, British Prime Minister Chamberlain reaffirms his policy of German appeasement.
- On November 9, following the assassination of a Nazi official by a German-born Polish Jew, Nazis conduct the worst pogrom in German history, destroying Jewish homes, synagogues, and shops and sending twenty thousand to thirty thousand Jews to concentration camps. It will become known as the Kristallnacht (Crystal Night).
- On November 10, the founder of the Turkish republic, Kemal Atatürk, dies from cirrhosis of the liver. He is succeeded by Ismet Inönü.
- On November 12, the German government levies a fine of one billion marks on Jews. The fines are to aid the poor, who supposedly have suffered economic losses at the hands of the Jews.
- On November 12, the Daladier government of France modifies the forty-hour workweek, provoking widespread labor unrest.
- On November 17, Great Britain, Canada, and the United States sign a trade pact.
- On November 26, Poland and Russia sign a nonaggression pact.

- On December 1, Great Britain begins voluntary registration for the draft.
- On December 6, Germany and France sign a diplomatic accord guaranteeing the inviolability of existing frontiers.
- On December 10, Germany and Romania sign an economic agreement providing Germany access to Romanian oil.
- On December 18, German physicists led by Otto Hahn produce the first nuclear fission of uranium.
- On December 24, twenty-one American republics adopt the Declaration of Lima, an affirmation of their intention to resist attacks on their sovereignty from outside the Western Hemisphere.

1939

- Marcel Carné's movie *Le Jour se lève* (Daybreak) is released.
- Aimé Césaire's long anticolonial poem *Cahier de retour au pays natal* (Return to My Native Land) is published in the French journal *Volontés.*
- C. S. Forester's novel *Captain Horatio Hornblower* is published.
- James Joyce's novel *Finnegans Wake* is published.
- Ernst Jünger's allegorical anti-Nazi novel *Auf den Marmorklippen* (On the Marble Cliffs) is published.
- Richard Llewellyn's novel *How Green Was My Valley* is published.
- Jean Renoir's movie *La Règle du jeu* (The Rules of the Game) is released.
- Italian political theorist Bruno Rizzi's *The Bureaucratization of the World,* a study of authoritarianism, is published.
- Jan Struther's novel *Mrs. Miniver* is published.
- César Vallejo's *Poemas humanos* (Human Poems) are published.
- On January 14, Norway claims approximately one million square miles of territory in Antarctica.
- On January 26, Franco's troops take Barcelona.
- On February 10, Pope Pius XI dies.
- On February 24, Hungary joins the Anti-Comintern pact.
- On February 27, Great Britain and France recognize Francisco Franco's regime as the government of Spain.
- On March 2, Papal diplomat Eugenio Pacelli becomes Pope Pius XII.
- On March 15, German troops occupy Bohemia and Moravia in violation of the 1938 Munich Pact. Hungary occupies Carpatho-Ukraine. Czechoslovakia ceases to exist.
- On March 18, Great Britain and France send envoys to the Soviet Union, Poland, Romania, Yugoslavia, Greece, and Turkey in an effort to form a military coalition against Germany.
- On March 23, Arabs and Jews in Palestine reject a British plan to gradually turn Palestine over to both groups.
- On March 28, Madrid and Valencia surrender to the fascists, ending the Spanish Civil War. Estimates place the number of dead at close to one million people.
- On March 31, Great Britain and France pledge to protect Poland from German territorial ambitions.
- On April 7, Spain joins Germany, Italy, and Japan in the Anti-Comintern Pact.
- On April 7, Italy invades Albania.
- On April 11, Hungary withdraws from the League of Nations.
- On April 13, Britain and France provide diplomatic guarantees of independence to Greece and Romania.
- On April 17, Stalin authorizes simultaneous Soviet diplomatic negotiations to form military alliances with either Great Britain and France or Germany.
- On April 27, the British government begins universal military conscription.
- On April 28, in an address to the Reichstag, Hitler denounces the 1935 Anglo-German naval agreement and the 1934 German nonaggression pact with Poland.
- On May 3, Hungary passes a series of drastic anti-Semitic laws.
- On May 17, a British white paper repudiates the Balfour Declaration of 1917 and limits Jewish immigration to Palestine.
- On May 20, following a victory parade in Madrid, German and Italian troops begin to withdraw from Spain.
- On May 22, Germany and Italy announce a military alliance they call the "Pact of Steel."
- On May 23, the SS *St. Louis* leaves Hamburg with 937 Jewish refugees. After its passengers are denied entry into Cuba and the United States, the ship will return to Hamburg, and most of those aboard will die in the Holocaust.
- From June 8 to June 11, King George and Queen Elizabeth of Great Britain visit the United States.
- On June 27, for the first time, Dubliners elect a woman mayor, Mrs. Tom Clarke. Her husband was killed by the British during the 1916 Republican Easter Uprising.
- On July 25, Britain and France dispatch envoys to Moscow to pursue negotiations for a military alliance with the Soviet Union.
- On July 26, the United States notifies Japan that it intends to abrogate the commercial agreement of 1911, opening the way to American trade restrictions.
- On August 23, the Soviet Union and Nazi Germany agree to two treaties: one to maintain military neutrality toward one another; the other to divide Poland and the Baltic states following a German attack on Poland in the autumn. The Anti-Comintern Pact is rendered null and void.
- On August 24, the Luftwaffe's new turbojet aircraft is tested at Rostock-Marienehe.
- On September 1, following a fabricated border clash, German troops invade Poland.
- On September 3, Great Britain and France declare war on Germany, beginning World War II.
- On September 17, Soviet troops invade Poland.

- On September 21, Romanian premier Armand Calinescu is assassinated by the fascist Iron Guard.
- From September 23 to October 3, representatives of Western Hemisphere nations meet in Panama to plan a Pan-American response to the European war.
- On September 27, Poland surrenders to Germany.
- On September 28, Germany and the Soviet Union partition Poland.
- On November 30, the Soviet Union invades Finland.

1

THE ARTS

JAMES N. CRAFT AND LORI HALL

Entries are arranged in chronological order by date of primary source. For entries with one primary source, the entry title is the same as the primary source title. Entries with more than one primary source have an overall entry title, followed by the titles of the primary sources.

Important Events in the Arts, 1930–1939

1930

- Edna Ferber's *Cimarron* is the year's best seller.
- Sinclair Lewis is the first American to win the Nobel Prize for literature.
- Americans go to the movies in unprecedented numbers, as the Vitascope widens screens and the new "talkies" provide an added dimension to the viewing experience.
- The "Golden Age" of radio begins.
- Grant Wood's painting *American Gothic,* in which he portrays his sister and his dentist as farmers, helps launch the American Regionalism style of painting. Other regionalist painters include John Curry, Thomas Hart Benton, Georgia O'Keefe, and Edward Hopper.
- Charles Sheeler, archetypal Precisionist, paints *American Landscape.*
- On January 7, *Children of Darkness,* by Edwin Justus Mayer, opens at New York's Biltmore Theater.
- On January 14, Bobby Clark and Red Nichols' band—including Benny Goodman, Glenn Miller, Jimmy Dorsey, and Jack Teagarden—perform songs by George and Ira Gershwin, such as "I've Got a Crush on You," in *Strike Up the Band,* which opens at New York's Times Square Theater. The musical is based on the book by George S. Kaufman.
- On February 18, *Simple Simon,* with music by Richard Rodgers and lyrics by Lorenz Hart, opens at New York's Ziegfeld Theater. Songs include "Ten Cents a Dance" and "I Still Believe in You."
- On February 21, Marc Connelly's play *Green Pastures,* an adaptation of a 1928 collection of tales by Roark Bradford depicting God and Heaven as envisioned by an African American country preacher, opens at New York's Mansfield Theater and runs for 640 performances, winning the Pulitzer Prize.
- On March 28, Walter Piston's *Suite for Orchestra* is first performed at Boston's Symphony Hall.
- On April 14, Philip Barry's *Hotel Universe,* starring Ruth Ford, Glenn Anders, Earle Larimore, and Morris Carnovsky, opens at New York's Martin Beck Theater.
- On May 3, Ogden Nash publishes his poem "Spring Comes to Murray Hill" in *The New Yorker.* Shortly thereafter, he joins the magazine's staff and becomes famous for his light verse.
- On September 24, the play *Once in a Lifetime,* by George S. Kaufman and Moss Hart and starring Spring Byington, opens at New York's Music Box Theater and runs for 401 performances.
- On October 14, *Girl Crazy,* starring Ethel Merman, with music by George Gershwin and lyrics by Walter Donaldson and Ira Gershwin, opens at New York's Alvin Theater and runs for 272 performances. Songs include "I Got Rhythm," "Embraceable You," and "Little White Lies."
- On October 16, *The Garrick Gaieties,* starring Sterling Holloway, Rosalind Russell, and Imogene Coca, opens at New York's Guild Theater. Songs include "I'm Only Human After All," by Vernon Duke, with lyrics by E.Y. Harburg and Ira Gershwin.
- On October 22, Ethel Waters and Cecil Mack's Choir perform songs such as Eubie Blake's "Memories of You" in *Lew Leslie's Blackbirds,* which opens at New York's Royale Theater.
- On November 13, W.A. Drake's play adaptation of the Vicki Baum novel *Grand Hotel,* starring Henry Hull and Sam Jaffe, opens at New York's National Theater and runs for 459 performances.
- On November 18, Bob Hope, Marilyn Miller, Eddie Foy, and Fred and Adele Astaire star in the musical *Smiles,* which opens at New York's Ziegfeld Theater.
- On December 8, *The New Yorkers,* starring Hope Williams, Ann Pennington, Jimmy Durante, Lew Clayton, and Eddie Jackson, and with music and lyrics by Cole Porter, opens at New York's Broadway Theater. Songs include "Love for Sale."

MOVIES: *Abraham Lincoln,* directed by D.W. Griffith and starring Walter Huston and Una Merkel; *All Quiet on the Western Front,* directed by Lewis Milestone and starring Lew Ayres; *Anna Christie,* directed by Clarence Brown and starring Greta Garbo; *The Big House,* directed by George Hill and starring Wallace Beery; *The Big Trail,* directed by Raoul Walsh and starring John Wayne (in his first role); *The Dawn Patrol,* directed by Howard Hawks and starring Richard Barthelmess and Douglas Fairbanks Jr.; *Hell's Angels,* directed by Howard Hughes and starring Ben Lyon and Jean Harlow; *Lightnin',* directed by Henry King and starring Will Rogers, Louise Dresser, and Joel McCrea; *Little Caesar,* directed by Mervyn LeRoy and starring Edward G. Robinson; *The Royal Family of Broadway,* directed by George Cukor and Cyril Gardner and starring Frederic March and Ina Claire; *Tom Sawyer,* directed by John Cromwell and starring Jackie Coogan and Mitzie Green.

FICTION: Max Brand, *Destry Rides Again*; Pearl Buck, *East Wind, West Wind*; Edward Dahlberg, *Bottom Dogs*; John Dos Passos, *The Forty-Second Parallel*; William Faulkner, *As I Lay Dying*; Edna Ferber, *Cimarron*; Michael Gold, *Jews Without Money*; Dashiell Hammett, *The Maltese Falcon*; Oliver La Farge, *Laughing Boy*; Katherine Anne Porter, *Flowering Judas.*

POPULAR SONGS: "Beyond the Blue Horizon," by Richard A. Whiting and W. Franke Harling, lyrics by Leo Robin; "Georgia on My Mind," by Hoagy Carmichael, lyrics by Stuart Gorrell; "It Happened in Monterey," by Mabel Wayne, lyrics by Billy Rose; "My Baby Just Cares for

Me," by Gus Kahn and Walter Donaldson; "Sing You Sinners," by W. Franke Harling, lyrics by Sam Coslow; "Three Little Words," by Harry Ruby, lyrics by Bert Kalmar.

1931

- Pearl Buck's *The Good Earth* and Ellery Queen's *The Dutch Shoe Mystery* are the year's best sellers.
- U.S. movie theaters begin showing double features to increase business. Many unemployed workers spend their afternoons at the movies.
- The Whitney Museum of American Art is founded by railroad heiress and sculptor Gertrude Vanderbilt Whitney.
- On January 26, *Green Grow the Lilacs,* by Lynn Riggs and starring Helen Westley, Lee Strasberg, and Franchot Tone, opens at New York's Guild Theater.
- On March 3, Congress votes to designate "The Star Spangled Banner" the national anthem.
- On April 3, in a concert celebrating the Boston Symphony's fiftieth anniversary, Paul Hindemith's *Concert Music for String Orchestra and Brass Instruments* is first performed at Symphony Hall.
- On May 1, Kathryn Elizabeth "Kate" Smith, who has played comic fat-girl roles on Broadway and performs in a singing role at New York's Palace Theater, makes her radio debut singing "When the Moon Comes over the Mountain."
- On May 19, *Billy Rose's Crazy Quilt,* starring Rose's wife, Fanny Brice, with music by Harry Warren and lyrics by Rose and Mort Dixon, opens at New York's Forty-Fourth Street Theater.
- On June 3, Fred and Adele Astaire make their final appearance together, on the first revolving stage to be used in a musical, in *The Band Wagon,* which opens at the New Amsterdam Theater.
- On July 1, *The Ziegfeld Follies,* starring Helen Morgan, Ruth Etting, and Harry Richman, with music by Walter Donaldson, Dave Stamper, and others, and lyrics by E.Y. Harburg and others, opens at New York's Ziegfeld Theater.
- On July 27, naked chorus girls are a part of the lineup for *Earl Carroll's Vanities,* which opens at the new 3,000-seat Earl Carroll Theater on Seventh Avenue at Fiftieth Street in New York City. In 1932, the show is modified and moved to the Broadway Theater, and stars Milton Berle and Helen Broderick.
- On October 5, *The House of Connelly,* by Paul Green and starring Stella Adler, Franchot Tone, Clifford Odets, and Rose McClendon, opens at New York's Martin Beck Theater.
- On October 13, *Everybody's Welcome,* starring Tommy and Jimmy Dorsey, Ann Pennington, and Harriet Lake (Georgia Sothern), opens at New York's Shubert Theater. Songs include Herman Hupfield's "As Time Goes By."
- On October 26, Eugene O'Neill's *Mourning Becomes Electra,* starring Alla Nazimova and Alice Brady, opens at New York's Guild Theater, where it runs for 150 performances.
- On November 22, Ferde Grofe's *Grand Canyon Suite* is first performed at Chicago's Studebaker Hall in a concert by Paul Whitman and His Orchestra.
- On December 26, with music by George Gershwin and lyrics by Ira Gershwin, *Of Thee I Sing,* starring Victor Moore and William Gaxton, opens at New York's Music Box Theater and runs for 441 performances, winning the 1932 Pulitzer Prize. Songs include "Love Is Sweeping the Country" and the title song.

MOVIES: *An American Tragedy,* directed by Josef von Sternberg and starring Sylvia Sidney, Phillips Holmes, and Frances Dee; *City Lights,* directed by and starring Charlie Chaplin; *Dishonored,* directed by Josef von Sternberg and starring Marlene Dietrich; *Dracula,* directed by Tod Browning and starring Bela Lugosi; *Frankenstein,* directed by James Whale and starring Boris Karloff; *Monkey Business,* directed by Norman Z. McLeod and starring the Marx Brothers; *Public Enemy,* directed by William Wellman and starring James Cagney, Jean Harlow, and Mae Clarke; *Scarface,* directed by Howard Hawks and starring Paul Muni and Ann Dvorak; *Skippy,* directed by Norman Taurog and starring Jackie Cooper; *Street Scene,* directed by King Vidor and starring Sylvia Sidney and William Collier Jr.; *Svengali,* directed by Archie Mayo and starring John Barrymore.

FICTION: Pearl Buck, *The Good Earth*; Willa Cather, *Shadows on the Rock*; Louis Colman, *Lumber*; James Gould Cozzens, *S.S. San Pedro*; Theodore Dreiser, *Newspaper Days*; E.E. Cummings, *ViVa*; William Faulkner, *Sanctuary*; Dashiell Hammett, *The Glass Key*; Henry Miller, *Tropic of Cancer*; Nathanael West, *The Dream Life of Balso Snell*; Edmund Wilson, *Axel's Castle.*

POPULAR SONGS: "All of Me," by Seymour Simons and Gerald Marks; "Dream a Little Dream of Me," by Fabian Andre and Wilbur Schwandt, lyrics by Gus Kahn; "Heartaches," by Al Hoffman, lyrics by John Klenner; "I Don't Know Why (I Just Do)," by Fred E. Ahlert, lyrics by Roy Turk; "I Love a Parade," by Harold Arlen, lyrics by Ted Koehler; "I Surrender, Dear," by Harry Barris, lyrics by Gordon Clifford; "(I'll Be Glad When You're Dead) You Rascal You," by Sam Theard; "Lazy River," by Hoagy Carmichael and Sidney Arodin; "Love Letters in the Sand," by J. Fred Coots, lyrics by Nick and Charles Kenny; "Mood Indigo," by Duke Ellington, lyrics by Albany "Barney" Bigard and Irving Mills; "Out of Nowhere," by Edward Heyman and John Green; "Sweet and Lovely," by Gus Arnheim, Harry Tobias, and Jules Lemare; "When It's Sleepy Time Down South," by Leon Rene, Otis Rene, and Clarence Muse; "When I Take My Sugar to Tea," by Sammy Fain, lyrics by Irving Kahal and Pierre Norman Connor; "Where the Blue of the Night (Meets the Gold of the Day)," by Fred E. Ahlert, lyrics by Roy Turk, performed by Bing Crosby.

1932

- Ellery Queen's *The Egyptian Cross Mystery* is the year's best seller.
- Sculptor Joseph Cornell exhibits his first boxes containing found objects, in New York City.
- *Death in the Afternoon,* Ernest Hemingway's extended essay on bullfighting, is published.
- Painter Ben Shahn produces *Sacco and Vanzetti,* the first of twenty-three gouaches inspired by the 1927 execution.

- Polaroid film, the first synthetic light-polarizing film, is invented by Harvard College dropout Edwin Herbert Land.
- Sculptor and painter Alexander Calder's motorized and hand-cranked "stabiles" are exhibited in Paris.
- Washington's Folger Library opens. Its vast William Shakespeare collection is funded by late Standard Oil chairman Henry Clay Folger.
- In February, Weston Electrical Instruments commercially introduces the Photronic Photoelectric Cell, the first exposure meter for cameras, developed by William Nelson Goodwin Jr.
- On April 4, George Bernard Shaw's *Too True to Be Good,* starring Beatrice G. Lilly, Hope Williams, and Claude Rains, opens at New York's Guild Theater.
- On April 30, Walter Piston's *Suite for Flute and Piano* premieres at the first Festival of Contemporary Music, held at the Yaddo artist colony, outside Saratoga Springs, New York.
- In July, *River Rouge Plant* is painted by Precisionist and photographer Charles Sheeler.
- On October 22, *Dinner at Eight,* by George S. Kaufman and Edna Ferber, and starring Constance Collier, opens at New York's Music Box Theater and runs for 232 performances. The next year, the play is made into a movie, directed by George Cukor and starring John Barrymore and Jean Harlow.
- On November 8, *Music in the Air,* starring Al Shean and Walter Slezak, with music by Jerome Kern and lyrics by Oscar Hammerstein II, opens at New York's Alvin Theater.
- On November 29, *Gay Divorce,* starring Fred Astaire and Claire Luce, and featuring music and lyrics by Cole Porter, opens at New York's Ethel Barrymore Theater and runs for 248 performances.
- On December 12, *Biography,* by S.N. Behrman and starring Earle Larimore and Ina Claire, opens at New York's Guild Theater and runs for 283 performances.
- On December 27, Radio City Music Hall opens in New York City's Rockefeller Center.
- On December 29, composer Roy Harris's *From the Gayety and Sadness of the American Scene* is first performed in Los Angeles.

MOVIES: *The Big Broadcast,* directed by Frank Tuttle and starring Kate Smith, George Burns, Gracie Allen, Cab Calloway, Bing Crosby, the Mills Brothers, and the Boswell Sisters; *A Bill of Divorcement,* directed by George Cukor and starring John Barrymore and Katharine Hepburn; *Blonde Venus,* directed by Josef von Sternberg and starring Marlene Dietrich, Herbert Marshall, and Cary Grant; *A Farewell to Arms,* directed by Frank Borzage and starring Cary Grant, Helen Hayes, and Adolphe Menjou; *Grand Hotel,* directed by Edmund Goulding and starring Greta Garbo, Joan Crawford, John and Lionel Barrymore, Lewis Stone, Wallace Beery, and Jean Hersholt; *Horse Feathers,* directed by Norman Z. McLeod and starring the Marx Brothers; *I Am a Fugitive from a Chain Gang,* directed by Mervyn LeRoy and starring Paul Muni; *Million Dollar Legs,* directed by Edward Cline and starring W.C. Fields and Jack Oakie; *The Mummy,* directed by Karl Freund and starring Boris Karloff; *Trouble in Paradise,* directed by Ernst Lubitsch and starring Miriam Hopkins, Kay Francis, and Herbert Marshall.

FICTION: Sherwood Anderson, *Beyond Desire*; Fielding Burke, *Call Home the Heart*; Erskine Caldwell, *Tobacco Road*; Edward Dahlberg, *From Flushing to Calvary*; John Dos Passos, *1919*; James T. Farrell, *Young Lonigan: A Boyhood in Chicago Streets*; William Faulkner, *Light in August;* Erle Stanley Gardner, *The Case of the Velvet Claws* (first Perry Mason detective novel); Grace Lumpkin, *To Make My Bread*; Laura Ingalls Wilder, *Little House in the Big Woods.*

POPULAR SONGS: "How Deep Is the Ocean?" by Irving Berlin; "I'm Gettin' Sentimental over You," by George Bassman, lyrics by Ned Washington; "(I Don't Stand) A Ghost of a Chance (with You)," by Victor Young, lyrics by Bing Crosby and Ned Washington; "(I'd Love to Spend) One Hour with You," by Richard A. Whiting, lyrics by Leo Robin; "It Don't Mean a Thing (If It Ain't Got That Swing)," by Duke Ellington, lyrics by Irving Mills; "I Wanna Be Loved," by John Green, lyrics by Billy Rose and Edward Heyman; "Minnie the Moocher," by Cab Calloway, lyrics by Irving Mills and Clarence Gaskill; "Say It Isn't So," by Irving Berlin; "Shuffle Off to Buffalo," by Al Dubin and Harry Warren; "That Silver Haired Daddy of Mine," by Gene Autry and Jimmy Long; "Willow Weep for Me," by Ann Ronell.

1933

- Hervey Allen's *Anthony Adverse* and Erle Stanley Gardner's *The Case of the Sulky Girl* are the year's best sellers.
- Justice John M. Woolsey of the U.S. District Court in New York rules that James Joyce's *Ulysses,* previously banned for reasons of obscenity, is acceptable for publication in the United States.
- Diego Rivera produces the mural *Man at the Crossroads,* which is destroyed because it portrays Russian Communist leader Vladimir Ilyich Lenin, for New York's Radio City Music Hall.
- Darryl Zanuck of Warner Bros. and other Hollywood executives organize 20th Century Pictures.
- An animated feature by Walt Disney, *The Three Little Pigs,* with songs such as "Who's Afraid of the Big Bad Wolf," by Frank E. Churchill, captures the imagination of children and adults.
- On January 24, Noel Coward's *Design for Living,* starring Coward, Alfred Lunt, and Lynn Fontanne, opens at New York's Ethel Barrymore Theater and runs for 135 performances. That year the play is made into a film directed by Ernst Lubitsch and stars Gary Cooper, Frederic March, and Miriam Hopkins.
- On May 27, to celebrate the Century of Progress, fan dancer Sally Rand appears at the Chicago World's Fair, attracting thousands.
- On June 6, Richard Hollingshead opens the first drive-in movie theater in Camden, New Jersey. Admission is twenty-five cents per car and twenty-five cents per person.
- On August 30, Samuel Barber's *School for Scandal Overture* is first performed at Philadelphia's Robin Hood Dell.
- On September 26, the Group Theatre production of Sidney Kingsley's *Men in White,* starring Morris Carnovsky,

Luther Adler, and Elia Kazan, opens at New York's Broadhurst Theater, where it runs for 367 performances.

- On September 30, Based on the book by Irving Berlin and Moss Hart, the musical *As Thousands Cheer,* with music and lyrics by Berlin, Edward Heyman, and Richard Myers, opens at New York's Music Box Theater on Broadway. The show, starring Marilyn Miller, Clifton Webb, and Ethel Waters, runs for four hundred performances.
- On October 2, Eugene O'Neill's only comedy, *Ah, Wilderness,* opens at New York's Guild Theater and stars George M. Cohan, William Post Jr., Elisha Cook Jr., and Gene Lockhart. The play runs for 289 performances.
- On October 24, *Mulatto,* by Langston Hughes, opens at New York's Vanderbilt Theater and stars Rose McClendon.
- On November 18, Ray Middleton, George Murphy, Bob Hope, and Fay Templeton star in *Roberta,* which opens at New York's New Ambassador Theater. With music by Jerome Kern and lyrics by Otto Harbach, songs include "Smoke Gets in Your Eyes" and "The Touch of Your Hand."
- On December 4, Jack Kirkland's adaptation of Erskine Caldwell's 1933 novel *Tobacco Road,* starring Henry Hull, opens at New York's Masque Theater and runs for 3,182 performances.

MOVIES: *42nd Street,* directed by Lloyd Bacon and starring Warner Baxter, Bebe Daniels, and Dick Powell; *Counsellor-at-Law,* directed by William Wyler and starring John Barrymore and Bebe Daniels; *Duck Soup,* directed by Leo McCarey and starring the Marx Brothers; *Flying Down to Rio,* directed by Thornton Freeland and starring Dolores Del Rio, Ginger Rogers, and Fred Astaire; *Footlight Parade,* directed by Lloyd Bacon and starring James Cagney and Joan Blondell; *Gold Diggers of 1933,* directed by Mervyn LeRoy and starring Ginger Rogers, Joan Blondell, and Dick Powell, with songs including "We're in the Money," by Al Dubin and Harry Warren; *International House,* directed by A. Edward Sutherland and starring W.C. Fields, George Burns, and Gracie Allen; *King Kong,* directed by Ernest Schoedsack and starring Fay Wray and Bruce Cabot; *Little Women,* directed by George Cukor and starring Katharine Hepburn and Joan Bennett; *Man's Castle,* directed by Frank Borzage and starring Spencer Tracy and Loretta Young; *Penthouse,* directed by W.S. Van Dyke and starring Warner Baxter and Myrna Loy; *Queen Christina,* directed by Rouben Mamoulian and starring Greta Garbo and John Gilbert; *She Done Him Wrong,* directed by Lowell Sherman and starring Cary Grant and Mae West (as Diamond Lil, who speaks the line "Come up and see me sometime"); *Sons of the Desert,* directed by William A. Seiter and starring Laurel and Hardy.

FICTION: Erskine Caldwell, *God's Little Acre*; Jack Conroy, *The Disinherited*; James Gould Cozzens, *The Last Adam*; William Faulkner, *A Green Bough*; Josephine Herbst, *Pity Is Not Enough*; Meyer Levin, *The New Bridge*; Gertrude Stein, *The Autobiography of Alice B. Toklas*; Nathanael West, *Miss Lonelyhearts.*

POPULAR SONGS: "Did You Ever See a Dream Walking?" by Harry Revel and Mack Gordon; "Everything I Have Is Yours," by Burton Lane, lyrics by Harold Adamson; "I Like Mountain Music," by Frank Weldon, lyrics by James Cavanaugh; "Lazybones," by Hoagy Carmichael, lyrics by Johnny Mercer; "Let's Fall in Love," by Harold Arlen, lyrics by Ted Koehler; "Love Is the Sweetest Thing," by Ray Noble; "It's only a Paper Moon," by Harold Arlen, lyrics by E.Y. Harburg and Billy Rose; "Sophisticated Lady," by Duke Ellington, lyrics by Irving Mills and Mitchell Parish; "Stormy Weather," by Harold Arlen, lyrics by Ted Koehler.

1934

- *The Case of the Curious Bride,* by Erle Stanley Gardner, and *The Chinese Orange Mystery,* by Ellery Queen, are the year's best sellers.
- The Berkshire Music Festival has its first season in Lenox, Massachusetts, on the 210-acre Tappan family estate, which accommodates 14,000 concert goers.
- Thomas Hart Benton produces several paintings, including *Lord, Heal the Child, Homestead, Ploughing It Under,* and *Going Home.*
- Chicago clock maker Laurens Hammond patents the Hammond organ, the world's first pipeless organ—an invention that leads to a whole generation of electrically amplified instruments.
- Fritz Lang, director of the acclaimed films *Metropolis* (1926) and *M* (1931), continues his career in the United States after fleeing Germany to avoid collaboration with the Nazi government.
- On January 4, *The New Ziegfeld Follies,* starring Fanny Brice, Jane Froman, Vilma and Buddy Ebsen, and Eugene and Willie Howard, opens at New York's Winter Garden Theater and runs for 182 performances.
- On January 18, Eugene O'Neill's *Days Without End,* starring Earle Larimore, Stanley Ridges, and Ilka Chase, premieres at Henry Miller's Theater in New York City and runs for only fifty-seven performances.
- On January 26, Harlem's Apollo Theater, opened by Leo Brecher and Frank Schiffman, admits African American patrons when Ella Fitgerald makes her Amateur Night debut. By booking performers like blues singer Bessie Smith, orchestra leader Count Basie, and singer Billie Holiday, the Apollo becomes the leading showcase for African American performers.
- On January 26, *Symphony-1933* by Roy Harris is first performed at Boston's Symphony Hall.
- On February 20, Gertrude Stein's opera, *Four Saints in Three Acts,* with music by Virgil Thomson, opens at New York's Forty-fourth Street Theater, adding to Stein's popularity with her use of bewildering lines.
- On July 1, the Hays Office, created by the U.S. film industry's Motion Picture Producers and Distributors of America (MPPDA), hires former Postmaster General Will H. Hays to administer an industry-wide production code that will curtail on-screen displays of sexuality.
- On August 13, Al Capp's *Li'l Abner* debuts in eight newspapers. Eventually, it runs in 500 and becomes the basis of a Broadway play and a Hollywood movie.
- On November 7, Sergei Rachmaninoff's *Rhapsody on a Theme of Paganini* written for piano and orchestra is first performed in Baltimore in a concert by the Philadelphia Orchestra.

- On November 20, *The Children's Hour,* by Lillian Hellman, premieres at Maxine Elliott's Theater in New York City, disturbing audiences with its references to a lesbian relationship.
- On November 21, *Anything Goes,* by Guy Bolton, P.G. Wodehouse, Howard Lindsay, and Russel Crouse, with music and lyrics by Cole Porter, and starring William Gaxton, Ethel Merman, and Victor Moore, opens at New York's Alvin Theater and runs for 420 performances. Songs include "The Gypsy in Me" and "I Get a Kick Out of You."
- On November 24, S. N. Behrman protests Nazi treatment of German Jews in *Rain from Heaven,* which opens at New York's Golden Theater.
- On December 25, Samson Raphaelson's *Accent on Youth,* starring Constance Cummings, premieres at New York's Plymouth Theater.

MOVIES: *Babes in Toyland,* directed by Gus Meins and Charles R. Rogers and starring Laurel and Hardy; *Bright Eyes,* musical directed by David Butler and starring Shirley Temple, who sings "On the Good Ship Lollipop"; *It Happened One Night,* directed by Frank Capra and starring Clark Gable and Claudette Colbert; *It's a Gift,* directed by Norman Z. McLeod and starring W.C. Fields; *The Lost Patrol,* directed by John Ford and starring Victor McLaglen and Boris Karloff; *Man of Aran,* documentary by Robert Flaherty; *She Loves Me Not,* musical directed by Elliott Nugent and starring Bing Crosby, Miriam Hopkins, and Kitty Carlisle; *Stand Up and Cheer,* musical directed by Hamilton McFadden and starring Shirley Temple, who sings "Baby Take a Bow"; *Tarzan and His Mate,* directed by Cedric Gibbons and Jack Conway and starring Johnny Weissmuller and Maureen O'Sullivan; *Treasure Island,* directed by Victor Fleming and starring Wallace Beery and Jackie Cooper; *Twentieth Century,* directed by Howard Hawks and starring John Barrymore and Carole Lombard; *What Every Woman Knows,* directed by Gregory La Cava and starring Helen Hayes and Brian Aherne.

FICTION: James M. Cain, *The Postman Always Rings Twice*; Robert Cantwell, *The Land of Plenty*; Edward Dahlberg, *Those Who Perish*; James T. Farrell, *The Young Manhood of Studs Lonigan*; F. Scott Fitzgerald, *Tender Is the Night*; Waldo Frank, *The Death and Birth of David Markand: An American Story*; Daniel Fuchs, *Summer in Williamsburg*; Dashiell Hammett, *The Thin Man*; Josephine Herbst, *The Executioner Waits*; Edward Newhouse, *You Can't Sleep Here*; John O'Hara, *Appointment in Samarra*; Henry Roth, *Call It Sleep*; William Saroyan, *Daring Young Man*; Tess Slesinger, *The Unpossessed*; Irving Stone, *Lust for Life*; Rex Stout, *Fer-de-lance*; Jerome Weidman, *I Can Get It for You Wholesale*; Nathanael West, *A Cool Million.*

POPULAR SONGS: "The Beer Barrel Polka (Roll Out the Barrel)," by Czech songwriters Jaromir Vejvoda, Wladimir A. Timm, and Vasek Zeman; "Blue Moon," by Richard Rodgers, lyrics by Lorenz Hart; "Deep Purple," by Peter De Rose, lyrics by Mitchell Parish; "I Only Have Eyes for You," by Harry Warren, lyrics by Al Dubin; "Little Man, You've Had a Busy Day," by Mabel Wayne, lyrics by Maurice Sigler and Al Hoffman; "Love Thy Neighbor," by Harry Revel, lyrics by Mack Gordon; "Miss Otis Regrets," "The Object of My Affection," by Pinky Tomlin, Coy Poe, and Jimmy Grier; "On the Good Ship Lollipop," by Richard A. Whiting, lyrics by Sidney Clare; "Solitude," by Duke Ellington, lyrics by Eddie De Lange and Irving Mills; "Stars Fell on Alabama," by Frank Perkins, lyrics by Mitchell Parish; "Tumbling Tumbleweeds," by Bob Nolan; "The Very Thought of You," by Ray Noble; "Winter Wonderland," by Felix Bernard, lyrics by Richard B. Smith; "You Oughta Be in Pictures," by Dana Suesse, lyrics by Edward Heyman.

1935

- Derived from a 1924 Edith Wharton novel, *The Old Maid,* by Zoe Atkins, plays at the Empire Theater in New York and wins the Pulitzer Prize.
- Andrew Mellon gives his twenty-five-million-dollar art collection to the American people and contributes ten million dollars for the construction of the National Gallery of Art in Washington, D.C.
- Robert E. Sherwood's play *The Petrified Forest,* starring Humphrey Bogart and Leslie Howard, opens at the Broadhurst Theater in New York.
- *Green Light*, by Lloyd Douglas, and *The Case of the Counterfeit Eye* are the year's best sellers.
- The Works Progress Administration (WPA) Federal Arts Projects are created, giving artists jobs to decorate post offices and other federal buildings.
- The Farm Security Administration is formed, and hires Dorothea Lange, Walker Evans, and Ben Shahn to publicize the living conditions of migrant farm workers via photography.
- Margaret Bourke-White is sent by *Fortune* magazine to photograph the Dust Bowl.
- From 1935 to 1939 low-priced theater productions tour the country under the Federal Theater Project directed by Hallie Flanagan.
- The Federal Music project, under the direction of Nikolai Sokoloff, employs 15,000 musicians, performs 225,000 concerts, and launches seven hundred projects between 1935 and 1939.
- On January 5, *Waiting for Lefty,* by Clifford Odets, premieres at New York's Civic Repertory Theater and runs for 168 performances. On March 26, the play is moved to Longacre Theater in a Group Theatre production, with the top price of $1.50 per seat.
- On February 19, Clifford Odets's *Awake and Sing!* premieres at the Belasco Theater, starring Stella Adler, Morris Carnovsky, and John Garfield. The show will run for 209 performances.
- In April, the radio show *Your Hit Parade* debuts with a lineup of top song hits.
- On July 1, Benny Goodman and his band record "The King Porter Stomp" for Victor Records, ushering in the Swing Era.
- On July 17, the show-business newspaper *Variety* headlines its issue with a report that rural audiences do not support movies that portray country folk and bucolic settings.
- On August 21, bandleader Benny Goodman's career takes a dramatic turn for the better when he opens at the Palomar Ballroom in Los Angeles, where he is dubbed the "King of Swing."

- On September 25, Maxwell Anderson's *Winterset,* starring Burgess Meredith and Richard Bennett, opens at New York's Martin Beck Theater. The play is based on the Sacco-Vanzetti case.
- On October 10, the opera *Porgy and Bess,* with music by George Gershwin and lyrics by Ira Gershwin and DuBose Heyward, opens at the Alvin Theater in New York, where it runs for 124 performances. Songs include "It Ain't Necessarily So," "Bess, You Is My Woman Now," and "Summertime."
- On October 12, with music and lyrics by Cole Porter and songs that include "Begin the Beguine" and "Just One of Those Things," *Jubilee,* starring Melville Cooper, Mary Boland, and Montgomery Clift, opens at New York's Imperial Theater.
- On November 16, Jimmy Durante stars in *Jumbo* with a live elephant at the New York Hippodrome. With music by Richard Rodgers and lyrics by Lorenz Hart, songs include "The Most Beautiful Girl in the World."
- On November 27, *Boy Meets Girl,* by Bella (Cohen) and Samuel Spewack, and starring Jerome Cowan, Garson Kanin, and Everett Sloane, opens at New York's Cort Theater and runs for 669 performances.

MOVIES: *Anna Karenina,* directed by Clarence Brown and starring Greta Garbo and Fredric March; *The Bride of Frankenstein,* directed by James Whale and starring Elsa Lanchester and Boris Karloff; *David Copperfield,* directed by George Cukor and starring Freddie Bartholomew, W.C. Fields, and Lionel Barrymore; *Gold Diggers of 1935,* musical directed by Busby Berkeley and starring Dick Powell, with music by Henry Warren and lyrics by Al Dubin, including "Lullaby of Broadway"; *The Good Fairy,* directed by William Wyler and starring Margaret Sullivan and Herbert Marshall; *The Informer,* directed by John Ford and starring Victor McLaglen; *Lives of a Bengal Lancer,* directed by Henry Hathaway and starring Gary Cooper and Franchot Tone; *The Man on the Flying Trapeze,* directed by Clyde Bruckman and starring W.C. Fields; *Mississippi,* musical directed by A. Edward Sutherland and starring Bing Crosby, W.C. Fields, and Joan Bennett, with music by Richard Rodgers and lyrics by Lorenz Hart; *Mutiny on the Bounty,* directed by Frank Lloyd and starring Charles Laughton, Clark Gable, and Franchot Tone; *A Night at the Opera,* directed by Sam Wood and starring the Marx Brothers; *Ruggles of Red Gap,* directed by Leo McCarey and starring Charles Laughton, Mary Boland, and Charles Ruggles; *The Story of Louis Pasteur,* directed by William Dieterle and starring Paul Muni; *Top Hat,* musical directed by Mark Sandrich and starring Fred Astaire and Ginger Rogers, with music by Irving Berlin, including "Cheek to Cheek."

FICTION: Nelson Algren, *Somebody in Boots*; James T. Farrell, *Judgment Day*; Zora Neale Hurston, *Men and Mules*; Tom Kromer, *Waiting For Nothing*; Sinclair Lewis, *It Can't Happen Here*; Horace McCoy, *They Shoot Horses, Don't They?*; John Steinbeck, *Tortilla Flat*; Clara Weatherwax, *Marching! Marching!*; Thomas Wolfe, *Of Time and the River* and *From Death to Morning.*

POPULAR SONGS: "About a Quarter to Nine," lyrics by Al Dubin, music by Harry Warren; "I'm Gonna Sit Right Down and Write Myself a Letter," by Fred E. Ahlert, lyrics by Joe Young; "I'm in the Mood for Love," by Jimmy McHugh and Dorothy Fields; "I Won't Dance," by Jerome Kern, lyrics by Otto Harbach and Oscar Hammerstein II; "In a Sentimental Mood," by Duke Ellington; "(Lookie, Lookie, Lookie) Here Comes Cookie," by Mack Gordon; "Moon Over Miami," by Joe Burke, lyrics by Edgar Leslie; "The Music Goes Round and 'Round," by Edward Farley and Michael Riley, lyrics by "Red" Hodgson; "Red Sails in the Sunset," by Hugh Williams, lyrics by Jimmy Kennedy; "She's a Latin from Manhattan," lyrics by Al Dubin and Harry Warren; "When I Grow Too Old to Dream," by Sigmund Romberg, lyrics by Oscar Hammerstein II.

1936

- *The Case of the Stuttering Bishop,* by Erle Stanley Gardner, and *Gone With The Wind,* by Margaret Mitchell, are the year's best sellers.
- *The Flowering of New England,* a study of U.S. literary history by Van Wyck Brooks, is published. It will win the 1937 Pulitzer Prize.
- Public-speaking teacher Dale Carnegie's book *How to Win Friends and Influence People* is published.
- Carl Sandburg's poem "The People, Yes" is published.
- Under the patronage of the Farm Security Administration, Dorothea Lange captures the suffering of an era with her photo of Florence Thompson and two of her children, titled *Migrant Mother, Nipomo California.*
- Songs such as "Good Night, Irene" by traveling blues singer Huddie "Leadbelly" Ledbetter are collected by Alan and John Avery Lomax and published in *Negro Folk Songs as Sung by Leadbelly.*
- Folksinger Woodrow Wilson "Woody" Guthrie is hired by the Department of the Interior to promote nationalistic feeling in the Northwest by traveling and performing his songs such as "Roll On, Columbia" and "Those Oklahoma Hills." Instead of his usual hitchhiking, he is chauffeured through several states and writes twenty-six songs in twenty-six days.
- On February 17, S. N. Behrman's *End of Summer,* starring Ina Claire, Osgood Perkins, Mildred Natwick, Van Heflin, and Sheppard Strudwick, opens at New York's Guild Theater.
- On March 14, *Triple-A Plowed Under,* a Living Newspaper written for the WPA Federal Theatre Project by the Living Newspaper staff, opens in New York at the Biltmore Theater.
- On March 29, Robert Sherwood's antiwar *Idiot's Delight* opens at New York's Shubert Theater and runs for 300 performances, winning the 1936 Pulitzer Prize for drama.
- On April 11, Richard Rodgers and Oscar Hammerstein II collaborate on music and lyrics for *On Your Toes,* which opens at New York's Imperial Theater, starring Ray Bolger, Tamara Geva, and George Church.
- On July 9, *The Women,* by Clare Boothe Luce and starring Ilka Chase, Jane Seymour, Arlene Francis, Doris Day, and Marjorie Main, opens at New York's Ethel Barrymore Theater and runs for 657 performances.
- On September 21, George Kelly's *Reflected Glory,* starring Tallulah Bankhead, opens at New York's Morosco Theater.

- On October 22, *Stage Door,* by George S. Kaufman and Edna Ferber, and starring Margaret Sullivan and Tom Ewell, opens at New York's Music Box Theater and runs for 169 performances. The next year it is made into a movie directed by Gregory La Cava and starring Katharine Hepburn, Adolphe Menjou, Lucille Ball, and Ginger Rogers.
- On October 27, *It Can't Happen Here,* by Sinclair Lewis and John C. Moffitt, produced under the auspices of the Federal Theatre Project, opens simultaneously in seventeen cities across the nation.
- On October 29, Songs such as "De-Lovely" highlight Cole Porter's music and lyrics for *Red, Hot and Blue,* which opens at New York's Alvin Theater and stars Ethel Merman, Jimmy Durante, Grace and Paul Hartman, and Bob Hope.
- On November 6, *Symphony No. 3 in A Minor,* by Sergei Rachmaninoff, premieres at Philadelphia's Academy of Music.
- On December 14, George S. Kaufman and Moss Hart's *You Can't Take It With You* opens at New York's Booth Theater, where it runs for 837 performances and wins the 1937 Pulitzer Prize.
- On December 16, *Brother Rat,* by John Monks Jr. and Fred F. Finklehoff, and starring Eddie Albert, Frank Albertson, Ezra Stone, and José Ferrer, opens at New York's Biltmore Theater and runs for 577 performances.

MOVIES: *Born to Dance,* musical directed by Roy Del Ruth and starring James Stewart and tap dancer Eleanor Powell, with songs by Cole Porter including "I've Got You Under My Skin"; *Camille,* directed by George Cukor and starring Greta Garbo, Robert Taylor, and Lionel Barrymore; *Dodsworth,* directed by William Wyler and starring Walter Huston and Paul Lukas; *Follow the Fleet,* musical directed by Mark Sandrich and starring Fred Astaire, Ginger Rogers, Randolph Scott, and Betty Grable, with songs by Irving Berlin including "Let's Face the Music"; *Fury,* directed by Fritz Lang and starring Sylvia Sidney and Spencer Tracy; *The Great Ziegfeld,* directed by Robert Z. Leonard and starring William Powell and Myrna Loy; *Mr. Deeds Goes to Town,* directed by Frank Capra and starring Gary Cooper and Jean Arthur; *Modern Times,* directed by and starring Charlie Chaplin; *My Man Godfrey,* directed by Gregory La Cava and starring Carole Lombard and William Powell; *Petrified Forest,* directed by Archie Mayo and starring Leslie Howard and Humphrey Bogart; *The Prisoner of Shark Island,* directed by John Ford and starring Warner Baxter; *San Francisco,* musical directed by W.S. Van Dyke and starring Clark Gable, Jeanette MacDonald, and Spencer Tracy; *Show Boat,* musical directed by James Whale and starring Paul Robeson, Irene Dunne, and Helen Morgan; *Swing Time,* musical directed by George Stevens and starring Ginger Rogers and Fred Astaire, with music by Jerome Kern and lyrics by Dorothy Fields, including "The Way You Look Tonight"; *Theodora Goes Wild,* directed by Richard Boleslawski and starring Irene Dunne and Melvyn Douglas.

FICTION: Djuna Barnes, *Nightwood*; Thomas Bell, *All Brides Are Beautiful*; James M. Cain, *Double Indemnity*; John Dos Passos, *The Big Money*; Walter D. Edmonds, *Drums Along the Mohawk*; James T. Farrell, *A World I Never Made*; William Faulkner, *Absalom, Absalom!*; Munro Leaf, *The Story of Ferdinand*; Henry Miller, *Black Spring*; Margaret Mitchell, *Gone With the Wind*; John Steinbeck, *In Dubious Battle.*

POPULAR SONGS: "Cool Water," by Bob Nolan; "Goody Goody," by Matt Malneck and Johnny Mercer; "I'm an Old Cowhand (from the Rio Grande)," by Johnny Mercer; "Moonlight and Shadows," by Frederick Hollander and Leo Robin; "The Night Is Young and You're So Beautiful," by Dana Suesse, lyrics by Billy Rose and Irving Kahal; "Pennies From Heaven," by Arthur Johnston and Johnny Burke; "Ramblings on My Mind," by Robert Johnson; "Sing, Sing, Sing," by Louis Prima; "Stompin' at the Savoy," by Benny Goodman, Edgar Sampson, and Chick Webb, lyrics by Andy Razaf; "Walkin' Blues," by Robert Johnson.

1937

- *The Case of the Dangerous Dowager* and *The Case of the Lame Canary,* by Erle Stanley Gardner, are the year's best sellers.
- Margaret Mitchell's *Gone With The Wind* wins the Pulitzer Prize.
- The Academy of Motion Picture Arts and Sciences awards the newly inaugurated Thalberg Memorial Award to the late M-G-M producer Irving Grant Thalberg.
- Dr. Seuss (Theodore Seuss Geisel) wins popularity with children learning to read with his imaginative rhyming and illustrations in *And to Think That I Saw It on Mulberry Street.*
- The six-and-a-half-minute *Porky's Hare Hunt,* the first Bugs Bunny cartoon, is released by Warner Bros. and features the voice of Mel Blanc as both Bugs Bunny and Porky Pig.
- Arturo Toscanini, seventy years old, is replaced as conductor of the New York Philharmonic but is hired by the National Broadcasting Company to conduct the NBC Symphony.
- Wallace Stevens's collection of poetry, *The Man with the Blue Guitar,* is published.
- On January 9, Maxwell Anderson's *High Tor,* starring Burgess Meredith and Peggy Ashcroft, opens at New York's Martin Beck Theater.
- On January 21, Ernest Bloch's *Voice in the Wilderness: Symphonic Poem for Orchestra and Violoncello Obbligato* premieres in Los Angeles.
- On January 29, Pearl Buck's play *The Good Earth* premiers in Los Angeles and opens in New York on February 2.
- On February 20, *Having a Wonderful Time,* by Austrian American playwright Arthur Kober, premieres at New York's Lyceum Theater.
- On April 14, Songs such as "My Funny Valentine" and "The Lady Is a Tramp," by Richard Rodgers and Lorenz Hart, are showcased in *Babes in Arms,* which premieres at New York's Shubert Theater.
- On May 19, John Murray and Allen Boretz's *Room Service,* starring Sam Levine, Eddie Albert, and Betty Field, opens at New York's Cort Theater and runs for five hundred performances.
- On June 20, Walter Piston's *Concertino* is premiered in a CBS radio broadcast from New York.
- On November 23, *Golden Boy,* by Clifford Odets, opens at New York's Belasco Theater. Starring Jules Garfield, Lee J.

Cobb, Karl Malden, and Elia Kazan, the play runs for 250 performances.

- On November 23, John Steinbeck's stage version of his new novel *Of Mice and Men* is polished by director George S. Kaufman and premieres at New York's Music Box Theater while Steinbeck gathers material for his next novel, *The Grapes of Wrath. Of Mice and Men* is made into a movie released in 1939, directed by Lewis Milestone and starring Burgess Meredith and Lon Chaney Jr.
- On November 27, *Pins and Needles,* with music and lyrics by Harold Rome and sponsored by the International Ladies Garment Workers Union (ILGWU), opens at New York's Labor Stage Theater and runs for 1,108 performances.
- In December, Disney's *Snow White and the Seven Dwarfs,* the first full-length animated feature in color and with sound, opens to become the biggest grossing film of the decade.

MOVIES: *The Awful Truth,* directed by Leo McCarey and starring Irene Dunne and Cary Grant; *Captains Courageous,* directed by Victor Fleming and starring Spencer Tracy and Freddie Bartholomew; *A Day at the Races,* directed by Sam Wood and starring the Marx Brothers; *History is Made at Night,* directed by Frank Borzage and starring Charles Boyer and Jean Arthur; *The Hurricane,* directed by John Ford and starring Dorothy Lamour, Jon Hall, and Raymond Massey; *The Life of Emile Zola,* directed by William Dieterle and starring Paul Muni; *Lost Horizon,* directed by Frank Capra and starring Ronald Colman, Sam Jaffe, and Thomas Mitchell; *Make Way for Tomorrow,* directed by Leo McCarey and starring Victor Moore and Beulah Bondi; *The Prisoner of Zenda,* directed by John Cromwell and starring Ronald Colman, Madeleine Carroll, and Douglas Fairbanks Jr.; *Shall We Dance,* musical directed by Mark Sandrich and starring Ginger Rogers and Fred Astaire, with music by George Gershwin and lyrics by Ira Gershwin, including "They Can't Take That Away from Me"; *Snow White and the Seven Dwarfs,* the first full-length animated feature by Walt Disney, with music by Frank Churchill and lyrics by Larry Mose, including "Heigh-Ho," "Some Day My Prince Will Come," and "Whistle While You Work"; *A Star Is Born,* directed by William A. Wellman and starring Fredric March and Janet Gaynor; *They Won't Forget,* directed by Mervyn LeRoy and starring Claude Rains and Lana Turner; *Topper,* directed by Norman Z. McLeod and starring Constance Bennett, Cary Grant, and Roland Young.

FICTION: James M. Cain, *Serenade*; Daniel Fuchs, *Low Company*; Ernest Hemingway, *To Have and Have Not*; Zora Neale Hurston, *Their Eyes Were Watching God*; Meyer Levin, *The Old Bunch*; John Phillips Marquand, *The Late George Apley*; Wallace Stegner, *Remembering Laughter*; John Steinbeck, *Of Mice and Men.*

POPULAR SONGS: "Blue Hawaii," by Leo Robin and Ralph Rainger; "The Dipsy Doodle," by Larry Clinton; "A Foggy Day," by George Gershwin, lyrics by Ira Gershwin; "Good Mornin'," by Sam Coslow; "Harbor Lights," by Jimmy Kennedy and Hugh Williams; "Hell Hound on My Trail," by Robert Johnson; "I've Got My Love To Keep Me Warm," by Irving Berlin; "In the Still of the Night," by Cole Porter; "I Can Dream, Can't I?" by Sammy Fain, lyrics by Irving Kahal; "The Joint Is Jumpin'," by Thomas "Fats" Waller, Andy Razaf, and James C. Johnson; "Me and the Devil Blues," by Robert Johnson; "The Moon of Manakoora," by Alfred Newman, lyrics by Frank Loesser; "Nice Work If You Can Get It," by George Gershwin, lyrics by Ira Gershwin; "Once in a While," by Michael Edwards, lyrics by Bud Green; "Rosalie," by Cole Porter; "Sweet Leilani," by Harry Owens; "That Old Feeling," by Sammy Fain and Lew Brown; "Too Marvelous For Words," by Richard A. Whiting, lyrics by Johnny Mercer.

1938

- *Fast Company* by Marco Page, *The Yearling* by Marjorie K. Rawlings, *Singing Guns,* by Max Brand, *The Case of the Substitute Face* by Erle Stanley Gardner, and *The Best of Damon Runyon* by Damon Runyon are the year's best sellers.
- In December, Regionalist Thomas Hart Benton exhibits his painting *Cradling Wheat.*
- The Cloisters, a medieval European nunnery filled with priceless art donated by the Rockefeller family to the Metropolitan Museum of Art, opens in New York's Tryon Park.
- The American Composers' Alliance is founded.
- Woody Guthrie releases his *Talking Union* album and makes appearances to support labor unions.
- Glenn Miller forms his own big band and begins touring after breaking from playing trombone and arranging music for Tommy and Jimmy Dorsey and Ray Noble.
- The samba and the conga are introduced to U.S. dance floors.
- Delmore Schwartz's first collection of poems, *In Dreams Begin Responsibilities,* is published.
- On January 17, Benny Goodman and his Orchestra, along with Duke Ellington, Count Basie, and members of their orchestras, give the first jazz performance in Carnegie Hall.
- On January 25, Ian Hay's *Bachelor Born* opens at New York's Morosco Theater and runs for four hundred performances.
- On January 26, Paul Vincent Carroll's *Shadow and Substance,* starring Cedric Hardwicke, Sara Allgood, and Julie Haydon, opens at New York's Golden Theater.
- On February 3, *On Borrowed Time,* by Paul Osborn and starring Dorothy Stickney, Dudley Digges, and Dickie Van Patten, premieres at New York's Longacre Theater.
- On February 4, *Our Town,* by Thornton Wilder, opens at Henry Miller's Theater in New York and runs for 336 performances, winning the 1938 Pulitzer Prize for drama.
- On March 26, Howard Hanson's *Symphony No. 3* is first performed in an NBC Orchestra radio concert.
- On March 30, Walter Piston's *The Incredible Flutist* is premiered at Boston's Symphony Hall.
- On September 22, Ole Olsen and Chic Johnson delight audiences with their slapstick comedy in the musical *Hellzapoppin',* which opens at New York's Forty-Sixth Street Theater and runs for 1,404 performances.
- On October 9, the ballet *Billy the Kid,* with music by Aaron Copland and choreography by Eugene Loring, opens at the Chicago Civic Opera House.

- On October 15, Robert Sherwood's *Abe Lincoln in Illinois,* starring Raymond Massey, opens at the Plymouth Theater and runs for 472 performances.
- On October 30, Orson Welles's radio broadcast *The War of the Worlds* creates hysteria as listeners believe that an interplanetary conflict has begun with Martians landing near Princeton, New Jersey.
- On November 9, Mary Martin simulates a striptease to Cole Porter's "My Heart Belongs to Daddy" in *Leave It to Me,* which premieres at New York's Imperial Theater.
- On November 11, On Armistice Day, Kate Smith sings Irving Berlin's "God Bless America" in a radio broadcast and later acquires exclusive air rights to the song, which Berlin originally wrote for his 1918 show *Yip-Yip Yaphank* but put aside.
- On December 7, Philip Barry's *Here Come the Clowns,* starring Eddie Dowling, Madge Evans, and Russell Collins, premieres at New York's Booth Theater.

MOVIES: *The Adventures of Robin Hood,* directed by Michael Curtiz and starring Errol Flynn; *The Adventures of Tom Sawyer,* directed by Norman Taurog and starring Tommy Kelly and Jackie Moran; *Bringing Up Baby,* directed by Howard Hawks and starring Katharine Hepburn and Cary Grant; *The Dawn Patrol,* directed by Edmund Goulding and starring Errol Flynn, Basil Rathbone, and David Niven; *Hard To Get,* musical directed by Ray Enright and starring Dick Powell and Olivia de Havilland, with music by Harry Warren and lyrics by Johnny Mercer, including "You Must Have Been a Beautiful Baby"; *Holiday,* directed by George Cukor and starring Katharine Hepburn and Cary Grant; *In Old Chicago,* directed by Henry King and starring Tyrone Power and Alice Faye; *Jezebel,* directed by William Wyler and starring Bette Davis, Henry Fonda, and George Brent; *Pygmalion,* directed by Anthony Asquith and Leslie Howard and starring Howard and Wendy Hiller; *Sing You Sinners,* musical directed by Wesley Ruggles and starring Bing Crosby, Fred MacMurray, and Donald O'Connor; *A Slight Case of Murder,* directed by Lloyd Bacon and starring Edward G. Robinson; *Three Comrades,* directed by Frank Borzage and starring Margaret Sullivan, Robert Taylor, and Franchot Tone; *You Can't Take It With You,* directed by Frank Capra and starring Jean Arthur, James Stewart, and Lionel Barrymore.

FICTION: Taylor Caldwell, *Dynasty of Death*; John Dos Passos, *U. S. A.*; James T. Farrell, *No Star Is Lost*; Albert Maltz, *The Way Things Are and Other Stories*; Kenneth Robeson (Lester Dent), *The Man of Bronze*; Wallace Stegner, *The Big Rock Candy Mountain*; Allen Tate, *The Fathers*; Richard Wright, *Uncle Tom's Children*; Leane Zugsmith, *The Summer Children.*

POPULAR SONGS: "A-Tisket, A-Tasket," by Ella Fitzgerald and Al Feldman; "Camel Hop," by Mary Lou Williams; "Cherokee," by Ray Noble; "F. D. R. Jones," by Harold Rome; "The Flat Foot Floogie," by Slim Gaillard, Slam Stewart, and Bud Green (who were forced to change the word "floozie" to "floogie" to gain radio airplay); "I Let a Song Go Out of My Heart," by Duke Ellington, lyrics by Irving Mills, Henry Nemo, and John Redmond; "Jeepers Creepers," by Harry Warren, lyrics by Johnny Mercer; "Love Walked In," by George Gershwin, lyrics by Ira Gershwin; "One O'Clock Jump," by William "Count" Basie; "Thanks for the Memory," by Ralph Rainger and Leo Robin (title song for a film starring Bob Hope, who makes it his theme song); "That Old Feeling," by Sammy Fain and Lew Brown.

1939

- *The Grapes of Wrath* by John Steinbeck is the year's best seller.
- Austrian-American Ludwig Bemelmans's new novel *Hotel Splendide* is soon overshadowed by the release of his children's book *Madeline,* which he illustrated himself.
- Thomas Hart Benton exhibits several paintings, including *Persephone, Threshing Wheat, Weighing Cotton,* and *Susannah and the Elders.*
- Virginia Lee Burton's children's book *Mike Mulligan and His Steam Shovel* is published.
- Dutch American painter Willem de Kooning exhibits his *Seated Man.*
- Grandma Moses (Anna Mary Robertson Moses) gains overnight fame for her primitivist paintings when art collector Louis Caldor buys her work and exhibits it at the Museum of Modern Art (MOMA) in New York City.
- The MOMA in New York City moves to a new building at 11 West 53rd Street.
- New Jersey roadhouse singer Frank Sinatra joins a new band formed by Harry James but leaves within a year to join the Tommy Dorsey band.
- *Gone With The Wind* is Hollywood's top grossing film.
- On January 10, Paul Vincent Carroll's *The White Steed,* starring Barry Fitzgerald and Jessica Tandy, opens at New York's Cort Theater.
- On January 20, *Sonata No. 1 for Piano and Orchestra,* by Charles Ives, is first performed at New York's Town Hall.
- On January 21, *The American Way,* by George S. Kaufman and Moss Hart and starring Fredric March and Florence Eldredge, opens at New York's Center Theater in Rockefeller Center.
- On February 15, Lillian Hellman's *The Little Foxes,* starring Tallulah Bankhead, Carl Benton Reid, Dan Duryea, and Patricia Collinge, opens at New York's National Theater and runs for 191 performances.
- On February 24, Roy Harris's *Symphony No. 3* premieres at Boston's Symphony Hall.
- On March 18, *The New Yorker* publishes "The Secret Life of Walter Mitty," by James Thurber.
- On March 28, Katharine Hepburn, Lenore Lonergan, Shirley Booth, Van Heflin, and Joseph Cotten star in Philip Booth's *The Philadelphia Story,* which opens at New York's Shubert Theater.
- On March 31, John and Ruby Lomax begin a 6,502-mile trip through the South recording twenty-five hours of folk music by three hundred performers.
- On April 13, William Saroyan's *My Heart's in the Highlands* premieres at New York's Guild Theater and has a short run of forty-three performances.

- On June 19, *The Streets of Paris,* starring Brazilian Carmen Miranda singing "South American Way," opens at New York's Broadhurst Theater.
- On August 28, the Three Stooges appear in the thirteenth and final version of *George White's Scandals* at New York's Alvin Theater. With music by Sammy Fain and lyrics by Jack Yellen, songs include "Are You Having Any Fun."
- On October 18, Desi Arnaz costars with Eddie Bracken, Van Johnson, Richard Kollmar, and Marcy Wescott in the New York Imperial Theater premiere of *Too Many Girls.* Richard Rodgers and Lorenz Hart's songs include "I Didn't Know What Time It Was."
- On October 25, *The Man Who Came to Dinner,* by George S. Kaufman and Moss Hart, opens at New York's Music Box Theater and runs for 739 performances.
- William Saroyan's *The Time of Your Life,* starring Eddie Dowling, Julie Haydon, Gene Kelly, and Celeste Holm, opens at New York's Booth Theater.
- On November 3, Clare Boothe Luce's *Margin for Error,* starring Otto Preminger, premieres at New York's Plymouth Theater.
- On November 8, *Life With Father,* a comedy by Howard Lindsay and Russel Crouse based on the book by Clarence Day, opens a run of 3,244 performances at New York's Empire Theater.
- On November 27, Maxwell Anderson's *Key Largo,* starring José Ferrer, Paul Muni, and Uta Hagen, opens at New York's Ethel Barrymore Theater.
- On December 6, *Du Barry Was a Lady* starring Bert Lahr, Ethel Merman, and Betty Grable, with music and lyrics by Cole Porter, opens at New York's Forty-Sixth Street Theater.

MOVIES: *Dark Victory,* directed by Edmund Goulding and starring Bette Davis; *Destry Rides Again,* directed by George Marshall and starring James Stewart and Marlene Dietrich; *Drums Along the Mohawk,* directed by John Ford and starring Henry Fonda and Claudette Colbert; *Goodbye, Mr. Chips,* directed by Sam Wood and starring Robert Donat and Greer Garson; *Gone With the Wind,* directed by Victor Fleming and starring Vivien Leigh, Clark Gable, Leslie Howard, and Olivia de Havilland; *Gunga Din,* directed by George Stevens and starring Cary Grant, Victor McLaglen, Douglas Fairbanks Jr., Joan Fontaine, and Sam Jaffe; *The Hound of the Baskervilles,* directed by Sidney Lanfield and starring Basil Rathbone and Nigel Bruce; *The Hunchback of Notre Dame,* directed by William Dieterle and starring Charles Laughton; *Love Affair,* directed by Leo McCarey and starring Irene Dunne and Charles Boyer; *Mr. Smith Goes to Washington,* directed by Frank Capra and starring James Stewart and Jean Arthur; *Only Angels Have Wings,* directed by Howard Hawks and starring Cary Grant, Jean Arthur, and Richard Barthelmess; *Stagecoach,* directed by John Ford and starring John Wayne and Claire Trevor; *The Stars Look Down,* directed by Carol Reed and starring Michael Redgrave and Margaret Lockwood; *The Wizard of Oz,* musical directed by Victor Fleming and starring Judy Garland, Ray Bolger, Bert Lahr, Jack Haley, Frank Morgan, and Margaret Hamilton, with music by Harold Arlen and lyrics by E. Y. Harburg, including "Somewhere Over the Rainbow," "Follow the Yellow Brick Road," and "We're Off to See the Wizard"; *Wuthering Heights,* directed by William Wyler and starring Laurence Olivier and Merle Oberon.

FICTION: Sholem Asch, *The Nazarene*; Raymond Chandler, *The Big Sleep*; Josephine Herbst, *Rope of Gold*; Norman MacLeod, *You Get What You Ask For*; John P. Marquand, *Wickford Point*; Henry Miller, *Tropic of Capricorn*; Katherine Anne Porter, *Pale Horse, Pale Rider*; John Steinbeck, *The Grapes of Wrath*; Dalton Trumbo, *Johnny Got His Gun*; Robert Penn Warren, *Night Rider*; Nathanael West, *The Day of the Locust*; Thomas Wolfe, *The Web and the Rock.*

POPULAR SONGS: "And the Angels Sing," by Ziggy Elman, lyrics by Johnny Mercer; "Ciribiribin (They're So in Love)" by composer A. Pestalozza, lyrics by Harry James and Jack Lawrence; "Heaven Can Wait," by Jimmy Van Heusen, lyrics by Eddie De Lange; "I'll Never Smile Again," by Ruth Lowe; "I Get Along Without You Very Well (except Sometimes)," by Hoagy Carmichael, lyrics by Jane Brown Thompson; "In the Mood," by Joe Garland, lyrics by Andy Razaf; "The Lady's in Love with You," by Burton Lane, lyrics by Frank Loesser; "Moonlight Serenade," by Glenn Miller, lyrics by Mitchell Parish; "Scatterbrain," by Kahn Keene, Carl Bean, Frankie Masters, and Johnny Burke; "Sent for You Yesterday (and Here You Come Today)," by Ed Durham, William "Count" Basie, and Jimmy Rushing; "South of the Border (Down Mexico Way)," by Jimmy Kennedy and Michael Carr; "Three Little Fishies (Itty Bitty Poo)" by Saxie Dowell; "Undecided," by Charles Shavers, lyrics by Sid Robin.

"The Production Code of the Motion Picture Producers and Distributors of America, Inc.—1930–1934"

Code

By: The Motion Picture Producers and Distributors of America

Date: March 1930–1934

Source: The Motion Picture Producers and Distributors of America. "The Production Code of the Motion Picture Producers and Distributors of America Inc.—1930–1934." Available online at http://home.earthlink.net/~davidp_hayes/prodcode/ProdCode.html; website home page: http://home.earthlink.net/~prodcode/index.html (accessed April 9, 2003).

About the Organization: The Motion Picture Producers and Distributors of America (MPPDA) was established in 1922 by the major Hollywood movie studios to develop an industry response to increasing calls for movie censorship. Now known as the Motion Picture Association of America, it continues to rate movies for the motion picture industry. ■

Introduction

By 1930, movies, like the radio and the automobile, had dramatically and permanently altered American lifestyles. In the early 1930s, the estimated weekly movie attendance was between 80 million and 110 million. (The U.S. population over five years of age was 111 million.) Clearly, Americans were infatuated with the movies.

Almost from the beginning of the motion picture industry, concerns over inappropriate content were raised. By the early 1920s, broad government censorship was a possibility. As it was, many local and state governments established censorship boards with the authority to ban local showing of offensive movies.

The concerns in the 1920s and 1930s were similar to those expressed today: sex, violence, substance abuse, vulgarity, the glorification of criminals, and affirmation of values contrary to American moral standards. Of particular concern, as today, was the impact these productions had on young people.

Fearing expanded government regulation, the industry made an attempt at self-regulation. The result was the creation of the Motion Picture Producers and Distributors of America (MPPDA) to enforce a self-regulation system. The system was initially consultative in nature. Studios voluntarily reviewed movie scripts with the MPPDA's regulating committee. By following the MPPDA's advice, the studios reduced confrontation with local censoring boards.

As the 1920s came to a close, it was becoming increasingly evident that self-regulation was not effectively addressing the problem, at least insofar as many socially conscious groups were concerned. What resulted was "The Production Code of the Motion Picture Producers and Distributors of America, Inc.—1930–1934," which remained, with minor changes, the movie rating standard until 1967. The code recognized the industry's responsibility for promoting "spiritual or moral progress, for higher types of social life, and for much correct thinking."

Significance

The details of the code satisfied public concerns. The difficulty was enforcement. The advent of the talkies and declining attendance because of the Depression prompted filmmakers to frequently ignore the voluntary standards in an effort to attract a larger audience.

The catalyst for further reform was the publication of *Our Movie Made Children* in 1933. Based on a series of studies on the movies' impact on the development of children and teenagers, *Our Movie Made Children* created a scientific basis for stricter regulation. Although the premise of the initial studies contained basic flaws and the book did not present an unbiased summary of those studies, the result was renewed clamor for tighter restrictions on movie content.

The Catholic Church created the most effective organization to bring pressure against the movie industry: the Legion of Decency. Supported by like-minded Protestant and Jewish groups and other civic and educational organizations, the Legion of Decency, by threatening movie boycotts, quickly forced the MPPDA into creating a new regulatory body, the Production Code Administration (PCA), to monitor and enforce the code.

Armed with the ability to levy fines of up to $25,000 against producers who distributed movies without the official MPPDA seal of approval, and the ability to review scripts in advance and recommend changes to ensure compliance with the code, the PCA quickly altered the character of movie-making in the United

A film still from the classic mobster movie *Little Caesar,* with Edward G. Robinson, 1931. Hollywood implemented and enforced its production code partly in response to movies like this one that glamourized crime. THE KOBAL COLLECTION/WARNER BROTHERS/FIRST NATIONAL. REPRODUCED BY PERMISSION.

States. For over thirty years, the movie industry adhered, though occasionally with ludicrous results, to a fairly rigid standard designed to produce movies in compliance with the generally accepted moral standards of the day.

Although the obvious threat to free speech began to come up in the 1940s, it was not until 1952 that a serious challenge to the PCA was made. In that year, *The Miracle,* an imported film criticized as sacrilegious, was shut down by the state of New York. A U.S. Supreme Court ruling reversed a lower court ruling and, citing the principles of free speech and freedom of religion, reinstated the movie. Over the next fifteen years, a series of Supreme Court rulings revolving around the issue of freedom of speech undermined "The Production Code of the Motion Picture Producers and Distributors of America, Inc.—1930–1934." It was finally replaced by a movie rating system that lacked the enforcement mechanism of the PCA.

Primary Source

"The Production Code of the Motion Picture Producers and Distributors of America, Inc.—1930–1934" [excerpt]

SYNOPSIS: This code was first published in 1930 and was not abandoned until 1967. The following is a portion of that code. It describes in considerable detail what was and was not acceptable. Once an enforcement mechanism was put in place in 1934, the code played a major role in shaping the content of American movies for over thirty years.

Preamble

Motion picture producers recognize the high trust and confidence which have been placed in them by the people of the world and which have made motion pictures a universal form of entertainment.

They recognize their responsibility to the public because of this trust and because entertainment and art are important influences in the life of a nation.

Hence, though regarding motion pictures primarily as entertainment without any explicit purpose of teaching or propaganda, they know that the motion picture within its own field of entertainment may be directly responsible for spiritual or moral progress, for higher types of social life, and for much correct thinking. . . .

On their part, they ask from the public and from public leaders a sympathetic understanding of their purposes and problems and a spirit of cooperation that will allow them the freedom and opportunity necessary to bring the motion picture to a still higher level of wholesome entertainment for all the people.

General Principles

1. No picture shall be produced which will lower the moral standards of those who see it. Hence the sympathy of the audience shall never be thrown to the side of crime, wrong-doing, evil or sin. . . .

I. Crimes Against the Law
These shall never be presented in such a way as to throw sympathy with the crime as against law and justice or to inspire others with a desire for imitation.

1. Murder
   (a) The technique of murder must be presented in a way that will not inspire imitation.
   (b) Brutal killings are not to be presented in detail.
   (c) Revenge in modern times shall not be justified. . . .

II. Sex
The sanctity of the institution of marriage and the home shall be upheld. Pictures shall not infer that low forms of sex relationship are the accepted or common thing.

1. Adultery and illicit sex, sometimes necessary plot material, must not be explicitly treated or justified, or presented attractively.
2. Scenes of passion
   (a) These should not be introduced except where they are definitely essential to the plot.
   (b) Excessive and lustful kissing, lustful embraces, suggestive postures and gestures are not to be shown.
   (c) In general, passion should be treated in such manner as not to stimulate the lower and baser emotions.
3. Seduction or rape
   (a) These should never be more than suggested, and then only when essential for the plot. They must never be shown by explicit method.
   (b) They are never the proper subject for comedy. . . .
6. Miscegenation (sex relationship between the white and black races) is forbidden.

III. Vulgarity
The treatment of low, disgusting, unpleasant, though not necessarily evil, subjects should be guided always by the dictates of good taste and a proper regard for the sensibilities of the audience.

IV. Obscenity
Obscenity in word, gesture, reference, song, joke or by suggestion . . . is forbidden.

V. Profanity
Pointed profanity (this includes God, Lord, Jesus, Christ—unless used reverently—Hell, S.O.B., damn, Gawd), or other profane or vulgar expressions, however used, is forbidden.

No approval by the Production Administration shall be given to the use of words and phrases in motion pictures including, but not limited to, the following:

. . . broad (applied to a woman); . . . God, Lord, Jesus, Christ (unless used reverently); . . . fanny; fairy (in a vulgar sense); finger (the); . . . hot (applied to a woman); . . . louse; lousy; . . . nerts; nuts (except when meaning crazy); pansy; . . . slut (applied to a woman); SOB; son-of-a; tart; . . . traveling salesman and farmer's daughter jokes; whore; [and] damn . . .

The Production Code Administration may take cognizance of the fact that the following words and phrases are obviously offensive to the patrons of motion pictures in the United States and more particularly to the patrons of motion pictures in foreign countries: Chink, Dago, Frog, Greaser, Hunkie, Kike, Nigger, Spic, Wop, Yid. . . .

VIII. Religion

1. No film or episode may throw ridicule on any religious faith.
2. Ministers of religion in their character as ministers of religion should not be used as comic characters or as villains. . . .

Reasons Supporting Preamble of Code

. . . The MORAL IMPORTANCE of entertainment is something which has been universally recognized. It enters intimately into the lives of men and women and affects them closely; it occupies their minds and affections during leisure hours; and ultimately touches the whole of their lives. A man may be judged by his standard of entertainment as easily as by the standard of his work. . . .

3.D. The latitude given to film material cannot, in consequence, be as wide as the latitude given to book material. In addition:

a. A book describes; a film vividly presents. One presents on a cold page; the other by apparently living people.
b. A book reaches the mind through words merely; a film reaches the eyes and ears through the reproduction of actual events.
c. The reaction of a reader to a book depends largely on the keenness of the reader's imagination; the reaction to a film depends on the vividness of presentation.

Hence many things which might be described or presented in a book could not possibly be presented in a film. . . .

In general, the mobility, popularity, accessibility, emotional appeal, vividness, straightforward presentation of fact in the film make for more intimate contact with a larger audience and for greater emotional appeal.

Hence the larger moral responsibilities of the motion pictures.

Further Resources

BOOKS

Sklar, Robert. *Movie-Made America: A Social History of American Movies.* New York: Random House, 1975.

Stanley, Robert H. *The Celluloid Empire: A History of the American Movie Industry.* New York: Hastings House, 1978.

All Quiet on the Western Front

Movie script

By: Lewis Milestone

Date: 1930

Source: *All Quiet on the Western Front.* The Greatest Films. Available online at http://www.filmsite.org/allq.html (accessed February 14, 2003), 3–5, 7–8.

About the Artist: Lewis Milestone (1895–1980) was born Lev Milstein in Kishinev, Russia, and immigrated to the United States just before World War I. Milestone got his early training in film during the war when he enlisted in the U.S. Signal Corps and worked as assistant director of Army training films. After the war, he went to Hollywood, to eventually become a film director. He won his first Academy Award in 1929 and his second in 1930 for *All Quiet on the Western Front.* His later films include *Of Mice and Men* (1939), *The Purple Heart* (1944), and *Awake in the Sun* (1945). ■

Introduction

Milestone's 1930 film *All Quiet on the Western Front* was based on the 1929 novel by Erich Maria Remarque (1898–1970), who was born Erich Paul Kramer in Germany. The name "Remarque" is a French adaptation of Kramer—"remark" spelled backwards. Remarque enlisted in the German army at age eighteen, fought on the western front in World War I (1914–1918), and was wounded several times. His firsthand war experiences produced the strong antiwar feelings that led to *All Quiet on the Western Front* and its 1931 sequel, *The Road Back.*

Remarque's pacifist books were banned in Germany in the 1930s. The Nazis ordered that they be publicly burned and ordered stores to stop selling them. Remarque lost his citizenship and moved to Switzerland in 1932. He immigrated to the United States in 1939, where he eventually became a citizen.

The novel attracted the attention of American film director Lewis Milestone and was adapted to the screen in 1930. The grainy black-and-white production was the first major antiwar film of the sound era. With a budget of $1.25 million, Universal Pictures used hundreds of acres of California ranchland for the battle scenes and employed more than two thousand extras.

All Quiet on the Western Front is about a young German soldier, Paul Baumer, and his war experience. The focus of the novel is the isolation, disillusionment, terror, and death of war. Baumer narrates the novel in the first person in a series of flashbacks fashioned as vignettes (short scenes).

In addition to winning Academy Awards for Best Picture and Best Director, the film was also nominated for Best Writing Achievement and Best Cinematography. Like the novel, it skillfully and graphically por-

A poster for the film version of *All Quiet on the Western Front,* the 1930 Academy Award winner for Best Picture and Best Director. **THE KOBAL COLLECTION/UNIVERSAL. REPRODUCED BY PERMISSION.**

trayed the senselessness and futility of war through the eyes of young German soldiers in the trenches of the western Front.

The film, like the book, met opposition, and its premier was disrupted by Nazi groups. It was denounced by the Germans as anti-German, by the Poles as pro-German, and by the French. Other controversy surrounded the film's actors. The film starred a young Lew Ayres as Paul Baumer. Deeply influenced by the antiwar message of the film, Ayres became a conscientious objector in World War II (1939–1945). The American public was outraged, and theaters vowed never to play his films again. He eventually served as a medic in the South Pacific and as a chaplain's aid in New Guinea and the Philippines, and he quietly returned to film after the war.

The skillful and creative cinematography of *All Quiet on the Western Front* is notable, specifically the tracking shots of soldiers attacking enemy lines and the dramatic final scene. In that scene, we find Paul in a trench just before the Armistice, exhausted and disoriented by the terror he has seen. He is alone following the gruesome death of every friend with whom he started out.

Significance

All Quiet on the Western Front was a powerful antiwar statement, reflecting and reinforcing the popular sentiment of the generation that had experienced the slaughter of World War I (1914–1918). There was a widespread sense in Europe and America that the war had been a terrible, pointless mistake. Many Americans felt that the United States had been tricked into a war that didn't even concern them by the schemes of arms merchants, war profiteers, and European politicians. The antiwar, isolationist sentiment from the war found frequent expression in the art and literature of the 1930s.

Avoiding war was the guiding principle of the foreign policy of Britain, France, and the United States throughout the 1930s. The totalitarian regimes of Germany, Italy, and Japan were far less reticent about threatening war and, as a result, were able to intimidate the Western democracies at every turn during their rise to power in the 1930s.

Primary Source

All Quiet on the Western Front [excerpt]

SYNOPSIS: These excerpts from the movie trace the maturation of Paul Baumer. They include a rousing speech by the schoolmaster to the young boys about to enter the war and a dialogue between the boys in the trenches.

Schoolmaster's Speech

You are the life of the Fatherland, you boys—you are the iron men of Germany. You are the gay heroes who will repulse the enemy when you are called to do so. It is not for me to suggest that any of you stand up and offer to defend his country. But I wonder if such a thing is going through your heads. I know that in one of the schools, the boys have risen up in the classroom and enlisted in a mass. If such a thing should happen here, you would not blame me for a feeling of pride. Perhaps some will say that you should not be allowed to go yet—that you have homes, mothers, fathers, that you should not be torn away by your fathers so forgetful of their fatherland . . . by your mothers so weak that they cannot send a son to defend the land which gave them birth. And after all, is a little experience such a bad thing for a boy? Is the honor of wearing a uniform something from which we should run? And if our young ladies glory in those who wear it, is that anything to be ashamed of? . . . To be foremost in battle is a virtue not to be despised. I believe it will be a quick war.

Actors Lew Ayers and Raymond Griffith in *All Quiet on the Western Front,* 1930. THE KOBAL COLLECTION. REPRODUCED BY PERMISSION.

There will be few losses. But if losses there must be, then let us remember the Latin phrase which must have come to the lips of many a Roman when he stood in battle in a foreign land: . . . Sweet and fitting it is to die for the Fatherland . . . Now our country calls. The Fatherland needs leaders. Personal ambition must be thrown aside in the one great sacrifice for our country. Here is a glorious beginning to your lives. The field of honor calls you. . . .

Commanding Officer's Speech to Recruits

The first thing to do is to forget everything you ever knew, everything you ever learned—Forget! See. Forget what you've been, and what you think you're going to be. You're going to be soldiers, and that's all. I'll take the mother's milk out of you, I'll make you hard-boiled. I'll make soldiers out of you, or kill you! . . .

Dialogue in the Trenches

Soldier: *(shocked)* Dead. He's dead.

Katczinsky: Why did you risk your life bringing him in?

Soldier: But it's Behm, my friend.

Katczinsky: *(admonishing)* It's a corpse, no matter whose it is. Now, don't any of ya ever do that again. . . .

Soldiers Question the War

Tjaden: Oh, that's it. I shouldn't be here at all. I don't feel offended.

Katczinsky: *(joking)* It don't apply to tramps like you.

Tjaden: Good. Then I can be going home right away . . . The Kaiser and me . . . Me and the Kaiser felt just alike about this war. We didn't neither of us want any war, so I'm going home. He's there already.

Soldier: Somebody must have wanted it. Maybe it was the English. No, I don't want to shoot any Englishmen. I never saw one 'til I came up here. And I suppose most of them never saw a German 'til they came up here. No, I'm sure they weren't asked about it.

Another Soldier: Well, it must be doing somebody some good.

Tjaden: Not me and the Kaiser.

Soldier: I think maybe the Kaiser wanted a war.

Tjaden: You leave us out of this.

Katczinsky: I don't see that. The Kaiser's got everything he needs.

Soldier: Well, he never had a war before. Every full-grown emperor needs one war to make him famous. Why, that's history.

Paul: Yeah, generals too. They need war.

A Third Soldier: And manufacturers. They get rich. . . .

How Wars Should be Fought

Katczinsky: I'll tell ya how it should all be done. Whenever there's a big war comin' on, you should rope off a big field (and sell tickets). Yeah, and, and, on the big day, you should take all the kings and their cabinets and their generals, put them in the center dressed in their underpants and let 'em fight it out with clubs. The best country wins.

Further Resources

BOOKS

Eyman, Scott. *The Speed of Sound: Hollywood and the Talkie Revolution.* New York: Simon & Schuster, 1997.

Firda, Richard Arthur. *"All Quiet on the Western Front": Literary Analysis and Cultural Context.* New York: Twayne, 1993.

Remarque, Erich Maria. *The Road Back.* Boston: Little, Brown, 1931.

WEBSITES

"All Quiet on the Western Front." Blackwell Web Development & Design. Available online at http://www.bwdd.com/allquiet (accessed February 14, 2003).

Frieden, James A., and Deborah W. Elliott. "Learning Guide to: *All Quiet on the Western Front.*" Teachwithmovies.org. Available online at http://www.teachwithmovies.org/guides/all-quiet-on-the-western-front.html (accessed February 14, 2003).

"Lewis Milestone." The Internet Movie Database. Available online at http://us.imdb.com/Name?Milestone,+Lewis (accessed February 14, 2003).

Early Sunday Morning

Painting

By: Edward Hopper

Date: 1930

Source: Hopper, Edward. *Early Sunday Morning.* 1930. In the collection of the Whitney Museum of American Art. Image number 109046.

About the Artist: Edward Hopper (1882–1967) is one of the best-known realist painters of the Depression era. Born in Nyack, New York, in 1882, Hopper studied with the renowned American realist Robert Henri and greatly admired the work of the Ashcan school of artists. He enjoyed significant success until abstract expressionism began to overtake realism in popularity. Except for regular summer trips to New England, Hopper confined himself to his New York studio for much of his life, dying there in 1967. ■

Introduction

Two branches of realist art emerged in the 1920s and 1930s in the United States. A reaction against the excesses of romanticism and classicism, they sought to represent realistic, everyday life.

One branch of realism was the American regionalist movement. It was characterized by artists painting rural American scenes. Grant Wood's famous 1930 painting, *American Gothic,* is perhaps the best-known example of this style. Other American regionalists included John Curry and Thomas Hart Benton who painted Plains-states landscapes and the plants and wildlife of rural America.

In contrast, the second branch of the realist movement, social realism, was more urban and sought to depict the social problems and hardships of everyday American life. Greatly influenced by Robert Henri and the Ashcan School, the artists of this movement included Jack Levine and Mexican muralist Diego Rivera.

Hopper's art combined elements of both the American regionalist and social realism movements and allowed him to form his own unique brand of realism—similar to yet very different from either branch. Because he lived and painted in his studio in New York City, his intimacy with city life often comes out in his work, but he had the unique ability to bring a rural feeling even to

Primary Source

Early Sunday Morning

SYNOPSIS: Hopper's *Early Sunday Morning,* painted in 1930, is an example of his striking use of light to create an ethereal mood. The painting is stark and efficient and conveys a sense of desolation, yet the lighting softens these characteristics. This theme is common in many of Hopper's other works, including *New York Movie* and *Cape Cod Afternoon.* In this, as in many of his paintings of the American scene, no people are included.

scenes from the heart of the city. He stripped the city of its skyscrapers, bustling crowds, and fast-paced traffic and replaced them with quiet scenes of sparsely populated movie theaters, train stations, cafés, and apartment rooms. He also brought this solitude to his authentically rural scenes, created from a composite of his impressions during summer travels to New England, as seen in *Cape Cod Afternoon, Lighthouse at Two Lights,* and *Monhegan Landscape.*

Significance

Although he was not exceedingly successful in his early years, Hopper had become well known by the 1930s, and his career was not significantly affected by

American painter Edward Hopper around 1940. Hopper is famous for his scenes of contemporary American life. © OSCAR WHITE/CORBIS. REPRODUCED BY PERMISSION.

the Depression. Major museums such as the Museum of Modern Art and the Whitney Museum of American Art bought a number of his paintings. In 1933, Hopper's *Early Sunday Morning* became the Whitney's most expensive purchase to date. In the same year, a retrospective exhibition of his work was given at the Museum of Modern Art. Later, in 1950, the Whitney gave a similar retrospective.

Hopper's depiction of loneliness and isolation reflected the feelings of the Depression-era United States, when people felt caught between nostalgia for the frontier life of the past and excitement over the progress of industrialism and burgeoning city migration. Hopper's art mirrored the paradoxical tendency for people to be with other people and yet feel isolated. This may have been Hopper's commentary on the isolation and pace of modern life.

Hopper created over forty important works that can still be seen in many major art museums across the country. His paintings and etchings reflect the sense of loss Americans were feeling as the landscape of the United States changed during the 1920s and 1930s. His style in such paintings as the celebrated image of a gas station can be viewed as foreshadowing the later American pop art movement that included such artists as Andy Warhol. Although he found success in his career while he was alive, his true impact has only been realized since his death.

Further Resources

BOOKS

Levin, Gail. *Edward Hopper: An Intimate Biography.* Berkeley and Los Angeles: University of California Press, 1995.

Lucie-Smith, Edward. *Lives of the Great Twentieth Century Artists.* New York: Rizzoli, 1986.

Needham, Gerald. *Nineteenth-Century Realist Art.* New York: Harper & Row, 1988.

WEBSITES

"Edward Hopper." Mark Harden's Artchive. Available online at http://www.artchive.com/artchive/H/hopper.html (accessed February 14, 2003).

AUDIO AND VISUAL MEDIA

"Streamlines and Breadlines." Episode 6 of the PBS series *American Visions.* PBS Home Video, 1996. VHS.

Poetry of Langston Hughes

"Scottsboro"; "Ballad of Roosevelt"; "Let America Be America Again"

Poems

By: Langston Hughes

Date: 1932; 1934; 1936

Source: Hughes, Langston. *The Collected Poems of Langston Hughes.* Edited by Arnold Rampersad. New York: Knopf, 1994, 234–237.

About the Author: Langston Hughes (1902–1967) was first published in a national magazine at age nineteen. Through his poetry, he became known as a major voice of the African American experience. Hughes often wrote about the plight of the oppressed, prejudice against African Americans, the American working class, or the struggle of peoples overseas. He traveled widely in the United States and abroad but considered Harlem his true home. Hughes died in a New York City hospital. ■

Introduction

The 1930s was a decade of great social unrest. Conditions were far from the American ideal, and Hughes' poetry expressed many of the injustices he saw in the American system. The Depression and the Roosevelt administration, with its New Deal programs, created the context for many of Hughes' works. Like those of other prominent writers of his time—Sinclair Lewis, John Steinbeck, Theodore Dreiser, and John Dos Passos, for example—Hughes' writings critically reflected the social upheaval of the Great Depression. He wrote in various genres: poetry, plays, essays, novels, short stories, newspaper columns, magazine articles, and song lyrics. All exposed the gap between what life in the United States could be and what Hughes witnessed in the everyday life of many Americans.

Because Hughes traveled overseas frequently, his writing also reflected his concern with the oppression he witnessed firsthand around the world. He supported the anti-Fascist and leftist Republican forces in the Spanish Civil War, supported Ethiopian independence from Italy, and spoke out against Jewish oppression in Germany. These and other global themes of injustice frequently appeared in his writing.

Although Hughes did not consider himself a Communist, his disenchantment with the capitalist system led him to consider and embrace Communist-influenced ideology. Nonetheless, Hughes was enthusiastic about American democracy and consistently expressed his confidence in progress in the United States. He and other Communist sympathizers in the 1930s believed that the Soviet Union's pact with Nazi Germany in 1939 revealed the true character of Communism. This revelation marked a turning point in his political views.

Langston Hughes, the famous African American poet and social critic, around 1930. © CORBIS. REPRODUCED BY PERMISSION.

Significance

Those who embraced his works did so because Hughes was a voice for the disenfranchised around the world and for his remarkable talent with vivid imagery. He was also an influential role model for the African American community, having achieved success in the literary world largely closed to African Americans. His success helped show others the possibilities.

Hughes' works were considered radical and controversial by some, and they were occasionally banned. Conservative political and religious groups cited such radical poems as "Goodbye Christ" as evidence of his Communist beliefs. As Hughes' political perspectives evolved, he attempted to dissociate himself from his earlier radical socialist poetry. This did not prevent him from being investigated by the FBI and the infamous House Un-American Acitivities Committee (HUAC) after World War II as a possible Communist or sympathizer. Hughes said in his statement to the committee that "although the United States still faces 'many problems,' it is also a significantly democratic nation that is young, strong, and beautiful."

Because of his controversial material, Hughes was called before HUAC for questioning about his possible Communist connections. The committee attempted to show that Communists were infiltrating every walk of American life. Suspecting strong Communist influence in the artistic community, HUAC questioned hundreds of actors, writers, and artists in the post–World War II years.

Primary Source

"Scottsboro"

SYNOPSIS: Published in 1932, "Scottsboro" is based on the trials of nine African American boys falsely accused of a 1931 rape of two white girls in Scottsboro, Alabama. Although one of the alleged victims confessed that she lied about the rape, the boys were sentenced to death. After a series of appeals and two Supreme Court decisions, the case ended with an agreement between the defense and prosecutors that four of the Scottsboro Boys would be released while five would serve prison sentences. The poem conveys Hughes' outrage at what he felt was a grave injustice.

8 BLACK BOYS IN A SOUTHERN JAIL.
WORLD, TURN PALE!

8 black boys and one white lie.
Is it much to die?

Is it much to die when immortal feet
March with you down Time's street,
When beyond steel bars sound the deathless drums
Like a mighty heart-beat as They come?

Who comes?

Christ,
Who fought alone.

John Brown.

That mad mob
That tore the Bastille down
Stone by stone.

Moses.

Jeanne d'Arc.

Dessalines.

Nat Turner.

Fighters for the free.

Lenin with the flag blood red.

(Not dead! Not dead!
None of those is dead.)

Gandhi.

Sandino.

Evangelista, too,
To walk with you—

8 BLACK BOYS IN A SOUTHERN JAIL.
WORLD, TURN PALE!

Primary Source

"Ballad of Roosevelt"

SYNOPSIS: "Ballad of Roosevelt" was published in 1934 during Franklin Delano Roosevelt's first term as president.

The pot was empty,
The cupboard was bare.
I said, Papa,
What's the matter here?
I'm waitin' on Roosevelt, son,
Roosevelt, Roosevelt,
Waitin' on Roosevelt, son.

The rent was due
And the lights was out.
I said, Tell me, Mama,
What's it all about?
We're waitin' on Roosevelt, son,
Roosevelt, Roosevelt,
Just waitin' on Roosevelt.

Sister got sick
And the doctor wouldn't come
Cause we couldn't pay him
The proper sum—
A-waitin' on Roosevelt,
Roosevelt, Roosevelt,
A-waitin' on Roosevelt.

Then one day
They put us out o' the house.
Ma and Pa was
Meek as a mouse
Still waitin' on Roosevelt,
Roosevelt, Roosevelt.

But when they felt those
Cold winds blow
And didn't have no
Place to go
Pa said, I'm tired
O' waitin' on Roosevelt,
Roosevelt, Roosevelt.
Damn tired o' waitin' on Roosevelt.

I can't git a job
And I can't git no grub.
Backbone and navel's
Doin' the belly-rub—
A-waitin' on Roosevelt,
Roosevelt, Roosevelt.

And a lot o' other folks
What's hungry and cold
Done stopped believin'
What they been told
By Roosevelt,
Roosevelt, Roosevelt—

Cause the pot's still empty,
And the cupboard's still bare,
And you can't build a bungalow
Out o' air—
Mr. Roosevelt, listen!
What's the matter here?

Primary Source

"Let America Be America Again"

SYNOPSIS: "Let America Be America Again," published in 1936, is a reflection of Hughes' broader appeal to the United States to live up to its ideal for democracy and economic justice for all. His collective voice represents farmers, the unemployed, workers, immigrants, Native Americans, and African Americans.

Let America be America again.
Let it be the dream it used to be.
Let it be the pioneer on the plain
Seeking a home where he himself is free.

(America never was America to me.)

Let America be the dream the dreamers dreamed—
Let it be that great strong land of love
Where never kings connive nor tyrants scheme
That any man be crushed by one above.

O, let my land be a land where Liberty
Is crowned with no false patriotic wreath,
But opportunity is real, and life is free,
Equality is in the air we breathe.

(There's never been equality for me,
Nor freedom in this "homeland of the free.")

Say, who are you that mumbles in the dark?
And who are you that draws your veil across the stars?

I am the poor white, fooled and pushed apart,
I am the Negro bearing slavery's scars.
I am the red man driven from the land,

I am the immigrant clutching the hope I seek—
And finding only the same old stupid plan
Of dog eat dog, of mighty crush the weak.

I am the young man, full of strength and hope,
Tangled in that ancient endless chain
Of profit, power, gain, of grab the land!
Of grab the gold! Of grab the ways of satisfying need!
Of work the men! Of take the pay!
Of owning everything for one's own greed!

I am the farmer, bondsman to the soil.
I am the worker sold to the machine.
I am the Negro, servant to you all.
I am the people, humble, hungry, mean—
Hungry yet today despite the dream.
Beaten yet today—O, Pioneers!
I am the man who never got ahead,
The poorest worker bartered through the years.

Yet I'm the one who dreamt our basic dream
In that Old World while still a serf of kings,
Who dreamt a dream so strong, so brave, so true,
That even yet its mighty daring sings
In every brick and stone, in every furrow turned
That's made America the land it has become.
O, I'm the man who sailed those early seas
In search of what I meant to be my home—
For I'm the one who left dark Ireland's shore,
And Poland's plain, and England's grassy lea,
And torn from Black Africa's strand I came
To build a "homeland of the free."

The free?

Who said the free? Not me?
Surely not me? The millions on relief today?
The millions shot down when we strike?
The millions who have nothing for our pay?
For all the dreams we've dreamed
And all the songs we've sung
And all the hopes we've held
And all the flags we've hung,
The millions who have nothing for our pay—
Except the dream that's almost dead today.

O, let America be America again—
The land that never has been yet—
And yet must be—the land where *every* man is free.
The land that's mine—the poor man's, Indian's,
  Negro's, ME
Who made America,
Whose sweat and blood, whose faith and pain,
Whose hand at the foundry, whose plow in the rain,
Must bring back our mighty dream again.

Sure, call me any ugly name you choose—
The steel of freedom does not stain.
From those who live like leeches on the people's lives,
We must take back our land again,
America!

O, yes,
I say it plain,
America never was America to me,
And yet I swear this oath—
America will be!

Out of the rack and ruin of our gangster death,
The rape and rot of graft, and stealth, and lies,
We, the people, must redeem
The land, the mines, the plants, the rivers.
The mountains and the endless plain—
All, all the stretch of these great green states—
And make America again!

Further Resources

BOOKS

Hughes, Langston. *Langston Hughes: Critical Essays Past and Present.* Henry Louis Gates Jr. and K.A. Appiah, eds. New York: Amistad, 1993.

———. *I Wonder as I Wander: An Autobiographical Journey.* New York: Hill & Wang, 1993.

Miller, R. Baxter. *The Art and Imagination of Langston Hughes.* Lexington, Ky.: University Press of Kentucky, 1989.

Ostrom, Hans. *A Langston Hughes Encyclopedia.* Westport, Conn.: Greenwood, 2002.

AUDIO AND VISUAL MEDIA

Langston Hughes: Poet. Produced and directed by Rhonda Fabian and Jerry Baber. 30 minutes. Schlessinger Video Productions, 1994.

Langston Hughes. New York Center for Visual History, Inc., 1999.

"Art: U.S. Scene"

Magazine article, Paintings

Date: December 24, 1934

Source: "Art: U.S. Scene." *Time,* December 24, 1934.

About the Publication: *Time,* first published in 1923, is still, in 2003, a frequently-read weekly newsmagazine. Created by journalists Henry R. Luce and Briton Hadden, the magazine was intended to provide information on national and international current events in a concise format later copied by other newsmagazines. By 1927, its circulation exceeded 175,000. ■

Introduction/Significance

On the eve of World War I (1914–1918), French artists clearly reigned in American art. The influential 1913 Armory Show (officially known as The International Exhibition of Modern Art) significantly advanced U.S. interest in modern art. While American artists were well represented, the exhibit was dominated by the French. Despite the evident French triumph, many American artists continued their pursuit of realism with a renewed enthusiasm that evolved into several influential schools of uniquely American art.

Artists in the Midwest began creating realist impressions of the American countryside instead of the more abstract images of the modernists. This new regionalist movement depicted everyday people doing everyday things. Midwest landscapes were often depicted. By the mid-1930s, American art patrons were often declining to buy French paintings in favor of regionalist art.

At the heart of the regionalist movement were three prominent painters: John Steuart Curry, Grant Wood, and Thomas Hart Benton. Although there were many regionalist artists in this era, this trio is considered the cornerstone of the movement.

John Steuart Curry (1897–1946)

John Steuart Curry grew up on a farm in Kansas, the landscape for many of his paintings. Educated in Kansas City, at the Chicago Art Institute, and then in Paris, Curry returned to the United States to teach at the Art Students' League in New York. His 1928 painting *Baptism in Kansas* began his fame as a regionalist painter. Curry's themes focused on rural life in Kansas, even when he lived in the eastern United States. His brief travels with the Ringling Brothers' circus reinforced his inclusion of animals in his paintings. He was preoccupied with natural disasters, as evidenced in his 1929 painting *Sanctuary.* The painting was a reflection of his experience in the Kaw River Flood near Lawrence, Kansas. He repeated the subject matter of natural disaster often, for example in *Kansas Tornado* (1929) and *Mississippi Noah* (1932). He frequently portrayed people and animals finding refuge on a small island of land surrounded by water. Some critics point out the apparent symbolism of Curry's paintings for the Depression era, when everyday people doing everyday things may have identified with the need to find refuge, an island in the middle of the symbolic flood.

Curry's popularity waned in the late 1930s and early 1940s. In 1941, the Kansas legislature, which had commissioned him to paint a mural, fired him because they did not like the mural he was painting. The mural, *Tragic Prelude,* was a depiction of the fiery abolitionist John Brown. One historian believed Curry's heartbreak over the issue contributed to his death. In 1997, the Kansas legislature issued a public apology on what would have been Curry's one-hundredth birthday and bought all of the drawings associated with the mural.

After Curry died, some museums began to remove his works from their walls as abstract expressionism became popular. Although his work never regained the popularity it enjoyed in the mid- and early 1930s, a revival of interest in his work occurred in the late 1990s. Americans looked back on the century then and gave credit to influential artists.

Grant Wood (1892–1942)

Born in Iowa, Grant Wood trained at the Chicago Art Institute and, as did many artists of the time, studied in Paris for a time. His work is heavily influenced by the German and Flemish Renaissance painters. But he is quoted as humorously evaluating the European influence another way:

> I found the answer [to what I know] when I joined a school of painters in Paris after the war who called themselves neo-meditationists. They believed an artist had to wait for inspiration, very quietly, and they did most of their waiting at the Dome or the Rotonde, with brandy. It was then that I realized that all the really good ideas I'd ever had came to me while I was milking a cow.

He returned from his studies abroad to teach in the Iowa public schools and was a spokesman for regionalist art in the 1930s.

Wood's most famous painting, *American Gothic* (1930), became a national icon. In 1934, approaching the peak of his career, Wood was appointed the head of Iowa's WPA Federal Arts Project. He continued painting rural scenes in such paintings as *Death on Ridge Row* (1935), *Spring Turning* (1936), *Seed Time* (1937), and *Iowa Cornfield* (1941). His works were satirical yet serene and often contained a suggestion of idealism. His cosmopolitan nature made his rural scenes almost paradoxical, but he always identified himself with his Iowa farmland.

Like Curry's, Wood's popularity suffered later in his career, especially in the years immediately following World War II (1939–1945). The public may have turned away from the regionalist painters when the crisis of the Depression and the war was over. They may not have wanted to be reminded of the era. Wood tried to save his career by starting again under a new name, to no avail.

Though many retrospective shows were held after Wood's death, the critics were merciless. Wood's art experienced a revival in the 1970s, and today his paintings are highly valued.

Thomas Hart Benton (1889–1975)

Like Curry and Wood, Thomas Benton was raised in the Midwest, the place that inspired many of his paintings. Born in Missouri, Benton studied at the Chicago Art Institute and then in Paris. Upon returning to New York, he taught at the Art Students' League. In the 1920s and 1930s, he taught at the Chelsea Neighborhood Association and became an important muralist. His early works include *Lonesome Road* (1927), *Political Business and the Intellectual Ballyhoo* (1932), and *Preparing the Bill* (1934).

In the mid-1930s, Benton returned to teach at the Kansas City Art Institute but was dismissed in 1941. Despite his disagreement with the institute, Benton went on to enjoy success during his career. Unlike Curry and Wood, Benton reached his peak later in his career. His later works include another *Lonesome Road* (1938), *Threshing* (1941), *June Morning* (1945), and *Wheat* (1967). Benton died painting a mural for the Country Music Foundation of Nashville.

Primary Source

"Art: U.S. Scene": Magazine article

SYNOPSIS: The following article and paintings from *Time*'s December 24, 1934, edition exposes regionalism as the new American art. Curry, Wood, and Benton are featured in the article, among a host of other regionalists. Although modern artists of the day like Stuart Davis rejected the apparent "sentimentality" of the regionalists, Benton said of the subject, "I am no sentimentalist either. I know an ass and the dust of his kicking." This quotation appeared on the cover of the magazine, with Benton's painting.

By last week, the U.S. art season was at its peak. In Manhattan there were no less than 70 exhibitions in progress. The public could see and buy practically anything it wanted. On 57th Street Edward Bruce was exhibiting the landscape technique and Chinese perspective he developed under the watchful eye of Maurice Sterne. Sir Francis Rose, Gertrude Stein's latest painter-protégé, was showing his sultry canvases. The Museum of Modern Art was aflame with Van Goghs, Cezannes, Toulouse-Lautrecs. At the New School for Social Research Yasuo Kuniyoshi, Robert Brachman, John Sloan and Alexander Brook were impressing their pupils with their craftsmanship.

In Chicago, the Art Institute was showing Degas and Manet prints. Pittsburgh was sending its big Carnegie International exhibition to Baltimore. San Franciscans were peering thoughtfully at Sculptress Malvina Hoffman's *Races of Man.* Los Angeles was holding its second annual California Modernists Exhibition. In Northampton, Mass., Smith College girls were giggling before Man Ray's Surrealist photographs.

Presented with their best year in five, dealers were again beginning to take cocktails with luncheon. The public's interest in art was proved by museum attendances which were uniformly up over last year. In one month in Manhattan, Ferargil Galleries' annual Artists' Relief Exhibition netted more than $2,000 with pictures priced at $5–$50. U.S. sales of the year were a Charles Willson Peale *Washington* to the Brooklyn Museum (price undisclosed); an early Rembrandt of *Christ Washing the Disciples' Feet* to the Chicago Art Institute; Jean Antoine Watteau's *Mezzelin* to the Metropolitan Museum for some $250,000 (*Time,* Dec. 17). The 1934 U.S. art turnover easily topped $126,000,000. (In 1928, the peak art year, the turnover was approximately $1 billion.)

As usual, top prices went for Old Masters whose value has survived many a depression. In London and Manhattan auctions of the 18th Century English portrait painters stood their customary ground as stolidly as oaks. But in U.S. sales of contemporary paintings, observers noted a significant difference. This year the French schools seem to be slipping in popular favor while a U.S. school, bent on portraying the U.S. scene, is coming to the fore.

In 1913 France conquered the U.S. art world. At the famed Manhattan Armory show arranged by the late Arthur B. Davies, the U.S. public got its first big dose of the arbitrary distortions and screaming colors which were making France's crop of artists the most spectacular in the world. The War took the public's mind temporarily off art but at its end, French artists were sitting on top of the world. U.S. painters, unable to sell at home or abroad, tried copying the French, turned out a profusion of spurious Matisses and Picassos, cheerfully joined the crazy parade of Cubism, Futurism, Dadaism, Surrealism. Painting became so deliberately unintelligible that it was no longer news when a picture was hung upside down.

In the U.S. opposition to such outlandish art first took root in the Midwest. A small group of native painters began to offer direct representation in place of introspective abstractions. To them what could be seen in their own land—streets, fields, shipyards, factories and those who people such places—became more important than what could be felt about far off places. From Missouri, from Kansas, from Ohio, from Iowa, came men whose work was destined to turn the tide of artistic taste in the U.S. Of these Earthy Midwesterners none represents the objectivity and purpose of their school more clearly than Missouri's Thomas Hart Benton.

At 17, Artist Benton gave up a job as surveyor's assistant in the lead and zinc district outside Joplin to do newspaper cartoons. A bad art student in Chicago, he went on to Paris where he speedily absorbed and copied all the latest French fads. Six Wartime months in the U.S. Navy knocked French Impressionism out of him, prompted him to develop a style of his own which he first exhibited in a series of realistic water-colors of War activities around Norfolk, Va.

Today Thomas Benton's fame rests chiefly on three murals. One is in the Library of Manhattan's Whitney Museum of American Art. Another is in the New School for Social Research. The third and best known, a huge panorama painted for the Indiana building at the Century of Progress Fair, is now stored

Primary Source

"Art: U.S. Scene": *The Ballad of the Jealous Lover of Lone Green Valley* by Thomas Hart Benton

(1 OF 4)

SYNOPSIS: "Thomas Benton's *The Jealous Lover of Lone Green Valley* . . . dips into fantasy but the story he tells is crisply clear. The three hillbillies sing and play an oldtime West Virginia ballad whose most dramatic incident—the stabbing of a bare-foot mountain wench by her jealous lover—is depicted in the background. The swirling rhythm of the road, repeated in the fence, the field and the sky, suggests the lilt of the music. Typical Americana are the jug of whiskey, the outhouse."—*Time,* December 24, 1934. SPENCER MUSEUM OF ART. REPRODUCED BY PERMISSION.

in an Indianapolis warehouse because the State lacks a suitable place to exhibit it. All three have a nervous electric quality which is peculiarly Benton's and which his pupils often try but fail to imitate. Painted from recognizable observations, all three portray such typical Americana as revivalists, bootleggers, stevedores, politicians, soda clerks.

Benton has had ample opportunity to study the U.S. he loves to paint. He was born in Neosho, Mo. in 1889. Says he: "My father [Congressman Maecenas Eason Benton] was a lawyer and politician. He came from Tennessee shortly after the Civil War, riding a horse and knocking snakes out of his path with a long stick. He was a great-nephew of Thomas Hart Benton, the Senator from Missouri and Andrew Jackson's lieutenant. My family table talk was entirely devoted to law and politics. Southwest Missouri was, and is yet in those parts in which the automobile road has not yet penetrated, a backwoods country with a characteristic backwoods culture. Turkey shoots, country school hoedowns, hunting (possum, squirrel, quail and other small

Primary Source

"Art: U.S. Scene": *The Tornado* by John Steuart Curry (2 OF 4)

SYNOPSIS: "Kansas does not like Kansan John Steuart Curry's pictures. Curry has aptly explained why: 'They have Kansas. They hardly need paintings of it.' But Curry has never painted Kansas with malice. He painted *Tornado* in 1929 after a tornado had passed a mile and a half from his father's farm. The son of devout Scotch Presbyterians, he made the picture represent man's elemental terror of nature, expressed in it his own boyhood fears and emotions."—*Time,* December 24, 1934. SPENCER MUSEUM OF ART. REPRODUCED BY PERMISSION.

game) and hay wagon parties were sports with which I was familiar."

Benton, in his murals and easel paintings, earnestly and almost ferociously strives to record a contemporary history of the U.S. A short wiry man with an unruly crop of black hair, he lives with his beauteous Italian wife and one small son in a picture-cluttered downtown Manhattan flat. To critics that have complained that his murals were loud and disturbing, Artist Benton answers: "They represent the U.S. which is also loud and not 'in good taste.'" "I have not found," he explains, "the U.S. a standardized mortuary and consequently have no sympathy with that school of detractors whose experience has been limited to first class hotels and paved highways. At the same time, I am no sentimentalist. I know an ass and the dust of his kicking when I come across it. But I have come across enough of it to be able to discover interesting qualities therein."

Thomas Benton has filled scores of notebooks with sketches of the U.S. scene which eventually find their way into his work. He boasts that all his burlesque queens, stevedores, Negroes, preachers, and college professors are actual persons. His vivid portraits of them are fast becoming collectors' items and the cost of Bentons has been steadily rising since the Navy put him on the right artistic track. Last week, Thomas Benton, who is usually jolly, had a special reason to be cheerful. He sold his oil, *Cotton Town . . . ,* to Marshall Field III.

If Thomas Benton is the most virile of U.S. painters of the U.S. Scene the honor of a pioneer

Primary Source

"Art: U.S. Scene": *New Gotham Burlesque* by Reginald Marsh (3 OF 4)

SYNOPSIS: "Sexy interiors of burlesque shows, along with city street scenes, amusement parks and beaches, are the specialty of this young tousle-headed artist. Here he presents the New Gotham Burlesque Theatre in Manhattan's Harlem. 'It is,' says [Reginald] Marsh, 'an accurate picture of that place.' Most critics agree that it is also an accurate picture of the interior of any other theatre given over to the art of the 'strip teaser.'"—*Time,* December 24, 1934. © BETTMANN/CORBIS. REPRODUCED BY PERMISSION.

in the movement belongs to Charles Ephraim Burchfield, 41, a tailor's son from Ashtabula Harbor, Ohio. In his childhood Burchfield found nothing so fascinating as tumble-down houses, freight trains, railroad tracks. Today most up-to-date museums have Burchfields. Not so spectacular a draughtsman as Benton, Burchfield manages to invest with a calm if somewhat dismal dignity and an exceptionally acute feeling for light and space. He lives in an eight-room frame house outside Buffalo, N.Y. with his wife and five children, amuses himself by tending his garden and building frames for his pictures.

A painter of the city is Reginald Marsh who was born 36 years ago to Muralist Fred Dana Marsh in

Paris. As a tousle-headed boy (he is now almost bald) he went to Lawrenceville, later to Yale. In spite of his very proper education, Artist Marsh thinks "well bred people are no fun to paint," haunts Manhattan subways, public beaches, waterfronts, burlesque theatres for his subjects. The Metropolitan and Whitney Museums thought enough of his work to purchase examples.

A friend who had not seen John Steuart Curry since he was a potent footballer at Geneva College in Beaver Falls, Pa. 15 years ago would hardly recognize him today. Apple-cheeked, fat, bald, he now weighs 187 pounds, lives quietly in Westport, Conn. He is so sensitive about his art that he frequently decides to give it up. But Curry is generally considered the greatest painter of Kansas and of the circus in the U.S. His two most famed works *Tornado* . . . and *Baptism in Kansas* won him important critical accolades in Chicago and Manhattan but only served to irritate his fellow Kansans who felt that such subjects were best left untouched. In 1932 John Ringling gave him permission to follow the "Greatest Show on Earth." The result was a spectacular group of canvases showing herds of elephants, the Flying Codonas, the Wallenda Family, Baby Ruth, the fat girl, etc.

Curry's art is simple and dramatic. Whether he likes it or not no Kansan who has looked at his State or been to a circus can fail to recognize the authenticity of Curry's subjects. Latest Curry is a two-panel mural for the Westport High School. In *Comedy* Artist Curry has included himself and his wife, has gaily jumbled Charlie Chaplin on roller skates, Mickey Mouse, Mutt & Jeff, Shakespeare's Bottom, Will Rogers, Popeye the Sailor. In *Tragedy* Uncle Tom prays by the bedside of Little Eva, Hamlet sulks, Lady Macbeth sleepwalks, Theodore Dreiser, Sherwood Anderson, Eugene O'Neill scowl, Aerialist Lillian Leitzel drops from her circus partner's arms to death.

The chief philosopher and greatest teacher of representational U.S. art is Iowa's chubby, soft-spoken Grant Wood. Like Benton, Grant Wood studied in France, turned out his share of *Blue Vase, Sorrento, House in Montmartre, Breton Market.* But in 1929 he radically changed his style. From his palette issued a series of rolling, tree-dotted Iowa fields done in a flat, smooth manner. His landscape of West Branch, Iowa (*Fortune,* Aug. 1932) got the birthplace of Herbert Hoover almost as much public attention as the infrequent visits of that President. Wood's credo: U.S. art suffers from a "Colonial attitude" to Europe, a feeling of cultural dependence upon the older continent. To combat this attitude Wood chose irony. His *American Gothic* . . . and his spectacular *Daughters of Revolution,* three prim spinsters against a background of *Washington Crossing the Delaware,* were his first attack. This year, what most critics consider his most important painting, *Dinner for Threshers* . . . , won no prize at the Carnegie International at Pittsburgh but was voted third most popular by the public. Simple and direct, the picture bears as genuine a U.S. stamp as a hotdog stand or baseball park.

Shy Bachelor Wood, 42, hates to leave his native Iowa where his fellow-citizens have been buying his pictures and singing his praise almost since he began painting. He is often convinced he is a better teacher than painter. In Munich, he once mastered in a few weeks the technique of glass painting when German artists insisted on making a bearded Civil War soldier (for a Cedar Rapids memorial window) look like Christ.

No man in the U.S. is a more fervid believer in developing "regional art" than Grant Wood. Long before Public Works Art Project started the Government's $1,408,381 program to give work to more than 3,000 artists, Wood had established his own Iowa art colony in Stone City. There for little more than $50 an artist could live and learn for a six-week session. When PWAP was established Wood became its Iowa leader, taught Iowa artists to paint the "U.S. scene"—prime purpose of PWAP. Today he is trying to continue the work PWAP started. He and a group of students are preparing a series of murals for the Iowa State University Theatre at Iowa City.

Wood's theory of regional art rests upon the idea that different sections of the U.S. should compete with one another just as Old World cities competed in the building of Gothic cathedrals. Only thus, he believes, can the U.S. develop a truly national art. Whether PWAP has sown the seeds of a national art no man can yet tell, but, beyond dispute, PWAP's investment has not only enormously stimulated the public's interest but has also revealed definite regional traits in art.

Some of these districts and their characteristics:

Chicago's leading artist is Ivan Le Lorraine Albright, 37, who likes to picture men whose skins are as wrinkled as a dirty handkerchief. His heavy Baroque style brought him local fame when he applied it to a loutish, hunched figure called *The Lineman.* Other noteworthy Chicago artists: Malvin Albright, twin of Ivan, who sculpts under the name of Zsissly; Aaron Bohrod (pronounced Bo-rod) who does sketches of Chicago streets and coal yards;

Primary Source

"Art: U.S. Scene": *American Gothic* by Grant Wood (4 OF 4)

SYNOPSIS: "To an Iowa lady who complained that this picture was an insult to Iowa ladies, Grant Wood was able to reply: 'It is a picture of my sister.' He might have added that the gentleman is a Stone City, Iowa dentist. *American Gothic,* painted in 1930, was Wood's first noteworthy stand against what he terms the U.S. 'colonial attitude,' a feeling of artistic dependence upon Europe. No critic could assert that Wood has not established his independence. The picture could have been painted nowhere outside the U.S."—*Time,* December 24, 1934. CORBIS/BETTMANN. REPRODUCED BY PERMISSION OF THE VISUAL ARTISTS AND GALLERIES ASSOCIATION, INC. FOR GRANT WOOD.

Jean Crawford Adams (landscapes); Archibald John Motley Jr., a Negro who gets a bright, sculpturesque quality in his portraits of fellow Negroes; Frances Foy, whose specialty is city parks and streets.

. . . Artist who has spent the most time with the most success portraying Detroit is a Philadelphian—Charles Sheeler. Commissioned by Edsel Ford in 1927 to do a series of paintings of the Ford River Rouge plant, Painter Sheeler turned out a series of meticulous, exact canvases that in black and white reproductions are almost indistinguishable from Photographer Sheeler's excellent camera studies of similar subjects. In spite of objecting to his photographic technique, most critics allow Sheeler a top place among U.S. painters of industrial scenes. Michigan's nearest approach to catching the U.S. scene in paint is a Flint school of artists led by Jaroslav Brozik which applies to industrial themes an impressionistic manner.

Boston remains conservative. Ten years ago Artists Harley Perkins, Charles Hovey Pepper and Carl G. Cutler started a minor revolt against what they called the "Museum [of Fine Arts] School" which was then turning out replicas of John Singer Sargent. The revolt sagged. Today Boston's best artist concerned with the contemporary U.S. scene is Molly Luce, wife of Alan Burroughs, X-ray art researcher for Harvard's Fogg Museum.

. . . The Pacific Coast has given its fair share of fame to San Francisco Artists Lucien Labaudt, Otis Oldfield, Jane Berlandina, Charles Stafford Duncan. Lately from Southern California have come two sturdy contenders for the title "best in the West"—Los Angeles' Millard Sheets and Pasadena's Paul Starrett Sample. At 19, husky blond Artist Sheets deliberately set out to win prize money to finance his painting, made $2,500 from ten prizes in two years. Today, at 27, he is head of the art department at Scripps College, Claremont. His PWAP canvas *Tenement Flats,* showing gossiping women against a design of bleak, wash-strung flats, was chosen by President Roosevelt to hang in the White House. Huge Paul Sample, a onetime Dartmouth tackle, divides his time between California and Vermont. He has sometimes shown the influence of Benton and Wood, like many another modern says his favorite painter is Breughel. A professor of painting at University of Southern California, he won two successive National Academy prizes with completely unacademic pictures.

Taos is in incredible country. The New Mexican sunlight is so intense that it casts shadows that would seem outrageous anywhere else. In Taos, reality is almost Cubism and Taos shadows are actually as elongated and mysterious as those in Salvador Dali's Surrealism (*Time,* Nov. 29). The Taos art colony was founded in 1898, today boasts some 54 painters. Most influential is barrel-chested Andrew Dasburg who looks like Beethoven and tortures himself in order to translate Taos light and form into oil paintings. Emil Bisttram is slowly working away from representation to symbolism but has never yet failed to produce a lucid canvas. Kenneth Adams thinks the Southwestern artist should evolve a formal design from the distortions of light, displays a strong feeling for form.

Probably no region in the U.S. can produce such distorted pictures as Taos and still claim that they record actuality. The fact that Taos artists are, as a rule, content not to exaggerate their region's natural exaggerations, puts them directly into the main stream of U.S. representationalism along with Grant Wood and his threshers, Burchfield and his gloomy houses, Benton and his squirming racketeers.

Further Resources

BOOKS

Dennis, James M. *Renegade Regionalists: The Modern Independence of Grant Wood, Thomas Hart Benton, and John Steuart Curry.* Madison, Wis.: University of Wisconsin Press, 1998.

Doss, Eric Lee. *Benton, Pollock, and the Politics of Modernism: From Regionalism to Abstract Expressionism.* Chicago: University of Chicago Press, 1991.

Guldon, Mary Scholz. *Regionalist Art: Thomas Hart Benton, John Steuart Curry, and Grant Wood: A Guide to the Literature.* Lanham, Md.: Scarecrow Press, 1982.

WEBSITES

Darman, Adrian. "Grant Wood: A Certain Misunderstanding." Artcult. Available online at http://www.artcult.com/wood.html (accessed February 15, 2003).

Haven, Janet. "Going Back to Iowa: The World of Grant Wood." University of Virginia American Studies Program. Available online at http://xroads.virginia.edu/~MA98/haven/wood/home.html (accessed February 15, 2003).

Composition

Painting

By: Stuart Davis

Date: 1935

Source: Davis, Stuart. *Composition.* 1935. In the collection of the National Museum of American Art. Image number 45061.

About the Artist: Stuart Davis (1892–1964) was a forerunner of modern American art. Son of a *Philadelphia Press* art editor, Davis was introduced early to artistic concepts. He studied in New York with Robert Henri. As a student in 1913, Davis exhibited paintings in the controversial abstract art Armory Show, and went on from there to become one of America's most influential abstract artists. His career included jobs as an illustrator and cartoonist for the radical journal *The Masses* and for *Harper's Weekly*. By 1935, he was president of the Artists Union. ■

Introduction

Abstract art in the United States had its beginnings at the Armory Show in 1913. This international show was held at the 69th Regiment Armory in New York City and showcased approximately 1,600 works, mostly European, embodying the modernist style, including cubism. The show was bashed by critics, who thought it epitomized the absurdity of the new art. Nonetheless, the show began to open people's minds to the future of art.

Stuart Davis was one American who took to abstract art early. A student in 1913, Davis exhibited watercolors in the Armory Show. He began to develop a distinctive cubist style in the late 1920s after studying in Paris. By the middle 1930s, he had established himself as one of America's most important abstract artists.

Davis was convinced that the object of the painting was not the physical object itself but the formal elements—especially line. Typical of other cubist artists, he arranged flat, two-dimensional shapes of color to form the objects in his paintings and separated objects with pronounced lines. He used sharp lines and vivid, contrasting colors adjoined in a way that communicates

Primary Source

Composition

SYNOPSIS: *Composition,* painted in 1935, is one of Davis's lesser-known works, but it conveys a strong sense of his distinctive style. The two-dimensional, contrasting objects and the heavy black lines used to separate them are characteristic of abstract style. Typically, Davis positions everyday objects together in a seemingly haphazard and incongruous way, like the artist's palette and the shovel—the idea being that when ordinary objects are shown in unusual ways, they are understood differently. PAINTING ON CANVAS BY STUART DAVIS, PHOTOGRAPH. NATIONAL MUSEUM OF AMERICAN ART, WASHINGTON DC/ART RESOURCE, NY. REPRODUCED BY PERMISSION.

a sense of balance and rhythm. Viewers can also recognize his love of jazz in the zestful rhythms and intense color patterns of his work. Like many of his American contemporaries, Davis depicted what he interpreted as the "American Scene." Asked about the subjects of his art, he was quoted as saying, "I paint what I see in America. In other words, I paint the American Scene." His subjects include landscapes from a New York waterfront and such everyday items as a percolator or an eggbeater.

Davis had a distinct distaste for what he called the sentimentality of the Realist artists of the time, including Thomas Hart Benton, Norman Rockwell, and Grant Wood. The realists, who were also painting the American scene, did so with a style distinctly different from the modernists. Realists attempt to represent objects as they appear in the physical world, whereas abstract artists such as Davis attempt to capture the fundamental elements in the object. The resulting artwork is reductive rather than representative.

Though Davis was an avowed Marxist and political activist, his artwork was not based on Marxist ideas. He did concede, however, that the concepts underlying modernist art and the reaction people had to it could serve the cause of revolution central to Marxist philosophies.

Significance

Davis played a major role in establishing modern, abstract, art in the United States. He was among the first American abstract artists, and the best. He also incorporated American themes into his work. An important style in itself, abstract art also set the scene for abstract expressionism, pop art, and post-painterly abstraction. Postmodern art took abstract art in new directions such as photorealism, conceptualism, new expressionism, assemblage, and performance and process art. Davis and his contemporaries built the foundation for these later movements in art.

In addition to his art, Davis made an impact through his support of artists' rights. He became president of the Artists Union in 1935 and designed covers for *Art Front,* the union's magazine. Through these roles he attempted to convince the public that artists are entitled to the same rights as other workers. In particular, he felt they should be allowed to unionize and take collective action.

Further Resources

BOOKS

Goosen, E.C. *Stuart Davis.* New York: G. Braziller, 1959.

Hills, Patricia. *Stuart Davis.* New York: Abrams, 1996.

Wilken, Karen. *Stuart Davis.* New York: Abbeville, 1987.

WEBSITES

Pioch, Nicolas. "Davis, Stuart." WebMuseum, Paris. Available online at http://www.ibiblio.org/wm/paint/auth/davis (accessed February 15, 2003).

"Stuart Davis." Artcyclopedia. Available online at http://www.artcyclopedia.com/artiats/davis_stuart.html; website home page: http://www.artcyclopedia.com/index.html (accessed February 15, 2003).

It Can't Happen Here

Novel

By: Sinclair Lewis

Date: 1935

Source: Lewis, Sinclair. *It Can't Happen Here.* New York: Doran, 1935, 74–83.

About the Author: American novelist Harry Sinclair Lewis (1885–1951) was a 1908 Yale graduate and editor of Yale's *Literary Magazine.* He began his writing career as a journalist and editor. Though his first five novels failed, he enjoyed success in the 1920s and 1930s with novels chiefly about the middle class. His best-known works include *Main Street, Babbitt, Arrowsmith,* and *Elmer Gantry.* Lewis traveled widely and spent his last days in Europe, where he died. ■

Introduction

Before *It Can't Happen Here,* Lewis had written six successful novels. For *Arrowsmith,* he was offered the Pulitzer Prize for literature but refused it. When he did accept the Nobel Prize for Literature in 1930, he chided the American Academy of the Arts, asserting his concern that writers might start to write to please the committee rather than writing from their own inner convictions. His own convictions were infused with compassion for the powerless, the basis for much of his writing.

In the early 1930s, when he was writing *Ann Vickers,* Lewis became concerned with the rise of totalitarian regimes in Europe. Hitler and Mussolini were evidence that the unthinkable could happen in the United States. The popularity of such demagogues as Father Charles Coughlin and Huey Long, as well as the appearance of blatantly fascist organizations, led many, including Lewis, to worry about the future of democracy in the United States.

In response to the perceived fascist menace, Lewis wrote *It Can't Happen Here,* a novel about the possibility of a fascist government in the United States. The story is about a 1936 presidential election in which President Franklin D. Roosevelt runs against Buzz Windrip, a dangerous fascist-disguised-as-savior. Doremus Jessup, the novel's protagonist, is an apathetic liberal until he is pushed into action by a rising fascist storm.

American author Sinclair Lewis wrote *It Can't Happen Here* as a cautionary tale against fascism. THE LIBRARY OF CONGRESS.

Characters in the story mirror real-life personalities of the time. Bishop Prang closely parallels Father Coughlin, and Windrip is modeled after Huey Long. By surrounding his fictional characters with real ones, Lewis subtly leads the reader into understanding how a figure like Buzz Windrip could in a volatile social climate persuade the masses in his favor.

Windrip is charming and charismatic. He makes outrageous promises, including a $5,000 grant to every family (much like Long's "Share the Wealth Plan"). Appearing to support both sides of any issue, he woos disenchanted throngs to his side. Meanwhile, Jessup warns his comrades about the threat of totalitarianism. Blinded by the promises of Windrip, they assure Jessup that "it can't happen here," until it does.

Windrip is elected president, and soon after, thousands of "disloyal" citizens are beaten, put into concentration camps, or executed by the fascist regime. Constitutional rights are abolished, educational systems are destroyed, and the military is expanded. Eventually, however, democracy begins to reappear in isolated sections of the country, but not before irreparable damage has been done to the fabric of American society. Countless lives, including those of Jessup and his family, are ruined.

Significance

It Can't Happen Here was a best-seller in 1936, a pivotal year in the expansion of fascism. Italy completed its conquest of Ethiopia, Germany remilitarized the Rhineland, and the Spanish Civil War began. Bolstered by Italian and German aid, Spanish Fascists emerged victorious two years later. In each case, Britain and France stood on the sidelines and refused to be drawn into the conflicts. The United States kept an even greater distance. It was, perhaps, the best chance that the Western democracies had to stop fascism before German rearmament moved into high gear and significantly raised the risks in challenging Hitler.

In this climate, Lewis wanted to write an antifascist play for the Federal Theatre Project, but the Roosevelt administration cancelled his production of "Ethiopia" because it might offend Italy. *It Can't Happen Here,* however, was adapted to the Federal Theatre stage. It opened in December 1936 in twenty-one locations and became one of the most popular Federal Theatre productions.

Lewis's great achievement is in making the unbelievable seem almost believable, if more than a little outrageous. In so doing, he successfully raises the question whether fascism could actually take root in the United States. Of course, what really happened in the 1936 election was nothing like Lewis's story. Huey Long, a possible rival to Roosevelt in 1936, was assassinated in September 1935. Father Coughlin, with some support from the disorganized Long followers, did form a third party—the Union Party—to challenge Roosevelt. The Union Party candidate, William Lemke, received only 875,000 votes out of nearly 45 million votes cast, and Roosevelt was overwhelmingly elected to a second term. While social and political change continued, the democratic process prevailed.

Primary Source

It Can't Happen Here [excerpt]

SYNOPSIS: This excerpt outlines the Fifteen Points of Buzz Windrip's presidential campaign platform. It was officially called "The Fifteen Points of Victory for the Forgotten Men." The points reveal diminished rights of Jews, blacks, women, and laborers, among others, and the outrageously embellished rights of the government.

■ ■ ■

I don't pretend to be a very educated man, except maybe educated in the heart, and in being able to feel for the sorrows and fear of every ornery fellow human being. Still and all, I've read the Bible through, from kiver to kiver, like my wife's folks say down in Arkansas, some eleven times; I've read all the law books they've printed; and as to contemporaries, I don't guess I've missed much of all the grand literature produced by Bruce Barton, Edgar Guest, Arthur Brisbane, Elizabeth Dilling, Walter Pitkin, and William Dudley Pelley.

This last gentleman I honor not only for his rattling good yarns, and his serious work in investigating life beyond the grave and absolutely proving that only a blind fool could fail to believe in Personal Immortality, but, finally, for his public-spirited and self-sacrificing work in founding the Silver Shirts. These true knights, even if they did not attain quite all the success they deserved, were one of our most noble and Galahad-like attempts to combat the sneaking, snaky, sinister, surreptitious, seditious plots of the Red Radicals and other sour brands of Bolsheviks that incessantly threaten the American standards of Liberty, High Wages, and Universal Security.

These fellows have Messages, and we haven't got time for anything in literature except a straight, hard-hitting, heart-throbbing Message!

Zero Hour, *Berzelius Windrip.*

During the very first week of his campaign, Senator Windrip clarified his philosophy by issuing his distinguished proclamation: "The Fifteen Points of Victory for the Forgotten Men." The fifteen planks, in his own words (or maybe in Lee Sarason's words, or Dewey Haik's words), were these:

(1) All finance in the country, including banking, insurance, stocks and bonds and mortgages, shall be under the absolute control of a Federal Central Bank, owned by the government and conducted by a Board appointed by the President, which Board shall, without need of recourse to Congress for legislative authorization, be empowered to make all regulations governing finance. Thereafter, as soon as may be practicable, this said Board shall consider the nationalization and government-ownership, for the Profit of the Whole People, of all mines, oilfields, water power, public utilities, transportation, and communication.

(2) The President shall appoint a commission, equally divided between manual workers, employers, and representatives of the Public, to determine which Labor Unions are qualified to represent the Workers; and report to the Executive, for legal action, all pretended labor organizations, whether "Company Unions," or "Red Unions," controlled by Communists and the so-called "Third International." The duly recognized Unions shall be constituted Bureaus of the Government, with power of decision in all labor disputes. Later, the same investigation and official recognition shall be extended to farm organizations. In this elevation of the position of the Worker, it shall be emphasized that the League of Forgotten Men is the chief bulwark against the menace of destructive and un-American Radicalism.

(3) In contradistinction to the doctrines of Red Radicals, with their felonious expropriation of the arduously acquired possessions which insure to aged persons their security, this League and Party will guarantee Private Initiative and the Right to Private Property for all time.

(4) Believing that only under God Almighty, to Whom we render all homage, do we Americans hold our vast Power, we shall guarantee to all persons absolute freedom of religious worship, provided, however, that no atheist, agnostic, believer in Black Magic, nor any Jew who shall refuse to swear allegiance to the New Testament, nor any person of any faith who refuses to take the Pledge to the Flag, shall be permitted to hold any public office or to practice as a teacher, professor, lawyer, judge, or as a physician, except in the category of Obstetrics.

(5) Annual net income per person shall be limited to $500,000. No accumulated fortune may at any one time exceed $3,000,000 per person. No one person shall, during his entire lifetime, be permitted to retain an inheritance or various inheritances in total exceeding $2,000,000. All incomes or estates in excess of the sums named shall be seized by the Federal Government for use in Relief and in Administrative expenses.

(6) Profit shall be taken out of War by seizing all dividends over and above 6 per cent that shall be received from the manufacture, distribution, or sale, during Wartime, of all arms, munitions, aircraft, ships, tanks, and all other things directly applicable to warfare, as well as from food, textiles, and all other supplies furnished to the American or to any allied army.

(7) Our armaments and the size of our military and naval establishments shall be consistently enlarged until they shall equal, but—since this country has no desire for foreign conquest of any kind—not surpass, in every branch of the forces of defense, the martial strength of any other single country or empire in the world. Upon inauguration, this League and Party shall make this its first obligation, together with the issuance of a firm proclamation to all nations of the world that our armed forces are to be maintained solely for the purpose of insuring world peace and amity.

(8) Congress shall have the sole right to issue money and immediately upon our inauguration it shall at least double the present supply of money, in order to facilitate the fluidity of credit.

(9) We cannot too strongly condemn the un-Christian attitude of certain otherwise progressive nations in their discriminations against the Jews, who have been among the strongest supporters of the League, and who will continue to prosper and to be recognized as fully Americanized, though only so long as they continue to support our ideals.

(10) All Negroes shall be prohibited from voting, holding public office, practicing law, medicine, or teaching in any class above the grade of grammar school, and they shall be taxed 100 per cent of all sums in excess of $10,000 per family per year which they may earn or in any other manner receive. In order, however, to give the most sympathetic aid possible to all Negroes who comprehend their proper and valuable place in society, all such colored persons, male or female, as can prove that they have devoted not less than forty-five years to such suitable tasks as domestic service, agricultural labor, and common labor in industries, shall at the age of sixty-five be permitted to appear before a special Board, composed entirely of white persons, and upon proof that while employed they have never been idle except through sickness, they shall be recommended for pensions not to exceed the sum of $500.00 per person per year, nor to exceed $700.00 per family. Negroes shall, by definition, be persons with at least one sixteenth colored blood.

(11) Far from opposing such high-minded and economically sound methods of the relief of poverty, unemployment, and old age as the EPIC plan of the Hon. Upton Sinclair, the "Share the Wealth" and "Every Man a King" proposals of the late Hon. Huey Long to assure every family $5000 a year, the Townsend plan, the Utopian plan, Technocracy, and all competent schemes of unemployment insurance, a Commission shall immediately be appointed by the New Administration to study, reconcile, and recommend for immediate adoption the best features in these several plans for Social Security, and the Hon. Messrs. Sinclair, Townsend, Eugene Reed, and Howard Scott are herewith invited to in every way advise and collaborate with that Commission.

(12) All women now employed shall, as rapidly as possible, except in such peculiarly feminine spheres of activity as nursing and beauty parlors, be assisted to return to their incomparably sacred duties as home-makers and as mothers of strong, honorable future Citizens of the Commonwealth.

(13) Any person advocating Communism, Socialism, or Anarchism, advocating refusal to enlist in case of war, or advocating alliance with Russia in any war whatsoever, shall be subject to trial for high treason, with a minimum penalty of twenty years at hard labor in prison, and a maximum of death on the gallows, or other form of execution which the judges may find convenient.

(14) All bonuses promised to former soldiers of any war in which America has ever engaged shall be immediately paid in full, in cash, and in all cases of veterans with incomes of less than $5,000.00 a year, the formerly promised sums shall be doubled.

(15) Congress shall, immediately upon our inauguration, initiate amendments to the Constitution providing (a), that the President shall have the authority to institute and execute all necessary measures for the conduct of the government during this critical epoch; (b), that Congress shall serve only in an advisory capacity, calling to the attention of the President and his aides and Cabinet any needed legislation, but not acting upon same until authorized by the President so to act; and (c), that the Supreme Court shall immediately have removed from its jurisdiction the power to negate, by ruling them to be unconstitutional or by any other judicial action, any or all acts of the President, his duly appointed aides, or Congress.

Addendum: It shall be strictly understood that, as the League of Forgotten Men and the Democratic Party, as now constituted, have no purpose nor desire to carry out any measure that shall not unqualifiedly meet with the desire of the majority of voters in these United States, the League and Party regard none of the above fifteen points as obligatory and unmodifiable except No. 15, and upon the others they will act or refrain from acting in accordance with the general desire of the Public, who shall under the new régime be again granted an individual freedom of which they have been deprived by the harsh and restrictive economic measures of former administrations, both Republican and Democratic.

■ ■ ■

"But what does it mean?" marveled Mrs. Jessup, when her husband had read the platform to her. "It's so inconsistent. Sounds like a combination of Norman Thomas and Calvin Coolidge. I don't seem to understand it. I wonder if Mr. Windrip understands it himself?"

"Sure. You bet he does. It mustn't be supposed that because Windrip gets that intellectual dressmaker Sarason to prettify his ideas up for him he doesn't recognize 'em and clasp 'em to his bosom when they're dolled up in two-dollar words. I'll tell you just what it all means: Articles One and Five mean that if the financiers and transportation kings and so on don't come through heavily with support for Buzz they may be threatened with bigger income taxes and some control of their businesses. But they are coming through, I hear, handsomely—they're paying for Buzz's radio and his parades. Two, that by controlling their unions directly, Buzz's gang can kidnap all Labor into slavery. Three backs up the security for Big Capital and Four brings the preachers into line as scared and unpaid press-agents for Buzz.

"Six doesn't mean anything at all—munition firms with vertical trusts will be able to wangle one 6 per cent on manufacture, one on transportation, and one on sales—at least. Seven means we'll get ready to follow all the European nations in trying to hog the whole world. Eight means that by inflation, big industrial companies will be able to buy their outstanding bonds back at a cent on the dollar, and Nine that all Jews who don't cough up plenty of money for the robber baron will be punished, even including the Jews who haven't much to cough up. Ten, that all well-paying jobs and businesses held by Negroes will be grabbed by the Poor White Trash among Buzz's worshipers—and that instead of being denounced they'll be universally praised as patriotic protectors of Racial Purity. Eleven, that Buzz'll be able to pass the buck for not creating any real relief for poverty. Twelve, that women will later lose the vote and the right to higher education and be foxed out of all decent jobs and urged to rear soldiers to be killed in foreign wars. Thirteen, that anybody who opposes Buzz in any way at all can be called a Communist and scragged for it. Why, under this clause, Hoover and Al Smith and Ogden Mills—yes, and you and me—will all be Communists.

"Fourteen, that Buzz thinks enough of the support of the veterans' vote to be willing to pay high for it—in other people's money. And Fifteen—well, that's the one lone clause that really does mean something; and it means that Windrip and Lee Sarason and Bishop Prang and I guess maybe this Colonel Dewey Haik and this Dr. Hector Macgoblin—you know, this doctor that helps write the high-minded hymns for Buzz—they've realized that this country has gone so flabby that any gang daring enough and unscrupulous enough, and smart enough not to *seem* illegal, can grab hold of the entire government and have all the power and applause and salutes, all the money and palaces and willin' women they want.

"They're only a handful, but just think how small Lenin's gang was at first, and Mussolini's, and Hitler's, and Kemal Pasha's, and Napoleon's! You'll see all the liberal preachers and modernist educators and discontented newspapermen and farm agitators—maybe they'll worry at first, but they'll get caught up in the web of propaganda, like we all were in the Great War, and they'll all be convinced that, even if our Buzzy maybe *has* got a few faults, he's on the side of the plain people, and against all the tight old political machines, and they'll rouse the country for him as the Great Liberator (and meanwhile Big Business will just wink and sit tight!) and then, by God, this crook—oh, I don't know whether he's more of a crook or an hysterical religious fanatic—along with Sarason and Haik and Prang and Macgoblin—these five men will be able to set up a régime that'll remind you of Henry Morgan the pirate capturing a merchant ship."

"But will Americans stand for it long?" whimpered Emma. "Oh, no, not people like us—the descendants of the pioneers!"

"Dunno. I'm going to try help see that they don't. . . . Of course you understand that you and I and Sissy and Fowler and Mary will probably be shot if I do try to do anything. . . . Hm! I sound brave enough now, but probably I'll be scared to death when I hear Buzz's private troops go marching by!"

"Oh, you will be careful, won't you?" begged Emma. "Oh. Before I forget it. How many times must I tell you, Dormouse, not to give Foolish chicken bones—they'll stick in his poor throat and choke him to death. And you just *never* remember to take the keys out of the car when you put it in the garage at night! I'm perfectly *sure* Shad Ledue or somebody will steal it one of these nights!"

■ ■ ■

Father Stephen Perefixe, when he read the Fifteen Points, was considerably angrier than Doremus.

He snorted, "What? Negroes, Jews, women—they all banned and they leave us Catholics out, this time? Hitler didn't neglect us. *He's* persecuted us. Must be that Charley Coughlin. He's made us too respectable!"

Sissy, who was eager to go to a school of architecture and become a creator of new styles in houses of glass and steel; Lorinda Pike, who had plans for a Carlsbad-Vichy-Saratoga in Vermont; Mrs.

Candy, who aspired to a home bakery of her own when she should be too old for domestic labor—they were all of them angrier than either Doremus or Father Perefixe.

Sissy sounded not like a flirtatious girl but like a battling woman as she snarled, "So the League of Forgotten Men is going to make us a League of Forgotten Women! Send us back to washing diapers and leaching out ashes for soap! Let us read Louisa May Alcott and Barrie—except on the Sabbath, of course! Let us sleep in humble gratitude with men—"

"*Sissy!*" wailed her mother.

"—like Shad Ledue! Well, Dad, you can sit right down and write Busy Berzelius for me that I'm going to England on the next boat!"

Mrs. Candy stopped drying the water glasses (with the soft dishtowels which she scrupulously washed out daily) long enough to croak, "What nasty men! I do hope they get shot soon," which for Mrs. Candy was a startlingly long and humanitarian statement.

■ ■ ■ *

"Yes. Nasty enough. But what I've got to keep remembering is that Windrip is only the lightest cork on the whirlpool. He didn't plot all this thing. With all the justified discontent there is against the smart politicians and the Plush Horses of Plutocracy—oh, if it hadn't been one Windrip, it'd been another. . . . We had it coming, we Respectables. . . . But that isn't going to make us like it!" thought Doremus.

Further Resources

BOOKS

Hutchisson, James. *The Rise of Sinclair Lewis, 1920–1930.* University Park, Pa.: Pennsylvania State University Press, 1996.

Lingeman, Richard. *Sinclair Lewis: Rebel from Main Street.* New York: Random House, 2002.

WEBSITES

"Sinclair Lewis." Bartleby.com. Available online at http://www.bartleby.com/people/LewisSin.html; website home page: http://www.bartelby.com/ (accessed February 15, 2003).

"The Nobel Prize in Literature 1930: Sinclair Lewis." Nobel e-Museum. The Nobel Foundation. Available online at http://www.nobel.se/literature/laureates/1930/index.html; website home page: http://www.novel.se.index.html (accessed February 15, 2003).

The Sinclair Lewis Homepage. Available online at http://lilt.ilstu.edu/separry/lewis.html (accessed February 15, 2003).

"Mouse & Man"

Magazine article

Date: December 27, 1937

Source: "Mouse & Man." *Time,* December 27, 1937.

About the Publication: *Time,* first published in 1923, is still a frequently-read weekly newsmagazine. Created by journalists Henry R. Luce and Briton Hadden, the magazine was intended to provide information on national and international current events in a concise format later copied by other newsmagazines. By 1927, its circulation exceeded 175,000. ■

Introduction

Born in Chicago, Walt Disney (1901–1966) moved to Los Angeles at age twenty-two and joined his brother, Roy, in creating Disney Bros. Studio. Advancing the style and technology of animation, this studio produced many popular films. Disney forever altered the mass media entertainment industry by pioneering product merchandising linked to his cartoon characters and by creating Disneyland, the theme park that quickly became a symbol of childhood innocence, American ingenuity, and rampant capitalism.

Short animated cartoons had become popular years before Walt Disney produced *Snow White and the Seven Dwarfs* in 1937. Mickey Mouse, Disney's most famous character, first appeared in 1928, amid many other cartoon figures of the Great Depression. As Americans needed to escape from economic difficulties, they increasingly sought the enjoyment of animated films. These shorts were played prior to full-length motion pictures in hundreds of theaters across the country. As the first feature-length animated picture with color and sound, *Snow White* marked a distinct break with the past.

Significance

In December 1937, *Time* magazine, the most popular newsweekly of its day, published a cover story on Walt Disney and the making of *Snow White.* The article traced Disney's personal history and examined how his company created the images and sounds that so mesmerized audiences. *Snow White* was not a simple film to make; in fact, at a cost of $1.6 million, the film was a gamble. Disney and his seventy-five animators spent three years creating the script, sketches, sound effects, and paintings needed for it.

Snow White made more than $4 million, easily paying for its cost and, more importantly, providing funds for future, even grander full-length productions. In the next few years, Disney repeated the success of *Snow White* with *Pinocchio* (1940), *Fantasia* (1940), *Dumbo* (1941), and *Bambi* (1942). These films established Disney's position at the vanguard of the animation industry and created the foundation for a media empire. Disney focused his studio's efforts on war propaganda during World War II (1939–1945), creating training films and the influential aviation documentary *Victory through Air Power* (1943). Following the war, his studio expanded its operations to produce a series for the booming medium of television and laid the groundwork for the Disneyland amusement park in California.

Disney's animation style reshaped the industry—rather than relying on plots based solely on jokes and sight gags, Disney's films created characters that displayed an emotional complexity and verve that others lacked. The studio composed its characters with a focus on fluidity of movement and emotion. Characters of all shapes and sizes, human or animal, possessed a dynamic range of personalities. The vividness of these cartoons led to their popularity, as viewers began to experience cartoons in a new way—as not only funny but also scary, awe-inspiring, and sad.

Walt Disney and Mickey Mouse examine a filmstrip together, 1935. **THE LIBRARY OF CONGRESS.**

Primary Source

"Mouse & Man" [excerpt]

SYNOPSIS: With the release of the full-length animated movie *Snow White and the Seven Dwarfs* in 1937, *Time* took the opportunity to evaluate the work of Walt Disney. In this excerpt, it declares him to be not only a commercially successful illustrator but also an artist.

Mr. Leon Schlesinger, Mr. Max Fleischer *et al.,* make most of the animated cartoons produced in the U.S. Of the man who makes the rest and the best, Mr. Schlesinger recently observed: "We're businessmen. Walt Disney's an artist. With us, the idea with shorts is to hit 'em and run. With us, Disney is more of a Rembrandt."

Even artists say that Walter Elias Disney is an artist. Some go farther, say that he is a great one. Certainly, his works are better known and more widely appreciated than those of any other artist in history. Three weeks ago, his Mickey Mouse created a minor government crisis in Yugoslavia. Last year, as "Miki-san," he was Japan's patron saint. In Russia the works of Disney are appreciated as "social satire" depicting the "capitalist world under the masks of mice and pigs." The late George V, it is said, would not go to a cinema performance unless it included a Disney film.

But Disney, the Artist, is nothing like as widely known as Mickey, the Mouse—or any of Mickey's score of charming fellow players in the Disney zoological stock company. In fact, when some art historian of the future sets out to chronicle the rise of the animated cartoon, the quest for original drawings by the man most responsible for it will be about as difficult as it is now to locate additional authentic Rembrandts. Walt Disney has not drawn his own pictures for nine years. To turn out the mass production issued nowadays under his name, he would have to have 650 hands. And 650 hands he has. With slim, 36-year-old Walt Disney as the guiding intelligence, his smooth-working cinema factory produces an average of twelve *Mickey Mouse* films and six *Silly Symphonies* every year. Were Disney to undertake the involved processes of drawing, coloring, photographing the 15,000 sketches that go into one of these shorts, the feat would approach Michelangelo's job on the Vatican ceiling. Released this week was the latest Disney venture, *Snow White and the Seven Dwarfs,* the most ambitious animated cartoon ever attempted. It took Disney's many hands over three years to make.

Snow White, like Mickey Mouse, was a creature of necessity. After sound came whooping in, Disney needed a character to replace silent Oswald The Rabbit. From a night of heavy thinking in an upper berth in 1928, Mickey Mouse was born. When the bulging

A still from Disney's groundbreaking feature length animated movie *Snow White and the Seven Dwarfs,* 1937. THE KOBAL COLLECTION. REPRODUCED BY PERMISSION.

double-feature movement began three years ago to crowd out the Disney shorts, Disney resolved to enter the feature field himself.

Disney's Folly

Wary Hollywood, which scoffed at sound ten years ago, scoffed at the idea of a seven-reel animated cartoon. The *Snow White* project was referred to as Disney's Folly. Rivals said he had bought a sweepstakes ticket. Shrewd older Brother Roy Disney, the business brain trust of the Disney enterprises, surveyed *Snow White*'s final bill of $1,600,000, observed: "We've bought the whole damned sweepstakes." . . .

Few changes have been made in the Grimm story. The dwarfs have been developed until each has a character of his own—that of Dopey so unexpectedly heart-winning that Disney may use the mute, youngest dwarf in a series of his own. Wood creatures have been animated with the same type of clever personalities that birds and animals acquire in the Disney shorts. Songs, dialogue in verse, dialogue in prose and silent sequences with incidental sound and music have been worked into a harmonious pattern. Catchiest tune: *Hi Ho,* as the dwarfs trudge home from work. Tunesmiths: Frank Churchill *(Who's Afraid of the Big Bad Wolf)* and Larry Morey. Technicolor is used with simpler and stronger effects than ever before in motion pictures, giving a vital, indelible reality to the fairyland locales.

Skeptical Hollywood, that had wondered whether a fairy story could have enough suspense to hold an audience through seven reels, and whether, even if the plot held up, an audience would care about the fate of characters who were just drawings, was convinced that Walt Disney had done it again. *Snow White* is as exciting as a Western, as funny as a haywire comedy. It combines the classic idiom of folklore drama with rollicking comic-strip humor. A combination of Hollywood, the Grimm Brothers, and the sad, searching fantasy of universal childhood, it is an authentic masterpiece, to be shown in theatres and beloved by new generations long after the current crop of Hollywood stars, writers and directors are sleeping where no Prince's kiss can wake them. . . .

Not long ago an interviewer spoke of *Snow White* as a cartoon, and reported that Mr. Disney retorted: "It's no more a cartoon than a painting by Whistler is a cartoon." The remark, if made, sounds pompous, out of character. The Rembrandt conception fits better—the conception of an artist, single of purpose, utterly unself-conscious, superlatively good at and satisfied in his work, a thoroughgoing professional, just gagging it up and letting the professors tell him what he's done.

Further Resources

BOOKS

Byrne, Eleanor, and Martin McQuillan. *Deconstructing Disney.* London and Sterling, Va.: Pluto, 1999.

Giroux, Henry A. *The Mouse That Roared: Disney and the End of Innocence.* Lanham, Md.: Rowman and Littlefield, 1999.

Maltin, Leonard. *The Disney Films.* New York: Disney Editions, 2000.

Thomas, Frank, and Ollie Johnston. *Disney Animation: The Illusion of Life.* New York: Abbeville, 1981.

Wasko, Janet. *Understanding Disney: The Manufacture of Fantasy.* Cambridge, N.J.: Polity, 2001.

AUDIO AND VISUAL MEDIA

Snow White and the Seven Dwarfs. Original release, 1937, Walt Disney Productions. Directed by William Cottrell, Walt Disney, David Hand, Wilfred Jackson, Larry Morey, Perce Pearce, Ben Sharpsteen, Webb Smith, Dorothy Ann Blank, Richard Creedon, Dick Richard, and Merrill de Maris. Platinum Edition DVD/VHS, 2001, Buena Vista Home Entertainment.

Songs of Woody Guthrie

"(If You Ain't Got The) Do Re Mi"; "I Ain't Got No Home"

Songs

By: Woody Guthrie

Date: 1937; 1938

Source: Guthrie, Woody. *Dust Bowl Ballads.* RCA Victor, 1940. Available online at http://www.geocities.com/Nashville/3448/guthrie.html (accessed February 15, 2003).

About the Artist: Woody Guthrie (1912–1967), a legendary American folksinger and songwriter, wrote more than a thousand songs, many chronicling his travels all across the Depression-era United States. Guthrie used his experiences to write songs about the people he encountered—migrant workers, unionists, the disenfranchised, and fellow wanderers. Having lived through the Great Depression, World War II (1939–1945), the McCarthy era, and the early civil rights movement, Guthrie also wrote several books, including autobiographies. He died after a long struggle with Huntington's disease. ■

Introduction

Woodrow Wilson Guthrie was raised in a poor working-class family in Okemah, Oklahoma, and remained poor for most of his life despite the success of his music. When Guthrie's mother was sent to the Central Hospital for the Insane in Norman, Oklahoma, his father soon after went to Texas to be with his own family. Guthrie joined him at age seventeen, a year before his mother's death.

Guthrie remained in Texas until he was driven from his home to California with thousands of other "dust bowl refugees," known as "Okies." The great dust storms of the mid-1930s devastated homes and farms across large parts of the United States, including Oklahoma, Kansas, Tennessee, Georgia, and Texas. It was widely believed that California offered jobs and a life of plenty, so Guthrie hitchhiked, rode the trains, and even walked to California.

Woody Guthrie, the famous American folksinger, experienced the hardships of the Great Depression and the Dust Bowl first hand. THE LIBRARY OF CONGRESS.

Guthrie and other migrants, however, were not welcome in California, and life there was often as hard as the lives they left. In many cases, they lived in poverty in migrant camps and were unable to secure jobs. Guthrie, one of the minority who landed a job, began writing for *The Light* newspaper. An assignment for the paper took him to the migrant camps to investigate working and living conditions. In 1939, he met actor Will Geer and began traveling with him to perform in the migrant camps. His journey from Texas to California and his time in the migrant camps produced the music in *Dust Bowl Ballads,* such as "I Ain't Got No Home," "Goin' Down the Road Feelin' Bad," "Talking Dust Bowl Blues," and "Hard Travelin'."

Guthrie's transient spirit later took him to New York City, where he wrote his famous "This Land Is Your Land" in reaction to Irving Berlin's "God Bless America." Living in New York allowed Guthrie to collaborate with other folksingers and songwriters on musical projects and socially conscious projects. Moving to Greenwich Village, he performed with the Almanac singers and wrote patriotic songs in the wake of Pearl Harbor. Guthrie moved back and forth several times from New York to California before his long series of hospitalizations and his death in New York.

Significance

Guthrie's music played an important role in giving voice to the poor and oppressed, both during and after the Great Depression. As a migrant and an "Okie" himself, Guthrie knew their hopes and their suffering first-hand. Guthrie's songs were so powerful that they have established him as a folksinging legend. He had a tremendous and lasting impact on the genre. Numerous artists met with success recording Guthrie's songs both before and after his death. His most famous disciple was a Minnesotan named Bob Dylan, who became Guthrie's friend in the last years of Woody's life.

In 1966, Guthrie was commended by the U.S. Department of the Interior for his Columbia River Songs and was presented with a Conservation Service Award. He was also honored by having a substation of the Bonneville Power Authority named after him. He was posthumously inducted into the Songwriters' Hall of Fame in 1971, the Nashville Songwriters Foundation, Inc., in 1977, and the Rock and Roll Hall of Fame in 1988, and he received a Lifetime Achievement Award from the North American Folk Music and Dance Alliance in 1996.

His son, Arlo, followed in his father's footsteps with a folk music career. Best known for "City of New Orleans" and "Alice's Restaurant," Arlo, like his father, became active in social causes.

Primary Source

"(If You Ain't Got The) Do Re Mi"

SYNOPSIS: "(If You Ain't Got The) Do Re Mi," written in 1937, exposes the dilemma, for dust bowl refugees, that California is only a Garden of Eden if they "got the dough" to make it so.

Lots of folks back East, they say, is leavin' home every day,
Beatin' the hot old dusty way to the California line.
'Cross the desert sands they roll, gettin' out of that old dust bowl,
They think they're goin' to a sugar bowl, but here's what they find—
Now, the police at the port of entry say,
"You're number fourteen thousand for today."

CHORUS:
Oh, if you ain't got the do re mi, folks, you ain't got the do re mi,
Why, you better go back to beautiful Texas, Oklahoma, Kansas, Georgia, Tennessee.
California is a garden of Eden, a paradise to live in or see;
But believe it or not, you won't find it so hot
If you ain't got the do re mi.

You want to buy you a home or a farm, that can't deal nobody harm,
Or take your vacation by the mountains or sea.
Don't swap your old cow for a car, you better stay right where you are,
Better take this little tip from me.
'Cause I look through the want ads every day
But the headlines on the papers always say:

If you ain't got the do re mi, boys, you ain't got the do re mi,
Why, you better go back to beautiful Texas, Oklahoma, Kansas, Georgia, Tennessee.
California is a garden of Eden, a paradise to live in or see;
But believe it or not, you won't find it so hot
If you ain't got the do re mi.

Primary Source

"I Ain't Got No Home"

SYNOPSIS: Guthrie wrote the parody "I Ain't Got No Home" in 1938 as a response to the Carter Family's popular rendition of "This World Is Not My Home." Guthrie did not like the message that "This World Is Not My Home" had for the migrants—namely, that they should be patient and wait until the afterlife for the rewards for their suffering.

I ain't got no home, I'm just a-roamin' 'round,
Just a wandrin' worker, I go from town to town.
And the police make it hard wherever I may go
And I ain't got no home in this world anymore.

My brothers and my sisters are stranded on this road,
A hot and dusty road that a million feet have trod;

Rich man took my home and drove me from my door
And I ain't got no home in this world anymore.

Was a-farmin' on the shares, and always I was poor;
My crops I lay into the banker's store.
My wife took down and died upon the cabin floor,
And I ain't got no home in this world anymore.

Now as I look around, it's mighty plain to see
This world is such a great and a funny place to be;
Oh, the gamblin' man is rich an' the workin' man is poor,
And I ain't got no home in this world anymore.

Further Resources

BOOKS

Garman, Bryan K. *A Race of Singers: Whitman's Working-class Hero from Guthrie to Springsteen.* Chapel Hill, N.C.: University of North Carolina Press, 2000.

Guthrie, Woody. *Pastures of Plenty: A Self Portrait.* Dave Marsh and Harold Leventhal, eds. New York: HarperCollins, 1990.

Yurchenco, Henrietta. *A Mighty Hard Road: The Woody Guthrie Story.* New York: McGraw-Hill, 1970.

WEBSITES

Helfert, Manfred. "Ballads from Deep Gap, North Carolina, and Okemah, Oklahoma." Available online at http://www.geocities.com/Nashville/3448 (accessed February 15, 2003).

"Woody Guthrie Folk Festival" home page. Available at http://www.woodyguthrie.com (accessed February 15, 2003).

AUDIO AND VISUAL MEDIA

Guthrie, Woody. *Dust Bowl Ballads.* BMG/Buddha Records, 2000.

———. *Dustbowl Ballads.* BMG International, 2001.

———. *The Greatest Songs of Woody Guthrie.* Vanguard Records, 1972.

———. *Library of Congress Recordings, Vols. 1–3.* UNI/Rounder, 1964.

"The Killer-Diller: The Life and Four-Four Time of Benny Goodman"

Magazine article

By: Frank Norris

Date: May 7, 1938

Source: Norris, Frank. "The Killer-Diller: The Life and Four-Four Time of Benny Goodman." *The Saturday Evening Post,* May 7, 1938, 22, 23.

About the Author: Frank C. Norris (1907–1967) was a Tennessee-born graduate of Princeton University. He joined *Time* magazine in 1929 as a staff writer and eventually became managing editor of the magazine. He later became a senior editor of *Newsweek.* Norris was the author of three novels. ■

Clarinetist and jazz band leader Benny Goodman became wildly popular in the 1930s, the so-called "King of Swing." ARCHIVE PHOTOS, INC. REPRODUCED BY PERMISSION.

Introduction

The life of Benny Goodman (1909–1986) was a rags-to-riches story. Born in a poor Chicago household, Goodman used his natural musical gift to pave the way to financial success. He received early training at the Kehelah Jacob Synagogue and then at Jane Addams' Hull House. His most influential teacher was the classically trained clarinetist Franz Schoepp. Goodman was also influenced early by the rhythms of New Orleans jazz musicians, especially clarinetists, and by Louis Armstrong.

Goodman's professional debut was at the Central Park Theater in Chicago at age twelve. At fourteen, he left for Los Angeles to join Ben Pollack's band, and he remained with him for the next six years. By the mid-1930s, Goodman had established himself as one of the country's leading musicians and had organized his first "big band." Among a wide array of other engagements, his band landed contracts with Columbia Records and NBC for the radio series *Let's Dance.*

In the late 1930s, the band reached its peak, with the three-year-long CBS radio series *The Camel Caravan* and a three-week engagement at the Paramount Theater in New York. They played to sellout crowds of primarily teenage audiences. It was during this popular success that Goodman was dubbed the "King of Swing."

As his popularity gained momentum, so did Goodman's musical maturity. He had by this time developed a distinct, controlled, and exacting style that required meeting high technical standards. Goodman expected this high-level performance of both himself and his sidemen. This standard for musical excellence helped him become the first popular jazz artist to achieve success performing his brand of classical music. This classical repertory became the focus of his performances in later years.

At age thirty-one, illness forced Goodman to disband his group. He recovered enough three months later to reform it with different members and a new sound. The compositions of Eddie Sauter, a Juilliard School graduate, established the new band's character. Goodman's new band enjoyed great success, playing with all the leading American orchestras.

In 1947, Goodman assembled his last and riskiest travel band. Although he had previously expressed a distaste for bop music, he and his new band accepted an engagement recording bop for Capitol Records. Goodman retained his classical style, however. He was the only member of the band to perform solo improvisations not in bop fashion but in classical mode. The group disbanded two years later at the end of the Capitol contract.

Significance

Goodman was a critical figure in popularizing jazz and, in particular, in ushering in the swing era of the 1930s. He found a wide and receptive audience whether he was playing solo or with groups. He enjoyed success in radio, movies, live performance, studio recording, and accompanying Broadway productions.

Goodman continued to tour and record late into his life, taking on the role of "jazz ambassador" during the 1960s and 1970s. His overseas tours took him to South America, Europe, the Soviet Union, and the Far East. In 1978, he and the original members celebrated the forty-year anniversary of his first trio's performance at Carnegie Hall. He was one of the five honorees at the Kennedy Center Honors awards in 1982.

Primary Source

"The Killer-Diller: The Life and Four-Four Time of Benny Goodman" [excerpt]

SYNOPSIS: It was apparent that swing music had arrived when Goodman performed his *Killer Diller* at Carnegie Hall in 1935. National Public Radio chose the song as one of the 100 most important American musical works of the twentieth century. Frank Norris, writer for *The Saturday Evening Post,* chose *Killer Diller* as the title for this article on Goodman published several months after Goodman's three-week engagement at New York's Paramount Theater in 1937.

When Benny Goodman opened at the Paramount in New York last winter, six or seven hundred people had already been waiting outside an hour when the sun came up. At six o'clock there were 3000 of them, mostly high-school kids from the Bronx and Brooklyn and Staten Island. Squeezing themselves in their windbreakers and leather jackets, they began to dance and shout and light fires in the gutters along Broadway to keep out the sting of a January morning. At 7:30 the West 47th Street precinct police station ordered Sergeant Harry Moore to saddle up and proceed with ten mounted men to the scene, and as he did so his tolerant Celtic intelligence must have dwelt on the ways of the world and the variety of a policeman's experience. This was the first time the sergeant had ever been sent on a riot call at daybreak to herd a crowd of children in to hear a jazz band play.

On the sergeant's advice, the management opened the theater at eight o'clock, for by this time Mr. Goodman's fans were multiplying by the minute, pouring up out of the Times Square subway exits like bees from a smoked hive. Fifty-five ushers, called for special duty, marshaled 3634 of them inside before the fire department ordered doors closed. The police detail was also increased and went into action on two fronts: Outside, where about 2000 disappointed youngsters were massed out into the streets, paralyzing early-morning traffic; and inside, where the luckier music lovers were stampeding around the lobbies and aisles. Never before in the city's history had police been called for duty *inside* a theater. But the cops had not seen anything yet.

On the screen, Mae West absorbed a number of gentlemen in high collars, but the audience viewed the proceedings with great restlessness, unbroken until Miss West ululated her final line, a rosy light prophetically suffused the orchestra pit and the sound of wailing clarinet was heard. The orchestra began to rise on its elevator platform, revealing first the brass section, Jess Stacey at his piano and Harry Goodman slapping his bass. Then, below them, Gene Krupa behind his alabaster drums, two rows of teeth flashing as they champed gum in four-four time. Then the reed section and—yes, the clarinet, the glittering spectacles, the smiling, Punch–like face of the veritable Goodman. Out in front, it sounded as though Navy had just completed a long forward pass for a touchdown.

Teenagers swing dancing at the 1939 New York World's Fair. © BETTMANN/CORBIS. REPRODUCED BY PERMISSION.

Radio people claim that three nights a week 2,000,000 people are listening to Benny Goodman broadcast. If you ever heard him, chances are you would not forget him. His chief characteristics are definition and power, the rhythm instruments—piano, drums, bass—sound and sure, solidly thumping out the time, while the melody, carried by the concerted brasses and reeds, pulses just a fraction ahead to give the urgent off-beat, the brasses a fine strong burr and the reeds swirling with improvisations on the tune. And then Goodman's clarinet, clear and unhurried and artful, playing a song that was never written and may never be heard again. No other band of this quality has ever had such popular acceptance. In the past year and a half it has sold more records, played longer runs and scored higher radio ratings than any band of its kind in the history of American popular music. When you hear it play over the radio, you want to beat your feet. When you hear it play in a dance hall or hotel ballroom, you want to dance. In an auditorium, the audience reaction is almost pure violence.

The Pied Piper of New York

Unhandicapped by either weight or age, the Paramount audience began clawing at the chairs before the band got through its first chorus of *Satan Takes a Holiday.* Gene Krupa's drums got off to an orgiastic uproar on the second chorus and certain shouts from the crowd became shrilly intelligible: "Feed it to me, Gene! Send me down!" Goodman took a chorus. "Get off, Benny! Swing it!" And then, trampling ushers, the children began to dance in the aisles. There were policemen in front of the bandstand, but some of the kids got by them and up on the stage. They did the Shag, the Lindy Hop, the Big Apple—all the leaping Harlem dances—while Goodman grinned and dodged them. This went on for a solid hour.

In fact, with the interludes of Mae West, it went on six times a day for three weeks. It cost only a quarter to get in for the morning show, so that was the one the kids mainly came to. But the platoon of experts who soon arrived on the scene to explain the phenomenon and put it down to juvenile hysteria overlooked the fact that when the old folks trooped in to the night performances, they raised Ned, too. Unlearned in the Big Apple, they tried to express their unity with the ceremony by clapping their hands and beating their feet in cadence. That, too, would begin with *Satan Takes a Holiday* and end with the long crashing finale—the "Killer-Diller," as Goodman calls any cumulative superlative—of the antiphonal *Sing, Sing, Sing!*

By the time the engagement was over, Goodman had smashed everyone's previous attendance records—including one of his own the year before—the director of the New York School of Music prepared a bill for the legislature making swing music illegal, and a New York University psychologist turned the light of pure science on the audience reaction. "It's simply that a combination of circumstances has made them one-minded and their inhibitory checks have broken down," he explained. "Some individuals are more suggestible than others, and those individuals start them piling into the aisles. They do sound like goats, don't they?" Other observers were reminded of a camp meeting, the crusades and the thirteenth-century dance madness.

And in the meantime, American popular music had reached and passed an important milestone. In its ups and downs, jazz had had plenty of devotion. But no other jazz band which had conscientiously and uncompromisingly stuck to playing the real stuff—supposedly unsalable to the public—had ever achieved such extraordinary popular reception.

Benny Goodman is a national, not a New York phenomenon. The autograph hunters, those telltale scavengers of the successful, keep him on the run in Los Angeles, Chicago, Detroit. In Philadelphia, not long ago, a strange mishap befell two Goodman fans. Waiting outside the theater all night in order to be among the first seated in the morning, they went to sleep standing up. An alarm clock in one of their pockets was set to arouse them at six A.M. When it went off, it spooked them so badly that they fell through a plate-glass window. The man who causes all this excitement is a highly talented, very effective and richly likable bundle of contradictions just past his twenty-eighth birthday. That makes him and jazz about the same age. In fact, they grew up together.

The Dixieland Jazz Band was just coming in off the street and looking around for a piano player who couldn't read music when Benny Goodman squealed his first note in the Chicago ghetto. The Dixieland had gone to Chicago, to New York, to London, had put jazz in the language and a fortune in its pockets. And now, with Art Hickman and the first wave of big bands calling the country's dance tunes, the Dixieland was on its last vaudeville tour when Benny's father heard that they were giving away musical instruments over at the synagogue. They were also giving away music lessons, so Father Goodman took Benny and two of his older brothers, Fred and Harry, to see what was going on. He figured they might want to make their living that way. Benny's father was a garment worker, but he hoped the boys would not have to spend their lives in a clothing loft. It wasn't a bad idea at all. With varying success, all the boys turned out to be musicians. Fred became the trumpet player on the old Ted Lewis band. He is now doing something else, having gone out with the high C. But when middle G was good enough for the customers, Fred was a pretty fair trumpet player. Harry took up the bass fiddle. He now plays it in Benny's band. And if Mr. Goodman were still alive, he would no doubt be glad to know that Benny, who chose the clarinet, paid income tax on $125,000 last year.

A Roaming Clarinet

The instruments were lined up around the wall in the synagogue basement, and Benny picked the clarinet because, with all its shiny nickel keys, it looked the prettiest.

In return for their lessons and the instruments, the boys were expected to play in the synagogue band. Benny, however, promptly made the first of the many shifts that were to take him and his clarinet all over the country. He left the synagogue and joined the Hull House outfit, for what inducement he no longer remembers.

When Benny was eleven, he was sent to a German music teacher named Frank Schepp. Notwithstanding the fact that he charged the Goodmans only a dollar a lesson—if it had been any more there wouldn't have been any lessons—Schepp was a rather famous Chicago musician. A number of members of the Chicago Symphony had studied under him, and Goodman recalls this opportunity with gratitude. "He taught me how to use the instrument right at the right time." Benny was eleven. This exposure to the classical tradition is just now beginning to take full effect, with the result that, while Goodman plays the music of each well enough to excite critics of serious music, he frankly states that whereas Mozart was a cat, for him Brahms is not in the groove.

But in 1921 Benny was not under the influence of dead Germans but live American Negroes. King Oliver had come up from New Orleans several years before—the general migration of American syncopation was up the Mississippi and turn right—and his protégé, Louis Armstrong, had his name in lights out in front of the Black Belt's famous Plantation. These two colored trumpeters strongly influenced all the musicians who listened to them. And Benny listened to them all he could. Chicago was a great place for a hot musician to grow up in the early 20's. It still is, but perhaps the giants seemed to be a little bigger then. Jimmy Dorsey had come out west from Scranton. Out of Davenport there was Bix Biederbecke, whose improvisations on the trumpet were often pure lyric poetry. He was not only interested in the colored men but hung around the College Inn a lot, listening to Tony Panico. The town was full of young ride musicians, and some a little older, who were showing them which way to go. Jazz music, in spite of the big, sweet, suffusing movie-house bands, was on its way to its second pinnacle.

Benny Goodman's first professional engagement was at the Central Park Theater on the far South Side. His act was an imitation of Ted Lewis. Ted got him the job. That summer Benny and some other kids began playing for dances at Electric Park in Waukegan, Goodman filling the engagement in short pants. He was still in short pants the following summer when the band got a job playing on a lake boat that left the Navy Pier at lunchtime and returned from Michigan City, across the horizon in Indiana, after supper.

To date, most Goodman biographies have been as riddled with small confusions as Mahomet's. Goodman himself often stops, when coaxed into an autobiographical conversation, to say, "Now let me see. Now wait a minute. Oh, *yeah*——." The middle 20's are particularly turgid. When talking about this period, he chiefly recalls that "things got going sort of fast in here."

But there are scenes that stick, like sitting in his bedroom at home, with the elevated clanging by outside and the door shutting off the rest of the family, the right foot beating the time, the clarinet crying the different ways in which Japanese Sandman, or Rose of the Rio Grande, or No, No, Nora—pop tunes of the day—were not written. His heart lifted up with the clearly reached high C, and it was good to feel the sure, increasing nimbleness of the fingers on a run of double notes. Then there is the scene of Bix coming down to the boat—he had worked on it the summer before—and, seeing Benny on the orchestra stand, telling the pudgy kid to keep away from the instruments. And then there was putting on long pants and joining Ben Pollack's orchestra, because by then they were already comparing Benny to Frankie Teschmaker and Milt Menirow and Peewee Russell. Jazz has its prodigies too. Benny was fifteen.

There is a picture of him, a fat boy of seventeen or eighteen, with the band outside the M-G-M Studios in California. That was the summer that Pollack played a dance hall in Venice; and in the long afternoons, in the cheap seaside hotel where they lived, Benny and Glenn Miller and the boys would sit in a bedroom and talk music and listen to Bix on the records, or the Cotton Pickers, or even old Dixieland records, for Benny liked, above anything else, the rich but inornate style of Rappolo.

Things got going even faster after that. Back to Chicago, on to New York at the Little Club, where the ginger-ale bottles wore bibs saying you mustn't pour them into gin. And there were the Princeton house parties and a long date on the Park Central roof, during which he doubled in the pit band of Hello, Daddy, and somebody downstairs in the hotel shot Mr. Rothstein.

In the Dixieland era and just after the war it was called jazz. Scott Fitzgerald used the word to describe an age. In the feverish late 20's it was hot music that Pollack's and Don Voorhees' and Goldkette's and Red Nichols' bands were playing. Now they call it swing, but it's the same kind of music.

Further Resources

BOOKS

Collier, James L. *Benny Goodman and the Swing Era.* New York: Oxford University Press, 1989.

Firestone, Ross. *Swing, Swing, Swing: The Life and Times of Benny Goodman.* New York: Norton, 1993.

WEBSITES

"Benny Goodman." *The New Grove Dictionary of Jazz.* Macmillan Publishers Ltd. Available online at http://www.pbs.org/jazz/biography/artist_id_goodman_benny.htm; website home page: http://www.pbs.org/ (accessed February 16, 2003).

Gottsegen, Ted. "Benny Goodman." The Red Hot Jazz Archive. Available online at http://www.redhotjazz.com/goodman.html (accessed February 16, 2003).

AUDIO AND VISUAL MEDIA

Battle of the Bands, Artie Shaw vs. Benny Goodman. New York: RCA Victor, 1998.

"Notes on a Cowboy Ballet"

Notes

By: Aaron Copland

Date: Unknown

Source: Copland, Aaron. "Notes on a Cowboy Ballet" in *The Aaron Copeland Collection.* New York: Aaron Copland Fund for Music. Reprinted online at http://memory.loc.gov/ammem/achtml/achome.html; website home page: http://memory.loc.gov (accessed April 9, 2003).

About the Artist: Aaron Copland (1900–1990), born in Brooklyn, studied with Rubin Goldmark, a well-known figure in New York music. He later studied with Nadia Boulanger in Paris, but developed an avant-garde style all his own that he characterized as distinctly American. Copland composed award-winning music for films, ballets, theater, and opera. In addition, he lectured, taught, conducted, wrote books about music, and as a concert pianist recorded his own piano concerto. ■

Introduction

Although Aaron Copland was not encouraged as a youngster, his parents financially supported his musical pursuits. He took piano lessons when he was young and traveled to Paris at age twenty. While there, he formed what would be a lifelong student-teacher relationship with Nadia Boulanger at the School of Music for Americans. Boulanger also taught Copland's American contemporaries Virgil Thompson and Roger Piston, among many others.

In 1923, Boulanger gave Copland his first break in the United States, with a request to compose what became his *Symphony for Organ and Orchestra,* to be played by the New York Symphony Orchestra. Boulanger was featured as solo organist in the performance. Because Copland's music was unique by traditional standards and contained unfamiliar rhythms, the performance caused a notably unpleasant stir. Walter Damrosch, conductor for the New York Symphony that day, burst out to the audience, "If a young man can write like that at age 23, in five years he will be ready to commit murder!"

Aaron Copland, one of America's most popular and distinguished classical composers. **COPLAND, AARON, PHOTOGRAPH.**

This notoriety had its advantages for the pioneering Copland. Although unpleasant, it focused attention on him and drew the curiosity of those who would eventually become his supporters and patrons. Copland earned one of the first Guggenheim grants and was supported by patron Paul Rosenfeld when he composed the concert piece *El Salon Mexico,* his *Piano Concerto,* and *Music of the Theatre.*

In the 1930s, Copland moved from the hard dissonance of his earlier days to a second phase when he began to write music "for useful purposes." At this point, his music became distinctly American and included the ballets *Billy the Kid* and *Rodeo,* two of his most readily recognized works along with 1944's *Appalachian Spring.* This era continued through the 1940s with his concert pieces *Fanfare for the Common Man* and *Lincoln Portrait.*

Copland's influence began to wane after World War II (1939–1945), when he shifted his attention to twelve-tone music. His compositions *Connotations* and *Inscape* embodied this shift. His friend Leonard Bernstein, on Copland's seventieth birthday, chided him in a magazine

Production photo from Aaron Copland's ballet *Billy the Kid,* 1938. **THE LIBRARY OF CONGRESS.**

article for abandoning his simpler style. But Copland saw it as yet another frontier to explore, a way to broaden his repertoire once again. This exploration of twelve-tone music, however, did not attain the popular appeal of his earlier works.

Though he stopped composing at the age of seventy, Copland often conducted and frequently appeared in tribute concerts.

Significance

Copland was an active supporter of modern music. In 1936, he founded the American Composers Alliance for the Promotion of New American Music. He was quoted as saying that "an ideal concert has three things: a classical piece, a contemporary piece, and something from an American composer." Howard Taubman, in a 1953 article, wrote that "he has taught innumerable composers, he has done missionary work for many more, he has written and lectured and even gone on goodwill tours for our Government to other countries. In short, he has been one of the most influential musicians on the American scene."

In addition to composing, Copland taught for twenty-five years at Tanglewood's Berkshire Music Center in Massachusetts, where he influenced thousands of budding musicians. He reached thousands more through the books he wrote based on his lectures. He fostered the careers of Leonard Bernstein, Roy Harris, Lukas Foss, Harold Shapiro, and Irving Fine—all notable figures in American music.

Copland was not a supporter of American music alone, however. He was creative and open, constantly exploring new possibilities in music. He had the unique ability to write many different kinds of music and to cross all music and party lines. His great range allowed him to influence a wide audience.

Ed. Note: Mr. Copland's ballet "Billy the Kid" will have its first performance this Wednesday evening, May 24th, as one of the American Lyric Theatre ~~Ballet presentations~~, by the Ballet Caravan.

NOTES ON A COWBOY BALLET
by Aaron Copland

~~xxxAaronxCopland~~

When Lincoln Kirstein, director of the Ballet Caravan, asks you to write a ballet for him it is a foregone conclusion that you are going to tackle an American subject. Still, when he suggested Billy the Kid as a proper hero for a native ballet, I had certain misgivings. Not about Billy the Kid, of course--for where could one find a better protagonist for an American work,--but about my own capabilities as a "cowboy composer." Lincoln Kirstein, however, thought differently --and since he is a very enthusiastic ~~fellow~~ young man, it wasn't long before I was convinced that fate had chosen me and none other to compose this folk-ballet about a young desperado of the Wild West.

I don't know how other composers feel, but as for myself, I divide all music into two parts--that which is meant to be self-sufficient and that which is meant to serve one of the sister arts--theatre, film or ballet. I have never liked music which gets in the way of the thing it is supposedly aiding. That is why I began with one single idea in writing Billy--a firm resolve to write simply. If it is a question of expressing one's soul, you can always write a symphony. But if you are involved in a stage presentation, then the eye is the thing, and music should play a modest role, helping when help is needed, but never injecting itself as if it were the main business of the evening.

There was one other reason for being simple--namely, our hero, Billy. No matter how complex a character he may have ~~had~~ been from the psychological standpoint, he makes a simple enough stage figure, this boy bandit who bragged that he had killed twenty-one men, "not counting Indians". Therefore my problem resolved itself into finding the porrect musical style to express the peculiar character of Billy

Primary Source

"Notes on a Cowboy Ballet" (1 OF 4)

SYNOPSIS: In 1938, Lincoln Kirstein, director of the Ballet Caravan, asked Copland to write the ballet *Billy the Kid.* The following are Copland's unpublished notes about the composition of the ballet. Copland offers his thoughts on tackling another frontier for him—cowboy songs—and shares his pleasure in being commissioned for the project. The ballet is one of Copland's most popular and well-known works.

2

the Kid.

To use or not to use cowboy songs as the basis for my ballet became a major issue. Mr. Kirstein said he didn't care,--and quietly tucked two slim collections of Western tunes under my arm. I have never been particularly impressed with the musical beauties of the cowboy song as such. The words are usually delightful and the manner of singing ~~it~~ needs no praise from me. But neither the words nor the delivery are of much use in a purely orchestral ballet score, so I was left with the tunes themselves, which I repeat, are often less than exciting. As far as I was concerned, this ballet could be written without benefit of the poverty -stricken tunes Billy himself must have known.

Nevertheless, in order to humor Mr. Kirstein, who said he did'nt really care whether I used actual cowboy material or not, ~~in this ballet, I~~ I decided to take his two little collections with me when I left for Paris ~~last~~ in the summer of 1938. It was there that I began working on the scenario as it had been outlined for me. Perhaps there is something different about a cowboy song in Paris. But whatever the reason may have been, ~~be,~~ it wasn't very long before I found myself hopelessly involved in expanding, contracting, rearranging and superimposing cowboy tunes on the rue de Rennes in Paris. If you listen closely ~~next Wednesday~~ you can hear in full or in part (in the order of their appearance) "Great Grandad", "Whoopee Ti Yi Yo, Git Along Little Dogies", "The Old Chisolm Trail", "Old Paint", "The Dying Cowboy", "Trouble for the Range Cook" and so forth. I can guarantee that I did not use "Home on the Range". (You see I had decided to draw the line someplace.)

"In rounding up this bunch of western songs from the plains and hills, we aren't aiming to educate you any". That's the way the editors of one of my source books introduces their collection. "We have only one object", they continue, " to be entertaining, and we

Primary Source

"Notes on a Cowboy Ballet" (2 OF 4)

Page two of Aaron Copland's notes for *Billy the Kid,* 1938. THE LIBRARY OF CONGRESS. REPRODUCED BY PERMISSION OF THE AARON COPLAND FUND FOR MUSIC, INC.

3

hope that our efforts will be considered from that angle". That is just about the way I would have put it myself. Except that I had the added difficulty of harmonizing these simple tunes without benefit of the usual accompanying chords. It is a rather delicate operation--to put fresh and unconventional harmonies to well known melodies without spoiling their naturalness. Its a moment for the composer to throw caution aside and to depend wholly on his instinct for knowing what to do. Courage and instinct are the only things that can be of help at that point.

Before leaving New York I had seen Jared French's lovely designs. The story around which the choreography was to be designed had been supplied to me after discussions with our choreographer Eugene Loring. In the finished script, the action begins and closes on the open prairie. The events which take place between the introduction and coda are merely typical of many such episodes on the long trek to the Pacific.

The central portion of the ballet concerns itself with significant moments in the life of Billy the Kid. The first scene is a street in a frontier town. Familiar figures amble by. Cowboys saunter into town, some on horseback, others with their lassoes. Some Mexican women do a Jarabe, which is interrupted by a fight between two drunks. Attracted by the gathering crowd, Billy is seen for the first time, as a boy of twelve, with his mother. The brawl turns ugly, guns are drawn, and in some unaccountable way, Billy's mother is killed. Without an instant's hesitation, in cold fury, Billy draws a knife from a cow-hand's sheath and stabs his mother's slayers. His short, but famous career begins.

In swift succesion we see episodes in Billy's later life. At night, under the stars, in a quiet card game with his outlaw friends. Hunted by a posse led by his former friend Pat Garrett, Billy is pur-

Primary Source

"Notes on a Cowboy Ballet" (3 OF 4)

Page three of Aaron Copland's notes for *Billy the Kid,* 1938. THE LIBRARY OF CONGRESS. REPRODUCED BY PERMISSION OF THE AARON COPLAND FUND FOR MUSIC, INC.

4

sued. A running gun battle ensues. Billy is captured. A drunken celebration takes place. Billy in prison is, of course, followed by one of Billys legendary escapes. Tired and worn in the desert, Billy rests with his girl. (Pas de deux). Starting from a deep xx sleep, he senses movement in the xxxx shadows. The posse has finally caught up with him. It is the end.

If we are ever to have a fully developed ballet company in America--the ballet company in the tradition of the Russians--it will come by way of just such companies as the Ballet Caravan, and just such subject matter as Billy the Kid. Speaking of the work of the Ballet Caravan in the pages of <u>Modern Music</u>, Edwin Denby, has this to say:..."they show that an American kind of ballet is growing up, different from the nervous Franco-Russian style..... Our own ballet has an easier, simpler character, a kind of American straightforwardness, that is thourough agreeable.... I think this is the highest kind of praise, because it shows the ballet has taken root and is from now on a part of our life."

Primary Source

"Notes on a Cowboy Ballet" **(4 OF 4)**

Page four of Aaron Copland's notes for *Billy the Kid,* 1938. THE LIBRARY OF CONGRESS. REPRODUCED BY PERMISSION OF THE AARON COPLAND FUND FOR MUSIC, INC.

Copland's awards included the Pulitzer Prize in 1944 for *Appalachian Spring,* a ballet written for and presented by Martha Graham and her company. He was honored at the Kennedy Center in 1979 for a lifetime of significant contribution to American culture and the performing arts.

Further Resources

BOOKS

Copland, Aaron. *The New Music, 1900–1960.* New York: Norton, 1968.

Copland, Aaron, and Vivian Perlis. *Copland: 1900–1942.* New York: St. Martin's, 1984.

———. *Copland Since 1942.* New York: St. Martin's, 1989.

Pollack, Howard. *Aaron Copland: The Life and Work of an Uncommon Man.* New York: Henry Holt, 1999.

WEBSITES

"The Aaron Copland Collection." American Memory: Historical Collections for the National Digital Library. Library of Congress. Available online at http://memory.loc.gov/ammem/achtml/achome.html; website home page: http://www.loc.gov/ (accessed February 16, 2003).

Chew, Robin. "Aaron Copland: American Composer." Lucidcafé. Available online at http://www.lucidcafe.com/lucidcafe/library/95nov/copland.html; website home page: http://www.lucidcafe.com/lucidcafe.html (accessed February 16, 2003).

Schwartz, Steve. "Aaron Copland." Classical Net. Available online at http://www.classical.net/music/comp.lst/copland.html; website home page: http://www.classical.net/welcome.html (accessed February 16, 2003).

AUDIO AND VISUAL MEDIA

Copland, Aaron. *12 Poems of Emily Dickinson.* Ocean, N.J.: Musical Heritage Society, 1984.

———. *The Complete Music for Solo Piano.* New York: Sony Classical, 1994.

———. *Copland the Modernist.* New York: BMG Classics, 1996.

One-Third of a Nation

Play script

By: Arthur Arent

Date: 1938

Source: Arent, Arthur, ed. "One-Third of a Nation." In *Federal Theatre Plays.* New York: Random House, 1938, 92–103.

About the Author: Arthur Arent (1904–1972) wrote plays for radio, television, and the Federal Theatre Project's Living Newspapers. His plays with Living Newspapers, in addition to *One-Third of a Nation,* include *Ethiopia, Injunction Granted,* and *Power.* His broader writing career included assignments for Warner Brothers and the U.S. Office of War Information. Arent was also a staff writer for CBS later in his career. ■

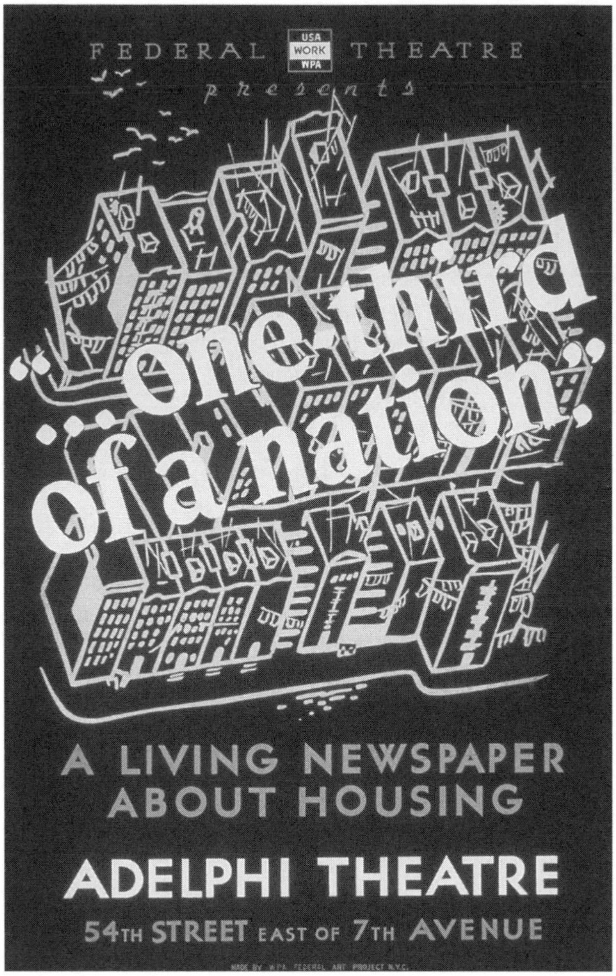

A poster for a 1939 performance of *One Third of a Nation,* the most famous of the Federal Theatre Project's Living Newspaper productions. **THE LIBRARY OF CONGRESS.**

Introduction

In response to the deep economic crisis of the early 1930s, the Roosevelt administration initiated a variety of relief programs. The Works Progress Administration (WPA), one of the signature programs of the New Deal, was created by the $4.8 billion Emergency Relief Appropriations Act of 1935. The WPA included several arts programs, one of which was the Federal Theatre Project (FTP). Like other WPA projects, the FTP was designed to put the unemployed back to work. Finding it hard to compete with the motion picture industry, many theater workers, actors, stagehands, technicians, musicians, and vaudeville performers found jobs in the FTP. It succeeded in employing about eight thousand theater professionals during its span from 1935 through 1939.

One of the FTP's special divisions was called Living Newspapers. The FTP's national director, Hallie Flanagan, developed the idea of producing Living Newspapers in response to the challenge of creating low-budget programs while employing as many people as possible.

The productions covered the dynamic social issues of the day and did so without the lavish sets that other plays required. Inviting the Newspaper Guild to collaborate, FTP created fast-moving sketches with a narrator cutting in to announce newsworthy facts and figures or to comment on an issue. The set often included maps, footage from current events projected on-screen, and excerpts from speeches, quotes, and reports. The productions covered issues such as labor, the law, and housing conditions.

Because the FTP was a government-sponsored program, issues regarding censorship arose when the FTP produced plays that were socially provocative. The Living Newspaper play *Ethiopia,* depicting the events surrounding the Italian invasion of Ethiopia, was banned. *Injunction Granted,* a chronicle of labor activity in the United States, outraged even Hallie Flanagan, who was disappointed in the director for "allowing his personal beliefs to endanger the life of the Living Newspaper." She felt the play was more an editorial comment than news and was contrary to the objectives of the FTP. The play was closed prematurely and ticket holders were issued refunds. Despite these problems, Living Newspaper productions continued to produce plays that were provocative and forced the audience to consider important social issues. *Power,* about the Tennessee Valley Authority and the influence of the utility industry, and *One-Third of a Nation* were two of the most successful.

Significance

Despite being reelected by a record-setting margin, Roosevelt knew that the Depression was not over and that serious social and economic issues still faced the country. In his second inaugural address, he indicated his intention to continue to correct the country's ills. The most memorable line from that speech, "I see one-third of a nation ill-housed, ill-clad, and ill-nourished," made clear the priority for his second administration.

When *One-Third of a Nation* opened in New York in 1938, it drew crowds of people from trade unions and some of the city's most disadvantaged populations. It ran for 237 performances and was the FTP's most successful Living Newspaper production.

The production drew attention to the slum housing conditions in New York City and exposed the unsavory behavior of slum landlords who profited from tenants' poverty. Public outrage at the conditions described in the play prompted an increased role for the federal government in housing. Most significant was the passage of the 1937 Housing Act, which authorized $500 million in loans for low-income housing. A modest beginning, the act helped establish a federal presence in public housing that continued into the twenty-first century.

Primary Source

One-Third of a Nation [excerpt]

SYNOPSIS: In these excerpts from *One-Third of a Nation*, the audience gets an idea of what it is like to rent or buy housing in the New York slums. A rent strike is enacted in the first excerpt, with the "Loudspeaker" interrupting intermittently with rent strike statistics. In the second excerpt, a "Little Man" tries to buy a house. The "Loudspeaker" interrupts in this scene to encourage the "Little Man" to stand up to the "bully" landlords, brokers, and building supply men.

(Music comes up.)

Loudspeaker: Harlem Rent Strike: New York, October 11th, 1936. Four thousand march in fight on Harlem rent rise! East Side Rent Strike—New York, January 28th, 1933—Three hundred tenants picket Landlord.

(*Light on fourth floor. Three women come out of the three doorways and stand in hallway.*)

First Woman *(pointing to gap in balustrade)*: Three dollars a month more rent! Look at that banister!

Second Woman: It's been just like this ever since I moved in!

First Woman: Some day somebody's going to get hurt.

Third Woman: Nobody did yet!

First Woman: That's right—nobody did yet! So let's not do anything until some kid falls and breaks his skull on the landing down there!

Second Woman: But what are we going to do?

First Woman: Let's just sit back and pray.

Third Woman: But what can we do about it?

First Woman: I'm not sure, but I've got an idea. . . .

Blackout

(Music comes up again.)

Loudspeaker: Bronx Rent Strike. New York, January 6th, 1933. Twenty families in Charlotte Street tenement picket Landlord.

(*Three women rush down steps and into third floor landing as light comes up. Three other women meet them.*)

Fourth Woman: I'm not going to pay it—that's what!

Fifth Woman: Three dollars a month more, beginning October first!

Fourth Woman: What about Mrs. MacNamara—where is she? *(Calling)* Mrs. MacNamara!

Mrs. MacNamara *(stepping out of shadows of landing)* : Here I am! And I just saw him!

Fourth Woman: Are you going to pay it?

Mrs. MacNamara: No!

Fifth Woman: Are you going to move?

Mrs. MacNamara: No!

Fifth Woman: What *are* you going to do?

Mrs. MacNamara: I'll tell you what I'm going to do—I'm going to picket—and so are you—and you . . . (*To* Sixth Woman) . . . and *you,* too!

Sixth Woman: Picket? We can't picket!

Mrs. MacNamara: Why not? All you have to do is walk up and down!

Sixth Woman: With signs?

Mrs. MacNamara: With signs and banners and everything! Sure—if the men can do it—so can we!

Blackout

(*Music comes up and continues throughout* Loudspeaker's *announcement.*)

Loudspeaker: Brooklyn Rent Strike. January 17th, 1933. Two hundred members of the Brooklyn Tenants' League picket the Landlord.

(*Lights come up on five or six* women *and* Tenants' League Organizer *in upper center cubicle.*)

Organizer: Do you know how much it'll cost him to evict each tenant? $25.00!—For forty apartments it'll cost him a thousand dollars!

Fourth Woman: A thousand dollars! He'll never spend it! *(There is a pause.)*

First Woman: But is it right for us to stay here without paying rent?

Organizer: Is it right for him to raise rents when there's a housing shortage? For us to be thrown out on the street? Is it?

Chorus of Voices: *No!*

Organizer: And so, I'm proposing right now that we, members of the Tenants' League, declare a rent strike of all the tenants in this house. That nobody move and nobody pay rent until the Landlord . . .

Fourth Woman: Until the Landlord is willing to let us stay for the old rent!

Chorus of Voices: Right!

Blackout

Scene Three

(What Price Housing?)

Characters

Guide

Little Man

Loudspeaker

Landlord

Real Estate Operators

- Landowner (Land Buying)
- First Broker—Mr. Salt (Land Buying)
- Second Broker—Mr. Spinach (Land Buying)
- First Building Supply Man (Construction)
- Second Building Supply Man (Construction)
- Contractor (Construction)
- Banker (Finance)
- Mortgage Company President (Finance)
- First Man—Government Taxes (Collector)
- Second Man—State Taxes (Collector)
- Third Man—City Taxes (Collector)
- Fourth Man—Insurance Agent (Operating Expense)
- Fifth Man—Coal Dealer (Operating Expense)
- Woman—Renting Agent (Operating Expense)
- Sixth Man—Janitor (Operating Expense)

Announcers—Government Housing Projects

- First Man
- Second Man
- Third Man
- Fourth Man

Nathan Straus, Administrator, United States Housing Authority

. . . (*Light on* Little Man *and* Guide *sitting on two-step, right. Black screen has been lowered behind them.*)

Guide: Say, that's a new one on me!

Little Man: Is it?

Guide: Never had anything like a rent strike in my day! Any good come out of it? Did they get the rent cut? Did they get rid of the roaches? Did they?

Little Man: Well, er . . . (*Looks at* Loudspeaker, *helplessly.*)

Loudspeaker: They did. In one case the rent was cut two dollars a month. In another, the Landlord was forced to comply with the Multiple Dwelling Laws. In other cases rent increases have been prevented, painting done, drains repaired and roaches exterminated. The City-Wide Tenants' Council has on its record thousands of instances where repairs were made and rent adjusted only after action was taken!

Guide: Well, well, well.

Little Man *(smiling happily)*: Well, well, well. *(Takes out paper and pencil)* I'll have to make a note of that. City-Wide Tenants' . . . *(He does.)*

Guide: Then all you've got to do is join the union and all your troubles are over. . . .

Little Man: Well, not exactly. . . . You see—er—Well, you see, all they can do for you is help keep the Landlord from raising the rent, and see that he obeys the laws. But they can't give you light and sunshine and a decent place to live! You need new houses for that! (*He looks up at the* Loudspeaker *for approbation.*)

Loudspeaker: That's telling him, Angus! (Little Man *smiles.*)

Guide: Well, why haven't you got these new houses? Why aren't they building new ones every day to replace the old ones?

(*Light on* Landlord, *who enters, left, crosses to center.*)

Landlord: I'll tell you why.

Little Man: Oh, hello. Who're you?

Landlord: I'm the fellow who can answer that question. I'm a Landlord.

Little Man: A Landlord. Well, well. (*He introduces him to* Guide) Mister Guide, I want you to meet a Landlord. (Guide *bows.*)

Landlord: Now the reason there's no incentive to the commercial builder to build for the low income group is this: there's no money in it. That's simple, isn't it?

Little Man (*crosses center to* Landlord): But why is there no money in it? I don't want a marble palace. All I want is a little light and air, fair-sized rooms, and a few modern plumbing gadgets!

Landlord: You got any ideas what goes into the building and operation of a house?

Little Man: Sure. First, the land has to be bought . . .

Landlord: Uh-huh.

Little Man: . . . and the Contractor and laborers paid . . .

Landlord: That's right.

Little Man: . . . there's taxes and the janitor, and . . . and . . .

Landlord: Go on.

Little Man: . . . and . . . and . . . well, I guess that's all.

Landlord: You guess that's all! Well, let me show you something! *(Beckons off)* Hey, come here! (*Light on fourteen men and a woman who enter left and right. Music.*)

Little Man *(puzzled)*: Say, who are all these people?

Landlord: Don't rush me. That's what I'm going to show you. (*To men and woman who stand upstage*) Line up over here, where everybody can see you. . . . That's right. (*Three men come to apron step and line up, left*——Landowner, *center*—First Broker, *right,* Second Broker, *left. To* Little Man *and* Guide) Now, you two get out of the way . . . (*Pause.* Little Man *and* Guide *stand at two-step, right*) Now, I'm a philanthropic sort of guy, see, and I love my fellow men. So I decide to build a house where they can have light—and air—and—and—what else do you want?

Loudspeaker: A few modern plumbing gadgets!

Landlord: A few modern plumbing gadgets. . . . Now I don't want to make anything out of it—much! Just a couple of dollars a year so I don't have to depend on the *Old Age Security Act. (Crosses in front of line below apron step)* Now I want to rent my apartments for about seven or eight dollars a room—remember that, seven or eight dollars a room!—that's for the low-income brackets. . . . So I draw my money out of the bank and I go to work. . . . (*Crosses to* Man *at end of line, left, who has just begun to whistle. This happens each time—the* Man *about to be approached whistles. To first in line*) I want to buy a piece of your land on the East Side.

Landowner: You'll have to consult my brokers—Pepper, Salt, Mustard and Cider, 220 Broadway! (*Indicates* Man *next to him, center.* Landlord *crosses.*)

Landlord: You Mister Pepper?

First Broker: No, I'm Salt. What can I do for you?

Landlord: I'd like to buy a piece of his property.

First Broker: Where's your broker?

Landlord: Do I have to have one, too?

First Broker: Certainly. I can highly recommend the firm of Beans, Beans, Beans and Spinach. (*Indicates* Man *next to him, right.* Landlord *crosses.*)

Landlord: You Mister Beans?

Second Broker: No, I'm Spinach. What can I do for you?

Landlord: I want to buy a piece of his property. Ask him how much he wants.

Second Broker (*to* First Broker): How much?

First Broker (*to* Landowner): How much?

Landowner (*to* First Broker): Ten dollars a square foot!

First Broker (*to* Second Broker): Ten fifty a square foot!

Second Broker (*to* Landlord): Eleven dollars a square foot!

Landlord (*to* Second Broker): But he said ten fifty!

Second Broker: That's my commission!

Landlord (*to* First Broker): And *he* said ten dollars!

First Broker: That's my commission!

Landlord *(doubtfully)*: Eleven dollars!

Landowner (*poking* First Broker *in the ribs*): Tell him I just sold a small piece for twelve dollars.

First Broker (*poking* Second Broker): He says he just sold a fairly large piece for sixteen dollars.

Second Broker (*poking* Landlord): He says he just sold a square block for nineteen dollars!

Landlord: But eleven dollars! That's an awful lot of money! Can't we shave it down just a little? (*He looks at* Second Broker *who turns to* First Broker, *who turns to* Landowner.)

Landowner: Ten dollars, that's my price.

First Broker: Ten fifty, that's his price.

Second Broker: Eleven dollars, that's his price. (*Three men step back. After group has spoken they remain frozen in their last positions.*)

Landlord *(a deep sigh)*: O.K. I'll take it. (*Hands over money to* Second Broker) Well, now I'm a man of property.

Little Man: What'd it cost you? (*Two men step to apron step; they stand right*—First Building Supply Man, *and left*—Second Building Supply Man.)

Landlord: Plenty. (*Crosses to* Man *right*—First Building Supply Man) I want to build a house. Four stories high, walk-up, plenty of light and air, and . . . and . . .

Little Man: Plumbing gadgets!

Landlord: Yeah. How much for the materials?

First Building Supply Man: Fifteen thousand dollars.

Landlord: Fifteen thousand! Too much.

First Building Supply Man: Why don't you try him? *(Indicates left)* There may be a lot of sand in his cement but he's cheap.

Landlord: Thanks. I will. (*Crosses to* Man, *left, a little tired*) Want to build a house. Four stories. Light. Air Gadgets. How much?

Second Building Supply Man (*looks at* First Building Supply Man, *inquiringly.* First Building Supply Man *holds up fifteen fingers.* Second Building Supply Man *nods,* Landlord *suspecting something, swings around at* First Man *but he's too late*): Fifteen thousand.

Landlord: That's what he said.

Second Building Supply Man: Did he? What a coincidence!

Landlord: He also said your cement was full of sand.

Second Building Supply Man: That's O.K. So is his.

Landlord *(hesitant)*: Well, I may as well go back to him. He saw me coming first. *(Crosses back)* Here you are. Fifteen thousand. (*Hands over money to* First Building Supply Man *and crosses to* Man *who has come down and stands, center*) You a Contractor?

Contractor: Yeah.

Landlord: Do I have to repeat it all or did you hear me talking to them?

Contractor: I heard you.

Landlord: How much?

Contractor: Twenty-four thousand.

Landlord *(indignant)*: Twenty-four . . .

Contractor: That's right. My carpenters get twelve dollars a day.

Landlord: Twelve dollars a . . .

Loudspeaker: Don't let him get away with that one. Sure they get twelve dollars a day. And they probably worked three days last month!

Landlord: Oh, well . . . *(Starts counting out money and stops in consternation)* Say, I haven't got enough money! (Contractor *languidly turns away and starts whistling*) What'll I do?

Contractor *(stops whistling)*: Try the bank. (*Steps up as two men come down and stand on apron step, right and left.*)

Landlord: Thanks. (*Crosses to* Man, *left*—Banker) I want a mortgage.

Banker: Sorry. Got too many!

Landlord: What'll I do?

Banker: Try the Mortgage Company.

Landlord: Thanks. (*Crosses to* Man, *right*—Mortgage Company President) I want a mortgage.

Mortgage Company President: Sure. We'll float bonds. Six per cent.

Landlord: Six per cent!

Mortgage Company President: Plus my commission!

Landlord: Your commission! O.K. Give me the money. (Mortgage Company President *hands over money.* Landlord *crosses back to* Contractor) Here you are. Twenty-four thou . . . (*Stops, hears whistling of* Man, *standing directly back of* Contractor. *His hand is outstretched. The* Collectors *follow* First Man, *circling past the* Landlord, *all with their hands outstretched, while he, in bewildered fashion, hands them money as they ask for it*) Who're you?

First Man: Government, taxes. (Landlord *pays him.*)

Landlord: Who're you?

Second Man: State, taxes. *(Same business.)*

Landlord: Who're you?

Third Man: City, taxes. *(Same business.)*

Landlord: Who're you?

Fourth Man: Insurance. *(Same business.)*

Landlord: Who're you?

Fifth Man: Coal. *(Same business.)*

Landlord: Who're you?

Woman: Renting Agent. *(Same business.)*

Landlord: Who're you?

Sixth Man: I'm the Janitor! *(The circle freezes.)*

Landlord: Thank God! *(He goes down and sinks, exhausted, center. There is a pause.)*

Loudspeaker: Well, now what?

Landlord: Wait a minute, will you?

Landlord (*he takes out a sign:* "APARTMENTS FOR RENT," *and hangs it around his neck.* Little Man, *seeing the sign, rushes to center.*)

Little Man: Have you got an apartment to rent? (Landlord *still exhausted, nods*) Pretty fair-sized rooms?

Landlord: Uh-huh.

Little Man: . . . and—er—modern plumbing gadgets?

Landlord: Uh-huh.

Little Man *(suddenly)*: Got a three-room apartment left?

Landlord: Uh-huh.

Little Man *(incredulous)*: Did you say, uh-huh?

Landlord: Uh-huh.

Little Man *(beside himself with excitement)*: Now lemme get this straight—fair-sized rooms, light, and airy, modern gadgets—And you've got an apartment for me?

Landlord: Uh-huh.

Little Man *(same)*: For the love of Mike, how much is the rent?

Landlord: Twenty-five dollars a room! *(Music.)*

Blackout

Further Resources

BOOKS

Browder, Laura. *Rousing the Nation: Radical Culture in Depression America.* Amherst, Mass.: University of Massachusetts Press, 1998.

De Hart, Jane Sherron. *The Federal Theatre, 1935–1939: Plays, Relief, and Politics.* Princeton, N.J.: Princeton University Press, 1967.

Hickock, Lorena. *One-Third of a Nation: Lorena Hickock Reports on the Great Depression.* Urbana, Ill.: University of Illinois Press, 2000.

WEBSITES

The New Deal Stage: Selections from the Federal Theatre Project 1935–1939. American Memory digital primary source collection, Library of Congress. Available online at http://memory.loc.gov/ammem/fedtp/fthome.html; website home page: http://www.loc.gov (accessed April 10, 2003).

"The Second Inaugural Address: January 20, 1937." Works of Franklin D. Roosevelt. New Deal Network. Available online at http://newdeal.feri.org/speeches/1937a.htm; website home page: http://newdeal.feri.org/index.htm (accessed February 16, 2003).

AUDIO AND VISUAL MEDIA

One-Third of a Nation. Directed by Dudley Murphy. United Home Studios, 1939, VHS.

The Grapes of Wrath

Novel

By: John Steinbeck

Date: 1939

Source: Steinbeck, John. *The Grapes of Wrath and Other Writings, 1936–1941.* Reprint, New York: Penguin Books, 1996, 290–294.

About the Author: John Steinbeck (1902–1968) was born in Salinas, California. Shortly after he began college, Steinbeck started writing, mostly about events taking place in California, and he finished his first novel in 1929. His 1937 novel *Of Mice and Men* was widely acclaimed, but it is 1939's *The Grapes of Wrath* that is considered his masterpiece. He won the 1940 Pulitzer Prize for that novel. His other works include many popular stories and novels, including *Cannery Row, East of Eden,* and *Travels With Charley: In Search of America.* One of America's most famous authors, Steinbeck won the Nobel Prize for literature in 1962. ■

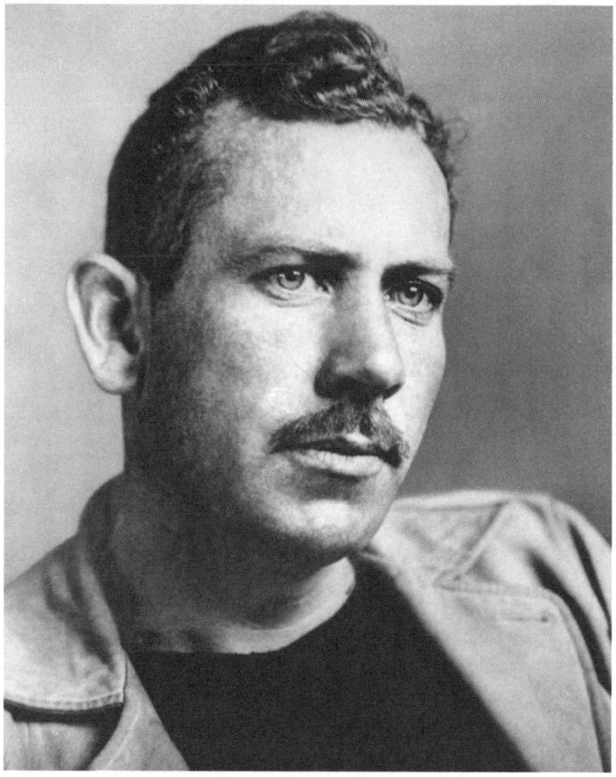

John Steinbeck authored many acclaimed novels, including the stark tale of the Great Depression: *The Grapes of Wrath.* NATIONAL ARCHIVES AND RECORDS ADMINISTRATION.

Introduction

The Great Depression and the dust storms, caused by erosion and drought, drove thousands of Great Plains farming families from their land. Census figures show that 440,000 left Oklahoma and 227,000 left Kansas during the 1930s. While most went into the cities, some joined an existing army (perhaps 2 million) of migrant workers who yearly followed a planting and harvesting cycle that took them all across the country in search of work. Many joined the permanent California migrant workforce of approximately 200,000. Ironically, many faced conditions as harsh and desperate as the ones they left on the Great Plains.

Steinbeck became involved in the plight of these migrant workers, and poor Americans in general. He wanted to write about their hardships, and to do so he felt that he had to live with them. So Steinbeck went to Oklahoma, joined a group of migrants, and journeyed with them to California, where he lived with them in the "Hoovervilles." He also visited migrant camps.

The result of Steinbeck's experience was the 1939 novel *The Grapes of Wrath,* a story about the Joads, a fictional extended family of Oklahoma tenant farmers who are forced off of their land by the Shawnee Land and Cattle Company. They hear there is work picking fruit in California and believe they have no choice but to go west, because to stay in Oklahoma means certain starvation. Loading a broken-down truck with what critical possessions they can fit in, they leave their home and head to California in search of work and a better life.

By telling the Joads' story, Steinbeck wanted his readers to understand the personal tragedies of dispossessed migrant workers. Readers are moved to sympathize with the Joads as they lose their home and land, lose family members along their journey, face poverty, starvation, ridicule, and rejection, and ultimately have their hopes for survival and a better life shattered by the hostile conditions in California.

Readers are also moved to respect the Joads' efforts to carry on with dignity. Glimmers of hope and demonstrations of great human strength and adaptability occur throughout the novel, with the underlying theme that by helping each other and extending human kindness, people find ways to survive even under the worst conditions. And it is in the worst conditions where readers find the remaining family members at the novel's end. Even though their situation is bleak, Steinbeck leaves readers with a glimmer of hope, planting seeds he hopes will bring social change.

Significance

Steinbeck's novel was an immediate sensation. It was widely read, and created considerable controversy. Some denounced his description of migrant conditions as greatly exaggerated, calling it "nothing but black lies," and voiced concern that the novel encouraged radical, even communist ideas. It was banned in some sections of California.

Others, however, rallied to testify to the accuracy of his portrayal and praised the novel's message. Regardless of the critics, Steinbeck helped draw public attention to the plight of migrant workers and, more generally, to the problems of the working poor in the United States. Ever since its publication, *The Grapes of Wrath* has been one of the most powerful literary images of the Great Depression. It evokes sympathy and understanding for the "Okies" and creates a vivid picture of the Depression.

The book was adapted to the screen and made into a movie in 1940. It won Academy Awards for Best Director (John Ford) and Best Supporting Actress (Jane Darwell), and was nominated for Best Picture and Best Actor (Henry Fonda).

Primary Source

The Grapes of Wrath [excerpt]

SYNOPSIS: Evicted from land the family has lived on for several generations, the Joads, having seen leaflets advertising for work at good wages, decide to move to California. After a difficult journey, the Joads arrive in California, where they stay in a work camp with other migrants. Here they are confronted by a reality that is unlike their dream.

Rose of Sharon closed her eyes. Ma turned over on her back and crossed her hands under her head. She listened to Granma's breathing and to the girl's breathing. She moved a hand to start a fly from her forehead. The camp was quiet in the blinding heat, but the noises of hot grass—of crickets, the hum of flies—were a tone that was close to silence. Ma sighed deeply and then yawned and closed her eyes. In her half-sleep she heard footsteps approaching, but it was a man's voice that started her awake.

"Who's in here?"

Ma sat up quickly. A brown-faced man bent over and looked in. He wore boots and khaki pants and a khaki shirt with epaulets. On a Sam Browne belt a pistol holster hung, and a big silver star was pinned to his shirt at the left breast. A loose-crowned military cap was on the back of his head. He beat on the tarpaulin with his hand, and the tight canvas vibrated like a drum.

"Who's in here?" he demanded again.

Ma asked, "What is it you want, mister?"

"What you think I want? I want to know who's in here."

"Why, they's jus' us three in here. Me an' Granma an' my girl."

"Where's your men?"

"Why, they went down to clean up. We was drivin' all night."

"Where'd you come from?"

"Right near Sallisaw, Oklahoma."

"Well, you can't stay here."

"We aim to get out tonight an' cross the desert, mister."

"Well, you better. If you're here tomorra this time I'll run you in. We don't want none of you settlin' down here."

Ma's face blackened with anger. She got slowly to her feet. She stooped to the utensil box and picked out the iron skillet. "Mister," she said, "you got a tin button an' a gun. Where I come from, you keep your voice down." She advanced on him with the skillet. He loosened the gun in the holster. "Go ahead," said Ma. "Scarin' women. I'm thankful the men folks ain't here. They'd tear ya to pieces. In my country you watch your tongue."

The man took two steps backward. "Well, you ain't in your country now. You're in California, an' we don't want you goddamn Okies settlin' down."

Ma's advance stopped. She looked puzzled. "Okies?" she said softly. "Okies."

"Yeah, Okies! An' if you're here when I come tomorra, I'll run ya in." He turned and walked to the next tent and banged on the canvas with his hand. "Who's in here?" he said.

Ma went slowly back under the tarpaulin. She put the skillet in the utensil box. She sat down slowly. Rose of Sharon watched her secretly. And when she saw Ma fighting with her face, Rose of Sharon closed her eyes and pretended to be asleep.

■ ■ ■

The sun sank low in the afternoon, but the heat did not seem to decrease. Tom awakened under his willow, and his mouth was parched and his body was wet with sweat, and his head was dissatisfied with

Steinbeck's fictional Joad family was inspired by the real life hardships faced by Americans displaced by drought and the Great Depression. This family was photographed by Dorothea Lange in 1935 as they fled the "Dust Bowl" in search of work. LIAISON AGENCY. REPRODUCED BY PERMISSION.

his rest. He staggered to his feet and walked toward the water. He peeled off his clothes and waded into the stream. And the moment the water was about him, his thirst was gone. He lay back in the shallows and his body floated. He held himself in place with his elbows in the sand, and looked at his toes, which bobbed above the surface.

A pale skinny little boy crept like an animal through the reeds and slipped off his clothes. And he squirmed into the water like a muskrat, and pulled himself along like a muskrat, only his eyes and nose above the surface. Then suddenly he saw Tom's head and saw that Tom was watching him. He stopped his game and sat up.

Tom said, "Hello."

"'Lo!"

"Looks like you was playin' mushrat."

"Well, I was." He edged gradually away toward the bank; he moved casually, and then he leaped out, gathered his clothes with a sweep of his arms, and was gone among the willows.

Tom laughed quietly. And then he heard his name called shrilly. "Tom, oh, Tom!" He sat up in the water and whistled through his teeth, a piercing whistle with a loop on the end. The willows shook, and Ruthie stood looking at him.

"Ma wants you," she said. "Ma wants you right away."

"Awright." He stood up and strode through the water to the shore; and Ruthie looked with interest and amazement at his naked body.

Tom, seeing the direction of her eyes, said, "Run on now. Git!" And Ruthie ran. Tom heard her calling excitedly for Winfield as she went. He put the hot clothes on his cool, wet body and he walked slowly up through the willows toward the tent.

Ma had started a fire of dry willow twigs, and she had a pan of water heating. She looked relieved when she saw him.

"What's a matter, Ma?" he asked.

"I was scairt," she said. "They was a policeman here. He says we can't stay here. I was scairt he talked to you. I was scairt you'd hit him if he talked to you."

Tom said, "What'd I go an' hit a policeman for?"

Ma smiled. "Well—he talked so bad—I nearly hit him myself."

Tom grabbed her arm and shook her roughly and loosely, and he laughed. He sat down on the ground, still laughing.

"My God, Ma. I knowed you when you was gentle. What's come over you?"

She looked serious. "I don' know, Tom."

"Fust you stan' us off with a jack handle, and now you try to hit a cop." He laughed softly, and he reached out and patted her bare foot tenderly. "A ol' hell-cat," he said.

"Tom."

"Yeah?"

She hesitated a long time. "Tom, this here policeman—he called us—Okies. He says, 'We don' want you goddamn Okies settlin' down.'"

Tom studied her, and his hand still rested gently on her bare foot. "Fella tol' about that," he said. "Fella tol' how they say it." He considered, "Ma, would you say I was a bad fella? Oughta be locked up—like that?"

"No," she said. "You been tried—No. What you ast me for?"

"Well, I dunno. I'd a took a sock at that cop."

Ma smiled with amusement. "Maybe I oughta ast you that, 'cause I nearly hit 'im with a skillet."

"Ma, why'd he say we couldn' stop here?"

"Jus' says they don' want no damn Okies settlin' down. Says he's gonna run us in if we're here tomorra."

"But we ain't use' ta gettin' shoved aroun' by no cops."

"I tol' him that," said Ma. "He says we ain't home now. We're in California, and they do what they want."

Tom said uneasily, "Ma, I got somepin to tell ya. Noah—he went on down the river. He ain't a-goin' on."

It took a moment for Ma to understand. "Why?" she asked softly.

"I don' know. Says he got to. Says he got to stay. Says for me to tell you."

"How'll he eat?" she demanded.

"I don' know. Says he'll catch fish."

Ma was silent a long time. "Family's fallin' apart," she said. "I don' know. Seems like I can't think no more. I jus' can't think. They's too much."

Further Resources

BOOKS

Gregory, James N. *American Exodus: The Dustbowl Migration and Okie Culture in California.* New York: Oxford University Press, 1989.

Stanley, Jerry. *Children of the Dust Bowl: The True Story of the School at Weedpatch Camp.* New York: Crown, 1993.

Worster, Donald. *The Southern Plains in the 1930s.* New York: Oxford University Press, 1979.

WEBSITES

"The Dust Bowl." Center for Earth and Planetary Studies, National Air and Space Museum, Smithsonian Institution. Available online at http://www.nasm.si.edu/ceps/drylands/dust.html (accessed February 16, 2003).

"The Dust Bowl." People and Environmental Change on the Great Plains. Available online at http://www.usd.edu/anth/epa/dust.html; website home page: http://www.usd.edu/anth/epa/index.html (accessed February 16, 2003).

"Lydia, the Tattooed Lady"

Song

By: E.Y. Harburg

Date: 1939

Source: Harburg, E.Y. "Lydia the Tatooed Lady," in *At the Circus.* Original release, 1939, MGM. Directed by Edward Buzzell. VHS.

About the Artist: Edgar Y. ("Yip") Harburg (1896–1981) wrote the lyrics to "Lydia" and all of the other songs in the Marx Brothers film *At the Circus.* After he lost his electrical appliance company in New York in the stock market crash of 1929, he began writing song lyrics. He wrote the lyrics for "Brother Can You Spare a Dime," an anthem for the Great Depression, *The Wizard of Oz*'s "Over the Rainbow," and "April in Paris." ■

Introduction

Born and raised in New York, the Marx brothers were noted for their zany slapstick comedy. Although Zeppo and Gummo, the two youngest brothers, left the act in 1935 to pursue other behind-the-scenes show business careers, Chico, Groucho, and Harpo went on to enjoy success as a team and are generally the individuals designated as the Marx Brothers. Late in their careers, they performed as solo musicians and comedians. Groucho starred as a solo film actor and hosted the television game show, *You Bet Your Life.* The brothers were notorious for being just as entertaining offstage as they were onstage.

Marx Brothers comedy borders on the insane. The slapstick humor and unexpected, often nonsensical punch lines gave their routines the right recipe for success in vaudeville, movies, and radio. Their exceptional musical talent added to the magic of their routines, and many of their movies have produced soundtracks that feature songs with zany lyrics sung by one brother accompanied by another playing an instrument.

Their genius was demonstrated in taking dignified settings, such as the opera, and turning them into chaos. While chaos was featured in acting out their wacky plots, there was predictability in the way they executed their parts. Chico generally played the restless huckster, Harpo the silent and childlike mime, and Groucho the deliverer of brash wisecracks and one-liners.

As early as 1910, the Marx Brothers were gaining popularity in vaudeville. Spanning into the mid-1930s, their vaudeville career included over twenty-one routines. This work became a valuable testing ground for their acts in front of a live audience before taking them to the movie screen. Consequently, several of their vaudeville routines were seen in later films, including *The Coconuts, Animal Crackers,* and *A Day at the Races.*

With the advent of movies, especially the "talkies," vaudeville gradually died out, and the Marx Brothers were one of many vaudevillian groups to try to take their acts to the big screen. They made at least fourteen feature films and guest-starred in many others. A typical plot takes Chico and Harpo on a heroic cause, where they run into the dishonest Groucho. One example is *Duck Soup,* a political satire in which Groucho plays Rufus T. Firefly, dictator of the tiny nation of Fredonia. Chico and Harpo play spies trying to steal his written plans for war on a neighbor nation. The following lines from *Duck Soup* provide an example of what the dialogue in a Marx Brothers movie is like:

Dumont: The plans of war are gone . . . They were taken right from under my nose.

Firefly: A fine place to keep the plans of war! Who was with you?

Dumont: The Secretary of War.

Firefly: What was he doing under your nose? What a fool I was to trust you—to listen to your siren song.

Dumont: But—

Firefly: You gratified your selfish whims, while nations tottered, dynasties rocked, and the world plunged headlong into a chasm of chaos and oblivion—I've read worse than that in three-dollar books. In fact, that's where I got it.

Chico: That's fine, now we gotta the plans—we take them right over to Trentino.

Firefly: Hands up!!!

Chico: Hey, you no got-a gun.

Firefly: Who said I had a gun. Keep your hands up and I'll get one . . . I'll be back in five minutes.

Chico: Wait a minute. . . . Can you use a knife?

Firefly: Well, a knife isn't as good as a gun, but this is no time to be choosy. Now—hand over those papers or I'll blow your brains out. You double-crossers—you traitors. You'll be court marshaled for this. You know what this is? This is treason—and you know what treason is?

Chico: Sure, my uncle he's-a got a hundred and sixty-five treason his back yard.

This wacky dialogue is typical of an interchange between Groucho and Chico in any of the Marx Brothers movies.

The Marx Brothers were also successful on the radio. Beginning in the mid-1930s, radio began to supplement the movies as a popular form of entertainment. It was free, convenient, and allowed for a much broader scope in programming. Families listened to the radio together as a traditional evening activity. As the Marx Brothers' popularity in the movies declined, they took full advantage of the radio and began to take more solo engagements. Their careers stretched into the late 1950s with such movies as *The Incredible Jewel Robbery.* The made-for-TV production was the last movie to include three Marx brothers performing together.

Still from the movie *At the Circus,* with Groucho Marx and Eve Arden dancing on the ceiling, 1939. **THE KOBAL COLLECTION/MGM. REPRODUCED BY PERMISSION.**

Significance

In a time of great economic and social unrest, particularly in the early part of the 1930s, the Marx Brothers, like other vaudeville comedians, turned into movie stars, providing temporary escapes from the seriousness of the times. Clips from a Marx Brothers movie or sound bites from one of their radio shows still inspire laughs.

Groucho recognized the paradox between the insanity portrayed in his comedy and the seriousness it could represent when he said, "The first thing which disappears when men are turning a country into a totalitarian state is comedy and comics. Because we are laughed at, I don't think people really understand how essential we are to their sanity."

Groucho's persona is arguably the most memorable of the Marx Brothers characters. His famous oversized mustache, exaggerated eyebrows, dark-rimmed glasses, and trademark cigar became a symbol of comedy. His one-liners are still imitated with the undeniable Groucho gestures. He was honored in 1974 with an Academy Award for lifetime achievement, and the Marx Brothers were inducted into the Motion Picture Hall of Fame in 1977.

Primary Source

"Lydia, the Tattooed Lady"

SYNOPSIS: In 1939, MGM released the movie *At the Circus,* featuring Groucho as crooked lawyer J. Cheever Loophole. The boys are trying to save the circus and look to a wealthy socialite, played by Margaret Dumont, to fund their efforts. The following song lyrics delivered by Groucho in the film, describe in detail the physical attributes of Lydia, the Tattooed Lady.

Oh Lydia, oh Lydia, say, have you met Lydia?
Lydia. The Tattooed Lady.
She has eyes that folks adore so,
And a torso even more so.

Lydia, oh Lydia, that encyclo-pidia.
Oh Lydia. The Queen of Tattoo.

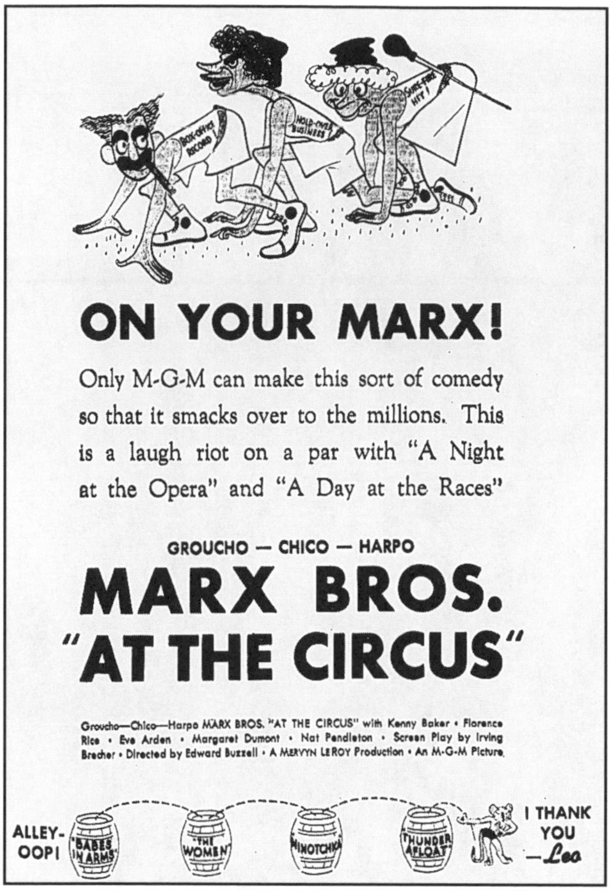

An advertisement for the MGM Marx Brothers film *At the Circus* from *Variety* magazine, Oct. 18, 1939.

On her back is the Battle of Waterloo.
Beside it, the Wreck of the Hesperus too.
And proudly above waves the red, white, and blue.
You can learn a lot from Lydia!

La-la-la . . . la-la-la.
La-la-la . . . la-la-la.

When her robe is unfurled she will show you the world,
If you step up and tell her where.
For a dime you can see Kankakee or Paree,
Or Washington crossing the Delaware.

La-la-la . . . la-la-la.
La-la-la . . . la-la-la.

Oh Lydia, oh Lydia, say, have you met Lydia?
Lydia. The Tattooed Lady.
When her muscles start relaxin',
Up the hill comes Andrew Jackson.

Lydia, oh Lydia, that encyclo-pidia.
Oh Lydia The Queen of them all.
For two bits she will do a mazurka in jazz,
With a view of Niagara that nobody has.
And on a clear day you can see Alcatraz.
You can learn a lot from Lydia!

La-la-la . . . la-la-la.
La-la-la . . . la-la-la.

Come along and see Buffalo Bill with his lasso.
Just a little classic by Mendel Picasso.
Here is Captain Spaulding exploring the Amazon.
Here's Godiva, but with her pajamas on.

La-la-la . . . la-la-la.
La-la-la . . . la-la-la.

Here is Grover Whelan unveilin' the Trilon.
Over on the west coast we have Treasure Isle-on.
Here's Nijinsky a-doin' the rhumba.
Here's her social security numba.

La-la-la . . . la-la-la.
La-la-la . . . la-la-la.

Lydia, oh Lydia, that encyclo-pidia.
Oh Lydia. The Champ of them all.
She once swept an Admiral clear off his feet.
The ships on her hips made his heart skip a beat.
And now the old boy's in command of the fleet,
For he went and married Lydia!

I said Lydia . . .
(He said Lydia . . .)
They said Lydia . . .
We said Lydia, la, la!

Further Resources

BOOKS

Adamson, Joe. *Groucho, Harpo, Chico, and Sometimes Zeppo: A History of the Marx Brothers and a Satire on the Rest of the World.* New York: Simon & Schuster, 1973.

Louvish, Simon. *Monkey Business: The Lives and Legends of the Marx Brothers: Groucho, Chico, Harpo, Zeppo, with added Gummo.* New York: St. Martin's Press, 2000.

WEBSITES

Timphus, Stefan, ed. "The Marx Brothers: Chico, Harpo, Groucho, Gummo, Zeppo." Available online at http://www.marx-brothers.org (accessed February 16, 2003).

Arena: The History of the Federal Theatre

Memoir

By: Hallie Flanagan

Date: 1940

Source: Flanagan, Hallie. *Arena: The History of the Federal Theatre.* 1940. Reprint, New York: Benjamin Blom, 1965, 340–346.

About the Author: Hallie Flanagan (1890–1969) was described by President Franklin D. Roosevelt as "the third most powerful woman in America, after my wife and Frances Perkins" (who was the first female cabinet member). Flanagan, however, earned this reputation with President Roosevelt by exerting her influence in the American theater, most notably as director of the Federal Theatre Project of the Works

Progress Administration (WPA) from 1935 to 1939. She later became dean of Smith College in Northampton, Massachusetts, and remained as professor of drama until her retirement in 1955. ■

Introduction

When Franklin D. Roosevelt (served 1933–1945) took office in 1933, the nation was reeling from the effects of the Great Depression. With the economic trouble much on his mind, Roosevelt said in his inaugural address, "I am prepared under my constitutional duty to recommend the measures that a stricken nation in the midst of a stricken world may require." These measures were called the New Deal, a massive governmental intervention composed of several major programs designed to put the unemployed back to work and provide relief for those badly in need. The WPA was part of this effort, and it included the Federal Theatre Project, one of five arts-related projects under its auspices.

Harry Hopkins, director of the WPA, recognized Flanagan's talent and contacted her about taking over the theater arm of the WPA's art programs. She and Hopkins agreed on the goal of democratizing the arts in the United States, increasing government activity in the arts, and creating a national arts program. Flanagan's original idea was to provide employment for approximately 7,500 professionals in theater arts. After consulting with theater professionals E.C. Mabie and Elmer Rice, she devised a much more elaborate plan. It provided employment for over thirty thousand people in state and regional centers and in drama departments of educational institutions. Regrettably, this plan stalled when it reached the WPA administrative staff, who doubted the WPA could fund the project.

Flanagan met with Eleanor Roosevelt at the White House in May 1935 to garner support for the plan, and she found Mrs. Roosevelt receptive. The scope of the project was still unresolved, however, when Flanagan was sworn in as director of the FTP in August. A final plan emerged in October, focusing on employment in the commercial theater centered in New York City but branching into regional theater all over the country.

When the Federal Theatre Project finally got under way, it encompassed forty cities in twenty-two states and produced a wide range of new plays, classical plays, vaudeville acts, marionette and puppet shows, and dance productions. FTP productions reflected what Flanagan and the company interpreted as the sentiments of the American people of that time.

One branch of the FTP, the Living Newspapers, was controversial. Living Newspapers was modeled after the international workers' theater movement in central Europe. Its goal was to dramatize current events. The initial idea crystallized when Elmer Rice, Flanagan's New York director, invited the American Newspaper Guild to work with the unit. The result was such socially conscious plays as *One-Third of a Nation* and *Triple-A Plowed Under,* demonstrating both the failure of Roosevelt's New Deal in healing the ills of the nation and giving voice to its unsatisfied constituents.

Hallie Flanagan Davis, the head of the Federal Theatre Project, in 1936. VASSAR COLLEGE LIBRARY.

Another especially controversial production, although not part of the Living Newspapers series, was a children's play entitled *Revolt of the Beavers.* In this play, a group of oppressed beavers rise against their leader. Critics felt it encouraged communism and revolution. Productions such as these made Senator Joseph W. Bailey of North Carolina and other lawmakers uncomfortable and would ultimately spell the end of the FTP. Flanagan, however, defended the integrity of FTP productions by contending that they only reflected the voice of the American people and were not intended as propaganda for leftist ideas.

Significance

The Federal Theatre Project, under Flanagan's direction, played to a total of twenty-five million Americans, produced a thousand plays with fifty thousand performances, and employed twelve thousand actors, directors, and stagehands.

Conservatives in Congress opposed the liberal direction of the Federal Theatre plays and began to cut funding in 1937. Clifton A. Woodrum led the opposition to the program in the House Committee of Appropriations, while Martin Dies investigated the alleged communist leanings of the FTP under the authority of the House Committee on Un-American Activities (HUAC). The HUAC was created in 1938 to investigate subversion, with a particular focus on communist infiltration of the federal government.

Though the Dies Committee did not uncover any direct connection with the Communist Party, the FTP was still shut down in 1939. Despite being relatively short-lived, the FTP made a significant impact on the direction of American theater and on the audiences who saw its plays.

Primary Source

Arena: The History of the Federal Theatre [excerpt]

SYNOPSIS: Following is an excerpt from the memoirs of Hallie Flanagan, in which she recounts her experience representing the Federal Theatre Project and defending her own intentions before the House Appropriations Committee in 1938. The hearings began in August, and Flanagan testified in early December. Following the hearings, Congress voted to end funding for the Federal Theatre Project, effective June 30, 1939.

On December 6, when Mrs. Woodward retired from the witness stand because the Committee wanted more specific information than she could give, I was called to testify. It was indeed much later than the W.P.A. thought. Could a few hours offset the months in which allegations had gone unanswered, and charges had been magnified by the press?

Before me stretched two long tables in the form of a huge T. At the foot was the witness chair, at the head the members of the Committee. At long tables on either side of the T were reporters, stenographers, cameramen. The room itself, a high-walled chamber with great chandeliers, was lined with exhibits of material from the Federal Theatre and the Writers' Project; but all I could see for a moment were the faces of thousands of Federal Theatre people; clowns in the circus . . . telephone girls at the switchboards . . . actors in grubby rehearsal rooms . . . acrobats limbering up their routines . . . costume women busy making cheap stuff look expensive . . . musicians composing scores to bring out the best in our often oddly assembled orchestras . . . playwrights working on scripts with the skills of our actors in mind . . . carpenters, prop men, ushers. These were the people on trial that morning.

I was sworn in as a witness by Chairman Dies, rangy Texan with a cowboy drawl and a big black cigar. I wanted to talk about Federal Theatre, but the Committee apparently did not. Who had appointed me? Harry Hopkins. Was that his own idea or did somebody put him up to it? I said I had no knowledge of any recommendations made in my behalf; I said that while the Committee had recently been investigating un-American activity, I had been engaged for four years in combating un-American inactivity. The distinction was lost on the Committee. I sketched the project's concern for the human values, the return of over 2,000 of our people to jobs in private industry, but the Committee was not interested in any discussion of the project. Wasn't it true I taught at Vassar? Yes. Went to Russia? Yes. Wrote a book about it? Yes. Praised the Russian theatre? In 1926 I had been appointed as a fellow of the Guggenheim Foundation to study the theatre in twelve European countries over a period of fourteen months; Russia was one of the countries in which I carried on such observations. What was it I found so exciting in the Russian theatre? It was at that time an interesting theatre about which little was known. It was my job at that time to study it. That, I pointed out, was twelve years ago. It was part of the background of my profession—the American theatre. The Committee was giving more time to the discussion of the Russian theatre than Federal Theatre had in the four years of its existence.

Mr. Starnes was curious about my visits to Russia. Had I gone there in 1931 as well as in 1926? Yes, for three weeks. Was I a delegate to anything? No, I had gone, as had many American theatre producers, to see the Russian theatre festival. Did I meet at the festival there any of the people later employed in the Federal Theatre? Certainly not.

Hadn't I written plays in Russian and produced them in Russia? I had not (I remembered my struggles to learn to order a meal or buy galoshes in Russian).

Then back to the project. Had communistic propaganda been circulated on the project? Not to my knowledge. Were there orders on my part against such activity? Yes, stringent orders which appear in the brief. Mr. Starnes took a different tack: Did I consider the theatre a weapon? I said the theatre could be all things to all men. "Do you see this?" Congressman Starnes suddenly shouted, waving a yellow magazine aloft. "Ever see it before?" I said it seemed to be an old *Theatre Arts Monthly.* This described a meeting of workers' theatres in New York in 1931. Hadn't I been active in setting them up? No. I had never been connected in any way with workers' theatres. I wrote a report on such theatres for *Theatre Arts Monthly* under the title "A Theatre Is Born." This theatre, however, was not born through me; I was simply a reporter.

How about these plays that had been criticized by witnesses before the Committee? Were they propaganda? For communism? "To the best of my knowledge," I told the Committee, "we have never done a play which was propaganda for communism; but we have done plays which were propaganda for democracy, for better housing. . . ."

How many people had we played to so far? Twenty-five million people, a fifth of the population. Where did our audience come from? Was it true that we "couldn't get any audiences for anything except communist plays"? No. The list submitted would show our wide audience support. Back to the article, "A Theatre Is Born," and the phrase where I had described the enthusiasm of these theatres as having "a certain Marlowesque madness."

"You are quoting from this Marlowe," observed Mr. Starnes. "Is he a Communist?"

The room rocked with laughter, but I did not laugh. Eight thousand people might lose their jobs because a Congressional Committee had so pre-judged us that even the classics were "communistic." I said, "I was quoting from Christopher Marlowe."

"Tell us who Marlowe is, so we can get the proper references, because that is all we want to do."

"Put in the record that he was the greatest dramatist in the period of Shakespeare, immediately preceding Shakespeare."

Mr. Starnes subsided; Mr. Thomas of New Jersey took over. How about this play, *The Revolt of the Beavers?* Didn't Brooks Atkinson of the *New York Times* disapprove of the play? Yes, he did. But Mr. Hearst's *New York American* thought it a "pleasing fantasy for children," and an audience survey by trained psychologists brought only favorable reactions from children such as "teaches us never to be selfish"—"it is better to be good than bad"—"how the children would want the whole world to be nine years old and happy."

Was it true that we had been rehearsing *Sing for Your Supper,* the musical in New York, for thirteen months? It was true and the delays were not of our choosing. We kept losing our best skits and our best actors to private industry. Was that, I asked, un-American? Mr. Mosier brought us back to the question of propaganda. Had we ever produced any anti-fascist plays? Some people claimed that Shaw's *On the Rocks* was anti-fascist and others thought it was anti-communist; Shakespeare's *Coriolanus* caused the same discussion.

"We never do a play because it holds any political bias," I declared. "We do a play because we believe it is a good play, a strong play, properly handled, with native material."

Was it true that Earl Browder appeared as a character in *Triple-A Plowed Under?* Yes. Did he expound his theory of communism? He did not; he appeared as a shadow on a screen along with Al Smith, Senator Hastings, and Thomas Jefferson. Had we ever produced plays that were anti-religious? On the contrary, we had produced more religious plays than any other theatre organization in the history of the country. Was I in sympathy with communistic doctrines? I said:

"I am an American and I believe in American democracy. I believe the Works Progress Administration is one great bulwark of that democracy. I believe the Federal Theatre, which is one small part of that large pattern, is honestly trying in every possible way to interpret the best interests of the people of this democracy. I am not in sympathy with any other form of government."

What percentage of the 4,000 employees on the New York project were members of the Workers' Alliance, Mr. Thomas wanted to know. We had no way of knowing. Was it a very large percentage? No, we knew it could not be large because the vast majority belonged to the standard theatrical organizations like Actors' Equity and the various stage unions, and these unions did not permit their members to join the Workers' Alliance.

Chairman Dies asked if we were out to entertain our audiences or to instruct them. I said that the primary purpose of a play is to entertain but that it can also teach.

"Do you think the theatre should be used for the purpose of conveying ideas along social and economic lines?"

"I think that is one justifiable reason for the existence of a theatre."

"Do you think that the Federal Theatre should be used for the purpose of conveying ideas along social, economic, or political lines?"

"I would hesitate on the political."

"Eliminate political, upon social and economic lines?"

"I think it is one logical, reasonable, and I might say imperative thing for our theatre to do."

Could I give the Committee one play, dealing with social questions, where "organized labor does not have the best of the other fellows"? Certainly. I mentioned *Spirochete,* the living newspaper on the history of syphilis, endorsed by the Surgeon General of the United States Public Health Service. I mentioned the living newspapers being prepared on flood control *(Bonneville Dam)*; the history of vaudeville *(Clown's Progress)*; the history of California real estate *(Spanish Grant)*. The Chairman waved these examples aside. Didn't *Power* imply that public ownership of utilities is a good thing? Is it proper for a government theatre to champion one side of a controversy? We do not choose plays by picking sides in a controversy.

On this matter of the writing of plays it was apparent that the Committee confused the Theatre and the Federal Writers' Project. Chairman Dies insisted that he had received admissions from Federal Theatre workers who were Communists, Communists who had placed their signatures openly in a book. I said this had not happened on our project.

"Well," declared the Chairman triumphantly, "Mr. De Solo said he was a Communist."

"But he is not on the Federal Theatre Project."

"He is on the Writers' Project."

"Yes, but not our project."

Suddenly Mr. Starnes remarked that it was a quarter past one, the Chairman announced an adjournment for an hour and said that Mr. Alsberg would be heard when they resumed.

"Just a minute, gentlemen," I interrupted. "Do I understand that this concludes my testimony?"

"We will see about it after lunch," the Chairman promised.

"I would like to make a final statement, if I may."

"We will see about it after lunch," the Chairman repeated and the gavel fell. We never saw about it after lunch.

As the hearing broke up I thought suddenly of how much it all looked like a badly staged courtroom scene; it wasn't imposing enough for a congressional hearing on which the future of several thousand human beings depended. For any case on which the life and reputation of a single human being depended, even that of an accused murderer, we had an American system which demanded a judge trained in law, a defense lawyer, a carefully chosen jury, and above all the necessity of hearing all the evidence on both sides of the case.

Yet here was a Committee which for months had been actually trying a case against Federal Theatre, trying it behind closed doors, and giving one side only to the press. Out of a project employing thousands of people from coast to coast, the Committee had chosen arbitrarily to hear ten witnesses, all from New York City, and had refused arbitrarily to hear literally hundreds of others, on and off the project, who had asked to testify.

Representative Dempsey, who throughout the hearing had been just and courteous, came up and told me that he felt my testimony had been "completely satisfactory." Congressman Thomas was jovial.

"You don't look like a Communist," he declared. "You look like a Republican!"

"If your Committee isn't convinced that neither I nor the Federal Theatre Project is communistic I want to come back this afternoon," I told him.

"We don't want you back," he laughed. "You're a tough witness and we're all worn out."

Further Resources

BOOKS

Bentley, Joanne. *Hallie Flanagan: A Life in the American Theatre.* New York: Knopf, 1988.

Sporn, Paul. *Against Itself: The Federal Theater and Writers Projects in the Midwest.* Detroit: Wayne State University Press, 1995.

Whitman, Willson. *Bread and Circuses: A Study of the Federal Theatre.* New York: Oxford University Press, 1937.

WEBSITES

Brown, Lorraine. *Federal Theatre: Melodrama, Social Protest, and Genius.* American Memory digital primary source collection, Library of Congress. Available online at http://international.loc.gov/ammem/fedtp/ftbrwn00.html (accessed April 10, 2003).

"Hallie Flanagan." Available at http://geocities.com/Broadway/Alley/5379/hallie.html (accessed February 17, 2003).

Marian Anderson

My Lord, What a Morning

Memoir

By: Marian Anderson

Date: 1956

Source: Anderson, Marian. *My Lord, What a Morning.* New York: Viking, 1956, 190–193.

About the Author: Marian Anderson (1897–1993) was born in Philadelphia and began singing at age six at the Union

Baptist Church. She later became a voice student and helped support her family by giving concerts. By 1917, she had become a noted contralto. She overcame global racism to become one of the truly outstanding performers of the twentieth century.

Marian Anderson: A Portrait

Memoir

By: Kosti Vehanen

Date: 1941

Source: Vehanen, Kosti. *Marian Anderson: A Portrait.* Westport, Conn.: Greenwood Press, 1941, 237–246.

About the Author: Kosti Vehanen (1887–1957), a classical pianist born in Finland, heard Marian Anderson for the first time in Berlin in 1931. He wrote: "It was as though the room had begun to vibrate, as though the sound came from under the earth . . . the sound I heard swelled to majestic power, the flower opened its petals to full brilliance; and I was enthralled by one of nature's rare wonders." Soon after they met, Vehanen began accompanying Anderson. Although Anderson and Vehanen encountered racist opposition, he accompanied her until 1940, when he returned to Finland due to illness. She went to Finland later in 1956 to perform with him one last time before he died. ■

Introduction/Significance

In the early 1930s, the Depression made it difficult for Anderson's manager to schedule performance dates for her in the United States. As a result, Anderson decided to live and study overseas. Her tour included studying and performing with musicians in England, France, and Germany. Accustomed to racism at home, Anderson could not completely escape it even in Europe. In 1933, for example, she was not allowed to complete her scheduled concert dates in Denmark.

Despite these obstacles, Anderson flourished in her 1934 and 1935 European tours and was a resounding success in Africa and South America. She returned to the United States and soon launched a grueling seventy-concert tour in 1938. Despite her success and widespread acclaim as a singer, however, she was unable to escape the country's deeply ingrained racism.

In 1939, Howard University arranged for her to sing at Constitution Hall in Washington, D.C. After initially agreeing to the date, the Daughters of the American Revolution (DAR), who owned the hall, cancelled her appearance because Anderson was black. The DAR had adopted a rule excluding African American artists from the Constitution Hall stage in 1932 following protests over "mixed seating" (blacks and whites seated together at concerts). This step contradicted one of the DAR's objectives: "to cherish, maintain, and extend the institutions of American freedom, to foster true patriotism and love of country, and to aid in securing for mankind all the blessings of liberty."

A disgusted Eleanor Roosevelt, who was on the board of the DAR, resigned her position in protest. Mrs. Roosevelt was a tireless worker for social causes, including youth employment and civil rights for blacks and women. Although she had never met Anderson, she led an effort to arrange for her to perform at the Lincoln Memorial in lieu of her cancelled date at Constitution Hall. Mrs. Roosevelt was supported by many local DAR members, artists, and public figures.

Over several days, Marian Anderson agonized over whether to perform. She was not a political activist and wished to maintain a noncontroversial public posture. In the end, however, she decided that it was her obligation to help draw attention to the treatment of African Americans. The concert at the Lincoln Memorial was a stunning success attended by over seventy-five thousand people. Four years later, the DAR attempted to atone for its narrow-mindedness by inviting Anderson to be part of a concert for China Relief at Constitution Hall. Her acceptance says much about her dignity and character.

Anderson's later career included additional politically and socially significant appearances. She sang for the Roosevelts at the White House and performed at the Eisenhower and Kennedy inaugurals. In 1955, in a much delayed debut, she became the first black soloist to perform with the Metropolitan Opera Company when she performed Ulrica in Verdi's *A Masked Ball.*

Anderson retired from singing in 1965, and she received a Grammy Lifetime Achievement Award for her contribution to music. She died in Portland, Oregon, in 1993.

Primary Source

My Lord, What a Morning [excerpt]

SYNOPSIS: The following excerpt is from the memoirs of Marian Anderson, recounting her recollection of the events surrounding the 1939 Easter performance at the Lincoln Memorial. She was awed by the sense of being present at a major event in the history of race relations in the United States.

We reached Washington early that Easter morning and went to the home of Gifford Pinchot, who had been Governor of Pennsylvania. The Pinchots had been kind enough to offer their hospitality, and it was needed because the hotels would not take us. Then we drove over to the Lincoln Memorial. Kosti was well enough to play, and we tried out the piano and examined the public-address system, which had six microphones, meant not only for the people who were present but also for a radio audience.

Marian Anderson performs the Easter concert at the Lincoln Memorial in 1939. Her pianist, Kosti Vehanen, is at left. **AP/WIDE WORLD. REPRODUCED BY PERMISSION.**

When we returned that afternoon I had sensations unlike any I had experienced before. The only comparable emotion I could recall was the feeling I had had when Maestro Toscanini had appeared in the artist's room in Salzburg. My heart leaped wildly, and I could not talk. I even wondered whether I would be able to sing.

The murmur of the vast assemblage quickened my pulse beat. There were policemen waiting at the car, and they led us through a passageway that other officers kept open in the throng. We entered the monument and were taken to a small room. We were introduced to Mr. Ickes, whom we had not met before. He outlined the program. Then came the signal to go out before the public.

If I did not consult contemporary reports I could not recall who was there. My head and heart were in such turmoil that I looked and hardly saw, I listened and hardly heard. I was led to the platform by Representative Caroline O'Day of New York, who had been born in Georgia, and Oscar Chapman, Assistant Secretary of the Interior, who was a Virginian. On the platform behind me sat Secretary Ickes, Secretary of the Treasury Morgenthau, Supreme Court Justice Black, Senators Wagner, Mead, Barkley, Clark, Guffey, and Capper, and many Representatives, including Representative Arthur W. Mitchell of Illinois, a Negro. Mother was there, as were people from Howard University and from churches in Washington and other cities. So was Walter White, then secretary of the National Association for the Advancement of Colored People. It was Mr. White who at one point stepped to the microphone and appealed to the crowd, probably averting serious accidents when my own people tried to reach me.

I report these things now because I have looked them up. All I knew then as I stepped forward was the overwhelming impact of that vast multitude. There seemed to be people as far as the eye could see. The crowd stretched in a great semicircle from the Lincoln Memorial around the reflecting pool on to the shaft of the Washington Monument. I had a feeling that a great wave of good will poured out from these people, almost engulfing me. And when I stood up to sing our National Anthem I felt for a moment as though I were choking. For a desperate second I thought that the words, well as I know them, would not come.

I sang, I don't know how. There must have been the help of professionalism I had accumulated over the years. Without it I could not have gone through the program. I sang—and again I know because I consulted a newspaper clipping—"America," the aria "O mio Fernando," Schubert's "Ave Maria," and three spirituals—"Gospel Train," "Trampin'," and "My Soul Is Anchored in the Lord."

I regret that a fixed rule was broken, another thing about which I found out later. Photographs were taken from within the Memorial, where the great statue of Lincoln stands, although there was a tradition that no pictures could be taken from within the sanctum.

It seems also that at the end, when the tumult of the crowd's shouting would not die down, I spoke a few words. I read the clipping now and cannot believe that I could have uttered another sound after I had finished singing. "I am overwhelmed," I said. "I just can't talk. I can't tell you what you have done for me today. I thank you from the bottom of my heart again and again."

It was the simple truth. But did I really say it?

There were many in the gathering who were stirred by their own emotions. Perhaps I did not grasp all that was happening, but at the end great numbers of people bore down on me. They were friendly; all they wished to do was to offer their congratulations and good wishes. The police felt that such a concentration of people was a danger, and they escorted me back into the Memorial. Finally we returned to the Pinchot home.

I cannot forget that demonstration of public emotion or my own strong feelings. In the years that have passed I have had constant reminders of that Easter Sunday. It is not at all uncommon to have people come backstage after a concert even now and remark, "You know, I was at that Easter concert." In my travels abroad I have met countless people who heard and remembered about that Easter Sunday.

In time the policy at Constitution Hall changed. I appeared there first in a concert for the benefit of China Relief. The second appearance in the hall, I believe, was also under charitable auspices. Then, at last, I appeared in the hall as does any other musical performer, presented by a concert manager, and I have been appearing in it regularly. The hall is open to other performers of my group. There is no longer an issue, and that is good.

It may be said that my concerts at Constitution Hall are usually sold out. I hope that people come because they expect to hear a fine program in a first-class performance. If they came for any other reason I would be disappointed. The essential point about wanting to appear in the hall was that I wanted to do so because I felt I had that right as an artist.

I wish I could have thanked personally all the people who stood beside me then. There were musicians who canceled their own scheduled appearances at Constitution Hall out of conviction and principle. Some of these people I did not know personally. I appreciate the stand they took.

Primary Source

Marian Anderson: A Portrait [excerpt]

SYNOPSIS: Anderson's good friend and accompanist gives an account of Anderson's 1939 Easter concert.

One day the newspapers carried the astonishing news that the Daughters of the American Revolution's headquarters in Washington objected to Marian Anderson's giving a recital in their Constitution Hall. This news seemed all the more strange to us, for we knew that Roland Hayes and also some colored dancers had appeared in the very same hall.

Why was this terrible insult put upon Marian Anderson? As we read the papers, we were sitting comfortably in her compartment on the train. A wonderful panorama of the great California mountains and forests was passing before our sight. Miss Anderson laid the paper down, kept looking out the window, and we both remained silent for some time. No one can tell the thoughts that were in her mind at that moment, I think not even herself. She did not discuss this serious question confronting her. There were too many good and beautiful things to talk about.

But the peace that Marian felt was soon disturbed by numerous newspaper reporters and many other people who constantly fired embarrassing questions at Miss Anderson, such as, "How do you feel?" "Do you feel insulted by this refusal?" "What is your attitude toward all this?" and "What do you intend to do?"

Miss Anderson's answer was, "I don't know anything except what you have all seen in the newspapers. I have no opinion to offer."

Then came the great announcement that Mrs. Eleanor Roosevelt had resigned from the D.A.R. A joyful look came into Marian's eyes, and she said to me, "What a wonderful woman she is! She not only knows what is right, but she also does the right thing."

The curious, bold questions these people kept asking Marian were never answered by her, and she still preserved the same attitude.

A proposal came from Washington that Miss Anderson should give an outdoor recital there. It so happened at this time that I was taken sick and was brought to a hospital in Washington.

There were many different opinions among Marian's friends about her giving a recital in the open. Some thought, why should she sing outdoors? It would be better not to sing at all. Others thought that it was a marvelous idea and that she should do it.

Miss Anderson telephoned me at the hospital every day from wherever she happened to be, and I knew that she was more against the idea than she was for it. She did not like the thought of doing anything sensational just because of the insult thrust upon her. Four days before the date announced for her appearance at the great Lincoln Memorial, which was to take place on Easter Sunday, 1939, she was still undecided and came very near canceling the arrangements. I have always thought that this was one of her most beautiful characteristics—she is so far removed from anything that might be considered sensational or in opposition to anyone or any organization that for her to oppose the idea of this extraordinary occasion was quite natural. She likes to win any victory purely with the implement of her great art and not mix anything that may oppose this holy gift.

She traveled to Washington just to see me during a few hours that she had free. Of course, the action of the D.A.R. had been given prominence in the papers, and when she arrived at the station there was a great crowd of people who were, no doubt, in sympathy with her. A police escort led her to the hospital. When she came to my room, we talked this important matter over and decided that it was too late to cancel the recital and step out. "But I do hope that you will be able to accompany me, Kosti," Marian said.

When the big day came, we were escorted to the Lincoln Memorial by several motorcycle police. Here we waited in an inner room. There were several people around us, including Marian's family, and a great feeling of anticipation was in the air. Marian was calm. She stood quiet and held her head high. I went to the piano first to fasten the music, for a soft wind was blowing. When I saw the immense crowd of seventy-five thousand people, then looked at the Steinway piano, I had a feeling that it would be of little use to begin to play, for I was sure that no one could possibly hear it. I also felt how really small a person seems when facing such a gathering, which stretched so far that I could scarcely see the end.

Those with special invitations were admitted to a platform that had been built for the occasion. Many prominent people were there, including Secretary Ickes, Supreme Court Justice Black, Secretary of the Treasury Morgenthau, and several members of Congress. The loud-speakers seemed to stretch their necks out, eager to heighten the sounds. All the important radio stations were represented, and their microphones stood like an army of soldiers guarding the elevated platform where Marian was to stand. Some yards in front of this was a special platform to accommodate the many film operators. The apparatus seemed to be looking with curious, anxious eyes at the place where she would be. Near by were countless photographers, with their cameras pointed in the same direction.

Secretary Ickes came forward and made a speech, in which he said: "There are those even in this great capital of our democratic republic who are either too timid or too indifferent to lift up the light that Jefferson and Lincoln carried aloft. Genius, like justice, is blind. For genius has touched with the tip of her wing this woman, who, if it had not been for the great mind of Jefferson, if it had not been for the great heart of Lincoln, would not be able to stand among us today a free individual in a free land. Genius draws no color line. She has endowed Marian Anderson with such a voice as lifts any individual above his fellows, as is a matter of exultant pride to any race. And so it is fitting that Marian Anderson should raise her voice in tribute to the noble Lincoln, whom mankind will ever honor."

Then Miss Anderson appeared within the central enclosure of the monument. She looked regal and dignified as she came forward with slow steps. She wore a long black velvet dress, her mink coat around her shoulders. When she came to the place where the steps began to descend, she stopped for a moment as she gazed over the enormous gathering of people. Her breath seemed to leave her for that fleeting moment; but I think that those persons who were privileged to see her at that time were much more moved than she was.

She looked slender and beautiful when she emerged between the high marble columns, directly in front of the great Lincoln Memorial, which was filled with shadow in the late afternoon light. The statue of Lincoln appeared to be alive on this occasion, and he seemed to be in deep thought, this great man with an exceptionally broad mind. Perhaps the most fitting and appropriate statement he would have made would have been to tell the assembled people that the appearance of Marian Anderson before this countless number of admirers was one of the greatest results of his efforts to make all people free and equal.

Miss Anderson was so deeply moved by the whole scene that she felt that it was not only a recital but something of much greater importance and value, which had a depth of meaning to all mankind. It was a message of peace, a message of understanding that she was destined to bring to a sinful world.

No one who saw her walking that day down the marble steps will ever forget this unusual and wonderful sight; and few can recall it without tears springing to their eyes.

She now stood ready. The first sounds of the piano were powerfully transmitted through the many loud-speakers, sounding as though ten organs were playing. Then she began to sing.

If human beings in their narrow wisdom closed the door of their small halls, then God in His great wisdom opened the door to His most beautiful cathedral, which was decorated that day as for a festival, with lovely green grass, cherry trees in blossom, the large pool mirroring the blue sky, and light clouds leisurely floating by, a soft wind caressing everyone, colored and white—every human being, rich and poor, the strong and the weak, the good and the bad sharing in the beauties so freely bestowed upon them that glorious Easter Sunday.

Further Resources

BOOKS

Keller, Alan. *Marian Anderson: A Singer's Journey.* New York: Scribner, 2000.

Newman, Shirley P. *Marian Anderson: Lady from Philadelphia.* Philadelphia: Westminster Press, 1966.

Salley, Columbus. *The Black 100: A Ranking of the Most Influential African-Americans, Past and Present.* Sacramento, Calif.: Citadel, 1999.

WEBSITES

Eleanor Roosevelt's resignation from the DAR. National Archives and Records Administration. Available online at http://www.archives.gov/exhibit_hall/american_originals/eleanor.html; website home page: http://www.archives.gov/index.html (accessed February 17, 2003).

Handy, D. Antoinette. "About Marian Anderson and Her Lincoln Memorial Concert." *Modern American Poetry.* Available online at http://www.english.uiuc.edu/maps/poets/s_z/taggard/anderson.htm (accessed February 17, 2003).

"Register of the Marion Anderson Papers, ca. 1900–1993." Annenberg Rare Book & Manuscript Library. University of Pennsylvania Library. Available online at http://www.library.upenn.edu/special/mss/anderson/anderson.html; website home page: http://www.library.upenn.edu/home.html (accessed February 17, 2003).

2

BUSINESS AND THE ECONOMY

JAMES N. CRAFT

Entries are arranged in chronological order by date of primary source. For entries with one primary source, the entry title is the same as the primary source title. Entries with more than one primary source have an overall entry title, followed by the titles of the primary sources.

Important Events in Business and the Economy, 1930–1939

1930

- Continental Baking introduces the world's first commercial sliced bread loaf, Wonder Bread.
- In January, the National Economic League, a group of business leaders, lists unemployment as only the eighth most serious problem in the United States. This belief underscores business leaders' lack of sympathy for workers during the Great Depression.
- On March 6, General Foods introduces Birds Eye Frosted Foods to stores in Springfield, Massachusetts. Frozen vegetables, fruits, and meats soon become a staple of grocery stores, despite high prices.
- On June 17, despite a petition signed by 1,028 economists, President Herbert Hoover signs the Smoot-Hawley Tariff—the highest in American history—into law. Other countries will retaliate by raising tariffs against the United States.
- In July, McGraw-Electric of Elgin, Illinois, introduces the first automatic toaster.
- On October 3, in Rusk County, eastern Texas, wildcatter Columbus M. Joiner opens a new oil field that will produce 3.6 billion barrels of oil.
- In November, 236 banks close.
- In December, an additional 328 banks close.
- On December 11, the Bank of the United States, with sixty branches and four hundred thousand depositors, closes, losing more than 200 million dollars in deposits.
- On December 20, Congress passes a $116 million public works bill and allocates 45 million dollars for drought relief.

1931

- Lucky Strike outsells Camel cigarettes for the first time. The two brands will spend the next twenty years alternating the lead in cigarette sales.
- The United States produces a record wheat crop, driving prices down and precipitating further financial crisis in the farm belt.
- On May 4, labor strife between the United Mine Workers and mine operators in Harlan County, Kentucky, leads to a gunfight that ends with three guards and one miner dead and many wounded.
- On June 20, President Herbert Hoover proposes a one-year moratorium on war debt and reparations.
- On August 4, Governor William H. "Alfalfa Bill" Murray of Oklahoma declares martial law and sends troops into the oil fields of the state to stop production in order to raise low prices for crude.
- On August 16, Governor Ross Sterling of Texas proclaims a state of insurrection and, like Governor Murray, sends troops into oil fields.

1932

- On January 22, Congress authorizes the Hoover administration's request to found the Reconstruction Finance Corporation (RFC) to loan money to businesses.
- On March 7, more than three thousand unemployed men march to Dearborn, Michigan, to ask Henry Ford for work. Police fire into the crowd, killing four and wounding more than one hundred.
- On March 23, Congress passes the Norris-La Guardia Act, prohibiting court injunctions against strikes and contracts that prohibit workers from joining labor unions.
- In June, the Federal Reserve Board reports that U.S. stocks and bonds had lost $25.3 billion since September 1929.
- On June 6, Congress increases income taxes by one-third to raise money for its economic programs, which Congress and President Franklin Roosevelt hoped would bring the United States out of the Great Depression.
- On July 2, President Franklin Roosevelt announces the New Deal, a series of programs to end the Great Depression.
- On July 7, the Dow Jones Industrial Average reaches its lowest point of 41.22.
- On July 21, Congress approves the Emergency Relief and Reconstruction Act, making $2 billion available to the states for relief and public works projects.
- On July 22, Congress passes a Home Loan Act, establishing twelve federal home loan banks to lend money to mortgage institutions.
- On August 9, the Iowa Farmers' Union begins a thirty-day strike to drive up farm prices.
- On October 31, Nevada is the first state to close its banks to prevent depositors from withdrawing their money, an action which would have caused banks to fail.
- On December 15, six nations, including France and Belgium, default on war debt payments to the United States.

1933

- In March, the U.S. Labor Department reports a 73 percent unemployment rate among construction workers.
- On March 6, in response to large numbers of people withdrawing their money from banks, President Franklin D. Roosevelt declares a national bank holiday. Congress grants Roosevelt power to regulate banking the next day; by the following week most American banks have resumed operations.
- On April 19, Congress abandons use of gold in international trade and investment. Instead Congress authorizes payment in dollars.

- On May 12, Congress passes the Federal Emergency Relief Act, disbursing 500 million dollars to states for economic assistance, and the Agricultural Adjustment Act, creating the Agricultural Adjustment Administration to raise farm prices.
- On May 18, Congress authorizes the Tennessee Valley Authority to operate a hydroelectric plant at Muscle Shoals, Alabama.
- On June 13, Congress establishes the Home Owners Loan Corporation to provide emergency loans for homeowners.
- On June 16, President Franklin D. Roosevelt signs the Glass-Steagall Act, establishing federal regulation of the banking industry. Congress approves the National Industrial Recovery Act, which for the first time upheld workers' right to bargain collectively, and the Farm Credit Act, which loaned money to farmers.
- On August 5, the Roosevelt administration establishes the National Labor Board to oversee labor's right to bargain collectively.
- On November 9, the Civil Works Administration, under former social worker Harry Hopkins, begins efforts to provide emergency jobs for 4 million unemployed Americans.
- From November 11 to November 13, a dust storm sweeps the drought-stricken plains, depositing Dakota soil as far east as Albany, New York.

1934

- On January 31, Congress passes the Farm Mortgage Refinancing Act to help farmers in danger of having the mortgages on their farms foreclosed.
- On February 5, Congress appropriates $950 million to the Civil Works Emergency Relief Act in an effort to create jobs for the unemployed.
- On February 12, the Export-Import Bank of Washington opens with funding from the Reconstruction Finance Corporation to finance trade.
- On April 13, Congress passes the Johnson Debt Default Act, prohibiting American loans to any country in default of debt payments to the United States.
- In May, dust storms strip the plains of 300 million tons of topsoil, blown as far east as the Atlantic Ocean.
- On May 9, President Franklin D. Roosevelt signs the Costigan-Jones Act into law to limit sugar imports, thereby protecting U.S. sugar plantations.
- On May 22, members of Teamsters' Local 574, which had gone on strike May 15, clash with Minneapolis police, leaving two dead, including a wealthy Minnesota businessman.
- On June 6, Congress establishes the Securities and Exchange Commission (SEC) to oversee investment in stocks and bonds. The first head of the commission is Wall Street speculator Joseph Patrick Kennedy Sr., the father of John F. Kennedy.
- On June 12, Congress passes the Reciprocal Trade Agreement Amendment to the Smoot-Hawley Tariff, reducing tariffs by up to 50 percent for nations willing to grant the United States reciprocal tariff reductions.
- On June 19, Congress creates the National Labor Relations Board (NLRB) to replace the National Labor Board.
- On June 21, President Roosevelt signs the Dill-Crozier Act into law, establishing a National Railroad Adjustment Board to guarantee railroad workers the right to organize.
- On June 28, Congress passes the Taylor Grazing Act to limit grazing and soil erosion in the West. The act was the first to restrict the freedom of ranchers to use land as they wished. Congress also passes the Frazier-Lemke Farm Bankruptcy Act, postponing some foreclosures for five years.
- On July 16, San Francisco is paralyzed by a general strike led by the International Longshoremen's Association, headed by Harry Bridges.
- In September, 376,000 textile workers go on strike, the largest that year.

1935

- On February 16, Congress passes the Connally Hot Oil Act, regulating the production of crude oil and providing penalties for overproduction.
- On April 8, Congress passes the Emergency Relief Appropriation Act, authorizing the disbursal of five billion dollars in work relief.
- On April 30, President Franklin D. Roosevelt creates by executive order the Resettlement Administration to move farmers from exhausted lands to fertile lands.
- On May 6, President Roosevelt creates the Works Progress Administration (WPA), headed by Harry Hopkins.
- On May 11, by executive order, Roosevelt establishes the Rural Electrification Administration to spread electricity to American farms.
- On June 26, Congress creates the National Youth Administration to provide jobs for young people.
- On June 27, in *Railway Retirement Board v. Alton Railway Co.,* the Supreme Court rules the Railway Pension Act of 1934 unconstitutional, a ruling that threatens other New Deal legislation.
- On July 5, Congress passes the Wagner Act, affirming the right of workers to collective bargaining.
- On August 9, Congress empowers the Interstate Commerce Commission to oversee interstate bus and truck lines.
- On August 14, President Roosevelt signs the Social Security Act into law, creating a nationwide system of old-age pensions and unemployment benefits.
- On August 23, President Roosevelt signs the Banking Act, increasing the power of the Federal Reserve Board to regulate banks.
- On August 30, Congress passes the Revenue Act, taxing inheritances and gifts heavily.
- On September 16, Morgan Stanley, an investment firm, opens. Because the Glass-Stegall Banking Act forbade the type of combined commercial and investment banking practiced by the J. P. Morgan Company, John P. Morgan II creates Morgan Stanley to handle investments, while the parent company continues commercial banking.

- On November 9, dissidents within the American Federation of Labor (AFL), form the Committee for Industrial Organization (later called the Congress of Industrial Organizations, or CIO). United Mine Workers president John L. Lewis is the first chairman.

1936

- Douglas Aircraft introduces the DC-3, a two-engine, twenty-one passenger workhorse of a plane that will revolutionize air travel. By 1938 it will have sold $28.4 million worth of the aircraft.
- On January 6, in *United States v. Butler* the Supreme Court strikes down the Agricultural Adjustment Act of 1933.
- On February 14, members of the United Rubber Workers of America refuse to leave the Goodyear Tire and Rubber Plant No. 2 after being laid off. This was the first sit-down strike.
- On February 17, the U.S. Supreme Court in *Ashwander v. Tennessee Valley Authority* upholds the constitutionality of the Tennessee Valley Authority.
- In March, the WPA estimates its workforce at 3.4 million people.
- On May 12, the first Super Chief locomotive leaves Chicago; the luxury liner will reduce Chicago-to-Los Angeles service to just under forty hours.
- On June 1, in *Morehead v. New York ex. rel. Tipaldo,* the Supreme Court strikes down a New York minimum wage law.
- On June 20, Congress passes the Robinson-Patman Act, supplementing the Clayton Anti-Trust Act of 1914 by forbidding price discrimination in advertising.
- In August, American Airlines introduces day-long, transcontinental service from Newark, New Jersey, to Glendale, California.
- On October 30, dockworkers paralyze American shipping by striking first on the West Coast and spreading to every port. The strike will last three months.
- On December 31, Workers at the General Motors Chevrolet body plant in Flint, Michigan, stage a sit-down strike.

1937

- In 1937, there are 4,740 work stoppages, working strikes, and lockouts in factories nationwide.
- On February 11, General Motors ends the sit-down strike in Flint, Michigan, by recognizing the United Auto Workers (UAW) as the bargaining agent for its employees.
- On March 2, United States Steel averts a strike by permitting the unionization of its workers.
- On March 29, in *West Coast Hotel v. Parrish,* the Supreme Court reverses itself and upholds the minimum wage for women.
- On May 24, the Supreme Court upholds the constitutionality of the Social Security Act.
- On May 30, following labor disputes, Chicago police attack a union picnic of Republic Steel workers, killing ten and injuring eighty-four in the Memorial Day Massacre.
- On December 13, the National Labor Relations Board accuses Henry Ford of blocking the right of workers to bargain collectively.

1938

- General Motors and Standard Oil organize Pacific Coast Lines, designed to lobby western cities to convert their streetcars to buses.
- On February 18, President Franklin D. Roosevelt signs the second Agricultural Adjustment Act. The act attempted to raise farm prices by paying workers to take land out of cultivation, thereby reducing the supply of food. Economic theory states that as supply decreases price increases.
- On May 27, Congress enacts the Revenue Act, reducing corporate taxes to encourage investment.
- On June 15, Congress passes the Fair Labor Standards Act, limiting workers to forty-four hours per week, after which they earn overtime. The act sets the minimum wage at 25 cents per hour. The new law covers 12.5 million American workers.
- On June 21, Congress passes the Emergency Relief Appropriations Act to continue government payments to the unemployed.
- On June 23, Congress creates the Civil Aeronautics Authority (CAA) to oversee the American aviation industry.
- On June 27, Franklin Roosevelt signs the U.S. Food, Drug and Cosmetic Act, updating the 1906 Pure Food and Drug Act and providing consumers greater protection.
- On November 18, John L. Lewis becomes president of the Congress of Industrial Organizations.
- On December 19, General Motors manufactures the first diesel engine.

1939

- The Department of Agriculture introduces food stamps.
- Pall Mall brand cigarettes introduce the first "king-size cigarettes."
- In February, private investors found the Hewlett-Packard electronic instrument firm.
- On February 27, the U.S. Supreme Court denies workers the right to use a sit-down strike as a tool to force concessions from an employer.
- On March 18, Congress increases tariffs 25 percent on German imports.
- On June 5, the U.S. Supreme Court affirms the right of the CIO to organize workers in New Jersey, reversing Governor Frank Hague's attempt to ban the CIO from the state.
- On June 28, Pan-American launches the first commercial transatlantic passenger air service. A flight takes 26.5 hours.
- In July, Howard Hughes buys control of Transcontinental and Western Airlines (TWA).
- On August 18, Henry Ford defies a National Labor Relations Board order to reinstate 24 workers he had fired for going on strike.
- In October, General Electric introduces fluorescent lighting.

"Statement of James C. Garland, of Pineville, Ky."

Testimony

By: James C. Garland and Edward P. Costigan

Date: 1932

Source: "Statement of James C. Garland, of Pineville, Ky." In *Hearings Before a Subcommittee of the Committee on Manufactures, United States Senate, 72nd Congress, 1st Session, on S. Res. 178.* Washington, D.C.: United States Government Printing Office, 1932, 6–7, 8–11, 12–13, 17–18.

About the Authors: James Garland was a coal miner from the Harlan Coal District. His family was from the region for as far back as Garland could recall. The twenty-seven-year-old miner had joined the United Mine Workers (UMW) union when he was thirteen.

Edward P. Costigan (1874–1939) was a Democratic Senator (1931–1937) from Colorado. The Harvard-educated lawyer began his career as a Progressive Republican. He helped form the Colorado Progressive Party in 1912 to support Theodore Roosevelt's presidential campaign of that year. Costigan held office in Woodrow Wilson's administration but did not formally join the Democratic Party until 1930. ■

Introduction

In 1930, one out of every forty employed males over the age of fourteen worked in coal mines. Coal fueled industry, heated homes, and generated electricity. Like the agricultural industry and despite steady demand, coal had already suffered through lean years by the time the Depression began. The number of miners had declined from 995,000 in 1920 to 892,000 by 1930. Wages had declined steadily in the dominant bituminous coal industry from ninety cents per hour in 1920 to sixty-six cents per hour in 1929.

Even in the best of times, coal miners lived a difficult life. The work was dangerous. In the 1920s an average of 2,250 miners were killed on the job each year. Mines were typically in isolated areas. There were very few alternatives to working in the local mines. The communities were often completely controlled by the mine owners. Miners lived in company-owned housing, bought everything from company-owned stores, and, in some cases, were even paid in company scrip. Troublemakers (i.e., union sympathizers) were fired, blacklisted, and evicted from their company-owned home.

There were few areas in the coal industry more isolated than the Harlan coal fields in the Appalachian Mountains of eastern Kentucky. Its inhabitants were old-stock Americans of Scotch-Irish and English descent. They were ancestors of early settlers typified by Daniel Boone. Until the opening of the coal mines, the inhabitants lived an independent, subsistence existence. Given the isolation and the independent character of the miners, it was relatively easy for the mine operators to keep the union at bay and the workforce controlled. And during boom times, with full employment and relatively high wages, the people of Harlan prospered.

Significance

This worker docility changed, however, as the demand for coal dropped at the outset of the Depression. By 1932, coal production had declined from the 1929 level by 42 percent. Work slackened and pay rates were slashed. Soon, desperate Harlan workers were driven into the arms of the United Mine Workers.

The catalyst that sparked the miners' revolt was yet another wage cut in February 1931. This enabled the UMW organizers to achieve some success in their efforts to enlist workers. Predictably, the mine operators fired miners identified as union sympathizers. In response, eleven thousand miners went on strike. Strikebreakers were brought in. Company guards assaulted strikers. Strikers looted stores for food. The cycle of violence reached new heights on May 4, when an open gun battle left three guards and one striker dead. The National Guard was brought in.

At this point, the UMW urged workers to return to work. With the full force of the law coming down on the strikers and an inadequate strike fund, the UMW felt there was no alternative but to settle the strike. Feeling betrayed, the Harlan miners were receptive to the overtures of the Communist-led National Miners Union (NMU).

At the same time, the miners' wretched condition, the virtually open warfare, and the specter of the communist menace attracted the attention of the nation. For a while, it was the topic of choice for a number of sympathetic writers.

Whereas the mine operators were initially on the defensive, the attention of left-oriented writers and the support of the Communist Party gave them sufficient rationalization to crush the workers. They were not, in their public position, oppressing struggling workers; they were protecting America from foreign radicals. It was ironic that the Harlan miners, many of whose ancestors had settled in the area before the American Revolution, were stamped as being un-American, foreign agitators. By late 1931 the NMU was routed.

With the backing of federal legislation, the UMW was gradually able to organize the workers, despite lingering distrust as a result of the UMW abandoning the fight in 1931. It was not until a successful strike in 1939, however, that coal operators were forced into recognizing the union and accepting collective bargaining.

Primary Source

"Statement of James C. Garland, of Pineville, Ky." [excerpt]

SYNOPSIS: As a result of the public attention and the violence of 1931 in Harlan County and the surrounding area, the Senate Committee on Manufactures launched its own investigation of the events in May 1932. The following excerpted testimony is from a miner turned union organizer.

Senator Costigan: Senator Cutting asked you to tell in your own way what you know about the conditions which have led to the request for this investigation.

Mr. Garland: Well, I guess I had better start at what first started the trouble. Is that what you want me to start with?

Senator Costigan: Start wherever you think will be most helpful to the committee.

Mr. Garland: I lived in Harlan County at the time. That was along the first of 1931. The operators gave a 25 per cent cut—no, hardly a 25 per cent cut—a cut from 40 cents to 32 cents a ton.

Senator Costigan: Were the miners organized in a union at the time of the cut?

Mr. Garland: No, sir.

Senator Costigan: What happened following the cut?

Mr. Garland: The miners were very dissatisfied with the cut; and the United Mine Workers of America in the month of March, I think, held a convention in Pineville, Ky.—not a convention, either; more of a mass meeting; and a vice president, Philip Murray—I think that is his name—addressed the meeting.

Senator Cutting: That is, he was vice president of the United Mine Workers?

Mr. Garland: Yes; of the United Mine Workers of America. He called on the men to organize, and told them to get a dollar some way or other and get in the union; and they began then to organize in the United Mine Workers of America. All that could get a dollar, I reckon, went in. I didn't have a dollar to join.

Senator Costigan: You did not join at the time?

Mr. Garland: No; I did not, although I attended the convention, the meeting. When I returned to the Coal Fork Coal Co. at Kitts, Ky., and applied for work, the boss told me he could not use me any more. I asked him what was the trouble. He said, "Well, it don't matter." I pressed him; I said, "Was it because I went to that meeting in Pineville?" and he said. "I guess that is right." . . .

Senator Costigan: What were the conditions in Bell County while you were there?

Mr. Garland: Well, the operator that I worked for, he run small mines, and he moved me, and I stayed there and worked every day that I could get to work, and it would average five days a week, and I never did make enough to pay for the moving bill, $8—that is, above what I ate. I couldn't get along there, and I went to another mine and got a job. This was at Arjay, Ky. I worked there three months. I made $27 one of these months and probably a few odd cents, and $25 each one of the other two.

Senator Costigan: How many days in each month were you working?

Mr. Garland: I could not specify the days, although it was not full time. It probably would average three days or four days a week.

Senator Costigan: What was your rate of pay?

Mr. Garland: I was driving entry, and it was a contract piece of work. My brother had the job. He got 55 cents, but we shot the top on up high, cut the slate and shot it and moved it. The regular scale was 40 cents. That is what they paid.

Senator Costigan: You were working under contract?

Mr. Garland: Yes.

Senator Costigan: Your brother having the contract?

Mr. Garland: Yes.

Senator Costigan: You were not employed as a regular miner by a coal-mining company?

Mr. Garland: Yes.

Harlan, Kentucky, miners go underground to work in spite of a strike called by the CIO in May 1939. © BETTMANN/CORBIS. REPRODUCED BY PERMISSION.

Senator Costigan: Oh, you were?

Mr. Garland: Yes. This job was driving entry, and they let a man or two or three men have it and work it. It was still under the company.

Senator Cutting: What company were you working for at this time?

Mr. Garland: Working for the Straight Creek Coal Co.

Out of this $27 one month and $25 the other two I paid stoppages amounting to $8 each month. That was house rent, doctor bill, borrow fund, coal, lights, and blacksmithing the tools you work with, and bought my own fuel, carbide that I burned in the lamp, and the powder to shoot the coal with. The carbide would amount to 5 cents a day, and the powder would amount to about 35 cents a week, I guess. This come out of the $27.

Senator Costigan: You paid rent on a company house?

Mr. Garland: Yes.

Senator Costigan: How large a house?

Mr. Garland: I had three rooms.

Senator Costigan: Frame?

Mr. Garland: A frame house—a box house.

Senator Costigan: What rent did you pay?

Mr. Garland: I paid $3.50, I think is what the rent was.

Senator Costigan: A month?

Mr. Garland: A month.

Senator Costigan: Do you know how your pay compared with that of other miners in that district?

Mr. Garland: Yes. It was about the average of the miners loading coal except on one entry. In one entry they had there that was on the side track, the men done a little bit better than that; but outside of the one entry I am satisfied my wages would have been the average.

Senator Costigan: Did you work longer than the three months?

Mr. Garland: No; I don't think I worked longer than three months. That was the months of July, August, and September. The month of October, the company tried to give the miners another cut. They wanted to cut the coal 3 cents a ton.

Senator Costigan: Did you continue when that cut was made?

Mr. Garland: We struck. There was five mines on the creek, on the left fork of Straight Creek.

Senator Costigan: All operated by the same company?

Mr. Garland: No; two of them by the same company. The Cary and Arjay mines was operated by one company, the Straight Creek Coal Co. There was the New Castro Coal Co. and the Coleman Mining Co. and Little & Sons. These mines struck for a month—the month of October.

Senator Costigan: What happened then?

Mr. Garland: At the Arjay mines, the miners gained the checkweighman, and instead of a 3-cent cut they got 2 cents, and the company agreed to meet with the mine committee to take up grievances.

Senator Costigan: Had you had no checkweighman up to that time?

Mr. Garland: We had not had any checkweighman.

Senator Costigan: Do you know whether the law of Kentucky required checkweighmen at mines?

Mr. Garland: Yes, sir.

Senator Costigan: Had you requested a checkweighman before, without having any designated?

Mr. Garland: Yes, sir.

Senator Costigan: Before that strike?

Mr. Garland: We made our demands before the strike, and asked for a checkweighman, and gave them to the company before even the strike was called.

Senator Costigan: Was anything else secured by the strike except that difference in the wage?

Mr. Garland: Yes; the 8-hour day.

Senator Costigan: The 8-hour day. If you know, what is the law of Kentucky about the 8-hour day?

Mr. Garland: The law of Kentucky says eight hours shall constitute a day's work.

Senator Costigan: That was the law at the time of the strike?

Mr. Garland: Yes; although the miners had been working 9 and 10 and as high as 12.

Senator Costigan: After the strike you were given the 8-hour day, if I understand your testimony?

Mr. Garland: Yes, sir; that is right.

Senator Costigan: Was anything else done as a result of the strike?

Mr. Garland: They promised to pay for draw slate. This draw slate has to be handled, you see, and thrown back out of the way.

Senator Costigan: It is dirt or rock which has to be separated from the coal?

Mr. Garland: Yes, sir. They promised to pay for this, which they did not.

Senator Costigan: Was that the first time you had received any consideration about separating the slate from the coal?

Mr. Garland: The first time we had for a long time. They used to pay as high as 15 cents an inch—an inch thick and a yard up and down—for this draw slate, although that had been discontinued.

Senator Costigan: How much did they allow you after the strike?

Mr. Garland: They never did pay us anything. They promised, but they didn't pay.

Senator Costigan: What did they agree to pay?

Mr. Garland: They agreed for the boss to come and examine it, and, where the draw slate was bad, to pay more on the ton for the places where the draw slate was—for the miners that handled it and the boss to agree on what it was worth to handle this draw slate.

Senator Costigan: Did you have a mine foreman at your property?

Mr. Garland: Yes, sir.

Senator Costigan: What did he say when the company refused to pay you for the expense of cleaning the coal?

Mr. Garland: He didn't say anything. He never did come around to examine it, even.

Senator Costigan: Did you talk to any officers of the company about payment for it?

Mr. Garland: I guess I had better continue this scale, because this was not drawn in writing. It was a verbal contract between us and the company, and it stood one week.

The company agreed to except the checkweighman's wages through the office—let him check from each man so many hundred pounds of coal to make his wages and accept his wages in the office on a tonnage rate the same as other men; and that went one week.

The boy worked three days, and they had the bookkeeper to come to the tipple and tell him that they wouldn't accept his wages, and what he had cut to put it back on the sheet, because they wouldn't accept his wages through the office; and three more days, each day—I was one of the mine committee that the company agreed to see—I went and saw the general mine foreman each day for three days, and he said he couldn't do anything about it. I asked him each time to see Mr. Humes, the general manager, so that we could come to some agreement, and for three days he wouldn't do it. So Monday morning the men struck again because they wasn't living up to the contract. This time the strike was broke, so what they gained they lost.

I was blacklisted just after this, though. During the week that we were not working, Theodore Dreiser and his committee came to Kentucky to investigate the conditions. At a meeting I made a speech before Theodore Dreiser on the conditions of the coal miners. There was a mass meeting. About 500 miners and operators and bookkeepers were there, and I was one of the speakers, and I was blacklisted. I don't know whether it was over my activity in this month's strike or over testifying before the Dreiser committee.

Senator Costigan: Do you know whether there is a law in Kentucky against blacklisting, as there is in some other States?

Mr. Garland: I do not.

Senator Costigan: How did you know that you were blacklisted?

Mr. Garland: I went to Lee Hollow, and the mine foreman gave me a job. He was a friend of mine, and he gave me a job at the mines, and he said he had me a house. I went in to sign up, and the superintendent, he started to write me out a house lease; and he said, "Wait a minute." He went and looked at the books, and he said, "You go outside," and told me I couldn't work; and from that I knew that as a usual thing he had my name. . . .

Senator Costigan: Let us return to your miners' union. You were telling us about it.

Mr. Garland: The miners organized, and by the time they got organized the operators were ready to cut them again. So on December 31, 1931, they had a convention in Pineville and voted to strike on January 1, and call the strike a "strike against starvation"; because they said they were starving while they worked.

On January 1 they struck.

Senator Costigan: January 1 of what year?

Mr. Garland: 1932.

Senator Costigan: What happened then?

Mr. Garland: Well, there wasn't anything much happened until January 4. The Workers' International Relief had some representatives—I believe it was the day the strike was called; yes, the day the strike was called, or the day before—there was some representatives of the Workers' International Relief came to Kentucky to give relief to the striking miners, and they did give relief the first day of the strike; and there was also some press representatives—that is what they said they were, writers for the papers—was there, and Joe Weber, a union organizer, was there, and Harry Simms, the boy that was killed, was in Pineville; and on January 4 the authorities—I don't know whether it was the deputy sheriff or the police—came into the National Miners' Union office at Pineville and arrested seven of these people and put them in Pineville jail.

Senator Costigan: Where were you at the time?

Mr. Garland: At the time they came in I was in the National Miners' Union office.

Senator Costigan: Were you arrested?

Mr. Garland: No, sir; I was not arrested. He told me to stand in the hall, although I disobeyed him and walked out, because I didn't see any need of my standing in the hall. If he arrested the rest, he would me.

Senator Costigan: Did they arrest all who were in the hall?

Mr. Garland: They didn't arrest any of the miners, I don't think. They arrested the seven other people that was in there.

Senator Costigan: What were the charges, if you know?

Mr. Garland: Well, I don't know exactly what the charges were at first. I heard later that when they brought them for examination and trial they didn't have any papers; but that is just what I heard.

Senator Costigan: By "papers" you mean warrants?

A mine at Dartmont, Kentucky, where the coal vein has run out, and the camp and mine has been abandoned. © BETTMANN/CORBIS. REPRODUCED BY PERMISSION.

Mr. Garland: Yes; but then I heard that the final charge is criminal syndicalism. That is what they say the charge is.

Senator Costigan: Are they still awaiting trial?

Mr. Garland: They are under bond now, awaiting trial.

Senator Costigan: Were they held in jail any time before they gave bond?

Mr. Garland: Yes; they were held in jail 11 or 12 weeks. We established a warehouse in Pineville for storing food and clothing that was shipped in by sympathizers from all over the United States. The authorities—I don't exactly remember the date—but, anyway, they came in and locked this warehouse up and drove the committee that was elected out.

Senator Costigan: The committee that had charge of the workers?

Mr. Garland: That had been elected by the miners to have charge of the warehouse. Then they appointed four fellows to stay in there.

Senator Costigan: Who appointed four fellows?

Mr. Garland: A deputy sheriff by the name of Walter Baker.

Senator Costigan: He appointed other deputies to stay in the warehouse?

Mr. Garland: He deputized them, according to what he said. He said he deputized them to stay in the warehouse that night.

Senator Costigan: What happened then?

Mr. Garland: These four fellows stole a truckload of the clothes out of the warehouse, and loaded them in a truck that they had.

Senator Costigan: Were the clothes taken away?

Mr. Garland: No. It rained so hard that night that the river got up in the town until they couldn't get out with it, and that is the reason why I tell it. My brother, Bill Garland, a preacher—Rev. W. M. Garland, a Baptist preacher—and Henry Williams and two more miners the next morning took the stuff out of the truck and put it back in the warehouse.

Senator Costigan: The clothes?

Mr. Garland: Yes; and so a warrant was issued for them for highway robbery in Pineville court. . . .

Senator Costigan: Mr. Garland, you stated early in your testimony that the strike was accompanied by charges that the miners were starving. Will you tell the committee what the conditions in Kentucky were when the strike, which began in January, 1932, was ordered?

Mr. Garland: Well, I think my statement about what I made was one pretty good say on the conditions; but a still more touching one, if not more impressive, was the amount of children that died in the spring of 1931 and throughout the summer; and the conditions had not got any better, although they had got the 2-cents-a-ton wage cut more.

Senator Costigan: What about the children?

Mr. Garland: There is approximately between five and six hundred people on the left-hand fork of Straight Creek. There was at least 25 young children died with one disease, known as flux, during that spring and early summer.

Senator Cutting: Was that due to lack of food?

Mr. Garland: That was due to the lack of food, or eating food, so the doctors told me, that it was caused by eating one diet, and the lack of milk or such food as a baby should have. The way the disease works, it inflames their stomach and entrails, and they bleed.

Senator Cutting: There was no milk for them?

Mr. Garland: No. The principal food of the miners is potatoes, beans, and bacon—this salt pork. Then, they make gravy. We call it "bull dog gravy." I guess sometimes they may get a meal different from that; but that is what you would say the staple food of the coal miners is in the camp where I lived, because there was families of as high as eight, and the men made no more than I made that had to live on that.

Senator Cutting: Where did you buy the food?

Mr. Garland: You buy the food in the company commissary. When you work your time goes into the company office. Then you go to the window and get what they call scrip. Some of it is metal scrip, round, and says, "25 cents." some of it "50 cents" or "$1" or "10 cents" and nickels, they have got. The other is on a cardboard, and it says on this, the one at the mine where I worked, "Good for $1 in merchandise only. Not transferable. One year after date, good for $1 in merchandise only." You can't trade this scrip anywhere but in the company commissary.

Senator Costigan: Do you know whether there is a law in Kentucky against company scrip?

Mr. Garland: I don't think so. That is, there may be, but it is not in the mining law, I don't think. That is the only law I know much about.

Senator Costigan: There is such a law in some coal-mining States.

Mr. Garland: Yes; there is, I hear, in Illinois.

If a miner is able to leave scrip in there for a month, then he will get it in money; but he will not get to work more than two weeks until they see, when he ain't taking it out in scrip, they fire him, like they told the men at Kitts, Ky. They said, "If you trade at Piggly Wiggly's, you can get your job at Piggly Wiggly's." That is what the superintendent got up at the drift mouth and made a speech to.

Senator Cutting: What kind of prices did they charge you in this commissary?

Mr. Garland: I will start on the dry goods first, because that is what we got little of.

A blue denim shirt cost a dollar. You can get a blue denim shirt in Pineville for 39 cents.

Overalls cost $1.25. You could get the overalls in Pineville at 49 cents.

Shoes that sold for $1.98 in Pineville you could get for $3.50.

Lard was 20 cents a pound at the commissary; 9 and 10 cents a pound in Pineville.

Flour, about the same grade, was around a dollar in the commissary; 42 cents in Pineville.

Meat was 20 cents in the commissary; 10 cents and 9 cents in Pineville.

Further Resources

BOOKS

Bernstein, Irving. *The Lean Years: A History of the American Worker, 1920–1933.* Baltimore: Penguin Books, 1960.

National Committee for the Defense of Political Prisoners. *Harlan Miners Speak: Report on Terrorism in the Kentucky Coal Fields.* 1932. Reprint, New York: Da Capo Press, 1970.

Watkins, Tom H. *The Hungry Years: A Narrative History of the Great Depression in America.* New York: Henry Holt, 1999.

WEBSITES

Dos Passos, John. "Harlan: Working under the Gun." Available online at http://newdeal.feri.org/voices/voce04.htm; website home page: http://newdeal.feri.org (accessed August 6, 2002).

"Coal Monument ~ Baxter, Kentucky." Black Diamond Net website. Available online at http://home.earthlink.net/~bela1/harlan.htm; website home page: http://home.earthlink.net/~bela1/index.html (accessed April 30, 2003).

"On the Bank Crisis"

Radio address

By: Franklin D. Roosevelt

Date: March 12, 1933

Source: Roosevelt, Franklin D. "On the Bank Crisis," Fireside Chat, March 12, 1933. Franklin D. Roosevelt Presidential Library and Museum. Available online at http://www.fdrlibrary.marist.edu/031233.html; website home page: http://www.fdrlibrary.marist.edu (accessed March 17, 2003).

About the Author: Franklin Delano Roosevelt (1882–1945) was the thirty-second president of the United States. Born to an old-stock, New York patrician family, Roosevelt was the Democratic vice presidential candidate in 1920. Stricken with polio in 1921, Roosevelt never regained full use of his legs. He was governor of New York between 1928 and 1932. Roosevelt was elected president four times and led the nation through two of the defining events of American history—the Great Depression and World War II. He died shortly before the German surrender in April, 1945. ■

Introduction

By 1933, into the fourth year of the Depression, the financial system of the United States was under great strain. Confidence in business in general, and the banking system in particular, was extremely low. There were legitimate reasons for this lack of faith.

During the boom years of the 1920s, many banks made unwise loans, often supporting speculation in the stock market. As the economy declined, banks were forced to write off an ever-increasing number of loans. Losses mounted. Bank failures became a daily event all across the country. From 1930 through 1932, more than five thousand banks failed. The total number of banks declined from twenty-five thousand to 18,700.

Equally important, confidence in banks was in free fall. Even in a country accustomed to a high rate of bank failures, the collapses of 1930–1933 were unprecedented. Worse, bankers themselves offered little hope that they could stem the tide of failures. Credibility of financial leaders was further eroded by the revelation of the unscrupulous behavior of some bankers, and credibility in banks was damaged by "runs" on banks rumored to be unstable.

By late 1932, the banking situation was grim. In October, Nevada closed its banks to give them a chance to shore up their ability to meet depositor demands. The real panic, however, began in Michigan on February 14, 1933. Michigan's governor, William Comstock, ordered the closure of every bank in the state until such time as their financial condition could be ascertained and certified as economically viable. In short order, similar "bank holidays" were proclaimed in Maryland, Kentucky, Tennessee, and California. By March 4, 1933, the date of Franklin Roosevelt's inauguration, thirty-eight states had declared bank holidays.

When, in his inaugural address, Roosevelt told the people of the United States: "We have nothing to fear but fear itself, " he had in mind the panic that had gripped the country as a result of the banking crisis. It was the first issue Roosevelt had to tackle. The next day, he called Congress into special session and, in a very liberal interpretation of his lawful authority, halted all transactions in gold and closed every bank in the United States.

Significance

The immediate impact of the "bank holiday" was a period of great inconvenience to every citizen in the country. While banks were closed, daily life took on a new and bizarre character. Cash was unavailable, so employers paid workers in scrip—Dow Chemical, for example, minted coins in Dowmetal. Foreign currency circulated. Many merchants accepted IOU's. Bus riders couldn't find nickels to pay for rides. No one could cash checks.

Nonetheless, a certain air of faith began to creep back into the American psyche. Roosevelt was doing something. He was specifically addressing a real problem. The inconvenience promised to be relatively short-lived. It affected everyone in the country. And the message was delivered by a president who exuded confidence and energy. In many ways, the "bank holiday" rallied Americans to combat a common enemy.

The specific action taken was to dispatch auditors to examine banks across the country. If a bank's soundness could be assured, it was allowed to reopen. If not, it remained closed. Starting with large regional institutions, banks began reopening on March 13. It was not until June, however, that the examinations were completed, and in the end, some four thousand banks never reopened. Thus in a period of four years, more than nine thousand banks failed and the total number of banks declined by more than eleven thousand.

However, overall confidence in the banking system returned. The banks that did open were solvent—and the American people believed they were. In addition, Roosevelt introduced legislation that increased regulation of the financial system and brought to it a much greater level of security. The most significant steps were the creation of the Federal Deposit Insurance Corporation and the Securities Exchange Commission.

Primary Source

"On the Bank Crisis"

SYNOPSIS: Perhaps one of Franklin Roosevelt's greatest assets was his ability to inspire confidence in the American people. His energy and faith in America was brought home to Americans most personally in his periodic radio addresses known as "Fireside Chats." His first such address explained to the country the causes, remedies and current status of the banking crisis. Both the consequence of the actions described in his address and the psychological impact on his listeners were enormous.

I want to talk for a few minutes with the people of the United States about banking—with the comparatively few who understand the mechanics of banking but more particularly with the overwhelming majority who use banks for the making of deposits and the drawing of checks. I want to tell you what has been done in the last few days, why it was done, and what the next steps are going to be. I recognize that the many proclamations from State Capitols and from Washington, the legislation, the Treasury regulations, etc., couched for the most part in banking and legal terms should be explained for the benefit of the average citizen. I owe this in particular because of the fortitude and good temper with which everybody has accepted the inconvenience and hardships of the banking holiday. I know that when you understand what we in Washington have been about I shall continue to have your cooperation as fully as I have had your sympathy and help during the past week.

First of all let me state the simple fact that when you deposit money in a bank the bank does not put the money into a safe deposit vault. It invests your money in many different forms of credit—bonds, commercial paper, mortgages and many other kinds of loans. In other words, the bank puts your money to work to keep the wheels of industry and of agriculture turning around. A comparatively small part of the money you put into the bank is kept in currency—an amount which in normal times is wholly sufficient to cover the cash needs of the average citizen. In other words the total amount of all the currency in the country is only a small fraction of the total deposits in all of the banks.

What, then, happened during the last few days of February and the first few days of March? Because of undermined confidence on the part of the public, there was a general rush by a large portion of our population to turn bank deposits into currency or gold.—A rush so great that the soundest banks could not get enough currency to meet the demand. The reason for this was that on the spur of the moment it was, of course, impossible to sell perfectly sound assets of a bank and convert them into cash except at panic prices far below their real value.

By the afternoon of March 3 scarcely a bank in the country was open to do business. Proclamations temporarily closing them in whole or in part had been issued by the Governors in almost all the states.

It was then that I issued the proclamation providing for the nation-wide bank holiday, and this was the first step in the Government's reconstruction of our financial and economic fabric.

The second step was the legislation promptly and patriotically passed by the Congress confirming my proclamation and broadening my powers so that it became possible in view of the requirement of time to entend [sic] the holiday and lift the ban of that holiday gradually. This law also gave authority to develop a program of rehabilitation of our banking facilities. I want to tell our citizens in every part of the Nation that the national Congress—Republicans and Democrats alike—showed by this action a devotion to public welfare and a realization of the emergency and the necessity for speed that it is difficult to match in our history.

The third stage has been the series of regulations permitting the banks to continue their functions to take care of the distribution of food and household necessities and the payment of payrolls.

This bank holiday while resulting in many cases in great inconvenience is affording us the opportunity to supply the currency necessary to meet the situation. No sound bank is a dollar worse off than it was when it closed its doors last Monday. Neither is any bank which may turn out not to be in a position for immediate opening. The new law allows the twelve Federal Reserve banks to issue additional currency on good assets and thus the banks which reopen will be able to meet every legitimate call. The new currency is being sent out by the Bureau of Engraving and Printing in large volume to every part of the country. It is sound currency because it is backed by actual, good assets. As a result we start tomorrow, Monday, with the opening of banks in the twelve Federal Reserve bank cities—those banks which on first examination by the Treasury have already been found to be all right. This will be followed on Tuesday by the resumption of all their functions by banks already found to be sound in cities where there are recognized clearing houses. That means about 250 cities of the United States.

Speculation that a bank was unstable often led to bank runs, such as this one at the Bowery Savings Bank in New York City. UPI/CORBIS-BETTMANN. REPRODUCED BY PERMISSION.

On Wednesday and succeeding days banks in smaller places all through the country will resume business, subject, of course, to the Government's physical ability to complete its survey. It is necessary that the reopening of banks be extended over a period in order to permit the banks to make applications for necessary loans, to obtain currency needed to meet their requirements and to enable the Government to make common sense checkups. Let me make it clear to you that if your bank does not open the first day you are by no means justified in believing that it will not open. A bank that opens on one of the subsequent days is in exactly the same status as the bank that opens tomorrow. I know that many people are worrying about State banks not members of the Federal Reserve System. These banks can and will receive assistance from member banks and from the Reconstruction Finance Corporation. These state banks are following the same course as the national banks except that they get their licenses to resume business from the state authorities, and these authorities have been asked by the Secretary of the Treasury to permit their good banks to open up on the same schedule as the national banks. I am confident that the state banking departments will be as careful as the National Government in the policy relating to the opening of banks and will follow the same broad policy. It is possible that when the banks resume a very few people who have not recovered from their fear may again begin withdrawals. Let me make it clear that the banks will take care of all needs—and it is my belief that hoarding during the past week has become an exceedingly unfashionable pastime. It needs no prophet to tell you that when the people find that they can get their money—that they can get it when they want it for all legitimate purposes—the phantom of fear will soon be laid. People will again be glad to have their money where it will be safely taken care of and where they can use it conveniently at any time. I can assure you that it is safer to keep your money in a reopened bank than under the mattress.

The success of our whole great national program depends, of course, upon the cooperation of the public—on its intelligent support and use of a reliable system. Remember that the essential accomplishment of the new legislation is that it makes it possible for banks more readily to convert their assets into cash than was the case before. More liberal provision has been made for banks to borrow on these assets at the Reserve Banks and more liberal provision has also been made for issuing currency on the security of those good assets. This currency is not fiat currency. It is issued only on adequate security—and every good bank has an abundance of such security.

One more point before I close. There will be, of course, some banks unable to reopen without being reorganized. The new law allows the Government to assist in making these reorganizations quickly and effectively and even allows the Government to subscribe to at least a part of new capital which may be required.

I hope you can see from this elemental recital of what your government is doing that there is nothing complex, or radical in the process.

We had a bad banking situation. Some of our bankers had shown themselves either incompetent or dishonest in their handling of the people's funds. They had used the money entrusted to them in speculations and unwise loans. This was of course not true in the vast majority of our banks but it was true in enough of them to shock the people for a time into a sense of insecurity and to put them into a frame of mind where they did not differentiate, but seemed to assume that the acts of a comparative few had tainted them all. It was the Government's job to straighten out this situation and do it as quickly as possible—and the job is being performed.

I do not promise you that every bank will be reopened or that individual losses will not be suffered, but there will be no losses that possibly could be avoided; and there would have been more and greater losses had we continued to drift. I can even promise you salvation for some at least of the sorely pressed banks. We shall be engaged not merely in reopening sound banks but in the creation of sound banks through reorganization. It has been wonderful to me to catch the note of confidence from all over the country. I can never be sufficiently grateful to the people for the loyal support they have given me in their acceptance of the judgment that has dictated our course, even though all of our processes may not have seemed clear to them.

After all there is no element in the readjustment of our financial system more important than currency, more important than gold, and that is the confidence of the people. Confidence and courage are the essentials of success in carrying out our plan. You people must have faith; you must not be stampeded by rumors or guesses. Let us unite in banishing fear. We have provided the machinery to restore our financial system; it is up to you to support and make it work.

It is your problem no less than it is mine. Together we cannot fail.

Further Resources

BOOKS

Burns, Helen M. *The American Banking Community and New Deal Banking Reforms, 1933–1935.* Westport, Conn.: Greenwood Press, 1974.

Leuchtenburg, William E. *Franklin D. Roosevelt and the New Deal, 1932–1940.* New York: Harper & Row, 1963.

Roosevelt, Franklin D. *The Public Papers and Addresses of Franklin D. Roosevelt.* Samuel I. Rosenman, comp. New York: Russell & Russell, 1969.

Whittlesey, Charles R. *Banking and the New Deal.* Chicago: The University of Chicago Press, 1935.

"Code of Fair Competition for the Men's Clothing Industry, as Amended"

Code

By: National Recovery Administration

Date: July 19, 1933

Source: "Code of Fair Competition for the Men's Clothing Industry, as Amended," 1933. Reprinted in Connery, Robert H. *The Administration of an N.R.A. Code: A Case Study of the Men's Clothing Industry.* Chicago: Public Administration Service, 1938, 162–173. ■

Introduction

One theory of the cause of the economic crisis of the 1930s was overproduction, insufficient worker wages, and a cutthroat competitive environment. Clearly, the United States had the resources and productive capacity to feed, house, and clothe its population. The problem, most agreed, was distribution—not production. A fundamental issue of the era was how to modify the "distribution system" in order to permanently solve the problems of unemployment and poverty.

One of the first programs to attack some of the root causes of the Depression was the National Industrial Recovery Act (NIRA). This act created the National Recovery Administration (NRA). It was an effort to address economic problems by creating a planned approach to managing the economy. The NRA tried to establish a cooperative relationship between employers, workers, and government in order to improve the economy for the good of all. Prices, wages, production, and working conditions would be established and enforced in a cooperative spirit. Competition would operate within established boundaries that would mutually benefit workers, management, and, in the long run, consumers.

While some critics immediately attacked the NRA, most Americans, eager to do something to solve the economic crisis, were anxious to comply.

To lead the NRA, Roosevelt appointed the well-respected General Hugh Johnson, a dynamic though somewhat eccentric former director of the Selective Service in World War I (1914–1918). His flamboyant style paid great dividends during the early months in building support and the voluntary cooperation needed for the NRA to achieve its goals.

The immediate objectives of the NRA were to increase employment, raise wages, and ensure business survival and profitability. Through the creation of industry-approved standards, the NRA attempted to reduce the level of destructive competition by establishing controlled prices, fair wage rates, and reduced hours. It also championed the elimination of child labor, the workers' right to organize unions, and improved working conditions.

Significance

Initially, the NRA made enormous strides. Johnson was able to create a spirit of cooperation; employers, employees, and the government together developed more than five hundred industry-specific codes. Spurred on by Johnson's emotional appeals, the general population eagerly supported the program. Almost immediately there were signs of progress: production increased; the stock market jumped; unemployment declined; wages rose; prices rose.

As the crisis seemed to ease, support for the NRA declined. The level of intervention necessary to enforce agreed-upon (and largely voluntary) standards doomed the program to failure. So, too, did the perception of the general population that prices had been kept artificially high.

In the end, the unwillingness of business owners to tolerate significant government intervention in business affairs, combined with the dubious legality of many aspects of the NRA, brought it to an end. By early 1934 its effectiveness had waned. It was finally put out of its misery in May 1935 when, in the famous "sick chicken" case *(Schechter v. U.S.)*, the Supreme Court declared the NRA to be unconstitutional.

Primary Source

"Code of Fair Competition for the Men's Clothing Industry, as Amended" [excerpt]

SYNOPSIS: The heart of the NRA was the creation of a series of industry standards that generally violated antitrust laws. These were agreements among businesses to set prices, wages, and production standards. The following excerpt from the "Code of Fair Competition for the Men's Clothing Industry" is representative of the NRA codes. A special problem it had to grapple with was reconciling the two main geographic centers of the industry: the urban, more unionized Northeast and the rural, antilabor South.

To effectuate the policy of Title I of the National Industrial Recovery Act, during the period of the emergency, by reducing and relieving unemployment, improving the standards of labor, eliminating competitive practices destructive of the interests of the public, employees, and employers, relieving the disastrous effects of overcapacity, and otherwise rehabilitating the Clothing Industry and by increasing the consumption of industrial and agricultural products by increasing purchasing power, and in other respects, the following provisions are established as a code of fair competition for the Clothing Industry:

I. Definitions

The term "Clothing Industry" as used herein is defined to mean the manufacture of men's, boys', and children's clothing, uniforms, single knee pants, single pants, and men's summer clothing (exclusive of cotton wash suits). . . .

The term "effective date" as used herein is defined to be the eleventh day of September, 1933.

The term "persons" shall include, but without limitation, natural persons, partnerships, associations, and corporations.

II.

On and after the effective date, the minimum wage paid by employers in the Clothing Industry to any of their manufacturing employees shall be at the rate of forty cents (40¢) per hour when employed in the northern section of the Industry, and at the rate of thirty-seven cents (37¢) per hour when employed in the southern section of the Industry; and to any nonmanufacturing employee the minimum weekly wage paid shall be fourteen dollars ($14.00) in the northern section and thirteen dollars ($13.00) in the southern section. "Southern section" shall include Alabama, Arkansas, Georgia, Louisiana, Mississippi, North Carolina, Oklahoma, South Carolina, Tennessee, and Texas.

The minimum wage paid by employers to employees working on single knee pants shall be at the rate of thirty-seven cents (37¢) per hour. . . .

a. On and after the effective date, the minimum wage which shall be paid to cutters shall be at the rate of One Dollar ($1.00) per hour, and the minimum wage which shall be paid to off-pressers shall be at the rate of seventy-five cents (75c) per hour. . . .

b. The existing amounts by which wages in the higher paid classes, up to classes of employees receiving Thirty Dollars ($30.00) per week, exceed wages in the lowest-paid substantial classes shall be maintained.

c. Any increase of the minimum wage made effective between the date of the filing of this Code, to wit, July 14, 1933, and the effective date, shall be disregarded and shall have no effect in connection with determining the wages to be paid in the higher-price classes as provided for in Section II (b) above.

d. The Men's Clothing Code Authority may appoint a committee to supervise the execution of the foregoing provisions.

e. The provisions for the minimum wage established in this Code shall constitute a guaranteed minimum rate of pay in connection with both a time rate or a piece work basis of compensation.

f. No increases in the amount of production or work shall be required of employees for the purpose of avoiding the benefits to employees prescribed by this Code in respect of wages and hours of employment. . . .

All requirements in respect of such increases shall be reported to the Men's Clothing Code Authority.

A poster promotes the National Recovery Administration code. COURTESY OF THE FDR LIBRARY.

III.

Three (3) months after the effective date a manufacturer shall not be permitted to have work done or labor performed on any garment or part thereof in the home of a worker. All work done for a manufacturer on a garment or part thereof shall be done in what is commonly known as an inside shop or in a contracting shop. . . .

IV.

On and after the effective date, the hours of employment for employees in the Clothing Industry, except repair shop crews, engineers, electricians, firemen, office and supervisory staff, stock clerks, shipping clerks, truck drivers, porters and watchmen, and except employees engaged in bona fide managerial or executive capacities shall not exceed thirty-six (36) hours per week nor eight (8) hours per day. Employers shall not operate productive machinery in the Clothing Industry more than one shift of thirty-six (36) hours per week. It is intended that the foregoing provisions for maximum hours shall establish the maximum hours of labor per week of every employee, other than those employees excepted therein, so that under no circumstances will an employee be employed or be permitted to work for any one or more employers in the Industry an aggregate in excess of the prescribed number of hours in any single week.

Repair shop crews, engineers, electricians, firemen, office and supervisory staff, stock clerks, shipping clerks, truck drivers, porters, and watchmen shall not work in excess of an average of forty (40) hours per week during any year beginning with the effective date.

It is intended that employees' wages shall not be reduced by reason of the reduction of the prescribed number of hours of employment.

Tailoring to the Trade and manufacturers of uniforms shall be permitted overtime at regular rates during peak seasons, the number of hours and the number of weeks to be determined by The Men's Clothing Code Authority. . . .

V.

All garments manufactured or distributed shall bear an N.R.A. label, which shall remain attached to such garments. Such labels shall bear a registration number specially assigned to each manufacturer in the Industry. The privilege of using such labels shall be granted and such labels shall be issued to any manufacturer from time to time engaged in the Clothing Industry upon application therefor to the Code Authority, accompanied by a statement of compliance with the standards of operation prescribed by this Code. The privilege of using such labels and the issuance thereof may be withdrawn and cease or may be suspended in respect of any such manufacturer whose operations, after appropriate hearing by The Men's Clothing Code Authority and review by the Administrator, shall be found to be in substantial violation of such standards. Manufacturers shall be entitled to obtain and use such labels if they comply with the provisions of this Code.

The Men's Clothing Code Authority may establish appropriate machinery for the issuance of such labels in accordance with the foregoing provisions.

VI.

On and after the effective date, employers in the Clothing Industry shall not employ any minor under the age of sixteen (16) years.

VII.

Safe, healthful, and otherwise satisfactory working conditions shall be provided for all employees, which conditions shall as a minimum comply with the highest standards respecting sanitation, cleanliness, light, and safety specified in the Factory Laws of any State in which the manufacturer operates.

VIII.

With a view of keeping the President informed as to the observance or nonobservance of this code of fair competition, and as to whether the Clothing Industry is taking appropriate steps to effectuate the declared policy of the National Industrial Recovery Act, each person engaged in the Clothing Industry will furnish every four weeks duly certified reports showing in substance:

a. Pay-roll data, showing by sex and occupation, number of people employed, number of hours worked, and the rates of wages paid.
b. Production data showing the number and type of garments cut and made up, in such form as may hereafter be provided by The Men's Clothing Code Authority.

The Men's Clothing Code Authority as hereinafter provided is constituted the agency to collect and receive such reports.

IX.

Where the costs of executing contracts already entered into in the Clothing Industry are increased as a result of the enactment of the National Industrial Recovery Act and by the provisions of this Code, it is equitable and promotive of the purposes of the Act that appropriate adjustments of such contracts to reflect such increased costs be arrived at by arbitral proceedings or otherwise and The Men's Clothing Code Authority, as hereinafter provided, is designated to assist in effecting such adjustments.

X.

On and after the effective date, it shall be unfair competition for any manufacturer in the Clothing Industry, either directly or indirectly, to sell its manufactured product at a price below its cost as determined without any subterfuge in accordance with sound accounting practice. Cost shall include the cost of piece goods consumed, trimmings, cutting, and making; and a percentage on the selling price to cover all overhead.

There shall be excepted, however, from the provisions of this Section, seasonal clearances of merchandise, and the following dates are fixed for such seasonal sales:

Wool Suits, Spring Season	On and after May 15th.
Wool Suits, Fall Season	On and after November 15th.
Summer Clothing	On and after June 15th.
Overcoats	On and after December 15th. . . .

Dropped lines or surplus stocks, sometimes designated as "closeouts," or inventories which must be converted into cash to meet immediate needs, may be sold on dates prior to those mentioned in the preceding clause, at such prices as are necessary to move the merchandise into buyers' hands. However, all such stocks must first be reported to the Men's Clothing Code Authority.

XI.

On and after the effective date, no contractor shall be permitted to contract for the manufacture of any garment or part thereof at a price below its cost as determined without any subterfuge in accordance with sound accounting practice, the cost

"The Spirit of the New Deal" cartoon by Clifford Berryman, July 25, 1933. GETTY IMAGES. REPRODUCED BY PERMISSION.

to include a percentage on the contract price to cover general overhead.

XII.

The following rules of fair trade practices are hereby established for the clothing industry:

a. The sale of garments on consignment is prohibited as an unfair method of competition. The term "consignment" as herein used shall include the delivery by a manufacturer to any distributor, as agent, purchaser, or otherwise, under any agreement or understanding, expressed or implied, pursuant to which the seller retains any lien upon or title to or interest in the goods delivered, or pursuant to which the distributor may at his option return any of the goods or claim any credits with respect thereto. This prohibition shall not apply to contracts entered into prior to July 14, 1933, the term of which expires within one year from the date of the enactment of the National Industrial Recovery Act.

b. A manufacturer or a contractor shall not make garments from fabrics, trimmings, and/or other materials owned or supplied by a retail distributor or the agent, representative, or corporate subsidiary or affiliate of such retail distributor; nor shall he manufacture garments from fabrics, trimmings, and/or other materials, the purchase of which is made upon the credit of or the payment for which is guaranteed by such retail distributor or the agent, representative, or corporate subsidiary or affiliate of such retail distributor. This section shall not prohibit the operations of retail distributors owning and operating their own plants, shops, or factories who distribute products manufactured therein directly to consumers. . . .

XIII.

A board known as The Men's Clothing Code Authority shall be established, and for the purpose of effecting membership therein representative of the entire industry, such Board shall be constituted as follows:

Ten (10) members representative of members of The Clothing Manufacturers' Association of the United States of America, and

Five (5) members representative of employers in the Clothing Industry who are not members of The Clothing Manufacturers' Association of the United States of America shall be appointed by this Association.

Two (2) members representative of other employers may be chosen by the foregoing members.

Five (5) members representative of labor shall be appointed by the Administrator on nomination by the Labor Advisory Board.

One (1) member may be appointed by the Administrator.

Subject to the approval of the Administrator, The Men's Clothing Code Authority shall have responsibility for the administration and the enforcement of the provisions of this Code, the standards of operation set forth therein, and all appropriate rules and regulations made pursuant thereto.

In connection with such responsibility The Men's Clothing Code Authority shall have the following authorities and powers:

a. Authority and power to examine all books of accounts and records of employers in the Clothing Industry so far as practicable for the purpose of ascertaining their respective observance or non-observance of the provisions of this Code and the standards of operation set forth therein.

b. Authority and power to cooperate, so far as possible, with the Administrator in making investigations as to the functioning and observance of the provisions of this Code and the standards of operation set forth therein, at its own instance or on complaint by any person affected, and to report its findings to the Administrator.

c. Authority and power to investigate and inform the Administrator, on behalf of the Clothing Industry, as to importation of competitive articles into the United States of America in substantial quantities or increasing ratio to domestic production, on such terms and under such conditions as to render ineffective or seriously to endanger the maintenance of this Code, and to make complaint, on behalf of the Clothing Industry, under the provisions of the National Industrial Recovery Act with respect thereto.

d. Authority and power to consider and to make recommendations to the Administrator and to the President of the United States in respect of the following matters:

1. Recommendations as to the requirement by the Administrator of such other and further reports from persons engaged in the Clothing Industry of statistical information and the keeping of uniform accounts as may be required to secure the proper observance of the Code and promote the proper balancing of production, distribution and consumption, and the stabilization of the industry and employment.
2. Recommendations for the setting up of a Service Bureau for engineering, accounting, credit, or any other purposes that may aid in the conditions of this emergency and the requirements of this Code.
3. Recommendations for the making of rules by the Administrator as to practices by persons engaged in the Clothing Industry as to methods and conditions of trading, the naming and reporting of prices which may be appropriate to avoid discrimination, to promote the stabilization of the Industry, to prevent and eliminate unfair and destructive prices and practices.

4. Recommendations for regulating the disposal of distress merchandise in a way that will secure the protection of the owners thereof and at the same time promote sound and stable conditions in the Industry.
5. Recommendations as to the making available to the suppliers of credit to those engaged in the Industry, all information regarding terms of and actual functioning of any or all of the provisions of the Code, the conditions of the Industry and regarding the operations of any and all persons engaged in the Industry and covered by this Code, to the end that during the period of the emergency, available credit may be adapted to the needs of the Clothing Industry, considered as a whole, and to the needs of the small as well as of the large units.
6. Recommendations for dealing with any inequalities that may otherwise arise that may endanger the stability of the Industry and/or production and employment. Such recommendations, when approved by the President of the United States, shall have the same force and effect as any other provision of this Code.

e. Authority and power to appoint such officers, agents, and other employees as may reasonably be required for the effective discharge of its functions.

Except for the purposes provided in Section VIII of this Code and except so far as may be necessary or appropriate for the enforcement of the provisions of this Code and the standards of operation set forth therein, the data in respect of employers in the Clothing Industry reported to or secured by The Men's Clothing Code Authority shall be treated as confidential and shall not be published or otherwise disseminated throughout the Industry, except as individually undisclosed portions of aggregate compilations.

None of the powers or authorities vested by this Code in The Men's Clothing Code Authority shall be utilized or availed of for any purpose other than the supervision and enforcement of the provisions of this Code or the standards of operation set forth therein, and for purposes of advice and information and recommendation substantially as provided for in this Code.

None of the powers or authorities vested by this Code in The Men's Clothing Code Authority in respect of the operations of employers in the Clothing Industry shall be made effective in such manner as to preclude an appropriate review thereof by the Administrator.

The expense of maintaining The Men's Clothing Code Authority shall be borne by employers in the Clothing Industry in such reasonable proportions and amounts and in such manner as may properly be allocated by the Administrator, upon the recommendation of The Men's Clothing Code Authority. . . .

XIV.

Employees shall have the right to organize and bargain collectively through representatives of their own choosing, and shall be free from the interference, restraint, or coercion of employers of labor, or their agents, in the designation of such representatives or in self-organization or in other concerted activities for the purpose of collective bargaining or other mutual aid or protection; no employee and no one seeking employment shall be required as a condition of employment to join any company union or to refrain from joining, organizing, or assisting a labor organization of his own choosing; and employers shall comply with the maximum hours of labor, minimum rates of pay, and other conditions of employment, approved or prescribed by the President.

XV.

This Code and all the provisions thereof are expressly made subject to the right of the President, in accordance with the provision of Clause 10 (b) of the National Industrial Recovery Act, from time to time to cancel or modify any order, approval, license, rule, or regulation, issued under Title I of said Act, and specifically to the right of the President to cancel or modify his approval of this Code or any conditions imposed by him upon his approval thereof.

XVI.

The Men's Clothing Code Authority shall designate the National Association of Uniform Manufacturers to aid the Administrator in the administration of this Code in respect of the manufacture and distribution of uniform apparel and shall make recommendations to the Administrator in respect of the trade practices desirable for this branch in the industry.

XVII.

Such of the provisions of this Code as are not required to be included therein by the National Industrial Recovery Act, may with the approval of the

President, be modified or eliminated as changes in circumstances or experience may indicate.

Further Resources

BOOKS

Bellush, Bernard. *The Failure of the NRA.* New York: Norton, 1975.

Bernstein, Irving. *A Caring Society: The New Deal, the Worker, and the Great Depression; A History of the American Worker, 1933.* Boston: Houghton Mifflin, 1985.

Cronon, Edmund David, ed. *Labor and the New Deal.* Chicago: Rand McNally, 1963.

"Statement of H.L. Lurie, Director of the Bureau of Jewish Social Research, New York City, New York"

Statement

By: H.L. Lurie

Date: 1933

Source: "Statement of H.L. Lurie, Director of the Bureau of Jewish Social Research, New York City, New York." In *Hearings Before a Subcommittee of the Committee on Manufactures, United States Senate, Seventy-second Congress, Second Session on S. 5125.* Washington, D.C.: United States Government Printing Office, 1933, 64, 65, 70–73.

About the Author: Harry L. Lurie (1892–1973) was the Director of the Bureau of Jewish Social Services in New York City. Lurie was also a member of the American Association of Social Workers, and it was in this capacity that he testified before the Senate Committee on Manufactures regarding unemployment, living conditions, and relief efforts. In this instance, thc so-called La Follette–Costigan committee was hearing testimony on Senate Bill 5125: A Bill to Provide for Cooperation by the Federal Government With the Several States in Relieving the Hardship and Suffering Caused by Unemployment, and for Other Purposes. ■

Introduction

Historically, relief to the needy was the concern of local government and charitable organizations. In fact, the traditional relief system was inadequate in urban settings, particularly during severe economic downturns. The system was completely overwhelmed by the poor economic conditions of 1931 and 1932. As a result, it became increasingly evident that federal funds were needed to maintain even the existing levels of relief.

Under the leadership of progressive Senators Robert La Follette, Jr. (R-Wis.), and Edward P. Costigan (D-Colo.), their Subcommittee of the Senate Committee on Manufactures heard extensive testimony over a two-year

Men walk in front of a billboard that reflects the conditions they are living in. 1930. COURTESY OF THE FDR LIBRARY.

Men wait to receive food from a soup kitchen during the Great Depression. COURTESY OF THE FDR LIBRARY.

period on a variety of legislative proposals to deal with the effects of the Depression. Sometimes clinical and detached in their presentation, witnesses were often graphic in their description of the conditions they found.

The liberal leanings of the La Follette–Costigan committee were quite evident from the strain of questioning and the types of witnesses that were called. Clearly, the intent was to gather evidence that would persuade and influence more aggressive federal involvement in dealing with the Depression.

Significance

The testimony from a variety of witnesses provided valuable information to Congress and the public about the depth of the problem, the breadth of the unemployed population's needs, and the effectiveness of various relief programs.

By 1932 local relief had exhausted the available resources. Local leaders and relief workers had completely lost confidence in the ability of a locally based system to meet the needs of the unemployed. These workers almost universally believed that federal action was essential. Congressmen were told repeatedly that unless the federal government stepped in, relief systems would collapse.

Another common point was the need for relief to extend beyond providing a subsistence diet. The unemployed were without shelter, fuel, and medical attention. The existing relief system focused on minimal food distribution while ignoring the health effects of the meager diet and, to a large extent, other basic human needs. While this was blamed in part on the lack of resources, witnesses also pointed out the philosophical limitations of local and charitable relief.

An important benefit of the testimony was the insight gained on procedural and administrative issues relief workers were experiencing. In H.L. Lurie's testimony, for example, he is critical of the lack of professional staff running the various local programs and the failure of the Reconstruction Finance Corporation (RFC) loans to fund such administrative functions.

Despite the voluminous testimony gathered in 1931 and 1932, federal involvement in relief remained limited and largely confined to the very tightly regulated RFC loans. While adequate federal legislation to deal with the Depression was not passed in Hoover's administration, much of the country and Congress was convinced of the need for action. When Roosevelt assumed office, he was met by a Congress prepared to approve dramatic legislation.

Primary Source

"Statement of H.L. Lurie, Director of the Bureau of Jewish Social Research, New York City, New York" [excerpt]

SYNOPSIS: Mr. Lurie presented a report prepared by the American Association of Social Workers, which summarized information from forty-four locations in larger communities across the country. In the excerpts below he advocates a dramatic expansion of federal involvement in relief efforts. The information presented was collected in December 1932.

The Chairman: The committee would be grateful if you would proceed in your own way to give us that material.

Mr. Lurie: The American Association of Social Workers, an organization with a membership of 6,000 professional workers from all parts of the country, by action of its executive committee, in November, 1932, appointed a special committee to concern itself with the problems of unemployment relief, present Federal relief policies, and proposed Federal legislation. . . .

This report summarizes information which has been received in the last week from this group of consultants and applies to 44 cities and adjacent areas in 25 States and the District of Columbia. Since few professional social workers serve the smaller communities and the industrial and mining areas not incorporated in large cities, we were able to obtain this information, therefore, primarily from populous communities which possess relatively well organized programs of relief and social service. . . .

With few exceptions none of the larger relief agencies in these cities is providing relief to pay electric-light bills. In thousands of families the use of electric lights has been entirely abandoned, although some families are permitted to purchase kerosene for light on their grocery orders. One of the exceptions is the city of Seattle, where the municipality owns the electric utility and has continued service to unemployed unable to pay their light bills.

Nearly all of the agencies are attempting to supply some amount of fuel during the winter months, although frequently in insufficient amounts. The usual amount of fuel given is one-half ton of coal during a three or four weeks' period, although in a number of cities the experience is similar to that of Lawrence and New Bedford, Mass., where only one-fourth of a ton of coal is given during the month. It is reported in many cities that the homes of the unemployed are poorly heated. Some cities attempt to supplement inadequate coal supplies by giving wood cut by the unemployed on work-for-relief projects. A few communities offer only wood as fuel to the unemployed.

It is only the exceptional agency which is providing any relief for rent to its unemployed clients, and it is reported that evictions are increasing and tax delinquencies are becoming more common among protesting landlords. The practice is general of not paying rent except in extreme emergencies. A number of agencies make an attempt to provide one month's payment of rent, rarely more than $12 a month, when a family has been evicted or is facing eviction and is suffering from serious illness. For example, San Francisco reports that it pays rents about 1 month out of 4; Denver pays practically no rent; Detroit is paying rent to 1 out of 8 families; it is reported from Philadelphia that no rents are paid with evictions occurring constantly and no help being given; Cleveland pays 25 to 60 per cent of the first month's rent in emergency situations. In a few cities the public agency is beginning to pay landlords sufficient rental to cover taxes and interest charges.

As a result of these prevailing policies on rent, there is a further doubling up of unemployed families with sympathetic relatives and friends frequently to the point of serious congestion and occasionally with demoralizing and disastrous consequences. It is reported from several cities that the relief agency is beginning to take over some abandoned and uninhabitable dwellings and is attempting to convert them for shelters with the aid of work relief clients. In several instances cities are resorting to congregate shelter of evicted families and an abandoned almshouse is being used for this purpose in one community.

The average amount of relief per family in these cities ranges from as little as $5 and $6 a month for food relief in Florida supplemented by a few miscellaneous items, such as wood, flour, and vegetables, to $10 and $12 per week for a family of five in some of the cities of medium size, such as in New York State, that have more adequate relief funds. In general, between $15 and $20 a month per family would be the total average relief for the current month in a group of cities included in this report. It is estimated that if essential relief were to be given on a minimum budgetary standard including food, clothing, rent, light, heat, and medical care, it would become necessary at least to double the present total relief expenditures of these cities. Instead of expending $17,500,000 they should be expending approximately $35,000,000 if they were using even a minimum standard budget. Only a minority of cities reported that their present relief expenditures are on a minimum subsistence basis. The relief expenditures in the others were from 20 to 60 per cent under a minimum relief budget for dependent families.

One city reports that relief had been so inadequate that the entire body of social workers protested and as a consequence an attempt is being made to raise the amount of relief from 50 cents per person per week to $1 per person per week.

In Stamford, Conn., grocery orders of $3, $4, and $5 are allowed, depending on the size of the family, but no family, no matter how many individuals it consists of, receives more than $5 a week.

In Grand Rapids the rate of food relief is reported to be 50 cents per person per week.

The Cleveland rate is $4.40 a week for a family of five for food.

In Toledo the same size family will receive $3 a week and in Cincinnati and Seattle $4 a week. In Dallas, Tex., the equivalent of $1.40 in groceries is given for one day's work a week. Attempts are being made now to improve this basis of relief to $4.50 in cash plus two sacks of groceries for five days' work a week. Other cities similarly are giving less than a minimum food ration.

Funds for relief programs are being supplied largely from governmental sources. It is estimated that for the next six months not more than 10 per cent of the relief expenditures can be secured from voluntary contributions, including community chest and emergency relief campaigns. Uncertainty concerning the sources of funds prevail. Few of the agencies are able to plan definitely for more than one month at a time and several of them are on a week-to-week basis because of the uncertainty of resources. The relief funds from private sources represent a very small proportion of the total amount needed and have been further decreased this year because of the failure in many cities of campaigns to reach the goal set and the necessity to use voluntary funds for established agencies for the care of aged, children, hospitals and clinics, and so forth. The outlook for local public funds is also extremely doubtful, and a number of the reporting communities are already depending principally upon funds from the Reconstruction Finance Corporation.

For example, Birmingham, Ala., estimates that $1,000,000 will be needed for the next six months on the present basis of relief and that only $42,000 is available from voluntary funds. It is expecting $150,000 a month from the R. F. C.

In Bridgeport, Conn., the public department has no funds until the beginning of the fiscal year in April, and it is hoped that credit may be obtained until that time. No loans are expected from the R. F. C., since Connecticut has no bonded indebtedness.

In Lawrence, Mass., where relief standards are even lower than average, it is reported that the city is almost bankrupt. Taxes have been greatly reduced, due to the closing of principal industries, and taxpayers are in rebellion against appropriations for public relief.

Columbus, Ohio, reports that the legislature and the R. F. C. will have to carry the entire relief burden in 1933. The State can only do this by providing some new sources of revenue to take the place of the utility tax bonds and the relief bonds. In any event, there will be a large gap between what the State and local bodies are able to supply and the minimum relief needs of the city.

Portland, Oreg.: This county spent $3,332,000 from all sources on organized relief in 1932 and will need $5,000,000 in 1933. The task is to get enough funds to carry present minimum standards, and if further cuts are made, more persons will be contributed to swell the transient group. Minimum funds for a balanced relief program which makes migration unnecessary is a fundamental need.

In Florida no community has raised enough money from voluntary subscriptions to continue the programs of the regular agencies, so that there are almost no funds available for unemployment relief from this source. Some cities have made small appropriations for road work and other projects although these appropriations are still well below normal expenditures for such public work. Many of the communities have defaulted on their bond issues. The State has a constitutional provision prohibiting the incurring of any indebtedness but will consider some sort of appropriation at the meeting of the legislature in January.

In Chicago it is estimated that at the present rate of relief expenditures $17,000,000 would be required for the next six months. Approximately $3,000,000 is available from voluntary funds and the emergency fund campaign. The State Legislature is permitting the Cook County Board of Commissioners to sell $17,000,000 in bonds, but the county commissioners have thus far received no bid for the bonds, and it is likely that the bonds will not be sold. The loan from the Reconstruction Finance Corporation runs out in December.

In Seattle a bond issue of $2,000,000 for county relief was passed by the electors, but it is reported that the bonds will probably not be saleable. The city has passed a bond issue of $1,000,000 for work relief which is probably marketable, and the proceeds will be available. The State of Washington can not legally pass any bond issue for relief until the general election of 1934. It is probable that the new state administration will develop public works program for funds already on hand and will perhaps find a way to make some relief available to counties. This is, however, problematical at present.

Many of the cities reporting have depended during the last few months to a large extent on Federal aid and nearly all of the others are counting upon making applications for such loans except in a few states which consider themselves unable to make such applications.

It is difficult to measure the effect of the depression and inadequate relief upon social conditions in these communities under consideration. Research on problems of malnutrition and family disorganization have been made in only a few of the communities. Several of the studies indicate a definite increase in malnourished and ill-nourished children of preschool and school age. In one or two instances no increase in malnutrition has been indicated and it is believed that the furnishing of school lunches is to be credited for this result. One city reports an increase in the tuberculosis rate.

The inadequacy of funds from voluntary contributions and the reduced tax resources in many communities have been followed by serious reductions and curtailments in essential services. There have been sharp reductions in the budgets of the social agencies, both public and private. Deep cuts have been made in a number of communities in the budgets for public education and recreation and in a number of communities budgets for health have also suffered. Reductions of 10 to 50 per cent in the budgets of private agencies are reported and from 5 to 30 per cent in the budgets of public agencies. Several cities report that public health nursing personnel has been reduced and in several communities family service and child welfare programs have suffered from lack of funds. Further decreases in the essential work of public and private welfare agencies are expected. An additional number of hospitals, particularly those under private auspices, are in danger of being closed in a number of cities because of lack of funds.

Further Resources

BOOKS

Bernstein, Irving. *The Lean Years.* Baltimore: Penguin Books, 1966.

Bremer, William W. *Depression Winters: New York Social Workers and the New Deal.* Philadelphia: Temple University Press, 1984.

Shannon, David A., ed. *The Great Depression.* Englewood Cliffs, N.J.: Prentice-Hall, 1960.

Watkins, Tom H. *The Hungry Years: A Narrative History of the Great Depression in America.* New York: Henry Holt, 1999.

Securities Exchange Act of 1934

Law

Date: 1934

Source: *Securities Exchange Act of 1934.* Reproduced by the Center for Corporate Law, University of Cincinnati College of Law. Available online at http://www.law.uc.edu/CCL/34Act/index.html; website home page: http://www.law.uc.edu (accessed April 17, 2003). ■

Introduction

The Stock Market Crash of 1929 and the growing uncertainty of the financial systems of the United States prompted critical examination of those systems. Spurred by the collapse of three thousand banks between 1930 and 1932 and by revelations of unscrupulous dealings by powerful financial leaders, greater regulatory control of key institutions seemed necessary.

Efforts to regulate financial institutions were helped by dramatic hearings of the Senate Banking Committee, which investigated Wall Street practices. The Pecora Committee (named for its chief counsel, Ferdinand Pecora) took on the leaders of Wall Street. He showed that they were motivated by self-interest and not inclined to operate in the best interests of the public.

The revelations of the Pecora Committee were instrumental in building support for the passage of the *Glass-Steagall Banking Act of 1933* and the Securities Exchange Acts of 1933 and 1934. The Glass-Steagall Act separated investing from commercial banking. The second Securities and Exchange Act created the Federal Deposit Insurance Corporation (FDIC), which guaranteed that deposits made into member banks would be available for withdrawal.

Before commencing work on a regulatory bill, its sponsors, Samuel Rayburn (D-Tex.) and Duncan Fletcher (D-Fla.) established the constitutionality of federal regulation of the stock exchanges. The basis of consitutionality was grounded in the fiscal authority of the government, the impact of the stock market on the credit of the government, and the national scope of the companies traded on the exchanges and their investors.

Significance

The primary objectives of the Securities and Exchange Acts were to prevent manipulation of stock prices by insiders, place the margin buying of stocks under tighter restrictions, and end misrepresentation of stock values by requiring full disclosure of information related to the securities sold on the stock exchanges. It gave the federal government regulatory responsibility over what had been known as laissez-faire economics. Laissez-faire, a French expression that means letting people do what they choose, in this case means letting the economic system operate without government interference.

One of the critical provisions of the act was the creation of the Securities and Exchange Commission (SEC). Charged with enforcing the provisions of the act, the SEC was granted broad powers to establish specific rules and regulations to enforce the general provisions of the act. This flexibility allowed the SEC to respond to the rapidly changing business environment and avoid the slow and cumbersome legislative process that previously had been necessary to conduct regulatory actions.

The first chairman of the SEC was Joseph P. Kennedy, father of future president John F. Kennedy. Under Kennedy, the SEC got off to a strong beginning. In the first year of operation, the SEC registered twenty-four stock exchanges while closing down ten exchanges of dubious credibility. In addition, the SEC investigated more than two thousand cases of fraud.

More than any other piece of New Deal legislation, the Securities and Exchange Acts turned business irrevocably against Roosevelt. Whatever hopes either side had of cooperating to combat the Depression ended with this

New York finance giant, J. P. Morgan (left), consults with Thomas W. Lamont, a partner in his banking house, and John W. Davis, Morgan's counsel, just before the Senate Banking Committee (Pecora) investigation opens into affairs of the House of Morgan in 1933. **AP/WIDE WORLD PHOTOS. REPRODUCED BY PERMISSION.**

legislation. Wrote the president of the New York Stock Exchange, Richard Whitney, "You gentlemen are making a great mistake. The Exchange is perfect." By tampering with this "perfect" institution, Roosevelt sent the clear message to business leaders that whatever they felt about so-called "natural laws" of economics, the financial institutions of this country must operate for the benefit of its citizens. (Note: In 1937, Richard Whitney's investment firm went bankrupt. Following an investigation, he pleaded guilty to grand larceny and was sentenced to ten years imprisonment.)

Primary Source

Securities Exchange Act of 1934 [excerpt]

SYNOPSIS: In this brief preamble to the 1934 Securities Act, the rationale and purposes of the bill are explained. The preamble is followed by excerpts that highlight the main functions of the law, which were to restrict buying on margin, ensure that information regarding listed companies was reported accurately, and prevent insiders from manipulating stock prices.

For the reasons hereinafter enumerated, transactions in securities as commonly conducted upon securities exchanges and over-the-counter markets are affected with a national public interest which makes it necessary to provide for regulation and control of such transactions and of practices and matters related thereto, including transactions by officers, directors, and principal security holders, to require appropriate reports, to remove impediments to and perfect the mechanisms of a national market system for securities and a national system for the clearance and settlement

The New York Stock Exchange, on Wall Street, New York City, in December 1930. © **HULTON-DEUTSCH COLLECTION/CORBIS. REPRODUCED BY PERMISSION.**

of securities transactions and the safeguarding of securities and funds related thereto, and to impose requirements necessary to make such regulation and control reasonably complete and effective, in order to protect interstate commerce, the national credit, the Federal taxing power, to protect and make more effective the national banking system and Federal Reserve System, and to insure the maintenance of fair and honest markets in such transactions:

1. Such transactions (a) are carried on in large volume by the public generally and in large part originate outside the States in which the exchanges and over-the-counter markets are located and/or are effected by means of the mails and instrumentalities of interstate commerce; (b) constitute an important part of the current of interstate commerce; (c) involve in large part the securities of issuers engaged in interstate commerce; (d) involve the use of credit, directly affect the financing of trade, industry, and transportation in interstate commerce, and directly affect and influence the volume of interstate commerce; and affect the national credit.
2. The prices established and offered in such transactions are generally disseminated and quoted throughout the United States and foreign countries and constitute a basis for determining and establishing the prices at which securities are bought and sold, the amount of certain taxes owing to the United States and to the several States by owners, buyers, and sellers of securities, and the value of collateral for bank loans.
3. Frequently the prices of securities on such exchanges and markets are susceptible to manipulation and control, and the dissemination of such prices gives rise to excessive speculation, resulting in sudden and unreasonable fluctuations in the prices of securities which (a) cause alternately unreasonable expansion and unreasonable contraction of the volume of credit available for trade, transportation, and industry in interstate commerce, (b) hinder the proper appraisal of the value of securities and thus prevent a fair calculation of taxes owing to the United States and to the several States by owners, buyers, and sellers of securities, and (c) prevent the fair valuation of collateral for bank loans and/or obstruct the effective operation of the national banking system and Federal Reserve System.
4. National emergencies, which produce widespread unemployment and the dislocation of trade, transportation, and industry, and which burden interstate commerce and adversely affect the general welfare, are precipitated, intensified, and prolonged by manipulation and sudden and unreasonable fluctuations of security prices and by excessive speculation on such exchanges and markets, and to meet such emergencies the Federal Government is put to such great expense as to burden the national credit.

Further Resources

BOOKS

De Bedts, Ralph F. *The New Deal's SEC: The Formative Years.* New York: Columbia University Press, 1965.

Koslow, Philip. *The Securities and Exchange Commission.* New York: Chelsea House Publishers, 1990.

Seligman, Joel. *The Transformation of Wall Street: A History of the Securities and Exchange Commission.* Boston: Houghton Mifflin, 1982.

WEBSITES

Chen, Zhun Dean. "Securities & Exchange Commission." Available online at http://www.geocities.com/Colosseum/Field/1633/sec.html (accessed August 7, 2002).

"Redistribution of Wealth"

Speech

By: George W. Norris

Date: February 25, 1935

Source: Norris, George W. "Redistribution of Wealth." Speech presented at the Charter Day celebration at the University of Nebraska, February 15, 1935. *Vital Speeches of the Day* I, no. 11, February 25, 1935, 327–329, 330–331.

About the Author: George W. Norris (1861–1944) was a senator from Nebraska from 1912 to 1943. Ohio-born, Norris settled in Nebraska in 1885. He practiced law and was elected to the House of Representatives in 1902. Norris was an independent-minded Republican with strong ties to the Progressive wing of the party. He was eventually pressured to resign from the Republican Party in 1936 for supporting Franklin Roosevelt. A person of high principles and integrity, Norris is particularly known for his advocacy of democratic election reforms, the Tennessee Valley Authority, labor, and a progressive tax structure. ■

Introduction

In the United States, the idea of an inheritance tax goes back at least to the Revolutionary era. Thomas

Senator George W. Norris, Republican Senator to Nebraska, November 30, 1929. Norris was an advocate of a progressive tax system. AP/WIDE WORLD PHOTOS. REPRODUCED BY PERMISSION.

Paine, for example, advocated it. Paine, who opposed inherited political power of monarchy in *Common Sense,* used a similar logic against hereditary wealth. While some American egalitarians agreed with Paine's arguments, in a society that held property rights in such high esteem, it is little wonder that the inheritance tax had little appeal to Americans.

At the federal level, the inheritance tax was briefly employed to help fund both the Civil War (1861–1865) and the Spanish-American War (1898). As the country became more industrialized, people of great wealth—Rockefeller, Morgan, and Vanderbilt, for example—seemed to dominate all aspects of American life and were in a position to continue that influence generation after generation. Many thought it was unfair that a handful of people could amass and retain such enormous wealth while wretched poverty was evident in the growing cities.

In these circumstances, limiting the transfer of wealth from one generation to the next began to have considerable appeal. Some felt it was necessary to preserve a democratic society. For others an inheritance tax was seen as an effective way to finance the cost of government by taxing those who were both the most able to pay and who received the greatest financial benefit from society. People like Andrew Carnegie, who gave away much of his accumulated fortune, thought the inheritance tax was a way to enforce the obligation of the wealthy to distribute that wealth to the benefit of society at large.

For all of these reasons, the inheritance tax was increasingly supported by Progressive reformers who favored a graduated tax system in the decades prior to World War I (1914–1918). Their major achievement was the 16th Amendment to the Constitution. Passed in 1913, it gave the federal government the authority to "lay and collect taxes on income from whatever source derived."

The threat of war and the cost of rearmament stimulated a more substantial tax package in 1916. It included a significant graduated income tax scale and an estate tax, similar to one proposed by President Theodore Roosevelt in 1906. The estate tax was supplemented by a gift tax in 1918 to close a loophole that allowed taxpayers to transfer wealth prior to death and thus avoid the estate tax.

Significance

The Depression revealed in stark terms a great failing of the American system: an inequitable distribution of that wealth. In response, there were a wide variety of ideas put forth to correct this imbalance. Some proposals, like Huey Long's "Share the Wealth" program, were revolutionary in consequence. By comparison, the inheritance tax, advocated by Senator Norris in the attached speech, was much less threatening.

Faced with the dual concerns of funding relief efforts and implementing basic reform, it was, perhaps, inevitable that the inheritance tax would be a part of Roosevelt's finance program. One part of that program, passed in August 1935, was the Revenue Act of 1935 (the so-called Wealth Tax Act). It included an aggressive 71 percent income tax rate for the highest income brackets as well as gift and estate provisions that in 1936 generated increased tax receipts from this source by nearly ten times the amount collected in 1933.

Although far more aggressive than previous tax measures—and necessary to help fund the various New Deal relief programs—Roosevelt's tax proposals could not seriously be called a radical wealth redistribution plan. The very wealthy paid more tax, to be sure, but it did very little to alter the relative position of the wealthy on the economic ladder.

Driven by the financial obligations of World War II (1939–1945) and the Cold War, estate and gift taxes remained high. It was not until 1981 that a serious move was made to permanently reduce the gift and estate tax rates. As a part of President Ronald Reagan's tax reform program, gift and estate tax rates were gradually reduced. Even under Reagan's plan the estate tax rate in the highest brackets remained at 50 percent. President Clinton reversed this trend, but the elimination of the estate tax was an important element of George W. Bush's tax reform bill passed in 2001.

Primary Source

"Redistribution of Wealth" [excerpt]

SYNOPSIS: Senator Norris delivered this speech on February 15, 1935, at the University of Nebraska. He could have delivered it at any time in his forty-year political career. Long an advocate of a progressive tax system, Norris found that the nation in 1935 was more prepared than ever to support his ideas.

An inheritance tax, as used in this discussion, means any tax which takes effect upon the death of the owner of the property taxed. . . . It is the least burdensome of any tax that has been devised by the mind of man. . . . It is a tax that cannot be shifted or successfully avoided. . . . It is a tax that is inexpensive to collect. . . . It is neither a hardship nor an injustice to beneficiaries. . . .

It has been in comparatively recent years, only, that a progressive inheritance tax has been advocated. . . . This movement has gained great headway because in the last 40 or 50 years people have begun to realize that the amassing of large fortunes in the hands of a relatively few individuals was detrimental to society in general.

In Revolutionary days, a millionaire was unknown. Today, they almost block the sidewalks. We are entering now upon a new class—the billionaire class. Economists and other students of government now realize that one of the great dangers to our civilization is the control by a few men of untold millions of property. Today, there is but little doubt in the minds of thinking people that the redistribution of wealth is a necessity, if we wish to preserve our civilization. This does not mean we should take the property of A and give it to B. It only means the taking of money from the estates of the very wealthy, where it can perform no real service for humanity, and the giving of it, in form of taxes, to all the people, from whom it was originally taken, and under whose laws it was accumulated.

We are rapidly becoming a nation of hired men; we are very rapidly drifting in the direction of wealth concentrated to such a degree that its evil effects are already influencing our economic world. Justice Brandeis, in a dissenting opinion in *Liggett v. Lee,* 288 U. S. Reports, page 566, has truly said:

> Other writers have shown that coincident with the growth of these giant corporations, there has occurred a marked concentration of individual wealth and that the resulting disparity in incomes is a major cause of the existing depression.

In 1929, about five hundred persons had more than one billion dollars, net income. This was practically the same as the gross, aggregate market value of all the wheat and all the cotton in the United States, grown by more than two million wheat and cotton farmers in 1930. Does any one believe that a free country can continue to exist under such unequal and unfair conditions? Here we have the net income in one year of five hundred persons equal to the total value of the two greatest farm crops produced in one year by more than two million farmers. This shows, in reality, that the net income of five hundred men, who for the most part neither "toil nor spin," is equal to the gross income of more than two million men, who by their unpaid toil feed and clothe the nation. It does not require an expert to see that such a condition cannot continue indefinitely, without bringing disaster.

The danger to our civilization from the accumulation of wealth was clearly foreseen by President Theodore Roosevelt. . . .

In an official message to Congress, December 4, 1906, President Theodore Roosevelt said:

> There is every reason why, when next our system of taxation is revised, the national government should impose a graduated inheritance tax, and, if possible, a graduated income tax. The man of great wealth owes a peculiar obligation to the state, because he derives special advantages from the mere existence of government. Not only should he recognize this obligation in the way he leads his daily life and in the way he earns and spends his money, but it should also be recognized by the way in which he pays for the protection the state gives him. . . .

There is a limit beyond which wealth can do no good, can bring no comfort or happiness. If you are possessed of a hundred million dollars, and I have only one million, there is nothing in this world which will bring you any happiness, contentment or pleasure that you can purchase, which I cannot also purchase, without any hardship, or without any injury to my estate. What, then is the good of this immense fortune, of this useless wealth? If money can do nothing to increase human contentment or happiness, then it is but worthless paper. It is true that you, with your hundred millions, might be more able to control legislatures, to control the selection of judges for our federal courts, to control conventions of the great parties, and to make yourself felt from one end of the country to the other, in the control of the election of public officials. But is it not conceded, to begin with, that such power is an evil? Do we not have to admit, at the outset, that one of the dangers to our country is the secret control of its officials by the use of such enormous blocks of wealth? Is it any injustice or injury to the man who is possessed of a large fortune, if, when he dies, after allowing an exemption sufficient to keep his dependents for life, the State then takes a goodly portion of the balance in the form of taxation, and returns it, in this way, to the public? Does such a man owe nothing to the government under whose laws he was permitted to amass such an enormous amount of wealth, and can it possibly be an injustice to him, if after he has used it during his lifetime, at his death, when it can under no condition be of any further value or use to him, it is taken for the benefit of society-at-large?

Conceive, if you can, that the property of the country was all owned by one man. Would it not follow that the rest of us would be his slaves? Would it not follow that he would be supreme—that he could fix the conditions under which all the rest of us would be permitted to even exist? I know this is an exaggerated illustration, because long before that time would arrive the country would be faced with a revolution such as the world has never known. But it is not necessary that one man should own all the property. Through combinations, especially through the organization of corporations, thousands of men may combine their wealth and do combine their wealth. This combination is controlled by one head, and, through the instrumentality of such a monopoly, reaching out with slimy fingers into every community and into every municipality of the land, a wonderful power is exerted over public officials, over business institutions, over political conventions, and, in a thousand different ways, the control of the country may be taken over and is being taken over today by combinations of great wealth.

In laying a tax upon property, it is always well to consider how much the owner of the property will have left, after he has paid the tax. The present federal inheritance tax is, unless we examine it carefully, somewhat misleading. It levies at increased rates greater burdens upon excessive portions of the estate. Its highest levy today, for instance, is a rate of sixty per cent on the excess of the estate over ten million dollars. But if you consider an estate of ten million dollars, at the various rates provided by law for the different brackets, you will find that the estate pays less than forty-five per cent upon the entire estate. Thus, an estate worth ten million dollars would have left, after all exemptions are allowed nearly six million dollars untaxed. Is not that a liberal amount? Would such a law do an injury to anyone? Would there be any danger of the widow or children going to the poorhouse, with an untaxed estate of six million dollars? Is there anything in this life in the way of comfort or even luxury that the beneficiaries under such an estate could not purchase, without any strain whatever upon their finances?

It must be remembered, in this illustration, that only the excess above ten million dollars is taxed at sixty per cent. If this excess were taxed at ninety per cent, as it should be, no possible injury could come to any beneficiary or to any individual, and such a tax would go a long way toward relieving society from the injury and the dangers that come from the gigantic and useless accumulation of wealth. . . .

We have the wealthiest country in the world, and yet one-third of our people are in beggary and want. We have millions of starving who must be fed. Whether we like it or not, we must raise billions in taxes. Are we, in this dire predicament, so foolish as to think that the money can be raised by taxing the beggar? Millions of others of our people, who are barely existing, will be taxed into starvation, if we increase the burden, already upon them. Can the men who have gathered together the fabulous riches of the wealthiest country on earth now defy the government to take a portion of their ill-gotten gains, after they are gone? . . .

Is there anything unjust or unfair that men of great wealth should be prohibited from passing on intact great fortunes which would result in such injury to society? When we make one billionaire, we make millions of paupers. Whenever a man is put in that class, we create an army of hungry children, ragged mothers, and broken-hearted fathers. We drag down our civilization to a point where, eventually, it must fail. If we would have a united country, we must have a country of homes. We must bring comfort and pleasure to the fireside. We must establish the home as the unit and in it must be maintained the comforts and pleasures of life. This can only come about if we prevent the accumulation of all the property in the hands of a few. Such a condition would, in the end, bring about a form of human slavery more bitter, more aggravated, and more heinous than any which have ever afflicted humanity. We have no right to bring children into this world, unless, in the struggle of life, they are

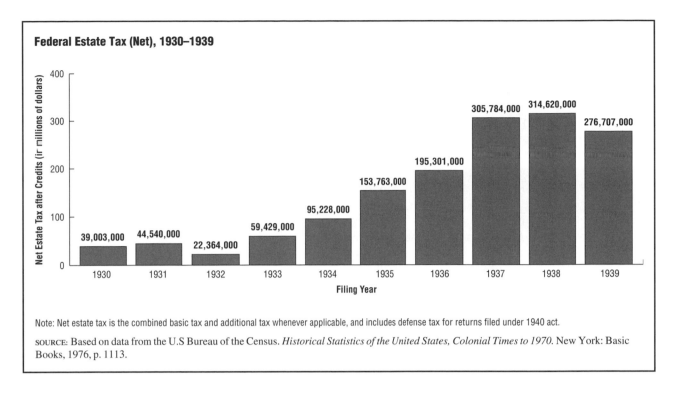

Federal Estate Tax (Net), 1930–1939

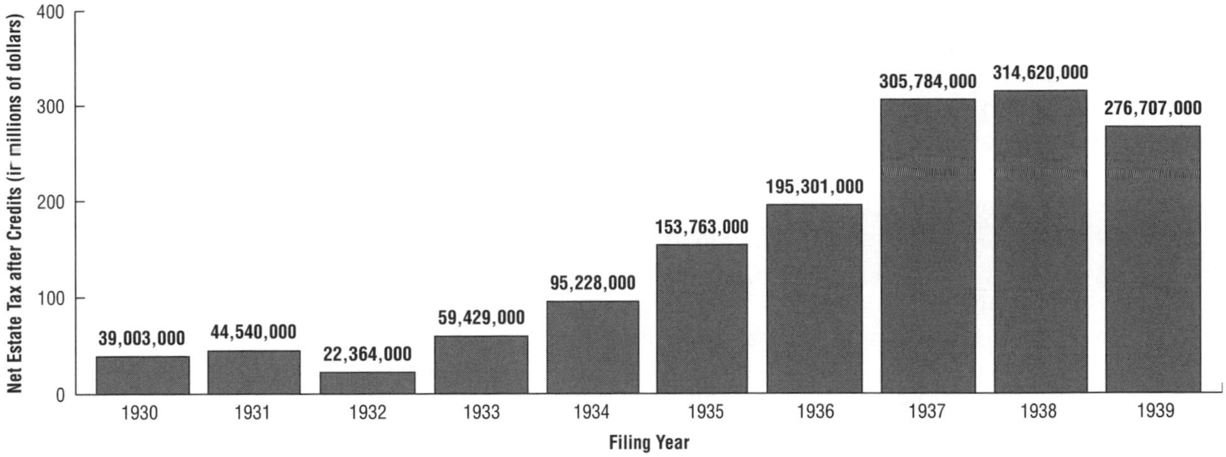

Note: Net estate tax is the combined basic tax and additional tax whenever applicable, and includes defense tax for returns filed under 1940 act.

SOURCE: Based on data from the U.S Bureau of the Census. *Historical Statistics of the United States, Colonial Times to 1970.* New York: Basic Books, 1976, p. 1113.

to be given a fair, honest chance to enjoy the pleasures and comforts which any civilization worthy of the name should provide. A society which is worth having, which is worth fighting for, and which is worth struggling to maintain, must be one in which the happiness of individuals, the comfort of the people, and the well-being of all men, is the object to be sought, and not the mad desire to obtain gold. In such a civilization, the necessity for unemployment insurance, or for the old-age pension, would to a great extent disappear. Such things, desirable in themselves, and which a civilized society should provide, would be confined for the most part to instances in which accidents of various kinds have brought affliction to worthy people for whom society must provide.

I make no complaint against any man, because of his wealth. Many of the noblest characters in history, not only of the past, but of the present, are men who have honestly acquired great wealth. Many of these men are true philanthropists. They do the best they can to handle this burden of immense weath in a way which will bring happiness and comfort to millions of their fellow men. But a progressive inheritance tax which would break up even fortunes of this kind carries no hardship. An inheritance tax law can be drawn in such a way as to permit the owner of the property during his life to provide for its disposition in bequests so small as to avoid the payment of the tax, altogether, but even such a law does not bring the justness and fairness which would come from a law which turned the property over to the government to be used for the happiness and comfort of all the people, instead of for a select few. No honest man can complain, if, after he has been permitted to provide for those near and dear to him, the excess of his estate is, at his death, given to the State under whose laws and under whose protection he has been allowed to accumulate it.

On the other hand, many large estates have been gathered together, sometimes by accident, sometimes by inheritance, and sometimes by other methods in which the labor, and the toil, and often the ability, of the owner has cut no figure whatever. Some of them have been accumulated by questionable means, some by dishonest and illegal means, and some by the inhuman oppression of those who earn their scanty living by toil and the sweat of their faces.

There is nothing sacred about a fortune gathered together by an Insull, who robs untold millions of honest investors of their hard-earned savings, and who, under the guise of law, takes pennies from the poor to create a fortune large enough to bribe a king. Other fortunes have been accumulated by men who, with other people's money have bought worthless stocks and bonds and then sold them at fabulous prices to thousands of honest men and women, scattered all over the land. There is nothing sacred about the fortune of a Doheny or a Sinclair, who with their ill-gotten gains, bribe high officials of the federal government and rob the nation of untold wealth, hidden in a Tea Pot Dome or an Elk Hills. And who can measure the evil influence upon the minds of common citizens when such representatives of great wealth steal from the poor and needy, rob the nation of its natural resources, and then are permitted to go scot free? It brings the blush of shame to the cheek of every patriotic citizen when he is compelled to admit that our criminal laws punish only the crimes of those who are poor, and furnish avenues and loopholes of escape for the criminal whose stealings amount to millions. It shocks the confidence of the ordinary citizen in his government, when he realizes that his country has permitted the building up of great fortunes, but has provided no way whereby the owner of such a fortune can be punished for his inhuman crimes. How long can a civilization continue to sustain in luxury a class of people who are above the law? Such conditions bring contempt for the law and they breed sentiments of disloyalty which will ultimately weaken and even destroy the hands which hold the scales of justice. The history of the past is written in burning letters upon the very canopy of Heaven, under the immutable law of God. Such a condition cannot indefinitely continue. . . .

It will do no good to heap abuse upon the heads of those who have the courage to tell the truth. The cry of Socialism, Anarchy, Communism, heaped upon the heads of those who are moved by the love they have for their fellow men to raise the danger signal will not stay the disaster which must follow, unless heed is taken of Nature's warning sign. Along the broad road of human progress stand the tombstones of nations that are dead because their people failed to heed the warning and rushed on in their godless luxury and worship of the Golden Calf. Anarchy cannot survive in a land of contented people. Communism is the result of oppression and injustice. Governments are destroyed, and civilizations are overthrown, when the accumulations of wealth in a few hands has brought starvation and misery into the land. There is no escape from the penalty when Nature's laws are violated. Such causes are tried in a court not controlled by any class and in its judgments wealth possesses no advantage over poverty. Hoarded wealth cannot prevent Nature's decrees. The judgment may be postponed, the stream may be impeded by artificial means, but the rising waters will eventually overflow any barriers made by man, and the greater the obstruction and the higher the water must rise to reach the crest, the greater will be the damage and devastation when eventually the floods come.

I speak not in anger, but in a spirit of friendship, when I warn hoarders of gold against the certain disaster which must follow such a course. I would not take away any legitimate happenings, comfort or even luxury that comes to men of great wealth. I would give to you and yours the full and legitimate fruits of your labors and the enjoyment during your life and the lives of those dependent upon you of all the money that can be usefully used or enjoyed. But I would take the balance to relieve the hardships, the sacrifices, and the suffering of your less fortunate brothers. Search your own hearts. Drive out of your soul that insatiable and unreasonable desire for gold. Let your hearts be filled with love for mankind, with a realization that those who love their fellow men are most beloved of God. Let equality reign for all classes of people in our tribunals of justice. Let the homes of those who produce the food that gives life to all of us be owned by those who till the soil and who constitute the foundation bulwark of our civilization. Let those homes be free from mortgage. Let the hideous face of desperation and want vanish forever. Let those who toil in our shops and in our factories and those who work at desks in our counting rooms be paid a living wage. Let the innocent little children in those homes and in all other homes in the land be clothed in comfort and placed beyond the reach of crushing misery, waste, and care. Let there be inscribed above every fireside in the land the burning words of the Lowly Nazarine—

> Suffer the little children to come unto me, and forbid them not, for of such is the Kingdom of Heaven.

Further Resources

BOOKS

Leff, Mark H. *The Limits of Symbolic Reform: The New Deal and Taxation, 1933–1939.* New York: Cambridge University Press, 1984.

Lowitt, Richard. *George W. Norris: The Persistence of a Progressive, 1913–1933.* Urbana: University of Illinois Press, 1971.

———. *George W. Norris: The Triumph of a Progressive, 1933–1944.* Urbana: University of Illinois Press, 1978.

Norris, George W. *Fighting Liberal: The Autobiography of George W. Norris.* Lincoln: University of Nebraska Press, 1992.

The National Labor Relations Act

Law

By: Senator Robert F. Wagner

Date: July 5, 1935

Source: *The National Labor Relations Act,* 49 Stat. 449, July 5, 1935. Reprinted in *The National Labor Relations Act: Should It Be Amended?* Julia E. Johnsen, comp. New York: H.W. Wilson, 1940, 355–356, 357, 359–360, 361–362, 363–365.

About the Author: Robert F. Wagner (1877–1953) was the chief architect of the National Labor Relations Act (NLRA) when he was representing New York in the Senate as a Democrat. German-born, Wagner became active in Democratic politics early in his career. He served as a justice of the New York Supreme Court before his election to the U.S. Senate in 1926. A strong supporter of labor, Wagner was a key congressional leader supporting the New Deal programs of Franklin Roosevelt. In addition to the NLRA, Wagner sponsored and helped draft such key legislation as the *National Industrial Recovery Act* (1933), the *Federal Emergency Relief Administration Bill* (1933), the *Social Security Act,* and the *Wagner-Steagall Act* that created the U.S. Housing Authority in 1938. ■

Senator Robert F. Wagner gives a speech over the radio on April 12, 1937. His pro-union bill became the National Labor Relations (or Wagner) Act in 1935. AP/WIDE WORLD PHOTOS. REPRODUCED BY PERMISSION.

Introduction

Since the late 1800s, unions representing skilled trades, primarily associated with the American Federation of Labor, had been reasonably successful. These skilled workers had sufficient bargaining power to force recognition of employers and enforce collective bargaining agreements. The situation for unskilled (industrial) workers was much different.

Employers in industries such as steel and automobile manufacturing were able to defeat every attempt on the part of unskilled workers to organize. Whereas skilled workers were able use their needed knowledge and skills to partially offset employer financial strength, unskilled and semi-skilled workers lacked that leverage. Employers could easily find unskilled workers to replace those who showed any inclination to organize.

The Depression generated a more sympathetic view toward the plight of labor. Previously unions, particularly of unskilled workers, were widely regarded as radical and un-American—opposed to the "rugged individualism" that was so much a part of the American ideal. The Depression convinced many Americans that individuals were not always in control of their economic destiny. Abject poverty in the midst of plenty forced the conclusion that collective action might be necessary to bring about a more equitable distribution of wealth.

The New Deal capitalized on the changing attitude toward labor. The *National Industrial Recovery Act,* a cornerstone of the early New Deal enacted in 1933, included a provision that guaranteed workers the right to collective bargaining. While Roosevelt was not strongly pro-union, he clearly recognized the need for workers to be able to offset the power of employers and the value unions had in raising wages.

In May 1935, the Supreme Court declared the NRA unconstitutional. Senator Wagner quickly found the necessary support, including Franklin Roosevelt, for his bill. On July 5, 1935, over the vehement opposition of business leaders and industrialists, the *National Labor Relations Act* (often called the Wagner Act) passed. This bill protected the rights of workers to form unions and set up guidelines to ensure that employers could not violate those rights. It also created the National Labor Relations Board for the purpose of ensuring compliance with the act. It has served in this capacity since that time.

Significance

The Wagner Act was a turning point in American labor history. For the first time the authority of the federal government was clearly behind workers, supporting their right to collective bargaining and to form unions. It was a catalyst to increased labor agitation. Union membership grew from 3.7 million (mostly skilled workers) in 1935 to 7.3 million in 1940. Most of this growth was among unskilled workers. By 1950, union membership was nearly 15 million.

Success, however, did not come overnight. Despite the Wagner Act, employers continued to fight unionization efforts. In part, this reflected a confidence in their ability to "divide and conquer" workers as they had in the past. In part, it was in the belief that the Supreme Court would declare the Wagner Act unconstitutional.

The first setback to employers came when the Supreme Court found the Wagner Act to be constitutional. Bolstered by this, labor became more confident. Beginning in late 1937, a long series of labor actions, highlighted by the appearance of a new tactic—the sit-down strike—resulted in unprecedented union successes by the middle of 1938. Labor had won.

Primary Source

The National Labor Relations Act [excerpt]

SYNOPSIS: This extract from the Wagner Act outlines the purposes of the legislation. It also defines unfair labor practices and describes, in part, the powers of the National Labor Relations Board. The Act remained as presented here until modified over the protests of labor—and the veto of President Harry Truman—in the 1947 *Taft-Hartley Act.*

An Act

To diminish the causes of labor disputes burdening or obstructing interstate and foreign commerce, to create a National Labor Relations Board, and for other purposes.

Be it enacted by the Senate and House of Representatives of the United States of America in Congress assembled,

Findings and Policy

Section 1. The denial by employers of the right of employees to organize and the refusal by employers to accept the procedure of collective bargaining lead to strikes and other forms of industrial strife or unrest, which have the intent or the necessary effect of burdening or obstructing commerce by (a) impairing the efficiency, safety, or operation of the instrumentalities of commerce; (b) occurring in the current of commerce; (c) materially affecting, restraining, or controlling the flow of raw materials or manufactured or processed goods from or into the channels of commerce, or the prices of such materials or goods in commerce; or (d) causing diminution of employment and wages in such volume as substantially to impair or disrupt the market for goods flowing from or into the channels of commerce.

The inequality of bargaining power between employees who do not possess full freedom of association or actual liberty of contract, and employers who are organized in the corporate or other forms of ownership association substantially burdens and affects the flow of commerce, and tends to aggravate recurrent business depressions, by depressing wage rates and the purchasing power of wage earners in industry and by preventing the stabilization of competitive wage rates and working conditions within and between industries.

Experience has proved that protection by law of the right of employees to organize and bargain collectively safeguards commerce from injury, impairment, or interruption, and promotes the flow of commerce by removing certain recognized sources of industrial strife and unrest, by encouraging practices fundamental to the friendly adjustment of industrial disputes arising out of differences as to wages, hours, or other working conditions, and by restoring equality of bargaining power between employers and employees.

It is hereby declared to be the policy of the United States to eliminate the causes of certain substantial obstructions to the free flow of commerce and to mitigate and eliminate these obstructions when they have occurred by encouraging the practice and procedure of collective bargaining and by protecting the exercise by workers of full freedom of association, self-organization, and designation of representatives of their own choosing, for the purpose of negotiating the terms and conditions of their employment or other mutual aid or protection. . . .

National Labor Relations Board

Sec. 3. (a) There is hereby created a board, to be known as the "National Labor Relations Board" (hereinafter referred to as the "Board"), which shall be composed of three members, who shall be appointed by the President, by and with the advice and consent of the Senate. . . .

Sec. 6. (a) The Board shall have authority from time to time to make, amend, and rescind such rules and regulations as may be necessary to carry out the provisions of this Act. Such rules and regulations shall be effective upon publication in the manner which the Board shall prescribe.

Rights of Employees

Sec. 7. Employees shall have the right to self-organization, to form, join, or assist labor organizations, to bargain collectively through representatives of their own choosing, and to engage in concerted activities, for the purpose of collective bargaining or other mutual aid or protection.

Sec. 8. It shall be an unfair practice for an employer—

(1) To interfere with, restrain, or coerce employees in the exercise of the rights guaranteed in section 7.

(2) To dominate or interfere with the formation or administration of any labor organization or contribute financial or other support to it: *Provided,* That subject to rules and regulations made and published by the Board pursuant to section 6 (a), an employer shall not be prohibited from permitting employees to confer with him during working hours without loss of time or pay.

(3) By discrimination in regard to hire or tenure of employment or any term or condition of employment to encourage or discourage membership in any labor organization: *Provided,* That nothing in this Act, or in the *National Industrial Recovery Act* (U. S. C., Supp. VII, title 15, secs. 701–712), as amended from time to time, or in any code or agreement approved or prescribed thereunder, or in any other statute of the United States, shall preclude an employer from making an agreement with a labor organization (not established, maintained, or assisted by any action defined in this Act as an unfair labor practice) to require as a condition of employment membership therein, if such labor organization is the representative of the employees as provided in section 9 (a), in the appropriate collective bargain unit covered by such agreement when made.

(4) To discharge or otherwise discriminate against an employee because he has filed charges or given testimony under this Act.

(5) To refuse to bargain collectively with the representatives of his employees, subject to the provisions of section 9 (a).

Representatives and Elections

Sec. 9. (a) Representatives designated or selected for the purposes of collective bargaining by the majority of the employees in a unit appropriate for such purposes, shall be the exclusive representatives of all the employees in such unit for the purposes of collective bargaining in respect to rates of pay, wages, hours of employment, or other conditions of employment: *Provided,* That any individual employee or a group of employees shall have the right at any time to present grievances to their employer.

(b) The Board shall decide in each case whether, in order to insure to employees the full benefit of their right to self-organization and to collective bargaining, and otherwise to effectuate the policies of this Act, the unit appropriate for the purposes of collective bargaining shall be the employer unit, craft unit, plant unit, or subdivision thereof.

(c) Whenever a question affecting commerce arises concerning the representation of employees, the Board may investigate such controversy and certify to the parties, in writing, the name or names of the representatives that have been designated or selected. In any such investigation, the Board shall provide for an appropriate hearing upon due notice, either in conjunction with a proceeding under section 10 or otherwise, and may take a secret ballot of employees, or utilize any other suitable method to ascertain such representatives. . . .

Presentation of Unfair Labor Practices

Sec. 10. (a) The Board is empowered, as hereinafter provided, to prevent any person from engaging in any unfair labor practice (listed in section 8) affecting commerce. This power shall be exclusive, and shall not be affected by any other means of adjustment or prevention that has been or may be established by agreement, code, law, or otherwise.

(b) Whenever it is charged that any person has engaged in or is engaging in any such unfair labor practice, the Board, or any agent or agency designated by the Board for such purposes, shall have power to issue and cause to be served upon such person complaint stating the charges in that respect, and containing notice of hearing before the Board or a member thereof, or before a designated agent or agency, at a place therein fixed, not less than five days after the serving of said complaint. Any such complaint may be amended by the member, agent, or agency conducting the hearing or the Board in its discretion at any time prior to the issuance of an order based thereon. The person so complained of shall have the right to file an answer to the original or amended complaint and to appear in person or otherwise and give testimony at the place and time fixed in the complaint. In the discretion of the member, agent or agency conducting the hearing or the Board, any other person may be allowed to intervene in the said proceeding and to present testimony. In any such proceeding the rules of evidence prevailing in courts of law or equity shall not be controlling.

(c) The testimony taken by such member, agent or agency or the Board shall be reduced to writing and filed with the Board. Thereafter, in its discretion, the Board upon notice may take further testimony or hear argument. If upon all the testimony taken the Board shall be of the opinion that any person named in the complaint has engaged in or is engaging in any such unfair labor practice, then the Board shall state its findings of fact and shall issue and cause to be served on such person an order requiring such person to cease and desist from such unfair labor practice, and to take such affirmative action, including reinstatement of employees with or without back pay, as will effectuate the policies of this Act. Such order may further require such person to make reports from time to time showing the extent to which it has complied with the order. If upon all the testimony taken the Board shall be of the opinion that no person named in the complaint has engaged in or is engaging in any such unfair labor practice, then the Board shall state its findings of fact and shall issue an order dismissing the said complaint.

(d) Until a transcript of the record in a case shall have been filed in a court, as hereinafter provided, the Board may at any time, upon reasonable notice and in such manner as it shall deem proper, modify or set aside, in whole or in part, any finding or order made or issued by it. . . .

Investigatory Powers

Sec. 11. For the purpose of all hearings and investigations, which, in the opinion of the Board, are necessary and proper for the exercise of the powers vested in it by section 9 and section 10—

(1) The Board, or its duly authorized agents or agencies, shall at all reasonable times have access to, for the purpose of examination, and the right to copy any evidence of any person being investigated or proceeded against that relates to any matter under investigation or in question. Any member of the Board shall have power to issue subpenas requiring the attendance and testimony of witnesses and the production of any evidence that relates to any matter under investigation or in question, before the Board, its member, agent, or agency conducting the hearing or investigation. Any member of the Board, or any agent or agency designated by the Board for such purposes, may administer oaths and affirmations, examine witnesses, and receive evidence. Such attendance of witnesses and the production of such evidence may be required from any place in the United States or any Territory or possession thereof, at any designated place of hearing.

(2) In case of contumacy or refusal to obey a subpena issued to any person, any District Court of the United States or the United States courts of any Territory or possession, or the Supreme Court of the District of Columbia, within the jurisdiction of which the inquiry is carried on or within the jurisdiction of which said person guilty of contumacy or refusal to obey is found or resides or transacts business, upon application by the Board shall have jurisdiction to issue to such person an order requiring such person to appear before the Board, its member agent, or agency, there to produce evidence if so ordered, or there to give testimony touching the matter under investigation or in question; and any failure to obey such order of the court may be punished by said court as a contempt thereof.

(3) No person shall be excused from attending and testifying or from producing books, records, correspondence, documents, or other evidence in obedience to the subpena of the Board, on the ground that the testimony or evidence required of him may tend to incriminate him or subject him to a penalty or forfeiture; but no individual shall be prosecuted or subjected to any penalty or forfeiture for or on account of any transaction, matter, or thing concerning which he is compelled, after having claimed his privilege against self-incrimination, to testify or produce evidence, except that such individual so testifying shall not be exempt from prosecution and punishment for perjury committed in so testifying.

(4) Complaints, orders, and other process and papers of the Board, its member, agent, or agency, may be served either personally or by registered mail or by telegraph or by leaving a copy thereof at the principal office or place of business of the person required to be served. The verified return by the individual so serving the same setting forth the manner of such service shall be proof of the same, and the return post office receipt or telegraph receipt therefor when registered and mailed or telegraphed as aforesaid shall be proof of service of the same. Witnesses summoned before the Board, its member, agent, or agency, shall be paid the same fees and mileage that are paid witnesses in the courts of the United States, and witnesses whose depositions are taken and the persons taking the same shall severally be entitled to the same fees as are paid for like services in the courts of the United States.

(5) All process of any court to which application may be made under this Act may be served in the judicial district wherein the defendant or other person required to be served resides or may be found.

(6) The several departments and agencies of the Government, when directed by the President, shall furnish the Board, upon its request, all records, pa-

pers, and information in their possession relating to any matter before the Board.

Sec. 12. Any person who shall willfully resist, prevent, impede, or interfere with any member of the Board or any of its agents or agencies in the performance of duties pursuant to this Act shall be punished by a fine of not more than $5,000 or by imprisonment for not more than one year, or both.

Limitations

Sec. 13. Nothing in this Act shall be construed so as to interfere with or impede or diminish in any way the right to strike.

Further Resources

BOOKS

Bernstein, Irving. *A Caring Society: The New Deal, the Worker, and the Great Depression; A History of the American Worker, 1933–1941.* Boston: Houghton Mifflin, 1985.

Cronon, Edmund David, ed. *Labor and the New Deal.* Chicago: Rand McNally, 1963.

Leuchtenburg, William E. *Franklin D. Roosevelt and the New Deal, 1932–1940.* New York: Harper & Row, 1963.

Progress in Michigan

Newsletter

By: Works Progress Administration

Date: December 1935

Source: Works Progress Administration. *Progress in Michigan* 1, no. 2, December 1935, 1, 8–11.

About the Organization: The passage of the Federal Emergency Relief Appropriations Act in 1935 allocated nearly $5 billion for work relief. The goal of the Roosevelt administration was to create employment rather than rely on direct relief to aid the unemployed. The Works Progress Administration (WPA), which produced this pamphlet, was created to administer those funds, finding appropriate projects upon which to employ millions of workers. ■

Introduction

Administration of the WPA was placed under the control of Harry Hopkins. Funds were allocated to states. They were responsible for identifying worthy projects and providing some of the funding, often as little as 5 percent. The balance was provided by the WPA.

In the first six months of the program, the state of Michigan was allocated $35 million. It was the responsibility of Harry L. Pierson, Michigan's WPA Administrator, to develop project ideas, arrange funding, and monitor project status. Priority was given to labor-intensive activities that required minimal capital investment. Given that WPA projects were not to conflict with either the private sector or with existing government agencies, creating meaningful work projects was often a challenge.

Michigan was one of the states hardest hit by the Depression. The automobile industry, by far the state's most important industry, was devastated. Automobile production dropped from 4.5 million in 1929 to just more than 1 million in 1932. The supplier base that provided the auto industry with parts, machinery, and raw materials was hit with equal force. The resulting unemployment was staggering.

In addition, the mining industry in Michigan's Upper Peninsula was hit very hard. As manufacturing plants curtailed operations, raw material orders dried up and the iron and copper mines in northern Michigan simply closed down. Thousands were laid off with no alternate employment available.

Significance

The activity of the WPA in Michigan is representative of that in other states. Road construction and repair was a major activity. This included building bridges and eliminating thousands of at-grade railroad crossings. Sidewalks were built in towns and cities across the state. (The sidewalk in front of the writer's present house was built by the WPA.) There was considerable effort to improve aviation in the state by the construction of airfields and hangars. Local communities built a variety of public buildings, schools, parks, swimming pools, and playgrounds. Sewage treatment and water purification plants along with sewer and water lines were constructed. Flood-control programs were undertaken.

The tourist industry, of particular importance to Michigan, received a considerable boost. WPA workers built cabins and campgrounds, improved state parks, constructed bathing beaches, laid out scenic drives, and built marinas and golf courses. A major expansion of the Detroit Zoological Park was among the WPA projects, as well as renovation of historic sites.

In addition, the Civilian Conservation Corps (CCC), created in 1933, fell under the control of the WPA. Among other activities, the one hundred thousand young men who served in Michigan's CCC planted nearly 500 million trees, cut thousands of miles of fire trails, built five hundred bridges, and fought hundreds of forest fires.

The most important result of the WPA was putting the unemployed to work. By December 1935, Michigan had employed ninety thousand people on more than one thousand WPA projects. These projects were funded by an initial WPA grant of $38 million covering the first six months of the program. Nearly a third of this money was earmarked for road construction.

WORKS PROGRESS ADMINISTRATION

PROGRESS — Christmas Greetings

IN MICHIGAN

FIRST DISTRICT EDITION

FIRST DISTRICT EDITION

HARRY LYNN PIERSON - ADMINISTRATOR

VOL. 1 NO. 2 — DECEMBER - 1935 — PUBLISHED MONTHLY

4,550 NOW EMPLOYED BY WPA

ERECTING GRAVEL CRUSHER AT NEWBERRY

ALL RELIEF WORKERS EMPLOYED

On December 1, 1935, the Works Progress Administration put an end to "the dole" in Michigan.

90,000 family heads were at work or had been summoned to work from relief rolls.

President Roosevelt's order: "To provide useful work for every able-bodied and destitute worker now on relief" had been carried out on schedule.

These 90,000 men and women, transformed from welfare dependents into family providers, are employed on approximately 1,200 WPA projects throughout the State and are receiving approximately $1,000,000 a week in security wages.

State Administrator Harry L. Pierson announced jobs and funds have been apportioned to the eight districts of the State as follows:

Dist.	Workers	Projects
1	4,554	$1,513,455
2	2,702	1,319,000
3	10,474	3,260,000
4	25,000	12,519,275
5	9,013	5,970,880
6	14,880	4,104,981
7	14,242	6,488,673
8	9,181	3,195,359
TOTALS	90,046	38,371,623

SECURITY WAGES TOTAL $200,000 A MONTH

CHEBOYGAN--4,550 men and women removed with their families from relief rolls and earning security wages amounting to nearly $200,000 a month.

This is the December picture of the WPA work-relief program in District 1, embracing 15 counties around the Straits of Mackinac.

Delayed in starting, the job drive in District 1 accelerated rapidly during November and produced work for every employable family head from welfare lists before December 1.

BENEFITS BY COUNTIES

On Monday, December 2, District Director Richard A. Lawson, reported 3,080 at work and jobs waiting for the remaining 1,474 assigned, but who had not yet reported for work.

WPA projects spread jobs and funds over the 15 counties as follows:

County	Workers	Projects
Alpena	326	$130,628
Antrim	273	94,098
Benzie	291	109,028
Charlevoix	376	177,775
Cheboygan	538	143,972
Chippewa	463	103,304
Emmet	325	135,227
Gd.Traverse	243	102,351
Leelanau	259	98,325
Luce	289	80,094
Mackinac	584	126,369
Montmorency	69	29,[illegible]80
Otsego	73	8,938
Presq.Isle	133	80,142
Schoolcraft	311	94,024

Primary Source

Progress in Michigan (1 OF 5)

SYNOPSIS: This page and subsequent pages are extracted from *Progress in Michigan,* a newsletter published by the Michigan WPA. It provided WPA workers and the general public with regular reports on specific projects and WPA issues. The articles included were published in the first twelve months of the WPA's existence and give a good view of the types of activities undertaken, the objectives of the WPA, and some of the problems encountered, as well as a steady stream of achievements.

WRITERS, ARTISTS, MUSICIANS GET JOBS

THREE PROJECTS NOW WELL UNDER WAY

Three projects providing jobs for unemployed writers, musicians and artists are well under way in Michigan.

The Writers' Project, under direction of Mrs. Cecil R. Chittenden, has requisitioned its quota of 200. Ninety-nine relief workers and 11 non-relief workers are employed in Wayne County. Twenty-nine relief and nine non-relief workers are employed out-state with requisitions made for 52 more.

More than two-thirds of the employees have had experience in writing and allied fields.

EMPLOY MUSICIANS

Guy Maier, regional director of the Musicians' Project has projects in operation or ready to start which will employ 222. In Grand Rapids 51 persons are employed in creating a traveling State orchestral and band library and 84 are in a symphony orchestra. Detroit has a band of 30 and Jackson a concert orchestra of 21. In addition 50 musicians in Wayne County will be placed in jazz bands, a string ensemble, copying, recreation and settlement projects.

In smaller communities projects will be started to improve rural church music.

SIXTY ARTISTS AVAILABLE

Clyde H. Burroughs, director of the Artists' Project has found that 50 or 60 artists are eligible for WPA jobs.

Ten artists from relief rolls, under 2 non-relief supervisors, are at work on four projects for schools in Wayne County. There are also projects in Grand Rapids, Flint and Kalamazoo.

Projects have also been planned in Washtenaw, Monroe and Oakland Counties and these will also be directed by Mr. Burroughs.

DIRECT WPA PROJECTS FOR WRITERS, ARTISTS AND MUSICIANS

Mrs. Cecil R. Chittenden, (top) is director of the Federal Writers' Project. Clyde H. Burroughs (center) is director of the Federal Artists' Project and Guy Maier is director of the Federal Musicians' Project.

KALAMAZOO CITY MANAGER GIVES HIGH PRAISE TO WPA PROJECTS

High praise of WPA projects was given by City Manager E.C. Ruts of Kalamazoo who attended the U.S. Conference of Mayors in Washington.

"WPA projects," he declared, "are accomplishing a lot of successful operations on very worth while public improvements. Our projects in Kalamazoo are distributed over the entire classification of programs mentioned by Harry L. Hopkins, Relief Administrator. It is a diversified program of different things essential to city life.

"I have no criticism to make of WPA work. It is an heroic effort on the part of those responsible for the care of the unemployed and indigent to meet a difficult and serious situation."

WOMEN MAKE BANDAGES

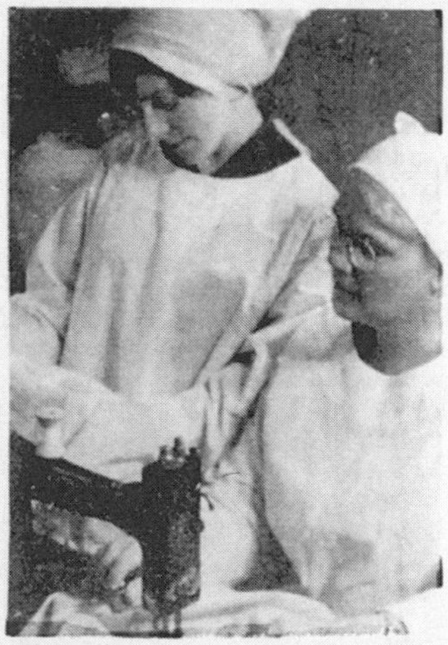

Jobs for 328 Detroit women have been provided in a $289,000 WPA allotment for the making of bandages, compacts and other types of surgical dressings. In the photo a Red Cross instructor is shown with a WPA woman worker.

Primary Source

Progress in Michigan (2 OF 5)

Page 8 of the WPA newsletter *Progress in Michigan*, Volume 1, Number 2. December 1935. REPRODUCED BY PERMISSION OF BENTLEY HISTORICAL LIBRARY, UNIVERSITY OF MICHIGAN.

WPA PROGRESS PAGE 9

101 PROJECTS FOR WOMEN UNDER WAY

9,754 REQUISITIONED BY WPA IN STATE

On Monday, December 2, all employable women with families had been requisitioned from relief rolls for jobs on WPA projects, Miss Catherine Murray, State Director, reported.

The women's program, slow in starting because of the stress in getting more than 80,000 men at work, picked up speed during the last half of November. On December 2, a total of 5,352 women were working and requisitions for a total of 9,754 had been issued throughout the State.

FIRST ESTIMATES HIGH

In the interval, the number of employable women had dropped from first estimates of 10,000 to approximately 7,000 so that requisitions far outnumbered the available workers.

Increased private employment was the greatest factor in reducing the employable load. But a considerable number of women were also found who could not leave their children and who must thus remain on relief rolls as unemployables.

EMPLOYMENT FIGURES

The record by districts on December 2:

Dist.	Requisitioned	Working
1	194	
2	145	145
3	1,110	912
4	4,196	1,493
5	601	450
6	943	447
7	1,700	1,380
8	875	525

One hundred one projects were under way. Most of them, outside Wayne County, were sewing projects designed to meet the clothing and household needs of families permanently on welfare rolls.

Largest women's project in the State is the rehabilitation of Detroit's public school books, employing 1,200.

Second largest, as the month began, was a huge sewing circle of 650 women in Grand Rapids.

Another project which may be duplicated elsewhere in the State is one in Detroit employing 300 women at the making of surgical dressings.

OFFERS TO WIELD SHOVEL FOR SICK FATHER

PATRICIA KELLY, DETROIT MISS, WON A WRITERS' PROJECT JOB AS THE RESULT OF HER OFFER TO TAKE HER SICK FATHER'S PLACE IN A PICK AND SHOVEL GANG. PHOTO SHOWS HOW SHE WOULD HANDLE A WHEELBARROW

WOULD TAKE SICK FATHER'S PICK AND SHOVEL JOB

It was the Irish in Patricia Kelly, 18, that won her a WPA job. Her father, who was ill had been called as a pick and shovel laborer. Patricia appeared in his stead and demanded his job. It developed that she is a good typist so a job was found for her in the Writers' Project.

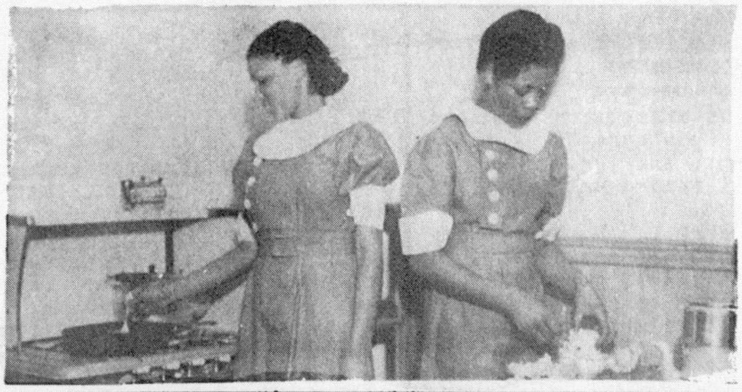

A "practice house" where young colored girls live for eight weeks and are thoroughly trained in domestic arts so that they may obtain positions in private homes is in operation at 307 Horton Ave., Detroit as a WPA project. Mrs. Elizabeth Evans is house mother. The girls are taught to cook, wash, iron, make beds, set table and the many other things a good housekeeper should know. They receive $6 a month.

Primary Source

Progress in Michigan (3 OF 5)

Page 9 of the WPA newsletter *Progress in Michigan*, Volume 1, Number 2. December 1935.

PAGE 10 **PROGRESS** WPA

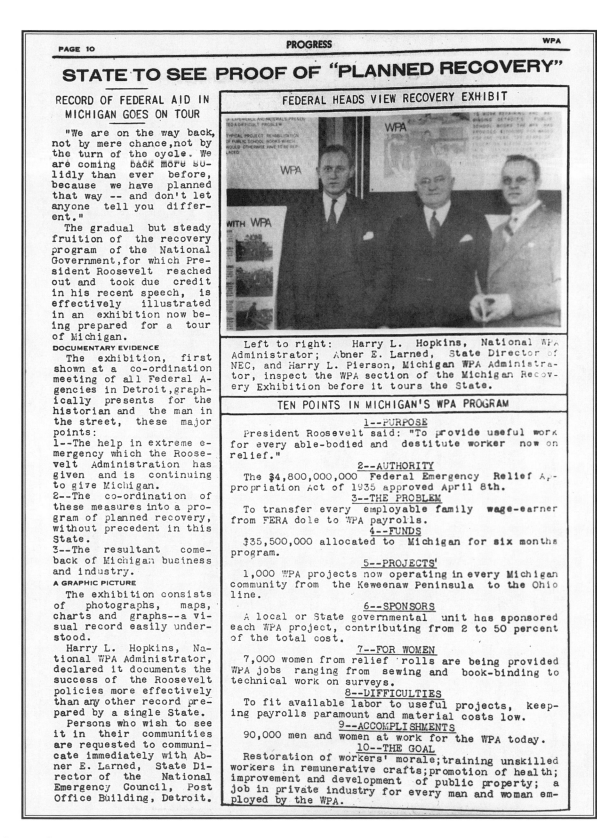

STATE TO SEE PROOF OF "PLANNED RECOVERY"

RECORD OF FEDERAL AID IN MICHIGAN GOES ON TOUR

"We are on the way back, not by mere chance, not by the turn of the cycle. We are coming back more solidly than ever before, because we have planned that way -- and don't let anyone tell you different."

The gradual but steady fruition of the recovery program of the National Government, for which President Roosevelt reached out and took due credit in his recent speech, is effectively illustrated in an exhibition now being prepared for a tour of Michigan.

DOCUMENTARY EVIDENCE

The exhibition, first shown at a co-ordination meeting of all Federal Agencies in Detroit, graphically presents for the historian and the man in the street, these major points:

1--The help in extreme emergency which the Roosevelt Administration has given and is continuing to give Michigan.

2--The co-ordination of these measures into a program of planned recovery, without precedent in this State.

3--The resultant comeback of Michigan business and industry.

A GRAPHIC PICTURE

The exhibition consists of photographs, maps, charts and graphs--a visual record easily understood.

Harry L. Hopkins, National WPA Administrator, declared it documents the success of the Roosevelt policies more effectively than any other record prepared by a single State.

Persons who wish to see it in their communities are requested to communicate immediately with Abner E. Larned, State Director of the National Emergency Council, Post Office Building, Detroit.

FEDERAL HEADS VIEW RECOVERY EXHIBIT

Left to right: Harry L. Hopkins, National WPA Administrator; Abner E. Larned, State Director of NEC, and Harry L. Pierson, Michigan WPA Administrator, inspect the WPA section of the Michigan Recovery Exhibition before it tours the State.

TEN POINTS IN MICHIGAN'S WPA PROGRAM

1--PURPOSE

President Roosevelt said: "To provide useful work for every able-bodied and destitute worker now on relief."

2--AUTHORITY

The $4,800,000,000 Federal Emergency Relief Appropriation Act of 1935 approved April 8th.

3--THE PROBLEM

To transfer every employable family wage-earner from FERA dole to WPA payrolls.

4--FUNDS

$35,500,000 allocated to Michigan for six months program.

5--PROJECTS

1,000 WPA projects now operating in every Michigan community from the Keweenaw Peninsula to the Ohio line.

6--SPONSORS

A local or State governmental unit has sponsored each WPA project, contributing from 2 to 50 percent of the total cost.

7--FOR WOMEN

7,000 women from relief rolls are being provided WPA jobs ranging from sewing and book-binding to technical work on surveys.

8--DIFFICULTIES

To fit available labor to useful projects, keeping payrolls paramount and material costs low.

9--ACCOMPLISHMENTS

90,000 men and women at work for the WPA today.

10--THE GOAL

Restoration of workers' morale; training unskilled workers in remunerative crafts; promotion of health; improvement and development of public property; a job in private industry for every man and woman employed by the WPA.

Primary Source

Progress in Michigan (4 OF 5)

Page 10 of the WPA newsletter *Progress in Michigan*, Volume 1, Number 2. December 1935.

WPA PROGRESS PAGE 11

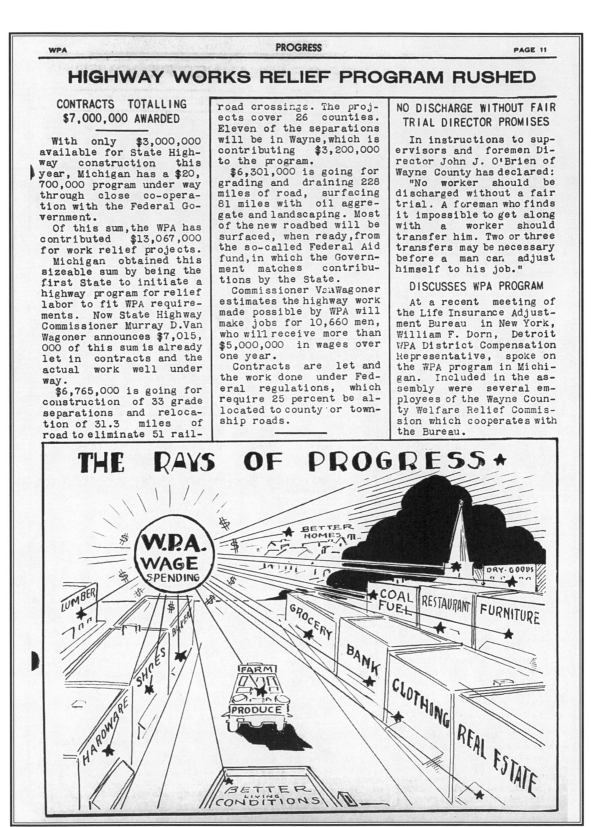

HIGHWAY WORKS RELIEF PROGRAM RUSHED

CONTRACTS TOTALLING $7,000,000 AWARDED

With only $3,000,000 available for State Highway construction this year, Michigan has a $20,700,000 program under way through close co-operation with the Federal Government.

Of this sum, the WPA has contributed $13,067,000 for work relief projects.

Michigan obtained this sizeable sum by being the first State to initiate a highway program for relief labor to fit WPA requirements. Now State Highway Commissioner Murray D. Van Wagoner announces $7,015,000 of this sum is already let in contracts and the actual work well under way.

$6,765,000 is going for construction of 33 grade separations and relocation of 31.3 miles of road to eliminate 51 railroad crossings. The projects cover 26 counties. Eleven of the separations will be in Wayne, which is contributing $3,200,000 to the program.

$6,301,000 is going for grading and draining 228 miles of road, surfacing 81 miles with oil aggregate and landscaping. Most of the new roadbed will be surfaced, when ready, from the so-called Federal Aid fund, in which the Government matches contributions by the State.

Commissioner VanWagoner estimates the highway work made possible by WPA will make jobs for 10,660 men, who will receive more than $5,000,000 in wages over one year.

Contracts are let and the work done under Federal regulations, which require 25 percent be allocated to county or township roads.

NO DISCHARGE WITHOUT FAIR TRIAL DIRECTOR PROMISES

In instructions to supervisors and foremen Director John J. O'Brien of Wayne County has declared:

"No worker should be discharged without a fair trial. A foreman who finds it impossible to get along with a worker should transfer him. Two or three transfers may be necessary before a man can adjust himself to his job."

DISCUSSES WPA PROGRAM

At a recent meeting of the Life Insurance Adjustment Bureau in New York, William F. Dorn, Detroit WPA District Compensation Representative, spoke on the WPA program in Michigan. Included in the assembly were several employees of the Wayne County Welfare Relief Commission which cooperates with the Bureau.

Primary Source

Progress in Michigan (5 OF 5)

Page 11 of the WPA newsletter *Progress in Michigan*, Volume 1, Number 2. December 1935.

An important objective of work relief was to get people off direct relief—the dole. It also provided retraining opportunities and added value to the community. On December 1, 1935, Harry Pierson announced that this objective was met: every able-bodied person in Michigan previously on direct relief was employed by the WPA.

Further Resources

BOOKS

Gerdes, Louise I., ed. *The 1930s.* San Diego, Calif.: Greenhaven Press, 2000.

Hill, Edwin G. *In the Shadow of the Mountain: The Spirit of the CCC.* Pullman: Washington State University Press, 1990.

Kurzman, Paul A. *Harry Hopkins and the New Deal.* Fair Lawn, N.J.: R.E. Burdick, 1974.

Works Progress Administration Reports

Report on the Works Program, 1936

Graph, Table

By: Works Progress Administration

Date: March 1936

Source: "Value of Projects Approved for W.P.A., by Types and by States, January 15, 1936"; "Works Program Employment by States, Dec. 28, 1935." In *Report on the Works Program.* Washington, D.C.: United States Government Printing Office, 1936.

Report on the Progress of the Works Program, 1937

Report, Illustration, Tables, Graph

By: Works Progress Administration

Date: March 1937

Source: "Security Programs"; "Selected Accomplishments on WPA Projects"; "Average Hourly Earnings of Persons Employed on WPA Projects"; "Employment on WPA Projects, Emergency Conservation Work, and Projects on Other Agencies, By States"; "Hours and Earnings of Persons Employed on W.P.A. Projects, Cumulative through Dec. 31, 1936, by Type of Project." In *Report on the Progress of the Works Program.* Washington, D.C.: United States Government Printing Office, 1937. ■

Introduction

Prior to the New Deal, direct relief in the United States combined the work of charitable organizations, often church- or faith-based, and that of local government. It was primarily directed at supporting children, widows, and the infirm. Modest work-relief programs—road repair, for example—were sometimes used during depressed times to provide support for able-bodied workers (who were otherwise left out of the equation).

American poor relief evolved from English practices. It was geared for rural/small-town communities where there tended to be a collective responsibility for the needy and a heavy reliance on families caring for their own. It worked reasonably well in stable, local economies where some form of employment, however modest, was available to community members. In the large and more impersonal urban environments that had been established by the 1930s, it was completely unsatisfactory.

Franklin Delano Roosevelt (FDR) believed in an activist government that had an obligation to improve the quality of life for its citizens—not sit on the sidelines and observe. Furthermore, as governor of New York, Roosevelt had seen the failure of traditional relief efforts and the need to enlist the power of the federal government to support and even initiate more effective relief programs.

Roosevelt's programs used both work relief and direct relief to attack abject poverty and unemployment. Specific programs designed to provide assistance included the Federal Emergency Relief Administration (FERA), the Civil Works Administration (CWA), the Civilian Conservation Corps (CCC), the Public Works Administration (PWA) and, most significantly, the Works Progress Administration (WPA). Direct and work-relief monies were funneled through the FERA to state and local governments. The other programs were work relief and remained under the direct control of the federal government.

At their peak, these programs provided direct relief to more than 6 million people and employment (work relief) to nearly 4 million workers. Billions were spent to provide direct aid and to fund massive public works programs to put people back to work.

Significance

When Roosevelt took office in 1933, morale of the American people was perhaps at the lowest point in history. The emotional turnaround that followed Roosevelt's inauguration was nothing short of miraculous. This turnaround was due in part to the infectious optimism with which FDR led the nation. More tangibly, however, Roosevelt initiated and sustained an enormous federal relief program that convinced the American people that they would not be allowed to starve and that prosperity would eventually return.

Perhaps the most widely recognized New Deal program was the WPA. Created in March 1935, following the passage of a $4.5-billion public works bill, the WPA came

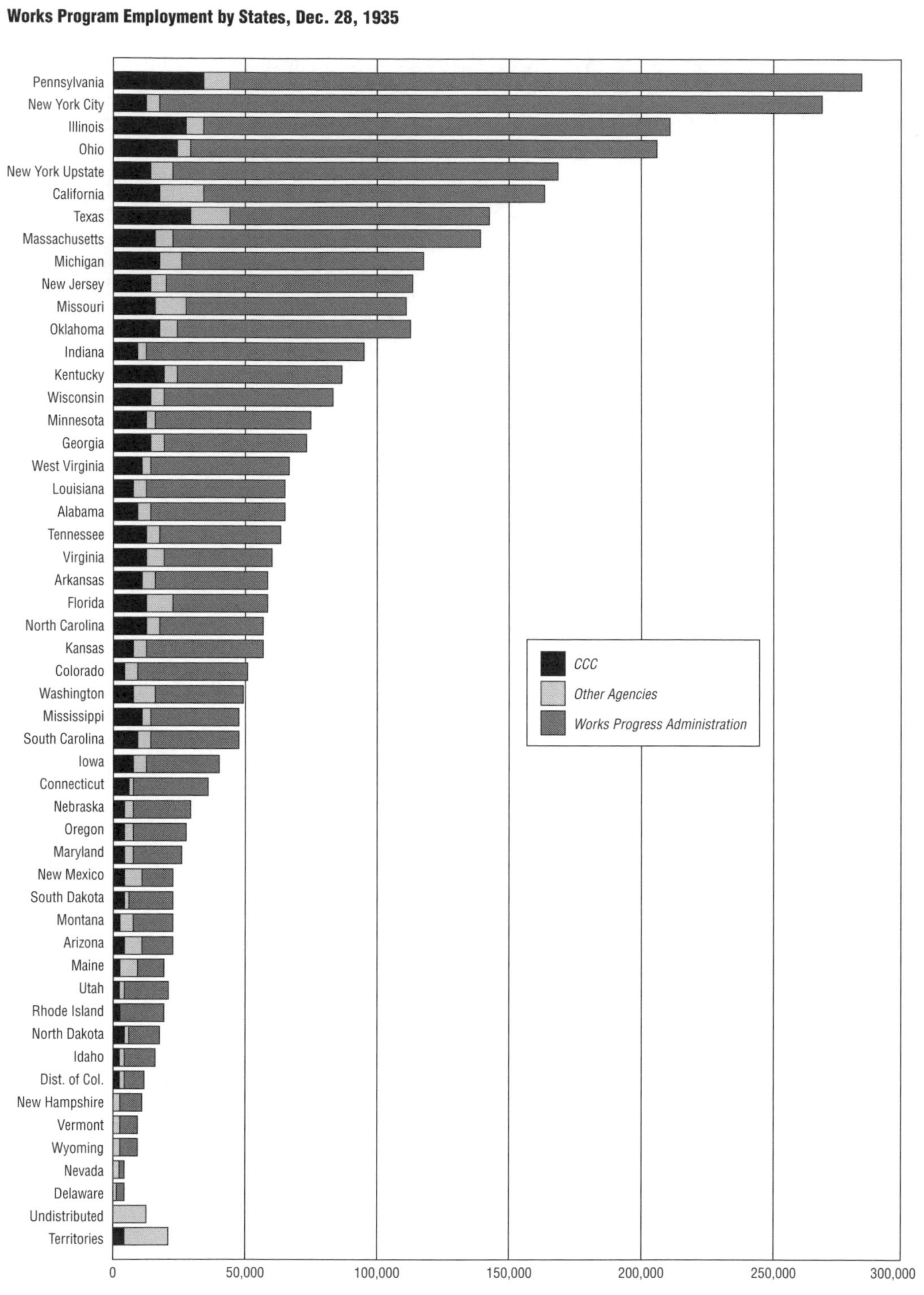

SOURCE: *Report on the Works Program.* Works Progress Administration, March 16, 1936, p.10.

Primary Source

Report on the Works Program, 1936: Graph (1 OF 3)

SYNOPSIS: "Works Program Employment by States, December 28, 1935," appeared in the 1936 *Report on the Works Program*, along with one other graphic illustration of the W.P.A.'s successes, "Value of Projects Approved for W.P.A., by Types and by States, January 15, 1936."

Value of Projects Approved for W.P.A., by Types and by States, January 15, 1936

	Grand total		Highways, roads and streets		Public buildings		Parks and playgrounds		Flood control and other conservation		Public utilities	
State (1)	Amount (2)	Percent (3)	Amount (4)	Percent (5)	Amount (6)	Percent (7)	Amount (8)	Percent (9)	Amount (10)	Percent (11)	Amount (12)	Percent (13)
Alabama	51,308,789	100	17,993,876	35.1	9,240,760	18.0	2,223,535	4.3	1,367,142	2.7	3,722,006	7.3
Arizona	14,623,695	100	4,898,907	33.5	3,434,776	23.5	1,772,551	12.1	1,463,428	10.0	143,117	1.0
Arkansas	45,560,829	100	28,739,638	63.1	3,794,961	8.3	2,112,109	4.6	2,665,734	5.9	1,020,096	2.2
California	221,902,939	100	39,850,565	17.9	22,351,759	10.1	19,759,498	8.9	11,702,250	5.3	68,249,461	30.8
Colorado	36,259,051	100	12,337,981	34.0	4,209,946	11.6	1,703,040	4.7	7,817,570	21.6	1,738,465	4.8
Connecticut	47,265,832	100	18,398,625	38.9	3,003,392	6.3	2,899,774	6.1	1,633,265	3.5	7,028,322	14.9
Delaware	3,616,936	100	1,125,928	31.1	233,282	6.4	235,995	6.5	382,725	10.6	534,420	14.8
District of Columbia	10,261,219	100	996,396	9.7	1,733,901	16.9	2,132,405	20.8	60,372	0.6	888,940	8.7
Florida	47,001,191	100	17,920,947	38.1	8,879,916	18.9	2,409,120	5.1	949,200	2.0	3,661,669	7.8
Georgia	59,639,865	100	20,688,173	34.7	10,359,764	17.4	2,515,172	4.2	800,846	1.3	8,242,886	13.8
Idaho	21,048,526	100	7,923,960	37.6	1,194,154	5.7	779,267	3.7	7,714,890	36.7	561,686	2.6
Illinois	300,904,998	100	96,426,177	32.0	26,779,571	9.0	40,678,653	13.5	11,233,866	3.7	62,565,132	20.8
Indiana	128,299,171	100	58,228,511	45.4	12,789,916	9.9	11,867,199	9.2	11,240,846	8.8	9,290,183	7.2
Iowa	62,682,057	100	27,802,587	44.4	5,503,333	8.6	5,882,852	9.4	2,736,032	4.4	5,934,644	9.5
Kansas	80,335,536	100	33,451,687	41.6	5,107,453	6.4	4,916,142	6.1	4,611,121	5.8	21,384,266	29.6
Kentucky	100,325,966	100	60,510,240	60.3	15,796,696	15.7	2,290,311	2.3	1,118,481	1.1	5,976,828	6.0
Louisiana	61,905,063	100	20,923,448	33.8	8,138,206	13.1	18,279,187	29.6	3,031,302	4.9	3,786,847	6.1
Maine	123,902,717	100	35,275,410	28.5	5,551,,827	4.5	15,360,054	12.3	155,259	.1	33,833,041	27.3
Maryland	32,886,260	100	11,698,841	35.6	4,419,028	13.4	2,040,521	6.2	556,074	1.7	6,389,952	19.4
Massachusetts	177,468,037	100	77,684,979	43.8	9,834,649	5.5	8,655,805	4.9	4,666,892	2.6	18,553,972	10.5
Michigan	137,945,019	100	65,065,652	47.2	13,797,122	10.0	7,786,100	5.6	8,049,133	5.8	16,573,852	12.0
Minnesota	103,788,718	100	48,132,323	46.3	11,528,297	11.2	11.187,406	10.8	14,641,930	14.1	3,473,487	3.4
Mississippi	59,834,325	100	24,811,530	41.5	14,071,578	23.5	1,393,605	2.3	3,168,262	5.3	1,496,729	2.5
Missouri	96,590,323	100	37,901,903	39.2	17,090,798	17.7	6,312,818	6.5	7,427,329	7.7	12,450,920	12.9
Montana	26,300,825	100	11,088,850	42.1	4,362,044	16.6	1,662,947	6.3	2,414,182	9.2	1,007,336	3.8
Nebraska	34,927,463	100	16,483,129	47.2	3,229,088	9.2	1,884,013	5.4	1,348,539	3.9	4,922,697	14.1
Nevada	2,931,925	100	752,619	25.7	615,408	21.0	337,154	11.5	102,676	3.5	47,447	1.6
New Hampshire	17,284,970	100	5,265,751	30.6	855,192	4.9	2,476,880	14.3	921,806	5.3	2,231,746	12.9
New Jersey	125,730,178	100	43,461,569	34.6	11,898,757	9.5	21,767,756	17.3	2,915,410	2.3	10,102,738	8.0
New Mexico	20,624,182	100	11,428,441	55.4	3,420,114	16.6	820,061	4.0	1,423,873	6.9	546,385	2.6
New York City	354,142,254	100	69,964,300	19.8	64,670,220	18.3	91,225,106	25.7	2,785,493	.8	25,938,382	7.3
New York (Excl. N.Y.C.)	470,805,028	100	277,221,100	58.9	18,800,909	4.0	19,283,727	4.1	22,842,925	4.9	45,058,886	9.6
North Carolina	61,225,628	100	19,316,337	31.6	8,942,283	14.6	2,219,313	3.6	2,704,444	4.4	2,535,121	4.1
North Dakota	21,276,277	100	12,598,924	59.2	1,782,320	8.4	1,768,271	8.3	457,989	2.2	472,340	2.2
Ohio	277,800,266	100	153,731,243	55.3	23,953,089	8.7	18,278,553	6.6	12,864,012	4.6	27,568,702	9.9
Oklahoma	125,508,918	100	44,525,472	35.5	21,238,995	16.9	9,709,877	7.7	14,758,939	11.8	8,917,694	7.1
Oregon	25,344,222	100	12,404,359	49.0	4,156,162	16.4	1,083,520	4.3	2,104,486	8.3	728,802	2.9
Pennsylvania	213.689,202	100	115,237,017	53.9	14,449,779	6.8	9,431,971	4.4	6,519,104	3.1	11,443,313	5.4
Rhode Island	34,309,059	100	15,828,571	46.1	2,255,376	6.6	2,489,493	7.3	723,995	2.1	2,450,208	7.1
South Carolina	28,963,539	100	6,572,662	22.7	5,854,273	20.2	1,194,779	4.1	2,078,019	7.2	736,948	2.5

[continued]

Primary Source

Report on the Works Program, 1936: Table (2 OF 3)

Part 1 of a table from the 1936 *Report on the Works Program.* It shows the amount of federal work relief aid going to each state or region, and how it was used.

Value of Projects Approved for W.P.A., by Types and by States, January 15, 1936 [CONTINUED]

	Grand total		Highways, roads and streets		Public buildings		Parks and play-grounds		Flood control and other conservation		Public utilities	
State	Amount	Per-cent	Amount	Per-cent	Amount	Per-cent	Amount	Per-cent	Amount	Per-cent	Amount	Per-cent
(1)	(2)	(3)	(4)	(5)	(6)	(7)	(8)	(9)	(10)	(11)	(12)	(13)
South Dakota	15,178,174	100	7.478,093	49.3	1,835,431	12.1	532,231	3.5	912,226	6.0	487,119	3.2
Tennessee	49,606,725	100	22,464,669	45.3	6,874,498	13.9	1,168,129	2.4	609,157	1.2	1,092,608	2.2
Texas	166,163,862	100	68,889,382	41.5	15,184,340	9.1	6,688,525	4.0	36,042,995	21.7	7,973,605	4.8
Utah	14,884,257	100	2,671,302	17.9	1,689,877	11.4	561,928	3.8	1,442,446	9.7	3,621,257	24.3
Vermont	9,926,246	100	5,084,763	51.2	1,206,427	12.1	409,360	4.1	55,604	.6	1,297,832	13.1
Virginia	48,157,339	100	14,928,247	31.0	12,314,536	25.5	1,677,108	3.5	734,245	1.5	3,254,809	6.8
Washington	47,287,272	100	13,325,332	28.2	4,689,205	9.9	4,105,719	8.7	8,482,838	17.9	3,645,518	7.7
West Virginia	110,628,344	100	64,236,847	58.1	22,775,871	20.6	1,538,555	1.4	1,576,876	1.4	4,193,439	3.8
Wisconsin	103,239,310	100	24,714,904	23.9	10,760,762	10.4	21,388,100	20.7	14,359,450	13.9	14,040,140	13.6
Wyoming	5,434,616	100	1,656,681	30.5	486,952	9.0	315,183	5.8	545,497	10.0	627,708	11.6
Nation-wide	142,631,715	100	–	–	–	–	–	–	42,885,959	30.1	–	–

SOURCE: *Report on the Works Program.* Works Progress Administration, March 16, 1936, p. 100.

Primary Source

Report on the Works Program, 1936: Table (3 OF 3)

Part 2 of a table from the 1936 *Report on the Works Program.*

Laborers work on a Works Progress Administration road construction project. © CORBIS. REPRODUCED BY PERMISSION.

to symbolize many of the good and bad things about the New Deal. Harry Hopkins, by this time the leading figure in Roosevelt's administration, was put in charge. The Civilian Conservation Corps (CCC), established in 1933, was brought under Hopkins' umbrella, as was the newly created National Youth Administration. Both programs were aimed at employing those between the ages of 18 and 25. The CCC employed young men in work camps, and the NYA especially targeted women and college students in the effort to provide relief and employment.

The WPA was the largest of the New Deal relief programs. It employed 8.5 million people at a federal government cost of $11 billion. For this, the WPA built or repaired 600,000 miles of roads, 24,000 miles of sidewalks, 1.2 million miles of culverts, over 100,000 schools, libraries, and other public buildings, 7,500 parks, playgrounds, and athletic fields, over 600 airports, 800 municipal swimming pools, 1,200 sewage treatment plants, 23,000 miles of sewer lines, and 75,000 bridges and viaducts.

In addition to the vast construction projects, the WPA funded a remarkable series of cultural programs. They included the Federal Arts Program, the Federal Theatre Project, the Federal Music Project, and the Federal Writers Project. Employing out-of-work painters, sculptors, musicians, writers, actors, and stagehands, they produced plays and public art, wrote state travel guides, performed puppet shows in city parks, gave concerts, and conducted historical research.

Concluding in 1943, when unemployment had been virtually eliminated due to wartime labor needs, the WPA had administered a public works program of unprecedented scale. During its eight-year existence, the WPA was the sole source of income for millions of families, and it significantly improved the infrastructure and quality of life for the entire country.

Primary Source

Report on the Progress of the Works Program, 1937 [excerpt]: Report

SYNOPSIS: "Security Programs" was the introduction to the March 1937 *Report on Progress of the Works Program,* a report prepared under the auspices of Harry Hopkins, administrator of the Works Progress Administration. It details the accomplishments of the various work-relief programs then in operation and summarizes the history of the various programs before and after 1933. It is a document written to extol the virtues of work relief and in particular the WPA. Nonetheless, it provides valuable commentary and statistical information on the various programs then underway. A few of the graphs and charts found in the 1937 and 1936 reports are included to illustrate the the scope of the WPA's programs.

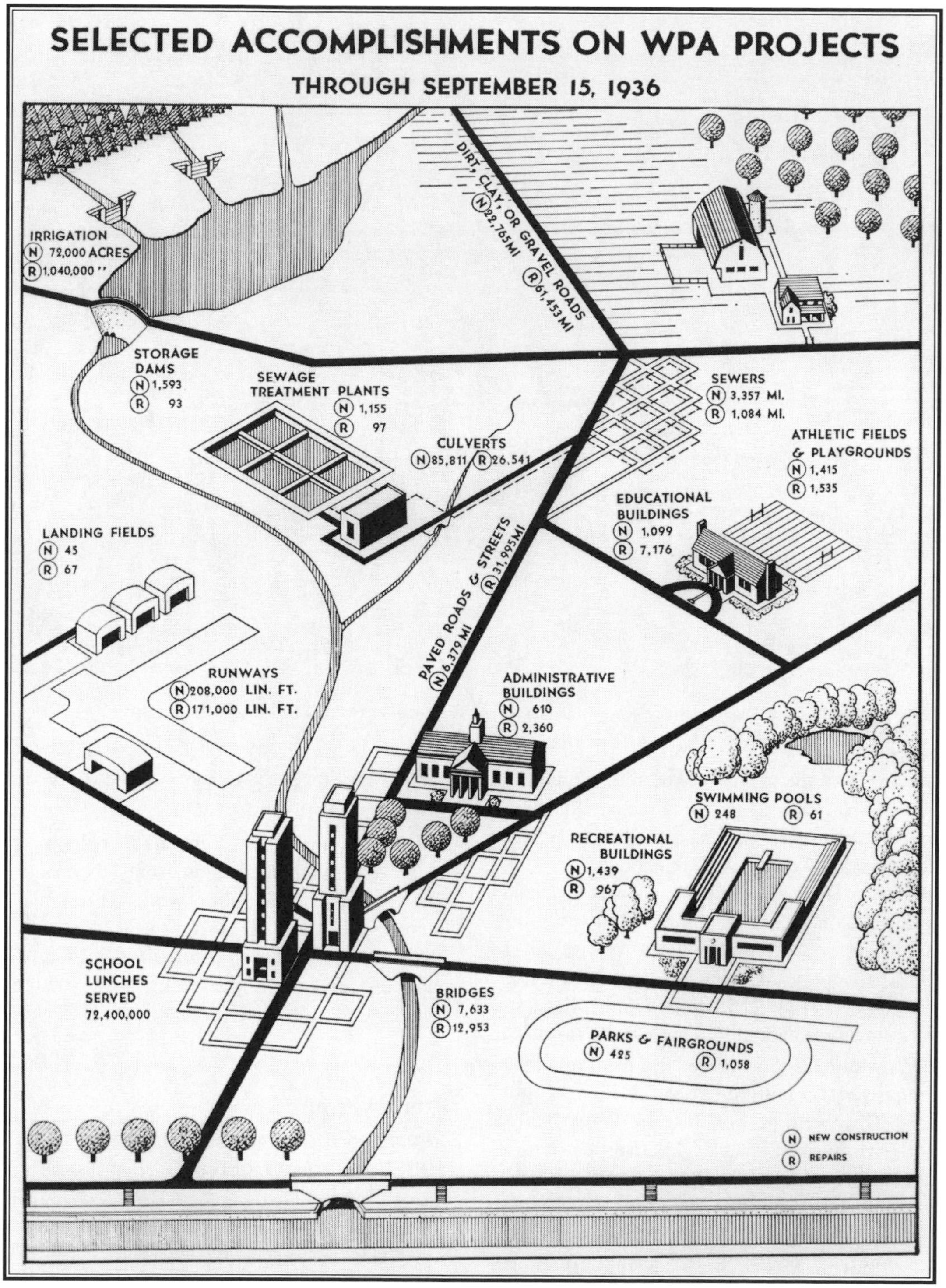

Primary Source

Report on the Progress of the Works Program, 1937: Illustration (1 OF 5)

SYNOPSIS: A map illustrating the selected accomplishments of WPA projects completed through September 15, 1936. This map originally accompanied Harry Hopkins' 1937 article "Security Programs," iterating the progress of the WPA. Tables and graphs illustrating similar progress appeared in both in the 1936 and 1937 *Report on Progress of the Works Program.*

Hours and Earnings of Persons Employed on W.P.A. Projects, Cumulative through Dec. 31, 1936, by Type of Project

Cumulative through December 31, 1936 [Subject to revision]

Type of project	Hours		Earnings		Average hourly earnings (cents)
	Number	Percent	Amount	Percent	
(1)	(2)	(3)	(4)	(5)	(6)
Grand total[1]	4,000,329,942	100.0	$1,829,494,192	100.0	45.7
Highways, roads, and streets	1,502,326,962	37.6	612,591,511	33.5	40.8
Highways	24,844,228	0.6	9,868,001	0.5	39.7
Farm-to-market and other secondary roads	522,135,973	13.0	183,140,300	10.0	35.1
Streets and alleys	335,619,531	8.4	152,428,964	8.3	45.4
Sidewalks, curbs, and paths	51,266,489	1.3	24,491,801	1.3	47.8
Roadside improvements	166,680,696	4.2	81,355,747	4.5	48.8
Bridges and viaducts	26,915,223	0.7	12,434,777	0.7	46.2
Grade-crossing elimination	2,180,061	0.1	1,250,833	0.1	57.4
Other[2]	372,684,761	9.3	147,621,088	8.1	39.6
Public buildings	338,420,837	8.4	190,264,176	10.4	56.2
Administrative	37,542,084	0.9	25,081,045	1.4	66.8
Charitable, medical and mental institutions	34,941,061	0.9	22,165,765	1.2	63.4
Educational	109,605,236	2.7	61,889,738	3.4	56.5
Social and recreational	52,488,285	1.3	26,070,005	1.4	49.7
Federal (including military and naval)	20,569,226	0.5	11,557,801	0.6	56.2
Improvement of grounds	47,733,318	1.2	20,447,160	1.1	42.8
Housing	8,326,728	0.2	5,145,494	0.3	61.8
Other[2]	27,214,899	0.7	17,907,168	1.0	65.8
Parks and other recreational facilities	428,986,856	10.7	225,231,575	12.3	52.5
Playgrounds and athletic fields	67,613,671	1.7	31,349,314	1.7	46.4
Parks	203,965,405	5.1	97,654,387	5.3	47.9
Other[2]	157,407,780	3.9	96,227,874	5.3	61.1
Conservation	206,633,710	5.2	87,607,105	4.8	42.4
Forestation	8,413,050	0.2	3,355,226	0.2	39.9
Erosion control and land utilization	14,045,174	0.4	6,422,715	0.4	45.7
Irrigation and water conservation	144,444,001	3.6	61,662,603	3.4	42.7
Plant, crop and livestock conservation	5,558,366	0.1	2,709,109	0.1	48.7
Other[2]	34,173,119	0.9	13,457,452	0.7	39.4
Sewer systems and other utilities	329,477,562	8.2	154,491,266	8.4	46.9
Water purification and supply	71,676,392	1.8	32,968,043	1.8	46.0
Sewer systems	238,080,071	5.9	112,472,116	6.1	47.2
Electric utilities	6,031,005	0.2	3,012,822	0.2	50.0
Other[2]	13,690,094	0.3	6,038,285	0.3	44.1
Airports and other transportation	80,736,578	2.0	39,214,801	2.1	48.6
Airports and airways	64,745,574	1.6	30,055,006	1.6	46.4
Navigation	10,377,088	0.3	6,338,443	0.3	61.1
Other[2]	5,613,916	0.1	2,821,352	0.2	50.3
White collar	373,087,058	9.3	234,868,670	12.9	63.0
Educational	75,069,137	1.9	48,708,005	2.7	64.9
Professional and clerical	298,017,921	7.4	186,160,665	10.2	62.5
Goods	484,456,301	12.1	182,603,140	10.0	37.7
Sewing	418,389,650	10.4	154,257,561	8.4	36.9
Canning	3,789,157	0.1	1,439,695	0.1	38.0
Other[2]	62,277,494	1.6	26,905,884	1.5	43.2
Sanitation and health	136,023,324	3.4	51,186,535	2.8	37.6
Elimination of stream pollution	4,120,381	0.1	1,885,594	0.1	45.8
Mosquito eradication	64,026,910	1.6	22.125,573	1.2	34.6
Other[2]	67,876,033	1.7	27,175,368	1.5	40.0
Miscellaneous	117,704,958	3.0	50,581,042	2.7	43.0

[1]Totals include 2,475,796 hours worked and $854,371 earned (each representing 0.1 percent of their respective totals) on W.P.A. projects in Hawaii, not distributed by types of projects.
[2]Includes projects classifiable under more than 1 of the headings.

SOURCE: *Report on Progress of the Works Program.* Works Progress Administration, March 1937.

Primary Source

Report on the Progress of the Works Program, 1937: Table (2 OF 5)

This table from the 1937 *Report on the Progress of the Works Program* details the hours devoted to various types of work relief in 1936. The earnings of people engaged in this work relief is also shown.

Employment on W.P.A. Projects, Emergency Conservation Work, and Projects on Other Agencies, By States

Quarterly–September 1935 to February 1937

State	Number of persons employed during week ending March 28, 1936				Number of persons employed during week ending June 27, 1936			
	Total	W.P.A.	Emergency Conservation Work	Other agencies	Total	W.P.A.	Emergency Conservation Work	Other agencies
(1)	(2)	(3)	(4)	(5)	(6)	(7)	(8)	(9)
Grand total	3,727,723	2,871,637	433,770	422,316	3,236,621	2,255,898	381,140	599,583
Total distributed by States	3,675,689	2,871,637	429,600	374,452	3,180,596	2,255,898	377,340	547,358
Alabama	61,330	39,977	7,231	14,122	56,613	32,398	7,415	16,800
Arizona	22,542	11,439	5,280	5,823	19,430	9.332	4,038	6,060
Arkansas	53,914	35,277	9,323	9,314	49,074	29,945	8,549	10,580
California	185,153	142,584	13,925	28,644	161,328	110,548	12,540	38,240
Colorado	47,628	39,033	4,392	4,203	37,633	28,328	4,679	4,626
Connecticut	34,861	27,810	4,749	2,302	33,034	22,508	3,966	6.560
Delaware	5,348	3,071	572	1,705	4,801	2,344	671	1,786
District of Columbia	13,586	8,983	2,559	2,044	12,001	7,546	2,150	2,305
Florida	57,494	32,514	8,041	16,939	48,695	27,124	8,079	13,492
Georgia	68.049	44,142	11,367	12,540	54,996	33,881	11,232	9,883
Idaho	18,546	12,634	3,126	2,786	17,954	6,380	2,525	9,049
Illinois	235,334	199,823	22,140	13,371	200,648	155,680	17,882	27,086
Indiana	97,938	84,715	7,586	5,637	87,281	68,287	6,674	12,320
Iowa	40,467	30,760	6,749	2,958	33,388	19,408	5,245	8,735
Kansas	60,314	45,076	6,784	8,454	44,497	30,402	5,599	8,496
Kentucky	82,407	62,134	15,843	4,430	65,884	45,911	10,706	9,267
Louisiana	62,711	50,508	7,205	4,998	47,776	36,510	6,873	4,393
Maine	18,395	9,913	3,179	5,303	17,156	7,971	2,251	6,934
Maryland	28,197	18,375	4,240	5,582	28,085	14,606	3,923	9,556
Massachusetts	141,283	120,372	12,970	7,941	128,343	104,557	12,407	11,379
Michigan	121,859	98,534	15,253	8,072	102,791	75,771	12,229	14,791
Minnesota	76,527	60,689	11,030	4,808	68,419	44,805	9,450	14,164
Mississippi	56,246	37,854	10,215	8,177	48,083	26,651	10,017	11,415
Missouri	112,774	87,727	14,726	10,321	94,058	66,602	13,129	14,327
Montana	29,400	19,861	3,221	6,318	19,792	10,489	2,767	6,536
Nebraska	31,121	21,497	4,637	4,987	27,048	14,512	3,926	8,610
Nevada	5,536	2,525	1,154	1,857	4,568	2,188	856	1,524
New Hampshire	12,854	9,557	1,819	1,478	11,977	7,607	1,653	2,717
New Jersey	110,492	92,136	10,709	7,647	98,794	79,811	10,816	8,167
New Mexico	23,615	10,274	5,176	8,165	21,684	7,899	5,193	8,592
New York City	254,805	236,723	9,792	8,290	225,929	205,490	9,705	10,734
New York (excluding New York City)	149,127	127,389	11,770	9,968	134,494	101,698	11,580	21,216
North Carolina	62,884	40,034	9,839	13,011	50,251	27,984	8,515	13,752
North Dakota	19,045	11,997	5,352	1,696	19,897	8,399	4,524	6,974
Ohio	214,984	186,358	19,245	9,381	184,060	152,850	15,126	16,084
Oklahoma	92,075	69,669	13,474	8,932	80,411	55,596	14,662	10,153
Oregon	29,946	19,972	4,898	5,076	26,480	14,469	3,740	8,271
Pennsylvania	323,355	287,847	26,009	9,499	277,748	235,047	19,998	22,703
Rhode Island	18,870	14,642	2,519	1,709	16,560	10,888	2,359	3,313
South Carolina	51,257	30,439	8,203	12,615	45,737	25,470	7,728	12,539
South Dakota	20,923	14,779	4,179	1,965	19,184	9,400	3,593	6,191
Tennessee	63,246	44,671	10,100	8,475	59,268	36,505	8,800	13,963
Texas	150,410	103,252	22,348	24,810	135,603	79,385	20,477	35,741
Utah	17,038	12,170	3,194	1,674	16,012	10,080	2,499	3,433
Vermont	10,446	6,697	2,131	1,618	9,633	4,400	1,777	3,456
Virginia	57,673	34,581	10,987	12,105	50,987	27,180	9,657	14,150
Washington	64,000	46,114	6,673	11,213	44,389	25,948	5,737	12,704
West Virginia	68,582	56,433	9,118	3,031	55,916	43,457	7,207	5,252
Wisconsin	82,548	63,179	13,113	6,256	74,123	48,862	10,764	14,497
Wyoming	8,554	4,897	1,455	2,202	8,083	2,789	1,452	3,842
Total distributed by Territories	40,010	–	4,170	35,840	43,067	–	3,800	39,267
Alaska	677	–	382	295	521	–	218	303
Hawaii	4,226	–	1,744	2,482	3,201	–	1,261	1,940

[continued]

Primary Source

Report on the Progress of the Works Program, 1937: Tables (3 OF 5)

A table from the 1937 *Report on the Progress of the Works Program.* It lists the number of people engaged in different kinds of work relief throughout the United States in early 1936.

Employment on W.P.A. Projects, Emergency Conservation Work, and Projects on Other Agencies, By States (CONTINUED)

Quarterly–September 1935 to February 1937

State	Number of persons employed during week ending March 28, 1936				Number of persons employed during week ending June 27, 1936			
	Total	W.P.A.	Emergency Conservation Work	Other agencies	Total	W.P.A.	Emergency Conservation Work	Other agencies
(1)	(2)	(3)	(4)	(5)	(6)	(7)	(8)	(9)
Panama Canal Zone	480	–	–	480	260	–	–	260
Puerto Rico	33,635	–	1,781	31,854	37,955	–	2,099	35,856
Virgin Islands	992	–	263	729	1,130	–	222	908
Not distributed by States or Territories	12,024	–	–	12,024	12,958	–	–	12,958

SOURCE: *Report on Progress of the Works Program.* Works Progress Administration, March 1937, p. 104.

Primary Source

Report on the Progress of the Works Program, 1937: Table (4 OF 5)

Part 2 of a table from the 1937 *Report on the Progress of the Works Program* listing the number of people engaged in work relief.

Security Programs

During the last several years the Federal Government has been formulating and putting into operation a program of security for the underprivileged of America, two principal features of which are the Social Security Act and the Works Program. In order to weigh the adequacy of these measures in achieving security, it is necessary to consider them in the light not only of their historical backgrounds and their recent progress, but also in the light of the unemployment problem with which they will have to cope either directly or indirectly.

Under the Social Security Act the Federal Government is providing financial assistance to States having approved plans for aid to such classes of unemployable persons as the destitute aged, the blind, and mothers with dependent children. Through these public-assistance provisions of the act, benefits were being provided, in January 1937, for 1,149,000 aged persons, 29,400 blind persons, and 115,000 families with dependent children. In future years, when the Social Security Act is in full effect, old-age benefits and unemployment compensation will also play an important part in the security system.

Under the Works Program 2,884,000 persons were receiving employment as of February 20, 1937; of these, 2,147,000 were employed by the Works Progress Administration. In addition to the persons benefiting under the Social Security Act and the Works Program, the Resettlement Administration was aiding more than 200,000 rural families by means of grants as well as a large number of additional families through loan agreements, and the States and localities were granting direct relief to over 1,600,000 families and single persons.

Relief Prior to 1933

The present status of the Federal programs to promote security is best understood in the light of antecedent conditions and measures. It is often overlooked in discussions of the relief problem that even prior to 1929 unemployment of varying intensity was an integral part of our economic order and that relief needs had been expanding steadily for decades. Estimates of unemployment by Paul Douglas covering the period from 1897 to 1926 for four major industries show an average of 10 percent unemployed. Even in such relatively prosperous years as 1923 and 1926 there were more than 1,500,000 persons out of work in the United States. Another fact not generally recognized is that in the decades preceding the recent depression relief expenditures rose constantly. Public relief expenditures in 16 major cities increased from $1,500,000 in 1911 to $20,000,000 in 1928.

In some respects the recent depression merely accentuated previous unemployment and relief difficulties, but the increased size of the problem forced a reorganization of the methods used in dealing with these difficulties. Changes were inevitable in any event; the depression merely hastened their development.

Prior to the depression which began in 1929, the poor laws of the various States alone provided legislation for the public care of needy persons.

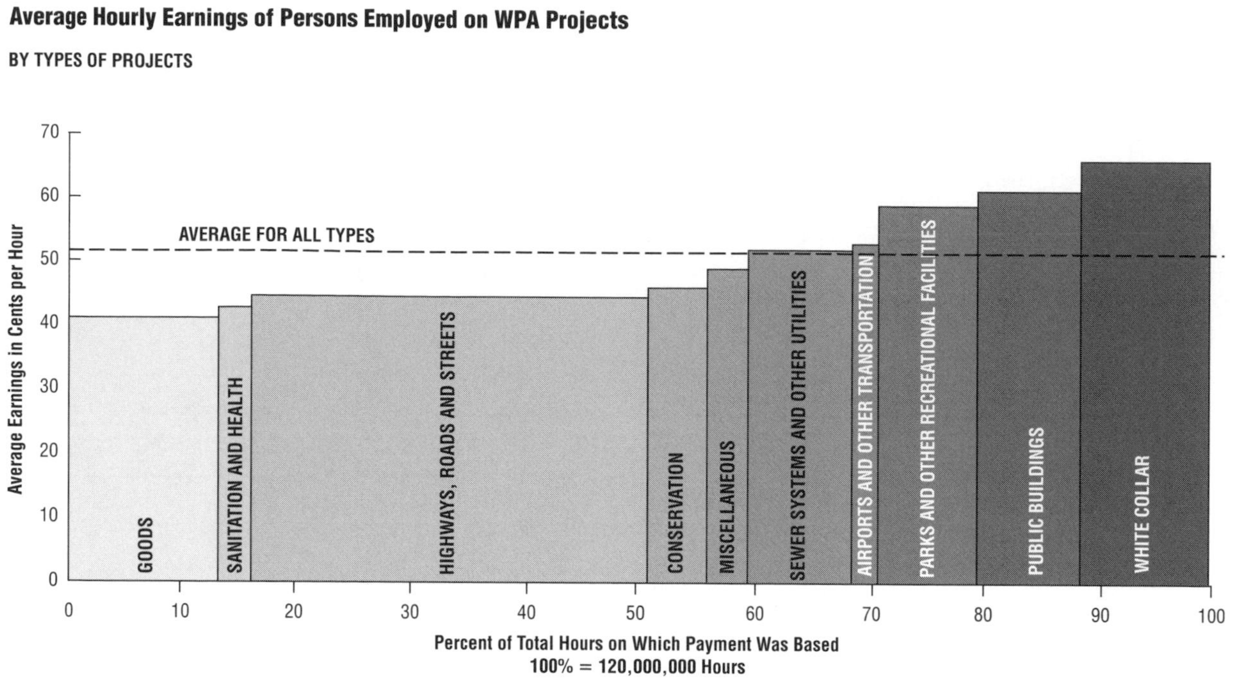

SOURCE: *Report on Progress of the Works Program.* Works Progress Administration, March 1937, p. 44.

Primary Source

Report on the Progress of the Works Program, 1937: Graph (5 OF 5)

The federal government's work relief programs were concentrated on building and maintaining public structures, but tried to provide employment for Americans of every background.

These statutes were designed primarily to care for unemployable persons and the aid given was usually limited to almshouse care, burial, medical care, and small amounts of outdoor relief. Administrative and financial responsibility for the operation of this system was centered in the political subdivisions of the States (the counties, towns, and cities) on the theory that destitution was distinctly a local problem and responsibility. In most urban localities this aid was supplemented by private charity.

Generally speaking, it was considered desirable to make public relief as unattractive as possible on the assumption that adequate relief would encourage idleness. Even before 1929, however, State legislatures were beginning to recognize that certain classes of needy individuals, such as mothers with dependent children, the blind, the aged, and veterans, were entitled to more adequate public assistance. Recognition of this resulted in the passage of special legislation for these classes in a number of States, a development which later was given added impetus through the Social Security Act.

The status of public relief in 1929 may be summarized briefly. All States had poor-relief laws. Veterans' relief legislation had been provided in 44 States and assistance for the blind in 22 States. Assistance to the aged was accorded in only 10 States. All but five States had provisions for aid to dependent children in their own homes, and all but three had laws making possible the care of children in foster homes and institutions. No State had enacted unemployment compensation legislation. With the exception of veterans' relief and care of dependent children by agencies or institutions, local political subdivisions generally were charged with responsibility for administering and financing the various types of aid.

This system soon proved incapable of meeting adequately the shock of a major depression. Shortly after the crisis of 1929 large numbers of the unemployed were forced to apply for relief. In the latter part of 1931 State emergency relief administrations were set up in four States, and many more were created in 1932. During this period States and localities found it increasingly difficult to collect taxes or to borrow money, and private contributions were inadequate to meet the new need.

It was not until 1932, however, that the Federal Government took steps implicitly recognizing the national character of the unemployment relief problem. In that year Federal cotton and wheat were donated to destitute persons through the Red Cross, and the Emergency Relief and Construction Act was passed authorizing the Reconstruction Finance Corporation to lend $300,000,000 to States and localities for emergency relief.

Relief Under the F.E.R.A. and the C.W.A.

The necessity of further and more substantial Federal aid was recognized in May 1933 with the passage of the Federal Emergency Relief Act. This act established the Federal Emergency Relief Administration and made available $500,000,000 for grants to the States. By the fall of 1933 State emergency relief administrations were functioning in every State and were receiving grants from the F.E.R.A. This grant-in-aid relationship for emergency relief continued in active operation through 1935. The program was essentially a local relief program, operated by local officials, but financed largely by Federal and State funds.

From the beginning of the F.E.R.A. program, several major objectives were continually stressed. Outstanding among these was the effort made to provide relief throughout the country in accord with adequate standards. Other major objectives included the encouragement of work programs for employable relief persons—already widely developed by local relief organizations—and a sufficient diversification of the program to insure differentiated care for the special groups of persons whose problems and needs merited such treatment.

One of the principal reasons for the establishment of the F.E.R.A. was the fact that relief funds in many localities were insufficient. The Administration therefore adjusted its grants to States so as to effect a gradual leveling upward of relief allowances in areas where relief was particularly inadequate. Under the F.E.R.A. the average amounts of relief extended per family for the country as a whole increased from $15.15 in May 1933 to a peak of $30.45 in January 1935. These averages obscure the differences between the amounts received by families wholly dependent on relief and by those receiving only supplementary assistance. They also ignore the fact that many families received relief during only part of the month and, therefore, understate the average amounts received by families completely dependent upon relief throughout the entire month. Generally, it may be said that although actual physical suffering was prevented under the F.E.R.A., adequate relief was not achieved.

Work Relief

During the summer of 1933 an average of more than a million persons were receiving aid through work on local work programs. This work relief, however, suffered from a number of defects. The earnings were low, some of the projects were of limited social value, and the projects in general were not sufficiently diversified to provide work in keeping with the past job experiences of the persons employed.

To remedy these defects, to meet the critical unemployment needs of the winter, and to promote recovery through the injection of purchasing power into the economic system in a short period of time, the Federal Government inaugurated the Civil Works Program early in the winter of 1933–34. In contrast with F.E.R.A. operations, this was a Federal program with Federal funds supplemented by State and local sponsoring agencies. The peak of employment under this first Federal mass employment program was reached during the week ending January 18, 1934, at which time 4,260,000 persons were at work. Approximately half of the persons employed were taken from relief rolls. The Civil Works Program had been designed primarily as a winter work-relief measure and its liquidation was practically completed by the early part of April 1934. It contributed valuable experience for the conduct of later work programs.

Although work relief was almost entirely discontinued by State emergency relief administrations during the period of active operation of the C.W.A., a large number of direct relief cases continued to be cared for by these agencies. With the close of C.W.A. activity the emergency work relief program of the F.E.R.A. and the States was begun. The total number of cases receiving emergency relief under the general relief program grew from 4,261,000 in June 1934 to a maximum of 5,276,000 in January 1935. Work relief employees averaged more than 2,000,000 per month from October 1934 through June 1935, with a maximum of 2,446,000 in January 1935.

Special Programs

In addition to the general relief program, the F.E.R.A. developed certain special programs to meet some of the problems peculiar to such special groups as farmers, teachers, transient persons, and youths. The rural rehabilitation program, inaugurated in April 1934, was one such undertaking. Its purpose was to enable farm families on relief, through direction and assistance in the form of tools, equipment, and working capital, to become wholly or largely self-sustaining. This activity was transferred to the Resettlement Administration on June 30, 1935, and has since been carried forward by that organization.

The emergency education program was begun in October 1933 to aid teachers who were both unemployed and destitute, and later included general adult education, literacy classes, vocational education and rehabilitation, parent and worker education, and nursery school work. Employment reached a peak in March 1935 of over 44,000 persons. This program was transferred to the Works Progress Administration under which it has been further developed.

In July 1933 the Transient Division of the F.E.R.A. was established. Forty States had instituted transient programs by January 1934, and the first mid-monthly census taken as of February 15, 1934, revealed that 92,000 transient families and single persons were under care. The number averaged almost 300,000 transient persons during the winter of 1934–35. Under the Works Program provision for transients is included in regular work project activities.

The special needs of young persons were recognized by the establishment of a college student-aid program, begun experimentally in Minnesota in December 1933 and extended throughout the country in February 1934. This program provided part-time employment for college students who otherwise would not have been able to continue their education. During the winter of 1934–35 an average of more than 100,000 students were aided per month. Since June 1935 student aid has been conducted by the N.Y.A., under which it has been expanded to include high-school and graduate college students.

In summary, the F.E.R.A. succeeded in raising relief standards throughout the country, in attaining diversification in programs, and in improving work-relief projects and extending them so that in the aggregate they provided work for a substantial proportion of the employable persons receiving relief.

Current Programs

In his message to Congress on January 4, 1935, President Roosevelt analyzed the relief situation and outlined the roles which he conceived should be played in the future by the States and localities, and the Federal Government. Unemployable persons were held to be a local responsibility, and States and localities were urged to resume their traditional responsibility for this group of relief persons. The President pointed out, however, that "the security legislation which I shall propose to the Congress will, I am confident, be of assistance to local effort in the care of this type of case." Employable persons, on the other hand, were held to be a Federal responsibility since "this group was the victim of a Nation-wide depression caused by conditions which were not local but national."

Congressional approval of the President's proposals was given through the passage of the Emergency Relief Appropriation Act of 1935 and the Social Security Act. During the latter part of 1935 Federal grants for direct relief were discontinued and the States and localities have since assumed sole responsibility for the care of unemployable persons (with Federal grants under the Social Security Act for certain types of assistance).

The Works Program

In order to achieve the purpose for which the Works Program was established—to provide jobs for 3,500,000 workers—various agencies of the Federal Government joined forces. The Federal units participating in the Works Program include bureaus of regular Government departments and independent establishments engaged in activities which could be expanded through the employment of relief workers, previously established emergency agencies such as the Public Works Administration and Emergency Conservation Work (Civilian Conservation Corps), and newly created agencies designed primarily for Works Program participation—the Resettlement, Rural Electrification, and Works Progress Administrations. The W.P.A. has the dual function of operating non-Federal, locally sponsored, work projects and of effecting the necessary coordination of all agencies participating in the Works Program.

These agencies undertook a wide variety of coordinated projects ranging from many kinds of construction work (which constitutes roughly three-quarters of the projects) to art, education, and research. In addition to the operation of regular projects employing as many as possible of the available workers at their accustomed occupations, Works Program activities include the provision of aid in cases of emergency and disaster. The services of many workers were used during periods of immediate danger from floods in both 1936 and 1937, and also to a large extent in the work of cleaning away debris and repairing damage after the floods had subsided. Similarly, during the serious drought of 1936, the W.P.A., the Resettlement Administration, and other agencies cooperated in providing financial aid, through work relief or other measures, to farmers in the emergency drought areas.

Funds for carrying out the Works Program have been provided under three appropriation acts. The Emergency Relief Appropriation Act of 1935, which initiated the Program, made available up to $4,880,000,000; the E. R. A. Act of 1936, $1,425,000,000; and the First Deficiency Appropriation Act of 1937, $789,000,000. Expenditures of Federal funds have been made largely for direct labor costs, with the sponsors of projects paying for varying proportions of the other expenses such as are incurred for materials, supplies, and equipment.

Total Works Program employment on projects of W.P.A., Emergency Conservation Work (C.C.C.), and all other Federal agencies reached a peak of approximately 3,840,000 persons during the latter part of February and early March 1936. About 78 percent of the total, or more than 3,000,000 persons, were employed by the W.P.A., more than 450,000 by E.C.W., and almost 400,000 by other Federal agencies. Throughout most of the period of Works Program operation the W.P.A. has provided between 70 and 80 percent of the total employment. From March through June 1936 the number of persons employed under the Works Program declined gradually, but the advent of the drought reversed the trend in July. By November 1936 the number of workers began to drop again and by February 20, 1937, total employment had fallen to 2,884,000. Of this number 2,147,000 were working on W.P.A. projects.

Further Resources

BOOKS

Gerdes, Louise I., ed. *The 1930s.* San Diego, Calif.: Greenhaven Press, 2000.

Hill, Edwin G. *In the Shadow of the Mountain: The Spirit of the CCC.* Pullman: Washington State University Press, 1990.

Kurzman, Paul A. *Harry Hopkins and the New Deal.* Fair Lawn, N.J.: R.E. Burdick, 1974.

Leuchtenburg, William E. *Franklin D. Roosevelt and the New Deal, 1932–1940.* New York: Harper & Row, 1963.

Louchheim, Katie. *The Making of the New Deal.* Cambridge, Mass.: Harvard University Press, 1983.

Settlement of a Sit-Down Strike

"General Motors Agreement: February 11, 1937"

Agreement

By: United Automobile Workers (UAW), represented by Wyndham Mortimer, first vice president of UAW; and General Motors (GM), represented by William S. Knudsen, president of GM. The chief mediator was Frank Murphy, governor of Michigan.

Date: February 11, 1937

Source: United Automobile Workers. "General Motors Agreement: February 11, 1937." Walter Reuther Papers, Box 18-1, Walter Reuther Library of Labor and Urban Affairs, Wayne State University, Detroit, Mich.

About the Authors: Wyndham Mortimer (1984–1966) was the chief United Auto Workers (UAW) representative in negotiating a settlement in the Flint sit-down strike. Mortimer, who was a Communist sympathizer, was also UAW vice president and a founder of the UAW. He initiated and led the Flint strike, and was backed by the more influential and dynamic John L. Lewis.

Frank Murphy (1890–1948) was an ardent New Dealer and supporter of Franklin Roosevelt. He was frequently mentioned as a successor to Roosevelt. Murphy, mayor of Detroit during the bleakest years of the Depression, had returned to Michigan in mid-1936 following a three-year assignment as Governor General of the Philippines. Pro-labor, Murphy was adamantly opposed to the use of violence to break strikes. He played a critical role in bringing about a peaceful settlement and one that resulted in GM's recognition of the UAW as the sole bargaining power for its workers.

Letter to Frank Murphy

Letter

By: William S. Knudsen

Date: February 11, 1937

Source: Knudsen, William S. Letter to Frank Murphy, February 11, 1937. Walter Reuther Papers, Box 18-1, Walter Reuther Library of Labor and Urban Affairs, Wayne State University, Detroit, Mich.

About the Author: William S. Knudsen (1879–1946) emigrated from Denmark to the United States in 1900. He forged a distinguished industrial career, opening assembly plants, directing a World War I boatbuilding program, and masterminding postwar European expansion for Ford Motor Company. He then served as president of Chevrolet and General Motors Corporation and finally guided America's World War II production effort. ■

Introduction

The sit-down strike had been used in the past in Europe. In 1936, however, it had a successful resurgence in

France. This attracted the attention of workers at the Goodyear Rubber Plant in Akron, Ohio, and at the Kelsey-Hayes Plant in Detroit in late 1936. Both strikes were successful, and local UAW organizers decided to use this tactic to force GM to recognize the union.

The object of the sit-down strike was for workers to gain physical control of a facility, evicting management and unsympathetic workers, and negotiating from a position of strength. Gaining physical control of a facility prevented management from bringing in strikebreakers and thus prevented the company from operating during a strike. Equally important was that workers were relatively safe from attack by company guards or regular police. On picket lines, workers were very vulnerable. Also, by occupying a location, strikers had control of considerable company property. Machinery, products, and the building itself were at risk, though in fact damage rarely occurred.

The Flint General Motors Strike started on December 30, 1936. If a key plant in the massive Flint complex could be shut down, it would quickly cripple the entire corporation. Although strikers did not initially seize such a plant, they managed to take control of the critical Chevrolet Engine Plant #4 on January 27, giving workers control of a needed "choke point" in Chevrolet's entire operation.

At the beginning of the strike, a violent end seemed likely, and in the opening days there were clashes between workers and local police. To preserve order, Governor Murphy called in the National Guard. On his instructions, they were used to keep workers and local police separated. Murphy had no intention of using the National Guard to forcibly evict the workers. Knudsen supported Murphy in pushing for a peaceful settlement.

After six weeks of difficult negotiation, an agreement was reached. It contained some face-saving clauses for General Motors, but the union had won. Henceforth, GM would negotiate with the UAW to establish wages and work rules.

Significance

The impact of the Flint sit-down strike was immediate and dramatic. Armed with an effective new tactic, nearly a half-million workers across the country were involved in sit-down strikes in the next several months. One after another, companies were organized. Union membership soared, growing from 4.1 million in 1936, the approximate level it had been for thirty years, to 6.1 million in 1938.

Nonetheless, there were failures. Two glaring setbacks were in the auto and steel industries. While Chrysler was soon organized following a successful sit-down strike, Ford Motor Company resisted and was not organized until 1941. In steel, industry giant United States Steel was peacefully unionized in March 1937, but the so-called Little Steel companies crushed union organizing attempts in 1937. They also held out until 1941.

The strikes in the spring and summer of 1937 were so widespread, so militant, so disruptive, and so effective that within a short time, sympathy for unions among the general population began to wane. Some even saw the sit-down strikes as the opening round of revolution.

The occupation of private property by sit-down strikers was particularly troubling. Most observers thought it was clearly illegal. Even many union sympathizers questioned the legality of the sit-down, but justified it on the grounds of a higher imperative. This point was soon resolved. In the Fanstock Steel case, decided in February 1939, the Supreme Court declared the sit-down strike illegal.

Nonetheless, once GM was broken, the dyke had been breached. Companies were inclined to accept the inevitable and were far more reluctant to fight union organization. The effectiveness of the sit-down strike combined with the legal right to organize as stated in the Wagner Act had tipped the scales in favor of the unions. While there were still several hard organizing years ahead, labor had won.

Primary Source

"General Motors Agreement: February 11, 1937"

SYNOPSIS: In this agreement that ended the strike, General Motors recognized the UAW as the sole bargaining power for GM workers. It was an important victory of the American labor movement.

Agreement entered into on this 11th day of February, 1937, between the General Motors Corporation (hereinafter referred to as the Corporation) and the International Union, United Automobile Workers of America (hereinafter referred to as the Union).

1) The Corporation hereby recognizes the Union as the Collective Bargaining agency for those employes of the Corporation who are members of the Union. The Corporation recognizes and will not interfere with the right of its employes to be members of the Union. There shall be no discrimination, interference, restraint or coercion by the Corporation or any of its agents against any employes because of membership in the Union.

2) The Corporation and the Union agree to commence collective bargaining negotiations on February 16th with regard to the issues specified in the letter of January 4th, 1937, from the Union to the Corporation, for the purpose of entering into a collective bargaining agreement, or agreements, cover-

Workers in a Flint, Michigan, General Motors auto plant read newspapers during a sit-down strike in 1937. **UPI/CORBIS-BETTMANN. REPRODUCED BY PERMISSION.**

ing such issues, looking to a final and complete settlement of all matters in dispute.

3) The Union agrees to forthwith terminate the present strike against the Corporation, and to evacuate all plants now occupied by strikers.

4) The Corporation agrees that all of its plants, which are on strike, or otherwise idle shall resume operations as rapidly as possible.

5) It is understood that all employees now on strike or otherwise idle will return to their usual work when called and that no discrimination shall be made or prejudices exercised by the Corporation against any employe because of his former affiliation with, or activities in, the Union or the present strike.

6) The Union agrees that pending the negotiations referred to in Paragraph Two, there shall be no strikes called or any other interruption to or interference with production, by the Union or its members.

7) During the existence of the collective bargaining agreement contemplated pursuant to Paragraph Two, all opportunities to achieve a satisfactory settlement of any grievance or enforcement of any demands by negotiations shall be exhausted before there shall be any strikes or other interruption to or interference with production by the Union or its members. There shall be no attempts to intimidate or coerce any employes by the Union and there shall not be any solicitation or signing up of members by the Union on the premises of the Company. This is not to preclude individual discussion.

8) After the evacuation of its plants and the termination of the strike the Corporation agrees to consent to the entry of orders, dismissing the injunction proceedings which have been started by the Corporation against the Union, or any of its members, or officers or any of its locals, including those pending in Flint, Michigan and Cleveland, Ohio, and subject to the approval of the Court to discontinue all contempt proceedings which it has instituted thereunder.

GENERAL MOTORS CORPORATION
William S. Knudsen
J. T. Smith
D. Brown

UNITED AUTOMOBILE WORKERS
Wyndham Mortimer, First Vice President
Lee Pressman, General Counsel, CIO
John L. Lewis, Chairman, CIO
Frank Murphy
James F. Dewey

THE DETROIT NEWS, FRIDAY, FEBRUARY 12, 1937.

A New Model

Purely Confidential

By PAUL MALLON

WASHINGTON, Feb. 12.—There are all kinds of ways of making congressmen see the broader aspects

The Public Letter Box

Too Old at 70?

To the Editor: If, as Mr. Roosevelt seems to think, a Supreme

Dog-Haters

To the Editor: In answer to J. V. A., the champion dog-hater, whose

Michigan governor Frank Murphy's role in facilitating the peaceful end of the Flint General Motors sit-down strike won him praise, as in this depiction of him in the February 12, 1937 edition of the *Detroit News*. **POLITICAL CARTOON "LAW, ORDER, COMMON, SENSE" FROM THE *DETROIT NEWS*, FEBRUARY 12, 1937, PHOTOGRAPH BY THE GRADUATE LIBRARY, THE UNIVERSITY OF MICHIGAN. COPYRIGHT © 2002, THE *DETROIT NEWS*. REPRODUCED BY PERMISSION FROM THE DETROIT NEWS.**

Primary Source

Letter to Frank Murphy

SYNOPSIS: This side letter from Knudsen to Governor Murphy assured him, and indirectly the UAW, that General Motors would not attempt to encourage competing unions. This letter was essential for the agreement to be acceptable to the UAW. Yet because of the strong philosophical opposition GM (and Knudsen) had maintained to compelling workers to join a union, it could not be included in the base agreement. Essentially, GM conceded to the UAW. They had come to accept the inevitability of a single union representing all hourly workers. The side letter allowed them to meet the UAW requirement that they be the sole bargaining agent without formally conceding the point.

The Honorable Frank Murphy
Governor of Michigan
Lansing, Michigan

Dear Governor:

We have been told that the United Automobile Workers of America, in justifying its demands for the bargaining privilege, state that they fear that without protection of some kind we might deliberately proceed to bargain with other groups for the purpose of undermining the position of this particular Union. We have said that we have no such intention.

On the other hand, we cannot enter into any agreement with anyone which can have the effect of denying to any group of our employes the rights of collective bargaining to which it is entitled, and which fails to protect them in the exercise of these rights.

On our part, therefore, we undertake not to seek or to inspire such activities on the part of other groups for the purposes of weakening this particular union.

This undertaking we assume on condition that the Union refrain from coercion and intimidation inside and outside the shop in its efforts to increase its membership.

As evidence of our intention to do all we can to hasten the resumption of work in our plants and to promote peace, we hereby agree with you that within a period of six months from the resumption of work we will not bargain with or enter into agreements with any other Union or representative or employes of plants on strike in respect to such matters of general corporate policy as referred to in letter of January 4th, without first submitting to you the facts of the situation and gaining from you the sanction of any such contemplated procedure as being justified by law, equity or justice towards the group of employes so represented.

Yours respectfully,
(Signed) W. S. Knudsen
Detroit, Michigan

Further Resources

BOOKS

Fine, Sidney. *Frank Murphy, Vol. 2: The New Deal Years.* Ann Arbor: University of Michigan Press, 1979.

———. *Sit-Down: The General Motors Strike of 1936–1937.* Ann Arbor: University of Michigan Press, 1969.

Brooks, Thomas R. *Toil and Trouble: A History of American Labor.* New York: Dell Publishing, 1964.

WEBSITES

BBC h2g2. "The 1936–37 Flint, Michigan Sit-Down Strike." Available online at http://www.bbc.co.uk/dna/h2g2/alabaster/A672310; website home page: http://www.bbc.co.uk (accessed August 9, 2002).

Local Legacies. "Sit-Down Strike." Available online at http://www.loc.gov/bicentennial/propage/MI/mi-09_h_kildee2.html; website home page: http://www.loc.gov (accessed August 9, 2002).

Michigan Department of Education, Educational Portal for Interactive Content. "Flint Sit-Down Strike: A Role-Playing Adventure." Available online at http://www.michiganepic.org/flintstrike/; website home page: http://www.michiganepic.org (accessed August 9, 2002).

"Progressive Labor Party Pamphlet, 'The Great Flint Sit-Down Strike against GM 1936–1937.'" Available online at http://www.plp.org/pamphlets/flintstrike.html; website home page: http://www.plp.org (accessed August 9, 2002).

"Armed Rebellion on the Right"

Editorial

By: Paul Y. Anderson

Date: August 7, 1937

Source: Anderson, Paul Y. "Armed Rebellion on the Right." *The Nation* 145, no. 6, August 7, 1937, 146–147. Available at the New Deal Network online at http://newdeal.feri.org/nation/na37145p146.htm; website home page: http://newdeal.feri.org (accessed March 17, 2003).

About the Author: Paul Y. Anderson (1893–1938) was a highly respected investigative journalist, described upon his death (by suicide) as the "last muckraker." Anderson spent most of his career with the *St. Louis Dispatch* and covered many of the great events of his era. He received a Pulitzer Prize for his reporting of the Teapot Dome Scandal in 1923–1924. ■

Introduction

Violence was an integral part of the labor movement. Management, often backed by local law enforcement, was frequently guilty of initiating attacks on union organizers, strikers, and union sympathizers. Crushing unions and all attempts at labor organization were deemed acceptable behavior among large segments of the population. During the Depression, however, popular support of unions and a more sympathetic stance by the federal government resulted in legislation such as the *National Industrial Recovery Act* (NIRA) and the

Wagner Act, which specifically granted workers the right to organize.

Despite the success of industrial union organization in early 1937, facilitated by the widespread use or threat of the sit-down strike, there remained significant areas of resistance to unionization. Ford Motor Company was one such anti-union bastion. The "Little Steel" companies were another. ("Little Steel" was a term applied to a handful of medium-sized steel companies, such as Republic, Bethlehem, and Inland. By comparison to industry giant U.S. Steel, they were "Little.")

In both cases, union organizing efforts resulted in some of the labor movement's most visible examples of flagrant violence by management, when unprovoked attacks on workers were captured on film. On May 26, 1937, in the so-called Battle of the Overpass, Ford's security force viciously attacked several United Automobile Worker organizers. Four days later, one of the most violent labor clashes in American history occurred during a union-sponsored Memorial Day picnic/rally near the Republic Steel plant in South Chicago. It left ten workers dead.

Ironically, the leading companies in automobile and steel manufacturing—General Motors, Chrysler, and U.S. Steel—had all agreed to union contracts several months earlier. Ford and the Little Steel companies were fighting a rear-guard action.

While the Little Steel companies were individually dwarfed by U.S. Steel, collectively they represented a significant part of the American steel industry. They adamantly opposed unions. Most vocal on this subject was the head of Republic Steel, Tom Girdler. In violation of the *Wagner Act,* the Little Steel companies refused to negotiate with the steel union, the CIO-sponsored Steel Workers Organizing Committee (SWOC). In response, the SWOC went on strike beginning in late May 1937, eventually idling more than seventy thousand workers.

Significance

In response to the SWOC's organizing efforts, Little Steel companies supplemented the traditional anti-union tactics of blacklisting, firings, spies, physical intimidation, and strikebreakers with a tactic known as the "Mohawk Valley Formula." Developed by James H. Rand Jr. and used to crush a strike at the Remington Rand Corporation in 1936, the Mohawk Valley Formula's main strategies were to undermine the union and rally popular support against "radicals." Frequently management was able to count on local government and law enforcement to support their union-busting efforts.

The initial local response to the events at Republic supported the company. As the facts became known and graphic film footage was made available, the obvious brutality of the police became evident. Nonetheless, the outcry was somewhat muted. The country had endured six months of debilitating labor strife—highlighted by hundreds of sit-down strikes—and there was a widespread belief that Communists were using the labor movement to engineer domestic turmoil or worse.

Even Roosevelt, to whom John L. Lewis and the CIO turned for support in backing the steel workers, had had enough. Roosevelt's oft-quoted Shakespearean response, "a plague on both your houses," demonstrated his frustration less with the steel situation than with labor's militancy and management's intransigence in the previous six months.

An investigation conducted by a Senate committee headed by Robert La Follette Jr. of Wisconsin concluded that the Memorial Day incident was the result of an unprovoked attack by the police on peaceful demonstrators. Nonetheless, Roosevelt's refusal to intervene left the workers isolated, and in July the strike collapsed.

The events of that summer brought an end to Lewis's support of Roosevelt. In 1940, John L. Lewis opposed Roosevelt's reelection. Following FDR's third-term election, Lewis resigned as president of the CIO.

It was not until 1941 that the SWOC was able to organize in the Little Steel companies.

Primary Source

"Armed Rebellion on the Right"

SYNOPSIS: *The Nation,* from which the following article was extracted, regularly covered the dramatic and often violent strikes of the 1930s. Wracked by months of labor unrest, popular pro-labor sentiment had lost some of its appeal. Nonetheless, this piece leaves no doubt about author Paul Anderson's strong opposition to management's arrogant, and even criminal, behavior. Anderson is particularly critical of Republic Steel's chairman, Tom Girdler.

For several months an important section of American industry, led by the Republic Steel Corporation, has been in a state of open, armed rebellion against the authority of the United States government as expressed in the *Wagner Act,* and its mercenaries have inflicted heavy casualties in dead, wounded, and captured, without suffering any appreciable losses. The explanation of this astonishing military success is to be found in the fact that the government thus far has refrained from sending regular troops against the insurgents, being content to rely on the efforts of citizen volunteers armed with nothing more deadly than moral

Striking workers march in between armed National Guardsmen and police outside of American Republic Steel Works in Chicago, Illinois. 1937. GETTY IMAGES. REPRODUCED BY PERMISSION.

suasion. And moral suasion is a poor defense against bullets.

The object of this dispatch is to parade recent incidents of the rebellion in a connected sequence, and thereby attempt to explain why the commission of mass murder in certain localities of the United States has become bolder, safer, and more systematically organized during the last two months than at any other period since Al Capone, Dion O'Banion, the Genna brothers, and Bugs Moran made Chicago their private battleground. The two periods are alike in one respect, that the motive was profit. But whereas the police were merely corrupt and quiescent when the gangsters were killing one another, they are now doing the killing themselves; and whereas all sides in the gang wars were well armed, the police victims have all been unarmed workingmen or innocent bystanders.

On the afternoon of Memorial Day Sunday a holiday crowd of some 2,500 men, women, and children attended a mass meeting several blocks distant from the South Chicago plant of the Republic Steel Corporation, where a strike was in progress. At its conclusion most of them proceeded to a point a few blocks removed from the plant, and there a group of about 400 detached themselves from the main body and walked along a dirt road across an open field in the general direction of the plant, with the intention of marching past the gates, displaying signs appealing to the non-striking workers to come out and join them.

At the far corner of the field, before the gates were in sight, the paraders were halted by a long line of uniformed Chicago policemen, numbering 200 or more. During a parley which lasted not more than four minutes individuals at the front of the procession asked the police for permission to proceed through the line and establish peaceful picketing, as had been promised by Mayor Kelly, and were told in reply to "get the hell out of here." Then, upon a signal which consisted either of the firing of a shot in the air or the tossing of a gas grenade into the midst of the crowd, police charged into the left flank of the crowd, clubbing its members ferociously. From back in the throng a shower of small stones and sticks was thrown toward the police.

Instantly there was a terrific roar of pistol shots from all along the police line, and as the front rank of the marchers went down in a bloody tangle the bluecoats charged with smoking guns and flying

Policemen battle with strikers outside Republican Steel plant, Chicago, Illinois. May 30, 1937. Ten strikers were killed during the battle, many others wounded. Three policemen were injured. AP/WIDE WORLD PHOTOS. REPRODUCED BY PERMISSION.

nightsticks. Total dead: ten, of whom seven were shot in the back. Total suffering from gunshot wounds: approximately 50, of whom 62 per cent were shot in the back. Total injured from all causes: approximately 75, of whom at least two will be crippled for life. Three policemen were hospitalized. No policemen were shot. Cook County authorities took the position that the victims, including those shot in the back, were killed by policemen acting in self-defense. The coroner's jury sustained that position. Among the 67 persons arrested by police and fortunate—or unfortunate—enough to recover from their wounds, a large number are to be prosecuted for "conspiracy to commit an illegal act," a penitentiary offense.

On June 19 a mediation board appointed by Secretary Perkins met in Cleveland. It consisted of Charles P. Taft, chairman, son of the late President and Chief Justice; Lloyd Garrison, dean of the law school at Wisconsin University, and Assistant Secretary of Labor Edward F. McGrady. Also present were Tom Girdler, chairman of Republic Steel, Eugene Grace, chairman of Bethlehem, and lower-ranking spokesmen for Inland and Youngstown Sheet and Tube. The mediators had undertaken their task under the impression—theretofore shared by virtually everyone else—that the only issue was whether the operators would sign an agreement with the union. They were promptly disillusioned.

Spouting purple profanity, Girdler took the floor to declare that John L. Lewis was a so-and-so, that the C.I.O. was a racketeering outfit, that he would never enter into any kind of an agreement, oral or written, in this connection, and that it was his determination to "make wages conform to the price of steel, if it involves changing them from hour to hour." The more delicate sensibilities of Mr. Grace appeared to shrink when exposed to the rigors of his colleague's vocabulary, but at no stage did he fail to support his position. Patiently the mediators strove to devise some formula, but each successive attempt ended when Girdler pounded the table and bellowed: "God damn it, I tell you the answer is no!" The atmosphere of tension eased somewhat when Girdler departed for Washington to stage his act before the Senate Post Office Committee, to the applause of Senator Bailey, patron saint of the North Carolina textile industry, but after a week the negotiations collapsed and the board members returned to Washington to report to Secretary Perkins.

After his appearance before the Post Office Committee Girdler presented himself at an exclusive press conference attended by six correspondents, and there he really took down his hair. His remarks about Governors Murphy and Earle, Myron Taylor, chairman of United States Steel, Secretary Perkins, McGrady, Taft, and Garrison cannot be printed here or in any other publication which is destined for the mails. They were not merely profane, they included insinuations which are not tolerated in ordinary locker-room conversation. He left a distinct impression that one of the things he needs most is to go to a competent psychiatrist and have his mind washed out with soap and water.

On June 29 President Roosevelt waived the rules of his press conference to allow himself to be quoted as follows: "Charlie Taft and I agreed that in the nation as a whole, in regard to the recent strike episodes, the majority of the people are saying just one thing— 'A plague on both your houses!'"

Four days later Representative Ditter, a Pennsylvania Republican who had been tormenting Secretary Perkins for an opinion on the legality of sit-down strikes, received a reply in which she "deduced" from an opinion by the Third Circuit Court of Appeals in the Apex Hosiery case "that strikers may not lawfully use the sitdown method." Two days later Secretary of Commerce Roper made a radio speech in which he said: "The right to strike must be safeguarded, but equally fundamental is the right to work. . . . Extremists on either side of the prevailing controversy should harmonize their views with the attitude of the majority."

Meantime "the prevailing controversy" had continued to prevail at Republic's struck plant in Massillon, Ohio, but something was being done to "harmonize" the situation. Just when President Roosevelt was washing his hands of the distasteful affair by calling for "a plague on both your houses," Carl Meyers, district manager for Republic in the Canton-Massillon district, was sending for Chief Switter of the Massillon police. Switter Later testified before the Labor Relations Board:

> Meyers wanted to know what the hell was going on over there—letting those hoodlums run the town. He wanted to know why we hadn't done like the Chicago police had done. They knew how to handle a situation, he said. He told me if the mills closed down Massillion would be nothing but a junction point, with no need for a mayor or a chief of police or any other city officials.

A Law and Order League, composed of Massillon's "leading" business men, was urging Switter to commission extra policemen for strike duty and offering to pay and equip them. General Marlin, who with a fine sense of impartiality had quartered two companies of the Ohio National Guard in the Republic plant, urged Switter to accept the offer. Harry Curley, a retired army officer, now in the contracting business, offered his services in organizing a larger police force. Finally two officials of Republic presented a list of "loyal" company employees and suggested that the proposed new policemen be selected from it!

Switter resisted valiantly for a few days. He emphasized that there had been no loss of life and no serious disorder. Local manufacturers held a luncheon and demanded action. The Law and Order League "climbed all over the mayor." General Marlin wanted to know why Switter wasn't "showing some signs of life," and when the chief of police explained that he was trying to select "neutral" men for the proposed new commissions the gallant general retorted: "This is no time to be neutral!"

On July 7 the city government and the chief of police capitulated, and thirty or forty Republic employees were sworn in as special policemen. Curley picked them from the proffered list. Republic indemnified their bonds. They were given badges and guns. On the evening of July 11 Chief Switter drove out of town on a picnic. Almost immediately, it appears from testimony, Curley took command of the department. He had no official standing. During the afternoon John Veto, a striker, passing a group of the new special policemen, heard Bill Henderson, a Republic foreman, remark: "We're going to clean them out tonight."

About eleven that night some fifteen or twenty of the "specials" arrived in front of strike headquarters and deployed in a line on the opposite side of the street. Two or three hundred strikers were loafing on the sidewalk in front of their building. An automobile occupied by a striker drew up, and the headlights shone on the police.

"Turn off those lights or we'll shoot them out, "ordered a policeman. The motorist turned them out; then, becoming frightened and wishing to drive away, he turned them on again. From among the police came a shout: "All right, they asked for it—let 'em have it!"

The order was obeyed. Wild screams and shouts filled the air as the hail of police bullets crashed into the dense crowd before the strikers' building and tear-gas grenades whizzed through the windows. A dozen men fell to the sidewalk and others staggered about in the street moaning with pain. Total dead:

two—one of them shot in the back of the head. Total wounded: 15. Total police injured: none.

In the hours following the killing, squads of police and special deputies raided rooming-houses in the vicinity, breaking down doors, dragging men from their beds, and questioning them as to whether they belonged to the union. Those who said they did—along with some who denied it—were loaded into National Guard trucks and carted off to the Massillon jail and the Canton workhouse. They were held two days, after which most of them were freed—but not before they had signed waivers releasing the city from any liability arising from property damage or false arrest. In that respect they fared better than their comrades at Chicago who will be tried.

Early this week a picket was killed before the gates of a Republic plant in Cleveland when he was run down by a truck operated by a "loyal worker." The latter has been arrested and may be tried for manslaughter. It would serve him right: he should know by now that under the rules of this game you are not permitted to kill a striker until you have been provided with a badge, and then you are expected to shoot him in the back—not run over him with a truck.

A few days ago the writer inquired of an authorized spokesman for the C.I.O. whether there had been a "break" with the Administration, and if not, whether one was anticipated. This was the reply:

> We don't want to "break" with the Administration. God knows we worked and sacrificed to keep it in office. But we don't understand its attitude in the steel strike, and we are resentful to find that suddenly we are no longer politically respectable in the eyes of the Administration. Labor's money and labor's votes were welcome enough last fall, when the Girdlers and the Graces and the reactionary press were damning Roosevelt from hell to breakfast. But now, when Girdler and Grace have their claws in labor's throat, all we hear from the White House is— "A plague on both your houses!"
>
> We could quote Shakespeare—and the Bible, too—in this situation. President Roosevelt is not the first magistrate to wash his hands when faced with an issue of innocence and guilt. Neutrality ceases to be a virtue when authority is confronted with wanton, cold-blooded, deliberately planned murder. Nor does our case rest on moral grounds alone. The Department of Justice is prosecuting nobody for violating the *Wagner Act.* It is prosecuting nobody for violating the *National Firearms Act.* It is prosecuting nobody for violating the act prohibiting the interstate transportation of strikebreakers.
>
> Yet, with Tom Girdler and Eugene Grace defying the law and spitting in the eye of Secretary Perkins's mediation board, Attorney-General Cummings rushes to indict eight men on charges of obstructing the mails, brought by Tom Girdler's lawyer, although the Post Office Department had informed the Senate that no violation has been reported.

We expected the Administration to be subjected to the drumfire of criticism, now being hurled at it by the Tory press and the vested interests who fought Roosevelt for reelection. Knowing him as we did and do, we expected him to yield a little. But there is a difference between giving ground for strategic reasons and beating a full retreat. There is a stage at which one degenerates into the other. Has that stage been reached? We shall wait a little longer to see.

Further Resources

BOOKS

Bauman, John F., and Thomas H. Coode. *In the Eye of the Great Depression: New Deal Reporters and the Agony of the American People.* DeKalb, Ill.: Northern Illinois University Press, 1988.

Bernstein, Irving. *A Caring Society: The New Deal, the Worker, and the Great Depression: A History of the American Worker, 1933–1941.* Boston: Houghton Mifflin, 1985.

Cronon, Edmund David, ed. *Labor and the New Deal.* Chicago: Rand McNally, 1963.

PERIODICALS

Stolberg, Benjamin. *The Nation* 145, no. 7, August 14, 1933, 168.

WEBSITES

Bork, William. "Massacre at Republic Steel." Illinois Labor History Society. Available online at http://www.kentlaw.edu/ilhs/republic.htm; website home page: http://www.kentlaw.edu (accessed September 11, 2002).

Fast, Howard. "Memorial Day Massacre." Trussel's EclectiC-ity. Available online at http://www.trussel.com/index.htm; website home page: http://www.trussel.com (accessed September 11, 2002).

Farmers on Relief and Rehabilitation

Monograph

By: Berta Asch and A.R. Mangus

Date: 1937

Source: Asch, Berta, and A.R. Mangus. *Farmers on Relief and Rehabilitation.* Research Monograph VIII. Washington, D.C.: United States Government Printing Office, 1937, 7–12.

About the Authors: Berta Asch and A.R. Mangus were part of a team of researchers for the Works Progress Administration's Division of Social Research. They helped produce a series of research monographs on various social aspects of the Depression. These monographs focused on rural life and the condition of migratory workers. ■

Introduction

The American farm underwent considerable change between 1910 and 1930. At the beginning of this period, farms were gradually becoming more mechanized, larger, and increasingly affected by global markets. These gradual trends were rapidly accelerated by World War I (1914–1918).

The demand for American farm products during the war caused tremendous growth. Unable to feed itself between 1915 and 1920, Europe turned to America. To meet this need, farmers took advantage of powered farm equipment (especially the tractor), increased fertilization, and brought marginal land into production. Tempted by high prices and short-term profits, they went heavily into debt to acquire the necessary resources to take advantage of the opportunity.

The boom years ended with the coming of peace and a return to normal production levels in Europe by 1921. As the European situation stabilized, demand for American products declined. Prices fell, and the financial position of farmers, now burdened with debt and able to operate more efficiently and with less manual labor, quickly became worse. While the Depression years were very difficult for the entire country, the farm depression began in the early 1920s. By the time of the stock market crash in 1929, the American farmer had already experienced nearly a decade of hard times.

The overall condition of the farm economy can be illustrated by a few key statistics: The price of wheat rose from 91¢ per bushel in 1910 to $2.16 in 1919 but lost value throughout the 1920s before plummeting to only 38¢ per bushel in 1932. Meanwhile, farm debt grew from $3.2 billion in 1910 to nearly $9.1 billion in 1932. Mechanization—there were more than a million tractors in use in 1932, whereas in 1910 there were less than one thousand—was a major cause of the mounting debt and increasing pressure on small farmers to remain competitive.

Significance

Increased productivity had allowed American farmers to meet the pressing needs of millions of Europeans during and immediately after World War I. That efficiency—the new standard of productivity which successful farmers needed to meet to remain competitive—came with considerable consequences. The cost of machinery and fertilizer had pushed farmers deep into debt, with their land often put up as collateral. When farmers could not pay their debts, thousands lost their farms.

Mechanization also put millions of farm workers at risk. Simply put, there was less need for manpower. While an absolute decline in farm population did not occur until after World War II (1939–1945), pressure on small and tenant farmers was intense. This was particularly true in the South as small farms became less and less profitable.

When the general economy collapsed in 1930, demand for farm products dipped further, followed by another sharp decline in prices. Weakened banks increased the rate of foreclosure.

Faced with a collapse of the farm economy, the federal government stepped in. Short-term relief, relocation efforts, work projects (often aimed at curbing erosion and expanding rural electrification), and a system of farm price supports initiated by the Agricultural Adjustment Act brought some stability to the farm sector by the mid-1930s. Nonetheless, the fundamental trends caused by increased productivity and global competition could not be changed. There were too many farmers. Those who survived would do so in a highly competitive, global market in which government played an increasingly larger role.

Primary Source

Farmers on Relief and Rehabilitation [excerpt]

SYNOPSIS: The following excerpt is from one of the many research papers prepared by the government during the New Deal in an effort to analyze social and economic conditions. *Farmers on Relief* describes federal efforts to assist farmers through direct relief, relocation and improving farm operations. This excerpt describes some of the basic causes of the farm crisis. By implication, it also outlines the scope of intervention required to address the needs of the farm sector.

Basic Farm Problems

Part of the vast volume of rural need was due directly to depression factors. Farmers who had done fairly well in the past were victims of bank failures and vanishing markets. City workers and workers in rural industries lost their jobs and, without farm experience or capital, tried to make a living from the soil. Youth who would normally have gone to the cities and towns to work in industry stayed on the farm, crowding into an already overcrowded agriculture.

The depression was not directly responsible, however, for all the rural distress reflected in the heavy re-

Net Income of Farm Operators from Farming, 1926–1939

AVERAGE INCOME PER FARM

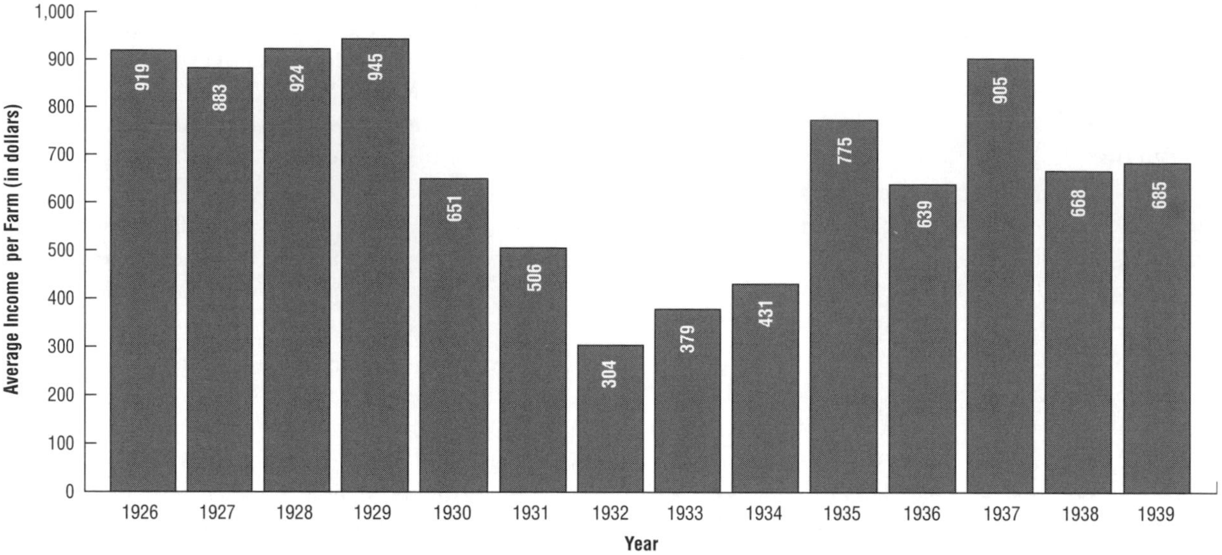

SOURCE: Based on data from the U.S. Bureau of the Census. *Historical Statistics of the United States, Colonial Times to 1970.* New York: Basic Books, 1976, p. 483.

lief rolls. Federal relief brought to light a much more numerous group of farmers whose distress arose from long-run factors, who had led a precarious existence for some years prior to the depression because of these factors, or for whom the depression was the last straw in an accumulation of troubles outside their control.

Some of the accumulating hazards of American agrarian life have been enumerated here. They show the variety and complexity of the forces which underlie rural distress and indicate the regional differences involved.

Farming on Poor Land

In many parts of the country, farmers have been attempting for years to cultivate soil which was never suitable for farming or which has deteriorated beyond redemption. Such soil has given them only the barest living and has made it impossible for them to better their condition. Had Federal relief not been made available, they might have continued more or less inarticulately to endure their extreme poverty unaided. The relief program served to bring their condition to light and to focus attention on the need for removing the impoverished land from cultivation.

The National Resources Board has estimated that about 450,000 farms in the United States, including 75 million acres, are of this submarginal type. They are to be found for the most part in the hilly, dry, or forested parts of the country and in sections where the soil is light and sandy or seriously eroded. Over one-half of the total acreage proposed for retirement from arable farming is in the Western Great Plains and the southeastern hilly cotton and tobacco regions, although scattered concentrations are found throughout the United States.

Excess Birth Rate in Poor Land Areas

Poor land in itself is a sufficient hazard to farming, but when, as in the Appalachian-Ozark highlands and parts of the cotton areas, it is coupled with an excessive birth rate, the problem is greatly aggravated, and individual and family suffering multiplied. In the past, the high farm birth rate served to populate new areas and the cities. But desirable free homestead land was exhausted years ago and the covered wagon is no longer a means of escape from an overcrowded shack in the hills. The depression shut off the opportunity to make a living by migrating to cities and towns. There was nothing for the surplus rural population to do but remain, causing serious unbalance between population and land in many sections.

All Wheat for Grain Prices, 1919–1939

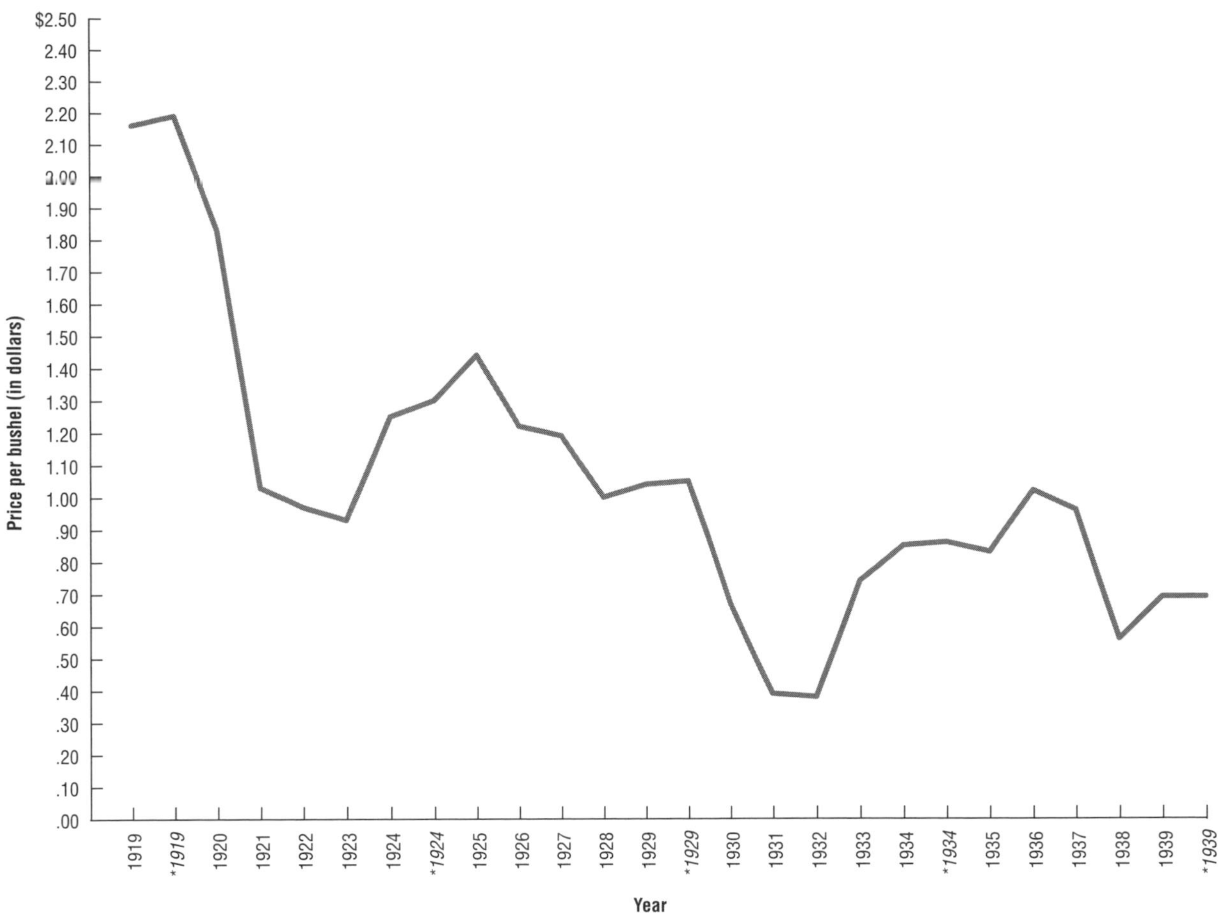

*Census figures in italics.

SOURCE: Based on data from the U.S. Bureau of the Census. *Historical Statistics of the United States, Colonial Times to 1970.* New York: Basic Books, 1976, p. 511.

Soil Erosion

Not only have some farmers been trying to grow crops on hopelessly poor soil, but others have been ruining good land by practices conducive to soil erosion or have failed to take necessary precautions to protect land subject to erosion. Warnings of soil erosion have been heard in many areas for years, but these have been ignored by farmers who were too eager for immediate results to care about the future. Other farmers could not afford the outlay necessary to prevent erosion or had such limited acreages that they had no choice but to use their land to the full, regardless of the danger of overcropping. In 1934, the National Resources Board reported that the usefulness for farming of 35 million acres had been completely destroyed, that the top soil was nearly or entirely removed from another 125 million acres, and that destruction had begun on another 100 million acres.

Excessive cropping has been especially destructive on the dry land of the Western Great Plains, where quarter sections allotted to the settlers under the homesteading laws were too small for economic use of the land. The farmers were further led astray during the World War when they were encouraged to break more and more sod in order to meet the world demand for wheat. No provision was made against the effects of the inevitable dry years, and vast acreages of dry soil were left unprotected by grass or trees against the ravages of wind and sun.

The southern and western corn belts also contain much easily eroded soil which is being destroyed because the many small farmers in the area have been concentrating on clean-cultivated row crops. In the hilly southeastern section, cotton and tobacco are being grown for the market on land from which the top soil has been completely worn away. Cultivating the subsoil requires extensive use of fertilizer, which makes farming on such land an expensive and precarious business. The cost of fertilizer consumes a large part of the farmer's income and credit, and when the crop fails he is ready for the relief rolls.

Inadequate Size of Farms

Small farms in areas which require large-scale methods often lead to practices conducive to soil erosion, as already pointed out. Even when soil erosion is not involved, the farms are often inadequate to make a stable income possible. Where productivity per acre is low, as in the western dry-farming regions and the hilly cotton areas, and where there is constant threat of drought, large acreages are required to compensate for low productivity and to build up reserves for years of crop loss. Farmers whose acreages are too small to provide such surpluses in good years are brought to dependency at the first year of crop failure.

Extension of the One Cash Crop System

The recent trend in American agriculture has been toward absolute dependence on a single cash crop—cotton, tobacco, corn, or wheat—to the exclusion of production of food and feed crops for home use. The small farmer who follows this practice is rarely able to accumulate reserves in good years for the year when his one crop fails or the market falls. When that time comes, he is left not only with no alternative source of income but also with no products for home consumption.

Overcapitalization of Farms

During the World War and post-war years, farmers borrowed money and bought large acreages of land at inflated values in order to take advantage of high prices for foodstuffs. They also invested heavily in machinery to be paid for at some future date. But before they could realize on their investment, the depression sent prices and land values tobogganing. Many were unable to meet real estate and chattel mortgage payments and were left in the hands of their creditors.

Decline of Rural Industries

Natural resources, such as timber, coal, and other minerals, have been progressively and often wastefully depleted in certain parts of the country. These formerly furnished small farmers with a means of earning the cash income necessary to supplement their limited agricultural production. When these industries declined, the farmers became completely dependent on farms too small or too unproductive to support them. This situation is found in the Lake States Cut-Over and Appalachian-Ozark Areas in particular, and accounts in part for the heavy relief loads in those regions.

The Tenant System

An extremely low standard of living has been characteristic of tenant farmers in various parts of the country since long before the depression. This has been particularly true of the South where the cotton tenant system, especially that phase of tenancy known as sharecropping, was developed to utilize the abundant supply of cheap and tractable labor.

Under the sharecropping system the tenant furnishes the labor of his entire family, as well as his own, for raising the cotton crop. The family receives in return the use of a piece of land, a house, work stock, equipment, subsistence goods, and the proceeds of half the crop, the other half being retained by the landlord. This system has become more and more widespread, until at the present time 50 percent of the tenants in some States are sharecroppers.

While cotton was booming, the extreme poverty of the southern cotton tenant attracted little attention, but the depression and pre-depression years brought a crisis in the cotton market. Cotton acreage was extended after the war. Increases in production, however, coincided with a relatively decreasing demand both at home and abroad. The competition of artificial silk, increased production in foreign countries since the World War, and increased tariffs were some of the factors responsible. The results were decreasing prices since 1925 and a large carry-over from one season to another.

When the depression brought these conditions to a climax, acreage was sharply reduced, and tenants, especially sharecroppers, were displaced from the land. With no resources of any kind, and accustomed to depend on the landlord for every want, large numbers of tenant farm families were left stranded, bewildered, and helpless.

The acreage reduction program of the Agricultural Adjustment Administration raised prices and helped the cotton growers by benefit payments. Most of the tenants' payments in the first years of the program, however, were applied by the landlords to old debts, and tenants continued to be displaced from the farms, although at a much slower rate than before.

Assuming a permanently decreased demand for cotton, the tenant system of the South has produced a "stranded" population, a group of landless people with undeveloped capacities, who, unless some scheme for rehabilitation is devised, will be permanently in need of public assistance.

Not so widely publicized, but more rapid of late, has been the increase in tenancy in the drought-stricken Great Plains Area, where discouraged owners are being replaced by tenants.

Farm Laborer Problem

Insofar as farm laborers have formerly been employed by farmers now on relief, their need for relief is caused by the same factors that caused the need of their former employers. The depression also led to unemployment of farm laborers through restricting the demand for farm hands by farmers still able to carry on. It may be reasonably assumed, therefore, that the relief problem of farm laborers is to a greater extent a function of the depression than the result of long-run tendencies.

In addition, the problem of migratory labor has grown markedly with the increase of large-scale one crop commercial farming. Since under this system laborers are needed for only a brief period while the one crop is being harvested, they must move on to other areas after a few weeks, and so on throughout the season. At best they can find employment for only a few months a year and their wages are not enough to carry them through the months of idleness. Because of their wandering existence, they are without roots in any community and cannot turn to neighbors or neighborhood grocers for help in off-seasons.

Further Resources

BOOKS

Holley, Donald. *Uncle Sam's Farmers: The New Deal Communities in the Lower Mississippi Valley.* Urbana: University of Illinois Press, 1975.

Saloutos, Theodore. *The American Farmer and the New Deal.* Ames: Iowa State University Press, 1982.

Watkins, Tom H. *The Great Depression: America in the 1930s.* Boston: Little, Brown, 1993.

John Maynard Keynes to President Roosevelt, February 1, 1938

Letter

By: John Maynard Keynes

Date: February 1, 1938

Source: Keynes, John Maynard. Letter to President Roosevelt, February 1, 1938. Reprinted in Current, Richard N., and John A. Garraty, eds. *Words That Made American History Since the Civil War.* Boston and Toronto: Little, Brown, 1965, 480–484.

About the Author: John Maynard Keynes (1883–1946) was an English economist whose revolutionary economic theories (Keynesian economics) have dramatically affected economic policy throughout the world since the early 1930s. His most important work, *The General Theory of Employment, Interest and Money* (1935), formalized his theories. In this work, Keynes sharply opposed traditional, laissez-faire doctrines that argued that the natural operation of the marketplace would correct economic downturns. Keynes played a major role in developing policies to fund World War II (1939–1945) and post–World War II economic recovery. ■

Introduction

At the time of the Depression, traditional economic theory held that the economy was self-correcting. It said that left alone, natural economic forces would restore prosperity within a relatively short time. Employment could be restored if workers accepted lower wages, and sales/production would return to appropriate levels if prices were cut. Above all, government should not intervene. Its role was to cut taxes, balance the budget, and let natural forces operate.

By the time Franklin Roosevelt became president, however, it had become evident to many Americans that these hands-off policies were not working. It was the English economist John Maynard Keynes who provided the theoretical explanation that demonstrated the flaws in traditional thinking and justified new policies.

Keynes strongly rejected the belt-tightening measures of most economists, business leaders, and politicians. He urged governments to undertake large-scale public employment projects to stimulate the economy during an economic downtorun. Keynes argued that private industry, driven by short term considerations of profit and loss, would be afraid to make major expenditures and investments during a severe downward cycle. Yet large expenditures are exactly what would be needed to end such a cycle and return to prosperity. Therefore only aggressive steps taken as a matter of public policy could reverse a severe recession.

In early 1933 Keynes began periodic communication with Franklin Roosevelt. It was initiated through the un-

British economist John Maynard Keynes works in his office in 1940.

usual device of an open letter addressed to Roosevelt but published in *The New York Times.* Although delivered in advance by Felix Frankfurter—a law professor, Roosevelt adviser, and future Supreme Court Justice—the letter was prepared "in response to *The New York Times*' request for his [Keynes'] views on the American outlook." The two met in 1934 and discussed Keynes' theories and their implications for government policy.

Roosevelt was not an economic scholar and did not fully grasp all of the complexities of Keynes' arguments. Nonetheless, Roosevelt came to accept many Keynesian ideas, perhaps less because of theoretical arguments than practical experience and necessity.

Significance

The most important aspect of Keynesian economic theory on the New Deal was the role he felt government should play in stimulating the economy. Keynes believed that government spending on such things as public works projects should be used to offset reduced activity in the private sector, even if it led to increasing government debt.

Opposition to amassing a large debt had been a major obstacle to public works projects and even providing basic relief in Hoover's administration. Roosevelt, too, placed emphasis on the need to balance the budget. In fact, in the last year of Hoover's administration the budget deficit was comparable to that which Roosevelt would incur during the balance of the 1930s. Hoover's debt, however, was primarily the result of declining tax revenues. Roosevelt substantially increased spending and revenues. The majority of those expenditures were on economic stimulus programs consistent with Keynesian ideas.

To what extent Keynes influenced Roosevelt is unclear. No doubt Roosevelt welcomed the support that Keynesian economic theory gave to many New Deal policies. And certainly Keynes' credibility and reputation helped win public support of the New Deal.

Nonetheless, Keynes cannot officially be called an adviser to Roosevelt. They met only once, and although they communicated periodically, Roosevelt never admitted to fully endorsing Keynes's ideas. Roosevelt seemed to follow a middle course. He abandoned any serious effort to balance the budget but was unwilling to undertake the more extensive programs urged by the Keynesians. This was particularly evident in 1938. Despite a return of high unemployment, Roosevelt's response was relatively modest. Roosevelt's reaction to the economic slide of 1937–38 can be explained in large part by his weakened political position. The deteriorating international situation and increased conservative pressure on the New Deal programs made it difficult for him to adopt the more aggressive spending measures.

In the end, the New Deal's incorporation of Keynesian thought created a federal government whose new role included supplementing the private sector in stimulating economic growth, particularly during depressed periods. While this philosophy has strong critics, it has become a generally accepted function of government.

Primary Source

Letter to President Roosevelt

SYNOPSIS: Keynes sent the following surprisingly blunt letter to President Roosevelt while the United States was in the midst of the so-called "Roosevelt Recession." After a period of recovery in 1935 and 1936, Roosevelt began to scale back federal programs. The private sector was unable to pick up the slack, and the economy went into a steep slide in 1937. Keynes urged, among other things, renewed public investment in large capital improvement projects.

February 1, 1938

King's College, Cambridge
Private and personal

Dear Mr. President,

You received me so kindly when I visited you some three years ago that I make bold to send you some bird's eye impressions which I have formed as to the business position in the United States. You will appreciate that I write from a distance, that I have not re-visited the United States since you saw me, and that I have access to few more sources of information than those publicly available. But sometimes in some respects there may be advantages in these limitations! At any rate, those things which I think I see, I see very clearly.

1. I should agree that the present recession is partly due to an "error of optimism" which led to an over-estimation of future demand, when orders were being placed in the first half of this year. If this were all, there would not be too much to worry about. It would only need time to effect a readjustment;—though, even so, the recovery would only be up to the point required to take care of the *revised* estimate of current demand, which might fall appreciably short of the prosperity reached last spring.

2. But I am quite sure that this is not all. There is a much more troublesome underlying influence. The recovery was mainly due to the following factors:—

(i) the solution of the credit and insolvency problems, and the establishment of easy short-term money;

(ii) the creation of an adequate system of relief for the unemployed;

(iii) public works and other investments aided by Government funds or guarantees;

(iv) investment in the instrumental goods required to supply the increased demand for consumption goods;

(v) the momentum of the recovery thus initiated.

Now of these (i) was a prior condition of recovery, since it is no use creating a demand for credit, if there is no supply. But an increased supply will not by itself generate an adequate demand. The influence of (ii) evaporates as employment improves, so that there is a dead point beyond which this factor cannot carry the economic system. Recourse to (iii) has been greatly curtailed in the past year. (iv) and (v) are functions of the forward movement and cease—indeed (v) is reversed—as soon as the position fails to improve further. The benefit from the momentum of recovery as such is at the same time the most important and the most dangerous factor in the upward movement. It requires for its continuance, not merely the maintenance of recovery, but always *further* recovery. Thus it always flatters the early stages and steps from under just when support is most needed. It was largely, I think, a failure to allow for this which caused the "error of optimism" last year.

Unless, therefore, the above factors were supplemented by others in due course, the present slump could have been predicted with absolute certainty. It is true that the existing policies will prevent the slump from proceeding to such a disastrous degree as last time. But they will not by themselves—at any rate, not without a large scale recourse to (iii)—maintain prosperity at a reasonable level.

3. Now one had hoped that the needed supplementary factors would be organised in time. It was obvious what these were—namely increased investment in durable goods such as housing, public utilities and transport. One was optimistic about this because in the United States at the present time the opportunities, indeed the necessity, for such developments were unexampled. Can your Administration escape criticism for the failure of these factors to mature?

Take housing. When I was with you three and a half years ago the necessity for effective new measures was evident. I remember vividly my conversations with Riefler at that time. But what happened? Next to nothing. The handling of the housing problem has been really wicked. I hope that the new measures recently taken will be more successful. I have not the knowledge to say. But they will take time, and I would urge the great importance of expediting and yet further aiding them. Housing is by far the best aid to recovery because of the large and continuing scale of potential demand; because of the wide geographical distribution of this demand; and because the sources of its finance are largely independent of the Stock Exchanges. I should advise putting most of your eggs in this basket, *caring* about this more than about anything, and making absolutely sure that they are being hatched without delay. In this country we partly depended for many years on direct subsidies. There are few more proper objects for such than working class houses. If a direct subsidy is required to get a move on (we gave our subsidies *through* the local authorities), it should be given without delay or hesitation.

Next utilities. There seems to be a deadlock. Neither your policy nor anyone else's is able to take effect. I think that the litigation by the utilities is senseless and ill-advised. But a great deal of what is alleged against the wickedness of holding com-

Federal Government Finances, 1930-1939

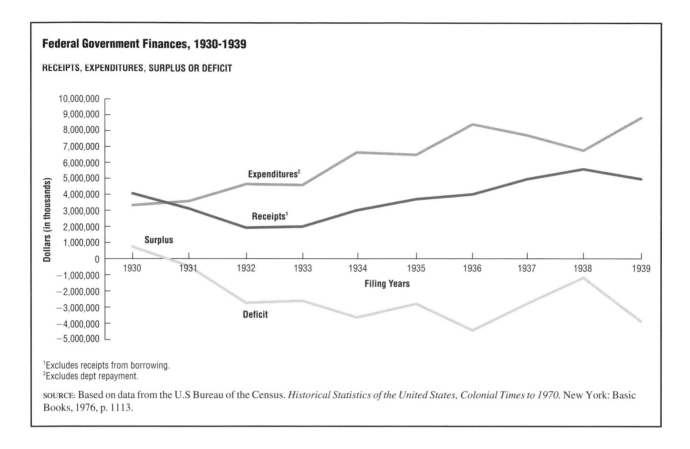

RECEIPTS, EXPENDITURES, SURPLUS OR DEFICIT

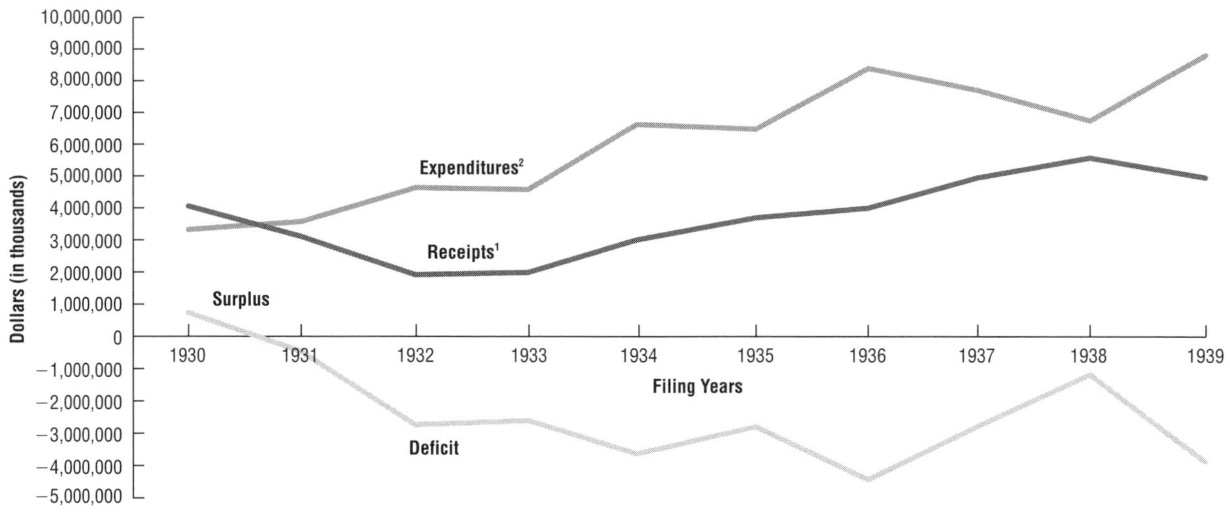

[1]Excludes receipts from borrowing.
[2]Excludes dept repayment.

SOURCE: Based on data from the U.S Bureau of the Census. *Historical Statistics of the United States, Colonial Times to 1970.* New York: Basic Books, 1976, p. 1113.

panies as such is surely wide of the mark. It does not draw the right line of division between what should be kept and what discarded. It arises too much out of what is dead and gone. The real criminals have cleared out long ago. I should doubt if the controls existing to-day are of much *personal* value to anyone. No-one has suggested a procedure by which the eggs can be unscrambled. Why not tackle the problem by insisting that the *voting power* should belong to the real owners of the equity, and leave the existing *organisations* undisturbed, so long as the voting power is so rearranged (e.g. by bringing in preferred stockholders) that it cannot be controlled by the holders of a minority of the equity?

Is it not for you to decide either to make real peace or to be much more drastic the other way? Personally I think there is a great deal to be said for the ownership of all the utilities by publicly owned boards. But if public opinion is not yet ripe for this, what is the object of chasing the utilities round the lot every other week? If I was in your place, I should buy out the utilities at fair prices in every district where the situation was ripe for doing so, and announce that the ultimate ideal was to make this policy nation-wide. But elsewhere I would make peace on liberal terms, guaranteeing fair earnings on new investments and a fair basis of valuation in the event of the public taking them over hereafter. The process of evolution will take at least a generation. Meanwhile a policy of *competing* plants with losses all round is a ramshackle notion.

Finally the railroads. The position there seems to be exactly what it was three or four years ago. They remain, as they were then, potential sources of substantial demand for new capital expenditure. Whether hereafter they are publicly owned or remain in private hands, it is a matter of national importance that they should be made solvent. Nationalise them if the time is ripe. If not, take pity on the overwhelming problems of the present managements. And here too let the dead bury their dead. (To an Englishman, you Americans, like the Irish, are so terribly historically minded!)

I am afraid I am going beyond my province. But the upshot is this. A convincing policy, whatever its details may be, for promoting large-scale investment under the above heads is an urgent necessity. These things take time. Far too much precious time has passed.

4. I must not encumber this letter with technical suggestions for re-revival of sources of demand. If demand and confidence re-appear, the problems of the capital market will not seem so difficult as they do to-day. Moreover it is a highly technical problem.

5. Businessmen have a different set of delusions from politicians; and need, therefore, different handling. They are, however, much milder than politicians, at the same time allured and terrified by the glare of publicity, easily persuaded to be 'patriots', perplexed, bemused, indeed terrified, yet only too anxious to take a cheerful view, vain perhaps but very unsure of themselves, pathetically responsive to a kind word. You could do anything you like with them, if you would treat them (even the big ones), not as wolves and tigers, but as domestic animals by nature, even though they have been badly brought up and not trained as you would wish. It is a mistake to think that they are more *immoral* than politicians. If you work them into the surly, obstinate, terrified mood, of which domestic animals, wrongly handled, are so capable, the nation's burdens will not get carried to market; and in the end public opinion will veer their way. Perhaps you will rejoin that I have got quite a wrong idea of what all the backchat amounts to. Nevertheless I record accurately how it strikes observers here.

6. Forgive the candour of these remarks. They come from an enthusiastic well-wisher of you and your policies. I accept the view that durable investment must come increasingly under state direction. I sympathise with Mr. Wallace's agricultural policies. I believe that the S.E.C. is doing splendid work. I regard the growth of collective bargaining as essential. I approve minimum wage and hours regulation. I was altogether on your side the other day, when you deprecated a policy of general wage reductions as useless in present circumstances. But I am terrified lest progressive causes in all the democratic countries should suffer injury, because you have taken too lightly the risk to their prestige which would result from a failure measured in terms of immediate prosperity. There *need* be no failure. But the maintenance of prosperity in the modern world is extremely *difficult*; and it is so easy to lose precious time.

I am, Mr. President, Yours with great respect and faithfulness,
[Signed] *JM Keynes*

Further Resources

WEBSITES

Keynes, John Maynard. "An Open Letter to President Roosevelt." Available online at http://www.geocities.com/ecocorner/intelarea/jmk6.html; website homepage at http://www.geocities.com (accessed August 9, 2002).

TIME 100: Scientists & Thinkers. "John Maynard Keynes." Available online at http://www.time.com/time/time100/scientist/profile/keynes03.html; website homepage at http://www.time.com (accessed February 26, 2003).

3

EDUCATION

NADINE PINÉDE

Entries are arranged in chronological order by date of primary source. For entries with one primary source, the entry title is the same as the primary source title. Entries with more than one primary source have an overall entry title, followed by the titles of the primary sources.

Important Events in Education, 1930–1939

1930

- On February 3, some 1.5 million schoolchildren listen to the first educational radio broadcast, transmitted on CBS by the American School of the Air.
- On July 1, Francis T. Spaulding at the Summer School for Engineering Teachers in New Haven, Connecticut, criticizes college and university faculty for teaching by lecture, leaving students to learn the information on their own.
- On October 15, festivities at colleges and in communities around the United States celebrate the Virgil Bimillennium, the two-thousandth anniversary of the birth of the Roman poet.
- On December 6, a grand jury in Westchester County, New York, accuses its public schools of fostering an increase in crime by failing to teach morals and character. No evidence indicates that crime increased in 1930 in Westchester County.

1931

- In January, funding cuts force Oregon State University not to offer contracts for the 1931–1932 academic year to 66 professors, leaving them unemployed at the end of the term. This was the first of a wave of depression-era cutbacks in higher education.
- In January, the William H. Spencer High School is dedicated in Columbus, Georgia. A model of the industrial-school movement, Spencer High is an all-black school designed to prepare students for industrial jobs rather than college.
- On March 18, Henry W. Holmes, dean of the College of Education at Harvard University, calls for public schools to educate only the best and brightest, leaving low-performing students to "special agencies outside the high school itself." This idea is fashionable among educators who see in Darwinism a justification for favoring smart students over mediocre ones, what one might call elitism.
- On March 19, Congress authorizes the National Survey of School Finance to take stock of the condition of schools in the United States.
- In April, Thomas E. Finegan estimates that taxpayers would spend $2.4 billion on public schools that year, a figure he put at 2.4 percent of Gross Domestic Product.
- In June, Harvard professor L. Leland Dudley estimates that the average public school teacher would earn $1,890 that year. This average hid the fact that some elementary school teachers would earn less than $1,300 that year. Because women taught at elementary schools, they suffered from the salary disparity.
- In November, Truman L. Kelley urges public schools to increase the number of science courses. The attack against evolution in the 1920s and the low esteem in which rural Americans held science had led public schools to reduce their science offerings, particularly in biology.
- In December, President Herbert Hoover's National Advisory Committee on Education issues its report on American schools, finding them in generally good condition.

1932

- On February 18, Columbia University professor George S. Counts delivers a speech to a teachers' convention in Baltimore on the topic "Dare Progressive Education Be Progressive?"—launching the social-reconstructionist movement in education.
- In March, psychologist John Brewer recommends that schools hire guidance counselors to meet the emotional needs of children.
- On August 12, African Americans in Philadelphia found the Educational Equality League to seek desegregation of public schools, the hiring of African American teachers, and the appointment of an African American to the school board.
- In September, Bennington College in Bennington, Vermont, holds its first classes.
- In November, a report from Harvard University urges public schools not to slash special-education programs to save money during the Great Depression, when nearly all states reduced appropriations to public schools.

1933

- In January, a social worker tells sociologist and recent immigrant Hans Morgenthau that he would never find a university professorship given Depression-era austerity and should instead settle for being an elevator boy. Morgenthau ignores this advice and finds part-time work teaching night classes at Brooklyn College of the City University of New York and later a tenure-track assistant professorship at the University of Chicago.
- On March 1, in an address before a school supervisors' convention in Minneapolis, John Dewey casts the U.S. Chamber of Commerce as an enemy of public education for having recently proposed radical cuts in American education as a Depression-era austerity measure.
- In April, William T. Foster, director of the Pollak Foundation for Economic Research, estimates that public schools had cut expenses 18 percent that year because of the Great Depression. He adds that since 1932 the Ohio General Assembly had reduced funding for new school construction by 99 percent.
- On April 17, the first Civilian Conservation Corps (CCC) camp opens. Although the CCC is a New Deal agency directed toward forestry and environmental work, it will also conduct educational programs for thousands from impoverished backgrounds. The program, the federal government

hopes, will reduce unemployment and train young men for jobs in the private sector.

- On April 24, five thousand Chicago schoolteachers march on city hall, demanding back pay after having been paid for ten months in scrip.
- In June, an American Association of University Professors report estimates that five thousand Ph.D.s were unemployed as a result of their inability to find professorships.
- On July 21, twenty-five thousand teachers and supporters fill Chicago Stadium, protesting budget cuts and firings by the Chicago school board.
- In September, the Institute for Advanced Study, a graduate institute that confers no degrees, opens at Princeton University. Educator Abraham Flexner is its first director.
- On December 14, ten children are killed and thirty injured when a school bus is struck by a freight train in Crescent City, Florida.

1934

- Indebtedness of school districts in the United States rises to $137 million, up from $93 million in 1930.
- Textbook purchases by public schools fall by one-third compared to 1930.
- The average public-school teacher's annual salary drops 13.6 percent from 1930 levels, from $1,420 to $1,227.
- On March 15, Harry E. Gardner, state supervisor of Teachers' Registration Bureau for the State of Massachusetts, warns that Massachusetts faces a teacher shortage as the number of pupils increased 13,000 in 1933, while the number of teachers fell by 315. He adds that Massachusetts schools were so desperate in fall 1933 that they hired 139 teachers who had not finished high school.
- On April 1, nearly twenty thousand schools, mostly in rural areas, are closed for lack of financing.
- Between May 1 and June 30, a total of 136,156 men and women graduate from a U.S. college or university.
- In June, the Progressive Education Association begins an eight-year study that it hopes will convince college to modernize their curricula.
- On August 6, a study shows that 98 percent of school superintendents were born in the United States and that 90 percent are from Anglo-Saxon backgrounds.
- In September, more than 1,300 teachers are unemployed in Michigan.
- In September, Berwyn, Pennsylvania, desegregates its schools after boycotts of segregated schools by the Educational Equality League of Philadelphia.

1935

- On January 18, Brookwood Labor College in New York celebrates its fifteenth anniversary with a commemoration involving more than five hundred graduates and trade unionists.
- On February 13, the Arkansas House of Representatives authorizes an investigation of alleged communist activities at Commonwealth College, a labor college in Mena, Arkansas.
- On March 16, the U.S. Supreme Court in *Murray v. Maryland* orders the University of Maryland Law School either to admit an African American student, Donald Murray, or to create a segregated law school for him alone. Murray is admitted to the law school.
- In April, Elgie Clucas of the Runkle School in Massachusetts estimates that taxpayers will spend more than $3 billion nationwide on public schools that year.
- In April, only 4.3 percent of the U.S. population is illiterate.
- In April, eight million students stay home because their schools had closed for repairs or lack of funds.
- On June 10, the Tennessee House of Representatives reaffirms the verdict of the 1925 Scopes "monkey trial" by passing a statute prohibiting the teaching of evolution.
- On June 26, Congress establishes the National Youth Administration (NYA) as part of the Works Progress Administration (WPA). The NYA will provide work and education for persons ages sixteen to twenty-five.
- Between July 2 and November 18, nineteen states succumb to pressure from the Daughters of the American Revolution, the American Legion, and other groups concerned about political subversion, passing laws requiring teachers to swear loyalty oaths to the United States.
- Between July 8 and July 11, a conference of the Harvard Summer School documents for the 1934–1935 academic year a 34.7 percent decrease in textbook purchases and a 38.3 percent decline in money spent on repairs at public schools nationwide.

1936

- On January 1, fewer than 20 percent of public high schools have laboratory equipment for experiments in science classes.
- On January 12, the National Association of Colored People (NAACP) declares a crisis in public education with black students four times more likely than white students to drop out of school.
- On March 3, the American Association for the Advancement of Science (AAAS) urges public schools to teach science by the scientific method and laboratory experiments.
- On May 19, the California Institute of Technology gives Nobel laureate Thomas Hunt Morgan, emeritus professor of zoology, its Distinguished Scholar Award.
- On June 11, the American Association of University Professors (AAUP) cautions American scholars against conducting research in Fascist Italy and Nazi Germany because of limits on academic freedom.
- In September, the U. S. Department of Agriculture (USDA) authorizes its scientists to teach at land-grant colleges and universities with approval from the Dean of the College of Agriculture at that college or university.

1937

- In January, historian and author Arthur M. Schlesinger, who would later serve in the Kennedy administration, criticizes the public-school history curriculum for focusing on kings and wars rather than on the lives of ordinary people. A focus on the lives of ordinary people is social history, of which Schlesinger is a founder.

- On February 9, Senators Pat Harrison of Mississippi and Hugo Black of Alabama introduce a bill providing $100 million in federal aid to schools. The bill will fail.
- In April, King William's School in Annapolis, Maryland, becomes St. John's College, under the leadership of Stringfellow Barr and Scott Buchanan.
- In May, a survey of graduating seniors in Massachusetts' public schools finds that half of those who wanted to attend college can't afford tuition.
- On May 28, President Franklin D. Roosevelt signs a bill repealing the infamous "red rider" to a Washington, D.C., appropriation bill. The rider had required teachers in the nation's capital to sign a loyalty oath.
- In July, the City University of New York founds Queens College in Flushing, New York.
- On July 16, Western Auto Supply magnate George Pepperdine funds Pepperdine College, a new school in Los Angeles.
- On August 15, Commonwealth College in Mena, Arkansas, formally affiliates itself with the Southern Tenant Farmers Union.
- In October, a Wellesley College report estimates the value of all U.S. public schools and their equipment at $9.9 billion.
- In October, enrollment in U.S. public schools peaks for the decade at 30.6 million students.
- In October, the Stanford-Binet intelligence test is revised.
- On November 21, Brookwood Labor College closes, the victim of the Depression and internal political divisions.

1938

- On February 6, a Carnegie Foundation for the Advancement of Teaching report condemns unfair competitive practices by colleges searching for tuition-paying students.
- On April 7, Albert Einstein of the Institute for Advanced Study at Princeton University joins the American Federation of Teachers, the largest union of public-school teachers and higher-education faculty.
- On April 18, Congress passes the George-Deen Act, appropriating $14.5 million for vocational education.
- On December 12, the U.S. Supreme Court, in *Missouri ex. rel. Gaines v. Canada,* orders the state of Missouri to provide equal educational accommodations for African American law students.

1939

- Only 4 percent of the professors at large state universities are women, but they hold 23.5 percent of the instructorships, the lowest academic rank.
- In March, George S. Counts begins a campaign to rid the American Federation of Teachers of communists.

"The Two Extremes"

Table

By: Helen Hay Heyl

Date: November 7, 1932

Source: Heyl, Helen Hay. "The Two Extremes." *Journal of Education,* November 7, 1932, 602. Reprinted in Tyack, David, Robert Lowe, and Elisabeth Hansot. *Public Schools in Hard Times: The Great Depression and Recent Years.* Cambridge, Mass.: Harvard University Press, 1984, 151.

About the Author: Helen Hay Heyl was born in Norfolk, Virginia, and received her M.A. from Teachers College, Columbia. Her long career as an educator included positions as a teacher, principal, and eventually as supervisor for the New York State Education Department in Albany, New York. ■

Introduction

Progressivism is a term that was used in many areas of American life. In politics, it was associated with the turn-of-the-century muckraking journalists who exposed government corruption and demanded reform. In education it was associated with a more scientific attitude to learning based on the discoveries of psychology and sociology.

Originally progressivism had its roots in the philosophy of pragmatism, which emphasized the real-life consequences of actions rather than people's intentions or abstract principles. One of its main proponents was John Dewey, a philosopher of education born in Vermont in 1859. After receiving his Ph.D. in philosophy from Johns Hopkins, Dewey set up an experimental school at the University of Chicago in 1894. Instead of memorizing and reciting, Dewey thought students should learn by doing. A "child-centered" curriculum should be developed by teachers rather than one imposed by tradition.

Dewey also thought that schools and democracy should be related: schools should not only teach reading, writing, and arithmetic, but should also prepare students to live as citizens of a democracy in a "Great Community." Two of his most influential works on progressivism and education are *School and Society* (1899) and *Democracy and Education* (1916). Dewey had an enormous influence on American education. After leaving the University of Chicago, he was a professor of philosophy at Teachers College from 1904 until his retirement in 1929, and he was actively involved in education until his death in 1952.

Various thinkers represented the traditionalist point of view in education, also called "essentialism." Among the most prominent was Robert M. Hutchins, who believed that a core curriculum of the "essential" great works of Western civilization was necessary to introduce students to the best in their culture. He and others championed the Great Books course. Unlike the progressives, traditionalists did not believe that schools needed to experiment to come up with better ways of teaching and learning or to prepare citizens for a democracy. Along with transmitting a liberal education for the academically talented, the purpose of the school, argued most essentialists, was to develop intellect and mental discipline,

Traditional vs. Progressive Schooling A Comparison from the 1930s

Traditional School	Progressive School
Child is sent to school and is kept until four o'clock, after which he is released home.	Child goes to school and cannot get there early enough, he lingers in shops, laboratories, yards, and libraries until dusk or urgent parents drag him homeward.
This is a school for listening.	This is a school for working.
Children are pigeonholed in long rows of desks.	Children are seated in groups at tables with comfortable chairs.
Children sit quietly studying their lessons.	Children sit working at projects, asking questions as needs arise. They "learn by doing" under wise teacher-guidance.
Movement means marching in rows at a teacher-directed and controlled signal.	Movement means purposeful activity, with consideration for the rights of others, and leads to self-direction and self-control.
Child learns unquestioning obedience to authority.	Child learns obedience through participation.
Keynotes: memorize, recite, pay attention.	Keynote: Experiences leading to growth.
Child's mind is submitted to the grindstone of an educational discipline which dwarfs his capacity to think for himself.	Child is taught to think, to develop tolerant understanding, to question critically, to evaluate.
Aim: Mental discipline, which it is believed will produce good citizens.	Aim: Growth and tolerant understanding, which it is believed will produce good citizens and the improvement of the social order.

Primary Source

"The Two Extremes"

SYNOPSIS: Heyl credits the progressive Harold Rugg for the ideas expressed in her chart. HEYL, HELEN HAY. "THE TWO EXTREMES." *JOURNAL OF EDUCATION,* NOVEMBER 7, 1932, 602.

Students work at the blackboard on a language exercise in a 1935 elementary school. GETTY IMAGES. REPRODUCED BY PERMISSION.

sometimes through subjects like Latin and Greek. Hutchins first presented his ideas for a classics-based curriculum in his 1936 book, *The Higher Learning in America.* Many, though, including Heyl, questioned whether the traditional approach was as effective as that proposed by Dewey several decades earlier. This chart is representative of the ideas of those who, like Heyl, thought that a progressive philosophy was better.

Significance

During the 1930s schools sometimes became a laboratory for social change, especially as society tried to cope with the changes brought on by the Great Depression. Ironically it was most often the private schools (or university laboratory schools such as the one founded by Dewey in Chicago) that could afford to be more experimental in their teaching methods. The overcrowded urban schools, or poor rural schools, often did not have the option of experimenting with progressivism in their curricula.

Some educators, like Lloyd Tireman, decided to bring progressive education to traditionally underserved populations. Tireman pioneered experiments in bilingual and bicultural education by setting up the San José Demonstration and Experimental School and the Nambé Community School in New Mexico. Others, like Jane Addams, found ways of bringing progressive ideas to immigrant families by providing adult education in Hull House, her settlement house on Chicago's South Side. Heyl also had a hand in bringing progressivism to the classroom. In 1941 the New York State Department of Education, where Heyl was a supervisor, approved a six-year experiment in schools embodying Dewey's progressive philosophy.

There were others who thought progressivism did not go far enough. George Counts, a social reconstructionist, argued that schools shouldn't just try to reform societies; they should try and change them. His ideas became very popular with intellectuals during the Great Depression, but most teachers continued to use a more familiar and traditional curriculum.

Whatever forms it took, progressivism and its offshoots helped inspire generations of educators and its influence is still felt today. Yet the debate between the traditionalists, who argue for a "back to basics" approach, and the modern-day progressives will probably continue well into the future.

Further Resources

BOOKS

Dewey, John. *School and Society.* Chicago: University of Chicago Press, 1899.

———. *Democracy and Education.* New York: Macmillan, 1916.

Hutchins, Robert. *The Higher Learning in America.* New Haven, Conn.: Yale University Press, 1936.

Krug, Edward A. *The Shaping of the American High School, Volume 2, 1920–1941.* Madison, Wis.: University of Wisconsin Press, 1972.

Reed, Ronald F., and Tony W. Johnson. *Philosophical Documents in Education.* New York: Addison Wesley Longman, 2000.

Rugg, Harold Ordway, and Ann Shumaker. *The Child-Centered School.* 1928. Reprint, New York: Arno, 1969.

Tyack, David, Robert Lowe, and Elisabeth Hansot. *Public Schools in Hard Times: The Great Depression and Recent Years.* Cambridge, Mass.: Harvard University Press, 1984.

Zilversmit, Arthur. *Changing Schools: Progressive Education in Theory and Practice, 1930–1960.* Chicago: University of Chicago Press, 1993.

PERIODICALS

Stern, Barbara Slater, and Karen Lea Riley. "Reflecting on the Common Good: Harold Rugg and the Social Reconstructionists." *The Social Studies* 92, no. 2, March 2001, 56.

WEBSITES

"Dr. John Dewey Dead at 92: Philosopher a Noted Liberal." Obituary in *The New York Times,* June 2, 1952. Available online at http://www.nytimes.com/learning/general/onthisday/bday/1020.html (accessed April 19, 2002).

"School: The Story of American Public Education." Available online at http://www.pbs.org/kcet/publicschool/index.html (accessed April 19, 2002).

AUDIO AND VISUAL MEDIA

"The American Pragmatists: C.S. Peirce, William James, John Dewey." Part of the BBC series *Great Philosophers.* Films for the Humanities and Sciences, 1987, VHS.

"As American as Public School: 1900–1950." Episode 2 of the PBS series *School: The Story of American Public Education.* Films for the Humanities and Sciences, 2001, VHS.

Dare the School Build a New Social Order?

Pamphlet

By: George S. Counts

Date: 1932

Source: Counts, George S. *Dare the School Build a New Social Order?* Carbondale, Ill.: Southern Illinois University Press, 1932. Excerpts reprinted in Reed, Ronald F., and Tony W. Johnson, eds. *Philosophical Documents in Education.* New York: Longman, 2000, 120–122.

About the Author: George Sylvester Counts (1889–1974) was born in frontier Kansas and taught high school before receiving the first Ph.D. in sociology of education awarded by the University of Chicago in 1916. By 1927 Counts was a professor of education at Teachers College, Columbia. Counts traveled extensively in the Soviet Union and throughout Europe in the 1920s. In 1932 he challenged the audience of the Progressive Education Association (PEA) with his speech, "Dare Progressive Education Be Progressive?" In his later years, Counts became an anticommunist, having seen the results of Joseph Stalin's regime when he revisited Russia in the 1930s. Counts became a faculty member at Southern Illinois University in Carbondale in 1961, where he would continue with his teaching and activism until his death in 1974. ■

Introduction

Counts was a member of what was known as the Teachers College Group, influential radical educators who included Harold Rugg in social studies education and William Heard Kilpatrick in philosophy of education. John Dewey, considered by many the father of philosophy of education, occasionally participated in their discussions and meetings. Counts himself felt he was a follower of Dewey, even though Dewey was not always happy with that claim.

The reform-minded educators of the 1930s, called progressives, were pushing for new goals and methods in education, where less emphasis would be placed on moral education in the schools, and more attention paid to the strengths and weaknesses of individual students. Counts and the others in the Teachers College Group believed that the reforms of the progressives had not gone far enough.

George S. Counts, who believed that schools and educators should use their influence to help form a better society. **THE LIBRARY OF CONGRESS.**

During his travels through the Soviet Union, Counts had been impressed with the centralized organization of the Russian schools and with the schools' commitment to building a new society, and the contrast with American schools was striking to him. He published *The Soviet Challenge to America* in 1931, well before he became aware of the cost in human lives of Stalin's political purges and forced industrialization policies. Viewed as an expert in Soviet education, Counts turned his critical eye to America's educational system. In his 1932 address to the PEA, Counts insisted that education be used for social change and that teachers be active participants in that change. The speech, along with two others given to professional groups, was published as a pamphlet, *Dare the School Build a New Social Order?*

Significance

Dare the School Build a New Social Order? was a direct call to arms. At the height of the terrible economic and social crisis of the Great Depression, Counts criticized progressive educators for focusing on a child-centered approach and ignoring the larger social role of the teacher, which he believed was to "reconstruct" society.

He urged teachers to organize themselves by joining unions and involving themselves in politics. He attacked what he saw as the upper-class liberal bias of the PEA, which did not struggle for social justice on behalf of the masses. Counts also argued that indoctrination and "imposition" might be a part of social reconstruction, much to the offense of the child-centered progressives.

He criticized the excessive individualism of the progressives and called for more collectivism, or more responsibility to the larger society's needs. Counts' speech was so provocative that the group suspended the rest of its agenda so it could discuss the issues raised by Counts. His message had special relevance during the Great Depression. Although he became an anticommunist in the 1940s and 1950s, pro-business conservatives labeled Counts a "red." During that period, he wrote several books concerning civil liberties and academic freedom.

Counts was forcibly retired from Columbia in 1955, but he lectured in Brazil and taught at the University of Pittsburgh and Michigan State University before his final faculty appointment at Southern Illinois University. Despite the completely transformed world order, *Dare the School Build a New Social Order?* is still relevant for the questions raised by Counts about the relation between schools and the societies in which they exist.

Primary Source

Dare the School Build a New Social Order? [excerpt]

SYNOPSIS: This excerpt examines one of what Counts calls the fallacies of education: that it is always impartial and unbiased. Instead, writes Counts, education should have a goal or direction in mind, or else it simply maintains the status quo.

There is a fallacy that the school should be impartial in its emphases, that no bias should be given instruction. We have already observed how the individual is inevitably molded by the culture into which he is born. In the case of the school a similar process operates and presumably is subject to a degree of conscious direction. My thesis is that complete impartiality is utterly impossible, that the school must shape attitudes, develop tastes, and even impose ideas. It is obvious that the whole of creation cannot be brought into the school. This means that some selection must be made of teachers, curricula, architecture, methods of teaching. And in the making of the selection the dice must always be weighted in favor of this or that. Here is a fundamental truth that cannot be brushed aside as irrelevant or unimportant; it constitutes the very essence of the matter under discussion. Nor can

This old, rickety building was typical of segregated African American schools in 1939. THE LIBRARY OF CONGRESS.

the reality be concealed beneath agreeable phrases. Professor Dewey states in his *Democracy and Education* that the school should provide a *purified* environment for the child. With this view I would certainly agree; probably no person reared in our society would favor the study of pornography in the schools. I am sure, however, that this means stacking the cards in favor of the particular systems of value which we may happen to possess. It is one of the truisms of the anthropologist that there are no maxims of purity on which all peoples would agree. Other vigorous opponents of imposition unblushingly advocate the "cultivation of democratic sentiments" in children or the promotion of child growth in the direction of "a better and richer life." The first represents definite acquiescence in imposition; the second, if it does not mean the same thing, means nothing. I believe firmly that democratic sentiments should be cultivated and that a better and richer life should be the outcome of education, but in neither case would I place responsibility on either God or the order of nature. I would merely contend that as educators we must make many choices involving the development of attitudes in boys and girls and that we should not be afraid to acknowledge the faith that is in us or mayhap the forces that compel us. . . .

As the possibilities in our society begin to dawn upon us, we are all, I think, growing increasingly weary of the brutalities, the stupidities, the hypocrisies, and the gross inanities of contemporary life. We have a haunting feeling that we were born for better things and that the nation itself is falling far short of its powers. The fact that other groups refuse to deal boldly and realistically with the present situation does not justify the teachers of the country in their customary policy of hesitation and equivocation. The times are literally crying for a new vision of American destiny. The teaching profession, or at least its progressive elements, should eagerly grasp the opportunity which the fates have placed in their hands.

Such a vision of what America might become in the industrial age I would introduce into our schools as the supreme imposition, but one to which our children are entitled—a priceless legacy which it should be the first concern of our profession to fashion and bequeath. The objection will of course be raised that this is asking teachers to assume unprecedented social responsibilities. But we live in difficult and dangerous times—times when precedents lose their significance. If we are content to remain where all is safe and quiet and serene, we shall dedicate ourselves, as teachers have commonly done in the past, to a role of futility, if not of positive social reaction. Neutrality with respect to the great issues that agitate society, while perhaps theoretically possible, is practically tantamount to giving support to the forces of conservatism. As Justice Holmes has candidly said in his essay on Natural Law, "we all, whether we know it or not, are fighting to make the kind of world that we should like." If neutrality is impossible even in the dispensation of justice, whose emblem is the blindfolded goddess, how is it to be achieved in education? To ask the question is to answer it.

To refuse to face the task of creating a vision of a future America immeasurably more just and noble and beautiful than the America of today is to evade the most crucial, difficult, and important educational task. Until we have assumed this responsibility we are scarcely justified in opposing and mocking the efforts of so-called patriotic societies to introduce into the schools a tradition which, though narrow and unenlightened, nevertheless represents an honest attempt to meet a profound social and educational need. Only when we have fashioned a finer and more authentic vision than they will we be fully justified in our opposition to their efforts. Only then will we have discharged the age-long obligation which the older generation owes to the younger and which no amount of sophistry can obscure. Only through such a legacy of spiritual values will our children be enabled to find their place in the world, be lifted out of the present morass of moral indifference, be liberated from the senseless struggle for material success, and be challenged to high endeavor and achievement. And only thus will we as a people put ourselves on the road to the expression of our peculiar genius and to the making of our special contribution to the cultural heritage of the race.

Further Resources

BOOKS

Bowers, C.A. *The Progressive Educator and the Depression: The Radical Years.* New York: Random House, 1969.

Dennis, Lawrence J. *George S. Counts and Charles A. Beard: Collaborators for Change.* Albany, N.Y.: State University of New York Press, 1989.

Gutek, Gerald Lee. *The Educational Theory of George S. Counts.* Kent, Ohio: Kent State University Press, 1970.

———. *George S. Counts and American Civilization: the Educator as Social Theorist.* Macon, Ga.: Mercer University Press, 1984.

PERIODICALS

Goodenow, Ronald, and Wayne Urban. "George S. Counts: A Critical Appreciation." *Educational Forum,* January 1977, 167–74.

WEBSITES

"George Counts (1889–1974)" Available online at http://www.nd.edu/~rbarger/www7/gcounts.html; website home page: http://www.nd.edu (accessed April 19, 2002).

Opinions on Federal Aid for Education

"Current Conditions in the Nation's Schools"

Tables

By: National Education Association

Date: November 11, 1933

Source: National Education Association. "Current Conditions in the Nation's Schools." *Research Bulletin*, November 11, 1933, 109, 111.

About the Author: Founded as the National Teachers Association in 1850, the National Education Association (NEA) acquired its current name in 1857. Its goal is to promote the welfare of professional educators and to advance public education. The NEA raises funds for scholarships, conducts workshops on issues that affect educators and support staff, lobbies Congress, files legal actions in support of academic freedom and the rights of educators, and provides training and technical assistance to its members.

"Why the Discrimination?"

Cartoon

By: National Committee for Federal Aid to Education

Date: February 1935

Source: *Phi Delta Kappan* 17, February 1935, 127 (originally published in a pamphlet by the National Committee for Federal Aid to Education). Reprinted in Tyack, David, Robert Lowe, and Elisabeth Hansot. *Public Schools in Hard Times: The Great Depression and Recent Years.* Cambridge, Mass.: Harvard University Press, 1984, 96.

"New Deal a Raw Deal for Public Schools"

Essay

By: Willard E. Givens

Date: 1935

Source: Givens, Willard E. "New Deal a Raw Deal for Public Schools." *Journal of the National Education Association* 24, January–December 1935, 198. Reproduced in "New Deal Document Library." New Deal Network. Available online at http://newdeal.feri.org/texts/649.htm; website home page: http://newdeal.feri.org (accessed April 21, 2002).

About the Author: Willard Earl Givens (1886–1971) was born in Anderson, Indiana, in 1886 and received his M.A. from Columbia University. His teaching career began in a rural Indiana one-room school, and he was a principal in Hawaii before eventually becoming the superintendent of schools in Oakland, California. In 1935 he became the executive secretary of the National Education Association (NEA) and remained in that position for seventeen years. Givens also served in many national and international posts, including advising the United Nations Educational, Scientific and Cultural Organization (UNESCO). The American Association of School Administrators recognized Givens's work with its highest award. He died in 1971. ■

Introduction

In 1918 the National Education Association (NEA) appointed a Commission on the Emergency in Education, when the wartime draft had shown just how badly educated and in bad health many of the draftees were. The commission pointed to under-financed rural schools, especially in the South, poorly trained teachers, and unequal school financing. It asked for $100 million in federal aid to attack these conditions, but nothing came of this. By the time of the Great Depression, conditions had only deteriorated, but the NEA had still not been successful in convincing the federal government of the need for help in reforming school finance. Some states proceeded on their own, but educators argued that migration from the South to the North made the quality of schooling a national issue. Yet opponents to federal aid to education pointed to the absence of education from the Constitution, and, especially in the segregated South, traditions of local control.

Most educators expected that the New Deal would help them in reforming and financing public education. But by 1935 the National Education Association (NEA) was protesting about the lack of federal support to education, especially in relation to other programs. The Office of Education had had its budget cut, while education programs were being established through new agencies like the Civilian Conservation Corps (CCC), National Youth Administration (NYA), and Works Progress Administration (WPA). The growing rift was not helped by President Roosevelt's preference for noneducation professionals as his advisers and administrators for these programs. The NEA, headed by professional education administrators, felt that credentialed professionals should administer the New Deal's education programs.

Reductions in Certain Types of School Training in City School Systems, 1931-1933

Schools or classes relating to:	Number of cities reporting	Percent of cities reducing or eliminating this work
Physically handicapped children	193	9.9
Homemaking	661	[illegible]
Industrial arts	630	13.0
Physical education	696	15.6
Mentally handicapped children	321	15.6
Art	632	16.2
Music	722	19.2
Kindergartens	404	19.8
Playgrounds and recreation	502	20.3
Continuation work	181	32.1
Americanization	247	34.5
Summer schools	240	41.3
Night schools and adult classes	266	42.5

SOURCE: National Education Association. "Current Conditions in the Nation's Schools." *Research Bulletin*, November 11, 1933, p. 109.

Primary Source

"Current Conditions in the Nation's Schools"

(1 OF 2)

SYNOPSIS: In its November 11, 1933, *Research Bulletin* the National Education Association provided statistics on reductions in school training and changes in school conditions in the early 1930s.

Significance

It was in this atmosphere that NEA Executive Secretary Willard Givens wrote his article, another demand for federal aid to education. He directly challenges the argument that there is no money for this, by pointing out that extravagant new education programs are being established while existing schools receive nothing. He displays contempt for the New Dealers entering the field of education and dismisses them as incompetent political appointees. The Works Progress Administration (WPA) is specifically attacked for taking control of education out of the hands of educators.

What the NEA wanted, to quote Givens, was "federal aid to education without federal control." To outsiders this might seem like teachers protecting their own jobs and salaries instead of working in the best interests of the nation during difficult times. Teachers marching for back pay may have felt they needed to defend their actions to a larger public that was also suffering from the

Changes in School Conditions by States, 1930-1934

	Rural schools: percent of change, 1930–1934			City schools: percent of change, 1931–1934			Higher education: percent of change, 1930–1934, in expenditures by state universities
States	Term	Staff	Total expenditures	Staff	Current expenditures	Capital outlay	
Continental U.S.	−4	−3	−23	−4.6	−19.5	−80.1	−17.7
Alabama	−36.0	+6	−47	−6.5	−32.4	−93.9	−27
Arizona	0.0	−15	−31	−16.3	−42.8	−62.6	—
Arkansas	−2.7	−14	−39	−15.6	−41.8	−20.5	—
California	−0.6	−1	−21	−4.6	−15.1	−80.6	−28
Colorado	−4.0	−4	−27	−11.6	−38.2	−97.8	−36
Connecticut	+0.5	−2	+3	−3.5	−19.5	—	−6
Delaware	0.0	+6	+15	—	—	—	—
Florida	−18.0	+3	−27	−1.3	−35.9	−84.3	−1
Georgia	−20.0	0	−23	−0.7	−18.4	—	+23
Idaho	−1.0	−10	−30	−6.5	−33.7	−66.1	−7
Illinois	−6.0	−2	−28	−7.9	−32.2	−68.0	−21
Indiana	−1.0	+1	−26	−8.7	−31.1	−79.8	−2
Iowa	+0.5	−4	−17	−7.4	−29.0	−54.1	—
Kansas	−0.6	−4	−29	−5.6	−28.8	−84.0	−39
Kentucky	−5.0	+6	−30	−3.6	−16.0	−50.2	−26
Louisiana	−24.0	+3	−18	+0.6	—	—	+59
Maine	−2.0	−2	−19	−1.8	−15.2	—	−7
Maryland	0.0	−1	−19	—	—	—	−8
Massachusetts	−0.6	−2	−11	−2.7	−4.9	−98.8	—
Michigan	−19.0	−6	−37	−13.0	−37.9	−91.1	+1
Minnesota	0.0	−1	−23	−3.1	−18.1	−94.3	−9
Mississippi	−4.0	−4	−42	−5.7	−23.5	—	−81
Missouri	−4.0	−1	−39	+0.9	−25.6	−93.2	−22
Montana	−2.0	−7	−35	−7.8	−9.7	−85.6	−23
Nebraska	0.0	−2	−35	−6.5	−14.0	−97.2	−31
Nevada	−5.0	+6	−3	—	—	—	—18
New Hampshire	0.0	−3	−22	−3.2	−11.9	+9.7	−11
New Jersey	−0.5	+2	−18	−0.8	−24.4	−54.7	—
New Mexico	−5.0	−3	−17	−6.3	−35.4	—	−18
New York	0.0	+2	−18	−2.3	−13.1	−97.0	—
North Carolina	+5.0	−3	−47	−2.2	−31.4	—	−1
North Dakota	−5.0	−7	−39	−7.7	−24.4	−86.3	—
Ohio	−9.0	−5	−31	−11.9	−20.1	−45.4	−11
Oklahoma	−10.0	−5	−26	−8.5	−24.9	−76.6	−21
Oregon	−4.0	−1	−14	−14.7	−36.1	−51.6	−56
Pennsylvania	0.0	0	−13	−2.0	−14.8	−71.2	−30
Rhode Island	0.0	+2	+3	+1.3	−12.7	−88.9	−12
South Carolina	−4.0	−9	−32	−5.2	−39.4	—	−43
South Dakota	−2.0	−21	−20	−10.1	−25.2	−89.1	−24
Tennessee	−2.0	+1	−23	−3.4	−17.0	+1.9	−40
Texas	+2.0	0	−15	−10.5	−28.4	−88.4	—
Utah	0.0	−6	−38	−2.4	−23.5	−99.6	−23
Vermont	+0.6	−5	−18	−7.1	−18.8	—	—
Virginia	−5.0	−3	−22	+2.2	−21.9	−90.6	+21
Washington	+3.0	−6	−29	−5.8	−29.5	+47.6	−42
West Virginia	−26.0	−3	−44	−13.3	—	—	—
Wisconsin	−0.6	−1	−27	−1.3	−15.6	−74.5	—
Wyoming	−4.0	−8	−25	−13.2	−22.2	−98.2	−17

SOURCE: National Education Association. "Current Conditions in the Nation's Schools." *Research Bulletin,* November 11, 1933, p. 111.

Primary Source

"Current Conditions in the Nation's Schools" (2 OF 2)

This table illustrates the reductions in staff, expenditures, and outlays that schools withstood in the early 1930s.

WHY THE DISCRIMINATION?

Primary Source

"Why the Discrimination?"

SYNOPSIS: The cartoon depicts Uncle Sam leading labor, farmers, banks, and industry to the "Recovery Show" at the fair. Left behind the ropes are libraries, schools, and recreation. It illustrates visually the sentiments expressed in the essay "New Deal a Raw Deal for Public Schools." *PHI DELTA KAPPAN* 17 (FEBRUARY 1935): 127 (ORIGINALLY PUBLISHED IN A PAMPHLET BY THE NATIONAL COMMITTEE FOR FEDERAL AID TO EDUCATION).

effects of the Great Depression. Unlike the 1920s, teacher union membership rose during the 1930s, but despite George Counts's calls for social reconstructionism, the unions' most important issues were job security and pay. The NEA never did receive the unrestricted federal aid it wanted, but by the end of the decade it had managed to help institute school finance reforms to help equalize the disparities among states and regions.

Primary Source

"New Deal a Raw Deal for Public Schools"

SYNOPSIS: In this piece, Givens asks why the federal programs for dealing with the Great Depression have not been extended to public education, accusing politics of entering the picture. He recalls President Roosevelt's words of tribute to America's schools, but questions why new agencies need to be formed to do the work usually performed by educators. Similarly, the National Committee for Federal Aid to Education expressed similar sentiments in a cartoon it published in the 1935 edition of *Phi Delta Kappan*, published a few months before Givens' essay.

Since it is known that no group [of] people in America is more in sympathy with the social ideals and objectives of the New Deal than are teachers, it becomes increasingly difficult to understand the raw deal given to the public schools.

When the disposing hand of the federal government began a program of financial aid to farm, factory, home, mine, and crippled business institutions, the schools closing by thousands asked for help. The Federal Emergency Relief Administration came to the rescue by organizing more schools—nurseries, adult classes, vocational training, parent education and rehabilitation centers—instead of aiding already organized institutions. Although emergency assistance was given to rural schools, the program was administered in such a way as to incur the disfavor of school officials and teachers.

In October 1933, President Roosevelt, after paying tribute to the schools, said "We need to make infinitely better the average education which the average child now receives." Instead of following this policy of improving the everyday educational offering of the average child, the New Dealers invented plain and fancy schooling, managed in a way to give the jitters to educators whose policy it is to shun waste. While a few youngsters were being taught harmonica playing, fancy lariat throwing, and boondoggling, some hundreds of thousands of less fortunate ones throughout the United States were being denied a decent health program or were doing without a full year's work in arithmetic, reading, and history. The millions expended in building a parallel system of education for relief purposes have done some good, but better results could have been achieved more economically by strengthening the already-established school systems.

The Works Progress Administration now announces that it, too, is to enter the field of education. Its July 25 bulletin, No. 19, advises the State Works Progress Administrator to "*consult with* the State Superintendent of Education" in outlining a program of utmost importance to local education and which wholly ignores—beyond the consultation point—the authorities which the people have themselves legally chosen to direct the schools. We quote from this bulletin:

> . . . The full responsibility for the successful state administration of Emergency Education is placed upon the State Works Progress Administrator. . . . From time to time the Works Progress Administration at Washington will prescribe the qualifications for and authorize the designation of certain State Supervisors of Emergency Education to have charge. . . . Final approval of State Assistant Directors and such state Supervisors of Emergency Education as may be authorized and appointed is with the Education Division of the Works Progress Administration at Washington. . . . It is *not permissible* to place unemployed teachers in the regular public schools as "helping teachers" to relieve so-called "over-crowded" conditions. . . . The possession of teaching certificates is not required for this program.

Thus once again the schools have been repudiated and their officers and their teachers placed among the untouchables of the present depression. Thus once again are the schools overshadowed by a Washington-centered political institution with an educational title, entirely removed from state or local control.

If anyone thinks that the wresting of educational administration from the hands of educators is a temporary move in a crisis, let him read the educational provisions of the Social-Security Act. This Act places in the Department of Labor responsibilities for handicapped children, and appropriates annually nearly $3,000,000 for services already performed for years in our best public schools. No new agency was needed to provide for these children. Why was this money not allocated to states thru the United States Office of Education, the federal government's agency for education since 1867, to be expended, not by a bureau in Washington, but thru the legally established educational agencies of the states and localities?

The government now steps forward with another proposal to aid young people from a central office in Washington. It had long been pointed out by educational leaders that between two million and four million boys and girls were without educational opportunities and without jobs. These leaders urged the United States Office of Education to outline a program for these neglected youth. The program was duly outlined by the Office of Education, accepted by the Emergency Administration—and then placed in the joint control of the United States Treasury Department and the Works Progress Administration!

With the $50,000,000 provided for this service much good, no doubt, will be accomplished, but it is quite evident that this work could be done more economically thru the United States Office of Education and the State Department of Education. The cost of the new administration is estimated as high as $2,225,000 and in the Washington office alone will perhaps reach $225,000, which is 80 percent of the cost of the entire Office of Education exclusive of vocational education. With $50,000 additional appropriation the Office of Education could manage the new program.

But the extravagance of the program is not its worst fault. It is being built around a staff of federal and state workers who are politically appointed. The responsibility to the people is so indirect as to be almost negligible. The long-established politically-free methods of school administration are being circumvented by the New Deal.

The National Education Association believes in federal aid to education without federal control. It asks that financial assistance be given to already-established schools. It believes that in the preparation of young people for the duties of citizenship, reading, writing, and arithmetic should take precedence over harmonica blowing, lariat throwing, and boondoggling. It would keep education in the hands of educators and formal educational opportunity in the schools. It is unalterably opposed to politics in education. The experience of certain foreign countries shows plainly that political domination of the schools and political administration of youth are inimical to democracy. They are dangerous steps to be taken by a people devoted to popular government.

Educators are aware of the danger, and yet the schools watch the stepchildren of a new political ideal fed and nourished while they starve with neglect. In the face of continued repudiation, is the voice of educational leadership to be only a plaintive wail or a vigorous demand for the rightful place of the American public schools in our democracy? There is courage and stamina and professional backbone in the men and women who have made the American school system what it is. They will protect it and lend their support only to those who befriend it.

Further Resources

BOOKS

Krug, Edward A. *The Shaping of the American High School, 1920–1941.* Madison, Wis.: University of Wisconsin Press.

Urban, Wayne, and Wagoner Jennings. *American Education: A History.* Boston: McGraw-Hill, 2000.

PERIODICALS

Wahlquist, John T. "An Evaluation of the New Deal in Education." *School and Society* 42, (December 21, 1935): 859–863.

WEBSITES

Roosevelt, Franklin D. "President Roosevelt Supports Federal Aid." *Journal of the National Education Association* 27, no. 6, September 1938, 163. Available online at http://newdeal.feri.org/schools/schools06.htm (accessed April 21, 2002).

AUDIO AND VISUAL MEDIA

Givens, Willard E. "The Reminiscences of Dr. Willard E. Givens," typescript, Oral History Research Office, Columbia University, 1980. (Transcription of tape-recorded interview by Paul Hopper, Washington, D.C., 1968.)

"Sample Outline of Adult Educational Programs"

Journal article

By: American Library Association

Date: December 1, 1933

Source: American Library Association. "Sample Outline of Adult Educational Programs." *Bulletin of the American Library Association* 27, no. 12, December 1933, 547. Reproduced in "New Deal Document Library." New Deal Network. Available online at http://newdeal.feri.org/ala/al33547.htm; website home page: http://newdeal.feri.org (accessed April 20, 2002). ■

Introduction

Adult education was a high priority for Franklin D. Roosevelt's New Deal. But instead of focusing on traditional schooling for their educational reforms, the New Dealers tried to reach unemployed adults, whose worsening situation could cause a social crisis. Federal Adult Schools were established around the country to encourage adults to return to school and learn new skills. Classes were often vocational, but they also included music and photography, which were taught by practicing artists through the Works Projects Administration (WPA). Evening classes were even offered for those who worked during the day.

New Deal programs like the Civilian Conservation Corps (CCC) were also experiments in adult education. Even more innovative than the CCC were the workers' education programs, established under the Emergency Education Division of the Federal Emergency Relief Administration (FERA). Unlike vocational training, wrote Hilda W. Smith,

> workers' education offers to men and women wage earners in industry, business, commerce, domestic service and other occupations an opportunity to train themselves in clear thinking through the study of those questions closely related to their daily lives as workers and as citizens. Its primary purpose is to stimulate an active and continued interest in the economic problems of our times and to develop a sense of responsibility for their solution.

Smith was a pioneer in workers' education, heading the Bryn Mawr Summer School for Women Workers in Industry, the first labor college in the United States. In 1933 she organized educational programs for FERA, which later became the WPA's Workers Education Service. For those who had previously been excluded from formal schooling, such as women factory workers, blacks, immigrants, and other minorities, workers' education, a branch of adult education, could be a significant experience. During the 1930s many American cities had labor colleges.

Another experiment in adult education during the Great Depression was the folk school. In folk schools, inspired by the Scandinavian example, teachers and students lived and worked together to operate and maintain the school. Highlander Folk School, founded by Myles Horton, was created to help Southern workers organize and unionize in some of the poorest and least unionized parts of the nation. Later on in the 1950s, its Citizenship Schools program would have a direct influence on grassroots organizing and the success of the Civil Rights

A Works Progress Administration poster advertises evening classes for adults. Adult education was a priority for Franklin Roosevelt's New Deal. **THE LIBRARY OF CONGRESS.**

movement in the South. In its own prospectus, the school clearly stated its aims:

> The Highlander staff is concerned actively with the solution of economic and social ills of the South. The whole purpose of our work is to help to find effective ways of dealing with social problems, improving living conditions, promoting human progress. Highlander believes that human welfare can best be promoted by the organization and education of working people. We believe that constructive action should be taken to secure greater prosperity, liberty, and opportunity for the southern people. Discussion of problems is useless unless it is followed by action which gets things done, which sets people in motion toward intelligent and lasting solutions.

Significance

The sample outline for adult educational programs in Cook County, Illinois, is representative of many that were proposed around the country. As a response to the Great Depression, it also represents the New Deal's ideal of communities trying to find solutions to their problems by working together for the common good. The public libraries, Northwestern University, and the Evanston school boards would contribute their expertise in education. The specific conditions of blacks in Evanston, who made up one out of six residents, would be addressed in a study with Northwestern's sociology department. For unemployed teachers, these new adult education classes could offer jobs, as well as the chance to try out new progressive teaching methods and aims. Countless adults benefited from these adult education programs, both as teachers for them and as students in them.

Primary Source

"Sample Outline of Adult Educational Programs" [excerpt]

SYNOPSIS: This letter is addressed to the Cook County, Illinois, director of the Federal Emergency Relief Administration, one of the major New Deal agencies. In it the professional educators of Evanston, Illinois, propose several different adult education projects for the city.

November 28, 1933

Dr. Martin Bickham
Director, Illinois–Cook County Division
Federal Emergency Relief Administration
Chicago, Illinois

My dear Dr. Bickham:

A work relief project to be carried out in Evanston under the Federal Emergency Relief Administration for the State of Illinois is herewith submitted jointly by the public educational agencies, namely, the Boards of Education of Districts 75 and 76, the Evanston Township High School, and the Board of Directors of the Evanston Public Library.

The program as a whole has been formulated by the Evanston Advisory Council on Adult Education, composed of the superintendents of schools, the public librarian, representatives of the Cook County relief Evanston division, the Family Welfare Association, the Central Council of Social Agencies, the churches, the Big Brother Movement, the American Library Association, Northwestern University–Departments of Sociology, Philosophy, and Recreation, and other interested groups.

Each project has been worked out by members of the council in conjunction with other specialists in their particular field. To carry out the various projects and provide clerical help, the services of teachers, librarians, activity workers, nurses, supervisors, file clerks, typists, and stenographers will be needed.

All of the agencies represented in the council, as well as many others in the city, have felt the urgent need for such community activities during this period of economic stress. Lack of funds has deterred action.

Evanston as a community stands ready to make a substantial contribution to the work. The school boards and private agencies have offered their buildings and equipment, including the additional cost for heating and lighting after regular hours. The library board will put all of its book facilities at the disposal of the workers. The Sociology, Philosophy, and Recreation departments of Northwestern University have already offered their expert advisory services. Other departments of Northwestern as well as the National College of Education and Garrett Biblical Institute have signified keen interest and will render equally valuable advisory service as the needs arise. It is anticipated that space in a downtown office building can be secured as central headquarters for the work.

With such expert advisory service available there is every reason to feel that the highest standards for the project can be maintained provided properly qualified workers are assigned to carry them out.

In Evanston there is a high percentage of the professional group who have long been out of employment. These persons have now reached the end of their resources and are in real need.

Were government funds available to finance the accompanying program of community educational activities, the results would, as we see them, be three fold:

1. Highly deserving educated persons out of employment would be put to work.
2. Adults with enforced leisure would be afforded opportunities for constructively utilizing such leisure.
3. Through pooling the interests of the many public and private agencies of Evanston in the conduct of a government project, a much better understanding of the social structure of Evanston will be had and lasting good for the community will thereby be accomplished. . . .

Project I

Program

Counseling and adjustment service to assist individuals to find themselves under present social conditions, to utilize the available social resources, and to educate them for new job requirements.

This service is designed primarily for two groups of people: (a) young people out of employment, and others who desire to come in, between the ages of 16 and 25, and (b) older men and women who are unemployed and need readjustment to new social and economic conditions. If possible, the group who are barely getting along, because of bad business conditions, should be included.

To carry out the program for:

a. *Young people.* The names of these young people will be secured through the schools. They will be brought together in groups for interviews and to register. This service will follow up those who drop out of the program as well as give counsel on the individual use of leisure and vocational problems to those enrolled in the community educational projects.

b. *Mature age group.* Special help will be given along lines of new job requirements, as well as for the mental disturbances peculiar to this group.

Personnel Required

a. Supervisor. A college graduate, trainee in personnel work.

b. Assistant supervisors. Four college-trained persons for the young peoples group four for the mature age group.

c. Two capable stenographers; two office workers, and office boy.

d. Director for training of interviewers.

Community assistance

a. Volunteers will form a community committee to guide these workers and a corps of interviewers will be trained in the technique of counseling and adjustment service.

b. Office space will be provided; three experienced workers (Polish, Negro, and South Evanston workers) will be provided part time by the Big Brothers Association; clinics and various departments at Northwestern University will be donated; some auto service and all office supplies will be secured.

Project II

Program

General education to include formal and informal instruction and guidance in:

a. Citizenship and elementary school subjects.

b. English, literature, history, economics, etc.

c. Vocational and business subjects in so far as equipment will permit.

d. Advanced adult education primarily for high school graduates out of employment.

e. Discussions on topics of special group interest, current social problems, etc.

Personnel Required

Fourteen teachers especially qualified to conduct classes and discussion groups in the special subjects assigned.

Three clerical assistants.

Project III

Program

Homemaking and health education to include instruction and guidance in:

a. Home economics, cooking, sewing, family budgeting, etc.

b. Parental education.

c. Child care and nutrition.

d. Community health projects.

Personnel Required

A staff distributed as follows:

a. Six persons, three for cooking, three for sewing and family budgeting. *Qualifications.* Training or experience in dietetics, visiting, housekeeping, nursing, domestic science.

b. Three persons with education in a kindergarten, normal school, or college (majoring in education, psychology, or sociology) or experience in teaching or leading study groups or both.

c. Three nurses—preferably with public health experience.

d. One clerical assistant.

e. One office worker.

The importance of training in home economics and the lack of such knowledge in all economic and social groups has been vividly brought out in these times by the inability of families to manage their households on minimum budgets—as social workers, nurses, and others can well testify. The stresses and strains in family relationships caused by hard times point to the need for better understanding and more knowledge of education for parenthood. This should include both instruction in health education and physical care, and methods of developing the emotional life of children. The desire and need for the above program was indicated by the large number of requests for sewing and cooking which a tentative survey revealed.

Further Resources

BOOKS

Adam, T.R. *The Worker's Road to Learning.* New York: American Association for Adult Education, 1940.

Altenbaugh, Richard J. *Education for Struggle: The American Labor Colleges of the 1920s and 1930s.* Philadelphia: Temple University Press, 1990.

Horton, Aimee Isgrig. *The Highlander Folk School: A History of its Major Programs, 1932–1961.* Brooklyn, N.Y.: Carlson Publishing Inc., 1989.

PERIODICALS

Counts, George. "Education—For What?" *The New Republic,* May 25, 1932, 38–41.

WEBSITES

Hill, Frank Ernest. "Laboratory for Adult Education." *Phi Delta Kappan* XIX, no. 9, May 1937, 302. Available online at http://newdeal.feri.org/schools/schools12.htm; website home page: http://newdeal.feri.org (accessed April 20, 2002).

Smith, Hilda W. "Workers' Education and the Federal Government." *Progressive Education,* April–May 1934, 239. Available online at http://newdeal.feri.org/schools/schools14.htm; website home page: http://newdeal.feri.org (accessed April 20, 2002).

Smith, Hilda W., and Barbara Donald. "Workers' Education Under the Federal Government." *Bulletin of the American Library Association* 30, no. 1, January 1936, 9. Available online at http://newdeal.feri.org/ala/al369.htm; website home page: http://newdeal.feri.org (accessed April 20, 2002).

Smith, Hilda W., and Nancy Hart. "Workers' Education in FERA." *Opportunity, Journal of Negro Life* 13, no. 1, January 1935, 19. Available online at http://newdeal.feri.org/opp/opp3519.htm; website home page: http://newdeal.feri.org (accessed April 20, 2002).

AUDIO AND VISUAL MEDIA

The Women of Summer: The Bryn Mawr Summer School for Women Workers: 1921–1938. New York: Filmmakers Library, 1985.

Land of the Spotted Eagle

Nonfiction work

By: Luther Standing Bear

Date: 1933

Source: Standing Bear, Luther. *Land of the Spotted Eagle.* Lincoln: University of Nebraska Press, 1933. Reprinted in *Native Americans.* William Dudley, ed. San Diego, Calif.: Greenhaven Press, 1998, 199–201.

About the Author: Luther Standing Bear (1868–1939), son of an Oglala Sioux chief, was born in December 1868 on the Pine Ridge Reservation in South Dakota. He was first educated on the reservation, but was later sent away to attend the Carlisle Indian School in Pennsylvania. Following graduation, Standing Bear worked as a teacher, clerk, minister, rancher, and interpreter for Buffalo Bill's Wild West Show before his success as a writer. He wrote several memoirs and was published widely during the 1930s, speaking out for Native American rights. Toward the end of his life, he worked in Hollywood as an actor. He died in 1939 in California. ■

Introduction

For many years before the 1930s, serious efforts had been made to erase all traces of Indian culture in Native American students. Assimilation was the goal, especially at the Indian boarding schools across the country. When children were taken from their parents to be indoctrinated in this way, they could often not return and live comfortably in the communities from which they came. Yet they were also not treated as full-fledged American citizens by white Americans.

In 1933, Franklin Roosevelt appointed John Collier to reform the corrupt Bureau of Indian Affairs. Unlike past commissioners, Collier was sympathetic to the Native Americans' demands for political autonomy and sensitive to their traditions. He ensured that Native Americans were hired in New Deal programs and even established special Indian Civilian Conservation Corps camps to provide jobs for the young unemployed. By 1934, he convinced Congress to pass the Indian Reorganization Act, which provided for Indian self-rule and put an end to the unfair land allotment system. It was accepted by three-quarters of the Indian nations.

Luther Standing Bear, a prominent advocate for Native American rights during the 1930s. **AP/WIDE WORLD PHOTOS. REPRODUCED BY PERMISSION.**

In education, Collier made sure that Indian students received loans, and most importantly, he closed down the sixteen federally operated boarding schools that had taken children from their parents and replaced them with eighty-four reservation day schools. Collier rejected assimilation as the aim of education and instead looked to anthropology as a tool for cross-cultural understanding.

Significance

Luther Standing Bear assumed his father's role of political leadership when he returned from Carlisle. Unlike some other graduates of this infamous school, he was able to successfully find a place for himself in the community. In 1928, when he was about sixty, he published his first book, *My People the Sioux,* which told of the changes he had seen over the decades while also being careful to preserve his own culture's traditions. It was reviewed favorably by such publications as *The New York Times.*

In 1931, Standing Bear published an account of his childhood, *My Indian Boyhood,* which was aimed at a younger audience. In it, he describes the coming-of-age rituals of the Sioux as well as the kind of education about life and nature that the Sioux children received from their elders. As in his earlier works, he took pains to dispel popular myths and misconceptions about Native Americans.

Land of the Spotted Eagle was a more critical look at the government's policies toward Native Americans under the Bureau of Indian Affairs, and it also compared the moral and political thought of the Sioux with those of white Americans. Among these comparisons were Standing Bear's reflections about his own education at Carlisle. One of the most renowned institutions of its kind, Carlisle was headed by a former U.S. Army captain who saw his mission as transforming "blanket Indians" into "civilized" Americans.

Standing Bear remembers his years at Carlisle with bitterness, recalling how he and the other young students were forced to have haircuts, wear uniforms, and eat an unfamiliar and debilitating diet of white bread with coffee and sugar. Such conditions, along with the cold weather, illness, and homesickness, resulted in the death of nearly half of the Plains children.

Despite the misery, he decided to stay at the school, urged by his father, who had come to visit him. Standing Bear's father warned him that the land was full of "Long Knives." "'They greatly outnumber us and are here to stay,' he said, and advised me, 'Son, learn all you can of the white man's ways and try to be like him.'"

Standing Bear recalls that his father did not say that white culture was better or that Standing Bear could be like a white man. Influenced by his father's advice, Standing Bear advocated an education based on both Native American cultural pride and knowledge of "the white man's ways."

Primary Source

Land of the Spotted Eagle [excerpt]

SYNOPSIS: In this section from his autobiography, Standing Bear explains his vision of Native American education, which is radically different from the education he received at Carlisle Indian School.

Teach Indians Old and New Ways

I say . . . that Indians should teach Indians; that Indians should serve Indians, especially on reservations where the older people remain. There is a definite need of the old for the care and sympathy of the young and they are today perishing for the joys that naturally belong to old Indian people. Old Indians are very close to their progeny. It was their delightful duty to care for and instruct the very young, while in turn they looked forward to being cared for by sons and daughters. These were the privileges and blessings of old age.

Many of the grievances of the old Indian, and his disagreements with the young, find root in the far-removed boarding school which sometimes takes the

Native American and white children in class on the Wind River Reservation, Wyoming, 1939. © CORBIS. REPRODUCED BY PERMISSION.

little ones at a very tender age. More than one tragedy has resulted when a young boy or girl has returned home again almost an utter stranger. I have seen these happenings with my own eyes and I know they can cause naught but suffering. The old Indian cannot, even if he wished, reconcile himself to an institution that alienates his young. And there is something evil in a system that brings about an unnatural reaction to life; when it makes young hearts callous and unheedful of the needs and joys of the old. . . .

To the end that young Indians will be able to appreciate both their traditional life and modern life they should be doubly educated. Without forsaking reverence for their ancestral teachings, they can be trained to take up modern duties that relate to tribal and reservation life. And there is no problem of reservation importance but can be solved by the joint efforts of the old and the young Indians. . . .

With school facilities already fairly well established and the capability of the Indian unquestioned, every reservation could well be supplied with Indian doctors, nurses, engineers, road- and bridge-builders, draughtsmen, architects, dentists, lawyers, teachers, and instructors in tribal lore, legends, orations, song, dance, and ceremonial ritual. The Indian, by the very sense of duty, should become his own historian, giving his account of the race—fairer and fewer accounts of the wars and more of statecraft, legends, languages, oratory, and philosophical conceptions. No longer should the Indian be dehumanized in order to make material for lurid and cheap fiction to embellish street-stands. Rather, a fair and correct history of the native American should be incorporated in the curriculum of the public school.

Caucasian youth is fed, and rightly so, on the feats and exploits of their old-world heroes, their revolutionary forefathers, their adventurous pioneer trail-blazers, and in our Southwest through pageants, fiestas, and holidays the days of the Spanish *conquistador* is kept alive.

But Indian youth! They, too, have fine pages in their past history; they, too, have patriots and heroes. And it is not fair to rob Indian youth of their history, the stories of their patriots, which, if impartially written, would fill them with pride and dignity. Therefore, give back to Indian youth all, everything in their heritage that belongs to them and augment it with the best in the modern schools. I repeat, doubly educate the Indian boy and girl.

What a contrast this would make in comparison with the present unhealthy, demoralized place the reservation is today, where the old are poorly fed, shabbily clothed, divested of pride and incentive; and where the young are unfitted for tribal life and untrained for the world of white man's affairs except to hold an occasional job!

Why not a school of Indian thought, built on the Indian pattern and conducted by Indian instructors? Why not a school of tribal art?

Why should not America be cognizant of itself; aware of its identity? In short, why should not America be preserved?

There were ideals and practices in the life of my ancestors that have not been improved upon by the present-day civilization; there were in our culture elements of benefit; and there were influences that would broaden any life. But that almost an entire public needs to be enlightened as to this fact need not be discouraging. For many centuries the human mind labored under the delusion that the world was flat; and thousands of men have believed that the heavens were supported by the strength of an Atlas. The human mind is not yet free from fallacious reasoning; it is not yet an open mind and its deepest recesses are not yet swept free of errors.

But it is now time for a destructive order to be reversed, and it is well to inform other races that the aboriginal culture of America was not devoid of beauty. Furthermore, in denying the Indian his ancestral rights and heritages the white race is but robbing itself. But America can be revived, rejuvenated, by recognizing a native school of thought. The Indian can save America. . . .

Regarding the 'civilization' that has been thrust upon me since the days of reservation, it has not added one whit to my sense of justice; to my reverence for the rights of life; to my love for truth, honesty, and generosity; nor to my faith in Wakan Tanka—God of the Lakotas. For after all the great religions have been preached and expounded, or have been revealed by brilliant scholars, or have been written in books and embellished in fine language with finer covers, man—all man—is still confronted with the Great Mystery.

So if today I had a young mind to direct, to start on the journey of life, and I was faced with the duty of choosing between the natural way of my forefathers and that of the white man's present way of civilization, I would, for its welfare, unhesitatingly set that child's feet in the path of my forefathers. I would raise him to be an Indian!

Further Resources

BOOKS

Coleman, Michael C. *American Indian Children at School, 1850–1930.* Jackson, Miss.: University of Mississippi Press, 1993.

Katz, William Loren. *A History of Multicultural America: The New Freedom to the New Deal.* Austin, Tex.: Raintree Steck-Vaughn Publishers, 1993.

Szasz, Margaret Connell. *Education and the American Indian: The Road to Self-Determination since 1928.* Albuquerque, N.Mex.: University of New Mexico Press, 1999.

PERIODICALS

Kramer, Max. "An Experiment in Indian Education." *Progressive Education* 12, January 1935, 155–159.

WEBSITES

"Luther Standing Bear (Ota Kte, Mochunozhin), 1868–1939." The Internet Public Library: Native American Authors Project. Available online at http://www.ipl.org/cgi/ref/native/browse.pl/A110 (accessed September 10, 2002).

AUDIO AND VISUAL MEDIA

In the White Man's Image. Produced by Christine Lesiak and Matthew Jones. 57 minutes. Alexandria, Va.: PBS Video, 1992.

Teachers and Teaching by Ten Thousand High-School Seniors

Survey, Tables

By: Frank William Hart

Date: 1934

Source: Hart, Frank William, ed. *Teachers and Teaching by Ten Thousand High-School Seniors.* New York: Macmillan, 1934, 72–73, 150–151.

About the Author: Frank William Hart (1881–1965) was born in Quincy, Indiana. He received his Ph.D. from Columbia University and began his career as a high school principal before returning to Columbia to teach. In 1920 he joined the faculty at the University of California, Berkeley, where he conducted numerous surveys of educational programs, organization and administration, school finances, and teachers' salaries. ■

Introduction

Part of progressive education was a growing confidence in the scientific expert to measure just about anything, and the survey was an instrument for this measurement. Educators might not be recognized by law as part of the government, but with their ability to measure and translate the results to the government, they still held a certain power.

The field of educational research was beginning to emerge as an important one. Experts and administrators came from the burgeoning schools of education. Intelligence testing, begun among recruits during World War I, had subsequently been used in schools, and a partnership had developed between some educators and the growing standardized testing industry. The school survey movement was yet another way that the administrative progressives, as they came to be known, could apply their ideas to education.

The survey usually consisted of a report by experts from outside the particular school district in question. In the report, the experts evaluated the work of the local schools and advised them on how to improve their practices. It was, of course, voluntary and left control to the local district, but the authority of the expert and his or her "scientific" research was not often ignored. In this way progressive administrators came to exert considerable influence on public education, above the fray of local politics. These experts often worked with business leaders and other professionals, and their surveys could be used by those groups for their own ends.

Significance

A survey of thousands of high-school seniors would seem to have little in common with the traditional school surveys. Everyone wanted to run the schools, but no one seemed to appreciate the labor of the teachers who toiled in them. In Chicago in 1933, thousands of teachers had marched in protest for their back wages, and all over the country teachers had been forced to work without pay because of budget shortages and calls for more tax cuts.

An article in the periodical *The Nation,* described the desperation of teachers:

> On April 27, according to the *New York Times,* Paul Schneider, aged forty-four, a sick and crippled Chicago school teacher, shot himself to death. His widow, left with three children, stated that he had not been paid for eight months, that his property had depreciated, groceries which his family needed could be bought only on wage assignment, and worry had aggravated his illness. Less than a month after Paul Schneider's discouragement drove him to suicide, the militant action of the Chicago teachers—patient no longer—in invading the banks and refusing to be distracted or amused by the picturesque profanity of Mr. Dawes resulted in the payment of $12,000,000 due them for the last months of 1932.
>
> Their pay for the five months of 1933 is still owed them. Four hundred of them are reported to be in asylums and sanitariums as a result of the strain, and are possibly beyond help by this very belated and partial payment . . . the plight of Chicago's teachers has received a relatively large amount of publicity, whereas the equally desperate, perhaps more hopeless condition of teachers in rural schools throughout the South and in many sections of the West and Middle West has gone almost unnoticed. Public education is threatened

To Seniors in Representative High Schools Throughout the United States

(Do not sign your name.)

Through the information you are asked to give, it is hoped that teaching in high schools may be made better. That would be a fitting memorial for your senior class to contribute to succeeding classes. To that end will you, therefore, carefully think through the issues raised below and record the results of your four years of experience frankly and accurately? You are not asked to sign your name, and these blanks will be collected by one of your classmates, sealed in your presence, and placed in the mail by the one collecting them. Your confidence will be respected.

(1) Considering all of the teachers you have had in high school, think of the one *you have liked best* and, without mentioning the teacher's name, write down in the space below as accurately as you can your *reasons for liking this teacher best.* Call this teacher "Teacher A." Note that this is to be the teacher you *liked best,* not necessarily the *best teacher.*

____

____

(2) Now think of the one *you have liked least of all,* and write down as accurately as you can your reasons for *not liking* this teacher. Call this teacher "Teacher Z."

____

____

(3) Was the teacher *you liked best* also the *best teacher,* that is, the one who taught you most effectively? __________

Was "Teacher Z" the *best teacher?*__________

(4) If neither "Teacher A" nor "Teacher Z" was the *best teacher* you have had, write down as clearly as you can just how your *best teacher differed from "Teacher A."* Call this teacher "Teacher H."

"Teacher H" differed from "Teacher A" in the following ways:

____

____

(5) Counting *all* the teachers you are *now* having work with:

(a) How many are *more like* "Teacher A" than "Teacher Z"? _____

(b) How many are *more like* "Teacher Z" than "Teacher A"? _____

Total __________

(This total should equal all the teachers you now have.)

SOURCE: *Teachers and Teaching by Ten Thousand High-School Seniors.* Collected, compiled, and analyzed by Frank W. Hart. New York: Macmillan, 1934, 3–5.

Primary Source

Teachers and Teaching by Ten Thousand High-School Seniors: Survey

SYNOPSIS: This survey of American high school seniors was designed to determine what made teachers likable, disliked, and effective in the eyes of students. Presented with this survey are two tables containing survey results as well as selected comments about their teachers.

with something little short of an absolute breakdown in vast areas of the country.

Teacher morale was clearly low, and in 1932 the educational scholar Willard Waller had published a book describing why teachers were unlikely activists who were often more conservative, suffering from the tension between dominance in the classroom and subordination elsewhere.

Unlike Waller, Hart did not look at any of these external factors in his work, published two years later. A questionnaire had been distributed to the seniors in sixty-six high schools all over the country, in large cities, small towns, and rural districts. They were filled out on the spot but apparently collected in a way that anonymity could be assured.

Students were asked to think of the teacher they liked best, least, and if neither one was the best teacher, then also their best teacher. Hart's conclusions seem to suggest that no matter what the external circumstances, a teacher's attitude to teaching should always be within her/his control.

Primary Source

Teachers and Teaching by Ten Thousand High-School Seniors: Survey [excerpt]

SYNOPSIS: This excerpt provides selected comments from students on the teachers they most liked and disliked, along with their reasons. The original survey questionnaire is here, as well as the two tables with survey results for Teachers A, Z, and H.

270. I considered Teacher A the one I liked best because he is of middle age and he was able to give me assignments, no matter how hard they seemed, and I would always enjoy them. He always had good discipline in his classes in a way which was enjoyable. He always seemed to be fair in his grading and class work. He was always ready to help anyone at any time possible for him. He was very neat and clean in dress at all times and on all occasions. As the last word, he taught his subjects in the most interesting way, and he treated all students alike, that is, realizing that no two students are alike.

271. Teacher A in my school, first, teaches an interesting subject. She is pretty to look upon, which is a change from most teachers. This Teacher A knows her subject and I am never in doubt as to whether she is right or not. She is sociable outside the classroom and seems to be glad to talk with

Reasons for Liking "Teacher Z" Least, Arranged in Order of Frequency of Mention, as Reported by 3,725 High School Seniors

Reasons for liking "Teacher Z" least	Frequency of mention	Rank
Too cross, crabby, grouchy, never smiles, nagging, sarcastic, loses temper, "flies off the handle"	1708	1
Not helpful with school work, does not explain lessons and assignments, not clear, work not planned	1025	2
Partial, has "pets" or favored students, and "picks on certain pupils"	859	3
Superior, aloof, haughty, "snooty" overbearing, does not know you out of class	775	4
Mean, unreasonable, "hard boiled," intolerant, ill mannered, too strict, makes life miserable	652	5
Unfair in marking and grading, unfair in tests and examinations	614	6
Inconsiderate of pupils' feelings, bawls out pupils in the presence of classmates, pupils are afraid and ill at ease and dread class	551	7
Not interested in pupils and does not understand them	442	8
Unreasonable assignments and home work	350	9
Too loose in discipline, no control of class, does not command respect	313	10
Does not stick to the subject, brings in too many irrelevant personal matters, talks too much	301	11
"We did not learn what we were supposed to"	275	12
Dull, stupid, and uninteresting	275	13
Too old-fashioned, too old to be teaching	224	14
Not "fair and square" in dealing with pupils	203	15
Knows the subject but "can't put it over"	193	16
Does not hold to standards, is careless and slipshod in her work	190	17
Too exacting, too hard, gives no chance to make up work	183	18
Does not know the subject	170	19
Does not respect pupils' judgments or opinions	133	20
Too changeable, inconsistent, unreliable	122	21
Lazy, not interested in teaching	115	22
Not friendly, not companionable	98	23
Shows boy or girl favoritism	95	24
Dresses unattractively or in bad taste	92	25
Weak personality	85	26
Insincere	75	27
Personally unattractive	65	28
Does not recognize individual differences in pupils	64	29
Voice not pleasant	63	30

SOURCE: *Teachers and Teaching by Ten Thousand High-School Seniors.* Collected, compiled, and analyzed by Frank W. Hart. New York: Macmillan, 1934, pp. 250-51.

Primary Source

Teachers and Teaching by Ten Thousand High-School Seniors: Table (1 OF 2)

SYNOPSIS: These survey results list reasons for liking "Teacher Z" least.

you. She seems to be interested in your future and willing to help you succeed. She is young and nearer our age, which makes her naturally closer to us. She takes an interest in town affairs and is always willing to help with a school activity. She is generally present at football and basketball games and rooting for our team. She doesn't pick out individuals to whom she grants special privileges.

272. Teacher A is a teacher I had during my Junior year. There were several reasons why I liked this teacher, but one of the most important was that he made everyone in the class feel he was a part of the class. Students often took charge of the class under his supervision and, when it was necessary for him to be absent, he gave charge of the class to the one who was the best student for the time being. He apparently had few favorites and disliked a student who thought himself above his classmates either in social standing or in intelligence. When something important in world affairs was going on, he led the class in a discussion of it. I thoroughly enjoyed the two hours I had classes under him every day because he made classes so very interesting. . . .

20. She was as nearly opposite to Teacher A as anyone could be. As far as I know she thought only of drumming knowledge of the subject into our heads any way possible—and didn't think of us as human beings at all. Her sense of humor was a bit misplaced—she laughed only at her own jokes (which were told annually) and couldn't hold on to her temper. Her temper became so common that finally she could frighten only the meekest of low sophomores. Her remarks during her tempers took the form of real insults.

21. I dislike Teacher Z because she acts about as lazy as some of her laziest students do. She doesn't seem to take a personal interest in the students. She says to do one thing one day and then forgets all about it the next. She is always yawning. Her explanations are never clear. She expects too much to be done without help. And I wish she could see the student's side of a question once.

22. Words can hardly express the faults of this teacher. Teacher Z always seemed to be sleepy; that is, she was continually yawning. Although this teacher knew her subject, she did not know how to present it. The class was strictly formal, no fraternal spirit whatever. Teacher Z was out of the room very frequently. This teacher was very old-fashioned; also rather sickly.

23. Of all the simple people, she is the worst I ever knew. Often she would act like a regular clown and I certainly have no respect for a teacher who thinks she is a star entertainer. She would waste all our class time and then give the stiffest tests about things she'd never mentioned. I never learned a thing in that class that I owe her any thanks for, as we practically had to teach ourselves. She was a misplaced joke. . . .

Differences between "Teacher H" and "Teacher A," Arranged in Order of Frequency, as Reported by 763 High School Seniors

"Teacher H" differed from "Teacher A" as follows:	Frequency of mention	Rank
More exacting in standards of work, stricter in marking, "we learned more"	267	1
Better at explaining lessons and assignments, work is better planned	155	2
Knows the subject better and can "put it over" better	95	3
Stricter, more rigid discipline	85	4
Makes the work more interesting	46	5
Is less friendly	39	6
More serious, more businesslike, keeps closer to the subject, more conscientious	38	7
Less understanding of pupils, less interested in pupils	13	8
More sarcastic	12	9
Less attractive	10	10
More cross and crabby	10	11
More aloof	6	12

SOURCE: *Teachers and Teaching by Ten Thousand High-School Seniors.* Collected, compiled, and analyzed by Frank W. Hart. New York: Macmillan, 1934, pp. 278-79.

Primary Source

Teachers and Teaching by Ten Thousand High-School Seniors: Table (2 OF 2)

More survey results list differences between two teachers.

Further Resources

BOOKS

Krug, Edward A. *The Shaping of the American High School 1920–1941,* Volume 2. Madison, Wis.: University of Wisconsin, 1972.

Tyack, David, Robert Lowe, and Elisabeth Hansot. *Public Schools in Hard Times: The Great Depression and Recent Years.* Cambridge, Mass.: Harvard University Press, 1984.

Waller, Willard. *The Sociology of Teaching.* New York: John Wiley, [1932] 1965.

PERIODICALS

Langdon, Eunice. "The Teacher Faces the Depression." *The Nation,* August 16, 1933, 182. Available online at http://newdeal.feri.org/texts/243.htm (accessed April 11, 2003).

WEBSITES

The First Measured Century. Available online at http://www.pbs.org/fmc (accessed April 19, 2002).

School: The Story of American Public Education. Available online at http://www.pbs.org/kcet/publicschool/index.html (accessed April 19, 2002).

Jane Addams and Education of Immigrants

"Jane Addams: A Foe of War and Need"

Obituary

By: *The New York Times*

Date: May 22, 1935

Source: "Jane Addams: A Foe of War and Need." *The New York Times,* May 22, 1935. Available online at http://www.nytimes.com/learning/general/onthisday/bday/0906.html; website home page: http://www.nytimes.com (accessed April 24, 2002).

Jane Addams Memorial

Painting

By: Mitchell Siporin

Date: 1936

Source: Siporin, Mitchell. *Jane Addams Memorial.* 1936. Tempera on paper. In the Fine Arts Collection, General Services Administration 8247589458423 293 A New Deal for the Arts. The National Archives. Reproduced in "A New Deal for the Arts." National Archives. Available online at http://www.archives.gov/exhibit_hall/new_deal_for_the_arts/rediscovering_america2.html; website home page: http://www.archives.gov (accessed February 10, 2003).

About the Artist: Mitchell Siporin (1910–1976) was born in New York City. He was a painter, educator, and illustrator who exhibited his works throughout the world and won numerous prizes. He died in 1976 in Newton, Massachusetts. ■

Introduction

By the turn of the century, many immigrants had entered America hoping to create a better life for themselves and their children. From 1870 to 1920, some 26 million immigrants came to the United States, making up close to a third of the populations of America's eight largest cities. Many of the more recent immigrants were from southern and eastern Europe, Italy, Russia, Austria-Hungary, and Greece. There was a wide diversity of languages, religions, and ethnic groups represented. By 1920 Chicago's population was about one-half foreign born. Public schools became more bureaucratic and standardized in response to this massive influx, using age-specific grades and the corresponding textbooks.

The public education system was not always equipped to meet the particular needs of immigrants, and local political machines often controlled the schools, rarely to the benefit of the newcomers. There were also tensions between school administrators and the local politicians. Many immigrants did not trust the public schools to educate their children. They often lived in ethnic enclaves like "Little Italy," "Greek town" and "Chinatown."

Progressive educators did not want the society fragmented into such ethnic groups and like John Dewey, preferred a "Great Community" dedicated to upholding democracy. Many educators, such as Ellwood P. Cubberley, believed that immigrant children should be assimilated into an "Anglo-Saxon" American way of life, conforming to the dominant social norms and abandoning their own heritage. They were taught in their classrooms that their ethnicity was something inferior, and Americanization was the process of getting rid of it as completely as possible.

Significance

Jane Addams had a very different view of the education of immigrants. Her commitment to public service led her to establish Hull House, a settlement house on Chicago's south side, whose impact was far-reaching. At Hull House, the idealistic Addams initially approached the immigrants—Italians, Bohemians, Poles, and Russian Jews—with a formal curriculum of lectures designed with moral uplift in mind. She soon discovered that the immigrants wanted more immediate things, such as practical help with finding jobs, paying the rent, health care, and educating their children. Addams changed her curriculum to reflect their needs, offering not only adult education courses but also less formal education as the immigrants came together to learn new skills. Since the women needed childcare, a nursery school was established; since they needed help with finances, a savings bank was set up, as was a health center. How the political process worked was taught as well, because Addams feared that the immigrants would become pawns of the political machines, and trade union meetings were held at Hull House.

In addition to educating immigrant women and children, Hull House offered a place where other women could learn and pursue their careers. Julia Lathrop, who would become the first chief of the Federal Children's Bureau, and Florence Kelley, who would become the chief factory inspector for the Illinois Bureau of Labor Statistics, were Hull House "alumna."

The nearby University of Chicago also benefited from Addams's work. Sociologists and educators interested in social reform came to Hull House to conduct research and

Primary Source

Jane Addams Memorial

SYNOPSIS: Mitchell Siporin's painting is a memorial to Jane Addams's work. It was painted for the Illinois Federal Art Project, sponsored by the Works Progress Administration (WPA), and shows Addams among the women and children she helped educate at Hull House. A worker and farmer shaking hands depict her support of labor. A soldier breaking a sword at her feet represents her peace activism. "JANE ADDAMS MEMORIAL," TEMPERA PAINTING ON PAPER BY MITCHELL SIPORIN. FINE ARTS COLLECTION, PUBLIC SERVICE BUILDING, GENERAL SERVICE ADMINISTRATION. (FA 216)

lecture. When John Dewey was still a professor at the University of Chicago, he became a trustee of Hull House and an advisor to Addams. As an educator of immigrants and urban educator, Addams developed a model for "socialized education." The settlement house, like the progressive school, was an experiment in using knowledge to solve real problems while creating a sense of community, unlike many of the public schools of that time.

Throughout her life, Addams was an influential advocate of progressive causes such as the reform of child labor laws and women's suffrage. As a member of the Chicago Board of Education, she urged closer ties between the public schools and immigrant families, opposing Americanization as an ideal. She was a multicultural educator before the term was invented. For her many achievements, including her activism for disarmament and peace, Addams was the first American woman awarded the Nobel Peace Prize in 1931.

Primary Source

"Jane Addams: A Foe of War and Need" [excerpt]

SYNOPSIS: This excerpt from Addams's lengthy obituary highlights the youthful idealism that led to her founding Hull House.

Of Quaker Ancestry

. . . As a child Miss Addams regarded herself as an ugly duckling. She said she was pigeon-toed and twisted in the back so that her head leaned slightly to one side and she didn't want to have any one know she was the daughter of so fine a man as her father. But surgery cured her deformities and she became a young woman described as "beautiful, not pretty," "beautiful because of her remarkable expression." She became, too, graceful, erect, with a fine carriage.

After she was graduated from Rockford College in 1881, Miss Addams went abroad to complete her education. It was not the Alps, the art galleries or the cathedrals that impressed her, but rather the slums of the great cities. More than ever she was determined to dedicate her life to the service of the poor.

She went to London and there saw Toynbee Hall, the first settlement house in the world. She was greatly impressed as she was by the European slums she visited. Returning to the United States, she was ill for some months and then, in 1888, she studied for a time in Philadelphia.

In 1889, when she was 29 years old, Miss Addams and Miss Ellen Gates Starr, her friend, founded Hull House at 800 South Halsted Street, Chicago, "in the midst of horrid little houses" of the slums. Four years previously the stately red brick mansion had been built by Charles J. Hull on the outskirts of the city. By 1889, however, it stood in the heart of one of the most miserable neighborhoods of the city. The owner, Miss Helen Culver, gave the two women a free leasehold to the house and later to the land about it, on which twelve additional buildings were built.

Hull House Opened in 1889

Miss Addams moved into Hull House in September, 1889, and it was her home thereafter. It was then between a saloon and an undertaking shop, and there was an annex to a factory in its rear. Thousands of the foreign born—Miss Addams always held welcoming arms to the strangers—including Poles, Jews, Russians, Italians, Greeks, Germans, Irish and Bohemians were welcomed there. Negroes were also cordially received.

Persons later to be famous lived there in those early days. Among them were Mr. and Mrs. Gerald Swope, who were married there, Mackenzie King, later Premier of Canada, Francis Hackett, and Professor John Dewey, dean of American philosophers, and his family.

Hull House grew to be known as one of the largest and best-known of the nation's settlements. It commenced with the ordinary activities of children's clubs and free kindergartens and later it sponsored courses in languages, literature, music, painting, history, mathematics, elocution, dancing, wood-carving, pottery, metal work, bookbindery, dressmaking, lacework, cooking and basketwork. A labor museum was also established at Hull House.

Dozens of clubs were organized to aid working women. A lunch room was opened, as was a nursery for the children of employed women. There was also a gymnasium, a natatorium, a penny savings bank, a lodging house, as well as a circulating library and an employment bureau. Miss Addams personally directed all these activities, which were models for hundreds of others throughout the world.

Further Resources

BOOKS

Addams, Jane. *The Second Twenty Years at Hull-House.* New York: Macmillan Publishing Co., 1930.

———. *Twenty Years at Hull-House.* New York: Macmillan Publishing Co., 1910.

Davis, Allen F. *American Heroine: The Life and Legend of Jane Addams.* New York: Oxford University Press, 1973.

Gutek, Gerald L. *Historical and Philosophical Foundations of Education: A Biographical Introduction.* Upper Saddle River, N.J.: Prentice-Hall Inc., 1997.

Lagemann, Ellen Condliffe, ed. *Jane Addams on Education.* New York: Teachers College Press, Columbia University, 1985.

WEBSITES

Jane Addams Hull House Museum at the University of Illinois at Chicago. Available online at http://www.uic.edu/jaddams/hull/hull_house.html (accessed April 24, 2002).

AUDIO AND VISUAL MEDIA

The Women of Hull-House. Chicago: University of Illinois at Chicago, 1992.

"Education"

Poem

By: Arthur Guiterman

Date: 1935

Source: Guiterman, Arthur. "Education." Published in *Death and General Putnam and 101 Other Poems.* New York: E.P. Dutton, 1935. Reprinted in *Unseen Harvests.* Fuess, Claude M., and Emory S. Basford, eds. New York: Macmillan, 1947, 351–52.

About the Author: Arthur Guiterman (1871–1943) was born in Vienna, Austria. A poet, editor, humorist, journalist, and librettist, he wrote thousands of poems for newspapers and magazines, publishing several collections in his lifetime. Guiterman was best known for his humorous verse. ■

Introduction

Guiterman graduated from the College of the City of New York in 1891. He accepted a clerical job with the trade publication *Jewelers' Weekly* and went on to work as an editor at *Woman's Home Companion* and the *Literary Digest.* His poetry did not gain recognition until 1906, when *Woman's Home Companion* magazine published his poem "Strictly Germ-Proof."

In the following year he published his first collection, *Betel Nuts,* and by 1918 he was publishing a book nearly every two years. From 1925 until his death, Guiterman was a frequent contributor to the *New Yorker,* as well as *Life, Saturday Evening Post, Scribner's,* and *Harper's.* He also contributed a poem, "The Cardinal Bird," to the popular Elson Reader primers. His witty verses often appear in collections of quotations. For example, on the Puritans, he wrote, "They fell upon their knees and then / Upon the aborigines." Guiterman, a founder of the Poetry Society of America, turned from humor to sentimental and patriotic themes in his later career, but these poems did not achieve the recognition of his earlier work.

Significance

In the poem "Education," Guiterman directly asks what the purpose of education is. Elsewhere, he had written, "Comparing Information and Knowledge is like asking whether the fatness of a pig is more or less green than the designated hitter rule." In making fun of the pretensions of the Latin and Greek still taught in elite college preparatory schools and colleges ("your splendid schools") Guiterman was reflecting the general spirit of his time. Ironically, President Franklin Roosevelt and his first lady were the very products of these elite institutions but had managed to identify themselves with the interests of the poor and working people. By contrasting the "farm boy" on one end of the log with Mark Hopkins, the one teaching, Guiterman makes this class distinction clear.

Students study in a rural Wisconsin school in 1937. THE LIBRARY OF CONGRESS.

He also distinguishes between the "things" that are taught, the curriculum, and the person doing the teaching. The innovations of progressive education based on a child-centered curriculum had been in vogue among the educated classes. Guiterman's poem is saying that no matter what the curriculum, it is the example of the teacher that has more force in education.

The teacher becomes a moral example, a living lesson: "No printed word nor spoken plea / Can teach young hearts what men should be." Guiterman's poem concludes that education is more than training the mind to think; it is a cultivation of character as well. Although published during the depths of the Depression, his are timeless words for the people of any generation, especially those who hope to teach.

Primary Source

"Education"

SYNOPSIS: The poem "Education" asks about the purposes of education and emphasizes the importance of the teacher's character. Mark Hopkins was a gifted nineteenth-century teacher, and James Garfield was elected the twentieth president of the United States in 1880.

Mark Hopkins sat on one end of a log
   And a farm boy sat on the other.
Mark Hopkins came as a pedagogue
   And taught as an elder brother.
I don't care what Mark Hopkins taught,
If his Latin was small and his Greek was naught,
For the farmer boy he thought, thought he,
   All through lecture time and quiz,
"The kind of a man I mean to be
   Is the kind of a man Mark Hopkins is."

Theology, languages, medicine, law,
Are peacock feathers to deck a daw
If the boys who come from your splendid schools
Are well-trained sharpers or flippant fools.
You may boast of your age and your ivied walls,
Your great endowments, your marble halls
   And all your modern features,
Your vast curriculum's scope and reach
And the multifarious *things* you teach—
   But how about your teachers?
Are they men who can stand in a father's place,
Who are paid, best paid, by the ardent face
When boyhood gives, as boyhood can,
Its love and faith to a fine, true man?

No printed word nor spoken plea
Can teach young hearts what men should be,
Not all the books on all the shelves,
But what the teachers are, themselves.
For Education is, Making Men;
So is it now, so was it when
Mark Hopkins sat on one end of a log
   And James Garfield sat on the other.

Further Resources

BOOKS

Anderson, Maggie, and Hassler, David. *Learning by Heart: Contemporary American Poetry about School.* Iowa City, Iowa: University of Iowa Press, 1999.

Dictionary of Literary Biography, Volume 2: American Humorists, 1800–1950. Farmington Hills, Mich.: Gale, 1982.

Swados, Harvey, ed. *The American Writer and the Great Depression.* Indianapolis, Ind.: Bobbs-Merrill, 1966.

Who Was Who in America, Volume II: 1943–1950. Chicago: Marquis, 1963.

PERIODICALS

Arthur Guiterman Obituary. *The New York Times,* January 12, 1943.

The National Youth Administration

Painting Depicting the Activities of the National Youth Administration

Painting

By: Alden Krider

Date: 1936

Source: Krider, Alden. *Painting Depicting the Activities of the National Youth Administration.* 1936. In the Franklin D. Roosevelt Library, National Archives and Records Administration. 44-107-1. Available online at http://www.archives.gov/exhibit_hall/new_deal_for_the_arts/work_pays_america.html; website home page: http://www.archives.gov (accessed April 24, 2002).

About the Artist: Alden Krider (1908–) was born in Newtown, Kansas. Krider taught at Kansas State University from 1949 to 1977 and was professor emeritus. The Krider Visual Resource and Learning Center, in the College of Architecture, Planning, and Design at Kansas State University is named for him.

"Evaluation of the Contributions of the National Youth Administration"

Report

By: Advisory Committee on Education

Date: 1939

Source: Advisory Committee on Education. "Evaluation of the Contributions of the National Youth Administration." *The National Youth Administration.* Washington, D.C.: U.S. Government Printing Office, 1939, 86–91. Reprinted in *Readings in American Educational History.* Edgar W. Knight and Clifton L. Hall, eds. New York: Appleton-Century-Crofts, 1951, 762–765.

About the Organization: President Roosevelt appointed an advisory committee on education that met from 1936 to 1939. Headed by Floyd Reeves, an author, educational consultant and professor at the University of Chicago, the committee was largely composed of people from labor, industry, agriculture, and government, with educators in the minority. In 1938 the committee issued what came to be known as the Reeves Report, which called for the national government to take a more activist role in using education for social reform. The committee also issued special reports on the work of New Deal agencies and on conditions in schools. ■

Introduction

Unemployment affected nearly every group during the Great Depression, including young people. Although public school administrators were at odds with New Dealers over funding education, the National Youth Administration (NYA) was one program through which many young people received an education. Led by a social worker and lay minister, Aubrey Williams, the NYA was more radical in its approach than the Civilian Conservation Corps (CCC).

Williams created a Division of Negro Affairs, headed by the noted African American Mary McLeod Bethune, which helped an estimated 300,000 African Americans. Neither the CCC nor public school advocates were particularly interested in helping African American youth, even though they were disproportionately hard hit by the Great Depression, many living in the rural South or the slums of northern cities and actively discriminated against in both areas. The NYA provided cash supplements to students so they could complete their studies, and, in return, students worked as teachers' assistants or in other jobs on school grounds.

For unemployed youth, the NYA offered a wide range of jobs, and nearly 2.6 million people participated in the program. Some lived at NYA resident centers, where they were taught particular skills or remedial courses in reading. The low-cost success of the NYA showed traditional educators that the children they had considered uneducable, those from poor, illiterate, and minority families, were capable of educational achievement.

Significance

As a program established to deal with youth unemployment, the NYA sponsored a wide range of activities. Unlike the CCC, which sent young men to residential military-style camps, the NYA was largely non-residential and more experimental. There were two ways in which the NYA dealt with education. First, the direct financial aid to students meant the difference between a student staying in school and dropping out. This was a preventative approach to youth unemployment. But by focusing on previously excluded groups, it made a substantial difference. The NYA helped 200 African Americans receive their Ph.D.s in the 1930s, which was 155 more than had received doctorates in the period prior to that.

Second, to help those young people already unemployed, the NYA developed a series of work and training programs that linked real-life work to education, unlike most public schools of the time. For example, young people working on a construction project might study blueprint reading as part of their training. The NYA placed young people in parks' departments, YMCAs, settlement houses, hospitals, preschools, and in community building projects.

Many educators were suspicious of NYA programs precisely because they offered a real alternative to public school education. The NYA's programs were directly targeted to young adults, 90 percent of who were from families on relief. The National Education Association (NEA), however, representing the voice of educational administrators, wanted general federal aid to existing schools and programs, and did not single out the poor or minority children as particularly needy. The conflict between educators and the New Dealers resulted in a 1941 report issued by the NEA, in which it recommended that the NYA and CCC be disbanded. Both organizations were defunct by 1943. However, the NYA would serve as a model for education programs during the Great Society reforms of the 1960s.

Primary Source

"Evaluation of the Contributions of the National Youth Administration" [excerpt]

SYNOPSIS: In this excerpt, the NYA's contributions to help alleviate unemployment are evaluated with a special focus on its training and education activities and the success of these programs in addressing the "urgent problems of youth." Some of the NYA's activities mentioned in this report are visually illustrated in a 1936 painting by Alden Krider.

The various programs of the National Youth Administration have been discussed in some detail in the preceding chapters of this study. In this chapter an effort will be made to evaluate the contributions of the youth administration and its programs to (1) the solution of the relief problem; (2) the establishment, development, and extension of educational concepts and policies; (3) the solution of urgent problems of youth; (4) co-operative activity in local communities; and (5) Federal administrative policy.

The Relief Problem

Adequate statistics from which to determine the extent to which the National Youth Administration has contributed to the solution of the relief problem are

Primary Source

Painting Depicting the Activities of the National Youth Administration

SYNOPSIS: This 1936 painting by Alden Krider shows the variety of programs sponsored by the NYA and serves as a visual illustration to the excerpted report "Evaluation of the Contributions of the National Youth Administration." Krider created this painting for an exhibit at the Kansas State Fair. The dark background represents some of the problems faced by young people during the Great Depression, including crime, poverty, and homelessness. In the foreground are the beneficial activities provided by the NYA, such as classes in sewing and construction. The words in the painting, "We can ill afford to lose the energy and skills of these young men and women," are Franklin Roosevelt's, spoken in 1935 when he established the NYA. COURTESY OF THE FDR LIBRARY.

not available. Only a rough estimate is possible. Of all persons registered in the unemployment census of November 1937, approximately 1,100,000 persons 16 to 19 years of age and about 1,300,000 persons 20 to 24 years of age were reported as either "totally unemployed" (but not necessarily on relief) or employed as "emergency workers" (necessarily on relief). "Emergency workers" alone constituted about one-fifth of the total within the age group 15 to 24. If it may be assumed that of the 15 to 19 year age group reported in the unemployment census roughly two-thirds are 18 to 19 years of age, it may be estimated that there were approximately 2,000,000 persons 18 to 24 years of age in the "totally unemployed or employed on emergency work" category, of whom approximately 400,000 were in "emergency work."

But in that same month, November 1937, the National Youth Administration employed approximately 122,000 youth aged 18 to 24 on (emergency) work projects. It thus provided for at least one-twentieth of all youth aged 18 to 24 who were totally unemployed or on emergency work, and about one-fourth of those on emergency (relief) work.

To what extent beyond the conservative measure here determined it is reasonable to go by the inclusion of youth aided on the student aid program it is impossible to estimate. Relief is not the only criterion of eligibility for student aid as it is for employment on work projects. It is obvious, however, that the estimates of the proportion of unemployed youth aided by the National Youth Administration are definitely conservative.

In view of the fact that the hourly wages of youth employed on the work projects are directly proportional to those paid to adult workers on the works program, and that the latter in turn are determined in accord with prevailing standard rates for employment in private industry, it not infrequently happens that work project youth receive hourly wages higher than the average available locally to youth in private industry. To this extent the National Youth Administration operates in conformity with the established Federal principle of security wage employment.

By adhering to accepted desirable policies relating to the minimum age for the participation of youth in gainful employment, it is probable that the National Youth Administration has helped to raise the level of wages and to lengthen the period of formal educational experience. By employing youth on public projects, the youth administration has helped to reduce pressure on the labor market and competition for jobs among adult workers. At the same time, it has provided youth with guidance, experience, and training against the time that they will join the ranks of adult applicants for employment.

Educational Concepts and Policies

As an emergency agency, flexible in its administration and with relatively large available funds, the National Youth Administration has been able to experiment in educational programs which, under ordinary circumstances, would have received little consideration by regular agencies of Government, and which even today are not fully recognized by the majority of educators.

Through the extension of educational opportunities to the underprivileged, the Youth Administration has uncovered a reservoir of competent youth desirous of continued education for whom almost no provision has been made in the past. It has demonstrated the possibility of providing educational opportunities at small cost which have proved of considerable advantage to the youth and to the institutions involved. And, by providing merely the essentials for the maintenance of youth, it has increased school and college enrollments by 300,000 to 400,000 without sacrificing quality to quantity.

Experimentation which grew out of the necessity for combining work with schooling has demonstrated possibilities of profound educational significance. Especially noteworthy in this connection are those work projects, sponsored by educational institutions, in which youth are maintained in residence at the institutions and undergo a course of training related to their employment on work of benefit to the institutions themselves. To the extent that the National Youth Administration has been successful in this combining work and schooling, the more pointedly by contrast does it emphasize the inadequacies of the conventional current curriculum and guidance policies at both high school and college levels.

Although the nominal aim of the National Youth Administration has been to serve as a relief agency, it has actually fulfilled an educational function as well. Because relief was the primary objective, the educational policy of the Youth Administration has of necessity been of a temporizing and exigent nature. Had the educational function been considered as of primary rather than of secondary importance, it is not unlikely that the policies and programs here reported would have been considerably altered. To the conflicting practices inevitably resultant from this confusion concerning the relative importance of the functions of relief and education may in large measure be attributed many of the apparent discrepancies and inconsistencies in the present program.

Urgent Problems of Youth

If there is today a "lost generation" of youth lacking work experience, lacking guidance, abandoned by the school, and disowned by industry, and if, as is often claimed, the new social and economic status of youth resultant from changes in the age composition of the population calls for national leadership in meeting the problems of youth, then it must be conceded that in large measure the National Youth Administration has contributed significantly toward the solution of these problems.

Without doubt the depression adversely affected the morale of youth. But by providing youth with an articulate agency for the expression of their needs and a focal point of direct action in meeting them, the National Youth Administration has helped to restore their morale. The indictment that actual achievement has failed to measure up to the demand for service becomes, therefore, a criticism not of inadequacy in function so much as of limitations in application. Through each of its major programs the National Youth Administration has provided youth with facilities for continued education, work experience, practical guidance, and, so far as possible, placement in employment in private industry. There is much to indicate that the morale and health of youth participating in student aid and work projects employment have improved.

By experimenting with youth of unrevealed potentialities in unusual situations, the National Youth Administration has drawn attention to many inadequacies in the current provisions for vocational guidance. Many unemployed youth, poorly educated and untrained, are to all appearances fit for nothing but unskilled or semiskilled work; nevertheless, time and again, reports are received concerning the surprising extent of their achievements when given the right environment, an encouraging and skillful supervisor or foreman, and the chance to do constructive work.

Further Resources

BOOKS

Johnson, Palmer Oliver. *The National Youth Administration.* New York: Arno Press, 1974.

Lindley, Betty Grimes. *A New Deal for Youth; the Story of the National Youth Administration.* 1938. Reprint, New York: Da Capo Press, 1972.

Salmond, John. *A Southern Rebel: The Life and Times of Aubrey Williams, 1890–1965.* Chapel Hill: University of North Carolina Press, 1983.

Tyack, David, Robert Lowe, and Elisabeth Hansot. *Public Schools in Hard Times: The Great Depression and Recent Years.* Cambridge, Mass.: Harvard University Press, 1984.

WEBSITES

New Deal Art. *ArtLex Visual Arts Dictionary.* Available online at http://www.artlex.com/ArtLex/n/newdeal.html; website home page: http://www.artlex.com (accessed April 24, 2002).

Records of the National Youth Administration. National Archives and Records Administration. Available online at http://www.nara.gov/guide/rg119.html; website home page: http://www.nara.gov (accessed April 24, 2002).

"Educational Contribution of the Civilian Conservation Corps"

Magazine article

By: Robert Fechner

Date: May 1937

Source: Fechner, Robert. "Educational Contribution of the Civilian Conservation Corps." *Phi Delta Kappan* 19, no. 9, May, 1937. Reproduced in the New Deal Network. Available online at http://newdeal.feri.org/texts/641.htm; website home page: http://newdeal.feri.org (accessed April 24, 2002).

About the Author: Robert Fechner (1876–1939), born in Chattanooga, Tennessee, was the grandson of German immigrants. At age sixteen he began his training as an apprentice machinist, joined a local union, and was elected secretary. He then worked as a traveling machinist for nine years, and eventually became a noted union leader who represented labor and helped settle many disputes. In 1933, Fechner was appointed by President Roosevelt to direct the Civilian Conservation Corps (CCC). He served as the CCC's director until his death in 1939. ■

Introduction

An estimated two million young people were unemployed in the early years of the Great Depression. At a time when only a minority of young adults went on to college, the majority could not find jobs, even when they had to quit school to support their families. Some became tramps and hobos, crisscrossing the country on the railroads in search of work.

The Civilian Conservation Corps (CCC) was an emergency program based on successful European models for peacetime "armies" of young people to carry out constructive tasks instead of military ones. Shortly after his election in 1932, President Franklin Delano Roosevelt announced his proposal for the CCC, "to be used in simple work, not interfering with normal employment, and confining itself to forests, the prevention of soil erosion, flood control and similar projects." All work was to be done on public land to avoid competition with private contractors.

Recruits had to be between eighteen and twenty-three and had to pass a physical exam. Many young men were malnourished but doctors accepted them anyway. The pay of a dollar a day plus room and board helped not only the recruit but his entire family: every recruit could enlist for the six-month term provided he accepted that twenty-four dollars of his salary would be sent home to his family each month.

Shortly after President Roosevelt appointed Robert Fechner to direct the CCC, camps were established in all forty-eight states and Puerto Rico, the Virgin Islands, Hawaii, and Alaska. The U.S. Army ran the camps, but instead of receiving military training, the recruits were to be treated as "soil soldiers." Although the unemployment rate was higher among young African American men, there were very few camps for them, and most camps were segregated despite legislation prohibiting discrimination. Young men in the CCC were responsible for creating thousands of miles of park trails, installing telephone lines, building erosion dams, planting trees in public parks, and fighting fires. As questions were raised as to whether or not the young men in the camps were receiving a quality education—or one at all—Fechner visited the camps and published his evaluation of just how the CCC contributes to the education of the nation's citizens.

Significance

In 1941, as young men were drafted into the army during World War II (1939–1945), the CCC camps officially closed. In the nine years of its existence, the CCC gave about two million young men jobs, taught around eighty thousand to read and write, and allowed a thousand to earn a high school degree. Many recruits attended classes at nearby colleges and close to one hundred earned their college degrees. Although CCC classes were only offered in the evening after a long day's work, many recruits voluntarily took advantage of the opportunity for an education.

The educational emphasis at CCC camps was on basic literacy training, discipline, and moral training. Some

Members of the Civilian Conservation Corps at work on a terraced outlet channel, 1937. THE LIBRARY OF CONGRESS.

educators felt the camps were too authoritarian with values that were inappropriate for a democratic society. Fechner himself banned a pamphlet he deemed "subversive" by a University of Chicago sociology professor. Yet the CCC offered an education and useful employment to many young men who probably would have had neither at that time, and it was largely regarded as one of the New Deal's most successful programs.

Primary Source

"Educational Contribution of the Civilian Conservation Corps" [excerpt]

SYNOPSIS: In this excerpt, Fechner argues for the value of a particular kind of education in CCC camps. Having visited almost all of the camps across America and its possessions, he concludes that the CCC should emphasize vocational education and basic literacy. Its broader purpose is character development and citizenship.

When the Civilian Conservation Corps was created in the spring of 1933, its premier objectives were the furnishing of employment to idle young men and the conduct of a sound conservation program in our forests, parks, and fields. After the CCC had been in operation for a few months it was found that in addition to achieving these two primary objectives, it was improving the citizenship, the character, the health and the all-around usefulness of young men enrolled in the Corps.

During the first summer that the Corps was in operation, I spent every free moment visiting in the CCC camps. Among the questions invariably put to camp officials were, "Are the enrollees interested in education?" "What are you doing to satisfy this demand where it exists?" "What sort of an educational program would be of most value to enrollees?" In some camps I found company commanders, project superintendents, and foremen were teaching as many as ten and twelve courses. Most of the subjects taught were in the elementary and high-school levels. Education that first summer, however, was largely of a catch-as-catch-can nature. In some camps, a wide variety of educational courses was offered. In others, very little was being done. . . .

What more should we teach the young men who enter the CCC than we are offering them at the present time? Should we attempt to turn out apprentices and finished mechanics? Should we devote a part of the workday to compulsory educational training? Should education be made a primary CCC objective

A poster promoting the New Deal's Civilian Conservation Corps, a specialized educational and employment program. **THE LIBRARY OF CONGRESS.**

ranking in importance with the conduct of work programs?

For my part I feel strongly that the Civilian Conservation Corps program should remain essentially a work program. I do not favor any reduction in the forty-hour work week now in force in the CCC camps. It is my opinion that substantial reduction of the work week in favor of the placing of greater emphasis on educational matters would deprive the young men sent to the CCC camps of one of the finest educational advantages which they now obtain. I refer to the disciplinary, morale- and character-building values of labor and the inner knowledge on the part of enrollees at the end of the day that they have done an honest day's work. One of the things in which I take the greatest pride is the knowledge that through the discipline of requiring the men to do a full day's work we have made them more employable, made them appreciate their fellow citizens, and inspired them with greater confidence in themselves. The knowledge that he can do a day's work helps make a man of a callow youth. It builds up his self-respect; it makes him more democratic. Instead of permitting the growth of idleness habits, we give the enrollees a concept of a world where men must work.

They return home feeling they have paid for their keep while in the camps. This serves to make the boys self-reliant, ambitious, and determined to get ahead through their own efforts. They want to be independent, not dependent.

At the same time I desire to give the boys every educational advantage consistent with the conduct of a forty-hour-a-week work program. Greater emphasis can and will be placed in the future upon the training of enrollees in the various types of work carried on in the camps and on work projects. Vocational training will be emphasized wherever practicable results can be attained. Every effort should be made to permit qualified enrollees to study at schools and colleges where such institutions are within reasonable distance of the CCC camps. We should make certain that illiterate enrollees are taught to read and write and that students in elementary-school levels have an opportunity to improve their education. Above all we should make our education as practical as possible.

I do not think it is practicable, under present conditions, to attempt to train apprentices or to turn out finished mechanics or graduate engineers. Enrollees, on the average, do not remain in the CCC camps long enough to carry out the training work necessary to become finished mechanics. Eight months is about the average time that boys remain in camp. This important fact, as well as the circumstance that most of these boys come to us inexperienced and often with a background of idleness, must be taken into consideration in the preparation of the future CCC educational program. Our major purpose is to help each boy to find himself, to arouse his ambition and to aid him in obtaining private employment. Every available part of the CCC organization and machinery should be utilized to that end.

Further Resources

BOOKS

Cole, Olen. *The African-American Experience in the Civilian Conservation Corps.* Gainesville, Fla.: University Press of Florida, 1999.

Melzer, Richard. *Coming of Age in the Great Depression: the Civilian Conservation Corps Experience in New Mexico, 1933–1942.* Las Cruces, N. Mex.: Yucca Tree Press, 2000.

Wormser, Richard. *Growing Up in the Great Depression.* New York: Antheneum, 1994.

PERIODICALS

Dearborn, Ned H. "Educational Opportunity for Enrollee." *Phi Delta Kappan.* 19, no. 9, May 1937, 300. Available online at http://newdeal.feri.org/schools/schools11.htm; website home page: http://newdeal.feri.org (accessed April 24, 2002).

Holland, Kenneth. "Education in CCC and European Camps." *Phi Delta Kappan* 20, October 1937, 317. Available online at http://newdeal.feri.org/schools/schools08.htm; website home page: http://newdeal.feri.org (accessed April 24, 2002).

Judd, Charles H. "Educational Activities in the CCC." *Phi Delta Kappan* 19, no. 9, May 1937, 299. Available online at http://newdeal.feri.org/schools/schools10.htm; website home page: http://newdeal.feri.org (accessed April 24, 2002).

———. "Educational Program of CCC Camps." *Phi Delta Kappan* 27, no. 2, December 1934, 49. Available online at http://newdeal.feri.org/schools/schools03.htm; website home page: http://newdeal.feri.org (accessed April 24, 2002).

Oxley, Howard W. "Growth and Accomplishments of CCC Education." *Phi Delta Kappan* 19, no. 9, May 1937, 299. Available online at http://newdeal.feri.org/schools/schools02.htm; website home page: http://newdeal.feri.org (accessed April 24, 2002).

Studebaker, John W. "Possibilities for Education Through the CCC." *Phi Delta Kappan* 19, no. 9, May 1937, 297. Available online at http://newdeal.feri.org/schools/schools09.htm; website home page: http://newdeal.feri.org (accessed April 24, 2002).

WEBSITES

The Civilian Conservation Corps Museum and Research Center. Available online at http://www.cccalumni.org/museum.html (accessed April 24, 2002).

Civilian Conservation Corps Museum. Michigan Historical Museum System. Available online at http://www.sos.state.mi.us/history/museum/museccc/index.html; website home page: http://www.sos.state.mi.us (accessed April 24, 2002).

AUDIO AND VISUAL MEDIA

Camp Forgotten—the CCC in Michigan. Forgotten Films & Video, 1993. Also available at Franklin D. Roosevelt Library & Digital Archives. Available online at http://www.fdrlibrary.marist.edu (accessed April 24, 2002).

Middletown in Transition: A Study in Cultural Conflicts

Study

By: Robert S. Lynd and Helen Merrell Lynd

Date: 1937

Source: Lynd, Robert S., and Helen Merrell Lynd. *Middletown in Transition: A Study in Cultural Conflicts.* New York: Harcourt, Brace and Company, 1937, 221–223, 228.

About the Authors: Robert Staughton Lynd (1892–1970) was born in New Albany, Indiana, and raised in Louisville, Kentucky. A graduate of Princeton, Lynd worked as an editor before entering Union Theological Seminary. Helen Merrell (1899–1982) was born in La Grange, Illinois, and attended Wellesley College. She taught in girls' schools in New York, where she met Robert Lynd. They were married in 1922. Together they published *Middletown: A Study in American Culture* (1929) and *Middletown in Transition: A Study in Cultural Conflicts* (1937). Robert became a professor of sociology at Columbia University, and Helen taught at nearby Sarah Lawrence College. ■

Introduction

After Robert Lynd received his divinity degree in 1923, the Lynds served as missionaries in the oil fields of Montana, where their interests shifted from religion to sociology. In the mid-1920s Robert Lynd directed a series of "Small City" studies for the Institute of Social and Religious Research, and the Lynds were then selected to conduct a study of religious life in Muncie, Indiana.

The study was to be an objective description of life in Muncie, chosen because it was thought to represent the "average" American town at the time. The Lynds and their researchers spent eighteen months conducting interviews, compiling statistics, and distributing surveys to the city's residents. *Middletown: A Study in American Culture* (1929) offered a portrait of the everyday life of a town. Chapter topics included earning a living, making a home, training the young, leisure, religious practices, and community activities. The Lynds were more interested in a precise "scientific" analysis and description of American society than in the moralizing of social reform.

But the book showed Muncie as a community divided by class and interested in status and materialism. It angered some of the residents of Muncie (although the town was never identified in the book), who thought it did not represent them well. However, it was an instant commercial and critical success. It was used by critics to illustrate the emptiness of the American way of life, and fueled the demand for more sociological surveys.

Middletown in Transition (1937) was the sequel intended to investigate how the Great Depression had changed Muncie. But unlike the original work, it was less dispassionate and focused more clearly on the economic and social power structure of the city, criticizing the leading families of the town for their dominance. Taken together, the Middletown books were the first elaborate studies of an American community done from the perspective of the social sciences rather than social reform.

In "Training the Young," the chapter on education, the Lynds review a wide range of issues, including Muncie's newly proclaimed status as a "college town," teachers' salaries, school budgets, the "hidden" curriculum,

Median Teacher Salaries, 1930-1931

Occupation	In 204 U.S. cities of 30,000 to 100,000 population (1)	In 19 cities in Middle-town's state (2)	In Middle-town (3)	Difference U.S. cities and Middle-town (Col. 1 less 3) (4)	Difference state cities and Middle-town (Col. 2 less 3) (5)
Sr. H.S. principal	$4,281.00	$3,965.28	$3,400.00	$881.00	$565.28
Jr. H.S. principal	3,353.00	3,146.21	2,525.00	828.00	621.21
Elem. principal	2,646.00	2,441.88	2,325.00	321.00	116.88
Sr. H.S. teachers	2,111.00	2,046.99	1,762.50	348.50	284.49
Jr. H.S. teachers	1,860.00	1,763.04	1,611.11	248.89	151.93
Elem. teachers	1,609.00	1,572.55	1,500.93	108.07	71.62

Note: These figures were published by the Board of Education in *How Much Do Our Schools Cost the Taxpayer?*

SOURCE: *Middletown in Transition: A Study in Cultural Conflicts.* By Robert Lynd and Helen Lynd. New York: Harcourt, Brace and Co., 1937, 228.

the struggle between individualism and conformity, and the fact that a high school course in sociology was dropped because of parental protest over discussion of sexual problems in class. The Lynds discuss in some detail the town's new focus on "education for individual differences," instituted by graduates from the teachers college. Much like progressive educators elsewhere, these educators wanted to provide a more relevant education than the "one size fits all" academic model. They introduced a new guidance program into the high school to help the students.

The Lynds agree that the high school guidance program was a necessity. But it only concerned itself with academic guidance, leaving aside the crucial issues of social and job guidance. Furthermore, write the Lynds, by not challenging the powerful businessmen and social elites who ran the town, such as the Daughters of the American Revolution, educators could never really expect to make significant changes to the educational system that could in turn challenge the town's class divisions. The Lynds conclude that despite the potential for change brought on by the Depression, in the struggle between administrative efficiency and "education for individual differences," the former was winning the battle.

Significance

The Lynds candidly described the nature of bureaucratic organization and the structure of power in *Middletown in Transition,* providing one of the first sociological analyses of bureaucracy and power in a local community setting. Sociology had been a burgeoning academic discipline in the 1920s, and although the Lynds had no formal academic training in it, their work came to be considered classics among sociological studies of communities. As proof of their popularity, a 1950 survey of introductory textbooks in which hundreds of sociology authors were indexed showed that Lynd was in the top thirty for the number of times cited.

Although he was never trained as a sociologist, the Middletown studies brought Robert Lynd to prominence, and he became the secretary of the Social Science Research Council, had a long teaching career, and helped establish sociology as an academic discipline. Helen was active in academic reform issues.

The Middletown studies also inspired a steady progression of social scientists who went to Muncie to either prove, disprove, or modify the Lynds' conclusions, making Muncie the most studied city of its size. Interest in Middletown continues: recently the National Science Foundation funded a fiftieth anniversary follow-up study, PBS aired a six-part documentary series by Peter Davis, and a Center for Middletown Studies was established at Ball State University in Muncie.

Primary Source

Middletown in Transition: A Study in Cultural Conflicts [excerpt]

SYNOPSIS: In this excerpt, the Lynds discuss one of the efforts of professional educators from Muncie's teachers college to introduce a new and progressive curriculum into the high school. In an attempt to respond to the needs of individual students, a guidance program is established, with mixed results.

[Ed. Note: the block quote below is from the opening pages of a report on educational planning in the Middletown] public schools, issued by the Department of Educational Research in 1933.]

During the past few years of educational endeavor in [Middletown], the Board of Education and its school administrators . . . have faced the problem of selecting the educational philosophy on which to build. . . .

The philosophy on which school authorities have attempted to build in [Middletown] may be made a bit clearer by first briefly contrasting it with that of the past. Our philosophy of education in America has been largely that of the pioneer. Prior to the last century, and during much of the nineteenth century, our philosophy was very largely nationalistic and aristocratic. We now believe in the education of the masses. We have spent too much time in transplanting to America the theories, practices, and educational traditions of European education.

Educational tradition from Europe furnished us with much that is outworn and ineffective. There are still many disciples of aristocratic European traditions. From the beginning of time until recent years, world change has developed slowly. As a result, knowledge was traditionally handed down. Such a process became authoritative and the accepted basis of knowledge. Many held to such a traditional philosophy and advocated that to learn is basically acquisition and acceptance on authority.

Ours is a different philosophy. It *advocates that the aim of education should be to enable every child to become a useful citizen, to develop his individual powers to the fullest extent of which he is capable, while at the same time engaged in useful and lifelike activities. . . . We believe in the doctrine of equal educational opportunity for every child to develop according to his abilities, interests, and aptitudes.* [Italics ours.]

In planning the educational work in [Middletown] in recent years, the Board of Education and school officials have tried to operate on the above basic philosophy of American Education. . . . The plan as at first laid out was to extend over a period of about ten years. The first five-year period has passed and it is the function of this Bulletin to briefly review what has been accomplished to date . . . and to look into the immediate future.

. . . While we do not desire [in the pages which follow in this Bulletin] to point to spectacular improvements, we do believe that the comparisons made will show a distinct advance from the practices of an earlier period. . . . The elements of the educational plan along which progress in varying degrees has been made, and upon which further thought and effort must be spent, are the following:

1. The personnel organization.
2. The gradual reorganization of the [Middletown] City Schools.
3. The reorganization and rearranging of curricular offerings in terms of pupil needs.
4. The revision of the courses of study and the development of technique of course-of-study construction.
5. The use of the appraisal and city-wide testing program.
6. Guidance program for counseling boys and girls of junior and senior high-school age.
7. The upgrading of teaching personnel.
8. Child accounting and holding power of the schools.
9. Budgetary procedure and the study of school costs and trends.
10. A survey of school sites.
11. Landscape plans for the school grounds.
12. A survey of school buildings.

Here speaks not the voice of the businessmen on Middletown's school board but that of the professional school of education, whose influence in the 1920's was pervading all American education and whose spirit had taken on flesh and fresh authority in Middletown in its own successful Teachers College.

In 1930 the Central High School adopted a new curriculum "devoted to the principle that the schools should fit the needs of the individual pupil instead of forcing the child to fit himself to the standard curriculum, as has been the practice in the past." Such radical changes in subjects taught, in methods of teaching, and in habits of teachers, as a literal putting into practice of such an educational credo involves, would require, according to some Middletown teachers, more knowledge of individual needs than at present exists, and more time to discover and meet these needs than administrators imagine. But, in response to this slogan, there is apparent today in the high school a slow diminution in the traditional emphasis upon factual courses and more emphasis upon exploratory work around main problems, supposedly closer to student needs. In chemistry, for example, individual supervised laboratory work is diminishing the role of class lectures. Mathematics is increasingly "shop math." There is, also, in the high school as in the grades, more grouping of students by ability, with more freedom and rapidity of progress for the more intelligent. Some of the abler children in the high school are receiving at the hands of unusual teachers a type of free-ranging training in social studies, wider than anything apparent in 1925, that is generally recognized in Middletown as answering these children's urgent questions and at the same time extending their horizon far beyond their local concerns.

Children walk home from a Decatur, Indiana, school in 1936. THE LIBRARY OF CONGRESS.

This new emphasis upon the development of the individual student, coming at the same time as the new problems raised by the heavy increase in the high-school and college populations, has forced Middletown into a revaluation of the role of "an education." With the high school and even the college no longer serving as a screen sifting out the "scholars" from the "nonscholars" even as roughly as they did before the World War, and with secondary education become a mass experience, the feeling has grown that education must not only be good but must be good for something—to the individual and to society. Otherwise, a culture believing so firmly in things' "paying their way" and being "worth what they cost" finds it hard to justify the increased cost to the taxpayers of the delay in children's "settling down to work" and the encouragement of "children's wild ideas" which prolonged education entails. "Culture," in the literary sense, is a luxury to most of these hard-working folk whose children are now pressing into the schools, and they want something more tangible—a better job, the ability to earn more money—as at least one dependable outcome of "an education." As a partial answer to this problem, a "guidance program" has been inaugurated as a part of Middletown's new educational planning.

The chief aim of this guidance program, according to Middletown's 1933 Bulletin on *Educational Planning,* cited above, "is to assure every child the advantages of individualization, which have always been provided by the best teachers for the most fortunate children under the most favorable circumstances, and to improve these services." Theoretically a combined social-, academic-, and vocational-guidance service, this work continues the old educational tradition by being strongest on the academic side. Every child, from grade 7 on, is seen by a counselor for ten minutes once each semester, with perhaps a quarter of the total being seen again during the year, there being one counselor for every eighty children in the junior high school and one for every 150 in the senior high school. A cumulative record for each student helps to give continuity to the process. The difficulties involved in incorporating into actual educational practices the aims of individual education set forth in the bulletin quoted from above are augmented by the fact that only ten minutes a semester are allowed for understanding and advising each child.

On the vocational side, the guidance work is as yet rudimentary, reflecting the general immaturity of the entire field of discovering vocational aptitudes.

Middletown does little more at present, according to one of the high-school counselors, than to urge its girls to develop a "second-string" skill in home economics or nursing and its boys who are "good in mathematics" to "go in for engineering," to discourage flagrant misfits, and generally to urge everybody of normal intelligence to "go on to college." The guidance of students in their social problems, the head of the guidance service reports, "while decidedly secondary in emphasis, is demanding more and more attention."

Middletown's attitude toward the guidance program is uneven. Some parents regard it as just another educational frill costing the taxpayers money; and some teachers criticize it as "not getting anywhere," since it must inevitably use counselors not adequately equipped to diagnose and prescribe for individual needs. Meanwhile, the need of Middletown's youth for guidance was probably never so great.

Further Resources

BOOKS

Caccamo de Luca, Rita. *Back to Middletown: Three Generations of Sociological Reflections.* Stanford, Calif.: Stanford University Press, 2000.

Krug, Edward A. *The Shaping of the American High School 1920–1941,* Volume 2. Madison, Wis.: University of Wisconsin, 1972.

Lynd, Robert S., and Helen Merrell Lynd. *Middletown: A Study in American Culture.* 1929. Reprint, New York: Harvest Books, 1956.

PERIODICALS

"Robert S. Lynd, Co-Author of 'Middletown,' Dies." *The New York Times,* November 3, 1970, 38.

WEBSITES

Center for Middletown Studies: Ball State University. Available online at http://www.bsu.edu/middletown/about.html; website home page: http://www.bsu.edu (accessed August 12, 2002).

"Middletown: A Study in Modern American Culture. Robert and Helen Lynd Measure Muncie, Indiana." Interviews from *The First Measured Century,* program segments 1900–1930. Available online at http://www.pbs.org/fmc/interviews/1seg4.htm; website home page: http://www.pbs.org (accessed April 25, 2002).

AUDIO AND VISUAL MEDIA

Middletown. New York: First Run/Icarus Films, 1982. Available online at http://www.frif.com/cat97/k-o/middleto.html; website home page: http://www.frif.com (accessed August 12, 2002).

Alfred Kinsey's Marriage Course

"Marriage"

Syllabus

By: Alfred C. Kinsey

Date: June 1938

Source: Kinsey, Alfred C. "Marriage." Syllabus for the course at Indiana University. June 1938. Archives for the Kinsey Institute for Research in Sex, Gender and Reproduction. Bloomington, Indiana.

"First Lecture of Marriage Course"

Lecture notes

By: Alfred C. Kinsey

Date: June 1939

Source: Kinsey, Alfred C. "First Lecture of Marriage Course." Indiana University. June 1939. Archives for the Kinsey Institute for Research in Sex, Gender and Reproduction. Bloomington, Indiana.

About the Author: Alfred Charles Kinsey (1894–1956) was born in Hoboken, New Jersey, and attended Bowdoin College in Maine, where he earned his degree in biology and psychology. He received a graduate degree in applied biology from Harvard, and he arrived at Indiana University in 1920 as an assistant professor of zoology. There, he established his academic reputation for work in taxonomy and evolution, and particularly for his studies of gall wasps. When he took over the university's new marriage course in 1938, Kinsey began gathering case histories of sexual behavior, which led to his research in sexuality. He published *Sexual Behavior in the Human Male* (1948), popularly known as "The Kinsey Report," and *Sexual Behavior in the Human Female* (1953). Kinsey founded the Kinsey Institute for Research in Sex, Gender and Reproduction in Bloomington, Indiana, in 1942 and directed it until his death in 1956. ■

Introduction

John Dewey's version of progressive education emphasized the scientific method of experimentation and verification with data, and also the significance of testing, measuring, and surveys. Until Kinsey's research, the scientific study of human sexuality did not exist in American higher education. Yet Kinsey did not begin his career with this kind of research in mind. He arrived at Indiana University as a zoologist specializing in taxonomy, the classification of species. He was also a naturalist who loved the outdoors and hiking with his wife.

His career was distinguished and without controversy until 1938, when Indiana University started its marriage course, considered a radical move for a university at that time. Kinsey became the chairman of a committee of seven faculty members who would decide what was to be taught and how to teach it. He began collecting individual case histories as part of a student questionnaire about the course and recognized the need for an objective study of human sexuality. He soon switched from questionnaires to face-to-face interviews to collect data, and by 1939, he was making weekend trips to Chicago to expand the size and diversity of his research population.

Kinsey interviewed his own friends about their sexual experiences and worked out statistical methods to calculate his findings. Indiana University, under the leadership of President Herman B. Wells, endorsed his research. After funding his early work himself, Kinsey received a grant from the National Research Council in 1940 and then annual funding from the Rockefeller Foundation.

Significance

Kinsey's research resulted in statistical analyses based on nearly 18,000 interviews with men and women, mostly white and middle class, though the group did include prisoners and African Americans. Kinsey found that petting and masturbation were very common and that premarital intercourse, extramarital sex, and homosexual experiences were more frequent than many Americans had believed. The results were controversial and aroused condemnation of his work. He was decried as a "menace to society," but the Kinsey Report sold almost 250,000 copies, and Kinsey's research challenged society's assumptions about what constitutes "normal" sexual behavior.

Kinsey's course was significant in laying the foundation for the scientific study of human sexuality. Indiana University's women students first requested the course and received the trustees' approval. As Kinsey's syllabus shows, the coeducational course was entitled "Marriage," but it was really a broad survey of the institution from economic, legal, reproductive, and psychological perspectives. Sexuality was only a part of the syllabus, but because sex was rarely discussed in classrooms, it was the most provocative part.

In a student newspaper article, "Cupid's Course" was described as extremely popular with its students, who also included townspeople and faculty. Most students said biology was the subject that interested them most, with economics a distant second. The course was described as a "noble experiment," and for the times, not only was it innovative in its subject matter, but also in its method of interdisciplinary team teaching. Eager to bring scholarly rigor to his subject, Kinsey carefully chose his lecturers from sociology, the law school, economics, biology, and history. He even brought in local physicians to discuss pregnancy and childbirth. Today the Kinsey Institute offers a wide array of undergraduate and graduate courses, including a Ph.D. in human sexuality.

Dr. Alfred C. Kinsey began his groundbreaking research into human sexuality during the 1930s. **THE LIBRARY OF CONGRESS.**

Primary Source

"First Lecture of Marriage Course" [excerpt]

SYNOPSIS: This excerpt from the lecture notes for Kinsey's first class session of his second year teaching the course reveals his practical as well as theoretical interest: he argues that a clear understanding of sexuality should help couples avoid marital problems. Kinsey approached the subject of marriage as an institution capable of being studied from a variety of perspectives, as can be seen in example of one of his course outlines, also provided.

A year ago last spring, a group of students on the campus became interested in the possibility of organizing such a program. Ultimately there were representatives of several organizations who requested the trustees to allow the organization of such a program. On the first of June, a year ago, the trustees authorized the course, and the program was pre-

MARRIAGE

BIOLOGIC BASES OF SOCIETY — KINSEY
Rarity and distribution of society; insect society based on nutritional castration; bases of human society in anthropoid backgrounds; cultural interferences with these bases.

THE FAMILY AS A SOCIAL INSTITUTION — MÜLLER

ECONOMIC BACKGROUND OF MARRIAGE — MOFFAT
The family as an economic unit; economic responsibility and marriage.

INCOME AND EXPENDITURE — MOFFAT
The family budget; costs of education; economics of health and medical care; recreation and travel.

LEGAL THEORY OF MARRIAGE — HARPER
Status of contract; competency; valid, void, voidable marriages; miscegenous, incestuous and bigamous marriages; extra-state marriages.

REPRODUCTIVE ANATOMY AND PHYSIOLOGY — KINSEY
Biologic significance of sexual reproduction; primary and secondary differentiation of sexes; embryologic homologies; functions of gonads and germ cells; genitalic structures and reflex behavior.

ENDOCRINE CHAIN IN HUMAN REPRODUCTION — KROC
Pituitary regulation of ovary; physiology of menstrual cycle; time of ovulation; ovarian structures and hormones; menopause; male hormone; temperature regulation; similarity in male and female hormones; occurrence in both sexes.

INDIVIDUAL VARIATION — KINSEY
Biologic signifcance of variation; normal and abnormal; variation in reproductive structure and physiology; consequent modifications in function.

PSYCHOLOGY — CONKLIN

PREGNANCY + AND BIRTH. Venereal Diseases. — SCHUMANN

STERILITY — KROC
Gradations and combinations of many factors; in both male and female; anatomic factors; endocrine imbalance; methods of diagnoses and therapy; age as most important single factor.

~~VENEREAL DISEASES~~ — ~~SCHUMANN~~

LEGAL ASPECTS — HARPER
Reciprocal rights and duties of husband and wife; contract and property relations; care and custody of children; legitimacy; protection of husband-wife and parent-child relation from interference by third persons, including alienation, seduction, criminal conversation;
Divorce: grounds, alimony; custody of children; ~~etc~~

Ethics — Kohlmeier

Primary Source

"Marriage"

SYNOPSIS: Alfred Kinsey's course syllabus shows how he divided the subject of marriage into an institution that could be studied from many disciplinary angles. KINSEY, ALFRED C. ARCHIVES FOR THE KINSEY INSTITUTE FOR RESEARCH IN SEX, GENDER AND REPRODUCTION, BLOOMINGTON, INDIANA.

Cupid's Course at I. U. Gains 30 Students in 2d Semester

12 of Last Term's Class Married During Year; Biology Most Popular Topic.

By PAUL BOXELL
Times Bloomington Correspondent

BLOOMINGTON, Feb. 9.—The marriage course launched at Indiana University this year has grown rapidly in popularity and will have an enrollment of 230 this semester as compared with 200 last semester, Dr. Alfred C. Kinsey, course chairman, said today.

The course is open to "all seniors and graduate students, other students 21 or older, students who are married or contemplate early marriage and others who have special and immediate desire for the course." The class meets twice weekly for lectures and discussions.

Last semester's class was made up of 108 men and 98 women. Twelve members of this group became married during the semester, Dr. Kinsey said. However, some of them were contemplating marriage before enrolling, he added.

* * *

THIRTY-TWO already were married and 39 engaged when they enrolled. Five were faculty members, 16 were townspeople and the rest were University students, including four freshmen.

In answering a questionnaire at the end of the semester, 102 said biology was the subject which interested them most; 37 named economics, 12 ethics, 28 law and nine sociology.

Fifty-six favoring giving more time to biology discussion; three, including a clergyman and his wife, favored decreasing biological material.

All favored continuing the course on a noncredit basis, giving as reasons: It should attract only serious students and discourage snap course hunters. It should avoid complications of credits, grades and departmental administration.

All except two upheld the mixed class and favored its continuance. Two unmarried faculty members recommended segregation of men and women.

Fifty-five thought small group discussions would improve the value of the course. Thirty-two were opposed to additional group discussions.

* * *

MOST students favored individual conferences with the staff. Seventy-eight personal-conferences were held last semester, and Dr. Kinsey predicted that many more will be requested this semester.

Thirty members of the class recommended that the course be thrown open to all University students, including freshmen.

Wrote one member: "These lectures probably are of more benefit to students than any other one course in the University. They should be continued on an enlarged scale. The problems in this course should be discussed freely without fear of University or outside interference."

Another labeled the course "a noble experiment."

Lectures this semester, will be given by faculty members of the economics, ethics and sociolgy departments, the School of Medicine and the School of Law.

Dr. Kinsey's course was unconventional and popular enough to attract media attention. *THE INDIANA TIMES*, FEBRUARY 9, 1939, 26.

sented for the first time in a series of twelve lectures last summer. The program was presented with some modifications and expansions during the fall and spring, and during the first three presentations, some 530 students were enrolled. Last summer there were 100 enrolled in the course; there are about 170 of you tonight.

This series of lectures is given by a group of men from several of the departments which are concerned with the various aspects of the problem of marriage. . . .

To the biologist, the phenomena of society is peculiar primarily because of its rarity in the animal kingdom. Out of two million different kinds of animals in the world, it is a fraction of 1 per cent of these species which is in a true sense social. By "social" the biologist refers to a group of individuals who live together, sharing a common food supply, using a common shelter which covers individuals of all ages and both sexes, and between whom there is a division of labor. The ants, the social wasps, bumble bees, honey bees, termites and the anthropoid apes, including man, are the only animals which live under conditions which fit that definition. The cattle of the field are not social; to a degree they may share a common food supply and shelter, but there is nothing like a division of labor which characterizes the truly social. The birds that fly in flocks and the fish that gather in the stream are not, strictly speaking, social. The number of social animals in the world is so small that if we were anything but social animals, we would be astonished.

The second peculiarity of society, at least from a biological standpoint, is its distribution in the animal kingdom. Termites are at one end of the insect world, ants, bees and wasps are at the other end and in no sense related to the termites. They are as remote, evolutionarily, as anything could be—in other words, society has originated at least three times and perhaps oftener in the animal kingdom. In order to analyze the basis of our own human society, I shall ask your indulgence for a moment while I analyze the basis of insect society; for it will introduce you to a biologic, materialistic analysis of a situation which you might never have faced objectively as far as it concerns the human. . . .

The culture which we have received is responsible for the prudish ideas which have done so much more than any other single factor to undermine the home. Studies indicate that some 34% of the whole married population is in trouble sexually at some time. The same studies indicate that 68% of the religiously devout and the highly educated have marital maladjustments. It is the development of ideas as to what is proper and what is not—what is fine and what is not—which interferes with the consummation of the biological relationship in marriage. Specifically, sexual difficulties in marriage originate through ignorance of sexual anatomy and physiology. In an uninhibited society, a twelve-year-old would know most of the biology which I will have to give you in formal lectures as seniors and graduate students. It is to make amends for the interference our social organization has imposed that a course like the marriage course is necessary. Sexual maladjustment in marriage originates also because of the ignorance in this day and generation of adequate contraceptives; and above everything else, originates because of prudish ideas of both men and women.

The biological material which we give you in this course will be designed to equip you to meet specific biological difficulties. It is the function of the marriage course to bring to you in a scholarly fashion, specific materials which you may utilize in the solution of your own problem. In any situation which has as many diverse aspects as marriage, it is inevitable that the solution of any problem will be different for each individual. I cannot—no one can tell you the answer to your own particular question. You will ask me many questions which I cannot answer for you; you would like to have my advice as to your own particular behavior—on your own particular problem. But I can tell you all the biology you need to know to solve that particular problem; Professor Harper will tell you the legal side; Professor Moffat can tell you what an economist knows about your particular problem; and at the end of the semester, we hope you will have enough material to put together for the solution of your own problem.

If any of you have legal, economic, or ethical questions and come to me, I can do nothing about them; that is not my function. I, individually, make no judgment ethically, socially, economically; it is the function of the other men who are contributing to the course to pass judgment in their own fields. I can be of more use to you in the individual conferences from the standpoint of the biologist.

We will take a few minutes for questions.

Further Resources

BOOKS

Christenson, Cornelia V. *Kinsey, a Biography.* Bloomington, Ind.: Indiana University Press, 1971.

Gathorne-Hardy, Jonathan. *Sex, The Measure of All Things: A Life of Alfred C. Kinsey.* Bloomington, Ind.: Indiana University Press, 2000.

Jones, James H. *Alfred C. Kinsey: A Public/Private Life.* New York: W.W. Norton, 1997.

Pomeroy, Wardell Baxter. *Dr. Kinsey and the Institute for Sex Research.* New York: Harper & Row, 1972.

PERIODICALS

Moke, Susan. "Learning from the Past—Looking to the Future." Originally published in *Research & Creative Activity* 20, no. 2 (September 1997). Available online at http://www.indiana.edu/%7Ercapub/v20n2/p6.html (accessed September 10, 2002).

WEBSITES

The Kinsey Institute for Research in Sex, Gender and Reproduction. Available online at http://www.kinseyinstitute.org (accessed September 10, 2002).

AUDIO AND VISUAL MEDIA

Reputations: Alfred Kinsey. Produced and directed by Clare Beavan. London: BBC, 1996.

Sex and the Scientist. Produced by Diane Ward. 90 minutes. Bloomington, Ind.: WTIU, 1989.

"Radio in a Modern School Program"

Radio address

By: Gertrude Metze

Date: March 20, 1939

Source: Metze, Gertrude. "Radio in a Modern School Program." Oshkosh State Teachers College radio program transcript. March 20, 1939. University of Wisconsin, Oshkosh Archives and Area Research Center. Oshkosh, Wisconsin. Audio available online at http://www.uwosh.edu/archives/radio/modern.htm; website home page: http://www.uwosh.edu (accessed March 6, 2003).

About the Author: Gertrude Metze (1909–1987) was born in Oshkosh, Wisconsin. She attended the Normal School's (teachers college) practice school and Oshkosh High School before getting her state teacher's college degree in 1931. For a time, Metze was an instructor at Oshkosh State Teacher's College, teaching second grade in the practice school. By 1941 Metze had moved to Illinois where she continued her teaching career. ■

Introduction

In the 1930s, technology was only beginning to make an impact on education. In the days before the "wired" classroom, wireless communication through radio was the most significant technology for education. Radio was already popular for listening to music, but it was first introduced to schools in Haaren High School, New York City, in 1923. At that time it was used for lessons in penmanship, accounting, math, and history.

In 1929, the first "School of the Air" began at Ohio State University. Children could listen to lessons in specially equipped classrooms, and radio in schools became more popular. That same year NBC introduced a Friday *Music Appreciation Hour* for schoolchildren, a series produced by the League of Women Voters, and the daily *National Farm and Home Hour,* produced by the Department of Agriculture.

On February 3, 1930, some 1.5 million schoolchildren listened to CBS's first *American School of the Air.* These daily half-hour lessons were created with the help

Students listen to school lessons on the radio, 1937. © BETTMANN/CORBIS. REPRODUCED BY PERMISSION.

of an advisory panel of prominent academics. By 1939 the CBS programs were heard across the country in more than 100,000 classrooms by about three million children a day.

Despite early efforts in the 1920s and continuing in the 1930s to organize colleges and schools into a coalition for independent educational radio, it was the commercial networks that won the struggle to enter the classrooms through the airwaves. They were able to outspend the educational institutions and to persuade the new Federal Communications Commission (FCC) in 1935 that independent noncommercial educational broadcasting was not necessary. Instead, the networks would cooperate with educational stations by providing them with programs like the *American School of the Air.*

Although Wisconsin was a leader in educational radio broadcasting with its station WHA, a voice of progressivism against the commercialism of the networks, it nevertheless experienced problems in producing its own programs and adequately exploiting the technology.

The future of radio in education was hotly debated during the 1930s. The National Committee on Education for Radio was established to promote radio for the public interest and education, while the National Advisory Council on Radio in Education represented the networks. The latter group was able to play on fears that the airwaves would be nationalized, like the British Broadcasting Corporation (BBC), while the former group attacked its opponents as monopolists. In the end, public radio would wait many years to be organized on a national level, and it would continue to suffer from lack of funding compared to commercial stations.

Significance

Today almost all educators are aware of technology's promise as well as its limitations. Computers in every classroom promise to help students learn better, while the Internet offers access to information at speeds that were unimaginable only a generation ago. Instructional Systems Technology is regularly offered at schools of education. Distance education—where a student never actually meets her teacher (or classmates) in person, but instead participates in a class that is conducted over the Internet—has its advocates and its detractors, but most professional educators in higher education see it as an inevitable part of the future.

But technology is a tool, and its use often brings its own problems. Metze's talk is an early exploration of the pros and cons of using the technology of her day. Metze writes that if a radio lesson is not introduced properly and given a context, it can easily be lost on students. It can enhance what is being taught but can seldom substitute for actual classroom teaching. A teacher must have the judgment to know when and how to use the tool of technology. Her argument and the debate over technology in the classroom is just as relevant today as it was when she gave her original broadcast.

Primary Source

"Radio In a Modern School Program" [excerpt]

SYNOPSIS: In this talk, Metze suggests the various ways in which technology can be used to enhance classroom education rather than detract from it. She also gives examples of how radio can provide even young children with a wider knowledge of politics and current events, enabling the education for citizenship stressed by Eleanor Roosevelt.

Not all radio lessons are used in the same way—let me tell you what I mean. Some lessons are used to introduce a new subject—"The Upside Down Man" was used in this way.

Other lessons are used to supplement material that has been studied. For example, the third grade children have been studying the chipmunk. They have done a lot of reading and had some class discussion. On March 15th they heard the story, "Time to Get Up Chippie." This lesson probably was used to supplement their previous lessons. However, it may have been used as a sort of summary or perhaps to clarify ideas over which the third graders had argued.

Frequently, the programs are used just for enjoyment and appreciation. Once a month, on the Peggy and Paul series, the Story Book Players dramatize a story. In addition to the mere pleasure of hearing the story, the boys and girls unconsciously get a great deal out of this. They begin to notice voice inflection and interpretation. They are aware that some voices are loud, some soft, some are clear, some are gruff, some pleasant, some unpleasant, depending on the characters in the story.

Besides the programs broadcast over station WHA, Monday through Friday, at 9:30, both NBC and CBS have some broadcasts for children in the lower grades. However, most of the NBC programs are for children above the third grade. There is one, though, at 2 o'clock, eastern standard time, on Tuesday called "Science Everywhere," which devotes the first 15 minutes to primary grades.

CBS programs are scheduled after school hours but, of course, the children could be encouraged to "listen in" at home.

While you are listening to your favorite news broadcast, musical program, continued story or whatever it may be, the children in your family are getting snatches of things to take to school,—all kinds of new ideas.

Some of this information is quite surprising. Not so long ago a youngster said, "Did you hear the President?" When I asked him what he meant, he said, "Why, Mr. Roosevelt, of course—and I always listen to what he says." I think he was disgusted with me because I hadn't kept up with him, for he was most patronizing. Although the child was only 7, he knew what was going on.

During a language lesson we were talking about interesting words. Someone mentioned "impersonate." He said, "I hear a story, and one man impersonates the Lone Ranger." Other words mentioned were *theme song, network, sub-zero, microphone, short wave*—all words heard over the radio.

Still another child in 2nd grade said, "Do you know what Guam is?" He then proceeded to tell what he knew about it, saying that he had heard about it in a news broadcast. He thought it had something to do with the fleet, and the United States and Japan.

The boys and girls in the modern school have added another source of information to their list. They used to say "Mother or Dad told me—I read it in a book—I saw it in the paper—I saw it in a show"—and to these they have added "I heard it on the Radio."

It is no task to interest boys and girls in radio or radio programs—they thoroughly enjoy these new lessons. They know that they must have time enough to get to the radio and get settled and they keep track of the time so that they will hear everything there is to be heard. It is interesting to watch their faces when they hear a familiar theme song. Some children clap, some sing, some keep time to the music, some whistle the melody. They are entirely unself-conscious and respond in different ways. It is really fun to see what happens. When the story teller asks them to raise their hands—up go the hands. They enter into the spirit of the thing without any hesitation.

If you should happen to visit our school at 9:30 in the morning and you cannot find your child—look in the radio room. He probably has found a good spot and is stretched out on his stomach listening to some kind of a story and having a fine time.

Further Resources

BOOKS

Hill, Frank Ernest. *Listen and Learn: Fifteen Years of Adult Education on the Air.* New York: American Association for Adult Education, 1937.

———. *Tune in for Education: Eleven Years of Education by Radio.* New York: National Committee on Education by Radio, 1942.

McChesney, Robert W. *Telecommunications, Mass Media and Democracy: The Battle for the Control of U.S. Broadcasting, 1928–35.* Oxford: Oxford University Press, 1993.

PERIODICALS

Leach, Eugene E. "Tuning Out Education: The Cooperation Doctrine in Radio, 1922–38." *Current,* January, February, and March 1983. Republished on the Internet, Dec. 13, 1999. Available online at http://www.current.org/coop (accessed April 26, 2002).

WEBSITES

School: The Story of American Public Education. "Evolving Classroom." Available online at http://www.pbs.org/kcet/publicschool/evolving_classroom/technology.html. (accessed April 18, 2003).

News about Public Broadcasting. Available online at http://www.current.org. (accessed April 26, 2002).

AUDIO AND VISUAL MEDIA

"As American as Public School: 1900–1950." *School: The Story of American Public Education.* Princeton, N.J.: Films for the Humanities and Sciences, 2001.

Stephan, Charlie, and Michael, three of Abbie Morgan Madenwald's students in Alaska, standing in front of their school. UNIVERSITY OF OKLAHOMA PRESS, 1992, NORMAN, PUBLISHING DIVISION OF THE UNIVERSITY. COPYRIGHT © 1992 BY MARY MADENWALD MCKEOWN. REPRODUCED BY PERMISSION.

Arctic Schoolteacher: Kulukak, Alaska, 1931–1933

Memoir

By: Abbie Morgan Madenwald

Date: 1992

Source: Madenwald, Abbie Morgan. *Arctic Schoolteacher: Kulukak, Alaska, 1931–33.* Norman, Okla., and London: University of Oklahoma Press, 1992.

About the Author: Abbie Morgan Madenwald (1908–1991) received most of her education at Washington State College. She was a lifelong teacher who began her career in a one-room schoolhouse. In 1931 she and her husband, Ed, accepted a contract to teach the Yup'ik Alaska Natives in a remote region of the Alaska territories. After the death of her husband, she returned home to Washington State to continue teaching, did graduate work at Columbia, and married Orville Madenwald. She never returned to Kulukak, but remained in contact with several of the Yup'ik while she worked for many years on the manuscript that would become *Arctic Schoolteacher.* She died in 1991, just as her book was to be published. ■

Introduction

For many decades women had ventured to unknown territories to teach. The image of the frontier "schoolmarm" was prevalent in American culture. But stereotypes about these teachers existed: they were spinsters who could not find a husband, or young women waiting until they were married to quit teaching. Many communities actually had laws about the personal behavior of women teachers, prohibiting them from marrying or from smoking in public. The teacher was expected to teach by example and to represent the standards of civilization in the midst of wilderness, but this meant her life could be open to the scrutiny of the community. On the other hand, on the frontier, there could often be more room for freedom. There was a greater chance for adventure for a woman teacher willing to take the risk, but also a greater chance of danger and disappointment. *Arctic Schoolteacher* is based on Madenwald's extensive diaries, which she later expanded into a book. She illustrated the book with the photographs Ed shot and developed in their kitchen sink.

Significance

In 1931 Alaska was still a part of the American frontier and not yet a state. Abbie and her husband, Ed, were living in eastern Washington State, where they struggled to make a living. In the midst of the Great Depression, the couple accepted a contract with the U.S. government to educate and offer medical care to the Alaska Natives in southwest Alaska. The region was also home to a herd of reindeer, and Abbie was to teach both children and adults, while Ed gave medical care and monitored the nearby herd.

The remote area had had trouble keeping schoolteachers because of the nomadic life of the Yup'ik Indians; the children moved with their families as they fished for herring. Most of the Yup'ik had never seen a white woman before. Abbie, unlike many of her colleagues, quickly adjusted to the new life, learning the language and customs of the Yup'ik. But sadly, Abbie's husband, Ed, froze to death on a trip crossing the River of Tears to transport supplies for the villagers, and Abbie returned alone to Washington State in 1933. The school was closed in 1936. Abbie's daughter, Mary, also a teacher, wrote the preface when the book was finally published in 1992, describing her parents as "the Peace Corps of their time."

Primary Source

Arctic Schoolteacher: Kulukak, Alaska, 1931–1933 [excerpt]

SYNOPSIS: In this excerpt from *Arctic Schoolteacher,* Abbie Madenwald—"Schoolarista," as the villagers called her—describes her attempts to communicate during her first days as a teacher in Kulukak.

The first morning the school bell rang, youngsters—twenty-three of them—popped over the top of the knoll before the ringing stopped. They removed their parkas and hung them in the hall, and the heavy odor of grass smoke and fish filled the room. Quietly, with covert glances at one another, they found seats to their size and liking.

The boys wore plaid gingham shirts and blue jeans. The girls wore several dresses each, with those beneath showing at hems and sleeves. The patterns of the dresses matched those of the boys' shirts. Evidently, when the men shopped after the fishing or trapping season, they bought entire bolts of plaid gingham. I learned later that the girls wore several dresses because they lacked underclothing. I also learned that inside the fur boots, feet and ankles were wrapped in rags or strips of burlap from coal sacks.

The children ranged in age (I guessed because the information wasn't in the records) from five to sixteen. To my delight, there were eight teenage girls with whom I would especially enjoy working. And there was a little boy, five years old, who didn't take his eyes from me and was brave enough to smile every time I looked his way. He was George Krause, Peter's son.

Abbie Morgan Madenwald and her first husband, Ed. This photo was taken in 1930, shortly before they left on Abbie's assignment as a schoolteacher for Native Alaskans.

Those first days in the classroom were frustrating and, at times, disheartening. At the end of the week I still wondered if the children could speak any English. Their expressionless faces remained as blank as clean paper when I spoke to them or asked a question. If there was any response at all, it was "*naamikika* [I don't know]."

Gradually, I discovered that when I asked, "Will someone close the door?" several children flew from their seats to the entryway. Later, when I asked who would like to do other tasks at the end of the day—take down the flag and carefully fold it and place it in the cupboard, or clean the blackboards and erasers, or fill the coal hods—hands waved wildly.

If I could just get a child to talk to Ed or me, and feel at ease doing so, I would be very happy. At night, I lay awake thinking of ways to break down that barrier of shyness. The children were more timid than any I had ever tried to teach.

Above all, never would I correct their grammar. When Nattia hesitantly whispered to me, "Please, I want headache," I gave her an aspirin tablet and several pieces of candy. Then, a few days later, with the aid of chalk and blackboard and a little printing set, I taught the children to say, "I have a headache," "I have a stomachache," "I am sick."

Whenever a child spoke to me, I gave my full attention, because having to repeat the message made him or her become silent and shy. My delight was unbounded one afternoon soon after school started, when I walked through the village and George caught up and walked along with me. Because I wanted him to be at ease, I only smiled and said, "Hello." He was silent, and then, mustering his courage, asked, "How you was?"

It was weeks before some of the children ever spoke a word to me other than *naamikika.* Ed said that their reserve would melt as they got to know us, and he suggested having parties for them in the schoolroom.

At first they sat and watched as Ed and I struggled to entertain them at the parties. We played the half-dozen scratchy records we had, and I did my best pumping the wheezy organ. Gradually, we got them into the games. We had taffy pulls in the kitchen, went on hikes, and played games in which they had to speak English. Children who thanked me with "*quyana*" won only a smile from me, while those who said "thank you" were praised. And they were anxious to earn the *schoolarista*'s favor.

The reading textbooks were inadequate, so with the little printing set and tagboard we made our own stories.

Stephan killed a seal.
It was a big spotted seal.
Stephan's mother skinned it.
She will make fur boots for Stephan.

Wassilia trapped a red fox.
He will take it to the trading post.

Chunook has a new parka.
Her mother and Anecia made it for her.

The reindeer herd is near the village.
We like to eat reindeer meat.

Stephan illustrated his story by drawing a seal and his new fur boots. Chunook made a picture of her parka, and Michael sketched beautiful reindeer. Around the room I fastened labels to objects, such as chair, desk, clock, door, window.

Then one day, as I noticed a stack of little notebooks in the cupboard, I thought of diaries. This was the best idea of all because the children became keenly interested in them. And I liked them, too, for as time went on, the children's statements gave me insights into their lives and interests outside the classroom. Sometimes they wrote about things they found difficult or were hesitant to say. One might write, "On my leg is bad hurt," and that would bring to light a tender, throbbing boil. Or perhaps "I am little bit stomachache." Many of the statements were precious bits of newly acquired English. Ocalena, desiring to say that baby Willie was always cheerful, wrote, "Willie, he is happying all the time."

Further Resources

BOOKS

Breece, Hannah. *A Schoolteacher in Old Alaska: The Story of Hannah Breece.* New York: Random House, 1995.

Holmes, Madelyn. *Lives of Women Public Schoolteachers: Scenes from American Educational History.* New York: Garland Pub., 1995.

Jacobsen, Steven A. *Central Yup'ik and the Schools: A Handbook for Teachers.* Juneau: Alaska Department of Education, Bilingual/Bicultural Program, 1984. Available online at http://www.alaskool.org/language/central_yupik/yupik.html#top (accessed April 15, 2002).

WEBSITES

"Map of Alaska Native Languages." Available online at http://www.alaskool.org/language/languageindex.htm (accessed April 15, 2002).

4

FASHION AND DESIGN

LISA R. LAWSON

Entries are arranged in chronological order by date of primary source. For entries with one primary source, the entry title is the same as the primary source title. Entries with more than one primary source have an overall entry title, followed by the titles of the primary sources.

CHRONOLOGY

PRIMARY SOURCES

Important Events in Fashion and Design, 1930–1939

1930

- In women's fashion, the chemise, popular in the 1920s, is now belted and lengthened. Cut on the bias, dresses hug and move with the body.
- Architect Raymond Hood completes the Daily News Building in New York City. With its lively cubist pattern of red and black bricks, it is one of the foremost examples of art deco architecture.
- Developer Hugh Prather plans and builds Highland Park Shopping Village in Dallas, Texas, the first unified commercial development where stores surround a parking lot rather than facing the street.
- In response to the stock-market crash, independent automakers Willy-Overland and Hudson produce one-third fewer cars than in 1929.
- Auto factories cut wages, shorten the workweek, institute periodic shutdowns, and fire thousands in an effort to cut costs.
- Ford's forty-horsepower Model A is hugely popular, and 1.15 million cars are sold.
- Reflecting a new interest in simple, ordinary fabrics, French designers Jean Patou and Gabrielle Chanel show elegant evening clothes made of cotton and cotton variants such as organdy.

1931

- The Chrysler Building opens in New York City. Designed by William Van Alen, it is a testimony to art deco with its crown of zigzag triangular windows. For a few months, it is the tallest building in the world.
- Architect Raymond Hood completes the 60-story McGraw-Hill Building in New York City.
- The world's longest suspension span, the George Washington Bridge, is completed across the Hudson River, connecting New York and New Jersey.
- The American West continues to be the fastest growing automobile market in the United States, with Los Angeles topping the list of cities with the highest number of cars each business day.
- On March 3, as the international depression deepens, the fashion world reels. *The New York Times* reports that French dress imports have dropped more than 40 percent since 1926.
- On April 30, although not as stylish as the Chrysler Building, the Empire State Building in New York City opens to the public as the tallest building in the world.

1932

- Hailed as the most advanced skyscraper of its time, the Philadelphia Savings Fund Society Building, designed by architects George Howe and William Lescaze, is completed.
- Eliel Saarinen is appointed president of the Cranbrook Academy of Art in Bloomfield Hills, Michigan.
- The Museum of Modern Art's International Exhibition of Modern Architecture, assembled by Henry-Russell Hitchcock and Philip Johnson, introduces modern architecture to America. Hitchcock and Johnson publish a monograph from the show, *The International Style,* the same year.
- Construction begins on Rockefeller Center, a proposed complex of modern high-rises in New York City.
- Congress appropriates more than thirteen million dollars to improve automobile access to the national parks, specifically targeting access roads and roads within the parks in an effort to stimulate tourism.
- To cut costs and boost efficiency, General Motors drops the Viking and the Marquette, companion cars to the Oldsmobile and Buick.
- Despite the popularity of the new Plymouth, the Chrysler Corporation's profits drop eleven million dollars from the previous year.
- The Ford Motor Company has its worst year on record, with production falling from a 1929 peak of 1.5 million cars to a low of 232,000. The company cuts its workforce from 170,502 in 1929 to 46,282 as the Depression worsens.
- Frank Lloyd Wright founds the Taliesin Fellowship for architecture students to live and work with him.
- First Lady Eleanor Roosevelt wears a Sally Milgron original to President Franklin D. Roosevelt's inaugural ball.
- In spring, Lord and Taylor begins window displays that identify American designers by name as a way to promote homegrown talent.
- On March 31, Ford introduces the V-8 convertible, notable for its powerful new engine.
- In August, as more and more roadside eateries, gas stations, and campgrounds spring up to meet the needs of American travelers, *Ladies' Home Journal* proposes an architectural contest to improve what it calls the "hideous American roadside spectacle."
- In October, General Motors sells a total of 5,810 cars for the fiscal year, a figure that all its dealers combined reached each week in 1929.

1933

- The Century of Progress Exposition, celebrating technology and modernity, opens at the Chicago World's Fair.
- Palm Beach and Miami Beach in Florida become boomtowns, as most Americans no longer travel abroad. Resort wear becomes fashionable, as do suntans.

- The term *supermarket* is introduced by Albers Super Markets of Cincinnati, Ohio, marking the long decline of mom-and-pop speciality stores and the rise of discount shopping.
- The federal government imposes a new gasoline tax to finance its road-construction projects across the country. Gas-station attendants claim it is the most popular tax they have ever seen.
- By January, Gordon B. Kaufmann presents his reworked design for the Hoover Dam to the Bureau of Reclamation. During the Great Depression, the dam becomes a symbol of the positive power of government.
- On January 11, *Business Week* announces that the 1933 Automobile Show features more radical changes in car design than seen since "the horseless carriage became a motor car." Lower, longer, and more unified, the new designs mark the beginning of a modern look for cars.
- On March 7, an autoworkers' union stages a march of the unemployed at the Ford River Rouge Plant in Dearborn, Michigan, to protest layoffs and deteriorating work conditions.
- On June 6, Richard M. Hollingshead Jr. opens the first drive-in movie theater in Camden, New Jersey.

1934

- The RCA Building, part of the three-block Rockefeller Center complex in downtown New York, is completed.
- Shoulder pads appear in women's clothing.
- The Ford Motor Company loses $120 million between 1931 and 1934.
- Much to the dismay of Detroit, Americans maintain their passion for automobiles by purchasing used cars, buying 171 used cars for every 100 new ones.
- In April, German chancellor Adolf Hitler announces that Germany should triple its number of cars in order to reach the "motorized glory" of the United States.

1935

- The United States Supreme Court building, designed by Cass Gilbert of New York, is completed.
- New retail display techniques include mannequins that look like Joan Crawford, Greta Garbo, Carole Lombard, Marlene Dietrich and Joan Bennett, designed by mannequin sculptors Cora Scovil and Lester Gaba.
- Howard Johnson opens his first roadside restaurant in Boston, Massachusetts.
- Detroit introduces the "passing beam" headlight, intended to redirect the headlight away from the oncoming driver's eyes.
- As automakers make bigger and better cars without pricing them higher, automobile executives start moving toward increased automation and mechanization as a way to hold down prices by cutting back on human labor.
- Fighting a valiant battle against the Big Three, independent car manufacturers record a year of good sales. Packard announces that sales are up 120 percent from 1934 levels; Auburn increases by 63 percent; and Nash increases by 61 percent.
- Designer Valentina features oriental details in her designs, including mandarin jackets and pointed coolie hats.
- Katharine Hepburn wears designer Muriel King's clothes in the movie *Sylvia Scarlett.*
- In April, Frank Lloyd Wright's designs for decentralizing urban America, Broadacre City, are exhibited in New York's Rockefeller Center to forty thousand viewers.
- On July 5, the National Labor Relations Act ensures the rights of workers to organize and bargain with employers for "fair labor practices," spurring the growth of unions and strikes in the auto industry.

1936

- Architect John Russell Pope wins approval for his designs of the Jefferson Memorial and the National Art Gallery.
- Architect Frank Lloyd Wright captures the new spirit of Streamline Moderne architecture in his Johnson Wax Company Administration Building in Racine, Wisconsin; it is completed in 1939. Its curved bands of brick walls and glass-tube glazing give the building the aerodynamic look of a Buick or an airplane.
- The San Francisco Bay Bridge is completed.
- General Motors reports that its annual profits are only ten million dollars short of its peak profits in 1929, proving to Detroit at least that the economy has turned a corner toward improvement.
- The automotive industry uniformly adopts steel tops and all-steel bodies that are longer and wider than on previous models, adding about one hundred pounds to the weight of 1937 models.
- Trailer manufacturing becomes the fastest-growing U.S. industry, as many Americans hit the road and tour the country.
- Red is popular with women, with matching rouge, lipstick, and nail enamel in such variations as "bright red," "gay red," "poppy," and "geranium."
- Run-proof mascara is invented.
- In October, despite an improving economy, the 1936 Cadillac Series 60 is priced at $1,645, seven hundred dollars less than Cadillac's lowest-priced 1935 model.

1937

- A poll taken by *Architectural Record* finds that the Colonial Style is still the most popular home in America, constituting 85 percent of homes costing less than ten thousand dollars.
- The Lincoln Tunnel under the Hudson River opens, connecting New York and New Jersey.
- German architect Walter Gropius is appointed head of the Harvard University School of Architecture.
- The Golden Gate Bridge near San Francisco is completed.
- *Business Week* announces that the luxury car is making a comeback, with the new Lincoln Zephyr, Cadillac LaSalle, and Chrysler Custom Imperial all selling at impressive rates.

- Frank Lloyd Wright designs the Kaufmann house known as Fallingwater. Perched on a waterfall, it becomes the symbol of far-out modern architecture.
- Independent automaker Nash's "Young Man's model" offers its drivers a bed-conversion option in its sedans.
- Americans who can afford to vacation do so by car, pushing the number of auto travelers from 45 million in 1929 to 52 million.
- Packard announces it expects to make and sell 130,000 cars in 1937.
- Solid-disk steel wheels replace steel-spoke wheels and secure the dominance of chrome-plated hubcaps on American cars.
- Muriel King designs dresses for Katharine Hepburn and Ginger Rogers for the movie *Stage Door,* introducing her designs to women across the country.

1938

- General Motors leads the American auto industry, claiming 43 percent of all passenger cars sold in the United States, with Chrysler second at 25 percent and Ford third with 22 percent.
- Designer Claire McCardell's "monastic dress" becomes her first commercial success, with its monklike cut that can be worn full, swinging from the shoulders, or belted.
- DuPont announces it has devised "whole new schools of fabrics," including rayon, synthetic silk, and an early version of nylon.
- As the Depression drags on, Macy's advertising states the obvious and proudly declares, "It's Smart to be Thrifty."
- Milliner Lilly Daché opens her design house on East Fifty-sixth Street in New York City and upholsters a room in silver for her brunette customers and one in gold for her blond ones.
- In January, *Architectural Record* devotes an entire edition to Frank Lloyd Wright's Usonia house designs, his utopian solution to the American housing shortage.
- On July 3, President Franklin D. Roosevelt formally dedicates the Gettysburg Memorial by lighting the eternal light, a flame intended to represent the nation's strength and unity.
- On July 30, auto manufacturer Henry Ford is presented with Germany's highest honor given to foreigners, the Grand Cross of the Supreme Order of the German Eagle, for making motorcars available to the masses.

1939

- The Museum of Modern Art in New York shows the work of the Bauhaus.
- *Vogue* shows trousers with pullovers for women.
- Surrealist painter Salvador Dali is hired by Bonwit Teller in New York to design a window display for the store. "Narcissus White" horrified customers and store executives, who altered it without the artist's consent.
- Eliel Saarinen designs the Crow Island School in Winnetka, Illinois, which is completed the following year.
- Heralded by some as a safety improvement, some American cars begin to feature gearshifts connected to the steering wheel instead of the floor of the car.
- Valentina designs Katharine Hepburn's costumes for Philip Barry's play *The Philadelphia Story.*
- In *An Organic Architecture,* Frank Lloyd Wright argues that a structure should be an integral part of its environment.
- Designed by Frank Lloyd Wright, the SC Johnson Wax Administration Building is completed in Racine, Wisconsin.
- In February, the Golden Gate World's Fair in San Francisco opens. This mile-long fair, erected on a man-made island, cost more than forty million dollars to construct.
- On April 30, New York World's Fair "Building the World of Tomorrow" opens in Flushing Meadows, ideologically promoting a belief in science and technology as the road to prosperity and freedom, while stylistically promoting a belief in clean lines and pure forms.

Federal Building Projects of the Depression Era

The National Gallery of Art

Architectural design

By: Eggers & Higgins

Date: 1941

Source: Gottscho-Schleisner, Inc. "National Gallery of Art, Washington, D.C., West Facade." *Gottscho-Schleisner Collection.* American Memory digital primary source collection, Library of Congress. Available online at http://memory.loc.gov/ammem/gschtml/gotthome.html (accessed March 25, 2003).

About the Architects: The famous architectural firm of Eggers & Higgins was comprised of Daniel Higgins (1886–1953) and Otto R. Eggers (1882–1964). Higgins left school to support his family after eighth grade, eventually learning accounting and architecture. Eggers was hired by John Russell Pope as a talented architect in 1912. Eggers and Higgins worked for Pope until he died in 1937; then the two formed their own firm. Higgins' business acumen and Eggers' fame as a designer earned them repeated work with prestigious clients. Their important projects included a number of hospitals, the Cardinal Hayes and Archbishop Stepinac high schools, and other assignments for the U.S. government. Higgins' death in 1953 brought an end to the famous partnership.

George Washington Bridge

Architectural design

By: Othmar H. Ammann

Date: October 25, 1931

Source: Rothstein, Arthur. "George Washington Bridge from New York City Side." 1941. *Farm Security Administration-*

Primary Source

The National Gallery of Art

SYNOPSIS: The construction of the National Gallery of Art (1937–1941) in Washington, D.C., revived the classical style of the early national buildings, making extensive use of American marble and white oak, and sparking a reassuring reconnection with the beginnings of the American experiment. THE LIBRARY OF CONGRESS.

Primary Source

George Washington Bridge

SYNOPSIS: In late 1929, Public Works Administration laborers began construction of the George Washington Bridge, which spans the Hudson River, linking upper Manhattan in New York City with Fort Lee, New Jersey. Designed by Othmar H. Ammann, Chief Engineer for the Port Authority at the time, the bridge was opened to traffic on October 25, 1931. Today, it is one of the most heavily traveled bridges in the world. THE LIBRARY OF CONGRESS.

Office of War Information Collection. American Memory digital primary source collection, Library of Congress. Available online at http://memory.loc.gov/ammem/fsowhome.html (accessed March 25, 2003).

About the Designer: Othmar Hermann Ammann (1879–1965) was born in Schaffhausen, Switzerland. There he studied under Wilhelm Ritter, an authority on suspension bridges. Hoping to gain experience in American bridge-building techniques, Ammann came to the United States in 1904. (He became a naturalized citizen in 1924.) In a career of over fifty years, Ammann secured his place as a leading designer of bridges through his work on the George Washington Bridge, the Walt Whitman Bridge in Philadelphia, and the Golden Gate Bridge in San Francisco. He died in New York.

U.S. Supreme Court Building

Architectural design

By: Cass Gilbert

Date: 1935

Source: Rothstein, Arthur. "The Supreme Court Building, Washington, D.C." *Farm Security Administration-Office of War Information Collection.* American Memory digital primary source collection, Library of Congress. Available online at http://memory.loc.gov/ammem/fsowhome.html (accessed March 25, 2003).

About the Architect: Cass Gilbert (1859–1934) was born in Zanesville, Ohio. He learned his craft during two years as an assistant at the Beaux-Arts firm of McKim, Mead and White. Gilbert was noted for his versatility, but was one of the most respected Beaux-Arts architects of the early twentieth century. He is most often remembered for designing the Woolworth Building (1913) in New York City, as well as the U.S. Treasury Annex (1919) and the U.S. Supreme Court building (1935) in Washington, D.C. He died at seventy-five, still at the height of his career. ■

Introduction

As the Depression of the 1930s deepened, President Franklin D. Roosevelt actively experimented with programs designed to stimulate the economy by addressing

Primary Source

U.S. Supreme Court Building

SYNOPSIS: Federal construction initiatives improved the public domain, but also inspired new design trends and revived old ones, such as the construction of the U.S. Supreme Court (1932–1935) in Washington, D.C. This photo was taken by famous photographer Arthur Rothstein (1914–1985) while he was working for the Farm Security Administration. THE LIBRARY OF CONGRESS.

the consequences of economic collapse at the point of its impact upon American citizens. In short, his programs created employment.

Those hardest hit by the Depression were unskilled workers. Federal work programs put thousands to work on projects that served important public purposes. The 1932 legislation that created the Public Works Administration (PWA) earmarked more than $3 billion in aid to states, counties, and municipalities for the construction of public buildings and public works projects. These included state and national buildings and monuments, hospitals, schools, water and sewage works, irrigation and soil protection projects, dams, bridges, road improvements, railway terminals, and national park improvements. In 1935, Roosevelt created a similar agency, the Works Progress Administration (WPA), by executive order.

Roosevelt's expansion of government was often criticized by his opponents, but he defended his philosophy. In a 1936 interview Roosevelt told one journalist that the New Deal's mission was

> to do what any honest government of any country would do; try to increase the security and happiness of a larger number of people in all occupations of life and in all parts of the country; to give them more of the good things of life, to give them a greater distribution not only of wealth in the narrow terms, but of wealth in the wider terms; to give them places to go in the summer time—recreation; to give them assurance that they are not going to starve in their old age; to give honest business a chance to go ahead and make a reasonable profit, and to give everyone a chance to earn a living.

Although his New Deal programs did not fundamentally restructure the American economic system, they did go far in fostering relief, reform, and recovery in the 1930s.

Significance

Mickey Kaus, in a March 1994 *Washington Monthly* article, argued in favor of the soundness of Roosevelt's logic, citing the favorable outcome of his federal employment programs and suggesting, in response to President Clinton's "workfare" proposal of the early 1990s, that Depression-era ideas could have modern applications. Kaus argued that Roosevelt's program worked "reasonably well," employing 3.3 million people in needed public works projects. He noted that, during its existence, the WPA alone constructed an estimated 40,000 buildings, including 8,000 schools; built or improved 650,000 miles of roads, 124,000 bridges and viaducts, 8,000 parks, 18,000 playgrounds, and 2,000 swimming pools. Such programs, Kaus suggested, could still offer feasible solutions to periodic economic downturns and a wiser "hand-up" to the poor. He noted that, by creating the WPA in 1935, Roosevelt effectively ended a relief program that had been giving cash to the able-bodied poor, saying, "To dole out relief in this way is to administer a narcotic."

Further Resources

BOOKS

Abbott, Berenice, and Bonnie Yochelson. *Changing New York: The Complete WPA Project.* New York: New Press, 1997.

Caro, Robert. *The Power Broker: Robert Moses and the Fall of New York.* New York: Vintage Books, 1975.

Schlesinger, Arthur M., Jr. *The Age of Roosevelt: The Politics of Upheaval.* Boston: Houghton Mifflin, 1960.

PERIODICALS

Micciche, Laura R. "More than a Feeling: Disappointment and WPA Work." *College English* 64, no. 4, March 2002, 432–458.

WEBSITES

"Construction/Engineering Projects." The Lilly Library, Indiana University. Available online at http://www.indiana.edu/~liblilly/wpa/construction.html; website home page: http://www.indiana.edu/~liblilly/index.html (accessed April 9, 2003).

"George Washington Bridge: Historic Overview." Nycroads.com. Available online at http://www.nycroads.com/crossings/george-washington; website home page: http://www.nycroads.com (accessed August 29, 2002).

Jennings, John K. *Final Report of the Indiana Work Projects Administration.* March 1943. Available online at http://www.indiana.edu/~libgpd/historical/digarc.html (accessed April 9, 2003).

The International Style: Architecture Since 1922

Nonfiction work, Architectural designs

By: Henry-Russell Hitchcock Jr. and Philip Johnson

Date: 1932

Source: Hitchcock, Henry-Russell, Jr., and Philip Johnson. *The International Style: Architecture Since 1922.* New York: W.W. Norton, 1932, 18–23.

About the Authors: Henry-Russell Hitchcock Jr. (1903–1987), widely considered the founder of modern architectural history, was born in Boston, Massachusetts, and educated at Harvard University, New York University, the Universities of Glasgow and Pennsylvania, and Wesleyan University. Throughout his career as an educator and architecture historian, he received numerous awards, wrote more than twenty books covering a wide range of topics, lectured extensively, and produced a number of influential architectural exhibits. He died in 1987 in New York.

Philip Johnson (1906–) was born in Cleveland, Ohio. He studied philosophy and architecture at Harvard. His activism has been recognized perhaps as much as his work. He served as the chairman of the department of architecture for the Museum of Modern Art from 1930 to 1934 and, again, from 1946 until 1954. He has embraced new trends in architecture, and his designs have often followed these trends; some are highly regarded, while others have provoked strong disapproval. He continues to speak at architectural forums, colleges, and universities. ■

Introduction

Between World War I (1914–1918) and World War II (1939–1945), a radical architectural style began to emerge in Europe. Dubbed "modernism," it proposed to be truly representative of a unique, technological age. Philip Johnson discovered it during a brief European tour in the 1920s.

In the early 1930s several proponents of this style who were fleeing Nazi Germany strengthened its influ-

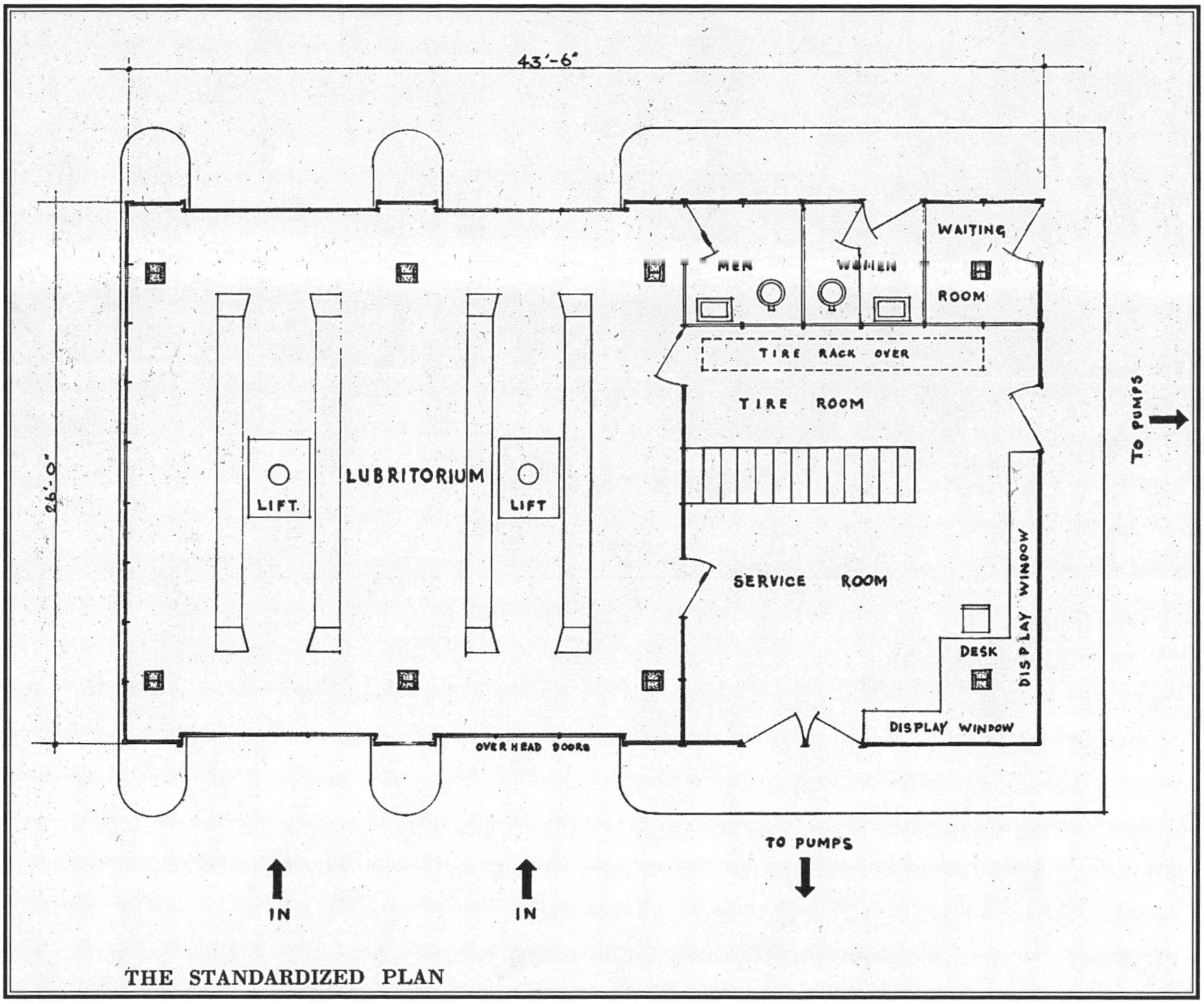

Primary Source

Ohio Filling Station Blueprint (1 OF 2)

SYNOPSIS: This design illustrates the international style of architecture that gained prominence in the early 1930s. BOOK ILLUSTRATION FROM *INTERNATIONAL STYLE: ARCHITECTURE SINCE 1922*, BLUEPRINT PLAN OF STANDARD OIL GAS STATION DESIGNED BY CLAUSS & DAUB, CLEVELAND, OHIO, 1931.

ence among American architects and educators. Hitchcock and Johnson met three of these men at Harvard University: Walter Gropius, founder of the Bauhaus in Berlin and head of the department of architecture at Harvard's Graduate School of Design; Marcel Breuer, a colleague of Gropius's at the Bauhaus; and Martin Wagner, former director of planning for the city of Berlin.

Hitchcock's and Johnson's working relationship began through a mutual acquaintance, Alfred Barr, director of New York City's Museum of Modern Art. In 1932 the two young men, anxious to launch their careers and make significant marks in their field, assumed leading and vocal roles at the forefront of the modern architectural movement by publishing one of the first definitions of the modernist style, *The International Style: Architecture Since 1922.* Along with Barr they enthusiastically embraced the style's aesthetic value of simple structures, devoid of any historical, local, or regional ornamentation, calling it the "International Style."

Significance

By the late 1940s the popularity of the International Style had begun to wane. In 1951, Hitchcock wrote an essay, "The International Style, Twenty Years Later," in which he acknowledged the shortcomings of his own earlier views and the need for greater latitude of style in architecture. In time, "postmodernism" responded to the sparse feel of the modernism of the 1920s and 1930s by

Primary Source

Ohio Fillling Station Photo (2 OF 2)

SYNOPSIS: One of a series of stations designed by Clauss and Daub, the sparse design is typical of the "modernist" or international style of architecture. Here is it applied to a small business. BOOK ILLUSTRATION FROM *INTERNATIONAL STYLE: ARCHITECTURE SINCE 1922,* STANDARD OIL GAS STATION AND PUMPS, DESIGNED BY CLAUSS & DAUB, CLEVELAND, OHIO, 1931.

pulling some elements from earlier forms but giving them a twist, often producing collages of many pieces of earlier styles.

By the 1980s some architects were exploring entirely new forms designed to deconstruct (or take apart from within and show how something is unstable) all previous structural traditions. Johnson took up the cause with great interest, writing of "the pleasures of unease." Others argued that, unlike the work of most artists, the work of architects served the public realm and, therefore, was under some obligation to society to provide environments that were "safe, secure, functional, and orderly." While the fervor of deconstructionist thought has since died down, it still exerts some influence among designers and still provokes mixed responses from the public.

Hitchcock was considered the founder of modern architectural history. Johnson was considered an icon of the modern movement, as well as one of its most celebrated and questionable figures. His impact on the architectural world since 1932 has been immense and largely facilitated by the connections he formed with Barr and Hitchcock at New York City's Museum of Modern Art in the 1930s, and by the credibility those associations bestowed upon him, even before he had produced significant designs of his own.

A *Commonweal* reviewer suggested, in response to *The International Style*'s reprinting in 1996, that there appears to be a resurgence of interest in the modern style, which he calls neomodernism: "[It] is seen in the current penchant for exposed steel I-beams, glass-and-steel canopies at street and roofline, and modernistic, slightly punky décor, with lots of exposed wire and metal, glass bricks, unmolded cherry-hued hardwood, lean track-lighting with tiny bulbs, and attenuated leather-and-metal furniture. Prominent in fashionable coffee-bars, the look is both retrospective and coolly, elegantly 'now,' like a Chanel suit or handbag. For my part, I am tempted to call it 'Millennial Modernism'—architecture for the age of CD-ROM, the Internet, and cellular telephones."

Primary Source

The International Style: Architecture Since 1922 [excerpt]

SYNOPSIS: In this excerpt from *The International Style: Architecture Since 1922,* Hitchcock and Johnson argue that architects of the 1910s and 1920s abandoned the imitative "styles" of the nineteenth century in favor of designs prompted by the vision of the individual architect. They suggest that this experiment produced, by the early 1930s, a distinct style, as sound and deserving of respect as some of the most revered styles of the past, including classical, Gothic, renaissance, and baroque. Examples of this new style accompanied the original text in the form of blueprints and designs and are reproduced here as well.

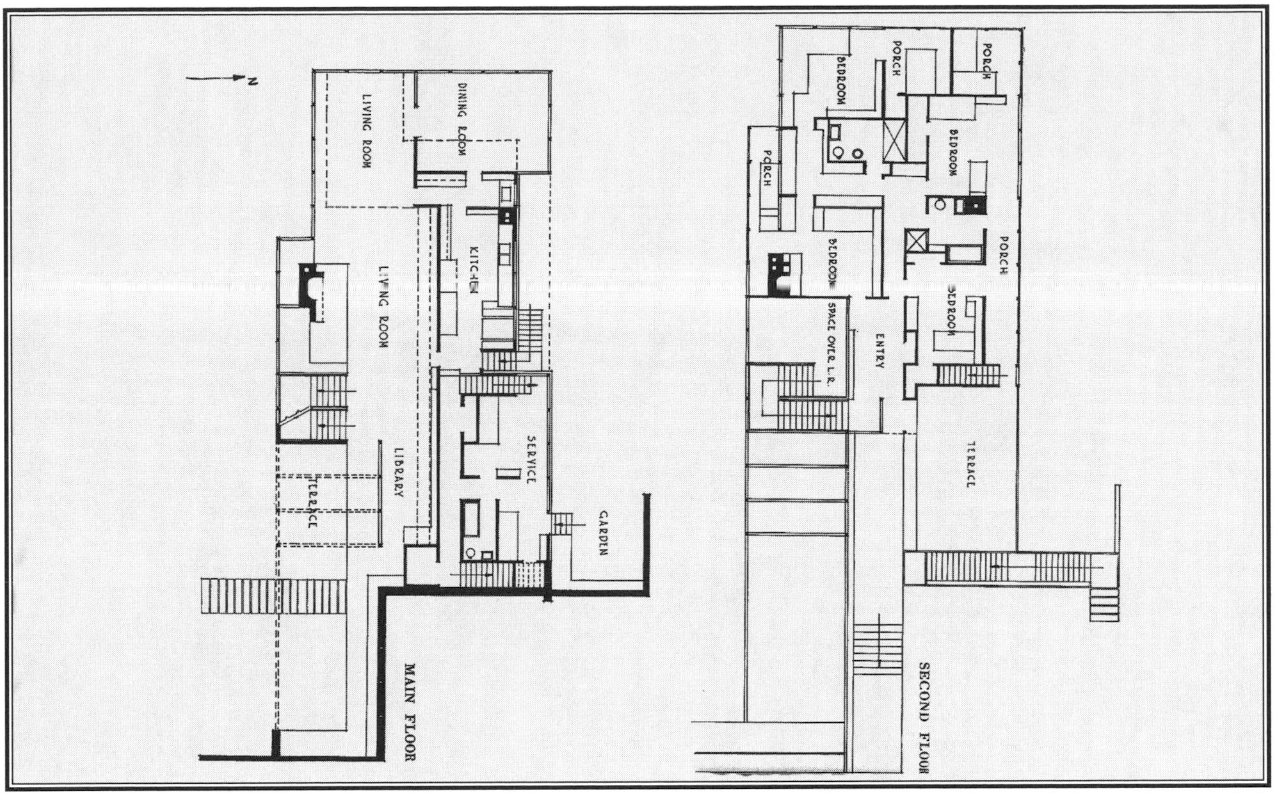

Primary Source

Lovell House Blueprints (1 OF 2)

SYNOPSIS: Designed by Richard J. Neutra. Here, the international style that Hitchcock and Johnson discuss in their book *The International Style: Architecture Since 1922* is applied to home living. BOOK ILLUSTRATION FROM *THE INTERNATIONAL STYLE: ARCHITECTURE SINCE 1922,* FLOOR PLANS FOR LOVELL HOUSE, DESIGNED BY RICHARD NEUTRA, IN 1929, SECOND FLOOR (TOP), MAIN FLOOR (BOTTOM).

The nineteenth century failed to create a style of architecture because it was unable to achieve a general discipline of structure and of design in the terms of the day. The revived "styles" were but a decorative garment to architecture, not the interior principles according to which it lived and grew. On the whole the development of engineering in building went on regardless of the Classical or Mediæval architectural forms which were borrowed from the past. Thus the chaos of eclecticism served to give the very idea of style a bad name in the estimation of the first modern architects of the end of the nineteenth and the beginning of the twentieth century.

In the nineteenth century there was always not one style, but "styles," and the idea of "styles" implied a choice. The individualistic revolt of the first modern architects destroyed the prestige of the "styles," but it did not remove the implication that there was a possibility of choice between one æsthetic conception of design and another. In their reaction against revivalism these men sought rather to explore a great variety of free possibilities. The result, on the whole, added to the confusion of continuing eclecticism, although the new work possessed a general vitality which the later revivalists had quite lost. The revolt from stylistic discipline to extreme individualism at the beginning of the twentieth century was justified as the surest issue from an impasse of imitation and sterility. The individualists decried submission to fixed æsthetic principles as the imposition of a dead hand upon the living material of architecture, holding up the failure of the revivals as a proof that the very idea of style was an unhealthy delusion.

Today the strict issue of reviving the styles of the distant past is no longer one of serious consequence. But the peculiar traditions of imitation and modification of the styles of the past, which eclecticism inherited from the earlier Classical and Mediæval Revivals, have not been easily forgotten. The influence of the past still most to be feared is that of the nineteenth century with its cheapening of the very idea of style. Modern architecture has

Primary Source

Lovell House Photo (2 OF 2)

SYNOPSIS: Richard Neutra's blueprint for a home in the international style is realized. BOOK PHOTOGRAPH FROM *THE INTERNATIONAL STYLE: ARCHITECTURE SINCE 1922*, LOVELL HOUSE, DESIGNED BY RICHARD J. NEUTRA, IN LOS ANGELES, CALIFORNIA, 1929.

nothing but the healthiest lessons to learn from the art of the further past, if that art be studied scientifically and not in a spirit of imitation. Now that it is possible to emulate the great styles of the past in their essence without imitating their surface, the problem of establishing one dominant style, which the nineteenth century set itself in terms of alternative revivals, is coming to a solution.

The idea of style, which began to degenerate when the revivals destroyed the disciplines of the Baroque, has become real and fertile again. Today a single new style has come into existence. The æsthetic conceptions on which its disciplines are based derive from the experimentation of the individualists. They and not the revivalists were the immediate masters of those who have created the new style. This contemporary style, which exists throughout the world, is unified and inclusive, not fragmentary and contradictory like so much of the production of the first generation of modern architects. In the last decade it has produced sufficient monuments of distinction to display its validity and its vitality. It may fairly be compared in significance with the styles of the past. In the handling of the problems of structure it is related to the Gothic, in the handling of the problems of design it is more akin to the Classical. In the preeminence given to the handling of function it is distinguished from both.

The unconscious and halting architectural developments of the nineteenth century, the confused and contradictory experimentation of the beginning of the twentieth, have been succeeded by a directed evolution. There is now a single body of discipline, fixed enough to integrate contemporary style as a reality and yet elastic enough to permit individual interpretation and to encourage general growth.

The idea of style as the frame of potential growth, rather than as a fixed and crushing mould, has developed with the recognition of underlying principles such as archæologists discern in the great styles of the past. The principles are few and broad. They are not mere formulas of proportion such as distinguish the Doric from the Ionic order; they are fundamental, like the organic verticality of the Gothic or the rhythmical symmetry of the Baroque. There is, first, a new conception of architecture as volume rather than as mass. Secondly, regularity rather than axial symmetry serves as the chief means of ordering design. These two principles, with a third proscribing arbitrary applied decoration, mark the productions of the international style. This new style is not international in the sense that the production of one country is just like that of another. Nor is it so rigid that the work of various leaders is not clearly distinguishable. The international style has become evident and definable only gradually as different innovators throughout the world have successfully carried out parallel experiments.

In stating the general principles of the contemporary style, in analyzing their derivation from structure and their modification by function, the appearance of a certain dogmatism can hardly be avoided. In opposition to those who claim that a new style of architecture is impossible or undesirable, it is necessary to stress the coherence of the results obtained within the range of possibilities thus far explored. For the international style already exists in the present; it is not merely something the future may hold in store. Architecture is always a set of actual monuments, not a vague corpus of theory.

The style of the twelfth and thirteenth century was the last before our own day to be created on the basis of a new type of construction. The break away from the High Gothic in the later Middle Ages was an æsthetic break without significant structural development. The Renaissance was a surface change of style generally coupled with actual regression in terms of structure. The Baroque and *a fortiori* the Romantic Age concerned themselves all but exclusively with problems of design. When a century ago new structural developments in the use of metal made their appearance they remained outside the art of architecture. The Crystal Palace at the London Exposition of 1851, Paxton's magnificent iron and glass construction, has far more in common with the architecture of our day than with that of its own. Ferroconcrete, to which the contemporary style owes so much, was invented in 1849. Yet it was at least fifty years before it first began to play a considerable part in architectural construction.

Metal had begun to be used incidentally in architecture before the end of the eighteenth century. Thenceforth it achieved a place of increasing importance, even in buildings of the most traditional design. Finally in the eighties it made possible the first skyscrapers. But on the whole the "arcades," the train sheds, the conservatories and the exhibition halls, of which the London Crystal Palace was the earliest and the finest, were adjuncts to, or substitutes for, conventional masonry buildings.

Behind the conventional story of nineteenth century revivals and eclecticism there are two further

Primary Source

The McGraw-Hill Building

SYNOPSIS: Designed by Hood and Fouilhoux in the international style, the McGraw-Hill building illustrates how this modern style of architecture could be used not only on small buildings and personal homes, but for tall skyscrapers as well. BOOK PHOTOGRAPH FROM *THE INTERNATIONAL STYLE: ARCHITECTURE SINCE 1922*, MCGRAW-HILL BUILDING, ON 42ND STREET, NEW YORK CITY, DESIGNED BY HOOD AND FOUILHOUX, 1931.

histories of architecture. One deals with the science of building alone. It traces the development of new engineering methods of construction and the gradual replacement of traditional masonry structure by successive innovations. The other history deals with the development of the art of architectural design regardless of specific imitations. Design was freed here and there from the control of the past. Some architects even sought novel forms and many aimed at a more direct expression of the new methods of construction. A new art of proportioning plane surfaces, a free study of silhouette, even a frank use of metal appear in the work of most of the leading nineteenth century architects. Soane in England, Schinkel and his followers in Germany, and Labrouste in France, were among these early precursors of modern architecture.

Further Resources

BOOKS

Johnson, Philip. *Architecture 1949–1965.* London: Thames & Hudson, 1966.

Johnson, Philip, with Mark Wigley. *Deconstructivist Architecture.* New York: Museum of Modern Art, 1988.

Schulze, Franz. *Philip Johnson: Life and Work.* Chicago: University of Chicago Press, 1996.

Searing, Helen, ed. *In Search of Modern Architecture: A Tribute to Henry-Russell Hitchcock.* Boston: MIT Press, 1982.

Stern, Robert. *New Directions in American Architecture.* New York: G. Braziller, 1977.

PERIODICALS

"Behind the Mirror: On the Writings of Philip Johnson." *Oppositions,* Fall 1977.

"Interview with Philip Johnson." *Archetype,* Winter 1983.

Kramer, Hilton. "Philip Johnson's Brilliant Career." *Commentary* 18, no. 3, September 1995, 38.

Thomas, Christopher. Review of *The International Style,* by Henry-Russell Hitchcock and Philip Johnson. *Commonweal* 15, no. 40, September 13, 1996.

WEBSITES

Hedges, Warren. "Using Deconstruction to Astonish Friends & Confound Enemies (In Two Easy Steps!)" Southern Oregon University. Available online at http://www.sou.edu/English/Hedges/Sodashop/RCenter/Theory/Howto/decon.htm (accessed April 9, 2003).

Keep, Christopher, Tim McLaughlin, and Robin Parmar. "Defining Postmodernism." The Electronic Labyrinth. Available online at http://www.iath.virginia.edu/elab/hfl0242.html; website home page: http://www.iath.virginia.edu/elab/elab.html (accessed April 9, 2003).

Klages, Mary. "Postmodernism." University of Colorado. Available online at http://www.colorado.edu/English/ENGL2012Klages/pomo.html; website home page: http://www.colorado.edu (accessed April 9, 2003).

A Century of Progress Exposition: Official Pictures in Color

"Ford Motor Company Building"; "The General Motors Building"; "The Chrysler Building"

Illustrations

By: Century of Progess International Exposition

Date: 1934

Source: Century of Progress International Exposition. *A Century of Progress Exposition: Official Pictures in Color.* Chicago: A Century of Progress, 1934, 33, 37, 39.

About the Organization: A Century of Progress was organized on January 5, 1928, as an Illinois corporation for the purpose of "the holding of a World's Fair in Chicago in the year 1933." The U.S. Congress authorized the president of the United States to invite the nations of the world to participate. The exposition imposed *no* tax burden on the American people already struggling under the weight of the Depression. Founders and sustaining members of the World's Fair Legion contributed all necessary funds. ■

Introduction

The Century of Progress Exposition, on 424 acres along the Lake Michigan shoreline edging Chicago, was a celebration of the modern history and of the future potential of science, exemplified by the machine. Exhibits illustrated the dependence of industry on scientific research by showcasing industrial processes, rather than finished products.

The "Big Three" American automakers—Ford, General Motors, and Chrysler—were especially enthusiastic participants. The Depression forced many carmakers out of business, and Ford, GM, and Chrysler, all of whom managed to remain marginally profitable during this time, dominated the auto industry. A few others, such as Packard, stayed in business through the 1930s but eventually declined. The Big Three hosted impressive exhibits at the exposition, which attracted almost 28 million visitors in 1933 and another 21 million in 1934.

The dazzling displays at the exposition, produced during the darkest days of the Depression, amounted to no small courage on the part of Ford, GM, and Chrysler, all of whom were walking economic tightropes at the time. Their dedication to creating a grand showcase for their products is illustrated by the watercolor sketches, rendered by Philip Lyford, of each company's exhibit hall.

Primary Source

"The Ford Motor Company Building" (1 OF 3)

SYNOPSIS: The Ford Motor Company Building sported a 200-foot-diameter dome, under which exhibits featured the development of wheeled vehicles throughout history, the automotive manufacturing process, and a collection of historical items related to the Ford Motor Company. An adjoining garden offered visitors shade, rest, and symphonic performances. A CENTURY OF PROGRESS EXPOSITION, 1933–1944, CHICAGO. OFFICIAL PICTURES IN COLOR. REPRODUCED BY PERMISSION OF THE CHICAGO HISTORICAL SOCIETY.

Primary Source

"The General Motors Building" (2 OF 3)

SYNOPSIS: A 177-foot tower dominated the General Motors Building's main structure, which was one of the outstanding exhibit buildings at the Fair. GM exhibits included a full assembly line in operation, automotive improvements designed and produced by the company, and a laboratory of micro-machining. A CENTURY OF PROGRESS EXPOSITION, 1933–1944, CHICAGO. OFFICIAL PICTURES IN COLOR. REPRODUCED BY PERMISSION OF THE CHICAGO HISTORICAL SOCIETY.

Primary Source

"The Chrysler Building" (3 OF 3)

SYNOPSIS: The Chrysler Building formed a large Maltese Cross with four pylons, 125 feet high, fronted by an impressive fountain, surrounded by comfortable outdoor seating. The company hosted an outdoor, quarter-mile exhibition and testing track, while indoor exhibits included a drop-forge steam hammer in operation and manufacturing demonstrations. A CENTURY OF PROGRESS EXPOSITION, 1933–1944, CHICAGO. OFFICIAL PICTURES IN COLOR. REPRODUCED BY PERMISSION OF THE CHICAGO HISTORICAL SOCIETY.

Significance

The 1933–1934 Chicago exposition celebrated the machine and tried to ease consumer anxieties about the chaos that many felt accompanied the machine age. Moving exhibits that demonstrated various industrial processes removed the mystery of the sciences, which were transforming American society at an increasingly rapid pace. The fair's success encouraged two other expositions during the 1930s: the 1935 California Pacific Exposition and the 1939 New York World's Fair. In all three, industry and science courted the American consumer.

Some of the Chicago exhibits led to new technological developments. The streamliner locomotive, for example, made its debut at the Chicago exposition and broke a nonstop railway record less than a year later. Other products—such as Chrysler's futuristic Dymaxion Airflow automobile, which was never marketed because of its inordinate manufacturing expense—generated a lot of public interest but proved impractical.

Further Resources

BOOKS

Batchelor, Ray. *Henry Ford, Mass Production, Modernism, and Design.* Manchester: University of Manchester Press, 1995.

Collier, Peter, and David Horowitz. *The Fords: An American Epic.* New York: Summit, 1987.

Cray, Ed. *Chrome Colossus: General Motors and Its Times.* New York: McGraw-Hill, 1980.

Curcio, Vincent. *Chrysler: Life and Times of an Automotive Genius.* New York: Oxford University Press, 2000.

Gelernter, David. *1939: The Lost World of the Fair.* New York: Free Press, 1995.

May, George S. *A Most Unique Machine: The Michigan Origins of the American Automobile Industry.* Grand Rapids, Mich.: W.E. Eerdmans, 1974.

WEBSITES

The Gottscho-Schleisner Collection. American Memory digital primary source collection, Library of Congress. Available online at http://lcweb2.loc.gov/ammem/gschtml/gotthome.html; website home page: http://memory.loc.gov (accessed April 8, 2003).

WPA Encourages Automotive Travel

"See America: Welcome to Montana"

Poster

By: M. Weitzman
Date: 1936
Source: Weitzman, M. "See America: Welcome to Montana." [1936?]. *By the People, For the People: Posters from the WPA, 1936–1943.* American Memory digital primary source collection, Library of Congress. Available online at http://memory.loc.gov (accessed March 24, 2003).

"They Like Winter in New York State: The State That Has Everything"

Poster

By: Jack Rivolta
Date: 1936
Source: Rivolta, Jack. "They Like Winter in New York State: The State That Has Everything." [1936?]. *By the People, For the People: Posters from the WPA, 1936–1943.* American Memory digital primary source collection, Library of Congress. Available online at http://memory.loc.gov (accessed March 24, 2003).
About the Organization: The Works Progress Administration (WPA) was created in 1935 by President Franklin Roosevelt as a federal work-relief program. Before its dissolution in 1943, it had employed almost nine million people at an average salary of $42 a month. The WPA employed laborers with a variety of skills for such projects as the construction of bridges and roads, the creation of archives, and visual advertisements and records of the period. ■

Introduction

Several WPA work-relief programs encouraged Americans to travel the country, in one of many attempts to jump-start the economy by enticing people to spend money. WPA workers built and improved roads, especially in and around national parks. WPA writers authored travel guides for each state, and WPA artists created travel posters advertising the special offerings of each of the mainland states. These initiatives were largely successful, as the Depression lowered the prices of automobiles and left many who were either unemployed or employed only part-time with more leisure time than ever before.

Significance

A transcript of Roosevelt's 1937 dedication of Timberline Lodge at Mount Hood, Oregon, records the President's personal encouragement of Americans to exercise their citizenship through travel within the United States. "I am very keen about travel for as many Americans as can possibly afford it, because those Americans will be getting to know their own country better; and the more they see of it, the more they will realize the privileges which God and nature have given to the American people."

The travel posters created by WPA artists for each state were widely distributed, much like the modern travel brochure. The automobile was more affordable than it ever had been, and Americans took up traveling in large numbers. Roadside food stands and motels abounded during these years—some, like the Howard Johnson's chain, enjoying a booming business. As an indication of the numbers of Americans on the road at the time, by the close of the 1930s, Howard Johnson's restaurants stretched the entire length of the Eastern Seaboard, from Maine to Florida.

Further Resources

BOOKS

DeNoon, Chris. *Posters of the WPA.* Seattle: University of Washington Press, 1987.

O'Gara, Geoffrey. *Long Road Home: Travels through America Today with the Great 1930s WPA Guides.* Boston: Houghton Mifflin, 1990.

Pyle, Ernie, and David Nichols. *Ernie's America: The Best of Ernie Pyle's 1930s Travel Dispatches.* New York: Random House, 1989.

Unrau, Harlan D., and G. Frank Williss. *Administrative History: Expansion of the National Park Service in the 1930s.* Denver: National Park Service, 1983. Available online at http://www.cr.nps.gov (accessed August 16, 2002).

Weisberger, Bernard A., ed. *The WPA Guide to America: The Best of 1930s America as Seen by the Federal Writers' Project.* New York: Pantheon Books, 1985.

PERIODICALS

Nassar, J. "1930s Travel Decals." *Americana,* 19, no. 13, August 1991, 52.

WEBSITES

Graphic Design from the 1920s and 1930s in Travel Ephemera. Available online at http://www.travelbrochuregraphics.com (accessed August 29, 2002).

Roosevelt, Franklin D. Address at Timberline Lodge, September 28, 1937. Reproduced in the New Deal Document Library. New Deal Network. Available online at http://newdeal.feri.org/speeches/1937d.htm; website home page: http://newdeal.feri.org (accessed April 8, 2003).

Primary Source

"See America: Welcome to Montana"

SYNOPSIS: This WPA poster, created in 1936, encouraged America's by-then-enthusiastic tourists to visit a little-known and mostly isolated region of the country, the wide open spaces of Montana. THE LIBRARY OF CONGRESS.

Primary Source

"They Like Winter in New York State: The State That Has Everything"

SYNOPSIS: This New York travel poster, created in 1936, appealed to tourists by advertising New York's winter recreational offerings. THE LIBRARY OF CONGRESS.

The Builders of Timberline Lodge

Nonfiction work

By: Oregon Writers' Project

Date: 1937

Source: Oregon Writers' Project. *The Builders of Timberline Lodge.* Portland, Ore.: Works Progress Administration, 1937.

About the Organization: The Oregon Writers' Project, partly funded by the Works Progress Administration (WPA), employed historians and writers in projects such as research and writing for state archives and the Oregon Historical Society; creating indexes of state newspapers and inventories of county archives; copying primary source materials, such as documents pertaining to pioneers of the state; and cataloging historical markers. ■

Introduction

The administrative staff of the Oregon Writers' Project completed the preparation, publishing, and distribution of *Timberline Lodge* and *The Builders of Timberline Lodge.* The publications' goals were to employ writers in a publicly beneficent endeavor, to advertise the success of WPA programs, and to celebrate the lodge itself as a travel destination. The Writers' Project wrote the text, and the Art Project of the Oregon Works Progress Administration prepared the drawings and illustrations. There is little background information on the primary documents themselves. However, they serve as examples of the kind of documentation produced by the WPA.

Timberline Lodge is an outstanding example of a Depression-era federal work project. President Franklin D. Roosevelt dedicated the Lodge on September 28, 1937. It was a unique counter to the design trends of the 1930s, which were wrapped up in the advent of the machine. The lodge was built over several months, almost entirely by hand and often in brutal weather conditions. The project employed several thousand laborers, artisans, and engineers and was jointly sponsored and financed by the Forest Service Division of the U.S. Department of Agriculture, the Works Progress Administration, federal appropriations, and local contributions raised by the Mount Hood Development Association. A 1930s WPA writer reported the total output of the completed project to be $1.5 million and 760,000 hours of labor.

The work included a six-and-a-half-mile road up to the lodge, which was built entirely with local materials. The exterior was made of wood and stone by unskilled laborers; and the courtyard was paved with flagstone from a local quarry. Interior details include hand-carved

The Timberline Lodge, Mount Hood National Forest, Oregon. Timberline Lodge was built entirely out of local materials by Works Progress Administration relief workers. NATIONAL ARCHIVES—PACIFIC ALASKA REGION, SEATTLE.

wood, extensive windows, large stone fireplaces, and unique furniture, all designed and built by artisans. Timberline Lodge is now a ski resort.

Significance

WPA documentation was widely distributed, as were the state travel guides. These publications were apparently useful in attracting tourists. (The presence of foreign visitors is noted in a portion of the following pamphlets not excerpted here.) However, the documents are much more extensive than modern travel brochures. They are literary essays in which, as the following excerpts illustrate, authors explored human, architectural, and historical details and issues, while painting a stirring portrait of the WPA in action.

Primary Source

The Builders of Timberline Lodge [excerpt]

SYNOPSIS: The following essay describes the natural beauty of Mount Hood as but a backdrop to the beauty of human minds and hands skillfully and enthusiastically employed in a cooperative and publicly beneficial endeavor. Many had known months of unemployment and hunger prior to working on the project. It goes on to describe the labor these artists and workers, noting the positive effects of architecture as a design is given concrete form through cooperative labor. The author suggests the individuals involved contribute to the greater social good and may perhaps even initiate an "American renaissance."

Each year the sun pauses in his steady pacing to the south, and for one brief dawn, presents a miracle on the slopes of Mt. Hood. His display on this particular morning, when he rolls up the ascent like a ball of fire and bursts in full splendor from the peak, is one for long anticipation, for awed witnessing silence and for subsequent contemplation. Hundreds greet that sunrise magic, turning their eyes toward the east in the traditional gesture of acknowledgement to the source of all the arts of civilization.

Those who view the magnificence of this solitary dawn and who salute the sun as a symbol of the renewal of life and the triumph of faith over darkness, have exemplified an age-old ritual. Moreover, in facing the east and its white mountain wedged into the roseate sky, they gaze toward Timberline Lodge, a recreational project which is a concrete manifestation of faith and of the triumph of intelligence over economic distress. . . .

In Mt. Hood Timberline Lodge the mystic strength that lives in the hills has been captured in wood and stone, and, in the hands of laborer and craftsman, has been presented as man's effort at approximating an ideal in which society, through concern for the individual, surpasses the standard it has unconsciously set for itself. . . .

In return for physical security supplied by a powerful social agency, they gave the best that was in them, cheerfully, with an eye to the finished project, realizing in the satisfaction of their work, though all unconsciously, that they were a part of something bigger than themselves. . . .

Each workman on Timberline Lodge gained proficiency in manual arts. He was a better workman, a better citizen, progressing infinitely slow steps to the degree above him. Perhaps he never reached it. Yet the unconscious but concerted effort of several hundred men to advance meant something, even if they failed. Its social values could not be estimated in monetary return for toil, nor man-hours of labor completed. . . .

A blacksmith, accustomed to working at the forge, but with no knowledge of the technique and artistry required in making ornamental wrought iron, enrolled at the foundry on Boise Street, where the hardware and decorative iron for Timberline Lodge were made. Encouraged by the foreman over a period of months, this blacksmith developed into an accomplished worker. He discovered in himself an artistic inclination he had not known he possessed. Then he was entrusted with carrying out the design prepared for the dining room grille gates at the Lodge, painstaking and intricate work, for which he forged every piece.

Another matter of interest as relating to the unskilled workmen at Timberline Lodge was the fact that its construction provided a suitable outlet for many whose intelligence quotient restricted them to the lower order of manual work. Yet even among these were found examples which heartened social workers. An illiterate Italian whose family had been a problem to Multnomah County, for the first time in years earned enough to support his children. . . .

Steam-fitters, carpenters, painters, wood carvers, and cabinet workers, identified with the skilled trades, many of whom were forced out of their craft through no responsibility of their own, discovered that government accepted this responsibility, and in accepting it was willing to prepare a place for them in the construction of Timberline Lodge.

Mechanized production with its emphasis on speed, which characterizes present day industry, places a serious handicap on age. The middle-aged and elderly men, though masters of their craft and skilled in proportion to their years of practice, find their muscles unequal to the tempo required. They lag behind. They are dismissed.

Rather than rewarding them for wisdom gained in years of work, our industrial scheme has penalized them. They have been left with but one asset—skill, and skill appears to be a drug on a mechanized market. Timberline Lodge, with its opportunity for the revival of dormant crafts and arts, offered employment to many men in this classification, and in their successful absorption suggested the possibility of a permanent program designed to perpetuate handicrafts and to make them serve a social need. . . .

Mallets drove chisels into clean-grained wood. Chips flew and the Thunderbird emerged from the pine, perpetuating not only the memory of a forgotten race, but the skill of earnest workers. This skill, which they had come to regard as almost worthless, was presented to them again as something valuable, something to be cherished and redeemed. They found it of dual concern: it was made to contribute to fulfillment of the social need for a recreational center, and in this fulfillment objectified the necessity for preserving the products of an active brain and a skillful hand. Old values these, and almost forgotten in the quickening tempo of the machine age. Old values, dear to the intimate soul of man, which respects the human body and the honest toil it may be made to perform. . . .

The crudity of evolving form, symbolic perhaps of the changing social order in which this recreational project has had a part, is evident not only in the exterior of Mt. Hood Timberline Lodge, with its projecting and rudely carved beams, its sturdy basaltic foundation, and its stalwart battens and shakes, but may be found in all the interior details. The only permanency, change, is exemplified in stone and wood. Cruel or beautiful, nature is shown in exquisite expressions of a universal power.

This sense of power, experienced by every person who visits the Mt. Hood recreational area, is the keynote of all construction and decoration. It is a realization of belonging to a vast freedom, of being fleetingly identified with natural force, with gigantic invisible form which is constantly varying in its manifestations. . . .

[D]ecoration is characterized by strength rather than by grace. It is identified by masses and substance and permits no confusing superfluity of line and color. A new and indigenous style was developed, a style that is more than a product of the forces that made Mt. Hood and the American ranges. It is the mountains themselves, this new Cascadian art. Artists have found their best expressions, not in the perfection of polished woods, but in the hewn strength and swift chiseling of natural figures. In murals, painters depicted the exaggerated comedy of the fisherman's lie, the bravado of the woodsman, and the paradox of the hunter washing grease-mottled dishes. Though amusing in theme, their spirit was drawn from the strength of the hills, a source that artists and craftsmen alike tapped and diverted to social and individual advancement. . . .

A young man was employed on the Timberline Lodge project to carve the newel posts on the massive stairway. Each post represents a bird or animal, characteristic of the Mt. Hood region. To be in keeping with the rough-hewn logs of the balustrades and the iron-bound steps, the designs required sturdiness and swift modeling. Convention-bound by the technique he had learned under a different social order the wood carver struggled with his old tools, his old methods. In despair he sought help from the source of his material. He learned the relation of the wood to the mountain upon which it grew, discovered the adventure and romance of Mt. Hood's past, and found at last a technique suitable for expressing the spirit of the place.

It was a new technique, bold in line and mass, and requiring specially made tools for its execution. These tools, made according to specifications, were forged at the WPA shop.

A painter, whose hobby is photography, made a pictorial record of construction during his employment on the project. He had over 200 pictures to tell of his participation in building the recreational center. His real story, however, could best be told by officials of the United States Forest Service, who were so pleased with the specially mixed paint which he originated for the Lodge, that they made the formula standard, not only for the northwest, but for the mid-mountain region as well. This paint, which simulates frost, is remarkable not only for its realism, but for its economy of cost.

The wood-carver's tools and the painter's formula were minor developments, yet each is indicative of Timberline Lodge's contribution to American progress in the arts. . . .

This disrespect for the ordinary has long eaten at the core of all American arts, and reflected in home decoration and domestic values, has, with alarmingly increasing pressure, set a false standard in American life. Radio, newspaper, and magazine advertising blare the advantages of the bizarre, the fantastic, the expensive, until the person of ordinary intelligence finds himself so bewildered he accepts what is thrust at him as valid. . . .

As the winding road leading to it represented progress by laborers, not the least of whose rewards was the daily inspiration of the enlarged and expanding view of mountain tops, so the building itself exemplifies a progressive social program which has revived dormant arts and pointed the way for their perpetuation. It presents concretely the evidence that men still aspire to the dream, often secret but always universal, of becoming greater than themselves through association with others in a common purpose.

Further Resources

BOOKS

Lowitt, Richard. *The New Deal and the West.* Norman: University of Oklahoma Press, 1995.

Murrell, Gary. *Iron Pants: Oregon's Anti-New Deal Governor, Charles Henry Martin.* Pullman: Washington State University Press, 2000.

Wrobel, David M. *The End of American Exceptionalism: Frontier Anxiety from the Old West to the New Deal.* Lawrence: University Press of Kansas, 1993.

WEBSITES

Timberline Lodge home page. Available online at http://www.timberlinelodge.com (accessed August 29, 2002).

"Timberline Lodge." Great Buildings Online. Available online at http://www.greatbuildings.com/buildings/Timberline_Lodge.html; website home page: http://www.greatbuildings.com (accessed August 29, 2002).

Fashion Is Spinach

Autobiography

By: Elizabeth Hawes

Date: 1938

Source: Hawes, Elizabeth. *Fashion Is Spinach.* New York: Random House, 1938, 3–6, 19.

About the Author: Elizabeth Hawes (1903–1971), born in New Jersey, studied anatomy and economics at Vassar College before apprenticing with fashion designers Bergdorf Goodman in New York and Nicole Groult in Paris. In 1931 Hawes staged the first American fashion show in Paris, and as the depression weakened American reliance upon expensive Parisian designs, she became increasingly successful, not only as a designer but also as an author and social activist. She died in 1971 in New York. ■

American clothing designer Elizabeth Hawes in 1941. AP/WIDE WORLD PHOTOS. REPRODUCED BY PERMISSION.

Introduction

The economic hardships of the worldwide depression of the 1930s eventually undercut Paris's longtime domination of the fashion industry, buoying the efforts of American designers such as Elizabeth Hawes, Charles James, Valentina, Nettie Rosenstein, Muriel King, Claire McCardell, and Hattie Carnegie. After Hawes's Paris debut of her work in 1931, the talent of American designers began to be recognized by the fashion industry and sought after by both status-conscious consumers of expensive, made-to-order clothing and manufacturers of more affordable, ready-to-wear apparel, designed for a mass consumer market.

Hawes's rising popularity among clothing manufacturers put her in an excellent position to begin to influence "that deformed thief," fashion. In 1938, she published *Fashion Is Spinach,* her view of the industry she had taken by storm, arguing in favor of style and comfort over blind adherence to fashion trends.

Hawes's venture into business alliances with manufacturers of ready-made clothing proved unsatisfactory (she severed these partnerships when she discovered her designs being produced in fabrics of poor quality). Yet she remained convinced that demand for ready-to-wear clothing would eventually outpace that of the made-to-order market, even among the socially elite. She was largely correct.

Significance

Hawes spent a lifetime in the fashion industry successfully promoting the ideal of self-expression through clothing designed with good lines and comfort as guiding principles. She believed that true style meant designs with both the requirements of living in a given age and the individual's unique needs in mind. *Fashion Is Spinach* made this argument convincingly, by exposing the essential basis of "fashion," a lifestyle of leisure made possible by a servant class, and by suggesting its inherently false nature, exposed by the Great Depression.

Hawes was passionately nonconformist and, in many ways, ahead of her time. Her vitality and articulate style of writing served her vision well in her own time and ensured its survival into the future. For example, the comfort-oriented American style of the present era, which has even replaced the traditional formality of the business setting, has addressed one of Hawes's great concerns. In 1939, she wrote an entire book, *Men Can Take It,* bemoaning the restrictive nature of business attire.

Primary Source

Fashion Is Spinach [excerpt]

SYNOPSIS: In the first chapter of her autobiography, *Fashion Is Spinach,* Hawes shares her thoughts about the fashion industry. She champions the ideal of timeless "style," which, she says, concerns itself with quality fabrics, good lines, and comfort, while deriding the frantic pace of "fashion," which she deems a "parasite on style." She explores the pros and cons of made-to-order versus ready-to-wear clothing. She also unmasks the concept of "chic."

The Deformed Thief, Fashion

There are only two kinds of women in the world of clothing. One buys her clothes made-to-order, the other buys her clothes ready-made.

The made-to-order lady frequents Molyneux, Lanvin, Paquin, Chanel, in Paris. In New York she is deposited by her chauffeur "on the Plaza," at the door of Bergdorf Goodman, or she threads through the traffic of Forty-ninth Street to Hattie Carnegie, less advantageously placed geographically but equally important where fashion is concerned. She may do her shopping out of the traffic, in a gray house on Sixty-seventh Street, Hawes, Inc., or just hit the edge of the mob at the Savoy-Plaza where Valentina holds sway.

In any case, the made-to-order lady can shop and dress to her entire satisfaction. Thousands of skilled craftsmen and women are ready to sew up her clothes. Tens of designers in London and Paris and New York and Los Angeles will work out her special sketches. Hundreds of salespeople are on tap at all hours of the day to watch over her fittings, advise her what not to buy, send shoppers to find that special color and material which really should be worn in her dining room.

She pays, yes. But it's worth it a thousand times. Her clothes are her own and correspond to her life as she understands it. She may spend hours fitting them, but in the end they are right.

Meanwhile, the ready-made lady shops. She too may want a special color to wear in her dining room. She may find that color after two weeks of hunting, or she may never find it, since very possibly "we are not using it this season." She may find a really warm and sturdy winter coat which will last her for the next six years and only cost $35—or she may discover that the coat she bought last year is not in fashion this year, that the material was, after all, not all wool.

Millions and millions of women go shopping year after year. They are tall and short, fat and thin, gay and depressed. They may clothe their bodies for the simple purpose of keeping warm or not going naked. They may choose their wardrobes with care for wintering in Palm Beach, or going to the races in Ascot. Their first necessary choice is, can they pay enough to get exactly what they want or are they at the mercy of mass production. Can they buy style—or must they buy fashion?

Lanvin and Chanel, Hawes and Valentina, are fundamentally occupied with selling style. The manufacturer and the department store are primarily occupied with selling fashion.

I don't know when the word fashion came into being, but it was an evil day. For thousands of years people got along with something called style and maybe, in another thousand, we'll go back to it.

Style is that thing which, being looked back upon after a century, gives you the fundamental feeling of a certain period in history. Style in Greece in 2000 B.C. was delicate outdoor architecture and the clothes which went with it. Style in the Renaissance was an elaborately carved stone cathedral and rich velvet, gold-trimmed robes. Style doesn't change every month or every year. It only changes as often as there is a real change in the point of view and lives of the people for whom it is produced.

Style in 1937 may give you a functional house and comfortable clothes to wear in it. Style doesn't give a whoop whether your comfortable clothes are red or yellow or blue, or whether your bag matches your shoes. Style gives you shorts for tennis because they are practical. Style takes away the wasp-waisted corset when women get free and active.

If you are in a position to deal with a shop which makes your clothes specially for you, style is what you can have, the right clothes for your life in your epoch, uncompromisingly, at once.

On top of style there has arisen a strange and wonderful creature called fashion. He got started at least as far back as the seventeenth century when a few smart people recognized him for what he was and is. "See'st thou not, I say, what a deformed thief this fashion is?" Mr. Shakespeare demanded in *Much Ado About Nothing.* But nobody paid any attention.

Now we have the advertising agency and the manufacturer, the department store and the fashion writer all here to tell us that the past, present, and future of clothing depends on fashion, ceaselessly changing.

Manufacturing clothes is the second largest business in the United States. Not one-half of one percent of the population can have its clothing made to order—or wants to for that matter.

This means that a large portion of $2,656,242,000 changes hands annually under the eye of that thief, fashion, who becomes more and more deformed with practice. Fashion is a parasite on style. Without style, he wouldn't exist, but what he does to it is nobody's business.

Fashion is that horrid little man with an evil eye who tells you that your last winter's coat may be in perfect physical condition, but you can't wear it. You can't wear it because it has a belt and this year "we are not showing belts."

Fashion gets up those perfectly ghastly ideas, such as accessories should match, and proceeds to give you shoes, gloves, bag, and hat all in the same hideous shade of kelly green which he insists is chic this season whether it turns you yellow or not. Fashion is apt to insist one year that you are nobody if you wear flat heels, and then turn right around and throw thousands of them in your face.

Fashion persuades millions of women that comfort and good lines are not all they should ask in clothes. . . .

We try very hard to have chic in America, but the ground is not fertile. We tried to substitute an English word, "smart." R. H. Macy took it right into the heart of our culture and decided it was "smart to be thrifty." That fixed that word. Nobody who knows anything about chic thinks you can have it and be thrifty. Nobody has ever seen a chic woman in thrifty $29.50 clothes.

If you are chic, you have your hair done every day or two. Your nails are perfect. Your stockings scarcely last an evening. Your shoes are impeccable. Your jewelry is real and expensive. Your clothes are made to order and to fit. They are *your* clothes made in your colors and not one of a thousand machine-made copies. Your hats are *your* hats with the brims exactly the right width and bend.

Chic is a combination of style and fashion. To be really chic, a woman must have positive style, a positive way of living and acting and looking which is her own. To this she adds those endless trips to the hairdresser, facial lady, shoemaker, and dressmaker. With infallible taste for her own problems, she chooses what is in her style and fashionable at the same time. If her style is not quite the fashion, the chic woman effects a compromise with the edge on the fashionable side.

Being chic was not only created "on the Continent" but it fundamentally can only flourish in that unhurried atmosphere. It takes a background of leisured people with secure bankrolls who don't have or want to worry about what's going on at the office, to produce chic and keep it alive. It takes large houses, in town and in country, with plenty of servants who run everything smoothly, without requiring too many orders.

Further Resources

BOOKS

Hawes, Elizabeth. *Men Can Take It.* New York: Random House, 1939.

———. *It's Still Spinach.* Boston: Little, Brown, 1954.

Lambert, Eleanor. *The World of Fashion: People, Places, Resources.* New York: R. R. Bowker, 1976.

Mahoney, Patrick R. "Elizabeth Hawes.'' In *Notable American Women: A Biographical Dictionary.* New York: Radcliffe Institute for Advanced Study and Harvard University Press, 1980.

Martin, Richard, ed. *Contemporary Fashion.* Detroit: St. James Press, 1995.

Milbank, Caroline Rennolds. *New York Fashion: The Evolution of American Style.* New York: Harry A. Abrams, 1989.

O'Hara, Georgina. *The Encyclopedia of Fashion.* New York: Harry A. Abrams, 1986.

PERIODICALS

Obituary of Elizabeth Hawes. *The New York Times,* September 8, 1971.

WEBSITES

"Elizabeth Hawes 1903–1971." *Very.* Available online at http://www.upandco.com/hawes.html; website home page: http://www.upandco.com (accessed April 20, 2003).

Magic Motorways

Nonfiction work, Illustrations

By: Norman Bel Geddes

Date: 1940

Source: Bel Geddes, Norman. *Magic Motorways.* New York: Random House, 1940, 3–4, 6, 9, 10, 41, 266, 267, 276–278, 280, 283, 287–288, 294–295.

About the Author: Norman Bel Geddes (1893–1958) lived to see the complete revolution in transportation effected by the automobile. A highly successful theatrical and industrial designer, he personified the balance between art and science espoused by such visionaries as Walter Gropius and Frank Lloyd Wright. He died in New York in 1958. ■

Introduction

The automobile was by far the most popular mode of transportation among Americans by 1930 and was already changing the style and pace of American life. The nation's system of roadways, however, did not keep pace with the automobile's increasing popularity and use. The consequent chaos of American roadways prompted Norman Bel Geddes to design and produce General Motors' "Futurama" exhibit, which showcased a plan for a national motorway system for the 1939 New York World's Fair. In 1940, he published *Magic Motorways,* a detailed discussion of this plan with photographs and diagrams.

Arguing that the implementation of a national motorway system was an urgent issue, Bel Geddes pointed to the overwhelmingly positive responses of visitors to

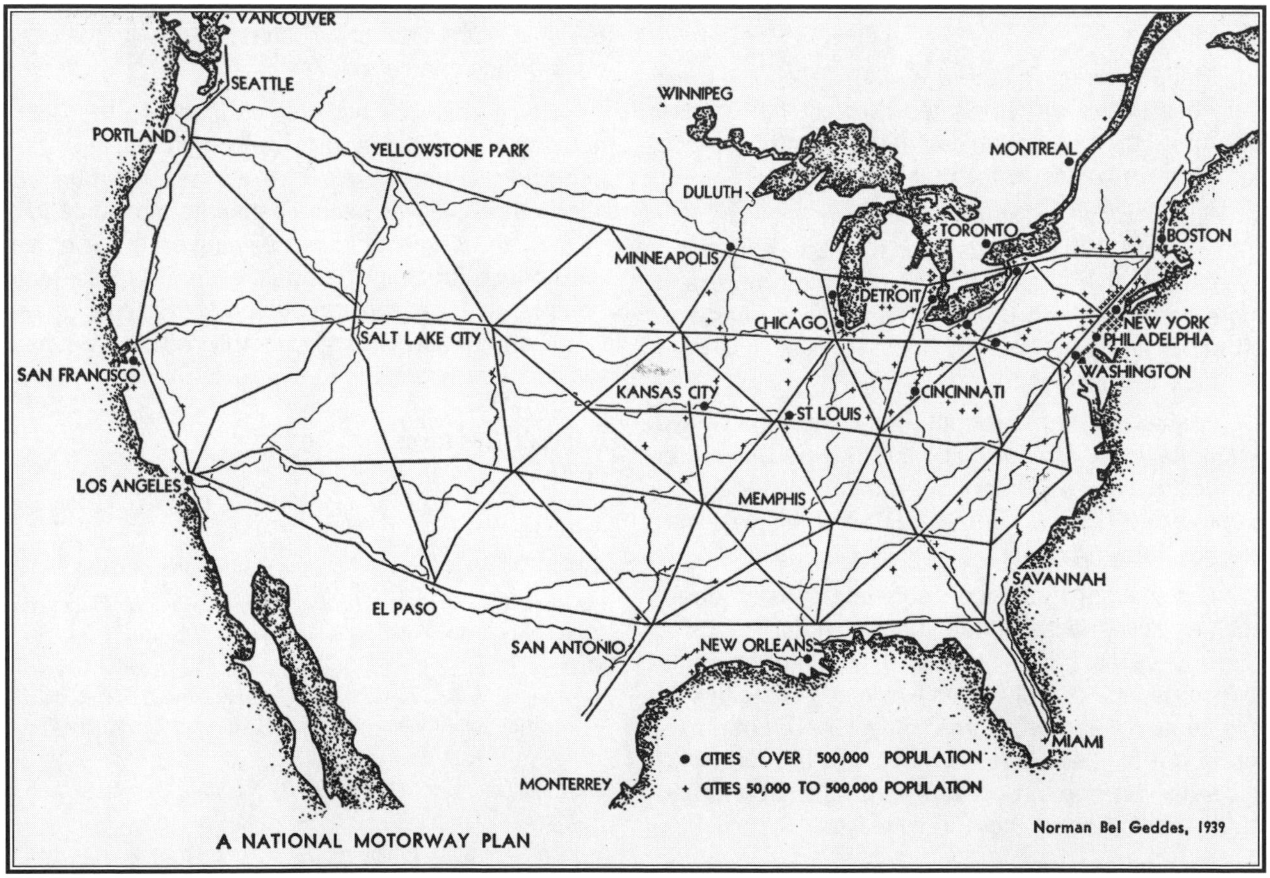

Primary Source

Magic Motorways: Illustration

SYNOPSIS: This map, included in Norman Bel Geddes' *Magic Motorways,* illustrates his plan for a national motorway, with lines for roads and circles and plus signs for cities. Bel Geddes' plan was part of the Futurama exhibit at the 1939 New York World's Fair. BOOK ILLUSTRATION FROM *MAGIC MOTORWAYS.* ILLUSTRATION BY NORMAN BEL GEDDES.

the Futurama exhibit, most of whom were all too familiar with the daily hassles of intersectional jams, congested bottlenecks, dangerous night driving, and the like. The exhibit was "a large-scale model, representing almost every type of terrain in America and illustrating how a motorway system may be laid down over the entire country—across mountains, over rivers and lakes, through cities and past towns—never deviating from a direct course and always adhering to the four basic principles of highway design: safety, comfort, speed, and economy." Bel Geddes also believed a free-flowing movement of people and goods nationwide was an essential requirement of modern living and prosperity.

Significance

The national motorway system Bel Geddes proposed in *Magic Motorways* undoubtedly influenced the designers of our present-day interstate highway system which makes it possible to travel from coast to coast, as well as from the Canadian to the Mexican borders, virtually unhindered by traffic congestion. This possible mobility, for citizens of all economic classes, since the implementation of Bel Geddes' ideas has exploded ancient restrictions on human interaction, especially commerce.

Bel Geddes' work also influenced the construction of recreational parkways, which were begun in earnest in the mid-1930s and largely funded by federal work programs. After a 1934 report of the Natural Resources Board of the National Park Service calculated that more than half of all highway traffic in 1933 was recreational, Congress began to authorize construction of national parkways. The first two projects were The Blue Ridge Parkway, connecting the Great Smoky Mountains and Shenandoah National Parks through the mountains of western Virginia and North Carolina, and The Natchez Trace Parkway, a five-hundred-mile, historically significant roadway connecting Nashville, Tennessee, and Natchez, Mississippi. Such roadways covered hundreds of miles of scenic and historical rural landscapes. A national parkway system, which coordinated all proposals, reviews, and projects, was in place by 1939.

Primary Source

Magic Motorways [excerpt]

SYNOPSIS: In *Magic Motorways,* Bel Geddes published illustrated details of the national motorway system he proposed, arguing that the speedy construction of such a system was not only imperative from the standpoint of convenience and safety, but was especially essential to the nation's economic structure. He anticipated far-reaching, positive consequences of such a system: expanded distribution routes, new communities, shifts in population centers, and, ultimately, greater human interchange resulting in sharing of mindset and culture. Along with this excerpt from his book are images of his designs and a map of the motorway plan he envisioned, also included in the book's original publication.

Five million people saw the Futurama of the General Motors Highways and Horizons Exhibit at the New York World's Fair during the summer of 1939. In long queues that often stretched more than a mile, from 5,000 to 15,000 men, women, and children at a time, stood, all day long every day, under the hot sun and in the rain, waiting more than an hour for their turn to get a sixteen-minute glimpse at the motorways of the world of tomorrow. There have been hit shows and sporting events in the past which had waiting lines for a few days, but never before had there been a line as long as this, renewing itself continuously, month after month, as there was every day at the Fair.

The people who conduct polls to find out why other people do things, and the editorial writers, newspaper men, and columnists who report daily on the doings of the human race, all had their theory as to why the Futurama was the most popular show of any Fair in history. And most of them agreed that the explanation was really very simple: All of these thousands of people who stood in line ride in motor cars and therefore are harassed by the daily task of getting from one place to another, by the nuisances of intersectional jams, narrow, congested bottlenecks, dangerous night driving, annoying policemen's whistles, honking horns, blinking traffic lights, confusing highway signs, and irritating traffic regulations; they are appalled by the daily toll of highway accidents and deaths; and they are eager to find a sensible way out of this planless, suicidal mess. The Futurama gave them a dramatic and graphic solution to a problem which they all faced.

Masses of people can never find a solution to a problem until they are shown the way. Each unit of the mass may have a knowledge of the problem, and each may have his own solution, but until mass opinion is crystallized, brought into focus and made articulate, it amounts to nothing but vague grumbling. One of the best ways to make a solution understandable to everybody is to make it visual, to dramatize it. The Futurama did just this: it was a visual dramatization of a solution to the complex tangle of American roadways. . . .

Much of the initial appeal of the Futurama was due to its imaginative quality. But the reason that its popularity never diminished was that its boldness

Primary Source

Magic Motorways: Illustration

SYNOPSIS: This model of the city of "Futurama" was displayed at the 1939 New York World's Fair. It was designed by Norman Bel Geddes to depict his vision of a city of 1960, and illustrated Geddes' belief that a national motorway would have a significant impact on the country. MODEL OF THE CITY "FUTURAMA," DEPICTING CITY DESIGN FOR 1960, AT NEW YORK WORLD'S FAIR OF 1939, DESIGNED BY NORMAN BEL GEDDES, FOR GENERAL MOTORS, PHOTOGRAPH BY RICHARD GARRISON.

was based on soundness. The plan it presented appealed to the practical engineer as much as to the idle daydreamer. The motorways which it featured were not only desirable, but practical.

As each spectator rode around the model in his comfortable, upholstered armchair, he listened to a description of it in a voice which came from a small speaker built into the back of the chair. This recorded description synchronized with the movement of the chairs and explained the main features of what was passing before the spectator's eyes. It directed his attention to the great arterial highways which were segregated into different speed lanes and which looked so different from the roads of today. It pointed out the overpasses, high-speed intersections and wide bridges over which tear-drop motor cars whisked by at a hundred miles an hour. It commented in passing on the surrounding scenery, the planned cities, decentralized communities, and experimental farms. But it did not describe in detail how any of this was to be accomplished. It did not explain how the highway system worked. It could not dwell at length on any specific points of interest because of the short time available. . . .

In designing the Futurama, we reproduced actual sections of the country—Wyoming, Pennsylvania, California, Missouri, New York, Idaho, Virginia—combining them into a continuous terrain. We used actual American cities—St. Louis, Council Bluffs, Reading, New Bedford, Concord, Rutland, Omaha, Colorado Springs—projecting them twenty years ahead. And we of course took already existing highways into account, making use of their most advanced features and, at the same time, projecting them also twenty years ahead. . . .

The Motorway System as visualized in the Futurama and described in this book has been arbitrarily dated ahead to 1960—twenty years from now.

But it could be built today. It is not too large a job for a generation which has replaced the plodding horse and buggy with the swift-moving automobile, which has grown wings and spanned the world with them, which has built skyscrapers a thousand feet high. Modern engineering is capable of magnificent accomplishments.

Already the automobile has done great things for people. It has taken man out beyond the small confines of the world in which he used to live. Distant communities have been brought closer together. Throughout all recorded history, man has made repeated efforts to reach out farther and to communicate with other men more easily and quickly, and these efforts have reached the climax of their success in the twentieth century. This increasing freedom of movement makes possible a magnificently full, rich life for the people of our time. A free-flowing movement of people and goods across our nation is a requirement of modern living and prosperity. . . .

The aim of highway engineers in the twentieth century should be to construct motorways instead of highways. It is an important task, and an inspiring one. It means pioneering, traveling over uncharted territory instead of following in the well-worn paths which tradition has laid down. But just as the horse and buggy have been replaced by the motor car, so must the highway be replaced by the motorway. . . .

The scope of men's lives has always been determined to a great extent by their facilities for movement. Without a highway system, for example, men were limited in their reach to an area of about 50 miles around them. Their whole point of view, their form of statehood, their trade and their philosophy differed entirely from that of men who were able to move out of their valleys and widen their horizon. . . .

Our generation has seen a basic revolution in transportation. It has taken thirty years. We stand now at the point where this major change has been completed. What is done in transportation in the future will consist of adaptations of experiments already proven, or of further developments in means that already exist. In this respect, our generation is at a particular vantage point. It can look back upon a vast task that has just been accomplished. It can look ahead and foresee to some extent the natural results of all this—the effects that such a change will have on future generations, on our grandchildren.

In 1960, if transportation in America continues to advance as it has to date, the average person will be flying about in a small mosquito plane, a roadster of the air. The average car will be smaller, safer, and more economical. Trains will be shorter, lighter, maintaining more frequent schedules. . . .

On the accompanying map such a Motorway Plan has been worked out. This plan is based on a relatively brief, preliminary study. But, although it is necessarily tentative, it is a key to a final comprehensive plan. Its design sums up the basic requirements of such a plan.

This map shows the country's principal population centers. Large black dots represent the larger cities, and cities with smaller population are shown as stars. Every city in the country with a population of 50,000 or over is indicated. The heavy lines represent the routes of the National Motorway System. Fine lines show the tentatively proposed superhighways of the Federal Bureau of Public Roads, for purposes of comparison. The scale on this map is so small that a pinpoint represents a distance of approximately ten miles. Because of this, only general routes are shown. Motorways won't really converge at the sudden angles which the map suggests. They will overpass and underpass each other, using wide-flowing developments of present-day cloverleafs; their traffic streams in the opposite direction will be completely separated, and individual lanes in the same direction will be segregated by separators. Although on the map they look like solid lines shooting across the country, actually they are complicated mechanisms which differentiate sharply between through traffic and maneuvering traffic, and which provide automatically safe means for entering and leaving the motorways. Their lanes are designed for three separate and constant speeds of 50, 75, and 100 miles an hour. Their grades are constant, never excessive. Their curving radii are constant, and always generous. All over the United States, the motorways are uniform and function in exactly the same way. . . .

The result of this National Motorway System is that traffic by car, bus, and truck can move swiftly, safely, comfortably, and economically over direct rights of way with a sufficient number of lanes to take care of the corresponding volume of traffic. This constitutes a new form of transportation. The principles behind it go beyond the immediate aim of linking sections of the country in the most direct and economical fashion. . . .

Road building must be viewed in an entirely different light than it has been up to now. It has to be considered as something far more than merely providing the means for getting people from one place

Primary Source

Magic Motorways: Illustration

SYNOPSIS: The entrance to General Motor's "Futurama" exhibit at the 1939 New York World's Fair. The wildly popular exhibit depicted a vision of a technologically advanced America of 1960 and was included in Bel Geddes' 1940 book *Magic Motorways.* ENTRANCE TO GENERAL MOTOR'S EXHIBIT AT NEW YORK WORLD'S FAIR, IN 1939, PHOTOGRAPH BY RICHARD GARRISON.

to the next. The motorways must be considered as an essential part of the entire economic system of the country. The problem of traffic flow is only a step removed from the problems of resources, conservation, national defense, education, and unemployment. As the American road builder of the future becomes a planner, he will grow into a key individual who is responsible to the whole nation. . . .

It is standard practice among highway engineers to calculate in figures the results—chiefly in terms of economies in time and fuel consumption—that will come from the building of a new road. With this motorway, the problem is the same only stepped up a thousandfold. The forecasting here rises to a very special plane. For these motorways, when added up together, do not amount to just so many thousand miles of new road. The principles behind their construction are those of freeing traffic and opening up land. What that amounts to isn't just "extension" or "improvement," but actually a new form of transportation.

It has been said before that every new form of transportation is, almost by definition, revolutionary. The effects of revolutions are felt through the entire economy. They may be shocks. They are also likely to be vast advances.

The coming of the automobile itself had revolutionary effects upon American industry. A vast new group of manufacturers came into existence. Millions of men and women found new employment. An undreamed-of increase took place in the production of related industries. Original and ingenious manufacturing methods were devised to fulfill newly created needs. By 1939, it was found that every fifth dollar spent in retail business represented purchases of or for automobiles. An even more impressive indication of the economic value of the automobile was that one out of every seven employed persons in the country was engaged in the motor transport field. Even the competing railroads benefited from the motor industry, carrying one carload of automotive equipment out of every seven carloads of freight.

These were some of the immediate effects of one new industry. The effects of a great motorway system must be calculated on an even broader basis. That the opening of new traffic arteries and the speeding-up of truck and passenger transport will result in greater use of automobiles and of the products that serve them is unquestionable. These new roads are not to be laid down for the motor car alone. As the national motorway system is built, distribution is also built. Travel radius increases. Travel habits are changed. Decentralized communities come into existence, population trends are changed. Cities tend to become centers for working, the country districts centers for living. . . .

This freedom of movement, this opening up of what is congested, this discarding of what is obsolete all add up to one thing: *interchange*—interchange of people, places, ways of life, and therefore modes of thought. The American nation is not going to be able to solve the major problems facing it until its people of various classes and regions—the workers, the intellectuals, the farmers, the business men—get to know each other better and to understand each other's problems.

An America in which people are free, not in a rhetorical sense, but in the very realistic sense of being freed from congestion, waste and blight—free to move out on good roads to decent abodes of life—free to travel over routes whose very sight and feel give a lift to the heart—that is an America whose inner changes may far transcend the alterations on the surface. If city dweller can know the land, Easterner know Westerner, the man who has lived among mountains know harbors and the sea, then horizons will be broadened, individual lives will grow. Along with the interchange, there will be plenty of diversity. And diversity—whether racial or geographic—is a basic heritage of America. And out of that very interchange of diversity will come another thing—something which in this era of misunderstanding and conflict and war may be the most essential thing of all. Our country was founded on it. We call it *unity.* It is not a unity imposed from above, such as exists under dictatorship, but a unity based on freedom and understanding.

Further Resources

BOOKS

Bel Geddes, Norman. *Miracle in the Evening.* W. Kelley, ed. Garden City, N.Y.: Doubleday, 1960.

Gelernter, David. *1939: The Lost World of the Fair.* New York: Free Press, 1995.

Unrau, Harlan D., and G. Frank Williss. *Administrative History: Expansion of the National Park Service in the 1930s.* Denver: National Park Service, 1983.

PERIODICALS

Bel Geddes, Norman. "Streamlining." *Atlantic Monthly,* November 1934.

Cogdell, Christina. "The Futurama Recontextualized: Norman Bel Geddes's Eugenic 'World of Tomorrow.'" *American Quarterly,* June 2000.

Strawn, Arthur. "Norman Bel Geddes." *The Outlook,* February 12, 1930.

Talking Through My Hats

Autobiography

By: Lilly Daché

Date: 1946

Source: Daché, Lilly. *Talking Through My Hats.* Dorothy Roe Lewis, ed. New York: Coward-McCann, 1946, 3–11, 13.

About the Author: Lilly Daché (1913–1989) was born in Beiles, France, and immigrated to America in 1924. By the mid-1930s, she had established herself as the milliner (hat de-

Lilly Daché was one of America's leading milliners (hat designers) during a time when hats were still a part of everyday apparel. **AP/WIDE WORLD PHOTOS. REPRODUCED BY PERMISSION.**

signer) of choice among wealthy American patrons from New York to Hollywood. She also designed for manufacturers, through whom her unique and flamboyant designs were marketed around the world. She died in Louveciennes, France, in 1989. ■

Introduction

Lilly Daché arrived in the United States during the 1920s, when it seemed that almost anything was possible. Her unique perspective and intuitive skill enabled her to rise to wealth and fame by taking full advantage of the fashion trends of the period. She, John Fredericks, and Sally Victor dominated the millinery industry of the period as New York's "Big Three." It was a time when millinery products carried far more weight in the fashion world than clothing.

Daché's products seem to have been an outgrowth of her own flamboyant personality. Her designs ran the gamut, from elegant simplicity to Carmen Miranda's outrageous turbans of birds and fruit. Daché was also unique in her approach to her clientele, which included individuals as well as manufacturers. She excelled at making her clients feel extremely special and important. She capitalized on Hollywood's heyday by designing her New York headquarters with the peculiar whims of the famous and pampered in mind: a silver fitting room for brunettes, a gold one for blondes. Wholesale buyers completed orders with Daché herself, draped in a leopard-skin jacket with matching slippers, seated on a leopard-skin divan in a circular room lined in pink satin.

Her marketing approach coupled with brilliant designs led to her company's enormous success. She operated numerous shops around the country, and her products, which eventually included clothing and perfumes, sold around the world. She published *Talking Through My Hats* in 1946 to reflect upon and share not only the story of her meteoric rise within the fashion industry, but also insights she had gained along the way.

Significance

The popularity of millinery was actually in its last phase during Daché's lifetime. In fact, the movement to going hatless had already begun. Always in tune with her market, she responded to this trend with her popular half-hat, which may very well have postponed the disappearance of the hat by a decade or two. Daché's ability to design courageously while also keeping a finger on the pulse of the consumer secured her position within the industry. Her skill at catering to the multitude without sacrificing originality and authenticity serves as a model worth studying.

Her autobiography, *Talking Through My Hats,* a highly readable account of her "rags to riches" experience, resounded with those who read it. She managed to communicate both the dazzling personality she had become and the down-to-earth woman who remembered her common origins.

Daché's designs seem to have passed the test of time. To this day, they remain popular with those who enjoy millinery and are highly valued as vintage collectibles.

Primary Source

Talking Through My Hats [excerpt]

SYNOPSIS: In the first chapter of *Talking Through My Hats,* Daché shares glimpses of the dizzying pace of the successful millinery business she created and of herself at work in the glamorous surroundings of her famous headquarters on Park Avenue in New York City.

Chapter 1: Keep This Under Your Hat

It all began one day in France when my mother slapped my hands and said:

"Lilly, you are a bad girl! You have cut up my best blouse to make a hat!"

That was when I was six, and the world stretched no farther than my father's fields in southern France. Now my world reaches from Park Avenue to the Champs Elysées, from Hollywood to Honolulu, Cairo, Ceylon, London—and still I am making hats.

So many hats I have made, it gives me a fright sometimes to think of them, and what a pile they would make—much higher than the Eiffel Tower, I am sure. Much higher than the Empire State Building. Much higher than my dreams when I was six.

Then I think of the women who have bought my hats. Some have been duchesses and some have been queens. Some have been famous actresses and some have been no better than they should be. Some have been great ladies of society, and some have been shopgirls and stenographers, not famous at all. These last I like to think of best, because a hat to them was worth going without lunches for a month.

So many hats. So many women. They would make a picture story of our times.

Marion Davies in a 1925 cloche, pulled down over the ears. That was New York in the days of lovely nonsense, ticker tape, parades, speak-easies, Mayor Walker, Lindbergh, Gertrude Ederle. Carole Lombard in a dashing big beret, pulled down over one eye. That was Hollywood in the thirties. Clark Gable, neon lights, full-dress openings, autographs, diaries.

Believe me, I have made many hats. Perhaps I have made more hats than any other one woman in the world. And with each hat is a story. It is the story of the woman who wore the hat, and why she bought it; the people she loved and the people she hated; the places she went and the things that happened to her, perhaps because of the hat.

You see, a woman's hat is close to her heart, though she wears it on her head. It is her way of saying to the world: "See, this is what I am like!" Or— "This is how I should like to be."

These things I think about sometimes in bed, in the mornings, when I am dictating letters to my secretary with one half my mind and with the other half designing a new hat. The bed is piled high with straw and flowers and ribbon and feathers. My assistant designers come in and out, bringing samples of this and that. My cook wants to know how many for dinner. My manager wants to know the day's schedules for the workrooms. My secretary wants to know how I am going to keep three appointments all at one o'clock.

It is a madhouse, really. But it is the most quiet spot in this building of mine which is a monument to hats.

I put a penny in the cornerstone when it was built, and watched it go up brick by brick, satin walls, circular rooms, leopard-skin upholstery and all. I picked the site carefully—just off Park Avenue and far enough uptown to be smart, near enough to be handy. On top of it I had the builders put a penthouse, so that I could live with my hats. And so I do.

The seven lower floors are given over to workrooms, showrooms, fitting rooms, reception rooms, even a perfume department. Here my 150 milliners turn out hats that are shipped all over the world, and make women happy in strange corners of the earth. Here my models parade in the newest creations of the season, and many customers all loaded with diamonds and furs order hats a dozen at a time.

My name is written big and bold, in my husband's handwriting, on the mat in front of the big glass doors of my building, on the millions of brown and cream hatboxes in the storerooms, on the satin perfume packages. It is not my own signature, as most people think, because I prefer the way my husband writes my name. It is much more dashing than my own handwriting. Perhaps he puts in it all the things he sees in me, which I myself cannot see.

When I look at my name in front of the door I know that this is mine—a house that is made of hats. Sometimes I walk around that so-elegant circular room that is the salon, all mirrors, with the silver fitting room for brunette celebrities and the gold fitting room for blondes, and I have to go out front to look at that name again, to be sure all this is really mine.

Sometimes I go on the wholesale floor, where all the buyers come to pick hats for stores in many places. I sit on my leopard-skin divan and I look at the round jewel box of a fitting room, with all the walls padded in tufted pink satin, and I say to myself:

"If sometime things get to be all too much, at least I'll have a beautiful padded cell!"

It is a great comfort, that pink satin padded room. That's really why I had it built—so I could bump my head in comfort.

You might think that making hats would be a ladylike and very calm business, with none of the hysterics that can be expected in someplace like the Stock Exchange, for instance. But in the season, my place is something you would not believe unless you could come and see for yourself what goes on.

On one floor, customers from Park Avenue and Broadway and Hollywood, each demanding the most beautiful hat in the world. On another floor, crowds of wholesale buyers ordering their spring or fall lines. In the workrooms, my girls going crazy trying to fill the orders faster and faster. Running back and forth between them all, me, completely mad. It is at times like these that I tear my hair, and the satin padded cell comes in handy.

Any morning, in or out of season, the telephone starts before I have my first cup of coffee.

It is the duchess wanting six hats for the South, wanting bags to match, wanting them now. . . . It is my manager saying Miss Loretta Young doesn't like the roses on her new turban because it makes her feel like Mrs. Miniver. . . . It is Maria Montez calling from the coast, to say she wants a wicked hat by air mail—that's what she *says*—wicked. . . . It's my secretary saying the buyer from Magnin's is on the way. . . . I have to see the models for my opening—six blondes, six brunettes. . . . It is my designer saying what kind of a hat should she make for Mrs. Vanderpoof, who has just been to see her astrologer and says it must be designed around the sign of Taurus. After all, says my designer, a bull just doesn't belong on a hat. . . .

My shoppers say there is a shortage of Tiger Lilly Pink ribbon in the market, and that the new felt is no good—it melted when the countess wore it out in the rain. . . .

I try to be calm in the middle of all this. I try to sip my coffee like a lady, and settle each thing as it comes, one at a time.

I say tell the countess next time she should take an umbrella. . . . I say all right, tell Miss Young she can have feathers instead of roses, and look like a chicken. . . . I say to Maria— "But darling, on you anything would look wicked!"

I tell myself that I cannot stand all this a minute longer. I say it is too much for any one woman. And then I think how bored I would be without it, and I admit, very quietly to myself, that I love it.

My day always begins with this "bedline," and there is a parade through my bedroom all morning of my secretaries, my milliners, my masseuse, my manager, even sometimes buyers.

I try to do as much work as possible in bed, as this is the only way I can conserve my energies. Most of my hats are designed in bed, my letters are dictated there, and often I buy materials from my bed, as manufacturers bring in their wares.

I suppose it would look strange to someone who did not know me to look in on this penthouse bedroom most any morning and see me sitting up in my bed, with a leopard-skin rug over my knees, a lacy bed jacket over my shoulders and my newest hat creation on my head, dictating to my secretary on one hand, consulting my designers on the other, sorting through piles of straw and lace and feathers and perhaps having a massage.

About eleven o'clock I usually go down to the workrooms. Always I used to wear leopard-skin slippers with bells on them, so that the girls would know when I was coming. For girls will be girls, you know, and I do not want to catch them in mischief.

Now I have given up the bells, but I always wear many jangling bracelets, and these serve the same purpose.

Up here in my skytop bedroom I can look out over this city that I love. On the east I can see the tall apartments of the rich, and far below the doormen looking like toy soldiers. On the west I can see Fifth Avenue and Central Park and the big green buses, like lumbering beetles.

At night I can see the lights of Broadway, and it is always as thrilling to me as it was when I first saw it, more than twenty years ago.

I live in a kind of stage setting most of the time, but underneath I am not like that. The setting—that is good business. I want to be honest, and so I must tell you that this building of chromium and pink satin and mirrors, of leopard skins and gold, is a sort of showcase for myself as well as for my hats.

My advisers have told me that I must live up to my legend. It would never do, they say, for Lilly Daché to look like a frump, or to have dull, drab things about her.

It is maybe fortunate that I do not like drab things anyway. I like bright colors around me always. Even when I do up my hair on rags, to curl it, I don't like to use just torn pieces of white rag, as is customary. It isn't decorative. Instead, I use bright pieces of yarn in many colors, and when I have finished I have what looks like a gay new hairdo—or even a new hat.

A friend of mine came upon me in the garden, at my home in the country one weekend, when I was wearing my yarn "curlers." She exclaimed:

"Why, Lilly! What a gay new hairdo!"

When I explained that it was only my way of doing my hair up on rags, she said:

"Nobody else in the world would have thought of that but you. I guess it's the artist in you."

It is true that I do not like to look ugly, even when I am working, or curling my hair. I like to work in my designing rooms in brilliant silk pinafores of shocking pink or green, worn over a plain black dress.

I like to have my hair, which is still dark auburn and very thick, done high and sleek, and I like to wear my own most sensational hats. I have been known to take a bath wearing a hat—at times it does something for my morale.

I like beautiful shoes in gay colors, with thick platforms and high heels. I like splashy jewelry that clinks when I walk, and I like my earrings big. I like green stones, like jade and emeralds, to match my green eyes.

All this is for five days a week, when I am being Lilly Daché, milliner de luxe.

But on weekends when I go to the country with my husband, I am Mrs. Jean Despres, a good wife. And then I can relax in a sweater and an old pair of slacks, and enjoy life.

Which of these is the real me I do not know. Perhaps it takes both to make me a whole person.

My husband says I am a dozen women rolled into one. If I were only one, perhaps he would not like me. If I can be a dozen, perhaps he will never want to look for more variety.

When I am in the country, I love to dig in the earth, and I have as much pride in a beautiful garden as I do in a successful hat collection. I belong to the garden club and the Red Cross, and every Sunday morning I go to mass at the little village church with its white spire like a finger pointing to Heaven. I scold the butcher and the grocer like any housewife. My husband and I plan great things for our farm, and worry over the rock garden. The peace I store up on these week ends is enough to take me through all the mad week in town.

Please do not think from this that I do not like my town life. It is just that I need the breathing spell between. Sometimes I have asked myself if I would rather make a beautiful hat or grow a perfect rose, and in all truth I cannot tell. This I know—the hats pay better.

And for every hat there is a woman to wear it, and for every woman there is a story. . . .

What's in a hat? A great deal besides so much straw or felt and so much trimming. Out of a hat have come love, success, a thousand adventures and a million friends for a frightened French girl who landed in New York in 1924 with $13 in borrowed money and no job. Out of a hat have come a worldwide business, a skyscraper building, and a certain fame.

Further Resources

BOOKS

Calasibetta, Charlotte. *Fairchild's Dictionary of Fashion.* New York: Fairchild Publications, 1975.

Daché, Lilly. *Lilly Daché's Glamour Book.* Philadelphia: J. B. Lippincott, 1956.

McDowell, Colin. *Hats: Status, Style and Glamour.* London: Thames & Hudson, 1992.

Morris, Bernadine, and Barbara Walz. *The Fashion Makers.* New York: Random House, 1978.

PERIODICALS

"Lilly Daché." *Current Biography,* July 1941.

"1940 Design Prizes Awarded to Four." *The New York Times,* April 30, 1941, 15.

Edward G. Budd Jr.'s Address to the Newcomen Society of England, January 16, 1950

Speech

By: Edward G. Budd, Jr.

Date: January 26, 1950

Source: Budd, Edward G., Jr. Address to the Newcomen Society of England, January 26, 1950. Reprinted in Budd, Edward G., Jr. *Edward G. Budd (1870–1946): "Father of the Streamliners" and the Budd Company.* New York: The Newcomen Society in North America, 1950, 18–19.

About the Author: Edward G. Budd, Jr. (1902–), was born in Philadelphia on March 23, 1902. Upon his graduation from Wesleyan University in 1923, he began work as an apprenticed operation worker for the Edward G. Budd Company, founded by his father, Edward Budd, Sr. He worked for Citroën, in Paris from 1925 to 1926, then returned to his father's employ in 1927. He was named vice-president and general manager of the Budd Company in 1934; executive vice-president in 1946; and president, upon his father's death, the same year. The American Society of Mechanical Engineers awarded Budd, Jr. their medal for "eminently distinguished engineering achievement" in 1944. He was also inducted into the Automotive Hall of Fame in 1985. ■

Introduction

Late nineteenth- and early twentieth-century experimentation had led to the development of new iron-working techniques—blasting molten iron with oxygen, reducing its impurities and carbon content—that produced a stronger, lighter, and more corrosion-resistant metal: steel. Adding other metals such as gold, tungsten, and chromium to steel both enhanced the metal's resistance to corrosion and strengthened the final product. Experimentation with alloy steels led to the discovery of a certain combination of chromium and carbon that produced a new form of steel. Called "stainless steel," this new steel was remarkably light, yet incredibly durable.

Industrialists quickly began to develop a wide variety of applications for the use of stainless steel. Edward Budd Sr.'s chief engineer, Col. Earl J. W. Ragsdale, devised a welding method that did not impair the material's structural strength. Using this "shotweld" method, Budd produced the first stainless steel airplane in 1931.

Edward Budd manufactured a stainless steel train, the Zephyr, for demonstration at the 1934 Chicago World's Fair, "A Century of Progress." The Zephyr wowed the crowds with its breathtaking design. Ralph Budd, president of the struggling Chicago Burlington & Quincy Railroad (CB&Q), saw this first Zephyr, as well as a new diesel-electric engine, and commissioned General Motors to build the engine and the Budd Company to manufacture the train. Nine diesel-electric streamliners were built by the Budd Company for the CB&Q (the company manufactured about five hundred such trains altogether) and remained in service until 1960.

Significance

The Zephyr proved to be the most popular passenger train of the 1930s—so popular, in fact, that it inspired an entirely new design trend in all fields of American manufacturing. Everything from modern transportation to household products began to be designed in the "streamline moderne" style. Mike Sarna, curator of the Pioneer Zephyr exhibit at Chicago's Museum of Science and Industry, suggests that the public's fascination with the streamliner is comparable to the wonder with which the first space shuttle was viewed: "The *Zephyr* was science fiction brought to life."

The train was 30 percent lighter than models built of other materials, was stronger and safer, and cost less to operate ($0.34 per mile, compared with $0.64 to operate a steam locomotive). In addition, it was significantly faster. On its first run, from Denver to Chicago on May 26, 1934, the Zephyr traversed 1,015 non-stop miles, averaging 77.5 miles per hour, in thirteen hours and five minutes, breaking the record for a non-stop run. The popular exterior design also inspired Philadelphia architect Paul Phillipe Cret's interior design—light, efficient, and functional—which quickly replaced the popularity of the dark and ornate Pullman cars.

In *Father of the Streamliners,* Budd, Jr., discussed the research and development of the streamliner, as well as his father's philosophy about the importance of transportation to the functioning of American democracy. His ideas were well received by Philadelphia members of the Newcomen Society, an international organization dedicated to the history of material civilization, as expressed in the British-American traditions. The Society published Budd, Jr.'s, comments, some of which follow:

> We have believed that widely available and relatively inexpensive transportation is one of the greatest civilizing forces in our modern Western world. In fact, fast, relatively inexpensive transportation is a characteristic of Western civilization. . . . Without modern transportation, a political unit as large as the United States probably could be governed only by ruthless dictatorship. . . . Perhaps most important of all, from a social standpoint, good and relatively cheap transportation has given the working man a mobility that more nearly approaches the mobility of capital than has ever been true in Man's history . . . he can go to the market that will pay the highest for his services.

The *Pioneer Zephyr* locomotive, circa 1934. Besides being a breakthrough in locomotive technology, the *Zephyr's* streamlined appearance and stainless steel materials had an immediate impact on designers in many fields. © BETTMANN/CORBIS. REPRODUCED BY PERMISSION

Primary Source

Edward G. Budd Jr.'s Address to the Newcomen Society of England, January 26, 1980 [excerpt]

SYNOPSIS: In the following excerpt, Edward G. Budd, Jr. recounts his father's pioneering use of a new form of stainless steel, as well as of a new welding technique required for its use. Both innovations led to many experimental applications (such as wheels, automobile bodies, trucks, and trailers) but ultimately to the modern, all–stainless steel passenger train.

Mr. Budd became aware, in 1928, of the stainless steel called *18-8.* It intrigued him, at first, only as a corrosion-resisting and decorative material. In producing sample lots at the Allegheny Steel Company, in 1932, however, they and we jointly stumbled on the cold-working characteristics of stainless. Thus was discovered a metal of very high strength with sufficient elasticity to permit formation by the use of dies and presses. It seemed that this material lent itself particularly to *moving* structures, where the ratio between the weight and strength was important, and where starting and stopping costs were great. Extensive structural testing proved that weight-strength ratios superior to any hitherto commercially possible could be achieved with stainless steel. Because of the austenitic characteristics of the steel, it was necessary to develop a more accurately controlled method of welding for joining purposes than had hitherto been known. Such a process which the company called *shot welding* was successfully developed by 1933.

On a Depression-bred need was built *the company's railroad car business.* Our particular art of forming and welding light-weight parts into strong structures again found expression in a new product with a new material. After experimentation in many fields, which included windmills, ship structures, chemical equipment, elevators, and airplanes, there finally evolved the belief that the best commercial application for our thinking, as expressed in terms of this marvelous new material, was the railroad passenger car.

■ ■ ■

Although there were earlier attempts, the first successful modern, streamlined, all stainless-steel train, *The Pioneer Zephyr,* delivered in April 1934, started *a revolution* in railway car building that has not yet reached its limits. The railroads were given a car that weighed 30 percent less than those built of other materials, and was stronger and safer, with lower maintenance cost. The new cars had a more beautiful exterior, and initiated an era of new interior decoration.

Although completely interrupted by the war, our car-building business is now 20 percent of our company's sales, and we now are the second largest passenger railroad car builder in the Country.

■ ■ ■

The second half of the 1930 decade, as industry began to emerge from the depths of the Depression, showed satisfactory growth and a return to somewhere near normal profits in our wheel and body business.

Further Resources

BOOKS

DeNevi, Don. *Tragic Train: "The City of San Francisco."* Seattle: Superior, 1977.

Heimburger, Byron, Donald J. Heimburger, and Carl R Byron. *The American Streamliner: Prewar Years.* Forest Park, Ill.: Heimburger House Publishing, 1997.

Welsh, Joe. *Pennsy Streamliners: The Blue Ribbon Fleet.* Waukesha, Wis.: Kalmbach Publishing, 1999.

WEBSITES

"All Aboard the Silver Streak." Museum of Science and Industry. Available online at http://www.msichicago.org/exhibit/zephyr; website home page: http://www.msichicago.org (accessed August 29, 2002).

"Streamliners: America's Lost Trains." American Experience Online. Available online at http://www.pbs.org/wgbh/amex/streamliners; website home page: http://www.pbs.org/wgbh/amex (accessed August 29, 2002).

AUDIO AND VISUAL MEDIA

Trains Unlimited: The American Streamliner. Produced by Greystone Communications for the History Channel, VHS, 1997.

Architecture and Design in the Age of Science

Pamphlet

By: Walter Gropius

Date: June 1952

Source: Gropius, Walter. *Architecture and Design in the Age of Science.* New York: Spiral Press, 1952, 1–3, 4–5, 6–7, 8, 9.

About the Author: Walter Adolf Georg Gropius (1883–1969) was born in Berlin. After studying architecture as an apprentice, he opened his own practice in 1910. He was later appointed to reorganize the Weimar Art School, which he reopened in 1919 as the Staatliches Bauhaus. In 1934, he immigrated to England and later to the United States, where he headed Harvard's Graduate School of Design. He became a U.S. citizen in 1944 and worked in architecture until his death in 1969. ■

Introduction

The "international style" of Walter Gropius and others swept away the previous generation's shallow caricatures of classical styles, in an attempt to give form to the ideal of human freedom in a technological age. Gropius celebrated the machine, especially its ability to free human effort for higher endeavors of thought and action, but argued vigorously for the necessity of a full baptism in the arts to balance the dehumanizing effects of technology. He found the plight of modern man troubling, and his experiences in Nazi Germany (from which he fled) no doubt had shown him the potential evils of modernity. Drawing upon this experience, he tried to demonstrate a path toward a balance between the arts and science.

In practice, this vision took the form of collaborative efforts between business owner, artist, and craftsman to design and build structures that made optimum use of modern construction methods to meet the functional requirements of human existence. Gropius's designs reflect some influence of Frank Lloyd Wright's use of symmetry and horizontal lines. His most significant architectural works represent what came to be defined as the "international style," which attempted to combine the rational and physical with the aesthetic and spiritual, though many critics found this vision forbidding and cold.

Significance

Gropius concluded *Architecture and Design in the Age of Science* by calling for the introduction of building teams composed of engineers, scientists, and contractors, as a new model for architectural design. He believed the goal of such teams should be "common expression," as opposed to "pretentious individualism," with the focus being to accommodate human life. Gropius's ideas about the purpose of architecture have been largely incorporated into modern thought, as much of private residential and public architecture is designed to facilitate human activity and interaction, though in a variety of styles.

Gropius's contributions to American architecture range from the simple grain silo, to the skyline of Manhattan, to designs of mass-housing and open-plan schools, all of which attest to his social concerns. His Siemensstadt Siedlung, a German housing complex, and an English college he designed with Maxwell Fry in 1934 while a refugee in England, are among his greatest European works. The Dessau Bauhaus in Germany is widely regarded as his masterpiece.

Primary Source

Architecture and Design in the Age of Science [excerpt]

SYNOPSIS: In the following excerpts from *Architecture and Design in the Age of Science,* Walter Gropius shares his thoughts about the changes to human existence effected by mechanization. Highly valuing the contributions of technology, he also expresses concern about its dehumanizing effects when the arts—which keep the human spirit alive—are neglected.

When I was a boy my family lived in a city apartment with open gas-jets and coal-heated stoves in each room. There was no electric streetcar, no automobile, no airplane; radio, film, gramophone, X-ray, telephone were nonexistent. The mental climate at that time was still of a more or less static character, rotating around a seemingly unshakable conception of the eternal truths. Everybody was still deeply conscious of the cultural heritage of a few generations ago when society was still of a piece and art and architecture developed organically as legitimate parts of the people's daily life in accordance with the slow growth of civilization.

With the advent of the age of science, with the discovery of the machine, this established form of our society went gradually to pieces. The means outgrew man. The sweeping changes which took place during the last half century of industrial development have achieved a deeper transformation of human life than all of the centuries since Jesus Christ combined. As the great avalanche of progress in science rolled on relentlessly, it left the individual bewildered and unhappy, unable to adjust, and lost in the whirlwind of those changes. Instead of striving for leadership through moral initiative, modern man has developed a kind of Gallup-poll mentality, a mechanistic conception relying on quantity instead of on quality and yielding to expediency instead of building up a new faith.

The vast development of science has thrown us out of balance. Science has overshadowed other components which are indispensable to the harmony of life. This balance must be re-established. What we obviously need is a re-orientation on the cultural level.

In today's universities we keep large departments under the name "Arts and Sciences," but when we scrutinize their activities, we find that science has everything; i.e., full information, complete facilities, and a training that develops individual inventiveness. But what about the Arts? Historical study of poetry and of musical composition, art appreciation and drafting-board architecture substitute for the real art of making poetry, composing music, creating art, and building architecture. This is the century of science; the artist is the forgotten man, almost ridiculed and thought of as a superfluous luxury member of society. Art is considered to be something which was accomplished centuries ago and is now being stored up in our museums from which we may tap as much as is needed. As science is supposed to have all the answers for our predominantly materialistic period, art is doomed to languish. Which so-called civilized nation today honestly promotes creative art as a substantial part of life?

Walter Gropius at his desk at Harvard University, 1937. CORBIS-BETTMANN. REPRODUCED BY PERMISSION.

This disintegrating society needs participation in the arts as an essential counterpart to science and to its atomistic effect on us. Made into an educational discipline—of which the Bauhaus was a beginning—it would lead to the unity of visible manifestations as the very basis of culture, embracing everything from a simple chair to the house of worship. Every one of us has to a greater or lesser degree innate artistic qualities with which to achieve harmony and dynamic equilibrium, if only our educational system would sufficiently emphasize the need for "equipoise" and recognize the necessity of train-

The Bauhaus Machine Shop. Designed by Walter Gropius, the Bauhaus Machine Shop is an excellent example of the international style of architecture that he helped popularize. **THE MUSEUM OF MODERN ART.**

ing head and hand simultaneously on all levels of education from the nursery on. In our era of expediency and mechanization, the predominant educational task is to call forth creative habits; vocational skill should be a by-product only, a matter of course. The student's mind, particularly that of the potential artist or architect will become increasingly inventive when he is guided not only by intellectual but also by practical, sensorial experiences, by a program of "search" rather than "re-search."

We certainly have recognized the essential value of the scientist for the survival of our society, but we are very little aware of the vital importance of the artist or, as we might call him, the creative designer or architect who has to control the visual manifestations of our productive life. . . .

When we analyze the character of the production of this world, we find similar opposites at work in the struggle of the individual versus the mass mind. In contrast to the scientific process of mechanized multiplication by the machine, the artist's work consists of an unprejudiced search for the forms that symbolize the common phenomena of life, which requires him to take an independent, uninhibited view of our whole life process. His work is most essential for a true democracy, for he is the prototype of the whole man. His intuitive qualities are the antidote against overmechanization. If mechanization were an end in itself, it would be an unmitigated calamity, robbing life of its fullness and variety by stunting men into sub-human robotlike automatons. But in the last resort mechanization can have only one purpose: to reduce the individual's physical toil in order that hand and brain may be set free for some higher order of activity. Our problem is to find the right balance and coordination between the artist, the scientist and the businessman, for only together can they create humanized standard products and build with them a harmonious entity of our physical surroundings. . . .

If the aim of true teamwork is to give the best possible service through closest integration of all the factors involved in manufacturing a product, then the professional work of each member of the team is of equal importance for the final result. Consequently, each member must be of equal rank, which makes for the specific technique of teamwork, "implying collaboration and not direction—freedom of initiative, not the impress of authority," as Herbert Read has outlined it. That approach does not exclude the selection of a job captain by the team itself, as the first among equals, whose task it is to control and schedule the processes of integration. The further development of teamwork, I believe, will bring the artist, the architect, back into the fold of the community. This will be decisive for the architecture of the future.

The complete separation of design and execution of buildings, for instance, as it is in force today, is rather artificial and unfortunate if we compare it to the methods of building during the great periods of the past. The changes in means and methods of production and the increase of building industrialization have posed completely new problems. The future architect can solve these problems only by initiating building teams together with the engineer, the scientist, and the contractor. Industrialization did not stop at the threshold of building; . . .

Democratic concepts cannot easily survive the assaults of our increasing mechanization and super-organization, unless a new approach is found which will protect the individual in his struggle against the leveling effect of the mass mind. Collaborating in teams without losing one's identity seems to be a most urgent task lying before the new generation—not only in the field of architecture and design, but in all our endeavors to create an integrated society. . . .

Through such mutual exchange a common language of architecture and design and its individual variations will be formed again, a humanized standard, fitting the whole of our community, but simultaneously satisfying also, by its modifications, the different desires of individuals; an achievement as exemplified in former times by the anonymous harmony and organic growth of a New England town or an Italian village. In short, the inspiration of the coming generation of architects will lead them in the direction of a common expression rather than to pretentious individualism.

The key to its success will be the determination to allow the human element to become the dominant factor. The biological principle must be paramount. Man is to be the focus for all design; then it shall be truly functional.

A new set of esthetics has already emerged from the genuine examples of modern architecture and design, defining the new architectural beauty as the result of a creative fusion between matter and spirit, absorbing both our scientific accomplishments and our new knowledge of man.

Architecture is becoming again an integral part of our life—a thing dynamic, not static. It lives, it changes, it expresses the intangible through the tangible. It brings inert materials to life by relating them to the human being. Thus conceived, its creation is an act of love.

Further Resources

BOOKS

Herdeg, Klaus. *The Decorated Diagram: Harvard Architecture and the Failure of the Bauhaus Legacy.* Cambridge, Mass.: The MIT Press, 1983.

Isaacs, Reginald R. *Gropius: An Illustrated Biography of the Creator of the Bauhaus.* Boston: Little, Brown, 1991.

Packard, Robert T. *Encyclopedia of American Architecture,* 2d ed. New York: McGraw-Hill, 1995.

Sharp, Dennis. *Twentieth Century Architecture: A Visual History.* New York: Facts on File, 1990.

PERIODICALS

Adlow, Dorothy. "Walter Gropius: An Architect Who Has Blazed a Way." *The Christian Science Monitor,* January 21, 1952, 9.

Burns, John Allen, and Deborah Stephen Burns. "The Bauhaus as You've Never Seen It." *American Institute of Architects Journal,* July 1981.

Fry, E. Maxwell. "Walter Gropius." *Architectural Review,* March 1955.

Jencks, Charles. "Gropius, Wright, and the International Fallacy." *Architectural Association Journal,* June 1966.

WEBSITES

"Gropius House." Great Buildings Online. Available online at http://www.greatbuildings.com/buildings/Gropius_House.html; website home page: http://www.greatbuildings.com (accessed August 29, 2002).

Times to Remember

Memoir

By: Rose Fitzgerald Kennedy

Date: 1974

Source: Kennedy, Rose Fitzgerald. *Times to Remember.* Garden City, N.Y.: Doubleday, 1974, 1, 89–90, 95, 186–87.

About the Author: Rose Elizabeth Fitzgerald Kennedy (1890–1995) was born in Boston. The mother of nine children, among them late president John F. Kennedy, she worked tirelessly supporting their political ambitions and public service initiatives, fund-raising for charitable organizations (especially those that helped the mentally challenged), and carefully recording her family's history. A woman of unswerving faith, she was named a papal countess by Pope Pius XII in 1951. She died in 1995 at the age of 104. ■

Introduction

Rose Fitzgerald married Joseph Patrick Kennedy in 1914. Both the Fitzgeralds and the Kennedys had emi-

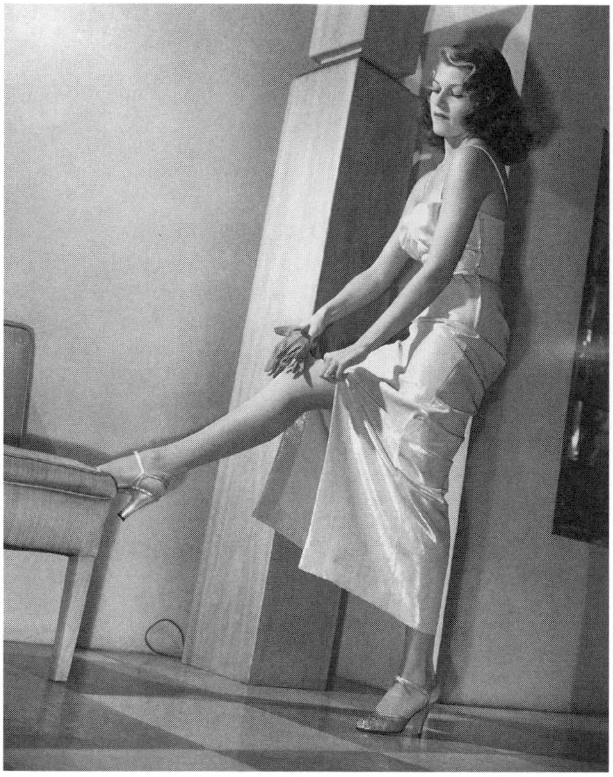

Rita Hayworth in a dress by Hollywood designer Howard Greer. Even during the Great Depression, a fashion industry catered to the rich and famous like Hayworth and Kennedy. THE LIBRARY OF CONGRESS.

grated from the same county in Ireland in the mid-1800s. The two families rose from poverty and, by the early decades of the 1900s, through grueling labor and in spite of severe hardships, had risen to positions of wealth and influence.

Typifying the second-generation success stories of the early twentieth century, Joseph Kennedy achieved significant financial success. (His wealth was estimated at $250 million in 1957.) Politically astute, Kennedy was the first chairman of the Securities and Exchange Commission (1934–1935) and the first Irish-Catholic U.S. ambassador to England (1937–1940).

During the early 1930s, "Joe," as he was generally known, operated his own independent film studio in Hollywood. It was highly successful, rivaling studios such as Goldwyn-Mayer and Fox. Rose, in her capacity as hostess, was called upon to entertain many of the most famous celebrities of the day. During summers at their home in Hyannis Port, Maine, the family enjoyed weekly "movie nights," to which they invited employees, neighbors, and friends, and watched many of the great films of the period.

During the years that her husband prospered in Hollywood, Rose enjoyed a standard of living far above that of the average well-to-do American family. Such wealth afforded her the opportunity to go on shopping excursions to Paris, sometimes accompanied by Joe or one of his Hollywood clients. This lifestyle stood in stark contrast to that of most Americans, who had to get their clothing from Sears Roebuck, or even from the cloth of sugar and flour sacks.

Significance

In sharing her experience of wealth and privilege, Rose Kennedy also informed us of its shadow. If those of her own generation suffered while she lived comfortably, fate appears to have addressed the inequity. Her oldest daughter, Rosemary, was born mentally challenged, and after a fairly normal childhood at home with the family, an unsuccessful lobotomy at age twenty-three left her permanently incapable of intelligible speech. Joe Jr., her eldest son, died in World War II (1939–1945). Rose's second-oldest daughter, Kathleen, died just a few years later, in a plane crash in Europe. Two other sons, Robert and John, were assassinated within five years of each other in the 1960s. Between their deaths, her husband, Joe, suffered a permanently debilitating stroke.

Rose Kennedy's experiences of both great joy and great sorrow produced in her a firm philosophy about wealth, perhaps her most important contribution to a history of the period:

> To whom much has been given, much will be required. Money is never to be squandered or spent ostentatiously. Some of the greatest people in history have lived lives of the greatest simplicity . . . money doesn't give you any license to relax. It gives an opportunity to use all your abilities, free of financial worries, to go forward, and to use your superior advantages and talents to help others—at school, in the neighborhood, and later in working for social gains in the community and in government.

When Rose died in 1995, her son, Senator Edward Kennedy, credited the "strength of her character, which was a combination of the sweetest gentleness and the most tempered steel" with her enormous impact on the family and, consequently, on the world. Numerous eulogies from outside the family echoed the same sentiment. A 1995 *Time* magazine article, commemorating her life and death, argued that it was Rose "more than her brash and dashing husband, more than the glamorous daughter-in-law she outlived, even more than her martyred sons, who forged the Kennedy character."

Primary Source

Times to Remember [excerpt]

SYNOPSIS: In the following passages from her memoir, Rose shares her experiences of a rarely explored, lighter side of life that flourished during a dark decade of international economic hardship. Rose's standard of living in general, and her shopping visits to Paris in particular, were direct results of the period's booming film industry, upon which her husband, Joe, was able to successfully capitalize.

"Golden Girls"

Diary entry:

"January 5, 1923

Ace of Clubs dance—wore blue and silver Hickson dress."

. . . [T]he 'Hickson dress,' that really was quite special.

I'd been brought up to dress well. My mother had a fine sense of style . . . I had been buying most of my clothes off the rack in Boston and Brookline shops and having them fitted. Others had been run up by local seamstresses working with patterns and my own ideas. But never had I splurged on the total luxury of *couture:* a dress made by a famous designer—as Hickson was—one of its kind, fabric chosen with only me in mind, design inspired by his artist's vision of what I should look like. It was wildly expensive: something like two hundred dollars, as I remember. But it was much complimented at the Ace of Clubs ball and much admired by Joe.

Joe always wanted me to dress well. It pleased him, in fact it delighted him, to have me turn up in something quite special. . . .

During Joe's years in the movie industry, he was surrounded daily by some of the most beautiful women in the world, dressed in beautiful clothes. Obviously, I couldn't compete in natural beauty, but I could make the most of what I had by keeping my figure trim, my complexion good, my grooming perfect, and by always wearing clothes that were interesting and becoming. And so, with Joe's endorsement, I began spending more time and more money on clothes. . . .

While we were in the Los Angeles area, we visited Hollywood, as most tourists did, for by that time the movies had become a national habit, and Hollywood was established in the public mind as a glamorous and fabulous place. That same year, Cecil B. De Mille released *The Ten Commandments,* one of the first of the silent superepics, advertised as having cost the then-staggering sum of more than a million dollars and "with a cast of thousands." The star system was then coming into its glory, too, and many a girl, I'm sure, sat in front of her mirror wondering if she might possibly resemble Mary Pickford or one of the reigning movie queens. . . .

Rose Fitzgerald Kennedy in high fashion, preparing to be presented at the English Royal Court in 1938.

Among the films Joe made for Gloria Productions [Gloria Swanson's own production company, managed by Joseph Kennedy, who was also an investor], I have special personal memories of *The Trespasser* (1928). Joe felt it had potentialities of becoming a great box office hit, and to that end he decided on a campaign of international publicity with successive premieres in Paris, London, New York and Los Angeles, building to a tremendous climax when the film was released to the general public.

Joe, his sister, Margaret Burke, and I, therefore, sailed in June 1928 for France and were joined by Gloria in Paris.

There was a lot of excitement, fun, and crises.

Much of the excitement revolved around clothes. Gloria and I both needed some things to wear. Gloria had to have something not only becoming, but spectacular, something that would draw gasps and ohs and ahs and would photograph well. Since there would be four different premieres, she needed four different outfits. . . .

The leading couturier of Paris in those times was Lucien Lelong. We went to his salon. I had bought some clothes in Paris when I was a schoolgirl traveling with Agnes and our father and later traveling with Joe, but this was my first full exposure to the *haute couture* at the height of its dazzling elegance. I sat fascinated as the beautiful mannequins slinked and slithered the length of the ornate salon showing M. Lelong's creations. And, of course, being with Gloria magnified the experience, for the *vendeuses* and management hovered around her, attentive to her every whim; and both the girls and the customers kept stealing glances at her. She was the great celebrity. I, by comparison, was a nobody, just the wife of the producer. But it was fun being with her and sharing in the excitement she generated.

My own special interest in clothes developed during this period, not just from this episode, but from the general circumstances of which it was an especially vivid part. . . .

There have been times when I felt I was one of the more fortunate people in the world, almost as if Providence, or Fate, or Destiny, as you like, had chosen me for special favors. Now I am in my eighties, and I have known the joys and sorrows of a full life. I can neither forget nor ever reconcile myself to the tragedies, [but] I prefer to remember the good times.

Further Resources

BOOKS

Amende, Coral. *Legends in Their Own Time.* New York: Prentice Hall, 1994.

Higham, Charles. *The Life and Times of Rose Fitzgerald Kennedy.* New York: Pocket, 1995.

Kennedy, Joseph P. *Hostage to Fortune: The Letters of Joseph P. Kennedy.* Amanda Smith, ed. New York: Viking, 2001.

Leamer, Laurence. *The Kennedy Women.* New York: Villard, 1994.

Siegel, Mary-Ellen. *Her Way: A Guide to Biographies of Women for Young People,* 2d ed. Chicago: American Library Association, 1984.

PERIODICALS

McCarthy, Kerry. "Happy 100th Birthday, Aunt Rose." *Ladies Home Journal* 107, no. 7, July 1990, 70.

Review of *Times to Remember,* by Rose Fitzgerald Kennedy. *Publishers Weekly* 242, no. 1, January 1995, 65.

5

GOVERNMENT AND POLITICS

JAMES N. CRAFT

Entries are arranged in chronological order by date of primary source. For entries with one primary source, the entry title is the same as the primary source title. Entries with more than one primary source have an overall entry title, followed by the titles of the primary sources.

Important Events in Government and Politics, 1930–1939

1930

- In January, the number of unemployed in America reaches four million.
- On February 10, in Chicago more than one hundred people are arrested for distributing whiskey. Bootlegging has increased as opposition grows to Prohibition, instituted in 1919 by the Eighteenth Amendment to the Constitution.
- On June 17, President Herbert Hoover signs into law the Smoot-Hawley Tariff Act, setting tariffs on imported goods at the highest rates in American history.
- On July 3, President Hoover signs into law an act establishing the Veterans Administration.
- On July 21, the Senate confirms the London Naval Treaty, in which the United States, Great Britain, and Japan agree to limitations on the size of their navies. The treaty supplements the Washington Naval Treaty of 1922, which also includes limitation agreements.
- On August 8, President Hoover makes public a federal report stating that one million farm families, who own 12 percent of all livestock in the country, are drought stricken.
- On November 4, in the congressional elections, the Democratic Party gains a majority in the House of Representatives. In the Senate, the Democrats gain eight seats, leaving the Republicans in the majority by 48-47. The remaining seat is held by a member of the Farmer-Labor Party.
- On December 11, one of the largest banks in the country, the Bank of the United States in New York, closes. Four hundred thousand depositors lose most of their savings.
- On December 20, Congress passes legislation appropriating $116 million for public-works projects.

1931

- On January 7, President Hoover's committee on unemployment reports that almost five million Americans are without work.
- On January 19, the Wickersham Committee, appointed by President Hoover, says Prohibition is not working and calls for repeal of the Eighteenth Amendment and federal laws that support its enforcement.
- On February 11, Ann Arbor police raid five fraternity houses at the University of Michigan. Eighty-four students are arrested and forty-two quarts of whiskey, five quarts of gin, three quarts of wine, and twelve cans of beer were seized.
- On February 27, Congress overrides President Hoover's veto of the Veterans' Bonus Act, which will lend World War I veterans 50 percent of a bonus they were promised in 1924.
- On March 3, President Hoover signs a bill making "The Star-Spangled Banner" the national anthem.
- On April 6, a federal court of appeals upholds former secretary of the interior Albert B. Fall's conviction of taking a bribe in the Teapot Dome Scandal.
- On June 10, the Tennessee House of Representatives pass a law prohibiting the teaching of evolution in public schools.
- On June 20, President Hoover proposes a moratorium on the payment of debts to the United States incurred by the allies during World War I.
- In July, Iowa and Kansas farmers stage strikes and demonstrations as prices for their crops continue to tumble.
- From September to October, hoarding of gold increases as the economic depression worsens; banks are failing in great numbers (522 close during October alone), and their depositors, uninsured by the government, lose most of their savings.

1932

- On January 7, Secretary of State Henry L. Stimson announces, "The United States cannot admit the legality nor does it intend to recognize" the puppet government Japan has installed in Manchuria after a successful invasion of that northern province of China. His assertion that the United States will not accept any Japanese action that endangers the sovereignty of China or the Open Door trade policy, by which the Western powers maintain equal trading rights in Asia, becomes known as the Stimson Doctrine.
- On February 2, Congress passes the Reconstruction Finance Corporation Act, giving it wide-ranging power to extend credit to private banks and businesses. In half a year, it authorizes more than a billion dollars in loans to banks, insurance companies, and farmers' credit corporations.
- On February 27, Congress passes the Glass-Steagall Credit Expansion Act, making $750 million of the government gold reserve available for industrial and business needs.
- On March 23, Congress passes the Norris-La Guardia Act. The legislation is hailed by labor for its restrictions on federal injunctions against strikers.
- On May 2, the U.S. Supreme Court rejects Al Capone's petition to have his conviction reviewed. Capone was convicted of tax invasion and sentenced to eleven years in prison and fined $50,000.
- On May 14, New York City Mayor James Walker leads a *We Want Beer Parade.* Similar parades occur in Detroit and Milwaukee.
- On May 29, calling themselves the "Bonus Army," a thousand World War I veterans arrive in Washington, D.C., hoping to persuade Congress to pay them all the bonus money promised them in 1924. Within weeks, about 20,000 of them are camped around the city in shanty towns.

- On July 15, President Hoover cut his salary by 20 percent. His vice president and nine cabinet officials cut their salaries by 15 percent.
- On July 18, the United States and Canada sign the St. Lawrence Treaty to develop the St. Lawrence River into a major shipping lane. Of the projected $543 million dollars it would cost to build it, the U.S. assumes responsibility for $272 million.
- On July 21, Congress passes the Emergency Relief and Reconstruction Act, increasing to $3 billion the amount of money the Reconstruction Finance Corporation can loan to states and businesses.
- On July 22, Congress passes the Federal Home Loan Bank Act, making $125 million available to financial institutions in an effort to reduce foreclosures and encourage new housing starts.
- On July 28, the remnant of the Bonus Army is routed from its camp at the Anacostia Flats in Washington, D.C., by U.S. Army troops under the command of Gen. Douglas MacArthur.
- On September 1, New York Mayor James Walker resigns while under corruption investigation.
- On October 31, President Hoover warns that "the grass will grow in streets of a hundred cities" if the Democratic presidential candidate, Governor Franklin D. Roosevelt of New York, wins the election.
- On November 8, Franklin D. Roosevelt is elected President of the United States, winning 472 votes in the Electoral College to Hoover's 59. In the landslide, Democrats assume control over both the House of Representatives and the Senate.

1933

- On January 23, the Missouri Legislature becomes the thirty-sixth state to ratify the *Lame Duck Act.* The Twentieth Amendment provides that Congress shall meet every year on January 3 and the President shall take office on January 20. As a result, the President-elect's term is shortened by forty-three days.
- On February 14, Michigan Governor W.A. Comstock declares an eight-day bank holiday. Twenty-one other states quickly follow suit.
- On February 15, in Miami, Florida, Italian immigrant Joseph Zangara fires six shots at President-elect Roosevelt. Though he misses Roosevelt, others in the party are wounded, and Chicago Mayor Anton J. Cermak dies a few days later.
- On February 25, the USS *Ranger,* the first U.S. aircraft carrier, is christened at Newport News, Virginia.
- On March 4, Franklin D. Roosevelt is inaugurated as President of the United States.
- On March 5, President Roosevelt declares a four-day national banking holiday and calls for a special session of Congress to open on March 9.
- On March 9, Congress convenes to deal with the banking crisis, beginning the "First Hundred Days" of the "First New Deal." The special session runs until June 16 and passes many bills designed to improve the economy and ease the suffering of the poor and unemployed.
- On March 9, Congress passes an act giving President Roosevelt complete power over all federal transactions in credit, currency, gold, and silver, including foreign exchange.
- On March 12, President Roosevelt's first "Fireside Chat" is broadcast over the radio.
- On March 15, the National Association for the Advancement of Colored People (NAACP) unsuccessfully sues the University of North Carolina on behalf of Thomas Hocutt. The suit serves as an opening salvo in the NAACP's drive against segregation in American higher education.
- On March 20, Congress passes the Economy Act, reducing government salaries and veterans' benefits and reorganizing some government agencies in the face of price deflation brought on by the Depression.
- On March 22, Congress legalizes alcoholic beverages with 3.2 percent or less alcohol content by weight, signaling the beginning of the end for Prohibition.
- On March 26, U.S. Secretary of State Cordell Hull attempts to assure the American Jewish community that violence against German Jews "may be considered virtually terminated."
- On March 27, 20,000 American Jews in New York City protest Adolph Hitler's atrocities against Jews.
- On March 31, Congress passes the Reforestation Relief Act, which establishes the Civilian Conservation Corps (CCC) to provide work for unemployed young men. By 1941, the act will have employed more than two million young men.
- On April 19, the United States officially abandons the gold standard.
- On May 12, Congress approves the Federal Emergency Relief Act, creating the Federal Emergency Relief Administration (FERA) to spend $500 million in grants to the states.
- On May 18, Congress establishes the Tennessee Valley Authority (TVA) to control flooding and provide electricity to the region.
- On May 22, Congress passes the Farm Credit Act to help farmers refinance the mortgages on their farms rather than lose them to foreclosure.
- On May 27, Congress passes the Truth-in-Securities Act, designed to keep investors informed about the stocks and bonds in which they invest.
- From June 12 to July 27, at the London Economic Conference, European nations and the United States are unable to develop a plan for international cooperation in ending the wide fluctuation of exchange rates and reducing trade barriers.
- On June 13, Congress passes the Home Owners' Refinancing Act, which creates the Home Owners' Loan Corporation (HOLC) to help people avoid foreclosure by refinancing their home mortgages.
- On June 16, Congress passes the Glass-Steagall Banking Act, which forbids banks to sell stocks and bonds and creates the Federal Deposit Insurance Corporation (FDIC) to insure deposits against bank failure; initially, the FDIC insures only deposits under $5,000.

- On June 16, Congress passes the National Industrial Recovery Act (NIRA), which establishes the Public Works Administration (PWA) and the National Recovery Administration (NRA). This act is the last major piece of legislation passed during President Roosevelt's "First Hundred Days."
- On August 1, President Roosevelt establishes the National Labor Board, authorized under the NIRA.
- On August 3, President Roosevelt approves $130 million for building twenty-one naval ships. At the time, the appropriation was the nation's largest naval expansion program.
- On October 20, the American Federation of Labor (AFL) begins a boycott of German-made goods in response to the rising Nazi antiunion sentiment in Germany.
- On November 7, Fiorello La Guardia is elected mayor of New York on a Fusion ticket.
- On November 8, Congress authorizes the Civil Works Administration (CWA) to provide unemployed adults with work.
- On November 16, the United States formally recognizes the Soviet Union, sixteen years after the Bolshevik Revolution.
- On December 5, the Twenty-first Amendment to the Constitution is adopted, repealing the Eighteenth Amendment. This ends the federal prohibition of alcohol.

1934

- On January 3, President Roosevelt, before a Joint Session of Congress, attempts to assure the American people that economic recovery is under way and that the "New Deal" is here to stay.
- On January 11, six U.S. Navy seaplanes fly non-stop 2,400 miles for twenty-four hours and fifty-six minutes from San Francisco to Pearl Harbor.
- On January 30, Congress passes the Gold Reserve Act of 1934, giving the government greater control over the value of the dollar.
- On January 30, South Carolina makes President Roosevelt's birth a state holiday.
- On February 15, Congress passes the Civil Works Emergency Relief Act, authorizing an additional $950 million to be spent on civil-works projects.
- On March 22, Congress passes the Philippine Independence Act, effective no later than January 1, 1945.
- On March 27, the federal government authorizes the building of a thousand airplanes and a hundred warships within five years.
- On April 12, the Senate authorizes the Gerald Nye Committee to look into profiteering by U.S. businesses during World War I.
- On April 27, the U.S. and twelve Pan American countries sign an anti-war pact at Buenos Aires, Argentina.
- On April 28, in an effort to revive the building industry, Congress passes the Home Owners' Loan Act to help people buy new houses or refinance their current homes.
- On May 21, the U.S Senate rejects a proposal to eliminate the Electoral College.
- On June 6, Congress passes the Securities Exchange Act, which creates the Securities and Exchange Commission (SEC) to regulate stock exchanges.
- On June 12, Congress passes the Trade Agreements Act, authorizing the president to cut tariffs for nations that grant the United States "most-favored-nation" trading status.
- On June 19, Congress creates the Federal Communications Commission (FCC) to oversee the telephone, telegraph, and radio industries.
- On June 25, the National Relief Administration announces that sixteen million Americans are on governmental relief.
- On August 1, the U.S. relinquishes control over Haiti, ending nineteen years of occupation.
- On November 6, the Democrats increase their congressional majorities by gaining nine seats in both the Senate and House.
- On December 29, the Japanese denounce the Washington Naval Treaty of 1922.

1935

- On January 4, the "Second New Deal" begins as President Roosevelt outlines a program for social reform that will benefit laborers and small farmers.
- On April 8, the Works Progress Administration (WPA) is created under the auspices of the Emergency Relief Appropriation Act; the WPA will employ more than eight million people in building parks, airports, and highways.
- On May 11, President Roosevelt by executive order establishes the Rural Electrification Administration.
- On May 22, Father Charles Coughlin, the popular "Radio Priest," attacks President Roosevelt and declares that if capitalism prevents social justice, then it should be "constitutionally voted out of existence."
- On May 22, President Roosevelt sets precedent by appearing before a Joint Session of Congress to veto in person the Patman Greenback Bonus bill.
- On May 27, the NIRA is declared unconstitutional by the U.S. Supreme Court.
- On July 5, Congress passes the National Labor Relations Act, which strengthens the National Labor Relations Board (NLRB) and restores the right of workers to form unions, which was part of the NIRA.
- On August 14, Congress passes the Social Security Act. The number of beneficiaries is estimated at over twenty-eight million people.
- On August 31, Congress passes the Neutrality Act of 1935, which outlaws shipment of arms to countries at war.
- On September 8, Senator Huey Long of Louisiana, founder of the "Share-Our-Wealth" Societies, is assassinated.
- On December 30, the United Auto Workers (UAW) begins a wildcat sit-down strike in Flint, Michigan.

1936

- On February 29, Congress passes the Neutrality Act of 1936, which extends and augments the Neutrality Act of 1935.

- On October 1, Alfred E. Smith, the former Democratic Governor of New York, calls President Roosevelt's administration "undemocratic and a failure." Smith announces his support for the Republican presidential nominee Alfred M. Landon of Kansas.
- On November 3, President Roosevelt is reelected in a landslide victory over Republican Alfred M. Landon. There are only 89 Republicans in the new House of Representatives and 16 in the Senate.
- On November 27, President Roosevelt, while aboard the U.S. warship *Indianapolis,* is cheered by 300,000 Brazilians at Rio de Janeiro. Roosevelt attends the Inter-American Conference.
- On December 8, the NAACP files *Gibbs v. Board of Education*; the Supreme Court decision in the case establishes the precedent of paying African American schoolteachers the same salaries as white schoolteachers.

1937

- On January 6, Congress outlaws supplying weapons to either side in the Spanish Civil War.
- On January 20, President Roosevelt begins his second term, declaring, "I see one-third of a nation ill-housed, ill-clad, ill-nourished."
- On February 5, President Roosevelt requests that Congress pass legislation to increase the number of justices on the U.S. Supreme Court to as many as fifteen. His proposal is decried by Democrats and Republicans alike as "court packing."
- On March 5, U.S. Secretary of State Hull expresses official regret to German Chancellor Hitler for remarks made by New York Mayor LaGuardia.
- On March 29, the U.S. Supreme Court rules constitutional a minimum wage law for women.
- On April 12, the U.S. Supreme Court upholds the constitutionality of the National Labor Relations Act.
- On May 1, Congress passes a third Neutrality Act, introducing the "cash-and-carry" policy, which allows warring nations to buy weapons (but not ammunition) if they pay for them in cash and carry them away on their own ships.
- On May 24, the U.S. Supreme Court declares the Social Security Act constitutional.
- On July 22, the Senate, on a vote of seventy to twenty, sends President Roosevelt's court-packing bill back to committee.
- On July 22, Congress establishes the Farm Security Administration (FSA), which offers low-interest loans to sharecroppers and farm laborers.
- On October 5, President Roosevelt urges an international "quarantine" of aggressor nations in an effort to preserve peace.
- On December 12, Japanese planes bomb and sink the U.S. gunboat *Panay* on the Yangtze River in China; two American sailors are killed. Two days later Japan formally apologizes for the incident, but relations between the Japan and the United States are further strained.

1938

- On January 28, President Roosevelt proposes major military spending in an effort to shore up the nation's defenses.
- On February 16, President Roosevelt signs the second Agricultural Administration Act, replacing the first AAA, which had been declared unconstitutional in 1936.
- On May 17, Congress authorizes a ten-year program to build up the U.S. Navy.
- On May 26, the House Un-American Activities Committee (HUAC) is established.
- On May 27, Congress reduces corporate taxes in an effort to stimulate the economy.
- On June 1, a special Massachusetts legislative committee reports that communists have infiltrated state maritime unions and are trained to sabotage engines, boilers, and steering gears.
- On June 4, Socialist Party presidential candidate Norman Thomas is pelted with eggs and tomatoes prior to a speech in New Jersey. Thomas is rescued by the police.
- On June 25, Congress passes the Fair Labor Standards Act, establishing federal standards for the length of the workweek (forty-four hours) and a minimum wage (initially forty cents an hour). It also prohibits the employment of children under sixteen.
- On July 4, President Roosevelt declares that the South is "the nation's No. 1 economic problem" in a message to the National Emergency Council.
- On September 27, President Roosevelt appeals to Hitler for a peaceful solution to the Sudetenland crisis.
- On September 29, the Munich Pact, signed by Hitler and Prime Minister Chamberlain of Great Britain, cedes the Sudetenland to Germany.
- On November 8, Republicans register their first congressional gains since the beginning of the Depression by gaining seven seats in the Senate and eighty in the House of Representatives; despite their loses, Democrats retain commanding majorities in both houses of Congress.
- On November 14, the U.S. recalls its ambassador from Germany in protest over the treatment of German Jews; the German ambassador to the U.S. is recalled four days later.

1939

- On January 4, in his State of the Union message, President Roosevelt stresses the dire international situation.
- On January 5, the president's budget calls for more than a billion dollars for national defense.
- On February 27, the U.S. Supreme Court rules illegal wildcat strikes (strikes in violation of a contract).
- On April 1, the United States recognizes the government of General Francisco Franco in Spain.
- On April 9, President Roosevelt, while leaving his vacation retreat at Warm Springs, Georgia, tells the waving crowd that he will be back in the fall if there is no war.
- On April 26, President Roosevelt asks Congress to appropriate $1.6 million to begin immediate construction of a chain of air bases in the Pacific, Alaska, Puerto Rico, and the mainland.

- On May 16, the U.S. Department of Agriculture introduces food stamps, which needy people can redeem for surplus agricultural goods.
- On July 22, Congress passes the Hatch Act, which prohibits federal employees from participating in political campaigns.
- On August 19, Mexico prohibits foreigners from owning land, water rights, or mining concessions within thirty-five miles of the Mexican-American border.
- On September 1, Germany invades Poland; the Second World War begins.
- On September 3, responding to the German invasion of Poland on September 1, Great Britain and France declare war on Germany. On the same day, thirty Americans are killed when Germany sinks a British passenger ship.
- On September 4, U.S. Secretary of State Hull asks Americans to keep their travel to Europe to a minimum.
- On September 5, President Roosevelt officially declares U.S. neutrality and bans the export of weapons to warring nations.
- On September 8, President Roosevelt declares a limited state of emergency, giving him the ability to act quickly if needed.
- On October 11, the NAACP Legal Defense and Education Fund is organized and pledges an all-out fight against discrimination.
- On October 18, President Roosevelt declares U.S. territorial waters off-limits to the submarines of the warring nations.
- On October 20, the U.S. government recognizes the Polish government in exile.
- On November 4, a fourth Neutrality Act repeals all but the "cash and carry" clauses of the previous restrictions on supplying belligerents with arms.
- On November 30, Thanksgiving Day is observed as a legal holiday in twenty-three states.
- On November 30, the United States declares its support for Finland as that nation is invaded by the Soviet Union.

"The Importance of the Preservation of Self-help and of the Responsibility of Individual Generosity as Opposed to Deteriorating Effects of Governmental Appropriations"

Press statement

By: Herbert Hoover

Date: February 3, 1931

Source: Hoover, Herbert. "The Importance of the Preservation of Self-help and of the Responsibility of Individual Generosity as Opposed to Deteriorating Effects of Governmental Appropriations." Press statement. February 3, 1931. Reprinted in Myers, William Starr. *The State Papers and Other Public Writings of Herbert Hoover, Volume 2.* New York: Kraus Reprint Co., 1970, 496–99. Originally published by Doubleday, Doran & Company, New York and Garden City, 1934.

About the Author: Herbert Hoover (1874–1964) was president of the United States from 1929-1933. A civil engineer by training, his international reputation as a humanitarian and administrator resulted in his appointment in 1914 as chief Allied relief administrator during World War I. He became Secretary of Commerce in 1921 and the Republican presidential candidate in 1928. A man of great integrity, intelligence, and compassion, Hoover was, in many ways, paralyzed by the depth of the Depression. He profoundly believed in the traditional American values of individualism, free enterprise and decentralized government. His primary objective was to sustain those values during the Depression, confident that the economy would recover quickest without tampering by the Federal government. ■

Introduction

Poor relief in the United States evolved out of a combination of overlapping practices and belief systems. It was an outgrowth of poor laws established in rural England in the eighteenth and nineteenth centuries that relied on local government, family responsibility, and local charity. They were supplemented by American

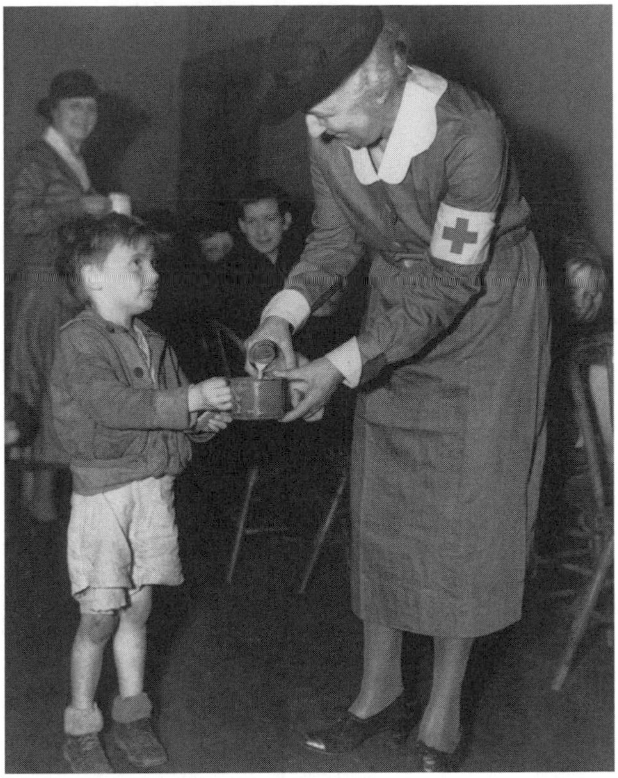

A young flood refugee has his cup filled with milk by a Red Cross worker in Cincinatti, Ohio, 1936. **AP/WIDE WORLD PHOTOS. REPRODUCED BY PERMISSION.**

ideals. These included a strong emphasis on what has been called the Protestant work ethic and a strong dose of the agrarian idea, which emphasized both the inferiority of urban life and the notion of "rugged individualism." In the post-Civil War years it was supplemented by the concept of Social Darwinism, in which it was assumed that in life's struggles the strong would survive and the weak would not.

In addition, it was widely held that in the U.S. federal system of government, the national government had no authority to directly intervene in the economic lives of its citizens. This was solely a responsibility of state and local governments and private charity.

When the Depression struck in late 1929, the systems in place to deal with the resulting unemployment reflected these beliefs. At all levels of government and business, the assumption was that local relief and charitable organizations would meet the needs of those displaced by a temporary downturn in the economy. It had been sufficient in the past and, they reasoned, it would suffice again.

As the economy worsened, proponents of the existing approach to relief increasingly emphasized the need to adhere to traditional American values. Taking a more aggressive approach in dealing with widespread unemployment, it was argued, would be fiscally irresponsible and, more importantly, would undermine the values and system that had made the United States a great nation.

President Hoover firmly believed in the U.S. system and was unwilling to damage the fabric of society by violating his basic principles to achieve short-term gain. Americans should not rely on the federal government to help them deal with their economic woes.

Significance

Initially, the most aggressive action Hoover was prepared to take was a modest expansion of federal construction programs. It was modest in part because, Hoover was very concerned with maintaining a balanced budget. Hoover also appointed the President's Emergency Committee for Employment (PECE) to encourage local responsibility for unemployment. It attempted to coordinate the activities of charitable organizations such as the Red Cross and the American Friends Service Committee. The PECE also encouraged companies to distribute existing work among as many employees as possible.

By the time Hoover delivered the following address, the systems he relied upon to aid the nation's unemployed were on the verge of collapse. Congressional pressure for federal action was rising, particularly from Progressives like Senators Robert LaFollette (R-WI) and Edward Costigan (D-CO). Hoover, however, clung to his principles. He was steadfast in his belief that for the federal government to intervene would be a severe blow to fundamental American values.

As conditions further deteriorated, Hoover finally supported a federal loan program known as the Reconstruction Finance Corporation (RFC.) Initially chartered to provide loans to selected industries (banks, insurance companies, agricultural credit associations, and railroads), it was eventually expanded to include state government loans to fund local relief programs.

Despite the fact that Hoover initiated several unprecedented programs, his efforts were done grudgingly and fell far short of what was required. He simply could not overcome his fiscal conservatism and, more importantly, the deeply held belief that federal relief programs would undercut core American values with irretrievable negative consequences.

Primary Source

"The Importance of the Preservation of Self-help and of the Responsibility of Individual Generosity as Opposed to Deteriorating Effects of Governmental Appropriations"

SYNOPSIS: In the following address, Hoover reasserted his political philosophy as it related to dealing with the economic crisis. From his perspective the existing systems were working. Local authorities, charitable organizations, and helping hands of neighbors were meeting the crisis. No one was going "hungry or cold." Hoover's specific objective was to undercut congressional efforts to pass what he considered to be extravagant and dangerous relief legislation. "The American people are doing their job," Hoover said. "They should be given a chance" to solve their problems within the "principles of individual and local responsibility . . . before they embark on . . . a disastrous new system."

Certain senators have issued a public statement to the effect that unless the President and the House of Representatives agree to appropriations from the Federal Treasury for charitable purposes they will force an extra session of Congress.

I do not wish to add acrimony to a discussion, but would rather state this case as I see its fundamentals.

This is not an issue as to whether people shall go hungry or cold in the United States. It is solely a question of the best method by which hunger and cold shall be prevented. It is a question as to whether the American people on one hand will maintain the spirit of charity and mutual self help through voluntary giving and the responsibility of local government as distinguished on the other hand from appropriations out of the Federal Treasury for such purposes. My own conviction is strongly that if we break down this sense of responsibility of individual generosity to individual and mutual self help in the country in times of national difficulty and if we start appropriations of this character we have not only impaired something infinitely valuable in the life of the American people but have struck at the roots of self-government. Once this has happened it is not the cost of a few score millions but we are faced with the abyss of reliance in future upon Government charity in some form or other. The money involved is indeed the least of the costs to American ideals and American institutions.

President Cleveland, in 1887, confronted with a similar issue stated in part:

> A prevalent tendency to disregard the limited mission of this power and duty should, I think, be steadfastly resisted, to the end that the lesson should be constantly enforced that though the people support the Government, the Government should not support the people.

Mothers receive clothes from Red Cross workers at a flood refugee headquarters in Memphis, TN. January 29, 1937. AP/WIDE WORLD PHOTOS. REPRODUCED BY PERMISSION.

> The friendliness and charity of our countrymen can always be relied upon to relieve their fellow-citizens in misfortune. This has been repeatedly and quite lately demonstrated. Federal aid in such cases encourages the expectation of paternal care on the part of the Government and weakens the sturdiness of our national character, while it prevents the indulgence among our people of that kindly sentiment and conduct which strengthens the bonds of a common brotherhood.

And there is a practical problem in all this. The help being daily extended by neighbors, by local and national agencies, by municipalities, by industry and a great multitude of organizations throughout the country today is many times any appropriation yet proposed. The opening of the doors of the Federal Treasury is likely to stifle this giving and thus destroy far more resources than the proposed charity from the Federal Government.

The basis of successful relief in national distress is to mobilize and organize the infinite number of agencies of self help in the community. That has been the American way of relieving distress among our own people and the country is successfully meeting its problem in the American way today.

We have two entirely separate and distinct situations in the country; the first is the drought area; the second is the unemployment in our large industrial centers—for both of which these appropriations attempt to make charitable contributions.

Immediately upon the appearance of the drought last August, I convoked a meeting of the governors, the Red Cross and the railways, the bankers and other agencies in the country and laid the foundations of organization and the resources to stimulate every degree of self help to meet the situation which it was then obvious would develop.

The result of this action was to attack the drought problem in a number of directions. The Red Cross established committees in every drought county, comprising the leading citizens of those counties, with instructions to them that they were to prevent starvation among their neighbors and, if the problem went beyond local resources, the Red Cross would support them.

The organization has stretched throughout the area of suffering, the people are being cared for today through the hands and with sympathetic understanding and upon the responsibility of their neighbors who are being supported in turn by the fine spirit of mutual assistance of the American people. The Red Cross officials whose long devoted service and experience are unchallenged, inform me this morning that except for the minor incidents of any emergency organization, no one is going hungry and no one need go hungry or cold.

To reinforce this work at the opening of Congress I recommended large appropriations for loans to rehabilitate agriculture from the drought and provision of further large sums for public works and construction in the drought territory which would give employment in further relief to the whole situation. These Federal activities provide for an expenditure of upward of $100,000,000 in this area and it is in progress today.

The Red Cross has always met the situations which it has undertaken. After careful survey and after actual experience of several months with their part of the problem they have announced firmly that they can command the resources with which to meet any call for human relief in prevention of hunger and suffering in drought areas and that they accept this responsibility. They have refused to accept Federal appropriations as not being consonant either with the need or the character of their organization. The Government Departments have given and are giving them every assistance. We possibly need to strengthen the public health service in matters of sanitation and to strengthen the credit facilities of that area through the method approved by the Government departments to divert some existing appropriations to strengthen agricultural credit corporations.

In the matter of unemployment outside of the drought areas important economic measures of mutual self help have been developed such as those to maintain wages, to distribute employment equitably, to increase construction work by industry, to increase Federal construction work from a rate of about $275,000,000 a year prior to the depression to a rate now of over $750,000,000 a year; to expand state and municipal construction—all upon a scale never before provided or even attempted in any depression. But beyond this to assure that there shall be no suffering, in every town and county voluntary agencies in relief of distress have been strengthened and created and generous funds have been placed at their disposal. They are carrying on their work efficiently and sympathetically.

But after and coincidently with voluntary relief, our American system requires that municipal, county and state governments shall use their own resources and credit before seeking such assistance from the Federal Treasury.

I have indeed spent much of my life in fighting hardship and starvation both abroad and in the southern states. I do not feel that I should be charged with lack of human sympathy for those who suffer but I recall that in all the organizations with which I have been connected over these many years, the foundation has been to summon the maximum of self help. I am proud to have sought the help of Congress in the past for nations who were so disorganized by war and anarchy that self help was impossible. But even these appropriations were but a tithe of that which was coincidently mobilized from the public charity of the United States and foreign countries. There is no such paralysis in the United States and I am confident that our people have the resources, the initiative, the courage, the stamina and kindliness of spirit to meet this situation in the way they have met their problems over generations.

I will accredit to those who advocate Federal charity a natural anxiety for the people of their states. I am willing to pledge myself that if the time should ever come that the voluntary agencies of the country together with the local and state governments are unable to find resources with which to prevent hunger and suffering in my country, I will ask the aid of every resource of the Federal Government because I would no more see starvation amongst our countrymen than would any senator or congressman. I have the faith in the American people that such a day will not come.

The American people are doing their job today. They should be given a chance to show whether they wish to preserve the principles of individual and local responsibility and mutual self help before they embark on what I believe is a disastrous system. I feel sure they will succeed if given the opportunity.

The whole business situation would be greatly strengthened by the prompt completion of the necessary legislation of this session of Congress and thereby the unemployment problem would be lessened, the drought area indirectly benefitted and the resources of self help in the country strengthened.

Further Resources

BOOKS

Bernstein, Irving. *The Lean Years.* Baltimore, MD: Penguin Books, 1966.

Mitchell, Broadus. *Depression Decade; From New Era through New Deal, 1929-1941.* New York: Rinehart, 1947.

McElvaine, Robert S. *The Great Depression: America, 1929-1941.* New York: Times Book, c1984.

The Proceedings and Transactions of a Conference of the Mayors of the State of Michigan

Proceedings

By: Mayors and Other Municipal Executives of the Cities of the State of Michigan

Date: May 18, 1932

Source: *The Proceedings and Transactions of a Conference of the Mayors and Other Municipal Executives of the State of Michigan, Held at the Invitation and in the Office of Honorable Frank Murphy, Mayor of the City of Detroit, Michigan, on Wednesday, May 18, 1932.* Burton Historical Collection, Detroit Public Library, Detroit, Mich., 4, 5, 11–13, 15, 16, 38, 39, 40.

About the Author: Frank Murphy (1890–1949) was a compassionate and activist mayor of Detroit from 1930 to 1933. Taking office at the outset of the Depression he led the city through the most desperate years of the economic crisis. His courageous battle against the entrenched conservative approaches to dealing with the Depression won the attention of the nation and grudging respect from his political enemies. It also attracted the attention of then New York governor and future U.S. president, Franklin D. Roosevelt (served 1933–1945). A bright young star in the Democratic Party, Murphy was appointed by Roosevelt to one of the most prestigious and challenging positions in the U.S. foreign service: governor general of the Philippines. After several successful years in the Philippines, Murphy was elected governor of Michigan. Roosevelt later appointed him U.S. attorney general and associate justice of the Supreme Court. ■

Introduction

The Depression hit Detroit very hard. Extraordinary unemployment, inadequate public and private relief resources, a dramatically declining tax base, and limited borrowing authority spelled disaster for the city. Detroit depended heavily on the automobile industry, and the collapse of the U.S. economy brought auto sales to a near standstill. By 1933 the director of the city's Department of Public Welfare estimated that 50 percent of the work force was unemployed and that many of the rest worked only part time. At the huge Ford Rouge plant, for example, employment dropped from 98,000 in 1929 to 29,000 in 1933. In the same period 25 percent of the city's factories closed and wages dropped 60 percent.

As mayor of Detroit from 1930 to 1933, Frank Murphy was an important and influential voice for national reform. THE LIBRARY OF CONGRESS.

To make matters worse, taxes could not be collected. The delinquency rate rose to 35 percent in 1933. Of the taxes collected, 43 percent went to pay back money the city had borrowed to expand its services to accommodate a population that had grown from 300,000 in 1910 to 1.5 million in 1930. To worsen the situation, state law severely restricted the borrowing power of cities. By 1932 Detroit, like most other major cities, had exhausted its limited borrowing capacity. It was left without the financial resources to provide basic government services, much less meet the staggering welfare burden.

Detroit's mayor, Frank Murphy—like the leaders in other cities across the country—believed that without federal assistance American cities would collapse. An outspoken advocate of federal assistance and mayor of one of the nation's hardest hit cities, Murphy was encouraged to lead the nation's mayors in urging Congress and the president to deal with this crisis. He argued that the only alternative was for the federal government to provide assistance. As the United States' financial condition continued to deteriorate in the spring of 1932, Murphy decided to take action. His first step was to organize a conference of 17 Michigan mayors and city managers to discuss the crisis and agree upon a united action.

Significance

The Michigan mayors and city managers met in Detroit on May 18, 1932. The one-day conference resulted in several specific resolutions concerning 1) direct Federal welfare relief to the cities; 2) amendments to the Reconstruction Finance Corporation's charter permitting loans to cities; 3) a national public works program.

The Michigan leaders also proposed that Murphy arrange a meeting of the nation's mayors to reinforce the need for federal action. This Murphy did, and on June 1, 1932, mayors of 48 large cities met in Detroit. It was an historic occasion. Never before had representatives of cities from multiple states met in formal session except to represent their respective states. It was indicative of the times that city leaders went over the heads of state authorities to seek federal aid directly.

The document prepared by the conference of Michigan mayors provided a basis of discussion for the June conference. There was near unanimous agreement that federal aid was essential and the mayors, eager for immediate action, were in no mood to quibble over details. The resolutions were easily adopted and a committee including Murphy and the mayors of Boston, Milwaukee, Grand Rapids, New Orleans, Cleveland, and Minneapolis soon headed for Washington to win congressional support for their proposals.

The immediate result was an amendment to the Reconstruction Finance Corporation that permitted loans to cities for welfare and other public works to ease unemployment. Although the resulting legislation was needlessly restrictive and limited the effectiveness of the amendment, it did facilitate the direct distribution of federal funds to the cities. This desperately needed cash permitted many welfare programs in the country to continue to operate.

Primary Source

The Proceedings and Transactions of a Conference of the Mayors of the State of Michigan [excerpt]

SYNOPSIS: The minutes of the Michigan Mayor's Conference held on May 18, 1932, are excerpted below. The purpose of the Conference was to develop recommendations to ease the financial and unemployment crisis facing the cities. The excerpts include a portion of Mayor Murphy's introduction; remarks by Dr. Frank D. Adams, pastor of the First Universalist Church in Detroit and Chair of the Mayor's Unemployment Committee; and the resolutions of the Conference as initially presented.

Mayor Murphy: You are called together at the request of the Mayor's Unemployment Committee, in order to discuss some of the fiscal affairs of the municipal governments of our state.

We have believed for some time that it was folly to go along on the theory that there would be some act of Providence, or some other act, that would bring about a sudden return to prosperity, or the business upturn and revival that is so frequently spoken of. We believe the Lord still helps those who help themselves; and that there are no sound reasons before us at the present upon which we may base the belief that any immediate return to conditions known two, three, four or five years ago, or during the past decade will be seen.

That being so, we think it is very wrong to let things drift, to be indifferent to the situation; but that we ought to plan for the immediate future, for the municipalities, as realists, knowing exactly what we are up against, and that we will do our utmost, individually, first, and, next, in co-operation with all other governments, such as the County, State and Federal, to bring the relief that we believe ought to be brought to the people of our communities.

The situation seems to become graver all the time. In a great city like Detroit for instance, at the present time, we have thousands of people who are actually reduced to a state of wretchedness and misery. These people are now not what has been so frequently called the unemployed, people who have lost their jobs, who had some resources; but I am speaking now of thousands of people in the municipal communities that are reduced to a state of almost wretchedness. In addition to them, there are thousands of others who are jobless, and whose life's earnings and savings have now disappeared; and whose homes and properties and possessions have gone into the hands of powerful interests and exploiters. The children and the aged folks, and the sick, who are dependent in our large municipalities on the bread winners and the wage earners of their families, find themselves in distressing conditions. . . .

We are not here to reach just the large cities of the State of Michigan. It was necessary to get a nucleus of thought, and, I assure you, the last thing that is in the minds of any of us is any selfish notion for the larger communities. Whatever principles we stand for, we must extend them, it seems to me, to all of the communities of our state, in accordance with their population and their problems.

We believe that direct Federal help could be given on unemployment. First, let me say, that lately the President, the chief executive of the country, has indicated in his messages and statements a change in attitude, and it is his present belief that help along certain lines, through the Reconstruction Finance Corporation, and through other legislation, might be given to the municipal governments. The leaders of both parties in Congress have indicated the same viewpoint recently, on both the administration and the opposition sides.

The question now seems to be what will be the form of the relief, and how will it be given. And it is because they have indicated their willingness to do this, and because we believe that it ought to be done, that some of us felt, including Mr. George Welsh, that there ought to be a meeting of the mayors of the cities to crystallize the sentiment of the municipal governments, swing it into action, make it articulate, muster our forces so that we will be heard on this question, and that we can further stimulate interest, encourage interest along these lines.

We believe that, first, Federal help may be given directly on the unemployment question, that is, for welfare relief, subject to the Government's limitations, and the Government's own problems. We believe this because the cities are limited, and we have not the capacity of either the State government or the Federal government to increase revenues and impose taxation. Therefore, we urge that this be done.

We believe, secondly, that the Reconstruction Finance Corporation is in a position to take up many of the refunding obligations, which will lighten the debt charges of cities, and thereby ease the credit situation, and preserve the credit of the municipalities. Any legislation, or any act that we can undertake in an executive way that eases the credit strain, and preserves our credit, puts us in a better position to give the fundamental services in the adequate way that we think they ought to be given, and puts us in a better position to do the welfare work which, in the minds of many of us, including this Unemployment Committee, is the first charge on the obligations of a municipal government set up to serve all of the people of a community.

Then we believe that legislation along the lines of the Prosperity Loan principle, which will encourage the creation of jobs and stimulate industry, is another important direction that we should be moving in. Welfare relief, the fiscal and credit situation of municipalities; the creation of jobs, and the stimulation of industry, all seem essential to erase the present blight that has settled upon our people.

So we are here to organize the sentiment of the municipalities. . . .

Dr. Frank D. Adams: Mr. Mayor, and gentlemen of the conference: I feel that it would be very presumptuous for me to occupy any considerable time, which is so valuable in a meeting of this sort.

I would like to emphasize, if I may, the salient points which Mayor Murphy has already put before us, and to say that the time has come, in my opinion, when nothing less determined and drastic than that which we hope to accomplish, will do anything in the solution of the problem which we are facing.

Those of us who for more than two years have been struggling with the situation, have been looking in every direction for aid and assistance in endeavoring to prevent actual starvation and death on the part of those who are victims of unemployment, know that we have come to the end of our resources, so far as our local governments are concerned. We know that we are bonded to the limit set by legal restrictions. We know that the long hoped for response on the part of the people and interests of wealth to an appeal for assistance has been practically a failure. We know that it is in the mind of everyone that some governmental means may be discovered by which the situation shall be dealt with.

We have left, then, gentlemen, it seems to us, in going carefully over the whole situation, only the Federal Government to which we can appeal; the Federal government, which has no limitations upon its power of taxation; the Federal government which has unlimited credit; the Federal government which is all of us, as the Mayor has so well said, and which has the confidence of all of its citizens; the Federal government which will find all of the substantial interests of the country behind it in any intelligent program looking to the relief of unemployment. . . .

Chairman Murphy: All right, gentlemen, the conference will come to order. Has the Committee on Resolutions a report prepared, Mr. Welsh?

Mr. Welsh: This is the report of the committee:

"The prolonged economic depression in this country, with the attending problems of unemployment and curtailment of credit, has precipitated a serious social and financial burden which has fallen largely upon municipalities.

"We, the executives of the greater cities of Michigan, representing industrial centers, have met in the City Hall, Detroit, Michigan, May 18th, 1932, to crystallize and organize the statement of the imperative needs and to express the concerted judgment of the people of this state towards assisting the Federal Government in its expressed desire to extend relief.

"The debt service of cities, alarming tax delinquencies, and necessary unemployment relief, have combined to exhaust the resources of our municipalities. Tax delinquency alone has increased to an extent that threatens not only welfare relief and essential governmental services, but the very foundations of our social order. The interest and principal payments on obligations contracted in normal or prosperous times are exacting a heavy toll disproportionate to debts incurred.

"A special session of the Legislature of the State of Michigan has been adjourned without making any provisions for the state's assistance in unemployment relief. The cities are finding it increasingly difficult, if not impossible, to borrow money against delinquent taxes. The issuance of new bonds has also been limited and greatly curtailed by legal restrictions and by the lack of a market.

"The sovereign government of the United States, of which we are citizens, unlike municipal governments, has no statutory financial limitations. It is the one remaining source to which we can turn in this emergency. In carrying their relief programs, our cities have employed their resources to the utmost limits permitted by legislative restrictions.

"We turn to the sovereign government of the United States for reasonable aid to supplement the full ability of our cities in their welfare relief programs; for adequate fiscal assistance which economically administered municipal governments require to preserve their credit; and for legislation that will help to stimulate an industrial revival.

"Specifically:

First, we urge a federal program for the direct relief of the unemployed; and we commend the growing recognition on the part of our constituted authorities in Washington of the seriousness of the unemployment situation and the obligation of the Federal Government.

We urge an amendment to the Congressional Act incorporating the Reconstruction Finance Corporation, or such other legislation as may be finally determined advisable, to permit such corporation to invest its assets in notes, debentures, bonds or other faith and credit obligations of cities for public welfare; and the refunding of bonds and obligations to release funds necessary to maintain the operation of municipal government.

Third, we endorse the proposal of the five billion dollar prosperity loan for an immediate program on a national scale that will create jobs and thus restore the purchasing power to millions of workers and be of immeasurable benefit to business and industry." . . .

Further Resources

BOOKS

Fine, Sidney. *Frank Murphy.* Vol. 1, *The Detroit Years.* Ann Arbor: University of Michigan Press, p. 19.

WEBSITES

Folsom, Burton W. "Michigan Resists the New Deal." March 2, 1998. Mackinac Center for Public Policy Research. Available online at http://www.mackinac.org/article.asp?ID=346; website home page http://www.mackinac.org (accessed April 17, 2003).

Press Statements and Related Correspondence on the Use of Troops to Control the So-called Bonus Marchers

Press statement, Correspondence

By: Herbert Hoover; Luther H. Reichelderfer

Date: July 1932

Source: Hoover, Herbert, and Luther H. Reichelderfer. Press statements and related correspondence on the use of troops to control the so-called Bonus Marchers. July 28–29, 1932. In Myers, William Starr, ed. *The State Papers and Other Public Writings of Herbert Hoover.* Vol. 2. Doubleday, Doran & Company, New York and Garden City, 1934; New York: Kraus Reprint Co., 1970, 242–45.

About the Author: Herbert Hoover (1874–1964) was president of the United States from 1929 to 1933. A civil engineer by training, his international reputation as a humanitarian and administrator resulted in his appointment in 1914 as chief Allied relief administrator during World War I (1914–1918). He became secretary of commerce in 1921 and the Republican presidential candidate in 1928. His administration and subsequent reputation were dominated by the Depression, which began in late 1929 and lasted until the early 1940s. While Hoover bears no responsibility for the Depression, his conservative political philosophy made him ill-suited to address the unprecedented economic collapse. His relatively hands-off approach to the crisis brought the scorn of millions of American citizens and he was soundly defeated in his reelection bid by Franklin D. Roosevelt (served 1933–1945). ■

Introduction

In gratitude for their service during World War I, Congress passed a bonus bill for war veterans, over the veto of President Calvin Coolidge (served 1923–1929). Valued at $400 in 1925, the bonus would appreciate to $1000 by the time the government actually paid it out in 1945. Congress intended it as a retirement supplement, but the Depression stimulated new ideas on the distribution of the bonus. Early in 1932 Wright Patman, a Texas Democrat in the House of Representatives, introduced a bill that would pay veterans the full bonus immediately. In a government desperately concerned with balancing the budget, the unanticipated payment of this bonus to an estimated 4,000,000 veterans had very little chance of success. Nonetheless the bill soon captured the attention of the desperate veterans the bill was designed to help.

In mid-May a small group of Oregon veterans began a trek to Washington, D.C., traveling by railroad and living on handouts. They arrived in Washington on May 29. Their goal was unclear, but they did vow to stay until Congress passed the Patman Bill.

Over the next few weeks between 15,000 and 23,000 veterans and their families arrived in Washington. They were well received, particularly by the very sympathetic Pelham D. Glassford, Washington's superintendent of police and a retired Army officer. Vacant government buildings were provided for lodging. Large vacant parcels of land—particularly in an area known as Anacostia Flats—were made available for the bonus marchers to set up temporary shacks. Fundraisers were held and food was provided.

The veterans who joined the "Bonus Expeditionary Force" were a cross section of the country. In addition to being veterans they had one more thing in common: they were beaten men. Most had not worked in months and joined the bonus marchers because they had lost hope and had nowhere to turn. The bonus was their only hope. Despite, or perhaps because of, their desperate condition, they were disciplined and peaceful, even docile. While the House passed the bill, the Senate soundly defeated it on June 17. Despite this most of the veterans stayed in Washington. It was not a gesture of defiance. Most simply had nowhere else to go.

Significance

As had happened in other places of social unrest, the Communist Party hoped to turn the incident to their advantage. The bonus marchers, however, did not provide very fertile recruiting ground. On a number of occasions the police needed to protect Communist spokesmen from being beaten by veterans. Nonetheless, the presence of "Reds" gave the opponents of the bonus march an excuse to act. In the weeks that followed the defeat of the Patman Bill, the federal government urged the veterans to leave the city. Increasingly, anti-bonus forces criticized Glassford for his conciliatory behavior. On July 21, he was ordered by the Washington, D.C., Commissioners to clear the bonus marchers from the vacant government buildings they were occupying. After several days of negotiation Glassford evacuated one building on July 28. He hoped to defer further action but several incidents ensued, one leaving a marcher dead. This gave the Commission the desired rationale to ask the U.S. Army, under the direct command of General Douglas MacArthur, to evict the marchers from the remaining buildings.

Military action had been discussed the previous day with President Hoover and MacArthur, but without Glassford, and when the Commission's request for help came the president immediately ordered MacArthur to act. Four cavalry troops and four infantry companies, supported by six small tanks and machine guns, moved in. Within a few hours the buildings were evacuated, the bonus marchers' encampments at Anacostia Flats and other locations were in flames, and the marchers them-

The U.S. Army violently expells the "Bonus Expeditionary Force" from Washington, D.C., July 28, 1932. ARCHIVE PHOTOS. REPRODUCED BY PERMISSION.

selves were fleeing Washington. Two veterans and an 11-week-old baby were killed.

The public reacted very strongly. Thomas L. Stokes, a reporter who witnessed the rout, expressed the feelings of many Americans:

> The United States Army turned on American citizens—just fellows like myself, down on their luck, dispirited, hopeless. It was an experience that stands apart from all others in my life. . . . I had nothing but bitter feelings toward Herbert Hoover that night.

Three months later Hoover lost his reelection bid to Franklin Roosevelt. While his handling of the Bonus Army cannot be singled out as the reason for his defeat, it was a severe blow to his personal credibility. Ironically, in 1936 Congress passed a bonus bill. It became law over the veto of President Roosevelt.

Primary Source

Press Statements and Related Correspondence on the Use of Troops to Control the So-called Bonus Marchers

SYNOPSIS: President Hoover released these two press statements on July 28 and July 29, 1932, respectively. They explain the decision to use troops to expel the bonus marchers. Also included are notes about the situation exchanged by Hoover and L. H. Reichfelderfer, president of the District of Columbia Board of Commissioners.

Press Statement, July 28, 1932

The President said:

For some days police authorities and Treasury officials have been endeavoring to persuade the so-called bonus marchers to evacuate certain buildings which they were occupying without permission. These buildings are on sites where Government construction is in progress and their demolition was necessary in order to extend employment in the District and to carry forward the Government's construction program.

This morning the occupants of these buildings were notified to evacuate and at the request of the police did evacuate the buildings concerned. Thereafter, however, several thousand men from different camps marched in and attacked the police with brickbats and otherwise injured several policemen, one probably fatally.

I have received the attached letter from the Commissioners of the District of Columbia stating that they can no longer preserve law and order in the District.

In order to put an end to this rioting and defiance of civil authority, I have asked the Army to assist the District authorities to restore order.

Congress made provision for the return home of the so-called bonus marchers who have for many weeks been given every opportunity of free assembly, free speech, and free petition to the Congress. Some 5,000 took advantage of this arrangement and have returned to their homes. An examination of a large number of names discloses the fact that a considerable part of those remaining are not veterans; many are communists and persons with criminal records.

The veterans amongst these numbers are no doubt unaware of the character of their companions and are being led into violence which no government can tolerate.

I have asked the Attorney General to investigate the whole incident and to cooperate with the District civil authorities in such measures against leaders and rioters as may be necessary.

Request of the President of the Board of Commissioners of the District of Columbia

The President:

The Commissioners of the District of Columbia regret to inform you that during the past few hours, circumstances of serious character have arisen in the District of Columbia which have been the cause of unlawful acts of large numbers of so-called "bonus marchers," who have been in Washington for some time past.

This morning, officials of the Treasury Department, seeking to clear certain areas within the Government triangle in which there were numbers of these bonus marchers, met with resistance. They called upon the Metropolitan Police Force for assistance and a serious riot occurred. Several members of the Metropolitan Police were injured, one reported seriously. The total number of bonus marchers greatly outnumbered the police; the situation is made more difficult by the fact that this area contains thousands of brickbats and these were used by the rioters in their attack upon the police.

In view of the above, it is the opinion of the Major and Superintendent of Police, in which the Commissioners concur, that it will be impossible for the Police Department to maintain law and order except by the free use of firearms which will make the situation a dangerous one; it is believed, however, that the presence of Federal troops in some number will obviate the seriousness of the situation and result in far less violence and bloodshed.

The Commissioners of the District of Columbia, therefore, request that they be given the assistance of Federal troops, in maintaining law and order in the District of Columbia.

Very sincerely yours,
L. H. Reichelderfer,
President, Board of Commissioners of the District of Columbia.

Reply of President Hoover to the Request

July 29, 1932.

Honorable Luther H. Reichelderfer,
Commissioner, District of Columbia,
Washington, D.C.

My dear Mr. Commissioner:

In response to your information that the police of the District were overwhelmed by an organized attack by several thousand men, and were unable to maintain law and order, I complied with your request for aid from the Army to the police. It is a matter of satisfaction that, after the arrival of this assistance, the mobs which were defying the municipal government were dissolved without the firing of a shot or the loss of a life.

I wish to call attention of the District Commissioners to the fact that martial law has not been declared; that responsibility for order still rests upon your commission and the police. The civil government of Washington must function uninterrupted. The Commissioners, through their own powers, should now deal with this question decisively.

It is the duty of the authorities of the District to at once find the instigators of this attack on the police and bring them to justice. It is obvious that, after the departure of the majority of the veterans, subversive influences obtained control of the men remaining in the District, a large part of whom were not veterans, secured repudiation of their elected leaders and inaugurated and organized this attack.

They were undoubtedly led to believe that the civil authorities could be intimidated with impunity because of attempts to conciliate by lax enforcement of city ordinances and laws in many directions. I shall expect the police to strictly enforce every ordinance of the District in every part of the city. I wish every violator of the law to be instantly arrested and prosecuted under due process of law.

I have requested the law enforcement agencies of the Federal Government to cooperate with the District authorities to this end.

There is no group, no matter what its origins, that can be allowed either to violate the laws of this city or to intimidate the Government.

Yours faithfully,
Herbert Hoover.

Press Statement, July 29, 1932

The President said:

A challenge to the authority of the United States Government has been met, swiftly and firmly.

After months of patient indulgence, the Government met overt lawlessness as it always must be met if the cherished processes of self-government are to be preserved. We cannot tolerate the abuse of Constitutional rights by those who would destroy all government, no matter who they may be. Government cannot be coerced by mob rule.

The Department of Justice is pressing its investigation into the violence which forced the call for Army detachments, and is my sincere hope that those agitators who inspired yesterday's attack upon the Federal authority may be brought speedily to trial in the civil courts. There can be no safe harbor in the United States of America for violence.

Order and civil tranquillity are the first requisites in the great task of economic reconstruction to which our whole people now are devoting their heroic and noble energies. This national effort must not be retarded in even the slightest degree by organized lawlessness. The first obligation of my office is uphold and defend the Constitution and the authority of the law. This I propose always to do.

Books

Bernstein, Irving. *The Lean Years.* Baltimore, Md.: Penguin Books, 1966.

Leuchtenburg, William E. *Franklin D. Roosevelt and the New Deal (1932–1940).* New York: Harper & Row, 1963.

Campaign Speech at Madison Square Garden, New York City

Speech

By: Herbert Hoover

Date: October 31, 1932

Source: Hoover, Herbert. Campaign Speech at Madison Square Garden, New York City, October 31, 1932. Reprinted in Myers, William Starr. *The State Papers and Other Public Writings of Herbert Hoover, Volume 2.* Doubleday, Doran & Company, New York and Garden City, 1934; New York: Kraus Reprint Co., 1970, 408, 410, 412–423, 428.

About the Author: Herbert Hoover (1874–1964) was president of the United States from 1929–1933. A civil engineer by training, his international reputation as a humanitarian and administrator resulted in his appointment in 1914 as chief Allied relief administrator during World War I (1914–1918). He became Secretary of Commerce in 1921 and the Republican presidential candidate in 1928. A man of great integrity, intelligence and compassion, Hoover was, in many ways, paralyzed by the depth of the Great Depression, which began during his presidency. He profoundly believed in the traditional American values of individualism, free enterprise, and decentralized government. He viewed his primary objective as sustaining those values during the Depression, confident that the economy would recover quickest without tampering. ■

Introduction

As the 1932 presidential campaign approached it was apparent that no previous sitting U.S. president had been less likely to be reelected than Herbert Hoover. He was enormously unpopular. While he was obviously not responsible for the Depression, an increasing number of Americans found his relative inaction unacceptable. He steadfastly adhered to political and economic beliefs that offered little immediate hope for helping millions of unemployed Americans. This doomed Hoover and the Republicans before the campaign even began.

The Republicans faced a political dilemma. Hoover was the sitting president elected by a large majority four years earlier. He did, in fact, accurately represent Republican ideology. By and large Republicans could offer nothing in addition to what Hoover had done as a solution to the country's economic woes. Finally no other viable candidate wanted the job. It was evident, even to Republicans, that barring a miraculous improvement in the economy, the Democrats would win the White House in 1932.

Despite the heavy odds against him, Hoover waged a passionate campaign. He certainly knew his chance of winning was remote. Nonetheless he felt compelled to focus the country's attention on what he saw as the fundamental issue of the campaign: the future direction of the U.S. political system. In Hoover's mind Democratic candidate Franklin D. Roosevelt (president 1933–1945) would overturn the fundamental values of what Hoover described as the American system.

Hoover's campaign, his mission, was to ensure that the American people understood the significance of the struggle being waged in the fall of 1932. His basic campaign strategy emphasized the fundamental differences between the Democrats and the Republicans. He saw the

Democratic program as nothing less than a full-scale assault on the finest political and economic system in the world. It was unique in both the liberties it granted citizens as well as the distribution of political power to the local, even individual, level. It was a system that had created the greatest, freest nation on earth.

Hoover believed the economic and social difficulties of past three years had resulted from international rather than domestic issues. Because of these difficulties, he maintained, the Democrats were prepared to destroy a system that had thrived for 150 years. In his opinion the existing system had prevented an even worse calamity. While he recognized that many were suffering he held fast to the idea that conditions were improving and that the changes proposed by Democrats would be counterproductive.

Significance

Based partly on fact and partly on intuition, Hoover's speech in New York during the final days of the presidential campaign gave a remarkably accurate description of the coming Roosevelt years. Point by point Hoover predicted what Roosevelt and the Democrats would do:

1. Dramatically increase the federal budget. I (In the next four years the budget would nearly double.)
2. Produce inflation and take the United States off the gold standard. (Within weeks after taking office the Unites States effectively went off the gold standard. Much of FDR's early policy was intended to counter the deflationary trend and introduce a more inflationary currency primarily to ease the pressure on debtors.)
3. Intervene in the banking system. (The day after his inauguration Roosevelt ordered a national "bank holiday" and within months the Glass-Steagall Act passed, creating a strong regulatory role for the federal government in the banking industry.)
4. Reduce the tariff on imports. (Not until late in his first term did Roosevelt cautiously move to reduce tariffs by negotiating a series of bilateral trade agreements. Nonetheless this practice was clearly the first step in moving the United States toward a free-trade philosophy and was the direct ancestor of today's trade policies.)
5. Bring the government into the power business. (On May 18, 1933, the Tennessee Valley Authority was established to produce a vast series of dams to control flooding and produce power for millions of Americans.)
6. Launch public works projects to offset unemployment. (By the end of the decade over ten million people had been employed on various work-relief programs.)

Hoover, of course, viewed Roosevelt and the Democrats as a threat to the American way of life. And, indeed, the 1932 election and Roosevelt's New Deal were turning points in the political, social, and economic structure of the United States.

The 1932 election ended in an overwhelming victory for Roosevelt and the Democrats. Roosevelt had 22.8 million popular votes to Hoover's 15.8 million. Roosevelt's victory in the electoral college was the largest in history, surpassing the previous record of Hoover over Al Smith in 1928. In a complete reversal of the pattern throughout the 1920s the Democrats were swept into power in both houses of Congress. It was a stunning repudiation of the conservative approach taken by Hoover and the Republicans and it gave Roosevelt an unprecedented mandate for change.

While it is unlikely that many voters on either side of the political spectrum fully appreciated the significance of Roosevelt's election in 1932, Herbert Hoover thought he did. For years after he remained a strong critic of the New Deal programs, which he continued to criticize as contrary to American values and harmful to the country.

Primary Source

Campaign Speech at Madison Square Garden, New York City, October 31, 1932 [excerpt]

SYNOPSIS: The following speech was delivered before a crowd of 22,000 people at Madison Square Garden in New York during the final days of the presidential campaign. It is the essence of the entire campaign. Hoover lays out not only his political philosophy but also a fairly accurate representation of Roosevelt's anticipated program. (Confident of victory, Roosevelt believed his best strategy was to say as little as possible about specific programs.)

This campaign is more than a contest between two men. It is more than a contest between two parties. It is a contest between two philosophies of government.

We are told by the opposition that we must have a change, that we must have a new deal. It is not the change that comes from normal development of national life to which I object, but the proposal to alter the whole foundations of our national life which have been builded through generations of testing and struggle, and of the principles upon which we have builded the Nation. The expressions our opponents use must refer to important changes in our economic and social system and our system of Government, otherwise they are nothing but vacuous

Herbert Hoover (right) and his vice president, Charles Curtis, during their successful campaign for the presidency in 1928. **AP/WIDE WORLD PHOTOS. REPRODUCED BY PERMISSION.**

words. And I realize that in this time of distress many of our people are asking whether our social and economic system is incapable of that great primary function of providing security and comfort of life to all of the firesides of our 25,000,000 homes in America, whether our social system provides for the fundamental development and progress of our people, whether our form of government is capable of originating and sustaining that security and progress.

This question is the basis upon which our opponents are appealing to the people in their fears and distress. They are proposing changes and so-called new deals which would destroy the very foundations of our American system. . . .

Let us pause for a moment and examine the American system of government, of social and economic life, which it is now proposed that we should alter. Our system is the product of our race and of our experience in building a nation to heights unparalleled in the whole history of the world. It is a system peculiar to the American people. It differs essentially from all others in the world. It is an American system.

It is founded on the conception that only through ordered liberty, through freedom to the individual, and equal opportunity to the individual will his initiative and enterprise be summoned to spur the march of progress.

It is by the maintenance of equality of opportunity and therefore of a society absolutely fluid in freedom of the movement of its human particles that our individualism departs from the individualism of Europe. We resent class distinction because there can be no rise for the individual through the frozen strata of classes, and no stratification of classes can take place in a mass livened by the free rise of its particles. Thus in our ideals the able and ambitious are able to rise constantly from the bottom to leadership in the community.

This freedom of the individual creates of itself the necessity and the cheerful willingness of men to act cooperatively in a thousand ways and for every purpose as occasion arises; and it permits such voluntary cooperations to be dissolved as soon as they have served their purpose, to be replaced by new voluntary associations for new purposes. . . .

I therefore contend that the problem of today is to continue these measures and policies to restore this American system to its normal functioning, to repair the wounds it has received, to correct the weaknesses and evils which would defeat that system. To enter upon a series of deep changes to embark upon this inchoate new deal which has been propounded in this campaign would be to undermine and destroy our American system.

Before we enter upon such courses, I would like for you to consider what the results of this American system have been during the last thirty years—that is, one single generation. For if it can be demonstrated that by means of this, our unequaled political, social, and economic system, we have secured a lift in the standards of living and a diffusion of comfort and hope to men and women, the growth of equal opportunity, the widening of all opportunity, such as had never been seen in the history of the world, then we should not tamper with it or destroy it; but on the contrary we should restore it and, by its gradual improvement and perfection, foster it into new performance for our country and for our children.

Now, if we look back over the last generation we find that the number of our families and, therefore, our homes, have increased from sixteen to twenty-five million, or 62 per cent. In that time we have builded for them 15,000,000 new and better homes. We have equipped 20,000,000 homes with electricity; thereby we have lifted infinite drudgery from women and men. The barriers of time and space have been swept away. Life has been made freer, the intellectual vision of every individual has been expanded by the installation of 20,000,000 telephones, 12,000,000 radios, and the service of 20,000,000 automobiles. Our cities have been made magnificent with beautiful buildings, parks, and playgrounds. Our countryside has been knit together with splendid roads. We have increased by twelve times the use of electrical power and thereby taken sweat from the backs of men. In this broad sweep real wages and purchasing power of men and women have steadily increased. New comforts have steadily come to them. The hours of labor have decreased, the 12-hour day has disappeared, even the 9-hour day has almost gone. We are now advancing the 5-day week. The portals of opportunity to our children have ever widened. While our population grew by but 62 per cent, we have increased the number of children in high schools by 700 per cent, those in institutions of higher learning by 300 per cent. With all our spending we multiplied by six times the savings in our banks and in our building and loan associations. We multiplied by 1,200 per cent the amount of our life insurance. With the enlargement of our leisure we have come to a fuller life; we gained new visions of hope, we more nearly realize our national aspirations and give increasing scope to the creative power of every individual and expansion of every man's mind. . . .

And in order to indicate to you that the proposals of our opponents will endanger or destroy our system, I propose to analyze a few of the proposals of our opponents in their relation to these fundamentals.

First. A proposal of our opponents which would break down the American system is the expansion of Government expenditure by yielding to sectional and group raids on the Public Treasury. The extension of Government expenditures beyond the minimum limit necessary to conduct the proper functions of the Government enslaves men to work for the Government. . . .

Second. Another proposal of our opponents which would destroy the American system is that of inflation of the currency. The bill which passed the last session of the Democratic House called upon the Treasury of the United States to issue $2,300,000,000 in paper currency that would be unconvertible into solid values. Call it what you will, greenbacks or fiat money. It was that nightmare which overhung our own country for years after the Civil War.

In our special situation today the issuance of greenbacks means the immediate departure of this country from the gold standard, as there could be no provision for the redemption of such currency in gold. The new currency must obviously go to immediate and constantly fluctuating discount when associated with currency convertible in gold. . . .

Third. In the last session the Congress, under the personal leadership of the Democratic Vice Presidential candidate, and their allies in the Senate, enacted a law to extend the Government into personal banking business. This I was compelled to veto, out of fidelity to the whole American system of life and government. . . .

Fourth. Another proposal of our opponents which would wholly alter our American system of life is to reduce the protective tariff to a competitive tariff for revenue. The protective tariff and its results upon our economic structure has become gradually embedded into our economic life since the first protective tariff act passed by the American Congress under the administration of George Washington. There have been gaps at times of Democratic control when this protection has been taken away. But it has been so embedded that its removal has never failed to bring disaster. Whole towns, communities, and forms of agriculture with their homes, schools, and churches have been built up under this system of protection. The grass will grow in streets of a hundred cities, a thousand towns; the weeds will overrun the fields of millions of farms if that protection be taken away. Their churches and school houses will decay. . . .

Fifth. Another proposal is that the Government go into the power business. Three years ago, in view of the extension of the use of transmission of power over state borders and the difficulties of state regulatory bodies in the face of this interstate action, I recommended to the Congress that such interstate power should be placed under regulation by the Federal Government in cooperation with the state authorities. . . .

I have stated unceasingly that I am opposed to the Federal Government going into the power business. I have insisted upon rigid regulation. The Democratic candidate has declared that under the same conditions which may make local action of this character desirable, he is prepared to put the Federal Government into the power business. He is being actively supported by a score of Senators in this campaign, many of whose expenses are being paid by the Democratic National Committee, who are pledged to Federal Government development and operation of electrical power. . . .

Sixth. I may cite another instance of absolutely destructive proposals to our American system by our opponents.

Recently there was circulated through the unemployed in this country a letter from the Democratic candidate in which he stated that he "would support measures for the inauguration of self-liquidating public works such as the utilization of water resources, flood control, land reclamation, to provide employment for all surplus labor at all times."

I especially emphasize that promise to promote "employment for all surplus labor at all times." At first I could not believe that anyone would be so cruel as to hold out a hope so absolutely impossible of realization to these 10,000,000 who are unemployed. But the authenticity of this promise has been verified. And I protest against such frivolous promises being held out to a suffering people. It is easily demonstrable that no such employment can be found. But the point I wish to make here and now is the mental attitude and spirit of the Democratic Party to attempt it. It is another mark of the character of the new deal and the destructive changes which mean the total abandonment of every principle upon which this government and the American system is founded. If it were possible to give this employment to 10,000,000 people by the Government, it would cost upwards of $9,000,000,000 a year.

The stages of this destruction would be first the destruction of Government credit, the value of Government securities, the destruction of every fiduciary trust in our country, insurance policies and all. It would pull down the employment of those who are still at work by the high taxes and the demoralization of credit upon which their employment is dependent. It would mean the pulling and hauling of politics for projects and measures, the favoring of localities, sections, and groups. It would mean the growth of a fearful bureaucracy which, once established, could never be dislodged. . . .

Eighth. In order that we may get at the philosophical background of the mind which pronounces the necessity for profound change in our American system and a new deal, I would call your attention to an address delivered by the Democratic candidate in San Francisco, early in October:

He said:

> Our industrial plant is built. The problem just now is whether under existing conditions it is not overbuilt. Our last frontier has long since been reached. There is practically no more free land. There is no safety valve in the western prairies where we can go for a new start. The mere building of more industrial plants, the organization of more corporations is as likely to be as much a danger as a help. Our task now is not the discovery of natural resources or necessarily the production of more goods, it is the sober, less dramatic business of administering the resources and plants already in hand establishing markets for surplus production, of meeting the problem of underconsumption, distributing the wealth and products more equitably, and adopting the economic organization to the service of the people.

There are many of these expressions with which no one would quarrel. But I do challenge the whole idea that we have ended the advance of America, that this country has reached the zenith of its power, the height of its development. That is the counsel of despair for the future of America. That is not the spirit by which we shall emerge from this depression. That is not the spirit that made this country. If it is true, every American must abandon the road of countless progress and unlimited opportunity. I deny that the promise of American life has been fulfilled, for that means we have begun the decline and fall. No nation can cease to move forward without degeneration of spirit.

I could quote from gentlemen who have emitted this same note of pessimism in economic depressions going back for 100 years. What Governor Roosevelt has overlooked is the fact that we are yet but on the frontiers of development of science, and of invention. I have only to remind you that discoveries in electricity, the internal-combustion engine, the radio—all of which have sprung into being since our land was settled—have in themselves represented the greatest advances in America. This philosophy upon which the Governor of New York proposes to conduct the Presidency of the United States is the philosophy of stagnation, of despair. It is the end of hope. The destinies of this country should not be dominated by that spirit in action. It would be the end of the American system. . . .

My countrymen, the proposals of our opponents represent a profound change in American life—less in concrete proposal, bad as that may be, than by implication and by evasion. Dominantly in their spirit they represent a radical departure from the foundations of 150 years which have made this the greatest nation in the world. This election is not a mere shift from the ins to the outs. It means deciding the direction our Nation will take over a century to come.

My conception of America is a land where men and women may walk in ordered liberty, where they may enjoy the advantages of wealth not concentrated in the hands of a few but diffused through the lives of all, where they build and safeguard their homes, give to their children full opportunities of American life, where every man shall be respected in the faith that his conscience and his heart direct him to follow, where people secure in their liberty shall have leisure and impulse to seek a fuller life. That leads to the release of the energies of men and women, to the wider vision and higher hope; it leads to opportunity for greater and greater service not alone of man to man in our country but from our country to the world. It leads to health in body and a spirit unfettered, youthful, eager with a vision stretching beyond the farthest horizons with an open mind, sympathetic and generous. But that must be builded upon our experience with the past, upon the foundations which have made our country great. It must be the product of our truly American system.

Further Resources

BOOKS

Steinberg, Alfred. *Herbert Hoover.* New York: Putnam, 1967.

WEBSITES

"Hoover Charges Roosevelt 'New Deal' Would Destroy Foundation of . . . ." Available online at http://www.nytimes.com/learning/general/specials/elections/1932/featured_article1.html (accessed August 29, 2002).

Hoover Online! Digital Archives. National Archives and Records Administration. Available online at http://www.ecommcode.com/hoover/hooveronline/hoover_and_the_depression/philosophy/ (accessed August 29, 2002).

"On the Purposes and Foundations of the Recovery Program"

Radio address

By: Franklin D. Roosevelt

Date: July 24, 1933

Source: Roosevelt, Franklin D. "On the Purposes and Foundations of the Recovery Program." Radio Address of the President, July 24, 1933. Fireside Chats of Franklin D. Roosevelt. Available online at http://www.fdrlibrary.marist.edu/042433.html; website homepage: http://www.fdrlibrary.marist.edu/ (accessed March 20, 2003).

About the Author: Franklin Delano Roosevelt (1882–1945) was the thirty-second president of the United States. He was elected to the presidency in 1932, during the worst year of the Great Depression. Only Lincoln assumed the presidency in a more desperate situation. In many ways, Roosevelt was the perfect president for the times. His unbounded optimism and energy gave the American people a sense of hope that they needed. His willingness to try a variety of programs to deal with the causes and consequences of the Depression demonstrated that their faith in him was well placed. Elected president four times, he led the nation through two of the defining events of American history—the Great Depression of the 1930s and World War II (1939–1945). He died shortly before the German surrender in April 1945. ■

Introduction

The First Hundred Days of Roosevelt's administration were a whirlwind of legislative activity. In the first three months of his administration, Congress passed legislation aimed at restoring the economy, providing relief to the unemployed, and instituting reforms that would prevent some of the causes of the Depression in the future. Many of these programs are still in effect in some form or another. Actions taken or initiated in the First Hundred Days included:

1. Emergency Banking Relief Act, to prop up the nation's banks
2. Reforestation Act, to create the Civilian Conservation Corp

3. Repeal of the Volstead Act, to allow the legal sale of alcoholic beverages of less than 3.2 percent alcohol
4. Federal Emergency Relief Act (FERA), to provide $500 million in state grants to provide direct relief to the unemployed
5. Abandoning the gold standard, to prevent a drain on the nation's gold reserves and to halt the deflationary spiral
6. Tennessee Valley Authority; to initiate a massive program to prevent flooding and generate electricity in the Tennessee River valley
7. Truth in Securities Act, to regulate the nation's stock exchanges
8. National Industrial Recovery Act, to create the National Recovery Administration (NRA) and initiate the major economic recovery plank of the First Hundred Days
9. Agricultural Administration Act (AAA), to curtail farm production and raise the price of farm products to an acceptable level
10. Home Owners' Refinance Act, to help stop the avalanche of home loan foreclosures
11. Farm Credit Act, to allow farmers to refinance their farms and stop foreclosures
12. Glass-Steagall Act, to create the Federal Depositors Insurance Corporation and guarantee deposits in most of the nation's banks

The energy exhibited by Roosevelt in the First Hundred Days was contagious. The renewed vigor was well expressed by a sign in the office of Charles Edison, President of Thomas A. Edison, Inc., that read:

> President Roosevelt has done his part: now you do something.
>
> Buy something—buy anything, anywhere: paint your kitchen, send a telegram, give a party, get a car, pay a bill, rent a flat, fix your roof, get a haircut, see a show, build a house, take a trip, sing a song, get married.
>
> It does not matter what you do—but get going and keep going. This old world is starting to move.
>
> *Time*, April 3, 1933.

Significance

Amazingly, things did get going. Spurred on by the general enthusiasm, the economy rallied. By July factory production had nearly doubled and industrial stock prices had climbed from 63 to 109. This initial flurry of activity, however, had more to do with Roosevelt's ability to rally the people than any direct impact of the Hundred Days' legislation. Before this could happen the programs needed to be put in place and given time to work.

Most visible was the dynamic head of the National Recovery Administration (NRA), Hugh Johnson. He generated an almost revivalist fervor as he criss-crossed the country negotiating NRA codes and signing up participants to voluntarily abide by measures designed to increase prices, wages, and employment.

In the farm sector Henry Wallace drove the implementation of the controversial Agricultural Adjustment Act (AAA). Wallace had planned his campaign before Roosevelt's inauguration. He knew that unless action was taken quickly the usual amount of crops would be planted; such overproduction would delay the benefits of the AAA another year. Despite the desperate condition of farmers, however, limiting production in order to raise prices in the face of widespread hunger was not popular. Wallace and the AAA bore the brunt of public and media criticism in the first year of Roosevelt's first administration.

The Civilian Conservation Corps (CCC) moved into full operation. Under the charge of officers from the U.S. Army and Army Reserves, the CCC got off to quick start and became one of the New Deal's most highly regarded programs. By mid-summer 300,000 young men were enrolled and at work across the country on various reforestation and conservation projects.

The desperate condition of local relief was abated by the infusion of funds from the Federal Emergency Relief Administration (FERA), administered by Harry Hopkins, a passionate and shrewd social worker who had directed Roosevelt's relief programs while the latter was governor of New York. When FERA funds proved inadequate, Hopkins pushed Roosevelt for more resources. He received them in the form of the Civil Works Administration. This short-lived public works program provided employment for over 4,000,000 during the winter of 1933–1934.

One by one New Deal programs came on line and with surprising speed began to remake the face of the United States. By the end of 1933 some level of confidence had been restored. The Depression, however, was far from over. Many hard years remained but the sense of desperation was gone. The economy showed modest signs of improvement. Farm prices began to creep up. Unemployment declined. Relief funds were available. Banks were stabilized. Home and farm foreclosures were checked. The journey down the long road back had begun.

Primary Source

"On the Purposes and Foundations of the Recovery Program"

SYNOPSIS: Roosevelt gave his third "Fireside Chat" radio broadcast on July 24, 1933. A feverish legislative session had recently ended. Dramatic steps had been taken to deal with the immediate economic issues and to implement permanent structural reform. In this address to the nation Roosevelt outlines some of the critical programs, explains their logic, and prepares the country for additional action. By firing the enthusiasm of the American people, Roosevelt hoped to rally the country to the programs that had been initiated.

After the adjournment of the historical special session of the Congress five weeks ago I purposely refrained from addressing you for two very good reasons.

First, I think that we all wanted the opportunity of a little quiet thought to examine and assimilate in a mental picture the crowding events of the hundred days which had been devoted to the starting of the wheels of the New Deal.

Secondly, I wanted a few weeks in which to set up the new administrative organization and to see the first fruits of our careful planning.

I think it will interest you if I set forth the fundamentals of this planning for national recovery; and this I am very certain will make it abundantly clear to you that all of the proposals and all of the legislation since the fourth day of March have not been just a collection of haphazard schemes but rather the orderly component parts of a connected and logical whole.

Long before Inauguration Day I became convinced that individual effort and local effort and even disjointed Federal effort had failed and of necessity would fail and, therefore, that a rounded leadership by the Federal Government had become a necessity both of theory and of fact. Such leadership, however, had its beginning in preserving and strengthening the credit of the United States Government, because without that no leadership was a possibility. For years the Government had not lived within its income. The immediate task was to bring our regular expenses within our revenues. That has been done. It may seem inconsistent for a government to cut down its regular expenses and at the same time to borrow and to spend billions for an emergency. But it is not inconsistent because a large portion of the emergency money has been paid out in the form of sound loans which will be repaid to the Treasury over a period of years; and to cover the rest of the emergency money we have imposed taxes to pay the interest and the installments on that part of the debt.

So you will see that we have kept our credit good. We have built a granite foundation in a period of confusion. That foundation of the Federal credit stands there broad and sure. It is the base of the whole recovery plan.

Then came the part of the problem that concerned the credit of the individual citizens themselves. You and I know of the banking crisis and of the great danger to the savings of our people. On March sixth every national bank was closed. One month later 90 per cent of the deposits in the national banks had been made available to the depositors. Today only about 5 per cent of the deposits in national banks are still tied up. The condition relating to state banks, while not quite so good on a percentage basis, is showing a steady reduction in the total of frozen deposits—a result much better than we had expected three months ago.

The problem of the credit of the individual was made more difficult because of another fact. The dollar was a different dollar from the one with which the average debt had been incurred. For this reason large numbers of people were actually losing possession of and title to their farms and homes. All of you know the financial steps which have been taken to correct this inequality. In addition the Home Loan Act, the Farm Loan Act and the Bankruptcy Act were passed.

It was a vital necessity to restore purchasing power by reducing the debt and interest charges upon our people, but while we were helping people to save their credit it was at the same time absolutely essential to do something about the physical needs of hundreds of thousands who were in dire straits at that very moment. Municipal and State aid were being stretched to the limit. We appropriated half a billion dollars to supplement their efforts and in addition, as you know, we have put 300,000 young men into practical and useful work in our forests and to prevent flood and soil erosion. The wages they earn are going in greater part to the support of the nearly one million people who constitute their families.

In this same classification we can properly place the great public works program running to a total of over Three Billion Dollars—to be used for highways and ships and flood prevention and inland navigation and thousands of self-sustaining state and municipal improvements. Two points should be made clear in the allotting and administration of these projects—first, we are using the utmost care to choose labor creating quick-acting, useful projects, avoiding the smell of the pork barrel; and secondly, we are hoping that at least half of the money will come back

President Franklin Delano Roosevelt prepares for one of his famous fireside chats. AP/WIDE WORLD PHOTOS. REPRODUCED BY PERMISSION.

to the government from projects which will pay for themselves over a period of years.

Thus far I have spoken primarily of the foundation stones—the measures that were necessary to re-establish credit and to head people in the opposite direction by preventing distress and providing as much work as possible through governmental agencies. Now I come to the links which will build us a more lasting prosperity. I have said that we cannot attain that in a nation half boom and half broke. If all of our people have work and fair wages and fair profits, they can buy the products of their neighbors and business is good. But if you take away the wages and the profits of half of them, business is only half as good. It doesn't help much if the fortunate half is very prosperous—the best way is for everybody to be reasonably prosperous.

For many years the two great barriers to a normal prosperity have been low farm prices and the creeping paralysis of unemployment. These factors have cut the purchasing power of the country in half. I promised action. Congress did its part when it passed the farm and the industrial recovery acts. Today we are putting these two acts to work and they will work if people understand their plain objectives.

First, the Farm Act: It is based on the fact that the purchasing power of nearly half our population depends on adequate prices for farm products. We have been producing more of some crops than we consume or can sell in a depressed world market. The cure is not to produce so much. Without our help the farmers cannot get together and cut production, and the Farm Bill gives them a method of bringing their production down to a reasonable level and of obtaining reasonable prices for their crops. I have clearly stated that this method is in a sense experimental, but so far as we have gone we have reason to believe that it will produce good results.

It is obvious that if we can greatly increase the purchasing power of the tens of millions of our people who make a living from farming and the distribution of farm crops, we will greatly increase the consumption of those goods which are turned out by industry.

That brings me to the final step—bringing back industry along sound lines.

Last Autumn, on several occasions, I expressed my faith that we can make possible by democratic self-discipline in industry general increases in wages and shortening of hours sufficient to enable industry to pay its own workers enough to let those workers buy and use the things that their labor produces. This can be done only if we permit and encourage cooperative action in industry because it is obvious that without united action a few selfish men in each competitive group will pay starvation wages and insist on long hours of work. Others in that group must either follow suit or close up shop. We have seen the result of action of that kind in the continuing descent into the economic Hell of the past four years.

There is a clear way to reverse that process: If all employers in each competitive group agree to pay their workers the same wages—reasonable wages—and require the same hours—reasonable hours—then higher wages and shorter hours will hurt no employer. Moreover, such action is better for the employer than unemployment and low wages, because it makes more buyers for his product. That is the simple idea which is the very heart of the Industrial Recovery Act.

On the basis of this simple principle of everybody doing things together, we are starting out on this nationwide attack on unemployment. It will succeed if our people understand it—in the big industries, in the little shops, in the great cities and in the small villages. There is nothing complicated about it and there is nothing particularly new in the principle. It goes back to the basic idea of society and of the nation itself that people acting in a group can accomplish things which no individual acting alone could even hope to bring about.

Here is an example. In the Cotton Textile Code and in other agreements already signed, child labor has been abolished. That makes me personally happier than any other one thing with which I have been connected since I came to Washington. In the textile industry—an industry which came to me spontaneously and with a splendid cooperation as soon as the recovery act was signed—child labor was an old evil. But no employer acting alone was able to wipe it out. If one employer tried it, or if one state tried it, the costs of operation rose so high that it was impossible to compete with the employers or states which had failed to act. The moment the Recovery Act was passed, this monstrous thing which neither opinion nor law could reach through years of effort went out in a flash. As a British editorial put it, we did more under a Code in one day than they in England had been able to do under the common law in eighty-five years of effort. I use this incident, my friends, not to boast of what has already been done but to point the way to you for even greater cooperative efforts this Summer and Autumn.

We are not going through another Winter like the last. I doubt if ever any people so bravely and cheerfully endured a season half so bitter. We cannot ask America to continue to face such needless hardships. It is time for courageous action, and the Recovery Bill gives us the means to conquer unemployment with exactly the same weapon that we have used to strike down Child Labor.

The proposition is simply this:

If all employers will act together to shorten hours and raise wages we can put people back to work. No employer will suffer, because the relative level of competitive cost will advance by the same amount for all. But if any considerable group should lag or shirk, this great opportunity will pass us by and we will go into another desperate Winter. This must not happen.

We have sent out to all employers an agreement which is the result of weeks of consultation. This agreement checks against the voluntary codes of nearly all the large industries which have already been submitted. This blanket agreement carries the unanimous approval of the three boards which I have appointed to advise in this, boards representing the great leaders in labor, in industry and in social service. The agreement has already brought a flood of approval from every State, and from so wide a cross-section of the common calling of industry that I know it is fair for all. It is a plan—deliberate, reasonable and just—intended to put into effect at once the most important of the broad principles which are being established, industry by industry, through codes. Naturally, it takes a good deal of organizing and a great many hearings and many months to get these codes perfected and signed, and we cannot wait for all of them to go through. The blanket agreements, however, which I am sending to every employer will start the wheels turning now, and not six months from now.

There are, of course, men, a few of them who might thwart this great common purpose by seeking selfish advantage. There are adequate penalties in the law, but I am now asking the cooperation that comes from opinion and from conscience. These are the only instruments we shall use in this great summer offensive against unemployment. But we shall use them to the limit to protect the willing from the laggard and to make the plan succeed.

In war, in the gloom of night attack, soldiers wear a bright badge on their shoulders to be sure that comrades do not fire on comrades. On that principle, those who cooperate in this program must know each other at a glance. That is why we have provided a badge of honor for this purpose, a simple design with a legend. "We do our part," and I ask that all those who join with me shall display that badge prominently. It is essential to our purpose.

Already all the great, basic industries have come forward willingly with proposed codes, and in these codes they accept the principles leading to mass reemployment. But, important as is this heartening demonstration, the richest field for results is among the small employers, those whose contribution will give new work for from one to ten people. These smaller employers are indeed a vital part of the backbone of the country, and the success of our plans lies largely in their hands.

Already the telegrams and letters are pouring into the White House—messages from employers who ask that their names be placed on this special Roll of Honor. They represent great corporations and companies, and partnerships and individuals. I ask that even before the dates set in the agreements which we have sent out, the employers of the country who have not already done so—the big fellows and the little fellows—shall at once write or telegraph to me personally at the White House, expressing their intention of going through with the plan. And it is my purpose to keep posted in the post office of every town, a Roll of Honor of all those who join with me.

I want to take this occasion to say to the twenty-four governors who are now in conference in San Francisco, that nothing thus far has helped in strengthening this great movement more than their resolutions adopted at the very outset of their meeting, giving this plan their instant and unanimous approval, and pledging to support it in their states.

To the men and women whose lives have been darkened by the fact or the fear of unemployment, I am justified in saying a word of encouragement because the codes and the agreements already approved, or about to be passed upon, prove that the plan does raise wages, and that it does put people back to work. You can look on every employer who adopts the plan as one who is doing his part, and those employers deserve well of everyone who works for a living. It will be clear to you, as it is to me, that while the shirking employer may undersell his competitor, the saving he thus makes is made at the expense of his country's welfare.

While we are making this great common effort there should be no discord and dispute. This is no time to cavil or to question the standard set by this universal agreement. It is time for patience and understanding and cooperation. The workers of this country have rights under this law which cannot be taken from them, and nobody will be permitted to whittle them away, but, on the other hand, no aggression is now necessary to attain those rights. The whole country will be united to get them for you. The principle that applies to the employers applies to the workers as well, and I ask you workers to cooperate in the same spirit.

When Andrew Jackson, "Old Hickory," died, someone asked, "Will he go to Heaven?" and the answer was, "He will if he wants to." If I am asked whether the American people will pull themselves out of this depression, I answer, "They will if they want to." The essence of the plan is a universal limitation of hours of work per week for any individual by common consent, and a universal payment of wages above a minimum, also by common consent. I cannot guarantee the success of this nationwide plan, but the people of this country can guarantee its success. I have no faith in "cure-alls" but I believe that we can greatly influence economic forces. I have no sympathy with the professional economists who insist that things must run their course and that human agencies can have no influence on economic ills. One reason is that I happen to know that professional economists have changed their definition of economic laws every five or ten years for a very long time, but I do have faith, and retain faith, in the strength of common purpose, and in the strength of unified action taken by the American people.

That is why I am describing to you the simple purposes and the solid foundations upon which our program of recovery is built. That is why I am asking the employers of the Nation to sign this common covenant with me—to sign it in the name of patriotism and humanity. That is why I am asking the workers to go along with us in a spirit of understanding and of helpfulness.

Further Resources

BOOKS

Lawson, Don. *FDR's New Deal.* New York: Crowell, 1979.

Leuchtenburg, William E. *Franklin D. Roosevelt and the New Deal (1932–1940).* New York, Harper & Row, 1963.

Letter to Major General Stuart Heintzelman

Letter

By: George C. Marshall

Date: December 4, 1933

Source: Marshall, George C. Letter to Major General Stuart Heintzelman, December 4, 1933. In Bland, Larry I., ed. *The Papers of George Catlett Marshall; The Soldierly Spirit, December 1880–June 1939*. Baltimore: Johns Hopkins University Press, 1981, 409–13.

About the Author: General George C. Marshall (1880–1959) was born in Uniontown, Pennsylvania. A descendant of U.S. Supreme Court Chief Justice John Marshall, he graduated from Virginia Military Institute and entered the United States Army in 1902. Over the course of his long and distinguished career Marshall served with distinction in World War I (1914–1918). ■

Introduction

Until the beginning of the Cold War in the mid-1940s the United States had no tradition of a standing army. The United States did not have any credible security threats in its own hemisphere, was protected by two broad oceans, and had had a substantial navy since the 1890s, so that the expense of a continually maintained army seemed unnecessary and contrary to democratic principles.

World War I (1914–18), however, demonstrated the risks associated with being ill-prepared in an age of mass armies and modern weapons. In 1916 the U.S. Army numbered 108,000. Following the United States' declaration of war on Germany in April 1917 the army grew to 2.5 million in 1918. It took a year, however, for U.S. troops to provide effective support to their allies on European battlefields. Furthermore, U.S. industry could not convert to war footing rapidly enough, forcing the army to rely on equipment provided by the British and French.

Appalled by the high number of casualties and the cost and apparent failure of these enormous sacrifices to advance the cause of civilization, the United States withdrew from international responsibilities after World War I. This isolationist posture was symbolized by the shrinking of the army to pre-World War I levels. In reality a large army was not justifiable in the years immediately following the war. Even as potential enemies appeared in the early 1930s, however, the United States failed to address military preparedness.

Most Americans preferred to ignore the possibility of future conflict, and the U.S. government continued to treat the military as an afterthought in the budgeting process. Nonetheless a handful of dedicated military professionals, their careers languishing in a largely unwanted military establishment, focused on preparing the Army

General George C. Marshall. Marshall's planning in the early 1930s helped establish an essential base for the success of the U.S. Army during World War II. **THE LIBRARY OF CONGRESS.**

and Navy for the next war. In the 1920s and 1930s they developed weapons, modern tactics and strategies, plans for converting civilian economy to a war footing, and approaches to creating an effective mass army of citizen soldiers capable of defeating the large professional armies of potential adversaries. Among the most important of these professionals was George C. Marshall. A highly regarded young officer in World War I, Marshall received several key assignments between 1918 and 1939 that allowed him to influence the future direction of the U.S. Army.

Significance

Among the most critical of Marshall's assignments was his posting to the Infantry School at Fort Benning, Georgia. During his five years as commander there, Marshall introduced young officers to important new ideas that would play a major role in the building of an effective army in World War II.

First, and most important, was the need to simplify. Simplify orders. Simplify tactics. Simplify supply systems. In the confusion of battle the ability to make and communicate decisions with limited information was critical. Second, the U.S. Army of the future would be one made up of citizen soldiers as it had been in World War

I. Reserve and National Guard units would support a small core of professional soldiers. The bulk of the future army, however, would be composed of draftees who would be placed into desperate situations after limited training and without the military background of professional soldiers. It would be necessary to develop officers and men quickly. Simplified systems and tactics were critical. Third, unlike the experience in World War I, the military must prepare for a war of movement. This would be especially critical in the opening months of a campaign when conditions were at their most fluid and the forces engaged were most vulnerable. Again, simplification enhanced the chances of success.

Upon completion of his tour of duty at Fort Benning in 1932, Marshall was given unit command and spent several years as commander of the Illinois National Guard. He also commanded several Civilian Conservation Corps districts, an experience he felt was very valuable for junior officers because it taught them how to deal with large numbers of young men. Marshall was appointed army chief of staff in 1939. His appointment took effect on September 1, 1939, the day Adolf Hitler launched the German invasion of Poland, beginning World War II (1939–45).

At that time the United States Army, which then included the air force, numbered 190,000 soldiers. It ranked seventeenth in the world. It still relied largely on equipment that had been used in 1918. The United States had virtually no capacity to produce the armaments and other supplies needed in war. In a nation where most people and congressmen still preferred an isolationist foreign policy, it was Marshall's job to prepare the army for the war that both he and Roosevelt knew was coming. Less than five years later the United States Army numbered 8,000,000 and was the best-equipped army in history. The officers and men were almost entirely the citizen soldiers Marshall had envisioned.

On June 6, 1944, which some historians have called the most important day of the twentieth century, the professionalism, devotion to duty, and operational theories of General Marshall and others like him showed their worth. Landing on the stormy coast of Normandy, France, a relative handful of citizen soldiers, pinned down and leaderless but schooled in the simplified systems developed by Marshall, rallied and fought their way off Omaha Beach. The landing they secured was the jumping off point for the Allied sweep across Western Europe that ended with the surrender of Nazi Germany ten months later.

Primary Source

Letter to Major General Stuart Heintzelman

SYNOPSIS: Marshall's experience as the director of instruction at Fort Benning was pivotal for his career and, perhaps, for the United States Army. His notions of simplified command, battlefield improvisation, and movement profoundly influenced and prepared the leaders of the army who served in World War II. In December 1933 he expressed some of his key points in the following letter to General Stuart Heintzelman, then Commandant of the Command and General Staff School at Fort Leavenworth, Kansas.

December 4, 1933

Chicago, Illinois

Dear General:

Since your arrival at Leavenworth I have written you three letters, none of which were mailed. I wrote the first on your assignment as Commandant; spent a great deal of time on it and finally decided I was simply borrowing trouble for myself. Later, the last month I was at Benning, I drafted, and redrafted many times, another letter of the same nature. I carried it to Fort Screven with me and finally came to the same decision and tore it up. Later my feelings again grew too strong and I painstakingly prepared another letter last spring on the eve of the Corps Area maneuvers, but again weakened and decided to let some one else pull the chestnuts out of the fire. But, since coming to Chicago and starting work here with this excellent National Guard Division, I have finally decided to let go and tell you, very confidentially I hope, what I have long wanted to say to you personally.

Briefly, my experience at Benning, especially my observation of two Corps Area maneuvers (about 7000 troops) most of which I was charged with staging, has lead me, not to the opinion, but to the firm conviction that our teaching and system has to be materially modified if we are to avoid a chaotic state of affairs in the first few months of a campaign with a major power. I think we have the best school system in the world, but I also think we are suffering acutely from a lack of practical experience in anything approximating warfare of movement at the outset of a campaign, with inexperienced officers and hastily recruited-up-to-war-strength organizations.

I might premise most of my observations on a preliminary statement of several personal beliefs, namely:

a. That the tactics and leadership of partially trained troops, is a much, much more difficult problem than for veteran organizations of full war strength. And that a different or much modified technique is required.

b. That handling troops with small scale and commercial maps—or no maps except the automobile type—is a much more difficult problem than doing the same thing with a Gettysburg map. And that a different technique is required.

c. That warfare of movement, except where the situation has temporarily stabilized for a day or more preliminary to a great assault, does not admit of orders one half or even one fourth as long as those turned out in our schools. And that, the shorter order, especially if oral, is a much more difficult problem than the elaborate, detailed order of the Gettysburg map variety. (We learnt that the modern German divisions are sometimes deployed on oral orders).

d. That the lack of troops, the infrequency of prolonged maneuvers, the tremendous number of desk jobs or non-command jobs now prevalent in the Regular Army, and the frequency of pure command post training, has led us into theoretical misconceptions that do not hold water in the actual business of handling large bodies of troops in protracted maneuvers.

I will briefly cite, in fragmentary fashion, a few of my experiences at Benning that led me to an almost complete revamping of the instruction and technique at that school. All of this I had to do quietly and gradually, because I felt so much opposition would be met on the outside that I would be thwarted in my purpose. General Collins and General Campbell King were in complete agreement with me, and both felt that general service publicity might bolt the business. Also, we had to educate our local constituency first, particularly the faculty, in order to have the necessary backing. In other words, we bored from within without cessation during my five years at Benning.

I found it next to impossible to convince instructors long absent from troops and steeped in school technique, of the urgent necessity for simplifying matters, no matter how great their war experience, and no matter how loyal they were. They had become unconscious creatures of technique, and lived in the experiences of the fourth year of a war. I made very little progress with these fellows until I stopped all rehearsed demonstrations of tactics, introduced a number of free maneuvers into the course and, finally, placed instructors in command in maneuvers, with all the Corps Area troops, and let them commit errors, some so gross as to be almost amusing, in their blind following of technique. I then endeavored to secure all replacements for the faculty from officers returning from foreign service where there were plenty of troops. This, even to the point of putting men in the tactical section who had not graduated from the Advanced Course or from Leavenworth. Incidentally, I found that the meticulous marking or grading methods caused instructors to draft problems from the view point of uniform and exact grading, rather than entirely with a view to getting across a certain lesson or example—tho they never would admit, or even seem to realize this.

I found that the technique and practices developed at Benning and Leavenworth would practically halt the development of an open warfare situation, apparently requiring an armistice or some understanding with a complacent enemy.

It was evident in many things that the real problem, the real difficulty, usually was not comprehended until too late. For instance, as a small example, all knew how to set up a command post but few understood the real problem, how to avoid a complete set up until the proper moment had arrived. The momentum of an operation was usually killed by the premature setting up of complete command posts. Or, prolonged thought would be given to reaching a tactical decision on purely tactical grounds, when the difficulties of execution or some entirely non-tactical matter, were the real dominant factors.

I found that the ordinary form of our tactical problems committed two deadly sins, relieving the student from the greatest difficulties of his tactical task in warfare of movement. The information of the enemy was about 80% too complete. And, the requirement called for his decision at a pictured moment, when the real problem is usually, *when* to make a decision, and not, *what* the decision should be.

I found no single officer in the entire Corps Area, including the school, ever found time or the map facilities to produce an order in the maneuvers one quarter of the length of a school order in similar situation—and all lacked the technique for preparing the briefer order, which requires much more skill than the voluminous, stereotyped variety.

I found the estimate of the situation had been so restricted to purely tactical questions and governed by so special a technique, suitable for such situations, that officers seldom properly estimated any situation or problem other than the tactical. They had been indoctrinated to the exclusion of orderly thinking habits regarding other matters (not involving the terrain, the enemy, etc.) where rapidity of thought was essential.

In the Corps Area maneuvers the mistakes were so numerous, and often so gross, that a critique was extremely difficult to handle with tact. Staff officers of brilliant reputation in the Army, graduates of Leavenworth and the War College, former instructors at those schools, committed errors so remarkable that it plainly indicated our school system had failed to make clear the real difficulties to be anticipated and surmounted in warfare of movement. The individual sank in a sea of paper, maps, tables and elaborate technique. Or, if he attempted to shorten the working method he confused everything because of lack of training in the more difficult—the simpler methods. Like women's clothes, the simpler the dress the more expensive the garment.

Now, if this was the case with highly trained officers and exceptionally trained troops, what will be the case in the event of a major mobilization and an immediate campaign, with partially trained national guard and theoretically trained reserve officers? I insist we must get down to the essentials, make clear the real difficulties, and expunge the bunk, complications and ponderosities; we must concentrate on registering in men's minds certain vital considerations, instead of a mass of less important details. We must develop a technique and methods so simple and so brief that the citizen officer of good common sense can readily grasp the idea.

The first "skin sheet" I checked at Benning had sixty-eight cuts. I limited it to twelve cuts, and later would not allow but two or three major cuts—the minor corrections being solely for the information of the student. One of the first problems I checked over started with a matter of Army Corps, and at the bottom of the third page I found it was a problem for a communication platoon. I limited this situation to six inches of typed space.

Witness the mass of documents and the months of work a Corp Area staff puts up for an Army Command Post Exercise, all of which could be cut 50% and the benefits of the exercise actually increased. But they are proud of the mimeographs!

I found the Infantry School mimeograph on supply was a prized document covering one hundred and twenty pages. After futile efforts to shorten and simplify it, I caused the entire thing to be thrown out and restricted the new pamphlet to ten pages. I required the supply procedure to be demonstrated completely on the ground. This took one and one-half days the first time and two and one-half hours when I left. The course became the most popular and effective in the school and worked a complete metamorphosis in the 29th Infantry in the field. Every cut or simplicity I imposed at Benning was opposed, often violently. And I think I am accurate in saying that all were enthusiastically approved once they were in effect.

I never got the G–2 business anywhere near what I thought it ought to be—generally, it was an elaborate, impracticable collection of data. I read a G–2 solution of a Leavenworth problem—before your time—in a situation depicting the *second day* of a war (on one of those damned river lines marking the boundary between Red and Blue states) in which fighting had occurred all day. The G–2 effort was *four,* small typed, printed pages! Imagine the tired distraught Division Commander the second day of a war, the first time under fire, trying to pore through such a report—if it ever could have been prepared—to find the meat of the matter.

I am dealing with this in a very fragmentary, disconnected fashion, but if I give you a general impression of any differences with the existing system I will have accomplished my purpose. I feel sure that if, say, every other year or every third year, your instructors could go through protracted divisional maneuvers, a few of them in command or top staff positions, the Leavenworth technique would automatically be simplified year after year until it was perfectly adapted to the practical business of open warfare, partially trained troops and citizen officers. At first I found my Instructors did not even want to go to Corps Area maneuvers at Camp Jackson near Columbia [South Carolina]. They preferred the even tenor of their theoretical ways. But, I must say now, that I think the faculty at Benning the last three years I was there was composed of the most brilliant, interesting and thoroughly competent collection of men I have ever been associated with. We all learned together, but we had a devil of a time getting started. We never got to the point of teaching tactics as General Morrison taught it—most of our supposed tactical instruction fell into the domain of technique.

It appears to me that Leavenworth should specialize on the tactics and technique specifically adapted to—

Partially trained troops;

Partially trained officers;

Mixed strength of organizations and lack of special troops;

and the first six months of a major war.

If this be thoroughly understood, there would be no difficulty whatever about handling veterans, static situations, unlimited ammunition supply and equipment, detailed maps instead of Geological Survey maps or similar affairs of commercial production. Honest to goodness simplicity would be achieved.

Now, having expressed myself far too freely, injected myself into the business of a Major General, and laid myself open to all kinds of trouble, I will close by saying this: I do not believe there is another General officer in the Army I would have chanced this letter with, except yourself. I ask you to consider it for your eye only. I do not want you to trouble to acknowledge it, or commit yourself to any expression regarding it. But simply believe that only my intense interest in the field efficiency of the national army has caused me finally to put myself on paper to the Commandant of Leavenworth.

This is not the carefully prepared production that any of the three previous drafts were. It is a first run of my pencil, and must go as first written. I have too little time and clerical assistance to do otherwise.

Further Resources

BOOKS

Pogue, Forrest C. *George C. Marshall.* Vol. 1, *Education of a General, 1880–1939.* New York: Viking Press, 1963.

WEBSITES

"About George C. Marshall." George C. Marshall Foundation. Available online at http://www.marshallfoundation.org/about_gcm/about_gcm.htm (accessed August 29, 2002).

"American Fascism in Embryo"

Magazine article

By: Harold Loeb and Selden Rodman

Date: December 27, 1933

Source: Loeb, Harold, and Selden Rodman. "American Fascism in Embryo." *The New Republic* 77, no. 995, December 27, 1933, 185–87.

About the Authors: Harold Loeb (1891–1974) graduated from Princeton University and had a brief and unrewarding experience in business before beginning a literary career. He wrote several novels and published a literary magazine. After a 1929 trip to Palestine raised his interest in Zionism, he published several articles on the subject. In the early 1930s, Loeb began working as an economist for the federal government. He went on to write four books on economics. Loeb became acquainted with author Ernest Hemingway and other American expatriates while living in Paris. Hemingway used Loeb as the model for the unflattering character of Robert Cohn in *The Sun Also Rises.*

Selden Rodman (1909–2002) was born in New York City. A graduate of Yale University, he edited two magazines during the 1930s and worked as a freelance writer. Following service in the Army during World War II (1939–1945), Rodman became increasingly interested in and wrote widely about Caribbean culture, particularly Haitian art. ■

Introduction

Fascism as a distinct political philosophy originated in Italy following World War I (1914–1918). In 1922 Benito Mussolini used the threat of revolution to gain control of the Italian government. Over the next twenty years fascist dictators came to power in Greece, Hungry, Spain, Argentina and, most notably, Germany.

The basic element of fascist ideology is an extreme nationalism in which the power of the state is considered absolute. An absolute dictator who is not subject to any constitutional restraint exercises that power. Personal freedoms become secondary to the interests of the state and personal satisfaction comes from the success of the state.

The extreme nationalism of fascism was consistent with another of its features, demagoguery or the targeting of "scapegoats" to rally support and gain power. By blaming "outsiders" for the problems of society fascists pandered to simple prejudices and infected supporters with a highly emotional enthusiasm that accepted the use of unilateral force to achieve state ends. Common "scapegoats" were communists, Jews, and international bankers.

Fascism was the antithesis of Western liberal thought that emphasized political democracy and individual rights. Indeed, fascists blamed the weakness of liberal ideas for the economic and political turmoil of the 1920s and 1930s. They claimed that governments paralyzed by their liberal, democratic philosophy were at the root of the problem. Fascists believed that in an essentially competitive world, nations had two choices. They could be strong and impose their will or be weak and dominated by their enemies. Power was everything and success required the will to use that power. Nations achieved greatness not by the ballot or political debate but by force.

In its crudest form fascism was government by thugs and bullies. It was a philosophy that could not sustain its position in rational argument. At the emotional level, however, it appealed to desperate people caught up in complex economic and political forces over which they had little understanding and even less influence.

Significance

The elements of fascism that made it so reprehensible did not originate in the years between World War I and World War II. Scapegoats, nationalism, and demagogues

Two men join the National Socialist Party, otherwise known as the Nazi Party, at the Party's recently opened New York headquarters. April 1, 1932. **AP/WIDE WORLD PHOTOS. REPRODUCED BY PERMISSION.**

had been around for a long time. In the United States, for example, the same group dynamics that led to fascism in Italy and Germany had led to the anti-immigrant Know Nothing movement of the 1840s and 1850s and the racist Ku Klux Klan in the 1870s. Rejuvenated in the 1920s, the Klan broadened its attack to include a wider range of "un-American" groups including Catholics, Jews, and communists.

As in Europe, the Great Depression gave rise to fascist impulses in the United States. Louisiana politician Huey Long and Roman Catholic priest Charles Coughlin, for example, led movements that used techniques and offered solutions similar to those employed by European dictators. Coughlin's message, which included powerful anti-Semitic rhetoric, was especially hateful. In addition to internal movements that included fascist elements, numerous American organizations patterned themselves directly after German and Italian fascists. While some were clearly marginal hate groups, Adolf Hitler's steady success in achieving international recognition and reinvigorating the German economy increased the appeal of blatant fascism in the United States.

Various isolationist groups also aided the fascist cause. Anxious to avoid war, the public posture of some isolationists gave credibility to fascist policies and ideas. The most significant of these, the America First Committee, was founded by reputable members of the U.S. establishment following the German invasion of Poland in 1939. The committee eventually boasted a membership of 800,000 and was effective in limiting President Roosevelt's efforts to aid Britain in the early 1940s. America First disbanded after Japan's attack on Pearl Harbor led the United States to enter the war in 1941.

The most notorious fascist groups in the United States were the German-American Bund, established in 1933, and the Silver Shirts, organized by William Dudley Pelham. Both claimed large but wildly exaggerated memberships. In one of the most sobering examples of fascist influence, 22,000 people attended a 1939 Bund rally in Madison Square Garden. Shortly afterward, however, the Bund's leader, Fritz Julius Kuhn, was arrested on charges of grand larceny and fraud. Like other fascist organizations the Bund disintegrated upon U.S. entry into World War II.

In retrospect, fascists in the United States were clearly fringe groups. They should not be dismissed too quickly, however. The same could have been said of the Hitler's Nazi Party as late as 1928. There is also a risk of missing the essential point: millions of Americans were attracted by the undemocratic, anti-Semitic, and essentially fascist appeals of various demagogues during the 1930s. While Americans eventually backed away from the abyss, the effectiveness of fascist ideas and techniques should not be ignored.

Primary Source

"American Fascism in Embryo"

SYNOPSIS: Published in late 1933, when Hitler had been German chancellor for less than a year, this article reflects the growing American concern over fascism and the associated anti-Semitism. One of the key objectives of the article is to emphasize the disdain with which opponents held Hitler during his rise to power. Despite being shrugged off as a marginal politician, he had come to power. It was, the authors believed, an important lesson.

When Adolf Hitler, after refusing to play second fiddle to von Schleicher and von Papen, turned the full blast of his propaganda trumpets upon the tiny state of Lippe, the whole world (and Germany in particular) remarked that the man was a fool and that the Nazi movement had come to the end of its tether. Whether this attitude, the sort of wishful thinking that had rendered intelligent men unprophetic, was the result of blind fear or whether the example of Italy had already become too much a matter of "history," is beside the point. The question now is: will the rest of the world, and for our purposes America, be able to cope with the menace of fascism? Bismarck was right when he laughed to scorn the oft-repeated proverb on learning things by experience. The clever man, he said, learns things by the experience of others.

Our government has been careful to extract from the envoy of Soviet Russia the most exacting promises in regard to communist propaganda. But although there are now some hundred and three separate fascist organizations operating in the United States, a few of them financed by German money and at least one preaching loyalty to Hitler and his barbarous ideas, not a promise has been exacted, not a protest lodged, with the government which constitutes such a menace to world peace.

One of us found himself last month at a symptomatic meeting. Unofficial representatives were present from Social Credit, the American branch of Major Douglas' economic school, from the Continental Committee on Technocracy, from the Farm Holiday and Farmer-Labor movements, as well as two former anarchists, an Equitist, a disillusioned banker, the former head of the disbanded New National party, a militant liberal, a Seventy-Sixer and the president of the Crusaders for Economic Liberty. One belief only seemed to be shared by those present, giving the meeting a basis for unity. All felt that the present monetary system had out-lived whatever usefulness it might have had in the past. The agreement ended here. The majority were evidently trying to preserve for the new order what they called economic liberty, and what seemed to mean the freedom to buy and to sell, to receive interest and to lend money. The Technocrats, who considered the freedom to be all important, and the right to sell for profit and to practise usury anachronisms in this age of potential plenty, were clearly in the minority.

Most of the individuals present expressed, in varying degrees, the unrest among many members of the middle class which is prevalent throughout the country. "Middle class" is loosely used to cover that vast heterogeneous body of Americans who are conscious neither of their proletarian nor of their capitalist status. Many members of this class, victims of the system no less than are the industrial workers, are revolting against it. Fascism, which is essentially conservative behind a smoke-screen of reform and hate, makes its appeal to this embittered multitude on two counts. In the beginning, as in the cases of Hitler and Mussolini, it makes an essentially radical appeal. It attacks the bankers and other vested interests of the profit system, urging unity of the working and middle classes. Then it attacks the existing working-class movements on the ground that they intend to take away from the middle class what little stake that class still retains in the profit system. In so doing it plays directly into the hands of the bankers and industrialists, who then deliberately finance it and lead it further and further to the right.

Some varieties of Fascism are local, some have branches in many parts of the country, some have sprung from the remnants of the Ku Klux Klan, others have spontaneously arisen to meet a momentary crisis or a labor threat. The organizations about to be described are typical.

The Khaki Shirts

The Khaki Shirts (U.S. Fascist) are, or were, led by "Commander-in-Chief" Art J. Smith. The movement grew out of the "Bonus Army" march on Washington and reached its finale on October 12 of this year in Philadelphia. The capture of the national capital by an "army," supposedly of 1,500,000 trained Khaki Shirts, had been scheduled for the following day. At first the plan had been to make Smith himself dictator, but by October the less ambitious scheme of investing Franklin D. Roosevelt with the job had been adopted. Publicity at any cost seems to have been the method. Smedley D. Butler, Huey Long and Louis McFadden were said to be hand in glove with Smith. When the day arrived only a few hundred men turned out, and Smith jumped out of the window as the police entered his headquarters. Embezzlement of funds and a good-sized "shirt racket" were exposed by the disgruntled "generals," "colonels" and lesser officers (if any).

The Khaki Shirts published a newspaper. Like most of the other fascist organizations about to be described, they freely circulated under the governmental postal frank Congressman McFadden's speech attacking the Jews. They have disappeared for a time. Some of their leaders are in jail. But the same was true of a certain Austrian corporal after a no less trivial piece of high comedy in Munich, *anno* 1923.

Order of '76

Unlike the Khaki Shirts, the Seventy-Sixers avoid publicity. Their work is done underground. Organizers are sent to trouble centers and members there enrolled. Their leader keeps himself in the background and calls himself organizer rather than chief. They have no program except a general antipathy to certain phases of capitalism such as racketeering, banking, politics. Hatred of Jews was for a time their mainspring. To get around the fact that Jews are actually a minor factor in American banking, they have told prospective members that Morgan and other prominent financiers have traces of Jewish blood.

This organization started in New York and claims to be enrolling 200 members a day. Its method of holding them is to assign specific tasks to each individual. These consist largely in petty espionage. Information is being compiled in order to be ready for "the day." Although it is to be doubted whether they uncover much "inside dope" on the bankers, they are successful in exposing petty graft—and in fingerprinting their own members.

The Silver Shirts

About the time that Hitler seized power, William Dudley Pelley came out into the open with his Silver Shirt national organization. Pelley has served the Y.M.C.A. in Siberia, has devoted much time to spiritualism and advocates a kind of cooperative commonwealth (The Christ Government) in which everyone will be a stockholder in the national industry. He says he converses frequently with spirits who have given him the key by which he reads the pyramids.

The first headquarters of the Silver Shirts were in Asheville, North Carolina. Their central office is now in Oklahoma City. Most of their strength—2 million claimed—lies in Southern California, and the first violent deed attributed to them occurred in Salt Lake City. A suspected Communist, Daniel Black, was kidnaped in the presence of officers, beaten and tied to a tree. At night he was beaten again and left for dead. Although the victim was found by a motorist and recovered to name his assailants, they have not been arrested.

The Silver Shirts, according to Mr. Pelley, not only sympathize with the aims of the Nazi movement but keep in close touch with Hitler's representatives. They accept the exposed forgery known as the Protocols of Zion as an authentic document and seem really to believe that a secret committee of Jewish elders is plotting to destroy civilization with such disparate tools as the Communist party and the international bankers. Mr. Pelley alleged in support of this story that Otto Kahn addressed in Yiddish a group of Jews in the Bronx, urging them to join the conspiracy.

The Crusaders

The Crusaders were organized in 1930 for the purpose of campaigning against prohibition. They have been seeking an excuse for continuing to exist and believe they have found it in "sound money." Their headquarters are in New York and they held their first big anti-inflation rally at Carnegie Hall on November 27.

It wasn't a great success. On the same night in the same city a monster meeting was being held at the Hippodrome for inflation. Unfortunately for the Crusaders, the competing rally was being addressed by a much better demagogue than they could offer. Father Coughlin, the "Radio Priest," stole their show. The Crusaders, with plenty of support from big business, are inclining toward a semi-military set-up, are making inroads upon the "good" preparatory schools

An American Nazi rally at New York's Madison Square Garden in 1935. © HULTON-DEUTSCH COLLECTION/CORBIS. REPRODUCED BY PERMISSION.

and colleges, and through their "sound-money" campaign are being forced to take a stand against further unemployment relief.

Crusaders for Economic Liberty

The Crusaders for Economic Liberty (White Shirts) have no connection with the Crusaders described above. An Idaho politician at a recent meeting of progressive leaders startled his colleagues by informing them that the White Shirts now constitute one of the major political problems not only in his state but in Oregon and Washington as well. They claim 2 million members and have recently announced that the Silver Shirts have decided to join their ranks in a body.

The president of the Crusaders for Economic Liberty is George W. Christians and their national capital is at Chattanooga, Tennessee. Mr. Christians has a panacea which gives a somewhat different character to his organization. The Gold Standard is his "source of all evil." Under the Gold Standard a certain amount of gold is needed as a basis for money and a certain amount of money is needed to run business. Obviously, the needs of business vary while the amount of gold is relatively constant. Mr. Christians recommends, in place of gold, a money that would "just be money," a kind of managed currency which would be expanded (credit to all askers) until every laborer was employed, and contracted, once this mark was attained, in order to prevent inflation. This equilibrium would be accomplished by controlling interest rates, not only by regulating the usual plus rates, but by offering money at minus rates when business was slack.

The White Shirts are the militant branch of the Crusaders for Economic Liberty. Mr. Christians has no inhibitions about the kind of mass appeal that a fascist organization must make. Consequently his organization tends to be radical when the community to be converted is radical, and fascist when the community leans toward reaction.

It is reported that Mr. Oscar C. Pfaus, commander of the German Alliance, thinks well of Mr. Christians. It is also said that a large fascist rally will soon take place in Chicago. Meanwhile general orders have been issued in preparation for a march on Washington. These instructions call for a perfectly drilled and disciplined membership and outline the tactics for taking control of the local governments. Members are to surround the government buildings, persuade the officials by force of numbers and patriotic appeal to resign, repudiate the public debt and bring dishonest officials to justice. The orders warn commanders against hanging politicians indiscriminately or using "pineapples" to loosen up the pocketbooks of those who will not contribute from patriotic motives.

No doubt these instructions are distributed for their psychological effect on White Shirts and others, and while they seem to indicate a sense of humor in Mr. Christians, this is not necessarily true. Mr. Christians uses psychology like a salesman who has taken a correspondence course. And in answer to the question whether he will convert the Nazis to his radical monetary system or the Nazis convert the White Shirts to medieval barbarism, it must be borne in mind that even while the Nazis are not noted for subtlety they possess the prestige which accrues from the subjection of a great nation. Recently one of their representatives closed a letter to Mr. Christians with the following greeting: "Let me salute you as you will be saluted in the days to come. Hail! Christians."

National Watchmen

The National Watchmen are a movement of a different character. No emotional appeal has been written into the "Plan for Economic Rehabilitation in the United States." The plan is detailed and radical, and includes the nationalization of all property except personal; abolishes all corporations for profit, establishes a graduated income tax reaching 100 percent on incomes above $10,000 a year, a minimum wage scale, fixed prices, etc. It seems to be an attempt to combine socialism and the profit system of the early nineteenth century. Just what function profit will retain when cost and price are fixed is not suggested. F. M. Cox, National Commander, says that members are enlisted by addressing factory employees with the permission of the management and claims half a million adherents in one city alone and numerous other units throughout the Middle West.

Many of the other fascist organizations in America are along somewhat similar lines. While fascism in its early manifestations springs from the bottom—from the ruined fringe of the middle class—it is also firmly established at the top. Certain features of the program of the present Democratic administration in Washington have all the economic earmarks of fascism, and it is significant that when Gerard Swope recently proposed his plan for absolute industrial dictatorship, General Johnson approved and added that the weapon of the strike should be taken away from labor.

Another indication of this trend-from-above is the paper recently published by Lawrence Dennis and Harold Lord Varney, The Awakener. Dennis, although a radical economist who has been predicting for some time the doom of capitalism, has now taken a fascist position of the most reactionary sort. The slogan of his paper is "Against Socialism of the Left!" and the bulk of the sheet is made up of attacks upon the administration in Washington for employing certain liberal and radical economists in the various government bureaus.

Fascism suffers from an inner contradiction. Organizations which seek to conserve cannot act against established powers as can true revolutionary movements. Since the rank and file demand action nevertheless, artificial enemies have to be created. Whatever the purpose of the leadership, it is not long before contemporary hates, bankers and Communists, and the traditional hate, the Jews, are dusted off and refurbished. But necessity forces the elimination of one of the triumvirate and concentration upon the other two. Organizing requires money, and neither the Communists nor the Jews can buy immunity by providing it. In Germany and Italy the bankers and industrialists came across. The movement has not reached this stage in America. The money powers seem insufficiently frightened to dig into their pockets to any serious extent, nor has anyone as yet assumed the mythical character with which heroes must be invested in order to put them across.

Fascism in this country is waiting. The leader has not yet emerged. A merger and concentration of forces will be necessary if the present independent movements are not going to cancel each other. The power of fascism will increase in direct proportion as the efforts of the present administration to bolster up the profit system fail. And last, the growth of a powerful radical movement, even faintly approaching the strength of the German labor movement in pre-Hitler days, would bring the battle into the open. This last, it need hardly be said, can work both ways. The development of a powerful radical movement is probably the only thing that can save this country from eventually going the way of Western Europe.

Further Resources

BOOKS

Bell, Leland V. *In Hitler's Shadow: The Anatomy Of American Nazism.* Port Washington, NY: Kennikat Press, 1973.

WEBSITES

Trotsky, Leon. "Fascism: What It Is and How To Fight It." Pamphlet, 1930–1932. Available online at http://eserver.org/history/fighting-fascism/ (accessed April 17, 2003).

"Carry Out the Command of the Lord"

Speech

By: Huey Long

Date: February 5, 1934

Source: Long, Huey. "Carry Out the Command of the Lord." February 5, 1934. Huey Long's Senate Speeches. Social Security On Line. Social Security Administration. Available online at http://www.ssa.gov/history/longsen.html; website home page: http://www.ssa.gov (accessed August 29, 2002).

About the Author: Huey Long (1893–1935) became governor of Louisiana in 1928 and exercised nearly dictatorial control over the state even after he was elected to the United States Senate in 1932. Long gained support from the rural whites of Louisiana, the poor, hardscrabble stock from which he came, through his dynamic and flamboyant style, in part by taking on the wealthy elite, and in part by delivering the basic services to a population that had been ignored by politicians for generations. Initially a supporter of President Franklin D. Roosevelt, Long played a pivotal role in Roosevelt's 1932 presidential nomination. After turning against the president, he was regarded by many as a threat to Roosevelt's reelection in 1936. Long was assassinated in September 1935. ■

Louisiana Senator Huey P. Long makes a point, 1933. CORBIS-BETTMANN. REPRODUCED BY PERMISSION.

Introduction

The disastrous economic conditions of the 1930s forced Americans to reexamine their fundamental political, social, and economic systems. Some, like President Herbert Hoover (served 1929–1933), concluded that salvation lay in the retention of traditional American values. No revolutionary himself, Franklin Roosevelt (served 1933–1945) favored retaining those traditional values but that they should not come before the basic well being of Americans. Consequently Roosevelt advocated greater participation of the federal government in the economic system to ensure fair play and to provide some measure of security to all Americans. In the end most Americans fell into the Roosevelt camp. For much of the 1930s, however, millions of Americans flirted with far more radical positions than those eventually implemented by the New Deal.

The range of radical options ran across the spectrum. At one end was the Moscow-directed Communist Party, openly advocating revolutionary change in the American system. At the other end were various fascist groups modeled, more or less, after the Mussolini's Italy or, later, Hitler's Germany. While the threat of these extremist groups frightened many, they never achieved significant popular support.

Far more appealing were the uniquely American movements, the most influential of which were led by several charismatic individuals including Francis Townsend, Father Charles Coughlin, and Louisiana Senator Huey Long. Initially supporters of Roosevelt, by 1934 each had decided the New Deal was too conservative and had begun to speak out against the president.

In a nation as wealthy as the United States, many Americans felt that the basic problem with the economic system was the inequitable distribution of wealth. Whether through stronger unions, progressive tax legislation, public works, liberal pension programs for the elderly, or the establishment of a communist state, the redistribution of wealth was the fundamental political issue of Depression.

Concern over the concentration of wealth was hardly new in 1930. Ever since the post–Civil War (1861–1865) industrial expansion and the associated accumulation of great wealth by a few, various reform movements had grappled with the problem as both an economic and political issue. Huey Long was raised in an impoverished section of northern Louisiana in a community highly sensitized to the great power of the wealthy elite. He resented it and long harbored ideas about the redistribution of wealth. In 1934 these ideas crystallized into Long's "Share the Wealth" program.

The primary component of this program called for a steeply graduated tax on wealth over $1 million, reaching 100 percent on all wealth over $8 million. This wealth would be redistributed based on a formula that guaranteed each family a minimum stake of one-third the national average of wealth. Based on a total national wealth of $400 billion, this would result in an initial distribution of $5,000 per family. That amount would allow each family "a fairly comfortable home, and automobile and a radio, with other reasonable home conveniences, and a place to educate their children." Long also promised that there would be sufficient annual revenue from his taxation plan to provide each family with a guaranteed yearly income of $2,000 to $2,500.

Significance

Ignoring faulty math and insurmountable practical implementation problems, down and out Americans were understandably drawn to Long's seductive plan. Under the direction of the equally flamboyant Reverend Gerald L. K. Smith, Share the Wealth Clubs were organized all across the country. By early 1935 Long boasted that there were twenty-seven thousand clubs with 7.5 million members. While this is undoubtedly an exaggeration, Long's political strength could not be disputed. It provided Long with a powerful political platform upon which to base a run for the presidency in 1936.

Coincident with Long's rise to prominence was that of Francis Townsend and Father Charles Coughlin. Townsend, a physician, came up with the "Townsend Recovery Plan." This program would redistribute wealth through a generous pension plan that would, Townsend claimed, care for the elderly and stimulate the economy. Coughlin, a Roman Catholic priest with a popular national radio program, established the National Union for Social Justice. Like Long, he attacked the wealthy manipulators of the U.S. economy and political system. All three men hoped to restore the country to the fundamental, egalitarian values that each associated with rural, small-town America. Combined, they claimed a following of nearly twenty million people.

By 1935, Roosevelt backers were genuinely concerned by the apparent popular support for Townsend, Coughlin, and Long. No doubt this prompted Roosevelt to sponsor such measures as the Social Security Act, an aggressive and progressive tax reform package, as well as a five-billion-dollar public works program. The impending 1936 election was turned on its head on September 9, 1935. On that day, the son-in-law of one of his political enemies assassinated Huey Long in the halls of the Louisiana capitol.

Despite efforts to continue the Share the Wealth crusade, Long's death ended it as a significant alternative to Roosevelt's New Deal. With Long out of the picture, a Coughlin-Townsend alliance was formed, encouraged by Reverend Smith, Long's former aide. They were able to run a candidate, William Lemke of South Dakota, for president under the Union Party banner. Out of nearly forty-five million votes cast, however, Lemke received less than nine hundred thousand. Roosevelt's dramatic victory—he captured 61 percent of the popular vote and all but eight electoral votes—ended Coughlin, Townsend, and the remaining Long contingent as serious threats to the New Deal.

Primary Source

"Carry Out the Command of the Lord"

SYNOPSIS: In early 1934 Huey Long began to publicize his Share the Wealth Plan. To the irritation of many senators, Long frequently requested that his radio speeches and other pronouncements be read into the congressional record. Such was the case with the following paper. Entitled "Carry Out the Command of the Lord," it outlines his recently announced Share the Wealth Plan and calls for citizens to form Share the Wealth Societies to push for his plan's adoption.

Mr. President, I send to the desk and ask to have printed in the RECORD not a speech but what is more in the nature of an appeal to the people of America.

There being no objection, the paper entitled "Carry Out the Command of the Lord" was ordered to be printed in the RECORD, as follows:

People of America: In every community get together at once and organize a share-our-wealth society—Motto: Every man a king.

Principles and platform:

1. To limit poverty by providing that every deserving family shall share in the wealth of America for not less than one third of the average wealth, thereby to possess not less than $5,000 free of debt.
2. To limit fortunes to such a few million dollars as will allow the balance of the American people to share in the wealth and profits of the land.
3. Old-age pensions of $30 per month to persons over 60 years of age who do not earn as much as $1,000 per year or who possess less than $10,000 in cash or property,

thereby to remove from the field of labor in times of unemployment those who have contributed their share to the public service.

4. To limit the hours of work to such an extent as to prevent overproduction and to give the workers of America some share in the recreations, conveniences, and luxuries of life.
5. To balance agricultural production with what can be sold and consumed according to the laws of God, which have never failed.
6. To care for the veterans of our wars.
7. Taxation to run the Government to be supported, first, by reducing big fortunes from the top, thereby to improve the country and provide employment in public works whenever agricultural surplus is such as to render unnecessary, in whole or in part, any particular crop.

Simple and Concrete—Not an Experiment

To share our wealth by providing for every deserving family to have one third of the average wealth would mean that, at the worst, such a family could have a fairly comfortable home, an automobile, and a radio, with other reasonable home conveniences, and a place to educate their children. Through sharing the work, that is, by limiting the hours of toil so that all would share in what is made and produced in the land, every family would have enough coming in every year to feed, clothe, and provide a fair share of the luxuries of life to its members. Such is the result to a family, at the worst.

From the worst to the best there would be no limit to opportunity. One might become a millionaire or more. There would be a chance for talent to make a man big, because enough would be floating in the land to give brains its chance to be used. As it is, no matter how smart a man may be, everything is tied up in so few hands that no amount of energy or talent has a chance to gain any of it.

Would it break up big concerns? No. It would simply mean that, instead of one man getting all the one concern made, that there might be 1,000 or 10,000 persons sharing in such excess fortune, any one of whom, or all of whom, might be millionaires and over.

I ask somebody in every city, town, village, and farm community of America to take this as my personal request to call a meeting of as many neighbors and friends as will come to it to start a share-our-wealth society. Elect a president and a secretary and charge no dues. The meeting can be held at a courthouse, in some town hall or public building, or in the home of someone.

It does not matter how many will come to the first meeting. Get a society organized, if it has only two members. Then let us get to work quick, quick, quick to put an end by law to people starving and going naked in this land of too much to eat and too much to wear. The case is all with us. It is the word and work of the Lord. The Gideons had but two men when they organized. Three tailors of Tooley Street drew the Magna Carta of England. The Lord says: "For where two or three are gathered together in My name, there am I in the midst of them."

We propose to help our people into the place where the Lord said was their rightful own and no more.

We have waited long enough for these financial masters to do these things. They have promised and promised. Now we find our country $10 billion further in debt on account of the depression, and big lenders even propose to get 90 percent of that out of the hides of the common people in the form of a sales tax.

There is nothing wrong with the United States. We have more food than we can eat. We have more clothes and things out of which to make clothes than we can wear. We have more houses and lands than the whole 120 million can use if they all had good homes. So what is the trouble? Nothing except that a handful of men have everything and the balance of the people have nothing if their debts were paid. There should be every man a king in this land flowing with milk and honey instead of the lords of finance at the top and slaves and peasants at the bottom.

Now be prepared for the slurs and snickers of some high-ups when you start your local spread-our-wealth society. Also when you call your meeting be on your guard for some smart-aleck tool of the interests to come in and ask questions. Refer such to me for an answer to any question, and I will send you a copy. Spend your time getting the people to work to save their children and to save their homes, or to get a home for those who have already lost their own.

To explain the title, motto, and principles of such a society I give the full information, viz:

> Title: Share-our-wealth society is simply to mean that God's creatures on this lovely American continent have a right to share in the wealth they have created in this country.

They have the right to a living, with the conveniences and some of the luxuries of this life, so long as there are too many or enough for all. They have a right to raise their children in a healthy, wholesome atmosphere and to educate them, rather than to face the dread of their under-nourishment and sadness by being denied a real life.

Motto: "Every man a king" conveys the great plan of God and of the Declaration of Independence, which said: "All men are created equal." It conveys that no one man is the lord of another, but that from the head to the foot of every man is carried his sovereignty.

Now to cover the principles of the share-our-wealth society, I give them in order:

1. To limit poverty:

We propose that a deserving family shall share in our wealth of America at least for one third the average. An average family is slightly less than five persons. The number has become less during depression. The United States total wealth in normal times is about $400 billion or about $15,000 to a family. If there were fair distribution of our things in America, our national wealth would be three or four or five times the $400 billion, because a free, circulating wealth is worth many times more than wealth congested and frozen into a few hands as is America's wealth. But, figuring only on the basis of wealth as valued when frozen into a few hands, there is the average of $15,000 to the family. We say that we will limit poverty of the deserving people. One third of the average wealth to the family, or $5,000, is a fair limit to the depths we will allow any one man's family to fall. None too poor, none too rich.

2. To limit fortunes:

The wealth of this land is tied up in a few hands. It makes no difference how many years the laborer has worked, nor does it make any difference how many dreary rows the farmer has plowed, the wealth he has created is in the hands of manipulators. They have not worked any more than many other people who have nothing. Now we do not propose to hurt these very rich persons. We simply say that when they reach the place of millionaires they have everything they can use and they ought to let somebody else have something. As it is, 0.1 of 1 percent of the bank depositors [own] nearly half of the money in the banks, leaving 99.9 of bank depositors owning the balance. Then two thirds of the people do not even have a bank account. The lowest estimate is that 4 percent of the people own 85 percent of our wealth. The people cannot ever come to light unless we share our wealth, hence the society to do it.

3. Old-age pensions:

Everyone has begun to realize something must be done for our old people who work out their lives, feed and clothe children, and are left penniless in their declining years. They should be made to look forward to their mature years for comfort rather than fear. We propose that, at the age of 60, every person should begin to draw a pension from our Government of $30 per month, unless the person of 60 or over has an income of over $1,000 per year or is worth $10,000, which is two thirds of the average wealth in America, even figured on a basis of it being frozen into a few hands. Such a pension would retire from labor those persons who keep the rising generations from finding employment.

4. To limit the hours of work:

This applies to all industry. The longer hours the human family can rest from work, the more it can consume. It makes no difference how many labor-saving devices we may invent, just as long as we keep cutting down the hours and sharing what those machines produce, the better we become. Machines can never produce too much if everybody is allowed his share, and if it ever got to the point that the human family could work only 15 hours per week and still produce enough for everybody, then praised be the name of the Lord. Heaven would be coming nearer to earth. All of us could return to school a few months every year to learn some things they have found out since we were there: All could be gentlemen: Every man a king.

5. To balance agricultural production with consumption:

About the easiest of all things to do when financial masters and market manipulators step aside and let work the law of the Lord. When we have a supply of anything that is more than we can use for a year or two, just stop planting that particular crop for a year either in all the country or in a part of it. Let the Government take over and store the surplus for the next year. If there is not something else for the farmers to plant or some other work for them to do to live on for the year when the crop is banned, then let that be the year for the public works to be done in the section where the farmers need work. There is plenty of it to do and taxes of the big fortunes at the top will supply plenty of money without hurting anybody. In time we would have the people not struggling to raise so much when all were well fed and clothed. Distribution of wealth almost solves the whole problem without further trouble.

6. To care for the veterans of our wars:

A restoration of all rights taken from them by recent laws and further, a complete care of any disabled veteran for any ailment, who has no means of support.

7. Taxation:

Taxation is to be levied first at the top for the Government's support and expenses. Swollen fortunes should be reduced principally through taxation. The Government should be run through revenues it derives after allowing persons to become well above millionaires and no more. In this manner the fortunes will be kept down to reasonable size and at the same time all the works of the Government kept on a sound basis, without debts.

Things cannot continue as they now are. America must take one of three choices, viz:

1. A monarchy ruled by financial masters—a modern feudalism.
2. Communism.
3. Sharing of the wealth and income of the land among all the people by limiting the hours of toil and limiting the size of fortunes.

The Lord prescribed the last form. It would preserve all our gains, share them among our population, guarantee a greater country and a happy people.

The need for such share-our-wealth society is to spread the truth among the people and to convey their sentiment to their Members of Congress.

Whenever such a local society has been organized, please send me notice of the same, so that I may send statistics and data which such local society can give out in their community, either through word of mouth in meetings, by circulars, or, when possible, in local newspapers.

Please understand that the Wall Street controlled public press will give you as little mention as possible and will condemn and ridicule your efforts. Such makes necessary the organizations to share the wealth of this land among the people, which the financial masters are determined they will not allow to be done. Where possible, I hope those organizing a society in one community will get in touch with their friends in other communities and get them to organize societies in them. Anyone can have copies of this article reprinted in circular form to distribute wherever they may desire, or, if they want me to have them printed for them, I can do so and mail them to any address for 60 cents per hundred or $4 per thousand copies.

I introduced in Congress and supported other measures to bring about the sharing of our wealth when I first reached the United States Senate in January 1932. The main efforts to that effect polled about six votes in the Senate at first. Last spring my plan polled the votes of nearly twenty United States Senators, becoming dangerous in proportions to the financial lords. Since then I have been abused in the newspapers and over the radio for everything under the sun. Now that I am pressing this program, the lies and abuse in the big newspapers and over the radio are a matter of daily occurrence. It will all become greater with this effort. Expect that. Meantime go ahead with the work to organize a share-our-wealth society.

Sincerely,
Huey P. Long,
United States Senator.

Further Resources

BOOKS

Brimkley, Alan. *Voices of Protest: Huey Long, Father Coughlin, and The Great Depression.* New York: Alfred A. Knopf, 1982.

Dethloff, Henry C., ed. *Huey P. Long: Southern Demagogue or American Democrat?* Boston: Heath, 1967.

Long, Huey P. *Every Man a King: The Autobiography of Huey P. Long.* Reprint. New York: Da Capo Press, 1996

WEBSITES

"Huey Long in Depth." Social Security Online. Social Security Administration. Available online at http://www.ssa.gov/history/hlong1.html; website home page: http://www.ssa.gov (accessed August 29, 2002).

Harry Hopkins Press Conference, February 16, 1934

Press conference

By: Harry Hopkins
Date: February 16, 1934

Source: "Harry Hopkins Press Conference, February 16, 1934." Civil Works Administration: Record Group 69, Series 737, Box 4. Available online at http://newdeal.feri.org/texts/787.htm (accessed August 29, 2002).

About the Author: Harry L. Hopkins (1890–1946) was born in Sioux City, Iowa. He worked as a social worker in New York City until 1931 when Franklin D. Roosevelt, then governor of New York, selected him to lead the New York State Temporary Emergency Relief Administration. In 1933 President Roosevelt (served 1933–1945) brought Hopkins to Washington to run the recently created Federal Emergency Relief Administration (FERA). Compassionate, confident, and a superb administrator, Hopkins became one of Roosevelt's most important advisors. ■

Introduction

When Franklin Roosevelt took office in March 1933, millions of Americans were on the verge of starvation. Local resources and charities were out of money. Determined to address this problem, Roosevelt pushed for a substantial federal relief package. In response, Congress passed the Federal Emergency Relief Act (FERA). Congress initially allotted FERA $500 million, half to be distributed to states on a matching grant basis, half to be used on a discretionary basis.

Harry Hopkins, FERA Administrator, was a truly progressive social worker. He despised the arrogance with which charity was usually dispensed and yet had serious reservations about an expansive direct relief program. Work relief was, to some degree, incorporated into the FERA. As the winter of 1933–1934 approached, Hopkins knew that a significantly expanded program would be necessary to see the unemployed through to the spring. In early November Hopkins presented the president with a proposal for an extensive, short-term work relief program. Almost immediately Roosevelt reallocated $400 million (eventual federal funds totaled $875 million) from other agencies, bringing the Civil Works Administration (CWA) into being.

Unlike FERA, which was primarily directed by the states using federal funds, the CWA was administered directly by the federal government. This was an important precedent. By early December, the CWA, in part by taking over FERA work projects, had two million workers on the payroll.

Significance

Although sharply criticized by conservatives, the CWA accomplished a great deal in just a few months. Its workers improved nearly 500,000 miles of roads, renovated thousands of public buildings and recreational areas, and built or improved over a thousand airports.

The CWA had high ambitions. While most of its projects were construction-related, the CWA also found suitable employment for nearly 400,000 white-collar workers, including 50,000 teachers. At the urging of the president's wife, Eleanor Roosevelt, a women's bureau was formed that coordinated work for 300,000 women. Foreshadowing the Federal Arts Program, the CWA created the Public Works of Art Program. It attempted to offset the drastic decline in donations and public funding that sustained cultural programs across the country.

As planned, the CWA began to wind down in March 1934. Layoffs began in the South and moved north with warm weather. Operations ceased on April 3. Projects in process were transferred to the FERA.

In the end, the CWA must be considered an important success. First and foremost it provided 4.2 million people and their families with the income to see them through the winter months. More importantly it reinforced Hopkins's belief, shared by social workers around the country, in the value of work relief over direct relief and in the ability of the federal government to manage such a program. Indeed, a contemporary noted that the civil works program successfully met the challenges of the 1933 crisis and illustrated that such a program may have long-term benefits in meeting the needs of the unemployed at any time.

The direct descendent of the CWA was the Works Project Administration (WPA), which was created in early 1935 with an initial budget of $4.8 billion. Lasting until 1942, the WPA eventually employed 8.5 million people on thousands of public works projects throughout the country.

Primary Source

Harry Hopkins Press Conference, February 16, 1934

SYNOPSIS: The self-assured Harry Hopkins gave frequent press conferences. Here he discusses the strategy for closing down the CWA.

Have you your high-power regulations?

Our regulations are not high-powered. You know, this is a great job. Here is a letter from a man who had a faithful wife, but he was unfaithful to her. He wants me to write her to take him back.

Well, you are the relief administrator, and he needs relief. How many pages did it take him to say that?

Only one to say that, but he took six pages to tell me why his wife should take him back.

Does the Federal Surplus Relief take care of things like that, under their broad powers?

No, I don't think it goes that far. They can't take care of that.

Are you going to write him a letter?

I think I will file it.

We are sending out our new rules and regulations today. In dropping CWA workers, all persons living in a household, where another member is working, will be dropped first.

What do you mean by working?

It means where another person has public or private employment.

How many people will that affect?

I do not know.

How will you find out about two people in a household working, through investigation?

Sure. Secondly, all persons who have other resources will be dropped. It is our intention to maintain CWA at its present strength in all industrial cities through the winter.

Next winter?

Through this winter.

When does the winter end? About March 21st, is it not?

It is our intention to begin demobilization in the rural areas of the country, beginning with next Friday, when about 400,000 will be dropped. The rate of decrease will be adjusted to weather conditions.

Weather and climatic conditions?

Yes, and the decrease will be accelerated with the beginning of Spring and the demobilization will be completed by the week ending May 1st.

Completed in the rural areas only?

Demobilization of the CWA will be completed by May 1st.

The wage regulations will read, substantially, as follows:

> Effective not later than March 1st, the wages paid on CWA work shall be a minimum of thirty cents an hour, and the prevailing rate of wage in each local community for the kind of work performed. The hours of work, for the present, will remain at twenty-four hours a week in the cities and fifteen hours in the rural areas. Any city which is authorized, for any reason, to add workers will add only workers that are in need of a job. Or, I think it would be better to say, who are in need.

It is our intention to develop, on a substantial scale, certain projects. One of these projects is the rebuilding, the extension and the building of new consolidated rural schools in those States that have a consolidated school system. Other similar major projects are under consideration which can be completed by May 1st.

Do you mean building new schools?

Yes, I mean that. Why not?

What is a consolidated school?

Why an eight or ten room building taking care of several townships. A consolidated rural school. I do not mean one, or two-room schools.

In other words, a community school, for several communities.

Yes, a community school limited to the population living in that particular rural section.

Will rural schools have pretty large bailiwicks? How far can you go as to the size of towns for these schools? Towns of five thousand maximum?

They will be rural schools, in rural territory—out in the country.

Will they be modern buildings, will they be fire-proof?

We will build modern schools.

Every time a school is built like that, you have to have a flock of buses for the pupils. How about that?

We will build them where maintenance will be assured. We will get the cooperation of local communities and get them to put up some money too.

In how many States do they have consolidated school systems?

About ten or twelve, but I do not want to give out a list of them.

Have you set an arbitrary date for the end of winter?

I think assurance can be given that the CWA, in industrial areas, will carry through the month of March, as now constituted.

When will demobilization reach non-industrial cities?

Very soon.

In two weeks?

I should think so.

You say that these regulations will be governed by climatic and weather conditions. That will make, practically, the first drops in the far South.

No, because I think that our regulations concerning more than one person in a family working, will drop them in other rural areas as well. It applies to rural districts throughout the country, and not solely in the South.

Will each State be given, before the end of the week, definite reductions in the number of men?

Yes, each State will be given a schedule of demobilization. Each State will also be given, at the same time, the total amount of money for materials which they will have during the balance of the period.

Harry Hopkins, head of the Federal Emergency Relief Administration and the Works Progress Administration, gives a speech at the United States Conference of Mayors on November 19, 1935. AP/WIDE WORLD PHOTOS. REPRODUCED BY PERMISSION.

Have these schedules been prepared yet?

Yes, but they are not available now.

Are these reductions in addition to the 150,000 which were dropped yesterday?

Well that drop simply started the demobilization.

Does this apply to Civil Works Service projects as well as Civil Works?

In some cases, yes.

These new schedules seem to indicate a reversal of policy, because the President said May 15th for the end of demobilization and now you say May 1st. On the other hand, there has been talk of extension beyond May 15th. Is there any significance to this? Does it mean that it is being done arbitrarily, without regard to conditions?

It simply means that this is our policy with regard to the CWA.

If you cannot take on new workers, what will you do in that school building plan?

There are many ways to kill a cat. Certainly, you can be assured, too, that consideration is being given to questions of long-range planning on this thing. This department is only one of several departments of the government that are concerned. This immediate enterprise which we have been prosecuting, has been one to give unemployed throughout the country decent jobs. I believe that has been done, the job has been done and we have nothing to apologize for in the way of giving unemployed workers a job and that goes for those unemployed who are not on the relief rolls. To give these people who have been fighting the battle through this winter, a chance to work, seems to me to be an essential part of not only intelligent but decent treatment of the unemployed.

There has been a suggestion that something will take the place of the CWA.

I think you must assume that the CWA, in itself, was intended as an emergency measure to meet the needs of this winter and that long time planning may include a number of devices, some of which are not now in operation, but, obviously, this concerns all departments of government. We have tried here to do an emergency job and we believe that it has been done, and these appropriations from Congress are for the purpose of meeting the emergency needs, and do not represent an indication of permanent government policy.

Will you take back on relief rolls, the workers who are dropped?

We will keep everyone on relief who is in need.

Can you tell us about the new methods?

No.

You said before that hours were cut because of lack of money. Is there any reason, other than that, for keeping them that way now?

We are faced with either increasing the hours, which would require a more rapid demobilization of the number of men, and, at the moment, it seems to the interest of the whole emergency and unemployed relief program to maintain more persons, rather than increase the hours for fewer workers.

Is this prevailing rate of wage calculated to bring about a reduction or increase?

I have no exact idea. In some cases it will mean an increase, but I do not think it will affect the totals a great deal.

How much will it take until demobilization?

Oh, I think it will cost something between $350,000,000 and $400,000,000.

When will you begin to demobilize in the very cold States?

In the rural areas, right away.

Do you mean that on this Friday, or rather, next Friday, February 23rd, 400,000 will be dropped?

Yes, that is right. Our pay-days run from Thursday to Thursday.

What will that make the total lay-off to that date?

There were between 150,000 and 200,000 dropped on Federal projects, and there will be at least 400,000 on the 23rd.

Have you given any instructions in letters to the state administrations about sending out social workers to examine into these situations?

Those will go out. Of course, they know these people and where more than one person is working in a household, it is known. That will not be so difficult.

Then you have revived your plan of letting them go in the South first and then working gradually towards the colder States?

Well, that will be the effect, substantially, because in the South, naturally, there would be a larger proportion, but we have many areas in the North where we have, apparently, more than one person in a household at work and in rural areas, men who have already earned six or seven weeks work.

How many on CWA works in rural areas?

I cannot figure that, but taking it as a whole, we had 3,850,000, at work and paid last week.

Are all cities regarded as industrial?

With but few exceptions.

This city, Washington, would be an exception?

I would think so.

Is the ten per cent dropping plan out?

That was simply a device in regard to Federal projects, but that plan will not be used throughout the country, for the whole thing.

What will be the percentage throughout the country?

It will not increase rapidly during the next few weeks. It will not be as fast as at a later date.

Will you make public the State schedules when you send them out? If you don't, they will come out at the other end.

Yes, that is right. Alright, we will give them to you.

If it appears that in some of the northern States, winter weather hangs on, will special dispensation be granted?

It might, but I do not think that will happen.

You say a minimum of thirty cents per hour. What is it now?

As a matter of fact, the minimum is now thirty cents an hour. And we will pay the local prevailing rate of wage for the kind of work performed. If they pay a bricklayer so much in any section, we will pay that, for example. This is not a device to break down wage scales.

When will we find out what States will get schools?

Just as fast as we make our decisions.

Any northern States?

We have one or two, yes.

In speaking of rural areas in general, who will designate the particular localities where demobilization will start?

We will leave that to the State administrations.

Do you consider a city of five thousand a rural area?

It might be. No one has ever made a satisfactory definition of a rural area.

Do these long-time projects you mention figure on taking care of large numbers of people thrown out of work?

Any long time plan, if it amounts to anything, takes care of the whole national economy.

Will half a million persons be demobilized weekly?

That would be high, particularly during the winter weeks. We are only going to demobilize 400,000 next week. It would not be as high as you saw during the winter weeks.

How about those schedules of demobilization? We will be kicked around if we do not get them.

You say you get kicked around! Well, so do I.

But you can take it.

Oh, can I? Is that so?

What will happen when these four millions are turned loose again?

Now you are asking me to speculate. I am here as part of this administration which believes that this recovery thing is working. This fellow over here makes things work.

How about that transplanting of people? Is that part of the idea?

I do not want to get into that. You all know perfectly well that this is only one department of the government.

How many will you drop the week ending March 30th?

I did not say anything about that week.

Have you received reports about demonstrations? Do they amount to anything?

I do not think they are serious.

Is it a good guess that the FSRC will be used as the agency for this long time planning?

I think that would be a very bad guess.

What would be a good guess?

Well, that is not important. The only thing that is important is over here a couple of blocks. As to who or what does it, that is a detail.

What will you do yourself after May 1st? Will you go to relief?

I will have some fun, whatever it is.

At this point, the conference adjourned.

Further Resources

BOOKS

Gill, Corrington. "Unemployment Relief." *Proceedings of the American Economic Association,* March 1935. In *The Hungry Years: A Narrative History of the Great Depression in America,* edited by T. H. Watkins. New York: Henry Holt and Company, 1999.

Hopkins, June. *Harry Hopkins: Sudden Hero, Brash Reformer.* New York: St. Martin's Press, 1999.

Kurzman, Paul A. *Harry Hopkins and the New Deal.* Fair Lawn, N.J.: R.E. Burdick, 1974.

Leuchtenburg, William E. *Franklin D. Roosevelt and the New Deal (1932–1940).* New York: Harper & Row, 1963.

Schwartz, Bonnie Fox. *The Civil Works Administration, 1933–1934: The Business of Emergency Employment in the New Deal.* Princeton, N.J.: Princeton University Press, 1984.

"Federal Emergency Relief"

Speech

By: Harry Hopkins

Date: 1934

Source: Hopkins, Harry. Speech before the National Democratic Club in New York. Printed in "Federal Emergency Relief." *Vital Speeches of the Day* 1, no. 7, December 31, 1934.

About the Author: Harry L. Hopkins (1890–1946) was a top advisor to President Franklin D. Roosevelt (served 1933–1945). He joined the Roosevelt administration in 1933 to lead the Federal Emergency Relief Administration. In 1935 he was put in charge of the Works Progress Administration (WPA) and from 1938 to 1940 served as secretary of commerce. During World War II (1939–1945) Hopkins was a special advisor on foreign affairs to the president and developed important relationships with leaders of the Allied powers. ■

Introduction

The relief programs of the New Deal were unprecedented in the history of the United States. As much as anyone, Harry Hopkins represented the goals and objectives of those programs. The first major hurdle to overcome in the relief program was the philosophical issue. Americans had to adjust to the idea of the federal government providing economic assistance, a function that had previously been performed by local governments and private charities. By the time Roosevelt came to office the country was in the depths of the Great Depression and it was clear that the traditional relief approaches needed to be supplemented by federal involvement.

A second obstacle was officials' typically condescending attitude toward the recipients of relief. This was born out of the belief that the poor and unemployed were responsible for their own situation and that they should be grateful for whatever the assistance they were given. A large percentage of the American population believed in the image of the "rugged individual" who was responsible for his or her own destiny and took full responsibility for overcoming adversity. It was a concept even more firmly held by the leaders of U.S. society, notably President Herbert Hoover (served 1929–1933). Hoover's firm belief in this concept had prevented him from initiating more liberal programs during the crisis of the Depression.

A third issue was the idea that relief should consist only of subsistence aid. This meant providing enough food to keep a person alive until they were able to fend for themselves. Housing, clothing, fuel, and other basic necessities often did not factor in the relief equation. Certainly traditional relief agencies did not consider the emotional needs of the recipient. To a large degree recipients were expected to feel degraded and ashamed. The idea of building or maintaining self-esteem was not a part of relief.

The relief programs of the New Deal changed the nature of relief assistance in the United States. It relied on and reflected the professionalization of social work, which introduced scientific casework, research, and analysis and replaced volunteer efforts often guided by a stern Protestant work ethic or the competitive aspect of Social Darwinism.

The person who best personified New Deal federal relief programs was Harry Hopkins. An important part of his role as head of the FERA and later the WPA was to persuade a skeptical United States that the expanded and more intrusive aid programs were the appropriate types of relief in general, and federal relief in particular.

Significance

Professional social workers of the era generally believed that welfare must promote the social good and the long-term benefit of the recipient. The objective should be to reinforce American values rather than undercut those values with a system that created a permanent class of welfare recipients.

The scope of the Depression reinforced the belief that the poor and unemployed were victims of a system over which they had little control. The extent of the problem, which affected the whole nation and quickly exhausted the resources of local and private agencies, helped New Dealers win wide support for new relief programs. This new approach included removing the stigma of relief. Payments should be made in cash rather than food or coal vouchers. Work relief should replace direct relief.

To Hopkins a critical element was the creation of extensive work relief programs to replace direct relief. They were more expensive and politically sensitive. Work relief programs ran the risk of competing with private business and were more susceptible to charges of corruption and waste. FERA included some work relief components but it was not until the start of the Civil Works Administration (CWA) late in 1933 that the federal government initiated a comprehensive work relief program to aid the unemployed. The CWA was, however, a temporary program to help see the country through the winter of 1933–1934. Thereafter federal aid reverted to the more traditional form of direct relief.

Buoyed by the success of the CWA, Hopkins pushed for additional work relief programs. This was accomplished in 1935 with the creation of the Works Progress Administration (WPA). Over the next eight years the WPA employed 8.5 million people on projects costing $11 billion.

Primary Source

"Federal Emergency Relief"

SYNOPSIS: In December 1934 Harry Hopkins addressed the National Democratic Club, and NBC radio broadcast his speech to the entire country. Hopkins chastises those who argue that "if you give the poor bathtubs, they'll only store coal in them . . . that poor people like being poor." He also makes a strong pitch for work relief as superior to direct relief.

Your chairman has permitted me to choose my own subject, but his suggestion was that I might like to talk about the relation of relief to the Christmas spirit. There are eighteen million people on relief who know better than I do what a difficult task that is. For one who still stands outside their ranks, even in a position so close to them as the Administrator of Relief, it seems like an effrontery.

It is a curious thing what a quantity of sickness, coldness, hunger and barefootedness we are willing to let other men suffer. It literally has no limit. You can hear it in the cautious tone of voice of a man who says, "We'd better be careful or we will have a major disaster." What, might we ask him, would he consider to be a major disaster? Obviously it has nothing to do with numbers. For eighteen million persons is a large enough number used in any connection to satisfy most men. Eighteen million men in an army is a large army. Eighteen million sick men is an epidemic larger than any we have ever recorded. Eighteen million criminals would turn the country into a jail. Eighteen million mad men would keep us locked in our rooms in a state of dithering terror. It is a figure large enough so that even in dollars we have to count carefully to know their full purchasing power. For most people large figures are as unusable to their reasoning processes as the astronomer's light-years are to a man with a piece of smoked glass. Yet we can easily roll across our tongues, without a reaction setting up in the heart or mind, the simple statement that eighteen million Americans are so poor of this world's goods that they are on relief.

Since these observers of the other man cannot easily visualize the truth by figures, or that is to say by quantity, are they able to think in terms of quality of destitution? Personally, I believe that it is only by comparison to his own estate as summed up in items of shoes, pants, shirts, toothbrushes, bread, beans, movies, meat, bed springs, plumbing, and leaking roofs, that a man can ever see the meaning of relief. If any one of you persons here should take a street car and get off at any block up and down Manhattan, go into the hall of a tenement house and up the steps through the hallways of the slums or into the more deceptive, newer, cleaner poverty of aspiring apartment houses, what would you see that would be intelligible to you? If any one of you should take a train and go up into Rhode Island or Massachusetts or Maine and get off either at local or express stops, seeing the poverty of little towns or big industrial cities what would you see? If you should take a train to Chicago, to Western Pennsylvania and get off at Steubenville, or get off at Wheeling, Pittsburgh or Indianapolis, what would you see? If you should take a train through the South and stop in Tennessee or go west to Mississippi, Arkansas and Texas; if you should take a plane to California, Washington or North Dakota, what would you see?

May I so impose upon your Christmas spirit as to tell you what you would see? You would see two kinds of poverty, new and old, and let me tell you that it is the old poverty as well as new poverty with which we should be concerned. Such poverty as you will see in the slums of New York has existed there for a century. People there have slept in rooms without windows, they have slept on chairs, they have slept on the floor, they have slept four and five in a bed since long before we ever heard of this depression. In 1929, an insurance collector who worked a district in a middle western city for several years, had seen during the most prosperous years of our country, that district go from a comfortable, home-owners' section in which each man sent his children to school well clothed and well fed and who had his check ready for the insurance man willingly upon the day when it was due, decline until the fathers of those families collectively were able to raise only enough money to keep the water supply turned on in one central house in the block. Their children were barefooted in winter. In 1929 a family of nine was supplied for the entire winter by the $7.00 which their fifteen year old son earned as an errand boy in the drug store, plus $3.80 which their father earned in one day from the city during a snow storm, and $10 which he received for putting a roof on a house. That winter their four year old child had pneumonia three times. In any state you wish to mention you can find thousands of people who have been underfed for so many years that it is a commonplace to believe that these people could not be induced to better standard of living. Give them a million dollars, it is said, and they will still want beans, pork and molasses. It is the well-fed who say it. They are the same people who say if you give the poor bathtubs, they'll only store coal in them. It is an old and popular fiction that poor people like being poor.

It is also important to remember, that although there is a difference in the living level to which people can aspire after fifty years of poverty and the living level to which they can aspire after a month of it, that poverty is not so very new after a year or two. We all recognize that one of the causes of our increasing load is the fact that things wear out. A pair of pants would have to be made of iron to last through three years of sitting. A pair of shoes would have to be made of concrete to resist three years of walking the streets in search of work. It is hard to remember a meal six hours after it is eaten. Therefore, although I say we have both new and old poverty, our depression poverty is really new no longer.

Many of you will say to me that these people like being on relief and that they are better off on relief than they have ever been before. We have heard that one very often. We are told they will not work any more. May I ask you one thing? When you know that a relief budget, for lack of funds, is placed at the very minimum of a family's needs and that in very few places it can take care of rent and that it can hope to do little more than keep body and soul together; and when you realize that this is a nominal budget only and because we lack funds, sometimes families are permitted to receive less than fifty per cent of that so-called ideal budget, which is in itself inadequate to life, may I ask you if this is an indictment of relief, that it is said to offer more than life offered before, or is it an indictment of something else? For myself, I do not call it an indictment of relief. I grant you that examples which you cite of chiseling, racketeering, politics, and laziness may be true, but I also say that we are in a position to know the proportions of these evils, and that it is a fact beyond contradiction that most men do not give up without a struggle that intangible thing they call their independence.

We have lately had a new kind of complaint from a very astute and humorous economist. He asks: "Why are you people in Federal relief always apologizing for straight relief, always talking about its being so demoralizing, and such a shameful thing, why are you always saying that as soon as you can, you are going to have work relief for all these people?" (For you know that we harp upon that a good deal in the Relief Administration. We are aware that it costs more in the beginning so we have to fight pretty hard for it.) This economist says: "Of course, you should be apologetic for the amount you give out. The whole matter would be righted and men could hold up their heads again if you gave them $30 a week and called it independent income."

The only trouble with this is that the unemployed themselves want work. We do not have to tell them that not having a job spoils a man for work. They go soft, they lose skill, they lose work habits. But they know it before you and I know it and it is their lives that are being wrecked, not ours.

We have certain preconceived notions as to how a man should act when he is out of a job. We would have him look, day in, day out, year in, year out, though he never caught sight of a job. We say they lose pride too, but pride is as relative as modesty and about as funny. There are old stock Americans mining tiff in the Ozarks. "Tiff" is a substance you put in high class paint. A whole family can make about $2 or $2.50 a week by digging for it. They have learned how to survive where foreigners (who it pleases us to think have lower standards of living than we do) have been beaten out. But these people still have pride left and, believe it or not, it is pride that they are Americans. So as I say pride is curious. Our own idea of pride for the other fellow is that he should be ashamed of being on relief. We want him to creep up back alleys with his head in his coat collar (if he has a coat) to the relief office. Well, he does do this for the first month. After that he decides, perhaps, it is best to take it on the chin with the other people who are in his own predicament and he walks up to the front door.

There are those who tell us that we should not have work relief. They say that straight relief is cheaper. No one will deny this contention. It costs money to put a man to work. Apparently, to the advocates of direct relief the primary object of relief is to save the Government money. The ultimate humane cost to the Government never occurs to them of a continued situation through which its citizens lose their sense of independence and strength and their sense of individual destiny. Work for the unemployed is something we have fought for since the beginning of the Administration and we shall continue to insist upon it. It preserves a man's morale. It saves his skill. It gives him a chance to do some thing socially useful.

Let me say again, that we should allow ourselves no smug feelings of charity at this holiday season to know that the Federal Government is attempting to take care of the actual physical wants of eighteen million people. We are merely paying damages for not having had a thought about these things many years ago. We will have to do a great deal of thinking from here out.

Work Relief vs. Direct Relief

A recipient of direct relief: "Maybe you think I like to come up here beggin'! I don't want no goddamn relief orders! I want work, I tell you! Work! Work! I got to have a job!"

A WPA worker in Texas: "Now I can look my children straight in the eyes. I've gained my self respect. Relief is all right to keep one from starving . . . but, well it takes something from you. Sitting around waiting for your case worker to bring you a check, and the kids in the house find that you contribute nothing toward their support, very soon they begin to lose respect for you. It's different now."

SOURCE: Watkins, T.H. *The Hungry Years: A Narrative History of the Great Depression in America.* New York: Henry Holt, 1999, 178, 262.

I should like to say a word right here about the housing which we have been allowed to stand as the shelter of American citizens. It is evil. It is unnecessary. No civilized nation needs to stand for it. Something has got to be done about housing and something is going to be done.

I know this minute of a farm family in which ten people have been sleeping in two beds until within six weeks. Now they sleep nine. Their father has been sent to a tuberculosis sanitarium. This family has no windows in its house, nothing but holes in the walls, and holes in the floor. They have nothing but a hoe with which to cut hay and nothing but broomstraw to cut. Their carefully tended garden yielded some corn and potatoes which they store in their three room house where big rats run in and out. In a city which boasts of its wealth, from six to twelve families will use common plumbing which is cut off when the rents of $1.50 a week up to $15 a month are behind for any of the tenants. The relief officials are buying wood at one cent a stick when natural gas is burning in the air. There wouldn't be fixtures to pipe it in, if the gas cost nothing. People are paying ground-rent for land in dumps where they build houses from flattened tin cans and shingle them with heavy cardboard. In a capital town there is a relief nursery school whose nearest available quarters are three miles from the district in which its children live because no rooms could be found there which had water, or heat, or plumbing. I could go on with this bill of particulars. Such poverty does not creep up on us over night.

It is safe to say that poverty in any city is as old as that city, and that it has grown in every city from little to big. It is part of its economic nature that poverty is infectious. It is like the old proverb of the shoemaker's children. The children of thousands of unemployed workers in the shoe district of New England are unshod. It would seem that the more you make the more you can't have. It is true, that while we have thousands of unemployed cotton textile workers there are literally hundreds of thousands of beds in the United States that have no sheets and that people sleep on pieces of old carpet placed upon bare springs, or stretch burlap out upon sawdust and lay their babies to sleep on gunny sacks filled with old rags.

I have painted you a very bleak picture. There are the facts with which we have to contend but even though we do not attempt to gloss them over, and it would be idle and even cruel to do so, there is in some ways a more hopeful color in it than any American Christmas has known before. In this country for the first time we have a President in the White House whose mind and heart are consecrated to the ending forever of such conditions. It has been one of the outstanding virtues of this administration that it has been willing to uncover the extent of the problem with which it has to deal. It is the motivating force behind the President and his aides to bring about a day when these men and women who have endured so much will come again, or even come, some of them, for the first time, into the inheritance which rightfully belongs to every citizen of the richest country in the world.

And this is not all still in the stage of hope. Much has been accomplished. It lacks some months of being two years since the President undertook a task which was years in preparing. Remember, that already at least three and a half million of unemployed persons have gone back to work. Remember, that in spite of the natural seasonal rise of unemployment in winter, and the additional physical needs that people experience in cold weather, and in spite of the fact that depleted family resources have forced newcomers to list themselves upon the relief rolls, there are fewer families on relief at this moment than there were in March, 1933. Besides this, new social movements have been begun that will protect and enrich our common life. These good effects are even now at the beginning of a long time program, substantial enough to be felt. Not only have pledges been made but pledges have been fulfilled.

To those who by chance throughout the country are listening to my words may I say something in the way of a Christmas greeting? This is the anniversary which we have celebrated every year for nearly 2,000 years of one who disliked poverty and injustice and believed that we were our brother's keeper. The wisdom and pleasure that comes from such deep conviction cannot be taken away from the most destitute, and for those who are comfortable such knowledge and the capacity to act upon it and to work toward an end where life will be a good thing for all men who live, it will be the truest assurance of a Happy Christmas.

Further Resources

BOOKS

Gerdes, Louise I., ed. *The 1930s.* San Diego, Calif.: Greenhaven Press, Inc., 2000.

Hopkins, June. *Harry Hopkins: Sudden Hero, Brash Reformer.* New York: St. Martin's Press, c 1999.

Kurzman, Paul A. *Harry Hopkins and the New Deal.* Fair Lawn, N.J.: R. E. Burdick, 1974.

WEBSITES

Work Relief Administration Press Releases. The New Deal Network. Available online at http://www.newdeal.feri.org/workrelief (Accessed August 29, 2002).

Old Age Revolving Pensions

Pamphlet

By: Francis E. Townsend

Date: c. 1934

Source: *Old Age Revolving Pensions: A Proposed National Plan.* Pamphlet. c. 1934. Available online at http://www.ssa.gov/history/towns5.html; website home page: http://www.ssa.gov (accessed August 29, 2002).

About the Author: Dr. Francis E. Townsend (1867–1960) was an elderly, country doctor who had relocated to California from South Dakota in 1919 for health reasons. He worked for the Long Beach Health Office until he lost his job in 1933. Sixty-seven years old and with barely enough money to get by, he developed an idea for a pension program to aid America's elderly which brought him to national attention. Townsend's plan attracted the attention of millions and was an important catalyst in the passage of the Social Security Act in 1935. Townsend, however, was not satisfied and continued his agitation for a more comprehensive old-age program until his death in 1960. ■

Introduction

In 1933 the United States was the only major industrialized nation in the world without a social security program for the aged. In the rural small-town America of the imagination, children cared for their elderly grandparents. This obligation belonged to the family, not the wider community. Never the universal picture of the aged, it certainly did not portray the reality in an urban, industrialized United States. When the Depression struck in 1929 the elderly were particularly hard hit.

Faced with his own financial problems and very aware of the financial condition of the elderly, Dr. Townsend developed a radical and impractical, but nonetheless appealing, plan to both solve the problem of impoverished elders and stimulate the economy.

The Townsend Plan called for a $200 monthly distribution to each person over sixty on two conditions. First, recipients had to spend the total amount each month. Second, they must stop all other employment. The plan was to be financed by a 2 percent tax on business transactions—basically a sales tax.

Initially Townsend promoted the value of his program as a needed support for the nation's elderly. Soon, however, the program's benefit as a perpetual economic and employment stimulus package carried equal weight and extended the plans appeal to a much broader segment of the population.

Critics regarded Townsend's plan as a fantasy. The proposed $200 per month payment, in a country with more than ten million people over sixty years old, would cost nearly $25 billion per year. In the Depression year of 1933 the Gross National Product was only $56 billion and the federal budget was $4.5 billion with tax revenues of less than $2 billion. The proposed monthly payment of $200 per person was more than double the average wage of workers in the manufacturing sector. Clearly Townsend's plan was not viable.

In 1933, Dr. Francis E. Townsend developed and promoted the plan for government funded old age pensions that bore his name, the "Townsend Plan." THE LIBRARY OF CONGRESS.

Significance

Despite the practical flaws in Towsend's plan, millions of Americans supported it. Led by the sincere, almost pious Dr. Townsend, the movement took on the aspects of a religious revival. By 1936 there were nearly seven thousand Townsend Clubs with 2.2 million paying members across the country, coordinated from the Townsend headquarters in California.

Somewhat reluctantly, Townsend was drawn into the political campaign of 1936. The Roosevelt administration, influenced in part by the popularity of Townsend's pension plan, pushed through the Social Security Act of 1935. This created a retirement program for most Americans but fell far short of Townsend's generous plan. It also lacked the economic stimulus component that was a critical piece of the Townsend Plan.

Frustrated by the passage of what he saw as an inadequate Social Security bill and his treatment by the Roosevelt administration, Townsend looked elsewhere for support. Sure of his strong popular base he became increasingly attracted to the political arena. He was drawn down this path by Reverend Gerald L.K. Smith, a follower of the recently assassinated Huey Long.

Smith brokered an alliance with Father Charles Coughlin. Coughlin, a highly controversial and politically active Roman Catholic priest from Detroit, had attracted a wide national audience to his weekly radio show. Initially a supporter of Roosevelt, by 1936 Coughlin had broken with the president and created the Union Party with William Lemke as presidential candidate. Townsend, Coughlin, Lemke, and Smith each had strong followings and initially appeared as though they might be a major force in the 1936 election. Internal rivalries, fundamental flaws in the various programs they backed, the eventual rejection by many followers of the demagogic style of the leaders, and Roosevelt's popularity combined to relegate the Union Party to a footnote in the election.

The failure of the Union Party and the general recognition that the Townsend Plan was unworkable resulted in the rapid decline of Townsend's influence. Nonetheless Townsend continued his crusade until his death in 1960 at age ninety-three.

Primary Source

Old Age Revolving Pensions [excerpt]

SYNOPSIS: The following excerpts are from Townsend's publication of his plan in 1934. It includes explanations of the plan as well as a large number of endorsements. One section not included here contains statements from President Roosevelt falsely implying his support for the plan.

The Townsend Plan . . . in Brief

Have the national Government enact legislation to the effect that all citizens of the United States—man or woman—over the age of 60 years may retire on a pension of $200 per month on the following conditions:

1. That they engage in no further labor, business or profession for gain.
2. That their past life is free form habitual criminality.
3. That they take oath to, and actually do spend, within the confines of the United States, the entire amount of their pension within thirty days after receiving same.

Have the National Government create the revolving fund by levying a general sales tax; have the rate just high enough to produce the amount necessary to keep the Old Age Revolving Pensions Fund adequate to pay the monthly pensions.

Have the act so drawn that such sales tax can only be used for the Old Age Revolving Pensions Fund.

Foreword by the Editor

The author of the plan for combining liberal retirement compensation for the aged with national financial recovery and permanent prosperity as described in the subsequent pages is a physician who has been employed by the city of Long Beach, California, for the past two years, through its health department, in caring for the indigent sick. A large percentage of his patients were old folks whose life savings have been swept away by the financial collapse of institutions in which their savings were invested.

With a suddenness that bewildered them these folks found themselves not only helpless but a burden to their financially embarrassed relatives. That was the last straw. To feel that they were not only helpless and useless but also in the way caused a rapid decline in their health and spirits and an actual, ardent wish for death as their only hope of relief.

This pathetic collapse of their morale with the hopeless apathy it produced in them made their care a double burden upon their anxious relatives who were impelled to stretch their already meager finances in an effort to provide little luxuries and means of amusement for their beloved elders. Many of the old folks went into a rapid decline and died, the sorrow for their loss and the added obligations of the funeral expenses but adding to the desperate situation faced by their sons and daughters.

Daily association with affliction, grim want and hopeless sorrow obsessed this physician with a consuming desire to provide a cure for the national folly of permitting blighting, destructive want in a land of superabundance.

He believes that he has found the cure. He believes with President Roosevelt that poverty and its useless horrors can be abolished. He believes that our nation with its vast creative power needs but one important principle to be established through legislation to banish poverty and its attendant evils forever.

This cure, or plan, is described in the following pages. Whether you agree with him or not, you will find intensely interesting food for thought in their perusal.

What the Old Age Revolving Pension Will Do

It will put about two billions of dollars more in circulation than has ever circulated before by creating important buying centers of poor communities that have never had buying power, thus insuring brisk trade in every section of the country. The old folks are to be found everywhere.

Analysis of Plan

Retirement at Age of Sixty

Insurance statistics show that only 8% of people reaching that age have achieved financial success to such a degree that they may live comfortably thereafter without depending upon further earnings. Eighty-five percent of the 92% of all people sixty years of age and over are still employed or are endeavoring in some manner to earn all or a part of their livelihood and the remainder are dependent upon public or private charity for their keep. Those of the 85% who are still earning are capable of producing only enough to partially pay for their living. A very small percentage actually earn enough for their total needs and but very few earn any surplus for their declining years

Approximately 8,000,000 people will be eligible to apply for the pension. Economists estimate that each person spending $200.00 per month creates a job for one additional worker. The retirement of all citizens of 60 years and over from all productive industry and gainful occupation, will thereby create jobs for 8,000,000 workers which will solve our national labor problem.

Retirement on a Monthly Pension of $200

The spending of $200 per month is for a constructive purpose. First, to place an adequate amount of buying power in the hands of these citizens which will permit them to satisfy their wants that have been so restricted for the past four years. Second, to create such a demand for new goods of all description that all manufacturing plants in the country will be called upon to start their wheels of production at full speed and provide jobs for all workers.

This money made suddenly available to the channels of trade will immediately start a tremendous flood of buying, since the country has been on short commodity rations for the past four years, and since all sections of the country will be affected alike (the old are everywhere) and the poorest sections will at once become important buying centers.

All factories and avenues of production may be expected to start producing at full capacity and all workers called into activity at high wages, since there will be infinitely more jobs available and many less workers to fill the jobs, the old folks having retired from competition for places as producers.

How Will This Money Be Spent

It will go into the regular channels of trade for food, clothing, homes, rent, furniture, automobiles—all manner and description of things dear to the human heart. It will go for travel, the pleasure of riding hobbies, theatre tickets, professional and servant employment and the thousand and one things which modern man demands.

How This Will Effect the Owners of Property or Business

Those of 60 years and over owning income property, whose income is greater than the pension, would not need or possibly care to apply for this pension, as it is not designed to be compulsory. Those whose income is less than the pension, undoubtedly would dispose of their interests in income investment to younger people and receive the pension for their declining years. Thus performing the two-fold function that the plan provides, that of relieving industry of their productiveness and increasing industry through their consumption of goods and farm products.

Establishment of homes by those now living with relatives or in institutions, either through ownership or rental, or the holding of homes, now occupied, are encouraged under this plan. Each new home established simply means greater consumption of goods and use of labor.

This plan will effect a marked reduction in the tax burden which they are now compelled to carry and make more secure the profits that should accrue from business and property investment, since it will be less expensive to collect and spend two billions of money monthly than it is to maintain the monthly present-day costs of organized charity in its multiple forms, plus much of the cost of crime and disease due to overcrowding and undernourishment. It will add immensely to the volume of business done and thereby make possible profits in greater amount without increasing the cost of goods.

Pensioners to Retire Without Further Gain from Labor or Profession

This is an important feature of the plan since the idea is to create jobs for the young and able, eliminating competition for such jobs and positions on the part of elderly people.

Consumption of the products of farm and factory is the vital problem now facing our nation. The success of this plan is based entirely on the creation of jobs of production and by retiring all those pensioned, with adequate spending power, that they may consume for all their need in comforts, necessities and pleasure.

Records Free From Crime

This clause is designed to have a strong effect in restraining the young and impatient from taking the short cut of criminal acitivty to obtain money. They will hesitate to jeopardize their future welfare for the sake of getting money now by criminal activities.

The desire to honestly earn is uppermost in the minds of American people. The records of our law enforcement departments show that crime is largely the result of lack of opportunity to provide necessities of life through the sale of labor. Provide these opportunities for our younger generations and the crime problem will be greatly lessened.

Saving for Old Age

We have been taught in the past that saving was essential in planning for security in old age. But recent experience has taught us that no one has yet been able to devise a sure method of saving. Statistical records show that ninety-two percent of all people reaching the age of sixty-five have, in spite of their best efforts, been unable to save enough to guard them from the humiliation of accepting charity in some form, either from relatives or from the state. Experience proves that no form of investment is infallible that human mind can devise which is based upon the small group or individual financing. The Townsend plan proposes that all who serve society to the best of their ability in whatever capacity shall not be denied that security in their declining years to which their services in active years have entitled them.

Costs of Maintaining the Huge Revolving Fund

The unthinking see a great increase in the cost of living due to the necessity for the retailer to raise his prices to meet the government tax for maintaining the pension roll. He fails to take into consideration the fact that the elimination of poor houses, organized state and county relief agencies, public and private pension systems, community chests, etc., are now costing the country the many millions of dollars per month that the Townsend plan would eliminate. And, too, would not the cost of crime and insane asylums be greatly reduced after the public became assured of the permanency of our prosperity? Further, the tremendous increase in the volume of the retail business which this huge revolving fund would insure makes certain that bigger profits would be possible to the retailer through his old rates than ever before and make unnecessary the advance in prices on any articles except those classed as luxuries. Estimated from the sources available a tax of 10% will be ample to raise this fund and the tax can be materially lowered as the volume of trade increases. Competition will still continue to operate and the profit hog will still find competitors who will hold him to a fair price rate. It is the logical foundation for our worthy President's NRA—National Recovery Act.

No one will object to paying the slight advance in price for commodities for the purpose of re-establishing prosperity and, in so doing, making it possible for the elderly people to retire and live comfortably the remainder of their days, since everyone in making his purchases will be providing for his own security when he reaches the age of sixty.

Sales Tax to be Used Exclusively for the Pensions

It is the intent of the plan to apply the sales tax solely to the one purpose of maintaining the pensions roll until such time as the public becomes fully assured of the beneficient and fair system of taxation involved in a universal retail tax. Here is the only fair system of taxation for all that can be devised. Every individual who enjoys the benefits of the numerous social agencies maintained for his benefit, such as schools, police protection, sanitation, public health supervision and the thousand and one functions of government, should be compelled to carry his share of the costs just in proportion to his ability to do so; that is, in proportion to his ability to spend money. This compels the child to become a taxpayer at an early age and accustoms him to the idea that he must do his share throughout his life.

No Change in Form of Government

This plan of Old Age Revolving Pensions interferes in no way with our present form of government, profit system of business or change of specie in our economic setup. It is a simple American plan dedicated to the cause of prosperity and the abolition of poverty. It retains the rights of freedom of speech and of press and of religious belief and insures us the right to perpetuate and make glorious the liberty we so cherish and enjoy.

The Meaning of Security to Humanity

Here lies the true value in the Townsend Plan. Humanity will be forever relieved from the fear of destitution and want. The seeming need for sharp practices and greedy accumulation will disappear. Benevolence and kindly consideration for others will displace suspicion and avarice, brotherly love and tolerance will blossom into full flower and the genial sun of human happiness will dissipate the dark clouds of distrust and gloom and despair.

A Permanent National Cure for Depression

We recognize the fact that the inventive genius of the world, and especially of the United States, has, through the perfection of labor-saving machines, created a condition in society which has resulted in a huge surplus of producers as well as a surplus of products. There is a constant standing army of unemployed.

Even in the boom days of 1929 there was a large number of them and their ranks have been steadily increased until today there are fifteen millions of them with their families who are without jobs. They can never be put to work again unless they are willing to accept the short day and the min-

A billboard in Welasco, Texas, advertises the Townsend Plan in 1935. © BETTMANN/CORBIS. REPRODUCED BY PERMISSION.

imum wage. Their labor will be too expensive. Machines will do the work of all of them in infinitely less time and at less cost. It will be the plan of organized society as constituted today to shunt this army of jobless aside on some sort of subsistence dole and do the work of the world with efficient and tireless machines. Mind, I say society as constituted today. We of this community say that this must be corrected. Are we a Nation of morons or imbeciles that we can solve the problems of production to a point where we have more products than we can consume and yet be eternally faced with the sight of an ever increasing number of citizens suffering form a lack of those same products to a point where they become mere human clods without ambition, content to wear the livery of serfs and eat the bread of grudging charity? This condition prevails today and nothing in the way of half-time employment, minimum wage plans or price fixing will alter the frightful state of affairs. It will grow steadily worse so long as we adhere to our present systemless lack of control of our monetary circulation. Money circulates under the present system or it does not circulate in accord with whims or fears or emotions of a few men or institutions that control the major portion of the money of the land.

We say that one of the chief functions of government should be the exercise of its power to insure a steady and sufficient flow of money through the channels of trade and commerce adequate to keep that trade at an even tempo free from fear of panic or boom. We say that our government must assume this function and adopt a system whereby money shall flow in a constant volume into the coffers of the U. S. Treasury and immediately start on a return flow back into the avenue of commerce whence it came.

The banking system of our country cannot do this. Money can flow into the Treasury by the taxation route but from there the stream can only reach the banks. There it stagnates. It cannot get back among the people where it is needed unless they have security to offer for it. This, when times are hard and the need for money greatest, the people cannot give and, as a consequence, business dies and the people have to accept charity or starve.

By what plan shall the government assume its rightful task of keeping the money of the Nation in circulation? The Old Age Revolving Pension Plan. Recognize the fact that we can spare the seven or eight millions of people over the age of sixty from the ranks of the producers and retire them with badges of honor and pensions of a size sufficient to keep them in affluence the rest of their days. These pensions should not be paltry. They should be large enough to make the recipient an envied individual and the aggregate of all the pensions great enough at all times to insure an abundant supply of money for all commercial needs as the pensioners spend it.

Let all citizens who become sixty years of age, and desire to retire, receive the pension upon two conditions: That they give proof of never having been criminals and that they solemnly promise to spend the entire amount of the pension during the current month in which it is received. Also that they retire from all productive or gainfull occupation or labor.

We shall request the government to assume a monopoly of the sales tax plan of collecting revenue for the pensions. This tax should be levied evenly and fairly upon all merchandise and commodities and be paid at a specific rate upon gross sales at the end of each month. A graduated "income" tax must be levied fairly so as not to discourage industry. And "inheritance" taxes must be increased. If these three forms of taxation are sensibly administered, real estate taxes can be greatly lowered. Under the sales tax plan of collecting government revenues, all classes of the population pay in proportion to their financial ability and none receive the benefits of government without assuming his share of the burden. A sales tax levied for the express purpose of paying pensions to the aged will meet with universal approval. Its beneficent purpose will be recognized by all; its two fold function (that of doing justice to those who have done a full life's work, and that of keeping and abundance of money circulating at all times) will be recognized and acclaimed by all. A rate of 10 per cent should be sufficient, if levied on all sales, to meet the pension roll. The pension system will relieve society of a tremendous burden of taxation now made necessary by the maintenance of poor farms, community chests and other charitable institutions. By keeping a healthy business condition throughout the Nation, it will remove to a large extent the incentive to crime and through lowering our prison population, reduce another huge taxation outlay. No doubt it will also reduce the number of unfortunates confined in our insane asylums. Pensions for the aged of sufficient size to assure a high standard of living will make the latter end of life a delightful golden autumn instead of the bleak and fearful winter which it represents for so many. Pensions for the aged will remove eight or ten millions of pensioners from the fields of productive effort and permit of the paying of high wages to younger workers. Prices will be stabilized at a level high enough to insure a fair profit to the producers at all times when the steady flow of money is assured from taxpayer to the government and from the government to the pensioners and thence to the channels of trade. Justice can be assured to all through this system and the injustice of permitting the wealth of the Nation to accumulate in the hands of a few will be eliminated.

If you believe, as we do, that buying power can be restored to the people who are now utterly without it and that the wheels of industry can be started throughout the entire Nation by the adoption of this system, join us in demanding its adoption.

Prosperity for All

There are ten million three hundred thousand odd persons in the U. S. above the age of sixty years according to the last census. They are quite uniformly proportioned throughout the population, this proportion, naturally, being greatest in the older settled sections where population is densest.

Two billions of dollars spend monthly in all sections of the country by these old folks would give the entire population of the United States an additional $14 per capita in spending ability each month. Enough to raise the standard of living very materially above the present low level but quite within the nation's ability to provide.

The constantly growing use of power by civilized man (largely electric) is increasing his power to produce the things man must use at an ever decreasing cost. Hence, an ever decreasing number of workers is required in production and an ever increasing number find themselves out of employment. If civilization is to be a blessing instead of a curse a sensible and just provision for their retirement must be devised.

The return to manufacturers in profits tends to increase as power displaces men (since machines are cheaper than men) only up to the point where buying power begins to diminish among the people through lack of paid jobs, thus decreasing market demands. Hence, manufacturers too begin to see the necessity of keeping up the buying power of the people by some such plan as the Old Age Revolving Pensions.

Poverty, once considered a natural curse which the human race was doomed to endure, can and will be abolished in the United States within the next five years never to return. Our country will show the way to other nations and poverty will be driven from the earth. No other construction can be given to the fact that man's ability to produce faster than he can consume is definitely established.

Poverty banished, the incentive to criminal activity will disappear and national, civic and individual standards of fairness and decency will become the natural order of the day.

Prosperity firmly established in America by this simple plan, the peoples of other countries will demand like opportunity and consideration from their governments and similar legislation may be expected to follow. When all civilized people are universally well off and contented there will be an end to warfare. Prosperous and contented people do not go to war.

What the Old Age Revolving Pension Will Do

It will insure the continuance of the profit system of doing business, that throughout the ages has been the mainspring of ingenunity and progress.

Last but not least, it will start the Golden Age of life for all who reach the age of sixty, making possible for all leisure to devote ourselves to doing the things we have always wanted to do.

Further Resources

BOOKS

Bennett, David Harry. *Demagogues in the Depression: American Radicals and the Union Party, 1932–1936.* New Brunswick, N.J.: Rutgers University Press, 1969.

Brimkley, Alan. *Voices of Protest: Huey Long, Father Coughlin, and The Great Depression.* New York: Alfred A. Knopf, 1982.

Leuchtenburg, William E. *Franklin D. Roosevelt and the New Deal (1932–1940).* New York: Harper & Row, 1963.

"On Social Security"

Message

By: Franklin D. Roosevelt

Date: January 17, 1935

Source: Roosevelt, Franklin D. "On Social Security." Message to Congress, January 17, 1935. Printed in *Vital Speeches of the Day* 1, no. 9, January 28, 1935, 258–259.

About the Author: Franklin D. Roosevelt (1882–1945) was elected president in 1932, the worst year of the Great Depression. While Roosevelt did not have a consistent strategy for dealing with the Depression, he was willing to experiment with various programs. This willingness to "try something" combined with his infectious enthusiasm and optimism, performed wonders in restoring the faith of the American people in themselves and their government. Roosevelt died while still in office. ■

Introduction

The first modern social security legislation was passed in Germany in 1883. Over the next several years the German government created a social security system that included health coverage, workers injury compensation, and an old age pension. Within twenty years these types of programs were implemented and expanded across Europe and in Australia, New Zealand, and Canada. In the 1920s various forms of social security began to appear in South America and Africa.

Restricted in part by constitutional issues but more significantly by philosophical opposition to government involvement in personal financial matters, the United States lagged far behind these countries in providing a social security system for its citizens. By 1930, the United States was the only important industrialized country without a government-mandated social security system.

The Depression was an important catalyst for change. Massive unemployment prompted a reassessment of government's responsibility in assuring some level of financial security for its citizens, particularly the elderly who were especially hard hit. While the first phase of the New Deal program focused on emergency relief and stimulating the economy, by 1934, the Roosevelt administration had begun to consider more fundamental reforms, including various social security measures.

Federal action was prompted by an old age pension plan suggested by a retired California doctor, Frances Townsend. The Townsend Plan called for a $200 payment to all Americans over the age of 65. This grant carried the stipulation that the recipient had ceased gainful employment and would spend the money immediately. Although wholly unworkable—the $25 billion cost would have been nearly half the gross domestic product of the entire United States in 1933—Townsend's proposal was very popular. It put considerable political pressure on Roosevelt to develop a federal old age pension program.

In June 1934 Roosevelt appointed Secretary of Labor Frances Perkins to chair the Committee on Economic Security (CES), which was charged with recommending appropriate legislation to address the broad question of social security. Specific issues to be considered were retirement pensions, unemployment insurance, national health insurance, disability protection, and aid to dependent children. The Committee's report was submitted to Congress in January 1935.

A poster from the 1930s explains the application process for benefits under the newly created system of Social Security. © BETTMANN/CORBIS. REPRODUCED BY PERMISSION.

Significance

Conservatives opposed the social security proposals as being contrary to the American principle of self-determination. Liberals, in contrast, thought the proposals were too limited. Despite coming under attack from both sides, the essential CES proposal was finally passed in June 1935.

The main components of the Social Security Act were:

1. A compulsory federally administered old age pension
2. A joint federal/state unemployment insurance program
3. Federal grants to states for old-age assistance, aid to the blind, and support for dependent children

In truth, the 1935 Act was not a particularly enlightened piece of social security legislation. It did not cover all workers and it was paid for through payroll deductions rather than a wealth redistribution program. Nonetheless the Social Security Act was a major New Deal achievement and represented a fundamental change in the U.S. philosophy of government. For the first time the federal government assumed some level of direct responsibility for the economic security of Americans.

Roosevelt recognized that the act did not go as far as it could have, and that employee payroll taxes may not have been the best funding approach. With regard to the funding mechanism, his explanation reflects both philosophical and practical considerations: "We put those payroll contributions there so as to give the contributors a legal, moral and political right to collect their pensions and their unemployment benefits. With those taxes in there, no damn politician can ever scrap my social security program." After nearly seventy years, the program remains unchanged in its basic structure.

Primary Source

"On Social Security"

SYNOPSIS: On June 8, 1934, Roosevelt sent a message to Congress citing the need for a broader economic security system for all Americans. The Committee on Economic Security was formed at that time and charged with recommending appropriate social security legislation. The Committee delivered its report to President Roosevelt in early January 1935. On January 17, 1935 Roosevelt forwarded the report to Congress along with this message.

To the Congress of the United States:

In addressing you on June 8, 1934, I summarized the main objectives of our American program. Among these was, and is, the security of the men, women and children of the nation against certain hazards and vicissitudes of life. This purpose is an essential part of our task.

In my annual message to you I promised to submit a definite program of action. This I do in the form of a report to me by a Committee on Economic Security, appointed by me for the purpose of surveying the field and of recommending the basis of legislation.

I am gratified with the work of this committee and of these who have helped it: the Technical Board on Economic Security drawn from various departments of the government, the Advisory Council on Economic Security, consisting of informed and public-spirited private citizens and a number of other ad-

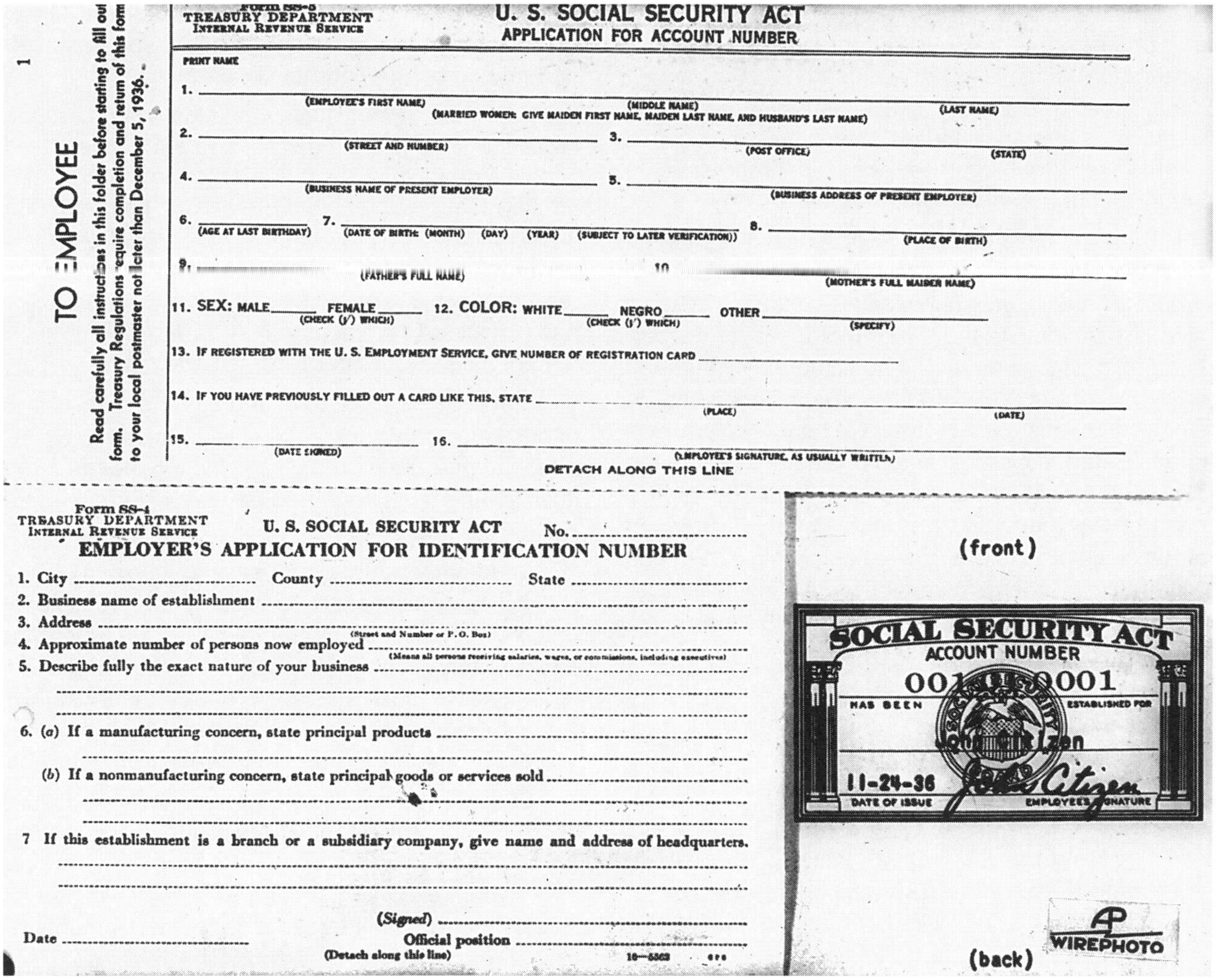
TO EMPLOYEE

Read carefully all instructions in this folder before starting to fill out form. Treasury Regulations require completion and return of this form to your local postmaster not later than December 5, 1936.

Form SS-5
TREASURY DEPARTMENT
INTERNAL REVENUE SERVICE

U. S. SOCIAL SECURITY ACT
APPLICATION FOR ACCOUNT NUMBER

PRINT NAME

1. (EMPLOYEE'S FIRST NAME) (MIDDLE NAME) (LAST NAME)
(MARRIED WOMEN: GIVE MAIDEN FIRST NAME, MAIDEN LAST NAME, AND HUSBAND'S LAST NAME)

2. (STREET AND NUMBER) 3. (POST OFFICE) (STATE)

4. (BUSINESS NAME OF PRESENT EMPLOYER) 5. (BUSINESS ADDRESS OF PRESENT EMPLOYER)

6. (AGE AT LAST BIRTHDAY) 7. (DATE OF BIRTH: (MONTH) (DAY) (YEAR) (SUBJECT TO LATER VERIFICATION)) 8. (PLACE OF BIRTH)

9. (FATHER'S FULL NAME) 10. (MOTHER'S FULL MAIDEN NAME)

11. SEX: MALE ___ FEMALE ___ (CHECK (✓) WHICH) 12. COLOR: WHITE ___ NEGRO ___ (CHECK (✓) WHICH) OTHER ___ (SPECIFY)

13. IF REGISTERED WITH THE U. S. EMPLOYMENT SERVICE, GIVE NUMBER OF REGISTRATION CARD

14. IF YOU HAVE PREVIOUSLY FILLED OUT A CARD LIKE THIS, STATE (PLACE) (DATE)

15. (DATE SIGNED) 16. (EMPLOYEE'S SIGNATURE, AS USUALLY WRITTEN)

DETACH ALONG THIS LINE

Form SS-4
TREASURY DEPARTMENT
INTERNAL REVENUE SERVICE

U. S. SOCIAL SECURITY ACT No.
EMPLOYER'S APPLICATION FOR IDENTIFICATION NUMBER

1. City ____ County ____ State ____
2. Business name of establishment
3. Address (Street and Number or P. O. Box)
4. Approximate number of persons now employed (Means all persons receiving salaries, wages, or commissions, including executives)
5. Describe fully the exact nature of your business
6. (a) If a manufacturing concern, state principal products
(b) If a nonmanufacturing concern, state principal goods or services sold
7 If this establishment is a branch or a subsidiary company, give name and address of headquarters.

(Signed)
Date ____ Official position
(Detach along this line)

(front)

SOCIAL SECURITY ACT
ACCOUNT NUMBER
001-[illegible]-0001
HAS BEEN ESTABLISHED FOR
John Citizen
11-24-36
DATE OF ISSUE
John Citizen
EMPLOYEE'S SIGNATURE

(back)

AP WIREPHOTO

The documents used in establishing the first Social Security accounts: a Social Security account card, an employer's application, and an employee application. November 1936. AP/WIDE WORLD PHOTOS. REPRODUCED BY PERMISSION.

visory groups, including a Committee on Actuarial Consultants, a Medical Advisory Board, a Dental Advisory Committee, a Hospital Advisory Committee, a Public Health Advisory Committee, a Child Welfare Committee and an Advisory Committee on Employment Relief.

All of those who participated in this notable task of planning this major legislative proposal are ready and willing, at any time, to consult with and assist in any way the appropriate Congressional committees and members with respect to detailed aspects.

It is my judgment that this legislation should be brought forward with a minimum of delay. Federal action is necessary to and conditioned upon the actions of States. Forty-four Legislatures are meeting or will meet soon. In order that the necessary State action may be taken promptly it is important that the Federal Government proceed speedily.

The detailed report of the committee sets forth a series of proposals that will appeal to the sound sense of the American people. It has not attempted the impossible, nor has it failed to exercise sound caution and consideration of all of the factors concerned; the national credit the rights and responsibilities of States, the capacity of industry to assume financial responsibilities and the fundamental necessity of proceeding in a manner that will merit the enthusiastic support of citizens of all sorts.

It is overwhelmingly important to avoid any danger of permanently discrediting the sound and necessary policy of Federal legislation for economic security by attempting to apply it on too ambitious a scale before actual experience has provided guidance for the permanently safe direction of such efforts.

The place of such a fundamental in our future civilization is too precious to be jeopardized now by extravagant action. It is a sound idea—a sound ideal. Most of the other advanced countries of the world have already adopted it and their experience affords the knowledge that social insurance can be made a sound and workable project.

Three principles should be observed in legislation on this subject. In the first place, the system adopted, except for the money necessary to initiate it, should be self-sustaining in the sense that funds for the payment of insurance benefits should not come from the proceeds of general taxation. Second, excepting in old-age insurance, actual management should be left to the States, subject to standards established by the Federal Government. Third, sound financial management of the funds and the reserves, and protection of the credit structure of the nation should be assured by retaining Federal control over all funds through trustees in the Treasury of the United States.

At this time I recommend the following types of legislation looking to economic security:

1. Unemployment compensation.
2. Old-age benefits, including compulsory and voluntary annuities.
3. Federal aid to dependent children through grants to States for the support of existing mother's pension systems and for services for the protection and care of homeless, neglected dependent and crippled children.
4. Additional Federal aid to State and local public health agencies and the strengthening of the Federal public health service. I am not at this time recommending the adoption of so-called health insurance, although groups representing the medical profession are cooperating with the Federal Government in the further study of the subject and definite progress is being made.

With respect to unemployment compensation, I have concluded that the most practical proposal is the levy of a uniform Federal payroll tax, 90 per cent of which should be allowed as an offset to employers contributing under a compulsory State unemployment compensation act. The purpose of this is to afford a requirement of a reasonably uniform character for all States cooperating with the Federal Government and to promote and encourage the passage of unemployment compensation laws in the States.

The 10 per cent not thus offset should be used to cover the costs of Federal and State administration of this broad system. Thus States will largely administer unemployment compensation, assisted and guided by the Federal Government.

An unemployment compensation system should be constructed in such a way as to afford every practicable aid and incentive toward the larger purpose of employment stabilization. This can be helped by the intelligent planning of both public and private employment. It also can be helped by correlating the system with public employment so that a person who has exhausted his benefits may be eligible for some form of public work as is recommended in this report.

Moreover, in order to encourage the stabilization of private employment, Federal legislation should not foreclose the States from establishing means for inducing industries to afford an even greater stabilization of employment.

In the important field of security for our old people, it seems necessary to adopt three principles—first, non-contributory old-age pensions for those who are now too old to build up their own insurance; it is, of course, clear that for perhaps thirty years to come funds will have to be provided by the States and the Federal Government to meet these pensions.

Second, compulsory contributory annuities which in time will establish a self-supporting system for those now young and for future generations. Third, voluntary contributory annuities by which individual initiative can increase the annual amounts received in old age.

It is proposed that the Federal Government assume one-half of the cost of the old-age pension plan, which ought ultimately to be supplanted by self-supporting annuity plans.

The amount necessary at this time for the initiation of unemployment compensation, old-age security, children's aid and the promotion of public health, as outlined in the report of the committee on economic security, is approximately one hundred million dollars.

The establishment of sound means toward a greater future economic security of the American people is dictated by a prudent consideration of the hazards involved in our national life. No one can guarantee this country against the dangers of future depressions but we can reduce these dangers.

We can eliminate many of the factors that cause economic depressions and we can provide the means of mitigating their results. This plan for economic security is at once a measure of prevention and a method of alleviation.

We pay now for the dreadful consequence of economic insecurity—and dearly. This plan presents a more equitable and infinitely less expensive means of meeting these costs.

We cannot afford to neglect the plain duty before us I strongly recommend action to attain the objectives sought in this report.

Franklin D. Roosevelt.
The White House, Jan. 17, 1935.

Further Resources

BOOKS

Leuchtenburg, William E. *Franklin D. Roosevelt and the New Deal (1932–1940).* New York, Harper & Row, 1963.

Lubove, Roy. *The Struggle For Social Security, 1900–1935.* Pittsburgh, Pa.: University of Pittsburgh Press, 1986.

U.S. Social Security Administration. *Pocket History of Social Security.* Baltimore: U.S. Department of Health, Education, and Welfare, Social Security Administration, 1976.

WEBSITES

History Page. Social Security Online. Social Security Administration. Available online at http://www.ssa.gov/history/ (accessed August 29, 2002).

Senator Lester J. Dickinson of Iowa, a firm opponent of President Roosevelt, in January 1936. **AP/WIDE WORLD PHOTOS. REPRODUCED BY PERMISSION.**

"What's the Matter with Congress?"

Magazine article

By: Lester J. Dickinson

Date: February 1936

Source: Dickinson, Lester J. "What's the Matter with Congress?" *The American Mercury* 37, no. 146, February 1936, 129–36.

About the Author: Lester J. Dickinson (1873–1968) was born and raised in Iowa. He served six terms in the House of Representatives (1919–1931) and one term in the Senate (1931–1937). A Republican and strong critic of President Franklin D. Roosevelt (served 1933–1945), Dickinson lost his bid for reelection to the Senate in 1936. ■

Introduction

Roosevelt entered the White House in a position to appeal to all gradations of the political spectrum. Sensing victory very early in the 1932 campaign, he had kept his program very vague. While he was known to be an active and liberal governor of New York, his aristocratic background and fairly conservative economic views led many Republicans and conservative Democrats to believe he was an essentially "safe" presidential nominee. During the campaign Roosevelt emphasized his vigor, confidence, and commitment to an undefined "New Deal" for all Americans. This approach won him a landslide victory and a fairly docile opposition, especially given the scale of his victory.

Consequently, Roosevelt found almost universal support for his programs during his first months in office. Even his potential opponents recognized the truth in the slogan, "Roosevelt or Ruin." His critics generally approved of his aggressive handling of the bank crisis and were generally agreeable to his actions in the First Hundred Days. His infectious confidence and can-do enthusiasm contrasted favorably with the dour, do-nothing public image of his predecessor, Herbert Hoover (served 1929–1933).

Even the National Recovery Administration (NRA), which eventually drew considerable criticism, was initially well received. Roosevelt's primary engine for recovery, the NRA, was intended to forge a cooperative relationship between labor, business, and government that would create a more orderly and mutually beneficial economic system. Desperate for leadership and acutely aware of the depth of the crisis, Americans united behind the NRA in particular, and Roosevelt's entire recovery efforts in general, in the first few months of his administration.

As 1933 wore on, however, this began to change. Some of the desperation that had created the crisis mentality began to wear off, in large part because of the New Deal programs and Roosevelt's leadership. In particular, conservatives quickly became very critical of his tampering with fundamental economic forces. This included taking the country off of the gold standard, regulation of the stock market and the banking system, and the intervention in the competitive market.

In addition, Roosevelt gradually came under fire from previous supporters. These included insiders such as former Democratic presidential candidate Al Smith and leading newspaper columnist Walter Lippman as well as radicals like Father Charles Coughlin and Senator Huey Long. While opponents couldn't agree on whether Roosevelt was a fascist dictator or a communist dictator, the incarnation of evil itself or the pawn of hidden forces, they agreed that the rapid expansion of federal and presidential power was absolutist in its tendency and had to be stopped.

In an age of totalitarian leaders such as Josef Stalin in the Soviet Union, Benito Mussolini in Italy, and Adolf Hitler in Germany, these concerns were not simply rhetorical. The preservation of the rule of law was a legitimate concern. Nonetheless it is also true that the accusations hurled at Roosevelt were often inspired by purely political motives.

As the 1936 presidential election approached, Roosevelt's "dictatorial" powers became one of the central issues of the campaign. While in hindsight there appears to have been little reason for concern, at the time Roosevelt's reelection seemed very uncertain.

Significance

The election of 1936 resulted in a landslide victory for Roosevelt and the Democratic Party in general. It was one of the most convincing endorsements of a president in the nation's history. It did not, however, end concerns over Roosevelt's dictatorial drift, an issue his opponents continuously raised.

Almost immediately after his second inauguration, two pieces of legislation focused attention on the question of Roosevelt's accumulation of power. The first dealt with Roosevelt's effort to create a more compliant Supreme Court. The existing Court, which included a number of conservative justices, had consistently declared key pieces of New Deal legislation unconstitutional. Roosevelt's proposal would have given the president the authority to expand the size of the court. By appointing judges more sympathetic to his programs, he hoped to protect the New Deal from the constitutional challenges that he felt undermined his recovery and reform efforts.

The second piece of legislation was a government reorganization bill put forward in 1938. A relatively innocuous bill initially supported by some leading conservatives, it eventually became a major issue in which Congress saw the bill as a shift of congressional authority to the president. While the reasons for opposition varied, the loudest voices belonged to those who saw the bill as one more step toward dictatorship. In both cases Roosevelt was defeated by a Congress less malleable than his critics feared.

As Roosevelt's second term wore on, his political power began to wane. Lost congressional seats in the 1938 election reflected this decline. Furthermore Roosevelt was not expected to run for an unprecedented third term. As a result, Democrats began looking out for their political future rather than obediently falling into line behind a lame duck president.

By 1940, of course, international events had altered the situation dramatically. Roosevelt did run for reelection. While many opposed his serving an unprecedented third term, Roosevelt did not face a frenzied opposition afraid of his dictatorial aspirations. By that time even his opponents had sufficient examples of foreign dictators to know Roosevelt did not pose that threat.

Primary Source

"What's the Matter with Congress?" [excerpt]

SYNOPSIS: Senator Dickinson's article appeared in *The American Mercury,* a relentless foe of Roosevelt and the New Deal. Dickinson is extremely critical of President Roosevelt, accusing him of acting as a dictator and buying the compliance of Congress. In his opinion, Roosevelt had masterminded a "transformation of American social and economic system into something closely akin to the collectivist societies of . . . Russia, Germany and Italy."

To the future historian the record of the first session of the Seventy-Fourth Congress will make strange reading. For that record will reveal that more legislation of far-reaching social and economic consequence was enacted last year than during any preceding session—and yet every one of the extraordinary new laws was passed by a Congress which operated for the most part in a complete fog and without any understanding of the ultimate meaning of its own actions. The chief distinction of the Congress was the docility with which it played the rubber stamp to Franklin D. Roosevelt, a performance never equalled in the history of legislatures since those rump Parliaments which, under the Stuarts, so seriously jeopardized English liberty in the seventeenth century. Bills clearly revolutionary in their effect upon future national welfare were brought before congressional committees for hearings which were casual and perfunctory. The Senate frequently adopted House reports as its own, thus omitting even the pretense of consideration for vital legislation. Debate was limited in the lower chamber by gag rules reminiscent of the worst days of Czar Tom Reed and Uncle Joe Cannon, without evoking protests from the supposed representatives of Democracy. An attitude of complete apathy and servility possessed the Congress. The duty of national legislation was neglected and forgotten.

The exultation which had ushered in the New Deal less than two years previously, expired before the manipulations of a Dictator-President. Instead of the early evangelistic fervor for the More Abundant Life, the atmosphere at the Capitol came to reflect a cynical indifference. Among the veterans of politics, the crusading spirit gave place to an almost sullen resentment against the "must" program of socialistic rather than democratic legislation, peremptorily ordered from the White House. These measures, concocted by the President's militant Brain Trusters, were enacted by a Congress which *did not believe in them* and which, in many instances, actually questioned the constitutionality of its own acts. As the session moved on to a bitter and acrimonious end during the summer's dog days, it became more and more evident that the one desire, on the part of majority members, was to evade personal responsibility for what was being done. The buck was passed to Mr. Roosevelt, and the ultimate fate of measures enacted in ignominious haste was left to the Supreme Court.

With barely a protest, the most jealously-guarded of all Congressional prerogatives—the control over appropriations—was surrendered to the Chief Executive, who proceeded to direct the raising and spending of the nation's resources as if a national legislature did not exist. More than fifteen billion dollars—a sum exceeding the entire cost of American participation in the World War—was frittered away in two years on scatter-brain recovery schemes and Utopian federal projects, conceived in the minds of the greatest group of spend-thrifts ever assembled—the Messrs. Hopkins, Ickes, Wallace, Tugwell, and their assistant wizards. The actual nature of these projects and how they were to be executed, appeared of small concern to Congress. Its only anxiety was directed toward the political allocation of the funds, that is, their division between the various states and congressional districts. The decisions of the Supreme Court, holding the delegations of power by Congress to the Executive unconstitutional, resulted not in an increase in congressional vigilance or a blunt reassertion of authority, but rather in an intensification of the search by the Administration's law experts for new legal devices and subterfuges by use of which the Court's interdicts might be evaded. And as if such abdication were not enough, Congress carried its own stultification even further: it conveyed to the President not only its power to regulate the currency and, by revision of treaties, to raise or lower tariff duties, but, under the AAA, it authorized the Secretary of Agriculture to draw upon the Treasury for unlimited billions and to impose internal taxes upon one class of citizens for the direct benefit of another class.

While this latter instance has been glibly explained away as a means of correcting disparities between agriculture and industry, the indefatigable Dr. Tugwell reveals that the real object of such levies is to provide an open political subsidy through which a permanent farmer-worker alliance will be created. This frank admission of revolutionary policy is an indication of what is going on behind the scenes in Washington. It is an introduction to the Tugwell theory of a sabotage of industry and government, which is to make possible the emergence of a socialistic collectivist state. When all the facts in the case are assembled they will prove conclusively that the chain of events which took place after the Democratic victory at the polls in November, 1932, was deliberately and consciously precipitated. The nation-wide banking moratorium and the almost complete shutdown of industry, which coincided with Mr. Roosevelt's inauguration, it will be discovered, were more than mere fortuitous circumstances providing opportunity for shrewd political exploitation.

That policy of refusing co-operation to the outgoing Hoover regime was undertaken deliberately, after frankly counting the risk of collapse of the nation's financial and economic machinery. To carry through the bold program envisioned even then by the New Deal, it was necessary to bring about a public psychology of panic and despair. Only thus could opposition from Congress to the acquisition of those broad powers for the Executive, already determined upon, be forestalled. The clever and thoroughly ruthless advisers of the President foresaw, accurately enough, that only through such a *fait accompli* would it be possible to attain that larger sphere of action which the Constitution prohibited. By projecting Franklin D. Roosevelt as the nation's savior in a time of national crisis, public and congressional acquiescence could be won for that dictatorship which was seen as necessary in establishing the regimentation of a system of planned economy.

Indeed, when the historian pieces together the events which have transpired since November, 1932, he is likely to be struck by the definite and logical pattern presented. In that carefully prearranged plan formulated by the Brain Trust, such a *coup d'état* played a necessary and vital part. This deduction arises naturally from the recent revelation of Professor Tugwell's own close acquaintance with the technique of revolution. While reform was to be used as a mask, the actual objective sought was the transformation of the American social and economic system into something closely akin to the collectivist societies which have emerged in post-war Russia, Germany, and Italy. . . .

To say that the Seventy-Fourth Congress should have been alert in opposing the revolutionary aims of the Roosevelt *putsch* is only to define the constitutional duties of a legislature. The principal reason for the existence of a Congress as the chosen representative body of the people is to protect the public interest against usurpation of power from any quarter. To plead a temporary emergency which supposedly forced the American people into such a desperate condition of mind that they were willing to accept a transfer of autocratic power to the President (which under any other circumstances they would have resisted vigorously), is to beg the question. The Supreme Court refused to countenance the plea of emergency; such appeals have been denounced as dangerous and subversive by every competent patriot from 1775 to the present day. It is a truism of democracy that liberty is most precious to a free people just at that moment when a usurper pleads emergency as an excuse for oppression.

In the face of the present crisis, Congress has been supine. And it has paid the penalty for dereliction in duty: American history offers few parallels of a legislature held in such low esteem by the public and the press. Not only did it sacrifice all standing as a deliberative body, but it ceased entirely to assert that traditional spirit of independence against attempts at dictation from the opposite end of Pennsylvania Avenue. This sensitiveness of Congress when its own prerogatives are threatened has always been one of the most wholesome safeguards for our constitutional government. While the Chief Executive may advise concerning legislation he thinks desirable, by means of messages to Congress, any effort to suggest specific phraseology or form has in the past created such resentment on the Hill as to prejudice seriously the proposed measure's chances of passage. It is a sadly different story today.

In calculating the completeness of present legislative subservience to the Executive, one has only to recall, in contrast, the bitter contests waged during the Wilson administration between Congress and the President. Those "wilful men" who opposed the War President's program, first on armed neutrality and subsequently on the League of Nations issue, were denounced from the White House almost as if they were public enemies. Yet it is generally conceded now that they performed a genuinely patriotic service, Likewise, this spirit of congressional independence was kept alive during the Coolidge and Hoover administrations by the activities of the Western Republicans who were condemned as "sons of the wild jackass". Nevertheless, their determined insistence upon relief for agriculture is now belatedly recognized, even in the industrial East, as having been based upon sound economic grounds. But these excursions into the past provide no explanation for the present nadir of congressional influence nor for the impairment of legislative authority which has taken place. The complete eclipse of the Congress behind that effulgent, thirty-billion-dollar Roosevelt smile, has now assumed such dimensions as to threaten seriously the very foundations of representative government.

Many political observers, commenting upon the current supineness of Congress—particularly in its callous indifference to those open breaches of Democratic platform pledges—usually place the blame upon two correlated causes: unwieldy Democratic majorities in both House and Senate, and the breakdown, in consequence, of the two-party system. While it is well to point out that minority opposition to unsound legislation is thus unquestionably handicapped, such observations ignore a factor of even greater importance. This is the shifting and distortion of that balance of power between the legislative, executive, and judicial branches of government which has reached such dimensions as to constitute one of the leading issues of the 1936 campaign. The past three years have provided sharp illustrations of how tyrannical the majority can be, imperiling, as it always does, the safety of democracy by nullification of those restrictions which the Constitution sets upon its power.

The plain duty of the Congress, its legal and moral responsibility, is to maintain a co-equal status with the Executive. The proper functioning of what is called the American system of government depends upon a vigorous and alert legislature, always concerned in protecting its own rights. Yet, when there arose the necessity for finding solutions to the most pressing economic problems in history, requiring the exercise not only of specifically defined duties but of the highest critical intelligence, Congress failed completely in its constitutional functions. In contrast to that searching and careful analysis of Administration proposals made by Democratic congressional leaders during the Wilson regime, there is now revealed an unexampled and almost fawning servility to the White House. . . .

The debauching of Congress reached its final culmination with the passage of the $4,800,000,000 Work Relief Bill. This measure may serve historically as a classic illustration of the methods by which democracies destroy themselves. By its terms, millions of the unemployed were regimented into a class of indigents who are rendered dependent upon the uncertainties of politics—and whose votes may be purchased with money from the federal Treasury. In Europe the dictators refer to their minions as Black Shirts, Nazis, or Comrades: the Roosevelt fascist state, if it is successful, can call its supporters by a simpler name—Reliefers. The potential power of this solid bloc of bought votes has not as yet been completely comprehended. But the indications have been numerous: Huey Long's militant organization, Father Coughlin's eight-million-member association, and, more recently, the preposterous Townsend clubs boasting an enrollment of twenty-five million, suggest a picture of what may come. Americans, while alert to the progress of dictatorships abroad, have been ignorant of events transpiring in their own country. And the Seventy-Fourth Congress is to blame for the existence of this ignorance. If the legislature had done its duty in Washington last year, the position of democracy today would not be so desperate. . . .

From this atmosphere of glib promising and easy spending, with the specter of inflation always hovering in the background, from this extension of government policing of industry and agriculture until all enterprise is strait-jacketed, two strong political currents have been set in motion. The first and most menacing relates to the Constitution itself. Since the Administration seemingly has embraced the doctrine that the end justifies any means whatever, it follows that those legal safeguards which place definite curbs upon federal authority are viewed with a growing impatience. This attitude reaches its extreme expression in various types of share-the-wealth movements, which would use the taxing power to level off the national income, or envisage the government possessed of a magic spring of credit which need only flow to produce a return of prosperity. Congress itself, judged by the staggering total of its appropriations, seems to have embraced this latter view. More recently, however, even the former supporters of the Administration have become alarmed by the extravagant claims now being put forward by enthusiasts for all-inclusive government paternalism. "It will be a bad day for democratic government in the world," declares one of their leaders, "if American progressives cease to understand and to stand by the American conception of government as a limited grant of power to public officials. What is the good of denouncing the despotisms of Europe if here at home we cultivate the idea that anything may be done which at the moment seems good to those in office?"

But the Constitutional question has a still graver implication. Many important New Deal measures are, at this writing, before the Supreme Court to be decided this winter and spring. What are the possibilities should the TVA be denied its announced function of serving as a yardstick to the public utility industry, should the processing taxes be declared invalid as restricting internal commerce between the states, should the Wagner industrial disputes bill, the Guffey bill, or the Social Security act be held unconstitutional exercises of Federal power? What is the Administration to do under such circumstances? Will it permit the issue to be joined between Utopian dreams and the actuality of economic law? The implications from such an impasse between the Executive and the judicial arm of the government would be grave enough under any circumstances. How much more serious must they be when the Administration, so challenged, is seeking re-election; when it asks, as it must, public ratification either upon its record or by excusing that record through attacks upon the Supreme Court? The strain so placed upon the Constitution is plainly evident.

The other outstanding political development is that, for the first time in our history as a nation, American citizens, American businessmen, and American farmers have actually become *afraid of their own government.* There now exists an atmosphere of fear more like that of Russia than of America. Punitive measures are to be employed against the slightest breaches of bureaucratic regulations imposed by the New Deal commissars. There has been set up the utterly un-American principle that to have knowledge of a so-called crime, and not to inform against a fellow citizen, is to make oneself guilty as of the original crime itself. The intent of such laws is not to gain information but to use such power for purposes of intimidation, to muffle criticism, and to make the individual wary of expressing his own views as a citizen lest he too suffer from reprisals. The American fascist state as contemplated by the militant Dr. Tugwell is already well under way.

Businessmen today are placed at the mercy of government to a degree that would have been regarded as incredible a few years ago. They are threatened, if they have borrowed from government agencies, with the calling of loans, or with the cancellation of government contracts. They are cracked down upon by the SEC, the FTC, the Treasury income tax bureau, or are subject to investigation by senatorial committees. Under such harassments, is it any wonder that great numbers of businessmen try to play safe? Is it any wonder that they succumb to the same influences which have reduced Congress to impotency? Or that the granting of amnesty in the form of a "breathing spell" brings great rejoicing? But what a commentary upon the Bill of Rights!

These questions pose the problem not only of what is the matter with Congress, but a deeper and more searching inquiry: What has happened to that spirit of liberty which we had thought was part of the American birthright?

Further Resources

BOOKS

Leuchtenburg, William E. *Franklin D. Roosevelt and the New Deal (1932–1940).* New York: Harper & Row, 1963.

Watkins, T. H. *The Hungry Years: A Narrative History of the Great Depression in America.* New York: Henry Holt and Company, 1999.

"I Have Seen War. . . . I Hate War"

Speech

By: Franklin D. Roosevelt

Date: August 14, 1936

Source: Roosevelt, Franklin D. "I Have Seen War. . . . I Hate War." Address at Chautauqua, N.Y., August 14, 1936. Printed in *The Public Papers and Addresses of Franklin Delano Roosevelt.* Vol. 5, *The People Approve, 1936.* New York: Macmillan, 1938; Random House, 1950, 285–292.

About the Author: Franklin D. Roosevelt (1888–1945) was appointed assistant secretary of the Navy by President Woodrow Wilson in 1913. He stayed in this position throughout World War I (1914–1918) and obtained valuable experience in the operation of the federal government, the conduct of a major war, military affairs, and international relations. In 1920, Roosevelt was the Democratic vice presidential candidate. His promising career seemed to end abruptly in 1921 when he was stricken by polio and left unable to walk. With the support of his wife, Eleanor, and advisor, Louis Howe, Roosevelt remained politically active and was elected governor of New York in 1928. As governor of the nation's largest state during the early years of the Great Depression, Roosevelt understood the depth of the problem and the need for federal intervention in providing relief and restarting the economy. The 1932 Democratic Convention nominated him as its presidential candidate and Roosevelt went on to win a landslide victory over President Herbert Hoover (served 1929–1933). ■

Introduction

When Roosevelt assumed the presidency in 1933, international affairs held little interest for the country or the new president. The high number of deaths in World War I (1914–1918) appalled most Americans as did the fact that, despite the United States' noble war aims, the world seemed no better as a result of its victory. Consequently, most Americans hoped to avoid involvement in international affairs as much as possible. In addition, the country was in the midst of a deep and prolonged economic depression and Roosevelt wanted to give his complete attention to the domestic situation.

Nonetheless the president had to deal with some important international issues, such as the regulation of international trade, because it had an immediate and direct impact on the United States' economic well-being. The Roosevelt administration placed particular emphasis on addressing international currency exchange policies and developing alternatives to the stifling trade effects of protective tariffs like the Smoot-Hawley Tariff of 1930.

At the time of Roosevelt's inauguration in March 1933, the international situation was bleak. Fascists had ruled Italy for ten years, Hitler was just coming to absolute power in Germany, and Japan was pursuing a very aggressive policy in China. While Americans wanted peace, they were generally unwilling to adopt an active role to preserve peace lest the country be drawn unwittingly into war.

American isolationism was reinforced by the 1934 investigation into the role the financial and munitions industries had played in drawing the United States into World War I. This investigation was conducted by Senator Gerald Nye, a Republican from North Dakota. Nye's committee arrived at the simplistic and sensationalist conclusion that U.S. involvement in the war resulted from the financial interests of a handful of companies. In response, Congress passed a series of Neutrality Acts, beginning in 1935, designed to keep the United States from repeating that mistake.

Significance

Sympathetic to the primary objective of the Neutrality Acts—the avoidance of war—and primarily concerned with maintaining the coalition necessary to support his domestic agenda, Roosevelt gave the acts public support. By 1935, however, he recognized the threat posed by Japan, Germany, and Italy. Lacking the political strength to override strong isolationist and antiwar sentiment, however, Roosevelt did not join the world community in its fight against totalitarian aggression, and approached the whole situation very cautiously in the mid- and late 1930s.

By the time of the Chautauqua speech, the international situation had grown critical. Japan was firmly in control of Manchuria and pressing further demands on China. Italy had invaded Ethiopia and German rearmament was well under way. The Spanish Civil War had broken out, threatening peace in Europe. While continuing to support the Neutrality Acts, Roosevelt pointed out that the United States must rely on "the wisdom of those who direct our foreign policy" to maintain the peace. He also reminded "remoter Nations that wish us not good but ill, that we are strong; they know that we can and will defend ourselves and our neighborhood."

In reality both Roosevelt and the "remoter Nations" knew that the United States had a weak military. The nation possessed a powerful navy but had a small and poorly equipped army, which at the time included the air force. In 1936 Roosevelt, confronted with strong antiwar sentiment and enormous domestic problems, was not in a position to take action. Not until early 1939 did he begin to raise the issue of enlarging the military in public.

German annexation of Austria and occupation of Czechoslovakia in 1938, combined with increasing German pressure on Poland, and Italy's invasion of Albania and implied threat to Greece in early 1939, impelled Roosevelt to take a more aggressive posture. He began to speak publicly about the need to adopt "methods short of war" that would allow the United States to support the victim of an aggressor.

Following the German invasion of Poland on September 1, 1939, Roosevelt pushed for ways to provide tangible support to the victims of fascist aggression. Despite strong opposition from isolationists, the Neutrality Acts were modified to allow the sale of arms, on a cash basis, to "the opponents of force." When the French were defeated in June 1940 Roosevelt engineered a variety of programs, short of war but in clear violation of strict neutrality, to assist the British and rearm the United States. These programs also met with stiff opposition. Not until the Japanese attack on Pearl Harbor and Germany's subsequent declaration of war on the United States did the country rally behind Roosevelt's foreign policy and rearmament plans.

Primary Source

"I Have Seen War. . . . I Hate War"

SYNOPSIS: Chautauqua was (and still is) a combination resort, religious retreat, and intellectual and educational community in western New York. Established in 1874, Chautauqua's summer encampments regularly featured lectures and speeches by important scholars and government leaders. Roosevelt visited it on August 14, 1936, to give an address defining American foreign policy. While he reaffirmed his commitment to some of the critical elements of isolationism, he also emphasized the importance of U.S. engagement in international affairs.

As many of you who are here tonight know, I formed the excellent habit of coming to Chautauqua more than twenty years ago. After my Inauguration in 1933, I promised Mr. Bestor that during the next four years I would come to Chautauqua again. It is in fulfillment of this that I am with you tonight.

A few days ago I was asked what the subject of this talk would be; and I replied that for two good reasons I wanted to discuss the subject of peace: First, because it is eminently appropriate in Chautauqua and, second, because in the hurly-burly of domestic politics it is important that our people should not overlook problems and issues which, though they lie beyond our borders, may, and probably will, have a vital influence on the United States of the future.

Many who have visited me in Washington in the past few months may have been surprised when I have told them that personally and because of my own daily contacts with all manner of difficult situations I am more concerned and less cheerful about international world conditions than about our immediate domestic prospects.

I say this to you not as a confirmed pessimist but as one who still hopes that envy, hatred, and malice among Nations have reached their peak and will be succeeded by a new tide of peace and goodwill. I say this as one who has participated in many of the decisions of peace and war before, during and after the World War; one who has traveled much; and one who has spent a goodly portion of every twenty-four hours in the study of foreign relations.

Long before I returned to Washington as President of the United States, I had made up my mind that pending what might be called a more opportune moment on other continents, the United States could best serve the cause of a peaceful humanity by setting an example. That was why on the 4th of March, 1933, I made the following declaration:

> In the field of world policy I would dedicate this Nation to the policy of the good neighbor—the neighbor who resolutely respects himself and, because he does so, respects the rights of others—the neighbor who respects his obligations and respects the sanctity of his agreements in and with a world of neighbors.

This declaration represents my purpose; but it represents more than a purpose, for it stands for a practice. To a measurable degree it has succeeded; the whole world now knows that the United States cherishes no predatory ambitions. We are strong; but less powerful Nations know that they need not fear our strength. We seek no conquest; we stand for peace.

In the whole of the Western Hemisphere our good-neighbor policy has produced results that are especially heartening.

The noblest monument to peace and to neighborly economic and social friendship in all the world is not a monument in bronze or stone, but the boundary which unites the United States and Canada—3,000 miles of friendship with no barbed wire, no gun or soldier, and no passport on the whole frontier.

Mutual trust made that frontier. To extend the same sort of mutual trust throughout the Americas was our aim.

The American Republics to the south of us have been ready always to cooperate with the United States on a basis of equality and mutual respect, but before we inaugurated the good-neighbor policy there were among them resentment and fear, because certain Administrations in Washington had slighted their national pride and their sovereign rights.

In pursuance of the good-neighbor policy, and because in my younger days I had learned many lessons in the hard school of experience, I stated that the United States was opposed definitely to armed intervention.

We have negotiated a Pan-American convention embodying the principle of non-intervention. We have abandoned the Platt Amendment which gave us the right to intervene in the internal affairs of the Republic of Cuba. We have withdrawn American marines from Haiti. We have signed a new treaty which places our relations with Panama on a mutually satisfactory basis. We have undertaken a series of trade agreements with other American countries to our mutual commercial profit. At the request of two neighboring Republics, I hope to give assistance in the final settlement of the last serious boundary dispute between any of the American Nations.

Throughout the Americas the spirit of the good neighbor is a practical and living fact. The twenty-one American Republics are not only living together in friendship and in peace; they are united in the determination so to remain.

To give substance to this determination a conference will meet on December 1, 1936, at the capital of our great Southern neighbor, Argentina, and it is, I know, the hope of all Chiefs of State of the Americas that this will result in measures which will banish wars forever from this vast portion of the earth.

Peace, like charity, begins at home; that is why we have begun at home. But peace in the Western world is not all that we seek.

It is our hope that knowledge of the practical application of the good-neighbor policy in this hemisphere will be borne home to our neighbors across the seas.

For ourselves we are on good terms with them—terms in most cases of straightforward friendship, of peaceful understanding.

But, of necessity, we are deeply concerned about tendencies of recent years among many of the Nations of other continents. It is a bitter experience to us when the spirit of agreements to which we are a party is not lived up to. It is an even more bitter experience for the whole company of Nations to witness not only the spirit but the letter of international agreements violated with impunity and without regard to the simple principles of honor. Permanent friendships between Nations as between men can be sustained only by scrupulous respect for the pledged word.

In spite of all this we have sought steadfastly to assist international movements to prevent war. We cooperated to the bitter end—and it was a bitter end—in the work of the General Disarmament Conference. When it failed we sought a separate treaty to deal with the manufacture of arms and the international traffic in arms. That proposal also came to nothing. We participated—again to the bitter end—in a conference to continue naval limitations, and when it became evident that no general treaty could be signed because of the objections of other

President Roosevelt and Brazilian President Getulio Vargas speak at a banquet in Rio de Janeiro. December 4, 1936. AP/WIDE WORLD PHOTOS. REPRODUCED BY PERMISSION.

Nations, we concluded with Great Britain and France a conditional treaty of qualitative limitation which, much to my regret, already shows signs of ineffectiveness.

We shun political commitments which might entangle us in foreign wars; we avoid connection with the political activities of the League of Nations; but I am glad to say that we have co-operated wholeheartedly in the social and humanitarian work at Geneva. Thus we are a part of the world effort to control traffic in narcotics, to improve international health, to help child welfare, to eliminate double taxation and to better working conditions and laboring hours throughout the world.

We are not isolationists except in so far as we seek to isolate ourselves completely from war. Yet we must remember that so long as war exists on earth there will be some danger that even the Nation which most ardently desires peace may be drawn into war.

I have seen war. I have seen war on land and sea. I have seen blood running from the wounded. I have seen men coughing out their gassed lungs. I have seen the dead in the mud. I have seen cities destroyed. I have seen two hundred limping, exhausted men come out of line—the survivors of a regiment of one thousand that went forward forty-eight hours before. I have seen children starving. I have seen the agony of mothers and wives. I hate war.

I have passed unnumbered hours, I shall pass unnumbered hours, thinking and planning how war may be kept from this Nation.

I wish I could keep war from all Nations; but that is beyond my power. I can at least make certain that no act of the United States helps to produce or to promote war. I can at least make clear that the conscience of America revolts against war and that any Nation which provokes war forfeits the sympathy of the people of the United States.

Many causes produce war. There are ancient hatreds, turbulent frontiers, the "legacy of old forgotten, far-off things, and battles long ago." There are new-born fanaticisms, convictions on the part of certain peoples that they have become the unique depositories of ultimate truth and right.

A dark old world was devastated by wars between conflicting religions. A dark modern world faces wars between conflicting economic and political fanaticisms in which are intertwined race hatreds. To bring it home, it is as if within the territorial limits of the United States, forty-eight Nations with forty-eight forms of government, forty-eight customs barriers, forty-eight languages, and forty-eight eternal and different verities, were spending their time and their substance in a frenzy of effort to make themselves strong enough to conquer their neighbors or strong enough to defend themselves against their neighbors.

In one field, that of economic barriers, the American policy may be, I hope, of some assistance in discouraging the economic source of war and therefore a contribution toward the peace of the world. The trade agreements which we are making are not only finding outlets for the products of American fields and American factories but are also pointing the way to the elimination of embargoes, quotas and other devices which place such pressure on Nations not possessing great natural resources that to them the price of peace seems less terrible than the price of war.

We do not maintain that a more liberal international trade will stop war; but we fear that without a more liberal international trade, war is a natural sequence.

The Congress of the United States has given me certain authority to provide safeguards of American neutrality in case of war.

The President of the United States, who, under our Constitution, is vested with primary authority to conduct our international relations, thus has been given new weapons with which to maintain our neutrality.

Nevertheless—and I speak from a long experience—the effective maintenance of American neutrality depends today, as in the past, on the wisdom and determination of whoever at the moment occupy the offices of President and Secretary of State.

It is clear that our present policy and the measures passed by the Congress would, in the event of a war on some other continent, reduce war profits which would otherwise accrue to American citizens. Industrial and agricultural production for a war market may give immense fortunes to a few men; for the Nation as a whole it produces disaster. It was the prospect of war profits that made our farmers in the West plow up prairie land that should never have been plowed, but should have been left for grazing cattle. Today we are reaping the harvest of those war profits in the dust storms which have devastated those war plowed areas.

It was the prospect of war profits that caused the extension of monopoly and unjustified expansion of industry and a price level so high that the normal relationship between debtor and creditor was destroyed.

Nevertheless, if war should break out again in another continent, let us not blink the fact that we would find in this country thousands of Americans who, seeking immediate riches—fools' gold—would attempt to break down or evade our neutrality.

They would tell you—and, unfortunately, their views would get wide publicity—that if they could produce and ship this and that and the other article to belligerent Nations, the unemployed of America would all find work. They would tell you that if they could extend credit to warring Nations that credit would be used in the United States to build homes and factories and pay our debts. They would tell you that America once more would capture the trade of the world.

It would be hard to resist that clamor; it would be hard for many Americans, I fear, to look beyond—to realize the inevitable penalties, the inevitable day of reckoning, that come from a false prosperity. To resist the clamor of that greed, if war should come, would require the unswerving support of all Americans who love peace.

If we face the choice of profits or peace, the Nation will answer—must answer—"We choose peace." It is the duty of all of us to encourage such a body of public opinion in this country that the answer will be clear and for all practical purposes unanimous.

With that wise and experienced man who is our Secretary of State, whose statesmanship has met with such wide approval, I have thought and worked long and hard on the problem of keeping the United States at peace. But all the wisdom of America is not to be found in the White House or in the Department of State; we need the meditation, the prayer, and the positive support of the people of America who go along with us in seeking peace.

No matter how well we are supported by neutrality legislation, we must remember that no laws can be provided to cover every contingency, for it is impossible to imagine how every future event may shape itself. In spite of every possible forethought, international relations involve of necessity a vast uncharted area. In that area safe sailing will depend on the knowledge and the experience and the wisdom of those who direct our foreign policy. Peace will depend on their day-to-day decisions.

At this late date, with the wisdom which is so easy after the event and so difficult before the event, we find it possible to trace the tragic series of small decisions which led Europe into the Great War in 1914 and eventually engulfed us and many other Nations.

We can keep out of war if those who watch and decide have a sufficiently detailed understanding of international affairs to make certain that the small decisions of each day do not lead toward war and if, at the same time, they posses the courage to say "no" to those who selfishly or unwisely would let us go to war.

Of all the Nations of the world today we are in many ways most singularly blessed. Our closest neighbors are good neighbors. If there are remoter Nations that wish us not good but ill, they know that we are strong; they know that we can and will defend ourselves and defend our neighborhood.

We seek to dominate no other Nation. We ask no territorial expansion. We oppose imperialism. We desire reduction in world armaments.

We believe in democracy; we believe in freedom; we believe in peace. We offer to every Nation of the world the handclasp of the good neighbor. Let those who wish our friendship look us in the eye and take our hand.

Further Resources

BOOKS

Bagby, Wesley Marvin. *America's International Relations Since World War I.* New York: Oxford University Press, 1999.

Cashman, Sean Dennis. *America Ascendant: From Theodore Roosevelt To FDR In The Century Of American Power, 1901–1945.* New York: New York University Press, 1998.

Dulles, Foster Rhea. *America's Rise To World Power, 1898–1954.* New York: Harper, 1955.

Powaski, Ronald E. *Toward An Entangling Alliance: American Isolationism, Internationalism, and Europe, 1901–1950.* New York: Greenwood Press, 1991.

"Hemingway Reports Spain"

Magazine article

By: Ernest Hemingway

Date: April 27, 1938

Source: Hemingway, Ernest. "Hemingway Reports Spain." *The New Republic,* April 27, 1938, 350–51.

About the Author: Ernest Hemingway (1899–1961) was one of the United States' best known authors of the twentieth-century. He began his career as a reporter, but soon found his way to writing novels and short stories. Following World War I (1914–1918) he moved to Paris and became part of a literary American expatriate group. Hemingway's best known novels include *The Sun Also Rises, For Whom the Bell Tolls,* and *A Farewell to Arms.* He received the Nobel Prize for literature in 1954. ■

Introduction

In the years following World War I, Spain was in a nearly continual state of turmoil. Although technically a constitutional monarchy the country was ruled by a relatively benign dictator, General Primo de Rivera, between 1923 and 1930. When he resigned the monarchy collapsed and Spain sank into chaos. An ongoing struggle between leftist sympathizers and conservative elements resulted in a steady stream of labor unrest, violence, and regional insurrections.

After several years of conservative control, the communist-influenced Popular Front achieved a majority in February, 1936. The republican government hoped to implement such measures as land reforms and the separation of Church and State. Conservative forces, however, would not tolerate these changes.

On July 18, 1936, General Francisco Franco launched a military coup against the Spanish Republic. Franco led the conservative elements of society: the military, large land owners, the Catholic Church, Royalists, and Spanish fascists (Phalangists.) The Republican government was supported by various leftist factions—communists, socialists, labor syndicalists—as well as separatists from the Basque and Catalonian regions of Spain. Expecting a quick victory, Franco was surprised by the popular reaction to the coup, which failed in critical areas of the country including Madrid. For the next three years Spain was griped in a ferocious civil war that threatened to engulf Europe.

Significance

Fearful that events in Spain would lead to a broader conflict, the international community, including all major powers, agreed to a policy of non-intervention. Despite having signed this agreement, Italy and Germany, both under fascist rule, soon began supplying Franco's forces, while the communist Soviet Union backed the Republic. In addition to material aid, Italian, German, and Soviet "volunteers" fought for their respective allies. In addition to being a struggle between competing ideologies, the war provided each of these countries a training ground to test new tactics and weapons. It was a prologue to World War II (1939–1945).

Meanwhile Britain and France remained neutral, preventing shipment of supplies to either side in the civil

Ernest Hemingway talks to refugees in Spain made homeless by the civil war in 1937. © HULTON-DEUTSCH COLLECTION/CORBIS. REPRODUCED BY PERMISSION.

war. The United States quickly modified its Neutrality Act to prevent the shipment of military goods to either side, anxious to avoid being drawn into the conflict as had happened in World War I. While Franco's army was reasonably well supplied by Italy and Germany, the distance between the Soviet Union and Spain limited the Soviets' ability to aid Spanish Republicans. Thus the embargo by the democracies of Britain, France, and the United States, imposed to ensure neutrality, actually aided the fascist-supplied rebels.

Although the western democracies stayed out of the conflict, many of their citizens volunteered to fight on behalf of the Republic in the so-called International Brigade. These volunteers included approximately 2,800 Americans in the Lincoln and Washington battalions. American volunteers were drawn primarily from the Communist Party and the ranks of radical labor unions. The ill-equipped Lincoln and Washington battalions suffered a high casualty rate, losing approximately 750 members before they were withdrawn in December 1938.

In January 1939 Franco's army entered Barcelona. Two months later Madrid fell, bringing the war to an end. Lasting not quite three years, the Spanish Civil War took the lives of almost a million people. It left the country devastated and under control of Franco, a fascist dictator who would remain in power until his death in 1975.

Primary Source

"Hemingway Reports Spain"

SYNOPSIS: Hemingway filed the following story while reporting for the North American Newspaper Alliance. It covers events in April 1938, primarily reporting on the situation of the Lincoln and Washington battalions. As a result of this campaign Franco's forces drove to the Mediterranean Sea at the small port town of Vinoroz. This effectively cut off the Republican forces in Catalonia, which collapsed several months later.

As we have done on two previous occasions, we present below selected passages from recent dispatches of Ernest Hemingway, who is reporting the Spanish war for the North American Newspaper Alliance. They have already been printed in various newspapers affiliated with the Alliance, but such publication has often been incomplete because of lack of space.—The Editors [of *The New Republic*]

Barcelona

It was a lovely false spring day when we started for the front this morning. Last night, coming in to Barcelona, it had been gray, foggy, dirty and sad, but today it was bright and warm, and pink almond blossoms colored the gray hills and brightened the dusty green rows of olive trees.

Then, outside of Reus, on a straight smooth highway with olive orchards on each side, the chauffeur from the rumble seat shouted, "Planes, planes!" and, rubber screeching, we stopped the car under a tree.

"They're right over us," the chauffeur said, and, as this correspondent dove headforward into a ditch, he looked up sideways, watching a monoplane come down and wing over and then evidently decide a single car was not worth turning his eight machine guns loose on.

But, as we watched, came a sudden egg-dropping explosion of bombs, and, ahead, Reus, silhouetted against hills a half-mile away, disappeared in a brick-dust-colored cloud of smoke. We made our way through the town, the main street blocked by broken houses and a smashed water main, and, stopping, tried to get a policeman to shoot a wounded horse, but the owner thought it was still possibly worth saving and we went on up toward the mountain pass that leads to the little Catalan

Newspaper correspondent Ernest Hemingway (right) talks with Captain Milton Wolfe, commander of the Lincoln-Washington Battalion of the American Brigade, near the front in Spain during that country's civil war. May 1938. **AP/WIDE WORLD PHOTOS. REPRODUCED BY PERMISSION.**

city of Falset. Soon we began passing carts loaded with refugees. An old woman was driving one, crying and sobbing while she swung a whip. She was the only woman I saw crying all day. There were eight children following another cart and one little boy pushed on a wheel as they came up a difficult grade. Bedding, sewing machines, blankets, cooking utensils and mattresses wrapped in mats, sacks of grain for the horses and mules were piled in the carts and goats and sheep were tethered to the tailboards. There was no panic, they were just plodding along.

On a mule piled high with bedding rode a woman holding a still freshly red-faced baby that could not have been two days old. The mother's head swung steadily up and down with the motion of the beast she rode, and the baby's jet-black hair was drifted gray with the dust. A man led the mule forward, looking back over his shoulder and then looking forward at the road.

"When was the baby born?" I asked him, as our car swung alongside. "Yesterday," he said proudly, and the car was past. But all these people, no matter where else they looked as they walked or rode, all looked up to watch the sky.

Then we began to see soldiers straggling along. Some carried their rifles by the muzzles, some had no arms. At first there were only a few troops, then finally there was a steady stream, with whole units intact. Then there were troops in trucks, troops marching, trucks with guns, with tanks, with anti-tank and anti-aircraft guns, and always a line of people walking.

As we went on, the road choked and swelled with this migration, until, finally, it was not just the road, but streaming alongside the road by all the old paths for driving cattle came the civilian population and the troops. There was no panic at all, only a steady movement, and many of the people seemed cheerful. But perhaps it was the day. The day was so lovely that it seemed ridiculous that anyone should ever die.

Barcelona

For two days, this correspondent has been doing the most dangerous thing you can do in this war. That is, keep close behind an unstabilized line where the enemy is attacking with mechanized forces. It's the most dangerous because the first thing you see is the tanks, and the tanks don't take prisoners; they don't give orders to Halt, and they use incendiary bullets on your car. And the only way you know they're there is when you see them.

We had been checking the front and trying to locate the Lincoln-Washington Battalion, from which no word had been heard since Gandesa was captured two days ago. The last time they had been seen, they were holding out on top of a hill outside Gandesa. On their right, the British battalion of the same brigade was holding up the Fascist advance all that day with them, and, after darkness came and both battalions had been surrounded, nobody had heard anything from the Lincoln-Washington outfit.

There were 450 men when they stood on that hill. Today we found eight of them and learned that probably 150 more had cut their way through. . . . Three of the eight, John Gates, Joseph Hecht, and George Watts, had swum the Ebro River opposite Miravet. When we saw them at noon they were barefoot and had just been given clothes. They had been naked since they had crossed the river at daylight. The Ebro, they said, was a fast-flowing, very cold river, and six others who had tried to swim it, four of whom were wounded, drowned.

Standing in the dusty brush beside a very nervous making road, already well up behind the Fascist advance down the Ebro, we listened to the story of their break through after the battalion had been surrounded. Of their stand before Gandesa, with the mechanized columns and tanks already past them. Of the wild night when the battalion was split into two parts, one going south, one east, and, from the scout officer who led one group which included the chief of staff, the brigade commissar and the battalion commissar, slightly wounded at Gandesa, and thirty-five others, of the possible capture of this group at Corbera, just north of Gandesa.

Of adventures through the Fascist lines, how, in wandering into the enemy lines at night, when challenged, they asked in Spanish, "What outfit are you?" and a sleepy voice answered in German, "We're the Eighth Division." Creeping through another camp, stepping on a sleeping man's hand, hearing him say in German, "Get off my hand." Of having to break across an open field toward the bank of the Ebro and being sniped at by artillery controlled by an observation plane overhead. Finally, the desperate swimming of the Ebro and wandering down the road, not to desert, not to try to reach the frontier, but looking for the remainder of the battalion so they could reform and join the brigade.

The scout officer, telling of the possible loss of the chief of staff, said: "I was ahead, going through an orchard just north of Corbera, when someone in the dark challenged. I covered him with my pistol and he called for the corporal of the guard. As the guard came, I shouted to those behind, 'This way, this way!' and ran through the orchard to pass north of the town. But no one followed. I could hear them running toward the town. Then I could hear commands of 'Hands up! Hands up!' and it sounded as though they had been surrounded. Perhaps they got away, but it sounded as though some were captured."

The British battalion, led by Waters, found boats further north on the Ebro and crossed successfully. Three hundred men, commanded by Waters, were marching down the road toward us, but we could not wait as we were due at Tortosa to check the situation there. . . .

Tortosa

Driving carefully between the boxes of dynamite set to mine the small stone bridges on the narrow road, we worked our way up the Ebro Valley. . . . Stopping to ask a soldier who was walking leisurely in the direction of the front where headquarters was located, we heard machine-gun fire hammering on ahead and the noise of shells bursting. Then, above these reassuring sounds that meant the front was located, came the drone of planes and the bung, bung, bung of bombs.

Leaving the car in the shade made by the steep left bank, we climbed to the top of a sheer, terraced ridge where we could see the planes. Below us was the river, the little town of Cherta in a bend between the river and the road, and, beyond, the planes were bombing where a road cut between mountains that looked as though they had been molded in gray paper-mâché for some fantastic stage-set.

Black puffs of anti-aircraft bursts blossomed around them and showed they were government planes. Government anti-aircraft bursts are white. Then, with a noise as though the sky was being hammered to pieces, more bombers came over. Crouched against a stone wall on the ridge-top, taking advantage of the shadow cast, you saw from the red wing-tips they were government, too.

As the droning faded, the machine-gun firing intensified ahead, and, as the shelling increased, you knew there was an attack a little way up the road. . . .

Beside the can was an Andalusian soldier from a division holding a line up the river. He was tall and gaunt and very cool and very tired.

"You can go on past the town, but there has had to be a little retirement today, so I wouldn't go too far," he said.

He said his brigade had been surrounded three times since the drive toward the sea had started, had cut its way out and drifted through at night and now had rejoined the division.

"We've held them here three days now," he said. "The Italian infantry is no good and we drive them back whenever we counter attack, but they've got so much artillery and planes and we've been fighting three weeks now with no rest. The men are all very tired."

Further Resources

BOOKS

DuPuy, R. Ernest, and Trevor N. DuPuy. *The Encyclopedia Of Military History.* New York and Evanston: Harper & Row, Publishers, 1970.

Pratt, Julius W. *A History of United States Foreign Policy.* Englewood Cliffs, N.J.: Prentice Hall, Inc., 1965.

WEBSITES

"About The Spanish Civil War." http://www.english.uiuc.edu/maps/scw/scw.htm (accessed August 29, 2002).

The Debate over Isolation

"Concerted Action against the Fascist States"

Speech [excerpted from a debate]

By: Frederick J. Libby

Date: May 24, 1938

Source: Libby, Frederick J. "Concerted Action against the Fascist States." In Johnson, Julia E., ed. *The Reference Shelf.* Vol. 12, no. 6, *United States Foreign Policy: Isolation or Alliance.* New York: H. W. Wilson, 1938, 69–73.

About the Author: Frederick J. Libby was a leading American pacifist and executive secretary of the National Council for the Prevention of War. His experience with the American Friends Service Committee during and immediately after World War I (1914–1918) convinced him to spend the rest of his life working to promote peace.

Address Before the Bar Association of Tennesee on the Spirit of International Law, June 3, 1938

Speech

By: Cordell Hull

Date: June 3, 1938

Source: Hull, Cordell. Address Before the Bar Association of Tennessee on the Spirit of International Law, June 3, 1938. In Johnson, Julia E., ed. *The Reference Shelf.* Vol. 12, no. 6, *United States Foreign Policy: Isolation or Alliance.* New York: H.W. Wilson, 1938, 89–94.

About the Author: Cordell Hull (1871–1955), a Tennessee-born lawyer, spent twenty years in Congress before serving as secretary of state from 1933 to 1944 under President Franklin D. Roosevelt (served 1933–1945). As secretary of state Hull led the implementation of several critical U.S. policies. He initiated the negotiation of bilateral trade agreements that moved the United States away from the protective tariff philosophy of the Smoot-Hawley Tariff. The consequence was a more cooperative trade policy that led to the present system established by the 1948 General Agreement on Tariffs and Trade. Hull was instrumental in implementing Roosevelt's Good Neighbor policy, which altered U.S. relations with Latin America as the nation drifted toward involvement in World War II (1939–1945). ■

Introduction

To understand the foreign policy issues of the 1930s one must fully realize the impact of World War I. The "Great War" had a devastating impact on the psyche of Europeans and Americans. The tremendous loss of life amid the horrors of trench warfare was burned into the minds of thoughtful citizens of every country who participated in the slaughter. The overriding sentiment was that it must never happen again. This fervent belief underlay the policies of the world's democratic nations between 1919 and 1939.

In addition to the obvious personal tragedy and cost of World War I, Europeans and Americans had to grapple with the implications the war had on the validity of the fundamental values of Western civilization. Europeans entered the war in the belief that Western values were the hope for the future of the entire world. The horror of war shook that self-confidence to its very roots.

For Americans, there was an added lesson. Many Americans, seeing the terrible loss of life in the war, felt

U.S. Secretary of State Cordell Hull. **U.S. SIGNAL CORP.**

they had been duped. The United States had been drawn into war by militarists and the naïve belief that victory would make the "world safe for democracy." Clearly this had failed. Never again, they felt, should the United States intervene in affairs that did not directly affect American interests.

The experience of World War I prompted a return to the more traditional U.S. foreign policy that had been in place since George Washington's Farewell Address in 1797, in which he urged the United States to avoid "foreign entanglements." This philosophy, many Americans reasoned, had served the nation well for 100 years. The country's foray into internationalism, which began with the Spanish-American War and subsequent acquisition of a colonial empire, was a disaster and must be reversed.

American withdrawal from foreign entanglements rested on the fact that the United States' geography allowed it to put thousands of miles of ocean between itself and any powerful enemies. Blessed with great natural resources and a huge internal market, the country had little need to project its power around the world. The United States could ensure its safety and happiness by retreating between the Atlantic and Pacific Oceans and, as founding father John Adams had argued in 1798, the "wooden walls" of a strong navy.

The foreign affairs of most of the years between the two world wars was a direct reflection of the experience born of World War I. There was a great effort to reduce armaments and diminish the threat of war through negotiation and treaty. A primary objective of U.S. foreign policy was the prevention of a costly naval arms race. This, it was hoped, would help deal with the particularly troubling and growing threat of Japanese expansion in the Far East. Naval conferences in Washington (1921) and London (1930) achieved some short-term results.

The Kellogg-Briand Pact (1928) was another step toward reducing the threat of war. In conjunction with French Foreign Minister Aristide Briand, the U.S. Secretary of State Frank B. Kellogg coordinated the pact to "renounce war as an instrument of national policy." This well meaning but naïve and unenforceable document was signed by fifteen nations including Germany, Italy, Japan, and the Soviet Union.

The United States was willing to engage in negotiated agreements in which countries voluntarily agreed to adopt measures to promote peace. The United States steadfastly refused to participate in international agreements that either restricted U.S. ability to act unilaterally or obliged the United States to act as a result of a treaty obligation. Most importantly the United States refused to sign the Treaty of Versailles, which concluded World War I, or join the League of Nations, an international organization devoted to preserving peace worldwide.

The rejection of the League is indicative of U.S. policy to reject cooperative action to preserve the peace during the interwar years. Aggression by Italy, Japan, or Germany may have been met by diplomatic notes expressing opposition, but the United States refused to participate in tangible, united efforts to enforce compliance. Instead, the country relied on the Atlantic, the Pacific, and John Adam's "wooden walls" to shield it from harm.

As tensions began to rise in the Far East and Europe in the early 1930s, so too did isolationist sentiments spurred by resentment over U.S. involvement in World War I. These were reinforced by a 1934 investigation into the munitions industry headed by Gerald Nye, a Republican senator from North Dakota. The conclusion, largely erroneous, was that financiers and the munitions industry, in pursuit of financial gain, were to blame for U.S. entry into World War I. Accurate or not, the well-publicized hearings intensified isolationist feelings at a time when the world was becoming increasingly dangerous.

Significance

By 1935 the international situation had become very serious. An arms control conference collapsed in 1933. Japanese aggression continued in China. Italy attacked

Ethiopia in 1935. Most ominous was Hitler's withdrawal of Germany from the League of Nations in late 1933 and his announcement in March 1935 that Germany was resuming compulsory military conscription and full rearmament. Although these actions specifically violated the Treaty of Versailles Britain, France, and the other signatories were content with filing formal protests.

In retrospect this was the best opportunity the democracies had to stop Hitler. The combined power of Britain and France would have been more than sufficient to bring Hitler to heel. Suffering from the same dread of war as the United States and lacking U.S. willingness to support intervention, Britain and France yielded to Germany's moves.

Meanwhile, in August 1935, the United States passed the first in a series of Neutrality Acts. These prevented the sale of military material to any participant in a war and aimed primarily to prevent the United States from being drawn into conflicts as a result of economic interests. While sustainable in situations in which there was mutual responsibility for war, the Neutrality Acts limited U.S. ability to support countries victimized by aggressive neighbors.

Despite, or perhaps because of, efforts on the part of the United States, Britain, and France to accommodate Germany, war came with the German invasion of Poland on September 1, 1939. Even Germany's blatant violations of international law and clear responsibility for starting World War II did not significantly decrease isolationist sentiment in the United States. Isolationists continued to resist efforts on the part of the Roosevelt administration to support the opponents of fascism.

Roosevelt, who clearly saw Hitler as a threat to the United States, needed to use all of his political power to bring the American people and Congress in line with his effort to support the enemies of Nazi Germany. During 1940 and 1941 he was able overcome resistance to U.S. rearmament and to modify the Neutrality Acts to permit the United States to support anti-fascist forces. By mid-1941 all pretense of neutrality had been dropped. An actual state of war, however, did not exist until after the Japanese attacked Pearl Harbor on December 7, 1941.

Primary Source

"Concerted Action Against the Fascist States" [excerpt]

SYNOPSIS: In "Concerted Action Against the Fascist States," Frederick Libby argues both against the futility of war, in general, and in support of the traditional American isolationist posture of looking out for our own interests behind the ocean barriers. He draws no distinction between the fascists of Germany and the empire builders of Britain and France.

I have spoken of this "concerted action" as perhaps to be undertaken by the "democracies." The prevailing war slogan is, "The democracies must unite against fascism." It would be profitable to analyze this slogan while we may. Who are these "democracies" that beckon us? They are the British empire, the French empire, and Russia, an imperialist-communist bloc, now pitted against three other nations, Germany, Italy, and Japan, who are challenging their supremacy in Europe and the world.

Great Britain is a democracy, but the empire is not a democracy; and it is the empire that is arousing the envy of its aspiring rivals. The same is true of the French empire which includes a great part of Northern Africa and a slice of China, taken before Japan thought of imperial expansion. Russia is the third member of the combination, a communist dictatorship in which only one party is permitted to exist. By my definition, this is no more a democracy than is fascist Germany. This slogan, like all war slogans, is false to the very core. Our government is being invited in reality to join in Europe's endless game of international poker, power politics, in which the chips of the players are the wealth and young manhood of nations. The President of the United States must not be allowed again to play this game which resulted so ruinously for our people last time, and with no benefit whatever to the rest of the world.

All that I have said hitherto regarding the folly of this highly academic theory of peace when jointly administered, applies with much greater force to unilateral action on the part of the United States. It would not stop the dictators, since they could and would get their supplies elsewhere; it would not overthrow the dictators but would establish them more firmly in power since they control the means of communications within their countries; it would stimulate fresh aggressions to the degree that the boycott became effective; and, for the psychological reasons to which I have alluded, it would lead our nation on the road straight to war, not with one nation but with three.

War, by which I mean the resort to the war method, has become the supreme enemy of mankind. Just follow thru a war with Japan, such as the advocates of concerted action ask us to risk. Military experts tell us that it would be an extremely difficult war to wage and a difficult war to win. It would necessarily be fought mainly if not entirely on Japan's side of the Pacific Ocean. Without going into the technical details to explain the almost insuperable problem of landing troops for the conquest of Japan and the neighboring portion of Asia, suffice it here to say that official estimates are that it would last five years or more; that it would cost us from forty to fifty billions dollars and an incalculable number of lives; and that victory, in the sense that Japan is trying to win a decision now in China, might not even then be won.

But assume for the sake of argument that we did win the war ultimately, both in the islands of Japan and on the adjacent continent. Our boys would want to come home when the war was over. We have no desire to annex any part of Asia with its vast poverty and age-old problems. When they came home, what improvement would they have made in the condition of the lands that they had conquered? They would leave behind them a land wasted and desolate, facing starvation and chaos. Whether communism or fascism would be their lot would be of little moment. Probably communism from Russia would sweep over Asia; but with nothing but misery to share.

To what conditions in America would our boys return? What system of government would they find here? The War Department's Mobilization Plan, of which the Hill-Sheppard Bill and its equally fascist successor, the May Bill, are significant expressions, is our answer. Our War Department has planned it all out for us. With the outbreak of any major war we go fascist. A totalitarian organization of the entire nation under a war dictator is to be our portion, with everybody in the army, from the farmer on his farm and the worker and manager alike in the factory, to the preacher in his pulpit. What is more, our War Department looks realistically beyond the period of the war and plans for the depression that will follow war. When the soldiers have been discharged from the army and the workers from the munition factories, when the bottom has dropped out of the world and when our dollar has lost its value as the German mark did after the World War, then our choice will be, or rather, the choice before our dictator will be, whether to let the nation sink down into a vast depression and chaos or to continue the control indefinitely to which we shall have become accustomed. Most well-informed men believe that the fascism of the war will remain as the fascism of the peace.

The futility of the war method of stopping dictators or promoting democracy or any other spiritual value ought by this time, with the World War and the present wars going on in Spain and China as our object lessons, to have sunk into our souls. Under no circumstances whatever has our government the right to involve us in another foreign war, whether in Asia or in Europe.

The best informed military experts agree that our country cannot be successfully attacked. Just as it is extremely difficult, if not impossible, for us successfully to attack Japan and land troops there for its conquest, so is it even more difficult and probably quite impossible for Japan or any other nation or combination of nations, during any period that can be foreseen, to make a successful attack upon the United States. This important fact having been clarified, we face next the question whether we can keep out of the wars of Europe and of Asia if we take reasonable precautions. We have the authority of our present ambassadors to Great Britain and Germany and of our former president, Herbert Hoover, to the effect that we definitely can. Norway and Sweden have not had a war for more than a hundred years. They stayed out of the World War for four-and-a-half years. So did little Denmark and Holland, with a war raging in their front and back yards. So did Switzerland. What is more, they are all making preparations and plans to stay out of the next war. So is Belgium. So is Poland. And so is Great Britain unless her vital interests are involved. It was Anthony Eden and not Neville Chamberlain who announced this fact in the House of Commons to the world.

When the nations of Europe are planning to remain neutral if war breaks out on their continent, why do the advocates of "concerted action" in our country preach a fatalistic doctrine that regards our involvement as "inevitable"? Even Canada intends to stay out of a European war if possible, whether Great Britain stays out or not, so Sir Herbert Marler told the Canadian Club of New York last fall. "Canada does not maintain that she can prevent war," he said. "She does intend if possible to avoid war."

What are the precautions that we must take to stay out? Briefly they are: (1) maintain and strengthen our neutrality law and elect an administration that will obey it; (2) pass the La Follette or some tighter war-referendum bill and add the war referendum to the Constitution of the United States; (3) establish a line in the Mid-Pacific beyond which our navy would have no responsibility, its recognized business being the defense of our soil from invasion; (4) set up an advisory commission for the State Department *now* to plan the steps necessary to maintain our neutrality in any war that may break out anywhere. The War Department has its War College planning with it how to win a war. Is it not high time that our State Department took the peace of the United States seriously and made its plans in advance for winning the peace?

Primary Source

Address Before the Bar Association of Tennesee on the Spirit of International Law, June 3, 1930

SYNOPSIS: No militarist, Secretary of State Cordell Hull believed that peace and security came from engagement in the international process. His long-range objective was the establishment of an international system of cooperation and the rule of law. Prudence, however, required adequate defense and a willingness to participate in the establishment of international order.

There was never a time in our national history when the influence of the United States in support of international law was more urgently needed than at present—to serve both our own best interests and those of the entire human race. The world is today in the grip of a severe upheaval, the outcome of which will affect profoundly the future of mankind.

There is again abroad, in more than one part of the earth, a spirit of international anarchy. Solemn contractual obligations are brushed aside with a light heart and a contemptuous gesture. Respect for law and observance of the pledged word have sunk to an inconceivably low level. The outworn slogans of the glorification of war are again resounding in many portions of the globe. Armed force, naked and unashamed, is again being used as an instrument of policy and a means of attaining national ends thru aggression and aggrandizement. It is being employed with brutality and savagery that outrage and shock every humane instinct.

In the face of these grim developments, there are some among our people who would have our nation withdraw into its own shell and isolate itself from the rest of the world. They would have us seek safety and security in a hermitlike existence among the nations of the world—in a voluntary surrender of legitimate rights and interests, which we have regarded for generations as essential to our national welfare, and a voluntary abandonment of our support of international law and of the instrumentalities for its application, which alone can make us secure in the exercise of such rights and the enjoyment of such interests.

Those who counsel this course of policy and action should pause in their fervent crusade to cast up an account of the possible benefits and injuries that its pursuance would entail.

On the side of benefits which, it is alleged, would accrue to our people from a policy of isolation would be, we are told, an assurance against our being called upon to engage in war. The proponents of this policy argue that by withdrawing from participation in world affairs, we would avoid conflicts or entanglements with other nations and would be free to pursue the tenor of our national life in peace and safety.

There is no worthier desire than to assure for our people the blessings of peace. But long and unmistakable experience offers abundant proof that the attainment of this precious end thru a policy of national isolation is wholly outside the realm of possibility.

It is my firm conviction that national isolation is not a means to security, but rather a fruitful source of insecurity. For while we may seek to withdraw from participation in world affairs, we cannot thereby withdraw from the world itself. Attempts to achieve national isolation would not merely deprive us of any influence in the councils of nations, but would impair our ability to control our own affairs.

Deliberate renunciation by us of any participation in international affairs would make for an easier triumph on this planet of lawlessness, brute force, and war. In a world growing internationally more and more disordered and chaotic, we would be compelled to increase our armed defenses on a scale that would impose a truly crushing burden on our people. And even so, we would have to live in constant danger that the rising wave of international anarchy would, sooner or later, reach and batter down our own walls and engulf us as well as the rest of mankind.

In this respect, a nation is not different from an individual. When a citizen declines to take an interest in the affairs of his community and refuses to cooperate in promotion and support of law and order, he helps to open the way for the forces of lawlessness to take control. Let us not forget that the present spread of lawlessness in international relations is a direct consequence of the recent drift toward national isolation.

As against the unattainable benefits claimed for the policy of isolation we must visualize the costs of such a policy. By embarking upon a policy of national isolation we would doom our nation to conditions of life under which it would inevitably become economically poorer, intellectually impoverished, morally decadent. We would deliberately deprive ourselves of the benefits of those numerous international relationships which have nourished the stream of human progress and enriched the lives of all peoples, including our own. Neither our political structure of democratic government nor our social and economic structure of free enterprise and individual freedom under law could long survive the material and spiritual decay which national isolation would inescapably impose upon the nation. Like the individual who would seek safety and security for himself thru escape from the responsibilities of organized society into hermitlike isolation, a nation pursuing a similar course—even if it were to succeed for a time in avoiding assault by and conflict with other nations—would soon find its dream of safety and security a bitter illusion.

The search for national isolation springs from the counsel of despair and an admission of defeat. Not thru a sudden and craven abandonment of our national traditions nor thru attempts to turn our backs upon our responsibilities as a member of the family of civilized nations, can we advance and promote the best interests of our people. That we can do only thru renewed devotion to those traditions; thru an ever more resolute determination to be guided by them in the ordering of our national affairs and our international relations; and thru a courageous facing of the facts by a united nation actuated by a vigorous, alert, and informed public opinion.

The task is not easy. Under conditions such as now prevail, disillusionment and despair are not unnatural human reactions. But mankind's progress has always been slow and its road has always been strewn with difficulties, interruptions, set-backs, temporary disappointments, and repeated, though transitory, reappearances of ghosts which seemed to have been laid forever.

Some of these ghosts are rising today. Two decades ago the concept of peace based upon competitive armaments seemed to have been buried under the wreckage caused by an otherwise utterly destructive world conflict. Out of that purgatory there emerged a profound realization that a new basis must be found for relations among nations. There arose a faith and a hope that a new spirit and a new system would come to prevail in the international structure of the world. The negotiation of numerous multilateral treaties and agreements, and the creation of appropriate regional and even worldwide organizations, were important steps in the direction of a system of true international cooperation—of a world order based upon international law; upon the principles of equality, justice, fairness, and mutual respect among nations; upon progressive disarmament; upon a determination to substitute for war as an arbiter of international relations, observance of the pledged word and willingness to compose international differences by pacific means.

The fact that today these efforts to establish, thru international cooperation, a world order under law are being challenged again by the doctrine of armed force and lawless self-aggrandizement, leads many people to the belief that the idea and principles of a peaceful and orderly world have proved to be unworkable. This belief is the product of a dangerous and unfortunate weakening of confidence. The challenge itself has arisen because the recent years have been characterized by a disastrous lowering of standards of conduct on the part of both individuals and nations—by a relapse in the spiritual and moral strength and driving power of vast masses of mankind and a consequent faltering of the march of human progress. Such relapses and such falterings have occurred before. That they are temporary in nature is amply attested by the lesson of history.

In the circumstances of today, it is a part of wisdom and prudence for a great nation like ours to provide adequately for its national defense. Security is essential, and peace is better than war, even when, under conditions of grave emergency, it has to be temporarily assured by adequate national armaments. But peace thus maintained is precarious and unenduring, a makeshift, at best. Stable and durable peace can be achieved only thru the universal enthronement of the spirit of respect for law and thru a resumption of determined efforts toward international cooperation, both of which in our lifetime have revealed themselves as attainable realities. Not until it is proved that these are no longer effective world forces will there be any justifiable grounds for the belief that armed force—and armed force alone—will rule international relations and that, therefore, the outlook for peace, progress, and civilization is devoid of all hope.

In the years which lie ahead, the chances that international anarchy and lawlessness will be replaced by order under law will largely depend upon the sincerity and firmness with which some nations, at least, maintain their devotion to the principles of international law, resting in turn upon the foundation of cooperation, justice, and morality. I can wish for our country no more glorious course than to be a leader in devotion to these principles and in service of their preservation and advancement.

Further Resources

BOOKS

Jones, Manfred. *Isolationism in America, 1935–1941.* Ithaca, N.Y.: Cornell University Press, 1966.

Powaski, Ronald E. *Toward An Entangling Alliance: American Isolationism, Internationalism, and Europe, 1901–1950.* New York: Greenwood Press, 1991.

Pratt, Julius W. *A History of United States Foreign Policy.* Englewood Cliffs, N.J.: Prentice Hall, 1965.

6

LAW AND JUSTICE

GLEN BESSEMER

Entries are arranged in chronological order by date of primary source. For entries with one primary source, the entry title is the same as the primary source title. Entries with more than one primary source have an overall entry title, followed by the titles of the primary sources.

Important Events in Law and Justice, 1930–1939

1930

- On February 3, President Herbert Hoover nominates Charles Evans Hughes to become the new chief justice for the U.S. Supreme Court. Hughes is nominated to replace William Howard Taft, who has left the bench due to failing health. Hughes, a former associate justice, had resigned his position in 1916 to run for the presidency.
- On February 10, massive crackdowns for Volstead Act violations take place in Chicago.
- On February 13, following a fierce debate in the Senate, the appointment of Charles Evans Hughes as chief justice is confirmed.
- On March 8, William Howard Taft, twenty-seventh president of the United States and retired chief justice of the Supreme Court, dies.
- On March 13, the trial of Edward Doheny begins in Washington, D.C. Doheny is accused of bribing former Secretary of the Interior Albert Fall to obtain leases for the Elk Hills naval oil reserve.
- On April 21, a conflagration breaks out in the Ohio state penitentiary in Columbus. The penitentiary was designed to hold a maximum of 1,500 prisoners, but holds 4,300 on the day of the fire. Of the prisoners, 318 die when efforts to contain the fire fail.
- On May 20, the Senate approves the nomination of Owen J. Roberts to the U.S. Supreme Court. Two weeks earlier, by a single vote, it had rejected President Hoover's first choice, Judge John J. Parker.
- On May 26, the Supreme Court issues a decision holding that the purchase of intoxicating liquor is not a violation of the Volstead Act.

1931

- On January 19, the Wickersham Commission, originally formed to study the problem of enforcing Prohibition, delivers its report recommending that Congress consider more effective means of control.
- On January 24, the Supreme Court defeats an attempt to declare the process in which the Eighteenth Amendment was adopted invalid by reversing a district court's ruling finding Prohibition unconstitutional.
- On March 17, Mayor James J. "Jimmy" Walker of New York City is charged with malfeasance and neglect of his official duties.
- On March 25, nine young black men, later to become known as the "Scottsboro Boys," are arrested in Alabama and charged with raping two white women.
- On June 1, the Supreme Court declares a Minnesota law unconstitutional because it amounts to prior restraint of the press, in *Near v. Minnesota ex rel. Olson.*
- On July 26, the Wickersham Commission delivers its final report, recommending major reforms in the federal prison system and greater use of parole.
- On October 17, Alphonse Capone is sentenced to an unprecedented eleven years in prison for income tax evasion.

1932

- On January 12, Associate Justice Oliver Wendell Holmes resigns from the Supreme Court after almost thirty years of service.
- On March 1, the twenty-month-old child of Charles and Anne Morrow Lindbergh is kidnapped from his parents' home in New Jersey.
- On March 3, the Twentieth or "Lame Duck" Amendment is submitted by Congress for ratification by the legislatures of the various states.
- On March 7, striking employees of the Ford Motor Company organize a demonstration at the company's Dearborn plant in Michigan. Violence erupts and four people are killed.
- On March 14, Benjamin N. Cardozo is appointed to the seat on the Supreme Court vacated by the retiring Justice Holmes.
- On March 23, Congress passes the Norris-LaGuardia Act, which prohibits the use of court injunctions to maintain antiunion employment contracts or to inhibit peaceful strikes.
- On November 7, the Supreme Court, in *Powell v. Alabama,* rules that the "Scottsboro Boys" were not properly represented at their trial, paving the way for a new trial.

1933

- On February 6, the Twentieth Amendment is adopted.
- On February 15, an attempt to assassinate Franklin D. Roosevelt in Miami, Florida, fails, but Anton J. Cermak, mayor of Chicago, riding in the president-elect's car, is killed by the bullets fired by a lone gunman, Giuseppe (Joseph) Zangara.
- On February 20, Congress votes to submit the Twenty-first Amendment, repealing Prohibition, to the states for ratification.
- On December 5, the Twenty-first Amendment is adopted, repealing the Eighteenth Amendment, and bringing an end to Prohibition.

1934

- On January 8, the Supreme Court holds that a Minnesota law extending the time debtors may pay back their debts on property is constitutional, in *Home Building and Loan Association v. Blaisdell.*

- On March 5, the Supreme Court upholds a New York regulation setting minimum retail prices for milk, saying the regulation does not violate the Commerce Clause, in *Nebbia v. New York.*
- On May 18, the Lindbergh Law, making the death penalty available for offenses involving cross-state kidnappings, is passed by Congress.
- On May 23, Bonnie Parker and Clyde Barrow, bank robbers believed to be responsible for thirteen murders, are killed by a posse of lawmen near Sailes, Louisiana.
- On July 16, in support of the striking members of the International Longshoremen's Association of San Francisco, unions in that city call for a "general strike" which, in violation of a court-issued injunction, is widely observed.
- On July 22, John Dillinger, "Public Enemy No. 1," is shot and killed outside a Chicago movie theater by agents of the FBI and local police.
- On October 22, Charles "Pretty Boy" Floyd is shot and killed by federal agents at a farm near East Liverpool, Ohio.
- On November 6, Nebraska, by means of an amendment of its state constitution, adopts a unicameral legislature.
- On November 27, George "Baby Face" Nelson, a bank robber responsible for the deaths of three FBI agents, is mortally wounded in a gun battle with law enforcement officers near Barrington, Illinois.
- On December 3, the right of land-grant colleges to require military training of students is upheld by the U.S. Supreme Court in *Hamilton v. Regents of the University of California.*

1935

- On January 16, Arizona Clark Barker, also called "Kate" or "Ma," and her son Fred are killed in a gun battle with police and FBI agents.
- On March 19, rumors and accusations of police brutality in the case of a sixteen-year-old black youth caught shoplifting in a department store touch off a riot in Harlem resulting in the deaths of three persons and damages in excess of two hundred million dollars.
- On May 27, the National Industrial Recovery Act of 1933, cornerstone of the New Deal program, is declared unconstitutional by the Supreme Court in the case of *Schechter Poultry Corp. v. United States.*
- On May 27, the Supreme Court rules that President Roosevelt could not fire a Federal Trade Commission commissioner for differences in political views in the case of *Humphrey's Executor v. United States.*
- On July 5, the National Labor Relations Board is created to protect the rights of workingmen to join labor unions, to vote for their own collective bargaining units, and to seek redress from the unfair labor practices of an employer.
- On July 29, Thomas E. Dewey is appointed as a special prosecutor in New York to lead a drive against crime and corruption, a crusade that quickly brings him national attention.
- On September 8, Senator Huey Long of Louisiana is shot during a visit to the state capital and dies two days later.
- On October 23, mobster Dutch Schultz, who is rumored to have been planning the murder of "gangbuster" Thomas Dewey, is killed by his fellow gangsters while dining in a Newark, New Jersey, tavern.

1936

- On February 17, the Supreme Court held that Congress did not exceed its power in implementing and administering the Tennessee Valley Administration in *Ashwander v. Tennessee Valley Authority.*
- On January 6, the Agricultural Adjustment Act of 1933 is declared unconstitutional by the Supreme Court in *United States v. Butler.*
- On April 3, Bruno Hauptmann, the convicted kidnapper of Charles Lindbergh, Jr., is electrocuted.
- On May 5, Bank robbers Alvin "Creepy" Karpis and Fred Hunter are arrested in New Orleans by J. Edgar Hoover and a small force of FBI agents.
- On May 18, the Supreme Court struck down the Bituminous Coal Conservation Act of 1935 in *Carter v. Carter Coal Company.*
- On June 1, the Supreme Court rules in *Morehead v. New York* that New York's minimum wage law for women is unconstitutional.
- On June 6, the Supreme Court rules in *United States v. Butler* that a processing tax in the 1933 Agricultural Adjustment Act is unconstitutional.
- On December 30, the United Auto Workers begin a strike against the General Motors Fisher Body plant in Flint, Michigan, employing a new tactic, the sit-down strike, in disregard of a state court's ruling that they are in violation of the law.

1937

- On March 1, Congress passes the Supreme Court Retirement Act, permitting justices to retire at the age of seventy with full pay.
- On March 26, William H. Hastie, the first African American federal judge, is sworn in.
- On March 29, the U.S. Supreme Court, in a complete reversal of the position it had taken in an earlier case, upholds a Washington State law establishing a minimum wage for women (*West Coast Hotel v. Parrish*).
- On April 12, the Supreme Court upholds the National Labor Relations Act (*NLRB v. Jones & Laughlin Steel Corporation*).
- On May 24, the Supreme Court upholds tax provisions in the Social Security Act (*Steward Machine Co. v. Collector of Internal Revenue*).
- On May 30, Chicago police kill 10 demonstrators and wound many more outside Republic Steel.
- On August 12, Senator Hugo Black of Alabama is nominated by President Roosevelt to replace retiring Supreme Court justice Van Devanter and wins Senate confirmation the following week.

- On August 26, Accepting the defeat of his original proposal to increase the number of justices in the Supreme Court, President Roosevelt signs into law a compromise bill that principally affects lower federal courts.
- On December 6, the Supreme Court rules that protection against double jeopardy is not a fundamental right under state law and is therefore not a right guaranteed by the Fifth and Fourteenth Amendments (*Palko v. Connecticut*).

1938

- Supreme Court associate justice George Sutherland retires.
- On January 31, Stanley F. Reed is sworn in as an associate justice for the United States Supreme Court.
- On April 25, the Supreme Court rules that federal courts could not ignore state common law in *Erie Railroad Co v. Tompkins.*
- On July 9, Supreme Court justice Benjamin Cardozo dies.
- On October 7, Comedians George Burns and Jack Benny are arrested and charged in New York City with smuggling gems into the country.

1939

- On January 7, Tom Mooney, widely believed to have been wrongly convicted of the 1916 Preparedness Day bombing in San Francisco, is given a full pardon and released from prison.
- Felix Frankfurter is sworn in as an associate justice of the U.S. Supreme Court.
- On February 13, Justice Louis Brandeis retires from the Supreme Court at the age of eighty-two.
- On February 18, the University of Wisconsin refuses to accept a donation that, by the stipulation of the donor, can only be used to benefit white students.
- On February 27, in its decision in the case of *NLRB v. Fansteel Metallurgical Corp.,* the U.S. Supreme Court rules that sit-down strikes are in violation of the Constitution.
- On March 2, a young man and woman, found together in a lover's lane outside of Atlanta, Georgia, are whipped to death for violating the "Moral Kode" of the Ku Klux Klan.
- On April 17, William O. Douglas is sworn in as an associate justice of the Supreme Court.
- On November 16, Supreme Court justice Pierce Butler dies.

Report on the Enforcement of the Prohibition Laws of the United States

Report

By: National Commission on Law Observance and Enforcement

Date: January 7, 1931

Source: National Commission on Law Observance and Enforcement. *Report on the Enforcement of the Prohibition Laws in the United States.* Volume 1, No. 2. Washington, D.C.: U. S. Government Printing Office, 1931. Available online at http://www.drugtext.org/reports/wick/Default.htm; website home page: http://www.drugtext.org (accessed March 1, 2003).

About the Organization: The National Commission on Law Observance and Enforcement, later called the Wickersham Commission, was formed when President Herbert Hoover (1874–1964) proposed, in his inaugural address of 1929, that a federal commission study the problem of crime. The commission was chaired by George W. Wickersham, who had been President William H. Taft's (1857–1930) attorney general. Its members included lawyers, judges, sociologists, and educators. Among these were Newton D. Baker, secretary of war under President Woodrow Wilson, and Roscoe Pound, dean of the Harvard Law School. ■

Introduction

Crime was pushed to the forefront as a national issue when the federal government attempted to enforce the Eighteenth Amendment to the Constitution. Put into effect on January 1920, the amendment prohibited the manufacture, sale, or transportation of alcohol. In addition, the 1919 National Prohibition Act, also known as the Volstead Act after its sponsor, Congressman Andrew Volstead of Minnesota, provided federal enforcement mechanisms to implement the amendment.

Initially, prohibition laws seemed to be effective in controlling the consumption of alcohol in the country. But by the late 1920s, public opinion had swayed toward favoring the repeal of Prohibition. The public openly disregarded the ban on alcohol. Meanwhile, some federal and local public officials accepted bribes in exchange for ignoring bootlegging (illegal liquor sale), especially among underground criminals. Some businessmen, police officers, and politicians participated in the manufacture, sale, and consumption of alcohol themselves. When organized-crime figures fought for dominance of the thriving bootlegging industry across the country, gang violence reached epidemic proportions.

By the 1930s, federal law enforcement agencies had reduced the effectiveness of bootleggers by jailing some of their more prominent members. Rival gangs had also weakened their own ranks in a wave of murders over the control of illegal activities.

Yet a significant constituency of Americans, especially rural Protestants, still defended Prohibition. Also, it was viewed as politically unwise for leaders to fight for repeal against the powerful interests that made up the constituency of "drys" (those opposed to the sale and consumption of alcohol). However, the Great Depression (1929–1939) changed the priorities of the nation. In 1933, as the country geared up to implement some of the most sweeping social programs in American history under President Franklin D. Roosevelt's New Deal, or reform and recovery program, the ineffective prohibition laws were no longer a high priority. In 1933, Prohibition opponents won the repeal of the Eighteenth Amendment. By the time prohibition was repealed, organized crime had increasingly turned its focus on other illegal activities, such as drug trafficking, racketeering (illegal money-making from fraud, intimidation, or bribery), gambling, extortion, bank robbery, and prostitution.

Significance

President Herbert Hoover's proposal of a national commission to study the crime problem across the nation marked a significant shift in federal policy. The president intended the fighting of crime to become a prominent national issue. In fact, Hoover was one of the first presidents to discuss crime in his inaugural address in 1929. Unfortunately, the start of the Great Depression changed the presidential agenda from fighting crime to overcoming economic crisis.

The Wickersham Commission published fourteen reports that studied everything from Prohibition to the causes of crime, police behavior, and penal institutions. Although the commission made an effort to stay out of the controversy over Prohibition enforcement, it issued harsh criticisms of the criminal justice system by exposing brutality, corruption, and inefficiency. In the end the Wickersham Commission's recommendations had little effect in reforming the criminal justice system.

Interestingly, the Wickersham Commission discovered an evolving public opinion toward Prohibition once the law went into effect. Initially when the enforcement of Prohibition resulted in the abolition of commercialized liquor trade and saloons, the American public applauded the law. However, once the public realized that Prohibition meant abstinence, those who approved and practiced moderate drinking started to look upon Prohibition as a governmental imposition on their individual freedom. The support for the repeal of Prohibition grew as some citizens experienced harassment from overzealous police, who had not received proper training and guidelines in enforcing the law. Corruption among public officials who were on the payroll of bootleggers (illegal liquor sellers) added to the support for the abolition of Prohibition.

Primary Source

Report on the Enforcement of the Prohibition Laws of the United States [excerpt]

SYNOPSIS: In this excerpt, the authors of the Wickersham reports discuss the corruption involved in the enforcement of the Prohibition law. In addition, the report stresses the changes in public opinion toward favoring the repeal of Prohibition, leading to the repeal of the Eighteenth Amendment in 1933.

Corruption

As to corruption it is sufficient to refer to the reported decisions of the courts during the past decade in all parts of the country, which reveal a succession of prosecutions for conspiracies, sometimes involving the police, prosecuting and administrative organizations of whole communities; to the flagrant corruption disclosed in connection with diversions of industrial alcohol and unlawful production of beer; to the record of federal prohibition administration as to which cases of corruption have been continuous and corruption has appeared in services which in the past had been above suspicion; to the records of state police organizations; to the revelations as to police corruption in every type of municipality, large and small, throughout the decade; to the conditions as to prosecution revealed in surveys of criminal justice in many parts of the land; to the evidence of connection between corrupt local politics and gangs and the organized unlawful liquor traffic, and of systematic collection of tribute from that traffic for corrupt political purposes. There have been other eras of corruption. Indeed, such eras are likely to follow wars. Also there was much corruption in connection with the regulation of the liquor traffic before prohibition. But the present regime of corruption in connection with the liquor traffic is operating in a new and larger field and is more extensive. . . .

The State of Public Opinion

From the beginning ours has been a government of public opinion. We expect legislation to conform to public opinion, not public opinion to yield to legislation. Whether public opinion at a given time and on a given subject is right or wrong is not a question which according to American ideas may be settled by the words, "be it enacted." Hence it is futile to argue what public opinion throughout the land among all classes of the community ought to be in view of the Eighteenth Amendment and the achieved benefits of national prohibition. So long as state cooperation is required to make the amendment and the statute enforcing it effectual, adverse public opinion in some states and lukewarm public opinion with strong hostile elements in other states are obstinate facts which can not be coerced by any measures of enforcement tolerable under our polity. It is therefore a serious impairment of the legal order to have a national law upon the books theoretically governing the whole land and announcing a policy for the whole land which public opinion in many important centers will not enforce and in many others will not suffer to be enforced effectively. The injury to our legal and political institutions from such a situation must be weighed against the gains achieved by national prohibition. Means should be found of conserving the gains while adapting, or making it possible to adapt, legislation under the amendment to conditions and views of particular states.

Improved personnel and better training of federal enforcement agents under the present organization may well effect some change in public opinion, especially in localities where indignation has been aroused by crude or high handed methods formerly in vogue. But much of this indignation is due, to the conduct of state enforcement, which affects opinion as to enforcement generally. A change in the public attitude in such localities should follow an overhauling of state agencies.

We are not now concerned with the various theories as to prohibition, or with public opinion thereon, except as and to the extent that they are existing facts and causes affecting law observance and enforcement.

It is axiomatic that under any system of reasonably free government a law will be observed and may be enforced only where and to the extent that it reflects or is an expression of the general opinion of the normally law-abiding elements of the community. To the extent that this is the case, the law will be observed by the great body of the peo-

Police confiscate equipment found in an illegal brewery during the prohibition era, Detroit, Michigan. NATIONAL ARCHIVES AND RECORDS ADMINISTRATION.

ple and may reasonably be enforced as to the remainder.

The state of public opinion, certainly in many important portions of the country, presents a serious obstacle to the observance and enforcement of the national prohibition laws.

In view of the fact, however, that the prohibition movement received such large popular support and the Eighteenth Amendment was ratified by such overwhelming legislative majorities, inquiry naturally arises as to the causes of the present state of public opinion. There appear to be many causes, some arising out of the structure of the law the conditions to which it was to be applied, and the methods of its enforcement. Others, inherent in the principle of the act, may now be stated.

The movement against the liquor traffic and the use of intoxicating liquors for beverage purposes was originally a movement for temperance. The organizations which grew out of this movement and were potent in its development, were generally in their inception temperance organizations having as their immediate objectives the promotion of temperance in the use of alcoholic beverages and, as a means to this end, the abolition of the commercialized liquor traffic and the licensed saloon, which were the obvious sources of existing abuses. In many of those states where prohibition laws were adopted and saloons abolished, provision was made for the legal acquisition of limited amounts of alcoholic liquors for beverage purposes. It was only when the Eighteenth Amendment was adopted that total abstinence was sought to be established by fiat of law throughout the territory of the United States or even in many of those states which had adopted limited prohibition laws.

There are obvious differences, both as to individual psychology and legal principle, between temperance and prohibition. Temperance assumes a moderate use of alcoholic beverages but seeks to prevent excess. Even though the ultimate objective may be total abstinence, it seeks to attain that objective by the most effective regulation possible and by the education of the individual to the avoidance of excess and gradual appreciation of the benefits of abstinence. To those holding this view, the field of legitimate governmental control over personal conduct is limited accordingly. Prohibition makes no distinction between moderate and excessive use. It is predicated upon the theory that any use of alcoholic liquors for beverage purposes, however moderate and under any conditions, is antisocial and so injurious to the community as to justify legal restraint. To those who entertain this view, the effort to enforce universal total abstinence by absolute legal mandate is logical. There is, therefore, a fundamental cleavage in principle between those who believe in temperance and those who believe in prohibition which it is difficult to reconcile under the traditional American attitude toward the law already discussed.

When the original temperance movement developed into one for prohibition, the immediate objective was the abolition of the commercialized liquor traffic and the legalized saloon. As between the alternatives of supporting prohibition or the saloon, those who favored the principle of temperance naturally supported prohibition; and, by a combination of the two groups, brought about the adoption of the Eighteenth Amendment and the National Prohibition Act.

When these measures became operative the situation was changed. The legalized liquor traffic and open saloon were abolished, and few desire their return. The question was no longer one between prohibition and the saloon but whether prohibition or the effort to enforce universal total abstinence by legal mandate was sound in principle or was the best and most effective method of dealing with the problem. On this question there was an immediate and inevitable cleavage between those who believed in prohibition and those who believed in temperance. Those who favored prohibition on principle naturally supported the law and demanded the most vigorous measures for its enforcement. Those who favored temperance on principle, while regarding the abolition of the legalized traffic and the saloon as a great and irrevocable step forward, yet looked upon the effort to require and enforce the total abstinence upon all the people, temperate and intemperate alike, by legal mandate, as unsound in principle and an unwarranted extension of governmental control over personal habits and conduct. They recognized and insisted upon the exercise of the right of the government to regulate and control the production, handling, and use of intoxicating liquors to the full extent necessary to prevent excessive use or other conduct which would be injurious to others or the community, but did not approve of the attempt to extend that power to the prevention of temperate use under conditions, not, in their view, injurious or antisocial. The abolition of the commercial traffic and the open saloon were so obviously steps in the right direction that for a time many of those holding this view acquiesced in the law or gave it passive support, but as its operations became more manifest and methods and efforts of enforcement developed, this acquiescence or indifference changed into nonobservance or open hostility. Thus an ever widening difference was developed between those groups who by their united efforts for the abolition of the saloon had made possible the adoption of the Amendment and the National Prohibition Act.

Of course, there had been at all times a very substantial portion of the normally law-abiding people who had actively opposed the Eighteenth Amendment on principle. Many of these accepted and observed the law when once it was passed. When it became apparent that the results expected were not being realized, when the effects of the operations of the law and of the methods of enforcement which they deemed invasions of private rights became manifest, their opposition became aroused. This opposition was now, for reasons stated above, largely increased from the ranks of those who had formerly supported the law to get rid of the saloons, but felt that it went too far—who really favored the principle of temperance but did not favor prohibition. The cumulative result of these conditions was that from its inception to the present time the law has been to a constantly increasing degree deprived of that support in public opinion which was and is essential for its general observance or effective enforcement. . . .

Geo W. Wickersham—Chairman
Henry W. Anderson
Newton D. Baker
Ada L. Comstock
William I. Grubb
William S. Kenyon
Frank J. Loesch
Paul J. McCormick
Kenneth MacIntosh
Roscoe Pound

Further Resources

BOOKS

Furnas, J.C. *The Life and Times of the Late Demon Rum.* New York: Putnam, 1965.

Gusfield, Joseph. *Symbolic Crusade: Status, Politics, and the American Temperance Movement.* Urbana, Ill.: University of Illinois Press, 1963.

Rose, Kenneth D. *American Women and the Repeal of Prohibition.* New York: New York University Press, 1997.

U.S. v. Alphonse Capone

Legal decision

By: U.S. District Court of Northern Illinois, Eastern Division.

Date: October 17, 1931

Source: *United States of America v. Alphonse Capone.* U.S. District Court of Northern Illinois, Eastern Division. 1931. Available online at http://www.archives.gov/exhibit_hall/american_originals/capverd.jpg; website home page: http://www.archives.gov (accessed February 5, 2003). ■

Introduction

The Chicago Crime Commission announced its "Public Enemies" list for the first time on April 23, 1930. Of the twenty-eight most-wanted men, Alphonse "Scarface" Capone headed the list as Public Enemy Number One. In the 1920s, Al Capone had risen to power as the boss of a major crime syndicate in Chicago. He had profited enormously from the illegal liquor trade during the Prohibition era, when it was against the law to manufacture, sell, or transport alcoholic beverages. Capone built a profitable empire from bootlegging (illegal liquor sale), prostitution, gambling, and racketeering (illegal money-making from fraud, intimidation, or bribery). In 1929, he was suspected of ordering the St. Valentine's Day Massacre, a revenge killing against his rival, crime boss George "Bugsy" Malone, and Malone's gang in Chicago.

By 1930, Capone had become a powerful symbol of urban gangsterism. Staying one step ahead of the law, he avoided federal prosecution for years. The government decided to pursue an extensive investigation in an area in which they had jurisdiction—tax evasion. Subsequently, Capone was indicted for income tax evasion in June 1930.

It was a highly publicized trial. Movie star Edward G. Robinson, who had played the part of a Capone-like gangster in the movie *Little Caesar,* observed Capone for a day at the trial. The Internal Revenue Service (IRS) estimated that Capone had personally made $10 million in 1927 alone. The jurors found Capone guilty of three felonies (serious crimes) and two misdemeanors (minor crimes) for failure to pay income taxes between 1925 and 1929. Judge James H. Wilkerson sentenced Capone to prison for eleven years. In 1932, Capone was sent to a federal prison in Atlanta, Georgia. In 1934, he became one of the first prisoners at Alcatraz Island, a new maximum-security prison in San Francisco Bay.

After eight years in prison Capone was paroled in 1939. He was released for both good behavior and because his health had severely declined. He had contracted syphilis (a sexually transmitted disease) sometime in the 1920s but had only been diagnosed after his incarceration. Capone died from a heart attack at his Florida estate in 1947.

The infamous mobster Al Capone. ARCHIVE PHOTOS, INC. REPRODUCED BY PERMISSION.

Significance

Issued by a district court of the United States, the verdict reflects the influence of organized crime on U.S. society in the 1920s and 1930s. During the early part of those years, outlaws were popularized and romanticized in gangster movies. The media portrayed mobsters as modern Robin Hoods, stealing from the rich to give to the poor. Although Al Capone was known for his violent

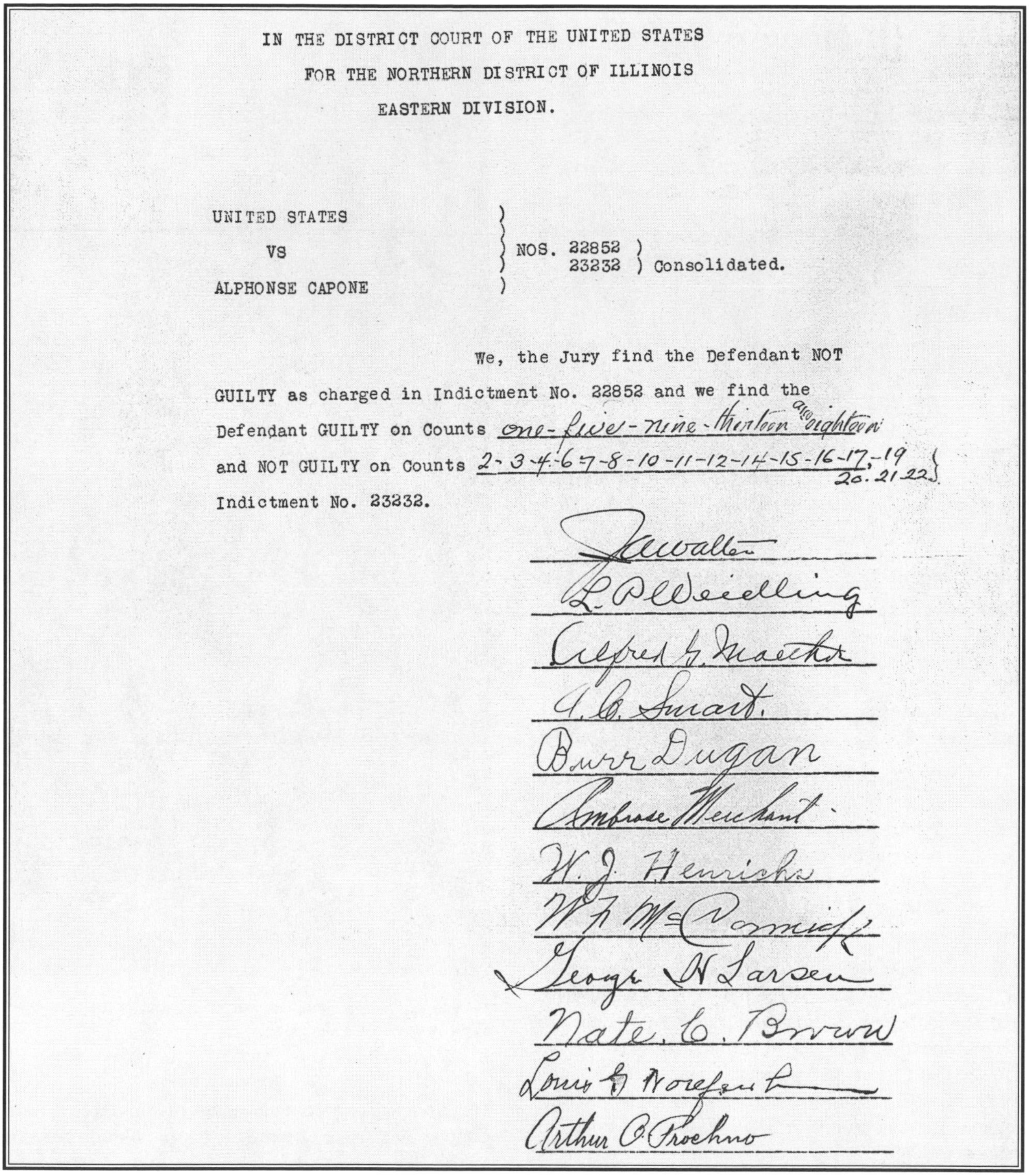

IN THE DISTRICT COURT OF THE UNITED STATES
FOR THE NORTHERN DISTRICT OF ILLINOIS
EASTERN DIVISION.

UNITED STATES)
VS) NOS. 22852) 23232) Consolidated.
ALPHONSE CAPONE)

We, the Jury find the Defendant NOT GUILTY as charged in Indictment No. 22852 and we find the Defendant GUILTY on Counts one-five-nine-thirteen and eighteen and NOT GUILTY on Counts 2-3-4-6-7-8-10-11-12-14-15-16-17,-19 20.21-22 Indictment No. 23232.

J. A. Walter
L. P. Weidling
Alfred G. Maetche
A. C. Smart
Burr Dugan
Ambrose Merchant
W. J. Henrichs
Wm. McCormick
George H Larsen
Nate. C. Brown
Louis G. Norefsen
Arthur O. Prochno

Primary Source

U.S. v. Alphonse Capone

SYNOPSIS: Verdict in *United States of America v. Alphonse Capone,* October 17, 1931. Al Capone's organization, illegally obtaining a list of potential jurors, had bribed and threatened them prior to the trial. However, on the first day of trial, Judge Wilkerson announced that he was switching his panel of jurors with that of another judge. The new jurors were not on Capone's list of people who had been bribed. In addition, to prevent jury tampering, the judge sequestered the jury overnight while the trial proceeded. The new jurors found Capone guilty of five counts of tax evasion and was subsequently sentenced to eleven years in prison and fined $80,000 in fines and court costs. COURTESY OF NARA'S GREAT LAKES REGION (CHICAGO). REPRODUCED BY PERMISSION. ARTLYNN PHOTOGRAPHY.

gangsterism, he also had a reputation for helping the ordinary people of Chicago. For example, he set up free soup kitchens that fed thousands of people a day. For some of the American public, Capone was a symbol of the Horatio Alger success story, a poor immigrant with an entrepreneurial spirit who pursued the American Dream.

Al Capone's downfall in 1931 illustrates a transition in American culture that was precipitated by the Great Depression (1929–1939). While Americans had been fascinated by the urban underworld of bootleggers during the Prohibition Era, also called the "Roaring Twenties," their attitudes toward these criminals gradually changed. After 1929, the rich and flamboyant lifestyles of gangsters did not resonate so well with a public engulfed in the worst economic recession in American history. Instead, by the 1930s the public's attention had turned to rural desperadoes and bank robbers, such as John Dillinger.

The verdict against Capone also signified the increased role of the federal government in fighting crime in the United States. Although the verdict showed the successful prosecution of Capone for tax evasion, it also illustrated federal law enforcement's inability to punish gangsters for their criminal activities at the local level.

Further Resources

BOOKS

Bergreen, Laurence. *Capone: The Man and the Era.* New York: Simon and Schuster, 1994.

King, Dave C. *Al Capone and the Roaring Twenties.* Woodbridge, Conn.: Blackbirch Press, 1999.

Potter, Claire Bond. *War on Crime: Bandits, G-men, and the Politics of Mass Culture.* New Brunswick, N.J.: Rutgers University Press, 1998.

Ruth, David E. *Inventing the Public Enemy: The Gangster in American Culture, 1918–1934.* Chicago: University of Chicago Press, 1998.

WEBSITES

"Exhibit: Al Capone Verdict." National Archives and Records Administration. Available online at http://www.archives.gov/exhibit_hall/american_originals/capone.html; website home page: http://www.archives.gov (accessed February 5, 2003).

"The New Deal (1933–late 1930s)." *History of the FBI.* Federal Bureau of Investigation. Available online at http://www.fbi.gov/libref/historic/history/newdeal.htm; website home page: http://www.fbi.gov (accessed March 1, 2003).

Response to San Franciscan Concerns Re: Alcatraz Island

Letter

By: U.S. Department of Justice

Date: November 6, 1933

Source: "Response to San Franciscan Concerns Re: Alcatraz." U.S. Department of Justice. November 6, 1933. Reproduced in "Alcatraz: The Warden Johnston Years (1933–1948)." Joel Gazis-Sax Website. Available online at http://www.notfrisco2.com/alcatraz/documents/openpr.html; website home page: http://www.notfrisco2.com (accessed February 5, 2003).

About the Organization: The U.S. Department of Justice, headed by the U.S. attorney general, was created in 1870 by Congress. The department enforces the law of the land in the name of the American people. Its functions include protecting the people through effective law enforcement and representing the national government in legal matters. ■

Introduction

The prison at Alcatraz Island in San Francisco Bay in California opened in 1934 as a maximum-security prison to house the most dangerous criminals in the United States. Alcatraz, or "The Rock," sits on a hill off the shores of San Francisco, with a thin but dangerous body of water serving as a natural barrier to prevent escapes. The prison was a grim and stark institution made of concrete and steel. No prisoners had ever been recorded to have escaped from the prison. Al Capone was probably the most infamous criminal to be incarcerated at Alcatraz.

After Alcatraz closed in 1963, it was occupied briefly, in symbolic protest, by American Indian Movement (AIM) militants, who claimed that the island was first inhabited by American Indians. Today, Alcatraz serves as a tourist attraction, bringing in hundreds of visitors every day.

Federal involvement in the prison system was a relatively recent development in American history, occurring when the federal prison population increased dramatically in the early twentieth century. As late as 1891, Congress authorized the building of three federal prisons. One was built at Fort Leavenworth, Kansas, in 1895; a second one in Atlanta, Georgia, in 1902; and a third on McNeil Island in Puget Sound, Washington, in 1909. By 1930, the government had five federal prisons to house offenders. In 1930, Congress passed a law that established the Federal Bureau of Prisons within the U.S. Department of Justice.

Alcatraz Island in San Francisco Bay. Bay area residents were concerned about the construction of a federal prison near them in 1933, but Alcatraz Prison would prove to be famously inescapable. **UPI/CORBIS-BETTMANN. REPRODUCED BY PERMISSION.**

Significance

The growth of the federal prison system reflected the increased role of the national government in fighting crime. The federal prison system expanded to accommodate the growing prison population in the country, which rose noticeably in the early twentieth century. In 1915, three thousand nonmilitary offenders were in federal prisons. Military personnel who committed crimes went through the military justice system. In 1930, there were thirteen thousand nonmilitary prisoners. By 1940, the number of nonmilitary prisoners had risen to twenty thousand. Much of the growth in inmate population in the 1920s and early 1930s was a result of arrests from Prohibition (illegal liquor manufacture, sale, or transport) enforcement.

In addition to illustrating the relatively recent expansion of the federal role in the punishment of criminals, the construction of Alcatraz in San Francisco Bay represented the controversial nature of putting prisons in the backyards of residential neighborhoods. The Department of Justice heard so many complaints from San Franciscans that it felt the need to address the community to publicly justify building the prison.

The Department of Justice's letter to the citizens of San Francisco promoted the view that there is a causal link between incarcerating more offenders and reducing crime. Such debate regarding this correlation has been ongoing throughout American history. In arguing for the need of an increased federal role in law enforcement, the department added that the citizenry needed to share the burden in their community by allowing the prison to be built in their city.

Primary Source

Response to San Franciscan Concerns Re: Alcatraz Island

SYNOPSIS: In this letter the Department of Justice rationalized the need for a maximum-security prison in San Francisco Bay. The grim concrete and steel penitentiary on a hill off the shores of San Francisco, California, was open from 1934 to 1963 to house some of the most infamous criminals in American history.

It has been wisely said that the people of this country can have as much or as little crime as they really want. It is likewise certain that the present unwholesome and dangerous conditions in many of our communities will not be materially improved until all of our citizens are prepared to make their share of sacrifice to bring about such a situation and to co-operate with the States and the Federal Government in the accomplishment of the important and difficult task of crime reduction.

On many sides it is being reluctantly admitted that law enforcing agencies in many of our States have fallen down and the demand is being made with increasing emphasis that the Federal Government take a hand in the situation. The power of Federal agencies in the detection, apprehension and treatment of criminals has long been respected. Through its freedom from local affiliations, its greater resources, and its generally trained personnel, the Federal Government is being recognized as an efficient ally of the local law enforcement agencies and the present campaign by the Department of Justice to curb the activities of racketeers is a natural development.

In the last two decades many Federal statutes have been passed broadening the scope of Federal activities in the apprehension of offenders. Twenty years ago there were 2,000 in Federal prisons, today there are 11,000, and the tendency today is to pass more Federal statutes, on the insistent demand of the communities themselves, giving greater power and opportunity to the central government along these lines.

In the case of its convicted offenders and in their reformation and rehabilitation wherever possible it is of fundamental importance that prisoners be properly classified and segregated. First offenders, boys, victims of circumstance, men with families, persons who have broken under the economic strain, and others who make up the great bulk of our criminal population should not be housed in the same institution with those who may be classed as enemies of society. The establishment by the Department of Justice of a Federal prison at Alcatraz Island is a necessary part of the Government's campaign against predatory crime.

Much misunderstanding has been engendered with reference to the operation of this prison. It will not be a Devil's Island. It will be an integral part of the Federal Prison System, operated in conformity with advanced ideas of penology and with the ultimate object in view of protecting all of our communities. Compared to the large State institutions such as San Quentin, with its 5500 inmates, and Folsom, it will house but a mere handful of men. The Department of Justice pledges itself to take every possible precaution, structurally and administratively, to prevent escapes.

The present plans call for the housing of not over 200 men at this point. It would be futile for relatives or friends of the inmates to find lodgement in the surrounding district, and even if they should, it would be to a very limited extent and their presence would have much less effect upon the urban population of the Bay District than those of the much larger numbers now housed in the State institutions of California.

It is difficult to see how the appearance of the Island or its effect upon the surrounding neighborhood will be in any way changed. The personnel of the institution will be carefully selected from trained prison officials. All modern scientific devices will be employed to insure the restraint of the inmates.

In brief, it seems to the Department of Justice that there is presented a splendid opportunity for the citizens of San Francisco to cooperate in a patriotic and public spirited manner in the Government's campaign against the criminal. The Department of Justice, while recognizing that civic pride and an interest in their community has prompted many of the recent communications which have come to the Department, nevertheless, bespeaks the cooperation and aid of this great community in the carrying on of this important and necessary activity.

Further Resources

BOOKS

Clauss, Francis J. *Alcatraz: Island of Many Mistakes.* Menlo Park, Calif.: Briarcliff Press, 1981.

Quillen, Jim. *Alcatraz from Inside: The Hard Years 1942–1952.* San Francisco, Calif.: Golden Gate National Park Association, 1992.

WEBSITES

AlcatrazHistory.com. Available online at http://www.alcatrazhistory.com/mainpg.htm (accessed April 16, 2003).

Alcatraz Island. Available online at http://www.nps.gov/alcatraz; website home page: http://www.nps.gov (accessed April 16, 2003).

"Date of Repeal of the Eighteenth Amendment"

Proclamation

By: Franklin D. Roosevelt

Date: December 5, 1933

Source: President. Proclamation. "Date of Repeal of the Eighteenth Amendment: By the President of the United States of America, A Proclamation." Presidential Proclamation 2065, Item PP2065, Series PRDOCPI159E23, Record Group 11. Old Military and Civil Records, National Archives Building, Washington, DC. Available online at http://www.archives.gov/digital_classroom/lessons/volstead_act/volstead_act.html; website home page: http://www.archives.gov (accessed February 18, 2003).

About the Author: Franklin D. Roosevelt (1882–1945) was president of the United States from 1933 to 1945. In the aftermath of the Great Depression (1929–1939), the president implemented an economic recovery program, called the New Deal, that provided jobs for the unemployed. His administration was instrumental in passing some of the most significant legislation in American history under the New Deal. Between 1941 and 1945, Roosevelt led the country in the war against fascism in Europe and Asia. ■

Introduction

The United States underwent dramatic social and economic changes between the time of the passage of the Volstead Act of 1919, which enforced the Eighteenth Amendment, and the repeal of Prohibition in 1933. The Eighteenth Amendment, ratified by three-fourths of the states in 1919, became effective in January 1920. The amendment prohibited the manufacture, sale, or transportation of alcoholic beverages in the nation. For years, a national temperance movement had been lobbying for the prohibition of alcoholic beverages.

At first it appeared as if the prohibition amendment was effective. In the years immediately after the amendment was ratified in the state legislatures, the sale and consumption of alcohol dropped, and crime rates declined noticeably across the country. But as the 1920s progressed, it became increasingly evident that many Americans simply ignored or worked around the ban. Even though the production of alcohol had been cut back, a wave of lawlessness soon spread across the country. Ironically, the Prohibition Era of the 1920s was also the "Roaring Twenties." A new youth culture had emerged, abandoning traditional values for a consumption-oriented lifestyle. By banning the legal sale and manufacture of alcohol, the government unwittingly provided criminal gangs the opportunity to make an easy profit from the illegal trade of alcohol. Bootleggers (illegal alcohol sellers) proliferated to supply a "wet" underworld (those who sold and consumed liquor) of "blind pigs" (after-hours clubs) and "speakeasies" (illegal saloons) in this new "jazz age."

Consequently, even though prisons across the country filled with Prohibition violators, law enforcement was unable to stem the flow of alcohol. When the Great Depression hit the country in 1929 and the nation was plunged into economic crisis, Prohibition ceased being a high priority on people's agendas. Public opinion had shifted so much in the 1930s that the Democratic Party included the repeal of Prohibition in its platform. After Franklin D. Roosevelt was elected president in 1932, Congress passed a resolution to repeal the Eighteenth Amendment. On December 5, 1933, the states ratified the Twenty-first Amendment, which repealed the Eighteenth Amendment.

Significance

President Roosevelt's signing of Presidential Proclamation 2065 ended a social experiment that attempted to enforce a ban on the sale and manufacture of alcoholic beverages. The legacy of Prohibition and its repeal had a lasting effect on American culture and its criminal justice system. While Prohibition produced unintended consequences in society on at least two fronts, its repeal left behind remnants that lasted well beyond the Prohibition Era.

In the 1920s, Prohibition created an opportunity for organized crime to develop a national network for bootlegging. After it was abolished, the criminal network did not disappear. The criminals simply shifted their business from bootlegging to drug trafficking, racketeering (illegal money-making from fraud, intimidation, or bribery), gambling, extortion, bank robbery, and prostitution.

In a parallel way, during the Prohibition Era the federal government responded to the needs created by the new law by expanding the role of federal law enforcement in fighting the illegal trade of alcohol. When bootleggers and bank robbers defied the law in the 1920s and 1930s, Congress responded by passing new federal laws to cover a whole range of crimes that previously had fallen under local jurisdictions. In 1934, when outlaws such as John Dillinger were avoiding capture by crossing state lines, Congress established a series of new federal offenses. As a result, the Federal Bureau of Investigation (FBI) was given more law enforcement power, including the authority to carry guns and make arrests. Under the new laws, it was a federal crime to rob a national bank; to extort by telephone, telegraph, or radio; to knowingly transport stolen property worth more than $5,000 across state lines; to flee across state lines to avoid prosecution for murder, kidnapping, burglary, robbery, rape, assault with a deadly weapon, or extortion with threats of violence; or to flee across state lines to avoid testifying in criminal proceedings.

Even after Prohibition was repealed, the expanded federal powers remained in place. Although the nation underwent dramatic political, social, and economic changes since the Eighteenth Amendment was ratified, many of the societal responses to the amendment continued into the following decades.

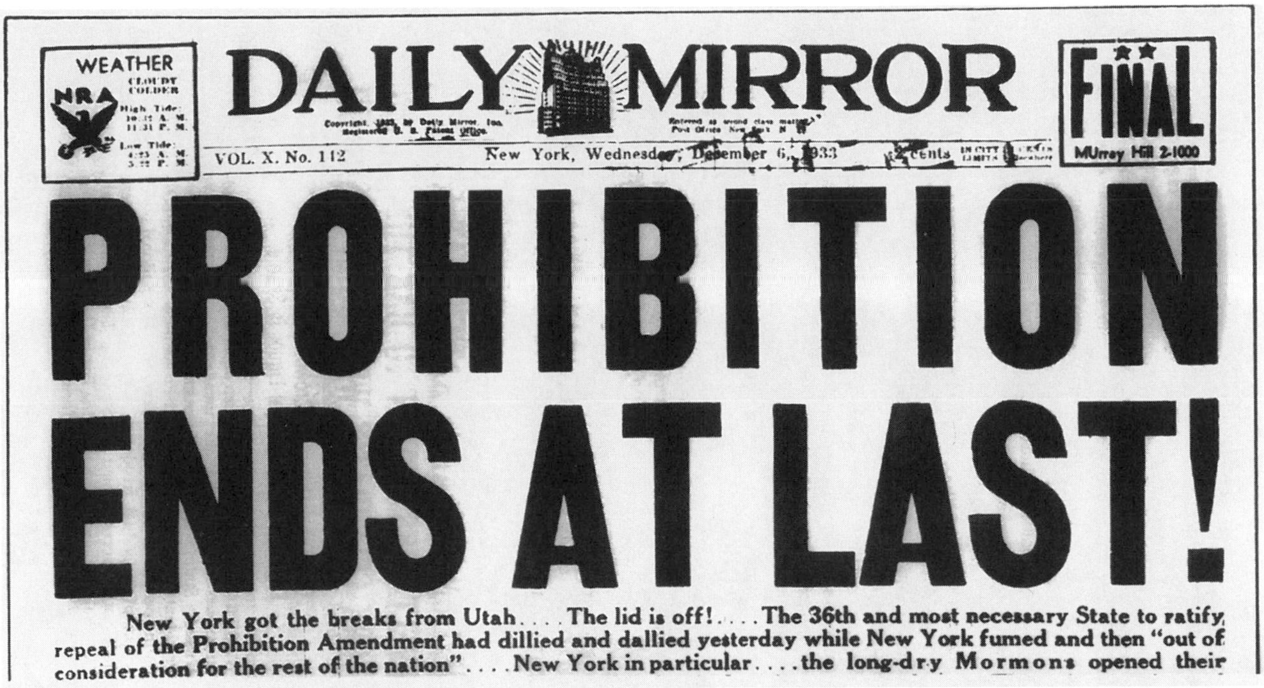
WEATHER Cloudy Colder

DAILY MIRROR

FINAL

MUrray Hill 2-1000

VOL. X. No. 112 New York, Wednesday, December 6, 1933 2 cents

PROHIBITION ENDS AT LAST!

New York got the breaks from Utah. . . . The lid is off! . . . The 36th and most necessary State to ratify repeal of the Prohibition Amendment had dillied and dallied yesterday while New York fumed and then "out of consideration for the rest of the nation" . . . . New York in particular. . . . the long-dry Mormons opened their

Headline from the *Daily Mirror,* December 6, 1933. Health factors were cited on both sides of the debate over prohibition, and experts still disagree whether the nation is healthier with alcoholic beverages being legal. AP/WIDE WORLD PHOTOS. REPRODUCED BY PERMISSION.

Primary Source

"Date of Repeal of the Eighteenth Amendment"

SYNOPSIS: Thirteen years after the Eighteenth Amendment ushered in the Prohibition Era, President Franklin D. Roosevelt signed Presidential Proclamation 2065, announcing the repeal of Prohibition. Many Americans supported the repeal because they feared that, through Prohibition, the federal government might curtail individual freedom.

Whereas the Congress of the United States in second session of the Seventy-second Congress, begun at Washington on the fifth day of December in the year one thousand nine hundred and thirty-two, adopted a resolution in the words and figures following, to wit:

Joint Resolution

Proposing an amendment to the Constitution of the United States.

Resolved by the Senate and House of Representatives of the United States of America in Congress assembled (two-thirds of each House concurring therein), That the following article is hereby proposed as an amendment to the Constitution of the United States, which shall be valid to all intents and purposes as part of the Constitution when ratified by conventions in three-fourths of the several States:

Article—

Section 1. The eighteenth article of amendment to the Constitution of the United States is hereby repealed.

Sec. 2. The transportation or importation into any State, Territory, or possession of the United States for delivery or use therein of intoxicating liquors, in violation of the laws thereof, is hereby prohibited.

Sec. 3. This article shall be inoperative unless it shall have been ratified as an amendment to the Constitution by conventions in the several States, as provided in the Constitution, within seven years from the date of the submission hereof to the States by the Congress.

Whereas section 217 (a) of the act of Congress entitled "An Act To encourage national industrial recovery, to foster competition, and to provide for the construction of certain useful public works, and for other purposes," approved June 16, 1933, provides as follows:

> Sec. 217. (a) The President shall proclaim the date of—
>
> (1) the close of the first fiscal year ending June 30 of any year after the year 1933, dur-

Bartenders pour a round of free drinks for a crowd of happy customers at Sloppy Joe's bar on December 5, 1933, the day prohibition was repealed. Chicago, Illinois. © **HULTON ARCHIVE/GETTY IMAGES. REPRODUCED BY PERMISSION.**

ing which the total receipts of the United States (excluding public-debt receipts) exceed its total expenditures (excluding public-debt expenditures other than those chargeable against such receipts), or

(2) the repeal of the eighteenth amendment to the Constitution, whichever is the earlier.

Whereas it appears from a certificate issued December 5, 1933, by the Acting Secretary of State that official notices have been received in the Department of State that on the fifth day of December 1933 conventions in 36 States of the United States, constituting three fourths of the whole number of the States had ratified the said repeal amendment;

Now, therefore, I, Franklin D. Roosevelt, President of the United States of America, pursuant to the provisions of section 217 (a) of the said act of June 16, 1933, do hereby proclaim that the eighteenth amendment to the Constitution of the United States was repealed on the fifth day of December 1933.

Furthermore, I enjoin upon all citizens of the United States and upon other residents within the jurisdiction thereof to cooperate with the Government in its endeavor to restore greater respect for law and order, by confining such purchases of alcoholic beverages as they may make solely to those dealers or agencies which have been duly licensed by State or Federal license.

Observance of this request, which I make personally to every individual and every family in our Nation, will result in the consumption of alcoholic beverages which have passed Federal inspection, in the break-up and eventual destruction of the notoriously evil illicit liquor traffic, and in the payment of reasonable taxes for the support of Government and thereby in the superseding of other forms of taxation.

I call specific attention to the authority given by the twenty-first amendment to the Government to prohibit transportation or importation of intoxicating liquors into any State in violation of the laws of such State.

I ask the whole-hearted cooperation of all our citizens to the end that this return of individual freedom shall not be accomplished by the repugnant conditions that obtained prior to the adoption of the eighteenth amendment and those that have existed since its adoption. Failure to do this honestly and courageously will be a living reproach to us all.

The Twenty-first Amendment

Section 1. The eighteenth article of amendment to the Constitution of the United States is hereby repealed.

Section 2. The transportation or importation into any State, Territory, or possession of the United States for delivery or use therein of intoxicating liquors, in violation of the laws thereof, is hereby prohibited.

Section 3. This article shall be inoperative unless it shall have been ratified as an amendment to the Constitution by conventions in the several States, as provided in the Constitution, within seven years from the date of the submission hereof to the States by the Congress.

SOURCE: U.S. Constitution. Amendment 21. Available online at http://caselaw.lp.findlaw.com/data/constitution/amendment21; website home page: http://caselaw.lp.findlaw.com (accessed March 17, 2003).

I ask especially that no State shall by law or otherwise authorize the return of the saloon either in its old form or in some modern guise.

The policy of the Government will be to see to it that the social and political evils that have existed in the pre-prohibition era shall not be revived nor permitted again to exist. We must remove forever from our midst the menace of the bootlegger and such others as would profit at the expense of good government, law, and order.

I trust in the good sense of the American people that they will not bring upon themselves the curse of excessive use of intoxicating liquors, to the detriment of health, morals, and social integrity.

The objective we seek through a national policy is the education of every citizen towards a greater temperance throughout the Nation.

In witness whereof, I have hereunto set my hand and caused the seal of the United States to be affixed.

Done at the city of Washington this fifth day of December, in the year of our Lord nineteen hundred and thirty-three, and of the Independence of the United States of America the one hundred and fifty-eighth.

Franklin D. Roosevelt
By the President:
William Phillips
Acting Secretary of State

Further Resources

BOOKS

Behr, Edward. *Prohibition: Thirteen Years That Changed America.* New York: Arcade, 1996.

Gusfield, Joseph. *Symbolic Crusade: Status, Politics, and the American Temperance Movement.* Urbana, Ill.: University of Illinois Press, 1963.

Lender, Mark Edward, and James Kirby Martin. *Drinking in America: A History.* Rev. ed. New York: Free Press, 1987.

Murdoch, Catherine Gilbert. *Domesticating Drink: Women, Men, and Alcohol in America, 1870–1940.* Philadelphia: Johns Hopkins University Press, 2002.

PERIODICALS

Thornton, Mark. "Alcohol Prohibition Was a Failure." *Policy Analysis,* July 17, 1991.

Home Building and Loan Association v. Blaisdell

Supreme Court decision

By: Charles Evans Hughes

Date: January 8, 1934

Source: *Home Building and Loan Association v. Blaisdell,* 290 U.S. 398 (1934). Available online at http://www2.law.cornell.edu (accessed February 6, 2003).

About the Author: Charles Evans Hughes (1862–1948), a conservative reformer, served as chief justice of the U.S. Supreme Court from 1930 to 1941. Earlier in his career, he began working for a law firm in 1884 and later taught at Cornell Law School. He gained a reputation as an independent-thinking Republican when he headed several investigations of corruption in industries during the Progressive Era, a period when a vibrant antitrust movement sought to regulate corporations. Hughes was elected governor of New York in 1906 and served two terms. He served as an associate justice to the Supreme Court from 1910 to 1916. He ran for president against incumbent Woodrow Wilson (served 1913–1921) and later served as secretary of state from 1921 to 1925. ■

Introduction

During the Great Depression of the 1930s many states enacted laws under "Little New Deals"—or social and economic legislation much like the national New Deal of Franklin D. Roosevelt's administration. Because they expanded the powers of government to regulate social and economic activities in the United States, some of these state laws were eventually challenged in the Supreme Court.

One case, *Home Building and Loan Association v. Blaisdell,* was appealed to the Supreme Court in November 1933. Minnesota legislators had passed the Mort-

During the Great Depression, many people became too poor to make their mortgage payments. They often lost their farms or houses as a result, leaving them homeless like this family. AP/WIDE WORLD PHOTOS. REPRODUCED BY PERMISSION.

gage Moratorium Law to provide relief to homeowners by exempting property from foreclosure. A property owner in Minneapolis, John Blaisdell, faced foreclosure on his property when he was unable to make payments to his lending agency, the Home Building and Loan Association. Under Minnesota's new law, Blaisdell attempted to prevent the foreclosure. Meanwhile the Home Building and Loan Association challenged the law, arguing that the law violated the contract clause of the U.S. Constitution as well as the due process and equal protection clauses of the Fourteenth Amendment. The Fourteenth Amendment had been ratified by the states in 1868, giving citizens of the United States equal protection under the law and empowering Congress to enforce it through legislation.

The Supreme Court upheld the constitutionality of the Minnesota law by a narrow 5-4 margin. The majority reasoned that "while emergency does not create power, emergency may furnish the occasion for the exercise of power." Chief Justice Charles Evans Hughes argued that because the contract clause of the Constitution was not absolute, a state had the authority to treat the clause with flexibility to protect the interests of its citizens. In a dissenting opinion, Justice George Sutherland argued that the contract clause of the U.S. Constitution should be interpreted literally and that even national emergencies could not justify states interfering with contracts. Sutherland stated, "If the provisions of the Constitution be not upheld when they pinch, as well as when they comfort, they may as well be abandoned."

In addition to upholding a state law as a precedent to the federal New Deal legislation to come, the narrow split between the justices illustrated the division on the Supreme Court over responding to the national crisis of the Great Depression.

Significance

For the Supreme Court of the United States, the period between 1930 to 1941 under Chief Justice Charles Evans Hughes was probably one of the most significant ones in the Court's history since its formative years. The landmark case *Home Building and Loan Association v. Blaisdell* highlighted a shift on the Court. A narrow majority willing to uphold congressional powers to regulate the economy was at odds with conservatives on the court. During the New Deal (from 1933 until the United States entered World War II in 1941), Hughes voted as a moderate reformer. While in 1935 the Court held that the National Recovery Act gave the federal government broader powers than were necessary, it supported state and federal regulatory powers in *Home Building and Loan Association v. Blaisdell.* In the late 1930s, the Court supported New Deal legislation in such cases as *National Labor Relations Board v. Jones and Laughlin Steel Corp.* in 1937, which upheld the National Labor Relations Act.

The Supreme Court's decision in *Home Building and Loan Association v. Blaisdell* provided an early example of how the groundswell of local demands for relief from the Depression eventually pressured the federal government to produce social and economic reforms.

Primary Source

Home Building and Loan Association v. Blaisdell [excerpt]

SYNOPSIS: In this excerpt from the landmark case *Home Building and Loan Association v. Blaisdell,* Chief Justice Charles Evans Hughes, who wrote the majority opinion, argues that in a time of national emergency states have the authority to exercise their powers to protect the interests of their citizens, even if in doing so they violate the contract clause of the Constitution. The case was decided on January 8, 1934.

Mr. Chief Justice Hughes delivered the opinion of the Court.

Appellant contests the validity of Chapter 339 of the Laws of Minnesota of 1933, p. 514, approved April 18, 1933, called the Minnesota Mortgage Moratorium Law, as being repugnant to the contract clause (Art. I, § 10) and the due process and equal protection clauses of the Fourteenth Amendment, of the Federal Constitution. The statute was sustained by the Supreme Court of Minnesota, 189 Minn. 422, 448, 249 N.W. 334, 893, and the case comes here on appeal.

The Act provides that, during the emergency declared to exist, relief may be had through authorized judicial proceedings with respect to foreclosures of mortgages, and execution sales, of real estate; that sales may be postponed and periods of redemption may be extended. The Act does not apply to mortgages subsequently made, nor to those made previously which shall be extended for a period ending more than a year after the passage of the Act (Part One, § 8). There are separate provisions in Part Two relating to homesteads, but these are to apply "only to cases not entitled to relief under some valid provision of Part One." The Act is to remain in effect "only during the continuance of the emergency and in no event beyond May 1, 1935." No extension of the period for redemption and no postponement of sale is to be allowed which would have the effect of extending the period of redemption beyond that date. Part Two, § 8.

The Act declares that the various provisions for relief are severable; that each is to stand on its own footing with respect to validity. Part One, § 9. We are here concerned with the provisions of Part One, § 4, authorizing the District Court of the county to extend the period of redemption from foreclosure sales "for such additional time as the court may deem just and equitable," subject to the above described limitation. The extension is to be made upon application to the court, on notice, for an order determining the reasonable value of the income on the property involved in the sale, or, if it has no income, then the reasonable rental value of the property, and directing the mortgagor

> to pay all or a reasonable part of such income or rental value, in or toward the payment of taxes, insurance, interest, mortgage . . . indebtedness at such times and in such manner as shall be determined by the court. The section also provides that the time for redemption from foreclosure sales theretofore made, which otherwise would expire less than thirty days after the approval of the Act shall be extended to a date thirty days after its approval, and application may be made to the court within that time for a further extension as provided in the section. By another provision of the Act, no action, prior to May 1, 1935, may be maintained for a deficiency judgment until the period of redemption as allowed by existing law or as extended under the provisions of the Act has expired. Prior to the expiration of the extended period of redemption, the court may revise or alter the terms of the extension as changed circumstances may require. Part One, § 5.

Invoking the relevant provision of the statute, appellees applied to the District Court of Hennepin County for an order extending the period of redemption from a foreclosure sale. Their petition stated that they owned a lot in Minneapolis which they had mortgaged to appellant; that the mortgage contained a valid power of sale by advertisement and that, by reason of their default, the mortgage had been foreclosed and sold to appellant on May 2, 1932, for $3,700.98; that appellant was the holder of the sheriff's certificate of sale; that, because of the economic depression appellees had been unable to obtain a new loan or to redeem, and that, unless the period of redemption were extended, the property would be irretrievably lost, and that the reasonable value of the property greatly exceeded the amount due on the mortgage, including all liens, costs and expenses.

On the hearing, appellant objected to the introduction of evidence upon the ground that the statute was invalid under the federal and state constitutions, and moved that the petition be dismissed. The motion was granted, and a motion for a new trial was denied. On appeal, the Supreme Court of the State reversed the decision of the District Court. 189 Minn. 422, 249 N.W. 334. Evidence was then taken in the trial court, and appellant renewed its constitutional objections without avail. The court made findings of fact setting forth the mortgage made by the appellees on August 1, 1928, the power of sale contained in the mortgage, the default and foreclosure by advertisement, and the sale to appellant on May 2, 1932, for $3,700.98. The court found that the time to redeem would expire on May 2, 1933, under the laws of the State as they were in effect when the mortgage was made and when it was foreclosed; that the reasonable value of the income on the property, and the reasonable rental value, was $40 a month; that the bid made by appellant on the foreclosure sale, and the purchase price, were the full amount of the mortgage indebtedness, and that there was no deficiency after the sale; that the reasonable total amount of the purchase price, with taxes and insurance premiums subsequently paid by appellant, but exclusive of interest from the date of sale, was $4,056.39. The court also found that the property was situated in the closely built-up portions of Minneapolis; that it had been improved by a two-car garage, together with a building two stories in height which was divided into fourteen rooms; that the appellees, husband and wife, occupied the premises as their homestead, occupying three rooms and offering the remaining rooms for rental to others.

The court entered its judgment extending the period of redemption to May 1, 1935, subject to the condition that the appellees should pay to the appellant $40 a month through the extended period from May 2, 1933, that is, that, in each of the months of August, September, and October, 1933, the payments should be $80, in two installments, and thereafter $40 a month, all these amounts to go to the payment of taxes, insurance, interest, and mortgage indebtedness. It is this judgment, sustained by the Supreme Court of the State on the authority of its former opinion, which is here under review. 189 Minn. 448, 249 N.W. 893.

The state court upheld the statute as an emergency measure. Although conceding that the obligations of the mortgage contract were impaired, the court decided that what it thus described as an impairment was, notwithstanding the contract clause of the Federal Constitution, within the police power of the State as that power was called into exercise by the public economic emergency which the legislature had found to exist. Attention is thus directed to the preamble and first section of the statute, which described the existing emergency in terms that were deemed to justify the temporary relief which the statute affords. The state court, declaring that it could not say that this legislative finding was without basis, supplemented that finding by its own statement of conditions of which it took judicial notice. The court said:

In addition to the weight to be given the determination of the legislature that an economic emergency exists which demands relief, the court must take notice of other considerations. The members of the legislature come from every community of the state and from all the walks of life. They are familiar with conditions generally in every calling, occupation, profession, and business in the state. Not only they but the courts must be guided by what is common knowledge. It is common knowledge that, in the last few years, land values have shrunk enormously. Loans made a few years ago upon the basis of the then going values cannot possibly be replaced on the basis of present values. We all know that, when this law was enacted, the large financial companies which had made it their business to invest in mortgages had ceased to do so. No bank would directly or indirectly loan on real estate mortgages. Life insurance companies, large investors in such mortgages, had even declared a moratorium as to the loan provisions of their policy contracts. The President had closed banks temporarily. The Congress, in addition to many extraordinary measures looking to the relief of the economic emergency, had passed an act to supply funds whereby mortgagors may be able within a reasonable time to refinance their mortgages or redeem from sales where the redemption has not expired. With this knowledge, the court cannot well hold that the legislature had no basis in fact for the conclusion that an economic emergency existed which called for the exercise of the police power to grant relief. 189 Minn. 429, 249 N.W. 336.

Justice Olsen of the state court, in a concurring opinion, added the following:

The present nationwide and worldwide business and financial crisis has the same results as if it were caused by flood, earthquake, or disturbance in nature. It has deprived millions of persons in this nation of their employment and means of earning a living for themselves and their families; it has destroyed the value of and the income from all property on which thousands of people depended for a living; it actually has resulted in the loss of their homes by a number of our people and threatens to result in the loss of their homes by many other people, in this state; it has resulted in such widespread want and suffering among our people that private, state, and municipal agencies are unable to adequately relieve the want and suffering, and congress has found it necessary to step in and attempt to remedy the situation by federal aid. Millions of the people's money were and are yet tied up in closed banks and in business enterprises. 189 Minn. 437, 249 N.W. 340.

We approach the questions thus presented upon the assumption made below, as required by the law of the State, that the mortgage contained a valid power of sale to be exercised in case of default; that this power was validly exercised; that, under the law then applicable, the period of redemption from the sale was one year, and that it has been extended by the judgment of the court over the opposition of the mortgagee-purchaser, and that, during the period thus extended, and unless the order for extension is modified, the mortgagee-purchaser will be unable to obtain possession, or to obtain or convey title in fee, as he would have been able to do had the statute not been enacted. The statute does not impair the integrity of the mortgage indebtedness. The obligation for interest remains. The statute does not affect the validity of the sale or the right of a mortgagee-purchaser to title in fee, or his right to obtain a deficiency judgment if the mortgagor fails to redeem within the prescribed period. Aside from the extension of time, the other conditions of redemption are unaltered. While the mortgagor remains in possession, he must pay the rental value as that value has been determined, upon notice and hearing, by the court. The rental value so paid is devoted to the carrying of the property by the application of the required payments to taxes, insurance, and interest on the mortgage indebtedness. While the mortgagee-purchaser is debarred from actual possession, he has, so far as rental value is concerned, the equivalent of possession during the extended period.

In determining whether the provision for this temporary and conditional relief exceeds the power of the State by reason of the clause in the Federal Constitution prohibiting impairment of the obligations of contracts, we must consider the relation of emergency to constitutional power, the historical setting of the contract clause, the development of the jurisprudence of this Court in the construction of that clause, and the principles of construction which we may consider to be established.

Emergency does not create power. Emergency does not increase granted power or remove or diminish the restrictions imposed upon power granted or reserved. The Constitution was adopted in a period of grave emergency. Its grants of power to the Federal Government and its limitations of the power of the States were determined in the light of emergency, and they are not altered by emergency. What power was thus granted and what limitations were thus imposed are questions which have always been, and always will be, the subject of close examination under our constitutional system.

While emergency does not create power, emergency may furnish the occasion for the exercise of power. . . .

Undoubtedly, whatever is reserved of state power must be consistent with the fair intent of the constitutional limitation of that power. The reserved power cannot be construed so as to destroy the limitation, nor is the limitation to be construed to destroy the reserved power in its essential aspects. They must be construed in harmony with each other. This principle precludes a construction which would permit the State to adopt as its policy the repudiation of debts or the destruction of contracts or the denial of means to enforce them. But it does not follow that conditions may not arise in which a temporary restraint of enforcement may be consistent with the spirit and purpose of the constitutional provision, and thus be found to be within the range of the reserved power of the State to protect the vital interests of the community. It cannot be maintained that the constitutional prohibition should be so construed as to prevent limited and temporary interpositions with respect to the enforcement of contracts if made necessary by a great public calamity such as fire, flood, or earthquake. See *American Land Co. v. Zeiss,* 219 U.S. 47. The reservation of state power appropriate to such extraordinary conditions may be deemed to be as much a part of all contracts as is the reservation of state power to protect the public interest in the other situations to which we have referred. And if state power exists to give temporary relief from the enforcement of contracts in the presence of disasters due to physical causes such as fire, flood or earthquake, that power cannot be said to be nonexistent when the urgent public need demanding such relief is produced by other and economic causes. . . .

When we consider the contract clause and the decisions which have expounded it in harmony with the essential reserved power of the States to protect the security of their peoples, we find no warrant for the conclusion that the clause has been warped by these decisions from its proper significance, or that the founders of our Government would have interpreted the clause differently had they had occasion to assume that responsibility in the conditions of the later day. The vast body of law which has been developed was unknown to the fathers, but it is believed to have preserved the essential content and the spirit of the Constitution. With a growing recognition of public needs and the relation of individual right to public security, the court has sought to prevent the perversion of the clause through its use as an instrument to throttle the capacity of the States to protect their fundamental interests. This development is a growth from the seeds which the fathers planted. It is a development forecast by the prophetic words of Justice Johnson in *Ogden v. Saunders,* already quoted. And the germs of the later decisions are found in the early cases of the *Charles River Bridge* and the *West River Bridge, supra,* which upheld the public right against strong insistence upon the contract clause. The principle of this development is, as we have seen, that the reservation of the reasonable exercise of the protective power of the State is read into all contracts, and there is no greater reason for refusing to apply this principle to Minnesota mortgages than to New York leases.

Applying the criteria established by our decisions we conclude:

1. An emergency existed in Minnesota which furnished a proper occasion for the exercise of the reserved power of the State to protect the vital interests of the community. . . .
2. The legislation was addressed to a legitimate end, that is, the legislation was not for the mere advantage of particular individuals, but for the protection of a basic interest of society.
3. In view of the nature of the contracts in question—mortgages of unquestionable validity—the relief afforded and justified by the emergency, in order not to contravene the constitutional provision, could only be of a character appropriate to that emergency, and could be granted only upon reasonable conditions.
4. The conditions upon which the period of redemption is extended do not appear to be unreasonable. . . . The relief afforded by the statute has regard to the interest of mortgagees as well as to the interest of mortgagors. The legislation seeks to prevent the impending ruin of both by a considerate measure of relief. . . .
5. The legislation is temporary in operation. It is limited to the exigency which called it forth. While the postponement of the period of redemption from the foreclosure sale is to May 1, 1935, that period may be reduced by the order of the court under the statute, in case of a change in circumstances, and the operation of the statute itself could not validly outlast the emergency or be so extended as virtually to destroy the contracts.

We are of the opinion that the Minnesota statute, as here applied, does not violate the contract clause of the Federal Constitution. Whether the legislation is wise or unwise as a matter of policy is a question with which we are not concerned.

What has been said on that point is also applicable to the contention presented under the due process clause. *Block v. Hirsh, supra.*

Nor do we think that the statute denies to the appellant the equal protection of the laws. The classification which the statute makes cannot be said to be an arbitrary one. *Magoun v. Illinois Trust & Savings Bank,* 170 U.S. 283; *Clark v. Titusville,* 184 U.S. 329; *Quong Wing v. Kirkendall,* 223 U.S. 59; *Ohio Oil Co. v. Conway,* 281 U.S. 146; *Sproles v. Binford,* 286 U.S. 374.

The judgment of the Supreme Court of Minnesota is affirmed.

Further Resources

BOOKS

Bartholomew, Paul C., and Joseph F. Menez. *Summaries of Leading Cases on the Constitution,* 13th ed. Savage, Md.: Rowman and Littlefield, 1990.

Hendel, Samuel. *Charles Evans Hughes and the Supreme Court.* New York: Russell and Russell, 1951.

WEBSITES

FDR and the Supreme Court. "The Little New Deal Goes to Court: *Blaisdell* and *Nebbia.*" Available online at http://newdeal.feri.org/court/essay02.htm; website home page: http://newdeal.feri.org (accessed March 3, 2003).

John Dillinger

Newspaper articles

"Dillinger—Public Enemy #1—Escapes;" "The End"

By: Associated Press

Date: March 3, 1934; July 23, 1934

Source: "Dillinger—Public Enemy #1—Escapes;" "The End." Associated Press, March 3, 1934; July 23, 1934. Available online at http://wire.ap.org/APpackages/20thcentury/34dillinger.html; website home page: http://wire.ap.org (accessed February 10, 2003).

About the News Agency: The Associated Press began in 1848 as a pool of reporting resources from several New York newspapers working together to relay events in Europe. The cooperate was so successful that it quickly spread to other parts of the country. By the end of the nineteenth century, the AP was positioned to become the world's most dominant newsgathering organization. It faced increased competition from other news agencies, such as United Press International, during World War I and World War II. By the end of the twentieth century, the Associated Press transmitted more than 20 million words per day in its work of disseminating the news to the public. ■

Introduction

In the popular culture of the 1930s, much of the American public saw outlaws such as John Dillinger as folk heroes. In 1924, twenty-one-year-old Dillinger started his bank-robbing career soon after befriending a pool shark named Ed Singleton in Mooresville, Indiana. On their first try, the men attempted unsuccessfully to rob a grocer and were arrested. Dillinger was convicted of assault and battery with intent to rob, as well as conspiracy to commit a felony. He received two sentences of two to fourteen years and ten to twenty years in the Indiana State Prison. He was paroled after serving eight and a half years of his sentence. While in prison, Dillinger became a hardened criminal, forming friendships with several serious offenders.

Soon after his release in May 1933, Dillinger went on a crime spree with his gang of ex-convicts, robbing banks in Indiana and Ohio. He was arrested in Ohio and jailed. In October of that year, his friends, who had escaped from Indiana State Prison, freed him from jail after killing the sheriff.

In late 1933, the Dillinger gang committed a string of bank robberies and raided several police arsenals. In January 1934 the gang killed a Chicago policeman during a bank holdup. When a fire broke out in a hotel where some of the gang members had been hiding under assumed names, firemen recognized them from photographs. Police arrested Dillinger and three others. Dillinger escaped from jail by forcing the guards to open his cell with what he would later claim was a wooden gun he had carved. Fleeing across the Indiana border to Chicago in the sheriff's car, Dillinger violated a federal law against such a crime. Consequently, the Federal Bureau of Investigation (FBI), under Director J. Edgar Hoover, got heavily involved in the search for the outlaw.

On July 21, 1934, FBI agents received a tip from a woman, who told the agents that she and a girlfriend would be with Dillinger at the Biograph Theater in Chicago the next night. On July 22, the FBI ambushed Dillinger as he was leaving the theater. He was shot three times, falling facedown on the ground. His death was a sign that the era of gangsters was at its end.

Significance

In 1934, when outlaws such as John Dillinger were avoiding capture by crossing state lines, Congress enacted laws to establish new categories of federal offenses, giving the FBI more power to enforce the law. The new laws made it a federal crime to rob a national bank; to extort by telephone, telegraph or radio; to knowingly transport stolen property worth more than $5,000 across state lines; to flee across state lines to avoid prosecution for murder, kidnapping, burglary, robbery, rape, assault with a deadly weapon, or extortion with threats of violence; or to flee across state lines to avoid testifying in criminal proceedings. In addition, the National Firearms Act taxed and regulated the sale of guns and made it a federal offense to violate the act.

The folksong about John Dillinger (sidebar) illustrates the significant impact gangsters had on popular culture in the 1920s and 1930s. People went to movies to escape the harsh realities of the long economic crisis. Gangster movies were especially popular. They glorified outlaws, who were portrayed as modern Robin Hoods coming to the aid of the poor. As with the movies, the escapades of the Dillinger gang distracted the public from their dire circumstances.

During Prohibition, Americans had been fascinated by the extravagant lifestyle of gangsters who got rich in enterprises involving the illegal sale of alcohol. But with the coming of the Great Depression, during which millions of Americans lost their life savings, people lost interest in the underground activities of such gangsters as Al Capone. Americans found new heroes in the likes of John Dillinger, who staged daytime robberies and daring prison escapes. Dillinger's death in 1934, however, signaled an end to the era of glamorous desperadoes.

Primary Source

"Dillinger—Public Enemy #1—Escapes"

SYNOPSIS: This first news report from the Associated Press, "Dillinger—Public Enemy #1—Escapes," dramatically details John Dillinger's escape from jail in March 1934. Dillinger's flamboyant style and criminal successes captured the public's imagination, and the outlaw's exploits were widely reported in the media. Despite intense efforts by law enforcement, Dillinger remained at large for another four months, until he was killed by federal law enforcement officers.

Crown Point, Ind. (AP)—John Dillinger, sworn "cop killer" and notorious desperado, made good his boast today, that he would escape any jail.

He walked out of the Lake county jail, known as "escape proof," cowing guards with a wooden pistol that he had whittled out in his cell, in a delivery unmatched for cold daring and sardonic cunning.

Almost unbelievable were the odds he surmounted, and the details of his break read like fantastic fiction.

Tonight he was at liberty, somewhere in the Chicago countryside, with a veritable army of law officials in pursuit, and on his trail grim-lipped Mrs. Lillian Holley, woman sheriff of Lake County, from whose custody he escaped.

"If I ever see John Dillinger, I'll shoot him through the head with my own pistol," Mrs. Holley said.

Authorities estimated as high as twenty thousand men were already engaged in the effort to catch Dillinger and his Negro jail center mate, Herbert Youngblood, who had been held for grand jury action of a murder charge.

As far east as Ohio and through out [sic] Indiana and Illinois authorities were on the alert. Central and southern Illinois tonight contributed frequent reports that a car answering the description of the sheriff's sedan in which they fled was spotted, generally adding it was traveling at a high rate of speed.

Sheriff Holley and Prosecutor Robert G. Estill were conducting an official inquiry into the escape during which Dillinger intimidated and temporarily imprisoned at least thirty-three deputies, jail employed [sic] and other prisoners. State authorities of Indiana were aiding in the quiz [sic].

A key witness was Deputy Sheriff Ernest Blunk who, after being carried as far as Peptone, Ill., along with Edwin Saager, Crown Point garage man, when the pair fled, hastily formed a posse near Joiliet to scout that section for his abductors.

Estill said no official statement would be given until all witnesses had been examined.

Meanwhile, reporters had spent most of the day endeavoring to get a correct account of the sardonically humorous coup. It was Blunk, whom the desperado jailed here after a manacled flight from Tucson, Ariz., following his capture there with three gangster pals [who was] compelled to call Warden Lewis Baker from the jail office.

After Baker was locked up along with Turnkey Sam Cahoon and several others who happened along Dillinger obtained the jail's two machine guns from the warden's office.

Shepherding Blunk and threatening all they encountered, he and Youngblood made their way out of the jail to the Main Street garage where they seized the sheriff's car and forced Saager to accompany them. While the trail, lost after the dumping of Blunk and Saager in the forenoon, near Peotone, was believed hottest in Illinois and reports flashed to Chicago police headquarters frequently that his car was sighted in the city or vicinity, machine guns were trained on Indiana highways and a barricade of sand bags was thrown up about the Lima (O.) prison where Dillinger's pals, Harry Pierpont, Charles Makley and Russell Clark, are held for trial.

Just where the desperado would strike next was problematical but Police Capt. John Stege of Chicago, who led the hunt for Dillinger here late last year, said he would likely attack a police station for additional arms and next would rob a bank Monday.

"John the Whittler" was the way fellow prisoners referred to Dillinger, the nation's No. 1 desperado held for trial March 12 on a charge of murdering William Patrick O'Malley, East Chicago policeman, killed Jan. 15 in a holdup of the First National Bank of East Chicago. Dillinger was charged with killing O'Malley with a machine gun. Seventeen witnesses had identified him and the state asserted he was certain to go to the electric chair.

Dillinger's apparently harmless pastime of whittling was a subject of much amusement on the part

"John Dillinger"

[This folksong, preserved by the Archive of American Folk Song (now the Archive of Folk Culture), illustrates the extent to which outlaws such as John Dillinger had become folk heroes in the popular culture and among working people of the early twentieth century. The authors of the song, Charles L. Todd and Robert Sonkin, New York sound recordists, documented the everyday life of residents of the Farm Security Administration (FSA) migrant work camps in central California in 1940 and 1941.]

John Dillinger, Johnnie Dillinger
The G-Men will chop you down
Some of the things that you've done done
Have been makin' the government frown.
Your numbers up, the words gone round
You won't be goin back to jail
You'll be a bull's eye for the police
And they'll throw the lead like hail.

John Dillinger, Johnnie Dillinger
The finger will be laid on you
And the G-Man watchin' with his gun
Is goin to get you too.
When he stops you Johnnie
He's gonna stop you dead
And head you out for the golden gate
Packin a load of lead.

O Billy the Kid and the Dalton Boys
And others of their kin
Were bad gun men outside the law
But they were brave gun men within
Now you know the old time story
How Billy met his end
It's too late to change you now
So long, old friend.

SOURCE: Lankas, Frank. "John Dillinger." 1941. *Voices From the Dust Bowl: The Charles L. Todd and Robert Sonkin Migrant Worker Collection, 1940–1941.* American Memory digital primary source collection, Library of Congress. Available online at http://memory.loc.gov (accessed March 2, 2003).

of guards and fellow prisoners. Little did they suspect that the outlaw would effect a jail delivery by means of his hobby.

After he had disarmed Ernest Blunk, the deputy, with the wooden pistol, the outlaw held it aloft laughed derisively and said: "Ha, ha, ha, I did it with a wooden pistol."

Locks Up All Guards

Subsequently, armed with a revolver taken from Blunk with an avenging hatred, he locked up all available guards, after disarming them, confiscated the two Thompson machine guns from the warden's office, commandeered the automobile and sped away with Blunk and Saager as hostages. Peptone where he released them, is twenty-five miles south of Joliet.

When he left the jail, five iron doors were locked behind him. With him was Youngblood, held for a Gary murder, who aided him in the escape.

Today's escape was Dillinger's second break from behind bars, and he engineered the delivery of ten convicts from the Indiana State Prison last Sept. 26. In his own previous escape, Dillinger broke from jail in Lima, Ohio, with the aid of companions from the outside, the sheriff being killed in the delivery, Dillinger earlier had engineered the Michigan City prison break of ten convicts. Some of these helped him escape and he took them with him as recruits to a gang which terrorized the mid-West for weeks, robbing banks and obtaining loot running into hundreds of thousands of dollars.

During that time, he and two of his gang, Harry Pierpont and John Hamilton, were among the most widely hunted criminals in America.

Hamilton is still at large. Dillinger and three members of his band; Clark, Pierpont and Makley, together with Mary Kinder, sweetheart of Pierpont, were captured in Tucson a few weeks ago. "Hick cops," Dillinger said disdainfully, after he was taken into custody.

All the time during the escape guards detailed outside the prison went about their duties in ignorance of what was going on. For more than a half hour, no one was able to gain entrance to the jail, due to Dillinger's thoroughness in locking all doors.

In the garage, Saager was on duty. He looked up to see Dillinger menacing him with a machine gun. "What's the fastest car?" barked the desperado.

Saager replied, "The sheriff's there," pointing to a small, black sedan. The car was equipped with a police short wave radio set and Dillinger could listen to broadcasts from police stations for his capture.

With the machine gun at his back, Blunk was forced to enter the car as driver. In the rear seat

John Dillinger (center) strikes a pose with Lake County prosecutor Robert Estill (left), while he is in jail at Crown Point, Indiana, 1934. **AP/WIDE WORLD. REPRODUCED BY PERMISSION.**

were Youngblood and Saager, and the automobile sped off toward Gary and Chicago.

Throughout the day, it was reported seen near Joliet, but no apparent definite clue as to the whereabouts of the desperado was available. Blunk and Saager were released at 11:30 o'clock and returned to Crown Point little the worse for their experience.

Dillinger began his break about 8:30 o'clock this morning. At that time, Blunk entered the cell to obtain fingerprints of Harry Jellenek, confined on a robbery charge. Youngblood was in the cell with Dillinger and Jellenek.

Dillinger, after disarming Blunk, forced him to call the five guards on duty in the jail, and one at a time, he disarmed them and locked them in a cell. Ironically, Guard Ernest Baar, who was off duty, was asleep on the third floor of the jail, armed with a .45 caliber pistol and twenty-one rounds of ammunition. He failed to awaken, as Dillinger locked up the guards in such a manner that they could not reach the alarm signals scattered throughout the jail. Had they reached any of the signals, Baar would have been awakened by the clamor and might have killed the outlaw.

With the guards all locked up and others outside unaware of the situation, Dillinger forced Blunk to accompany him, singing out to Jellenek as he left, "Come on, Harry, let's go."

"Go to h—." replied Jellenek. "I wouldn't walk two feet with you."

Dillinger, Youngblood and Blunk proceeded to the warden's office, which was untenanted, and the outlaw snatched two heavy Thompson machine guns, the only weapons of that type owned by the sheriff's office.

Then the group, with Blunk in front of the menacing machine gun, began a slow and careful march to freedom.

To the jail kitchen Dillinger proceeded, there encountering Mrs. Mary Lincoln, matron and cook. "Be a good little girl," Dillinger said facetiously to her, "and we won't kill you." The woman obeyed in frozen horror and down to the jail garage marched the outlaws and their hostage.

There were several cars in the garage, but all were locked, and Dillinger, unable to start one to make a getaway, carefully tore out the ignition wires in each.

A mailman named Robert Volk was in the Main street public garage at the time Dillinger and his escaping confederates came in and demanded "the fastest car you got."

"I just drove my truck into the garage, which is a couple of doors away from the county jail," Volk related excitedly. "I was standing there talking to Saager, a mechanic, and Loran Rader, salesman. The door opened and in came three fellows, a big Negro and two white men. One fellow walked up to Saager and all at once I saw he had a machine gun. He said, 'Gimme the fastest car you got, garage man, and make it snappy.' I didn't realize until a minute or so that it was Dillinger.

"Then this fellow Blunk—I found out afterward who he was he's a fingerprint fellow—said to the garage man, 'He means business.'

"I looked around and this big Negro had a machine gun, too. So after a minute Saager says the sheriff's car is the fastest thing he's got in the garage. They took the sheriff's car and they took Blunk and the garage man with them. The car went out the door lickety-split. They went north toward Gary.

"So I jumped to a telephone and called the Gary police. Then we ran to the Criminal Courts building, which is between the garage and the county jail, and told the watchman there. They wanted to chase us out.

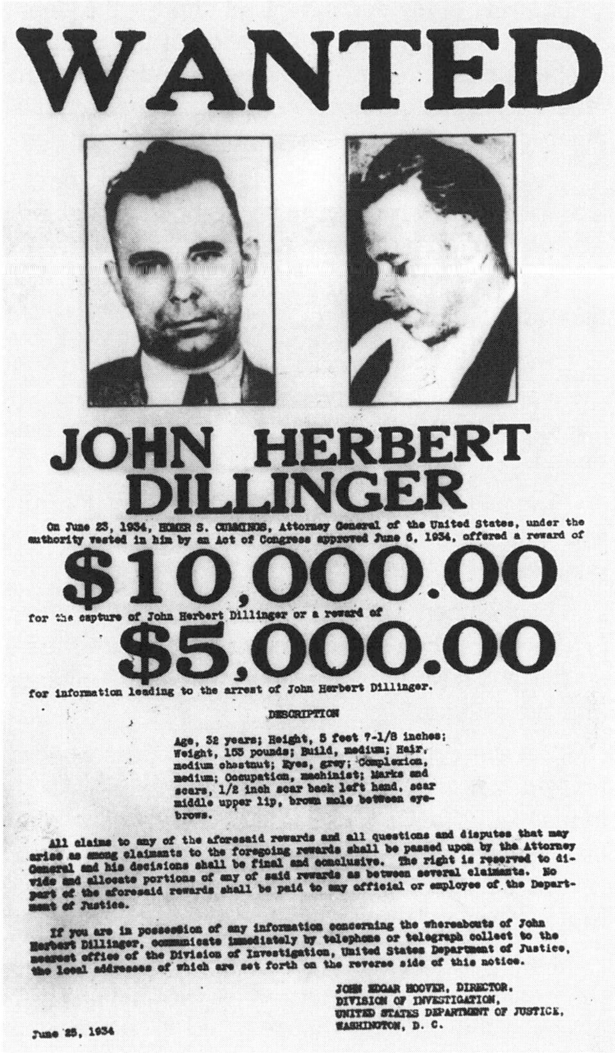

A "Wanted" poster for John Herbert Dillinger, 1934. CORBIS-BETTMANN. REPRODUCED BY PERMISSION.

They told me we were crazy and got sore and told us to quit kidding. Finally they went over to the jail, and sure enough Dillinger was gone and the jail locked up."

Primary Source

"The End"

SYNOPSIS: This Associated Press article details the events leading up to and immediately following the death of John Dillinger.

Chicago, (AP)—John Dillinger lay on a cold slab in the Cook county morgue today.

He was slain by three bullets fired by unnamed federal operatives last night after they had been "tipped off" by a woman.

Crowds of the curious milled through the gloomy building, seeking to view the body of the notorious desperado and to verify to their own satisfaction that federal crack shots had finally ended the incredible crime career of the internationally-known hoodlum.

In a drab coroner's office just removed from the ice filled vault where Dillinger's body lay a solemn jury wrote the last chapter.

It read: "Justifiable homicide by officers of the federal government."

The man who ran him down was not present; the man whose bullet killed him was not named, and the informant who led him to his death was not mentioned.

The entire investigation of the life of the man who was sought for months lasted less than twenty minutes.

Two women were held incommunicado as having been the thug's companions at a movie theater on Chicago's North Side and from which he emerged into the federal trap.

But the dogged government operatives who had tracked him from coast to coast did not wait for the formalities of an autopsy. They began a drive immediately to bring in all the headlong henchmen who had ranged the Midwest with the leering Hoosier leader who had turned from a quiet farmer to a ruthless killer.

Melvin H. Purvis, chief of the Chicago staff of the federal department of investigation, who arranged the ambush that resulted in the phantom fugitive's death, announced a wide search for Homer Van Meter, gunner-in-chief for the Dillinger mob, George (Baby Face) Nelson, John Hamilton, Alvin Karpis, Fred Barker and the other raiders.

"Bring them in," was his tense order to his forces.

Captain John Stege, head of the Chicago police department's Dillinger detail, echoed the command to his charges.

The pace of the hunt for the gangsters, never relaxed during long months of futile effort, was stepped up to a new high speed and placed on a "dead or alive" basis.

Purvis said, however, that he had not determined whether the gang champion was accompanied when he went into the show house. A file of film fans entered and left the place at the same time as Dillinger did precluding definite establishment of whether he was alone. Earlier, Purvis had said that Dillinger was by himself, and he denied that two girl friends of the outlaw had been seized by his operatives as reported by two Chicago detectives who witnessed the slaying of Dillinger.

Concerning the information that led to the trap. Purvis said: "All I can say is that the tip was not given by a sweetheart of Dillinger. The name of the man who gave us the information will never be known."

The "finger woman" was reported to have gone to the movie on Dillinger's pistol arm but to have tarried behind as he sauntered from the lobby to his tryst with death a few hours later. Despite police stories of the woman involved, Purvis insisted that his version was correct.

"The bullet that killed Dillinger," Jerome Kearns, coroner's physician, announced, "was the one that entered the back of his neck right at the shoulder, ripped through into the head, cutting the spinal column, and emerged through the right eye."

He also said he believed that only two bullets had punctured the desperado, one in the neck and the other in the left side.

"This slug," he continued, "cut through the eighth rib, missing the heart by two inches and emerging from the left side."

There were rumors that Purvis fired the shots which dropped Dillinger, but Purvis denied it. Known as a crack shot, the slight young southerner collects guns as a hobby.

East Chicago police in the raiding squad said "two department of justice men" executed the desperado, but would not name them.

Dillinger had been planning his biggest escape when federal agents killed him, it was reported. The desperado was trying to obtain a fake passport, police were informed, which would have let him flee the country. Presumably he intended to go to South America, in view of his known ambition to retire from crime and become a rancher there.

Dillinger swaggered from the neighborhood theater into the raking fire of government guns. Too late he saw the gleaming steel of the trap set for him.

His hand went for his gun. Too late. Three bullets tore into him—one in the neck, two in the body. He staggered, fell.

The hour was 9:40 p.m. central standard time. The place was just outside the Biograph theater, a neighborhood movie at Fullerton and Lincoln avenues, on the northwest side, in territory where the blood of many a Chicago gangster has flowed before.

Had the climax of this bank robber-desperado-killer's career been prearranged, it could have been no more sensational. There was even an audience, loitering about the vicinity of the theater, drawn by the presence of so many department of justice agents, that for a time some believed a holdup was planned.

Dillinger, his hair dyed a darker hue, telltale scars on his cheeks lifted by plastic surgery, gold-rimmed spectacles framing his shifty eyes, his nose straightened, a carefully groomed black mustache adorning his leering lip, and the whorls of his finger tips obliterated by acid strode through the lobby and sauntered down the street.

He passed, apparently without recognition. Purvis seated in a parked car, moved his right arm in a casual signal. Several agents leaped forward, their pistols glistening in the garish light.

Suddenly the mask of insolence dropped from the phantom freebooter's countenance. He darted into an alley, reaching for a pistol as a five-shot fusillade cut him down. Three of the bullets struck him. Two missed their mark and whizzed past him, striking the legs of two gaping women spectators.

The infamous fugitive sprawled on the pavement in a crumpled heap. There was a tense silence, then the scores of horrified witnesses, the agents, two Chicago detectives and five officers from East Chicago, Ind., hurried forward. A cordon was thrown about the body. The curious were herded away, despite their efforts to crowd closer for a glance at the broken gangster. Eerie rays of the blinking marquee lamps flickered over his gray visage. Dark splotches spread over the broad expanse of his silk shirt and natty tie and soiled his flannel trousers and white sports shoes.

The vehicle transporting the wounded Dillinger made for the Alexian Brothers Hospital. He died without a word or motion, before medical aid could be administered, at a street crossing en route to the hospital.

The body was laid on the green lawn of the hospital. Four government operatives stood guard. A deputy coroner arrived, and the dead outlaw was borne to the county morgue. Stripped, cold and colorless as marble, the body was put on a slab. A small group gathered. A surgeon spoke. The slug which ended an amazing crime career had struck in the neck and coursed up to emerge beneath the right eye. The others had pierced the left breast, one cleaving the tip of the heart, the third striking two inches farther down.

One federal man, Purvis said, had fired five shots. He declined to reveal his identity. Officials searched through the clothing. In one of Dillinger's pockets, into which the lion's share of the estimated thousands of loot he and his brigands had gathered in daring raids was reputed to have gone, was found just $7.80.

Further Resources

BOOKS

Potter, Claire Bond. *War on Crime: Bandits, G-men, and the Politics of Mass Culture.* New Brunswick, N.J.: Rutgers University Press, 1998.

Ruth, David E. *Inventing the Public Enemy: The Gangster in American Culture, 1918–1934.* Chicago: University of Chicago Press, 1998.

WEBSITES

"John Dillinger." *Famous Cases.* Federal Bureau of Investigation. Available online at http://www.fbi.gov/libref/historic/famcases/dillinger/dillinger.htm; website home page: http://www.fbi.gov/homepage.htm (accessed March 3, 2003).

Norris v. Alabama

Supreme Court decision

By: Charles Evans Hughes

Date: April 1, 1935

Source: *Norris v. Alabama,* 294 U.S. 587 (1935). Available online at http://www2.law.cornell.edu (accessed February 7, 2003).

About the Author: Charles Evans Hughes (1862–1948), a conservative reformer, served as chief justice of the U.S. Supreme Court from 1930 to 1941. Earlier in his career, he began working for a law firm in 1884 and later taught at Cornell Law School. He gained a reputation as an independent-thinking Republican when he headed several investigations of corruption in industries during the Progressive Era, a period when a vibrant antitrust movement sought to regulate corporations. Hughes was elected governor of New York in 1906 and served two terms. He served as an associate justice to the Supreme Court from 1910 to 1916. He ran for president against incumbent Woodrow Wilson (served 1931–1921) and later served as secretary of state from 1921 to 1925. ■

Introduction

On March 25, 1931, about twenty-five youths who were searching for employment had taken a freight train south from Chattanooga. During the Great Depression millions of unemployed Americans migrated across the country to seek work by hopping trains from town to town. While on the train, African American youths had confrontations with white teenagers, forcing the whites

"Letter to the Editors: Plea From a Scottsboro Boy"

Dear Sirs:

I am quite sure you all have read the outcome of my trial, and seen that I was given a miscarriage of justice. I feel it is my duty to write you all the facts of my case, which you perhaps overlooked, or perhaps it was not published in the papers. I was framed, cheated, and robbed of my freedom. First, beginning March 25, 26, and 27, 1931, I wasn't charged with criminal assault on either girl, and was carried through the first, second, and third degree, and even on the basis I would gain my freedom by turning state evidence against the other eight boys. Just because I didn't know nothing, nor neither would I lie on the other boys the charge of rape was framed and placed against me on the 28th day of March, 1931.

I was tried, convicted, and given the death sentence, and in November, 1932, the Supreme Court of the United States reversed the sentence and a retrial ordered. The 19th day of July, 1937, I was retried and sentenced to 99 years' imprisonment.

Now I wish to call your attention to how the judge charged the jury. He charged them in a perjury way. Out of his one hour and twenty-five minutes summation he only mentioned acquittal three times and each time he contradicted it by saying if you juries find a doubt which goes to me reconsider it. Never did he mention a single defense witness in his hour and twenty-five minutes summation to the jury.

How can I receive justice in the state of Alabama, especially of Morgan County, when perjury is used against me and my attorneys too? And I beg you, dear friends, readers, all stick together and work and struggle together and see that justice be brought to light. Let us all pull and struggle together and see that justice be done. It is not that I hate to go to prison, but I am innocent, and the slander is being thrown on our race of people and my family, is my reason of wanting to fight harder than ever.

Andy Wright
Montgomery, Ala., July 24

SOURCE: "Letter to the Editors: Plea From a Scottsboro Boy." *The Nation,* August 7, 1937, 159–160. Available online at http://newdeal.feri.org/nation/na37145p159.htm; website home page: http://newdeal.feri.org (accessed February 10, 2003).

off the train. When the white teenagers notified the police, the authorities ordered the train to stop near Paint Rock, Alabama. A sheriff took custody of the nine African American teenagers and two white women. When the young women realized they might be arrested, the women accused the black teenagers of raping them at knifepoint.

When the nine youths were taken to the Paint Rock jail, crowds gathered outside. With the possibility of a lynching imminent, the sheriff moved the arrested youths to a jail in Scottsboro. Meanwhile, the governor of Alabama sent twenty-five National Guardsmen to the scene in case of a riot. In only two weeks, an all-white grand jury indicted the nine teenagers for forcible rape, and the court tried and found all of them guilty. Even though the trial had proceeded hastily and the women gave contradictory testimony, in what amounted to a "legal lynching," eight of the boys were sentenced to death by electrocution. Only the youngest one had been spared the death penalty.

With the Communist Party rallying behind the Scottsboro boys, the case became well known around the world, as the European press covered the ensuing story on a consistent basis. The nine youths received a groundswell of support from all over the world, and the injustices they suffered became one of the most searing indictments of Jim Crow laws (the system of white supremacy used to subjugate African Americans) in the South to surface in the United States up to that point.

The International Labor Defense (ILD), an organization associated with the Communist Party, fought a legal campaign to reverse the Scottsboro decision. Later, the National Association for the Advancement of Colored People (NAACP) joined in the defense as well. After the Alabama Supreme Court upheld the convictions, except for that of the youngest defendant, two Scottsboro cases were eventually appealed to the U.S. Supreme Court. A week after Franklin D. Roosevelt was elected president, the Supreme Court reversed the verdict in *Powell v. Alabama,* arguing that the youths had not received effective legal counsel and had not gotten a fair trial, both of which were mandated by the due process clause of the Fourteenth Amendment.

When the cases were retried in Alabama, one of the nine defendants, Clarence Norris, received the death sentence once again. When the *Norris v. Alabama* case reached the Supreme Court, the decision was reversed again on the grounds that African Americans had been systematically excluded from serving on the juries. Both the *Powell* and *Norris* cases were groundbreaking because the due process clause of the Fourteenth Amendment was used to challenge the lack of effective counsel and all-white jury trials, which historically had been used in the South to systematically enforce white supremacy. The cases were the most impressive civil rights victories to date that had been won before the Supreme Court. The last Scottsboro defendant was released from prison in 1950.

Significance

In the early twentieth century, when it came to questions of race, the record of the Supreme Court was uneven at best. Although the Court was more active than before in protecting the rights of racial minorities, significant changes in constitutional doctrine would not occur until Chief Justice Earl Warren headed the Court after 1953. In the 1930s, Chief Justice Charles Evans Hughes generally supported civil liberties and the rights of the accused. Although by no means free of racism, Hughes tended to side with victims of racial discrimination when presented with stark evidence that the rights protected by the Constitution had been violated or skirted. A rigorous defender of the legal process, he was angered by the blatant racism in the criminal justice system.

Although the vindication of the Scottsboro boys did not bring fundamental changes to legal doctrine, the case brought about the use of the due process clause of the Fourteenth Amendment. In addition to the *Norris* case, the *Powell* decision was the first time the Supreme Court had held that the due process clause required that the state provide counsel to indigent defendants if doing otherwise would result in an unfair trial.

One of the turning points in the emergence of a modern civil rights movement in the United States, the Scottsboro cases represented a common tactic among progressive civil rights groups: mass defense and legal action. Organizations such as the NAACP used legal action to gradually chip away at legal segregation and disenfranchisement in the South. Finding that the legal avenues were not working, by the 1950s more militant civil rights activists, who had formed organizations such as the Southern Christian Leadership Conference (SCLC), initiated nonviolent direct actions such as the Montgomery bus boycott of 1955 on a massive scale across the South.

Primary Source

Norris v. Alabama [excerpt]

SYNOPSIS: In this excerpt from *Norris v. Alabama,* Chief Justice Charles Evans Hughes argues that Clarence Norris, one of the Scottsboro boys who had been sentenced to death for the rape of two white women, was denied the right to due process. This right, guaranteed under the Fourteenth Amendment of the Constitution, was violated when African Americans were systematically excluded from serving on the jury. The case was decided on April 1, 1935.

Mr. Chief Justice Hughes delivered the opinion of the Court.

Petitioner, Clarence Norris, is one of nine negro boys who were indicted in March, 1931, in Jackson County, Alabama, for the crime of rape. On being brought to trial in that county, eight were convicted. The Supreme Court of Alabama reversed the conviction of one of these, and affirmed that of seven, including Norris. This Court reversed the judgments of conviction upon the ground that the defendants had been denied due process of law in that the trial court had failed, in the light of the circumstances disclosed, and of the inability of the defendants at that time to obtain counsel, to make an effective appointment of counsel to aid them in preparing and presenting their defense. *Powell v. Alabama,* 287 U.S. 45.

After the remand, a motion for change of venue was granted, and the cases were transferred to Morgan County. Norris was brought to trial in November, 1933. At the outset, a motion was made on his behalf to quash the indictment upon the ground of the exclusion of negroes from juries in Jackson County where the indictment was found. A motion was also made to quash the trial venire in Morgan County upon the ground of the exclusion of negroes from juries in that county. In relation to each county, the charge was of long-continued, systematic and arbitrary exclusion of qualified negro citizens from service on juries solely because of their race and color, in violation of the Constitution of the United States. The State joined issue on this charge, and, after hearing the evidence, which we shall presently review, the trial judge denied both motions, and exception was taken. The trial then proceeded, and resulted in the conviction of Norris, who was sentenced to death. On appeal, the Supreme Court of the State considered and decided the federal question which Norris had raised, and affirmed the judgment. 229 Ala. 226; 156 So. 556. We granted a writ of certiorari. 293 U.S. 552.

First. There is no controversy as to the constitutional principle involved. That principle, long since declared, was not challenged, but was expressly recognized, by the Supreme Court of the State. Summing up precisely the effect of earlier decisions, this Court thus stated the principle in *Carter v. Texas,* 177 U.S. 442, 447, in relation to exclusion from service on grand juries:

> Whenever, by any action of a State, whether through its legislature, through its courts, or through its executive or administrative officers,

Eight of the nine Scottsboro boys sit in jail after being convicted on false charges of rape. UPI/CORBIS-BETTMANN. REPRODUCED BY PERMISSION.

> all persons of the African race are excluded solely because of their race or color, from serving as grand jurors in the criminal prosecution of a person of the African race, the equal protection of the laws is denied to him, contrary to the Fourteenth Amendment of the Constitution of the United States. *Strauder v. West Virginia,* 100 U.S. 303; *Neal v. Delaware,* 103 U.S. 370, 397; *Gibson v. Mississippi,* 162 U.S. 565.

This statement was repeated in the same terms in *Rogers v. Alabama,* 192 U.S. 226, 231, and again in *Martin v. Texas,* 200 U.S. 316, 319. The principle is equally applicable to a similar exclusion of negroes from service on petit juries. *Strauder v. West Virginia, supra; Martin v. Texas, supra.* And although the state statute defining the qualifications of jurors may be fair on its face, the constitutional provision affords protection against action of the State through its administrative officers in effecting the prohibited discrimination. *Neal v. Delaware, supra; Carter v. Texas, supra.* Compare *Virginia v. Rives,* 100 U.S. 313, 322, 323; *In re Wood,* 140 U.S. 278, 285; *Thomas v. Texas,* 212 U.S. 278, 282, 283.

The question is of the application of this established principle to the facts disclosed by the record. That the question is one of fact does not relieve us of the duty to determine whether, in truth, a federal right has been denied. When a federal right has been specially set up and claimed in a state court, it is our province to inquire not merely whether it was denied in express terms, but also whether it was denied in substance and effect. If this requires an examination of evidence, that examination must be made. Otherwise, review by this Court would fail of its purpose in safeguarding constitutional rights. Thus, whenever a conclusion of law of a state court as to a federal right and findings of fact are so intermingled that the latter control the former, it is incumbent upon us to analyze the facts in order that the appropriate enforcement of the federal right may be assured. *Creswell v. Knights of Pythias,* 225 U.S. 246, 261; *Northern Pacific Ry. Co. v. North Dakota,* 236 U.S. 585, 593; *Ward v. Love County,* 253 U.S. 17, 22; *Davis v. Wechsler,* 263 U.S. 22, 24; *Fiske v. Kansas,* 274 U.S. 380, 385, 386; *Ancient Etian Order v. Michaux,* 279 U.S. 737, 745.

Second. The evidence on the motion to quash the indictment. In 1930, the total population of Jackson County, where the indictment was found, was 36,881, of whom 2,688 were negroes. The male population over twenty-one years of age numbered 8,801, and of these, 666 were negroes.

The qualifications of jurors were thus prescribed by the state statute (Alabama Code, 1923, § 8603):

> The jury commission shall place on the jury roll and in the jury box the names of all male citizens of the county who are generally reputed to be honest and intelligent men, and are esteemed in the community for their integrity, good character and sound judgment, but no person must be selected who is under twenty-one or over sixty-five years of age, or who is an habitual drunkard, or who, being afflicted with a permanent disease or physical weakness, is unfit to discharge the duties of a juror, or who cannot read English, or who has ever been convicted of any offense involving moral turpitude. If a person cannot read English and has all the other qualifications prescribed herein and is a freeholder or householder, his name may be placed on the jury roll and in the jury box. . . .

Defendant adduced evidence to support the charge of unconstitutional discrimination in the actual administration of the statute in Jackson County. The testimony, as the state court said, tended to show that, "in a long number of years, no negro had been called for jury service in that county." It appeared that no negro had served on any grand or petit jury in that county within the memory of witnesses who had lived there all their lives. Testimony to that effect was given by men whose ages ran from fifty to seventy-six years. Their testimony was uncontradicted. It was supported by the testimony of officials. The clerk of the jury commission and the clerk of the circuit court had never known of a negro serving on a grand jury in Jackson County. . . .

That testimony, in itself, made out a *prima facie* case of the denial of the equal protection which the Constitution guarantees. See *Neal v. Delaware, supra.* The case thus made was supplemented by direct testimony that specified negroes, thirty or more in number, were qualified for jury service. Among these were negroes who were members of school boards, or trustees, of colored schools, and property owners and householders. . . .

We are of the opinion that the evidence required a different result from that reached in the state court. We think that the evidence that, for a generation or longer, no negro had been called for service on any jury in Jackson County, that there were negroes qualified for jury service, that, according to the practice of the jury commission, their names would normally appear on the preliminary list of male citizens of the requisite age, but that no names of negroes were placed on the jury roll, and the testimony with respect to the lack of appropriate consideration of the qualifications of negroes established the discrimination which the Constitution forbids. The motion to quash the indictment upon that ground should have been granted.

Third. The evidence on the motion to quash the trial venire. The population of Morgan County, where the trial was had, was larger than that of Jackson County, and the proportion of negroes was much greater. The total population of Morgan County in 1930 was 46,176, and, of this number, 8,311 were negroes.

Within the memory of witnesses long resident there, no negro had ever served on a jury in that county or had been called for such service. Some of these witnesses were over fifty years of age, and had always lived in Morgan County. Their testimony was not contradicted. A clerk of the circuit court, who had resided in the county for thirty years, and who had been in office for over four years, testified that, during his official term, approximately 2,500 persons had been called for jury service, and that not one of them was a negro; that he did not recall "ever seeing any single person of the colored race serve on any jury in Morgan County."

There was abundant evidence that there were a large number of negroes in the county who were qualified for jury service. Men of intelligence, some of whom were college graduates, testified to long lists (said to contain nearly 200 names) of such qualified negroes, including many businessmen, owners of real property, and householders. . . .

We find no warrant for a conclusion that the names of any of the negroes as to whom this testimony was given, or of any other negroes, were placed on the jury rolls. No such names were identified. The evidence that, for many years, no negro had been called for jury service itself tended to show the absence of the names of negroes from the jury rolls, and the State made no effort to prove their presence. . . .

For this long-continued, unvarying, and wholesale exclusion of negroes from jury service, we find no justification consistent with the constitutional mandate. We have carefully examined the testimony of the jury commissioners upon which the state court based its decision. . . .

The general attitude of the jury commissioner is shown by the following extract from his testimony:

> I do not know of any negro in Morgan County over twenty-one and under sixty-five who is generally reputed to be honest and intelligent and who is esteemed in the community for his integrity, good character and sound judgment, who is not an habitual drunkard, who isn't afflicted with a permanent disease or physical weakness which would render him unfit to discharge the duties of a juror, and who can read English, and who has never been convicted of a crime involving moral turpitude.

In the light of the testimony given by defendant's witnesses, we find it impossible to accept such a sweeping characterization of the lack of qualifications of negroes in Morgan County. It is so sweeping, and so contrary to the evidence as to the many qualified negroes, that it destroys the intended effect of the commissioner's testimony. . . .

We are concerned only with the federal question which we have discussed, and, in view of the denial of the federal right suitably asserted, the judgment must be reversed and the cause remanded for further proceedings not inconsistent with this opinion.

Further Resources

BOOKS

Carter, Dan T. *Scottsboro: A Tragedy of the American South.* Baton Rouge, La.: Louisiana State University Press, 1969.

Hine, Darlene Clark. *The Path to Equality: From the Scottsboro Case to the Breaking of Baseball's Color Barrier, 1931–1947.* New York: Chelsea House, 1995.

Patterson, Haywood and Earl Conrad. *Scottsboro Boy.* New York: Collier, 1969.

A. L. A. Schechter Poultry Corp. v. U.S.

Supreme Court decision

By: Charles Evans Hughes

Date: May 27, 1935

Source: *A.L A. Schechter Poultry Corp. v. United States.* 295 U.S. 495 (1935). Available online at http://www2.law.cornell.edu (accessed February 7, 2003).

About the Author: Charles Evans Hughes (1862–1948), a conservative reformer, served as chief justice of the U.S. Supreme Court from 1930 to 1941. Earlier in his career, he began working for a law firm in 1884 and later taught at Cornell Law School. He gained a reputation as an independent-thinking Republican when he headed several investigations of corruption in industries during the Progressive Era, a period when a vibrant antitrust movement sought to regulate corporations. Hughes was elected governor of New York in 1906 and served two terms. He served as an associate justice to the Supreme Court from 1910 to 1916. He ran for president against incumbent Woodrow Wilson (served 1913–1921) and later served as secretary of state from 1921 to 1925. ■

Introduction

In 1935, the U.S. Supreme Court unanimously rejected the government's case to uphold the National Industrial Recovery Act (NIRA), which was the first significant attempt by the Franklin D. Roosevelt administration to stimulate economic recovery and lower unemployment. This decision, in *Schechter Poultry Corp. v. United States,* effectively abolished the NIRA programs of the early New Deal.

The agency set up by the NIRA, the National Recovery Administration (NRA), used codes of fair competition, which industries voluntarily drafted and Roosevelt then signed for approval. Within two years the codes covered about twenty-three million Americans. In fact, the codes had helped to raise wages and limit unfair labor practices.

However, violations of the codes were quite common because the program was largely voluntary. In what would later become the *Schechter* case, Brooklyn slaughterhouse operators were found guilty of violating the wage and hour provisions of the industrial code, along with other offenses, such as selling "unfit chicken." Although the poultry was transported from another state, the Schechters only operated their business locally.

When the *Schechter* case was appealed to the Supreme Court, the Court unanimously rejected the government's argument for supporting the program. Chief Justice Charles Evans Hughes rejected the government's claim that the national emergency justified the legislation, even though in the 1934 case *Home Building and Loan Assoc. v. Blaisdell* Hughes had found that the economic crisis allowed for mortgage relief for farmers in Minnesota. Having held what some saw as the opposite view in 1934, Hughes now stated in *Schechter* that "extraordinary conditions do not create or enlarge constitutional power." In addition, Hughes found that the NIRA granted the president legislative power, violating the separation of powers required by the Constitution. Furthermore, the Constitution grants Congress the power to regulate trade only when it crosses state borders, but the poultry code regulated local business exchanges, not interstate commerce.

Even though the early New Deal legislation was struck down in 1935, far more progressive legislation was passed later to provide relief to the poor as well as to lower unemployment and improve work conditions and guarantee the rights of organized labor. The legislation of the later New Deal has continued to function to this day.

Significance

The landmark *Schechter* case had a lasting effect on the balance of power between the branches of government.

Although President Roosevelt criticized the Court for its interpretation of the Constitution in the *Schechter* decision, in fact, when the National Recovery Administration (which was set up under the NIRA) was abolished, it cleared the way for New Deal legislation such as the National Labor Relations Act (NLRA), which was later upheld by the Supreme Court.

After the *Schechter* decision, the Roosevelt administration responded by proposing a plan to increase the number of justices on the Court. Roosevelt's "court-packing plan" was intended to moderate the Supreme Court's conservatism by adding justices who agreed with the president's politics. Although the plan was defeated, it may have reached its goals. After 1937, the Court dropped its attempts to restrict the growth of national power.

When the NRA programs had to be dismantled, the Roosevelt administration wrote regulatory legislation that would pass constitutional muster. In what became known as the Second New Deal, the government passed a whole set of regulatory and benefit programs to alleviate unemployment, provide a safety net for the nation's poor, and reinvigorate the economy. After 1937, the Supreme Court upheld New Deal legislation that guaranteed the right to collective bargaining, a forty-hour work week, and a minimum wage of forty cents an hour. To this day, the New Deal legislation continues to function to regulate the economy and guarantee labor standards.

Primary Source

A. L. A. Schechter Poultry Corp. v. U.S. [excerpt]

SYNOPSIS: In this excerpt from *A. L. A. Schechter Poultry Corp. v. U.S.,* Chief Justice Charles Evans Hughes wrote the unanimous decision that rejected the government's case for the program established by Congress in the National Industrial Recovery Act (NIRA), one of many legislative acts passed during the early New Deal that attempted to stimulate an economic recovery and lower unemployment. The court found that the statute had unconstitutionally delegated power to the president and that the poultry code of the NIRA regulated local business, not interstate commerce, which would have appropriately fallen under congressional authority. The case was decided on May 27, 1935.

Mr. Chief Justice Hughes delivered the opinion of the Court.

Petitioners in No. 854 were convicted in the District Court of the United States for the Eastern District of New York on eighteen counts of an indictment charging violations of what is known as the "Live Poultry Code," and on an additional count for conspiracy to commit such violations. By demurrer to the indictment and appropriate motions on the trial, the defendants contended (1) that the Code had been adopted pursuant to an unconstitutional delegation by Congress of legislative power; (2) that it attempted to regulate intrastate transactions which lay outside the authority of Congress, and (3) that, in certain provisions, it was repugnant to the due process clause of the Fifth Amendment.

The Circuit Court of Appeals sustained the conviction on the conspiracy count and on sixteen counts for violation of the Code, but reversed the conviction on two counts which charged violation of requirements as to minimum wages and maximum hours of labor, as these were not deemed to be within the congressional power of regulation. On the respective applications of the defendants (No. 854) and of the Government (No. 864), this Court granted writs of certiorari, April 15, 1935.

New York City is the largest live poultry market in the United States. Ninety-six percent of the live poultry there marketed comes from other States. Three-fourths of this amount arrives by rail and is consigned to commission men or receivers. Most of these freight shipments (about 75 percent) come in at the Manhattan Terminal of the New York Central Railroad, and the remainder at one of the four terminals in New Jersey serving New York City. The commission men transact by far the greater part of the business on a commission basis, representing the shippers as agents and remitting to them the proceeds of sale, less commissions, freight and handling charges. Otherwise, they buy for their own account. They sell to slaughterhouse operators, who are also called marketmen.

The defendants are slaughterhouse operators of the latter class. A. L. A. Schechter Poultry Corporation and Schechter Live Poultry Market are corporations conducting wholesale poultry slaughterhouse markets in Brooklyn, New York City. Joseph Schechter operated the latter corporation and also guaranteed the credits of the former corporation which was operated by Martin, Alex and Aaron Schechter. Defendants ordinarily purchase their live poultry from commission men at the West Washing-

The Schechter brothers, left to right, Martin; Aaron; Joseph; and Alex, raise their attorney, Joseph Heller, in the air. New York, 1935. They are celebrating their Supreme Court victory. **UPI/CORBIS-BETTMANN. REPRODUCED BY PERMISSION.**

ton Market in New York City or at the railroad terminals serving the City, but occasionally they purchase from commission men in Philadelphia. They buy the poultry for slaughter and resale. After the poultry is trucked to their slaughterhouse markets in Brooklyn, it is there sold, usually within twenty-four hours, to retail poultry dealers and butchers who sell directly to consumers. The poultry purchased from defendants is immediately slaughtered, prior to delivery, by *schochtim* in defendants' employ. Defendants do not sell poultry in interstate commerce.

The "Live Poultry Code" was promulgated under § 3 of the National Industrial Recovery Act. That section—the pertinent provisions of which are set forth in the margin—authorizes the President to approve "codes of fair competition." Such a code may be approved for a trade or industry, upon application by one or more trade or industrial associations or groups, if the President finds (1) that such associations or groups "impose no inequitable restrictions on admission to membership therein and are truly representative," and (2) that such codes are not designed to promote monopolies or to eliminate or oppress small enterprises and will not operate to discriminate against them, and will tend to effectuate the policy. . . .

First. Two preliminary points are stressed by the Government with respect to the appropriate approach to the important questions presented. We are told that the provision of the statute authorizing the adoption of codes must be viewed in the light of the grave national crisis with which Congress was confronted. Undoubtedly, the conditions to which power is addressed are always to be considered when the exercise of power is challenged. Extraordinary conditions may call for extraordinary remedies. But the argument necessarily stops short of an attempt to justify action which lies outside the sphere of constitutional authority. Extraordinary conditions do not create or enlarge constitutional power. The Constitution established a national government with powers deemed to be adequate, as they have proved to be both in war and peace, but these powers of the national government are limited by the constitutional grants. Those who act under these grants are not at liberty to transcend the imposed limits because they believe that more or different power is necessary. Such assertions of extraconstitutional authority were anticipated and precluded by the explicit terms of the Tenth Amendment—

> The powers not delegated to the United States by the Constitution, nor prohibited by it to the States, are reserved to the States respectively, or to the people.

The further point is urged that the national crisis demanded a broad and intensive cooperative effort by those engaged in trade and industry, and that this necessary cooperation was sought to be fostered by permitting them to initiate the adoption of codes. But the statutory plan is not simply one for voluntary effort. It does not seek merely to endow voluntary trade or industrial associations or groups with privileges or immunities. It involves the coercive exercise of the lawmaking power. The codes of fair competition which the state attempts to authorize are codes of laws. If valid, they place all persons within their reach under the obligation of positive law, binding equally those who assent and those who do not assent. Violations of the provisions of the codes are punishable as crimes.

Second. The question of the delegation of legislative power. We recently had occasion to review the pertinent decisions and the general principles which govern the determination of this question. *Panama Refining Co. v. Ryan,* 293 U.S. 388. The Constitution provides that

> All legislative powers herein granted shall be vested in a Congress of the United States, which shall consist of a Senate and House of Representatives Art I, § 1. And the Congress is authorized "To make all laws which shall be necessary and proper for carrying into execution" its general powers. Art. I, 8, par. 18. The Congress is not permitted to abdicate or to transfer to others the essential legislative functions with which it is thus vested. . . .

Accordingly, we look to the statute to see whether Congress has overstepped these limitations—whether Congress, in authorizing "codes of fair competition," has itself established the standards of legal obligation, thus performing its essential legislative function, or, by the failure to enact such standards, has attempted to transfer that function to others. . . .

To summarize and conclude upon this point: Section 3 of the Recovery Act is without precedent. It supplies no standards for any trade, industry or activity. It does not undertake to prescribe rules of conduct to be applied to particular states of fact determined by appropriate administrative procedure. Instead of prescribing rules of conduct, it authorizes the making of codes to prescribe them. For that legislative undertaking, § 3 sets up no standards, aside from the statement of the general aims of rehabilitation, correction and expansion described in section one. In view of the scope of that broad declaration, and of the nature of the few restrictions that are imposed, the discretion of the President in approving or prescribing codes, and thus enacting laws for the government of trade and industry throughout the country, is virtually unfettered. We think that the code-making authority this conferred is an unconstitutional delegation of legislative power.

Third. The question of the application of the provisions of the Live Poultry Code to intrastate transactions. Although the validity of the codes (apart from the question of delegation) rests upon the commerce clause of the Constitution, § 3(a) is not, in terms, limited to interstate and foreign commerce. From the generality of its terms, and from the argument of the Government at the bar, it would appear that § 3(a) was designed to authorize codes without that limitation. But, under § 3(f), penalties are confined to violations of a code provision "in any transaction in or affecting interstate or foreign commerce." This aspect of the case presents the question whether the particular provisions of the Live Poultry Code, which the defendants were convicted for violating and for having conspired to violate, were within the regulating power of Congress. . . .

The question of chief importance relates to the provisions of the Code as to the hours and wages of those employed in defendants' slaughterhouse markets. It is plain that these requirements are imposed in order to govern the details of defendants' management of their local business. The persons employed in slaughtering and selling in local trade are not employed in interstate commerce. Their hours and wages have no direct relation to interstate commerce. . . .

It is not the province of the Court to consider the economic advantages or disadvantage of such a centralized system. It is sufficient to say that the Federal Constitution does not provide for it. Our growth and development have called for wide use of the commerce power of the federal government in its control over the expanded activities of interstate commerce, and in protecting that commerce from burdens, interferences, and conspiracies to restrain and monopolize it. But the authority of the federal government may not be pushed to such an extreme as to destroy the distinction, which the commerce clause itself establishes, between commerce "among the several States" and the internal concerns of a State. The same answer must be made to the contention that is based upon the serious economic situation which led to the passage of the Recovery Act—the fall in prices, the decline in wages and employment, and the curtailment of the market for commodities. Stress is laid upon the great importance of maintaining wage distributions which would provide the necessary stimulus in starting "the cumulative forces making for expanding commercial activity." Without in any way disparaging this motive, it is enough to say that the recuperative efforts of the federal government must be made in a manner consistent with the authority granted by the Constitution.

We are of the opinion that the attempt, through the provisions of the Code, to fix the hours and wages of employees of defendants in their intra-state business was not a valid exercise of federal power. . . .

In view of these conclusions, we find it unnecessary to discuss other questions which have been raised as to the validity of certain provisions of the Code under the due process clause of the Fifth Amendment.

On both the grounds we have discussed, the attempted delegation of legislative power, and the attempted regulation of intrastate transaction which affect interstate commerce only indirectly, we hold the code provisions here in question to be invalid and that the judgment of conviction must be reversed.

Further Resources

BOOKS

Baker, Leonard. *Back to Back: The Duel Between FDR and the Supreme Court.* New York: Macmillan, 1967.

Bartholomew, Paul C., and Joseph F. Menez. *Summaries of Leading Cases on the Constitution,* 13th ed. Savage, Md.: Rowman and Littlefield, 1990.

Hendel, Samuel. *Charles Evans Hughes and the Supreme Court.* New York: Russell and Russell, 1951.

Leuchtenburg, William E. *Franklin D. Roosevelt and the New Deal, 1932–1940.* New York: Harper and Row, 1963.

WEBSITES

FDR and the Supreme Court. "The Little New Deal Goes to Court: *Blaisdell* and *Nebbia.*" Available online at http://newdeal.feri.org/court/essay02.htm; website home page: http://newdeal.feri.org (accessed March 2, 2003).

Eleanor Roosevelt to Walter White, March 19, 1936

Letter

By: Eleanor Roosevelt

Date: March 19, 1936

Source: Roosevelt, Eleanor. Letter to Walter White, March 19, 1936. Reproduced as "Letter, Eleanor Roosevelt to Walter White detailing the First Lady's lobbying efforts for federal action against lynchings, 19 March 1936." *Words and Deeds in American History.* American Memory digital primary source collection, Library of Congress. Available online at http://memory.loc.gov/cgi-bin/query/r?ammem/mcc:@field(DOCID+@lit(mcc/015)); website home page: http://memory.loc.gov (accessed April 20, 2003).

About the Author: Eleanor Roosevelt (1884–1962), the wife of President Franklin D. Roosevelt (served 1933–1945), had been involved in the settlement house movement of the Progressive Era and became a strong advocate for social justice in the interests of women, children, African Americans, and working people during the Roosevelt administration. In addition, she lobbied and spoke publicly about reform issues that were important to her. As one observer in Washington stated, she was "a cabinet member without portfolio." ■

Introduction

The Great Depression increased racial tensions across the country because of tightening competition for scarce jobs, especially in the agricultural South. An increase in the number of lynchings in the South came with the heightened conflicts. From the late nineteenth century to World War I (1914–1918), hundreds of blacks had been lynched in the South. According to the Tuskegee Institute, the number peaked at twenty-eight in 1933, a record high after it had fallen to a low of ten the year before. Horror stories abounded of lynch mobs mutilating victims in unspeakable ways and the enthusiastic crowds participating in carnivalesque violence.

Civil rights activists responded to the marked increase by reinvigorating the campaign to pass a federal anti-lynching law. The National Association for the Advancement of Colored People (NAACP) had tried unsuccessfully for years to get a federal anti-lynching law passed. In the 1920s, the campaign for federal legislation had died out after the defeat of the Dyer Anti-Lynching Bill. When Walter White became executive secretary of the NAACP in 1930, he took up the drive for a federal anti-lynching law again. The surge in lynchings had forced the NAACP to put the New Deal's commitment to civil rights for African Americans to the test.

Eleanor Roosevelt and Secretary of the Interior Harold Ickes, who had once been the president of the Chicago chapter of the NAACP, supported the revived anti-lynching campaign. However, President Franklin Roosevelt was less enthusiastic. Above all, the president wanted to garner and maintain support from conservative southern Democrats for his New Deal programs. He risked losing their tenuous support with civil rights legislation that intervened in the affairs of states and would have had a significant impact on the South.

PERSONAL AND CONFIDENTIAL.

THE WHITE HOUSE
WASHINGTON

Mrs. Roosevelt

March 19, 1936

Rec'd W.W. 3-21-36

My dear Mr. White:

Before I received your letter today I had been in to the President, talking to him about your letter enclosing that of the Attorney General. I told him that it seemed rather terrible that one could get nothing done and that I did not blame you in the least for feeling there was no interest in this very serious question. I asked him if there were any possibility of getting even one step taken, and he said the difficulty is that it is unconstitutional apparently for the Federal Government to step in in the lynching situation. The Government has only been allowed to do anything about kidnapping because of its interstate aspect, and even that has not as yet been appealed so they are not sure that it will be declared constitutional.

The President feels that lynching is a question of education in the states, rallying good citizens, and creating public opinion so that the localities themselves will wipe it out. However, if it were done by a Northerner, it will have an antagonistic effect. I will talk to him again about the Van Nuys resolution and will try to talk also to Senator Byrnes and get his point of view. I am deeply troubled about the whole situation as it seems to be a terrible thing to stand by and let it continue and feel that one cannot speak out as to his feeling. I think your next step would be to talk to the more prominent members of the Senate.

Very sincerely yours,

Eleanor Roosevelt

Primary Source

Eleanor Roosevelt to Walter White, March 19, 1936

SYNOPSIS: In this letter to NAACP executive secretary Walter White, First Lady Eleanor Roosevelt explained why the president was not supporting the anti-lynching bill for which civil rights advocates had been pushing. The First Lady's letter illustrated the role she played in advocating reform issues important to her as well as serving as a voice of her allies to be heard in the White House. THE LIBRARY OF CONGRESS.

African Americans protest in front of DAR Memorial Hall against the crime conference's neglect to include lynching in its program. Washington, D.C., 1934. © BETTMANN/CORBIS. REPRODUCED BY PERMISSION.

The new legislation, sponsored by Edward P. Costigan of Colorado and Robert F. Wagner of New York, addressed the problem of enforcement by bringing the offenders to trial and punishing culpable officials. The Costigan-Wagner Act also included federal trials for individuals who participated in a mob when local authorities refused to act, as well as fines or jail terms for officers who did not fulfill their duties.

However effective the bill would have been, it faced stiff opposition and was defeated. Lynchings continued into the 1950s even though not at the frequency as before World War II (1939–1945). Although the federal anti-lynching measure was defeated, civil rights workers did have limited successes. The number of lynchings in the South declined significantly by the late 1930s.

Significance

Eleanor Roosevelt's letter to Walter White, the NAACP executive secretary, suggested the extent to which the cause of civil rights was beholden to the conservative southern Democrats' willingness to compromise over issues that were important to them. As long as the president needed the southern Democrats to move forward on New Deal programs, he was unable to push them to prevent lynching in their own states. Yet many southern states passed anti-lynching measures on their own to avoid federal intervention and an infringement on the cherished principle of states rights. President Roosevelt was well aware that federal intervention on such a matter would only antagonize southern states.

In addition, Roosevelt had already experienced the thorny issue of federal intervention in the internal affairs of states with New Deal legislation that was declared unconstitutional. Unless a crime involved crossing state lines, the federal government was constitutionally limited in its ability to enforce laws otherwise under the jurisdiction of states.

Despite the defeat of the federal anti-lynching bill in the 1930s, civil rights activists benefited from the work by building a coalition that was the basis for future struggles for equality for African Americans in the United States. Having reduced the actual number of lynchings in the South, activists in the anti-lynching campaign helped to reduce the suffering of African Americans caused by white supremacists.

Further Resources

BOOKS

Brundage, W. Fitzhugh, ed. *Under Sentence of Death: Lynching in the South.* Chapel Hill, N.C.: University of North Carolina Press, 1997.

Dray, Philip. *At the Hands of Persons Unknown: The Lynchings of Black America.* New York: Random House, 2002.

Kearney, James. *Anna Eleanor Roosevelt: The Evolution of a Reformer.* Boston: Houghton Mifflin, 1968.

Margolick, David. *Strange Fruit: Billie Holiday, Café Society and an Early Cry for Civil Rights.* Philadelphia, Pa.: Running Press, 2000.

Tolnay, Stewart and Emory. *A Festival of Violence: An Analysis of Southern Lynching, 1882–1930.* Urbana, Ill.: University of Illinois Press, 1995.

Wells-Barnett, Ida B. *Southern Horrors and Other Writings: The Anti-lynching Campaign of Ida B. Wells, 1892–1900.* Boston: Bedford, 1997.

WEBSITES

"The Anti-Lynching Conference at Baltimore." *The Charlottesville Reflector.* Available online at http://www.iath.virginia.edu (accessed April 16, 2003).

"The Supreme Court and the Constitution"

Pamphlet

By: Robert E. Cushman

Date: 1936

Source: Cushman, Robert E. "The Supreme Court and the Constitution." *Public Affairs Pamphlet* 7, 1936, 1–36. Available online at http://newdeal.feri.org/court/cushman.htm (accessed February 7, 2003). ■

Introduction

In February 1937, President Franklin D. Roosevelt (1882–1945) surprised most people in Congress when he sent them a bill to increase the number of justices on the Supreme Court. Soon to be called the "court-packing bill," Roosevelt hoped to increase the number of justices he could nominate to ensure that the body would uphold the New Deal legislation's constitutionality.

After conservative justices had been appointed to the Court in the 1920s, a majority on the body held a restrictive interpretation of the regulatory power of the federal government. The justices could potentially undermine the reforms he thought were necessary for economic recovery. The Court had upheld reform legislation in some cases, but in May 1935 the Court struck down vital components of the New Deal reforms. In one of the cases, *Schechter Poultry Corporation v. United States,* the Court struck down the National Industrial Recovery Act, arguing that Congress could not delegate overly broad powers to the executive branch.

Even though Roosevelt was shocked by the Supreme Court's decisions, he chose not to confront the Court because the presidential election was approaching. The Court then struck down more New Deal programs, including the Agricultural Adjustment Act (AAA). When Roosevelt won a landslide reelection victory, he ordered the attorney general to devise a plan to reform the court so that a majority would uphold the constitutionality of the New Deal's regulatory reforms. Roosevelt and Attorney General Homer Cummings agreed to a plan that would add one new justice for each current Supreme Court justice over the age of seventy. Roosevelt justified the plan by arguing that the new justices would improve the efficiency of the Court.

Having consulted very few people about the plan, it was broadly condemned from both ends of the political spectrum. Not only Republicans, conservative and moderate Democrats, and newspapers, but also liberal Supreme Court justices roundly criticized the plan. Even though the plan was denounced from many sides, Roosevelt continued to push for it and urged Congress to sway votes in favor of it.

The plan appeared to have backfired, creating such a controversy as to make it even more difficult to move forward on New Deal reforms. Yet despite the political damage that the Roosevelt administration suffered from the loss, after the controversy the Supreme Court began to rule much more favorably on Roosevelt's New Deal agenda. Most significantly, the Court upheld the constitutionality of the National Labor Relations Board.

Significance

Robert Cushman's *Public Affairs Pamphlet* argued for amending the Constitution to adapt to modern times rather than "tinkering" with the Supreme Court a year before President Franklin D. Roosevelt proposed the "court-packing plan." Cushman sided with liberals in the public controversy about whether the power of the central government should be expanded to deal with the economic depression that gripped the country.

It was a sign of the times that during the Great Depression, commentators such as Robert E. Cushman entertained the idea of amending the Constitution to account for contingencies that the founding fathers could not have imagined at the time. The hardships that Americans confronted in the 1930s forced them to question the very basis upon which society was organized. What may have seemed only a decade ago to be a president overreaching the legitimate boundaries of his power appeared in the 1930s to be an attempt to deal with the economic crisis by reforming old institutions to adapt to newer, more modern times.

Despite the shift in discussion to possibilities that were unthinkable before the Great Depression, both Roosevelt's opponents and allies saw the court-packing plan as an opportunistic attempt to sway the Court toward his

Vehement Opposition to "Court-Packing"

In this letter, sent to the Office of the Solicitor in the Justice Department, Frank Gannett, publisher of Gannett Newspapers, criticizes President Roosevelt's plan to pack the Supreme Court as a move toward absolute power and a threat to the integrity of the Supreme Court.

President Roosevelt has cleverly camouflaged a most amazing and startling proposal for packing the Supreme Court. It is true that the lower courts are slow and overburdened, we probably do need more judges to expedite litigation but this condition should not be used as a subtle excuse for changing the complexion and undermining the independence of our highest court. Increasing the number of judges from nine to fifteen would not make this high tribunal act any more promptly than it does now, but it would give the President control of the Judiciary Department.

A year ago I predicted that this is exactly what would happen if Roosevelt was reelected. The Supreme Court having declared invalid many of the administration measures the President now resorts to a plan of creating a Supreme Court that will be entirely sympathetic with his ideas. Provision has been made for amending the Constitution. If [it] is necessary to change the Constitution it should be done in the regular way. The President is mistaken, if he thinks he can conceal his real purpose of packing, influencing and controlling the Supreme Court by confusing that objective with a long dissertation on the slow action of our various courts.

The Supreme Court has been the anchor that has held America safe through many storms. Its absolute independence and integrity must never be in doubt.

Our Government is composed of three departments, Legislative, Executive and Judiciary. These are the foundations of our Democracy. As a result of the election and the transfer of powers by so-called emergency measures, the Executive now dominates the Legislative Department. The President now proposes also to dominate the Judiciary. Do we want to give to this man or any one man complete control of these three departments of our Government which have from the beginning of the Republic been kept entirely separate and independent?

This proposal should give every American grave concern for it is a step towards absolutism and complete dictatorial power.

SOURCE: Gannett, Frank E. A Statement by Frank E. Gannett, publisher, Gannett Newspapers. National Archives and Records Administration. Records of the Justice Department. Record Group 60. Available online at http://www.archives.gov/digital_classroom/lessons/separation_of_powers/images/gannett_letter.jpg; website home page: http://www.archives.gov (accessed February 7, 2003).

political agenda. The court-packing battle was the turning point for the Roosevelt administration. Having pushed the New Deal agenda even further to the left from its beginning in 1933 to the president's landslide reelection in 1936, the political loss from the court-packing clashes led the administration to implement a retrenchment with many of the more progressive aspects of the New Deal. What appeared to be a sound mandate after the presidential reelection faded away in the controversy over the courts. It was also one of the most controversial struggles between the judicial and executive branches in American history.

Primary Source

"The Supreme Court and the Constitution"

SYNOPSIS: In the following pamphlet, Cushman examines the question of whether the Constitution should be amended to "narrow the field of judicial review by sharpening the vague clauses of the Constitution under which the Supreme Court is now engaged."

The average citizen has a very wholesome respect for the Constitution of the United States. His respect does not usually come from any clear or accurate knowledge of the document itself, but grows out of the belief that the Constitution sanctions those policies which he approves and forbids those which seem to him dangerous or oppressive. His reaction to the Supreme Court is similarly direct and forthright; its decisions are sound if he likes them and unsound if he does not. While this solution of our constitutional problems by the "hunch" method has the advantage of simplicity, it is rather too simple to be helpful in answering two very vital questions now before the country: (1) Is our Constitution adequate to the demands of our present day national life? (2) Is the Supreme Court preserving our Constitution or obstructing its normal and healthy expansion?

It is well to remember that the "fathers" who framed the Constitution were no more competent to manage their affairs than we are to manage ours. They relied upon what political experience they had, but much of their work was frankly experimental. Some parts of the Constitution in which they took the greatest pride, such as the intricate method of electing the President, failed completely to work as they intended.

Certain inadequacies in the original document, as interpreted by the Supreme Court, had to be met

The U.S. Supreme Court in 1937. Chief Justice Charles Evans Hughes sits in the center. © **HULTON ARCHIVE/GETTY IMAGES. REPRODUCED BY PERMISSION.**

by constitutional amendments. But the basic features of the Constitution of 1936 are those of the Constitution of 1787. For purposes of the present discussion those basic features may be summed up as follows: 1. The Constitution set up the outlines of a structure of national government, while at the same time it left intact the state governments. 2. The Constitution worked out a division of powers between the new national government and the states. It did this by delegating to the new national government the powers deemed necessary for national purposes, and by declaring that the powers not thus given to the new nation were left to the states unless specifically forbidden to them. The national government had only the powers positively given to it; the states kept all the powers not taken away from them. 3. The Constitution, with its added amendments, carefully listed certain vital civil liberties which the new federal government might not invade. Most of these were set out in the Bill of Rights added in 1790. Other guarantees of civil liberty were set up as limitations upon the states. Here we find prohibition against impairment of the obligation of contracts and later the all-important due process and equal protection clauses of the Fourteenth Amendment. 4. The new Constitution declared itself to be the "supreme law of the land a fundamental law binding upon state and federal officers alike." To make effective this concept of the Constitution, the Supreme Court, after putting out one or two hesitant feelers, boldly announced in 1803 in the case of *Marbury v. Madison* that it was the organ of government to maintain the supremacy of the Constitution and that in the exercise of its judicial work of applying the law in cases brought before it, it would invalidate acts of Congress which were in conflict with the Constitution. Since the Constitution itself declared its supremacy over conflicting state legislation, the power of the Supreme Court to invalidate state law deemed to violate that Constitution were even easier to defend. Whether the framers of the Constitution intended the Supreme Court to exercise this power of "judicial review" in enforcing the supremacy of the Constitution, or whether the Court "usurped" it, has evoked bitter argument which we need not enter into here. Whether "usurped" or not, and the weight of historical argument is against the charge of "usurpation," the Supreme Court has exercised this important power of declaring statutes unconstitutional ever since Marshall established the precedent in 1803, and it is now as much a part of the working American Constitution as the provision

A political cartoon alludes to President Roosevelt's court packing plan. May 28, 1935. S.J. RAY/THE KANSAS CITY STAR. REPRODUCED BY PERMISSION.

that Senators shall be chosen for six years or that the President may veto bills sent to him by Congress.

Nation Changed since 1789

Thus the basic nature of our constitutional system has not changed since 1789. But the nation which it governs has vastly changed. From a fringe of jealous and struggling colonies on the Atlantic seaboard it has become a great continental empire, national in its thinking and its impulses, with an economic life pulsating through nationwide systems of markets, transportation, and communications. Congress still has its delegated power to regulate commerce, and we are told that the power is unchanged; but what a difference between the commerce of 1787 and 1936! And so with the other delegated powers: they have not shrunk, they have not expanded, but they apply to concrete problems and situations beyond the wildest imagination of the founding fathers.

This is also true of the guarantees of civil liberty found in the Constitution. No longer do they restrict the simple activities of an 18th century government, but they are used to measure the validity of the many complex rules and restrictions which the modern nation and state impose upon the daily life of the citizen. What many thoughtful people have been asking is: How adequate is the old Constitution to the needs of a 20th century nation? Are the delegated powers broad enough to permit the federal government to deal with all truly national problems? Are the old limitations on behalf of civil liberty too strict or too loose? To what extent has the Supreme Court in construing the Constitution been able to adapt its provisions to the demands of modern life? If the Constitution, as interpreted by the Court, prevents the proper solution of our social and economic problems, should we do something to the Constitution to meet the difficulty, or should we do something to the Supreme Court? . . .

Proposals for Constitutional or Judicial Reform

Whatever we may feel about the wisdom of the statutes involved it is a sobering thought that Congress cannot proceed with its program for agriculture rehabilitation because six of our nine Supreme Court justices so rule, and that neither the nation nor the states can protect women and children from starvation wages because five of the same nine justices find something in the words "due process of law" which prevents it. And this pushes to the front the question whether, viewing the whole situation, we think something ought to be done about it. And if we assume that something ought to be done, that raises a whole row of questions as to what can be done. Let us, then, examine the various positions which an intelligent citizen might take on this important question and see what ways are open to him to make his view effective. 1. In the first place there is the view point that the Constitution is fully adequate to present day needs and that the Supreme Court is performing wisely and efficiently its difficult task of interpreting it. Those holding this opinion, and there are many, will naturally propose no changes in our constitutional or judicial system, but will, on the contrary, fight any changes that may be proposed. 2. In the second place there are those who view with concern the whole constitutional picture presented in the earlier pages but who feel that no change in the Constitution is needed and that any "tinkering" with the Supreme Court will be dangerous and unsatisfactory. These critics of the present system believe that the Constitution with its broad and generous clauses is sufficiently flexible to meet the changing demands of the modern nation. That flexibility must be recognized and accepted by the Supreme Court in the work of constitutional construction. And we must "educate" the Court through criticism, public discussion, and the various techniques of an informed public opinion to a more enlightened view of their task. A person thus minded is apt to quote Mr. Dooley's comment that the Supreme Court follows the election returns and, if more fully informed, alludes to the fact that the Supreme Court has actually reversed or drastically modified its decisions in about forty cases. This shows that judicial opinions can be and sometimes are changed gradually and it is urged that such a process of evolution and adjustment is likely to be more satisfactory than any jerky and uncertain results attained by altering either the Constitution or the Court. In reply it is urged that few, if any reversals of the decisions of the Court have come about in answer to any immediately expressed public opinion, that the recent decisions indicate a trend toward judicial ruthlessness rather than judicial tolerance of legislative policies, and that such a program of judicial education is at best slow and uncertain. This, however, is no valid argument against employing the method as vigorously as possible in the hope of securing substantial results. 3. A third position is that the Constitution, properly interpreted, is fully adequate to our present day national needs, that the Supreme Court is at fault either in assuming the vast power it exercises, or in the way in which it uses it, and that we should, therefore, let the Constitution alone and reform the Court. Having agreed that something ought to be done to the Court, these reformers split up into at least five groups on the question of what to do.

"Packing" the Court

One thing that can be done to the Court is to "pack" it. By this is meant to increase the number of judges on the Court and fill the new places with men who have a more "liberal" point of view. For those who like speedy action this plan has the advantage of getting immediate results and of being a change which can be made by Congress without the aid of a constitutional amendment. The Constitution provides that there shall be a Supreme Court but leaves it to Congress to determine its size by statute. We started out with six justices, we have had as many as ten, and since 1869 we have had nine. There is no constitutional reason why we should not have fifteen or twenty-five. This scheme to "pack" the Court has a certain child-like simplicity. If we have judges whom we regard as bad, let us add to the Court enough good judges to outvote the bad ones and all will be well.

Newspaper tycoon Frank Gannett in 1938. Gannett was one of many supporters of Roosevelt who were outraged by his court packing plan.

In 1870 the Supreme Court declared the Legal Tender Act invalid by a vote of four to three. There were two vacancies on the Court at the time. President Grant filled these places with two men who promptly voted with the minority of three to reverse the decision by a vote of five to four. Historians still argue as to whether Grant "packed" the Court, a question which we are not called upon to settle. It is more important to note that the incident cost the Court heavily in public confidence. Mr. Hughes calls the reversal under these circumstances "a self-inflicted wound." Those who urge that we "pack" the Supreme Court should bear in mind that packing may well be a two-edged sword. If we "pack" the Court with liberals there is nothing to prevent reprisal by the conservatives when they come into power, and the process may go on until all sound traditions of judicial independence are undermined. Furthermore, the packing of the Court with justices of a particular breed or color of view promises very uncertain results. If these men are really the kind whose judicial work will be directly governed by their political and economic affiliations, who will in short live up to the implied understanding which led to their appointment, they would appear to be unfit for judicial service. Nothing

This 1937 political cartoon shows President Roosevelt proposing to massively increase the size of the Supreme Court building, a reference to his plan to "pack" the Court with more justices. **THE LIBRARY OF CONGRESS/CORBIS. REPRODUCED BY PERMISSION.**

but calamity can be expected from a definitely biased Court. If, on the other hand, judicially-minded men are appointed in the expectation that their known predilections and hunches will color their work on the bench, it should be noted that experience does not bear this out sufficiently to make the method a very reliable instrument of specific reform. The history of the Supreme Court is full of cases in which Presidents appointed men to the bench in the hope that they would give effect to a certain point of view. Such efforts were almost always disappointing in their results. In virtually every case the justice so appointed failed to do his "duty" in this regard and settled down to be a judge and not a partisan.

But it is not necessary to swamp the Court in order to change its personnel. Five justices are now over seventy-four years of age and a sixth is over seventy. The President elected in 1936 will hardly escape the responsibility of appointing one or more justices. In doing so he will affect the trend of the Court's decisions for many years. If he appoints men with the broad judicial tolerance of a Brandeis, Stone, or Cardozo, the Constitution may prove flexible enough to meet the demands we are making on it. If he appoints hard-minded judicial dogmatists from the ultra-conservative school, we may find ourselves facing the issue of drastic constitutional revision. Those who believe the Constitution is adequate to our present needs, if flexibly construed, will do well to exert every ounce of influence toward the selection of justices who share their views, not on specific questions, but on the broad principles of liberal construction. . . .

Must the Constitution Be Amended?

This brings us to the fourth and final position which may be taken by those who believe that our constitutional and judicial system calls for some change. This position is that we should change our Constitution to meet new demands rather than change the Court. Accepting judicial review as a going concern we can all agree that it is most open to attack where the Supreme Court is interpreting the vague and general clauses of the Constitution or is applying an ancient provision to conditions lying beyond the contemplation of the founding fathers. This is clear from our earlier analysis of the New Deal decisions. Now it is wholly intelligent to suggest that if the results we are getting from judicial review under these circumstances are not satisfactory then the thing to do is to sharpen and clarify the constitutional provisions which the Court has to interpret. Since wise men disagree as to whether the due process clause forbids the enactment of a minimum wage, a simple solution would be to put into the Constitution a definite grant of authority to fix wage and working conditions. That would take the matter out of the realm of judicial debate and put it where it belongs, in the field of political debate. Are there to be no limits to the amount of "stretching" of the delegated powers of Congress to meet the growing demands of our national life? Must they inevitably be construed to cover all the emerging problems calling for centralized control?

In demanding that the Supreme Court permit the commerce clause, the taxing clause, or other constitutional clauses to serve as constitutional pegs upon which to hang new and drastic regulatory programs penetrating into hitherto unoccupied fields of governmental power we are asking them to exercise very broad discretion. If they refuse to do the necessary stretching we may well consider whether the powers of Congress ought not to be frankly and openly increased rather than stretched. The writer is one of those who finds the dissenting opinions in the A.A.A. and Guffey Act cases much more convincing on constitutional grounds than the opinions of the Court. At the same time if American agriculture and mining demand national regulation there is much to be said for giving to Congress clearly and unmistakably the powers we feel it should have. It will hardly be denied that if Congress ought to have the power to prohibit child labor we should do much better to ratify the pending child-labor amendment than to use the backstairs method of driving child labor out of existence by destructive taxation or by denying the employers of children the privileges of interstate commerce.

The Court now occupies the position of exercising a very broad discretion in drawing the limits of governmental power granted in vague terms and under vague limitations. If we do not like the way it does that job it is quite possible to change the Court's job by defining those powers with some precision and sharpening the terms of the limitations. We might give to Congress, free from all doubt, the powers which it needs in order to deal with the pressing problems of present day national life. The uncertainties of the due process limitation may be met by specific clauses clarifying its application.

It is no adequate objection to this proposal to point out the difficulty of drafting such amendments. It is always difficult to draft constitutional provisions which mean exactly what we wish them to mean—and no more. The difficulty, though great, is not insuperable. To refrain from making such grants of power merely because of the difficulty of phrasing them is to confess either lack of skill in the art of draftsmanship, or our inability to make up our minds what we wish to accomplish. But if we do not really know what new powers we wish to grant we should probably refrain from granting them.

There are many, however, who are skeptical of this proposal. They ask whether we can give Congress enough power to control industry and handle all our truly national problems effectively without destroying the basis of federalism, without virtually destroying the states. This may be met by suggesting that we are merely making a formal transfer from state to nation of powers of economic and social control which by their very nature and scope the states have never exercised and never can. A more serious criticism is that which urges, in the light of the history of the Child Labor Amendment, that it is politically impossible to secure the adoption of any constitutional amendment affecting vital economic questions. But while argument can be made for an easier method of constitutional amendment, those who favor constitutional change by the present process of amendment will hardly be shaken from their position by being told that the amendments they propose will not be readily adopted.

Conclusion

The New Deal cases emphasize the position of supremacy which the Supreme Court occupies in the American constitutional system. Chief Justice Hughes is doubtless bored by the constant repetition of his epigram "We are under a Constitution, but the Constitution is what the judges say it is." It is a practical man's appraisal of the realities of the constitutional system under which we live. This judicial supremacy has arisen in part from the very nature of the judicial process of interpreting and applying the law, and it has been increased by the vagueness and generality of the constitutional clauses which have to be construed.

If we are satisfied with the present system and its results we will naturally have no proposals to make. If we feel that the constitutional wreckage left by the New Deal decisions is due to the abuse of judicial power rather than to the inadequacy of the Constitution to modern needs, then we may logically demand some limitation on the power of the Supreme Court. We shall in this case need to be cautious to see that we do not create more problems than we solve. We may, however, feel that our present difficulties are due partly to an over-zealous extension of judicial power and partly to the failure of an 18th century Constitution to meet adequately the demands of the 20th century. In this case we may attempt to solve both problems by clarifying amendments to the Constitution. This will not only modernize the Constitution, but it will also narrow the field of judicial review by sharpening the vague clauses of the Constitution under which the Supreme Court is now engaged, almost of necessity, in the work of national policy determination.

This plan might well be tried before anything is "done to" the Court, since it promises not only an immediate adjustment of the Constitution to the current of our present national life, but also a forced retirement of the Court from the fields of constitutional construction in which it faces the greatest difficulty and incurs the sharpest criticism.

Further Resources

BOOKS

Les Benedict, Michael. *The Blessings of Liberty: A Concise History of the Constitution of the United States.* Lexington, Mass.: Heath, 1996.

Steiner, H. Arthur, ed. *Significant Supreme Court Decisions, 1934–1937.* New York: Wiley, 1937.

Letter of Resignation from the Daughters of the American Revolution. February 26, 1939

Letter

By: Eleanor Roosevelt

Date: February 25, 1939

Source: Roosevelt, Eleanor. Letter of resignation from the Daughters of the American Revolution. February 26, 1939. American Originals Collection. National Archives and Records Administration. Reprinted online at http://www.archives.gov/exhibit_hall/american_originals/eleanor.html; website home page: http://www.archives.gov (accessed February 7, 2003).

About the Author: Eleanor Roosevelt (1884–1962), the wife of President Franklin D. Roosevelt (served 1931–1945), had been involved in the settlement house movement of the Progressive Era and became a strong advocate for social justice in the interests of women, children, African Americans, and working people during the Roosevelt administration. In addition to having her own staff to manage, she spoke publicly on reform issues that were important to her. As one observer in Washington stated, she was "a cabinet member without portfolio" in the White House. ■

Introduction

When the Daughters of the American Revolution (DAR), a patriotic organization of descendents of the founding citizens of the United States, prohibited world-famous African American singer Marian Anderson from performing at Constitution Hall in Washington, D.C., First Lady Eleanor Roosevelt responded by resigning from the organization. In a stern letter, Roosevelt criticized the DAR for having "failed" to "lead in an enlightened way" on the issue.

In 1932 the DAR had implemented a rule that barred African American artists from performing at Constitution Hall after the organization received complaints about "mixed" seating (blacks and whites seated together) at concerts of African American artists.

The controversy triggered broad public condemnation of the DAR. Supreme Court justices, state, Senate, and House leaders, and major religious and labor organizations issued statements that condemned the racial discrimination. Following the First Lady's controversial stand against racial segregation in a public space at the nation's capital, the federal government invited Anderson to sing on the steps of the Lincoln Memorial on Easter Sunday. On April 9, 1939, an interracial crowd of seventy-five thousand people attended the free recital. Anderson reflected on that day in her autobiography: "All I knew then was the overwhelming impact of the vast multitude . . . I had a feeling that a great wave of good will poured out from these people." Although such moments where the color barrier had broken down remained infrequent in the coming decades, racial integration was increasingly becoming a national issue of concern to many Americans.

Significance

With controversies such as Eleanor Roosevelt's resignation from the DAR surfacing, signs had cropped up of an emerging modern civil rights movement in the early twentieth century. Cracks had begun to appear in the public's silence about repression and racial segregation across the country. Through legal and informal actions, civil rights workers were slowly chipping away at the color line that separated whites from African Americans and that relegated people of color to the status of second-class citizens.

Organizations such as the National Association for the Advancement of Colored People (NAACP) had been pushing the federal government to include more African Americans in leadership positions. Compared to unresponsive administrations in the past, having Eleanor Roosevelt as an advocate in the White House provided an opportunity to achieve progress on a national level. During the Great Depression, civil rights workers had made some strides in racial integration. Several civil rights leaders were appointed to government positions with the expanded programs of the New Deal.

However, critics rightly pointed out that widespread racial discrimination prohibited the vast majority of unemployed African Americans from benefiting from the array of New Deal social programs. Gradually, the federal government was forced to recognize the problem of widespread racism that created institutions that produced an inferior education, a lack of job opportunities, and denial of basic civil rights to the vast majority of African Americans. The government incrementally and haphazardly took steps to promote equal rights. For example, President Harry S. Truman (served 1945–1952) signed an executive order to integrate the armed forces. But discriminatory institutions allowed the continued treatment of people of color as second-class citizens until the civil rights movement of the 1950s and 1960s dismantled the system of white supremacy.

February 26, 1939.

My dear Mrs. Henry M. Robert: Jr.

I am afraid that I have never been a very useful member of the Daughters of the American Revolution, so I know it will make very little difference to you whether I resign, or whether I continue to be a member of your organization.

However, I am in complete disagreement with the attitude taken in refusing Constitution Hall to a great artist. You have set an example which seems to me unfortunate, and I feel obliged to send in to you my resignation. You had an opportunity to lead in an enlightened way and it seems to me that your organization has failed.

I realize that many people will not agree with me, but feeling as I do this seems to me the only proper procedure to follow.

Very sincerely yours,

Primary Source

Letter of Resignation from the Daughters of the American Revolution. February 26, 1939

SYNOPSIS: In this letter First Lady Eleanor Roosevelt took a public stand to resign as a member from the Daughters of the American Revolution because the organization refused to allow Marian Anderson, an African American singer, to perform at Constitution Hall. After a public outcry, the federal government invited Anderson to sing at the Lincoln Memorial on Easter Sunday in 1939. [Editor's note: Signature not present on original.] COURTESY OF THE FDR LIBRARY.

Marian Anderson, holding a bouquet of flowers, and her mother, Mrs. Anna D. Anderson, following Marian's concert at the Lincoln Memorial on April 9, 1939. © BETTMANN/CORBIS. REPRODUCED BY PERMISSION.

Further Resources

BOOKS

Broadwater, Andrea. *Marian Anderson: Singer and Humanitarian.* Berkeley Heights, N.J.: Enslow, 2000.

Kearney, James. *Anna Eleanor Roosevelt: The Evolution of a Reformer.* Boston: Houghton Mifflin, 1968.

Keiler, Allan. *Marian Anderson: A Singer's Journey.* New York: Scribner, 2000.

"Angelo Herndon Comes Back from Georgia"

Essay

By: Theodore Poston

Date: c. 1939

Source: Poston, Theodore. "Angelo Herndon Comes Back from Georgia." *American Life Histories: Manuscripts from the Federal Writers' Project, 1936–1940.* American Memory digital primary source collection, Library of Congress. Available online at http://memory.loc.gov (accessed March 3, 2003).

About the Author: Theodore Roosevelt Augustus Major Poston (1906–1974) was born in Hopkinsville, KY. He worked various odd jobs until landing his first writing job as a reporter for the New York daily *Amsterdam News* in 1929, where he was the first black to work full time at a white-owned daily. He became city editor of the paper in 1934, but was fired for organizing a strike in 1936. He then worked as a writer for the Works Progress Administration until being hired as a reporter for the *New York Post,* a job he held until his retirement in 1972. ■

Introduction

In June 1932, nineteen-year-old African American Angelo Herndon, a self-professed Communist, was arrested in Atlanta, Georgia, for violating an insurrection law, sparking a wave of publicity around the world. Herndon was arrested for leading an interracial demonstration for the unemployed at the Fulton County Courthouse. The insurrection law had originally been used to avert slave uprisings before the Civil War (1861–1865). Facing the blatant racism of the judge, Herndon was found guilty of incitement to insurrection and received the draconian sentence of eighteen to twenty years on a chain gang. Much like the Scottsboro boys in Alabama (nine young blacks accused of allegedly raping two white girls), Herndon through his plight helped publicize the injustices of the white supremacist system in the South.

For the next five years Communists built a broad-based coalition of progressives, African Americans, liberals, and organized labor to fight for Herndon's freedom. Thousands of important people who signed on in support helped to give the case international publicity. Legal defense committees raised public awareness by holding public forums, raising defense funds, signing petitions, and issuing proclamations in support of Herndon.

The persistent public pressure produced results. Initially, Herndon faced a setback when in May 1935, the U.S. Supreme Court dismissed the case upon appeal. However, in 1937 the Supreme Court took a liberal turn when the swing votes, Chief Justice Charles Evans Hughes and Owen Roberts, joined Louis Brandeis, Benjamin Cardoza, and Harlan Fiske Stone and agreed to

Civil rights activist and Communist Angelo Herndon. His imprisonment and eventual release by the U.S. Supreme Court drew attention to the pervasive racism of the South. © BETTMANN/CORBIS. REPRODUCED BY PERMISSION.

hear the appeal. On April 26, 1937, the Supreme Court, in *Herndon v. Lowry* (301 U.S. 242), ruled that Herndon's Fourteenth Amendment rights had been violated.

Significance

Poston's essay was submitted as part of the Federal Writers' Project (FWP), a work relief program that was started under President Franklin D. Roosevelt's New Deal, a recovery program established during the Great Depression (1929–1939). The president had funded massive work relief programs across the country in the hopes of jump-starting the economy by pumping money into the system. One of the agencies established in 1935 was the Works Progress Administration (WPA), which provided an average of over two million federal jobs to unemployed workers through 1941. The agency constructed or refurbished public buildings and built roads, airports, and bridges. The WPA also offered assistance to unemployed writers in the FWP by giving them a chance to work in their field of expertise while receiving a government salary. The writers collected volumes of invaluable historical and cultural materials by documenting the day-to-day experiences of ordinary people around the country. For example, they interviewed migrant workers in California, as well as former slaves in the South. Their invaluable work produced volumes of folklore, songs, and cultural artifacts that are preserved in the country's archives.

The narratives highlight the day-to-day lives of working people and the hardships they faced during the economic crisis. Herndon's interview documented the brutality and repression that African Americans faced in the segregated South, where separation of blacks and whites was enforced. Herndon also shares his individual experience in a state prison in Georgia. The southern penal system was notorious for its brutality and harsh conditions. Subjected to grueling manual labor for long hours, exposed to the elements, and made to sleep in makeshift, squalid cages (like circus animals), convict laborers suffered high mortality rates. Herndon claimed he experienced harsh treatment in prison because of his civil rights activism. His experience in the Georgia prison system showed the conscious attempt of southern authorities to dissuade African Americans from fighting for equal rights by imposing laws originally crafted to control the enslaved population before the Civil War.

Primary Source

"Angelo Herndon Comes Back from Georgia"

SYNOPSIS: The interview recounted in Poston's essay was conducted by a reporter from the *Amsterdam News,* an African American newspaper based in Harlem, New York, in one of the nation's largest African American communities. The newspaper had been an integral part of the flourishing artistic and intellectual life of the Harlem Renaissance during the 1920s. Theodore Poston submitted this essay to the Folklore Project of the Federal Writers' Project, a WPA program. It highlights the brutality that prisoners suffered, as well as the intense repression African American radicals and civil rights workers suffered under southern white supremacy.

New York
1938–9

References:
Personal Interview (August 7, 1934)
Memory refreshed from Amsterdam News files

He was tired. Very tired and very sick. His sagging muscles, pallid face, drooping shoulders and nervous fingers proclaimed it. And as the train headed for Pennsylvania Station where 6,000 people waited impatiently to hail him, Angelo Herndon turned wearily to the reporter who had met him at Manhattan Transfer.

"Oh, the Amsterdam News? I remember it. It was one of the five papers which came to me regularly at Fulton Tower prison, but which they never let me read. The Daily Worker, Amsterdam News, New York Times, Atlanta World and Wall Street Journal." He smiled slowly. "No, they wouldn't let me read even the Wall Street Journal. They poured ink on it."

"How was prison?" the reporter asked. "How did they treat you?"

"It was hell," he answered simply and shrugged his thin shoulders. After a pause he continued:

"They tortured me. Oh, they tried to be clever about it. They insisted they were giving me 'special attention,' but they did things to me under that pretense. They cooked up that lie that I tried to escape. They searched my cell twice for steel saws. They found some rusty bits of tin which had been in there for years, and used this as an excuse to move me into a damp cell where water dripped from the ceiling.

"I pointed to the water and told them I was sick. (He looks tubercular) They said: 'We don't give a damn if you drown.' and left me there. Later they put me in the death cell. They put special guards near my door. They taunted me."

"Didn't they give you regular treatment?" the reporter asked. "There was a letter in the Nation from a young white woman who said she visited you and found you were treated all right. She said you looked fine."

"Regular treatment?" he smiled again, wearily, fleetingly. "They took my medicine away from me."

He looked down at his thin bloodless fingers. "Do I look fine?"

"I remember that young woman. They let her in to see me. I wasn't allowed any other visitors, except my lawyers. I think she was fine. She was a Socialist though. (Herndon is a Communist) As she was leaving she said: 'We are so far apart.'"

Was there a demonstration when he left Fulton Tower prison? What did the other prisoners and guards say? Were they surprised?

"The authorities were dumbfounded. They never expected that we could raise the money. That's why they made the bail $15,000. The boys were surprised too. They were glad to see me go. They wished me good luck. The turnkey said: 'Hope to see you back soon—for good.'"

"We left quietly. There had been some talk about a lynching. They are conducting a campaign throughout the state against Communists. They didn't bother us though."

"If the United States Supreme Court reverses your conviction," the reporter asked, "and you are freed at a later trial, will you continue to work in the South?"

"Why not?"

"Won't the publicity attendant your case make it impossible for you to continue there? Won't it be too dangerous?"

The wry smile again. "Its dangerous to be a worker anywhere—if you're trying to better your condition."

The train was pulling into Pennsylvania Station. Bob Minor, grizzled Communist leader, was the first to reach Herndon. Awkwardly he threw his arms about the youth's frail shoulders and kissed him. James Ford, Negro candidate for the Vice Presidency of the United States in 1932, was second. He too kissed Herndon clumsily. Ruby Bates, one-time accuser but later chief defense witness in the Scottsboro case, was next. She hugged him and held her cheek to his.

Milton, Angelo's young brother, stood a little to the side. The two boys gazed quietly at each other. Silently they shook hands and embraced. On the upper level, 6,000 persons, mainly white, strained against the police lines and yelled for their hero.

Angelo Herndon had come back from Georgia.

Further Resources

BOOKS

Herndon, Angelo. *Let Me Live.* New York: Random House, 1937.

Kelley, Robin D.G. *Race Rebels: Culture, Politics, and the Black Working Class.* New York: Free Press, 1994.

Lichtenstein, Alex. *Twice the Work of Free Labor: The Political Economy of Convict Labor in the New South.* London: Verso, 1996.

Martin, Charles H. *The Angelo Herndon Case and Southern Justice.* Baton Rouge, La: Louisiana State University Press, 1976.

7

Lifestyles and Social Trends

James N. Craft

Entries are arranged in chronological order by date of primary source. For entries with one primary source, the entry title is the same as the primary source title. Entries with more than one primary source have an overall entry title, followed by the titles of the primary sources.

CHRONOLOGY

PRIMARY SOURCES

Important Events in Lifestyles and Social Trends, 1930–1939

1930

- The number of miles of paved roads in the United States has doubled since 1920, reaching 695,000. Gasoline consumption is at 16 billion gallons per year, up from 2.7 billion gallons in 1919.
- With smoking glamorized by the movies, 124 billion cigarettes are produced in the United States, up from less than 9.7 billion in 1910.
- The United States has 6.3 million farms, and a quarter of its population either lives on farms or grew up on farms.
- For the first time in history, emigration from the United States exceeds immigration.
- On February 10, a major bootlegging operation is shut down in Chicago. The operation has done some fifty million dollars in business while providing over seven million gallons of illegal whiskey to customers across the nation.
- On March 6, General Foods introduces Birdseye Frosted Foods: frozen peas and spinach, three kinds of berries, fish, and various meats. Because the prices of these products are relatively high (thirty-five cents for a package of peas, as opposed to ten to thirteen cents for a pound of dried navy beans) and because they are hidden away in grocers' ice cream freezers, frozen foods are not immediately successful.
- On March 7, commenting on the stock market crash of October 1929, President Herbert Hoover tells the American public: "All evidences indicate that the worst effects of the crash upon unemployment will have passed during the next sixty days." Unemployment has grown from 1.5 million to 3.2 million in the five months since the crash.
- On March 30, nearly one million people take part in "hunger marches" across the country.
- On May 15, the first airline stewardess, Ellen Church, begins work for United Airlines. Her primary task is to ease passengers' fears of flying. The job requirements are female, single, over twenty-one, no taller than 5 feet 4 inches, under 115 pounds, and with a friendly personality.
- On May 24, a poll indicates that two thirds of Americans favor the repeal of Prohibition.
- In August, King Kullen Grocery, the nation's first modern supermarket, opens in Queens, New York.
- On August 7, President Hoover tells governors from the drought-stricken Midwest to establish local and state committees to handle the problem.
- In September, the immigration of foreign workers to the United States is banned.
- In October, with unemployment at 4.5 million, President Hoover appoints a Committee for Unemployment Relief.
- On December 11, the Bank of the United States in New York, with sixty branches and 400,000 depositors, collapses. It is one of more than 1,300 banks to close in 1930.
- On December 20, Congress responds to President Hoover's request for funding for public works construction by authorizing a $116 million public works loan. It also authorizes $45 million in drought loans for farmers in the Midwest and South.

1931

- To generate income by attracting visitors from other states, Nevada legalizes gambling and institutes a six-week residency period for divorces (far shorter than elsewhere in the nation).
- Sales of glass jars increase dramatically while sales of canned goods decline—indicating that people are saving money by preserving food at home.
- Schick Dry Shaver, Inc., begins marketing the first electric shaver, selling three thousand at twenty-five dollars apiece in 1931 and more than ten thousand in 1932. Other new products introduced to consumers during this year include Hostess Twinkies, Alka-Selzer, Beech-Nut baby food, and Breck shampoo.
- Hundreds of unemployed workers in New England dig clams and sell them door to door for twenty-five cents a peck.
- In January, President Hoover insists, "No one is going hungry and no one need go hungry or cold."
- The New England Telephone and Telegraph Company lays off all of its married women workers.
- In February, a group of 6,024 Americans of Mexican origin leave Los Angeles for Mexico on the Southern Pacific Railroad at a cost of $77,247 to the city of Los Angeles. These *repatriados* are the first of some 400,000 to repatriate voluntarily or be deported forcibly to Mexico under a program initiated by the U.S. Department of Labor.
- On March 3, Congress designates "The Star Spangled Banner" the national anthem.
- On May 1, the Empire State Building, the world's tallest building at the time, opens in New York City. Government officials hail the structure as a symbol of confidence in the economy.
- On October 7, President Hoover acts to shore up the nation's banks, some eight hundred of which have failed to date.
- In November, Hattie T. Caraway is the first woman to be elected to the U.S. Senate.

1932

- New products available to Americans this year include Skippy peanut butter, Frito corn chips, Zippo lighters, and Johnson Glo-Coat floor wax.
- Wheat prices reach a new low of thirty-two cents a bushel. This contrasts with the 1920 price of $2.33 a bushel.

- In January, some 18,000 unemployed men from the Pittsburgh area march on Washington, D.C., to plead for relief for the nation's growing number of poor.
- On March 12, six thousand dissidents march in Detroit, while the band plays the Communist anthem, "The Internationale."
- On May 29, the first of World War I veterans known as the "Bonus Army" arrive in Washington, D.C., to demand early payment of a bonus for their wartime service that is not due until 1945. They set up camp in the city, and over the next month their number grows to seventeen thousand.
- On June 18, *The New York Times* reports that eleven thousand hungry Chicago children are depending on their teachers for food. The teachers' help is made more difficult by the fact that the board of education has failed to pay them.
- In July, home foreclosures reach twenty-five thousand per month. Most public aid has fallen below five dollars a week. St. Louis has cut its relief roles in half. Dallas is denying aid to African Americans and Hispanics.
- On July 28, General Douglas MacArthur, acting under orders from President Hoover, uses infantry, cavalry, and tanks to drive the "Bonus Army" from Washington, D.C. MacArthur's aide, Major Dwight D. Eisenhower, criticizes the attack on the veterans.
- In August, dairy farmers in the Midwest go on strike.
- On October 13, a Colorado theater owner introduces "Bank Night." These drawings for cash prizes are designed to increase attendance in his movie houses. The idea catches on and rapidly spreads across the country.
- In November, the Iowa Farmers' Union stages a thirty-day strike, urging supporters to "Stay at Home! Buy Nothing! Sell Nothing!" They hope to force the federal government to institute a farm program to stabilize prices and provide mortgage relief.
- On November 8, Franklin D. Roosevelt is elected to his first term as president of the United States with 22,800,000 popular votes to 15,750,000 for Herbert Hoover.
- In December, unemployment reaches thirteen million. Nearly one in four workers is without a job. Wages for those who have employment are down an average of 60 percent from 1929 levels.

1933

- One survey estimates that illness is 40 percent higher among the jobless.
- Hoping to raise prices by cutting supply, farmers kill six million young pigs and plow under thousands of acres of cotton.
- New products this year include Sanka, Ritz crackers, Campbell's chicken noodle and cream of mushroom soups, and Windex.
- The marriage rate is down 40 percent from the 1920s level. However, average life expectancy has risen to 59 years, ten more than in 1900.
- On March 7, New York Life Insurance Company refuses to allow the people it insures to borrow any more money against their policies.
- On March 9, Congress passes the Emergency Banking Act. Within three days, more than a thousand banks reopen across the nation.
- In May and June, the first New Deal legislation passes: the Federal Emergency Relief Administration (FERA) is created to give direct relief to the unemployed; the Public Works Administration (PWA) is established, utilizing private contractors for dams and bridges; the Civil Works Administration (CWA) authorizes employment for civic purposes, such as parks, roads, and schools. The National Industrial Recovery Act sets up National Recovery Administration (NRA) to regulate prices and wages. The Farm Credit Act makes low-interest loans available to farmers.
- On May 27, the Century of Progress World's Fair opens on the south side of Chicago.
- On August 17, Secretary of Labor Frances Perkins, the first female Cabinet member in American history, reports that a million jobless workers have found employment since March. Unemployment is now at October 1931 levels, In addition, farm prices are up 60 percent and industrial production has nearly doubled since March.
- In September, some two thousand schools fail to reopen. More than two hundred thousand teachers are unemployed. It is estimated that nearly three million children are not attending school.
- On November 30, Eleanor Roosevelt convenes the White House Conference on the Emergency Needs of Women, "to pay attention that women are employed wherever possible."
- On December 5, the prohibition of the sale of alcoholic beverages, in effect since 1920, is repealed. Six southern states, as well as Kansas and North Dakota, remain dry.

1934

- Food shopping patterns shift, as Americans buy more red meats, fruits, green vegetables, and dairy products.
- Coca-Cola sales drop with the repeal of Prohibition.
- Americans hope the Depression may be ending. Some four million more workers have found jobs, and the purchasing power of industrial workers is up 25 percent.
- Only 58 banks fail during the year, compared to the recent annual average of 901.
- On March 13, automaker Henry Ford shows his faith in the economy by raising the minimum wage in his factories to $5 a day.
- On April 28, President Roosevelt signs the Home Owners Loan Act to augment the Home Owners Refinancing Act of 1933. The two laws are intended to revive the home building industry.
- On May 10 and 11, dust storms expand the "Dust Bowl" to Arkansas, Kansas, Colorado, Oklahoma, and Texas. Eventually, some 300 million tons of topsoil will blow away in the Plains states.
- On June 12, the Farm Mortgage Foreclosure Act provides aid for farmers who are threatened with loss of their farms because they can't pay their loans.
- On June 28, the Federal Housing Administration (FHA) is created to provide federal loans to people who want to buy

homes or improve their current houses. The Federal Farm Bankruptcy Act puts a freeze on farm foreclosures.

- On July 5, police clash with striking San Francisco waterfront workers, fatally shooting two workers.
- On July 16, some twelve thousand West Coast longshoremen and seamen strike.
- On September 3, sixty-five thousand textile workers strike in North Carolina.
- In October, the Federal Surplus Relief Corporation, the Commodity Credit Corporation, and the Jones-Connally Farm Relief Act pass, responding to the farm crisis and expanding government's role in farming.
- On October 2, the American Federation of Labor calls for the length of the work week to be reduced to five days. However, the general lack of work has already made the five-day week widespread throughout the nation.

1935

- One out of four households is on relief; 750,000 farms have been foreclosed since 1930.
- Thousands of migrants from Oklahoma, Texas, and Missouri move to the West Coast.
- Bingo begins in movie houses and becomes popular with charities.
- The ten-cent chain letter fad begins. Denver postal employees work at night to sort thousands of letters.
- Twenty million Monopoly sets are sold in one week.
- The first canned beer is introduced by Krueger Beer of Newton, New Jersey. Eastman Kodak introduces Kodachrome for sixteen-millimeter movie cameras. The first hearing aid is introduced.
- Large numbers of Americans are learning to dance the rhumba.
- On April 8, the Emergency Relief Appropriation Act is signed, establishing the Works Progress Administration to create relief jobs in public works. This development marks the start of the "Second New Deal."
- On May 11, President Roosevelt creates the Rural Electrification Association to provide inexpensive power for rural America. Just 10 percent of the nation's farms have electricity, but estimates are that the REA will add another 30 percent by 1941.
- On June 10, in New York, former alcoholic Bill Wilson and drinking companion Dr. Robert H. Smith found Alcoholics Anonymous.
- On July 5, Roosevelt signs the National Labor Relations Act, known as the Wagner Act, boosting organized labor.
- On August 14, Roosevelt signs the Social Security Act of 1935, a historic turning point in government responsibility for the welfare of its citizens.
- On October 26, corn and hog farmers in sixteen states vote by a margin of six-to-one to continue voluntary production quotas in order to raise farm prices.
- On November 22, Pan Am's flying boat, the *China Clipper,* leaves Alameda, California, for the Philippines, inaugurating transpacific commercial air and mail service.
- On December 3, the nation's first public housing project opens on New York's Lower East Side.
- On December 5, the National Council of Negro Women, founded by Mary McLeod Bethune, begins advocating civil rights.
- On December 21, American Airlines unveils the DC-3, the first reliable passenger plane for non-stop transcontinental travel. With a soundproofed and heated cabin, the plane can carry twenty-one seated passengers (or fourteen in overnight sleeper berths) in relative luxury. With a cruising speed of 160 mph, travel time is fifteen hours.

1936

- A U.S. Circuit Court of Appeals judge rules that shipping contraceptives by mail does not violate anti-obscenity Comstock Laws.
- Dust storms denude vast farmlands of Kansas, Oklahoma, Colorado, Nebraska, and the Dakotas. A Colorado farm survey shows that half of the six thousand farmhouses in one region are abandoned.
- The nation's unemployment rate is almost 17 percent, down from a high of nearly 25 percent during the winter of 1932–1933.
- A *Fortune* magazine poll reports that 67 percent of the respondents favor birth control.
- Herbert LeRoy Hechler runs a flea circus on New York City's Forty-second Street. For thirty cents viewers can watch trained fleas juggle, dance, walk a tightrope, and operate a carousel.
- Although movies enjoy their best year since the Depression started, 80 percent of the year's films lose money. Even the introduction of Technicolor does not bring people back to theaters in large numbers.
- Products introduced this year include the fluorescent light tube, Tampax, and Vitamin Plus, the first vitamin pill.
- Seven million women pay more than two billion dollars for thirty-five million hair permanents.
- A sleeper berth from Newark to Los Angeles costs $150; the Fifth Avenue double-decker-bus fare goes up from five cents to ten cents.
- The WPA Federal Art Project provides work for more than five thousand artists in forty-four states. They produce more than six hundred murals for government buildings, as well as countless oil and watercolor paintings. The Federal Music Project employs some eighteen thousand musicians and sponsors thousands of free concerts in communities across the nation.
- In May, the streamline train passenger *Super Chief* sets a new time record for train service from Chicago to Los Angeles: 39.75 hours.
- In November, the annual auto show in New York City is held two months early in an effort to ease seasonal unemployment in the auto industry. For the first time, automakers begin emphasizing style changes to stimulate sales.
- On December 8, the case of *Gibbs v. Board of Education* of Montgomery Country, Maryland, is filed. The eventual de-

cision sets a precedent for equalizing the salaries of black and white teachers.

- On December 11, press and public alike thrill to British king Edward VIII's announcement that he is renouncing the throne in order to marry an American divorcée, Wallis Warfield Simpson.

1937

- The George A. Hormel company introduces the canned meat Spam. Other products available to consumers for the first time include ALCOA aluminum foil and Aqua Velva aftershave.
- The introduction of the shopping cart—a shopper's basket on wheels—encourages consumers to buy more items when they go to the store.
- A *Fortune* poll reports that 50 percent of college men and 25 percent of college women have had premarital sex. In addition, two-thirds of the women say that they would engage in premarital sex for "true love."
- A Gallup poll shows that 80 percent of respondents approve of relief through paid work rather than a dole.
- One study reports that people spend an average of 4.5 hours a day listening to the radio.
- Thousands of Americans join the Abraham Lincoln Battalion to fight with the Loyalists against Francisco Franco's fascist forces in the Spanish Civil War. Among the writers who go to Spain are John Dos Passos, Ernest Hemingway, Malcolm Cowley, and Upton Sinclair.
- On January 1, an average of twenty-five travel trailers an hour are counted crossing the state line into Florida. The age of the auto camper is in full swing. By the end of the year, some 160,000 trailers will be on the nation's highways.
- On January 11, General Motors shuts off the heat at its Fisher Body Plant No. 2 in Flint, Michigan, in an effort to force the striking workers out of the factory. Previous attempts to prevent food from reaching the "sit-down" strikers have failed. This effort fails, too. On February 3, the company accepts the workers' union and agrees to sign a contract with it. The following month, U.S. Steel comes to terms with the steelworkers' union. Both developments are major triumphs for organized labor.
- On March 15, the first state contraceptive clinic opens in Raleigh, North Carolina.
- On March 26, the Supreme Court in the case of *West Coast Hotel v. Parrish* upholds a minimum wage law for women.
- On May 6, the dirigible *Hindenburg,* the world's largest airship, explodes and burns in less than a minute in Lakehurst, New Jersey, while docking after a transatlantic flight. Thirty-five of the ninety-seven people on board are killed. The disaster marks the virtual end of commercial lighter-than-air transport.
- On May 27, the Golden Gate Bridge is officially opened across San Francisco Bay.
- In June, the number of workers who had participated in sit-down strikes across the country since the previous September rises to 484,711.
- On July 22, Congress establishes the Farm Security Administration to make four-year loans at 3 percent interest to aid sharecroppers, tenant farmers, and farm laborers in buying their own land.
- On August 2, President Roosevelt signs the Marijuana Traffic Act, outlawing the sale and possession of the drug.
- On September 1, Congress creates the U.S. Housing Authority (USHA) to remedy the nation's housing shortage.

1938

- A Gallup poll indicates that 65 percent of Americans approve of the Munich Pact, by which Britain and France gave in to Hitler's demands in hope of avoiding war in Europe.
- More than a million fans go to professional football games, and some 10 million attend major league baseball. However, movie attendance is down about 40 percent.
- DuPont's new toothbrush makes the first commercial use of nylon. Other new products introduced during the year include Teflon and Fiberglas. Americans are also able to copy documents on a Xerox machine for the first time.
- In March, in a new economic crisis, known as the "Roosevelt Recession," unemployment rises to nearly 20 percent of the labor force.
- On April 12, the first state law requiring marriage license applicants to take a blood test is passed in New York. It is intended to prevent the spread of syphilis. The law follows a similar one passed in March requiring the same test for all pregnant women.
- On May 26, Texas congressman Martin Dies is given congressional approval for his Special Committee to Investigate Un-American Activities, with "Un-American" principally meaning communist.
- On June 24, Congress passes a law that requires disclosure of the ingredients of food, drugs, and cosmetics on their labels.
- On June 25, Congress passes the Fair Labor Standards Act. The law raises the federal minimum wage from 25 cents to 40 cents an hour. It also sets the length of the work week at 44 hours, to be reduced to 40 hours in three years time. Work by children under age 16 is outlawed.
- In July, at a conference of twenty-seven European and Latin American countries on the question of Jewish emigration, Roosevelt says that the United States will not raise its immigration quotas to the victims of Hitler's Nazi regime.
- On September 21, a hurricane devastates Long Island and southern New England, killing 680, leaving 63,000 homeless, and causing four hundred million dollars in damage.
- On December 12, in the NAACP-supported case *Missouri ex re Gaines v. Canada,* the U.S. Supreme Court declares that states must provide equal, even if separate, educational facilities for blacks within their boundaries.
- On December 13, the Works Progress Administration reports that the number of Americans receiving federal relief has fallen from 3.2 million in 1937 to 2.1 million.

1939

- Packard introduces the first air-conditioned automobile.
- Unemployment continues to hover around 17 percent of the workforce.
- A Gallup poll indicates that 58 percent of Americans believe the United States eventually will be drawn into World War II.
- Current fads include Chinese Checkers, knock-knock jokes, and dancing the chicken scratch, the chestnut tree, and the boomps-a-daisy. Among college students, swallowing live goldfish is popular. The individual record is 210.
- On February 22, a rally of the pro-Nazi Bund organization at Madison Square Garden in New York is disrupted when Jewish activist Isadore Greenbaum attempts to pummel Bund founder Fritz Kuhn.
- On February 27, the Supreme Court declares sit-down strikes unconstitutional. However, increasingly hostile public opinion has already prompted labor unions to largely abandon their use.
- On April 9, African American contralto opera singer Marian Anderson performs to an audience of seventy-five thousand at the Lincoln Memorial. When the Daughters of the American Revolution refused to give permission for Anderson to perform in Constitution Hall, Eleanor Roosevelt resigned from the group in protest. Secretary of the Interior Harold Ickes invited Anderson to perform at the Lincoln Memorial in Washington, D.C., on Easter Sunday in an event cosponsored by Mrs. Roosevelt.
- On April 30, the New York World Fair opens as war clouds continue to gather. Germany is not among the sixty nations with exhibits.
- On May 16, Rochester, New York, begins a program to distribute the nation's surplus food to the needy. Within two years, this "food-stamp" plan spreads to 150 other cities.
- On June 28, Pan American Airways launches the first passenger air service between the United States and Europe. Flying time from New York to Lisbon, Portugal, is 24 hours.
- On July 17, the proposed Brooklyn-Battery Bridge over the East River is rejected by the War Department, which fears it could pose a hazard to Navy ships in the event of war.
- On October 25, the first nylon stockings go on sale in the United States.
- On November 23, by presidential proclamation Thanksgiving Day is celebrated on the fourth Thursday in the month rather than on the last, in order to lengthen the Christmas shopping season.

Statement of Mrs. Margaret Sanger

Statement

By: Margaret Sanger

Date: May 1932

Source: Statement of Mrs. Margaret Sanger, National Chairman, Committee on the Federal Legislation for Birth Control. *Birth Control: Hearings Before a Subcommittee of the Committee on the Judiciary, United States Senate, 72nd Congress, 1st Session on S. 4436.* Washington, D.C.: Government Printing Office, 1932, 6–12.

About the Author: Margaret Higgins Sanger (1879–1966) argued for family planning education for all. As a nurse and one of eleven children (her mother had eighteen pregnancies and died at the age of fifty), Sanger saw firsthand how poor mothers were affected by having numerous children. Sanger established the first birth control clinic in 1916, which evolved into the Planned Parenthood Federation of America. ■

Introduction

Various forms of birth control, including abortion, have been practiced since ancient times. While it is difficult to generalize, until the mid-nineteenth century, birth control was usually regarded as a personal issue. As stricter moral codes evolved in nineteenth century America, legislation at all levels of government began to restrict birth control and even the dissemination of information on the subject.

A particularly energetic moral reformer, Anthony Comstock led a post-Civil War crusade to stamp out obscenity. His efforts led to "Comstock" laws in various states and the passage of a federal Comstock law in 1873 that outlawed the shipping of obscene material through the U.S. mail. This category included birth control material and contraceptives.

The growth of cities in the late nineteenth century was accompanied by the growth of slums. Packed into squalid living conditions, desperately poor women often had numerous children. Ignorant of birth control methods, many women either continued to have unwanted children or sought the services of back-alley abortionists with often devastating results.

Streetwise medical practitioners and social workers saw the relationship between uncontrolled family size and the unending cycle of poverty and began to support birth control. Margaret Sanger was one of these professionals who determined to take action. Among Sanger's objectives was the education of women and giving them the ability to employ birth control methods under the care of a physician. Given the restrictive nature of the various Comstock laws, these actions were usually illegal. As a result, Sanger fought for many years to repeal this legislation at the state and federal level.

Significance

Throughout the 1920s and early 1930s, Sanger led the effort to repeal the restrictive Comstock Law and to permit the importation of birth control material and its distribution through the mail. Sanger's basic argument was that children and mothers were far more susceptible to physical and mental illness as a result of living in squalid conditions brought on in part by the large numbers of children. In addition, the "handicapped" children became less productive members of society and tended to repeat the mistakes of their parents, thus increasing an already vast social problem.

Sanger's appeals to the U.S. Congress failed, and the 1873 Comstock Law and restrictive clauses of the 1930 tariff legislation remained in force. It was not until 1936 that the U.S. Court of Appeals ruled that the law did not apply to physicians exercising medical responsibilities. The case was the outgrowth of the seizure by the U.S. Customs of contraceptive material being imported from Japan. On Sanger's initiative, the seizure was challenged with the resulting favorable decision. The practical effect was to give doctors the right to prescribe and distribute contraceptives. It was a major victory for Sanger and the birth control movement.

Primary Source

Statement of Mrs. Margaret Sanger [excerpt]

SYNOPSIS: Beginning in the early 1920s, Margaret Sanger attempted to convince lawmakers to amend the Comstock Law of 1873. Although amendments passed in the House on several occasions, they never passed in the Senate. In May 1932 Sanger testified before the Senate Judiciary Committee in support of a proposed amendment to the 1873 Comstock Law and the 1930 Smoot-Hawley Tariff. These amendments would have ended the bans on the importation and shipping of birth control material via the U.S. mail.

Mrs. Sanger: Mr. Chairman and gentlemen of the committee, this bill, S. 4436, directly affects the health, the future development and the

Margaret Sanger testifies before a Senate subcommittee in 1932, arguing unsuccessfully that the federal ban on selling birth control materials should be lifted. Despite this setback she continued her efforts, leading to a favorable Supreme Court decision in 1936. **AP/WIDE WORLD PHOTOS. REPRODUCED BY PERMISSION.**

happiness of 25,000,000 married women of child-bearing age in this country.

It further affects indirectly the health, happiness, and future welfare of 45,000,000 children in this country, of which 10,000,000 are said to be handicapped, according to the reports of 1,400 experts who came to this city at the call of President Hoover at the White House conference about a year ago. . . .

Now, Mr. Chairman, you might say how does this bill affect these handicapped children. It directly affects the handicapped children because as some of our experts here to-day will show the mothers of these handicapped children are needed for the care of these children.

Furthermore, according to these reports, it is stated that a large percentage of these children were handicapped from causes due to ignorance, poverty, and neglect.

Even the most optimistic of us will not claim that we are going to do away with poverty, ignorance, and neglect in the next few years, and yet these 1,400 experts did not emphasize that the parents of these 10,000,000 children should have the knowledge and means and instruction to prevent the coming of 10,000,000 more children, who may be handicapped from the same causes of poverty, ignorance, and neglect.

To me it is just a simple piece of common sense that people who can not take care of children to-day, because they are ignorant, or because they are too poor, or because they neglect them, certainly should not be encouraged to have more children.

In my own experience, both as the mother of three children, and as a trained nurse for many years in New York City, I came in contact with all kinds of people, representing the poor of all races, all creeds, and all religions.

I found that there are a certain number of people, perhaps we can say 20 per cent of our population to-day, who in spite of these laws have availed themselves of some kind of knowledge by which they have controlled the size of their families. Of the other 80 per cent, I found that about half are struggling to find something to control the size of their families, while the other half are those generally classed as unfit, mentally and physically, and include morons and mental defectives who usually come upon our social vista as permanent unemployables and dependents. It is for this other 40 per cent you might say, or half of the 80 per cent, that we are talking about today. It is these people that this bill will directly affect.

Mr. Chairman, you asked Senator Hatfield a few questions that I wonder if I may cover. These parents, if they can afford to go to a private physician, if they have a family doctor, may get some kind of information as to the means of controlling the size of their families. It may not be the best advice, but nevertheless it is something, and it has enabled a certain percentage of our population to control the size of their families. It is better than nothing, but the majority of women, those who are too poor to have a family physician, have to go to the hospitals and public institutions. They have to go to the dispensaries and to public wards to get their medical care and it is right here that this law operates. While a physician may in his private office do and say as he wishes; he may give some device and no one can ask him where he gets it; as soon as he is connected with an institution the situation is entirely changed. In the first place the hospital would have to order and pay for any contraceptive supplies which he might prescribe. In the second place he would be accountable to the laws of the country for his action in that institution, and he can not thus jeopardize his own license nor the charter of the institution which operate legally under the State laws.

There is where this law operates, because the law, section 211, definitely forbids the transportation of articles or of information through the United States mails or common carriers. Unless every hospital has a manufacturing plant associated with it, or in the city where it is located, you will see that they must get their articles either from New York or Chicago or some large city where the articles are manufactured.

The tariff act, section 305, affects such articles coming in from other countries.

Many physicians do not know that there is a great deal of research going on in this particular field in England, in Oxford, and Cambridge, also the University of Edinburgh, Scotland. A great deal is being accomplished there because they are unhampered by restrictive laws and are free to do research, while we in this country are years behind in medical research in this particular field. . . .

May I say again that the Federal law, section 211, makes no exception for physicians. It makes no exception for hospitals to get such supplies. It makes no exception for anyone. Any one convicted under this law is subjected to five years in prison and $5,000 fine.

In this country the laws of 47 States allow a physician to give contraceptive information in his practice. Some of them are limited.

In New York State he can only give information "for the cure or prevention of disease." In New Jersey he can give it "for a just cause." In 24 States the subject of contraception is not mentioned in their laws at all.

Senator Hastings: This law does not help there, does it?

Mrs. Sanger: It does by allowing them to transport the articles through the mails, also common carriers.

Senator Hastings: Yes; but of course these State laws remain in effect.

Mrs. Sanger: Absolutely; but there is only one State in the Union where the giving of advice would be doubtful, and that is Mississippi. All the other States give a physician the right to give such information in his private practice provided he can get the things from the manufacturer. That is what our amendment provides for.

When this law was passed in 1873 there was very little known concerning the whole subject; certainly there was no real information concerning the medical and sociological importance of the practice of contraception. The subject of birth control or contraception was wrongly classed with indecency, obscenity, and abortion. The passage of this law in 1873 really closed the avenues of proper scientific information and research by the medical profession, medical schools, and medical universities in this country.

It has done untold harm to classify contraception in that category. It is an insult to every decent married woman in the country who wants to bring up her family intelligently: it prevents her from applying the benefits of science to the cultivation of her children and the bringing up of her family; and, furthermore, to all intents and purposes it classifies every married woman in this country as a "child-bearing conscript." Unless a woman has some means of preventing conception and spacing her children, she is forced to bear children like an animal, and in fact animals are not allowed to breed in sickness and with diseased bodies as the women of this country are made to do to-day, as I will show you a little later on.

This bill is simple; it is conservative; it is constructive, because it simply allows the physician at a hospital, or licensed clinic, to receive such supplies and to give such information.

The passage of this bill would be the first attempt on the part of the Congress to place the responsibility of giving contraceptive instruction in the hands of the medical profession, where it rightly belongs.

It would be the first attempt on the part of Congress to give the medical profession the control of such knowledge, which we know is very promiscuously scattered about to-day. It would let physicians regulate the kind of devices used, and thus wipe out the present traffic in wrong and harmful devices. The poor mothers, the people who should have the information, are uninformed and are denied the proper kind of devices suitable to their own individual requirements.

Senator Hastings: If you do not mind me interrupting you—

Mrs. Sanger: No.

Senator Hastings: It occurs to me paragraph numbered 3 might be a little uncertain "by any druggist in his legitimate prescription business."

What is intended by that?

Mrs. Sanger: That the physician would prescribe certain devices, tested by research and experience in our clinics. The druggist should be able to supply these devices. We have found that contraceptives, to be properly safe and harmless, should be prescribed according to the individual requirements, just as eyeglasses must be individually fitted by oculists.

Senator Hastings: What I was interested in was whether it was intended that a person might apply to the druggist without going to the physician at all.

Mrs. Sanger: No. According to that I would understand that a person must have a physician's prescription.

Senator Hastings: I am anxious to find out what is your intent.

Mrs. Sanger: That is our intent, that it should be by prescription.

Senator Hastings: By prescription only?

Mrs. Sanger: Yes.

I do not wish to go into great detail concerning different methods and devices for contraception. However, there are certain articles, which are commonly used as contraceptives, but which may also be used for the cure and prevention of disease. These articles, according to a recent court decision may be legally transmitted through the United States mails. However, there are certain other articles which are used only for the prevention of conception, which are now excluded from the mails. These articles must be prescribed by a physician, and only after a thorough physical examination, so that the prescription varies with the individual. It is like any other medical advice, highly individual and adapted to the particular requirements of the patient. It is to such articles that we refer, and it is for these that the law must be changed.

Senator Hastings: There would be no objection to changing that to read "by any druggist upon a written prescription of a licensed physician"?

Mrs. Sanger: There would be no objection whatever.

Senator Hastings: I wanted to get your thought, so that after all what you are seeking here is all limited to physicians or medical colleges, which are really controlled by physicians.

Mrs. Sanger: Yes; they are already controlled by physicians. In many States the medical colleges are free to instruct their young graduates and physicians in this particular art, as they are instructed in other departments, but this has not generally been done up to the present time. There are comparatively few medical colleges that include a course in contraception in their regular curriculum.

I want to say in passing that where the laws allow a physician within the State to give information, some clinics have been established.

Some of the social agencies and some of the forward-looking physicians are to-day struggling to solve their immediate problems, not only health problems, but social problems as well. The problem of unemployment, the whole question of congestion, is coming before them as never before. Birth control helps to solve some of these problems, but even where clinics are already in operation, it is difficult to obtain either the best information or supplies, under the present law. The proposed amendment would release the physician and make this information available, also, in public institutions such as clinics and hospitals.

Mr. Chairman, if I may digress for a moment, I want to go into an even broader aspect of the question.

Birth control is not a new idea. It is as old as nature itself. In fact, even in the period of savagery there was some means, some knowledge, of controlling the numbers in the tribes. It is only the methods that have changed.

Instead of infanticide and killing off the old and sick as has been done at various stages in the development of civilization, the only means of controlling the size of her family which is left to woman is abortion.

The number of abortions in this country is colossal, and we are convinced that only through a proper knowledge of contraception shall we do away with this abortion practice, one which is extremely detrimental to the health and happiness of women.

Let us now consider the two groups of people, those who practice birth control and those that do not. If you will look into every community, and every city and every town, you will see on the one hand small groups who have controlled the size of their families and on the other hand you will see a larger group who have not been able to avail themselves of any information whatever. In the first group, we have the educated, cultured, well-to-do citizens; professors, doctors, lawyers, ministers, scientists, artisans, and skilled laborers. Here we find the spacing of children an adopted rule, the mother's health being the first consideration and the earning power of the father a close second. From this group come almost all of our social movements. Civilization is directly benefited and advanced through this low birth rate group. In the other large family group we have overcrowding, illiteracy, ignorance, slums, infant and maternal mortality, and child labor. Almost all our social problems are entrenched in this group and these conditions and their problems are perpetuated from generation to generation.

I, myself, have found that the mothers in both groups are equally desirous of bringing into the world only the number of children they can properly care for. I find that even women of the very lowest grade of intelligence are willing to avail themselves of information to prevent conception at any cost and at any trouble to themselves. I have, during the past several years, received over a million letters, the great majority of these letters coming from mothers and from women, especially in this second group. I should like to read a few of these letters which are rather typical of the conditions that prevail throughout the country—conditions that the passage of this bill would help:

Twenty-nine years old, mother of nine children: "I am a Catholic 29 years old. I was married at 17 years of age and the first baby was born after 9 months 1 day. I have now been married 12 years have had 9 children, 6 are living and 3 are dead. I have had children every year since 1925. My husband is out of work now, so you see how hard it is to keep going and to pay one's debts and expenses for hospitals and doctors."

Seventeen children at 35: "I am 35 and the mother of 17 children, the last one not yet 2 months old, and I am in great hopes you can help me some way. Our net income during the winter has been $28 a month and out of that we have had to pay all our groceries, fuel, and clothes.

"I had the fond hope of becoming a teacher, but all I could do was six grades in the public school, then out to work, fitted for nothing, so all I could do was housework at $1 a week. So I married hoping to resume my studies at night school, but almost at once there was a pregnancy. Is it necessary to have my children grow up with no more hope or vision for their future than I've had? So many babies, never a time between them; why, one year I had one baby in January and twins the next December.

"I am pleading with you to help me some way."

Seven children at 30: "Will you please tell me about birth control? Our doctor refuses to tell us. I am 30 years old and have been married 11 years. My oldest child is 10 years old and I have 7 children and expect another baby next month. I had my last baby born dead last October. She was crippled and deformed. We are poor people trying to get along at $90 a month. Please help me."

Thirty-four years old; 12 pregnancies: "I am only 34 years old and have given birth to 12 children, only 3 of them living. They die so quickly after they are born, it seems they don't have strength to live long. My husband is a good, hard-working man, but the best he ever made was $1.50, and never for long. We're poor people, Mrs. Sanger, and the coffins of the last two are not paid for yet; it's hard on a woman to see them go like that and I think if I did not have any for a while I could keep the three I've got and give them better than we ever had. Please help me. I'll be watching the postman, waiting for your answer. Please don't fail me."

Eight years in pregnancy for three children. Cruelty beyond belief! Nine little coffins. The United States Government would help her rear and breed pigs, cows, chickens, but makes laws to deprive mothers of knowledge to perfect and develop the human race.

A 75 per cent loss; sordid; a business man would shut up his shop. We are paying to-day for these laws of nearly 60 years ago. We are paying for them by the multiplication of the unfit, the diseased, the feeble-minded. We are paying for them in our high maternal mortality, in the hordes of death-doomed infants who never see their first birthday, in the widespread practice of abortions, in child labor, in the waste of mother power and creative energy. We are paying the cost in increasing billions and piling up huge debts for unborn generations to pay.

Further Resources

BOOKS

Chesler, Ellen. *Woman of Valor: Margaret Sanger and the Birth Control Movement in America.* New York: Simon & Schuster, 1992.

Kennedy, David M. *Birth Control in America: The Career of Margaret Sanger.* New Haven, Conn.: Yale University Press, 1970.

WEBSITES

London, Kathleen. "The History of Birth Control." Yale–New Haven Teachers Institute. Available online at http://www.yale.edu/ynhti/curriculum/units/1982/6/82.06.03.x.html; website home page: http://www.yale.edu (accessed August 8, 2002).

"Margaret Sanger." Planned Parenthood Federation of America, Inc. Available online at http://www.plannedparenthood.org/about/thisispp/sanger.html; website home page: http://www.plannedparenthood.org (accessed August 8, 2002).

"The Margaret Sanger Papers Project." Available online at http://www.nyu.edu/projects/sanger/index.html; website home page: http://www.nyu.edu (accessed August 8, 2002).

Statement of Miss Helen Hall, University Settlement, Philadelphia, Pa.

Statement

By: Helen Hall

Date: January 1933

Source: Statement of Miss Helen Hall, University Settlement, Philadelphia, Pa. *Federal Aid for Unemployment Relief: Hearings Before a Subcommittee of the Committee on Manufactures, United States Senate, 72nd Congress, 2d Session, on S. 5125* Washington, D.C.: Government Printing Office, 1933, 380–385.

About the Author: The prominent social worker Helen Hall was director of the University Settlement in Philadelphia at the time of the testimony reported below. In 1933 she became the director of the Henry Street Settlement on Manhattan's Lower East Side. Hall became president of the National Federation of Settlements and was a member of the Advisory Council at the Conference on Economic Security. This committee produced the draft that resulted in the Social Security Act of 1935. ■

Introduction

By 1932 an estimated one-third of the workforce was unemployed. Many of those who still had jobs were working reduced hours. American farmers were being pushed to their limits by record low prices for their products and high debts. The numbers were staggering, but worse was the human misery that accompanied the economic slump.

Never before had the United States witnessed such widespread hardship. For those who did not personally experience the helplessness of unemployment, poverty, or eviction, most knew friends, neighbors, or relatives who did. Or they saw it.

The unemployed wandered the streets and slept in parks, vacant lots, and in hobo jungles. Shantytowns, derisively called Hoovervilles, appeared all across the country.

> The police, with apologies and good feelings on both sides, arrested for vagrancy twenty-five inhabitants of Hoover Valley, the shantytown that sprang up in the bed of the old lower reservoir of Central Park . . . Police and Park Department officials say none of them are hoboes. They repair in the morning to comfort stations to shave and make themselves as clean as they can.
>
> *The New York Times,* September 22, 1932

Stories of people in desperate straits were commonplace.

> Constable Simon Glaser found a young couple starving. Three days without food, the wife, who

is twenty-three, was hardly able to walk. The couple . . . invested all they had, except 25 cents for food, in bus fare to this region in search of work. Finding none, they went into the cottage, preferring to starve rather than beg. They said they had "resigned themselves to dying together."

The New York Times, December 25, 1931

Reported in newspapers and magazines and the subject of innumerable studies by private welfare and charity organizations as well as government commissions, poverty, hunger, and hopelessness seemed to pervade the United States. This knowledge made many conservative Americans far more inclined to accept changes that a few years or even months earlier they would have considered radical.

Most business and political leaders, however, clung to the conservative view that the economy would correct itself and that outside meddling would only make matters worse.

Significance

While Hoover did more to address an economic slump than any previous president, his were half-measures done halfheartedly. By 1932 the nation clamored for more action. A handful of midwestern progressives and urban liberals attempted to push through Congress more aggressive relief and public works programs than Hoover would accept. They had limited success, but their efforts led to a series of legislative hearings before a subcommittee of the Senate Committee on Manufactures, cochaired by two of these midwestern progressives: Senators Robert La Follette, Jr. (R-Wis.) and Edward P. Costigan (D-Colo.).

The La Follette–Costigan Committee took testimony from social workers, economists, educators, and other professionals confronting Depression conditions on a number of pieces of relief legislation. These reports included graphic anecdotal stories describing the plight of the unemployed and how the existing relief systems were nearing collapse.

In late 1932, in response to the inadequacy of Hoover's Reconstruction Finance Corporation's loan policy to either stimulate the economy or address relief needs, Senator Robert Wagner (D-N.Y.) resurrected earlier relief proposals. These incorporated direct aid to states for relief purposes and federally funded public works programs. It was in consideration of this proposal that Helen Hall, whose partial testimony appears below, went before the La Follette–Costigan Committee in early 1933.

By this time, however, Franklin Roosevelt had been elected president. He would not be sworn in until March 4. During this lame-duck period of Hoover's administration, very little was accomplished as Congress waited on direction from the incoming Roosevelt. Once he took office, a flurry of activity dramatically expanded the relief legislation then in process, and Congress scrambled to keep pace with the aggressive programs of the First Hundred Days of Roosevelt's administration.

Men in Cleveland wait in a long line to receive potatoes through government relief. **AP/WIDE WORLD PHOTOS. REPRODUCED BY PERMISSION.**

Primary Source

Statement of Miss Helen Hall, University Settlement, Philadelphia, Pa. [excerpt]

SYNOPSIS: Helen Hall came before the La Follette-Costigan Committee in part because of her recent study of the British welfare system and in part as a result of her role as the director of Philadelphia's University Settlement. The portion of her testimony printed below includes anecdotal stories that reveal the condition of her clients. One of her themes was that these people were not idle poor. They were the very people who fit Hoover's notion of the "rugged individual," stranded for reasons beyond their control.

Miss Hall: I testified three years ago, giving some of our committee's earlier material, but since then we have made a study of the effect of the depression on our neighborhood families during these last three years, and I will be glad to give you some of that material.

The Chairman: We will be very glad to have that.

Miss Hall: The stories come from all over the country, Senator, because the study is a national one, and I can just give you glimpses here and there of how our relief methods have borne down on the individuals. Necessarily there are only a few excerpts, but they come from a background of hundreds of studies that the National Federation of Settlements has made, and a great many of the families I myself have interviewed.

The Chairman: Would you say that they were fair examples?

Miss Hall: I would say they are very fair examples.

The Chairman: They are fair examples of the 3,000,000 families, let us say, that are now on relief in the United States?

Miss Hall: Yes; I should say they were very fair examples, as our material comes from all over the United States. They are neighbors of the settlement people and people that we have known over a long period of time, people whom we have known when they were working and getting along well, and we have seen at close hand what has happened to them since the depression. . . .

A year ago the statistics of the Children's Bureau pointed to the fact that the weights of miners' children were very low. Upon learning this an appropriation was made for West Virginia, Kentucky and Pennsylvania from funds which, I understand, were left from flood relief and amounted to $300,000. This was given to the Red Cross to distribute through grocery orders, and the American Friends' service committee was asked to work with the children, putting milk into the schools and sending it to babies.

The men and women told me about this, numbers of them, and on one particular occasion I remember they described how they had been helped when the groceries came and when the milk came, and one of the women said, "The children fattened like little pigs all over the county when they got that pint of milk. It's wonderful how a child perks up when it gets enough to eat."

"Then," they said, "In the spring the groceries stopped and the Quakers went home, and there wasn't any more milk for the babies." They said it was not so bad for the people who had gardens, because they could perhaps get along, but it was bad for the babies.

I turned to one of the women and said, "Just exactly what did you do; how did you manage?" And one of them said, "Honey, it seems like it would be easy to say, but I don't know as you would understand our ways."

And I said, "Well, I would like really to know how you have managed"; and one of them said, "Well, tell her how we manage," and the other one said, "Well, I will tell you; there was lots of times when there was just gravy soup"; and I said, "What is gravy soup?" And she said, "Well, you puts flour in a pan and browns it and stirs water into it."

I said. "Do you feed babies on gravy soup?" The babies looked as though they had been fed on gravy soup. And one woman said, "No, honey; not when I could help it. A neighbor up Pidgeon Creek way had a cow, and whenever she had any milk left over she sent me down half a pint. That was sometimes every other day, and sometimes once a week, but it was mighty helpful."

I said, "Is that what you are feeding the baby now?" And she said, "No; we are feeding it bean soup from beans in the garden."

The milk had stopped coming. The money from the flood relief had been exhausted in the spring, and at the time I was there in October I understood that the counties were negotiating with the Reconstruction Finance Corporation for loans. But the babies waited for their milk from May until November.

I could not but feel that it would have been cheaper for us, in the end, to have given the children milk during that period, particularly when I looked at the babies and saw them sick and undernourished.

The Chairman: Did they give outward evidences of malnutrition and undernourishment?

Miss Hall: Yes; they most certainly did.

I should like to give just a few excerpts, Mr. Chairman, from the neighborhood reports, just as they have come to me, as a part of our settlement study. I think it is just as easy, probably, as telling the story. The first is from Detroit, but I am not using it as an example because I consider it necessarily more tragic than hundreds of others but merely because its cost to the State is perhaps more obvious than some, where the future costs may be greater but are more difficult to evaluate. The report, just as it came to me, starts with the family situation in May, 1929. The family consisted of a man 42 years old, a woman 42 years old, and six children ranging from 4 to 19 years. Man a hard-working, unassuming type. Very fond of his wife and children. Family lives in a frame building which they own and which they have divided into three apartments. They receive $27 a month for the rent of the two apartments. The man was employed at Ford Motor Co., averaging $32.75 a week in wages. John, the oldest boy, was employed at the General Box Factory, earning $20 a week.

June, 1929, one month later: Man put on part-time work three days a week, earnings averaged $16 a week.

December, 1929, six months later: John laid off at box factory.

November, 1930, 11 months later: Tenants not paying rent. Mother gets job as janitress.

May, 1931, six months later: John went to work for farmer for room and board. Mother develops varicose veins in legs from being on feet so much.

June, 1931, one month later: Man laid off altogether. Comes to settlement office asking for card referring him to other factories. Worried over wife's health.

October, 1931, four months later: Department of public welfare refused family relief, but offered to get tenant for one of their apartments and pay rent. Department of public welfare paid $12 rent for one month.

December 18, 1931, two months later: Man applied to department of public welfare because no rent was paid on apartment after first month. Was told by worker that under new ruling no rents were being paid to landlords where city taxes were overdue. Man came home very desperate and despondent. Christmas was very near and he hoped to buy necessities for children. Children being fed at fire house.

December 19, 1931, next day: Son, Stanley, aged 7, went to wood-shed for some wood to build fire in house and found his father had hanged himself.

December 22, 1931, three days later: Insurance policies not kept up, so man buried by department of public welfare.

December 23, 1931, next day: Woman came to office asking for help. She is destitute and not able to work. Since husband's death appears very broken down. Veins in legs worse.

December 24, 1931, next day: $3 emergency relief from department of public welfare.

December 24, 1931: Christmas basket delivered to family.

January 5, 1932, 12 days later: $3 emergency relief from department of public welfare. New Year's basket delivered to family. Woman appears very nervous and broken hearted. Cries whenever man is mentioned and seems bewildered. Advised woman to apply for mother's pension.

December 12, 1932, 11 months later: Family living on widow's pension when I visited them. . . .

In arguments against Federal aid for the unemployed, the words "local responsibility" appear often and have a convincing ring. Unfortunately, the words are used with more earnestness in combating Federal aid than in facing just how adequately the community itself is meeting that local responsibility.

Surely, no city which does not consider rent as a definite part of its local relief program, can fairly claim that its relief needs are being met. We can well question the right that a community has to say that it is taking care of its own, when what it means by care is little more than payment of a grocery order. We may be sure that those who have lived under the fear of the constable and the sheriff for these past years have no such conviction.

There is a game of eluding the landlord which is being played all over the United States today. Unemployed wage earners and their families are forced to play it, social agencies and emergency relief funds are playing it, and municipalities are playing it. It brings not only suffering and hardship in its wake, but great demoralization.

I want to give just a few instances of the kind of thing that happens in our system of nonpayment of rents. These few tell the story of so many, many others.

The Reiters, a family of seven, were getting grocery orders from the unemployment relief fund in Philadelphia, and were evicted from their home in December.

The Chairman: Of what year?

Miss Hall: This was last year.

The Chairman: 1931?

Miss Hall: 1931; yes. A neighbor took them in and for two months the father, mother, and five children, the oldest of whom is a girl of 13, lived in one room. The mother was expecting a baby at the time of eviction.

The Careys were evicted just before Christmas and relatives offered them one room. For over two months the mother, father, and four children slept in one bed until another bed was given them which they were scarcely able to squeeze into the room.

Mrs. Green, who lives just around the corner from University House in Philadelphia, left her five small children alone one morning while she went to get her grocery order filled. While she was away the constable arrived and padlocked her house with the children inside. When she came back she heard the 6-weeks old baby crying. She did not dare touch the padlock for fear of being arrested, but she found a window open and climbed in and nursed the baby and then climbed out. The mother was a schoolteacher before her marriage.

Another neighbor of mine, Mrs. Fleer, had a husband who was dying of tuberculosis. When she lost her job they had no means of support and were given food from unemployment relief funds. But weekly the rent collector found his way back into the alley in which she lived. She had been told that her husband had only a short time to live, and she wanted to keep it peaceful for him until he died. She had never been back in her rent before and both she and her husband were panic-stricken when she could not keep the collector quiet.

The Lazars live in Cleveland. They were determined to give their children a good schooling and be independent in their old age. In spite of the fact that Mr. Lazar had worked all his life at unskilled labor, they saved enough to buy a 2-family house which they remodeled to accommodate four families, and later bought a 2-family house next door. Besides this they had a $1,000 in the bank when Mr. Lazar lost his work. Soon after he lost his own work his tenants lost theirs and stopped paying their rent. Some of them were getting relief in grocery orders, but at that time it was not the policy in Cleveland to pay rents except upon eviction. No rent was paid Mr. Lazar. After his savings were gone he borrowed on his property until the borrowing power was exhausted. The two oldest girls left school to save carfare and shoes. The youngest children were refused milk in school because their family owned property.

We sometimes feel that property owners, who have done all of the things we have wanted them to do, who have saved and bought homes, are almost worse off than renters. I want to tell you now of a family in Chicago. This story illustrates the confusion that individuals feel in our complicated set-up and our haphazard methods of relief. There were, last year, 1932, 3,611 evictions in Chicago, in spite of the fact that it has been their policy to pay rent upon notice of eviction. The Ricardos have four young children. John is 31 and his wife, Rose, is 24. Would you like to have me give you this whole story?

The Chairman: Yes; we would like to have it. But if you see any objection, I do not see any reason why you should give their names.

Miss Hall: I do not give any of their real names. The families know their records are taken; that names are not to be used. We always use a name of the same nationality as the family, but never the same name.

Rose is a good housekeeper and their home has always been neat and attractive in spite of four young children. In 1930 the father was earning $34 a week as a chauffeur on a truck for a cartage company for whom he had worked 11 years. Their furniture was all paid for, and, as they described it, they were "getting along fine."

The father was discharged in May, 1930. In four months their savings were exhausted and their relatives began to help them. In November they were served with an eviction notice. They went to court, but their relatives gave them enough for the two months' back rent, and continued to help them until the first of that year when they began to be pressed themselves and felt they could help no longer. The Settlement House to which they came gave the man some made work which covered their rent, coal, milk, some groceries, and electricity from January until spring. In addition to this the county supplied staples amounting to $6.75 a month.

It has been complicated in Chicago because, until recently, the county supplied the staples and the private relief agencies, which were subsidized by public funds, issued grocery orders and gave other forms of relief. So the families were confused by the fact that there were two agencies working with them, and it was difficult for them to know exactly where they stood or to whom to turn.

In May, 1931, when there was still no sign of work and the settlement funds were exhausted the family applied to the United Charities. At this time, from May to November, of 1931, the United Charities were paying rent, so that the family's rent was taken care of and the county's staples were supplemented with a grocery order and coal. In November the policy of paying rents was discontinued and by January, 1932, the landlord was pressing them hard for rent again. John Ricardo said at this time "A fellow doesn't know what to do with hisself. There is no use looking for work any longer. I still ask my friends, but all they do is to give you sad news—more lay-offs. I just sit around and help around the house, then about 6 I go out. I hang on the corner or I walk downtown, just to see something different. It just chills you when you hear the talk about the funds giving out. They don't want a fellow to steal, but what would anyone do if they didn't get it for their children?"

Further Resources

BOOKS

Bremer, William W. *Depression Winters: New York Social Workers and the New Deal.* Philadelphia: Temple University Press, 1984.

Shannon, David A. *The Great Depression.* Englewood Cliffs, N.J.: Prentice-Hall, Inc., 1960.

Watkins, T.H. *The Hungry Years: A Narrative History of the Great Depression in America.* New York: Henry Holt, 1999.

"Will the New Deal Be a Square Deal for the Negro?"

Journal article

By: Jesse O. Thomas

Date: October 1933

Source: Thomas, Jesse O. "Will the New Deal Be a Square Deal for the Negro?" *Opportunity, Journal of Negro Life* 11, no. 10, October, 1933, 308. Available online at http://newdeal.feri.org/opp/opp33308.htm; website home page: http://newdeal.feri.org (accessed August 29, 2002).

About the Author: Jesse O. Thomas (1883–1972) was an educator and social worker who helped create and administer educational, health management, and job-related programs aimed at improving the quality of life for African Americans. A graduate of Tuskegee Institute, Thomas spent most of his career with the Urban League and later the American Red Cross. He also served in a variety of special roles including as a member of the Mississippi Flood Relief Committee in 1928 and as the prime mover in establishing the School of Social Work at the University of Atlanta. ■

Introduction

The second-class status of African Americans in U.S. society is well documented. Excluded from the fruits of American democracy by law and personal prejudice, African Americans were especially vulnerable during economic recessions. The Great Depression was, of course, no exception.

Although New Deal programs offered great opportunity to blacks, their implementation was often in the hands of local administrators who were not always in agreement with the color-blind spirit of federal legislation. In addition, the New Deal was primarily aimed at rejuvenating the economy. This goal did not always work to the equal benefit of all members of society. The National Industrial Recovery Act (NIRA) was an example of a program that was potentially harmful to African Americans.

In the early years of the Roosevelt administration, the primary engine of recovery was the NIRA. Managed by the National Recovery Administration (NRA), the NIRA was intended to create a more planned economy that would ensure higher employment, stable wages, and reasonable profits. The basic approach was for business and labor to establish, under government auspices, codes that would set production quotas, wage rates, working conditions and hours, minimum prices, etc.

Hundreds of codes were developed. Different local conditions and the fluidity of the economy, however, made creating codes that were effective for the entire country a difficult, if not impossible, task. Naturally protective of what they perceived to be their own advantage,

African American and white WPA workers work together on a project in New York City. Although New Deal relief programs provided work for African Americans, they were often segregated. © JOSEPH SCHWARTZ COLLECTION. CORBIS. REPRODUCED BY PERMISSION.

various interest groups struggled to achieve acceptable compromises.

One consistent problem related to wage rates. The differences between wage rates in the urbanized North and the more rural South were significant. Southerners often felt a lower wage scale was the only way they could remain competitive. They used this device, in particular, to justify discriminatory wage rates that disproportionately affected African Americans.

Another argument was based in the dual problems of antipathy toward blacks and the belief that they were less productive than whites. If business owners were forced to pay equal wages to blacks and whites, so the reasoning went, they would hire whites. It was only by giving blacks lower wages that white business owners would tolerate black employees and could afford to employ them given the perceived difference in productivity. It was, therefore, in the interest of blacks to allow discriminatory wages to continue, since that way they could at least work.

Whatever the objectives of the NRA, black leaders were caught in an apparent dilemma. While disgusted with discriminatory wages, they were equally aware that, especially in a depressed economy, lower wages did help blacks compete for jobs.

Significance

A number of the NRA codes did include de facto discriminatory wage clauses that affected blacks. In the end, however, the NRA failed to achieve its objective of sustained economic growth. It also ran afoul of the Constitution and was declared unconstitutional by the Supreme Court in 1935. The more fundamental question of equitable treatment of blacks by New Deal programs remained.

Generally, those programs that were directly administered by the federal government were less discriminatory than those run locally. Early New Deal programs, such as the Federal Emergency Relief Administration (FERA), were funded by the federal government but managed locally with little federal oversight. As might be expected, the local prejudices prevailed, and black participation, particularly in the South, was sometimes limited. More successful was the Works Progress Administration (WPA), a federally managed program that included African Americans at rates at least proportionate to their numbers in society.

In the end, New Deal programs, such as the Civilian Conservation Corps (CCC), WPA, and National Youth Administration (NYA), provided substantial relief and training for blacks. While these programs were not without significant flaws, they were positive steps in combating discrimination in the United States.

Harold Ickes on Discrimination in CCC Camps

September 26, 1935

The Secretary of the Interior
Washington

My dear Mr. Fechner:

I have your letter of September 24 in which you express doubt as to the advisability of appointing Negro supervisory personnel in Negro CCC camps. For my part, I am quite certain that Negroes can function in supervisory capacities just as efficiently as can white men and I do not think that they should be discriminated against merely on account of their color. I can see no menace to the program that you are so efficiently carrying out in giving just and proper recognition to members of the Negro race.

Sincerely yours,
Harold Ickes
Secretary of the Interior

SOURCE: Ickes, Harold L. Letter to Robert Fechner, September 20, 1935. "CCC Negro Foremen" file, Box 70O, General Correspondence of the Directory, Record Group 35, National Archives, College Park, Maryland. Available online at http://newdeal.feri.org/texts/825.htm; website home page: http://newdeal.feri.org (accessed March 21, 2003).

Primary Source

"Will the New Deal Be a Square Deal for the Negro?"

SYNOPSIS: *Opportunity, Journal of Negro Life* was the publication of the National Urban League. The Urban League was established in 1911 and by the 1920s had spread to most large cities in the country. The initial purpose of the League was to help blacks arriving in northern industrial cities from the rural South. Although it avoided direct involvement in political affairs, the Urban League was and continues to be a leading representative of black economic and social interests. The following article from this publication presents the fundamental concerns African Americans had with regard to the NRA and, more generally, the application of New Deal legislation.

Through the various channels of the recovery program propelled by the New Deal as a mobilizing slogan, American industry, both agricultural and manufacturing, is being revolutionized. President Roosevelt, the author of the New Deal, is attempting to lift the nation out of this widespread and prolonged depression, which has been so devastating to our social and economic life for the past three years, by reducing unemployment and increasing the buying power of wage earners.

In support of this campaign, there has been set in motion, governmental machinery, whose principle function is to reduce hours per working day, to establish a minimum wage above the starvation level; and at the same time, to increase the price of commodities utilized to meet normal human needs. Codes have been and are still being worked out to cover different types of industries in different population centers. But the universal acceptance of the blanket code is made difficult by the twelve million Negroes in our population.

The perplexing question to the employing class in all parts of America is, "Can the National Recovery Act operate in such a manner as to prevent the Negro from sharing equally with other wage earners?" It is the most important element in the whole recovery set-up to the captains of industry in the South. It has caused a sharp division in the alignment of the white world in this area. Many white people in the South are dogmatically opposed to Negroes participating on equality with white people in any beneficial measures; and they insist that in the administration of relief and in the application of the minimum wage scale there must be an exception to the general rule when it comes to Negroes. Spokesmen for this school of thought insist that the NRA can only be made a success by making exceptions wherever it is applied to the status of Negroes.

There is still another group who insists that this is the opportunity for the South to be lifted above the starvation level by paying the minimum wage as provided by the several codes to all employees regardless of race. They further prophesy that the NRA will be a failure to the extent that it attempts to establish a differential wage based on race.

Expressing the sentiment of the former, the Thomasville (Georgia) *Times-Enterprise* on Monday, July 31, spoke editorially as follows:

> The various groups in Thomasville have all met, elected their chairman and gone to work studying to see how far they can go in meeting the full requirements. It is safe to say that no store in town with delivery or porter service will sign an agreement to pay that boy fourteen dollars per week. If he does the messenger will be some white boy who will do the work satisfactorily.
>
> In that event we will have all white jobs and the Negroes out of work except in domestic circles. Many of them are unskilled and can not earn enough to produce the wage even at greatly exalted prices. A delivery boy in a drug store would make fifty trips per week. That is at the rate twenty-five cents per trip, while a Western Union boy will do it for a dime. See where we are, not considering the bicycle furnished and things of that kind?
>
> When the Negroes get the idea that they are all going to be paid fourteen dollars per week, they are being poorly led, misinformed. They cannot hope to get that and any organization to attempt to put that over will meet with a form of resistance that will prove very very unfortunate to many of them. The house servants are not affected for they get a certain amount of subsistence that counts heavily in their living expenses. It is to be hoped that this question will be soon settled and that no drastic steps will be necessary. Business must be operated ably to win. The government cannot afford to penalize any business in a way that will bring on bankruptcy and that is just what many fear, for they cannot come up to that scale where they hire a hundred or more Negroes and keep going for even a month unless they have great financial reserves. The modifications in that regard are being studied. The labor differential in the South is all that keeps us in competition.

In an editorial appearing in the Atlanta Constitution, under date of August 24th, we find the following in support of the position taken by the Thomasville *Times-Enterprise:*

> Undoubtedly, the lack of wage differentials, based on the difference in living costs between whites and Negroes, would result in a wide increase in Negro unemployment. This is so clearly true that the recovery administration has already evidenced its realization of the situation, as indicated in the laundry code recently agreed upon.
>
> When the president's agreement for reemployment was submitted, wages for all manual labor were fixed at $13.50 a week minimum. When the laundry code was submitted by the laundries, the wages for female colored help were fixed at 14 cents per hour for a 45-hour week, which was an increase of 86 per cent. This wage scale was first approved by the NRA, and subsequently revoked, the NRA offering 20 cents minimum, or $9 per week. It was pointed out that the President's agreement of $13.50 per week was prohibitive and would deprive colored women of this class of employment, and that white labor would be substituted.
>
> The danger of the situation was recognized by the NRA administration and a differential in favor of manual labor of this type was allowed.
>
> In view of the cheaper living conditions among the Negroes, they are done no injustice by such differentials. Comparatively they can receive the same improvement in condition by a small wage increase that a larger increase would bring to white labor.
>
> Unless such differentials are granted, the Negro is certain to suffer, because many would lose employment if a common minimum wage for both white and Negro labor was enforced.
>
> That is a condition that the white people of the South do not wish to see and are certain to protest, for after all, the Negroes, as the New York Times comments, have no better friends than the white people among whom they live and who will not willingly see them done an injustice.
>
> The national reconstruction act is sufficiently flexible to permit the warding off of this danger to the Negro manual labor of the country, and the recovery administration will no doubt follow the precedent set in this respect in the laundry code.

The Norfolk *Virginia-Pilot* has the following to say on the same subject:

> To these poor folk the Blue Eagle may be a predatory bird instead of a feathered messenger of happiness.
>
> A Norfolk restaurant, obliged to raise its minimum wage under the code—a wage that had been acceptable to Negro workers—dismissed them and employed Caucasians in their place. This newspaper fears that thousands of Negroes, engaged as porters, janitors, elevator men, messengers, drivers and the like, will be ousted throughout the country by employers who hire Negroes at present because they can get them cheaper.

Speaking for the other side, Mr. W. T. Anderson, editor of the Macon *Telegraph,* writes under date of August 5th, perhaps the strongest editorial that has appeared in any paper in the United States in opposition to the differential wage minimum. This editorial was provoked by a letter written to Mr. Anderson by a subscriber in regard to his advocacy of justice being done to the Negro. We quote a paragraph from the letter to Mr. Anderson because it has a significant bearing on this whole subject:

> Your speeches and editorials on the greater things promised the South in the new deal are fine, and every word is gospel; but when you talk about being fair and generous toward the Negro you are on an unpopular side, and you had better watch out.

The Macon *Telegraph* editorial follows:

> Twenty years ago this newspaper cast about to see if there were not some undeveloped resources, some acres of diamonds, right at our doorsteps that might be utilized to its own advantage and eventually to the advantage of the city and state—and perhaps the South. Analyzing the matter of business done in Macon and Georgia, and comparing it to cities and states of similar population in Northern sections of this country, it was found that we were away below the standard. Sales of all kinds of goods from our stores were away below stores selling similar goods in other sections.
>
> Soliciting advertising for nationally-sold goods, manufacturers pointed out that the Southern country was a poor field for advertising—that results were not comparable with those obtained in other sections of the country. Our population might be fully equal to other sections or cities under comparison—what was the matter?
>
> "Oh, well," the Telegraph man would reply, "you see about 40 per cent of our population is Negro, and these people don't earn enough to enable them to keep up their part of the buying percentage—that's why our average is low. They don't earn enough to enable them to subscribe for papers, or buy books, or buy good clothes, or do any of the things that make other cities good for advertising."
>
> "Oh, I see," said the space-buyer, "you count them in the census, but they have no other value! Well, then, instead of your town being a 50,000 city as you claim, so far as business and advertising are concerned, your 40 per cent Negro population deducted leaves you with only 30,000. And that is too small a town for an advertising campaign. Our advertising is not placed in any cities of less than 50,000. It simply doesn't pay, and you have explained this matter of the Negro population not having money enough to buy goods like other cities of 50,000—that's something we never understood before. Good day."
>
> The *Telegraph* began at that time trying to find a way by which the Negro could be counted in other ways than simply in the census; to make a buyer out of him; to give him a hopeful, orderly, law-abiding outlook on life; to improve his condition by improving his information and efficiency. We counted it as a great achievement if this 40 per cent population could be converted into buying power so as to make Macon rank with industrial towns of 40,000 to 50,000 of the North. It was the only way to help these people up so they might quit pulling white people down. We either had to transform them into population that could make Macon 50,000, or we had to be content with having them hold us down to a city of [3]0,000.
>
> We began publishing a section of the *Telegraph* for Negroes, containing the news they were especially interested in, placing in their hands a newspaper published by white people who knew their value if they were developed in the right attitude and along the right lines. Where 300 Negroes formerly took The *Telegraph,* there developed a list of approximately 5,000. These Negroes pay their subscriptions promptly, there is the least trouble with them from all standpoints, and their records for general character, behavior and observance of law, we believe excel that of any other city in this country.
>
> They have placed Macon in the 50,000 class from a standpoint of subscribers to the two Macon papers. We do not now go to the space-buyer for national advertising and have to explain why we haven't as large a percentage of subscribers to population as other cities.
>
> We want to go on with this thing, not so much for the benefit of the Negro, as we have said a thousand times, but for the benefit of Macon and Georgia. If his earnings are increased, he becomes a buyer of advertised goods, and Macon rates accordingly—and The *Telegraph* prospers accordingly. We are selfish in it. It's good business to uncover these acres of diamonds at our own door-step.
>
> And what the Negro has done for The *Telegraph* and Macon he will do for Georgia—for the merchants and every other interest in this state, if he is given the chance. He had been spending $2,700 per year with The *Telegraph* before he was given any special consideration; after that he increased his business to $45,000 per annum, not to speak of the additional advertising from national accounts that were brought in by the increased subscriptions.
>
> All of the above is set down as a living, actual experience in business, so that other busi-

nesses and people may profit by it in seeing how much constructive effort might affect their own. Our attitude has been largely one of race prejudice, hatred, jealousy. We have felt that we must hold the Negro back in the matter of wages and everything else, otherwise he might get out of his place, become bigoted. And in holding him back we failed to go forward ourselves, or he held us back with him. It has been argued that we are so blinded with our prejudice and jealousy of the Negro that if in some way it was proposed that all of the Southern Whites and Negroes were to be paid $10,000 each without any cost whatsoever to a Southerner, and it were left to a vote of the Southern whites as to the Negroes receiving it, the whites would vote against it, for fear of spoiling the Negroes, or letting them get away from some of their poverty. We would lose sight entirely of the advantage that would accrue to us by reason of this new money. We would deny them and ourselves because "it would ruin them, make them bigoted, they wouldn't work."

It is grand and glorious that so many of the poorly paid white people have been given benefits under the new deal, such as increased wages, shorter hours and better living conditions. That will have its effect upon the entire section. But this other race that is ever with us must be carried along to better things also. They will help us or they will hinder us. It depends upon our decision. What they did to put Macon on the map from a newspaper standpoint, remove her handicaps, they will do for every other business in Macon—if wages are paid them ungrudgingly which will afford some spending money beyond a bare living.

Dr. W. W. Alexander, of the Interracial Commission, spoke thus for the interracially minded white South:

> Employers of labor who are urging a lower wage level for Negroes under the Code of the N. R. A. are offering a dangerous proposal. If put into effect, it would undermine the President's program of economic recovery in the South, and at the same time would cut the economic foundations from under the feet of white working men. Negroes, pressed to accept and even to ask for such a differential, are vigorously and, I think, quite properly objecting. They are unwilling to be put in the role of "scabs," under-cutting the white man's wage and standard of living. There can be no economic recovery for the South that does not include the Negro. The wiser economic leaders will not acquiesce in a plan so obviously unsound.

As a threat of intimidation to its Negro employees, a pencil factory in Atlanta put a pink slip in the pay envelope in all of its more than one hundred Negro employees during the first week of September, which contained, among other things, the following:

> If the "false friends" of the colored people do not stop their propaganda about paying the same wages to colored and white employees this company will be forced to move the factory to a section where the minimum wage will produce the greatest production. Stop your "friends" from talking you out of your job.

The automobile dealers of Florida appeared before the Recovery Commission of that state contending that if they were compelled to pay their Negro filling station attendants more money and work them less hours than competing stations, it would make unfair competition. Their request for exemption from the code paying the minimum wage to Negro labor was granted. The exemption asked by T. R. Williams, of the Florida Service Station, was disapproved. He desired to work a Negro porter 84 hours a week for $7.

In contrast to the above, a number of employers have complied with both the spirit and letter of the law. As a result, many Negroes are beneficiaries of the minimum wage schedule set by the NRA. It is true that many others have lost their jobs on account of the enforcement of the minimum wage scale. We have not gone far enough and there is not enough authentic information available for anyone to state with any degree of scientific authority just to what extent the Negro will benefit or how much he will suffer as a result of the enforcement of these codes.

It must be recognized that the President and his administration have departed from the usual custom of appointing political demagogues as heads of these several important missions. The highest type of men and women the nation can afford, with Northern and Southern background, have been chosen. Mr. A. L. Johnstone, of Newberry, South Carolina, Regional Director of the Relief of the Southeastern Sea Board, is an example of the calibre of men chosen to interpret the policies of the administration as well as charged with the responsibility of their enforcement. Mr. Johnstone is a man of great courage, foresight, wisdom and understanding.

The Federal Government, however, finds itself in a paradoxical situation. It has virtually conceded that it cannot stop lynching, that it is powerless to enforce the provisions of the 11th and 15th Amendments. Beyond a Supreme Court decision, it cannot nullify the almost universal practices of residential segregation, or render ineffective the discriminatory practices of the Democratic primary. Too many of the employers of labor whom the government, through its National Recovery Act and the several codes, is insisting upon paying the minimum wage, are members of school boards and otherwise identified with business corporations and industrial concerns in this area whose policy in dealing with Negroes runs counter to the equalization provision of the minimum wage schedule. In the public schools, Negro teachers receive from 50 to 75 per cent of the salary of the white teachers with the same qualifications and a teacher-load invariably much heavier.

The double economic standard makes itself manifest in the relationship of the Negro wage earners to whites in every department of our economic and political life in this section. This has become such an established and accepted policy that the proposed shift required to meet the provisions of the NRA is little less than revolutionary.

Further Resources

BOOKS

Kirby, John B. *Black Americans in the Roosevelt Era: Liberalism and Race.* Knoxville: University of Tennessee Press, 1980.

Packard, Jerrold M. *American Nightmare: The History of Jim Crow.* New York: St. Martin's Press, 2002.

Wolters, Raymond. *Negroes and the Great Depression: The Problem of Economic Recovery.* Westport, Conn.: Greenwood Publishing, 1970.

Lorena Hickok to Harry L. Hopkins

Letter

By: Lorena Hickok

Date: October 30, 1933

Source: Hickok, Lorena. Letter to Harry L. Hopkins, October 30, 1933. Reprinted in Lowitt, Richard, and Maurine Beasley, eds. *One Third of a Nation: Lorena Hickok Reports on the Great Depression.* Urbana, Ill.: University of Illinois Press, 1981, 55–59.

About the Author: Lorena Hickok (1893–1968) was a reporter and author best known for her coverage of and friendship with Eleanor Roosevelt. The product of a difficult childhood, Hickok became an important political reporter at a time when female reporters were usually confined to the social page. While working for the Associated Press, Hickok began covering Eleanor Roosevelt during the 1932 presidential campaign. They developed a close friendship that lasted until Mrs. Roosevelt's death in 1962. ■

Lorena Hickok, left, with Eleanor Roosevelt in Puerto Rico, 1934. The two were close friends for nearly three decades. © CORBIS. REPRODUCED BY PERMISSION.

Introduction

In 1933, the federal government was small by contemporary standards. Nearly half of all government employees worked for the post office. The data-gathering capacity of the government was largely confined to the census bureau and congressional committees. The number of unemployed, for example, was an estimate. As the Roosevelt administration expanded its role, the absence of reliable information was a serious problem. Without good data, it was very difficult to assess need or evaluate the effectiveness of new programs.

To fill this void, information was gathered, analyzed, and stored at an unprecedented pace. In many cases, the work was done by the various work-relief programs. The Works Progress Administration (WPA), for example, employed out-of-work professionals on numerous studies that would help policymakers. College students employed by the National Youth Administration (NYA) were another resource at the disposal of the administration to perform much needed research and analysis of conditions.

Harry Hopkins, assigned to head the Federal Emergency Relief Administration (FERA) in 1933, recognized that without reliable field reports, he could not hope to understand needs or assess program effectiveness. As

FERA primarily distributed funds to local agencies for the actual administration of relief programs, Hopkins was dependent on organizations over which he had no direct authority to provide information. In Hopkins' mind, this situation was unacceptable.

Lacking the time, resources, or authority to implement more sophisticated programs that could provide him with reliable and consistent information, Hopkins sought outside help. He hired fifteen reporters, including Lorena Hickok, to travel the country and provide firsthand, unbiased feedback on the impact of the Depression on the average citizen and on the effectiveness of the various aid programs. This approach provided Hopkins with a "feel" for what was going on in the country as a supplement to hard data and, in many cases, in the total absence of any other reliable information.

Hopkins' directions to "Hick" were clear: "I don't want statistics from you. I don't want the social worker angle. I want your own reactions, as an ordinary citizen. Go talk with preachers and teachers, businessmen, workers, farmers. Go talk with the unemployed, those who are on relief and those who aren't . . . Tell me what you see and hear. All of it. Don't ever pull your punches."

It was the perfect assignment for a reporter of Hickok's ability, tenacity, and social conscience.

Significance

Between 1933 and 1936, Hickok traveled thousands of miles, visited thirty-two states, and sent hundreds of letters to Hopkins. She talked to embattled miners in the Harlan County coalfields, Dust Bowl migrants in California, "hailed out" farmers in North Dakota and Tennessee, and hill folk on the impact of the Tennessee Valley Authority. Her letters to Hopkins contained some of the most insightful and descriptive observations on Depression conditions that can be found.

One of her duties was to assess the effectiveness of the various relief agencies charged with the distribution of FERA funds. Hopkins was concerned not only with the efficiency of the relief efforts, but also with the impact local politics had in developing and implementing relief policy at the local level. The information Hickok and other reporters provided confirmed Hopkins' belief that these programs would be more effective under federal management. He successfully achieved this control in the creation of the short-lived Civil Works Administration and the more extensive WPA.

Primary Source

Lorena Hickok to Harry L. Hopkins

SYNOPSIS: Hickok's letter of October 30, 1933, found her in Dickinson, North Dakota. It is a depressing letter describing a desperate situation. Like other farmers of the Great Plains, the North Dakota farmers had been beaten down by years of low prices, heavy debt, foreclosures, and drought. In this county, hailstorms had ground their crops to nothing. Expecting to find militant and defiant farmers, Hickok found instead beaten men hoping for some kind of help that would allow them to survive the coming winter and retain their farms. It was a dismal place.

Dickinson, N.D., October 30, 1933

Dear Mr. Hopkins:

I just wound up my first day's work in North Dakota. I must say there was nothing particularly joyous about it.

This afternoon, with a couple of Morton County Commissioners, from Mandan, I drove over a road so full of ruts that you couldn't tell it from ploughed fields up to a shabby little country church, standing bleakly alone in the center of a vast tawny prairie land.

Grouped about the entrance to the church were a dozen or more men in shabby denim, shivering in the biting wind that swept across the plain.

Farmers, these, "hailed out" last summer, their crops destroyed by two hail storms that came within three weeks of each other in June and July, now applying for relief.

Most of them a few years ago were considered well-to-do. They have land—lots of land. Most of them have 640 acres or so. You think of a farmer with 640 acres of land as being rich. These fellows are "land poor." A 640-acre farm at $10 an acre—which is about what land is worth hereabouts these days—means only $6,400 worth of land. Most of them have a lot of stock, 30 or 40 head of cattle, 12 or 16 horses, some sheep and hogs. Their stock, thin and rangy, is trying to find a few mouthsful of food on land so bare that the winds pick up the top soil and blow it about like sand. Their cows have gone dry for lack of food. Their hens are not laying. Much of their livestock will die this winter. And their livestock and their land are in most cases mortgaged up to the very limit. They are all away behind on their taxes, of course. Some of them five years!

After a succession of poor crops—this whole area apparently is in process of drying up and becoming a desert—these fellows had a good one last year. But wheat in North Dakota last year brought about 30 cents a bushel. It costs 77 cents a bushel to raise it.

This year they had no crop at all. I sat in with an investigator who was taking their stories. Again and again on the applications appeared the statement: "Hailed out. No crop at all." One man had sown—I believe, at that, they say "sowed" when they refer to planting of crops—140 acres of wheat, 25 acres of oats, 20 acres of rye, 30 acres of corn, and 20 acres of barley. All he harvested was a little corn. He was lucky, at that. I drove past cornfields today that had never grown up at all. There lay the immature stalks on the ground as the hail had beaten them down—half-starved cattle rooting around among them. From 800 acres of land one old German had harvested this year 150 bushels of wheat and seven bushels of rye.

Of the men I saw this afternoon none had any income except a little here and there from cream checks. And this will soon be stopped, for their cows are going dry for lack of food.

For themselves and their families they need everything. Especially clothing. "How about clothes?" the investigator asked one of them. He shrugged. "Everything I own I have on my back," he said. He then explained that, having no underwear, he was wearing two pairs of overalls, and two, very ragged, denim jackets. His shoes were so far gone that I wondered how he kept them on his feet. With one or two exceptions none of the men hanging about the church had overcoats. Most of them were in denim—faded, shabby denim. Cotton denim doesn't keep out the wind very well. It was cold enough today so that I, in a woolen dress and warm coat, was by no means too warm when I stood out in the wind. When we came out to get into the car, we found it full of farmers, with all the windows closed. They apologized and said they had crawled in there to keep warm. . . . The women and children are even worse off than the men. Where there has been any money at all, it has gone for shoes for the children and work clothes for the men. The women can stay inside and keep warm, and the children can stay home from school.

I am quite sure that anything that could be done in the way of getting clothing out to these people IMMEDIATELY—shoes, overshoes, warm underwear, overcoats—would do quite a bit toward clearing up unrest among North Dakota farmers!

The plight of the livestock is pitiable. All these people have got to keep their stock alive this winter is roughage—and darned little of that. They've even harvested Russian thistle to feed to their horses and cattle. Russian thistle, for your information, is a thistle plant with shallow roots that dries up in the fall and is blown across the prairies like rolls of barbed wire. The effect on the digestive apparatus of an animal, if it were fed the dried plant, would be, I should imagine, much the same as though it had eaten barbed wire! However—"We tried to cut it while it was still green," one of the farmers said.

There is a good deal of complaint about the inflexibility of our rules governing the granting of livestock relief. The rules were made applicable, I was told, to farms in Wisconsin, for instance, smaller farms, with less stock. They point out to me here that they can't find a market for their stock—that, to conform to our rules for providing food for the stock, they will have to kill most of it. Or they'll cheat on us—pretend to sell it, but not actually do so. If they get rid of most of their stock, they say, they'll probably be on relief next winter, too, since they need the stock in normal times to get a living. It doesn't take much, they say, to keep this stock alive. One man said he lost seven milch cows last winter, and that $15 worth of feed would have kept them alive. I'm going to find out more about this Friday when, in Bismarck, I'm to see a man named Wilson, who, they tell me, knows all about it.

In the county I visited this afternoon the Federal Relief Administration, through the North Dakota State Relief Committee, is doing a 100 percent job. The county's financial resources are exhausted, and nobody will take their tax warrants. The job, as I wired you tonight, is shamefully inadequate.

I don't know exactly what is wrong. I'm going to try to find out when I return to Bismarck Friday. But what is actually happening, I was told, is this:

In the county there are now 1,000 families—a third of the population—on relief. Mostly farmers. To handle the job the County Commissioners are given $6,000 a month. That means $6 per family. And most of the families are huge—eight or ten children. The set-up in this county is different from that in most other counties in the state. The relief here is being handled by the County Commissioners. Bismarck apparently suspects them of using relief for political purposes. They are constantly after the commissioners, I was told, to cut down the load. Whether there's any politics in the show in that county I don't know. But this I do know—those people at that church applying for relief today certainly looked as though they needed relief.

The commissioners told me they had tried to work out a plan whereby the men could work on county roads this fall for more adequate relief—in order that they might get enough to buy clothing and fuel now, when they need it. To do this, the commissioners said, the families should be getting at least $15 a month for the next three months. That doesn't sound like much to me. They went ahead, on the advice of the state highway department, they said, and put the men to work. But today the State Relief committee told them to cease all road work and that they would get $6,000 a month for relief and no more. The commissioners say that, if they could have $15,000 a month these next three months—until the people get clothed and stocked with fuel—they might be able to get along, by half-starving them, on $6,000 a month the rest of the winter! . . . Well, anyway, it's our money that is being spent, and we're getting the blame. I'll try to get the other side of the story in Bismarck on Friday. But on the face of it, it looks as though somebody was responsible for a pretty rotten job.

I was told in Bismarck that in the county I visited this afternoon I would find a good deal of unrest—"farm holiday" spirit. I can't say that I did. They seemed almost too patient to me. I went to see one farmer who was supposed to be a chronic kicker. I found him doing the family washing! His wife died five years ago and left him with eight children, the eldest now 14. Somehow he has kept that family together—doing the washing and cooking himself, besides farming! With an expression of utter hopelessness on his face he was puttering around a dilapidated old washing machine. The rolls on the wringer were entirely worn away—right down to the iron bars. He said he had done some kicking. He wanted his boy (14) to substitute for him on road work. The boy was no good at housework, he explained, and, if he went out to work on the roads himself things went to pieces at home!

In Bismarck this morning I had a long talk with the chief justice of the North Dakota Supreme Court, who is also chairman of the state relief committee. He and the commissioners with whom I spent the afternoon, while not quite so bitter or so gloomy as Floyd Olson and some of the farm people in the Twin Cities, were not any too cheerful.

Chief Justice [Adolph Marcus] Christianson told me that "in most counties" no farm loans had been granted at all—that he had heard of cases where applications made last May had still received no action. He blamed it on red tape and inadequate personnel. I am trying to find out just what a farmer has to go through to get a federal loan, but didn't get much help from him. He said most of the applications had to be made in writing and sent to St. Paul, which would of course slow things up. The whole machinery is so complicated! I heard of organizations today that I didn't know existed. . . .

In the county I visited this afternoon farmers had received federal loans, but the impression was that the loans were granted to pay back the Twin City bankers. . . . When I pointed out that, even though the money did go to the banks, it probably saved their farms for them, someone remarked, "Well, the farms aren't worth saving now."

They are not at all impressed with Mr. [Henry A.] Wallace's acreage reduction plan. This, they say is why:

Twenty-five years ago they used to get 21 bushels to the acre of wheat in this territory. If they get 10 bushels to the acre nowadays, it's a bumper crop. They insist that what they need is not reduction in production, but a decent price for what they do produce. Wheat was selling in North Dakota for 70 cents a bushel today. They say it costs 77 cents a bushel to raise it.

"In order to make a living," one farmer told me, "we've got to get 7 cents a pound for hogs, 9 cents a pound for beef, and $1 a bushel for wheat."

Further Resources

BOOKS

Hopkins, June. *Harry Hopkins: Sudden Hero, Brash Reformer.* New York: St. Martin's Press, 1999.

Saloutos, Theodore. *The American Farmer and the New Deal.* Ames, Iowa: Iowa State University Press, 1982.

Watkins, T.H. *The Great Depression: America in the 1930s.* Boston: Little, Brown, 1993.

WEBSITES

"Letters from the Field: Lorena Hickok Reports on the State of the Nation." New Deal Network. Available online at http://newdeal.feri.org/tva/lorena1.htm; website home page: http://www.newdeal.feri.org (accessed August 8, 2002).

"Subsistence Farmsteads"

Magazine article

By: Eleanor Roosevelt

Date: April 1934

Source: Roosevelt, Eleanor. "Subsistence Farmsteads." *Forum* 91, April 1934, 199–201. Available online at

The Farm Labor Homes and Allotment Gardens in Thornton, California. This was one of several subsistence farmstead developments sponsored by the federal government during the Great Depression. **COURTESY OF THE FDR LIBRARY.**

http://newdeal.feri.org/texts/532.htm; website home page: http://newdeal.feri.org (accessed August 9, 2002).

About the Author: Eleanor Roosevelt (1884–1962), niece of President Theodore Roosevelt, married her distant cousin Franklin Delano Roosevelt in 1905. Eleanor assisted her polio-stricken husband as he served as governor of New York and president of the United States (served 1933–1945). Following her husband's death, as a delegate to the United Nations, Mrs. Roosevelt was chairperson of the U.N. Commission on Human Rights and led the drafting and adoption of the Universal Declaration of Human Rights (1948). ■

Introduction

"The country needs and, unless I mistake its temper, the country demands bold, persistent experimentation. It is common sense to take a method and try it: If it fails, admit it frankly and try another. But above all, try something." Franklin Roosevelt spoke these prophetic words in May 1932 at Oglethorpe University in Georgia. When Roosevelt became president less than a year later, he initiated a variety of creative programs, many plainly experimental, in an effort to stimulate the economy and reform society to the benefit of average U.S. citizens.

Few of these programs were closer to the hearts of the president and Mrs. Roosevelt than subsistence homesteads. An owner of several farms and thus having an extensive agricultural background, Roosevelt was traditional in his faith in the value of living close to the land. He saw great potential in communities of families who could be self-sufficient by feeding themselves with food they grew on their own small farms and who supplemented their income with wages earned in nearby factories, mines, or various handcraft workshops.

This concept of self-sufficiency did not originate with Roosevelt. The Depression stimulated a popular back-to-the-land movement. Often naïve and almost utopian in their plans, advocates of agrarian solutions to the nation's problems were numerous.

Roosevelt wanted to experiment with this idea and enlisted the help of Senator George Norris (R-Neb.) to push a bill through Congress authorizing $25 million to create subsistence homesteads for twenty-five thousand people. It was eventually attached to the National Industrial Recovery Act that was passed in June 1933.

Significance

The Subsistence Homestead program was experimental. Planners hoped to develop an alternative lifestyle that would blend farm and city in order to give residents stable prosperity in a community with a high quality of life. Built from scratch, new communities would provide families with enough land to produce much of their own

Eleanor Roosevelt, an advocate for subsistence farmsteads, addresses a group at Cumberland Farmsteads in Tennessee. **COURTESY OF THE FDR LIBRARY.**

food. Residents would also work, at least part-time, in local industries to earn enough cash to meet other needs and have a decent standard of living. There was an expectation that a strong sense of communalism would unite these settlements and further their prosperity.

Secretary of the Interior Harold Ickes described the program as an attempt at "decentralization of industry; opening up of congested factory areas; and a demonstration of the social benefits of sound community life based on a combination of part-time industrial employment and small-scale farming" (T.H. Watkins, *The Hungry Years: A Narrative History of the Great Depression in America*).

Mrs. Roosevelt was a great supporter of subsistence homesteads. She became a guardian angel for one such community, Arthurdale, near Reedsville, West Virginia, in a depressed coal mining area. Mrs. Roosevelt had previously visited Reedsville and seen the wretched poverty and hopelessness of the people. She saw Arthurdale as an opportunity to help people in desperate need and simultaneously create a community that might provide a model for people all across the country. She contributed thousands of dollars of her own money and solicited much more to support the Arthurdale experiment.

The federal government established approximately one hundred subsistence communities across the country. Some never became operational. None achieved permanence as subsistence settlements. Few attracted or were close enough to industry to provide the needed supplemental wages to support the community. Since the communities lacked a solid economic base, government subsidies were often more than originally anticipated. Most residents were probably drawn to the communities in desperation. Once the economy improved, they preferred a more traditional wage-supported lifestyle rather than the semi-agricultural existence envisioned by the planners.

In the 1940s the property, originally owned by the government and leased to residents, was sold to the residents at favorable long-term rates. Vestiges of these communities can still be found scattered about the country.

Primary Source

"Subsistence Farmsteads"

SYNOPSIS: Eleanor Roosevelt was a frequent contributor to magazines and newspapers. She wrote a syndicated daily column ("My Day") throughout and after her White House years candidly expressing her opinions. In this article from *Forum* magazine, she describes the goals of the subsistence homesteads and the progress at Arthurdale.

It was a bright and sunny day in a mining camp in West Virginia, and a relief worker was walking down between two rows of houses, talking to a stranger as she went.

"In this house here, where we are going now," she said, "lives a young couple with two children. They have done remarkably well with the garden they started. He was a farmer before he came to the mines, and she is a very energetic young woman. She has canned dozens and dozens of things and sold all she is able in a nearby town. But their neighbors are not so fortunate. Right next door there is a family where the children undoubtedly have tuberculosis."

By this time we had reached the steps. We found the interior of the house clean, although the young woman who let us in apologized for the fact that her children were rather dirty, and her kitchen full of the mess which canning creates. It was easy to see that here was a young woman who was trying hard to bring up a healthy family and who had the standards of good and well-planned farm living in her mind. Before we had talked ten minutes, she asked the relief worker eagerly, "Is there any chance that we can get some land?" She knew that an effort was being made to persuade either the state or the mining companies to divide some land amongst the unemployed miners and she was most anxious to remove her children from the danger of tuberculosis and the family across the way, where the men spent a good deal of time drinking.

The case worker answered, "Yes, we hope that something will be done." As she emerged, she sighed a little and said, "I wonder when it will be done or if it will be done in time to serve any of these people." They had never heard of "Subsistence Farms," but they were the kind of people ideally suited to go and live on one.

The objective of subsistence farming is not to compete with regular farming or add to the burden of agricultural overproduction. The idea is that families engaged in subsistence farming consume their own garden products locally instead of sending them to distant markets. They are not expected to support themselves entirely by raising food, like the successful commercial farmers of the country. The plan is that they shall be situated near enough to an industry for one member of the family to be employed in a factory a sufficient number of days in the year to bring in the amount of money needed to pay for the things which the families must have and cannot produce for themselves. In this way farming will be helped by industry, and industry will be helped by farming. There will be no competition with agriculture nor with industry. Industry must be centralized in order to clear up the congested slum areas of our big cities. Subsistence farms will make possible shorter hours of work in the factories as well as the decentralization of crowded populations.

This new self-supporting manner of American living is being projected under the direction of the Division of Subsistence Homesteads of the Department of the Interior. Last spring $25,000,000 was appropriated for study and practical illustration of this idea of new social and economic units. We have several models to build upon in this country, and there is always the example of the self-sufficiency of village life in France. Round about the country various model projects are being planned. In Monmouth County, New Jersey, a community is being projected for two hundred families of Jewish needle workers from nearby crowded manufacturing cities. A factory is to be built for their use; the best soil is to be set aside for homesteads; and the less fertile land is to be devoted to cooperative agriculture to serve solely the consumption of this community.

Recently I have observed at first hand the subsistence-farming project near Reedsville, West Virginia. In that state a great many mines have closed down; some will probably never reopen; some may reopen for a certain number of days a week during part of every year. It is being urged upon the owners of these mines that they use the land which they own above the ground for this new type of subsistence farm. The miners can still work in the mines even though their jobs may not be steady day in and day out.

The government experiment near Reedsville is designed to provide for one hundred twenty-five families especially chosen from those miners who are permanently out of work. The West Virginia College of Agriculture had made a study of unemployed miners' families and found that many of them had come to the mines only within the last few years and because they were attracted by the very high wages paid. The high wages, alas, lasted in some cases not even long enough to pay for the cheap car bought on the installment plan, and these homes are devoid of all improvements. Living conditions in the mining villages are so bad that many of the families who have come from farms long to get back again. There is good land available for the Reedsville project, with watershed hills and a certain amount of valley bottom, typical of much of the West Virginia farming land. A factory will supply the industry, and every homestead will have five acres. There will be some land suitable for pasture only, which will be owned by the community and operated on model co-operative principles. The houses, while very simple, are being planned to meet the needs and aspirations of comfort of the people who are going to live in them. They want certain very definite things, among these a chance to be clean, a shower or a bathtub in every house, a suitable tub in which to wash clothes, enough room so that each member of the family can have a bed of his own. These desires suggest some of the things which the miners lack in their present houses.

Some of the men who have been building the foundations for the first fifty houses, which are now nearing completion, will probably occupy them. You hear one builder saying, "I want to live on a hill," while another man declares emphatically, "I don't like hills." Each farm family will plan for crops suited to its own land: the man who chooses to live down in the valley will grow one thing, and the man on the hillside another. Both men will have, during the first year, the advantage of expert advice and direction from the State College of Agriculture.

These new farming families will all remain on public relief until the factory is opened and the first crops are harvested; but when a family makes its first payment the title to the land will pass to the individual homesteader. In twenty or thirty years the individual will own it free and clear of debt. This plan varies in different projects.

Plowing was going on near Reedsville all through last autumn. Now roads are being built. The question of the type of government which the community wishes to set up is a difficult one, but it is hoped that some way will be found to organize a town-meeting type which may be changed easily to fit into the state government at the end of the first year.

There are in the vicinity a number of high schools which can accommodate the children who will be sent to them. An old barn is to be converted into a local grammar school and made attractive under the direction of the Department of Education. In this building a number of experiments will be tried: for instance, it may be possible to give more vocational guidance and more handicraft work than is usually done in schools. It may also be feasible to have a nursery school to which the mothers themselves may come for a couple of hours at definite times during the week to cooperate with the teachers and learn how best to feed and discipline their children.

All these things are being discussed, and some will be actually tried out. There is the possibility that one hundred twenty-five families will be too few for this community of graduate miners, and that the population will have to be enlarged. Eventually there may be two or three factories instead of one, but in any case the farms will be kept out of competition with those farms which are run for profit.

If the West Virginia experiment succeeds it may be the model for many other similar plans throughout the United States. It is easy to see in advance, however, that the people living on these subsistence farms will be far more secure than the unemployed people living today in towns, whether small or large. It is possible, too, that on these farmsteads home crafts of different kinds may be started which will furnish added income. The Editor has asked me not to fail to mention in passing the modest village furniture industry of which I have for several years been chairman in Dutchess County, New York.

If directed from some central point where good designs and color schemes may be furnished by really good artists, and the products marketed in some cooperative way, a limited but still a good and remunerative occupation may be furnished to those who stay at home on the farms and yet can find spare time to do hand work.

We shall know more about subsistence farming when the first new projects have been working for a number of years. Already there is hope that this program will solve the difficulties of a good many people throughout our country who are now suffering from unemployment or the inability to better the poor standards of living imposed on them by slums and congested areas.

Further Resources

BOOKS

Holley, Donald. *Uncle Sam's Farmers: The New Deal Communities in the Lower Mississippi Valley.* Urbana: University of Illinois Press, 1975.

Watkins, T.H. *The Hungry Years: A Narrative History of the Great Depression in America.* New York: Henry Holt, 1999.

WEBSITES

"The Cumberland Homestead Project." Available online at http://plateauproperties.com/home.html (accessed August 9, 2002).

"The Farm Security Administration and Subsistence Homesteads." Available online at http://xroads.virginia.edu/~UG99/lane/fsa.html; website home page: http://www./xroads.virginia.edu (accessed August 9, 2002).

Harriet Craft and John Craft to President Franklin D. Roosevelt

Letter

By: Harriet Craft and John Craft

Date: November 22, 1934

Source: Craft, Harriet and John Craft. Letter to President Franklin D. Roosevelt, November 22, 1934. Private collection of John P. Craft.

About the Authors: Harriet and John Craft came to the United States from England in 1915. They settled in Detroit, Michigan. A bricklayer by trade, John Craft struggled to find work during the depression of the early 1920s, and the family considered moving back to England. Working steadily by 1923, they built a house in Highland Park, Michigan. When the Great Depression hit, steady work ceased, and they nearly lost their home. It was years before John was able to return to his trade on a regular basis. He died in 1948. Harriet lived until 1978. ■

Introduction

The Depression hit homeowners all over the country very hard. When homeowners were unable to make payments, homes were foreclosed upon at an alarming rate. With roughly eleven million nonfarm homeowners in the country, an average of over two hundred thousand were evicted each year from 1930 to 1937.

A similar condition occurred on American farms. In 1930 there were 6.2 million farms in the United States. By 1933 over 150,000 farm mortgages were being foreclosed each year. Eventually, some farmers began taking matters into their own hands. They used threats and actual violence to stop auctions, or they converted the sale process into "penny auctions" in which items were sold to sympathetic bidders and then given back to the original owners.

Unemployment and low prices for farm goods were, of course, the obvious causes of the problem. In addition, however, the Depression was a period of serious deflation. The combined effect of overproduction and unemployment drove prices and wages down. For people who were in debt, declining income—regardless of the cost of goods—increased the difficulty of meeting fixed loan payments incurred during normal times.

Stopping this deflationary spiral and creating a controlled inflationary economy was an important objective of several New Deal programs. The purpose was to ease pressure on debtors.

When Franklin Delano Roosevelt (served 1933–1945) took office, the need for action was critical. Even conservative business leaders realized that a moderate debt relief program was preferable to continued defaulting and the prospect of a more radical debt repudiation

Real Estate Foreclosures of Non-Farm Properties, 1926–1939

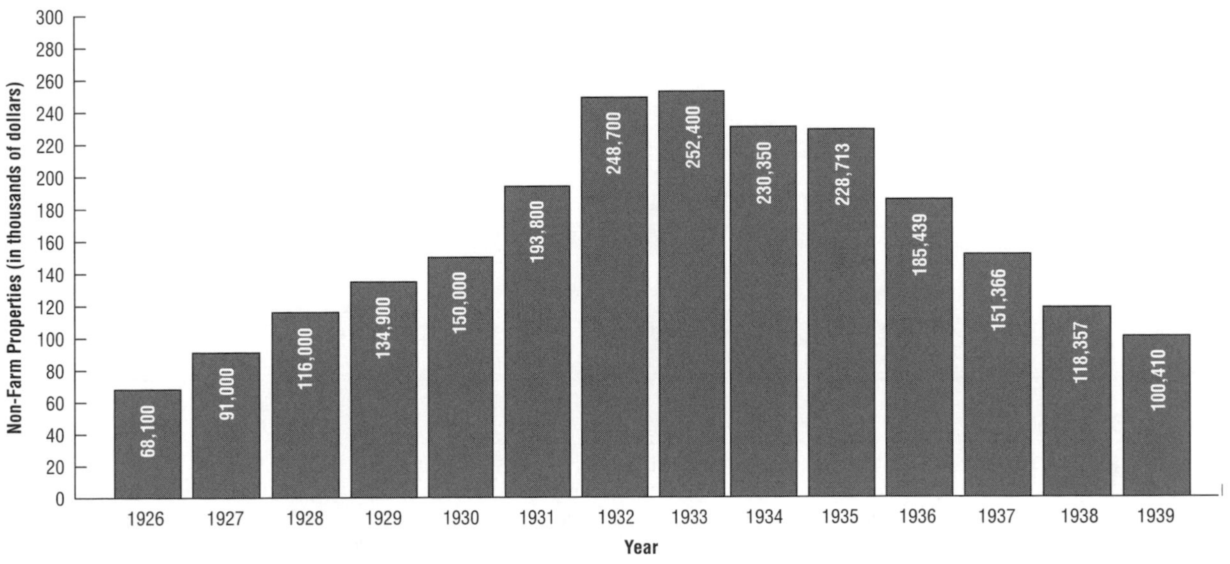

SOURCE: Based on data from the U.S. Bureau of the Census. *Historical Statistics of the United States, Colonial Times to 1970.* New York: Basic Books, 1976, p. 651.

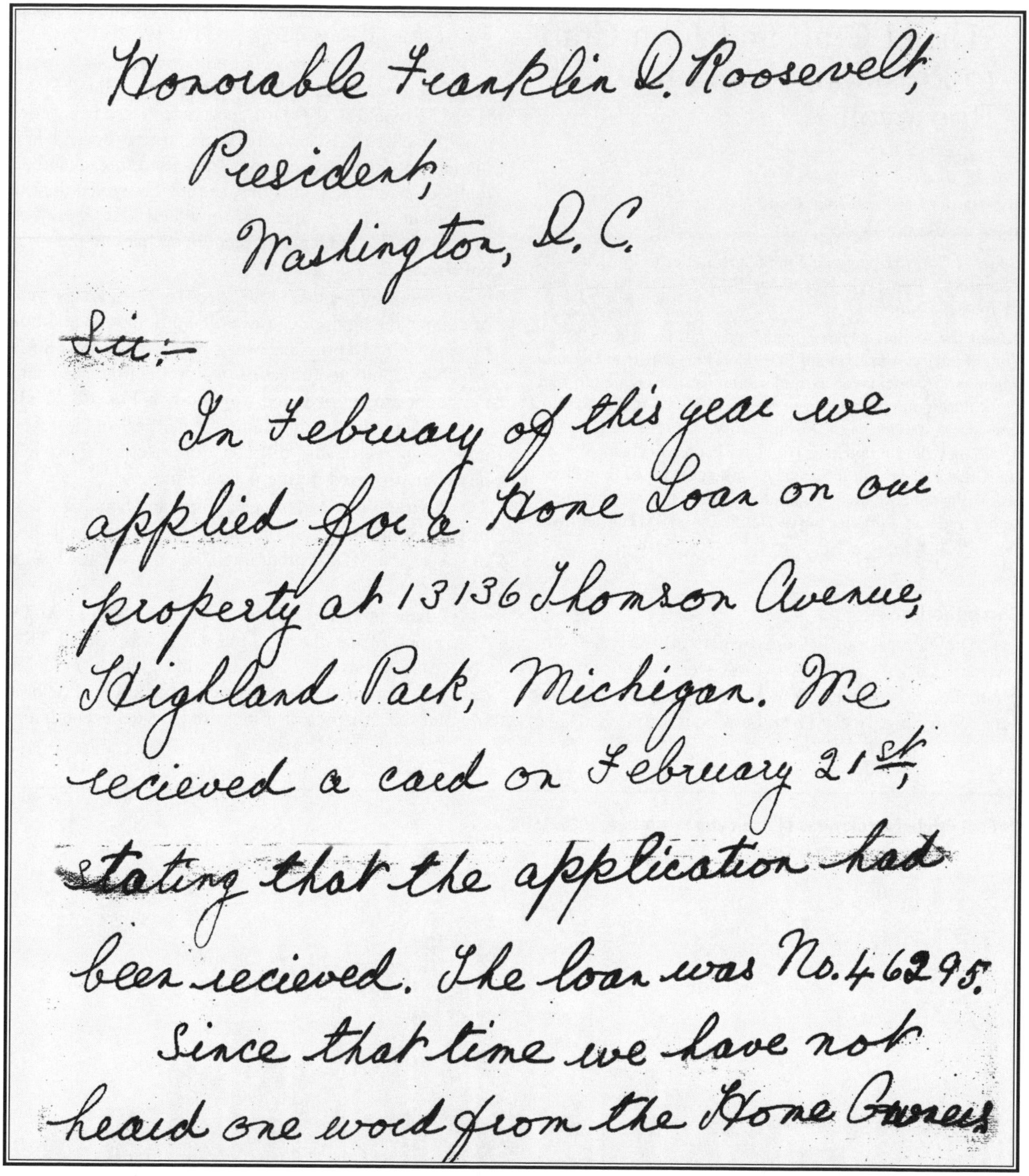

Honorable Franklin D. Roosevelt;
President;
Washington, D.C.
Sir:-
In Febuary of this year we applied for a Home Loan on our property at 13136 Thomson Avenue, Highland Park, Michigan. We recieved a card on February 21st, stating that the application had been recieved. The loan was No. 46295.
Since that time we have not heard one word from the Home Owners

Primary Source

Harriet Craft and John Craft to President Franklin D. Roosevelt (1 OF 2)

SYNOPSIS: Mr. And Mrs. John Craft wrote the following letter to President Roosevelt after waiting months for a reply to their HOLC refinancing application. Although no response has been found, they were eventually approved for the loan and managed to keep their home. Many years later, the thankful Harriet Craft spoke fondly of President Roosevelt for saving their home. COURTESY OF JAMES CRAFT.

Loan Corporation.
We do not know why. We are very anxious to get this matter straightened out, and so worried because we do not know whether our loan will be taken care of.

Will you please tell someone in charge to look after our loan and see what has happened to it.

With great respect, we are

Yours very truly,

Mr. and Mrs. John Craft

13136 Thomson Avenue,

Highland Park,

Michigan.

November 22nd 1934.

Primary Source

Harriet Craft and John Craft to President Franklin D. Roosevelt (2 OF 2)

The second page of a letter from Mr. And Mrs. John Craft to President Franklin Roosevelt. COURTESY OF JAMES CRAFT.

program. In response, the Farm Credit Act and the Home Owners' Loan Act were passed in June 1933. Both measures offered people federal refinancing of loans at reasonable terms. This provision gave them a way to retain their homes and farms.

Significance

Within eighteen months, 20 percent of the nation's 2.5 million farm mortgages were refinanced by the Farm Credit Administration (FCA). By the time the Home Owners' Loan Corporation (HOLC) ceased making loans in 1936, an additional 3 million homeowners, including 20 percent of all urban mortgage holders, had refinanced their homes.

The HOLC and FCA were among the New Deal's more successful programs. They gave Americans time to recover from the effects of the Depression without losing their homes and farms.

They were not, however, giveaway programs. Loan applications were critically reviewed, and new loans were made with the expectation of full repayment. Over time, the HOLC and FCA were also forced to foreclose on properties in which the owners had defaulted. They were examples of the essential conservatism of the Roosevelt program. No revolutionary, the president wanted the capitalist system to work. He believed that in a fair economic system in which the government helped balance the playing field previously tipped in favor of business, individuals would succeed.

The HOLC and FCA brought the federal government into the housing market. Over the next several years, the Roosevelt administration expanded that involvement by creating various organizations that have had a permanent effect on housing in the United States. The 1934 Federal Housing Act (FHA) insured private lenders who were making certain types of loans for home improvement and home purchase. The Housing Act of 1937 subsidized low-rent public housing by local authorities. The Federal National Mortgage Association ("Fannie Mae") was created in 1938 to provide a secondary market for mortgage loans by standing ready to buy mortgages from other financial institutions. It became a private organization in 1968.

As in other areas, the New Deal rewrote the basic rules of home ownership in the United States.

Further Resources

BOOKS

Harriss, C. Lowell. *History and Policies of the Home Owners' Loan Corporation.* New York: National Bureau of Economic Research, 1951.

Leuchtenburg, William E. *Franklin D. Roosevelt and the New Deal, (1932–1940).* New York: Harper & Row, 1963.

Watkins, T.H. *The Hungry Years: A Narrative History of the Great Depression in America.* New York: Henry Holt, 1999.

Boy and Girl Tramps of America

Study

By: Thomas Minehan

Date: 1934

Source: Minehan, Thomas. *Boy and Girl Tramps of America.* New York: Farrar and Rinehart, 1934, 46–48, 62–65, 74–77, 92–93, 95–96.

About the Author: Thomas Minehan was a graduate student when he took to the rails in 1932 to research migrants in the Depression. He was surprised to find a large number of young people—boys and girls—among the transient population. The result of his research was a classic study of the impact of the Great Depression in the United States: *Boy and Girl Tramps of America.* ■

Introduction

The drifter has long had a part in American mythology, from Daniel Boone to Johnny Appleseed. It was such a notable phenomenon that one philanthropist, Thomas McGregor of Toledo, planned to open a series of shelters for transient men in every major Great Lakes city to help meet their needs. The mission he opened in Detroit in 1890 provided shelter for fifteen thousand men per year during the forty years of its existence.

The Depression, however, changed the profile of American transients. Hundreds of thousands of people, usually unemployed men, took to the road. They did so not from the fabled wanderlust but from a sense of failure and destitution and in hopes of finding work elsewhere.

Estimating the exact number of transients was difficult. Some indication of the magnitude of the problem can be found in testimony given to the Senate Committee on Manufactures in 1933 on the transient problem. An agent of the Southern Pacific Railway stated that in 1929 the railroad had ejected approximately eighty thousand trespassers (i.e., transients hopping freights) from their trains and rail yards. Four years later, trespassers evicted numbered nearly seven hundred thousand. A Missouri Pacific agent estimated the numbers over the same period on his company property grew from 14,000 to 150,000.

Although they were welcomed nowhere, this new breed of transient appears to have been docile and honest. They were forced on the road not by choice but by desperate circumstances, and most hoped to discover stable employment and a permanent home.

Remarkable among the transients was the large number of young people, boys and girls, who had left home. In some cases, they had left because of problems with their parents or with a boy or girl friend. Usually, however, they left because of the hard times. They may have been told by their parents to leave or, not wanting to be a burden, left of their own accord. Whatever the reason, an estimated two hundred thousand teenagers were on the road in 1932.

Significance

In the early 1930s, welfare or poor relief was a local matter. The states were only marginally involved and the federal government not at all. While in normal times local relief and charity might have effectively helped transients, during the Great Depression years these agencies were overwhelmed. (The inadequacy of local relief was, of course, one reason so many at home left for other places.) Unable to care for their own needy, relief organizations had little sympathy for transients passing through their districts. Instead, communities posted signs that read: "No jobs for transients." "Transients, keep moving." In California transients became such a problem the state attempted to forcibly stop them at the state line.

Recognizing the immediate need to provide help to transients and the inability and unwillingness of local relief to provide that aid, the Federal Emergency Relief Administration (FERA) created the Federal Transient Service (FTS) in the spring of 1933 to establish and run work camps for itinerants. The FTS provided shelter, food, and a modest weekly stipend in exchange for work on various short-term construction or maintenance projects. Experimental in nature, the FTS was phased out as other federal programs stabilized relief services across the country.

An important part of the federal relief effort was addressing the specific needs of the young. The Civilian Conservation Corps (CCC) and the National Youth Administration (NYA) were key programs aimed at young Americans. Established in 1933, the CCC was housed in camps scattered across the country; it put nearly three million young men to work on various conservation and reforestation projects. The NYA, a broader-based program that began operation in 1935, provided work for young people, often on a part-time basis so they could also attend school. NYA was one of the more successful programs in providing balanced opportunities for men and women, whites and blacks. In the end, over five million young people participated in NYA programs. It was an important factor in keeping youth in school and in increasing college attendance in the late 1930s.

Improving the general level of employment was, of course, the ultimate solution to the transient problem. As full employment returned with the coming of World War II (1939–1945), both the CCC and NYA were dismantled.

A young man hitches a ride on a freight car in Bakersfield, California. NATIONAL ARCHIVES AND RECORDS ADMINISTRATION.

Primary Source

Boy and Girl Tramps of America [excerpt]

SYNOPSIS: Extracted from Minehan's study of young "boy and girl tramps" are descriptions of the day-to-day matters of finding food, finding shelter, and catching a freight. Minehan was struck by their youthfulness and how, in different circumstances, they would be at a high school football game or dance.

Why Did They Leave Home?

It is the middle of September and already a tinge of winter haunts the air in spite of the mellow sun of autumn and the warmth of early-changing, reddening leaves. Twelve boy tramps and three little girl companions sit in a natural clearing in a woods a hundred yards from a railroad grade fourteen miles south of Chicago. A spring bubbles from the ground in one corner, running away in a tiny stream to the woods. Here the child tramps wash their clothing. Bushes are hung with drying shirts, socks, underwear, and pants. Two boys try to bend a shoe nail with rocks as last and hammer. A Titian-haired girl of fifteen, extremely pretty and extremely thin, sews a patch on the seat of a boy's pants. The boy stands very still on a hummock. The girl sews very business-like, as she turns in the edges of the patch and reenforces the center. A second, blond girl boils coffee and potatoes and directs the barbecuing of a small hog. Except for the disproportionate ratio of boys to girls, the drying clothes and the deshabille of many, the gathering seems very much like a high school wiener roast, or a Sunday school barbecue. Nature has been kind to the farmers, and the farmers, with crops rotting in the fields, have been kind to the child tramps. There is food enough in the jungle to feed forty. Vegetables have been collected by the sack. Cantaloupes and apples stand in a pyramid on the ground. The hog, of course, was not a gift. But, then, he might have been hit by a truck.

Ragged, smiling Texas, merry as usual, is returning with a knapsack full of bread which he has begged uptown. He recounts his experiences and success gustily and with the pardonable braggadocio of one who has accomplished something.

" . . . and one woman asked me why did I leave home, and I answers, 'Hard times, lady!' Just like that. 'Hard times, lady, hard times!'"

His auditors laugh.

And hard times it seems to be, lady.

Three hundred and eighty-seven out of four hundred and sixty-six boys and girls stated definitely that hard times drove them away from home.

Yet there were other reasons.

Twenty-six of the remaining seventy-nine were on the road because of some trouble with a girl. . . .

How They Get Food

At another mission, in another city, I sat at a bench with four men. My meal was a bowl of soup, a cheese sandwich, a piece of corn cake, and a cup of insipid coffee. I raised the coffee to my lips. As I did, the man to my left grabbed the sandwich and the piece of cake with the filthiest hands I have ever seen.

"You don't want them, do you, brother?" he asked, and as he spoke he pawed, crumbling the bread, cheese and cake into a dirty mass. Before I could remove the cup from my mouth and protest, he had spoiled the dinner for which I had worked four long and hard hours. . . .

Whether adult or young tramp, you learn rapidly on the road. You learn to eat at a "hungry" mission with your eyes wary, your attention concentrated on rapidly consuming the small portions of food, and one hand and arm half-circling the plate much as a dog throws a paw protectively around a bone.

For girls there are less accommodations than for boys. Boys can slip in front of a mission for a meal. Girls on the road can appeal to but a few agencies and those agencies are swamped with demands from local cases. Generally they get their food in other ways. And these ways are woman's age-old ways of using her own body and a man's desire to attain her ends. The boys, in the majority of cases, provide the girls with food, even as men in the upper world provide their women with food. The methods by which the boys secure food for themselves and for the girls are begging, stealing, and very rarely indeed, working.

Begging is by far the most common occupation of the young tramps. Even in the country where it is easy to raid a farmer's garden or henyard, begging is more common than stealing. It is easy for a young tramp to beg food. Few back doors refuse a hungry boy bread. If then at a butcher shop he can get a hunk of bologna or a few wieners, he has a meal. Storekeepers, too, are solicited and less frequently restaurateurs. Housewives, especially in the smaller towns, are "hit" regularly and successfully. Bakeries always have some stale returns.

The techniques for ordinary begging are simple. The boys appear at the back door of a bakery or a house—preferably a small, individually owned one—and ask for something to eat.

"A good way," explained Lady Lou—a boy with the complexion of a girl and one of the most successful younger "promoters"—as we stood before a bakeshop, our nostrils tantalized by a yeast-sweet smell, "is to ask for just a little. Hit a guy for a nickel or a couple pennies and he'll give you a dime. Hit him for a dime and he'll give youse the stony stare. I always ask a baker if he has any old half-loaves that he is going to throw away. He pretty near always gives me something good. I even get pie slices that way." Pie, the boy tramp's idea of manna! "Ask a butcher for some old scraps of dog meat and first thing you know he'll be handing you a ring of fresh bologna. I went into a swell joint in Chicago one time and asked the cook if I couldn't clean up the plates that were coming back from a banquet upstairs; you know, the stuff the big guys weren't eating. First thing you know I was having chicken, ice cream, and pie. And before I left I got a buck from a big fat guy."

"Ask a woman in a house if she's got anything left over," said Boris, handing me half a raisin pie he had just received from a woman, "and pretty soon she'll be cooking you a meal. Ask her for a meal and she'll give you the stony stare."

"Another thing you always want to do," advised Happy Joe as he tried to initiate me into the niceties of panhandling in an Iowa town, "is to tell a baker or a woman you got a kid brother down the stem a ways. Then maybe when you are leaving you'll get something to take along. In that way you'll have a nice lunch for later."

"Or," he continued as we munched apples donated by a German grocer, "if it is a bakery you are hitting you can even do better than that. Tell them you got a sick mother and a lot of younger kids at home hungry."

"Before I hit anybody," Texas is describing his methods as we ride a gondola west, "I always ask if there isn't something I can do for a meal or a piece of bread. . . ."

Where They Sleep

Near a small jungle between a railroad track and the Mississippi, a gigantic sewer spues a city's filth into the river. Rains and floods have bit deep holes into the gravel and cinder bank, leaving the sewer's mouth projecting like a huge cannon. Along the north side of the sewer young tramps have constructed a rude shelter, ten by fourteen feet. Decked over with tin and utilizing the sewer and river bank as two walls, the lean-to opens on the water and the West. Sacks of burlap filled with straw lie on the ground. A small narrow bunk held erect by limestone rock runs along the sewer wall. Three cedar posts uphold the tin roof which slants at a crazy angle as though at any moment it might lose its precarious hold on the land and slide off into the Mississippi.

To the front and side of the lean-to smudge fires smoke in a foredoomed effort to keep mosquitoes away from six who have just finished supper in the jungle. The day has been swelteringly hot with the intense unallayed heat of "good corn-growing days" in August in Iowa. Not a wisp of air deflects the smudge smoke which arises straight as the flame of a tallow candle toward the unclouded stars. Long since the sun has disappeared behind the cliffs. Supper is over. The tins are cleaned and stacked under the bunk. Every person in the city not detained by work has gone to the beaches.

"No use to pound the pavements tonight," says Slim Jim, a tall, gangling youth from Tennessee. His face is as red and sunburned as a tomato from riding on the roof of a freight all afternoon. "With a face like mine I'd scare 'em, besides they are all out to the lake."

"Why didn't you have sense enough to come down off the roof?" mocked Helen, a slight but cunning lass of fifteen. She has just finished washing her socks and underwear in the river. With only dirty patched trousers on she has difficulty standing close enough to the smudge to keep the mosquitoes away from her white and tender skin. Her small breasts have blue marks on them and a livid sunburnt scar across one shoulder records a rent in her shirt.

"I couldn't," Slim defends himself, long hands and powerful wrists gesturing, "I couldn't. I fell asleep at Willmar, and I didn't wake up until I was damn' near to Minneapolis and then I thought somebody was frying me in a pan."

"Well, you shoulda been in the gondola coming up from Dubuque with me yesterday. That was hot." Fred, a stubby German with red face and fair hair, is speaking. "Was it hot! Cripes! We thought we must be in hell." He pounds a nail in the sole of one shoe with a rock, using another smaller stone as last. "The rubber heels on these shoes, I put them on the iron in the sun and they begin to melt." . . .

The fire smolders and dies down. Mosquitoes rally to the feast. Sand fleas crawl out of the gravel and onto the young tramps. Lice and other miscellaneous vermin deposited by other tramps attack the sleepers. But the sleepers care not. Nor do they heed any bites or crawling things until the morning sun strikes Slim Jim's lobster-red face, and he awakes with a curse.

A quarter of a mile down the railroad tracks thirty-four boys and girls are waking in another jungle. Here are no lean-tos but a growth of willows and cottonwoods on an old sand bar. Paths lead in from the railroad tracks in three directions to a clearing sixty by eighty sheltered by small trees. Grass, fed by moisture from below, grows luxuriantly and high. Tramped by many feet and bodies, it still pushes its way up, making a soft natural bed. In the center of this clearing a huge smudge has smoked all night long, watched carefully by pairs of boys serving turns.

As we continue down the tracks we find other camps. Some are near the right of way, others a quarter of a mile removed. Five or six girls and boys are bunking here. Twenty-five or thirty men and women, boys and girls there. Any thicket, any grove along the railroad track may be a burrow for a boy, a moll, or a bum.

Although they would be a welcome relief from the heat, caves along the river are unoccupied. The tramps believe that sleeping in them in summer "will make you cough."

Uptown, migrant youths sleep unconcernedly in city parks side by side with tenement families driven out by the heat. Here is a child tramp pillowed on his knapsack next to a mother and her babe. Over there is a transient girl who has removed her shoes and tied them to her wrist, sleeping peacefully alongside a fat Jewish clothing worker.

Until late fall the young tramps sleep outside, with the sky as their roof and a camp-fire vigil light. There comes a day, however, when mercury in the thermometer drops low, snow covers the ground, and the young tramps must seek shelter. All older transients, too, must find cover, and the boys and girls who have been living in the rural districts during summer and fall gravitate inevitably toward the cities and the main drag. Relief facilities are swamped. New bread lines form. Old ones are extended. Mission annexes spring up. New municipal lodging houses are opened. Still the relief facilities are inadequate. Without enough accommodations for the local homeless men and women, transients must be squeezed in as circumstances dictate. In the squeezing-in process, child tramps are usually squeezed out. . . .

How They Travel

In traveling in box cars the child tramps ordinarily require no techniques. They merely climb into a box car and wait until the train pulls out. Some cities and towns and some railroads do not permit the transients to board a train so openly. The boys and men must sneak on. In other places the railroad police are inflexible about enforcing the rule that the hoboes must not board a train until it is in motion. After it is in motion, it is the task of the train crew to keep the transients off—a task obviously impossible. It is not at all unusual to see several hundred men and boys lined up beyond the railroad property fence. A train is being made up a track or two away. The intervening space is patrolled by railroad police.

"Get back there, I tell you, get back," shouts an officer to a pair of boys crossing the tracks.

"Don't let me catch a one of you," warns another as he swings a club in our faces, "putting a foot upon railroad property until that train gets in motion."

The transients are silent. Box cars buckle and bump. A brakie connects the last air hose. From a station near the caboose, the conductor gives the highball. Imperceptibly the train moves as the fireman rings the bell. Like a group of race horses springing the barrier, or football players surging forward when the ball is snapped, the boys and girls surge en masse across the tracks. They alight and swarm all over the train as a cloud of locusts alight and swarm over an orchard. Some climb ladders to the roofs. Others pile into gondolas. The majority choose box-car doors.

And here is one fertile source of the accidents which daily cripple boy and girl tramps for life. The train is in motion. Scores of boys and girls crowd, boost and shove one another. Youths in the car reach down and lift others. Boys on the ground boost friends or try to leap up themselves, and all the time the speed of the train is accelerating. First you walk, but soon you must trot to keep up with it. The ones near the door are trying to get in. The ones away from the door are pushing forward, fearing they may be left. And in the jumble and confusion, the stumbling over cinders and tripping over ties, someone may fall. Fortunately the train is moving so slowly that in most cases the youth has time to recover and slide out of the way. But not always—and another homeless girl is crippled for life, another boy killed.

The railroad police justify their efforts to keep the transients out of the yards by saying that they are not only protecting the companies' property but the youths themselves. Boys and girls straying between cars and across switching tracks are in danger, it is true, but they are certainly in less danger than when trying to board a moving train. Inasmuch as they are going to ride anyway, why not let them board the train openly and safely? Many towns do.

Other towns do not. Not only do they prevent the transients from boarding a freight before it is moving, but they make every effort to keep the men off after the train has started. In these towns the child tramps must drop off and board a train far from the yards and often beyond the city limits. A grade near a block signal is the favorite flipping place. Here the freights slow up or stop and the boy or girl can, with a little skill and more luck, board the train.

Box cars are the favorite riding place of child tramps, but they ride anywhere. On tops of cars, between cars, in reefers, in gondolas, on open cars, and in with cattle and stock they ride. I have never seen a boy or a girl riding the rods underneath a car. Deception isn't necessary on freights.

Further Resources

BOOKS

Reiman, Richard A. *The New Deal and American Youth: Ideas and Ideals in a Depression Decade.* Athens, Ga.: University of Georgia Press, 1992.

WEBSITES

"'Dear Mrs. Roosevelt': Cries for Help from the Depression Generation, and the American Youth Crisis of the 1930s." New Deal Network. Available online at http://newdeal.feri.org

/eleanor/cohen.htm; website home page: http://www.newdeal.feri.org (accessed August 9, 2002).

Riding the Rails. The American History Project. Available online at http://www.albany.edu/jmmh/vol2no1/ridingrails.html; website home page: http://www.albany.edu (accessed February 27, 2003).

Springer, Gertrude. "Men Off the Road." *Portrait of America: Survey Graphic in the Thirties.* Available online at http://xroads.virginia.edu/~MA01/Davis/survey/articles/relief/relief_sep34.html; website home page: http://www.xroads.virginia.edu (accessed on August 9, 2002).

Flash Gordon, Episode 2

Radio script

By: Alex Raymond

Date: May 4, 1935

Source: Hearst Corporation. *Flash Gordon.* Episode 2, May 4, 1935. Radio program transcript. Available online at http://www.genericradio.com/flashgordon2.htm; website home page: http://www.genericradio.com (accessed March 24, 2003).

About the Artist: Alex Raymond (1909–1956), an influential comic strip artist, created the popular strip "Flash Gordon." The artistry of the panels was the special attraction of Raymond's work. Drawing for King Features, Raymond teamed with writer Don Moore to create a competitor to a rival syndicate's popular science fiction comic strip, "Buck Rogers." The result, "Flash Gordon," appeared in January 1934. Raymond was killed in an automobile accident in 1956. ■

Introduction

The first commercial radio program was broadcast in November 1920. By 1922 there were fewer than sixty thousand homes with radios. That number grew to ten million homes by 1929 and nearly twenty-eight million by 1939. The radio revolutionized how people in the United States and much of the rest of the world entertained themselves, learned about world events, and decided what products to buy.

In the 1930s, the radio supplanted the newspaper as the primary source of news. Faster and far more dramatic, radio became the news medium of choice for most Americans. A beleaguered nation heard President Franklin Delano Roosevelt (served 1933–1945) deliver his comforting "Fireside Chats" as if he were in the armchair across the room. They heard the fiery rhetoric of arch-demagogues Huey Long and Father Charles Coughlin. They thrilled at Joe Louis knocking out Hitler's representative of the "master race," Max Schmelling, in the first round of their much ballyhooed rematch. Audiences were moved to tears by Herb Morrison's emotional description of the *Hindenburg*'s explosion. And they listened in dread of war as Edward R. Murrow described Nazi troops occupying Austria in 1938. Never before had whole nations been so aware and felt so much a part of a larger world.

In the 1920s, radio was in its infancy. By the 1930s, however, the technology had advanced, and the industry was learning how to deliver programming the country wanted. Well funded by advertisers, radio was supreme, and by the 1930s it had entered its "Golden Age."

Radio entertainment took many forms. It included live broadcasts from concert halls and studio orchestras. A myriad of musicians and singers filled the air from morning till night. Will Rogers, humorist, irreverent commentator of world events, and film star, was one of the country's most popular radio stars as he regularly lampooned politicians, bankers, and just about anyone else. Comedians like George Burns and Gracie Allen or the Marx Brothers brought variations of their vaudeville routines to the air. Americans listened to Amos and Andy each week to find out how Andy's next harebrained scheme was going to land him and Andy in another mess of trouble.

For children, the radio was an escape to a make-believe world. Each evening would find them sitting on the floor in front of their radio sets waiting eagerly for the next episode in their favorite adventure program: "The Lone Ranger," "The Green Hornet," or "Buck Rogers." Representative of these serials was a radio version of the popular comic strip "Flash Gordon."

Significance

Created as a comic in 1934, the first series of twenty-six weekly Saturday radio episodes of "Flash Gordon" began in April 1935. It was the unlikely tale of Flash and his girlfriend, Dale Arden, struggling against incredible odds to save the world from annihilation.

The initial episode begins with the Earth threatened by collision with a new planet. Flash, a Yale graduate and world-renowned polo player, is a passenger on an airplane that is struck by a meteor. He saves Dale, a fellow passenger and girlfriend, from certain death by leaping from the plane. (He appears to have been coincidentally wearing a parachute.)

They land, again coincidentally, near the laboratory of the brilliant scientist Dr. Zarkov, who is trying to save Earth from imminent destruction. Believing Dale and Flash are spies, Dr. Zarkov takes the two on his rocket ship in an effort to divert the planet Mongo from its collision course with Earth. On Mongo the three must contend with evil Ming, Emperor of the Universe, and a vast array of villains including Hawk Men, Monkey Men, and Shark Men.

Happily for the people of Earth, Flash, Dale, and Dr. Zarkov succeed in fending off the evil Ming and saving

Dale Arden and Flash Gordon as they appeared in the *Flash Gordon* comic strip, 1935.

the Earth from destruction. But as the episode ends, listeners find Dale being dragged to the bottom of a lake by "two powerful green, scaly arms." Will Flash be able to save her?

Primary Source

Flash Gordon, Episode 2

SYNOPSIS: Episode Two of the Flash Gordon radio series was broadcast on May 4, 1935. The announcer explains the ending of Episode One by informing us that Flash and Dale had been captured by the Shark Men and rescued by Ming's daughter, Aura. The action begins in Episode Two with Flash trying to rescue Aura, by now infatuated with the handsome Earthman, from a carnivorous plant.

Music up

Announcer: Last week you may remember, Flash Gordon and Dale Arden saved the Earth from destruction by shooting a rocket at a planet which threatened to collide with it. They became marooned on the planet, called Mongo. The Emperor, Ming the Merciless, ordered Flash killed, and commanded Dale to marry him. The royal princess, loving Flash, saved him. Thun, Prince of the Lion Men, helped Flash prevent Ming from marrying Dale, by breaking up the marriage ceremony and escaping underground. Now, we continue the story.

Flash and Dale are captured by the Sharkmen. Princess Aura appears and again saves Flash, who in turn, tries to free Dale, but Thun's father, searching for his princely son, captures the Princess and Flash. Rather than remain a captive, the proud Aura hurls herself over the cliff, only to be caught by the terrible leaves of a constrictor plant. Flash hastens to her aid.

Aura: Ooooh. Oh . . .

Flash: Don't struggle Princess Aura. I'll free you.

Aura: Oh, hurry! The leaves are crushing me.

Flash: I'll cut them with my sword.

Aura: Oh, be careful! Ah! Oh, careful Flash! The plant may touch you.

(*Sound of sword chopping*)

Flash: Arrgh, this devilish plant!

Aura: . . . Oh!

Flash: . . . Arrgh! There!.

Aura: . . . Oh Flash! It's got you too.

Flash: Yes. Yes, I didn't think it could. . . . I think that's a tough break.

Aura: What shall we do now?

Flash: I don't know . . . yet.

Aura: Oh, Oh, Flash!

Flash: What is it Princess? Are you in pain?

Aura: No. Look—look down there. Out there a door in the ship . . . has opened!

Flash: So it has. There are soldiers coming out. With strange looking guns. Are those your father's men?

Aura: No. No, I never saw them before. They must have seen us, and come to make us captives.

Flash: Well at least they'll get us out of the clutches of this terrible plant!

Barin: (*Off mike*) Soldiers! Attack that plant and kill it, but don't injure its victims . . . I want them brought to me alive.

Flash: Don't be afraid, Princess. Those men will catch you.

Aura: Oh!

Barin: (*Off mike*) Be ready to catch her men.

(*Aura drops to ground*)

Barin: Now, the other one.

Flash: Here I come!

(*Flash drops to ground*)

Aura: We're safe on the ground. But what will happen now?

Flash: It's up to the leader of those soldiers.

Barin: (*coming on mike*) Soldiers, you did that well. Ahh, Princess Aura . . .

Aura: Yes. How do you know me? I do not know you.

Barin: I know your father.

Aura: Oh!

Barin: So, what's this? Another white stranger?

Captain: Yes, Prince Barin.

Barin: Blindfold him. And prepare our other white prisoner for the ordeal of the poisoned daggers.

Captain: As you command, Prince Barin.

Aura: What are you going to do with me?

Barin: Guard, take the Princess to my quarters.

Guard: As you command, Prince Barin.

Barin: Ahh, here comes our other white prisoner. Perhaps you know him, youth?

Flash: How can I tell, he's got a hood over his head. I can't see his face.

Barin: He says he is from the Earth. I suppose you are from there, too?

Flash: I am.

Barin: I don't believe you. But no matter. Our hiding place must remain a secret so both of you must die. Are the white prisoners prepared guard?

Guard: They are, Prince Barin. Their left forearms are tied together.

Barin: And the poisoned daggers? Are they ready?

Guard: Yes, they are.

Barin: Now listen prisoners. I am dipping these two daggers in dragon's blood. The slightest scratch from these blades means certain death. Guard, give these to the prisoners. On the count of three you will commence fighting. One . . . two . . . three!

Announcer: As Prince Barin utters the words, Flash steps back, jerking his mysterious antagonist off balance. He flings aside his dagger and then causes his opponent to drop his poisoned weapon. Picking up the dagger, Flash severs the cords binding him to his opponent, and as the two whip off their blindfolds and reveal themselves to each other . . .

Zarkov: Flash Gordon!

Flash: Dr. Zarkov!

Barin: So you do know each other.

Flash: I should say we do. I am mighty glad to see you, doctor. I thought you were dead after our rocket crashed on this planet.

Zarkov: I was badly hurt, Flash. These fellows, they picked me up and brought me here. They made me act as their servant. Well, we saved the Earth, didn't we lad?

Flash: We certainly did, doctor. Now Prince Barin, maybe you'll believe that we are from the Earth. This man was the most brilliant scientist in the world. He was D———

Barin: Stop! My admiration for both of you is boundless. I would be honored to have you shake my hand and call me friend.

Flash: Your friend?

Barin: Yes.

Flash: Why, of course. Here is my hand.

Zarkov: And mine.

Barin: Good. Now come to my quarters. (*sound of walking*) My friends, I have invented an electric mole with which I intend to burrow underground into the palace of Ming the Merciless and overthrow his tyrannical government. Are you with me?

Zarkov: Certainly!

Flash (Buster Crabbe) battles a tribe of martians in the 1936 film, *Flash Gordon Goes to Mars.* © UNDERWOOD & UNDERWOOD/CORBIS. REPRODUCED BY PERMISSION.

Flash: You bet we are! We've got to rescue Dale and Thun from that fiend.

Barin: Princess Aura! You heard what I plan to do, Aura?

Aura: Yes. Please take me back to my father's palace with you.

Barin: You?! Why it is because of you that I am a hunted man with a price on my head. You will remain here as my prisoner. Come, my friends . . . come. (*they exit*)

Aura: Oh I will, Will I? Guard!

Guard: What is it?

Aura: What is your name?

Guard: Ronkel, my Princess.

Aura: Ronkel. I thought I recognized your face. You fled into exile from my father's guard when you were caught stealing.

Guard: Yes.

Aura: Listen, Ronkel.

Guard: Princess.

Aura: If you would help me warn my father of what those men plan to do, I will make you not only wealthy, but also a Duke.

Guard: For one so lovely as my Princess, how could I refuse? Come with me.

Music up and out

Announcer: Unaware of what has happened in the hiding place, and racing underground toward the palace of Ming the Merciless in their electric mole, Prince Barin, Dr. Zarkov, and Flash Gordon encounter a fierce Gwakko, or armor plated dragon. Flash climbs out of the mole and gives battle, saving his companions. For this Prince Barin promises that if they succeed in overthrowing Ming, Flash will be made a Prince of Mongo and anything he desires will be his. Finally . . . (*sound of crash*) . . . the electric mole breaks through the floor of the central hall in Ming's palace. The door opens and the three emerge from the metal burrowing machine.

Barin: Come my friends, we have arrived.

Zarkov: Ah, so we have. What is our next move, Prince Barin?

Barin: Hmm. This is the central hall of Ming's palace. We will go up those stairs, Dr. Zarkov, and surprise the inner guards.

Flash: Prince Barin, look.

Barin: Ming's armored men!

Flash: We've been betrayed.

Barin: Yes.

Flash: But how could the news have reached here before us?

Zarkov: Let us get our ray guns.

Barin: It's no use, doctor. The armor of those soldiers is ray-proof.

Zarkov: Here comes Ming the Merciless with his High Priest.

Dale: (*Off mike*) No . . . Flash!

Flash: Dale! Thank heavens she is all right.

Ming: Welcome back to my palace, Flash Gordon. And welcome to your companions. Soldiers, lash them to the pillar over there and execute them.

Dale: Oh, Flash darling. I love you so much.

Flash: Dale, my dear. We did our best to save you, but we've been betrayed. I guess they have us now.

Dale: Let them shoot. They will kill me, too, and we will be together, forever.

Ming: Very well, Dale Arden. You can have him in death. Captain!

Captain: Sire!

Ming: Proceed with the execution.

Flash: Shoot, you yellow dogs. We aren't afraid to die.

Captain: Ready . . . aim . . .

Zogi: Captain, hold your fire!

Ming: Zogi! What is this? If you were not the High Priest, I would have your tongue torn out for your insolence.

Zogi: I ask you to remember, Sire, that according to the writ of Pau-oo even a traitor has the right to choose between the firing squad and the terrible pit.

Ming: True, Zogi. And on second thought such deaths would provide greater amusement.

Zogi: Yes, Sire. We must abide by the sacred writs. And I see no reason . . . uh . . . why the girl should be killed.

Ming: Captain.

Captain: Sire.

Ming: Release the prisoners. They shall undergo the terrible test. Bring them over to the pit.

Captain: All right. Come on. Move along

(*Sound of walking*)

Ming: This is the test of the torture pit. Flash Gordon, you and Barin will stand at each end of the narrow platform and with long whips try to topple each other into the pit where a surprise will be awaiting you. Take your places!

Announcer: The two mount the platform. Flash ducks as Barin's whip whines over his head. Flash's whip hits Barin with such force as to knock him off balance and into the pit. Dropping his whip, Flash leaps after him. As he throws the unconscious former Prince Barin over his shoulder and prepares to climb out, a transparent metal sheet slides over the top of the pit, trapping them. At the same time, Flash hears a growl, and looking around sees three snarling tigrons. Placing Barin on the floor, Flash turns on the fierce beasts.

The first one charges. Leaping high in the air, Flash comes down on the tigrons back and with a powerful wrench, breaks its neck. The other two tigrons leap at each other to fight for possession of the body. Furiously the battle rages. (*Beast snarls*) Finally, both animals are down, wounded unto death. Then Prince Barin regains consciousness.

Barin: Oooo. Where . . . where are we?

Flash: It's alright Prince Barin. Stand up. We are in the pit. But they've trapped us with that transparent metal lid.

Barin: And you . . . you saved us from these beasts. Why you are superb, Flash.

Flash: That was easier than figuring how we are going to get out of here.

Barin: Look up there.

Flash: Prince Thun! He's just in time. Thun! Roll that metal lid back. (*He nods that he understands*)

Barin: There, he's done it. We are free!

Flash: Come along!

Music up and under

Announcer: Meanwhile in the Temple of Pau-oo Ming and Dale are about to be married by Zogi, the High Priest.

(*Gong over Ming's music*)

Ming: By now, Dale Arden, my saber toothed tigrons have torn your hero to pieces.

Dale: Oh, poor Flash. He died trying to save me. Nothing matters now.

Ming: Here comes Zogi to perform the ceremony.

Zogi: Oh mighty Ming, ruler of Mongo and the universe, does your Supreme Intelligence take this Earthwoman to be your wife and Empress of Mongo?

Ming: I most certainly do.

(*Sound of gong*)

Zogi: And you, Dale Arden, do you take this just and brilliant man to be your Lord and Master?

Dale: I . . . I don't care what happens now.

(*Sound of gong*)

Zogi: As you have accepted each other in matrimony before the great god Pau-oo, I pronounce . . .

VO: Wait! Stop!

Zogi: The idol speaks!

VO: I, Pau-oo forbid this marriage.

Crowd: (*Gasps and murmurs*)

Ming: It is a trick! Fools! A stone idol cannot talk! Zogi, swing back the statue.

Zogi: At once, Sire.

(*Sound of stone door creaking open*)

Ming: Flash Gordon!

Dale: Flash, darling! They told me you were dead.

Zogi: The Earthman and two companions arrive!

Ming: Guards! Shoot them down! The marriage must go on.

Zogi: Wait! Sire! The sacred writs say you cannot execute the man who has passed the test of the tigrons. Guards! Drop your weapons or Pau-oo will curse you all.

Ming: What! You dare defy me!

Zogi: I only quote the sacred writ, sire. As High Priest, it is my duty to interpret and enforce its dictates.

Ming: Guard, give me your sword. Zogi, I will shut your jabbering mouth forever.

Zogi: (*Screams*)

Dale: Oh, how awful. He's killed the High Priest.

Ming: Carry his body away, guards.

Dale: Flash, my darling. I thought I'd lost you.

Flash: Never as long as I have strength in these two arms and a breath of life in my body.

Ming: So Pau-oo forbids me to slay you, huh? Well Pau-oo and I will both laugh while you rebels slave in the prison city of the Hawkmen.

Flash: Death would be more desirable.

Ming: As for you, Dale Arden, you shall be taught to act like my Empress.

Music up and under

Announcer: Doomed to a fate worse than death among the cruel Hawkmen, what terrifying adventures await our friends? Be sure to listen in again next week and hear the further Amazing Adventures of Flash Gordon and Dale Arden!

Further Resources

BOOKS

MacDonald, J. Fred. *Don't Touch That Dial!: Radio Programming in American Life, 1920–1960.* Chicago: Nelson-Hall, 1979.

Nachman, Gerald. *Raised on Radio: In Quest of the Lone Ranger.* New York: Pantheon Books, 1998.

WEBSITES

The Old Time Radio Script Collection. Available online at http://www.genericradio.com (accessed August 9, 2002).

Employed Women Under N.R.A. Codes

Study

By: Mary Elizabeth Pidgeon

Date: 1935

Source: Pidgeon, Mary Elizabeth. *Employed Women Under N.R.A. Codes.* Bulletin of the Women's Bureau, no. 130. U.S. Department of Labor. Washington, D.C.: Government Printing Office, 1935, 1–5, 129–33.

About the Author: Mary Elizabeth Pidgeon (1890?–1979) was an economist for the Department of Labor's Women's Bureau. ■

Introduction

The National Recovery Administration (NRA) was created in 1933 to establish an economic planning and management system based on a cooperative relationship between labor, business, and government. The short-term objective was to increase wages and employment, ensure businesses a fair profit, eliminate destructive competition, and improve working conditions. The anticipated increase in purchasing power was expected to stimulate the economy and help bring the country out of the Depression.

The primary vehicle for achieving these objectives was the voluntary creation of and adherence to NRA codes that established guidelines regarding hours, wages, prices, and working conditions. Nearly six hundred codes, each affecting a different market or industry, were ultimately approved. They were developed jointly by business and labor with representatives of the federal government facilitating the process.

Issues affecting women reflected their disadvantaged place in the workforce. In a society strongly committed to the traditions of a nuclear family and a Victorian view of gender roles, women in the workforce were generally regarded as temporary workers (between school and marriage) or as unmarried women with only themselves to support. Even if they could obtain the same job as a man, usually women were not believed to be entitled to the same wages since they were not expected to support a family.

These assumptions had a major impact on women in the workplace. Nearly 40 percent of female workers in 1930 were under twenty-five years of age, though this age group represented only 20 percent of the male work force. Women were far less likely to be unionized. Typically they worked in limited and highly segregated roles, either by industry or occupation. Moreover, they were paid less than men, even when working in the same job.

Younger, more isolated, and, with regard to pay equity, lacking popular sympathy, women had long been the victims of blatantly discriminatory wage and labor practices. Many industries exploited the common practice of paying women lower wages and argued that their competitiveness in the marketplace was dependent on using the unequal wage structure. The establishment of NRA codes forced some of these inequities into open view and presented the opportunity to address some of the most serious problems.

Effect of the N.R.A. on Women's Wages

	Selling price of dress		
	$3.75 and less	**$4.75 and $5.75**	**$10.75 and $12.75**
Number of women reported (inside operators only)	170-187	150	154-177
Median week's earnings:			
Before code	$19.10	$28.00	$26.75
After code	$30.35	$36.50	$36.05
Percent increase	58.8	30.3	34.7

SOURCE: Mary E. Pidgeon. *Employed Women under N.R.A. Codes.* Bulletin on the Women's Bureau, U.S. Department of Labor, p. 130.

Significance

Because women were more vulnerable in the workplace, they received important benefits from the NRA, particularly as it established minimum wages and restricted hours. Nonetheless, these achievements fell far short of what was needed. The immediate issues included the inequality of pay, the exclusion of female-dominated employment groups from the NRA codes, and the frequency with which exceptions were made to groups with large female representation.

As initially developed, many codes authorized different rates of pay for men and women performing identical jobs. These discrepancies were almost immediately challenged by Mary Anderson, director of the Women's Bureau of the Department of Labor, and Secretary of Labor Frances Perkins, the first female Cabinet member in U.S. history. Within the first year, 119 codes were modified, bringing about greater pay equity.

Perhaps the greatest deficiency of the NRA from the perspective of women workers was its failure to include critical industries and occupations in which women were disproportionately represented. In some cases, occupations simply were not covered. By law the NRA could only develop codes for industries engaged in interstate commerce. This restriction, for example, precluded the establishment of codes for domestic workers. In other cases, codes were simply never developed. The work of telephone operators, an occupation that employed women almost exclusively, was never included.

Despite the initial wave of enthusiasm, the NRA was soon beset by insurmountable and often self-inflicted problems. Realizing that it was not the solution he had hoped it would be, Franklin Delano Roosevelt (served 1933–1945) was almost relieved when the Supreme Court declared the NRA unconstitutional in early 1935.

While the NRA codes were short-term in their practical effect, strengthening the case for pay equity and enlisting the federal government in achieving this goal, this legislative action constituted a significant step in the women's labor movement. Subsequent New Deal programs bolstered this effort, although certainly none fully achieved the desired results.

Primary Source

Employed Women Under N.R.A. Codes [excerpt]

SYNOPSIS: The following excerpt comes from a 1935 study by the Women's Bureau of the U.S. Labor Department on the impact of the NRA on women in the workforce. While reporting favorably on the overall impact, the study recognized significant shortcomings. The report pointed out the exclusion of groups with large female populations from the NRA, continued wage discrimination, and inadequate protection offered by many existing codes.

Women work in the cramped space of a textile factory during the 1930s. © **HULTON-DEUTSCH COLLECTION/CORBIS. REPRODUCED BY PERMISSION.**

Introduction

The National Recovery Act originally was passed for a 2-year period, going into effect June 16, 1933. By January 1, 1934, it was estimated that codes had been approved covering about 90 percent of all industrial workers, the most important of them having been promulgated within the first 6 months.

The primary effort of the present study is to summarize the provisions of codes that affected large numbers of women. The code provisions discussed are those approved by July 1, 1934. The report gives some data indicating effects of codes on employed women as shown by such Federal and State figures as are available.

The general purposes of the act included advantages to labor as well as to industry and business. Among these purposes as stated in the act are the following: (1) To increase purchasing power; (2) to reduce and relieve unemployment; (3) to improve standards of labor. Moreover, the President said, when he signed the act, June 16, 1933:

> Its goal is the assurance of a reasonable profit to industry and living wages for labor with the elimination of the tyrannical methods and practices which have not only harassed honest business but also contributed to the ills of labor.

Briefly, the plan followed in preparing the codes was to encourage persons "truly representative" of any industry in or affecting interstate or foreign commerce to draw up the code of fair competition proposed for that industry, after which public hearings were held to allow labor, industry, and consumers to protest anything they objected to. Final approval was sealed by signature of the President, who was empowered "as a condition of his approval" to impose conditions "for the protection of consumers, competitors, employees, and others, and in furtherance of the public interest." . . .

Gains of Employed Women under The N.R.A.

The outstanding gains made under the N.R.A. in the development of standards of employment that affect women *never can be lost sight of.* This is most keenly appreciated in the Women's Bureau, which, under its legal mandate to "formulate standards and policies to promote the welfare" of wage-earning women, has labored continuously toward the very ends that, through the N.R.A., have been more closely incorporated into the thinking of the American people.

Even in this period of time, which is exceedingly short for the development of so broad a program of social reconstruction, enormous advances were made for employed women in a raising of their wages, a shortening of their hours, and an increase in their employment.

Increase in women's wages

In connection with wage increases, instances continually appear to show the wide-spread effect of code minima in bringing up the earnings of very large numbers of women who were at the lowest wage levels. Obviously this is very true of hourly earnings, but—still more important—there were definite additions to the pay envelop for the week. To cite but a few of these from Women's Bureau material not yet in complete published form:

> In a recent survey of the New York dress industry, weekly wage increases under codes of from 30 to nearly 60 percent are shown in the earnings of inside operatives.
>
> In a recent survey of employed women in Michigan, week's earnings had increased for the most part from 20 to 40 percent in the various industries and this was true even though hours were shorter. While median earnings in 1932 ranged from $3.85 to $14.95, the lowest median in 1934 was $10 and the highest $19.65.
>
> In a study of men's work clothing made in certain areas, the number of women in such factories in 12 cities in Georgia who received $12 or more a week, increased from 11.8 percent before the code to 56.2 percent after the code. (For Atlanta, Savannah, and Macon this increase was from 16.8 percent to 66.5 percent, and in 9 other cities it was from 7.7 to 48.1 percent.) In New Orleans, 9.2 percent of the women in factories making men's work clothing received $12 or more a week before the code, while 61.2 percent of the women employees received such amounts after the code. In 7 cities in California, the proportion of women receiving $13 or more a week in work clothing factories increased from 62.6 percent before the code or the President's Reemployment Agreement to 67 percent after.

A further point to be noted in the improvement of women's wages is that the few available data indicate a very definite narrowing of the pay differential between women and men. This was fully to be expected, since it so frequently is the women employed who are at the lowest pay levels, and consequently they would be the ones brought up to the minimum and somewhat nearer the wage paid to men.

Shortened hours of work for women

In the matter of hour standards, the 40-hour week has been proposed for immediate action and definite progress toward its establishment has been made. Never before has the universal shortening of hours received such far-reaching governmental backing nor has the ideal of attaining a work week as short as 40 hours been seriously proposed on so wide a scale; no State had legislated for a week shorter than 48 hours, and only about one-fifth of the States for work time even so short as that, most of these laws covering only certain industries.

Increased employment of women

In the third line of advance for women—increased employment—such data as are available show the definite benefit of the recovery program, and there also is some indication of greater regularization. For example, in the Michigan survey referred to, there was a 23 percent increase in the number of women in general mercantile firms and a 25 percent increase in manufacturing employment, though naturally the extent of the latter varied with different industries.

Advance in standards for the employment of women

A gain under the N.R.A. that is even more important than specific code provisions is the direction of public thinking along constructive social lines—the popular realization of the importance not alone to the individual employee but to the entire scheme of American life of definite advances in wage and hour standards for wage earners.

Further needs

It was to be expected that women stood to receive a large share of the gain from the inauguration of so constructive a social policy as that provided for employed persons under the N.R.A., since in the past women have represented one of the chief groups most subject to the vagaries of the labor market, massed heavily in low-wage and long-hour employments, forming large proportions of those having jobs in seasonal industries, for the most part receiving considerably less for their services than men received, in many cases working in unsanitary and unhealthful surroundings.

Social development always is a matter of growth, and a complete program naturally takes a long time for accomplishment. The rapidity with which the N.R.A. program was carried forward was phenomenal, and it is inevitable that there remained problems to be solved, certain unanticipated effects to be adjusted, and efforts to be undertaken toward following further certain of the lines that were inaugurated.

In view of this and of the inestimable benefit to employed women represented by the standards proposed in many of the codes, a distorted view would be given if the Women's Bureau, in line with its legal duty to wage-earning women, did not point out certain defects that were developed.

As the codes were confined to industries in or affecting interstate or foreign commerce, nearly one-half of all employed women did not come under codes . . . ; furthermore, some of the more important woman-employing groups to which the law applied had no codes in effect at the close of the first year, though many of these came under the President's Reemployment Agreement.

Besides those women not under codes and those not provided for until quite late, very many were affected in some codes by the lowered minimum wages fixed on various differential bases, such as geographic location, sex, or size of city; by lower minima for handicapped workers and for learners sometimes not carefully defined; by lack of provisions for eliminating home work in some of the codes covering industries in which home work is done; and by the allowance of many exceptions from the hour maxima. Moreover, if the idea was to bring about increases in employment there is no doubt that the hour standards in many codes were too long. Another problem not solved was that of providing adequately for the maintenance of wage standards for those who received, or who in view of their type of work should have received, more than the minimum. This however, could be done more effectively through collective bargaining and was done in some codes where collective bargaining was strongly developed prior to adoption of the code.

In calling attention to the matters suggested above, the Women's Bureau is fully sensible of the magnitude of the problems the N.R.A. had to face, of the inestimable value and importance of the objectives sought, and of the real benefits that resulted. In the many phases of the problem that must be considered, perfection along any one line in such a very short period of time scarcely could be expected. Still it is the obvious function of the Women's Bureau to direct attention to further needs in connection with woman employment.

The fact that women form more than one-fifth of all employed persons makes the consideration of their situation under the codes one of great importance. While certain of the problems to be discussed here are especially connected with woman employment—such as sex differentials in the wage, or industrial home work—yet these are not isolated conditions, since a wage scale depressed by such situations likewise affects the men in an industry. It usually is found that in an industry where women's wages are low or where the bulk of the employees are women, men's wages also are low. . . .

Extent to which Codes Covered Employed Women

Since codes covered only industries in or affecting interstate and foreign commerce, they covered only about half of all employed women, mainly those in the manufacturing industries, trade, communication, clerical, and certain large service groups. The chief classes of women that it may be estimated came under codes are shown in appendix tables I and III, and may be summarized as follows:

Manufacturing	1,313,792
Clerical	1,244,526
Trade	855,699
Service	683,869
Communication	235,259
Total	4,333,145

Among the women not covered by codes were those in certain industries in which the worst employment conditions too often have prevailed. Codes did not cover household employees ("servants in homes"), nearly 1½ million, a number approaching the total of all women in manufacturing. This is a group whose conditions of work in many instances have been very unsatisfactory. Nor could the codes provide for the more than 1½ million women in professional service, whose experience has been that they were paid considerably less than men were paid for work of the same amount and caliber. . . .

■ ■ ■

APPENDIX C

Extracts from Women's Bureau Testimony . . .

Examples of Beneficial Effects of Code Provisions

Under the codes the following outstanding advantages have accrued to gainfully occupied women:

1. The material shortening of standard hours in some industries, with the effort to place legal safe-

guards around a Nation-wide and fairly uniform standard of hours for factory operatives all over the country.

2. An increase in employment in manufacturing, and some slight indications of a tendency toward more regular employment, both of which are indicated by attached figures from the one State regularly publishing such data by sex (New York). A striking example showing increases in employment corresponding to hour reductions under codes in 10 Michigan industries is afforded by a recent survey the Women's Bureau made in that State. Before the codes, from nearly 40 to 90 percent of the women reported worked over 40 hours, but after the codes less than 10 percent worked over 40 hours (except in one industry), in 6 of the 10 less than 5 percent worked over 40 hours. This was accompanied by employment increases of more than 50 percent in three industries, of practically 20 percent or more in four others.

3. Very definite increases are found in the earnings of many of those at the lowest wage levels, a good illustration being in the earnings reported by the Women's Bureau from pay rolls in the dress industry in New York showing increases under the code of from 30 to nearly 60 percent in the earnings of inside operatives (depending on the selling price of dress made). . . .

Where such increases have occurred to women, it is largely because so many have been paid at shockingly low rates before the code. The effect of the codes has been just what is expected of the minimum wage—that numbers who were in the most hopeless abyss have been brought up at least to some bottom level.

Having indicated all too briefly the lines of great advantage that have resulted from codes, it is my purpose now to mention certain main points of essential improvement that must be worked toward as rapidly as possible. The need for each of these lines of action can be supported from the experience of trained observers of the Women's Bureau in the field, and from investigations made by this Bureau during the past months, with testimony of too great length for presentation in full at this time.

1. The need for a better standard of hours, especially in some industries.
2. The importance of bringing under more complete code coverage certain very large woman-employing groups that have been very inadequately provided for, as well as others that have no codes at all.
3. The necessity of lessening the ways in which the substandard wage groups and the many exceptions to code provisions are being allowed to undermine wage standards.
4. The importance of provision for wages above the minimum. . . .

Summary

In final summary of the points here made it may be said that:

First: Code provisions for hours and wages represent a definite move in the right direction, that should be continued and perfected.

Second: In regard to hours—

These should be further shortened in some industries.

"Averaging" provisions should be eliminated.

Overtime, if allowed, should be rigidly safeguarded.

Fewer exemptions should be permitted and these only on strong evidence of a true emergency.

Third: More satisfactory code provisions should be worked out for certain large woman-employing groups not satisfactorily covered or not under any codes, such as those in certain service trades, in some remaining manufacturing industries, in telephone exchanges, and in many clerical occupations.

Fourth: Further steps should be taken to minimize the number of those to whom industries are permitted to pay a wage below a standard minimum for unskilled work, such as women, learners, and those employed on industrial home work.

Fifth: Further efforts should be made to bring into more uniform groups, under the better standards, industries similar in character of products and processes.

Sixth: To counteract a tendency toward general depression of wage levels, a strong movement should be made to fix definite limits to the proportions of workers that may be paid at the minimum, and below various gradations above the minimum, at least until more scientific study can be made of the degrees of skill that actually are required for occupations above the unskilled level for which a minimum is primarily intended to apply.

Break-downs in the code system have come chiefly from two sources, from a definite minority within certain industries and from a few entire industries largely unwilling to afford from their abundant coffers an adequate measure of living to those upon whose labor their profits depend. Throughout the period of code existence, sincere efforts to develop the system on a satisfactory basis have been evident on the part of the great majorities in the forces both of industry and of labor. With the continued cooperation of these forces we believe further steps can be taken toward perfecting a system that will operate for the increased employment, the more untrammelled leisure, the more adequate pay envelops, and in general the fuller living of the great majority of the people.

Further Resources

BOOKS

Foner, Philip S. *Women and the American Labor Movement.* New York: The Free Press, 1979–1980.

Kessler-Harris, Alice. *Out to Work: A History of Wage-Earning Women in the United States.* New York: Oxford University Press, 1982.

"The Ethics of Living Jim Crow: An Autobiographical Sketch"

Autobiography

By: Richard Wright

Date: 1937

Source: Wright, Richard. "The Ethics of Living Jim Crow: An Autobiographical Sketch." *American Stuff: An Anthology of Prose and Verse by Members of the Federal Writers' Project.* New York: The Viking Press, 1937, 39–52. Available online at http://newdeal.feri.org/texts/608.htm; website home page: http://newdeal.feri.org (accessed March 24, 2003).

About the Author: Richard Wright (1908–1960), novelist and short-story writer, was born near Natchez, Mississippi, to an impoverished family. Largely self-educated, he was one of the first writers to describe white treatment of blacks. His best known works, *Native Son* and *Black Boy,* are classic studies of racism in America. Wright, who had become a Communist in 1933, grew increasingly disenchanted with the United States and moved to Paris in the late 1940s. Later, Wright often wrote about colonialism in Africa. ■

Introduction

During the Reconstruction period following the Civil War (1861–1865), progress was made in extending social and political equality to freed slaves. Backed by federal troops, southern state governments were controlled by Republicans, the best of whom were legitimately interested in helping blacks become productive members of an egalitarian society. After federal troops withdrew, conservative white governments came to power. Over the next generation a legal and social system evolved, known as Jim Crow, which deprived African Americans of their basic rights and created a social structure that made them second-class citizens.

Richard Wright had to overcome the repressive segregation of the Jim Crow South before becoming a famous author. **REPRODUCED BY PERMISSION OF THE CARL VAN VECHTEN TRUST.**

Jim Crow laws constituted legalized segregation. Noted historian C. Vann Woodward wrote:

> [The] code lent the sanction of law to racial ostracism that extended to churches and school, to housing and jobs, to eating and drinking. Whether by law or by custom, that ostracism extended to virtually all forms of public transportation, to sports and recreation, to hospitals, orphanages, prisons, and asylums, and ultimately to funeral homes, morgues, and cemeteries.
>
> The Strange Career of Jim Crow. *London: Oxford University Press, 1966, p. 7.*

Sanctioned by blatantly discriminatory laws and a legal system that enforced their racist spirit, an oppressive social system emerged. It was one in which the daily humiliation and degradation of blacks was standard practice.

And behind it all were the night riders who firebombed, murdered, and held public lynchings to ensure that African Americans did not challenge the system. It was difficult enough to combat the legalized enemy in broad daylight; the largely unseen, criminal enforcers of Jim Crow were a critical prop to this heinous system.

Significance

By the 1930s, Jim Crow was deeply ingrained in the South and to a lesser extent established in other parts of the country. Several generations of African Americans had grown up under a system hardly less odious than slavery.

Progress toward eliminating Jim Crowism was very slow, but as the twentieth century progressed, an increasing militancy developed among African Americans. The rising expectations of several hundred thousand blacks returning from service during World War I (1914–1918) added pressure. The Great Migration of southern blacks into northern industrial cities was another major factor that increased the sense of urgency for change. Freed from the worst effects of Jim Crow, blacks found opportunity for expression.

The 1930s brought new factors. The turmoil caused by the Depression created an environment ripe for social change. The general success of labor unions was an important catalyst also. The inclusive character of the Congress of Industrial Organizations (CIO) in organizing unions in the auto and steel industries, for example, was in marked contrast to the racist policies of the American Federation of Labor (AFL) craft unions. By the end of the decade African Americans were beginning to play important roles in integrated unions.

The New Deal, of course, had an enormous influence on black Americans. While the program did not include specific civil rights reforms, it did include a strong commitment to equal treatment, in both its philosophy and its legislation. Despite the impact of local prejudices on the implementation of New Deal programs, overall these programs were a significant step forward for blacks and other disenfranchised groups.

The overarching objective of the Roosevelt administration, however, was economic recovery and the implementation of fundamental reforms in the economic system. While civil rights were important, Roosevelt did not want to take up that fight at the risk of losing valuable political support. President Roosevelt believed he needed the support of the southern Democrats to sustain his New Deal programs.

Roosevelt did bring into his administration liberals such as Harry Hopkins and Harold Ickes who had strong civil rights credentials. He also included blacks in his administration and sought their advice to a far greater degree than any previous president had.

Eleanor Roosevelt often carried forward the fight on equal rights for blacks. Speaking more candidly than her husband could, she pushed opponents more aggressively and devoted more attention to these matters than her husband could. Mrs. Roosevelt was an influential advocate for African American rights.

In a decade of turmoil, influential black voices were heard among those who advocated social change. Richard Wright, Langston Hughes, Paul Robeson, W.E.B. Du Bois, and many others were able to publicize the concerns of African Americans in a way not previously possible. After World War II (1939–1945), which increased the sense of urgency among African Americans, the civil rights movement steadily eroded the Jim Crow system Richard Wright describes below.

Primary Source

"The Ethics of Living Jim Crow: An Autobiographical Sketch" [excerpt]

SYNOPSIS: Wright's essay, "The Ethics of Living Jim Crow: An Autobiographical Sketch" was first published in *American Stuff: An Anthology of Prose and Verse by Members of the Federal Writers' Project* in 1937. It includes a number of incidents from Wright's youth that demonstrate the demeaning and violent nature of the black experience in the segregated South.

It was a long time before I came in close contact with white folks again. We moved from Arkansas to Mississippi. Here we had the good fortune not to live behind the railroad tracks, or close to white neighborhoods. We lived in the very heart of the local Black Belt. There were black churches and black preachers; there were black schools and black teachers; black groceries and black clerks. In fact, everything was so solidly black that for a long time I did not even think of white folks, save in remote and vague terms. But this could not last forever. As one grows older one eats more. One's clothing costs more. When I finished grammar school I had to go to work. My mother could no longer feed and clothe me on her cooking job.

There is but one place where a black boy who knows no trade can get a job. And that's where the houses and faces are white, where the trees, lawns, and hedges are green. My first job was with an optical company in Jackson, Mississippi. The morning I applied I stood straight and neat before the boss, answering all his questions with sharp yessirs and nosirs. I was very careful to pronounce my sirs distinctly, in order that he might know that I was po-

"Colored Only" drinking fountains were the norm in the segregated, Jim Crow, South. CORBIS-BETTMANN. REPRODUCED BY PERMISSION.

lite, that I knew where I was, and that I knew he was a white man. I wanted that job badly.

He looked me over as though he were examining a prize poodle. He questioned me closely about my schooling, being particularly insistent about how much mathematics I had had. He seemed very pleased when I told him I had had two years of algebra.

"Boy, how would you like to try to learn something around here?" he asked me.

"I'd like it fine, sir," I said, happy. I had visions of "working my way up." Even Negroes have those visions.

"All right," he said. "Come on."

I followed him to the small factory.

"Pease," he said to a white man of about thirty-five, "this is Richard. He's going to work for us."

Pease looked at me and nodded.

I was then taken to a white boy of about seventeen.

"Morrie, this is Richard, who's going to work for us."

"Whut yuh sayin' there, boy!" Morrie boomed at me.

"Fine!" I answered.

The boss instructed these two to help me, teach me, give me jobs to do, and let me learn what I could in my spare time.

My wages were five dollars a week.

I worked hard, trying to please. For the first month I got along O.K. Both Pease and Morrie seemed to like me. But one thing was missing. And I kept thinking about it. I was not learning anything, and nobody was volunteering to help me. Thinking they had forgotten that I was to learn something about the mechanics of grinding lenses, I asked Morrie one day to tell me about the work. He grew red.

"Whut yuh tryin' t' do, nigger, git smart?" he asked.

"Naw; I ain' tryin' t' git smart," I said.

"Well, don't, if yuh know whut's good for yuh!"

I was puzzled. Maybe he just doesn't want to help me, I thought. I went to Pease.

"Say, are you crazy, you black bastard?" Pease asked me, his gray eyes growing hard.

I spoke out, reminding him that the boss had said I was to be given a chance to learn something.

"Nigger, you think you're white, don't you?"

"Naw, sir!"

"Well, you're acting mighty like it!"

"But, Mr. Pease, the boss said . . ."

Pease shook his fist in my face.

"This is a white man's work around here, and you better watch yourself!"

From then on they changed toward me. They said good-morning no more. When I was just a bit slow in performing some duty, I was called a lazy black son-of-a-bitch.

Once I thought of reporting all this to the boss. But the mere idea of what would happen to me if Pease and Morrie should learn that I had "snitched" stopped me. And after all, the boss was a white man, too. What was the use?

The climax came at noon one summer day. Pease called me to his work-bench. To get to him I had to go between two narrow benches and stand with my back against a wall.

"Yes, sir," I said.

"Richard, I want to ask you something," Pease began pleasantly, not looking up from his work.

"Yes, sir," I said again.

Morrie came over, blocking the narrow passage between the benches. He folded his arms, staring at me solemnly.

I looked from one to the other, sensing that something was coming.

"Yes, sir," I said for the third time.

Pease looked up and spoke very slowly.

"Richard, Mr. Morrie here tells me you called me Pease."

I stiffened. A void seemed to open up in me. I knew this was the show-down.

He meant that I had failed to call him Mr. Pease. I looked at Morrie. He was gripping a steel bar in his hands. I opened my mouth to speak, to protest, to assure Pease that I had never called him simply Pease, and that I had never had any intentions of doing so, when Morrie grabbed me by the collar, ramming my head against the wall.

"Now, be careful, nigger!" snarled Morrie, baring his teeth. "I heard yuh call 'im Pease! 'N' if yuh say yuh didn't, yuh're callin' me a lie, see?" He waved the steel bar threateningly.

If I had said: No, sir, Mr. Pease, I never called you Pease, I would have been automatically calling Morrie a liar. And if I had said: Yes, sir, Mr. Pease, I called you Pease, I would have been pleading guilty to having uttered the worst insult that a Negro can utter to a southern white man. I stood hesitating, trying to frame a neutral reply.

"Richard, I asked you a question!" said Pease. Anger was creeping into his voice.

"I don't remember calling you Pease, Mr. Pease," I said cautiously. "And if I did, I sure didn't mean . . ."

"You black son-of-a-bitch! You called me Pease, then!" he spat, slapping me till I bent sideways over a bench. Morrie was on top of me, demanding:

"Didn't yuh call 'im Pease? If yuh say yuh didn't, I'll rip yo' gut string loose with this f—kin' bar, yuh black granny dodger! Yuh can't call a white man a lie 'n' git erway with it, you black son-of-a-bitch!"

I wilted. I begged them not to bother me. I knew what they wanted. They wanted me to leave.

"I'll leave," I promised. "I'll leave right now."

They gave me a minute to get out of the factory. I was warned not to show up again, or tell the boss.

I went.

When I told the folks at home what had happened, they called me a fool. They told me that I must never again attempt to exceed my boundaries. When you are working for white folks, they said, you got to "stay in your place" if you want to keep working.

2

My Jim Crow education continued on my next job, which was portering in a clothing store. One morning, while polishing brass out front, the boss and his twenty-year-old son got out of their car and half dragged and half kicked a Negro woman into the store. A policeman standing at the corner looked on, twirling his nightstick. I watched out of the corner of my eye, never slackening the strokes of my chamois upon the brass. After a few minutes, I heard shrill screams coming from the rear of the store. Later the woman stumbled out, bleeding, crying, and holding her stomach. When she reached the end of the block, the policeman grabbed her and accused her of being drunk. Silently I watched him throw her into a patrol wagon.

When I went to the rear of the store, the boss and his son were washing their hands at the sink.

They were chuckling. The floor was bloody, and strewn with wisps of hair and clothing. No doubt I must have appeared pretty shocked, for the boss slapped me reassuringly on the back.

"Boy, that's what we do to niggers when they don't want to pay their bills," he said, laughing.

His son looked at me and grinned.

"Here, have cigarette," he said.

Not knowing what to do, I took it. He lit his and held the match for me. This was a gesture of kindness, indicating that even if they had beaten the poor old woman, they would not beat me if I knew enough to keep my mouth shut.

"Yes, sir," I said, and asked no questions.

After they had gone, I sat on the edge of a packing box and stared at the bloody floor till the cigarette went out.

That day at noon, while eating in a hamburger joint, I told my fellow Negro porters what had happened. No one seemed surprised. One fellow, after swallowing a huge bite, turned to me and asked:

"Huh. Is that all they did t' her?"

"Yeah. Wasn't that enough?" I asked.

"Shucks! Man, she's a lucky bitch!" he said, burying his lips deep into a juicy hamburger. "Hell, it's a wonder they didn't lay her when they got through."

3

I was learning fast, but not quite fast enough. One day, while I was delivering packages in the suburbs, my bicycle tire was punctured. I walked along the hot, dusty road, sweating and leading my bicycle by the handle-bars.

A car slowed at my side.

"What's the matter, boy?" a white man called.

I told him my bicycle was broken and I was walking back to town.

"That's too bad," he said. "Hop on the running board."

He stopped the car. I clutched hard at my bicycle with one hand and clung to the side of the car with the other.

"All set? "

"Yes, sir," I answered. The car started.

It was full of young white men. They were drinking. I watched the flask pass from mouth to mouth.

"Wanna drink, boy?" one asked.

I laughed, the wind whipping my face. Instinctively obeying the freshly planted precepts of my mother, I said:

"Oh, no!"

The words were hardly out of my mouth before I felt something hard and cold smash me between the eyes. It was an empty whisky bottle. I saw stars, and fell backwards from the speeding car into the dust of the road, my feet becoming entangled in the steel spokes of my bicycle. The white men piled out, and stood over me.

"Nigger, ain' yuh learned no better sense'n that yet?" asked the man who hit me. "ain' yuh learned t' say sir t' a white man yet?"

Dazed, I pulled to my feet. My elbows and legs were bleeding. Fists doubled, the white man advanced, kicking my bicycle out of the way.

"Aw, leave the bastard alone. He's got enough," said one.

They stood looking at me. I rubbed my shins, trying to stop the flow of blood. No doubt they felt a sort of contemptuous pity, for one asked:

"Yuh wanna ride t' town now, nigger? Yuh reckon yuh know enough t' ride now?"

"I wanna walk," I said, simply.

Maybe it sounded funny. They laughed.

"Well, walk, yuh black son-of-a-bitch!"

When they left they comforted me with:

"Nigger, yuh sho better be damn glad it wuz us yuh talked t' the' way. Yuh're a lucky bastard, 'cause if yuh'd said the' t' somebody else, yuh might've been a dead nigger now."

4

Negroes who have lived South know the dread of being caught alone upon the streets in white neighborhoods after the sun has set. In such a simple situation as this the plight of the Negro in America is graphically symbolized. While white strangers may be in these neighborhoods trying to get home, they can pass unmolested. But the color of a Negro's skin makes him easily recognizable, makes him suspect, converts him into a defenseless target.

Late one Saturday night I made some deliveries in a white neighborhood. I was pedaling my bicycle back to the store as fast as I could, when a police car, swerving toward me, jammed me into the curbing.

"Get down and put up your hands!" the policemen ordered.

I did. They climbed out of the car, guns drawn, faces set, and advanced slowly.

"Keep still!" they ordered.

I reached my hands higher. They searched my pockets and packages. They seemed dissatisfied when they could find nothing incriminating. Finally, one of them said:

"Boy, tell your boss not to send you out in white neighborhoods this time of night."

As usual, I said:

"Yes, sir." . . .

9

I had learned my Jim Crow lessons so thoroughly that I kept the hotel job till I left Jackson for Memphis. It so happened that while in Memphis I applied for a job at a branch of the optical company. I was hired. And for some reason, as long as I worked there, they never brought my past against me.

Here my Jim Crow education assumed quite a different form. It was no longer brutally cruel, but subtly cruel. Here I learned to lie, to steal, to dissemble. I learned to play that dual role which every Negro must play if he wants to eat and live.

For example, it was almost impossible to get a book to read. It was assumed that after a Negro had imbibed what scanty schooling the state furnished he had no further need for books. I was always borrowing books from men on the job. One day I mustered enough courage to ask one of the men to let me get books from the library in his name. Surprisingly, he consented. I cannot help but think that he consented because he was a Roman Catholic and felt a vague sympathy for Negroes, being himself an object of hatred. Armed with a library card, I obtained books in the following manner: I would write a note to the librarian, saying: "Please let this nigger boy have the following books." I would then sign it with the white man's name.

When I went to the library, I would stand at the desk, hat in hand, looking as unbookish as possible. When I received the books desired I would take them home. If the books listed in the note happened to be out, I would sneak into the lobby and forge a new one. I never took any chances guessing with the white librarian about what the fictitious white man would want to read. No doubt if any of the white patrons had suspected that some of the volumes they enjoyed had been in the home of a Negro, they would not have tolerated it for an instant.

The factory force of the optical company in Memphis was much larger than that in Jackson, and more urbanized. At least they liked to talk, and would engage the Negro help in conversation whenever possible. By this means I found that many subjects were taboo from the white man's point of view. Among the topics they did not like to discuss with Negroes were the following: American white women; the Ku Klux Klan; France, and how Negro soldiers fared while there; French women; Jack Johnson; the entire northern part of the United States; the Civil War; Abraham Lincoln; U.S. Grant; General Sherman; Catholics; the Pope; Jews; the Republican Party; slavery; social equality; Communism; Socialism; the 13th and 14th Amendments to the Constitution; or any topic calling for positive knowledge or manly self-assertion on the part of the Negro. The most accepted topics were sex and religion.

There were many times when I had to exercise a great deal of ingenuity to keep out of trouble. It is a southern custom that all men must take off their hats when they enter an elevator. And especially did this apply to us blacks with rigid force. One day I stepped into an elevator with my arms full of packages. I was forced to ride with my hat on. Two white men stared at me coldly. Then one of them very kindly lifted my hat and placed it upon my armful of packages. Now the most accepted response for a Negro to make under such circumstances is to look at the white man out of the corner of his eye and grin. To have said: "Thank you!" would have made the white man think that you thought you were receiving from him a personal service. For such an act I have seen Negroes take a blow in the mouth. Finding the first alternative distasteful, and the second dangerous, I hit upon an acceptable course of action which fell safely between these two poles. I immediately—no sooner than my hat was lifted—pretended that my packages were about to spill, and appeared deeply distressed with keeping them in my arms. In this fashion I evaded having to acknowledge his service, and, in spite of adverse circumstances, salvaged a slender shred of personal pride.

How do Negroes feel about the way they have to live? How do they discuss it when alone among themselves? I think this question can be answered in a single sentence. A friend of mine who ran an elevator once told me:

"Lowd, man! Ef it wuzn't fer them polices 'n' them ol' lynch-mobs, there wouldn't be nothin' but uproar down here!"

Further Resources

BOOKS

Packard, Jerrold M. *American Nightmare: The History of Jim Crow.* New York: St. Martin's Press, 2002.

Woodward, C. Vann. *The Strange Career of Jim Crow,* 2nd ed. London: Oxford University Press, 1966.

Wormser, Richard. *The Rise and Fall of Jim Crow: The African American Struggle Against Discrimination, 1865–1954.* New York: Franklin Watts, 1999.

WEBSITES

"Examples of Jim Crow Laws." Available online at http://academic.udayton.edu/race/02rights/jcrow02.htm; website home page: http://www.academic.udayton.edu (accessed August 9, 2002).

Cultural and Social Aspects of the New York World's Fair, 1939

Pamphlet

By: National Advisory Committee on Women's Participation
Date: 1939
Source: National Advisory Committee on Women's Participation. *Cultural and Social Aspects of the New York World's Fair,* 1939, 8, 9, 13–18, 19–51. ■

Introduction

The first world's fair was the 1851 Crystal Palace Exhibition in London, England. The glass-and-iron structure housed exhibits from around the world, but, as might be expected, focused on the accomplishments of Great Britain and the British empire. Enormously popular, the London Exhibition set the tone for subsequent fairs in which a common theme was the celebration of technological achievement.

Two years later, New Yorkers opened their own Crystal Palace exhibition with a similar theme. Thereafter, a steady stream of "World's Fairs" and other significant exhibitions appeared every few years in Europe and the United States. In the United States, the most notable World's Fairs were the 1876 Centennial Exposition in Philadelphia, the 1893 Columbian Exposition in Chicago, and the St. Louis World's Fair in 1904.

The 1930s saw a resurgence of these great fairs in the United States with exhibitions in Chicago (1933–1934), San Diego (1935–1936), San Francisco (1939–1940), and New York (1939–1940).

The New York World's Fair was the largest and included several exhibits that were etched in the country's collective memory for several decades. Ostensibly a celebration of the 150th anniversary of George Washington's inauguration as president, held in New York in 1789, the fair's theme was embodied in its slogan: "Building the World of Tomorrow."

As expressed by the fair's Committee on Theme:

> The New York World's Fair is planned to be "everyman's fair"—to show the way toward the improvement of all the factors contributing to human welfare. We are convinced that the potential assets, material and spiritual, of our country are such that if rightly used they will make for a general public good such as has never been known. In order to make its contribution toward this process the Fair will show the most promising developments of production, service and social factors of the present day in relation to their bearing on the life of the great mass of the people. The plain American citizen will be able to see here what he could attain for his community and himself by intelligent coordinated effort and will be made to realize the interdependence of every contributing form of life and work.

The two great symbols of the fair were the Trylon (a 610-foot-high triangular obelisk) and the adjacent Perisphere (a dome with a diameter of 180 feet). The Perisphere housed the fair's signature exhibit: Democracity. Incorporating the current technology and theories of urban planning, Democracity was a core city surrounded by five satellite towns. It was a model of how the U.S. city of the future could look.

Many of the exhibits were corporate-sponsored. Two of the more prophetic were from General Motors (GM) and RCA. At the RCA exhibit, millions of people caught their first glimpse of the appliance that would dramatically alter American lifestyles in the 1950s and beyond: television.

Perhaps the most impressive exhibit was General Motors's Futurama. GM's vision of the future—America in 1960—was a nation of cars, suburbs, and highways. Futurama was a 36,000-square-foot scale model complete with futuristic homes, urban centers, landscape, and, most important, an advanced highway system on which cars traveled at speeds of one hundred miles per hour. Visitors viewed the exhibit from moving chairs that circled the impressive view of the future.

Significance

Impressive though the fair was, it never reached the attendance expectations of its president, New York adman Grover Whalen. The nearly 45 million visitors were insufficient to cover expenses, and when the fair closed its gates for the final time, in November 1940, it was millions of dollars in debt.

But by November 1940 the world was a very different place than it had been when the fair opened in April 1939. The world was at war. Poland had been occupied by Germany and the Soviet Union. France had fallen to the Germans. England, having already endured the German aerial bombardment for months, was battling the Nazis alone.

When the fair opened in the spring of 1940, the Czechoslovakian, Polish, and Russian pavilions were gone. Soon the French flag was flying at half-mast. The optimistic theme of 1939, "Building the World of Tomorrow," was replaced by a new 1940 theme: "For Peace and Freedom."

Although still at peace, Americans could not look to the future with confidence. Soon the brutal global war would, like the last one, destroy millions of lives and reshape the world. After peace finally did come, however, it was not long before many of the images of the 1939 World's Fair began to materialize.

Primary Source

Cultural and Social Aspects of the New York World's Fair [excerpt]

SYNOPSIS: The following are excerpts from *Cultural and Social Aspects of the New York World's Fair, 1939.* Included are descriptions of Democracity and Tomorrow Town, an exhibit that demonstrated new housing and urban planning ideas. Partially funded by the federal government, the fair reflected the government's increasing involvement in remedying the inadequate housing situation in the United States.

A Statement by President Roosevelt

"It is an inspiring thing for nations and communities to have high objectives, to unite their energies in self-appraisal, and boldly plan for the future.

"The World's Fair to be held in New York beginning in 1939 is a challenge to all Americans who believe in the destiny of this nation, and who welcome the knowledge that the exposition is to focus upon one central theme: Building the World of Tomorrow.

"At this great Fair all the world may review what the United States has achieved in the 150 years since George Washington was first inaugurated as President of the United States. Here millions of citizens may visualize the national life which is to come.

"That it will be a memorable and historic Fair, that it will profoundly influence our national life for many years to come, and that success may attend every phase of its activities—these are the hopes of the people of the United States. All power to your sponsors."

"The Fair—A Social Force"

Excerpts from Mr. Grover Whalen's Address at the Dedication of the Theme Center, August 16, 1937

"This day we have reserved as the dedication of dedications, for at the spot where we are gathered will rise the towering Trylon and the massive Perisphere which will dominate and give vivid significance to the entire exposition. Today, as we stand here on the brink of futurity, we hold tomorrow in our hands.

"It is fitting on this occasion to review the progress we have already achieved; for we have overcome many material obstacles, and we have already brought into being many superb material things. But no matter how successful these things are, or will be, they represent only the half of what we are determined to do. It is a monumental task to build the exposition we have planned; it is even more difficult to breathe into it a soul, to suffuse it with an idea, to provide it with social and philosophical significance. Ideas must ever shape, dominate, and give meaning to mere material things. The theme which permeates the New York World's Fair is noble and inspiring. This is the time, and this the place to restate our fundamental purpose, and to pledge the Fair anew to its consummation.

"The Fair will celebrate the 150th anniversary of the inauguration of Washington as the first President of the new American nation under the Federal constitution. This was a momentous event not only in the history of the United States, but in the history of Western civilization. Even now it is of the highest interest to America and to the world. May it remain so for the years to come! The founders of the Fair were early persuaded that this anniversary presented more than the opportunity to build a great exposition on a purely commemorative theme. To us, the future, pregnant with high destiny, seemed as meaningful as the past, with all its fateful achievements. Washington and his contemporaries, in their time, had, with courage and vision, plotted a course for the future; they builded better than the most optimistic had dared to hope.

"The contemporaries of George Washington were able to see life clearly and to see it whole because they lived the uncomplicated existence of a community that was primarily agricultural, but even this era saw the first beginnings of our modern scientific and industrial civilization. Science, in revolutionizing industry, has enriched and complicated every phase of living. Within the short space of several generations the world that men had known and

The Trylon and Perisphere, the symbols of the 1939 New York World's Fair. AP/WIDE WORLD PHOTOS. REPRODUCED BY PERMISSION.

understood for many hundreds of years rapidly disappeared. Never has civilization suffered such a profound change. The world was enlarged, enriched, and plunged into bewildering complications. We must, and we will, come to understand the world as one whole, integrated and complete—a single entity such as is depicted in our great Perisphere.

"So, in rendering homage to Washington and his illustrious colleagues, we determined to pattern our conduct upon their brave example. They solved the problems which threatened to destroy them. So we, in our time, resolved to gather together the genius and the imagination of the twentieth century to respond to those living questions which clamor for answers from living men and women.

"What is the deep significance of the dazzling scientific and material achievements of our age? What are the relationships of the various diverse elements of modern society? How can mankind work and live in peace and harmony? How can life be made more secure, more comfortable, more significant, for the average man and woman? This Fair, our Fair, your Fair, is determined to exert a social force and launch a needed message." . . .

We Approach a New Era

About 1850 the Queen of England, sensing that she had one small foot over the threshold of what has since become the Victorian era, set about planning the First International Exhibition, with her beloved consort, Prince Albert. It was to be a glorification of a new energy which was rapidly transforming civilization from an agricultural to an industrial basis. Everywhere people were excited by the change and opportunities, wrought by the harnessing of steam and the wonders of machinery. Human hands, which had toiled since the beginning at rough, hard tasks, seemed about to be released for pleasanter occupations. Steam trains, steam ships were taking some of the hazard and hardship out of transportation, and the shrinkage of distances had begun. It was a time of bright prospects, fine plans, and great ambitions. The Victoria and Albert Museum in London still stands as a monument to the acumen of the British rulers and the tremendous success of the first organized effort to appraise man's progress and indicate his future.

Eighty-eight years after the first International Exhibition the New York World's Fair, with its audacious purpose, to take inventory of civilization's present resources and project a possible better World of Tomorrow, may well be the beginning of another new period. Airplanes and zeppelins now represent the steam trains and steam ships of Queen Victoria's youth. Skeptical we may be of rocket transportation for the future but not nearly so skeptical as people eighty-eight years ago were of horseless carriages and airplanes, if indeed they thought at all of such fantastic possibilities. So much scientific, industrial and intellectual progress has been made that we now speak with familiarity of the stratosphere, take pleasure trips in airplanes, regard automobiles as commonplaces, and have even begun to predict human behavior and hold off death. We have learned how to make cloth without cotton, wool or silk and how to grow food without soil. We take vapors apart and put them together again so that gas masks have become household equipment, like fire extinguishers, in some parts of the world. We can smash an atom, pick sound out of the air and send it on its way again, flash pictures around the world, keep the human heart alive and beating outside the human body and do a great many other astonishing things.

But the major portion of the world's population is still underfed, badly housed and ill clothed. Even in enlightened countries the preponderance of people are undernourished. Many millions of people in the United States of America . . . rich democracy which boasts a progressive viewpoint . . . live in communities blighted by poverty, crime and disease. And the nations of the world, instead of being brought to closer cooperation and increased happiness by the world-wide development of transportation, communication, production and distribution facilities, grow increasingly suspicious of their neighbors.

To the tremendous task of presenting a picture of more orderly, happier living, that can be brought out of progress so rapid it has frequently brought about maladjustment of individuals, communities and nations, the New York World's Fair 1939 is dedicated. While its primary object is to present to the world a vivid and integrated expression of the expanding American social scene, the cooperation and viewpoint of sixty-three foreign governments have been enlisted. Prominent men and women from the fields of science, art, philosophy, architecture and design decided the pattern of the Fair after a small group had procured the vast capital necessary to realization of the grandiose plan. They agreed that the theme of the Fair was to be:

> A happier way of American living through a recognition of the interdependence of man and the building of a better world of tomorrow with the tools of today.

To its anticipated sixty million visitors the Fair will say, here are the new materials, ideas and forces at work in the world. These are the tools with which the World of Tomorrow can be made, or can be wrecked. With these instruments we can achieve a happier, richer way of living.

There seems to be a misguided impression that the Fair has been using the word "theme" as a synonym for some kind of poetic theory. Actually, as soon as the sponsoring group had accepted the principle of the Fair's message a profoundly practical problem arose. How could the message best be given out? National fairs, and even international fairs, psychologists warned, are popularly regarded as amusement jags. The problem was the difficult one of presenting a social message to a vast and various assemblage of sightseers from all parts of the country whose primary desire would be release through amusement from the cares and responsibilities of routine living. How to impress fun-seeking millions with a social message they could never forget, that would influence them subconsciously to strive for a new concept of living? How to impress upon everyone the realization that the future of social, economic and political peace in the world depends upon recognition of the interdependence of individuals, groups, cities, states and nations? It was essential to show that the farmer needs the miner, the miner needs the educator, who, in turn, needs the man that makes his clothes in the factory. Each needs for his welfare the functional contribution of the other.

If people could be made to understand more fully the relation between the functions they themselves perform and the great world around them; if they could be made aware of causes of difficulties which they face in everyday living; if the complexities of modern living could be broken down and analyzed so dramatically that the least social minded citizen understood the reasons for his perplexities, much maladjustment between individual and modern conditions, with resultant unhappiness, could be rectified. The Fair's planning group gave the problem months of consideration and research.

A spectacle was the obvious solution. But it must be a spectacle appealing to the mind rather than the emotions: drama so new and forceful that its social message would shine out as a climax overtopping everything else seen or heard at the Fair. The answer was the Theme Show which the Fair will present within the Perisphere. In the brief space of six minutes it portrays twenty-four hours in the life of Democracity, a city of the immediate future. The spectacle must necessarily be brief in order to get its message to the many millions of visitors anticipated at the Fair. By showing Democracity to 8,000 people an hour, for the period of the Fair, this can be accomplished.

The important task of designing a theatre for such a spectacle, and, at the same time providing a center of architectural interest at the Fair was entrusted to the architects who devised the Music Hall in Rockefeller Center: Wallace K. Harrison and J. Andre Fouilhoux. Their answer was the Trylon, the Perisphere and the Helicline. These are "made" words taken from Greek architectural and geometrical terms. The Trylon is a symbol of the Fair's lofty purpose, a triangular steeple of steel whose top is often lost in the clouds 700 feet above Flushing Meadow. Alongside it, seemingly floating on the spray of fountains at its base, the Perisphere symbolizes a complete plan; unity. The Helicline is the long spiral ramp which serves as exit from the Perisphere. These unescapable reminders of the Fair's social message dominate the 1200 acres occupied by the projected World of Tomorrow.

Democracity

To Henry Dreyfuss, famous industrial designer, was assigned the task of planning Democracity, a city of the immediate future, and making it so vivid to the millions who are to gaze upon it that each will feel it is a practical possibility and be stimulated to new interest in social and city planning. It was a job for a dreamer involving tremendous research, with great mechanical difficulties, and the creation of a new theatre technique. To begin with, no producer of a spectacle, however simple, has ever before been presented with an empty sphere and told that it was a theatre, and that within it was to be produced an unforgettable spectacle of a possible metropolis seen by thousands of spectators each hour like a mirage glimpsed in a flight through space.

Undaunted, Mr. Dreyfuss set to work with the architects and Robert D. Kohn, Chairman of the Committee on Theme. Difficulties were overcome one by one. The problems of entrance to and departure from the Theme Show within the Perisphere were solved by a double moving stairway giving access through the Trylon, and a long spiral exit ramp, called the Helicline. The Helicline is a descending curved platform from which a splendid view of the Fair's panorama provides a fitting climax to the spectacle of Democracity. Within the Perisphere two spectator platforms, one revolving clockwise and one counterclockwise, will carry audiences from Trylon entrance to Helicline exit. The six-minute interval within the Perisphere concentrates twenty-four hours in the life of Democracity and illustrates the interdependence of man.

To animate the world within the sphere, William Grant Still, Negro composer, has written a symphonic poem suggesting the city as a living thing, vibrant with the work and the lives of its inhabitants. Clouds float above the metropolis, and, as daylight fades and the city is illuminated, the stars appear, reproducing exactly the constellation of the heavens on the opening night of the Fair. This is the contribution to the Fair of Charles A. Federer, Jr. of the Hayden Planetarium.

Democracity is Mr. Dreyfuss' conception of how we should be living today. It is a city of light and air and green spaces. Stretching out in all directions are fine roads crossing broad green areas and connecting various industrial towns to the metropolitan center. Each industrial town is a complete unit of factory, homes and schools relying on the central city only for its general administration, its amusements and the things, commercial and cultural, that it cannot provide as a smaller community. The city has a vast transportation center where ocean liners, limited trains, airplanes and dirigibles report to a single terminal. In a vast basin nearby amphibians and speedboats find harborage.

From his safe vantage point on almost imperceptibly moving platforms that are seemingly suspended in space but are actually gliding smoothly on unseen struts projecting from the walls, the spectator can imagine himself dwelling in Democracity which seems to be above, below, and all about him.

The walls of the Perisphere form the largest screen on which technicians have ever attempted to project motion pictures. Ten different films will be projected simultaneously, with sound effect. At the climax of the drama columns of marching humanity approach from a great distance singing the triumphant Marching Song of the Fair. These are workers of all kinds, representing the cooperation essential to the building of a World of Tomorrow and complete realization of the interdependence of man.

A radiance in the sky develops into a blazing curtain of polaroid light in which the vision dissolves as though fire poured over it slowly. The transported spectators emerge from the world of the sphere. The Helicline brings them gently back to earth and the Fair's broad bright reality. . . .

Tomorrow Town

Tomorrow Town, on the edge of the Community Interests zone, consists of fifteen demonstration homes ranging in price from low cost houses to houses costing around $20,000, and the Domestic Utilities Building, which contains a series of modern basements and utility rooms adaptable to these demonstration homes or to any type of new or modernized homes. These homes will exemplify the proper use of nationally available materials, equipment and methods for home building or home modernization.

The instruction given to the architects who designed these houses stated that they "should be consistent with the conditions of the Atlantic Coast States. This section as a whole should neither be traditional nor modernistic in design. It should be modern." The arrangement of the houses is not intended to represent a model neighborhood plan, as neither the circulation requirements nor the available ground area make it possible, but the houses will be representative of those that might be found in a satellite town, such as Democracity dramatizes in the Theme Show.

A special feature of each demonstration home will be that one room on the ground floor will be given over to a comprehensive exhibit of the "hidden" materials which have been used in that particular house. Here will be free-standing sections of walls, roofs, and floors showing their construction, including sheathing, insulation and special structural systems for walls, floors and roofs. There will also be models of framing systems, layouts of plumbing, wiring and other domestic utilities and special service systems.

Visitors to Tomorrow Town will receive a directory of the village, listing all exhibitors, their products and locations. In the demonstration homes booklets will be distributed giving complete plans for all the houses and listing participating manufacturers. This is in line with the Fair policy of stressing consumers' interests and assisting prospective home builders to obtain more value for their money.

Town Planning and Housing

The Committee on Theme, which was the original planning group for the Fair, visualized, as an integral part of the program, significant exhibits showing the economic factors involved in the improvement of living conditions of the American people and the fundamental aspects of the problem that will have to be considered in any cooperative effort by agencies, public or private, to bring about this social advance.

An important and original contribution in this field will be the first showing of a motion picture depicting the life and death of American cities. The film was prepared at the instigation of the Committee on Theme under the direction of Robert D. Kohn, through a grant from the Carnegie Foundation and will be shown in the auditorium of the Science, Education and Medicine and Public Health Building. It shows changes in housing conditions from the early years of the Republic to the present time and indicates further program for better town and city planning and housing methods. The American City Planning Institute appointed a special committee to cooperate with the producers of the motion picture, in the selection of material and preparation of the scenario on which it is based. The picture vividly contrasts the crime, poverty and disease of blighted and dying cities with the happier way of living in communities developed under large-scale planning.

The large part played by Government in the housing field is emphasized in a section devoted to Shelter in the Federal Building. The story of Government's aid in housing is told by the use of dynamic exhibits dramatized by a large sculptural work symbolizing federal housing aid. On each side of the sculptural mass are two large dioramas: one showing the Government's contribution toward the betterment of farm areas through farm rehabilitation, replanning and electrification. By means of colored transparencies, the work of Governmental financing agencies in relation to rural Housing is shown. On the right-hand side of the sculptural mass is another large diorama twenty feet long showing the Government's contribution in urban and suburban replanning. This diorama contrasts the bad conditions existing in some of our city's dwelling areas with the replanned, modernized sections reconditioned through Government. Toward the suburban part of the diorama is shown a replanned town such as a "greenbelt" town with its planned streets, houses, underpasses, play areas and community centers. All this emphasizes what an important part the Government agencies play in the modernization and improvement of our city dwelling areas.

While "Tomorrow Town" is in no way intended to be an exhibit of low-costing housing, it makes its contribution to necessary information on that difficult problem through exhibits of new processes and the methods by which some well-known materials can be made more effective.

This exhibition includes only a section of a town and represents the adaptation to modern living conditions of dwellings for the American family of more than average income. It is meant to point the obsolescence of much small dwelling construction and show the home owner how to obtain more comfort, more value and more pleasure from his house, his garden and his community.

Further Resources

BOOKS

Gelernter, David. *1939: The Lost World of the Fair.* New York: Free Press, 1995.

Rosenblum, Robert. "Introduction." *Remembering the Future: The New York World's Fair from 1939–1964.* New York: Rizzoli, 1989.

WEBSITES

"1939 New York World's Fair." Available online at http://www.geocities.com/hepcat_paul/1939nywf.html; website home page: http://www.geocities.com (accessed August 8, 2002).

"Cultural Contradictions of a Consumer Society." Available online at http://www.sjsu.edu/faculty/wooda/149/149syllabus12susman.html; website home page: http://www.sjsu.edu (accessed August 9, 2002).

"Images of the 1939 New York World's Fair." Available online at http://www.sjsu.edu/faculty/wooda/wfcard.html; website home page: http://www.sjsu.edu (accessed August 9, 2002).

"New York World's Fair." Available online at http://www.geocities.com/Paris/Tower/9826/1939ny-ingles.html; website home page: http://www.geocities.com (accessed August 9, 2002).

The Grapes of Wrath

Novel

By: John Steinbeck

Date: 1939

Source: Steinbeck, John. *The Grapes of Wrath.* New York: Viking Penguin, 1939; 1992, 3–7.

About the Author: John Steinbeck (1902–1968), California-born and Stanford-educated, wrote novels about working-class people in the West. *The Grapes of Wrath* tells the story of migrants from Oklahoma who try to escape the combined disaster of the Dust Bowl, Depression, and farm consolidation by heading for California. In 1940 Steinbeck received the Pulitzer Prize for *The Grapes of Wrath.* In 1962 he received the Nobel Prize for literature. ■

Introduction

Dust Bowl is a term that specifically applies to an area of western Oklahoma, western Kansas, and northern Texas that was frequently struck with severe dust storms in the 1930s. More generally, but perhaps less accurately, the term is applied to the entire Great Plains. Though properly confined to one section of the country, the term is useful in drawing attention to the broader problem of farmland erosion that was graphically illustrated in the photos of huge black clouds descending on isolated farming communities of the central Great Plains.

The United States is a vast and rich agricultural land. From the earliest colonial times, settlers often used this abundance through wasteful agricultural practices, assuming they were safe in having more land available to the west. For nearly three hundred years, it always was. By the late nineteenth century, however, the frontier was gone. The wasteful practices often continued.

Coincidentally, the final push to the agricultural frontier in the late 1890s coincided with a period of relatively abundant rainfall in the western Great Plains that created a false impression of fertility. The plow broke land that could not support agriculture, and oversized herds were put to graze on grasslands that could not properly sustain them. When the inevitable drought cycle returned, the natural grasses with their deep root structures had been destroyed. There was nothing to hold the fragile topsoil in place, and permanent erosion resulted.

The tendency to overuse land increased during World War I (1914–1918). With Europe desperate for U.S. food products, marginal land was put into production. As peace returned, farmers—many of whom were heavily mortgaged to pay for expansion and machinery to meet the demands of the war years—continued to work this land in an effort to pay off their debt and offset the steady decline in agricultural prices.

Significance

This agricultural phenomenon had national scope. When droughts began, first in the Mississippi Delta in 1930, farmers paid a steep price for years of neglecting the needs of the land. The drought spread to the Midwest in 1931. It then moved across the Great Plains to the Rockies and east into the Ohio River Valley. But the worst

Alexander Hogue's painting *Dust Bowl.* SMITHSONIAN AMERICAN ART MUSEUM, GIFT OF INTERNATIONAL BUSINESS MACHINES CORPORATION.

was yet to come. Between June 1933 and May 1934, the Great Plains experienced some of the lowest rainfall on record.

The heat, too, climbed to record levels. Grasshoppers emerged from years of dormancy and blanketed sections of the plains, devouring every stalk of grass in their path. The wind was incessant. It scooped up dry soil—millions of tons—and blew it eastward. The dust storms were so intense that evidence was seen as far away as New York and Washington. Prairie dust was even reported to have settled on ships three hundred miles out in the Atlantic.

On the plains, the conditions became unbearable. Huge storms destroyed the land, killed livestock, trapped people in their homes, and resulted in untold deaths due to respiratory ailments brought on by breathing the dust.

Many farmers simply left. It is estimated that 3.5 million people left Great Plains farms in the 1930s. Beaten by the drought, as tenants forced off the land by eviction and farm consolidation or simply by financial failure, farmers left the land in droves.

Some of the lasting achievements of the New Deal were the efforts made to reverse the destructive soil-eroding farming and grazing practices that had led to the Dust Bowl and the nationwide erosion of valuable land. Measures such as the 1936 Soil Conservation and Domestic Allotment Act, the Taylor Grazing Act (1934), and the creation of the Soil Erosion Service (1933) pointed in the right direction. The Civilian Conservation Corps eventually put 2.5 million young men to work on conservation projects all across the country. The great dam projects such as the Tennessee Valley Authority and those on the Colorado, Columbia, and other western rivers were launched in part to aid conservation efforts.

By design or luck, the consequence of these and other conservation programs have helped prevent a recurrence of the erosion-caused disasters of the 1930s.

Primary Source

The Grapes of Wrath [excerpt]

SYNOPSIS: The following is chapter one of Steinbeck's novel *The Grapes of Wrath.* This powerful de-

The surreal landscape of an Oklahoma farm buried under loose, dry sand. It is representative of the countless farms ruined by drought and poor land management in the Dust Bowl. NATIONAL ARCHIVES AND RECORDS ADMINISTRATION.

scription of a dust storm mirrors the experience of people from Texas to the Dakotas in the Dust Bowl years of 1933–1936.

To the red country and part of the gray country of Oklahoma, the last rains came gently, and they did not cut the scarred earth. The plows crossed and recrossed the rivulet marks. The last rains lifted the corn quickly and scattered weed colonies and grass along the sides of the roads so that the gray country and the dark red country began to disappear under a green cover. In the last part of May the sky grew pale and the clouds that had hung in high puffs for so long in the spring were dissipated. The sun flared down on the growing corn day after day until a line of brown spread along the edge of each green bayonet. The clouds appeared, and went away, and in a while they did not try any more. The weeds grew darker green to protect themselves, and they did not spread any more. The surface of the earth crusted, a thin hard crust, and as the sky became pale, so the earth became pale, pink in the red country and white in the gray country.

In the water-cut gullies the earth dusted down in dry little streams. Gophers and ant lions started small avalanches. And as the sharp sun struck day after day, the leaves of the young corn became less stiff and erect; they bent in a curve at first, and then, as the central ribs of strength grew weak, each leaf tilted downward. Then it was June, and the sun shone more fiercely. The brown lines on the corn leaves widened and moved in on the central ribs. The weeds frayed and edged back toward their roots. The air was thin and the sky more pale; and every day the earth paled.

In the roads where the teams moved, where the wheels milled the ground and the hooves of the horses beat the ground, the dirt crust broke and the dust formed. Every moving thing lifted the dust into the air: a walking man lifted a thin layer as high as his waist, and a wagon lifted the dust as high as the fence tops, and an automobile boiled a cloud behind it. The dust was long in settling back again.

When June was half gone, the big clouds moved up out of Texas and the Gulf, high heavy clouds, rain-heads. The men in the fields looked up at the clouds and sniffed at them and held wet fingers up to sense the wind. And the horses were nervous while the clouds were up. The rain-heads dropped a little spattering and hurried on to some other country. Behind them the sky was pale again and the sun flared. In the dust there were drop craters where the rain had fallen, and there were clean splashes on the corn, and that was all.

A gentle wind followed the rain clouds, driving them on northward, a wind that softly clashed the drying corn. A day went by and the wind increased, steady, unbroken by gusts. The dust from the roads fluffed up and spread out and fell on the weeds beside the fields, and fell into the fields a little way. Now the wind grew strong and hard and it worked at the rain crust in the corn fields. Little by little the sky was darkened by the mixing dust, and the wind felt over the earth, loosened the dust, and carried it away. The wind grew stronger. The rain crust broke and the dust lifted up out of the fields and drove gray plumes into the air like sluggish smoke. The corn threshed the wind and made a dry, rushing sound. The finest dust did not settle back to earth now, but disappeared into the darkening sky.

The wind grew stronger, whisked under stones, carried up straws and old leaves, and even little clods, marking its course as it sailed across the fields. The air and the sky darkened and through them the sun shone redly, and there was a raw sting in the air. During a night the wind raced faster over the land, dug cunningly among the rootlets of the corn, and the corn fought the wind with its weakened leaves until the roots were freed by the prying wind and then each stalk settled wearily sideways toward the earth and pointed the direction of the wind.

The dawn came, but no day. In the gray sky a red sun appeared, a dim red circle that gave a little light, like dusk; and as that day advanced, the dusk slipped back toward darkness, and the wind cried and whimpered over the fallen corn.

Men and women huddled in their houses, and they tied handkerchiefs over their noses when they went out, and wore goggles to protect their eyes.

When the night came again it was black night, for the stars could not pierce the dust to get down, and the window lights could not even spread beyond their own yards. Now the dust was evenly mixed with the air, an emulsion of dust and air. Houses were shut tight, and cloth wedged around doors and windows, but the dust came in so thinly that it could not be seen in the air, and it settled like pollen on the chairs and tables, on the dishes. The people brushed it from their shoulders. Little lines of dust lay at the door sills.

In the middle of that night the wind passed on and left the land quiet. The dust-filled air muffled sound more completely than fog does. The people, lying in their beds, heard the wind stop. They awakened when the rushing wind was gone. They lay quietly and listened deep into the stillness. Then the roosters crowed, and their voices were muffled, and the people stirred restlessly in their beds and wanted the morning. They knew it would take a long

"Dust Bowl Blues"

[This song, written by folksinger/songwriter Woody Guthrie in the 1930s, poetically describes the difficult times encountered by those living in the Dust Bowl.]

I just blowed in, and I got them dust bowl blues,
I just blowed in, and I got them dust bowl blues,
I just blowed in, and I'll blow back out again.

I guess you've heard about ev'ry kind of blues,
I guess you've heard about ev'ry kind of blues,
But when the dust gets high, you can't even see the sky.

I've seen the dust so black that I couldn't see a thing,
I've seen the dust so black that I couldn't see a thing,
And the wind so cold, boy, it nearly cut your water off.

I seen the wind so high that it blowed my fences down,
I've seen the wind so high that it blowed my fences down,
Buried my tractor six feet underground.

Well, it turned my farm into a pile of sand,
Yes, it turned my farm into a pile of sand,
I had to hit that road with a bottle in my hand.

I spent ten years down in that old dust bowl,
I spent ten years down in that old dust bowl,
When you get that dust pneumony, boy, it's time to go.

I had a gal, and she was young and sweet,
I had a gal, and she was young and sweet,
But a dust storm buried her sixteen hundred feet.

She was a good gal, long, tall and stout,
Yes, she was a good gal, long, tall and stout,
I had to get a steam shovel just to dig my darlin' out.

These dusty blues are the dustiest ones I know,
These dusty blues are the dustiest ones I know,
Buried head over heels in the black old dust, I had to pack up and go.
An' I just blowed in, an' I'll soon blow out again.

SOURCE: Lyrics as recorded by Woody Guthrie, *Dust Bowl Ballads.* Camden, N.J.: RCA Studios, 1940. Transcribed by Manfred Helfert.

time for the dust to settle out of the air. In the morning the dust hung like fog, and the sun was as red as ripe new blood. All day the dust sifted down from the sky, and the next day it sifted down. An even blanket covered the earth. It settled on the corn, piled up on the tops of the fence posts, piled up on thc wircs; it settled on roofs, blanketed the weeds and trees.

The people came out of their houses and smelled the hot stinging air and covered their noses from it. And the children came out of the houses, but they did not run or shout as they would have done after a rain. Men stood by their fences and looked at the ruined corn, drying fast now, only a little green showing through the film of dust. The men were silent and they did not move often. And the women came out of the houses to stand beside their men—to feel whether this time the men would break. The women studied the men's faces secretly, for the corn could go, as long as something else remained. The children stood near by, drawing figures in the dust with bare toes, and the children sent exploring senses out to see whether men and women would break. The children peeked at the faces of the men and women, and then drew careful lines in the dust with their toes. Horses came to the watering troughs and nuzzled the water to clear the surface dust. After a while the faces of the watching men lost their bemused perplexity and became hard and angry and resistant. Then the women knew that they were safe and that there was no break. Then they asked, What'll we do? And the men replied, I don't know. But it was all right. The women knew it was all right, and the watching children knew it was all right. Women and children knew deep in themselves that no misfortune was too great to bear if their men were whole. The women went into the houses to their work, and the children began to play, but cautiously at first. As the day went forward the sun became less red. It flared down on the dust-blanketed land. The men sat in the doorways of their houses; their hands were busy with sticks and little rocks. The men sat still—thinking—figuring.

Further Resources

BOOKS

Saloutos, Theodore. *The American Farmer and the New Deal.* Ames, Iowa: Iowa State University Press, 1982.

Watkins, T.H. *The Hungry Years: A Narrative History of the Great Depression in America.* New York: Henry Holt, 1999.

Saga of the CCC

Poem

By: John D. Guthrie

Date: 1942

Source: Guthrie, John D. *Saga of the CCC.* Washington D.C.: American Forestry Association, 1942, 11–45.

About the Author: John D. Guthrie was a member of the United States Forest Service. He collected and published poems about forestry and the Forest Service. He wrote *Saga of the CCC* in 1942. ■

Introduction

Franklin Roosevelt's immediate objective upon taking office on March 4, 1933, was providing relief to the needy. One of the most popular New Deal programs was the Civilian Conservation Corps (CCC). The aim was to put young unemployed men to work on much-needed conservation programs.

Roosevelt proposed the CCC on March 21, 1933. It was signed into law on April 5, and the first recruit enlisted on April 7. The first camp began operation on April 17. By July, some 275,000 "boys" were at work in 1,300 camps all across the country.

Workers made $30 per month, with $22–$25 being sent home to their families. They were housed in barracks of 40 to 50 men with several barracks per camp. The camps were established and administered by U.S. Army officers. The work was usually supervised by the U.S. Forestry Service and "local experienced men" (LEMs). Work began at 7 A.M. and ended at 4 P.M. The "tree boys" learned valuable job skills, and in the evening an educational adviser (teacher) provided classroom education.

The average age was eighteen and a half years upon enlistment. They typically had an eighth-grade education and stayed in the CCC for nine months. Sixty percent were from farms or small towns. For most, it was their first full-time job and the first time away from home.

For those escaping urban and rural poverty, the CCC often provided better living conditions than at home. Some had indoor plumbing and electricity for the first time. Many were better fed and better clothed. Perhaps most importantly, CCC workers had the satisfaction of sending much-needed financial support to their families.

Significance

Over the nine-year life of the CCC there were nearly three million participants. The service they performed for the preservation and improvement of U.S. resources cannot be overstated. Over 300,000 "check dams" and 65,000 miles of terracing were built to help control erosion. Over 1.5 billion trees were planted. The men cut

Recruits line up for lunch at the Civilian Conservation Corps (CCC) camp at Fort Slocum, New York, April 1933. **AP/WIDE WORLD PHOTOS. REPRODUCED BY PERMISSION.**

fire trails, built 3,000 watch towers connected by 65,000 miles of telephone wire, and spent 4 million man-hours fighting forest fires. Campgrounds, parks, and museums were built. Mosquito-infested bogs were drained. Lakes and streams were stocked with millions of hatchery fish. The workers fought floods and grasshopper infestations. In nine years of operation, the CCC transformed much of the American landscape and left a legacy citizens continued to enjoy into the twenty-first century.

The use of the Army to run the camps, however, was not always popular. Isolationists suspected it was a ploy to train young men for the military. Roosevelt's most cynical opponents even charged it was Roosevelt's attempt to build up a fascist paramilitary force like Mussolini's Black Shirts or Hitler's Brown Shirts (SA). The simple truth was far more mundane. The Army was the only agency in the federal government capable of taking on the responsibility in short order. It was the type of task at which the Army excelled.

Few in the Army liked the assignment. Future chief of staff and general of the Army George C. Marshall, however, saw the CCC as excellent training for the day when Army officers would have to create a citizen army composed of soldiers identical to those who came into the CCC.

As with any program of this scale, there were problems. More than 10 percent of the workers left without permission, most in the first few days. They were homesick and simply left. There were incidents of corruption, mismanagement, and harsh treatment. African Americans, approximately two hundred thousand of whom joined the CCC, were underrepresented and were usually assigned to segregated camps. Women were totally excluded.

Still, by any measure, the CCC was a great success. The tangible results speak for themselves, as does the more than $600 million in wages that was sent back to the needy families of the CCC men. For the three million participants, however, there was more. There was the pride of accomplishment. There were the skills and self-discipline they learned. There was learning to work together and experiencing a world most had never seen—one that was very different from the farms or streets where they had grown up. It was a place to mature and learn important life skills.

Primary Source

Saga of the CCC

SYNOPSIS: *Saga of the CCC* is a romanticized but instructive poem about the Civilian Conservation Corps. Published in the year the CCC was closed, Guthrie's poem presents a fascinating social history of one of Franklin Roosevelt's favorite programs.

The Call

Every State, every County,
Every township and parish in the United States,
Sent its Youth
In answer to that April call,
The April, 1933, call, that said—
"Here is a chance for meals, clothes, shelter,
For a job, for self-respect, for pride,
And a chance to help the folks back home."
A new call, a long call,
A call to adventure,
A call Youth always hears.
And the boys came, 250,000 of them at first, then 300,000.
Then 350,000, then 500,000 came.
Bright boys, dull boys, pleasant boys, homesick boys,
Suspicious and sullen boys, hopeful boys, down-and-out boys,
Boys who had well-nigh given up,
Boys gaunted by days and nights of hunger.
They flocked into the CCC camps.

They Came from America

Boys from the big cities, from the slums,
From small towns and country villages,
From cross-roads and gullied farms,
Boys from mining towns, ghost towns and lumber towns,
Boys from the pool halls, the "jungles,"
From good homes and shacks,
All coming into the CCC.
Boys of Cavalier and Puritan stock, English, Scotch-Irish,
Boys from Swedish, Danish, and Norwegian families,
Boys with blood strains of German, Italian, Swiss, Greek, Spanish,
Jewish, Chinese, and Japanese, Negro boys,
Letts, Finns, Russkys, Polocks and Hunkies,
French from Canada, 'Cajuns from Louisiana,
French-speaking Negro boys in the Virgin Islands,
Spanish-speaking Puerto Ricans, polyglots of Hawaii.
Hosteen Begay, the Navajo, Eagle Feather, Nez Perce,
No Indian CCC camps, but living in wickieup, tepee, hogan,—
But all in the CCC.
Many-strained husky Alaskans, Thlinget Alaska Indians,
Working out of totem-pole villages,
Eskimos from Point Barrow, reindeer herders,
Already born brown by Arctic sun.
All stocks, all strains, all races that make America,
All in the CCC.

What They Looked Like

Tall boys from Oklahoma,
Undernourished share-cropper boys from Alabama,
Soft-voiced Mexican boys from Arizona,
Husky farm boys from hot Kansas,
Hungry, dark-skinned boys from Chicago's slums,
Pale-faced boys from New York's eastside,
Clear-eyed boys from the Green Mountains,
Webfoot boys from Oregon's foggy coast,
High-cheeked Mormon boys from Utah,
Fair-haired Swedish boys from Minnesota,
Finnish boys from Dakota,
Tall, shy boys from Georgia's red hills,
French-talking boys from Louisiana,
Big raw-boned boys from Texas, some working barefoot—
They all came into the CCC camps.

Sorting

These 250,000, and the 3,000,000 who followed
Were sorted out into Companies, 200 men each,
Issued blue "fatigues," heavy shoes, mess kits,
Given shovels and axes and grubhoes and picks.
Many boys didn't know what they were, nor what to do with them.
They put up tents, squad tents, and cots and blankets,
And towels and sheets were issued out.
Bathhouses, latrines, garbage pits, grease traps,—
Shower baths and toothbrushes puzzled many a backwoods boy.
First they went into tents, Army tents,
Then into barracks, like the Army,
First issued OD, then spruce green CCC uniforms.
Pacifists raved with "We told you so"—
But these weren't Army camps, but a new kind of camps,
New to America,
They were CCC Camps.
There were Reveille and Mess Call and Taps,
And the Flag went up, all over America,
But no drilling, no saluting, no squads east or west,
Though all Army officers were "Colonels" or "Sergeants" to the boys.
Order came out of that first confusion.
The Camp Commander, the Lieutenant, and the Doctor were everywhere
In these first CCC camps.

Being Shown

Project Superintendent, Foreman, Technicians, Foresters, Engineers,

Took the boys out,
To the woods, to the fields, to what was to be a park.
They told the boys how to hold a shovel, and why,
How to swing an ax, how to carry a double-bitted ax,
How to pull and how to carry a cross-cut saw,
How to drill a hole in a rock,
How to fell a tree, and to run and yell "Timber."
How to drive a truck, a "cat," a bulldozer,
What poison oak looked like, rattlesnakes and water moccasins.
This was life, life in the open, a man's life.
This was something like it, the boys said.
The boys went to work,
Stripped to the waist, soon became
Brown-armed, brown-shouldered, chests, backs, and legs—
Like Indians, modern American Redmen.
The boys set the stripped style,
CCC boys-stripped-to-waist-style, all over America.
Best way to work, clean, healthy,—
All in CCC Camps.

Forest Work

All the boys went to work.
In spruce and white pine of New England and New York,
In the Pine Barrens of New Jersey,
In the hemlocks of Pennsylvania,
In the hardwood coves of Virginia and Carolina,
In the longleaf pines of Alabama,
In the yellow pines of Arizona,
The hickories and oaks of Illinois and Ohio,
In the red and jack pines of the Lakes States,
The lodgepole pines of Montana,
In the high mountain forests of Colorado and Wyoming,
In the open pinyons of Nevada,
The redwoods of California, the Douglas firs of Washington—
All working,
To protect, to improve these forests,
To plant new forests,
To make green again the cut-off and burned hillsides
Of gutted America.

By Many Names

The boys are called the Triple C's, the Three C Boys, the C-Men,
The Tree Nurses, the Peavys, Roosevelt's Boys, the Woodpeckers,
The Conservation Gang, Uncle Sam's Trouble Shooters,
The Acorn Planters, the Pension Robbers, the CCC.
They go by many names.
They've had much "foolishness knocked out of them,"
They have grown in girth and stature,
Their biceps became visible;
Now they hold up their heads, their muscles bulge,
Their shoulders are thrown back,
Their pride and self-respect are restored,
They have gained the respect of women, of men, of their families,
Of bankers, of Rotarians, of Congress.
They left home and pool hall and slums and country store,
Eroded hills and sand flats,
Callow or timid, or sullen kids.
Summer suns sweated and browned them,
Winter's cold and snows hardened them.
They have become men,
Out there in the sun, the wind and the rain,
Under the lightning, the clouds, the fogs,
Out there under the stars,
In the CCC camps.

What They Did

The boys built trails and bridges,
Telephone lines and fire breaks,
They fought forest fires on a thousand fronts,
They built cabins, fire towers,
Built up public campgrounds and parks,
Piped in pure water, built dams and dykes,
They terraced eroded farms and planted young trees in the gullies,
They built ponds and brought back water to waterfowl marshes,
Counted the deer, and planted deer feed,
Restored marshes for mallards and Canada honkers.
They climbed trees for nuts and seed,
They cleared land for forest nurseries,
Planted the forest seed they collected,
Watered and weeded the young seedlings,
They set out young trees by hundreds of millions
On bare lands that knew no shade.
All working for America.

For National Conservation

For nine years now these boys have worked,
Put in millions of man-hours in Conservation,
With Conservation, and for Conservation of Natural Resources,
And Conservation of Historical Resources.
They cleared snow from forest roads in Maine, 'way below zero,
They gathered gypsymoth egg-clusters in Massachusetts,
They trenched and dried out mosquitoes on Jersey's flats,
They built lean-tos in New York's Adirondacks,
They filled up again the Mattamuskeet
And dyked marshes on wildfowl flyways,
Built seashore parks mid Gulla negroes on Edisto Island,
Made firebreaks through Georgia's longleaf pines,
And made green rest spots in Florida's sands.
They filled and levelled off Tennessee's red gullies,
Set young locust trees out to hold soil,
Sweated along Louisiana's levee banks
Building roads for flood times,
Watched from high towers for forest fires in Mississippi;
They drained clogged farmlands in Arkansas and Missouri;

They were the first to be called to Ohio's flooded banks,
Filling sandbags, lifting sandbags, piling up sandbags,
Days in and days out.
They "scalped" sandy cut-overs of Michigan,
Set out millions of young jack pines,
Built portage canoe landings in Minnesota's Superior country,
Threw up earth dams in Dakota to hold water against drought,
Dug waterholes in western Kansas,
Planted trees on Nebraska's sandhills,
Created antelope refuges in Eastern Oregon,
Put out coal fires on Wyoming's public domain,
Manicured National Park roadsides in Montana.
Swinging in wire baskets,
They ran jackhammers on Grand Canyon's steep slopes,
Built brandnew state parks all over Texas,
Held in check gypsy moths in New England,
Grubbed and pulled wild currant bushes all over Idaho
To stop blister-rust spores from *pinus monticola.*
They landscaped and dug up bits of china and glass,
And uniform buttons at old Jamestown and Williamsburg,
Old rum and wine bottles from Cornwallis' sunken ships at Yorktown,
They restored its fortifications.
They brought back history,
Visualized American history for Americans.
Restored forts, headquarters of early Colonial days,
French and Indian Wars, Revolutionary War,
War of 1812, Mexican War,
War Between the States, the Civil War,
Indian Wars, forts on pioneer westward trails.
They restored breastworks, trenches, craters,
Showed gaping tourists about the stockades.
CCC boys lived these wars over again,
CCC boys learned American history first-hand,
So now Americans can see American history.
In doing all this, they became men,
Trained men; they learned skills,
Skills useful to them on later jobs,
Skills useful to their country;
An "Army with Shovels,"
For National Defense,
When War comes.

Emergencies

When big emergencies came,—
Wind, rain, dust, floods, blizzards, fires, insect pests—
Always the public turned to the CCC.
The boys came, they would help,
Organized into cheerful work and salvage crews—
They always came.

A hurricane swept Florida's southern point—
Many CCC Veterans killed.
The CCC boys buried the dead,
Cleaned things up.

A tornado spiraled over North Alabama.
The CCC pulled dead and wounded from the wreckage,
Fed the hungry, put them under shelter,
Cleaned up the wreckage.

Swarms of grasshoppers and big Mormon crickets
Crowded over Idaho and Utah farms.
The CCC boys came,
Ditched, piled up, burned the crawling masses.

Blizzards swept sage flats and pinyon hills of Utah,
Cutting off sheep, snowbound herders, prospectors,
Back in the hills, away from food and fuel.
The CCC boys opened roads, dug out sheep,
Cattle, herders, and prospectors,
Got them out to food and safety.

Big forest fires broke in Oregon, California, Wyoming—
"Calling CCC," "Calling CCC," "Calling CCC."
The CCC came in long truck caravans,
With shovels, axes, back and gas pumps,
Blankets, first-aids, chuck,
With ready arms and legs and backs.
They fought on a thousand fire fronts.

Winds blackened out the Dust Bowl
Blinding men and beasts,
Caught travelers, covered crops, fences, houses.
The CCC boys came.
Through hot months they built water holes,
Ponds and tanks,
From Dakota clear to Texas.
They did their bit to keep the soil in place.

Heavy long rains raised the rivers,
Potomac, Susquehanna, Ohio, Mississippi.
The waters knew no bounds,
Rose, lapped, and spread out.
The CCC boys came,
In trucks, in companies, organized,
Ready, strong, and willing.
They saved children, women, men,
Chairs, bedding, trucks, cows and chickens,
Dogs and horses.
Hauled them out to high land,
Put them under tents, fed them,
Passed pure water around, food and first-aids,
Kept things sanitary for days.

When the waters went down
There was mud to dig out of third floors,
From front parlors, from kitchen sinks.
The Red Cross and the Legion got the credit
But the CCC did the work.

Camp Nights

Supper is over.
The flag has been lowered.
Too dark to play softball or baseball any longer,
Camp lights are on.
Boys leaning over the PX counter,
Boys shooting pool.
A boy tuning in on New York or England,
Another banging on the camp piano.
Four boys at a table, drinking "coke."
All in the Rec Hall.

Lights in the Mess Hall.
KP's peeling breakfast potatoes in the kitchen,

Cooks taking off their whites.
Lights in the Infirmary.
Two patients in bed,
One with a mashed toe, on his cot, reading
"Adventure."
The other with a sore appendix—
Going out tomorrow to the Vet Hospital,
Just lying there wondering about that operation.
How will the ether taste?
Will he feel the knife?
Hoping Ma won't worry about him, nor Marie.
Lights in the Forestry Quarters.
Foremen writing up the day's notes
On timber survey, TSI, and lecture outlines.
Superintendent and Enrollee Clerk working,
On Form 7, due tomorrow in Supervisor's office.
Lights in the Barracks.
One boy propped on his cot reading TIME,
Another HAPPY DAYS.
Big Tom, the Hillbilly,
Twisting his mouth, shoulders, his toes,
Writing his first letter home.
Short and misspelled, but proud of it.
Proud of that signature—
He learned to do *that* in the CCC!
Another boy quiet on the end bunk,
Writing home too.
First time he's ever been away as long as a month.
How long it seems, how far away is home!
He's homesick.
Boy reading a tree picture book from the Camp Library.
Gee! He never knew there were so many oaks,
And so many different kinds of pines too.
They do look different. Leaves different, too.
"Gee! This is interestin'.
Wonder what kind o' oak is that near the front door
at home?"
He'd never thought of that before.
It was an oak all right—it had acorns—
He'd eaten them.
He'd ask the Forestry Foreman in the morning.
Gee! There's Taps.
And barracks lights going out soon.

They Have Learned

Over nine years old now is the Corps.
Over 3,000,000 boys have passed through the
camps,
From all over America.
Some boys didn't like it, they never would;
They didn't fit,
The highbrows called them "anti-social,"
They couldn't take it.

Most of them stayed a year, two years,
Saw America;
Her vastness, her beauty, her grandeur, her
nakedness,
Her raped forests and soils and wildlife and waters.
They have learned about America.

The CCC boys have seen visions, dreamed dreams;
They will never be the same boys.
They have learned many things about nature,
About themselves, about their fellows,
How to get on with people,
About work, how to work, the dignity of work,
They're no longer afraid of work—
They'll tackle any job, the harder the better.
They have learned sanitation and health,
Personal hygiene and safety;
Learned respect for those over them, they now say
"Sir";
They have learned respect for their families,
For women, and little children
They have learned many things,
How to read and write, to study, to ask questions,
Learned to get on their feet and talk.
They have got what it takes.
They have learned many kinds of jobs,
Practical jobs,
Jobs which the world wants done.
They will give a good account of themselves,
When called on, in daily life,
In a national emergency.
They have learned
In the CCC camps.

Now They Are Men

CCC was no place for panty-waists,
No place for boondogglers nor goldbrickers.
If they got in, they didn't last;
They reformed or went over the hill,
Back to popper and mommer, or to corner pool hall.
The Corps had real work to do,—
No idle gestures,
No pointless experiments,
But work, 8 hours per.
Real conservation jobs
To save forests, soils, waters, and wildlife.
Jobs with blue-prints and specifications.
Jobs had to stand up, to last.
Bridges, dams, phone lines
Had to be built right, for use not looks.
Boys took pride in their work.
CCC fought forests fires, no kid's play,
Hard work, hot work.
Foremen trained CCC fire fighters,
Taught them safety, watched over them,
Lived in danger every minute.
CCC boys gave their lives on fires
In Jersey, in Pennsylvania,
In Wyoming, in Nevada.
Boys fought fires like men—
Old-timed rangers and lumberjacks said so.
The Corps took them in as boys
Turned them out as men.

The CCC Vets

The CCC was set up for idle youth,
But thousands of Veterans were also idle
Back in March, 1933,—and
They had started their Second March on Washington.
So,—Veteran CCC Camps
Sprang up all over the U.S.
In nine years 220,000 Vets

Have served in the Corps.
They have done a good job.
They built the Winooski Dams,
And dams in Central New York,
To hold back flood waters.
They've built roads, bridges, public camps,
All over the country.
They liked to build things.
They weren't too good as tree planters,—
Too much stooping and bending—
Nor at thinning out old forests—
Couldn't see the good sense of that;
They weren't fitted for fire fighting,
But at construction jobs,—
A bit slow but sure—
They built well what they built.
The Juniors got the spotlights
But the Vets were also in the CCC.

Taps

Uncle Bob, the Old Man, the Director,
Modest Robert Fechner, headed the Corps for six years.
Made it unique in history,
Made "America a strong nation
Because of the CCC."
He called them his boys,
Took them in as kids
Turned them out as men,
Saw them in camps from Ocean to Ocean,
North, East, South, and West,
Alaska, Hawaii, Virgin Islands, Puerto Rico.
Worked for them, fought for them,
Laughed with them, worried over them.
And at last gave his all
For the CCC.

Further Resources

BOOKS

Hill, Edwin G. *In the Shadow of the Mountain: The Spirit of the CCC.* Pullman, Wash.: Washington State University Press, 1990.

WEBSITES

"Civilian Conservation Corps." Available online at http://www.cccalumni.org (accessed February 27, 2003).

Golden, Randy. "Civilian Conservation Corps." About North Georgia. Available online at http://www.ngeorgia.com/feature/ccc.html; website home page: http://www.ngeorgia.com (accessed April 20, 2003).

8

The Media

Dan Prosterman

Entries are arranged in chronological order by date of primary source. For entries with one primary source, the entry title is the same as the primary source title. Entries with more than one primary source have an overall entry title, followed by the titles of the primary sources.

Important Events in the Media, 1930–1939

1930

- *The Smart Set* magazine ceases publication.
- The first issues of *Astounding Science-Fiction* are published.
- On January 13, the *Mickey Mouse* daily comic strip, drawn by Floyd Gottfredson until 1975, makes its debut. A Sunday page is added on January 10, 1932.
- On January 20, radio station WXYZ in Detroit airs the first episode of the drama *The Lone Ranger.*
- In February, the first issue of Henry Luce's *Fortune* magazine is published.
- In April, Ham Fisher's comic strip *Joe Palooka* makes its debut, reflecting a contemporary interest in boxing and in adventure comics.
- On July 30, *Death Valley Days* debuts on the NBC-Blue Network. The series moves to CBS in 1941 and continues until 1945.
- On September 8, Chic Young's *Blondie* first appears in newspapers.
- On September 29, Lowell Thomas begins a nightly radio news program. NBC carries the program until 1946, when it moves to CBS, which carries it until 1974.

1931

- The first issues of *Apparel Arts* (later *Gentleman's Quarterly,* or *GQ*) are published.
- On February 7, New York publisher George Putnam marries aviator Amelia Earhart with the condition that she may continue to pursue her flying.
- On April 6, the NBC-Blue Network introduces *Little Orphan Annie,* a radio adaptation of Harold Gray's popular comic strip.
- On May 5, the *Atlanta Constitution* receives the Pulitzer Prize for its exposure of corruption in Atlanta city government.
- On July 21, CBS experimental television station W2XAB begins broadcasting in New York City with twenty-eight hours of programming a week. About eight thousand receivers exist in the area. The station ceases operations in February 1933.
- On June 1, in *Near v. Minnesota,* the U.S. Supreme Court rules that a 1925 Minnesota law banning publication of a "malicious, scandalous and defamatory newspaper, magazine or other periodical" is unconstitutional.
- On October 4, Chester Gould's *Dick Tracy* begins appearing in newspapers.
- On December 22, NBC's experimental TV station, W2XBS, begins operations in New York. Its first broadcast is "Felix the Cat." In Los Angeles, W6AXO begins broadcasting the next day. It is on the air an hour a day except Sundays. Its signal can be received for a radius of thirty miles.

1932

- German photographer Erich Solomon takes an illegal picture of the U.S. Supreme Court in session.
- Walt Disney receives a special Academy Award for his creation of Mickey Mouse, who first appeared in 1928.
- On March 19, Carl Anderson's *Henry* begins in the *Saturday Evening Post.*
- On May 2, the radio comedy *The Jack Benny Show* premieres on NBC. The program featuring the violinist-comedian will run for twenty-three years on radio and for ten more years on CBS television.
- On May 22, the first national gathering of the Communist-sponsored John Reed Clubs convenes in Chicago. The clubs are organized to promote the dissemination of Communist propaganda in music, film, and magazines.
- In September, *Family Circle,* the first magazine marketed exclusively through grocery stores, begins publication; by 1939 it will have a circulation of 1.44 million.
- On October 23, the radio program *The Fred Allen Show* premieres on CBS and will be on the air until 1949.
- On November 7, the radio adventure drama *Buck Rogers in the Twenty-Fifth Century* premieres on CBS. The program will air until 1947.
- On December 4, *New York Daily Mirror* columnist Walter Winchell starts broadcasting his enormously popular radio program, which begins, "Good evening, Mr. and Mrs. America and all the ships at sea."

1933

- *Reader's Digest,* which has reprinted previously published articles since its formation in 1922, publishes its first original signed articles.
- *U.S. News & World Report* is founded.
- Dorothy Day's magazine *Catholic Worker* is first published.
- Ernie Bushmiller introduces Nancy to his *Fritzi Ritz* Sunday comic; she and her friend Sluggo become so popular that the strip is renamed *Nancy* in 1938.
- Milton Caniff's *Dickie Dare* first appears in the comics.
- On February 17, British-American journalist Thomas John Cardel Martyn publishes the first issue of *News-Week* magazine, a newsweekly designed to compete with Henry Luce's *Time.*
- On February 17, Blondie Boopadoop and Dagwood Bumstead marry in *Blondie.*

- In March, the first issue of *Doc Savage* magazine is published.
- On March 12, President Franklin D. Roosevelt delivers the first of his radio addresses known as "fireside chats."
- On June 1, the bankrupt *Washington Post* is bought by California chemical millionaire Eugene Meyer, who will ultimately turn over the paper to his daughter, Katharine Graham.
- On July 31, WBBM of Chicago airs the first episode of the enormously popular radio adventure program *Jack Armstrong, the All-American Boy.*
- On August 7, V. T. Hamlin's comic strip *Alley Oop* makes its debut in daily newspapers. It first appears in Sunday newspapers on September 9, 1934.
- In October, *Esquire,* at first a men's fashion magazine, begins publication. The first issue features a story by Ernest Hemingway, and the magazine quickly establishes a reputation for publishing exceptional writing.
- In December, the American Newspaper Guild is founded.

1934

- The Wagner-Hatfield bill, proposing that 25 percent of radio channels be reserved for educational purposes, is defeated.
- WLW in Cincinnati begins broadcasting at 500,000 watts, becoming one of the most influential radio stations in the Midwest.
- Alex Raymond and Don Moore's *Flash Gordon* first appears in newspapers.
- Whitman Publishing offers an unauthorized book about L. Frank Baum's Oz, *The Laughing Dragon of Oz,* in a Big Little Book.
- In January, the comic strip *Secret Agent X-9,* written by Dashiell Hammett and drawn by Alex Raymond, first appears in newspapers. Both leave it in other hands in 1935.
- On April 15, Dagwood and Blondie have a baby, Alexander.
- On June 9, Donald Duck makes his screen debut with a small part in "The Wise Little Hen," one of Disney's *Silly Symphonies.* On August 11, he is a featured character in a Mickey Mouse cartoon, "The Orphans' Benefit."
- On June 19, Congress authorizes the creation of the Federal Communications Commission (FCC) to oversee the nation's mass-communications industry.
- On June 16, FM (frequency modulation) radio is tested for the first time.
- On August 13, Al Capp's *Li'l Abner* debuts in eight newspapers. By 1939 it has been picked up by four hundred.
- In September, the Mutual Broadcasting Network is created.
- In October, the soap-opera strip *Apple Mary* first appears in newspapers. It is later renamed *Mary Worth.*
- On October 8, in a decision widely condemned by engineers and scientists, the U.S. Supreme Court rules that the patent rights to the superregeneration circuit, an essential component of radios, belong to Lee De Forest rather than its inventor, Edwin Howard Armstrong.

1935

- The verdict in the Lindbergh baby kidnapping trial is broadcast over radio.
- The American Institute of Public Opinion is established by George H. Gallup to measure reader response to newspaper features. The following year it accurately predicts the results of the presidential election.
- The Federal Writers' Project is created to provide jobs for unemployed editors, journalists, and other writers.
- The cost of network radio advertising on NBC is $300 a minute.
- On February 23, Marjorie "Marge" Lyman Henderson creates Little Lulu for the *Saturday Evening Post.*
- On April 16, NBC-Blue Network airs the first episode of the radio comedy-drama *Fibber McGee and Molly.* The program will run until 1952. *Flash Gordon, Dick Tracy,* and *Your Hit Parade* are other radio programs premiering during the year that will enjoy long and popular runs.
- On May 13, attacked throughout the early 1930s for its many laxative commercials, CBS announces that it will ban ads for laxatives and other products for which the "good taste" of ads could be questioned.
- In November, FM pioneer Edwin Howard Armstrong demonstrates his invention for the press.

1936

- The Republican Party produces a radio "dramatization," *Liberty at the Crossroads,* as part of the 1936 presidential campaign.
- RCA begins television field tests.
- *The Shadow* and the *Kate Smith Show* premiere during the year and become quick hits with radio listeners.
- Moses L. Annenberg purchases the *Philadelphia Inquirer* for a reported fifteen million dollars.
- *Consumer Reports* is first published.
- In a poll relying on Republican-heavy telephone and automobile owners, *Literary Digest* inaccurately predicts the defeat of Franklin D. Roosevelt in the presidential election. The magazine folds in 1937.
- In November, a harsh critic of the Roosevelt administration, Father Charles Coughlin, the "radio priest," temporarily leaves the air as promised following Roosevelt's landslide reelection.
- The Clock, the first masked crime fighter to appear in comic books, simultaneously makes his debut in *Funny Pages* and *Funny Picture Stories.* In December, he also appears in *Detective Picture Stories.*
- On November 23, the first issue of Henry Luce's *Life* is published.

1937

- Martyn's *News-Week* becomes *Newsweek* and becomes a far more effective competitor to *Time.*
- *Des Moines Register* publisher Gardner Cowles launches *Look,* a pictorial bi-weekly, to compete with Henry Luce's *Life.*

- A&P begins publication of *Woman's Day* magazine.
- *Popular Photography* begins publication.
- NBC hires Arturo Toscanini to conduct its new NBC Symphony. Its first concert is broadcast in December.
- The American Bar Association adopts Canon 35, barring microphones and photographers from courtrooms.
- On January 25, NBC airs the first episode of its soap opera *The Guiding Light.* It will run as a radio program until 1956, after which it will become a television program.
- In March, *Detective Comics,* which becomes the longest-running comic book in existence, first appears on newsstands.
- On March 4, CBS broadcasts its *Columbia Workshop* production of Archibald MacLeish's radio verse play *The Fall of the City.* Its cast includes Burgess Meredith and Orson Welles.
- On May 6, the first coast-to-coast radio broadcast takes place when Herbert Morrison reports the *Hindenburg* disaster.
- On May 9, NBC debuts *The Charlie McCarthy Show,* featuring ventriloquist Edgar Bergen with his dummy Charlie McCarthy. The program will air on NBC until 1948 and then on CBS until 1954.
- On May 12, the first worldwide radio program heard in the United States provides live coverage of the coronation of King George V of England.
- On June 6, Walter Piston's piano concertino is broadcast by CBS from New York.
- On December 21, Disney's *Snow White,* the first feature-length animated motion picture, is released.

1938

- CBS purchases Columbia Records.
- Bugs Bunny makes his screen debut.
- Adolf Hitler's *Mein Kampf* is published in English.
- In January, movie star Mae West arouses controversy after she makes sexually suggestive remarks in a skit on the Edgar Bergen-Charley McCarthy radio show. The public outcry prompts an investigation by the FCC. NBC apologizes for the incident, but 130 stations ban even the mention of West's name.
- On March 13, Edward R. Murrow and William L. Shirer describe the German annexation of Austria from Vienna for American radio audiences.
- In June, *Action Comics* #1 introduces Jerry Siegel and Joe Shuster's Superman.
- In September, Jerry Iger and Will Eisner's Fiction House introduces Sheena, Queen of the Jungle, in the first issue of *Jumbo Comics.*
- On October 30, on his Mercury Theatre on the Air radio show, Orson Welles broadcasts "Invasion from Mars," a dramatization based on H. G. Wells's "The War of the Worlds," and panic-stricken listeners think Martians have landed in New Jersey.

1939

- FM radio receivers go on sale for the first time.
- The National Association of Broadcasters adopts a code that promotes objectivity in news broadcasts.
- The FCC ends WLW's superpower broadcasts at 500,000 watts; the Cincinnati station scales back to 50,000 watts.
- *Philadelphia Inquirer* publisher Moses L. Annenberg is indicted on charges of income-tax evasion. He ends up paying some $9.5 million in taxes, penalties, and interest and is sentenced to the federal prison in Lewisburg, Pennsylvania.
- Pocket Books, the first modern American paperback company, is founded.
- *Grapes of Wrath,* a novel by John Steinbeck, traces the sufferings of an Oklahoma family that loses their farm in the dust bowl and relocates to California, where they become migrant workers. The book soon becomes a best-seller.
- On January 21, *Public Opinion* by William Albig, an important study of propaganda and censorship, is published.
- On April 30, NBC televises the opening of the New York World's Fair.
- In May, Bob Kane and Bill Finger's Batman is introduced in *Detective Comics* #27.
- In Summer, the first issue of *Superman Comics* appears.
- In August, the Blue Beetle makes his comic-book debut in *Mystery Men Comics* #1.
- On August 6, *The Dinah Shore Show* premieres on NBC radio.
- On October 14, Broadcast Music Incorporated (BMI) is founded to provide musicians an alternative licensing agent to the American Society of Composers, Authors, and Publishers (ASCAP).
- On October 26, sportscaster Red Barber announces the first televised major league baseball game, between the Brooklyn Dodgers and the Cincinnati Reds. The broadcast goes out on NBC's experimental TV station W2XBS to about 400 television sets.
- In November, *Marvel Comics* make their debut with stories featuring the Human Torch and the Sub-Mariner.

Fortune Magazine Covers

Magazine covers

Date: February 1930

Source: *Fortune,* February 1930, September 1930, December 1937, May 1938, July 1939, front covers. Available online at http://xroads.virginia.edu/~1930s/PRINT/fortune/fortunethumbs.html; website home page: http://xroads.virginia.edu/~1930s (accessed March 12, 2003). ■

Introduction

Fortune magazine hit the newsstands during one of the most tumultuous periods in American history—the Great Depression. Four months after the stock market crash of 1929, *Fortune* appeared before a weary, disgruntled public that was threatened with complete economic downfall. Despite the misfortune, millions of Americans struggled through during the 1930s. The publishers of *Fortune* decided that a market would remain for readers interested in understanding the intricacies of the financial markets and who desired to join the ranks of the upper class.

Significance

The *Fortune* magazine covers displayed below provide a sense of how the magazine focused on the "machinery" of the United States and its symbols of technological innovation and even prosperity during the height of the Depression. These cover displays alternated between somewhat idyllic depictions of rural, farm-based America and industrial urban centers. Rather than presenting readers with realistic artwork concerning the travails they faced, *Fortune*'s editors opted for imagery of better times. The September 1930 and May 1938 editions, for instance, presented visions of agricultural production that passed over the devastation, disease, and death faced by farming families.

The presentation of urban life was similar in its obliviousness toward the Great Depression. Cover art for the December 1937 and July 1939 issues presented cities with motifs of progress and apparent prosperity. Drawings of rural life displayed common images with no specific geographic location implied other than an increasingly machine-dominated "American Heartland." Urban life, on the other hand, revolved around the country's greatest metropolis—New York City.

Peering at the New York cityscape on the cover of the July 1939 issue, readers saw the majesty of capitalism and industrialization. This scene refused to delve into the decade's hundreds of slums. The December 1937 cover offered readers perhaps the most idyllic representation of all: skyscrapers joined together in the formation of a gigantic Christmas tree. The city actually glistened in stardust rather than appear choked on poverty and inequality.

Perhaps, then, the magazine's popularity was linked with its ability to transport readers to an American nation far different from the troubled one people encountered during the decade. For rich and nonrich alike, *Fortune* provided a means to exist temporarily in a more prosperous time and place, working on the perfect farm or marveling at the greatest city on earth.

Although the Great Depression forced millions out of work, the publication industry witnessed the birth of several of its most enduring magazines—*Fortune* (1930), *Newsweek* (1933), *Esquire* (1933), *Life* (1936), and *Look* (1937). In the midst of the greatest economic downturn in U.S. history, millions of readers spent a few of their precious coins to be transported to faraway places, meet famous stars, and, in *Fortune,* get an optimistic glimpse at the future of the U.S. economy.

Further Resources

BOOKS

Baughman, James L. *Henry R. Luce and the Rise of the American News Media.* Baltimore, Md.: Johns Hopkins University Press, 1987.

Elson, Robert T. *Time Inc.: The Intimate History of a Publishing Enterprise,* vol. 1 (1923–1941). New York: Atheneum, 1968.

Herzstein, Robert E. *Henry R. Luce: A Political Portrait of the Man Who Created the American Century.* New York: Scribner's, 1994.

Primary Source

Cover of first issue of Fortune Magazine (1 OF 5)

SYNOPSIS: The cover of the first issue of *Fortune* was designed by Thomas Maitland Cleland. Published in February 1930, the cover depicts the wheel of fortune. Subsequent covers appearing throughout the rest of the decade depicted Americans' economic fortunes resembling a roller-coaster ride: while some citizens experienced a general improvement in their financial stability, the Great Depression remained paramount during the period, especially for the working-class. Workers' and their families' grip on stability, much less prosperity, remained tenuous until the 1940s ushered in a new crisis for the American public to face, World War II.

Primary Source

Cover of Fortune Magazine, Sept. 1930 **(2 OF 5)**
Fortune, September 1930, cover designed by Peter Helck.

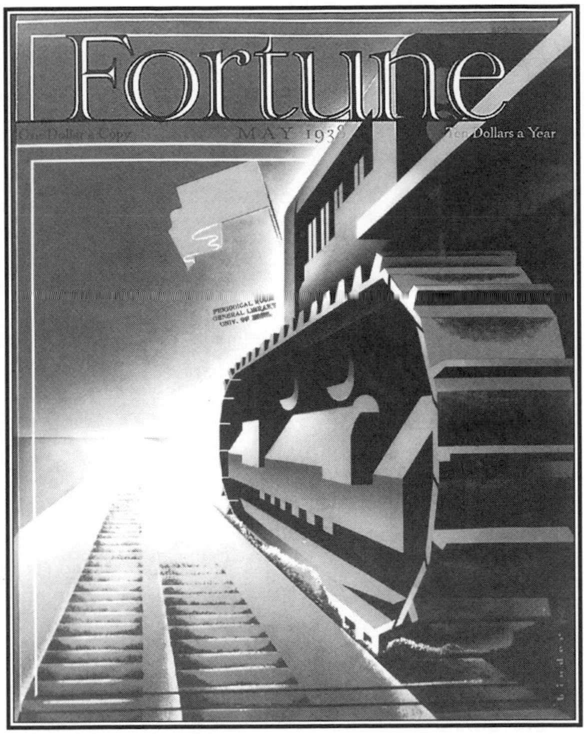

Primary Source

Cover of Fortune Magazine, May 1938 **(4 OF 5)**
Fortune, May 1938, cover designed by Joseph Binder.

Primary Source

Cover of Fortune Magazine, Dec. 1937 **(3 OF 5)**
Fortune, December 1937, cover designed by Joseph Binder.

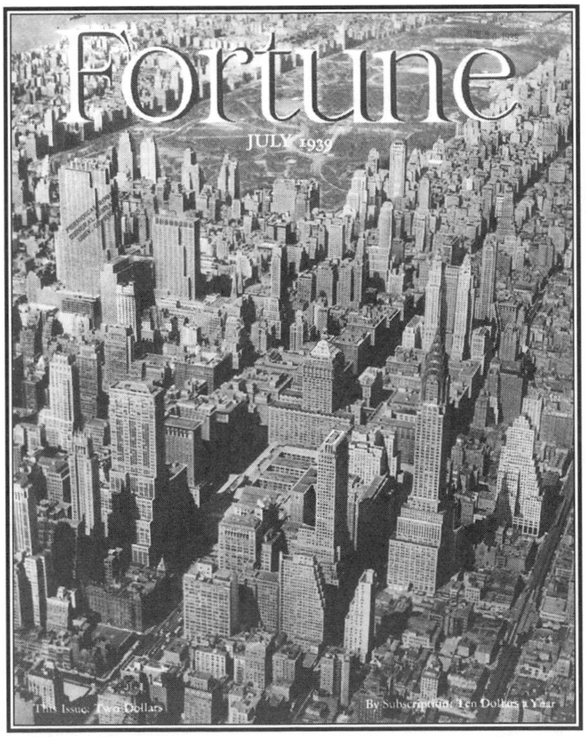

Primary Source

Cover of Fortune Magazine, July 1939 **(5 OF 5)**
Fortune, July 1939, cover designed by Bernice Abbott.

Amos 'n' Andy Radio Episode 920

Radio script

By: Charles J. Correll and Freeman F. Gosden

Date: March 5, 1931

Source: Correll, Charles J., and Freeman F. Gosden. *Amos 'n' Andy,* episode 920, syndicated radio broadcast, March 5, 1931. Reprinted online in McLeod, Elizabeth. *Amos 'n' Andy in Person.* http://www.midcoast.com/~lizmcl/aa920.html/; website home page: http://www.midcoast.com/~lizmcl/aabp.html (accessed March 14, 2003).

About the Authors: Freeman Gosden (1899–1982) was born in Richmond, Virginia, at the turn of the century, the son of a Confederate army officer. He met Charles Correll (1890–1972) as a member of a traveling vaudeville group in North Carolina in the early 1920s. From these fairly inauspicious beginnings, the pair went on to write, direct, and star in perhaps the most famous, and most controversial, radio program of the twentieth century—*Amos 'n' Andy.* ■

Introduction

Correll and Gosden worked in radio production and secured positions with WGN in Chicago in the early 1920s. By 1926, the two middle-aged white men had produced their first hit. In *Sam 'n' Henry,* Correll and Gosden portrayed two African American teens whose comedic adventures provided the main plot lines and the basis for the show's popularity. This brand of humor, where Caucasians portrayed themselves as African Americans, had a long history in the United States and was known as blackface minstrelsy—named for the black paint white actors would use to cover their faces to imitate blacks. While live-action minstrel theater performances diminished in popularity in the early twentieth century, the practice saw increased appeal in motion pictures and, with Correll and Gosden, in radio.

Following a contract dispute, the pair moved to WMAQ in Chicago and began their most famous radio venture—*Amos 'n' Andy.* The show became an instant success, running fifteen minutes a night, five nights per week. By 1929, *Amos 'n' Andy* was a nationally syndicated hit, reaching upwards of forty million listeners on a nightly basis. By 1943, CBS doubled the show's length as its popularity increased during World War II (1939–1945). The franchise grew in popularity to such an extent that it spun off several motion pictures and, beginning in the early 1950s, television sitcoms. Despite this mass appeal, the mounting civil rights movement of the postwar era helped cause the downfall of the stereotypical duo. Protests by civil rights groups, especially the National Association for the Advancement of Colored People (NAACP), increased following the television series' debut in 1951. Freeman and Correll contended that *Amos 'n' Andy* contained no racist or prejudicial depictions of African Americans. But these contentions were to no avail. The pair's popularity declined over the course of the decade and, having lost national syndication, the radio show's final broadcast came in 1960.

Significance

The script transcribed below conveys the flavor of how Correll and Gosden performed the wildly popular program in its heyday during the Great Depression. The show's plots revolved primarily around the exploits of Amos Jones and Andrew Brown, two African Americans who had recently migrated from the American South to the North (Chicago, then Harlem) in search of wealth. The pair managed the Fresh-Air Taxicab Company, named as such for the company's lone automobile, a broken-down jalopy missing a roof. The characters seemed polar opposites, with Andy often running afoul of the law, women, and common sense, while Amos remained good natured, virtuous, and steadfastly loyal to his friend. Using this skeleton framework, Correll and Gosden created hundreds of radio broadcasts that captivated listeners longing to avoid the troubles of depression and war.

At the same time, though, the pair's gags and punch lines often revolved around racist stereotypes of African Americans as lazy, childlike, and uneducated. The following excerpt provides a sense of one such joke:

> Lawyer: And I don't want you to do anything that will incriminate you.
>
> Amos: An' git dat in yo' head.
>
> Andy: Whut kin I do dat'll make 'em cre-mate me?
>
> Lawyer: No, I said incriminate.
>
> Andy: Oh.
>
> *From March 5, 1931, program*

In another scene, a lawyer representing Andy's fiancée noted that he closed one love letter by labeling his would-be bride, "Mrs. Andrew H. Brown, eskimo." Andy was quick to point out the error, "Dat's es-ki-quire." Lawyer: "Well, you have on this paper, Andrew H. Brown, eskimo." These excerpts, following the original scripts' presentation of African-American vernacular English, underscore the troubling nature of Correll and Gosden's humor. *Amos 'n' Andy*'s popularity during the 1930s reveals the double-edged influence of mass media in U.S. society—radio entertainment perpetuated racist stereotypes at the same time that it entertained millions of listeners.

Primary Source

Amos 'n' Andy Radio Episode 920

SYNOPSIS: The "Breach of Promise" storyline ran from December 27, 1930, until March 12, 1931. The series' plot revolved around Andy's promise to marry Madam Queen and his subsequent attempts to avoid the marriage. The court scenes transcribed from the March 5th episode below focus on Andy's testimony concerning the nature of his relationship with Queen and his justification for reneging on his promise. In a later show, listeners learned that Queen had actually still been married to another man at the time of Andy's engagement, thus prohibiting a "breach of promise" lawsuit. This storyline prompted the *Pittsburgh Courier,* the nation's second largest black newspaper, to mount an unsuccessful campaign to ban the program for its negative depiction of African American men and women. Correll and Gosden acted all of the characters, including Madam Queen.

Today Andy is scheduled to take the witness stand in his own behalf. He has spent many hours with his attorney getting instructions as to his action on the stand. Attorney Smith, representing Madam Queen, has endeavored to locate Prince Ali Bendo, a crystal gazer, who was instrumental in having the original date of Andy's wedding postponed. As the scene opens now we find Amos, Andy and Lawyer Collins just outside of the court room during a short recess. Here they are:—

Amos: If yo' just stop shakin' Andy, ev'ything's goin' be alright. Ain't no use to git nervous.

Andy: I can't he'p from gittin' nervous, kin I?

Collins: I want you to remember everything I told you Andy.

Amos: Yo' heah dat?

Amos: Well, if you don't remember how you gotta act on dere, den you IS out o' luck.

Collins: I want you to think of all the things I've told you and during the direct examination I will ask you questions that you know how to answer. The only thing I do want you to do is to be careful under cross examination because the cross examination is very important.

Amos: Yo' heah dat?

Collins: And I don't want you to do anything that will incriminate you.

Amos: An' git dat in yo' head.

Andy: Whut kin I do dat'll make 'em cre-mate me?

Collins: No, I said incriminate.

Andy: Oh.

Amos: Well, don't worry 'bout dat—just think how yo' goin' act when yo' git on de witness stand—ain't dat right Mr. Collins?

Collins: Yes, if you can give a testimony that will help you as much as Amos did when he was on the stand, I think you'll come out alright.

Amos: De trouble is wid him, he's nervous, look at him.

Andy: Who wouldn't be? I gotta sit on dat chair in front o' Madam Queen an' all dat stuff.

Collins: The only thing I want to warn you about is the cross examination. Remember what you have said and don't contradict yourself.

Andy: Don't whut?

Collins: Contradict yourself.

Amos: You better 'splain dat to him too Mr. Collins.

Collins: In other words Andy, stick to your original statement and when you are being cross examined don't let Smith get you mixed up.

Andy: Oh, I kin handle dat sichiation alright. De only thing I'se worried 'bout is when I'se on de witness stand.

Amos: Well, dat's whut he's talkin' 'bout.

Andy: Oh.

Amos: Mr. Collins, you got a hard job—I feel sorry fo' yo'.

Andy: I wish somebody'd feel sorry fo' me—I got a hard job too.

Amos: I say you is.

Andy: Dis is de worst picklement dat I was eveh in.

Amos: You been in a lot of 'em too.

Collins: The whole idea is the thing we talked over today. You didn't want to marry Madam Queen.

Amos: Dat's de truth too.

Andy: Well, why was I regaged to her?

Collins: Because she led you on.

Andy: Yeh, dat's right, ain't it?

Amos: An' don't fo'git dat she ast you to write dem letters.

Andy: Whut lettehs?

Amos: De letters dat you writ her.

Andy: Well, whut's dat gotta do wid it?

Amos: Wid whut?

Andy: Yo' see dere, Mr. Collins—I wear myself out 'splainin' things to Amos. By de time I git on de witness stand I'll be weak in de head from 'splainin' to him.

Amos: 'Splainin' whut to me?

Andy: Dat boy kin ast mo' questions.

Collins: Well, at the present time Andy, you better confine your efforts to your own testimony on the witness stand.

Andy: At de present time—I got dat much—whut was dat stuff afteh dat?

Amos: In other words—

Andy: Shut up, will yo'? Mr. Collins, YOU 'splain ev'ything to me.

Collins: I think we better go in and take a seat.

Amos: Come on.

Andy: I'm comin', ain't I? Ev'ybody's always hollerin' at me, "Come on somewhere."

Amos: An' don't talk so loud, yo' heah?

Collins: Take the same seats you've always had.

Amos: Yessah.

Andy: I wish I could stay in dat seat.

Amos: You is always wishin' sumpin', ain't yo'?

Andy: Dem mens on de jury—dey act like dey mad about sumpin'.

Amos: Sit down.

Collins: Don't forget everything I've told you.

Andy: Oh, I ain't goin' fo'git nuthin' dat you told me. (quietly to Amos) Amos, whut is he told me?

Amos: Well, just wait till yo' git in dat chair an' do de best yo' kin.

Andy: Dat judge—he acts like he's mad. Ev'ybody's mad at me, an' I ain't done nuthin'. I'se regusted.

Amos: Quiet.

Collins: Alright Andy, don't forget what I told you.

Andy: 'Bout 'em cre-matin' me?

Judge: (raps) Quiet please. Mr. Collins, call your witness please.

Collins: Andrew Brown, take the witness stand.

Andy: Yessah.

(*pause*)

Bailiff: Do you swear that the testimony that you are about to give in this case is the truth, the whole truth, and nothing but the truth, so help you God?

Judge: Will the people in the back part of the court room be quiet?

Collins: Whut is your name?

Andy: Andrew Brown, wid a "H" in it—in de middle.

Collins: Andrew H. Brown. What is your occupation?

Andy: Nosah, I did not.

Collins: No, no, I say whut do you do for a living?

Andy: Oh.

Judge: Will the witness answer the questions promptly. We've had enough delay in this trial.

Collins: Whut do you do for a living?

Andy: I runs de Fresh Air Taxicab comp'ny of America incorpulated, I runs a lunch room, of America—but dat ain't incorpulated. Den I doos a lot o' figgerin', like income tax.

Collins: Are you successful in business?

Andy: Whut's de matteh?

Collins: Have you made a success of your business?

Andy: Oh, sho'.

Collins: You are aware of the fact that Madam Queen is suing you for breach of promise.

Andy: Whut did yo' say I wear?

Collins: I say, you KNOW that the plaintiff in this case, Madam Queen, is suing you for breach of promise.

Andy: Yessah.

Collins: How long have you known Madam Queen?

Andy: Oveh a yeah. WAY oveh.

Collins: Now you first met her, where?

Andy: Gittin' a manana-cure.

Collins: Did Madam Queen say anything to you about coming back for another manicure?

Andy: Yes—an' no. Mostly yes.

Collins: What do you mean by that?

Andy: I did not—I mean-a—whut is it?

Collins: Did she ask you to come back to her beauty shop?

Andy: Oh sho', she told me dat I ought to have mo' manana-cures dan I is been gittin'. Dat's when I give her 50 cent.

Collins: In other words, she suggested that you should come back to the beauty shop for another manicure.

Andy: Yessah.

Collins: Did she ever ask you to write her a letter?

Andy: Yessah, she ast me to write her a letteh.

Collins: Is that why you wrote the letters?

Andy: Whut lettehs?

Collins: You said you wrote her letters. I'm asking you if you wrote her because she requested you to do so.

Andy: Yes, an' no—mostly yes.

Collins: Did you spend any money by taking her out to dinner?

Andy: All de time.

Collins: Did you ever eat at her home?

Andy: If I would stop by de butcher shop an' bring de food, I'd eat dere.

Collins: And did you intend to marry her?

Andy: Well, to tell yo' de truth Mr. Collins, I said I did, but in de back paht o' my head, sumpin' kept tellin' me "don't do it." You know how dat is.

Further Resources

BOOKS

Dunning, John. *On the Air: The Encyclopedia of Old-Time Radio.* New York: Oxford University Press, 1998.

Ely, Melvin Patrick. *The Adventures of Amos 'n' Andy: A Social History of an American Phenomenon.* New York: Free Press, 1991.

PERIODICALS

"Actor Charles J. Correll, Andy of 'Amos 'n' Andy' Radio Show, Dies on Sept 26; Was 82." *The New York Times,* September 27, 1972.

Treaster, Joseph B. "Freeman F. Gosden Is Dead at 83; Amos in Radio's 'Amos 'n' Andy." *The New York Times,* December 11, 1982.

WEBSITES

Broadcasting History Resources. Available online at http://simplyscripts.com (accessed March 1, 2003).

Near v. Minnesota

Supreme Court decision

By: Charles Evans Hughes

Date: June 1, 1931

Source: *Near v. Minnesota.* 283 U.S. 697 (1931). Available online at http://www.civnet.org/resources/teach/basic/part7/45.htm; website home page: http://www.civnet.org/ (accessed March 12, 2003).

The only existing photo of Jay M. Near, editor of Minnesota's *Saturday Press* in the 1920s and 1930s. **MINNESOTA HISTORICAL SOCIETY. REPRODUCED BY PERMISSION.**

About the Author: Charles Evans Hughes (1862–1948) served two terms as governor of New York. From 1910 to 1916, he served as an associate justice on the U.S. Supreme Court. In 1916, incumbent president Woodrow Wilson narrowly defeated Hughes in one of the closest presidential elections in history. After serving as U.S. secretary of state under Presidents Harding and Coolidge from 1921 to 1925, President Herbert Hoover nominated Hughes to serve as chief justice of the Supreme Court. ■

Introduction

Hughes' most significant ruling with regard to freedom of the press was in a lawsuit filed against *The Saturday Press,* a Minnesota tabloid newspaper that specialized in titillating, and often unsubstantiated, rumors about public figures in local politics and business. A police chief had sued the publication in response to several front-page articles that charged him with corruption and links to organized crime. The publication responded to the suit with further inflammatory headlines

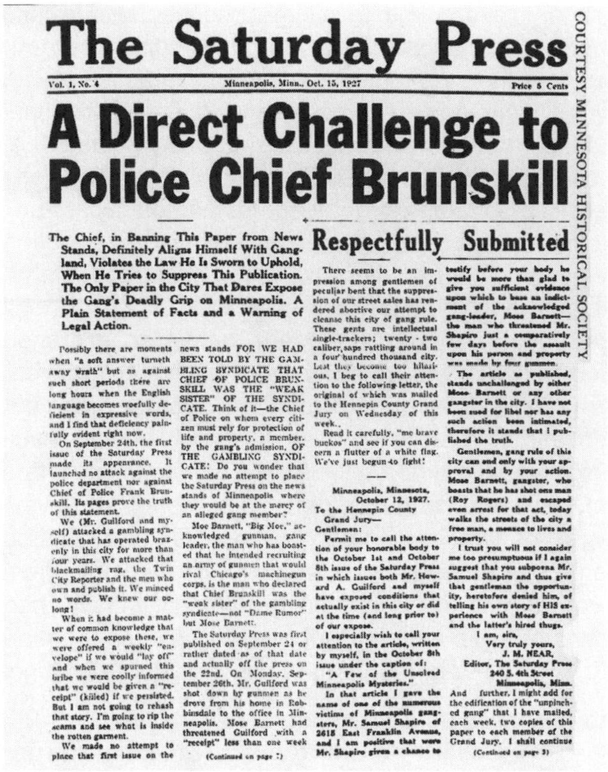

The Saturday Press

Vol. 1, No. 4 | Minneapolis, Minn., Oct. 15, 1927 | Price 5 Cents

A Direct Challenge to Police Chief Brunskill

The Chief, in Banning This Paper from News Stands, Definitely Aligns Himself With Gangland, Violates the Law He Is Sworn to Uphold, When He Tries to Suppress This Publication. The Only Paper in the City That Dares Expose the Gang's Deadly Grip on Minneapolis. A Plain Statement of Facts and a Warning of Legal Action.

Possibly there are moments when "a soft answer turneth away wrath" but as against such short periods there are long hours when the English language becomes woefully deficient in expressive words, and I find that deficiency painfully evident right now.

On September 24th, the first issue of the Saturday Press made its appearance. It launched no attack against the police department nor against Chief of Police Frank Brunskill. Its pages prove the truth of this statement.

We (Mr. Guilford and myself) attacked a gambling syndicate that has operated brazenly in this city for more than four years. We attacked that blackmailing rag, the Twin City Reporter and the men who own and publish it. We minced no words. We knew our oolong!

When it had become a matter of common knowledge that we were to expose these, we were offered a weekly "envelope" if we would "lay off" and when we spurned this bribe we were coolly informed that we would be given a "receipt" (killed) if we persisted. But I am not going to rehash that story. I'm going to rip the seams and see what is inside the rotten garment.

We made no attempt to place that first issue on the news stands FOR WE HAD BEEN TOLD BY THE GAMBLING SYNDICATE THAT CHIEF OF POLICE BRUNSKILL WAS THE "WEAK SISTER" OF THE SYNDICATE. Think of it—the Chief of Police on whom every citizen must rely for protection of life and property, a member, by the gang's admission, OF THE GAMBLING SYNDICATE: Do you wonder that we made no attempt to place the Saturday Press on the news stands of Minneapolis where they would be at the mercy of an alleged gang member?

Moe Barnett, "Big Moe," acknowledged gunman, gang leader, the man who has boasted that he intended recruiting an army of gunmen that would rival Chicago's machinegun corps, is the man who declared that Chief Brunskill was the "weak sister" of the gambling syndicate—not "Dame Rumor" but Mose Barnett.

The Saturday Press was first published on September 24 or rather dated as of that date and actually off the press on the 22nd. On Monday, September 26th, Mr. Guilford was shot down by gunmen as he drove from his home in Robbinsdale to the office in Minneapolis. Mose Barnett had threatened Guilford with a "receipt" less than one week

(Continued on page 7)

Respectfully Submitted

There seems to be an impression among gentlemen of peculiar bent that the suppression of our street sales has rendered abortive our attempt to cleanse this city of gang rule. These gents are intellectual single-trackers; twenty-two caliber saps rattling around in a four hundred thousand city. Lest they become too hilarious, I beg to call their attention to the following letter, the original of which was mailed to the Hennepin County Grand Jury on Wednesday of this week.

Read it carefully, "me brave buckos" and see if you can discern a flutter of a white flag. We've just begun to fight!

Minneapolis, Minnesota,
October 12, 1927.

To the Hennepin County Grand Jury—

Gentlemen:

Permit me to call the attention of your honorable body to the October 1st and October 8th issue of the Saturday Press in which issues both Mr. Howard A. Guilford and myself have exposed conditions that actually exist in this city or did at the time (and long prior to) of our expose.

I especially wish to call your attention to the article, written by myself, in the October 8th issue under the caption of:

"A Few of the Unsolved Minneapolis Mysteries."

In that article I gave the name of one of the numerous victims of Minneapolis gangsters, Mr. Samuel Shapiro of 2618 East Franklin Avenue, and I am positive that were Mr. Shapiro given a chance to testify before your body he would be more than glad to give you sufficient evidence upon which to base an indictment of the acknowledged gang-leader, Mose Barnett—the man who threatened Mr. Shapiro just a comparatively few days before the assault upon his person and property was made by four gunmen.

The article as published, stands unchallenged by either Mose Barnett or any other gangster in the city. I have not been sued for libel nor has any such action been intimated, therefore it stands that I published the truth.

Gentlemen, gang rule of this city can end only with your approval and by your action. Mose Barnett, gangster, who boasts that he has shot one man (Roy Rogers) and escaped even arrest for that act, today walks the streets of the city a free man, a menace to lives and property.

I trust you will not consider me too presumptuous if I again suggest that you subpoena Mr. Samuel Shapiro and thus give that gentleman the opportunity, heretofore denied him, of telling his own story of HIS experience with Mose Barnett and the latter's hired thugs.

I am, sirs,
Very truly yours,
J. M. NEAR,
Editor, The Saturday Press
240 S. 4th Street
Minneapolis, Minn.

And further, I might add for the edification of the "unpinched gang" that I have mailed, each week, two copies of this paper to each member of the Grand Jury. I shall continue

(Continued on page 3)

COURTESY MINNESOTA HISTORICAL SOCIETY

The front page of *The Saturday Press,* October 15, 1927. ***THE SATURDAY PRESS*, OCTOBER 15, 1927. MINNESOTA HISTORICAL SOCIETY. PUBLIC DOMAIN.**

on October 15, 1927: "The Chief, in Banning This Paper from News Stands, Definitely Aligns Himself With Gangland, Violates the Law He Is Sworn to Uphold, When He Tries to Suppress This Publication. The Only Paper in the City That Dares Expose the Gang's Deadly Grip on Minneapolis. A Plain Statement of Facts and a Warning of Legal Action."

The Minnesota Supreme Court ruled that authorities could halt the publication of the newspaper or any other "malicious, scandalous or defamatory" journal. The U.S. Supreme Court accepted the case for review in 1931. The national news media regarded the case as a critical moment for the future of journalism, for an adverse ruling by the Court could result in a dramatic decline in investigative reporting and exposés of government corruption. Proponents of the lower courts' decisions argued that the press had overstepped its bounds and needed to be prevented from printing unfounded rumors.

Significance

In the majority opinion, Chief Justice Charles Evans Hughes concluded that the state of Minnesota was forcing the publication to prove the truth of its articles prior to publishing them. When the state court deemed the paper's reporting uncorroborated, it forbid the publication of these stories. Hughes found that this practice amounted to "the essence of censorship" and ruled in favor of *The Saturday Press.* In the face of a growing economic depression and charges of business and government misdeeds, Hughes strengthened the freedom of the press guaranteed in the First Amendment to the U.S. Constitution.

Hughes quoted Sir William Blackstone, an influential British jurist, who had argued years before that the "liberty of the press is indeed essential to the nature of a free state; but this consists in laying no previous restraints upon publications, and not in freedom from censure for criminal matter when published." Thus, news media organizations could still be sued for libel, but these lawsuits needed to occur after the reports were published. Hughes was careful not to overrule the Court's earlier decisions in *Schenck v. United States* (1919) and *Abrams v. United States* (1920). These decisions upheld the constitutionality of the Sedition and Espionage Acts passed by Congress during World War I; these laws permitted the censorship of treasonous or seditious publications.

Hughes nevertheless concluded that the subject matter of the Minnesota tabloid still did not allow for prior restraint or censorship: "The fact that the liberty of the press may be abused by miscreant purveyors of scandal does not make any the less necessary the immunity of the press from previous restraint in dealing with official misconduct." Hughes argued that the practice of judges deciding which articles should be published and which should not rested "but a step [from] a complete system of censorship."

The Court's ruling in *Near* did not lessen the federal government's scrutiny of media organizations. In fact, Congress actually increased regulation over the press, particularly radio stations, during the liberal Roosevelt administration. The Communications Act of 1934, passed by Congress on June 19, 1934, established the Federal Communications Commission (FCC) "for the purpose of regulating interstate and foreign commerce in communication by wire and radio so as to make available, so far as possible, to all the people of the United States a rapid, efficient, Nation-wide, and world-wide wire and radio communication service with adequate facilities at reasonable charges, for the purpose of the national defense, and for the purpose of securing a more effective execution of this policy by centralizing authority. . . ."

The FCC's actual directives included contradictory language prohibiting censorship but permitting heightened restrictions on language deemed unsuitable for public broadcast:

> SEC. 326 (Censorship; Indecent Language). Nothing in this Act shall be understood or construed to give the Commission the power of censorship over the radio communications or signals

transmitted by any radio station, and no regulation or condition shall be promulgated or fixed by the Commission which shall interfere with the right of free speech by means of radio communication. No person within the jurisdiction of the United States shall utter any obscene, indecent, or profane language by means of radio communication.

Thus, according to Section 326, the FCC did not possess the power to censor radio broadcasts, but the commission did have the authority to forbid the use of "obscene, indecent, or profane language" over the airwaves. These confusing powers over broadcasting continue to pose dilemmas for a government body designed specifically to regulate speech under a Constitution calling for that very freedom.

Primary Source

Near v. Minnesota [excerpt]

SYNOPSIS: Brought before the Supreme Court at the height of the Great Depression, *Near v. Minnesota* raised a central concern over the First Amendment's protection of freedom of the press: Should the news media possess the ability to print unproven allegations and, on the other side, does the U.S. Constitution protect all journalistic freedom in the Bill of Rights? In the following excerpts from the Court's decision, Chief Justice Hughes maintains that the state does not have a right to prior restraint of publications. The case was decided on June 1, 1931.

Chief Justice Hughes delivered the opinion of the Court.

If we cut through mere details of procedure, the operation and effect of the statute in substance is that public authorities may bring the owner or publisher of a newspaper or periodical before a judge upon a charge of conducting a business of publishing scandalous and defamatory matter—in particular that the matter consists of charges against public officers of official dereliction—and unless the owner or publisher is able and disposed to bring competent evidence to satisfy the judge that the charges are true and published with good motives and for justifiable ends, his newspaper or periodical is suppressed and further publication is punishable as a contempt. This is of the essence of censorship.

The question is whether a statute authorizing such proceedings in restraint of publication is consistent with the conception of the liberty of the press as historically conceived and guaranteed. In determining the extent of the constitutional protection, it has been generally, if not universally, considered that it is the chief purpose of the guaranty to prevent previous restraints upon publication. The struggle in England, directed against the legislative power of the licenser, resulted in renunciation of the censorship of the press. The liberty deemed to be established was thus described by Blackstone: "The liberty of the press is indeed essential to the nature of a free state; but this consists in laying no previous restraints upon publications, and not in freedom from censure for criminal matter when published. Every freeman has an undoubted right to lay what sentiments he pleases before the public; to forbid this, is to destroy the freedom of the press; but if he publishes what is improper, mischievous or illegal, he must take the consequence of his own temerity." The criticism upon Blackstone's statement has not been because immunity from previous restraint upon publication has not been regarded as deserving of special emphasis, but chiefly because that immunity cannot be deemed to exhaust the conception of the liberty guaranteed by state and federal constitutions. . . .

The objection has also been made that the principle as to immunity from previous restraint is stated too broadly, if every such restraint is deemed to be prohibited. That is undoubtedly true; the protection even as to previous restraint is not absolutely unlimited. But the limitation has been recognized only in exceptional cases. No one would question but that a government might prevent actual obstruction to its recruiting service or the publication of the sailing dates of transports or the number and location of troops. On similar grounds, the primary requirements of decency may be enforced against obscene publications. The security of the community life may be protected against incitements to acts of violence and the overthrow by force of orderly government . . . These limitations are not applicable here. . . .

The exceptional nature of its limitations places in a strong light the general conception that the liberty of the press, historically considered and taken up by the Federal Constitution, has meant, principally although not exclusively, immunity from previous restraints, or censorship . . . Public officers, whose character and conduct remain open to debate and free discussion in the press, find their remedies for false accusations in actions under libel laws providing for redress and punishment, and not in proceedings to restrain the publications of newspapers and periodicals. The fact that the liberty of the press may be abused by miscreant purveyors of scandal does not make any the less necessary the immunity of the press from previous restraint in dealing with official misconduct. Subsequent punishment for such abuses as may exist is the appropriate remedy, consistent with constitutional privilege.

The statute in question cannot be justified by reason of the fact that the publisher is permitted to show, before injunction issues, that the matter published is true and is published with good motives and for justifiable ends. If such a statute is valid, it would be equally permissible for the legislature to provide that at any time the publisher of any newspaper could be brought before a court, or even an administrative officer (as the constitutional protection may not be regarded as resting on mere procedural details), and required to produce proof of the truth of his publication, or of what he intended to publish and of his motives, or stand enjoined. If this can be done, the legislature may provide the machinery for determining in the complete exercise of its discretion what are justifiable ends and restrain publication accordingly. And it would be but a step to a complete system of censorship. We hold the statute, so far as it authorized the proceedings in this action, to be infringement of the liberty of the press guaranteed by the Fourteenth Amendment. . . .

Judgment reversed.

Further Resources

BOOKS

Friendly, Fred W. *Minnesota Rag: The Dramatic Story of the Landmark Supreme Court Case That Gave New Meaning to Freedom of the Press.* New York: Random House, 1982.

Irons, Peter H. *A People's History of the Supreme Court.* New York: Viking, 1999.

WEBSITES

"Communications Act of 1934." Available online at http://showcase.netins.net/web/akline/1934act.htm (accessed March 1, 2003).

"An Emergency Is On!"

Editorial

By: T. Arnold Hill

Date: September 1933

Source: Hill, T. Arnold. "An Emergency Is On!" *Opportunity, The Journal of Negro Life,* 11, no. 9, September 1933, 280. Available online at http://newdeal.feri.org/opp/opp33280.htm; website home page: http://newdeal.feri.org/ (accessed March 1, 2003).

About the Author: T. Arnold Hill (1888–1947) became one of America's foremost civil rights leaders decades before the movement's 1960s heyday. He moved up through the ranks of the National Urban League, eventually becoming the organization's general secretary. Formed as the Committee on Urban Conditions Among Negroes in 1910, the National Urban League still stands as one of this country's most influential civil rights associations. ■

Introduction

Although the New Deal created dozens of programs geared at alleviating the depression's impact, the programs did not come close to eliminating the depravation caused by the economic downturn. This was especially true for women and minority groups. Influential social advocacy groups, such as the National Association for the Advancement of Colored People and the National Urban League, used their own publications to provide accounts of the Depression and press for greater aid for its victims.

Significance

T. Arnold Hill's editorial "An Emergency Is On!" took aim at what many groups believed were racist provisions in certain New Deal programs. Policies creating minimum wage laws, Social Security, and temporary employment opportunities, Hill argued, discriminated against African Americans. He found that the wage scale instituted by the National Industrial Recovery Act provided different pay rates for workers in traditionally minority-concentrated employment areas. He declared, "In leaving agricultural and domestic workers out of the code formula, the bulk of Negro workers, some 3,000,000 out of a total of 5,500,000, will continue to live under a system which is little better than slavery." Driving the point home, Hill exclaimed, "Are we to have a New Deal for whites and an old deal for Negroes?" Hill concluded that policies to improve blacks' economic well-being would also improve the health and stability of the entire national economy, giving Americans ambivalent toward civil rights a concrete reason for supporting equal treatment.

Hill also criticized the Roosevelt administration for funding programs that perpetuated racial inequality at home while the federal government decried racist regimes abroad. This "hypocrisy" of supporting freedom abroad and repression at home would become the rallying cry of millions of African Americans during World War II. The Double-V campaign, first advocated by a black editor of the *Pittsburgh Courier,* called for defeating racism on the home front and the battlefront—"Victory at home! Victory abroad!" T. Arnold Hill's dissatisfaction with the Roosevelt administration mounted during the decade, reaching its peak with the movement to march on Washington, D.C., during World War II, for equality in the workforce. On September 27,

1940, President Roosevelt finally met with A. Philip Randolph, president of the Brotherhood of Sleeping Car Porters; Walter White, executive secretary the NAACP; and T. Arnold Hill, then acting secretary of the National Urban League, to discuss their complaints about discrimination in war production employment practices, as well as the proposed desegregation of the armed forces. This meeting resulted in the creation of the Fair Employment Practices Commission, the federal government's first program specifically designed to prohibit job discrimination on the basis of race.

Primary Source

"An Emergency Is On!"

SYNOPSIS: Less than one year after the initiation of President Franklin D. Roosevelt's New Deal policies to combat the Great Depression, the national economy remained on the verge of complete collapse. Millions of Americans, particularly African Americans, continued to endure poverty of money and spirit. The journal of the National Urban League, *Opportunity, Journal of Negro Life,* published the following editorial about the ongoing problems being experienced by African Americans during the Roosevelt administration.

Negro workers are being discharged by employers whose belief in white supremacy will not tolerate their paying Negroes a wage equal to that paid whites. Fearful that such practices will force many Negroes now employed into idleness, some are suggesting that the codes of the National Industrial Recovery Act provide a dual wage scale—one that will allow the option of paying a smaller wage to Negroes than to whites.

Such a position is economically unsound and socially unjust. Few employers will pay more for their labor than they have to. If they can get Negroes cheaper than they can whites, the latter will often find themselves unwanted and unemployed. This condition will tend to perpetuate the age-old strife between the two groups and make for actual warfare at a time when it takes little to foment either racial or industrial discord.

Moreover, it is impossible to have national recovery as long as one-ninth of the nation's workers are not given the opportunity to recover. If high wages are essential to an improved economic and social state, then recovery of business and public welfare is retarded to the extent that low wages are permitted. In leaving agricultural and domestic workers out of the code formula, the bulk of Negro workers, some 3,000,000 out of a total of 5,500,000, will continue to live under a system which is little better than slavery. Wages now for domestic workers in the South are down to as low as $1.50 per week, and three dollars a week is regarded as a good wage.

It has been contended that what the nation needs to lift it out of the depression is adequate consumption for normal production of goods. Because we are not able now to consume all products farmed, it is costing the government millions to subsidize farmers who are turning crops back into the soil rather than harvest them for a market overstocked with farm products. If the 2,500,000 Negroes in the North and the 9,500,000 in the South earned more they would buy more. The masses of Negroes have never purchased enough food, clothing, furniture, transportation, hospitalization, and the like. Twelve million people would greatly expand production if they were employed and paid according to their economic value rather than their social status.

If a correlation were established between the wages paid Negro workers and the minimum wage level for all workers, it would undoubtedly show that the starvation wages received by Negroes have been directly responsible for limiting the economic security of all workers, as well as for contracting the market for consumer goods. Thus, Mississippi and South Carolina must forever be backward states as long as one-half the members of their population are not allowed sufficient livelihood to purchase their normal share of their state's products.

If employers are unwilling to pay Negroes wages equal to those paid whites, then let them be discharged. There should be no wage distinction based upon race in the NRA codes. To the extent that people are unemployed, to that same extent will those who work have to take care of them. This fits Negroes as well as whites. If all Negroes are discharged in the South, so that whites may work, then the employed whites will have to support the idle Negroes. It is unfair, of course, that the race should be forced into mendicancy, but it is better that Negro workers insist upon wages equal to those paid whites, even if it means their ultimate discharge, than to accept smaller wages and thereby perpetuate the class distinctions that now exist. Neither position is a satisfactory one for the Negro, but it is fair to assume that if the burden of support for the maintenance of Negroes were thrown upon the State, conditions would tend to right themselves much more quickly than if Negroes submitted to a smaller wage.

Three mechanics at work for the National Youth Administration. CORBIS. REPRODUCED BY PERMISSION.

But more than this, the Government of the United States and the Recovery Administration, must put an end to this hypocrisy for the sake of national integrity. At some point this system of exploitation must cease. It impedes prosperity and disqualifies the government as a democracy fit to pass sentence upon other nations. President Roosevelt cannot permit the United States to rush to the protection of Cuba and at the same time tolerate the enslavement of its own fellow-citizens. Neither can our economic experts permit race prejudice to nullify all the thinking, planning and work that have gone into the agricultural and industrial plans for business recovery. Is the New Deal departing from the conventional in all important national issues, to be listless to the plight of twelve million persons, merely because they are darker than the other 110,000,000? Are we to have a New Deal for whites and an old deal for Negroes? The United States cannot possibly remain an international arbiter if it continues to neglect to arbitrate its own domestic affairs.

As serious a national blunder as the neglect of Negroes is, it is not as disturbing as the failure of Negroes to rouse themselves on behalf of their own salvation. This is largely because Negro leaders have not agreed upon a program. They are in agreement that something is wrong; and while they suspect that it has its foundation in economics, they are not sure what the "something" is, nor how to get rid of it. Those who have been leading are unwilling to try new ideas or new personnel. Ignorance and custom are not the only drawbacks. Traditional enmities, factional differences, organizational loyalties, personal likes and dislikes all stand in the way of a united front at the time when the most potent weapon is the impact upon governmental authority of a solidified public opinion representative of Negroes everywhere and of every activity in life. There has been no honorable attempt to bring this about. When efforts are undertaken with the same bias and selfishness that have so often characterized projects of this sort heretofore, then we can expect weak organizations, weak support, and weak results.

An emergency is on. It calls for forthright leadership that will indoctrinate Negro masses with an awareness of the effect of economic relationships upon other aspects of life. It demands leadership that will provide a program for insulating Negroes with industrial and occupational information and firing them with devotion to a cause that is just and fruitful. This leadership is needed to compel the respect of the Administration and to build an esprit de corps among the masses of Negroes who are ready psychologically for a program as they have never been before.

Further Resources

BOOKS

Cook, Robert. *Sweet Land of Liberty?: The African-American Struggle for Civil Rights in the Twentieth Century.* New York: Longman, 1998.

Davis, Kenneth S. *FDR: The New Deal Years, 1933–1937: A History.* New York: Random House, 1986.

Dubofsky, Melvyn, and Stephen Burwood, eds. *Women and Minorities During the Great Depression.* New York: Garland, 1990.

Egerton, John. *Speak Now Against the Day: The Generation Before the Civil Rights Movement in the South.* New York: Knopf, 1994.

WEBSITES

National Urban League. Available online at http://www.nul.org/ (accessed March 1, 2003).

Roosevelt and the Media

"Mr. Roosevelt's Magic"

Editorial

Date: January 15, 1936

Source: "Mr. Roosevelt's Magic." *The Nation* 142, no. 3680, January 15, 1936, 60.

About the Publication: Since its first issue in 1865, *The Nation* has provided Americans with consistently strong leftist opinion about all facets of American culture and politics. It has not hesitated to criticize even the most popular and influential liberals, including four-term president Franklin D. Roosevelt. *The Nation* continues to offer readers progressive views into the twenty-first century.

"The Presidency and the Press"

Editorial

By: J. Fred Essary

Date: June 1936

Source: Essary, J. Fred. "The Presidency and the Press." *Journalism Quarterly* 13, no. 2, June 1936, 177–178.

About the Author: J. Fred Essary (1881–1942) was a popular correspondent for the *Baltimore Sun* during the 1920s and 1930s. In 1943, a net cargo ship bearing his name was acquired by the U.S. Navy. ■

Introduction

In November 1936, President Franklin D. Roosevelt won reelection by the largest margin in history at that time. Not all Americans, though, were satisfied with the president's performance in domestic and foreign policy. Consistently derided by conservatives for overexpanding the federal government with his New Deal policies, FDR also encountered enormous criticism from liberals for not going far enough in combating the economic devastation wrought by the Great Depression.

The following article from the leftist opinion journal *The Nation* provides a sense of how liberals often chafed at what they deemed Roosevelt's refusal to go further in aiding victims of the Depression. *The Nation* and other leftist publications argued that Roosevelt remained "frozen in his tracks." At the same time, this editorial and scores of others continued to marvel at the President's media and political savvy.

Significance

"Mr. Roosevelt's Magic," written in response to Roosevelt's radio message to Congress, characterized his "radio oratory [as] a magnificent achievement." *The Nation,* though, contended that his rhetorical "magic" had begun to wear thin and that its substance was not matching his style. Ever since his rise to the White House in 1932, Roosevelt had consistently attacked whom he considered the perpetrators of the nation's economic turmoil, "the finance-capitalists, the holding-company wizards, the corporation lawyers, and the whole resplendent array of big-business statesmanship." *The Nation* and other leftist organizations endorsed Roosevelt's powerful condemnations of big business. But, with the Depression continuing well into its sixth year, *The Nation* concluded, "Mr. Roosevelt must go farther. If he has not entirely shot his bolt, if he is not more adept at showmanship than at statesmanship, he must affix to the speech a real legislative program."

Although Roosevelt's popularity continued to rise during the election campaign of 1936, this January 1936 editorial examined the Supreme Court's rejection of a crucial New Deal program—the Agricultural Adjustment Act (AAA). The Court's 1935 decision foreshadowed a tumultuous period in American constitutional history, as the Roosevelt administration battled with Congress, the Supreme Court, and the press over whether the executive should have the power to arbitrarily expand and make additional appointments to the Court. With a conservative judiciary striking down many of the New Deal's critical components, Roosevelt decided to fight to increase the Court's membership and thereby gain the ability to appoint like-minded justices.

A political cartoon from the *New York Herald Tribune,* March 22, 1937.

The court-packing plan, as its critics dubbed the proposal, cost the president valuable media support. Conservative, moderate, and even some liberal journalists charged the president with blatantly attempting to usurp the Constitution—many political cartoons of the era illustrate the rancor with which newspapers regarded the president and his controversial, eventually unsuccessful plan. The drawings depicted Roosevelt as so power hungry as to overthrow constitutional government in the United States.

Primary Source

"Mr. Roosevelt's Magic" [excerpt]

SYNOPSIS: As the editorial below makes clear, President Roosevelt and the American people faced significant choices in the winter of 1936. With the Supreme Court outlawing central provisions of the New Deal, should Roosevelt attempt to overthrow the Court? What should the president do about fascist aggression by Hitler's Germany and Mussolini's Italy? Encountering enormous dilemmas in domestic and foreign policy, the news media debated with the president over which options would prove best for a weary, embittered American public.

Mr. Roosevelt's amazing radio message to Congress has undoubtedly strengthened his campaign fortunes, but leaves his program as unclear as ever. Politically adroit, and from the standpoint of radio oratory a magnificent achievement, it was intellectually a confused and straddling performance. Unlike most "historic" events with such an enormous publicity build-up, the thing somehow managed to come off—judging not so much by the applause of Congress and the galleries, which formed the studio audience, as by the talk of the plain men and women in their homes and on the street. The common man wanted to be let in on a dramatic occasion, and he had his wish. He wanted a fighting speech, and he got it. He was tuning in on history-in-the-making, and the President took pains to make it a good show. Even the *Herald Tribune* has had to admit grudgingly that this puts Mr. Roosevelt in a dominating position for the campaign. The President has again used some sort of magic to increase his stature, and by comparison every Presidential possibility on the Republican side seems puny and frustrate. They can talk only of outraged "taste"—these men whose stomachs have not been turned by their association with Hearst and all the revolting exploitation of a company universe.

But a sober rereading of the speech shows how consummately Mr. Roosevelt displayed his talent for

President Franklin Delano Roosevelt delivers a radio address from his home in Hyde Park, New York. Roosevelt made regular radio addresses to the nation to calm fears about the Depression and build support for his programs. AP/WIDE WORLD PHOTOS. REPRODUCED BY PERMISSION.

leaving almost all the important things unsaid. Not that the speech lacked importance for what it did say. It was Mr. Roosevelt's first significant and sustained official utterance on the international situation since his ill-starred incursion into the London conference in the mad July days of 1933. It carried on two Wilsonian traditions: that of seeking to distinguish between European rulers and the desires of the people themselves, and that of reading a vigorous lecture on democracy and autocracy. It was, however, Wilson with a difference. Since Wilson's time the national and international scenes have more clearly emerged. It was possible for Mr. Roosevelt to draw a clear relationship between the fascist imperialism of Hitler, Mussolini, and the Japanese militarists and the fascism of the American plutocrats. We may of course be overestimating the clarity with which Mr. Roosevelt sees this relation. Quite conceivably his main purpose was to capitalize on the widespread anti-war and anti-fascist sentiment in the country, and to bolster his failing prestige in domestic affairs by vigorous leadership in foreign affairs.

But generously interpreted, the President's international stand is more than a clever political device. Despite its overemphasis on the personal and ideological factors and its too easy assumption that Europe needs nothing more than an inner conversion on the part of Hitler and Mussolini, it does face the overwhelming reality of today. It is a recognition of the relation between fascism abroad and at home, between fascism and war, between fascism and the economic plutocracy. If the President had meant only to repeat the well-worn distinction between democracy and dictatorship, he would not so studiously have avoided mention of Soviet Russia. That he did so avoid, it is a tribute to his good sense, and proof of his intent to single out the fascist dictators as the imperialist war-makers.

In the domestic field Mr. Roosevelt's message was better as a manifesto than as a preface to legislative action. It was here that the speech became, as Paul Ward describes it elsewhere in this issue, a political rally, with the business of state being transacted under the klieg lights. It was here that the President showed himself complete master of the grammar of vituperation. Never has an American President so clearly attacked the finance-capitalists, the holding-company wizards, the corporation lawyers, and the whole resplendent array of big-business statesmanship. His attack, coming at a period of capitalistic crisis, is the most significant Presidential utterance we have had on the concentration of financial power in a capitalist state. There have been leftwing attacks on big business in abundance. But when an American President who is politically astute, realistic, sensitive to opinion, directs his Presidential message to such a sustained and considered attack, that becomes news—and history. It becomes an official recognition of the strains within our economic system, and of a basic inner cleavage of interest between those who would freeze the structure as it stands, even at the cost of destroying our culture, and those who still hope to take advantage of whatever flexibilities the system offers.

But Mr. Roosevelt must go farther. If he has not entirely shot his bolt, if he is not more adept at showmanship than at statesmanship, he must affix to the speech a real legislative program. This he reveals little intention of doing. The Supreme Court's invalidation of the AAA will force him and Congress into some sort of action on the agricultural issue. But his essential temper will still be that of a cautious administrator seeking to conserve and consolidate the gains he has already achieved, rather than of an aggressive leader pushing ahead with a program well begun.

The President's speech may be called his "standstill agreement." He has gone as far as the economic necessities of capitalist crisis coerced him into going, and as far as the outer limits of his patrician training and character have permitted him to go. By his references to taxation, the budget, and relief, by his very pointed emphasis upon the New Deal as a finished achievement rather than a fragmentary and incomplete program, he is serving notice that he will go no farther. His right foot is not to be budged a step backward, and his left foot is planted with equal firmness against any forward movement. History may find him frozen in his tracks. That is the meaning of his agile bows to both disarmament and a big navy, to a moratorium on taxes and an attack on big business, to a reduced relief budget and unctuously rhetorical questions on our duty to the unemployed. No man has ever shown greater dexterity in facing both ways than Mr. Roosevelt. Whether such a talent will be adequate either in saving the country or winning a campaign remains to be seen. Mr. Roosevelt got the jump on the Republicans; the Supreme Court has now got the jump on Mr. Roosevelt.

Primary Source

"The Presidency and the Press"

SYNOPSIS: This essay discusses the belief that Washington correspondents are serving the Roosevelt Administration, as well as other presidential administrations, as a type of propaganda organization. This essay looks at whether the president is consciously promoting this propaganda concept. Journalists are viewed as professionals who must weed out the propaganda and distinguish it from legitimate news.

An impression prevails in many quarters—a conviction in some—that the press of the country, as represented by the corps of correspondents in Washington, is lending itself to wholesale propaganda in behalf of the Roosevelt policies. It is frequently asserted that a gigantic publicity organization has been created here, expensively manned, equipped and financed to popularize the New Deal and to overwhelm and defeat the critics of the Administration.

It is further asserted that the President himself is the arch propagandist of the lot; that by the exercise of personal charm, an ingratiating candor and a measure of Machiavellian adroitness, he prostitutes his press conferences to base uses. There are some who affect to believe that he draws about him twice a week from one to two hundred ordinarily hard-boiled news writers, that he captivates or perhaps hypnotizes them, and through them successfully glorifies his own acts and purposes and spreads the poison that confounds his opponents.

Specifications are lacking, it is true. Concrete instances of the colored or misleading news matter that flows from us here in Washington to the reading public are rarely if ever cited. Only the vague or generalized notion exists that a conspiracy has been entered into between the head of the party in power and a section of the press to hoodwink the country.

But quite enough is said to prove disquieting. And if what is said were true and were widely believed, the American people might well be alarmed. The facts of government, which is another way of saying the news of government, are important. They have never been more so. Never in my lifetime, at least, have these facts touched so intimately the livelihood and the general well-being of so many millions of people.

And it goes without saying that if those of us who are daily writing the news of government are being deluded, either consciously or unconsciously, by designing public officials; if we are falling for all the inspired publicity that is dished up to us; in other words, if we are being used to betray the reading public, then we are unfit to be here.

I suppose it will always be true, however, that the narrow-gauged partisan who is out of power will complain bitterly of space given by the press to the activities of those temporarily in power. We long observed the anguish, for example, of the hungry Democrats in this connection during the Coolidge and Hoover Administrations. Also we observed the suffering of the Republicans when Woodrow Wilson dominated the Washington scene. This sort of political wretchedness is perhaps inevitable and the blame for inflicting it must be borne, I suppose, by journalists with such fortitude as they can summon.

It would be absurd to argue that Presidents do not use all available means to inspire publicity and to feed to the country only that line of information or of opinion most advantageous to themselves. Presidents do seize these opportunities. They use them for all they are worth. They seek to strengthen themselves politically and to make their policies more appealing. It is the human thing for them to do. And no President whose news I have handled has been above this practice.

But the extent to which Presidents get away with this sort of propaganda depends entirely upon the writers themselves. It is ridiculous to place the blame for what goes out upon the Roosevelts or the Hoovers or the Coolidges. One President, to be sure, may be more dexterous or crafty than another in giving out his stuff, but that is no excuse. It should merely put the reporter more on his guard.

It is the reporter's business to know propaganda as distinguished from legitimate news, wherever and whenever he encounters it. And if he does not know when he is being imposed upon by a propagandist, whether that propagandist be a President, or a Congressman or a Liberty Leaguer, that reporter should be withdrawn from the Washington field.

Further Resources

BOOKS

Best, Gary Dean. *The Critical Press and the New Deal: The Press Versus Presidential Power, 1933–1938.* Westport, Conn.: Praeger, 1993.

Davis, Kenneth S. *FDR, the New Deal Years, 1933–1937: A History.* New York: Random House, 1986

WEBSITES

New Deal Network. Available online at http://newdeal.feri.org (accessed March 1, 2003).

Photography of the Great Depression

"Migrant Mother"

Photograph

By: Dorothea Lange

Date: February or March 1936

Source: Lange, Dorothea. Illustrative photo in "Ragged, Hungry, Broke, Harvest Workers Live in Squaller." *San Francisco News,* March 10, 1936. Reprinted in "Dorothea Lange's 'Migrant Mother' Photographs in the Farm Security Administration Collection: An Overview." Library of Congress. Image no. 36583. Available online at http://lcweb.loc.gov/rr/print/128_migm.html; website home page: http://memory.loc.gov/ammem/fsowhome.html (accessed March 19, 2003).

About the Photographer: Dorothea Lange's (1895–1965) ability to capture the despair and isolation of her subjects arose, seemingly, from her own life's travails. At the age of seven, she contracted polio and was left with a limp for the rest of her life. At twelve, her father deserted her mother and left the two to fend for themselves in turn-of-the-century New York City. Following the stock market crash of 1929, Lange and her husband lost their home; she coped by refocusing her trade on depictions of life during the Depression. During World War II, she documented the internment of Japanese Americans for the War Relocation Board.

Photograph from *Let Us Now Praise Famous Men*

Photograph

By: Walker Evans

Date: 1936

Source: Agee, James, and Walker Evans. *Let Us Now Praise Famous Men.* Boston: Houghton Mifflin, 1939. Reprinted online at http://lcweb2.loc.gov/ammem/fsowhome.html; website home page: http://lcweb2.loc.gov/ (accessed March 20, 2003).

About the Photographer: Born to a well-off family in St. Louis, Walker Evans (1903–1975) began his career in photography in 1928. He soon became known for the honesty and realism of his photos. During the Great Depression he worked for the Farm Security Administration as well as *Fortune,* documenting the Depression in pictures. His photography for the 1941 book *Let Us Now Praise Famous Men* is his most famous and influential work. Following its publication he continued to document American life as a photographer and editor for *Fortune* until 1965. From 1965 on he taught photography at Yale University.

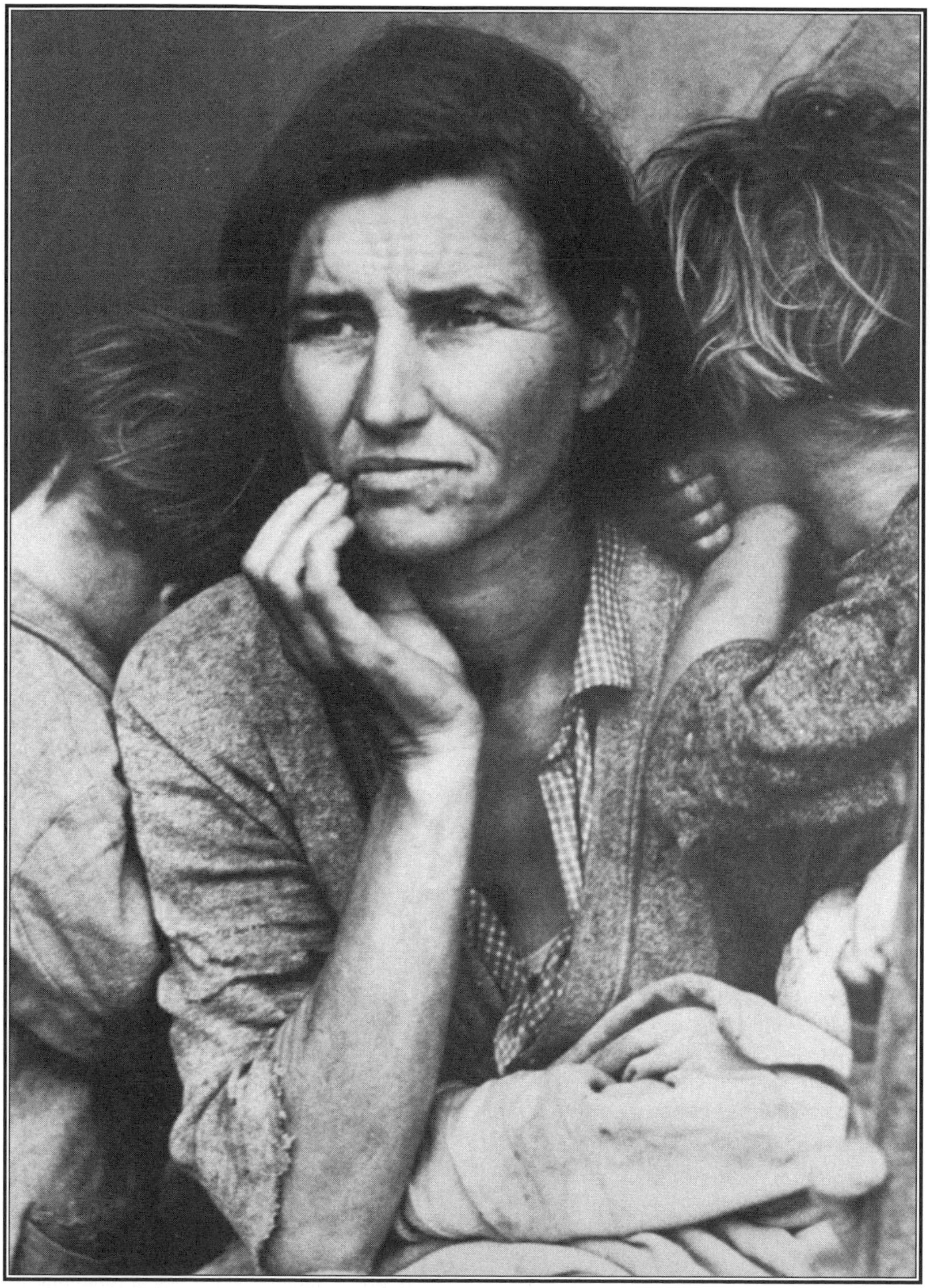

Primary Source

Migrant Mother

SYNOPSIS: "Migrant Mother," 1936, is Dorothea Lange's signature piece. Combined with the other major pictures from the era, it marks a turning point in the history of documentary photography. Interviewed in *Popular Photography* in February 1960, Lange explained how she created the photograph: "I saw and approached the hungry and desperate mother, as if drawn by a magnet. I do not remember how I explained my presence or my camera to her, but I do remember she asked me no questions. . . . There she sat in that lean-to tent with her children huddled around her, and seemed to know that my pictures might help her, and so she helped me." THE LIBRARY OF CONGRESS.

Primary Source

Photograph from *Let Us Now Praise Famous Men*

SYNOPSIS: James Agee and Walker Evans's book focused on a few families struggling to get by in Alabama during the Great Depression. Allie Mae and Floyd Burroughs were sharecroppers living in a small cabin in Hale County. This photo is of the washstand in the dog run and kitchen of Floyd Burroughs' cabin, from *Let Us Now Praise Famous Men.* THE LIBRARY OF CONGRESS.

Primary Source

"Farmer and Sons Walking in the Face of a Dust Storm"

SYNOPSIS: Arthur Rothstein describes his photograph of a father and his sons suffering through a 1936 dust storm in Oklahoma in Hank O'Neal's *A Vision Shared: A Classic Portrait of America and Its People, 1935–1943.* Rothstein related, "I could hardly breathe because [of] the dust. . . . I saw the farmer and his two sons. . . . As they pressed into the wind, the smallest child walked a few steps behind, . . . covering his eyes to protect them." AP/WIDE WORLD PHOTOS. REPRODUCED BY PERMISSION.

"Farmer and Sons Walking in the Face of a Dust Storm"

Photograph

By: Arthur Rothstein

Date: 1936

Source: Rothstein, Arthur. "Farmer and Sons Walking in the Face of a Dust Storm. Cimarron County, Oklahoma." Reprinted online at http://lcweb2.loc.gov/ammem/fsowhome.html; website home page: http://lcweb2.loc.gov/ (accessed March 20, 2003).

About the Photographer: Arthur Rothstein (1915–1985) was born in New York City, the son of immigrants. He developed an interest in photography while studying at Columbia University. After graduating, his friend Roy Stryker hired him to work as a photographer for the FSA. Rothstein became famous for his photos of the Dust Bowl. In 1940 he was hired by *Look* magazine. He remained there until 1971, eventually becoming director of photography for the photo-journal. Rothstein was also the author of seven books, a founder of the American Society of Magazine Photographers, and taught photography at Columbia and at the Newhouse School of Communications. ■

Introduction

During the 1930s, the Resettlement Administration (RA)—a New Deal program later transferred to the Farm Security Administration—hired a number of prominent photographers. Besides providing employment to these photographers during a difficult time for the arts, the purpose of the program was to document the experience of the group hit hardest by the Great Depression: farmers.

America's farming centers were devastated by the Great Depression. Even before the crash of 1929, farmers throughout the United States had already suffered through years of dwindling crop prices and drought during the 1920s. The stock market fall only heightened the impact of the Depression on agricultural laborers. By the mid-1930s, millions had been forced to abandon their farms and migrate between labor camps in the hopes of finding work. The Midwest was especially hard hit. The prolonged drought there destroyed not only crops but the land itself, with parched soil blowing up into the air on the wind, creating great clouds of dust that gave the region the nickname "the Dust Bowl."

The FSA's photographers came from a variety of backgrounds. Dorothea Lange had decades of experience and her work for the California Rural Rehabilitation Administration had helped inspire the formation of the FSA's photography unit. Arthur Rothstein, on the other hand, was hired fresh out of college. Walker Evans came to photography after a failed attempt at a writing career. What these three, and the other photographers of the FSA, had in common was a commitment to depicting the harsh realities of the Great Depression with simple, unstaged, photographs of the individuals who were suffering through it.

Significance

The work of FSA's photographers had broad and powerful effects almost as soon as it had begun. Dorothea Lange's most enduring portrait was "Migrant Mother," taken in early 1936. It captured the hunger, weariness, and solemn dignity of a migrant worker and her children, living in a ragged tent in Nipomo, California. Published in the *San Francisco News* shortly after it was taken, "Migrant Mother" raised a public outcry about the impoverished conditions of migrant camps throughout the West. The federal government swiftly authorized additional funds for the Nipomo, California, camp where the mother and her seven children struggled to survive on peas and dead birds. "Migrant Mother" came to symbolize the Great Depression.

Arthur Rothstein took his camera to the central United States. Most Americans were already well aware of the drought and wind storms there, the dust from which was being blown all the way to the Atlantic Ocean. Rothstein's photos brought home the human dimension of this devastation, showing families struggling to survive amidst incredible devastation.

Walker Evans also worked for the FSA in the 1930s, but his most famous photos were taken during this same time period for *Fortune*. In 1936, the magazine hired photographer Walker Evans and writer James Agee to produce a report of rural life during the Depression. *Fortune* ultimately decided not to run the series, but in 1941 Evans and Agee had their work published in book form. This book, *Let Us Now Praise Famous Men* quickly became a best-seller, providing a mass audience with sympathetic portraits of three families living in hard times in Alabama. The New York Public Library currently lists *Let Us Now Praise Famous Men* as one of the most influential books of the twentieth century. As Agee described in his preface, "The photographs are not illustrative. They, and the text, are co-equal, mutually independent, and fully collaborative. By their fewness, and by the impotence of the reader's eye, this will be misunderstood by most of that minority which does not wholly ignore it. In the interests, however, of the history and the future of photography, that risk seems irrelevant, and this flat statement necessary" (p. xi).

The work of the FSA photographers also had a significant impact on photography. The photographers of the FSA, and others like them such as Charles Evans, were at the forefront of modern photojournalism. They captured their subjects in real life and used these photos to dramatically illustrate the problems of their day.

Further Resources

BOOKS

Agee, James, and Walker Evans. *Let Us Now Praise Famous Men.* Boston: Houghton Mifflin, 1941. Reprinted, New York: Mariner Books, 2001.

Heyman, Therese Thau, et al. *Dorothea Lange: American Photographs.* San Francisco: San Francisco Museum of Modern Art, Chronicle Books, 1994.

O'Neal, Hank. *A Vision Shared: A Classic Portrait of America and Its People, 1935–1943.* New York: St. Martin's Press, 1976.

Scott, William. *Documentary Expression and Thirties America.* New York: Oxford University Press, 1973.

WEBSITES

"The 1930s in Print: Documentaries." American Studies at the University of Virginia. Available online at http://xroads.virginia.edu/~1930s/PRINT/documentaries.html (accessed March 1, 2003).

The Lindbergh Case and the Media

"The Lindbergh Case in Its Relation to American Newspapers"

Speech

By: Walter Lippmann

Date: April 18, 1936

Source: Lippmann, Walter. "The Lindbergh Case in Its Relation to American Newspapers." Speech presented at the Fourteenth Annual Convention of the American Society of Newspaper Editors, April 16–18, 1936.

About the Author: Walter Lippmann's (1889–1974) sixty-plus years in journalism spanned the twentieth century from the beginning of World War I until the end of the Vietnam War. Chosen at twenty-four as the first editor of the weekly journal *The New Republic,* Lippmann eventually rose to become one of the nation's most respected, nationally syndicated columnists.

"Have You Seen This Baby?"

Photograph

By: Anonymous

Date: March 1932

Source: "Have You Seen This Baby?" March 1932. AP/Wide World Photos. Image no. 1752634. Available online at http://www.apwideworld.com/ (accessed April 30, 2003). ■

Introduction

In March 1932, Charles and Anne Lindbergh's eighteen-month-old son was kidnapped from their New Jersey estate. For four years, the ensuing ransom demands, investigation, arrest, murder trial, conviction, and execution of the alleged perpetrator stayed in the public consciousness on an almost daily basis. Newspaper headlines and radio bulletins blared story after story about the "Lindbergh Baby" case, with hundreds of reporters covering it. The story even inspired a comic strip, entitled "The Crime of the Century." Run in twenty-four installments, and distributed by King Features Syndicate, the strip gave readers an overview of the case.

Bruno Richard Hauptmann, a German immigrant, was arrested for the kidnapping two years after it occurred, in the fall of 1934. Following his conviction for kidnapping, extortion, and murder in February 1935, Hauptmann exhausted his appeals until he was executed on April 3, 1936. Historians now conclude that Hauptmann certainly was involved in the extortion of ransom money from the Lindberghs, but the evidence remains murky with regard to whether he kidnapped and murdered the Lindberghs' baby. Through countless pages of irresponsible news coverage and rumor mongering, the American public had by and large convicted Hauptmann long before the trial began.

Significance

Using his position as one of the nation's preeminent journalists, Walter Lippmann urged the news profession to reform its reporting practices to prevent such sensational coverage in the future. He called for editors to search for methods that "will greatly reduce, if they do not entirely prevent, sensational murder cases from becoming a public scandal." What Lippmann described as the "irregular popular process" of reporting high-profile cases "interferes with, distorts and undermines the effectiveness of the law and the people's confidence in it." Reflecting sentiments that media critics continue to offer, he abhorred the situation where "the self-appointed detectives get in the way of the regular detectives, the self-appointed judges and jurymen and advocates for the prosecution get in the way of the officers of the law, and the official verdict becomes confused with the popular verdict, often in the court itself, almost always in the public mind."

Rather than focusing exclusively on the press and overly eager reporters, Lippmann chastised the criminal justice system for being too quick to assign innocence or, more often, guilt to individuals who had yet to appear before a judge and jury. In the Lindbergh case, where lawyers on both sides issued subpoenas so that friends could be forced into the courtroom to view the proceedings, a damaging, public media circus evolved. The overreporting of the case biased the public and potential jury pool by publicly assigning guilt prior to trial. This central criticism plagued the media profession throughout the century—the Sacco and Vanzetti and O.J. Simpson murder trials being primary examples.

Lippmann also railed against unscrupulous journalists who participated in the "circulation of malicious rumors and the invasion of the privacy of the Lindbergh family." The commentator, though, staunchly defended the freedom of the press against censorship. In fact, Lippmann focused his concluding statements on arguing that the press should focus on officers of the court who aid in sensationalizing certain cases. The press, according to Lippmann, should not be held accountable for printing what it learns. Rather, it is the press's duty to force the criminal justice system to operate fairly and truthfully, "For here the whole process of justice and the dignity of American life are at stake."

Primary Source

"The Lindbergh Case in Its Relation to American Newspapers"

SYNOPSIS: Two weeks after the execution of Bruno Hauptmann, Walter Lippmann addressed the annual convention of the American Society of Newspaper Editors at the National Press Club in Washington, D.C. In his speech, titled "The Lindbergh Case in Its Relation to American Newspapers," he focused his remarks on the Lindbergh baby kidnapping and ensuing media free-for-all that forced the Lindberghs to leave the United States and resulted in the execution of the primary suspect, Hauptmann. To prevent future feeding frenzies, Lippmann called for reform of reporting methods and the criminal justice system itself. An example of media coverage of the kidnapping is included in a sidebar of a newspaper headline and Associated Press article.

Mr. Patterson, Ladies and Gentlemen: Although most of us would, I believe, willingly forget the horrors that began with the kidnaping of the Lindbergh baby and are perhaps not ended even now, the American public will be glad to know that the larger aspects of the case are being studied by the American Bar Association, by this Society and by the other organizations representing the newspaper profession. We are under obligation to do that and to see whether the American bar and the American press cannot jointly reach practical conclusions which will greatly reduce, if they do not entirely prevent, sensational murder cases from becoming a public scandal.

It goes without saying that we are not concerned with the law and the facts of Hauptmann's arrest, trial, conviction, appeal and execution. We are concerned with a situation spectacularly illustrated in this case, but typical of most celebrated criminal cases in the United States, which may be described by saying that there are two processes of justice, the one official, the other popular. They are carried on side by side, the one in courts of law, the other in the press, over the radio, on the screen, at public meetings—and at every turn this irregular popular process interferes with, distorts and undermines the effectiveness of the law and the people's confidence in it.

Because there are two pursuits of the criminal, two trials and two verdicts—the one supposed to be based on the law and a thousand years of accumulated experience, the other totally irresponsible—the self-appointed detectives get in the way of the regular detectives, the self-appointed judges and jurymen and advocates for the prosecution and defense get in the way of the officers of the law, and the official verdict becomes confused with the popular verdict, often in the court itself, almost always in the public mind.

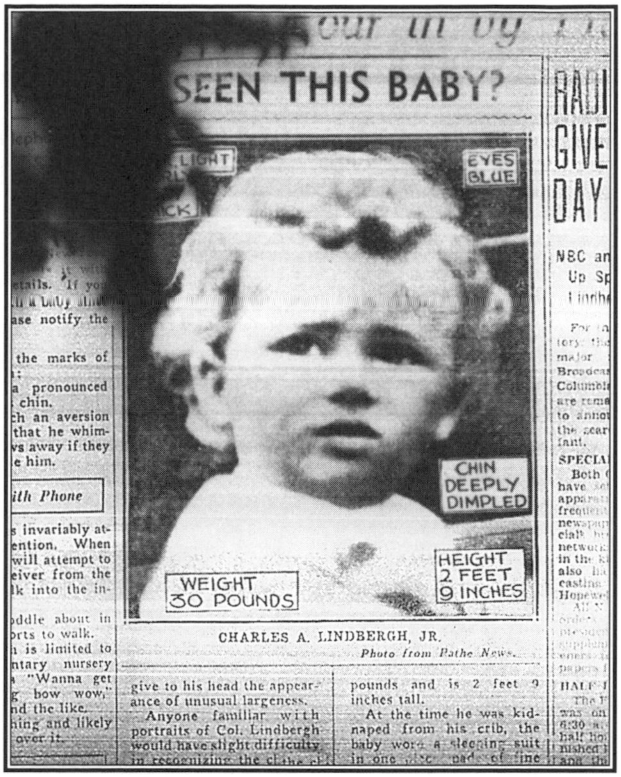

Primary Source

"Have You Seen This Baby?"

SYNOPSIS: A newspaper announces the kidnapping of Charles A. Lindbergh, Jr., in March 1932. News coverage of the Lindbergh baby kidnapping was criticized for sensationalism by Walter Lippmann in his 1936 address "The Lindbergh Case in Its Relation to American Newspapers." AP/WIDE WORLD PHOTOS. REPRODUCED BY PERMISSION.

We can examine the problems best, I think, by examining a few concrete instances. Hauptmann was arrested on September 20, 1934, and within a week there was a headline in a New York paper saying that "clues build iron-clad case against Bruno, police claim," and a few days later it announced that "twelve men and women selected at random" by a reporter had decided, according to the headline: "Bruno guilty but had aids, verdict of man in street."

Here we find that the police, unless the newspaper was lying, which I doubt, made an appeal to the public to believe their evidence before that evidence had been submitted to a court of law. That was an interference by the police with the lawful process of justice. It is for the jury to determine whether a case is "iron-clad," and since juries have to be selected from the newspaper reading public,

Colonel Charles A. Lindbergh is mobbed by reporters as he leaves the Bronx County Courthouse on September 26, 1934. **AP/WIDE WORLD PHOTOS. REPRODUCED BY PERMISSION.**

such a positive statement on the authority of the police is deeply prejudicial. I do not for a moment think that Hauptmann was innocent. But that does not alter the fact that he had a right to be tried before a jury and to be tried nowhere else. Because he was tried in two places at once, thousands of persons came to believe that he was not tried fairly. But in the administration of justice it is of the highest importance not only that the right verdict should be reached but that the people should believe that it has been reached dispassionately.

In the two headlines I have cited, and you will recognize them as being by no means exceptional, we see the police rendering a verdict on their own evidence and a newspaper establishing a verdict among the potential jurors.

Let us pass to the trial in Flemington. It had, of course, to be a public trial. But if it was to be a reputable trial, it had also to be a trial in which the minds of the judge, the jury, the lawyers and the witnesses all concentrated on the evidence, were as little influenced as possible by excitement or prejudice. The court room at Flemington is said to have a maximum seating capacity of 260 persons. On January 2, according to The *New York Times,* the constables on duty admitted to an already overcrowded courtroom 275 spectators without passes. A few weeks later it was learned that attorneys for both sides were issuing subpoenas to favored friends in order to force their admission as spectators in the court room, more than a hundred having been issued for one day's session. The authorities permitted the installation of telegraph wires in the court house itself, and one of the telegraph companies alone had to have a hundred men on hand. Although it was forbidden to take pictures during the trial, pictures were taken, and the authorities took no action.

Now there is no use pretending that a case can be tried well in an overcrowded court room with every actor knowing that every word he speaks, every intonation of his voice, every expression of his face, will instantly be recorded, transmitted to the ends of the earth, and judged by millions of persons.

This brings us to the actual trial of the case outside the court room. As a sample from the press, we may take a report in which it was said that Hauptmann on the stand "made senseless denials," and he was described as "a thing lacking human characteristics." This, let us not forget, was during his trial and before the jury had rendered its verdict. We should not delude ourselves into thinking that comment of this sort is of no effect simply because the jury is locked up and is not allowed to read the papers. The witnesses read them, the spectators read them, and no newspaper man needs to be told that the sentiment of a crowd communicates itself more or less to every one. There is no way of isolating a jury in such a way as to protect it from the feeling of the crowd.

We have next to consider the conduct of the lawyers. They began trying the case in the newspapers almost from the day of Hauptmann's arrest. The counsel for the defense, Mr. Reilly, appeared in the news reels two days after his appointment and declared his belief that Hauptmann was innocent. A few days after the opening of the trial he announced to the press that he would name the kidnapers and that they were connected with the Lindbergh household. Two weeks after the trial, while the case was set for appeal, he addressed the Lions Club of Brooklyn and denounced the verdict, and the next day he addressed a mass meeting at which, during the course of his speech, the crowd booed Colonel Lindbergh.

Hauptmann himself issued newspaper statements during the course of the trial, the statements being given out by his lawyers. The prosecution also tried the case in the newspapers. On January 3 Mr. Wilentz said at his press conference that Mrs. Lindbergh's testimony would be "loaded with importance"; on January 22 he told a reporter that he would "wrap the kidnap ladder around Hauptmann's neck," and so on and so on.

Finally, we cannot omit the Governor of New Jersey, who, on December 5, 1935, while the case was still pending before the Supreme Court of the United States, let it be known that he was conducting his own investigation. I do not criticize him for that. The governor of a state has a right and, I think, an obligation to satisfy himself that justice had been done in his state. But the governor, who is a member of the New Jersey Court of Pardons, a quasi-judicial body, proceeded to try the case not before the court but in the newspapers. On December 8 his investigators let it be known that rail 16 of the ladder had, in their opinion, been planted against Hauptmann, and the governor was quoted as saying that he thought so, too. He also gave his opinion about fingerprints and was reported as saying that his personal investigator was "convinced that Hauptmann is not the man."

I must apologize for devoting so much time to these specific instances. I have done so because mere generalities cannot lead to practical conclusions. The instances I have cited are, I believe, typical, and taken together they illustrate the problem which the bar and the press have undertaken to deal with. Perhaps I should say: can deal with. For nothing that we can say here today, or embody in a policy, can meet directly some of the most shocking incidental aspects of the case: for example, the

"Lindbergh Baby Kidnapped" [excerpt]

[The kidnapping of the Lindbergh baby elicited a great deal of journalism that emotionally colored the public's perception of the case. Although the publication of the child's diet is not the same as trying the case in the press, it did contribute to the emotional atmosphere that made a dispassionate examination of the evidence difficult.]

The Child's Diet

Hopewell, N.J.—With a prayer that it might reach the persons who hold the fate of her baby boy in their hands and the hope that it might find in them some spark of human compassion, Mrs. Charles A. Lindbergh today sent a mother's appeal to the kidnapers of her child.

It concerned the baby's diet. The child is sick. It has a bad cold.

One quart of milk during the day, she cautioned in a message broadcast through the press.

Three tablespoons of cooked cereal morning and night.

Two tablespoons of cooked vegetables once a day.

One yolk of egg daily.

Half a cup of orange juice on waking.

Half a cup of prune juice after the afternoon nap.

Fourteen drops of viosterola during the day.

No Blankets Taken

That's the diet the baby was receiving until it was snatched from its crib in the forepart of last night—a slim one, but such as a baby of 20 months with a severe cold should have.

A search of the nursery disclosed no blankets had been taken, giving rise to Mrs. Lindbergh's fears that the child was taken away improperly clad.

SOURCE: Blackman, Samuel. "Lindbergh Baby Kidnapped." Associated Press. March 2, 1932. Available online at http://wire.ap.org/APpackages/20thcentury/32lindberghbaby.html; website home page: http://wire.ap.org (accessed February 5, 2003).

circulation of malicious rumors and the invasion of the privacy of the Lindbergh family. All that I can say for the present about them is that in so far as we can succeed in restoring the administration of justice to the police and the courts, eliminating the irregular, irresponsible, popular process, we shall create a radically different atmosphere for cases of this sort.

Now I should like to point out that all of the instances I have cited have a common denominator. The regular officers of the law acted irregularly. I do not say this as a newspaper man trying to vindicate the press at the expense of the police, the bench, the bar, and public officials. Far from it. I should regard it as insulting to the press to claim that it has not great responsibilities in the administration of justice. I say it because a recognition that the abuses of this case are due to the fact that the regular officers of the law acted irregularly is the only way to arrive at practical conclusions as to what can be done about the abuses.

So let us fix in mind the facts.

1. That the police published and commented on the evidence before the trial.
2. That the officers of the court did not provide an orderly court room for the trial.
3. That no effective action was taken by officers of the court against spectators and reporters who took a hand in the trial.
4. That the attorneys on both sides by their public statements violated No. 20 of the Canons of Ethics of the American Bar Association.
5. That the governor, acting in a quasi-judicial capacity, made ex parte statements to the press. And I conclude that without the connivance of the regular officers of the law the intolerable abuses of publicity would have been reduced to manageable proportions. It is, therefore, upon the officers of the law that we must place the primary responsibility for effective action which will prevent a repetition of these abuses in the future.

In respect to the police this is a matter of discipline. The Army does not grant interviews describing its war plans: there is no more reason why the police should tell the criminals they are pursuing how they hope to capture them or what they think of the evidence that the grand jury and the petit jury may have to pass upon. Reform will begin here whenever a chief of police decides to enforce it.

In respect to the trial in court, it is the right and it is the duty of the judge to keep order in his court and around it. He does not have to admit more spectators than can be seated comfortably or more than a reasonable number of representative newspaper men. He does not have to admit cameras, radio broadcasting machinery, special telephone and telegraph apparatus to the court house. The streets can be cleared of crowds and the traffic can be kept moving.

Moreover, he does not have to submit to having the case tried simultaneously in the newspapers. Under any realistic conception of the judicial process, comment on the evidence by newspapers, speakers on the radio, by the lawyers, is contempt of court. It should be treated as such. This is the English law, developed not by statute but by judicial decision, and no one, I think, will wish to say that the English have any less respect for freedom of speech than we have. . . . Yet when in the Crippen case, The Daily Chronicle published an article hinting that Dr. Crippen, who was in custody awaiting trial, had purchased poison before his wife's murder, the editor was held for contempt of court. The principle, as laid down by Mr. Justice Wells in an earlier case was as follows: "It is not because the comments might damage the accused person that the court would interfere, but on a broader and higher ground—namely, that it was the province of the tribunal before whom the case was tried to determine as to his guilt or innocence." (In re Stead, Reg. vs. Balfour, 11 Times Law Review 492.)

As for a chief executive official who tries a case in the press when it is before a quasi-judicial body like the Court of Pardons, this, too, is in spirit a contempt of court.

It will be said at once that in arguing that we must look to the police and the bench and the bar to see that criminal cases are tried only before the regular tribunal, I have failed to take account of the fact that these public officials are dependent on public favor, and that they would have to be heroes to refuse to let these cases be exploited by the press.

This is where we as professional newspaper men have our primary responsibility. Hitherto we have generally taken the attitude that if we refrained from participating in the worst of it, we had done our full duty. I believe that we must now recognize that this is not our full duty. It is our duty, I believe, to make it plain to the regular officers of the law that we expect them to administer justice in an orderly way, that we shall attack them if they do not, and that we shall defend them if they do. Then let them choose between the yellow press and the reputable press, and let them find out whose favor counts the more.

I am convinced that this would be sound editorial practice, that the way to meet the competition of the sensationalists is to make an issue, publicly and dramatically, not against the yellow press as such, for we are not our brothers' keepers, but against public officials who play its game. I believe we shall find an interested audience. I am certain we shall have the support of a multitude of quiet men and women who are sick at heart over this whole business. And I believe that gradually, as has been done by the press in its long fight against corruption, we shall raise the standards on which American criminal justice is administered.

I do not suggest, you will note, that we piously deplore the sensationalism of the Lindbergh case and then indulge only in so much of it as we think we have to have to compete for circulation. I suggest that we challenge the police, the judges, the lawyers, who connive at it, that we declare that they are subverting the processes of law, that they are acting corruptly, and center public attention on them rather than on the criminal in the dock. There is a newspaper crusade waiting to be conducted here which is every bit as important and far more interesting than crusades about whether an official has taken a bribe. For here the whole process of justice and the dignity of American life are at stake.

I claim too that the program I have sketched meets the specific evils exemplified in the Lindbergh case without the slightest suggestion of censorship, without the necessity of passing any new laws, without any self-righteous and impracticable attempt on our part to lay down rules as to what any newspaper shall print. We cannot edit the yellow press directly or indirectly and we have no business to try. But we have every right as American citizens to call upon the police, the bench and the bar to administer the law in a lawful way. That is asking no special favor for ourselves. It will deprive all the newspapers of whatever commercial advantage may flow from exploiting a corruption of the judicial process. But it will enable us to sleep better at night. (Applause)

Further Resources

BOOKS

Ahlgren, Gregory, and Stephen Monier. *Crime of the Century: The Lindbergh Kidnapping Hoax.* Boston: Branden Books, 1993.

Bak, Richard. *Lindbergh: Triumph and Tragedy.* Dallas: Taylor, 2000.

Berg, A. Scott. *Lindbergh.* New York: Berkley, 1999.

Steel, Ronald. *Walter Lippmann and the American Century.* New York: Little, Brown, 1980. Reprinted, Somerset, N.J.: Transaction Publishers, 1999.

Waller, George. *Kidnap: The Story of the Lindbergh Case.* New York: Dial Press, 1961.

PERIODICALS

Whitman, Alden. "Columnist and Author Walter Lippmann Dies on Dec. 14 at Age of 85, NYC." *The New York Times,* December 15, 1974.

———. "Lindbergh Dies of Cancer in Hawaii at the Age of 72." *The New York Times,* August 27, 1974.

WEBSITES

Charles Lindbergh: An American Aviator. Available online at http://www.charleslindbergh.com/ (accessed March 1, 2003).

"Lindbergh." American Experience. Available online at http://www.pbs.org/wgbh/amex/lindbergh/; website home page: http://www.pbs.org/ (accessed March 1, 2003).

The Lindbergh Case. *Hunterdon Online: From the Hunterdon County Democrat.* Available online at http://www.lindberghtrial.com/html/comic.shtml (accessed March 1, 2003).

"The Lindbergh Kidnapping." *Famous Cases.* Federal Bureau of Investigation. Available online at http://www.fbi.gov/libref/historic/famcases/lindber/lindbernew.htm; website home page: http://www.fbi.gov/homepage.htm (accessed March 1, 2003).

"Landon 1,293,669; Roosevelt, 972,897: Final Returns in the *Digest*'s Poll of Ten Million Voters"

Journal article, Table

By: *Literary Digest*

Date: October 31, 1936

Source: "Landon 1,293,669; Roosevelt, 972,897: Final Returns in the *Digest*'s Poll of Ten Million Voters." *Literary Digest,* October 31, 1936. Available online at http://historymatters.gmu.edu/d/5168/; website home page: http://historymatters.gmu.edu (accessed March 13, 2003).

About the Publication: Although the publication's title connoted a strict focus on literature and the arts, *Literary Digest* began in 1890 as a magazine devoted to current events and opinion in the United States and the world. The weekly journal quickly became popular, making it all the more embarrassing when it incorrectly predicted the outcome of the 1936 presidential election. This misuse of public opinion polls created a firestorm of controversy, causing the downfall of the magazine within two years. ■

Alfred M. Landon and his wife pose confidently during the 1936 presidential campaign. Landon, the Republican candidate for president in 1936, was soundly defeated by Franklin Roosevelt despite a widespread prediction by the *Literary Digest* that Landon would win by a large margin. AP/WIDE WORLD PHOTOS. REPRODUCED BY PERMISSION.

Introduction

The science of public opinion polling was not entirely new in 1936, the year of President Franklin D. Roosevelt's run for reelection against Alfred (Alf) Landon, a virtually unknown Republican governor from Kansas. By 1936, *Literary Digest* considered itself an expert in the rapidly evolving practice of polling public opinion prior to elections. In fact, the publication had correctly predicted the results of the presidential elections of 1916, 1920, 1924, 1928, and 1932. Unfortunately, *Literary Digest*'s estimate for the 1936 contest proved to be one of the worst miscalculations in U.S. political history.

Significance

Coming off of his victory in 1932 and the installation of his massive New Deal policy network to combat the Great Depression, Franklin Delano Roosevelt appeared to many pundits to be an unbeatable candidate in 1936. Republican governor Alf Landon possessed little national name recognition, as most prominent Republicans refused to compete against the Roosevelt steamroller. Hailing from Kansas, one of the most sparsely populated states in the union, Landon seemed to pose little threat to the wildly popular Roosevelt. Although conservatives, primarily business leaders, despised Roosevelt's monumental expansion of the federal government, moderates and liberals from all classes, especially those impoverished by the Depression, idolized the president for his frontal assault on the Depression that began under Republican Herbert Hoover.

The *Literary Digest* thought differently. The publication sent millions of post cards to be filled out by readers and returned with their choice for president in the 1936 election. According to the boastful article transcribed below, the poll's results were clear—Landon would soon defeat Roosevelt in a "landslide." Out of the more than two million cards received, nearly 1.3 million chose Landon, about 973,000 chose Roosevelt. The publication predicted that Landon would crush Roosevelt with 57 percent of the national vote and 370 electoral votes. According to the poll, only the staunchly Democratic South would back the president, with nearly every other state, including Roosevelt's home state of New York, opting for Landon.

Despite the article's opening protestations that the poll numbers were "neither weighted, adjusted, nor interpreted," *Literary Digest*'s editors felt that the results needed to be justified and explained fully. The report even went so far as to defend its poll to a reader who wagered $100,000 that the actual outcome would be quite different from the *Digest*'s conclusion. While the publication may have provided exact figures about reader replies, the poll's methodology spelled doom for these estimates.

Americans reelected President Roosevelt by the greatest margin in history at that time: 60.8 percent of the vote and 523 electoral votes versus Landon's 36.5 percent of the vote and 8 electoral votes. Landon won only in the tiny states of Vermont and Maine. The wide disparity between prediction and outcome greatly embarrassed the *Literary Digest* and continues to be regarded as one of the low points in media opinion polling. The poll cost the publication subscribers and credibility—the *Literary Digest* folded less than two years after the election, in February 1938, largely because of public outcry from the erroneous 1936 presidential poll.

Nonetheless, in the following decades, media organizations of all types continued to use public opinion polls during election campaigns. In fact, one of the major criticisms of election coverage at the end of the twentieth century focused on the media's *overuse* of such polls. This "horse-race" mentality, critics argue, concentrates too much media attention on estimates of popularity

***Literary Digest* Poll, 1936 Presidential Election: Questionnaire Results, Landon vs. Roosevelt**

Predicted Electoral and Total Votes for States

State	Electoral Vote	Landon 1936 Predicted Total Vote For State	Roosevelt 1936 Total Vote For State	State	Electoral Vote	Landon 1936 Predicted Total Vote For State	Roosevelt 1936 Predicted Total Vote For State
Alabama	11	3,060	10,082	Nebraska	7	18,280	11,770
Arizona	3	2,337	1,975	Nevada	3	1,003	955
Arkansas	9	2,724	7,608	New Hampshire	4	9,207	2,737
California	22	89,516	77,245	New Jersey	16	58,677	27,631
Colorado	6	15,949	10,025	New Mexico	3	1,625	1,662
Connecticut	8	28,809	13,413	New York	47	162,260	139,277
Delaware	3	2,918	2,048	North Carolina	13	6,113	16,324
Florida	7	6,087	8.620	North Dakota	4	4,250	3,666
Georgia	12	3,948	12,915	Ohio	26	77,896	50,778
Idaho	4	3,653	2,611	Oklahoma	11	14,442	15,075
Illinois	29	123,297	79,035	Oregon	5	11,747	10,951
Indiana	14	42,805	26,663	Pennsylvania	36	119,086	81,114
Iowa	11	31,871	18,614	Rhode Island	4	10,401	3,489
Kansas	9	35,408	20,254	South Carolina	8	1,247	7,105
Kentucky	11	13,365	16,592	South Dakota	4	8,483	4,507
Louisiana	10	3,686	7,902	Tennessee	11	9,883	19,829
Maine	5	11,742	5,337	Texas	23	15,341	37,501
Maryland	8	17,463	18,341	Utah	4	4,067	5,318
Massachusetts	17	87,449	25,965	Vermont	3	7,241	2,458
Michigan	19	51,478	25,686	Virginia	11	10,223	16,783
Minnesota	11	30,762	20,733	Washington	8	21,370	15,300
Mississippi	9	848	6,080	West Virginia	8	13,660	10,235
Missouri	15	50,022	38,267	Wisconsin	12	33,796	20,781
Montana	4	4,490	3,562	Wyoming	3	2,526	1,533

SOURCE: *Literary Digest,* October 31, 1936.

Primary Source

Literary Digest Poll Results: Table

SYNOPSIS: The results of the *Literary Digest*'s famously inaccurate poll, reported in the article "Landon 1,293,669; Roosevelt, 972,897: Final Returns in the *Digest*'s Poll of Ten Million Voters," predicted that Alf Landon would defeat Franklin Roosevelt in the 1936 presidential election.

rather than how the candidates view more substantive foreign and domestic policy issues.

Primary Source

"Landon 1,293,669; Roosevelt, 972,897: Final Returns in the *Digest's* Poll of Ten Million Voters"

SYNOPSIS: The following article appeared in the *Digest*'s last edition prior to the 1936 election. Many pundits charged that the publication's conservative leanings had gotten the better of its editorial judgment, as the attack about Republican control of the magazine made clear in the fourth paragraph. Roosevelt supporters feared that the article would convince voters that Landon would win, thereby diminishing their desire to vote and giving Landon's supporters greater confidence in the election's closing days. Roosevelt and his backers, though, had nothing to fear. The statistical table of the poll's results, which accompanied the original article, is also reproduced here.

Well, the great battle of the ballots in the poll of 10 million voters, scattered throughout the forty-eight states of the Union, is now finished, and in the table below we record the figures received up to the hour of going to press.

These figures are exactly as received from more than one in every five voters polled in our country—they are neither weighted, adjusted, nor interpreted.

Never before in an experience covering more than a quarter of a century in taking polls have we received so many different varieties of criticism—praise from many and condemnation from many others—and yet it has been just of the same type that has come to us every time a Poll has been taken in all these years.

A telegram from a newspaper in California asks: "Is it true that Mr. Hearst has purchased the *Literary Digest* ?" A telephone message only the day

Comparison of Polls

This article printed the day before the election shows that the Institute of Public Opinion (now Gallup) was much more successful in estimating the election results.

November 2, 1936

The American Institute of Public Opinion forecasts the reelection of President Roosevelt in tomorrow's voting, while the *Literary Digest* shows a victory for Governor Landon in the battle of the pre-election polls.

The *Digest,* after sending out more than 10,000,000 ballots, finds Governor Landon polling 57 percent of the major party vote and leading in 32 states with 370 electoral votes.

The Institute of Public Opinion, operating on a sampling method which calls for a representative cross section of voters, predicts Roosevelt's reelection with approximately 56 percent of the major party vote, and shows him leading in 40 states, of which 31 with 315 electoral are called "sure," and the others too close for positive prediction.

Literary Digest Final Poll

Landon	57%
Roosevelt	43%
States for Landon	32
States for Roosevelt	16

A.I.P.O (Gallup) Final Poll

Roosevelt	55.7%
Landon	44.3%
States for Roosevelt	40
States for Landon	6
On the line	2

SOURCE: *The Gallup Poll: Public Opinion 1935–1971.* New York: Random House, 1972.

before these lines were written: "Has the Republican National Committee purchased the *Literary Digest*?" And all types and varieties, including: "Have the Jews purchased the *Literary Digest*?" "Is the Pope of Rome a stockholder of the *Literary Digest*?" And so it goes—all equally absurd and amusing. We could add more to this list, and yet all of these questions in recent days are but repetitions of what we have been experiencing all [over] the years from the very first Poll.

Problem

Now, are the figures in this poll correct? In answer to this question we will simply refer to a telegram we sent to a young man in Massachusetts the other day answer to his challenge to us to wager [$]100,000 on the accuracy of our Poll. We wired him as follows:

For nearly a quarter century, we have been taking Polls of the voters in the forty-eight States, and especially in Presidential years, and we have always merely mailed the ballots, counted and recorded those returned and let the people of the Nation draw their conclusions as to our accuracy. So far, we have been right in every Poll. Will we be right in the current Poll? That, as Mrs. Roosevelt said concerning the President's reelection, is in the "lap of the gods."

We never make any claims before election but we respectfully refer you to the opinion of one of the most quoted citizens today, the Hon. James A. Farley, Chairman of the Democratic National Committee. This is what Mr. Farley said October 14, 1932:

> Any sane person cannot escape the implication of such a gigantic sampling of popular opinion as is embraced in the *Literary Digest* straw vote. I consider this conclusive evidence as to the desire of the people of this country for a change in the National Government. The *Literary Digest* poll is an achievement of no little magnitude. It is a Poll fairly and correctly conducted.

In studying the table of the voters from all of the States. . ., please remember that we make no claims at this time for their absolute accuracy. On a similar occasion we felt it important to say:

In a wild year like this, however, many sagacious observers will refuse to bank upon appearances, however convincing. As for the *Digest,* it draws no conclusions from the results of its vast distribution of twenty million ballots. True to its historic non-partizan policy—or "omni-partizan," as some editor described it in 1928—we supply our readers with the facts to the best of our ability, and leave them to draw their own conclusions.

We make no claim to infallibility. We did not coin the phrase "uncanny accuracy" which has been so freely applied to our Polls. We know only too well the limitations of every straw vote, however enormous the sample gathered, however scientific the method. It would be a miracle if every State of the forty-eight behaved on Election day exactly as forecast by the Poll.

We say now about Rhode Island and Massachusetts that our figures indicate in our own judgment too large a percentage for Mr. Landon and too small a percentage for Mr. Roosevelt, and although in 1932 the figures in these two States indicated Mr. Hoover's carrying both, we announced:

> A study of the returns convinces us that in those States our ballots have somehow failed to come back in adequate quantity from large bodies of Democratic voters.

Our own opinion was that they would be found in the Roosevelt column, and they were. We will not do the same this year; we feel that both States will be found in the Landon column, and we are reaching this conclusion by the same process that lead to the reverse conclusion in 1932.

Pennsylvania is another State which requires special mention. Four years ago, our figures gave the State to Mr. Roosevelt, and Mr. Hoover carried it on Election day. In comparing our ballot this year with that of 1932, we find that in many cities in Pennsylvania our figures showed a much higher trend toward Mr. Roosevelt than was justified by the election figures on Election day in 1932. In examining the very same cities now we discover the reverse trend, and in cities that in 1932 indicated an approximately 60–40 percent relationship between Roosevelt and Hoover, we now find 60 percent for Landon and 40 percent for Roosevelt.

That's the plain language of it. Many people wonder at these great changes in a State like Pennsylvania, and we confess to wonderment ourselves.

On the Pacific Coast, we find California, Oregon, and Washington all vote for Mr. Landon in our Poll, and yet we are told that the Pacific Coast is "aflame" for Mr. Roosevelt.

A State like California is always a difficult State to get an accurate opinion from by the polling method, and we may be far astray, yet every one should remember that in the Gubernatorial campaign a few years ago, we took a Poll of California when it was believed by most of California citizens that Mr. Upton Sinclair would be elected Governor, and the result of our Poll showed that Mr. Sinclair would not be elected Governor and the Poll was correct.

The State of Washington seems to be more favorable to Mr. Landon than either Oregon or California. We cannot in our Poll detect anything that would indicate a reason for this difference.

Seattle

Right here we wish to say that in 1932 our Poll in Seattle gave Mr. Roosevelt 65.43 percent of the vote, and he carried that city by 61.58 percent of the vote. In the current Poll, 1936, Seattle gives Mr. Landon 58.52 percent and Mr. Roosevelt 40.46 percent. Our readers will notice we overestimated Mr. Roosevelt in 1932—are we overestimating Mr. Landon now? We see no reason for supposing so. And the three Pacific Coast States which now show for Mr. Landon and which millions believe will vote for Mr. Roosevelt (they may be right) in 1924, 1928, and 1932 were correctly forecast in the *Literary Digest* Polls.

In the great Empire State, New York the figures for so large a State are what might be called very close. After looking at the figures for New York in the column at the left, remember that in 1932 we gave Mr. Roosevelt 46.1 percent and Mr. Hoover 43.9 percent, even closer than it is to day. And yet we correctly forecast that Mr. Roosevelt would carry the State.

And so we might go on with many States that are very close, and some not so close, but in which local conditions have much to do with results, not in polls such as our Poll but on Election day.

The Poll represents the most extensive straw ballot in the field—the most experienced in view of its twenty-five years of perfecting—the most unbiased in view of its prestige—a Poll that has always previously been correct.

Even its critics admit its value as an index of popular sentiment. As one of these critics, the *Nation,* observes:

> Because it indicates both the 1932 and 1936 vote, it offers the raw material for as careful a prognostication as it is possible to make at this time.

Further Resources

BOOKS

Davis, Kenneth S. *FDR, the New Deal Years, 1933–1937: A History.* New York: Random House, 1986.

Webber, Michael J. *New Deal Fat Cats: Business, Labor, and Campaign Finance in the 1936 Presidential Election.* New York: Fordham University Press, 2000.

WEBSITES

"Landon in a Landslide: The Poll That Changed Polling." *History Matters.* Available online at http://historymatters.gmu.edu/d/5168/?PHPSESSID=bec471c0f77501bc7ecce9677c116efe (accessed March 1, 2003).

New Deal Network. Available online at http://newdeal.feri.org (accessed March 1, 2003).

The Rise of National Magazines

First Issue of *Life*

Magazine cover, Photograph, Essay

By: *Life*

Date: November 23, 1936

Source: *Life,* November 23, 1936.

First Issue of *Look*

Magazine cover, Magazine article

By: *Look*

Date: January 1937

Source: *Look,* January 1937.

About the Publications: *Life* was founded in 1936 as a pictorial news magazine by publisher Henry R. Luce (1898–1967), who also founded *Time* in 1923, *Fortune* in 1930, and *Sports Illustrated* in 1954. It published weekly until 1972, and beginning in 1978 it shifted to publishing monthly issues. *Look* magazine was launched in 1937, shortly after the debut of *Life.* Like *Life,* its focus was on photojournalism, using photos to tell its readers about the world. *Look* was *Life*'s major competitor until the 1970s. By then the growing popularity and availability of television caused the downfall of *Look* and significantly diminished the appeal of *Life.* ■

Introduction

Life magazine released its first edition on November 23, 1936, only a few weeks after the reelection of President Franklin Roosevelt in one of the largest election landslides in U.S. history. *Look* magazine followed in January 1937. Americans craved news throughout the 1930s as they attempted to overcome the Great Depression that dominated the decade and worried about the international conflict that continued to spread through East Asia and Europe.

Although readers had choices for which newsmagazine they read each week, the birth of *Life* marked a bold shift. *Life*'s appeal came from its design and style rather than from its investigative reports or editorial opinions. It was the full-color, larger-than-life pictures that lured millions of Americans to the pages of *Life.*

Significance

Life's photography served as the publication's core editorial content—reporters' texts provided the context, but the grand pictures served as the focus. Given the magazine's concentration on photography, it was no surprise that *Life* hired some of the industry's foremost artists to contribute stunning photo-documentaries for every weekly edition. Margaret Bourke-White, Thomas D. McAvoy, Peter Stackpole, and Alfred Eisenstaedt served as the magazine's original group of dedicated photographers.

As Bourke-White's cover article on a small town in Montana for *Life*'s first issue made clear, the publication's photographs presented human stories from a variety of perspectives, from industry and architecture to candid portraits of working families. This variety of photographic subject matter, and the dramatic form in which these subjects were depicted, provided readers with an unmistakably innovative and alluring product.

In its early editions, the monthly *Look* explained to readers the publication's objective under a picture of a bull biting a matador's leg: "*Look* Gives You 1000 Eyes to See Round the World. LOOK is an educational picture magazine for EVERYONE. It is the belief of the editors of LOOK that the news of the world can best be told today in well edited pictures—not in long columns of type. LOOK will bring current events, science, sports, beauty, education, all in interesting pictures, to both the Colonel's Lady and Mrs. O'Grady (and their respective husbands and children) to make them better informed on what's happening in the world." Similar justifications would later be used for the educational use of television programs. Pictures, these publications argued, overpowered words.

Life and *Look* were the television of their day. Their style, especially that of *Life,* would remain in vogue for decades, though television's growing popularity eventually hampered the publication's ability to maintain its high popularity. This loss of allure came as television's live, video depictions of life began to replace the need for photo-based magazines such as *Life.* At the beginning of the twenty-first century, any visit to the newsstands, though, reveals the great appeal still garnered by photo magazines in U.S. print media.

Further Resources

BOOKS

Doss, Ericka, ed. *Looking at Life Magazine.* Washington, D.C.: Smithsonian Institution Press, 2001.

Stolley, Richard B., and Tony Chiu, eds. *Life: Our Century in Pictures.* Boston: Little, Brown, 1999.

WEBSITES

Life. Available online at http://www.life.com (accessed March 1, 2003).

Primary Source

First Issue of *Life*: Cover (1 OF 3)

SYNOPSIS: As the editors explained in their "Introduction to the first issue of *Life,*" published on November 23, 1936: "Photographer Margaret Bourke-White had been dispatched to the Northwest to photograph the multi-million dollar projects of the Columbia River Basin. What the Editors expected—for use in some later issue—were construction pictures as only Bourke-White can take them. What the Editors got was a human document of American frontier life which, to them at least, was a revelation." Millions of readers became hooked with the first issue and returned week after week, drawn by pictures that revealed the condition of humanity. MARGARET BOURKE-WHITE/TIMEPIX. GRADUATE LIBRARY, UNIVERSITY OF MICHIGAN. REPRODUCED BY PERMISSION.

LIFE BEGINS

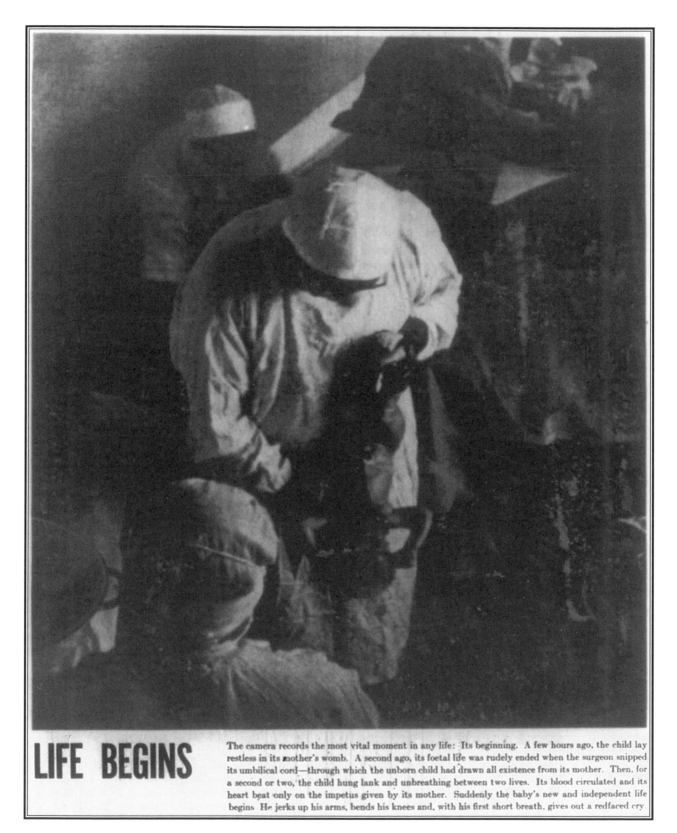

The camera records the most vital moment in any life: Its beginning. A few hours ago, the child lay restless in its mother's womb. A second ago, its foetal life was rudely ended when the surgeon snipped its umbilical cord—through which the unborn child had drawn all existence from its mother. Then, for a second or two, the child hung lank and unbreathing between two lives. Its blood circulated and its heart beat only on the impetus given by its mother. Suddenly the baby's new and independent life begins He jerks up his arms, bends his knees and, with his first short breath, gives out a redfaced cry.

Primary Source

First Issue of *Life*: Photograph (2 OF 3)

The second page of the first issue of *Life* magazine, November 23, 1936. REPRODUCED BY PERMISSION OF THE ESTATE OF ANDRE DAMIANO. GRADUATE LIBRARY, UNIVERSITY OF MICHIGAN.

Introduction to this first issue of

LIFE

If any Charter Subscriber is surprised by what turned out to be the first story in this first issue of LIFE, he is not nearly so surprised as the Editors were. Photographer Margaret Bourke-White had been dispatched to the Northwest to photograph the multi-million dollar projects of the Columbia River Basin. What the Editors expected—for use in some later issue—were construction pictures as only Bourke-White can take them. What the Editors got was a human document of American frontier life which, to them at least, was a revelation.

Having been unable to prevent Bourke-White from running away with their first nine pages, the Editors thereafter returned to the job of making pictures behave with some degree of order and sense. So there follow, not far apart, two regular departments:—Life On The American Newsfront, and the President's Album. The first is a selection of the most newsworthy snaps made anywhere in the U. S. by the mighty picture-taking organization of the U. S. press. The President's Album is a kind of a picture diary—a special focus on the personality-center of the nation's life. Luckily for LIFE, it can start its diary with a President who is a marvelous camera actor and is not above demonstrating his art.

So strong is the President's hold on the attention of the people that a hint from him is enough to bring even South America crashing into the headlines. South America is the continent Americans *ought* to be most interested in, and usually just plain won't be. But a month ago LIFE decided to do its duty and be interested—a duty which turned out to be surprisingly easy to take. This week, Brazil. Next week, The Argentine.

On looking over what happened to the issue, the Editors are particularly pleased that Art is represented not by some artfully promoted Frenchman but by an American, and that the Theatre is here in the person of an American lady who is being called the world's greatest actress. Hollywood's No. 1 Screen Lover is also here due to sheer coincidence of release dates. But that he is an American, is inevitable.

As is the case with too many able American artists, the name of John Steuart Curry of Kansas is known where his works are not. An active exciting painter who has heard the trumpeting of elephants and tornadoes, Curry records the kind of American life that does not require a trip to the circus or to Kansas to appreciate and understand.

For Helen Hayes, LIFE went directly to the theatre where she is daily adding to her own glory as well as Queen Victoria's—and, of course, to the ties that bind the English-speaking peoples. Miss Hayes kindly lent LIFE her private album from which to select pictures of her little daughter, Mary. Thus LIFE is able to contrast the childhoods of a famous mother and of a daughter who created a commotion on Broadway before she was born.

Sooner or later every great actress plays *Camille*. The Great Garbo has just got around to that teary role. For millions of people, however, a more exciting fact will be that Robert Taylor is playing opposite her. Who is Robert Taylor? His high school class at Beatrice, Nebraska, could tell you something. Pomona College could add more. Sam Goldwyn's scout and the screen test that followed would be a likely source of information. To all of these LIFE sent emissaries so that you may know, once and for all, who Robert Taylor really is.

LIFE's camera also went, as any good camera must these days, up into the air. And from the air it saw for the first time the world's two most notable forts—Fort Knox soon to be the home of America's fantastic gold hoard; Fort Belvedere, favored home of a King-Emperor's romance.

Black Widow spiders are no more news this week than they were last week or the week before. But that they make news steadily, every newspaper reader knows. It just happened that George Elwood Jenks made this deadly insect his hobby and recently took what LIFE's editors think is a remarkable set of photographs. Can any brow-beaten husband follow the sad career of the Black Widow's mate without a fellow feeling for the poor little creature?

Besides the sections already discussed, Charter Subscribers will find in this issue beginnings of several regular departments. The Drawing is of and about a place called Overweather—an interesting locale which is definitely out of Bourke-White's or Eisenstaedt's range. The Camera Overseas begins on page 54. And, on page 90—LIFE Goes To A Party. It almost didn't—because just this week it couldn't find anything interesting enough to invite itself to, until at the last minute it sighted Sir George Clerk and some dead rabbits.

Hundreds, perhaps thousands, of people contribute their photographic presence to the pages of this issue. French aristocrats, New York stock brokers, Montana barkeeps, gooney-golfers, English judges at prayer and English ladies in the rain, babies, farmers, sailors, doctors, crowds, a high school class, a one-legged man, a strip-artist, a bearded Russian, The President of the U. S. and the late Sarah Bernhardt—to one and all the Editors of LIFE are grateful. And most of all they are grateful to the little Chinese girls on page 26 who go about their lessons with an almost breathless grace. For sheer charm LIFE's Editors during the week saw no picture which could match those taken recently by a staff photographer at the only Chinese parochial school in the U. S. Lafcadio Hearn might have described these little students at length—but Eisenstaedt's camera, in this case, beggared words.

The first issue of a magazine is not the magazine. It is the beginning. The Editors anticipate a strenuous and exciting year of growth and adventure. To Charter Subscribers they express again their deep appreciation and their hope that this new relationship of Editor and Subscriber may continue through many years.

THE EDITORS

Nov. 23rd

LIFE is published weekly by Time Inc. at 350 East 22nd Street, Chicago, Ill. Entry as second-class matter applied for at the post office at Chicago, Ill., under the act of March 3, 1879. *Subscription rates:* One year in United States and Possessions, $3.50; Canada and Countries of the Pan-American Postal Union, $5, elsewhere $7
LIFE, November 23, 1936 Volume I Number 1

Primary Source

First Issue of *Life*: Essay (3 OF 3)

Introduction page, *Life* magazine, November 23, 1936.

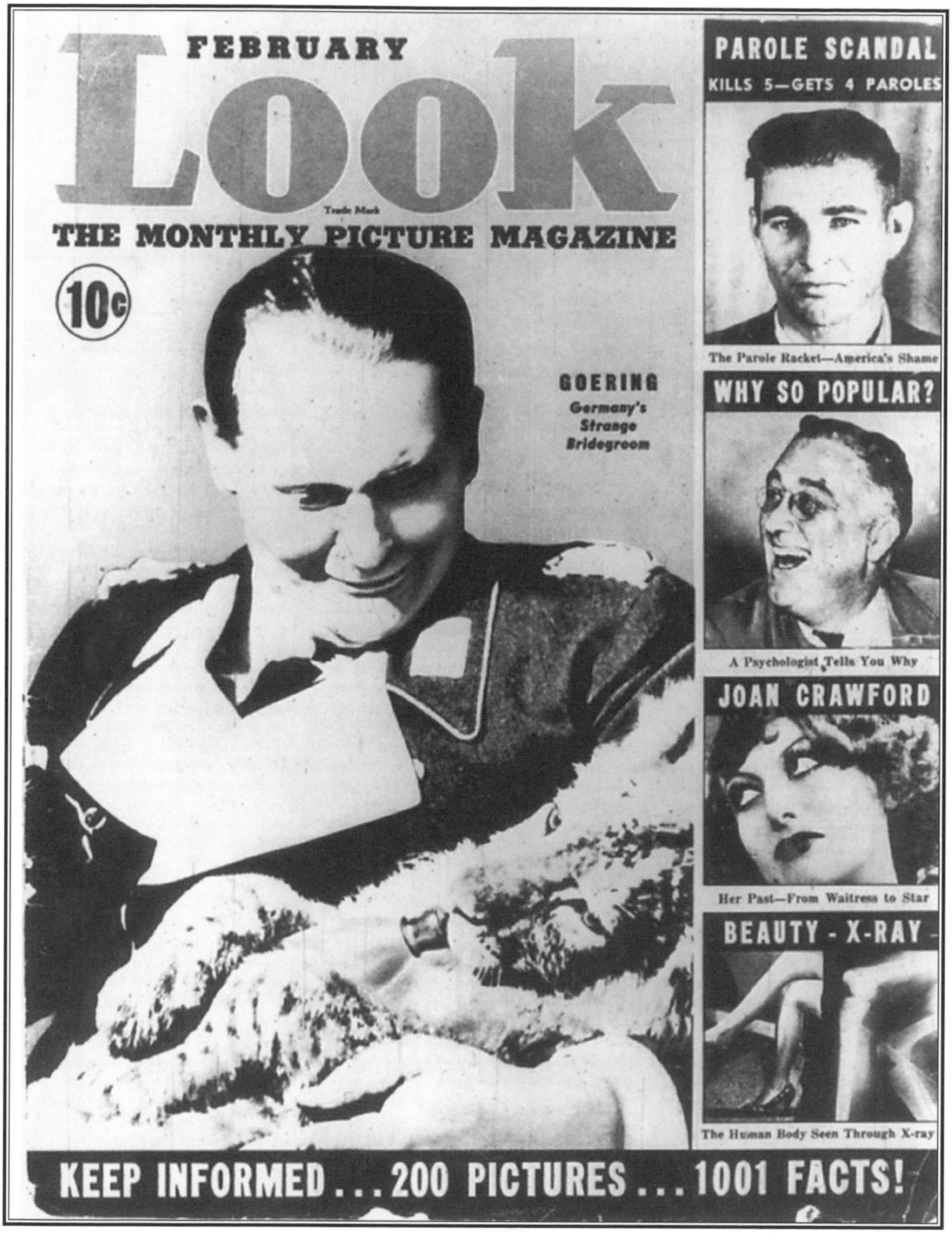

Primary Source

First Issue of *Look*: Cover (1 OF 2)

SYNOPSIS: The cover and first page of *Look* reveal another aspect of photojournalism. There are photos of the famous: President Roosevelt and actress Joan Crawford; the infamous: Nazi official Hermann Goering, a murderer; and the eye-catching: "Bull bites man!" "Beautiful legs, X-Rayed!" Exciting, sensationalistic photos like these are just as important a part of photojournalism's appeal as the more artistic work of master photographers like Bourke-White. PUBLIC DOMAIN. GRADUATE LIBRARY, UNIVERSITY OF MICHIGAN. REPRODUCED BY PERMISSION.

Look Gives You 1000 Eyes to See Round the World

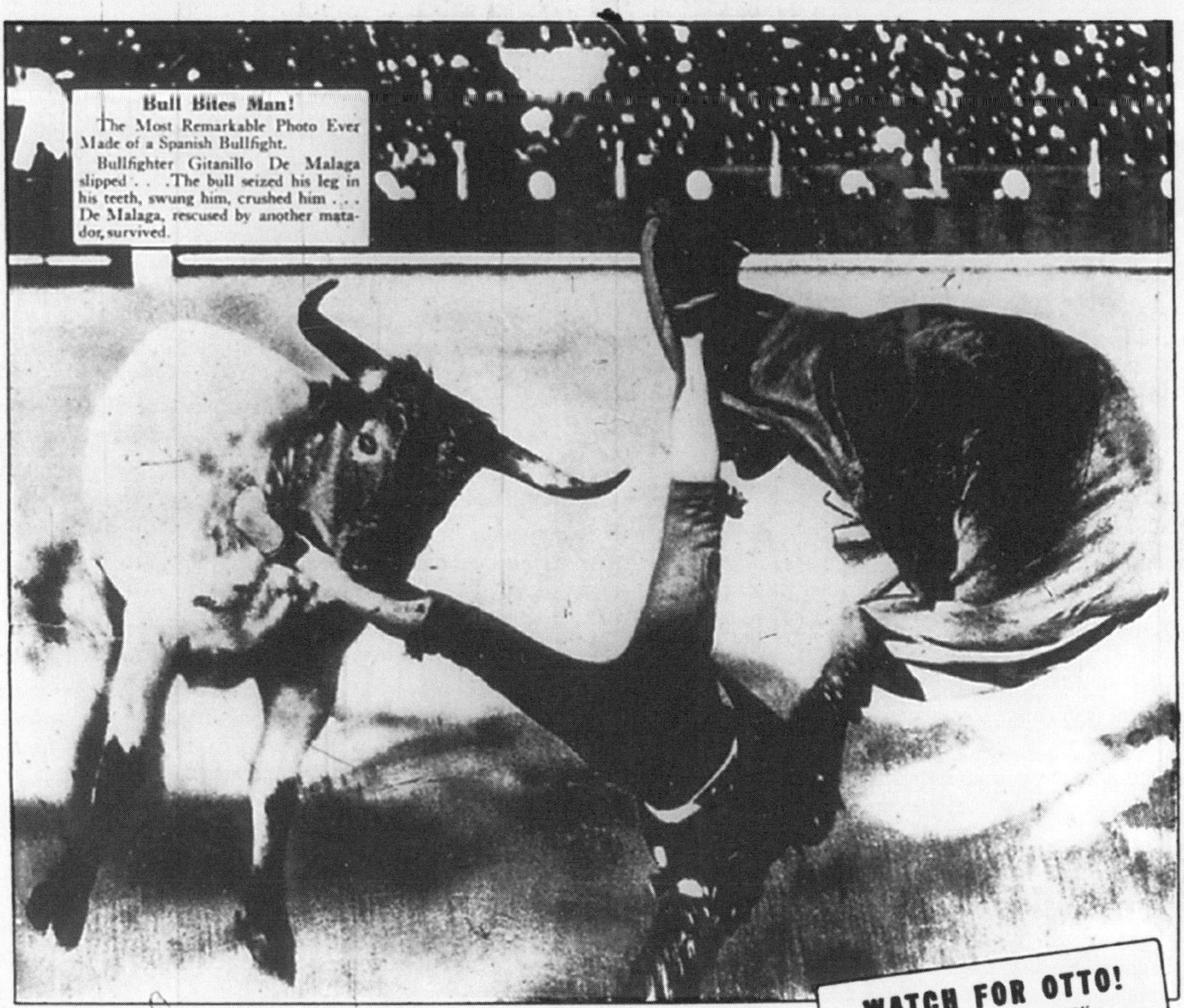

Bull Bites Man!

The Most Remarkable Photo Ever Made of a Spanish Bullfight.

Bullfighter Gitanillo De Malaga slipped . . . The bull seized his leg in his teeth, swung him, crushed him . . . De Malaga, rescued by another matador, survived.

LOOK is an educational picture magazine for EVERYONE. It is the belief of the editors of LOOK that the news of the world can best be told today in well edited pictures—not in long columns of type. LOOK will bring current events, science, sports, beauty, education, all in interesting pictures, to both the Colonel's Lady and Mrs. O'Grady (and their respective husbands and children) to make them better informed on what's happening in the world.

Watch for LOOK on the first day of each month at your newsstand.

LOOK has no advertising department; is accepting no advertising.

WATCH FOR OTTO!

I'm Otto Look, the office boy of LOOK.

Maybe the editor won't like it, but I'm going to give you my comments on these swell pictures as you turn the pages of LOOK.

LOOK is published monthly by LOOK, Incorporated, at 715 Locust Street, Des Moines, Iowa. Entry as second class matter applied for at the post office at Des Moines, Iowa, under the act of March 3, 1879. Subscription rates. Twelve issues in United States and possessions, $1.00. Single copy, 10c. The following picture agencies are represented in this issue of LOOK: Acme, Black Star, European, Globe, International, Pictures, Inc., Pix and Wide World. Entire contents copyrighted. Reproduction in whole or in part prohibited. LOOK February, 1937 Volume 1 Number 2

Look THE MONTHLY PICTURE MAGAZINE

PRINTED IN U. S. A.

Primary Source

First issue of *Look*: Magazine article (2 OF 2)

First page of *Look* magazine, January 1937. PUBLIC DOMAIN. GRADUATE LIBRARY, UNIVERSITY OF MICHIGAN. REPRODUCED BY PERMISSION.

"Are We Going Communist? A Debate"

Debate

By: Everett Dean Martin and Earl Browder

Date: November 1936

Source: Martin, Everett Dean, and Earl Browder. "Are We Going Communist? A Debate." *Forum and Century,* 96, no. 25, November 1936, 202–208.

About the Authors: Everett Dean Martin (1880–1941), a New York-based newspaper columnist early in his career, achieved his greatest influence as a social philosopher in the 1920s and 1930s. He despised the notion of revolution as a solution to societal ills and urged instead the pursuit of democracy for the improvement of humanity.

Earl Russell Browder (1891–1973) joined the newly formed American Communist Party after being imprisoned for refusing to be drafted in World War I. Browder advanced through the ranks of the party, eventually leading it during the Great Depression and World War II. ■

Introduction

The Great Depression caused enormous social turmoil throughout the world in the 1930s. In the United States, laborers protested decreasing wages and increasing unemployment by striking in hundreds of cities nationwide. The American Communist Party (CPUSA) and other leftist groups argued that the federal government needed to take greater control of the economy, regulate big business more severely, and offer aid to the millions of workers left destitute by the Depression. Under Earl Browder's leadership, though, the CPUSA generally approved of President Roosevelt's New Deal programs and urged that they be expanded as the downturn continued through the decade. Anti-Communists focused their charges on Communists and socialists, but they also set their sites on liberals and moderates who supported the New Deal.

According to conservatives, the New Deal represented the first step toward communism in the United States. This view echoed the propaganda of the Red Scare following World War I and foreshadowed the rise of McCarthyism during the cold war. In response, Republican congressmen formed the House Committee on Un-American Activities (HUAC) in 1937 to investigate subversive threats to democracy in the United States. The Dies Committee, named for its chairman, Representative Martin Dies, often alleged Communist infiltration in the Roosevelt administration. The HUAC continued its dubious career long after the Depression ended, gaining its greatest fame at the cold war's height during the 1940s and 1950s.

Significance

The debate excerpted below provides some of the arguments for and against communism offered in the mass media during the Great Depression. Social philosopher Everett Dean Martin argued that communism contradicted the philosophical underpinning of American society: its historical focus on individual liberty and its anti-authoritarian mindset. Martin rebutted the Communists' argument that democracy could not survive the Depression, "This entire dilemma is based on two fallacies—first, that liberal democracy is dead and, second, that there is a real difference between communism and fascism." As fascism rose in Spain, Italy, and Germany during the decade, Martin asserted that Communists intended to soon bring their brand of repression to America. Martin concluded that, far from improving the functioning of democratic self-government, communism would destroy American freedom.

Martin concluded that Americans rejected communism: "They will put up with a great deal of disturbing radical propaganda, but do not try to 'take them over.' The evidence is strong that Americans do not want communism." Yet, Martin's discussion did not provide any evidence or investigation of public opinion. Rather, he accepted the idea that Americans abhorred communism as a matter of fact, especially given his characterization of the movement as destructive to individualism and freedom. His argument ignored the hundreds of thousands of Americans who had already rebelled against the status quo in wave after wave of strikes. Whether these individuals believed in communism per se did not seem to matter quite as much as the larger struggle to feed one's family and survive in the midst of economic decay.

Browder, responding as the leader of the American Communist Party, asserted that fascism had already taken over "the upper circles of monopoly capital," that is, the leaders of big business. These individuals, who leftists believed caused the Great Depression, now threatened to take over the United States and destroy it in the process. Browder dismissed Martin's definition and framed communism as an essentially American program. Communists, Browder argued, "advocate the widest democracy; universal suffrage; direct and secret election of all government officials, including the judiciary; equality of representation; the principle of recall and referendum; the equality of peoples; unconditional freedom of worship, speech, press, and assemblage; and governmental guarantee of work, education, and leisure to every citizen." Unfortunately, Browder's communist ideology did not match Soviet leader Josef Stalin's version. Throughout his reign during this period, Stalin forbid many of the proposals at the heart of Browder's optimistic plan. This repression, though, was only sporadically covered in the American news media, as the United States and the Soviet Union remained tenuous allies prior to and during the Second World War.

Interestingly, the growing conflict in Europe overshadowed both of these interpretations. For Communists and anti-Communists alike, the rise of Nazi Germany represented a significant threat to freedom and prosperity. Although the United States did not enter the war until several years later, intellectuals and political leaders were already considering the impact of war abroad on security at home.

Throughout the Depression, conservatives and leftists used the mass media as an implement of intense propaganda. The economic crisis shook the foundation of American society, and leaders from both ends of the political spectrum attempted to manipulate the Depression for their own political ends. The Popular Front, as the CPUSA named its public relations campaign, employed radio broadcasts, artwork, theater, film, newspapers, magazines, and opinion journals such as *Forum* to sway the public. Conservatives likewise attempted to focus media attention on what they saw as the Communist takeover of the country by the "New Deal Order." One of the central attacks on the Roosevelt administration focused on its expansion of federal government power, especially as seen in the New Deal programs aimed at alleviating the impact of the Great Depression. The right portrayed these policies as unconstitutional threats to liberty; Communists described them as first steps toward guaranteed security for all citizens. Millions of ordinary Americans, battered by the Depression and the threat of world war, were left to ponder which side to take in an increasingly acrimonious debate.

Primary Source

"Are We Going Communist? A Debate" [excerpt]

SYNOPSIS: In November 1936, the same month in which the debate appeared in *Forum,* President Roosevelt won reelection by the largest margin in history. The massive popularity of Roosevelt's New Deal programs brought FDR over 60 percent of the popular vote and all but two states in the Electoral College. Although the president's appeal did not stay at this high level, the New Deal appeared to most Americans to be a fitting solution for the Great Depression. Liberalism's success blocked the expansion of communism and, with the outbreak of World War II, the Constitution remained the governing framework in the United States.

America Rejects Communism, by Everett Dean Martin

A man is known by the dilemmas he keeps. Communist propagandists in America are the victims of a viciously false dilemma. They have deluded them-

American demonstrators rally for the communist cause during the 1930s. GETTY IMAGES. REPRODUCED BY PERMISSION.

selves into believing that the American people must inevitably decide whether this nation is to be communist or fascist. This is like asking an innocent man whether he prefers to spend his life in Sing Sing or Dannemora. This entire dilemma is based on two fallacies—first, that liberal democracy is dead and, second, that there is a real difference between communism and fascism.

Apparently there is most violent antagonism between communists and fascists, but it is a verbal and accidental difference, rather than a conflict of basic principles. Communism and fascism have in common three fundamental principles, all so destructive of the values of modern civilization that once their principles are established it makes little difference which pressure group puts them into operation. These principles in which communists and fascists agree are (1) revolution, (2) the dictatorship of a faction, (3) the corporate state.

Communism and fascism are both, wherever they appear, revolutionary movements. Both hold that the existing forms of constitutional government, the liberal state, must be destroyed. Both advocate resort to violence as a means of establishing the control of a desperate minority faction over the entire community. Both hold that the bullying and terrorism necessary to such revolutionary behavior are justified on the ground that the revolutionary party is the self-appointed representative of the masses. They differ as to the terms they use for the masses. The fascists prefer to speak of the masses as "the nation"; the communists prefer the name "proletariat." Both alike would exterminate the "bourgeois liberals." It is necessary only to study the revolutionary techniques of these rival groups to see that the techniques are the same and are derived from the same source. The procedure is to build up a political party which is to become a state within the state, to force the liberals to compromise themselves by concessions granted under pressure, to organize the revolutionary party with military regimentation under one central committee, to force the party central committee on the nation as its government and concentrate in its hands all executive, legislative, judicial, and military power.

Communists would persuade us that fascist or Nazi dictatorship is that of the big reactionary capitalists, while that of the communists is a dictatorship of all the workers and so a dictatorship of the great mass of the nation. Neither argument has the support of fact. Fascist and Nazi leaders may have had at the beginning the support of a few capitalists, but the great majority of industrialists in both Germany and Italy were, according to communist theory as well as in fact, "bourgeois liberals" and supported neither fascists nor communists but the *status quo.* Industrialists in Italy and Germany soon discovered that they had lost under dictatorship all constitutional and legal guarantees of the rights of private property. This is not surprising, for there are no rights under a dictatorship. Moreover, it should not be forgotten that Mussolini is a former socialist and that the Nazis are National Socialists.

On the other hand, it is not true that communism means the dictatorship of the workers. It is a dictatorship over the workers by a gang of radical politicians who themselves love Labor and hate work. Russian communism was not in fact established by a spontaneous uprising of the working class but by a conspiracy in which Bolshevik politicians manipulated a force made up of deserting soldiers and land-hungry peasants. The workers rule in name only. Communist bureaucracy is daily entrenching the rule of a new class of labor politicians over the mass of Russian workers. . . .

Neither does communism represent the organized workers of America. The American worker is neither class-conscious nor is he revolutionary. The longer democracy endures, the more "bourgeois" becomes the mind of the worker. He sends his children to high school, along with the children of other groups; he has bourgeois ambitions; he enjoys bourgeois movies; he wants to have his own home and motorcar—and many thousands do. He is a superpatriot. He votes for the New Deal or for the protective tariff and he reads the Hearst papers. . . .

You cannot put dictatorship over on a nation with a Puritan background. Our people have learned from the united opinion of the great political teachers of the English-speaking world—Hobbes, Locke, Hume, Burke, Adam Smith, Jefferson, Jackson, Lincoln—that dictatorship is tyranny, the worst of all forms of government. They have had ample opportunity to see how dictatorship works in both Nazi Germany and communist Russia—concentration camps, nightly arrests, innocent people held without trial, condemned by revolutionary tribunes without opportunity to know what they are accused of or who is the accuser, cruel and unusual punishments, terror, suspicion, and favoritism. I would remind communists that we have a Bill of Rights in this country, formulated to prevent precisely the inevitable practices of all dictatorships. If you think that Americans do not prize the Bill of Rights, just try to take it away from them. I note that communists are among the first to seek the protection of this Bill of Rights whenever their right to make radical propaganda is challenged.

Finally, communism, like fascism, means a corporate state—all for the state and nothing outside the state. In this respect the two are becoming more alike every month—that is, both are forms of state capitalism. Now many Americans, both rich and poor I regret to say, would like to live on the Government of the United States at somebody else's expense. But the bulk of American people has a deep-rooted fear and suspicion of the extension of the power of government. Americans have more often than not abused the creed of individualism, but they are at heart individualists, especially so when government attempts to regulate them.

The dilemma of fascism or communism is therefore a false dilemma. Americans have no intention of making choice between these evils, nor is American liberalism a middle-of-the-road position between tweedledee and tweedledum. We are not on that road at all, for it is a road which would lead to our destruction. . . .

Out on the California desert in August one frequently sees a rattlesnake which to the tenderfoot looks dead. Natives have learned to be very sure the snake is dead before they try to pick it up and "take it over." Americans are, as nations go, a tolerant people. They will put up with a great deal of disturbing radical propaganda, but do not try to "take them over." The evidence is strong that Americans do not want communism.

Communism Is on the Way, by Earl Browder

Mr. Martin takes the easy way to find the answer that he wants to this question. If he had been writing in the early 1770's, he could have made the same case against American independence. In the days when the issue of independence was maturing, no doubt the overwhelming majority, if asked to vote for or against a long revolutionary war against the mother country, would have voted against. Today, when the vast majority of our population has not yet faced the issue fundamentally, it is easy to prove that Americans do not want communism or socialism (which is really what communists propose as the next stage of social development).

The question really is whether Americans desire deeply such things as the present capitalist system cannot or will not give them and whether their struggle for these things will finally lead them to socialism. To such a formulation of the question, I would answer unequivocally, "Yes."

Mr. Martin evades a crucial question, when he ignores the Communist Party declaration that today the issue is democracy vs. fascism, that the issue is not socialism vs. capitalism or communism vs. fascism. He puts into our mouth this last slogan, which we have definitely repudiated as the immediate issue. That makes his task easier, but only at the expense of completely falsifying the question.

Communists in America and in every country where traditional democratic institutions are endangered by the rise of fascism are completely on the side of democracy against fascism, up to the point of unhesitatingly laying down their lives for democracy.

We do not say that democracy is dead; but we do say that the upper circles of monopoly capital have decided to try to kill it, that they have turned to fascism. We point out Hearst in the United States, together with the Liberty League, whose strategy has been adopted by the Republican Party, as the example of the fascist trend in our country. Mr. Martin's "three fundamental principles," which he says are common to fascism and communism, are only three further confusions. Communists most emphatically are *not* advocates of violence as a means to the "control of a desperate minority faction over the entire community"; communists have always warned that violence comes from the desperate minority of reactionaries against the mass of the people. For communists, the "principle" of revolution was taught in its entirety by the Declaration of Independence, by Thomas Jefferson and Tom Paine, and all we have had to add has been the deeper understanding of the role of classes, the forces of production, and the details of modern society.

Communists do not advocate the dictatorship of a faction. They advocate the widest democracy: universal suffrage; direct and secret election of all government officials, including the judiciary; equality of representation; the principle of recall and referendum; the equality of peoples; unconditional freedom of worship, speech, press, and assemblage; and governmental guarantee of work, education, and leisure to every citizen. If Mr. Martin can identify these principles under a single heading with the fascist terroristic dictatorship and with the corporate state, on behalf of monopoly capital, then his principles are elastic enough to cover with equal validity any kind of combination he might desire to make.

I imagine there are few literate people who could agree with Mr. Martin's philosophy of history, which explains the greatest revolution of all time as the result of a "conspiracy" by a "gang of radical politicians." The only way to answer such naïveté is to refer him to the universally acknowledged control of social development (acknowledged, I emphasize, by literate circles of all classes) by forces which transcend all groups, individuals, cliques, or "conspiracies." . . .

The American people have created a tremendous system of productive forces, almost equal to that of the rest of the world combined. But the potentiality of well-being for all people which is inherent in this tremendous national wealth is denied realization, and periodically the whole system stalls in a crisis that brings intense suffering to tens of millions. The American people are conscious of this problem, and are conscious that its source is the monopolistic ownership and control of our productive system by a small group of rich families, the monopolists, Wall Street. . . .

We communists believe that the majority of the people . . . will eventually come to see the truth of the communist contention, that the final solution of the problem must be the social ownership and control of the productive forces, that is, that new social and economic order known as socialism, which is the transitional stage between capitalism and communism. That change from capitalism to socialism is what is known as the revolution.

Mr. Martin thinks of revolution as the source of all evil. Thereby he involves himself in a dilemma; since Mr. Martin has informed us that a man is known by the dilemmas he keeps, this one should let us know what kind of a man is Mr. Martin. Basing himself upon the Constitution, which was produced by revolution, he argues against revolution in principle, against revolution as essentially evil and productive of nothing but evil.

The charge that communists advocate violence is merely a repetition of an old slander. It is not true. Communists do not advocate force and violence but on the contrary want to abolish it from the social world. The Communist Party is a legal party and defends its legality. Of course, communists are not pacifists; they believe in fighting when necessary to defend democracy and liberty. I am sure Mr. Martin, being a patriotic citizen, does not cross his fingers when he sings the *Star Spangled Banner* and therefore will not take issue with us on our rejection of pacifism.

But Mr. Martin has plunged into a dilemma even deeper than this one. He accepts the premise that communism is a terrible menace to American democracy; he therefore enrolls in the army of defense by attempting to prove that communism is the sum of all human stupidities, which he proceeds to refute. If communism were the stupidities he says it is, it would be no menace and not worth his valuable time to write about; if it is not and he is only slaying straw men, then his services are of little value to anyone. In either case, the question is left open as to why such an article should be written—or printed—or answered. Frankly, the only reason I have engaged to answer it is that it gives me another opportunity to refute some current misrepresentations about the Communist Party.

It is precisely such muddle-headed thinking, on the part of supposed defenders of democracy, which opens up the gates to fascism and brings all those horrible alternatives before which Mr. Martin shudders. If he and his kind were really bold and uncompromising defenders of democracy against all attacks, they would have no reason to fear the communists and could easily defeat the fascists. It is not the communists who would make the issue communism vs. fascism. We repudiate that issue as the practical question of 1936. We reject even the milder slogan of socialism vs. capitalism as the central issue of the present elections. We say that at present the dominant issue is the defense of democracy against the rising forces of reaction, fascism, and war. On this issue, the communists are without reservation on the side of democracy and call for the broadest united front in its defense.

We say, no, the American people are not ready to make the decisive choice of the change from capitalism to socialism (and eventual communism). But through the necessary organization and struggle to defend their living standards and democratic rights, under the conditions of a capitalist system which more and more breaks down and refuses to function, the American people will in the not distant future not only learn the necessity of socialism but will have found the power to make their choice effective. And, when the majority of Americans want socialism, they will get it, all the arguments of Mr. Martin to the contrary notwithstanding. So long as he thinks the majority will not want socialism, he has nothing to worry about.

Further Resources

BOOKS

Denning, Michael. *The Cultural Front: The Laboring of American Culture in the Twentieth Century.* London and New York: Verso, 1996.

Kennedy, David M. *Freedom from Fear: The American People in Depression and War, 1929–1945.* New York: Oxford University Press, 1999.

Klehr, Harvey. *The Heyday of American Communism: The Depression Decade.* New York: Basic Books, 1984.

Ryan, James G. *Earl Browder: The Failure of American Communism.* Tuscaloosa, Ala.: University of Alabama Press, 1997.

WEBSITES

Red Ink: Records of the Communist Party USA Opened. Available online at http://www.loc.gov/loc/lcib/0102/red_ink.html (accessed April 11, 2003).

"How to Stay Out of War"

Journal article

By: *Forum and Century*

Date: February–April 1937

Source: "How to Stay Out of War: An Open Forum of Opinions on Keeping America Neutral." *Forum and Century* 97, nos. 2–4 (February–April, 1937), 89–92; 165–166, 168–169; 249–253.

About the Publication: To provide a balanced survey of informed opinion on how to avoid U.S. entry into a second world war, *Forum and Century* printed responses from leaders in industry, government, journalism, social activism, literature, and academia. Informed readers of this high-brow journal would probably have instantly recognized many of the prominent respondents. *Forum and Century* began as separate publications in 1886 and 1913, respectively. As the Great Depression reached its peak in 1930, the publications merged to avoid closing. The increasing popularity of full-color, photo-based weekly magazines, including *Time, Newsweek,* and *Life* decreased readership of traditional journals that focused on social commentary. *Forum and Century* merged with *Current History* in 1940, but the newly titled *Current History and Forum* ceased publication one year later. ■

Introduction

By the spring of 1937, Adolf Hitler's Nazi Party in Germany had built a substantial military force and was almost ready for full-scale invasions into eastern and western Europe. In 1936, Germany annexed Austria and by the end of 1937 had finalized plans for the takeover of Czechoslovakia. In 1939, Germany attacked Poland, officially beginning World War II in Europe, and soon began its assaults on the Soviet Union, France, and Great Britain. The Roosevelt administration, along with the rest of the country, faced serious questions over whether to enter the European conflict. Many Americans bitterly recalled U.S. involvement in World War I and resolved never again to be embroiled in a distant conflict caused by Europeans. Also, given the resources needed to fight the Depression that would be devoted to a foreign war, public opinion opposed involvement. In 1935, 1936, and 1937, the president signed Neutrality Acts designed specifically to forbid U.S. interests from dealing with belligerent nations. By curtailing loans, trade, and transportation to nations involved in war, Roosevelt sought to prevent entanglement in another world war. Just as Roosevelt refused to label any specific nation, even Germany, as belligerent, most of *Forum*'s contributors remained vague as to which nations would be allies or foes in a possible war.

Though many of the authors focus exclusively on the mounting conflict in Europe, a few referred to the conflict already under way between China and Japan in East Asia. In 1931, Japanese troops invaded Manchuria in northeastern China, beginning fifteen years of near constant conflict throughout the Pacific Rim.

Significance

Forum and Century posed a question both direct and haunting: "If a new and gigantic war should threaten civilization, what policies should the United States pursue in order to avoid being drawn into the conflict and to safeguard and conserve her physical and spiritual resources?" The responses reflected Americans' diversity of opinion concerning how the United States should respond to mounting foreign aggression. The journal classified the ideas into several different groups, which reflected the variety of authors and, perhaps more importantly, the range of possibilities at the start of 1937. Within just two years, the debate became far narrower, with policy options dwindling and war seen as virtually unavoidable. *Forum*'s categories often included authors from opposing ends of the political spectrum:

1. "Mandatory Neutrality": The respondents included Carrie Chapman Catt, a women's rights leader and pacifist; and a member of the American Legion, who argued that America's armed services should be increased dramatically. On the whole, though, those who favored mandatory neutrality sought to avoid war at all costs.
2. "Defend Democracy!": These interventionists concluded that war could be the only means of preserving democracy in Europe. Rather than seeking to evade conflict, the United States should strongly advocate and protect liberty where necessary.
3. "Co-operate!": These authors contended that the U.S. must involve itself immediately in negotiations to avoid the outbreak of international conflict.
4. "Strong National Defense": For these contributors, only a strong national defense could intimidate aggressors and thus prevent U.S. involvement in war.
5. "Economic Readjustment": Similar to pacifist rhetoric during World War I, this leftist argument declared that capitalist imperialism drove the desire for war. Journalist George Seldes concisely defined the origins of global conflict: "All modern wars are commercial."

Primary Source

"How to Stay Out of War" [excerpt]

SYNOPSIS: The discussion excerpted below presents multiple strategies for U.S. policymakers to pursue in order to avoid American involvement in a foreign conflict. At that time, Nazi aggression in Europe had only recently begun and the threat of war seemed distant. As the likelihood of U.S. participation in the war increased during the next few years, the mass media became engulfed in a ruthless, polarized debate between isolationists and interventionists over whether to enter the war.

Can the United States keep out of future wars? Can we help other nations to settle their differences without war? In no country are there greater divergences of opinion regarding national policy toward war and peace than in the United States. At one extreme are the conscientious objectors, determined to face punishment rather than fight in another war. At the other pole are the heroic patriots who demand armed protection for American property as well as American lives in every quarter of the globe.

In general, however, the conviction is growing that the problem is not a negative one but a positive one, that the United States is not only responsible for keeping the peace with her neighbors but, as one of the greatest powers, inextricably affected by the welfare of the whole planet, is culpable also if she does not seek to mitigate the menace or the prosecution of wars between other nations. The question is, then, of ways and means. It is probable that the year 1937 will see the passage by Congress of a new neutrality law of world importance.

In co-operation with the Foreign Policy Association *The Forum* recently sent a questionnaire to a number of outstanding observers of foreign affairs. We publish in the following pages the answers of two groups: those who favor absolute neutrality by economic insulation against war—mandatory embargoes—and those who favor discretionary neutrality. In subsequent issues we shall present opinions from those who suggest other means of facing the future in our foreign relations.

The question we have asked is this: *If a new and gigantic war should threaten civilization, what policies should the United States pursue in order to avoid being drawn into the conflict and to safeguard and conserve her physical and spiritual resources?*

"Mandatory" Neutrality

Charles A. Beard, Professor of political science

. . . If our efforts to right historic wrongs and bring peace and reason to Europe in 1917–1919 have not taught American citizens anything, no words of mine can add to their education. My program of action for the perils of the Far East and of Europe is to preserve neutrality and to preserve it by drastic limitations on selling munitions and lending money to all belligerents. It may be chimerical, given the posture and propensities of American interests. But surely it is no more chimerical than belief in the power of our words or our arms to heal the wounds of a mad world. If we preserve a little bit of sanity ourselves amid the madness we may at least set the world an example, even if we have no influence on its conduct.

Carrie Chapman Catt, Lecturer

The United States can keep out of the much predicted next war provided a working majority of the administration, the Congress, and the people so determine. The real question facing the nation in case of war would be: Are we civilized enough to pay the price of neutrality? What is the price?

■ ■ ■

Given a majority, however, convinced that war is an outworn, barbarous, and indefensible custom which it is the duty of civilized people to abolish, no power on earth could break our neutrality.

Harry W. Colmery, National Commander of the American Legion

The American Legion recommends for immediate action: (1) maintenance of an adequate national defense; (2) legislation to equalize the burdens of and eliminate the profits from war; and (3) adoption and strict adherence to a policy of neutrality.

■ ■ ■

The enactment into law of the American Legion's universal-service plan, to equalize the burden of war by providing that in a crisis the nation shall bring into its service capital and industry as well as man power, with *special privilege and profit for none,* and to protect against the loss on the economic front due to speculation, inflation, etc. by taking the profits out of war, will remove danger of war. By making all our resources available in a crisis, it will strengthen our defense and by making war a personal service and sacrifice for every citizen it will discourage war and promote peace. . . .

Wilbur L. Cross, Governor of Connecticut

With our present laws relating to neutrality, the steady development of the Administration's present foreign policy of the "good neighbor" would seem to me the best way of safeguarding the nation against being drawn into any possible general European war. At the same time we need to remind ourselves, as private citizens of a democratic country, that, no matter how wisely conceived or executed a policy of neutrality may be, it cannot pull its weight unless it is enforced by public opinion. We must further remind ourselves that in the event of a conflict between major European powers, our feelings, prejudices, and selfish motives would all naturally become more violent than they are today. It would therefore be necessary for us individually to exercise restraint in word and act and to put the good of the nation above personal gain or loss, in order to mobilize public opinion effectively behind whatever official position of neutrality might be deemed advisable for the best interests of the Republic.

Oswald Garrison Villard, Journalist

The greatest safeguard would be having a man in the White House firmly and immovably resolved not to let the country get into war under any conditions whatsoever. Until the power of the president to put us into war is controlled adequately by the requirement of a referendum on war nationwide in scope, no amount of neutrality legislation will prevent our being drawn into a conflict if a president again yields to pressure of war profiteers and bankers who through loans have become identified with the cause of another nation. . . .

Defend Democracy!

H. M. Kallen, Teacher of philosophy

Just as it takes two to make a quarrel, it takes two to keep the peace. In Europe today, with Germany and Italy trying to make a quarrel and England and France trying to keep the peace, the Nazi and Fascist war-threatening powers have the upper hand over the democratic pacifist ones. They have compelled a general resumption of competitive armament and are forcing Europe toward war. I foresee this war as being started not later than September, 1938, and at any time before this date. The pretense of the last war was to "make the world safe for democracy." The pretense of the next one is to "make the world safe from communism." It is a far more hypocritical pretense, for its drive comes from the endeavor to subject the world to fascism.

How can we Americans save ourselves from being drawn into this war? How can we protect our democratic heritage and our American way of life and government.

■ ■ ■

So far as I know, there exists no way to accomplish that insulation which could save America from the emotional and economic disturbances that a European war would generate, and precedent is against our devising any methods successfully to offset them. Under the circumstances, therefore, the most important thing is, while so far as possible minimizing occasions for fighting, to be prepared fully to fight. . . .

D. F. Fleming, Professor of political science

What we are now witnessing is a desperate race of the fascist powers to reach the peak of their armed strength before Britain and France can do so. The democracies have been retreating steadily for five years. Some day they will be compelled to stand their ground. When that hour comes, free men everywhere will have to choose whether they wish to live in a world in which there is no law except the will of the strongest, a world in which war is not only relegalized but enthroned as the sublime means of extending the sway of the fit peoples.

Faced with this elemental issue it is impossible to believe that any free nation anywhere will be neutral in its heart. Until the blighting hand of an all-powerful censorship fastens its hold on us also, the choice between civilization and anarchy, between liberty and despotism, between the rule of law and the rule of brute force will have to be made. . . .

Co-operate!

Josephine Schain, Peace worker

In order to avoid being drawn in, we should act to keep the conflict from starting. As a nation we have mainly pursued a negative policy of saying we would not take part in another war. Passive resistance is not enough. What we need is a constructive policy whereby we would be working with other nations to create channels for handling difficulties that arise in the world.

■ ■ ■

Our government should take immediate steps to help to bring about a world economic conference in order to see what can be done about some of the pressing problems that are causing international irritations. We should throw our powerful influence to help straighten out the snarls in which the modern economic world has entangled itself.

One cannot watch with equanimity the on-slaught being made on peace and democracy by the forces of reaction. I believe that as a nation we should lose no time in aligning ourselves with the forces striving to help both to survive.

Ray Lyman Wilbur, University president

Apparently all the efforts we have made to isolate ourselves by failing to participate officially in the co-operative efforts of the world toward peace have given us no security and no sense of security. Neutrality legislation which is now part of our program seems to me more likely to cause trouble than to prevent it. It is a poor time to try to avoid being brought into war when a war starts.

The hope that I see is in working from the standpoint of prevention of war and the promotion

A crowd outside the U.S. State Department reads the newspaper headlines announcing the beginning of World War II in Europe, Washington, D.C. September 1, 1939. AP/WIDE WORLD PHOTOS. REPRODUCED BY PERMISSION.

of understanding between and among nations. I feel that we should take an active and constructive part in the World Court, in the League of Nations, and in similar measures that will make the chances of war more remote. We cannot do this without accepting definite responsibility and joining in some form of collective security.

The idea that we can pass some special legislation that will give us insurance against war seems to me to be as futile as to make whipping boys of munitions manufacturers.

Strong National Defense

William Hovgaard, Professor of Naval Construction

. . . The best safeguard against those dangers is fully to be prepared for war. If the United States in 1917 had been so prepared, it is likely that Germany would never have declared the unrestricted submarine warfare. Hence, besides following an impartial policy of neutrality based on revised international regulations, the United States should possess an armament of the same order as that now being built up by other great powers. Even then, under certain circumstances, the country may be forced into war. . . .

Economic Readjustment

Peter Molyneaux, Editor

The various possible policies among which the United States would have to choose if a new and gigantic war should threaten civilization in Europe, seem to me to be about equally futile. Those that could be successfully and effectively applied at all present prospects of equal frightfulness. I think I have explored all the possibilities thoroughly and I have found none which gives any measurable assurance of safety in the event of such a war. The impression that there is such a policy is a delusion and a very dangerous one. For even if we succeeded in avoiding actual participation in the conflict altogether, a possibility which I seriously question, we could not escape the economic and social collapse and prostration, approaching chaos, which would be the inevitable consequence of such a war. . . .

George Seldes, Journalist

To avoid being drawn into a new and gigantic war threatening civilization the United States could do one of many things generally listed as impractical, fantastic, idealistic, and naïve—as, for example, making the necessary constitutional changes in government so that we became a co-operative commonwealth, employing man, the machine, and the natural resources of America for the purpose of supplying every person with all that he requires, thereby preventing the bankers and financiers from forcing us into a position which eventually drags us into war and preventing the munitions makers and plain dirt farmers from even desiring to profit by it.

I do not think there are any easy, practical formulae for keeping out of war. One practical thing I should advocate: a voluntary oath from every boy and girl in America, *I swear I will never fight in a commercial war.*

All modern wars are commercial. The only war worth fighting is the war against fascism.

Upton Sinclair, Author

Wars, when they come, are merely the automatic working out of the competition between nations, which today are nothing but competitive commercial groups, each using the slogans and shams of patriotism to delude the people into serving their exploiters. I do not believe that America will keep out of the next world war and I do not believe that there is anything that can be done to keep us out of that war, unless and until we are willing to socialize our industries and abolish the profit motive in our economy. The breakdown of capitalism has proceeded to the point where we are drifting into bankruptcy because of the burden of supporting the unemployed. Cutting off our foreign trade and profits would multiply this distress, and the people would never stand it. Add to that the ability of big-scale profit takers to raise a clamor and influence the public mind and you have forces which will automatically and inevitably take us into the next world war.

Further Resources

BOOKS

Kennedy, David M. *Freedom from Fear: The American People in Depression and War, 1929–1945.* New York: Oxford University Press, 1999.

WEBSITES

The Era of Isolationalism, 1939–1941. Available online at http://www.ww2homefront.com/isolationism.html (accessed April 11, 2003).

The Perilous Fight: America's World War II in Color: Isolationism. Available online at http://www.pbs.org/perilousfight /home_front/isolationism/ (accessed April 11, 2003).

"The Crash of the *Hindenburg*"

Radio broadcast

By: Herb Morrison

Date: May 6, 1937, broadcast on May 7, 1937

Source: Morrison, Herb. "The Crash of the *Hindenburg*." NBC Radio broadcast. May 6, 1937. Reprinted in Garner, Joe. *We Interrupt This Broadcast: Relive the Events That Stopped Our Lives.* Naperville, Ill.: Sourcebooks, 1998.

About the Author: Herbert (Herb) Morrison (1906–1989), born in Pennsylvania, began his radio news career as a broadcaster at a small rural station in nearby West Virginia. Though journalism later took him to assignments in Chicago and New York, Morrison never forgot about the area where he first hit the airwaves. After serving as news director for a Pittsburgh television station, he returned to West Virginia in the 1960s to help the state university in Morgantown develop a broadcasting department. He died in Morgantown, West Virginia, in 1989 at the age of eighty-three. ■

Introduction

On a gloomy, rainy day in New Jersey, thirty-one-year-old radio reporter Herb Morrison stood with his

We Saw the "Hindenburg" Disaster! [excerpt]

[George Willens and his son were scheduled to take the *Hindenburg* on its return flight to Europe to attend the May 12 coronation of King George VI in London. The attached narrative was published as a small pamphlet at Willens' printing company in a limited run of four hundred copies.]

I was busy with my movie camera—taking pictures here and there—when a spectator at my elbow cried, "There she is!" I looked and, sure enough, through the rain and mist the Hindenburg was approaching slowly, majestically from the West. It loomed suddenly out of the sky like a ship at sea, in a fog. It was almost upon us before we knew it. The ground crew caught the lines she threw out and were plodding through the rain soaked field with the big ship in tow. The crowd moved toward the mooring mast—some waving to friends on the ship. Here and there a cry of welcome.

"Getting it?" the man at my left asked as I looked through the sights in my camera, taking a movie in color of the landing. "I guess so," I said. "The light is pretty bad." I was glad Harvey had stayed in New York—glad because in such weather he couldn't have seen the Hindenburg in all the glory of her immense silver hull. Not much of a thrill watching a drab monster settle, slowly, through the gathering dusk—and rain.

Then—as I worked my camera, I saw a streak of flame shoot from the upper seam of the ship, back near the tail. "Strange," I thought, never dreaming that tragedy and disaster were seconds away. I kept on working the camera. The flames, more intense in volume, continued to roll along the ship's seam. The man beside me clutched my arm. "What is it?" he shouted in my ear. Suddenly there was a terrific explosion. Then another. Then the ship burst into flames and settled, like a stricken mastodon—not sagging in the middle or crumpling—but nose down like a living thing mortally hurt.

From the crowd came, at first, a long drawn sigh—then silence except for the crackling of the flames and the scream of a woman here and there. I saw two men catapulted out of the ship—several jumped—and the crowd scurried back as the heat from the flames, now enveloping the entire ship, became more and more unendurable. It was all so sudden—so unexpected—so without precedent—that for precious moments no one knew what to do or what to say. It seemed as if no living thing could pass unscathed through that hell of flames—as if all must have perished. But, thank God, while many were fatally burned—and many suffered grievous injuries—through the mercy of a Divine providence, most were saved.

Presently ambulances, doctors and nurses began coming on the field. Crowds of people sprung up as if by magic. The roads were blocked with cars and people hurrying to the scene. And all the time the ship, now prostrate, was burning furiously while the work of rescue went on.

SOURCE: Willens, George. *We Saw the "Hindenburg" Disaster!* Detroit: George Willens, 1937? Burton Historical Collection, Detroit Public Library, Detroit, Mich.

engineer, waiting for the German airship *Hindenburg* to make its landing at Lakehurst Naval Station. On assignment for WLS radio in Chicago, Morrison intended to focus his report on the ship's magnificent design and luxurious interior. The *Hindenburg* then appeared a testament to German brilliance in aviation technology and was a powerful symbol of the Third Reich's technical wizardry. At the time, dirigible, or blimp, transportation stood at the forefront of air travel. This ship had made the transatlantic journey from Germany to the United States many times before, but the May 1937 flight remained a significant news event. What transpired over the next few minutes changed the course of aviation, and radio, history.

Herb Morrison stood at the landing field as thousands of spectators gathered to witness the *Hindenburg*'s arrival. What followed was one of the most memorable aviation tragedies in history—memorable for the loss of life—thirty-six of the ninety-seven passengers—and because of Morrison's reporting and the terrifying films and photographs that recorded the disaster at the moment it occurred.

Significance

Expecting a routine landing, Morrison began his report by describing the ship's interior and luxurious amenities. The scene changed without any warning: "[T]he back motors of the ship are just holding it just enough to keep it from—it burst into flame! It burst into flame and it's falling, it's fire . . ." During the next few moments, Morrison continued to describe the scene, struggling to regain his composure amidst the flames, smoke, and screaming. Out of breath and nearly in tears, Morrison screamed the most famous lines of his coverage, "Oh, the humanity, and all the passengers. Screaming around me, I'm so—I can't even talk, the people, it's not fair, it's—it's—oh! I can't talk, ladies and gentlemen, honest . . ."

Media critics and some reporters later charged that Morrison had lost his composure and become too emo-

The *Hindenburg* explodes into flames, May 6, 1937. **PUBLIC DOMAIN.**

tional during this report. Radio news reporters were supposed to be sharp and calm during times of crisis, not overly dramatic and self-absorbed. Morrison exclaimed breathlessly, "There's not a possible chance for anyone to be saved," though two-thirds of those aboard were saved. Yet, given Morrison's background and his expectation that the *Hindenburg* story would be just like any other, his report does not appear contrived. In fact, his description affected Americans precisely because it came across from the perspective of an ordinary person witnessing a horrible tragedy.

One lingering misconception about Morrison's emotional report is that it was broadcast live to a nationwide radio audience. It was not. Morrison and his engineering assistant recorded the scene as they viewed it, but listeners did not hear the report until the following day. At that time, most radio networks prohibited taped news reports and preferred to offer listeners only live broadcasts. Given the drama of the *Hindenburg* explosion and the fact that Morrison was the only radio reporter on the scene, NBC decided to feature this story as the network's first nationally broadcast, taped news story. Though taped, this report gave rise to the modern style of dramatic, live, on-the-scene reporting that continued into the twenty-first century to dominate broadcast news.

Primary Source

The Crash of the *Hindenburg*

SYNOPSIS: The *Hindenburg* had been in sight for several minutes over the airfield, and mooring lines were being dropped to crews on the ground to anchor the ship. Passengers gazed at the spectacle below as the crowd of spectators swelled for the landing. The following transcript excerpt begins as Morrison moved from inside the naval station to describe the news outside, his own excitement building by the moment. As listeners heard, "Now they're coming in to make a landing of the Zeppelin. I'm going to step out of here and cover from the outside, so as I move out would you stand by for a second."

Well here it comes, ladies and gentlemen, we're out now, outside of the hangar, and what a great sight it is, a truly one, it's a marvelous sight. It's coming down out of the sky pointed directly towards us and toward the mooring mast. The mighty diesel motors just roared, the propellers biting into the air and throwing it back into a gale-like whirlpool. No wonder this great floating palace can travel through the air at such a speed with these powerful motors behind it.

The sun is striking the windows of the observation deck, on the eastward side, and flashing like glittering jewels on a background of black velvet. And every now and then the propellers are caught in the rays of the sun their highly polished surfaces reflect surfaces of gold. The field that we thought active when we first arrived has turned into a moving mass of cooperative action. The landing crews have rushed to their posts and spots, and orders are being passed along, and last-minute preparations are being completed, for the moment we have waited for so long.

The ship is ridin' majestically toward us, like some great feather. Riding as though it is mighty good—mighty proud of the place its claimed in the world's aviation. The ship is no doubt bustling with activity, frequency, orders are being shouted to the crew, the passengers are probably lining the windows looking down and ahead of them, getting a glimpse of the mooring mast.

And these fine flagships standing here, the American Airlines flagships awaiting directions to all points in the United States when they get the ship moored. There are a number of important persons that's on board, and no doubt the new commander, Captain Max Bluth is thrilled too for this is his great moment, the first time he's commanded the Hindenburg on previous flights he was chief officer under Captain Lehmann.

It's practically standing still now, they've dropped ropes out of the nose of the ship, and it has been taken ahold of down on the field by a number of men. It's starting to rain again, the rain had slacked up a little bit, the back motors of the ship are just holding it just enough to keep it from—it burst into flame! It burst into flame and it's falling, it's fire, watch it, watch it, get out of the way, get out of the way, get this Charley, get this Charley, it's fire and it's rising, it's rising terrible, oh my god

About Zeppelins

Dirigibles are fixed-frame airships. The first powered dirigible was flown in 1852 in France. The German Count Ferdinand von Zeppelin (1838–1917), the most famous advocate of dirigibles, made his first successful flight in 1900. In this early stage of aircraft development, the dirigible (often known as the Zeppelin) had distinct advantages of range and altitude over fixed-wing airplanes. The German military seized upon these advantages and built a fleet of nearly one hundred Zeppelins during World War I (1914–1918). Filled with hydrogen, the great airships were highly vulnerable, however, and their career as an offensive weapon was short-lived.

Following the war, the Zeppelin Company, at the time headed by Hugo Eckener, produced airships as commercial carriers. The *Graf Zeppelin,* launched in 1928, was over seven hundred feet long. Its long and successful career ended with its 1937 decommissioning after nearly six hundred flights, 144 ocean crossings, and a 1929 around-the-world flight.

The massive *Hindenburg* was launched in 1936. It measured 804 feet in length with a diameter of 135 feet. (By comparison, the *Titanic* measured 885 feet. A Boeing 747 has an overall length of approximately 240 feet.) As a safety measure, Eckener planned to fill the *Hindenburg* with helium, a nonflammable gas, rather than the highly explosive hydrogen used in all previous German airships. (The United States had used helium in its airships since the early 1920s.) By 1936, however, the United States, the sole source of large quantities of helium, had reservations about the military aims of Nazi Germany and refused to allow the sale of helium to the Zeppelin Company. Reluctantly, the company used hydrogen.

In its first year of operation, the *Hindenburg* completed twenty transatlantic flights from Germany to Lakehurst, New Jersey, and to Rio de Janeiro, Brazil, without incident. It was a highly visible symbol of both luxurious travel and the technical skill of Nazi Germany.

The flight of May 3–6, 1937, although delayed by headwinds and local storm activity at Lakehurst, was uneventful. Arriving at 7 p.m., the *Hindenburg* was in the midst of its landing procedure when a small flame was noticed in the tail section. Within seconds, the ship was completely engulfed in flames and had collapsed to the ground at the base of the mooring tower.

what do I see? It's burning-bursting into flame, and it's falling on the mooring mast and all of the folks agree that this is terrible, this is one of the worst catastrophes in the world, oh the flames are rising, oh, four or five hundred feet into the sky. It's a terrific crash, ladies and gentlemen, the smoke and its flames now and the frame is crashing to the ground, not quite to the mooring mast, oh the humanity, and all the passengers. Screaming around me, I'm so I can't even talk, the people, it's not fair, it's—it's—oh! I can't talk, ladies and gentlemen, honest, it's a flaming mass of smoking wreckage, and everybody can hardly breathe . . . I'm concentrating. Lady, I'm sorry, honestly, I can hardly breathe, I'm going to step inside where I cannot see it. Charley that's terrible. I, I can't . . . listen folks I'm going to have to stop for a minute, just because I've lost my voice, this is the worst thing I've ever witnessed. . . .

Ladies and gentlemen I'm back again, I've sort of recovered from the terrific explosion, and the terrific crash that occurred just as it was being pulled down to the mooring mast it's still smoking and flaming and crashing and banging down there, and I don't know how many of the ground crew were under it when it fell, and there's not a possible chance for anyone to be saved. The relatives of the people who are waiting here ready to welcome their loved ones as they came off that great ship . . . oh . . . are broken up . . . They're carrying them in to give them first aid and to restore them. Some of them have fainted and the people are rushing down to the uh, burning ship the uh . . . have all have gone down to see if they can extinguish any of the blaze whatsoever but the terrible amount of hydrogen gas in it just caused the tail surface broke into flame first, then there was a terrific explosion, and that followed by the burning of the nose and the crashing nose into the ground, and everybody carrying back at breakneck speed to get out from underneath it because it was over the people at the time it burst into flame.

Now whether it fell on the people who were witnessing it, we do not know, but as it exploded they rushed back and now it's smoking, a terrific black smoke flooding up into the sky, the flames are still leaping maybe thirty, forty feet from the ground, the entire eight hundred and eleven feet length of it. They're frantically calling for ambulances and things, the wires are being, humming with activity, and I've lost my breath several times during this exciting moment here.

Will you pardon me just a moment? I'm not going to stop talking, I'm just going to swallow several times until I can keep on.

Further Resources

BOOKS

Archbold, Rick, and Ken Marschall. *"Hindenburg": An Illustrated History.* New York: Warner Books, 1994.

Dick, Harold G., with Douglas H. Robinson *The Golden Age of the Great Passenger Airships, "Graf Zeppelin" and "Hindenburg."* Washington, D.C.: Smithsonian Institution Press, 1985.

PERIODICALS

"Herbert Morrison, 83, *Hindenburg* Reporter." Obituary. *The New York Times,* January 11, 1989.

WEBSITES

"Afterglow of a Myth: Why and How the *Hindenburg* Burnt." Available online at http://www.dwv-info.de/pm/hindbg/hbe.htm#LZ129 (accessed March 1, 2003).

"*Hindenburg* (LZ-129)." *Navy Lakehurst Historical Society.* Available online at http://www.nlhs.com/hindenburg.htm; website home page: http://www.nlhs.com (accessed August 9, 2002).

"LZ-129, *Hindenburg.*" *Zeppelin Library Archives.* Available online at http://www.ciderpresspottery.com/ZLA/greatzeps/german/Hindenburg.html; website home page: http://www.ciderpresspottery.com (accessed August 9, 2002).

Widner, James F. "*Hindenburg* Disaster." Radio Days. Available online at http://www.otr.com/hindenburg.html (accessed March 1, 2003).

Action Comics No. 1

Comic book

By: Jerome Siegel and Joe Shuster

Date: June 1938

Source: Siegel, Jerome, and Joe Shuster. *Action Comics* No. 1, June, 1938, cover, 1. Available online at http://xroads.virginia.edu/~UG02/yeung/actioncomics/cover.html; website home page: http://xroads.virginia.edu/~UG02/yeung/home.html (accessed March 13, 2003).

About the Authors: High-school classmates Jerry Siegel (1915–1996) and Joe Shuster (1914–1996), in a period of only a few years, went from scribbling comic strips after homework to creating arguably the most famous comic book character of all time, Superman. Siegel wrote the stories and Shuster drew them. In 1934, just out of high school in Cleveland, Ohio, the pair finalized the Superman serial and began submitting it to newspapers. Four years later, an editor at DC Comics picked up the idea and agreed to publish *Action Comics* featuring Superman. Siegel and Shuster wrote Superman comic books for DC Comics from 1938 until 1947, when they sued DC for more compensation. Siegel died in 1996 at the age of eighty-one, and Shuster died in 1992 at the age of seventy-eight. ■

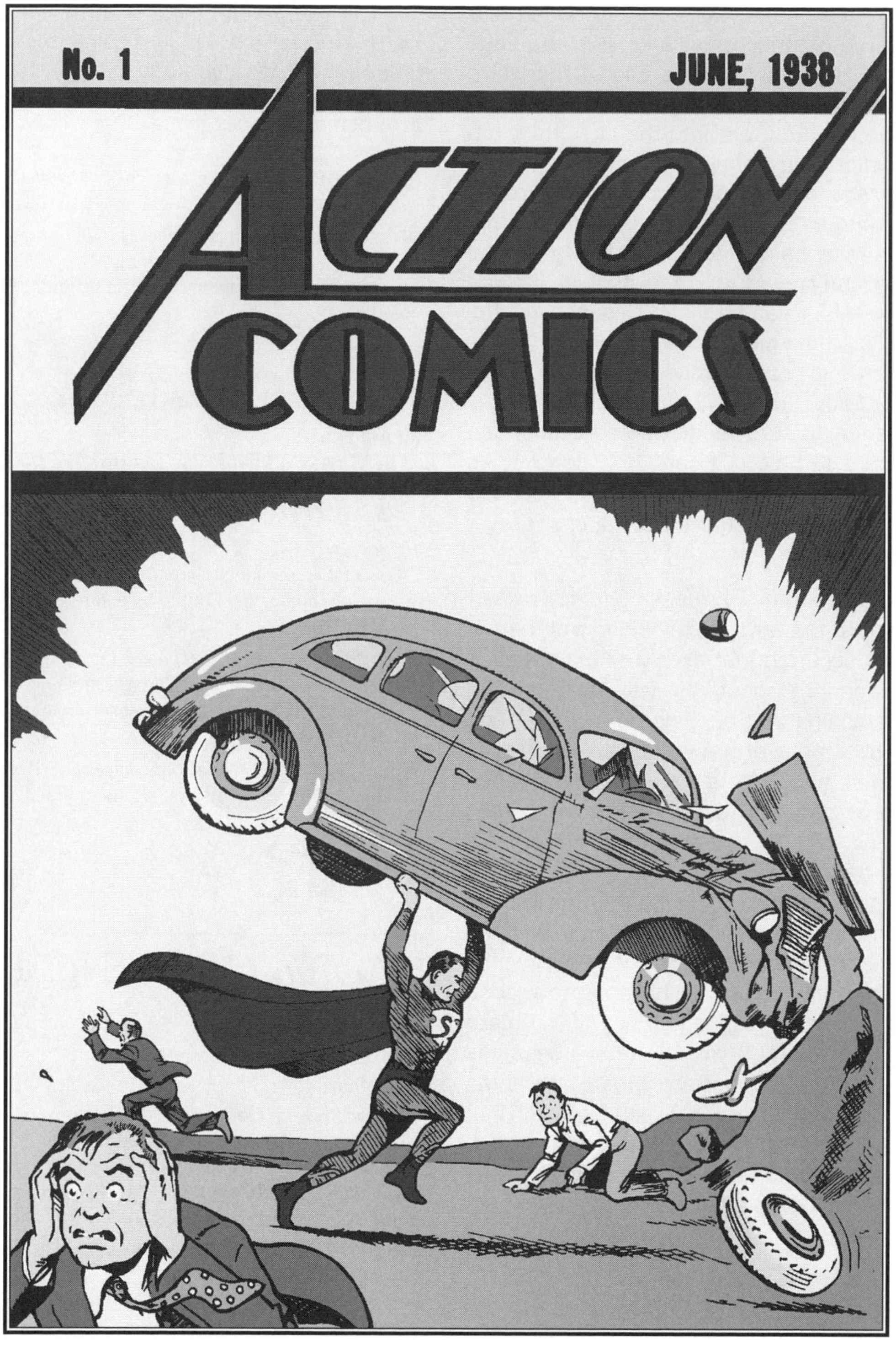

Primary Source

Action Comics No. 1, Cover (1 OF 2)

SYNOPSIS: The following images are the cover and first full page text of the very first appearance of Superman. The story begins with the origins of Superman, including the famous descriptions of his ability to leap over tall buildings and run faster than a locomotive. The comic continues with several different storylines involving Clark Kent's attraction to Lois Lane, a pair of last-minute, life-saving adventures, and a cliffhanger conclusion involving government corruption. DC COMICS, INC. REPRODUCED BY PERMISSION.

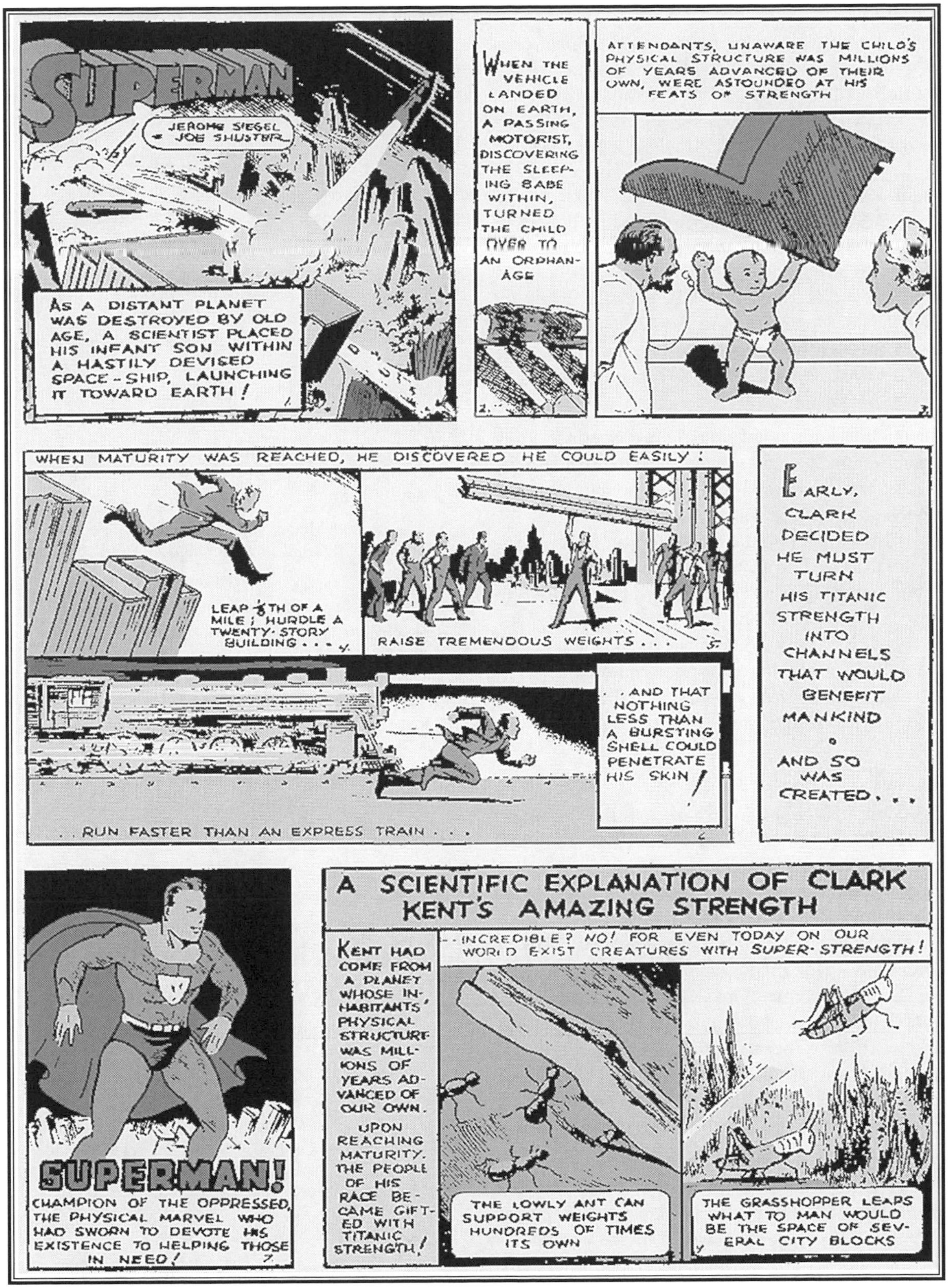

Primary Source

Action Comics No. 1, First Page (2 OF 2)

First full page of Superman in *Action Comics,* No. 1, June 1938. Superman's birth, voyage to Earth, and supernatural abilities are briefly explained. DC COMICS, INC. REPRODUCED BY PERMISSION.

Introduction

When *Action Comics* appeared in 1938, Americans remained in the grips of the Great Depression and the advancing threat of the Second World War. A severe recession gripped the countryside in 1937–1938, as unemployment rates rose to their highest levels since the start of the Depression. In Europe, Adolf Hitler annexed Austria in 1938 and took over Czechoslovakia in the spring of 1939; and the German invasion of Poland in September 1939 would mark the beginning of World War II in Europe. The Japanese army continued its destruction of China and threatened to take over the nation by the end of the decade. In December 1937, Japanese troops sank the USS *Panay* off the coast of Nanjing, China, leaving the Roosevelt administration to consider whether to declare war on Japan.

The public sought relief from daily concerns in mass media entertainment such as magazines, radio programs, newspapers, and comic books. Though comic strips and comic books had existed for decades, the 1930s saw the creation of the most popular characters in history, Superman (1938) and Batman (1939). Superman and Batman, among other famous comic book heroes, strove to preserve "law and order" and defend the American way of life. These characters would make the comic book industry a multibillion-dollar enterprise and provide readers of all ages with amazing new heroes and villains every month for the rest of their lives.

Significance

The debut of *Action Comics* marked the beginning of the "Golden Age" of comic books. By 1941, DC Comics sold nearly one million copies of Action Comics every month, and the bimonthly *Superman* comic, created in 1940, sold more than 1.25 million copies every edition. The Superman character became ubiquitous in popular culture—Superman saved the day, every day, in newspaper strips, comic books, radio programs, and, later, television shows and movies. Siegel and Shuster allegedly sold the rights to *Action Comics,* No. 1, for $10 per page, or $130. The current estimated value of *Action Comics,* No. 1, in near mint condition, is $350,000. Only one copy is known to exist in this condition.

Shuster and Siegel's original comic book provides modern readers with a glimpse into American society at the end of the 1930s. Superman was portrayed as a "champion of the oppressed," providing Depression-weary Americans with protection against violence and injustice. The Superman in *Action Comics,* No. 1, is not warm and forgiving; he taunts foes and threatens them with his awesome powers. With war beginning to rage across the Atlantic, this Great Depression-era superhero seeks to prevent a government conspiracy that may lead the United States into war in Europe, reflecting the concerns of many Americans. Superman and other comic book heroes, like millions of Americans, would soon find World War II unavoidable and rally against the Axis powers.

Further Resources

BOOKS

Daniels, Les. *Superman, The Complete History: The Life and Times of the Man of Steel.* San Francisco: Chronicle Books, 1998.

Goulart, Ron. *Comic Book Culture: An Illustrated History.* Portland, Ore.: Collectors Press, 2000.

A Smithsonian Book of Comic-Book Comics. Edited by Michael Barrier and Martin Williams. New York: Smithsonian Institution Press and Harry N. Abrams, 1981.

PERIODICALS

Lambert, Bruce. "Joseph Shuster, Cartoonist, Dies; Co-Creator of 'Superman' Was 78." *The New York Times,* August 3, 1992.

Thomas, Robert McG., Jr. "Jerry Siegel, Superman's Creator, Dies at 81." *The New York Times,* January 31, 1996.

WEBSITES

Barnes, Erin, Dave Hendrick, and Chris Yeung. "Superman in Identity Crisis: The Many Faces of the Man of Steel." Available online at http://xroads.virginia.edu/~UG02/superman/home.html (accessed March 1, 2003).

Brown, Mitchell. "The 100 Greatest Comics of the 20th Century." Available online at http://www.geocities.com/mbrown123/greatest_comics/ (accessed March 1, 2003).

Younis, Steven, ed. Superman Homepage (unofficial). Available online at http://www.supermanhomepage.com (accessed March 1, 2003).

"Radio Listeners in Panic, Taking War Drama as Fact"

Newspaper headline, Newspaper article

Date: October 31, 1938

Source: "Radio Listeners in Panic, Taking War Drama as Fact." *The New York Times,* October 31, 1938, 1, 4. Reprinted online at http://www.jd.gosling.btinternet.co.uk/wotw/docs.htm; website home page: http://www.jd.gosling.btinternet.co.uk/wotw/ (accessed March 13, 2003). ■

Introduction

News reports grew increasingly tense during the 1930s. The United States teetered on the brink of complete economic devastation following the stock market crash of 1929. Then, following the rise of Adolf Hitler and the Nazi Party in Germany in 1933, the threat of war mounted year by year. By the fall of 1938, Germany had annexed Austria, taken over Czechoslovakia, and was openly planning for a greater European invasion the following year. American radio listeners consistently heard breathless radio announcers break into entertainment programs to report on dramatic developments at home and abroad. Orson Welles' Mercury Theatre designed its production of *The War of the Worlds* to take full advantage of this tension with its mock, though seriously styled, news coverage of a Martian invasion.

Significance

The CBS broadcast of the Mercury Theatre's performance of H.G. Welles' *The War of the Worlds* on October 30, 1938, exposed the dramatic influence of mass media in American culture. Americans trusted their radio news reports, and many immediately accepted broadcasters' descriptions of a Martian invasion as actual fact.

During the hour-long program, the Mercury Theatre portrayed invading Martians wreaking havoc, killing thousands of people, and moving to take over the entire planet. CBS included only a few (three or four) clarifications explaining that the broadcast was fictitious and meant for entertainment. These fifteen-second notices read, "You are listening to a CBS presentation of Orson Welles and the Mercury Theatre on the air in an original dramatization of *The War of the Worlds* by H.G. Welles. The performance will continue after a brief intermission. This is the Columbia . . . Broadcasting System." Any audience member who missed such brief announcements tuned in to hear seemingly real reports of chaos and destruction.

Although CBS and the Mercury Theatre claimed that it was not their "intention to mislead any one," Welles concluded the program by describing it as a fairly serious attempt at pulling a Halloween prank over millions of listeners: "This is Orson Welles, ladies and gentlemen, out of character to assure you that *The War of the Worlds* has no further significance than as the holiday offering it was intended to be." The ensuing turmoil wrought by the broadcast revealed the significant role radio played in American society. A transcript of the original broadcast can be viewed at http://www.waroftheworlds.org/wow_script.htm.

Primary Source

"Radio Listeners in Panic, Taking War Drama as Fact": Newspaper article

SYNOPSIS: The following front-page headline and report from the next day's *The New York Times* examined the immediate "mass hysteria" caused by Welles' prank. The article included numerous accounts of individuals panicking throughout the Eastern Seaboard.

Orson Welles delivers his famous radio broadcast of the *War of the Worlds* on October 30, 1938. **AP/WIDE WORLD PHOTOS. REPRODUCED BY PERMISSION.**

In small towns and large cities alike, listeners leapt from their chairs and prepared to defend themselves against spaceships and flame-spouting alien invaders. While these reactions may seem unbelievable, their very real context of worldwide economic and social devastation perhaps gives a sense of the times in which this confusion occurred.

A wave of mass hysteria seized thousands of radio listeners throughout the nation between 3:15 and 9:30 o'clock last night when a broadcast of a dramatization of H. G. Wells's fantasy, "The War of the Worlds," led thousands to believe that an interplanetary conflict had started with invading Martians spreading wide death and destruction in New Jersey and New York.

The broadcast, which disrupted households, interrupted religious services, created traffic jams and clogged communications systems, was made by Orson Welles, who as the radio character, "The Shadow," used to give "the creeps" to countless child listeners. This time at least a score of adults required medical treatment for shock and hysteria.

In Newark, in a single block at Heddon Terrace and Hawthorne Avenue, more than twenty families rushed out of their houses with wet handkerchiefs and towels over their faces to flee from what they believed was to be a gas raid. Some began moving household furniture.

Throughout New York families left their homes, some to flee to nearby parks. Thousands of persons called the police, newspapers and radio stations here and in other cities of the United States and Canada seeking advice on protective measures against the raids.

The program was produced by Mr. Welles and the Mercury Theatre on the Air over station WABC and the Columbia Broadcasting System's coast-to-coast network, from 8 to 9 o'clock.

The radio play, as presented, was to simulate a regular radio program with a "break-in" for the material of the play. The radio listeners, apparently, missed or did not listen to the introduction, which was: "The Columbia Broadcasting System and its affiliated stations present Orson Welles and the Mercury Theatre on the Air in 'The War of the Worlds' by H. G. Wells."

They also failed to associate the program with the newspaper listing of the program, announced as "Today: 8:00–9:00—Play: H. G. Wells's 'War of the Worlds'—WABC." They ignored three additional announcements made during the broadcast emphasizing its fictional nature.

Mr. Welles opened the program with a description of the series of which it is a part. The simulated program began. A weather report was given, prosaically. An announcer remarked that the program would be continued from a hotel, with dance music. For a few moments a dance program was given in the usual manner. Then there was a "break-in" with a "flash" about a professor at an observatory noting a series of gas explosions on the planet Mars.

News bulletins and scene broadcasts followed, reporting, with the technique in which the radio had reported actual events, the landing of a "meteor" near Princeton N. J., "killing" 1,500 persons, the discovery that the "meteor" was a "metal cylinder" containing strange creatures from Mars armed with "death rays" to open hostilities against the inhabitants of the earth.

Despite the fantastic nature of the reported "occurrences," the program, coming after the recent war scare in Europe and a period in which the radio frequently had interrupted regularly scheduled programs to report developments in the Czechoslovak situation, caused fright and panic throughout the area of the broadcast.

Telephone lines were tied up with calls from listeners or persons who had heard of the broadcasts. Many sought first to verify the reports. But large numbers, obviously in a state of terror, asked how they could follow the broadcast's advice and flee from the city, whether they would be safer in the "gas raid" in the cellar or on the roof, how they could safeguard their children, and many of the questions which had been worrying residents of London and Paris during the tense days before the Munich agreement.

So many calls came to newspapers and so many newspapers found it advisable to check on the reports despite their fantastic content that The Associated Press sent out the following at 8:48 P.M. :

"Note to Editors: Queries to newspapers from radio listeners throughout the United States tonight, regarding a reported meteor fall which killed a number of New Jerseyites, are the result of a studio dramatization. The A. P."

Similarly police teletype systems carried notices to all stationhouses, and police short-wave radio stations notified police radio cars that the event was imaginary.

Message From the Police

The New York police sent out the following:

"To all receivers: Station WABC informs us that the broadcast just concluded over that station was a dramatization of a play. No cause for alarm."

The New Jersey State Police teletyped the following: "Note to all receivers—WABC broadcast as drama re this section being attacked by residents of Mars. Imaginary affair."

From one New York theatre a manager reported that a throng of playgoers had rushed from his theatre as a result of the broadcast. He said that the wives of two men in the audience, having heard the broadcast, called the theatre and insisted that their husbands be paged. This spread the "news" to others in the audience.

The switchboard of *The New York Times* was overwhelmed by the calls. A total of 875 were received. One man who called from Dayton, Ohio, asked, "What time will it be the end of the world?" A caller from the suburbs said he had had a houseful of guests and all had rushed out to the yard for safety.

Warren Dean, a member of the American Legion living in Manhattan, who telephoned to verify the "reports," expressed indignation which was typical of that of many callers.

"I've heard a lot of radio programs, but I've never heard anything as rotten as that," Mr. Dean said. "It was too realistic for comfort. They broke into a dance program with a news flash. Everybody in my house was agitated by the news. It went on just like press radio news."

At 9 o'clock a woman walked into the West Forty-seventh Street police station dragging two children, all carrying extra clothing. She said she was ready to leave the city. Police persuaded her to stay.

A garbled version of the reports reached the Dixie Bus terminal, causing officials there to prepare to change their schedule on confirmation of "news" of an accident at Princeton on their New Jersey route. Miss Dorothy Brown at the terminal sought verification, however, when the caller refused to talk with the dispatcher, explaining to her that "the world is coming to an end and I have a lot to do."

Harlem Shaken By the "News"

Harlem was shaken by the "news." Thirty men and women rushed into the West 123d Street police station and twelve into the West 135th Street station saying they had their household goods packed and were all ready to leave Harlem if the police would tell them where to go to be "evacuated." One man insisted he had heard "the President's voice" over the radio advising all citizens to leave the cities.

The parlor churches in the Negro district, congregations of the smaller sects meeting on the ground floors of brownstone houses, took the "news" in stride as less faithful parishioners rushed in with it, seeking spiritual consolation. Evening services became "end of the world" prayer meetings in some.

One man ran into the Wadsworth Avenue Police Station in Washington Heights, white with terror, crossing the Hudson River and asking what he should do. A man came in to the West 152d Street Station, seeking traffic directions. The broadcast became a rumor that spread through the district and many persons stood on street corners hoping for a sight of the "battle" in the skies.

In Queens the principal question asked of the switchboard operators at Police Headquarters was whether "the wave of poison gas will reach as far as Queens." Many said they were all packed up and ready to leave Queens when told to do so.

Samuel Tishman of 100 Riverside Drive was one of the multitude that fled into the street after hearing part of the program. He declared that hundreds of persons evacuated their homes fearing that the "city was being bombed."

"I came home at 9:15 P.M. just in time to receive a telephone call from my nephew who was frantic with fear. He told me the city was about to be bombed from the air and advised me to get out of the building at once. I turned on the radio and heard the broadcast which corroborated what my nephew had said, grabbed my hat and coat and a few personal belongings and ran to the elevator. When I got to the street there were hundreds of people milling around in panic. Most of us ran toward Broadway and it was not until we stopped taxi drivers who had heard the entire broadcast on their radios that we knew what it was all about. It was the most asinine stunt I ever heard of."

"I heard that broadcast and almost had a heart attack," said Louis Winkler of 1,322 Clay Avenue, the Bronx. "I didn't tune it in until the program was half over, but when I heard the names and titles of Federal, State and municipal officials and when the 'Secretary of the Interior' was introduced, I was convinced it was the McCoy. I ran out into the street with scores of others, and found people running in all directions. The whole thing came over as a news broadcast and in my mind it was a pretty crummy thing to do."

The Telegraph Bureau switchboard at police headquarters in Manhattan, operated by thirteen men, was so swamped with calls from apprehensive citizens inquiring about the broadcast that police business was seriously interfered with.

Headquarters, unable to reach the radio station by telephone, sent a radio patrol car there to ascertain the reason for the reaction to the program. When the explanation was given, a police message was sent to all precincts in the five boroughs advising the commands of the cause.

"They're Bombing New Jersey!"

Patrolman John Morrison was on duty at the switchboard in the Bronx Police Headquarters when, as he afterward expressed it, all the lines became busy at once. Among the first who answered was a man who informed him:

"They're bombing New Jersey!"

"How do you know?" Patrolman Morrison inquired.

"I heard it on the radio," the voice at the other end of the wire replied. "Then I went to the roof and

The New York Times.

Copyright, 1938, by The New York Times Company.

Entered as Second-Class Matter, Postoffice, New York, N. Y.

NEW YORK, MONDAY, OCTOBER 31, 1938.

PP

MEAD STANDS PAT AS A NEW DEALER IN BID FOR SENATE

Democratic Candidate Opposes Any Except Minor Changes in Labor and Security Laws

UPHOLDS THEORY OF TVA

Wants Budget Balanced, but Not if This Means 'Misery,' He Tells The Times

Text of Representative Mead's reply is printed on Page 6.

From a Staff Correspondent

BUFFALO, N. Y., Oct. 30.—Representatives James M. Mead, Democratic candidate for the short-term Senatorial seat in the election Nov. 8, today answered in a statement the six questions on campaign issues propounded by THE NEW YORK TIMES to the four New York nominees of the two major parties in an editorial Oct. 20.

Mr. Mead's answer, in the main, was a broad and little qualified defense of the New Deal legislation which he, as a member of the House of Representatives, had a part in formulating and passing.

The principles of the Social Security and National Labor Relations Acts he defended stoutly, seeing

Radio Listeners in Panic, Taking War Drama as Fact

Many Flee Homes to Escape 'Gas Raid From Mars'—Phone Calls Swamp Police at Broadcast of Wells Fantasy

A wave of mass hysteria seized thousands of radio listeners throughout the nation between 8:15 and 9:30 o'clock last night when a broadcast of a dramatization of H. G. Wells's fantasy, "The War of the Worlds," led thousands to believe that an interplanetary conflict had started with invading Martians spreading wide death and destruction in New Jersey and New York.

The broadcast, which disrupted households, interrupted religious services, created traffic jams and clogged communications systems, was made by Orson Welles, who as the radio character, "The Shadow," used to give "the creeps" to countless child listeners. This time at least a score of adults required medical treatment for shock and hysteria.

In Newark, in a single block at Heddon Terrace and Hawthorne Avenue, more than twenty families rushed out of their houses with wet handkerchiefs and towels over their faces to flee from what they believed was to be a gas raid. Some began moving household furniture.

Throughout New York families left their homes, some to flee to near-by parks. Thousands of persons called the police, newspapers and radio stations here and in other cities of the United States and Canada seeking advice on protective measures against the raids.

The program was produced by Mr. Welles and the Mercury Theatre on the Air over station WABC and the Columbia Broadcasting System's coast-to-coast network, from 8 to 9 o'clock.

The radio play, as presented, was to simulate a regular radio program with a "break-in" for the material of the play. The radio listeners, apparently, missed or did not listen to the introduction, which was: "The Columbia Broadcasting System and its affiliated stations present Orson Welles and the Mercury Theatre on the Air in 'The War of the Worlds' by H. G. Wells."

They also failed to associate the program with the newspaper listing of the program, announced as "Today: 8:00-9:00—Play: H. G. Wells's 'War of the Worlds'—WABC." They ignored three additional announcements made during the broadcast emphasizing its fictional nature.

Mr. Welles opened the program with a description of the series of

Continued on Page Four

OUSTED JEWS FIND REFUGE IN POLAND AFTER BORDER STAY

Exiles Go to Relatives' Homes or to Camps Maintained by Distribution Committee

REVEAL CRUELTY OF TRIP

Others Sent Back to Germany Pending Parleys on Issue by the Two Governments

Wireless to THE NEW YORK TIMES.

WARSAW, Poland, Oct. 30.—The evacuation from frontier areas of thousands of Polish Jews—8,000 according to official reports and 12,000 according to an estimate by Jewish Relief Committee—deported from Germany began today after they had been massed at frontier stations up and down the border for twenty-six hours. Their terrible ordeal is nearing its end.

Polish authorities have permitted officials of the Joint Distribution Committee to send the victims to relatives' homes in Poland or to special camps the committee maintains. The refugees spent a sleepless night in barracks, crowded station buildings or empty freight cars; many spent the night in the open in the no man's land between the frontiers.

The Joint Distribution Committee supplied food and will also pay spe-

B. C. VLADECK DIES: DALADIER PREPARES

LETTER EARLE

Has Right Campaigns Misused

Primary Source

"Radio Listeners in Panic": Newspaper headline

SYNOPSIS: The front page of the *The New York Times,* on October 31, 1938, the day after Orson Welles' infamous radio broadcast of the *War of the Worlds*, which confused many radio listeners into believing the events were real. *THE NEW YORK TIMES*. GRADUATE LIBRARY, UNIVERSITY OF MICHIGAN. REPRODUCED BY PERMISSION.

I could see the smoke from the bombs, drifting over toward New York. What shall I do?"

The patrolman calmed the caller as well as he could, then answered other inquiries from persons who wanted to know whether the reports of a bombardment were true, and if so where they should take refuge.

At Brooklyn police headquarters, eight men assigned to the monitor switchboard estimated that they had answered more than 800 inquiries from persons who had been alarmed by the broadcast. A number of these, the police said, came from motorists who had heard the program over their car radios and were alarmed both for themselves and for persons at their homes. Also, the Brooklyn police reported, a preponderance of the calls seemed to come from women.

The National Broadcasting Company reported that men stationed at the WJZ transmitting station at Bound Brook, N. J., had received dozens of calls from residents of that area. The transmitting station communicated with New York and passed the information that there was no cause for alarm to the persons who inquired later.

Meanwhile the New York telephone operators of the company found their switchboards swamped with incoming demands for information, although the NBC system had no part in the program.

Record Westchester Calls

The State, county, parkway and local police in Westchester County were swamped also with calls from terrified residents. Of the local police departments, Mount Vernon, White Plains, Mount Kisco, Yonkers and Tarrytown received most of the inquiries. At first the authorities thought they were being made the victims of a practical joke, but when the calls persisted and increased in volume they began to make inquiries. The New York Telephone Company reported that it had never handled so many calls in one hour in years in Westchester.

One man called the Mount Vernon Police Headquarters to find out "where the forty policemen were killed"; another said her brother was ill in bed listening to the broadcast and when he heard the reports he got into an automobile and "disappeared." "I'm nearly crazy!" the caller exclaimed.

Because some of the inmates took the catastrophic reports seriously as they came over the radio, some of the hospitals and the county penitentiary ordered that the radios be turned off.

Thousands of calls came in to Newark Police Headquarters. These were not only from the terror stricken. Hundreds of physicians and nurses, believing the reports to be true, called to volunteer their services to aid the "injured." City officials also called in to make "emergency" arrangements for the population. Radio cars were stopped by the panicky throughout that city.

Jersey City police headquarters received similar calls. One woman asked detective Timothy Grooty, on duty there, "Shall I close my windows?" A man asked, "Have the police any extra gas masks?" Many of the callers, on being assured the reports were fiction, queried again and again, uncertain in whom to believe.

Scores of persons in lower Newark Avenue, Jersey City, left their homes and stood fearfully in the street, looking with apprehension toward the sky. A radio car was dispatched there to reassure them.

The incident at Hedden Terrace and Hawthorne Avenue, in Newark, one of the most dramatic in the area, caused a tie-up in traffic for blocks around. The more than twenty families there apparently believed the "gas attack" had started, and so reported to the police. An ambulance, three radio cars and a police emergency squad of eight men were sent to the scene with full inhalator apparatus.

They found the families with wet cloths on faces contorted with hysteria. The police calmed them, halted those who were attempting to move their furniture on their cars and after a time were able to clear the traffic snarl.

At St. Michael's Hospital, High Street and Central Avenue, in the heart of the Newark industrial district, fifteen men and women were treated for shock and hysteria. In some cases it was necessary to give sedatives, and nurses and physicians sat down and talked with the more seriously affected.

While this was going on, three persons with children under treatment in the institution telephoned that they were taking them out and leaving the city, but their fears were calmed when hospital authorities explained what had happened.

A flickering of electric lights in Bergen County from about 6:15 to 6:30 last evening provided a build-up for the terror that was to ensue when the radio broadcast started.

Without going out entirely, the lights dimmed and brightened alternately and radio reception was also affected. The Public Service Gas and Electric Company was mystified by the behavior of the lights, declaring there was nothing wrong at their power plants or in their distributing system. A spokesman for the service department said a call was made to Newark and the same situation was reported. He believed, he said, that the condition was general throughout the State.

The New Jersey Bell Telephone Company reported that every central office in the State was flooded with calls for more than an hour and the company did not have time to summon emergency operators to relieve the congestion. Hardest hit was the Trenton toll office, which handled calls from all over the East.

One of the radio reports, the statement about the mobilization of 7,000 national guardsmen in New Jersey, caused the armories of the Sussex and Essex troops to be swamped with calls from officers and men seeking information about the mobilization place.

Prayers for Deliverance

In Caldwell, N. J., an excited parishioner ran into the First Baptist Church during evening services and shouted that a meteor had fallen, showering death and destruction, and that North Jersey was threatened. The Rev. Thomas Thomas, the pastor quieted the congregation and all prayed for deliverance from the "catastrophe."

East Orange police headquarters received more than 200 calls from persons who wanted to know what to do to escape the "gas." Unaware of the broadcast, the switchboard operator tried to telephone Newark, but was unable to get the call through because the switchboard at Newark headquarters was tied up. The mystery was not cleared up until a teletype explanation had been received from Trenton.

More than 100 calls were received at Maplewood police headquarters and during the excitement two families of motorists, residents of New York City, arrived at the station to inquire how they were to get back to their homes now that the Pulaski Skyway had been blown up.

The women and children were crying and it took some time for the police to convince them that the catastrophe was fictitious. Many persons who called Maplewood said their neighbors were packing their possessions and preparing to leave for the country.

In Orange, N. J., an unidentified man rushed into the lobby of the Lido Theatre, a neighborhood motion picture house, with the intention of "warning" the audience that a meteor had fallen on Raymond Boulevard, Newark, and was spreading poisonous gases. Skeptical, Al Hochberg, manager of the theatre, prevented the man from entering the auditorium of the theatre and then called the police. He was informed that the radio broadcast was responsible for the man's alarm.

Emanuel Priola, bartender of a tavern at 442 Valley Road, West Orange, closed the place, sending away six customers, in the middle of the broadcast to "rescue" his wife and two children.

"At first I thought it was a lot of Buck Rogers stuff, but when a friend telephoned me that general orders had been issued to evacuate every one from the metropolitan area I put the customers out, closed the place and started to drive home," he said.

William H. Decker of 20 Aubrey Road, Montclair, N. J., denounced the broadcast as "a disgrace" and "an outrage," which he said had frightened hundreds of residents in his community, including children. He said he knew of one woman who ran into the street with her two children and asked for the help of neighbors in saving them.

"We were sitting in the living room casually listening to the radio," he said, "when we heard reports of a meteor falling near New Brunswick and reports that gas was spreading. Then there was an announcement of the Secretary of Interior from Washington who spoke of the happening as a major disaster. It was the worst thing I ever heard over the air."

Columbia Explains Broadcast

The Columbia Broadcasting System issued a statement saying that the adaption of Mr. Welles's novel which was broadcast "followed the original closely, but to make the imaginary details more interesting to American listeners the adapter, Orson Welles, substituted an American locale for the English scenes of the story."

Pointing out that the fictional character of the broadcast had been announced four times and had been previously publicized, it continued:

"Nevertheless, the program apparently was produced with such vividness that some listeners who may have heard only fragments thought the broadcast was fact, not fiction. Hundreds of telephone calls reaching CBS stations, city authorities, newspaper offices and police headquarters in various cities testified to the mistaken belief.

"Naturally, it was neither Columbia's nor the Mercury Theatre's intention to mislead any one, and when it became evident that a part of the audience had been disturbed by the performance five announcements were read over the network later in the evening to reassure those listeners."

Expressing profound regret that his dramatic efforts should cause such consternation, Mr. Welles said: "I don't think we will choose anything like this again." He hesitated about presenting it, he disclosed, because "it was our thought that perhaps people might be bored or annoyed at hearing a tale so improbable."

Scare Is Nation-wide

Broadcast Spreads Fear In New England, the South and West

Last night's radio "war scare" shocked thousands of men, women and children in the big cities throughout the country. Newspaper offices, police stations and radio stations were besieged with calls from anxious relatives of New Jersey residents, and in some places anxious groups discussed the impending menace of a disastrous war.

Most of the listeners who sought more information were widely confused over the reports they had heard, and many were indignant when they learned that fiction was the cause of their alarm.

In San Francisco the general impression of listeners seemed to be that an overwhelming force had invaded the United States from the air, was in the process of destroying New York and threatening to move westward. "My God," roared one inquirer into a telephone, "where can I volunteer my services? We've got to stop this awful thing."

Newspaper offices and radio stations in Chicago were swamped with telephone calls about the "meteor" that had fallen in New Jersey. Some said they had relatives in the "stricken area" and asked if the casualty list was available.

In parts of St. Louis men and women clustered in the streets in residential areas to discuss what they should do in the face of the sudden war. One suburban resident drove fifteen miles to a newspaper office to verify the radio "report."

In New Orleans a general impression prevailed that New Jersey had been devastated by the "invaders," but fewer inquiries were received than in other cities.

In Baltimore a woman engaged passage on an airliner for New York, where her daughter is in school.

The Associated Press gathered the following reports of reaction to the broadcast:

At Fayetteville, N. C., people with relatives in the section of New Jersey where the mythical visitation had its locale went to a newspaper office in tears, seeking information.

A message from Providence, R. I., said: "Weeping and hysterical women swamped the switchboard of The Providence Journal for details of the massacre and destruction at New York, and officials of the electric company received scores of calls urging them to turn off all lights so that the city would be safe from the enemy."

Mass hysteria mounted so high in some cases that people told the police and newspapers they "saw" the invasion.

The Boston Globe told of one woman who claimed she could "see the fire," and said she and many others in her neighborhood were "getting out of here."

Radio and Its Powerful Influence

At the end of the nineteenth century inventors harnessed radio waves, a type of electromagnetic radiation invisible to the human eye, to carry information. In 1899 the inventor Guglielmo Marconi used radio waves to carry the dots and dashes of the Morse code. This invention was the radio telegraph. In 1906 radio waves carried the human voice, ushering in the era of the radio telephone. Since both inventions sent information via radio waves rather than through wires, people called them "wireless." In 1912 the U.S. Navy replaced the term "wireless" with radiotelegraphy and radiotelephony, though Americans simplified terminology by using "radio" for any transmission by radio waves.

In 1920 Frank Conrad, a Westinghouse engineer in East Pittsburgh, Pennsylvania, started the first commercial radio station, KDKA. In addition to sharing news with listeners, Conrad played phonograph records, and local department stores began selling radio receivers. By 1922, 508 radio stations existed, and Americans owned 60,000 radios. In 1923 American businesses sold $46 million of radio equipment, a five-fold increase over sales in 1921. In 1926 American businesses sold $400 million of radio equipment, and in 1929 this number increased to $850 million. By 1930 Americans owned nearly 14 million radios, and in 1933 this number leapt to nearly 20 million.

The first stations transmitted information by modifying the amplitude or height of radio waves. This method was amplitude modulation, abbreviated as AM. In 1929 the inventor Edwin Armstrong developed a second way of transmitting information. He varied the frequency, that is, the number of waves that passed a fixed point per second, of radio waves. This method was frequency modulation, better known as FM.

The rapid growth of radio during the 1920s and 1930s made it possible for broadcasters to influence the behavior of listeners, as advertisers were quick to appreciate. Nothing underscored this fact more than the "War of the Worlds." On Oct. 30, 1938 listeners had tuned into a local station in Chicago for an evening of dance music. The host Orson Welles periodically interrupted the music with fictitious news bulletins describing an invasion of earth by Martians.

Minneapolis and St. Paul police switchboards were deluged with calls from frightened people.

The Times-Dispatch in Richmond, Va., reported some of their telephone calls from people who said they were "praying."

The Kansas City bureau of The Associated Press received inquiries on the "meteors" from Los Angeles, Salt Lake City, Beaumont, Texas, and St. Joseph, Mo., in addition to having its local switchboards flooded with calls. One telephone informant said he had loaded all his children into his car, had filled it with gasoline, and was going somewhere. "Where is it safe?" he wanted to know.

Atlanta reported that listeners throughout the Southeast "had it that a planet struck in New Jersey, with monsters and almost everything and anywhere from 40 to 7,000 people reported killed." Editors said responsible persons, known to them, were among the anxious information seekers.

In Birmingham, Ala., people gathered in groups and prayed, and Memphis had its full quota of weeping women calling in to learn the facts.

In Indianapolis a woman ran into a church screaming: "New York destroyed; it's the end of the world. You might as well go home to die. I just heard it on the radio." Services were dismissed immediately.

Five students at Brevard College, N. C., fainted and panic gripped the campus for a half hour with many students fighting for telephones to ask their parents to come and get them. A man in Pittsburgh said he returned home in the midst of the broadcast and found his wife in the bathroom, a bottle of poison in her hand, and screaming: "I'd rather die this way than like that."

He calmed her, listened to the broadcast and then rushed to a telephone to get an explanation.

Officials of station CFRB, Toronto, said they never had had so many inquiries regarding a single broadcast, the Canadian Press reported.

Further Resources

BOOKS

Brady, Frank. *Citizen Welles: A Biography of Orson Welles.* New York: Scribner, 1989.

Callow, Simon. *Orson Welles.* New York: Viking Press, 1996.

———. *Orson Welles: The Road to Xanadu.* New York: Viking, 1996.

Fitzgerald, Martin. *The Essential Orson Welles.* London: Pocket Essentials, 2000.

Higham, Charles. *Orson Welles: The Rise and Fall of an American Genius.* New York: St Martin's Press, 1985.

McBride, Joseph. *Orson Welles.* New York: Da Capo Press, 1996.

Welles, Orson, and Peter Bogdanovich. *This Is Orson Welles.* Jonathan Rosenbaum, ed. NewYork: Da Capo Press, 1998.

Wells, H.G. *The War of the Worlds.* Toronto and New York: Bantam, 1988.

PERIODICALS

Orson Welles Obituary. *The New York Times,* October 11, 1985.

WEBSITES

R Cubed Productions. "Orson Welles Resource Page." Available online at http://www.rcubedproductions.com/orson.html; website home page: http://www.rcubedproductions.com/ (accessed October 16, 2002).

The War of the Worlds—The Script. Available online at http://members.aol.com/jeff1070/script.html; website home page: http://members.aol.com/jeff1070/wotw.html (accessed March 18, 2003).

AUDIO AND VISUAL MEDIA

Koch, Howard, and John Houseman. "War of the Worlds." Directed by Orson Welles. The Mercury Theater on the Air program transcript. October 30, 1938. Available online at http://www.unknown.nu/mercury; website home page: http://www.unknown.nu (accessed October 16, 2002).

KTSA Broadcast: "Orson Welles Meets H.G. Wells (October 28, 1940)." Available online at http://www.unknown.nu/mercury/40128.ra; website home page: http://www.unknown.nu/mercury/ (accessed October 16, 2002).

Original *War of the Worlds* 1938 Broadcast. The Official Grover's Mill War of the Worlds. Available online at http://www.waroftheworlds.org/the_broadcast.htm (accessed March 1, 2003).

"Television in the 1930s"

Magazine article

By: Ranger

Date: June 1939

Source: Ranger. "Television in the 1930s." *Esquire,* June 1939. Reprinted online at http://www.tvhistory.tv/1939-June-Esquire.jpg; website home page: http://www.tvhistory.tv/ (accessed March 1, 2003).

About the Publication: Begun in the fall of 1933, *Esquire* remains a monthly magazine marketed towards males and includes commentary on trends in American culture—from fashion and entertainment to politics, technology, and fitness. In more recent years the *Esquire* publishers have put out a line of guide books titled *Things a Man Should Know* that cover topics such as personal style and marriage. ■

Introduction

Although Americans first heard of television years before its much-publicized appearance at the 1939 World's Fair, the celebration marked a turning point for the history of the medium. Herbert Hoover, the secretary of commerce and later president, starred in the first public demonstration when he gave a speech in Washington, D.C., that American Telephone and Telegraph transmitted to viewers in New York City in 1927. But on April

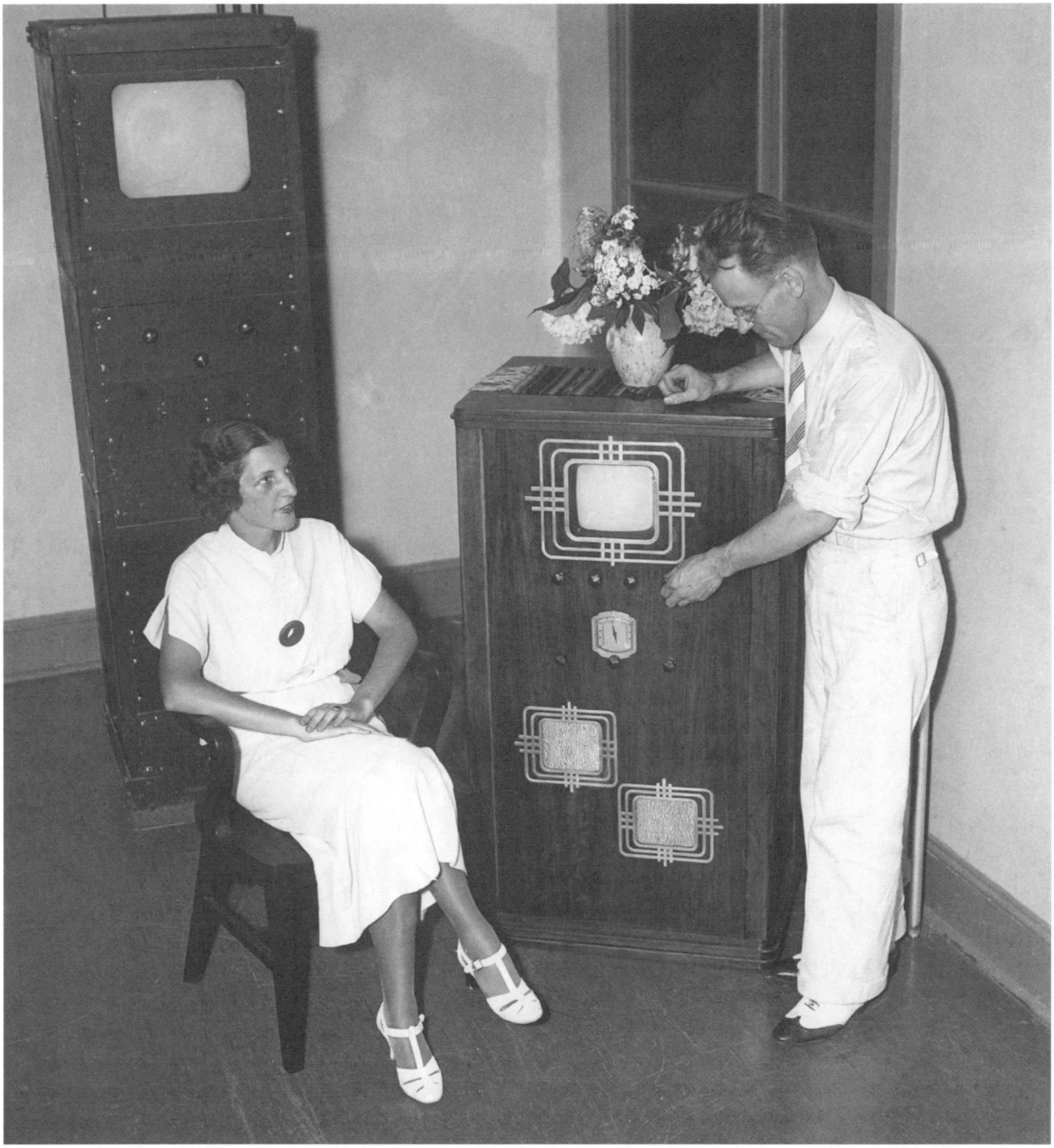

Television pioneer Philo T. Farnsworth demonstrates his combination radio and television in 1935. © **BETTMANN/CORBIS. REPRODUCED BY PERMISSION.**

30, 1939, Franklin D. Roosevelt became the first sitting president to utilize television to make a public address. In grandiose displays, the fair depicted the "radio with pictures" as the wave of the future. Yet, as the *Esquire* article written above the name "Ranger" below makes clear, television remained far outside the reach of most Americans technically and economically in the 1930s.

Significance

Esquire paid special attention to the problems that hindered television's growth during the Depression, as "in the east, television on a weekly basis is available only to those living within a fifty mile radius of Manhattan." Paling in comparison to the widespread enjoyment of radio, television broadcasts were few and far

A boy watches a baseball game on television on September 6, 1939. Sports broadcasts were among the earliest television programs. © SCHENECTADY MUSEUM; HALL OF ELECTRICAL HISTORY FOUNDATION/CORBIS. REPRODUCED BY PERMISSION.

between during the 1930s. Except for Chicago and New York City, virtually the entire U.S. population lived outside of the receiving range of television transmissions. Even New Yorkers rich enough to purchase a television could watch programs only a few hours per day on select days of the week.

The Great Depression dominated American life in this decade and certainly helped postpone television's boom until well into the next decade. World War II freed Americans from the bonds of economic devastation, but the great conflict also stopped virtually all nonmilitary research and development. The Federal Communications Commission stopped most television broadcasts, and viewers waited until after the war to see TV's most dramatic evolution.

Primary Source

"Television in the 1930s"

SYNOPSIS: True to its positioning as a publication in sync with developments in the arts, politics, and consumer technology, *Esquire* covered the 1939 World's Fair in New York City with a keen interest in how the fair's exhibits may impact readers. Given television's prominent role in the fair and its growing appeal in American society, *Esquire* published the following article to provide a brief history of the technology and, it seems, hint at the possibly pivotal role it would soon play in the world.

Long awaited, but always just a step around the corner, television has finally arrived. Ever since 1817, when a Swedish pharmacist discovered a strange element he named selenium, television enthusiasts have worked steadily to eliminate its perplexing engineering problems. This year, New York witnessed the results of this century of experimenting and planning when for the first time, a major radio company went "on the air" with a regular television program. On April 30th, coincidental with the World's Fair opening, a two hour weekly schedule of public telecasts began.

It is true that the field is still definitely limited, for in the east, television on a weekly basis is available only to those living within a fifty mile radius of Manhattan. Its costs are also somewhat above the level that permits mass consumption. But the price of television sets is rapidly being lowered, and they now range anywhere from $100 to $1000, depending upon the size of the image and several other factors. The usual radio outlets, including department and radio stores, carry them. The experimental sets were rather formidable with an array of fourteen tuning knobs, but the 1939 model is practically as simple to operate as the ordinary radio set. The clarity with which both image and voice come in is an unfailing source of surprise to those seeing a telecast for the first time. Newspapers and magazine photographs are misleading, as the camera catches the lines on the screen, which move too quickly for the eye to see. In addition, the screen's light values are too weak to produce a strong photographic impression.

Experimentations with program material have covered a wide range of possibilities. This summer, the more important ceremonies out in Flushing Meadows will be a major part of the schedule, television doing what amounts to a newsreel job on the Fair. These outside pick-ups are handled by a telemobile unit consisting of two large vans, one a transmitter, the other a control room. There will also be some studio productions and telecasts from Radio City. In the past, scripts and entertainers from the theatre, cinema and radio have been used. Simple program material has been the rule—one-act plays, newsreels, vaudeville and the like. Finding the type of material most suited to the medium, and finding it in sufficient variety and scope has been the crux of the problem.

Experts, readying television for public consumption, have had to iron out many other problems of a less prominent nature. Make-up, which today is similar to that used in movies, in 1930 involved painting the face white and the lips black. Although several inventors have claimed success in the production of color television, a few peculiarities remain. Red photographs as a light grey, and a young dancer, recently performing before the camera in a wide red sash, appeared on the screen with her midriff completely bare. Television does not however, as some would seem to believe, have any x-ray potentialities.

Because the possibility of broadcasting full length film features is limited, television will have little effect on the movies. Its use of motion picture material should expand rather than curb the popularity of the movies. It is a separate and distinct medium, and with little interference to existing forms of public diversion, may well become the most comprehensive means of wholesale entertainment and education.

Further Resources

BOOKS

Barnouw, Erik. *Tube of Plenty: The Evolution of American Television.* New York: Oxford University Press, 1975.

Greenfield, Jeff. *Television: The First Fifty Years.* New York: Crescent Books, 1981.

Kisselhoff, Jeff. *The Box: An Oral History of Television, 1929–1961.* New York: Viking, 1995.

PERIODICALS

Melniker, Joanne. "1948 Is Television's Big Boom Year." *Look,* July 20, 1948, 28–33.

WEBSITES

Boyd, Lydia. "Brief History of the Television Industry." Ad*Access. Duke University. Available online at http://scriptorium.lib.duke.edu/adaccess/tv-history.html (accessed March 1, 2003).

"The Iconography of Hope: The 1939–40 New York World's Fair." American Studies at the University of Virginia. Available online at http://xroads.virginia.edu/g/1930s/DISPLAY/39wf/front.htm (accessed March 1, 2003).

"Television in the World of Tomorrow." MZTV Museum. Available online at http://www.mztv.com/worldhome.html (accessed March 1, 2003).

9

MEDICINE AND HEALTH

SUSAN P. WALTON

Entries are arranged in chronological order by date of primary source. For entries with one primary source, the entry title is the same as the primary source title. Entries with more than one primary source have an overall entry title, followed by the titles of the primary sources.

CHRONOLOGY

PRIMARY SOURCES

Important Events in Medicine and Health, 1930–1939

1930

- Anesthesia is advanced with the increased use of Avertin, originally developed in Germany.
- Tincture of merthiolate gains widespread popularity for painting cuts and scratches after adding alcohol to sanitize the cut and vegetable dye to make it show on the skin.
- Spleen X rays are accomplished by injecting emulsions of iodized nutrient oils into the bloodstream.
- *The Human Mind* by Menninger Clinic psychiatrist Karl Menninger popularizes psychiatry as a source of help for the mentally ill.
- On January 28, Prohibition reaches its tenth anniversary as the Metropolitan Life Insurance Company reports that deaths from alcoholism are soaring.
- In February, scientists at the U.S. Public Health Service begin growing the rickettsia bacterium as a prelude to developing a typhus vaccine.
- On April 8, Congress creates the National Institutes of Health.
- In April, isolation of the hormone cortin from the cortex of the suprarenal glands proves useful in the treatment of Addison's disease.
- In May, Harvard Medical School scientists find a lack of vitamin B in the diet causes a paralysis in animals similar to that of humans suffering from pernicious anemia.
- On May 24, a *Reader's Digest* poll shows the majority of Americans favor repeal of Prohibition laws.
- On May 30, the first International Congress of Mental Hygiene is held in Washington, D.C.
- On June 6, frozen food arrives on the market.
- In June, scientists at Texas A&M University discover that viruses cause the common cold.
- On June 27, Diathermy—an electrical method of elevating body temperature—is used to treat patients with paresis, a disease of the central nervous system caused by syphilis.
- In August, Johns Hopkins University scientists develop a new method for diagnosing brain tumors by injecting air into the brain under local anesthesia, then using X rays.
- In September, the *American Journal of the Diseases of Childhood* reports that a balanced diet rich in vitamin D prevents dental cavities in children but that antiseptic mouthwashes are of little value.
- In September, Duke University Hospital and Medical School open.
- On October 25, an artificial respirator treats acute respiratory failure of infantile paralysis, newborn asphyxia, and other diseases.
- In November, Cornell University scientists discover that injected adrenaline increases blood pressure and is valuable in treating traumatic shock, bronchial asthma, hives, and hay fever.

1931

- Alka-Seltzer gains acceptance for treating headaches, hangovers, and upset stomachs.
- Death rates from childbirth are greater in the United States than in any other of the twenty nations with available statistics; doctors attribute this to the isolation of pregnant women from medical care.
- In January, rheumatoid arthritis is identified as a streptococcal infection.
- On March 20, the U.S. Federal Council of Churches approves the use of limited birth control.
- In June, New York obstetricians report the drug pernocton makes childbirth nearly painless without the possible harm to babies from other drugs.
- On June 20, Ernest Goodpasture adopts the technique of inoculation on the chorioallantoic membrane of a chick for use in virology.
- In July, Max Theiler infects monkeys with the poliomyelitis virus.
- In August, Metropolitan Life Insurance Company statistics show that deaths from appendicitis continue to increase.
- In August, *The Journal of the American Medical Association* reports early diagnosis of pregnancy by injecting small quantities of a woman's urine into a castrated female mouse; if it goes into heat the woman is pregnant.
- On September 3, chemists find a growth hormone in the pituitary gland.
- On October 17, the National Advisory Council on Radio in Education begins a series of fifteen-minute radio talks called *Psychology Today.*
- On December 31, Dr. Frederick Eberson of the University of California Medical School announces that he has grown the poliomyelitis virus and has reproduced the disease in monkeys; he hopes his discovery will lead to a vaccine for the disease.

1932

- In January, the U.S. Public Health Service begins the Tuskegee Syphilis Experiment on African Americans in Alabama that seeks to chronicle the progression of untreated syphilis.
- In February, a serum is developed to treat yellow fever.
- In March, scientists at the Missouri Agricultural Experiment Station discover the B vitamin riboflavin.
- On April 4, vitamin C is identified and isolated.
- In June, the Benzedrine inhaler is introduced as a nasal decongestant with amphetamine as its active ingredient.

- In July, the poliomyelitis virus is grown in a petri dish.
- On August 29, Harvey Williams Cushing describes the syndrome that bears his name.
- In September, scientists at Northwestern University School of Medicine demonstrate that extract of the gastric mucous membrane of swine, served in ice cream, malted milk, or fruit juices, can cure stomach ulcers.
- In November, the Chicago Institute for Psychoanalysis is established.

1933

- In January, sodium pentothal, an intravenous barbiturate, is used to anesthetize a patient before surgery.
- In February, Blue Cross introduces insurance to cover hospital costs.
- In April, scientists present a new method for treating certain forms of chronic heart disease; the metabolic rate is lowered by removing the thyroid gland, decreasing the body's demand on the heart.
- On April 5, the first successful surgery to remove a cancerous lung is performed.
- In August, a dysentery epidemic in Chicago demonstrates that the disease is not limited to tropical areas, as had been thought.
- From August 7 to September 10, an encephalitis epidemic in Saint Louis kills more than 100 people.
- On September 18, the U.S. Children's Bureau estimates that half of all preschoolers and schoolchildren suffer malnutrition and lack of medical care.
- On November 4, scientists report success in treating obesity by using the drug alpha-dinitrophenol to increase the patient's metabolism but caution against the drug's potential lethality.
- On December 11, physicians report a new technique to transplant portions of the thyroid and parathyroid glands from one patient to another.
- On December 21, the first dried human blood serum is prepared.

1934

- On September 4, Evipan, a new German anesthetic, is first tried in the United States in a George Washington University Medical School postgraduate clinic.
- In October, the Rockefeller Institute for Medical Research develops a vaccine for psittacosis (parrot fever).
- On December 12, George Hoyt Whipple, George Minot, and William P. Murphy win the Nobel Prize for medicine or physiology for liver therapy against anemia.
- Liver extract cures agranulocytosis, a blood disease that kills all untreated victims.

1935

- In January, chemists synthesize Riboflavin (Vitamin B2).
- In May, the Board of Education of New York City reports 18 percent of the city's pupils are malnourished.
- In June, the first hospital for drug addicts is founded at Lexington, Kentucky.
- On June 10, Alcoholics Anonymous is founded in New York City.
- On June 20, Dr. Alexis Carrel, surgeon and biologist, with the assistance of aviator Charles A. Lindbergh, announces the perfection of the first mechanical "heart," a pumping device that can keep different types of tissues and organs alive outside the body.
- Between June and July, epidemics of polio occur throughout the country.
- In July, stomach ulcers are attributed to pure gastric juices.
- In August, Yale University scientists observe that primates who have had a bilateral prefrontal lobotomy are calm, even when presented with difficult problems.
- On August 9, Congress passes the Social Security Act, which includes funds to states for setting up public health programs.
- In October, polio vaccine trials inoculate three thousand children—several contract polio and one dies, leading the public to fear vaccination.
- On October 7, Edward Calvin Kendall and Tadeus Reichstein isolate cortisone.

1936

- In January, the Federal Children's Bureau notes a decrease in infant mortality but calls attention to the fact that fifty-nine per ten thousand women die during childbirth in 1934, a rate higher than that in many European countries.
- In January, chemists synthesize Thiamine (Vitamin B1).
- In February, Long and Bliss introduce sulfa drugs in the United States.
- In March, schizophrenic patients are treated with insulin doses to create hypoglycemic shock.
- On May 14, Missouri doctors criticize the use of drugs for painless childbirth.
- In June, scientists at the Rockefeller Institute grow poliovirus in human brain cells.
- On August 14, the Social Security Act calls for setting aside funds for grants-in-aid to states for maternal and child-health services, especially in poor and rural areas.
- In October, Dilantin (diphenylhydantoin) comes on the market as the first successful anticonvulsive treatment for epilepsy since phenobarbital and is also used to treat abnormal heartbeats.
- On November 30, birth control under medical direction is recognized as legal by the U.S. Circuit Court of Appeals for the Second Circuit.
- In December, the alkaloid ergonovine is used to treat postpartum uterine bleeding.

1937

- In March, German scientists develop a yellow-fever vaccine. Max Theiler criticizes its toxicity in humans.
- In March, Ochsner and DeBakey attribute lung cancer to cigarette smoking.

- On March 15, the first modern blood bank is established at the Cook County Hospital in Chicago.
- In April, children die after treatment with an elixir of the antibacterial drug sulfanilamide.
- On April 1, forty-two states approve plans for crippled children under the Social Security Act.
- In June, the American Medical Association approves birth control as an essential part of medical practice and education.
- On June 14, the National Cancer Institute is established.
- On June 23, Yale University professors announce the isolation of the pituitary hormone.
- In August, zinc protamine, the most important advance in treating diabetes since Sir Frederick Grant Banting's discovery of insulin in 1922, is introduced.
- In August, a Federal Children's Bureau study announces the mortality rate of African American infants for the years 1933 to 1935 is 86 per 1,000 live births as compared to 53 per 1,000 for white infants.
- From August 30 to August 31, the first meetings of the American Association of Applied Psychologists are held.
- On September 23, the National Foundation for Infantile Paralysis is founded in Warm Springs, Georgia.
- In October, a new closed-plaster method for treating compound fractures reduces infections.
- In December, niacin treats pellagra, a niacin-deficiency disease.
- In December, sulfanilamide (para-amino-benzene-sulfonamide) is used to treat streptococcus infections.

1938

- On February 24, the first commercial product using the synthetic fabric nylon—toothbrushes with nylon bristles—goes on sale in New Jersey.
- In March, physicians increase the prothrombin content of the blood by administering vitamin K derived from fish meal, bile, and bile salts to treat bleeding in jaundice patients.
- On April 12, New York becomes the first state to require medical tests for marriage license applicants.
- On April 20, birth-control movement pioneer Margaret Sanger declares birth control is finally legal in the United States, except for Connecticut, Mississippi, and Massachusetts.
- In May, coccidioidomycosis, or "valley fever," common in California, is discovered to result from inhaling dust containing the fungus coccidioides, which infects the upper respiratory tract.
- On June 27, after more than 100 people die from an antibiotic, Congress enacts the Food, Drug, and Cosmetic Act, which bans potentially dangerous drugs.
- In November, sodium diphenyl hydantoinate is used to treat epilepsy.
- On November 27, Congress enacts the Venereal Disease Control Act, which provides federal funds for the prevention, treatment, and control of venereal diseases.

1939

- In January, the steroid diethylstilbestrol treats menopause in women.
- In February, the U.S. Justice Department charges the American Medical Association, the Medical Society of the Washington, D.C., and other medical societies and hospitals with creating a monopoly in the heath-care industry.
- On February 28, the U.S. Senate debates the Wagner Health Bill but does not vote on it.
- In March, Blue Shield introduces insurance to pay for physicians' charges.
- State public-health agencies receive federal payments totaling $3,724,362 under the Social Security Act Amendments of 1939.
- On May 1, President Franklin D. Roosevelt proclaims this day as Child Health Day.
- On May 9, the New York City Department of Health reports success in curing syphilis in its first stage with massive doses of neoarsphenamine, a chemotherapeutic agent.
- In June, Australian scientist Howard Walter Florey purifies penicillin.
- In June, the Rh factor in human blood is discovered.
- In July, the U.S. Census Bureau reports the lowest maternal and infant mortality rates on record for the United States in 1938.
- In October, Addison's disease is treated with the hormone desoxycorticosterone acetate.

Opinions on Mental Health

Dr. Karl A. Menninger, February 7, 1935. Dr. Menninger's advice column for *Ladies Home Journal* entitled "Mental Hygiene in the Home" was a pioneering effort to make mental health theory applicable to the public. AP/WIDE WORLD PHOTOS. REPRODUCED BY PERMISSION.

Exchange of Letters Between an Anonymous Patient and Dr. Karl Menninger

Letters

By: Anonymous and Dr. Karl Menninger

Date: 1930

Source: Anonymous, and Dr. Karl Menninger. Exchange of Letters Between an Anonymous Patient and Dr. Karl Menninger, 1930. Originally published in *Ladies' Home Journal,* 1932. Reprinted in Faulkner, Howard J., and Virginia D. Pruitt, eds. *Dear Dr. Menninger: Women's Voices from the Thirties.* Columbia, Mo.: University of Missouri Press, 1997, 47–50.

The Human Mind

Guidebook

By: Dr. Karl Menninger

Date: 1930

Source: Menninger, Karl A. *The Human Mind.* New York: Knopf, 1930.

About the Author: Dr. Karl Menninger (1893–1990), author of *The Human Mind,* studied medicine at Harvard and helped establish the still well-known Menninger Clinic. From 1930 to 1932, he had an advice column in the *Ladies' Home Journal.* American women living during the Great Depression sent him letters. The writers asked for advice about various personal problems, and Dr. Menninger answered each of them. ■

Introduction

In the early 1930s, two theories of mental illness were common. One held that mental illness could be cured through physical treatment. The other held that mental illness could be cured through a process called mental hygiene. The idea of mental hygiene grew out of the experience of Clifford Beers. In the first years of the century, Beers had what was then termed a "nervous breakdown" and spent several years undergoing treatment in mental hospitals until he finally recovered spontaneously. His account, *A Mind That Found Itself,* described the harsh treatment he had received. To replace this treatment with a humane and compassionate approach, Beers founded the first society for mental hygiene in Connecticut. In 1909, he established the National Committee for Mental Hygiene. In 1930, the First International Congress on Mental Hygiene was held in Washington, D.C., with Beers as a speaker.

Mental hygiene was drawn from various schools, including psychiatry, psychology, and psychoanalysis. The *Psychiatric Dictionary* (Oxford, 1996) defines it as an approach designed "to develop optimal modes of personal and social conduct in order to produce the happiest utilization of inborn endowments and capacities" and also to prevent mental disorders. In contrast, one contemporary practitioner, writing in the journal *Social Forces* in 1930, notes that mental hygiene is not psychiatry. "Mental hygiene is mental sanitation. It involves the intellectual grasp, the emotional acceptance, and the continuous utilization of certain principles and techniques of wholesome living which enable one to employ his abilities and capacities more fully and effectively in work and enjoyment."

Menninger believed that mental health depended on the interplay of several factors. In the introduction to *Dear Dr. Menninger,* Howard Faulkner and Virginia Pruitt describe Menninger's view as "his conviction . . . that mental diseases are not fixed or static conditions that can be isolated from environmental factors but rather can be understood only in the total context of an individual's history, relationships, and continuous attempts at adjustment."

Menninger was well known when he began writing his column "Mental Hygiene in the Home" for the *Ladies' Home Journal.* Newspaper advice columns were common by the 1930s. An advice column in which the sender would remain anonymous served as a sympathetic ear for problems that writers would not share with people they knew. Menninger was especially attractive because he was a doctor. During the eighteen months he wrote the column, he received thousands of letters from women all over the United States.

Significance

The Human Mind was the first book aimed at explaining the workings of the mind to the general reader that captured readers' attention. The book was a bestseller and a selection of the Literary Guild, with a first printing of seventy thousand copies. Sydney Smith, a psychologist, writes in the introduction of a book honoring Menninger's work that "no such treatise accessible to the intelligent layman had been previously written." After living through the horror of World War I (1914–1918) and the economic rise and fall of the 1920s, the public felt the need to understand human behavior.

The book was also groundbreaking in that it dealt with mental illness as treatable, sometimes curable. Menninger favored psychoanalysis, and if that was not available to his readers (which often it was not), he suggested intense self-examination.

Menninger's use of real people as examples also set a precedent. This practice made sense. Readers who grew bored with abstract descriptions would be more likely to follow the story of a person whose problems might be like their own. The technique of mixing these stories with theory has become standard in modern self-help books. Libraries and bookstores have entire sections devoted to self-help, a term that Menninger did not use but which clearly shows his influence.

Primary Source

Exchange of Letters Between an Anonymous Patient and Dr. Karl Menninger

SYNOPSIS: This excerpt from *Dear Dr. Menninger: Women's Voices from the Thirties* reflects some of the concerns presented by women with regard to mental health and Dr. Menninger's opinions regarding some of their causes.

Missouri

Nov. 15, 1930

Dear Sir,

I am coming to you with my own mental problem, whether it is based on a bodily ailment I do not know, anyway I think my problem is one commonly known as "nerves."

I am twenty eight years old, the wife of a farmer in very moderate circumstances and the mother of four children.

My first mental trouble came upon me when I was sixteen years old. After a busy day I went to bed, only to experience a feeling that I had never had before, that of a great oppression coming over me; I could not get my breath and I thought I was dying. I rushed to my parents' bedroom in great fear and tried to explain to them what I was going through. Then I was afraid to go to sleep for fear I would die. The next morning I had a headache and temperature and suffered an attack of the "flu." That was the year during the war when influenza was so prevalent.

After I was well again I resumed my high school work, but that awful fear came over me when I went to bed at night. Some of the same sensations came over me. No one whom I told seemed to understand me. So my nights were horrors and my days came to be days of brooding. I dreaded to be by myself for my thoughts seemed to always turn toward that "something the matter with me." I constantly sought something to take my mind off of my troubles, somewhere to go or something to do. I was a rather highstrung child, my parents always said, my father was on that order, too. I had diseased tonsils which were removed just a few months before the occurrence which I have already mentioned.

I gradually overcame my trouble within the next few years. At the age of twenty I married. When I was twenty-one my first child was born. Then by the time three years and eight months had elapsed I had had my fourth child.

When my second baby was four months old I again had a similar experience to that of my girlhood. Lying in bed one night I thought I was dying. Then after that sensation was over, everything seemed blurred to me, that is, my senses were dulled, my head having great pressure in it, a horrible depression came over me, and I decided then that I must be losing my mind or having something happening to it. I went into hysterics one day and the doctor was called. He told me it was just my "nerves" and not to worry. He told me also that I had a simple goiter.

It took me a year to gain much strength and I had that feeling that there was something the matter with me and I was different from others. I was so afraid I would not be right.

My husband was not very sympathetic with me. I realize he did not understand my trouble. Every winter since I have had more or less trouble in the same manner. Every once in a while I have one of those sinking, swimming, "falling away" sensations but I try not to let them frighten me. Last winter I became so depressed one night that I went into hysterics. Then for a couple of months I was dull and depressed. Horrible thoughts entered my mind. I was afraid I might lose control of myself and harm someone. At times my spirits would rise and I would be happy.

Now this winter I am threatened again with thoughts which come without my bidding and almost paralyze me. I have a sharp pain in the region of my goiter at times, and often a feeling as if I had something tied around my neck. I am also constipated most of the time.

It is my desire to make a happy home and rear good Christian children. But I do not seem to be able to handle children right, and they quarrel so, which only upsets me and makes me nervous and weak. I suffer far more in a way than I did a few years ago. I like beauty, neatness and order in my home and it is not possible. That frets me. I work hard, do every bit of the housework and laundering and help my husband when he needs me, out-of-doors.

I teach a Sunday school class and am the president of the Neighborhood Club. I like to do these things, but so often I find myself dull and weary, irritable and cross. I feel that my life needs adjustment. I want to learn to know the true values of life.

For years I felt that my marriage was unsatisfactory for all my friends were starting professional work, while I was drudging away bearing children too fast and working too hard, worrying and fretting, with it. My disposition changed from one which was seldom ruffled outwardly to a "crosspatch."

I am getting away from some of those old ideas and now I want a set of mental hygiene rules which will help me to be happy. I know happiness is in the reach of all, but I do not seem to know how to find it.

May the Lord greatly enrich you if you can help me.

Yours truly,
[Anonymous]

Dec. 12, 1930

My dear Mrs. ———:

Your letter of November 15 addressed to me in care of the *Ladies' Home Journal* has been carefully read.

From your description I should say that there is not very much doubt about the type of trouble from which you suffer. Your description is almost classically that of the nervous disease which we know as anxiety neurosis. Now that I have told you the name of it I don't know that I have helped you very much. You may want to read about it; I have written about it myself in my book called *The Human Mind* which is about the mind and its afflictions and which I think you might enjoy reading.

The particular things that you ought to know about your trouble are these. In the first place, you will never die in one of these attacks, terrible as they seem at times. You will be amused at the story about the policeman in my book on page 251, who was not afraid of anything in the world and yet used to get so frightened at nothing at all. You will not die, you will probably not do anything horrible either to yourself or to anyone else, you will not lose your mind. But you will suffer the tortures of the damned. Nothing is more distressing than this sense of anxiety and fear which is so typical of these attacks or panics.

They are caused by disturbances in the depths of the mind, the part which is known as the subconscious or unconscious part of the mind. A good deal can be done by a skilled specialist in the way of eradicating the cause of them. But you do not live anywhere near a good psychoanalyst and if you can possibly get along without taking treatments I know you want to do so. I think perhaps my reassurance that nothing terrible will come of them, in spite of the way you feel, will help you some and then I also want to make another suggestion which is rather difficult to make clear in a letter but which I shall attempt. In some instances these attacks come because of the lack of satisfaction in the sexual life. You did not mention anything about this in your letter and of course I know nothing about it in your particular instance. Sometimes, however, it is very helpful for the husband to talk this over very frankly with a doctor and get him to help you both to arrange your sexual life in such a way that it gives you complete satisfaction if possible. Some husbands do not realize how important it is for their wife's health. They are apt to be so engrossed in their own satisfaction that they forget their wives. This is not due to unkindness or meanness on their part but usually due to a lack of understanding. I think, perhaps, if your husband had his attention called to it and perhaps had a little help in the matter, it would do you both a great deal of good. There are a number of books discussing such things; I often refer people to some books by Dr. Robie; next time you are in Kansas City stop in to a second hand bookstore and any book by Dr. Robie is a good one. I believe one of them is called *Rational Sex Ethics* and another one is called *Love and Life* or something of the sort. I don't remember just the titles but the books all deal in general with the same thing. Most sex books are not very satisfactory in their discussion of it. Of course, I have taken a long shot in the dark because I don't know whether this applies in your case but it does in some.

May I add a final word about your children. All children quarrel; it is a part of the battle of life on a small scale. They have to learn the technique of fighting as well as other forms of life. Don't be too disturbed about it. I think it might reassure you and help you a little to read some of the books on child culture which are now so numerous. Particularly one by Garry Myers called *The Modern Parent* and one which Mr. Crawford and I have edited called *The Healthy-Minded Child.* If I can find one I will enclose a circular describing it.

Sincerely yours,
[Signature] Dr. Karl Menninger

Primary Source

The Human Mind [excerpt]

SYNOPSIS: This excerpt from *The Human Mind* summarizes Menninger's approach to mental health.

When a trout rising to a fly gets hooked on a line and finds himself unable to swim about freely, he begins a fight which results in struggles and splashes and sometimes an escape. Often, of course, the situation is too tough for him.

In the same way the human being struggles with his environment and with the hooks that catch him. Sometimes he masters his difficulties; sometimes they are too much for him. His struggles are all that the world sees and it usually misunderstands them. It is hard for a free fish to understand what is happening to a hooked one.

Sooner or later, however, most of us get hooked. How much of a fight we have on our hands then depends on the hook, and, of course, on us. If the struggle gets too violent, if it throws us out of the water, if we run afoul of other strugglers, we become "cases" in need of help and understanding. Statistics say that one out of every twenty of us is, or has been, or will be, in a hospital for mental illness; and the other nineteen of us don't feel any too comfortable all of the time, even if we have no fears of such an extremity. The minor symptoms of the struggle are legion; mental ill health is certainly as common as physical ill health and probably much more so. Cicero said: "The diseases of the mind are more numerous and more destructive than those of the body." He was right. But they are not always recognized as such.

When a man is promoted to a new job and it worries him so much that he has to quit it; when a woman gets married, finds herself unfitted for married life, and becomes depressed; when a student goes to college with high hopes, but fails in half his subjects; when a soldier goes to war and develops shell-shock at the sound of the first gun; when a lad of promise spurns opportunities of achievement in favour of cheque-forging or automobile-stealing—then these people are mentally unhealthy; they are unable to adjust themselves to their environment. They are inept and they are unhappy; some of them will end their lives in tragedy.

Consider some more specific examples of hooked fish. Remember that you might not have thought of them so. "Eccentric," you might have said, "queer," perhaps even "just mean." But these are the sorts of struggle that indicate to the psychiatrist a fish hooked and in peril.

The Man Who Is Always Sick

Henry Clay is a clerk. He has always been a clerk. He will always be a clerk. When he isn't clerking, which he does mechanically, accurately, satisfactorily, he is contemplating his imminent death. He regards himself as suffering from tuberculosis, diabetes, rheumatism, heart-trouble, and goitre. He confidently expects that one or all of these will get the upper hand any minute and put him in his grave. He has never been able to get married because he spends all his savings on doctors' bills and new remedies.

The Scoffer

Weston Williams was the brilliant and handsome son of a wealthy father. Everything was done to afford opportunity for developing his intellectual talent. He was sent to the best schools and provided with the best of companions.

At twenty-seven he was a hard-boiled, scoffing, idle cynic. To exemplify his contempt for sentiment he married a girl thirty minutes after he met her; he did not even know her name. He divorced her and married a derelict, whom he picked up from the street, and upon whom he spent thousands of dollars, only to have her elope with another man after she became a presentable human being. He contemptuously rejected an opportunity to take the lead in a large business owned by his family and now lives anonymously on a small allowance sent to him by his family on condition that he stay away from home.

The Nagging Wife

Mrs. Watson is regarded by the women of her community as a brilliant, talented, charming woman. She presides over her committees, her clubs, and her parties with enviable grace and poise. Everyone assumes and believes that she is a beautiful wife and mother.

At home she nags the children, quarrels with her husband, mismanages her household, and points to her outside success as an indication that the fault is anyone's but hers.

The Incendiary

Helen Wilson had married well. Her husband made money and she made friends who were prominent in the social circles of her city. It was not until several fires had occurred that it dawned upon her husband that his wife had deliberately set them. When he accused her of it, she calmly and demurely denied it; even when indisputable proof was brought, she remained obdurate in her denials. For a time the fires ceased, but one night her husband awoke to see their garage in flames and to find his wife's place in bed empty.

The Merchant Turned Criminal

Howard Gilchrist is the false name for a well-known prisoner in the Kansas state penitentiary. Four years ago he was the owner of a Ford agency, which was making him about forty thousand dollars a year. He played pool in the evenings for amusement and met at the pool-room some gentlemen of fortune who induced him to lend them a car and later join them in half a dozen escapades of bank-robbing and car-stealing which netted him about five hundred dollars and ten years in the state prison.

The Man-haters

Mary's parents had done everything they could to break up a crush between her and her pal Nell, but in spite of tears and lectures and threats and scoldings Mary and Nell were steadfast. No other girls interested them; all men disgusted them. They were happy with each other even when they were quarrelling most bitterly. . . .

The Evolution of the Devil: What Is the Matter with These People?

Ever since the dawn of history society has been trying to decide. They have been called one thing and another; they have been pushed from pillar to post. All sorts of explanations have held popular sway.

Two thousand years ago it was *devils.* Persons and things were "possessed of devils." Jesus and others in the Bible cast out these devils. Some of the native Australians and Africans still interpret misbehaviour as demoniac possession.

But this Devil has undergone evolution. In the Middle Ages some of these people would have been called *witches* and others *bewitched.* The witches had sold themselves to Satan. And this amiable theory of misbehaviour and unhappiness still persists, not only in certain parts of Africa, but among certain groups in civilized countries.

A little later the Devil became *original sin.* Sincere, devout people still exist who regard the misbehaviour of mankind as nothing but the evidence of sinfulness. Their solution is religious salvation. Instead of burning and exiling these strange actors as the devil-believers did, or hanging them and drowning them as the witch-believers did, they would have them prayed with, exhorted, cajoled, threatened, frightened, and told to repent and believe in God.

Then there is a less religious but more practical-minded point of view which regards all misbehaviour as representing *orneriness, or pure cussedness.* Because this is simple, because it is less pretentious, it has a great following, especially among policemen, army sergeants, and the superintendents of girls' reformatories. Unfortunately it, too, is much of a pessimistic theory based on a sentimental rather than on an intellectual attitude toward the problem, so that its application is as fruitless as the application of the theories of witchcraft and devil-possession.

A little more recent in origin were the moralists. They linked up all behaviour, good and bad, with a mystical metaphysical essence called responsibility. According to this solemn theory, it isn't God or lack of God, or sin or the Devil or witches or anything celestial or mundane that makes men saints or sinners. It is a single, solemn imponderable called *responsibility.* Millions of dollars are spent annually to determine who has it or who hasn't it. If one is found to have it, he is locked up; if he is found not to have it, he is also locked up. Thus is demonstrated the pragmatic beauty of the doctrine, which is neither fish nor fowl, but which is still the shibboleth and the fallacy of the lawyers just as the doctrine of original sin was the fallacy of the clergy.

And next came the fallacy of the psychologists. When they discovered tests a few years ago which in a general way measured the amount of intelligence a person has, and began applying this test to people far and wide, they found out that many people had less of it than had been supposed. Accordingly they began to suspect that a person who got into trouble did so because he hadn't enough brains to keep out of trouble. *Feeblemindedness* became the explanation of all the woes of mankind, from bed-wetting to bootlegging. The psychologists no longer cling, officially, to this fallacy. They know, as does everyone else, that there is far more to the human mind than intelligence.

Then came the eugenists, for whom the Devil took the form of bad *heredity.* The fact that the children of feeble-minded parents sometimes become college professors and the fact that superior parents are often afflicted with inferior progeny has discouraged most of them.

The philosophers all this while were explaining it all as *human nature* (to which they assign numerous titles). Nations may rise and fall, social forms and economic systems may change ever so much, but something called human nature—so they insisted—remains unchanged. But what is this human nature? The same old Devil we have been discovering in the fallacious thinking of every group. . . .

We have good reasons for believing that there is no such thing as human nature, certainly not in the sense of a human nature independent of social-psychological-biological laws. And these are not something we can get moralistic about. This is a long-time philosophical fallacy.

And finally there came the great fallacy of the psychiatrists, who found yet another cloak for His Satanic Majesty. His new name was *insanity.* People who misbehaved seriously must be crazy, sometimes with craziness type A, sometimes craziness type X; sometimes benign, sometimes malignant. But always human misbehaviour was explained on the assumption that something from the outside world got into the inside of a hapless soul and made him do and feel as he shouldn't do and feel.

And this in general is the trouble with all these theories. They all assume that something mysterious and malignant floating in the ether or transmitted in the germ plasm gets into the individual and makes him go wrong. And then he gets called names. Calling people witches or devils or psychopathic personalities doesn't help. To do so doesn't indicate any real understanding or why they are what they are, why they do what they do, or what can be done to help matters. If any names are to be called, they ought to be names which imply something as to treatment.

Further Resources

BOOKS

Burnham, William H. *The Wholesome Personality.* New York: Appleton, 1932.

Smith, Sydney. *The Human Mind Revisited: Essays in Honor of Karl A. Menninger.* New York: International Universities Press, 1978.

PERIODICALS

Elder, Glen H., Jr. "Hard Times in Women's Lives: Historical Influences across Forty Years." *American Journal of Sociology* 88, 2, 1982, 249–261.

Jensen, Howard E. "Mental Hygiene and Family Counselling." *Social Forces* 17, 1: 90–98.

White, William A. "The Origin, Growth, and Significance of the Mental Hygiene Movement." *Science* 72, 1930, 77–81.

WEBSITES

Menninger Clinic home page. Available online at http://www.menningerclinic.com (accessed July 1, 2003).

Menninger's Move. *Topeka Capital-Journal.* Available online at http://www.cjonline.com/webindepth/menninger/; website home page: www.cjonline.com/ (accessed July 1, 2003).

Radio Address on a Program of Assistance for the Crippled

Radio address

By: Franklin D. Roosevelt

Date: February 18, 1931

Source: Roosevelt, Franklin D. Radio Address on a Program of Assistance for the Crippled, February 18, 1931. Available at the New Deal Network online at http://newdeal.feri.org/speeches/1931a.htm; website homepage http://newdeal.feri.org (accessed March 17, 2003).

About the Author: Franklin Delano Roosevelt (1882–1945) was the governor of New York State in 1931, and in 1932 was elected president of the United States. Roosevelt is famous for leading the nation through the Great Depression and World War II (1939–45), in the process serving longer than any other president (1933–45). At age thirty-nine, Roosevelt was cripled by polio. Although he spent seven years working to regain the use of his legs, his rehabilitation efforts failed, and he was left unable to walk independently. He took great pains to hide the extent of his disability from Americans and never used a wheelchair in public. ■

Introduction

The first major epidemic of polio, then called infantile paralysis because most of its victims were children, struck the United States in 1916, with twenty-seven thousand reported cases and six thousand deaths. The year that Roosevelt made this speech, New York City experienced an epidemic. In 1932, the year he won the presidency, an epidemic in Los Angeles left the streets in front of hospitals filled with polio patients on wheeled stretchers, turned away by hospital employees who were afraid of contracting the disease.

It is not clear why polio surfaced in epidemic form in the early decades of the twentieth century. Naomi Rogers, a historian and author of *Dirt and Disease: Polio Before FDR,* notes that in earlier years, the polio virus was present, but most children became immune through maternal antibodies or had a mild case of the disease as infants, which conferred lifelong immunity. In an ironic twist, major improvements in sanitation and public health made middle-class children more vulnerable because they were not exposed to the disease as infants.

The disease's unpredictable path was frightening enough. There was also no way to protect against it, and no effective way of treating or lessening its effects. These effects were unpredictable; once a person contracted polio, the disease ran its course. The possible outcomes ranged from complete recovery to death, with degrees of paralysis in between.

Polio was terrifying because it killed children (and older people, though most of its victims were under five years old). Almost as terrifying, though, was the realization that its victims could be left permanently and severely crippled. Some who survived were relatively lucky and could get around on crutches or in leg braces. Others used wheelchairs. The truly desperate cases were those victims who were confined to "iron lungs," machines that through mechanical pressure forced the person within to continue breathing even when he or she could not do so independently. Such equipment became increasingly sophisticated, but the early versions resembled large iron coffins.

Significance

Franklin Roosevelt was both a powerful politician and a polio victim. This speech marks the first step in what was to become his national crusade against the disease, one that was funded almost entirely by charitable organizations. His initial effort, outlined in this speech, seemed modest enough: to help children crippled by polio. The speech was, however, more than that; it represented the first time a politician championed the idea that people with physical disabilities should, in his words, be put "back on their feet." This idea was contrary to conventional wisdom, which held that people who were disabled by polio could no longer be useful. What is now known as rehabilitation was termed "after care" by Roosevelt, and it was a pioneering concept.

In his 1931 speech, Roosevelt outlined what would subsequently be viewed as normal practice with disabled people. He recognized that although the costs of a year or so of rehabilitation were relatively high, they were far lower than the cost of maintaining for life a disabled person who could not work. He used financial figures to argue his case, a practice now known as a cost/benefit analysis. Roosevelt showed that the benefits outweighed the costs. A thousand dollars spent on rehabilitation, or after care, would result in forty years of useful work from the person who had been rehabilitated. At the same time, once polio victims had received enough rehabilitation so that they could earn an income, the cost of rehabilitation was quickly eclipsed by their ability to support themselves.

Roosevelt's point of view had far-reaching effects. In the coming decades, Congress would enact laws that required facilities to be accessible to the handicapped. These laws changed handicapped people's lives in several ways. In education, the state was required to provide them, whatever their disability, with a "free and appropriate public education." In terms of logistics, Congress mandated that cities and towns that received federal funding make their public facilities accessible to people in wheelchairs. Though not a complex change, accessibility dramatically improved the self-sufficiency of wheelchair users.

Roosevelt was a major influence on Americans' attitude toward the disabled. Had Roosevelt not taken that first step toward acknowledging the rights of the "crippled children," the needs of the handicapped might have remained unmet for much longer.

Primary Source

Radio Address on a Program of Assistance for the Crippled

SYNOPSIS: In this 1931 radio address, Franklin Delano Roosevelt describes the plight of crippled children and gives his views on how their physical rehabilitation could make them productive members of society.

I believe it was announced that I was going to talk today on why it pays to do things for crippled children

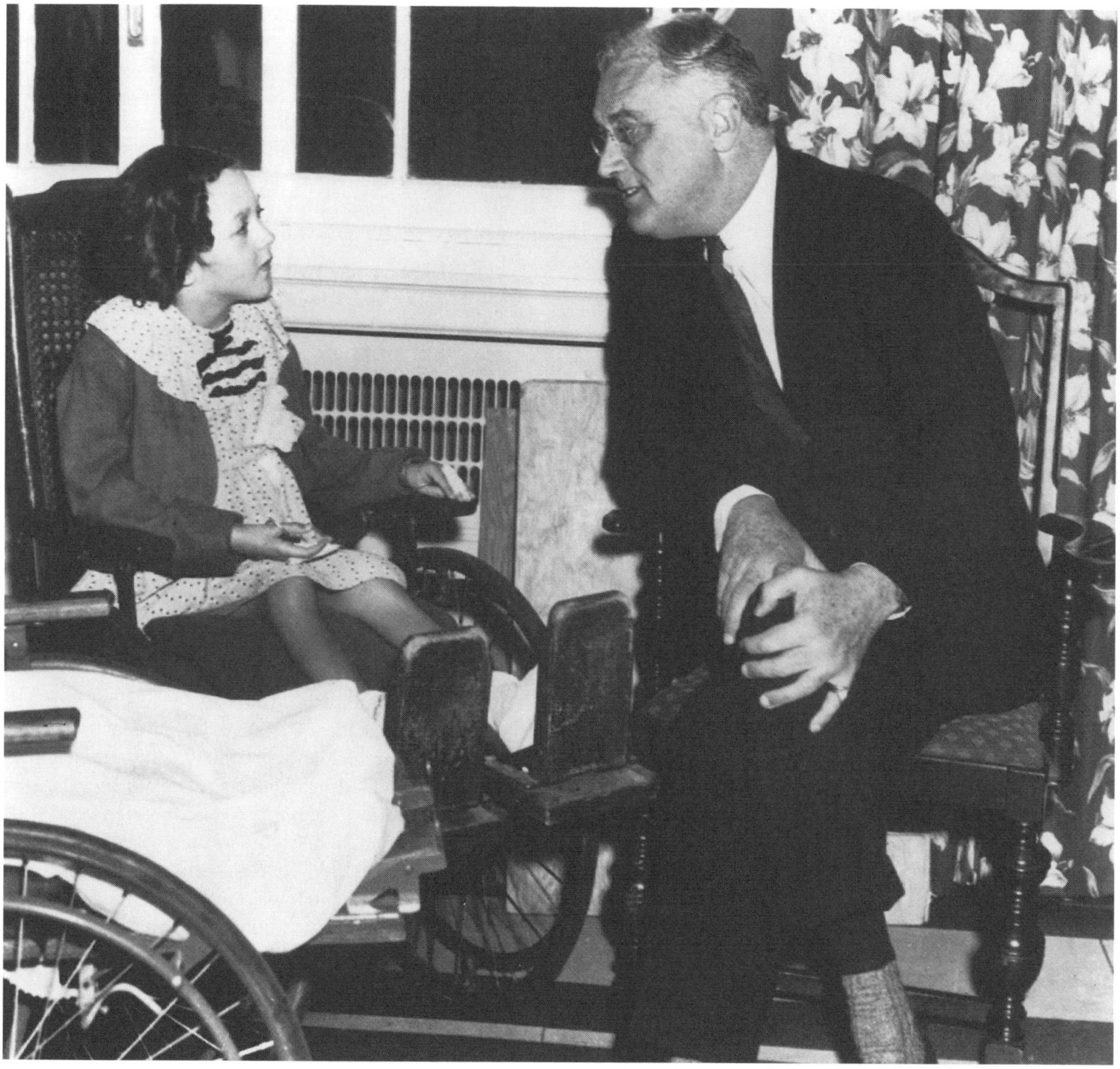

President Franklin D. Roosevelt talks with Renee Daly, Warm Springs, Georgia, April 2, 1938. A polio victim himself, Roosevelt led a national crusade against the disease. He also pioneered the idea that people with disabilities can still be productive members of society. CORBIS-BETTMANN. REPRODUCED BY PERMISSION.

and, I might add to that, other kinds of cripples—grown-up cripples as well. I want to talk, of course, about the big human side of relieving distress and helping people to get on their feet, but at the same time I think there is another phase of the broad question of looking after cripples to which some people have never given much thought—the financial side. For instance, I am told that there are somewhere between three and four hundred thousand cripples in this country today—I mean cripples who are pretty thoroughly put out of business, who cannot get around, who cannot perform any useful task—people, in other words, most of them children, who have to be looked after by other people. Think of it, three or four hundred thousand people out of our total population. This is a tremendous percentage.

Now let us figure for a minute in simple terms. Suppose for the sake of argument that three hundred thousand people are out of useful work when they grow to be older and that each one of them, if he could work, could produce one thousand dollars' worth of new products every year. In other words, if the productive value were one thousand dollars a year apiece, three hundred thousand of them would mean three hundred million dollars added to the annual productive capacity of the United States. That is worth thinking about from the purely money end of things. If we could restore every cripple in this country to some kind of useful occupation it would do much to help the general wealth and well-being of the United States.

People know well that restoring one of us cripples—because as some of you know, I walk around with a cane and with the aid of somebody's arm myself—to useful occupation costs money. Being crippled is not like many other diseases, contagious and otherwise, where the cure can be made in a comparatively short time; not like the medical operation where one goes to the hospital and at the end of a few weeks goes out made over again and ready to resume life. People who are crippled take a long time to be put back on their feet—sometimes years, as we all know. Take it from that angle. Suppose for the sake of argument it costs one thousand dollars a year for a crippled child to be put back on his feet and that it takes five years to do it. The cost to the community—because it has to be community effort in most cases, for most families cannot afford it—is five thousand dollars to put that one individual back on his feet. Remember that most of the cripples can in some shape, manner or form be brought back to useful life. Suppose they are brought back so that at the time they are 20 or 21 they have before them the expectation of a long and useful life, perhaps at least 40 years more. During those 40 years each one of them ought to be able to earn one thousand dollars a year. There is forty thousand dollars added to the country's wealth, at a cost of only five thousand dollars. So the net saving or profit to the State or country as a whole is thirty-five thousand dollars. That shows it pays from the money point of view, if from no other.

At the present time in the United States, they tell me, there are about thirty thousand new cases every year of people who become crippled for one reason or another. The first thing we are trying to do everywhere is to cut down that number of new cases; and I have a letter from my old friend Daddy Allen, whom a great many people all over the United States know as the man who started the International Society for Crippled Children which has branches in every civilized country of the world. He tells me that work is going on in every State in this Union to prevent people from getting crippled, and he hopes that as a result, within a short time, instead of having thirty thousand cases, we shall be able to cut it down to 20,000. It would be a tremendous saving if by preventive measures we can keep ten thousand children every year from becoming crippled.

Of course, modern medical science is trying to prevent diseases and troubles of all kinds just as much as it is trying to make cures. This calls for better understanding on the part of the people, for better education on the part especially of the parents, for better conditions surrounding the birth of children, better care in the home, and, equally important, prevention of many unnecessary accidents of all kinds—automobile accidents, train accidents, and so on. So the first step is to work for the prevention of crippling. This covers the great advances that have been made in preventing industrial accidents—unnecessary injuries that come to people who are at work not only in factories, but also in the field, in nearly every State of the Union. The United States now is working hard and spending much money to prevent these industrial accidents. They are far too common, but much has been accomplished and more will be accomplished in the years to come.

Now for the second step—the work of finding cripples all over the United States. We in the State of New York have had surveys made not only in the cities, but also in the country districts and even out to the remote farms that are not reached by R.F.D. carriers. We have had surveys made and have found literally thousands of children and grown-ups who were crippled and had no medical care of the right kind. There are probably today not only hidden away in the big cities, but also in the agricultural and mountainous parts of the United States, other thousands and thousands of crippled children who have never had any proper care, who have never been to a doctor, who have never been to a hospital or been looked over to see whether they could be brought back to useful life. That second step of finding the cripples is gradually being carried out.

Then the third step—the matter of diagnosing what the trouble is. This step is primarily for the doctors; and yet it is true that our good doctors—even the general practitioners—cannot in many cases consider themselves experienced in what is really orthopedic work. In other words, the average practitioner has to go to a specialist when it comes to treating certain types of patients. All over the United States we are establishing, more and more, clinics run by cities, schools, counties or the State, clinics

White House employees open letters with contributions for the National Infantile Paralysis Foundation. President Roosevelt's crusade on polio led to public awareness and many efforts to rehabilitate people with the disease. AP/WIDE WORLD PHOTOS. REPRODUCED BY PERMISSION.

that are within reasonable travel distance of every home, clinics to which the crippled children can be taken. After they have become crippled or after the people in search of them have found them they are taken to the clinic and the case is diagnosed. Great strides have been made in the past few years in providing facilities for the operations that are essential in some cases. But the medical profession is also realizing that many operations can be avoided through a system of plaster casts, massage exercise and other forms of treatment. The main point is to get the case properly diagnosed by the right kind of doctor in the first instance. Then comes the treatment.

The next medical step, which up to this time has not been developed far in this country, is "after care." After the cause of the trouble is known and the first remedies for it have been applied and the child is able to go home, the treatment must not stop; the parents must be taught what to do. Visiting nurses go in occasionally to see how the child is getting on, and furthermore we are developing new methods by which "after care" is being given in schools for crippled children. We do not want to take the children away from their education, of course, and many schools are putting in special facilities for crippled children where along with their education they can be given the right kind of medical treatment. The point to remember is that the overwhelming majority of children who become crippled can with proper treatment be restored to a useful, active life in the community. It seems to me from somewhat wide experience not only of my own, but of other people, the average cripple in this country has about the finest natural disposition of anyone in the community. There is something that comes to crippled children that gives to them happier, better dispositions. They are seldom cross, they are seldom fretful; we nearly always find them ready to cooperate; we find that they turn out well as scholars and that they are ready to assist in every way in the treatment provided for them.

I want to repeat that we owe to every crippled child in the United States a chance to come back, not merely from the big, broad point of view of humanity. I want to emphasize again that by restoring all of these tens of thousands of children to useful, normal lives, we shall be doing a fine thing, carrying out a great objective for the Nation. I know that we shall have your cooperation. From you who are crippled and you who are absolutely normal we shall have help in furthering this great purpose; we must search out the cripples from every nook and corner of the land; we must do through education everything possible to prevent crippling; we must provide the right medical care; we must spread "after care" to the homes throughout the land.

I am glad to have had this opportunity to say these few words today. We are enlisted in a great cause, one of the greatest causes of humanity that exists in America today.

Further Resources

BOOKS

Rogers, Naomi. *Dirt and Disease: Polio Before FDR.* New Brunswick, N.J.: Rutgers University Press, 1992.

Seavey, Nina Gilden. *A Paralyzing Fear: The Triumph over Polio in America.* New York: TV Books, 1998.

Smith, Jane S. *Patenting the Sun: Polio and the Salk Vaccine.* New York: William Morrow, 1990.

AUDIO AND VISUAL MEDIA

A Paralyzing Fear. Directed by Nina Gilven Seavey. PBS Home Video. Videocassette, 1998.

Sister Kenny. Fictionalized Account of the Life of the Australian Nurse, Sister Elizabeth Kenny. Directed by Dudley Nichols. RKO, 1946.

"Preventing Disease in the Nation"

Letter

By: Joseph E. Ransdell

Date: August 4, 1931

Source: Ransdell, Joseph E. "Preventing Disease in the Nation." *The New York Times,* August 4, 1931.

About the Author: Joseph E. Ransdell, a U.S. senator from Louisiana, wrote the Ransdell Act, which transformed the National Hygienic Laboratory into the National Institute of Health. Ransdell was a proponent of publicly funded biomedical research, and he joined forces with scientists who also believed in the creation of an institute to supply such funding. ■

Introduction

The U.S. government has had a role in medical research since 1887. The first small institution was the Marine Hospital Institute (MHI), created to provide health care for merchant seamen. The physicians who worked there also screened arriving passengers for signs of contagious disease. Because infectious disease was perhaps the most significant health problem of the time, the MHI researchers followed the findings of European researchers. To pursue its investigations, the MHI opened a one-room laboratory staffed by one physician/bacteriologist. This was called the "laboratory of hygiene" (*hygiene* was a term made popular by German physicians). Many scientists, though, continued to rely on private patrons or university resources to carry out their research.

In the decades that followed, the laboratory was given more and more responsibility. In 1902, legislation was passed making the National Hygienic Laboratory–Marine Hospital Institute (PL-MHI) responsible for screening vaccines and antitoxins. In 1912, in recognition of the expanded role of the laboratory, its name was changed to the Public Health Service (PHS). The National Hygiene Laboratory continued its work under this name. World War I brought the work of the PHS to the fore, as physicians investigated sources of infectious disease around military bases.

The year the war ended, 1918, chemists who had worked on chemical warfare for the U.S. government proposed the idea of federal funding for basic biological and medical problems. Some years later, they found a champion in Ransdell. Established in the early years of the Great Depression, the National Institute of Health was not heavily funded. Its founding, though, made possible research funding that the workers at the original laboratory would have found stunning. The NIH moved to its current location in Bethesda, Maryland, in 1938.

Significance

The immediate result of the creation of the National Institute of Health was that it brought the government into funding biomedical research. Scientists could apply for grants by submitting a proposal for their project, and they could then use the money to carry out the research at their own institutions. In a positive editorial about the new institute, *The New York Times* noted that the cost of health care in the United States was $1 billion and that Congress was allocating substantial sums to other areas of national interest, such as agriculture, mining, and industry.

The creation of the NIH, though, was also an acknowledgment that the federal government had a role in improving and maintaining the U.S. population's health through basic and applied research. As physicians and scientists were alerted to the spread of various diseases, the Public Health Service responded by slowly creating new institutes dedicated to particular diseases. The first of these was the National Cancer Institute (NCI), established in 1937 and formally made part of NIH in 1944.

At the same time, the NIH continued to address particular crises. During World War I, the physicians who worked for the MHS had been borrowed to treat victims of the 1918 influenza pandemic. In contrast, during World War II, the NIH contributed much to war-related health issues. They analyzed why 43 percent of the men

The National Institutes of Health, Bethesda, Maryland. The National Institutes of Health was created by the U.S. government to improve and maintain the population's health through biomedical research. © BETTMANN/CORBIS. REPRODUCED BY PERMISSION.

called up to serve in the military were found unfit. Bad teeth and syphilis were the primary reasons. After that, though, the institute focused its efforts on finding ways to combat the diseases that troops faced, such as malaria. The researchers also investigated health problems that might occur among workers who manufactured war-related materials, such as explosives.

After World War II, the NIH began to expand in new directions. The Division of Research Grants was established in 1946, followed by the National Heart Institute in 1948, the National Microbiological Institute in 1948, the Experimental Biology and Medicine Institute in 1948, the National Institute of Dental Research in 1948, and the National Institute of Mental Health, established in 1946 and funded in 1948.

The names of these institutes changed in the years following, and more were created, reflecting the progress of the NIH. Both staff scientists and outside researchers who won grants identified specific medical problems and did basic biomedical research, for example, in allergy and infectious diseases. They learned that both problems needed to be addressed at a fundamental level within the immune system. The NIH now has a National Institute of Allergy and Infectious Disease.

In the last decades of the twentieth century, the NIH made key discoveries in such areas as the human immunodeficiency virus (HIV), which causes AIDS. Their work has saved the lives of cancer patients, whose disease was arrested by new drugs developed at NIH. The creation of the modest research institute had long-term effects that would give its founders great satisfaction.

Primary Source

"Preventing Disease in the Nation"

SYNOPSIS: In this 1931 letter to the editor of *The New York Times,* Joseph E. Ransdell describes the National Institute of Health and informs readers of its features.

Institute of Health, With Government Backing, Has Important Task in Which All Can Help.

To the Editor of the *New York Times* :

The *New York Times* has expressed such a deep and intelligent interest in the National Institute of Health of the United States Public Health Service that I write to thank you; also to tell your readers something about the institute.

The National Institute of Health was created by Congress in 1930. The act contains three distinct features:

1. It establishes the National Institute of Health in the Public Health Service under the administrative direction and control of its Surgeon General, for the special purpose of pure scientific research to ascertain the cause, prevention and cure of diseases affecting human beings. The Hygienic Laboratory was merged in the institute and an appropriation of $750,000 was authorized
2. It authorizes the Treasury Department to accept gifts for research in problems "relating to the health of man and matters pertaining thereto," with the provision that if donations in the sum of half a million dollars or more are made, the name of the donor shall be perpetuated by suitable memorial in the institute
3. It provides for the establishment and maintenance in the institute of a system of fellowships in scientific research.

There is no conflict between the learned professions in their research work in schools, private institutions and foundations on the one hand, and the Institute of Health on the other. All professions connected in any way with problems of the health of plants, lower animals and human beings will profit by the researches carried on in the institute.

Not only the organization but the physical facilities are being enlarged. Congress has authorized appropriations, and has wisely afforded the opportunity for individuals to participate in this great movement by permitting them to make donations for:

1. Acquisition of ground and erection, equipment and maintenance of buildings and promises;
2. Fellowships in aid of research; and
3. Study and investigation in fundamental problems of diseases of man and matters pertaining thereto.

The Federal Government has made provision for administrative buildings and grounds, together with costs of operation. These improvements are being devised so as to insure large future growth. Separate laboratory buildings will be required for the conduct of investigations in the basic sciences.

Through specific private donations, opportunity is provided for gifts for fellowships in aid of research, also for the purchase of grounds and the establishment of permanent laboratories on or near the premises of the National Institute of Health in the city of Washington, these to become an integral part of the institute. The number of these laboratories at first will be few. Their cost will depend on the character of the buildings and their equipment. They will bear the names of the donors when built with private contributions, and be permanent memorials in the nation's capital to those whose foresight and humanity make them possible.

All gifts, by will or otherwise, must be delivered to the Secretary of the Treasury, who will expend them as desired by the donors, or hold them in trust and invest them in proper securities of the United States, the income thereof to be administered by the Surgeon General of the Public Health Service, with all the safeguards attendant upon Federal appropriations.

Recently a wealthy American made the following statement: "What is a business man to do with a fortune of several million dollars when, having provided for all his dependents and met all his worldly obligations, he comes eventually to that passing on which ends his need of money and his power to direct its use? . . . I fully understand that it will make no difference to me what is done with my money after I am gone. But the more I think about it, the more I am convinced that it does make a great deal of difference now: that I am under an obligation to see that it is made continuously useful. . . . I want to contribute my share toward making a better and happier world."

That man is a worthy steward of his wealth. He and others like him should be assisted in solving the vital question of how to dispose of a portion of their wealth so as to make it "continuously useful," and to contribute "toward making a better and happier world."

I respectfully suggest that they cannot make wiser disposition of a part of their wealth while living, or by last will, than to give generously to the National Institute of Health.

Such benefactions would insure effective scientific efforts in the National Institute of Health to the end of time. By making these bequests, there is opportunity not only to alleviate suffering and promote happiness, but to place our government and people in the forefront of scientific research. What greater opportunity could present itself for making this a "better and happier world"?

Jos. E. Ransdell
Executive Director
Washington, D. C.
Aug. 4, 1931

Further Resources

WEBSITES

National Institutes of Health. Available online at www.nih.gov (accessed March 3, 2003).

National Library of Medicine. Available online at www.nlm.nih.gov (accessed March 3, 2003).

"Children Hurt at Work"

Journal article

By: Gertrude Folks Zimand

Date: July 1932

Source: Zimand, Gertrude Folks. "Children Hurt at Work." *The Survey,* July 1932.

About the Author: Gertrude Folks Zimand (1894–1966) was the director of research and publicity for the National Child Labor Committee, a private organization founded in 1904 and dedicated to controlling child labor, establishing fair laws, and protecting working children. The committee continued to operate in the early years of the twenty-first century. ■

Introduction

The work of children is integral to the history of the United States. They worked on family farms and for family businesses. With the industrial revolution, however, they also began to labor in mills, mines, and factories. The 1900 U.S. census showed that almost two million children between the ages of ten and fifteen were employed. The National Child Labor Committee's work reduced the number of child workers during the 1920s. With the onset of the Great Depression, however, child labor increased. Employers could get away with paying children less than they would pay adult workers. Families needed money from whatever source, and if the only way they could survive was by sending a child out to work in a textile mill, factory, or coal mine, they would do so.

The employment of children affected their futures and their health. A child working in a factory could not attend school regularly, if at all. His or her early life as an industrial worker spelled out a grim future. Without education, most working children were doomed to spend their adult lives continuing with the same sort of work that broke both backs and spirits. They were at risk for diseases related to their occupations. With minimal legal protection and indifferent employers, children were severely injured and killed on the job.

The laboring children suffered subtler health effects as well. They inhaled dust that caused lung disease and were at times infected with tuberculosis. They spent so many hours closed in that they rarely saw the sun and so suffered vitamin D deficiencies. The close quarters in which they worked made infectious disease spread rapidly. And still, many did not earn enough to eat a nutritious diet, which debilitated them further.

Significance

The National Child Labor Committee (NCLC) was an important force for change in the area of child employment, and thus health, but effecting change was a long struggle. "Children Hurt at Work" exemplifies the committee's work. Children's advocates tried several avenues before they succeeded in convincing Congress to enact protective legislation. Before that, other measures of varying usefulness were put into effect. One was the Code of Fair Competition for the Cotton-Textile Industry, which President Franklin Roosevelt (served 1933–1945) signed in July 1933. That code barred children under the age of sixteen from working in textile mills. It was the first step taken by the federal government to prevent the exploitation of children as workers.

Even with that law in effect, however, it was clear that further controls were needed. In Pennsylvania, for example, some twenty-two thousand employment certificates were issued to children aged fourteen and fifteen in 1932. Some sought summer or after-school employment, but at least nineteen thousand were issued to children who were leaving school for full-time employment.

State laws on the ages for compulsory schooling of children did something to control illegal employment of children and thus reduce the general effects of working, as well as of injuries and deaths. In situations of economic need and corporate greed, however, families and employers both ignored these laws. New York State, for example, passed legislation in the late nineteenth century that required children between the ages of eight and fourteen to attend school. In 1911, a fire at the Triangle Shirtwaist Factory in New York City took the lives of many girls and young women between those ages who were working there.

The NCLC was also a force behind a proposed amendment to the U.S. Constitution, described in this article, that would have set limits on child labor. Although at least fifteen states ratified the proposed amendment, it never secured the support of the two-thirds of all states needed to allow it to be transformed into law.

The committee and other children's advocates, however, did succeed during President Franklin Roosevelt's second term of office. In 1938, the Congress passed the Fair Labor Standards Act, which controlled employment for children under the age of sixteen. Young workers over sixteen were then given the same protections if injured as were all workers.

The long-term effect of the NCLC, probably the most visible and active child-labor advocacy group, was that states began controlling child labor by the permit system. The legal age at which a child can legally began working varies, and the number of allowable hours rises with age.

Primary Source

"Children Hurt at Work"

SYNOPSIS: In this article Gertrude Folks Zimand, an NCLC official, describes the number of children injured and killed on the job and the scarcity of resources to help them.

One of the many tragic aspects of the industrial exploitation of children is the army of boys and girls who, at the outset of their industrial careers, fall victims to the machine. Each year, in the sixteen states which take the trouble to find out what is happening to their young workers, no less than a thousand children under eighteen years are permanently disabled and another hundred are killed.

It was Florence Kelley, the pioneer in this field, who first maintained that the term "industrial accidents" as applied to children was a misnomer and insisted that we speak of industrial *injuries.* For an accident, she pointed out, implies something which just happens, which cannot be prevented, whereas such wholesale maiming of children by industry constitutes criminal negligence. But unfortunately permitting half-grown youngsters to assume the risk of accident is but the first step in a general laissez-faire policy.

Charles E. Gibbons, assisted by Chester T. Stansbury, has been making for the National Child Labor Committee a follow-up study of children who were seriously injured in industry four or five years ago. So far 108 children have been studied in two states, Illinois and Tennessee. These children, now nearly adult, had been maimed physically, often to the extent of a lifelong handicap, and had undergone the experience of seeing their whole future jeopardized just as they were emerging from childhood to adulthood—a period at best of emotional stress and strain. Yet in this crisis, the protecting arm of the state had not been extended, and the children had been left to make their adjustments as best they might.

The children for a variety of reasons did not receive the full amount to which they were entitled.

The Illinois law permits, but does not require, that in cases of permanent injury a child's future earning capacity be taken into account in determining the wage basis for the compensation award. In practice however this is rarely done. In Tennessee the law does not permit such consideration. At the time of this study the Tennessee law limited payment for medical care to $100; later another $100 was provided. Some children not only had to use their entire compensation award for medical expenses, but to draw on other funds or go in debt. In both states the age of the child affects the amount of compensation received. Illinois allows extra compensation to children under sixteen injured while illegally employed; in Tennessee such children are excluded from the Compensation Act and must sue at common law, and a guardian is required for minors under eighteen. Yet the ages of half the children in Tennessee were reported higher on the accident records than they actually were and in Illinois in 27 per cent of the cases age had not been verified.

In spite of the fact that one of the chief reasons for workmen's compensation is to prevent the uncertainty, delay and cost incidental to litigation, nevertheless two out of every five children in Illinois had felt the need of hiring attorneys. The fees for such services varied from less than 20 per cent to 47 per cent of the compensation award.

In most cases the compensation money was neither used for the child's education or immediate benefit nor invested for his future.

Some children received a comparatively small amount of compensation, but in most cases it was several hundred dollars and in a considerable number well over a thousand dollars. Of the $62,000 received by the 108 injured children, only 2.5 per cent was used for education—the paramount need of a child with an industrial handicap; and only 22 per cent was placed in banks or invested. Most of it was frittered away on non-essentials, often foolishly, and in some cases the existence of this temporary source of income blinded the child and his parents to the need for vocational education. Yet if these children are not trained for self-support, they are likely to become dependent upon relatives or recipients of charity, with the possibility of ending up as beggars on the street, using their handicap as the chief stock in trade.

These children had not received vocational re-education and few knew of the state rehabilitation service.

The study demonstrates that the accidents children suffer seriously handicap them for industry. Of the 108 children, only 44 had returned to their former jobs, and 35 stated that they felt unable to continue in the kind of work in which they were previously engaged either because of physical incapacity or fear resulting from the accident. An even larger number experienced difficulty in securing work directly attributable to their injury.

Nevertheless in spite of the fact that in both Illinois and Tennessee there is a state rehabilitation service, only 7 of the 108 children had even heard of this service and only one thoroughgoing case of rehabilitation which benefited the child was found. This boy had learned of the service through a newspaper.

The study on the whole presents a disheartening picture; children injured, often needlessly, permanently handicapped for work at the outset of their industrial careers; ignorant of their rights under the compensation law; sometimes at the mercy of unscrupulous employers; left without advice or counsel in planning for the future; groping in the dark for something that will enable them to regain their power of self-support, but drifting oftentimes into discouragement and despondency if not into definitely anti-social behavior. "I've about decided I cannot make an honest living and will go to bootlegging," said one youth who had been turned down repeatedly because "we can't afford to take a boy with three fingers off."

But the machinery is already in existence which, if properly administered, can transform the picture. More care in checking up on age and legality of employment, advising the child of his compensation rights, assistance in securing his award and in its collection, extension of guardianship provisions and a closer tie-up between the compensation department and the rehabilitation service—this is the program which should not be difficult to achieve but remarkably fruitful in results.

Further Resources

BOOKS

Hobbs, Sandy, Jim McKechnie, and Michael Lavalette. *Child Labor: A World History Companion.* Santa Barbara, Calif.: ABC-CLIO, 1999.

Trattner, Walter I. *Crusade for the Children: A History of the National Child Labor Committee and Child Labor Reform in America.* Chicago: Quadrangle Books, 1970.

Zelizer, Viviana A. *Pricing the Priceless Child: The Changing Social Value of Children.* New York: Basic Books, 1985.

WEBSITES

McConnell, Beatrice. "The Shift in Child Labor." *The Survey,* May 1933. Available online at http://www.newdeal.feri.org /survey/s335.htm; website home page: http://www.newdeal .feri.org (accessed March 4, 2003).

NCLC Fact Sheet. National Child Labor Committee. Available online at http://www.kapow.org/nclc.htm; website home page: http://www.kapow.org (accessed March 4, 2003).

The Tuskegee Syphilis Experiment

Letters

By: Taliaferro Clark; Hugh S. Cumming

Date: August 29, 1932; September 20, 1932

Source: Clark, Taliaferro, Letter to J. N. Baker. August 29, 1932; Cumming, Hugh S. Letter to R. R. Morton. September 20, 1932. Reprinted in Reverby, Susan M., ed. *Tuskegee's Truths: Rethinking the Tuskegee Syphilis Study.* Chapel Hill, N.C.: University of North Carolina Press, 2000.

About the Authors: Dr. Taliaferro Clark was the assistant Surgeon General in charge of the Venereal Disease division of the Public Health Service in 1932. He developed the idea of the Tuskegee Syphilis Experiment and oversaw it for a year before retiring.

Hugh S. Cumming (1869–1948) was born in Virginia and graduated from medical school there in 1894. He then joined the Marine Hospital Service, later to be known as the Public Health Service (PHS). He worked up through the ranks and was appointed Surgeon General in 1920. He held this position until retirement in 1936. As Surgeon General, Cumming oversaw the expansion of the PHS. He was also ultimately responsible for the Tuskegee Syphilis Experment. ■

Introduction

Syphilis is a sexually transmitted disease that can now be cured with antibiotics. For centuries, however, it was incurable, though various remedies were tried. Syphilis has three stages: primary, secondary, and tertiary. In the primary stage the victim has sores and other lesions that clue medical practitioners to the presence of the disease. The sores disappear without treatment, though, leading to the secondary stage of the disease. During this time, the disease remains alive in a person's body but he or she does not display any symptoms. Decades may pass before the third, or tertiary stage begins. At that point, the syphilis has affected the central nervous system and causes mental and physical deterioration.

The Tuskegee Syphilis Experiment was started in Macon County, Alabama, to "determine the natural course of untreated, latent syphilis in black males," according to Allan M. Brandt, writing in *Tuskegee's Truths.* Beginning in the early 1930s, the United States Public Health Service (USPHS) recruited black males in Macon County, chosen because it had the highest rate of untreated syphilis in a multi-county area surveyed by the USPHS.

When the national media broke the news of the Tuskegee Experiment in 1972, the public was outraged that these men had not been treated after penicillin became available in the 1940s. This judgment, though, does not put the experiment in the context of the beliefs of the times. When the experiment was started, blacks were viewed as being genetically endowed with an excess sex drive. Physicians at the time also noted that blacks with syphilis tended to seek treatment in the primary stage but, after that passed, did not visit doctors until the symptoms of the third stage became apparent. At that point, there was little that medical science could do. The high rates of syphilis among the black population had caused some physicians to argue that the disease was fundamentally different in blacks and treatment was futile.

When penicillin became available as a cure for syphilis in the early 1950s, the Tuskegee subjects did not receive it from the Public Health Service, although some sought treatment on their own. Given the nature of the study, which involved regular examinations by physicians, the men believed that they *were* being treated. The physicians cited a Norwegian study of untreated syphilitics carried out in the early twentieth century, which had by then been discredited. The authors of that study argued that it was useless, perhaps dangerous, to treat people in the tertiary stage of the disease.

Racism, however, is the only plausible reason that the USPHS and its Alabama counterparts withheld treatment. A reading of the correspondence and other documents from the study leaves the impression that the men in the study did not receive treatment because to treat them would have meant that the study was a wasted effort. When the federal Department of Health, Education, and Welfare (HEW) issued a final report in 1974, researchers at the time argued that withholding treatment had been justified for several reasons. One was that the population was sufficiently uneducated that they never would have known to seek treatment anyway (which was not true). Others argued that blacks had a "different" form of the disease (which was also not true).

Nurse Eunice Rivers and the Tuskegee Experiment

Nurse Eunice Rivers was the "scientific assistant" and public-health nurse for the Tuskegee Experiment during its entire forty years (1932–1972). She became a trusted friend of the subjects, ferrying them back and forth for their examinations in what became known as "Nurse Rivers's Taxi." The physicians who worked on the study changed, but Nurse Rivers was a constant.

Eunice Rivers was also African American, and her participation in a project that left poor blacks with untreated syphilis for forty years illuminates the attitudes of black health-care professionals and academics at the time. She wrote a report in 1953, after the subjects could have been treated with penicillin. In her report, "Twenty Years Followup Experience in a Long-Range Medical Study," Nurse Rivers gives a clear, clinical description of the "care" given to the subjects (they did receive medicine, but not for syphilis). Her job was to keep the study going, and she did.

Nurse Rivers' participation in the project is another reason that modern students must consider Tuskegee a product of its time. The early fifties marked the very beginning of the Civil Rights era but greatly predated the time when black professionals were expected to show solidarity with poor people solely on the grounds of race. Nurse Rivers' writings suggest that her first loyalty lay to her profession, and that she viewed her participation in the experiment as a perfectly acceptable—indeed, useful—way of practicing that profession.

Significance

The men who corresponded about the Tuskegee Experiment did not know what the historical significance of their work would be. It was not their findings on untreated syphilis that changed medical research. Rather, it was several aspects of the study that had nothing to do with the findings. The first was that they misled their subjects into thinking that they were being treated. The second was that they never offered treatment. Initially, the treatment available was not a cure, but it did cut the death rate from syphilis. After the introduction of penicillin, their failure to offer treatment went beyond unethical. The researchers not only let the people enrolled in the study die without treatment, but they also left a community at risk of further spread of the disease by failing to treat the subjects. They did so as late as 1969, when a committee from the Centers for Disease Control decided to continue the study (one physician argued against doing so). All of these behaviors are now illegal.

Beyond its effects on the men and their community, the Tuskegee experiment both generated change in the requirements for "informed consent" and created a climate of suspicion in parts of the black community about medical treatment and research. Some black victims of the AIDS virus, in particular, were reluctant to take part in government treatment trials because they feared that they would be used as had the Tuskegee subjects. For people who agreed to take part in trials of experimental medications, the changes implemented since Tuskegee mean that if in the middle of a double-blind trial, a medication proves highly effective, the researchers stop the trial and treat all participants with the medication instead of a placebo.

John A. Andrew Memorial Hospital at Tuskegee Institute, Alabama, 1939. This hospital was the site of the infamous Tuskegee Syphilis Experiment, which led to many questions regarding the ethics of medical research. **AP/WIDE WORLD PHOTOS. REPRODUCED BY PERMISSION.**

Primary Source

The Tuskegee Syphilis Experiment

SYNOPSIS: The letters between a federal and a local public health official marked the start of a forty-year study in which the researchers at no point looked clearly at the well-being of the subjects. These letters were followed by many more, as well as by reports and journal articles.

August 29, 1932

Doctor J. N. Baker
State Health Officer
Montgomery, Alabama

Dear Doctor Baker:

I have for some time wished to talk over with you a piece of research work that might be carried out on syphilitic Negroes in Macon County, the expense of which is to be bourne by the Public Health Service. If you are likely to be in Montgomery about the middle of September I should like to arrange to leave Washington on the afternoon of September 12th en route for Montgomery to talk this matter over with you in person and then proceed to Tuskegee with a view of securing the cooperation of the Andrews Memorial Hospital of Tuskegee Institute.

In working up the data for the final report to the Julius Rosenwald Fund I was particularly impressed with the fact that a negligible number, something less than 35, of the Negroes under treatment in Macon County during the period of the demonstration had ever had any previous treatment. It seems to me that this situation in a very heavily infected population group affords an unparalleled opportunity of studying the effect of untreated syphilis on the human economy. If you think you will be interested in this subject, but nevertheless cannot arrange to be in Montgomery on the date or dates specified above, I shall arrange to visit you on any date that may be mutually satisfactory.

Very Sincerely Yours,
Taliaferro Clark
Assistant Surgeon General
Division of Venereal Diseases

Hugh S. Cumming. Dr. Cumming was Surgeon General of the U.S. Public Health Service and served during the beginning of the Tuskegee Syphilis Experiment. AP/WIDE WORLD PHOTOS. REPRODUCED BY PERMISSION.

September 20, 1932

Doctor R. R. Moton
Tuskegee Institute
Alabama

Dear Doctor Moton:

I regret your unavoidable absence from Tuskegee that prevented your meeting Assistant Surgeon General Taliaferro Clark at the time of his recent visit to Tuskegee because I wanted him to explain to you at firsthand the proposed study of the effects of untreated syphilis on the human economy with the cooperation of your hospital. It is expected the results of this study may have a marked bearing on the treatment, or conversely the non-necessity for treatment, of cases of latent syphilis. For this reason I shall be grateful if you shall be able to extend the splendid cooperation offered by Doctor Dibble contingent on your approval.

The recent syphilis control demonstration carried out in Macon County, with the financial assistance of the Julius Rosenwald Fund, revealed the presence of an unusually high prevalence rate in this county and, what is still more remarkable, the fact that approximately 99 per cent of this population group was entirely without previous treatment. This combination, together with the expected cooperation of your hospital, offers an unparalleled opportunity for carrying on this piece of scientific research which probably cannot be duplicated anywhere else in the world. No doubt Doctor Dibble has explained our plan of procedure to you that contemplates, among other things, an intensive physical and serological examination of untreated cases having positive Wassermann, which may not be carried out in the necessary scientific detail except in a hospital. You can readily see, therefore, that the success of this important study really hinges on your cooperation.

Sincerely,
H. S. Cumming
Surgeon General

Further Resources

BOOKS

Jones, James H. *Bad Blood: The Tuskegee Syphilis Experiment.* New York: Free Press, 1981.

U.S. Department of Heath, Education, and Welfare. *Syphilis: A Synopsis.* Atlanta, Ga.: National Communicable Disease Center, 1968.

Morale: The Mental Hygiene of Unemployment

Pamphlet

By: George K. Pratt, M.D.

Date: 1933

Source: Pratt, George K. *Morale: The Mental Hygiene of Unemployment.* New York: The National Committee for Mental Hygiene, 1933, 5, 7, 8, 9, 10, 11, 12, 13.

About the Author: George K. Pratt, a physician who specialized in mental disorders, wrote various popular books on mental hygiene, including *Your Mind and You.* Pratt contributed to the government's efforts to fight all effects of the Great Depression by writing this pamphlet, which acknowledged that economic hardship affected people's mental health. ■

Introduction

The Great Depression of the 1930s was not the first such economic downturn in U.S. history, but it was the first to occur in an era when the mental health of average people was taken seriously. The "mental hygiene" movement promoted the idea that people could, through a combination of self-help, professional health care, and clean living, improve their emotional and psychological well-being.

The Great Depression, however, posed a challenge to the mental hygiene movement. The movement was based, in large part, on the idea that once people understood the causes of their emotional pain, they could end it. The emotional distress that the Great Depression brought was caused by a global economic crisis over which the average person had no control. He or she could pound the pavements seeking employment for months on end and still remain unemployed. Raised in a country where the prevailing ethic was that those who worked hard would succeed, many Depression-era would-be workers found that their best efforts meant nothing in a country in which there were more workers than jobs.

A 1931 article in the magazine *The New Republic* summed up the situation. "As part of the widespread slump, the people who thought themselves secure have been thrown into it. The people who have been able to have a college education suddenly find themselves out of a job. No one can take a census of this misery. It doesn't walk the street. It sits and shivers in cold houses. It hides itself."

Low morale, which today might fall into the category of clinical depression, could have severe effects. Walter A. Lunden, a sociologist, correlated suicide rates with different aspects of economics. He found that between 1929 (the year that the stock market crashed) and 1932, the suicide rate rose an alarming 29 percent. It did not drop in a major way until 1944, well into World War II (1939–1945), when it fell to 34 percent below the 1932 high.

At the same time, while the Great Depression created mental health problems in many people, it also countered the idea that people were unemployed because they were inferior. A program pioneered by the University of Minnesota to work with the unemployed found that it was "impossible to state that a certain percentage of the unemployed are inferior or superior people. Each case is unique." This novel concept took the blame off those who could not find work, although one program could not eliminate the sense of despair that people felt about being unable to provide for their families.

While the Great Depression diminished men's abilities to provide for their families, it also changed the role of women in a curious way. The standards of the time were that men were expected to be the primary earners in families, while women looked after the home and family. The Great Depression had a decisive effect on women and their roles, one that made them more resilient and independent, although it did not make their lives any easier. They were often faced with severe losses. Glen H. Elder, in "Hard Times in Women's Lives," notes that family experience during the Depression often involved "severe income reductions and prolonged unemployment; the irretrievable loss of a family home and furnishings; the collapse of educational plans for a child; the trauma of financial dependence and shared living quarters; the disability, death, or separation of a spouse. A way of life had come to an end for many."

Significance

Morale acknowledged that along with alleviating the material needs caused by the Great Depression, the government and health professionals needed to make efforts to meet the "equally vital need for relieving the emotional strains and raising the morale of those who are made insecure." The mental hygiene of "those who are reacting to fear and deprivation" was deemed a matter of concern on a par with physical needs. It was an official government statement that unemployment had psychological as well as economic effects.

The 1920s was an era of economic good times, which made the Depression of the 1930s even more difficult for people to accept. But at the same time, the end of that prosperous way of life also marked the beginning of the recognition that achieving good "mental hygiene" was not purely a matter of eliminating despair by understanding what caused it. Dr. Pratt describes the unconscious reactions to unemployment that men who have always been employed might display. These included physical symptoms, such as headaches, as well as increased irritability with family members. He notes that during economic hard times, children become more competitive with one another, particularly if the family's living situation has become more crowded through the arrival of other relatives or married siblings. Dr. Pratt espoused the then-unusual recommendation that each family member have an opportunity for privacy, time alone, and space away from others.

Morale and later works on the psychological effects of unemployment and economic hard times broke the longstanding notion that each person could, through hard work, control his or her destiny. Acknowledging that sometimes this was not true, that some forces were larger and stronger than individuals, allowed the involuntarily unemployed to retain both dignity and perspective on their situation.

Primary Source

Morale: The Mental Hygiene of Unemployment [excerpt]

SYNOPSIS: *Morale* describes the effects of the economic depression on individuals' mental health and on family life.

Introduction

Along with the organized work of relieving hunger, cold and sickness in these times of unemployment, there must not be forgotten the equally vital need for relieving the emotional strains and raising the morale of those who are made insecure. More than ever before are social workers, unemployment relief officials, community chest executives and members of boards of charitable and character-building agencies finding it necessary to deal not only with problems of material relief, but also to understand something of the mental hygiene of people who are reacting to fear and deprivation.

It must be obvious to almost everyone that this present crisis holds the most critical of possibilities, either for progress or regress, psychologically speaking. Indeed, it is not unwarranted to believe that the future of re-invigoration of our whole nation will depend to an astonishing degree equally on the ways in which the material relief and the mental health problems of the unemployed are handled today. Whether these fellow citizens of ours are to be turned into paupers or malcontents filled with self-pity and a grudge against society, or whether they are to be helped back to their former self-respect and efficiency as useful members of the community—this is the problem as well as the opportunity which faces every person whose professional work touches at any point these vitally human affairs of our times. . . .

Chapter 1

How We Act in the Face of Adversity

To adapt one's self reasonably well to strange or unpleasant experiences is a sign of good mental health. Likewise, failure to adjust to these experiences indicates some degree at least of mental ill-health. Men and women whose morale and mental health are threatened because of difficulty in adapting themselves to unemployment conditions are individuals who, when multiplied by thousands in the same boat, set the pattern for the morale and mental health of the whole community.

It is obvious that loss of employment, reduction of income and the necessity for a lowered standard of living thwart some of our needs, desires or emotions. If the need for lowering our standards is not particularly great, or if our ambitions and desires are simple, then we can adjust ourselves to this thwarting without much difficulty. But, on the other hand, if we are endowed with more than the average amount of ambition, if our desires for material comforts or for power happen to be strong, or if we have built up over the years of prosperity a conception of comfort-needs greater than necessary, then we find it hard to adjust to frustration and our attitudes and behavior reflect this in varying degrees of unadjustment to the situation.

How Mental Health Is Affected

The principal way in which unemployment affects mental health is by imposing strains and anxieties on people. The adaptive capacities of human beings can stand just so much. When stresses boiling up from within (such as pent-up feelings) or when those impinging from without (such as painful factual experiences) become too great, something has to give. Some persons seem naturally more free from internal stresses and better able to resist external ones than do others. But even with these sturdy men and women, some experiences beyond their control (like mortal danger, war, grave illness, and, just now, the economic crashing of our times) may become so severe or so prolonged that the staunchest of adaptive capacities falter and at last surrender. When this happens, regardless of the cause, the mental health of such individuals is impaired. Moreover, it seems probable that many others who may have been on the borderline of mental ill-health for some time before unemployment will now go under. . . .

What Mental Health Is

The modern conception of mental health may be summed up as the adjustment of one's self to inner and outer strains in a manner that will be reasonably satisfactory, both to the individual and to the customs of the society in which he lives.

How It Differs from Mental Disorder

Departures from an average state of mental health constitute some degree of mental disorder and these departures are usually caused by an unsuccessful adjustment to the stresses of the experiences that assail one. The mental disorder that results from this failure to adjust may be very mild and expressed in nothing more that frequent ups-and-downs in mood, continued irritability or perhaps in "queer" attitudes toward people or customs. But in some other cases it may find more serious expression in spells of depression so black that suicide is welcomed; or in extravagant, violent behavior; in delusions that others are trying to harm one; or sometimes in the development of a shut-in and seclusive personality that forsakes the world of reality for one of sterile daydreams.

Why Unemployment Affects Mental Health

Fortunately statistics so far available do not seem to indicate that serious mental disease or "insanity" (which is merely an advanced degree of poor mental health) has increased as a result of the suffering caused by our times. However, suicide unmistakably has grown more frequent and a great many lesser departures from average mental health also are being observed. It is especially these latter unhealthy types of mental ill-health with which social workers are daily forced to content.

No Sharp Line Divides Mental Health from Mental Disease

Obviously there is no clear-cut line in this conception that separates mental health from mental disease. Mental health, for example, may be thought of as excellent, good, fair or poor, grading imperceptibly downward on an imaginary scale toward the point where mental disease may be said to enter the picture. This point is extremely difficult to locate on the scale because standards differ in various groups and what might pass for a merely poor or even a fair degree of mental health among one group might be labeled a mild grade of mental disorder in another. It is only when mental disease has progresses down the scale from mild to extreme that we are justified in calling a person "insane."

What "Insanity" Is

"Insanity" is purely a legal term. It has no medical standing. It merely means that a given person's symptoms of mental disease have grown so serious and his sense of judgement has become so impaired that the law makes it possible for others to decide for him what measures are necessary for his proper treatment or cure. Although in the United States today there are more than 300,000 such "insane" men and women in mental hospitals, there are probably twenty to thirty times as many others who display some signs of mental disorder (but not necessarily legal "insanity") of such types as probably will never bring them to a hospital. Although not in good mental health and often making trouble and hard to get along with, the overwhelming majority of these people are mentally sick. And yet, according to modern psychiatric conceptions of what constitutes mental disorder, their worries, fears, eccentricities, and what-not are made of precisely the same stuff, although in lesser degree, as that from which obvious mental disease is made. . . .

Some Examples of These Common Mental Disorders

. . . When, therefore, having lost his job, John Jones or his wife comes to a relief bureau seeking aid, and when either of them is noted on the record card as acting surly, defiant, bitter, suspicious, "cocky," depressed, hopeless, or in any of the dozens of other ways to which people resort when faced with fear and hardship, the social worker will be wise to regard these attitudes as *symptoms* which indicate a growing difficulty in making an emotional adjustment to the situation. These symptoms are the more readily understandable when it is realized what it means to a man who has striven for position and proper care for his family to be cut off from his job and income. This loss and the resulting shock tend to destroy his belief in his capacity to live up to his self-appointed standards and to achieve whatever goals in life he has set for himself. When these things are destroyed his sense of security and his morale are lessened, and the insecurity that now grips him finds expression in some of the unhealthy attitudes just described.

Disturbing Attitudes Are Usually Symptoms of Poor Adjustment

It is important to understand that these attitudes are not just the casual expressions of sheer cussedness (as some people still believe) nor the earmarks of a chronically disgruntled personality. They are, instead, the signs that John Jones and his wife are inwardly frantic with fear and are nearing the end of their rope in the struggle to adjust their needs for food and shelter, as well as their conceptions of themselves, their normal wills-to-power and their self-esteem to the thwarting that loss of job necessitates. These attitudes (defiance, suspicion, depression, etc.) are just as infallible symptoms of a state of mental health that is beginning to crack under the strain of trying to adjust, as physical pain or fever are symptoms of some approaching illness. Both need immediate and understanding attention if the disease process is not to grow serious.

Further Resources

BOOKS

Boardman, Fon W., Jr. *The Thirties: America and the Great Depression.* New York: Henry Z. Walck, 1967.

McElvaine, Robert S. *The Great Depression: America, 1929–1941.* New York: Times Books, 1984.

Terkel, Studs. *Hard Times: An Oral History of the Great Depression.* New York: Pantheon Books, 1970.

PERIODICALS

Elder, Glen H., Jr., and Jeffrey K. Liker. "Hard Times in Women's Lives: Historical Influences Across Forty Years." *American Journal of Sociology* 88, no. 2, 1982, 241–268.

Perrott, J., and Edgar Sydenstricker. "Causal and Selective Factors in Sickness." *American Journal of Sociology* 40, no. 6, 1935, 804–812.

"Dear Mr. Hopkins"

Reports

By: Henry W. Francis and Martha Gellhorn

Date: November 19, 1934, and December 7, 1934

Source: Francis, Henry W., and Martha Gellhorn. "Dear Mr. Hopkins." November, December 1934. Hopkins Papers, National Archives/New Deal Network. Available at New Deal Network online at http://newdeal.feri.org/hopkins/hop04.htm; website homepage http://newdeal.feri.org (accessed March 17, 2003).

About the Authors: Henry W. Francis and Martha Gellhorn (1908–1998) were among the writer/reporters sent by Federal Emergency Relief administrator Harry Hopkins to travel around the United States and report on conditions that did not make the headlines of the national newspapers. On this project, he sent his observers out with instructions to describe conditions vividly and honestly. ■

Introduction

The crowded, disease-ridden slums of American cities drew the attention of philanthropists and social activists at the beginning of the twentieth century, and they continued to be subjects of relief efforts throughout the Great Depression. People in rural areas, however, received less attention, although they were living in conditions that were as bad as those in the cities, perhaps worse, because they lacked access to some of the relief resources that city dwellers could use.

Malnutrition was an enormous problem. Families who lived on cornbread and hominy, a grain, were likely to develop pellagra, caused by a shortage of B vitamins. They did not drink enough milk or eat other dairy products, which left them vulnerable to stunted growth and weak bones. Syphilis was rampant and getting more pervasive. People spent their money on quack cures, then continued often unknowingly to spread the disease. In the hollows of West Virginia, as Henry Francis notes, virtually every disease one could think of was active. Martha Gellhorn bluntly stated she could not understand why everyone had not died of waterborne diseases, and perhaps they would be better off if they had.

Significance

Such grinding rural poverty and the health problems that went with it were not caused by the Depression but had been decades in the making. With the loss of jobs, however, the Depression greatly worsened the plight of the rural poor. Just as rural poverty had taken decades to

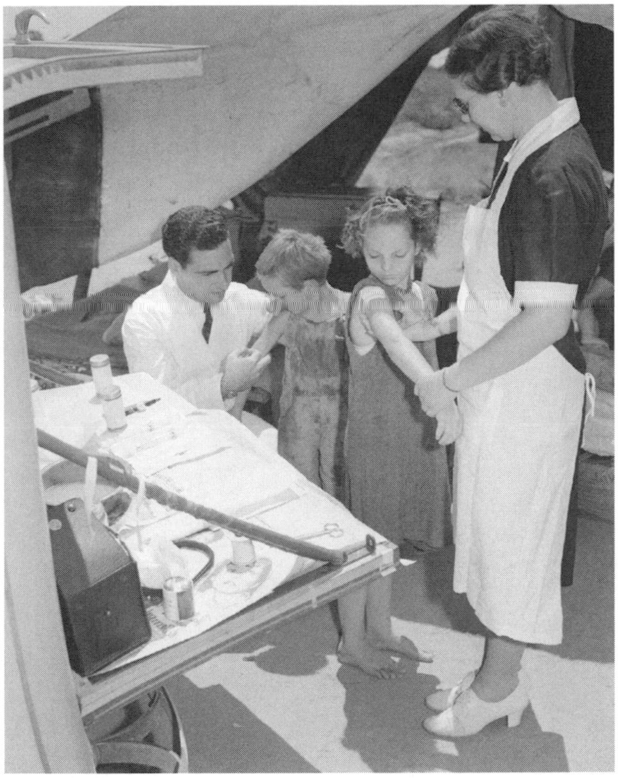

A doctor and nurse vaccinate migrant farm workers' children in Visalia, California, 1939. Some of the first efforts to improve the health of the population and prevent epidemics consisted of auto-clinics set up to immunize children from smallpox. © BETTMANN/CORBIS. REPRODUCED BY PERMISSION.

develop, it would take decades to improve, and few believed (correctly, as it turned out) that it could be eradicated any more than urban poverty could.

The precise impact of these "Dear Mr. Hopkins" reports is difficult to gauge. Since Hopkins was one of the president's closest advisors, the reports generated by Gellhorn, Francis, and others were a factor in crafting the programs and policies of the Social Security Act. The reports brought rural poverty to the attention of the often powerful southern congressmen who represented these states and possibly influenced their willingness to enact the social legislation.

For the people who lived in these areas, the New Deal brought some relief. Southern poverty pockets were among the first to adopt the notion of a free, hot lunch for schoolchildren. Relief workers began making grocery deliveries to the needy.

Hopkins' reporters also described gross deficiencies in education. Schools lacked the most basic supplies. At the same time, children who lacked decent clothing and shoes could not go to school. Many letters that Eleanor Roosevelt received from poor people asked if the Roosevelts could send them old clothes, requests that the First Family could

A coal miner's family in West Virginia, September 1938. Disease and malnutrition were widespread in poverty-stricken rural areas during the Depression, though the urban slums drew most of the attention of social activists. © CORBIS. REPRODUCED BY PERMISSION.

not fill. Nevertheless, the presence of reporters such as Gellhorn and Francis probably increased rural residents' knowledge of what the president was trying to do.

Some provisions of Roosevelt's Social Security Act did address the needs of the rural poor, particularly in the areas of maternal and child health and mortality. The government paid traveling nurses to visit mothers and children, to give checkups, and to advise mothers on child care. The nurses at the same time were up against more than disease and dirt. They also tried, and often failed, to correct the long-standing beliefs that led poor rural mothers to care for children as they did. Modern methods of hygiene often could not compete with decades of cultural tradition.

When World War II ended the Depression, it also improved the lives of many poor rural residents. Some joined the military, although many were undoubtedly turned away because of physical defects caused by malnutrition, as well as because of venereal disease and tuberculosis. The people who remained had better chances for employment.

Many, however, did not escape the cycle of poverty. Hopkins' reporters were not the only ones to document rural conditions, and some of their colleagues are better remembered today. In 1936, photographer Walker Evans and writer James Agee were hired under a New Deal program to document conditions in the rural South in pictures and words. They talked to and photographed people whose lives were characterized by hard work, poverty, and despair. Their work was preserved in the now classic book, *Let Us Now Praise Famous Men.* Fifty years later, in 1986, two journalists traveled the same route that Evans and Agee had taken and interviewed some of the surviving families and their children. In *And Their Children After Them,* Michael Williamson, a photojournalist, documented their stories in pictures; Dale Maharidge wrote their stories. They found that many people's lives were almost as dismal as they had been in 1936.

Primary Source

"Dear Mr. Hopkins" [excerpt]

SYNOPSIS: In these excerpts from reports to Harry Hopkins, reporters Gellhorn and Francis vividly describe rural southerners whose lives were filled with hunger and disease and who lacked the resources to improve their situations. In the first excerpt, Francis reported on conditions in West Virginia; in the second, Gellhorn wrote from North Carolina.

Report to Mr. Hopkins on West Virginia from Henry W. Francis

Dr. R. L. Farley, whom I met at Delbarton, said:

> Health conditions here are worse than anywhere in the United States. You folks in the cities get excited over slum conditions—they're nothing compared to conditions in these hollows. In Williamson Hollow, just out of town, children are sleeping on the floor in corners of old shacks, rat-ridden, filthy and open to the four winds of Heaven. They're marked for death here—marked by the hundreds. We have everything in the way of disease. All forms of venereal rampant, tuberculosis, cancer—everything. Intermarriage has depleted the stock to begin with, malnutrition has further weakened it. It falls an easy prey to disease. Right now pneumonia is raging throughout these hills. People, lacking clothes but having relief coal or digging it in the hills, heat their hovels to suffocating temperatures. When the fires go out at night the temperature inside the shacks, open as they are, is the same as that outside. Bed clothing is scant and they sleep cold. Children, sleeping on floors, can't help getting pneumonia. I've half a dozen cases to see to-day.

Miss Cushman, Visiting Nurse said:

> Another case of typhoid to-day; we've had quite a lot of it. Due to unsanitary conditions. Water supply, usually wells, became polluted from toilet seepage. We fill up the wells with rocks and make them get water elsewhere. Sometime they have to carry it from wells a quarter of a mile away. I don't know how many cases of typhoid there are in the county. I have only this one now. But I've had a dozen.

C.O. Batson, Chairman of the Relief Welfare Board and Superintendent of Schools, said:

> Lack of clothing is causing suffering but it always has. The children have never been adequately clothed even in prosperous days. Malnutrition always has been a problem, too. More than a year ago the Kiwanis arranged for lunches to be served to needy children at school. The lunches were offered; not one child accepted. Pride prevented them from eating to their need. I believe that has all vanished now. We are planning to start serving hot lunches again on January 1st.
>
> Lack of clothing and a good deal of sickness is keeping children out of school. Our attendance is down to around seventy per cent. I think some children stay away because the parents feel that they can learn nothing without books. We have hardly any books. We have just reorganized the state school system into county units. The old district school system broke down due to political graft. Under the new system we cannot allow free books although I hope this soon will be changed. It is impossible for our teachers to hold the pupils without books. In the lower Jenny Street School, in Harvey District, we have sixty children and three books. You cannot blame parents for keeping their children home, especially when the children have to walk long distances in bad weather without shoes or proper clothing.

Report to Mr. Hopkins on North Carolina from Martha Gellhorn

The medical set-up in this area is non-existent; and I think my last report adequately stressed the terrific health conditions. Syphilis uncured and unchecked; spread by ignorant people who have no conception of the disease, and no special interest in getting cured. One doctor in Gastonia, who handles our relief cases, said, "syphilis has reached the point of being an epidemic here." The doctors all talk of malnutrition and fear the present and future effects. Birth control is needed here almost more than in any other area I have ever seen; there is one mill village where half the population is pathologic, and reproducing half wits and with alarming vigor. None of this is surprising; Gaston County has one health office and that's all in the way of public medicine. He himself is a total loss. The private doctors do what they can which isn't much. And all are appalled by what the future holds for these people, who are absolutely unequipped for life.

Further Resources

BOOKS

Agee, James, and Walker Evans. *Let Us Now Praise Famous Men.* New York: Houghton Mifflin, 1939.

Katz, William Loren, ed. *These Are Our Lives.* Chapel Hill, N.C.: University of North Carolina Press, 1939; reprinted, Arno, 1969.

Maharidge, Dale, and Michael Williamson. *And Their Children After Them.* New York: Pantheon, 1989.

Prenatal Care for Rural Poor

Social Security Act of 1935

Law

By: U.S. Congress

Date: 1935

Source: *Social Security Act of 1935.* Available at the Social Security Administration online at http://www.ssa.gov/history/35actv.html; website homepage at: http://www.ssa.gov (accessed March 17, 2003).

An African American woman holds her child in a slum apartment, Washington, D.C., 1937. Prior to the New Deal, black women and children were largely ignored by health care programs. THE LIBRARY OF CONGRESS.

"The County Health Nurse"

Interview

By: Chlotilde R. Martin

Date: January 31, 1939

Source: Ingram, Mattie. Interview by Chlotilde R. Martin. "The County Health Nurse," January 31, 1939. South Carolina Writers' Project. Available online in a search for "The County Health Nurse" at http://memory.loc.gov/ (accessed March 17, 2003).

About the Author: Chlotilde R. Martin was one of many writers employed by the Works Project Administration to document conditions in the United States during the Great Depression. ■

Introduction

The Social Security Act of 1935 included many provisions, one of which was for maternal and child health. In poor and rural areas, this was a need that had long gone unmet for a variety of reasons. There were not enough doctors and nurses, and people often could not afford to pay doctors even if any were available. Many were unaware that they had long-standing conditions that were dangerous to their health, syphilis being the primary example. Many had chronic conditions of which they were completely unaware (high blood pressure, diseases of malnutrition, and the like). Many faced such a struggle simply to survive that their only true health concern was being able to work.

Infant and maternal morbidity and mortality were particularly severe among poor rural African Americans (although they were also major problems among poor whites). The United States was at the time a racially segregated nation, and health care, too, was segregated. Most of these families had many children and no access to or knowledge of birth control. In fact, until 1937, physicians could not legally provide birth control information to their patients. Malnourished women gave birth to sickly infants, many of whom died. Syphilis was rampant, and children born to syphilitic mothers were likely not to survive.

Within this general population, however, people varied in their standard of living, ways of caring for children, and knowledge of hygiene. Some lived clean, orderly lives; others lived in utter squalor.

Significance

Under the New Deal, public health nurses were dispatched to work with poor black women and children and try to provide them with some prenatal care. The nurses also ran clinics for these women (where they could be seen by a doctor), instructed the midwives who would assist in the birthing process, tried to monitor such conditions as high blood pressure and, a particularly difficult task, attempted to get pregnant women into the clinics for "the shots" for syphilis or "bad blood." The treatments did not cure the disease, but they did reduce the rate of transmission to infants.

The nurses' own descriptions of their work with this population indicate that they faced a difficult task, yet their narratives also brought to public attention the variety that existed among a population that was assumed to be all alike. A few such narratives could not end years of stereotyping about how "they" lived, but these writings did modify some of the negative images. The nurses could not change situations caused by years of poverty, neglect, and lack of education. But their presence and effort were of enormous significance in both symbolic and practical terms.

In symbolic terms, the public health nurses' weekly rounds to visit their black prenatal patients marked for most of the patients the first time the white health care system had paid them the slightest bit of attention. As far back as they could remember, they had looked after their own, using practices passed down through the generations. Understandably, not all poor blacks welcomed the nurses. People who had never bothered with them were suddenly showing up and telling them how to live and how to treat their children, and resentment would seem a normal reaction. But some did welcome the nurses and tried to follow advice, visit the clinics, and have their children checked.

In practical terms, the nurses' work was a matter of achieving small victories. One mother might, as in the narrative quoted here, burn the clothes of an infant who had died rather than save them for her next born, or she might refuse to prepare for a baby's arrival in advance because it was bad luck. But others followed the nurses' suggestions about preparing for babies. Lacking clean linen and having only rudimentary washing facilities, the expectant mothers used the old newspapers that the nurses brought to cover the bed during birth, perhaps reducing the risk of infection from unsanitary conditions. The nurses also spotted health problems in the pregnant mothers' other children and urged visits to the clinic for treatment.

The work of these nurses during the Depression set the stage for the visiting nurse services that in the early 2000s operate all over the United States. The Depression-era nurses carried tins of donated milk; the much later Women, Infants, and Children government feeding program provides extra nutrition for these vulnerable groups. The nurses did not achieve sweeping change. They achieved slight change and, in doing so, improved the lives of some people.

Works Project Administration poster from the Cook County Public Health Unit. The Social Security Act of 1935 was a major first step in national maternal and child health care. THE LIBRARY OF CONGRESS.

Primary Source

Social Security Act of 1935 [excerpt]

SYNOPSIS: This Act included many provisions, one of which was for maternal and child health: public health nurses were dispatched to work with poor black women and children and try to provide them with some prenatal care.

Part 1—Maternal and Child Health Services

Appropriation

SECTION 501. For the purpose of enabling each State to extend and improve, as far as practicable under the conditions in such State, services for promoting the health of mothers and children, especially in rural areas and in areas suffering from severe economic distress, there is hereby authorized to be appropriated for each fiscal year, beginning with the fiscal year ending June 30, 1936, the sum of $3,800,000. The sums made available under this section shall be used for making payments to States which have submitted, and had approved by the Chief of the Children's Bureau, State plans for such services.

Primary Source

"The County Health Nurse" [excerpt]

SYNOPSIS: This account of a county health nurse presents, in the words of the nurse and her clients, the problems they both faced and the modest measures that eased some of these problems.

Date of First Writing: January 31, 1939
Name of Person Interviewed: Miss Mattie Ingram
Fictitious Name: Miss Brunson
Street Address: Port Republic
Place: Beaufort, S. C.
Occupation: County Health Nurse
Name of Writer: Chlotilde R. Martin

She stopped the car in front of Rosa Webb's house. "This is one more case where birth-control would be a blessing. Rosa isn't married—very few of these young mothers are. It's a funny thing, but parents will forbid their daughters to marry if they consider them too young, but they take motherhood as a natural event no matter how young they are. Rosa's mother has a house full of children herself and the burden of Rosa's child will fall on her."

We found Rosa bare-footed in the front room. This room, in contrast to the usual newspapered walls, was papered with regular wall paper, but it was furnished only with a table and a few chairs.

While Miss Brunson was taking Rosa's blood pressure, a flock of six small boys, ranging in ages from about ten to three, gathered in the door which led into the kitchen. They arranged themselves conveniently in steps so that the larger ones could look over the heads of the smaller ones and they stood staring with eyes like round black marbles.

When Rosa left the room to get a specimen of her urine, Miss Brunson tried to engage the boys in conversation. "How is your mother's baby?" she inquired.

There was no reply and she repeated the question, smiling. Still, there was no reply. "Why, can't any of you talk?" the nurse asked.

"'E daid," said one of the boys solemnly.

Rosa came back into the room and Miss Brunson turned to her. "Is your mother's baby really dead?"

Rosa nodded.

"That's too bad," Miss Brunson sympathized. "Have you made any clothes for your baby?"

Rosa shook her head. "Bad luck to mak clothes for chillen 'fo dey bawn."

Miss Brunson frowned. "But, Rosa, it isn't at all—you just think that." She smiled at Rosa. "Well, anyway, you'll have your little brother's clothes—they'll do nicely for your baby, won't they?"

Rosa look startled. "Us done bu'n dem."

Miss Brunson gasped. "Why, Rosa, you didn't really burn the baby's clothes!"

"'E bin sich a puny baby," Rosa explained.

"But that wouldn't have mattered—you could have boiled them, you know. Oh, Rosa, I'm so disappointed!"

But Rosa only shook her head. "Bad luck to dress live baby een puny daid baby clothes."

Miss Brunson sighed. "Come out to the car with me, Rosa, I want to give you something." She took some of the newspapers from the back seat and laid them in Rosa's arms. "They are to use on your bed when the baby comes—now, Rosa, don't burn them or paper your house with them. Your baby is coming next month and you'll need them—will you remember?"

Further Resources

BOOKS

Bauman, John F., and Thomas H. Goode. *In the Eye of the Great Depression: New Deal Reporters and the Agony of the American People.* DeKalb, Ill.: Northern Illinois University Press, 1988.

Katz, William Loren, ed. *These Are Our Lives: As Told by the People and Written by Members of the Federal Writers' Project of the Works Progress Administration in North Carolina, Tennessee, and Georgia.* Chapel Hill, N.C.: University of North Carolina Press, 1939. Reprint: New York: Arno Press and *The New York Times,* 1969.

Westin, Jeanne. *Making Do: How Women Survived the '30s.* Chicago: Follett, 1976.

Consumer Protection Expands

American Chamber of Horrors

Nonfiction work

By: Ruth deForest Lamb

Date: 1936

Source: Lamb, Ruth deForest. *American Chamber of Horrors.* New York: Farrar and Rinehart, 1936, 123–127.

About the Author: Ruth deForest Lamb was the chief education officer at the U.S. Food and Drug Administration during at era when the public was being deluged with advertisements for quack remedies and useless and sometimes dangerous devices, cosmetics, and regimes. Her book, along with the work of other FDA officials, was instrumental in convincing the U.S. Congress to pass the *Food, Drug, and Cosmetic Act of 1938.*

Food, Drug, and Cosmetic Act of 1938

Law

By: U.S. Congress

Date: 1938

Source: *Food, Drug, and Cosmetic Act of 1938.* Sec. 351.—Adulterated drugs and devices. Available at the Legal Information Institute online at http://www4.law.cornell.edu/uscode/21/351.html; website homepage at: http://www4.law.cornell.edu (accessed March 18, 2003). ■

Introduction

With modern medicine, Americans can feel fairly confident that their ills can be effectively treated, if not cured. If they really want to change their appearance or eliminate the visible effects of aging, they can, provided they are willing and able to spend the money. And they can also go shopping for food, feeling secure that the products they buy are free of harmful ingredients and additives.

In the 1930s, none of the above was true. In 1906, Congress had passed the so-called *Wiley Act* that prohibited the manufacture and interstate transport of adulterated and misbranded foods and drugs. The government could take action against a suspect manufacturer, but the law contained no components that would prevent these foods and drugs from being manufactured in the first place.

Medical research brought some advances, but many illnesses remained untreatable, and people turned to quacks who sold patent medicines (the formulas were patented) that they claimed could cure disease. People were willing to pay for "miracle cures." In the quest for a young and beautiful appearance, they also swallowed the outrageous claims of some cosmetic advertisements. Moreover, hit by the economic hardships of the Great Depression, housewives bought adulterated food (cut with poisonous or impure ingredients) because it was sometimes all that they could afford.

The 1930s were also part of the "medicine show" era. Medicine showmen (and women) traveled from town to town touting their "cures," many of which were common substances with fancy labels. Although profits dwindled as fewer people were able to afford patent medicines, the medicine shows still sold to people who could not afford doctors. In *Snake Oil, Hustlers, and Hambones,* Ann Anderson describes a gimmick used with a tapeworm "remedy." Part of the cure involved swallowing a gelatin capsule that contained an artificial tapeworm, then it would be excreted by the patient, thus "proving" that the person was cured of this parasite.

The public's willingness to believe these claims was only part of the problem. Congress had enacted the first *Food, Drug, and Cosmetic Act* in 1906 but had undone most of its effectiveness in 1912. That year, it passed an amendment that still outlawed false therapeutic claims but required that the government prove that the claims were indeed false. The requirement was not for scientific evidence that the claim was false. Rather, Congress asked only that the person who was charged with selling false remedies did in fact believe that they worked. Few people charged with selling ineffective medicine were going to stand up in a court of law and say, in effect, "You're right, your Honor. It doesn't work." One of President Franklin D. Roosevelt's first initiatives was to rewrite the law, but powerful opposition from the industries involved and the advertising agencies they paid kept it from passing in 1933. Soon after, legislators, pro-consumer factions and organizations, and the administration began to craft a new bill.

Well-publicized tragedy provided the push that Congress needed to pass the bill. A substance called "Elixir Sulfanilamide" (diethylene glycol) was sold as a prescription cure for childhood infections. The elixir had not been tested for safety or toxicity (amount of poison in it), an omission that proved fatal to many children who died of kidney failure caused by the drug. Five years after the first legislation failed to pass, Roosevelt signed the *Food, Drug, and Cosmetic Act of 1938.*

Significance

The new law, although not perfect, protected consumers from a good many of the practices that had been legal. Drug manufacturers had to test drugs for safety before selling them to the public. Factories that produced any consumer goods that fell within the act could be inspected. The government no longer had to prove fraud against manufacturers who made false claims. Food processors were forbidden from adding poisonous substances to foods in most cases.

The gaps in the law set the stage for stronger legislation. The 1938 legislation protected consumers from substances known to be toxic. A new substance could be added without testing. In 1949, after two years of congressional hearings and work on chemicals in food, Congress amended the 1938 act to require manufacturers to prove a substance was safe before adding it to foods (and later, cosmetics). The Delaney Amendments, so-called for Congressman James Delaney, who chaired the hearings, provided the FDA with a powerful weapon with which to protect consumers.

Beyond its immediate effects, the 1938 act was an important step in what was to become an ongoing effort to protect the American public from untried drugs and false claims about food and cosmetic products. The law's passage marked the emergence of the "consumer" as an influence on product legislation. One of the groups promoting the law was Consumer's Research, the first such group and the precursor of what is now a powerful consumer lobby. Americans routinely consult *Consumer Reports* before choosing brands of food or buying new goods and appliances.

Primary Source

American Chamber of Horrors [excerpt]

SYNOPSIS: In this chapter of *American Chamber of Horrors,* the author describes some fraudulent weight-loss plans.

Those 62 pounds of lost fat that Margaret George chalked up to the credit of *Germania Herb Tea* make a pretty good showing; but for all that, the Grand Prize in the Reducing Racket Sweepstakes must go to *Kruschen Salts,* for Miss Nellie Simpson of Swissvale, Pa., testified that by taking this mixture of Epsom, table, and other common salts (with its dash of potassium iodide, presumably to act upon the thyroid and speed up metabolism) she had succeeded in reducing her avoirdupois as much as 102 pounds. Though this cathartic has since gone high-hat and crashed the aristocratic pages of *Vogue* and *Harper's Bazaar,* it was with just such old-time circus stuff as Nellie Simpson's testimonial and before-and-after pictures that *Kruschen* started the present epidemic of reduction-by-purging.

Jad Salts, which had suffered a head-on collision with the meat industry some years before ("Too Much Meat Hurts Kidneys") as well as multiple seizures under the Food and Drugs Act, was delighted with this new selling appeal and lost no time in getting a ride on the vast sums spent to advertise *Kruschen.* Promising to reduce your weight "a pound a day on a full stomach" if you but follow directions, the manufacturer, like all the other reducing racketeers, has been careful to recommend a regimen of diet and exercise, and to include in every advertisement a significant note to this effect:

> The *Condensed* JAD Salts, remember, is urged as a poison-banishing agent and to banish unhealthy bloating . . . not as a reducing one.

The most elaborate of all the reducing programs, however, is the one which accompanies *Dr. McCasky's Prescription Tablets.* It has the distinction, moreover, of originating with a real M. D.—Donald Gilbert McCasky, a graduate of Fordham, with a medical degree from Pennsylvania. Dr. McCasky, according to the advertising, is "an internationally recognized authority on weight control, basal metabolism, electro-cardiography and blood chemistry." The regime he advises includes not only the usual diet and exercise, but also Epsom salt baths (presumably *Fayro,* in which he takes a kindly interest) and the Fro-tage Treatment. This is a daily stiff brushing with Epsom salts—a handful to a basin of water. His *Prescription Tablets* used to be compounded of potassium chloride, cane sugar, potato starch, saccharin and aromatics—in other words a diuretic with filler and flavoring. It was harmless enough unless you happened to have a kidney disease or some other ailment in which salt would be contraindicated, and the taking of it, if you were one of his idle-rich patients, gave you something to think about while the unwonted exercise and restrictions in diet were doing the work.

But then Dr. McCasky fell in with some clever promoters, James M. Marner and M. H. Sloman, who had been making a good thing out of *Fayro,* despite such setbacks as seizures by the Food and Drug Administration and trouble with the Post Office and the Federal Trade Commission. Marner, president of the *Fayro* concern, professed to have got the *Fayro* formula from Lillian Russell, but being skeptical, so he says, of its merits, added a diet list. Sloman, the advertising representative and former president, has been mixed up with a variety of medicine rackets, slipping in and out with quick thrusts and getting rid of his interests whenever the proposition threatened to become too hot to handle or had been milked dry. His first venture of any note was *Tanlac,* a wine and bitter-herb mixture for "catarrh"—meaning what have you. Sloman was supposed to be handling the advertising, but took a one-fourth interest in the business to pay for his services. His partner was an old-time medicine-show man by the name of Cooper, who mortgaged his wife's house to float the enterprise. When a Cincinnati newspaper notified Sloman that one of the *Tanlac* testimonials had been published two weeks after the writer's death, he became alarmed and sold out to Cooper.

Over a million and a half packages of *Fayro* were sold in 1931—at $1.25 apiece. On the basis of ingredients they cost about 3 cents and contained enough of the pine-scented mixture of common rock and Epsom salts for three baths. Though the stuff was obviously a fake, it had also to be proved a fraud before it could be taken off the market. Seizure was possible only because the promoters had carelessly slipped up with some therapeutic claims for rheumatism, neuralgia and gout in the labeling.

While the Post Office can issue a fraud order, and the Federal Trade Commission a cease-and-desist order, without going to court, the Food and Drug Administration, before it can make a seizure—the action fairly comparable to these orders—must first have the United States attorney file a libel in the Federal court of the district where the goods are found and later, if the manufacturer chooses to contest the action, fight it out before a court and jury. Though it does not happen often, it is always possible that the court may refuse to permit the filing of the libel. To establish fraud in the *Fayro* case, it was to the advantage of the Administration to provide evidence for the Post Office and the Commission to act first. Then, when the manufacturer had stipulated to stop using the mails to defraud, and had also been on the receiving end of a cease-and-desist order, there was a much better chance of getting a favorable verdict from the jury. Under the treacherous fraud joker, the Administration can never be too careful in preparing its cases, for it is not authorized to throw away taxpayers' money on hopeless court actions just for the sake of making a gesture.

Since Dr. McCasky joined forces with the *Fayro* outfit, his *Prescription Tablets* seem to have been changed. For while they still contain potassium chloride, and a bit of starch and milk sugar with oil of peppermint to flavor, they now depend for action, not on suggestion, but on *yellow phenolphthalein* at the rate of a grain a day. In other words, you are supposed to dose yourself constantly with a powerful laxative of the poisonous type in order to reduce!

Differ though they may in some respects, there is one thing that all the reducing racketeers have in common, aside from a talent for exploiting the public, and that is a cordial dislike of having the facts about their products made known. They always complain bitterly whenever such information is given out. But would the manufacturer have the Food and Drug Administration ignore a letter like this:

> I have been told that Marmola contains the head of a tapeworm.
>
> Would you be kind enough to analize Marmola. If there is a charge for this please let me know at your earliest.

This tapeworm story, by the way, seems to be one of those imperishable bits of American folklore that turn up every so often in different parts of the country. Usually it is told about *Marmola,* for this thyroid preparation is the most widely advertised reducing agent put out in tablet form. Another reason why *Marmola* is singled out for this dubious honor may be that thyroid, by making the consumer "live" faster than normally, has a depleting effect on the system. According to one popular version, the presence of the tapeworm is discovered when the tablets become lively after lying on the window sill in the sun; in another, they hop around at any time like Mexican jumping beans. There is no scientific evidence to show that the tapeworm ever cavorts in this fashion. Though it is a pity to scotch the legend, the sad truth is that while the story has been circulating for years no Federal agency has ever been able to find any product, whether *Marmola* or another, that contained any part of a tapeworm. Of course, if *Marmola* carried an honest and straightforward label, it would not lay itself open to such canards.

Much as they dislike to tell you the truth about what their products contain and how they really act to reduce weight—that is to say, the whole truth, for some of them do list the scientific names of their ingredients on the package—the manufacturers do not hesitate to say, in superior fashion, what their products are not. Isabella Laboratories, for instance, advertises that

> Formula 281 is a scientifically safe reducing remedy that has *no laxative* effect and can be used with complete confidence.

This nostrum, as it happens, is anything but "safe"; for though it may not be a laxative, its active ingredient is deadly, tissue-consuming dinitrophenol, which even the *Drug and Cosmetic Industry* concedes to be too dangerous to use in a patent medicine.

A more ingenious type of fake comprises the foods sold as fat-reducers. In the case of *Stardom's Hollywood Diet,* you are assured that

> The possibilities of your having an exciting type of Hollywood figure is now so real as to be actually breath-taking, and to gain it you won't have to go hungry, engage in violent exercises, use drugs or resort to laxatives; all of these methods are taboo.

Primary Source

Food, Drug, and Cosmetic Act of 1938 [excerpt]

SYNOPSIS: With the introduction of this new bill, drug manufacturers had to test drugs for safety before selling them to the public; factories that produced any consumer goods that fell within the act could be inspected. Consumers were now protected from substances known to be toxic.

A drug or device shall be deemed to be adulterated—

(a) Poisonous, insanitary, etc., ingredients; adequate controls in manufacture

(1) If it consists in whole or in part of any filthy, putrid, or decomposed substance; or

(2A) If it has been prepared, packed, or held under unsanitary conditions whereby it may have been contaminated with filth, or whereby it may have been rendered injurious to health; or

(2B) If it is a drug and the methods used in, or the facilities or controls used for, its manufacture, processing, packing, or holding do not conform to or are not operated or administered in conformity with current good manufacturing practice to assure that such drug meets the requirements of this chapter as to safety and has the identity and strength, and meets the quality and purity characteristics, which it purports or is represented to possess; or

(2C) If it is a compounded positron emission tomography drug and the methods used in, or the facilities and controls used for, its compounding, processing, packing, or holding do not conform to or are not operated or administered in conformity with the positron emission tomography compounding standards and the official monographs of the United States Pharmacopoeia to assure that such drug meets the requirements of this chapter as to safety and has the identity and strength, and meets the quality and purity characteristics, that it purports or is represented to possess.

Further Resources

BOOKS

Anderson, Ann. *Snake Oil, Hustlers, and Hambones: The American Medicine Show.* Jefferson, N.C.: McFarland, 2000.

McCoy, Bob. *Quack! Tales of Medical Fraud.* Santa Monica, Calif: Santa Monica Press, 2000.

Peiss, Kathy. *Hope in a Jar: The Making of America's Beauty Culture.* New York: Henry Holt, 1998.

WEBSITES

Museum of Questionable Devices. Available online at http://www.mtn.org/quack (accessed on March 4, 2003).

Food and Drug Administration home page. Available online at http://www.fda.gov (accessed online at March 4, 2003).

"Surgery Used on the Soul-Sick; Relief of Obsessions is Reported"

Newspaper article

By: William L. Laurence

Date: June 7, 1937

Source: Laurence, William L. "Surgery Used on the Soul-Sick; Relief of Obsessions is Reported." *The New York Times,* June 6, 1938.

About the Author: William Laurence (1888–1977), science reporter, was born Leid Siew in the village of Salantai, Lithuania. He wrote about many important scientific breakthroughs in the 1930s and 1940s, one of which demonstrated his rare gift for reducing modern scientific theory to easily comprehended terms. Largely on the strength of that story, *The New York Times* hired him as its full-time science reporter in 1930. Later he became science editor, a position he held until his retirement in 1964. Known also as "Atomic Bill," Laurence wrote several books on atomic energy. ■

Introduction

Insanity, lunacy, paresis, and *dementia praecox* were some of the names used to describe what is now termed mental illness. Until the early years of the twentieth century, people afflicted with what would now be called schizophrenia, depression, and other diseases were sent to asylums where they were looked after, although not treated; if a family could afford it, they were kept at home.

In the early twentieth century, physicians began to view these ailments as treatable. The treatment came in two forms, the psychological and the physiological. The first was pioneered by followers of the Austrian psychoanalyst Sigmund Freud and was talk therapy. The second took multiple forms. Psychiatrists in various countries began to experiment with physiological modes of intervention. One of the first was insulin therapy, pioneered by German physician Manfred J. Sakel, who found that overdosing his schizophrenic patients with insulin caused convulsions, which reduced their schizophrenic symptoms. Sakel brought his therapy to the United States in 1934. The so-called convulsive therapy was tried with various drugs, but insulin proved the safest and most effective. A few years later, an Italian neurologist began using electric shocks to produce convulsions. Electroconvulsive therapy, or ECT, was widely used.

Convulsive therapy, however, did not produce lasting results. Psychosurgery did. Psychosurgery had its origins in the United States, when neurologists noted that damaging or removing the frontal lobes of the brain in chimpanzees eliminated aggressive behavior. Portuguese neurologist Antonio Moniz applied their findings to humans and reported in 1936 that the operation that he termed a leucotomy, or cutting of the white matter in the brain, greatly reduced the symptoms of some severely agitated or depressed patients. The operation did not lead to improvement in other patients, however, and Moniz advised that it be used only in extreme cases.

American neurologist Walter Freeman initially issued the same cautions as Moniz. But by 1938, two years after he first tried the operation, he was promoting the surgery and conducting many operations. Freeman and his colleague, neurosurgeon James Watts, traveled around the United States performing the surgery, which they called the prefrontal lobotomy. Freeman, however, thought that the operation was too time-consuming and developed a new technique. The technical name was the "transorbital approach"; it was known popularly as the "ice-pick lobotomy" because a tool that greatly resembled an ice pick was inserted through the patient's eye socket until it penetrated the brain. The surgeon then moved it around to destroy the brain cells that were presumably causing the unacceptable behavior. Watts did not approve of the technique and separated from Freeman.

Significance

The lobotomy became the new miracle cure for mental illness. Freeman overcame the initial objections of the medical community and persuaded many of his colleagues that the lobotomy was the solution to ills that ranged from schizophrenia to depression. By 1942, for example, Connecticut medical officials were terming the operation "a major contribution to psychiatry" in their state, according to a March 22 article in *The New York Times.* West Virginia conducted mass lobotomies on mental patients, the *Times* also reported. R.M.E. Sabbatini, in his article on the history of the lobotomy, notes that the psychiatric casualties of World War II were filling the mental asylums. The lobotomy promised a way to deliver them from their demons. Between 1939 and 1951, according to Sabbatini, at least eighteen thousand lobotomies were performed in the United States.

In 1949, Freeman was still promoting the lobotomy in medical journals and attributing failure to poor choice of patients and unskilled surgeons. Evidence contrary to his arguments was piling up, though. By 1950, it was acknowledged that one-third of lobotomy patients improved, one-third stayed the same, and one-third got worse, according to Sabbatini. Given that one-third of mental patients recover without treatment, these statistics were not a ringing endorsement for lobotomy. By the early to mid-1950s, lobotomy had lost most of its luster, and even Freeman acknowledged its limitations.

The legacy of the lobotomy extended beyond the many lives it destroyed. It also created an enduring suspicion of any kind of psychosurgery. Freeman and his followers used a technique that was imprecise to an extreme. They had no idea what cells they were wiping out. By the end of the twentieth century, however, advances in several fields of medicine made the prospect of psychosurgery much more precise. First, physicians gained considerable understanding of the structure of the brain and which parts affected which kinds of behavior. At the same time, advances in imaging techniques allowed physicians to see, as they performed surgery, the precise area of the brain that they wanted to influence. The lobotomy and the way it was massively abused, however, have made both neurologists and patients extremely suspicious of surgical intervention for psychiatric problems.

Primary Source

"Surgery Used on the Soul-Sick; Relief of Obsessions is Reported"

SYNOPSIS: This article by the science reporter William Laurence describes what was viewed as a sanity-saving operation for people with psychiatric illnesses.

New Brain Technique Is Said to Have Aided 65% of the Mentally Ill Persons on Whom It Was Tried as Last Resort, but Some Leading Neurologists Are Highly Skeptical of It.

Atlantic City, N.J., June 6.—A new surgical technique, known as "psycho-surgery," which, it is claimed, cuts away sick parts of the human personality, and transforms wild animals into gentle creatures in the course of a few hours, will be demonstrated here tomorrow at the Comprehensive

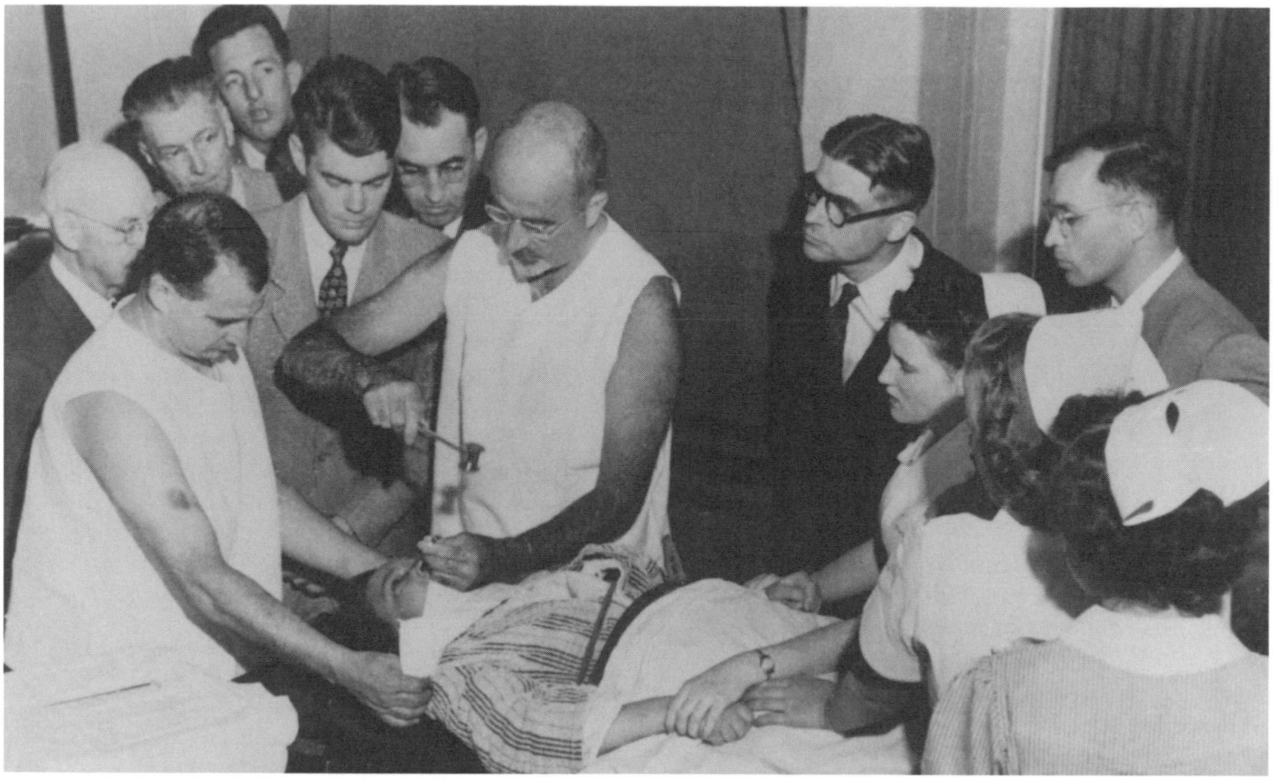

Dr. Walter Freeman performs the "ice pick" lobotomy he perfected on a mentally-ill patient. Lobotomy experiments flourished in the mid-1930s and became a common surgical procedure by the 1940s. UPI/CORBIS-BETTMANN. REPRODUCED BY PERMISSION.

Scientific Exhibit of the American Medical Association, which is holding its eighty-eighth annual assembly here this week.

The new "surgery of the soul" has been applied to twenty mentally ill human beings, 15 per cent of whom, it is claimed, were "greatly improved," with an additional 50 per cent "moderately improved." It is asserted the mental symptoms relieved by this new brain operation, often performed under local anaesthesia, include tension, apprehension, anxiety, depression, insomnia, suicidal ideas, delusions, hallucinations, crying spells, melancholia, obsessions, panic states, disorientation, psychalgesia (pains of psychic origin), nervous indigestion and hysterical paralysis.

When performed on wild monkeys, two of which were placed on exhibition here today, the brain operation changed the apprehensive, anxious and hostile creatures of the jungle into creatures as gentle as the organ grinder's monkey.

The new "soul surgery" was originally announced last year in a French scientific publication by Dr. Egas Moniz of Lisbon, Portugal. The results obtained by him appeared so startling that they were repeated in this country on cases in which every recognized form of treatment had been employed without improvement.

The exhibit is presented by Dr. James W. Watts, Dr. Walter Freeman and Dr. Ralph W. Barris of George Washington University Medical School. A supplementary paper will be presented by Drs. Watts and Freeman before the section on nervous and mental diseases on Wednesday. The title of the paper is "Psycho-Surgery: Effect on Certain Mental Symptoms of Surgical Interruption in the Pathways in the Frontal Lobe."

The new surgery consists in separating twelve small cores of the white matter in the brain, underlying the gray matter of the two frontal lobes, from the rest of the brain's white matter. The cores, each one centimeter in diameter, are not taken out of the brain, but are left in their places after the surgical instrument, known as the leucotome, has separated them from their original environment.

The twelve cores are separated in two groups of six each, one group below the gray matter of each of the two frontal lobes, which are regarded as the seat of intellectual integration. Only two holes, however, are drilled in the scalp, each hole being sufficient, by proper manipulation of the instrument, for the separation of six cores.

Case Histories Are Cited

Here are a few of the cases to be described by Drs. Freeman and Watts before the meeting:

"Mrs. A. H., housewife, aged 63. Two previous nervous breakdowns. Always meticulous and exacting. Increasing apprehension, anxiety, insomnia, agitation and tension for one year, so that the patient was confined to her home with special day and night nurses.

"After the operation (prefrontal lobotomy), Sept. 14, 1936, the symptoms disappeared immediately. Now manages home and household accounts, enjoys people, attends theatre, drives her own car. Great improvement.

"Case 2. Mrs. E. A., bookkeeper, aged 59. In bed since nervous breakdown May, 1936. Complained of anxiety and agitation, fear of being poisoned, constant mourning and weeping. Disoriented. Confined to hospital with special day and night nurses. Immediate disappearance of anxiety, apprehension and pain after a prefrontal lobotomy Oct. 7, 1936. Has been working in old position as bookkeeper continuously since Jan. 1, 1937. Great improvement."

After citing a number of other cases, some of which were only moderately improved, while 35 per cent of the others showed no improvement, Drs. Freeman and Watts state:

"After cutting the pathways in the prefrontal area, there was a disappearance or a reduction of tension, apprehension, anxiety, depression and agitation in all but two cases. The relief of the symptoms has persisted to the present time in more than half of the patients. Ten of the twelve patients having ideas of suicide before operation no longer consider self-destruction. Crying spells have ceased in six of nine patients. Hallucinations have gradually cleared up in the seven patients who had them.

"More than half of the patients are unresponsive for a week or two after the operation. They answer questions, but speak only when spoken to. The change in behavior which persists is slight and may be described as emotional, flattening, diminished spontaneity, lack of attention and indifference.

"Seven patients, on the contrary, were very talkative and definitely euphoric for two or four weeks after operation. Transient perseveration of speech and disorientation have occurred a few times."

Two Died After Operation

One patient died several months after the operation and another patient died on the sixth day after the operation, the physicians report.

On the other hand, some of the leading neurologists who viewed the exhibit today expressed themselves as being very skeptical about the new "psycho-surgery" and they predicted that the method would meet with considerable criticism.

In devising his new technique, Dr. Moniz worked on the assumption, Drs. Freeman and Watts said, "that while there are no detectable abnormalities of the brain in certain of the functional psychoses, the symptoms might be due to the development of stereotypy in cortical association centers, i. e., fixed patterns of response tending to perpetuate themselves to the detriment of the personality as a whole.

"By forcibly breaking up the connections over a large area, an opportunity would be given, Dr. Moniz argued, for reintegration of cortical activity along different lines."

Further Resources

BOOKS

Grob, Gerald N. *The Mad Among Us: A History of the Care of America's Mentally Ill.* New York: Free Press, 1994.

Kalinowsky, Lother B., and Paul H. Hoch. *Shock Treatments, Psychosurgery, and Other Somatic Treatments in Psychiatry,* rev. ed. New York: Grune & Stratton, 1952.

Whitaker, Robert. *Mad in America: Bad Science, Bad Medicine, and the Enduring Mistreatment of the Mentally Ill.* New York: Perseus, 2001.

PERIODICALS

Freeman, Walter. "Psychosurgery: Retrospects and Prospects Based on Twenty Years' Experience." *Psychosurgery,* February 1949.

WEBSITES

"History of Lobotomy." Available online at http://www.epub.org.br/cm/n02/historia/lobotomy.htm; website home page: http://www.epub.org.br (accessed March 4, 2003).

"Moniz develops lobotomy for mental illness." Public Broadcasting System information. Available online at http://www.pbs.org/wgbh/aso/databank/entries/dh35lo.html; website home page: http://www.pbs.org/ (accessed March 4, 2003).

March of Dimes Poster

Poster

By: National Foundation for Infantile Paralysis

Date: 1937

Source: "National Foundation for Infantile Paralysis Campaign." Poster, 1937. Available at the New Deal Network online at http://newdeal.feri.org/library/w23.htm; website homepage http://newdeal.feri.org (accessed March 17, 2003).

About the Organization: In 1937, President Frankin D. Roosevelt announced the creation of the National Foundation for Infantile Paralysis, a private organization headed by his former law partner, Basil O'Connor. The campaign to raise private funds became known as the "March of Dimes" during a fundraiser in Hollywood, California, when radio personality Eddie Cantor suggested the name based on the idea that most Americans, even in the Depression, could afford to send ten cents to support the cause. (The name was also a take-off on the song "The March of Time.") ■

Introduction

When Franklin Delano Roosevelt took office as president of the United States in 1933, he was a man who had already profoundly affected public opinion about polio, known then as infantile paralysis. As governor of New York, he had taken on the cause of crippled children. But he himself was a powerful symbol and agent of change. Polio had long been viewed as a disease that struck poor, dirty children. Roosevelt, who was rich and came from a privileged family, contracted the disease in his thirties. Despite his handicap (he was never able to walk unassisted, even after years of rehabilitation), he went on to become president of the United States.

Roosevelt's situation raised public awareness of polio, and events in his honor raised money for research into its causes. The first such effort was the "birthday balls," held on January 30, the president's birthday. The first birthday ball was held in 1934 and raised $1 million, a stunning amount given the economic circumstances of the time. Although linked to Roosevelt's birthday, the birthday balls were nonpartisan. They set the stage for later fundraising for polio by not-for-profit agencies that used what one historian deemed "sophisticated advertising techniques." One of these was the March of Dimes, the fund-raising effort of the National Foundation for Infantile Paralysis

Singer and comedian Eddie Cantor's suggestion that the effort be called March of Dimes caught on. It resulted in an avalanche of ten-cent pieces mailed to the White House. As the historian Naomi Rogers noted, "The Foundation's campaigns were a stunning success, based on the premise that polio had the potential to attack any child, despite class or ethnicity."

Significance

The National Foundation for Infantile Paralysis had both short- and long-term effects. The most immediate effect was an influx of funds from ordinary Americans. These monies went to scientists who were already engaged in the fight against polio. Many were unaccustomed to being part of a high-profile campaign, but "flamboyant publicity" was the name of the game. The foundation maintained close ties with celebrities and Hollywood; the disease touched the lives of even the rich and glamorous.

The foundation also made a major contribution toward the eventual development of a vaccine for polio. In the process, it nurtured the emerging science of virology (the science that studies viruses). It was a grant from the foundation that funded the work of John Enders, Thomas Weller, and Frederick Robbins. The researchers used a different strain of the polio virus and were able to grow it in cells other than nerve cells and in cultures rather than only in animals. This, noted Rogers, "cleared the way for safe vaccine production." In 1954, the team was awarded the Nobel Prize for their work. The post-World War II years brought foundation-sponsored debates on the virology of polio. These conferences (as well as other scientific communications) marked the emergence of what was to be perhaps the most controversial aspect of the development of the vaccine. Jonas Salk believed that immunity could be achieved using a so-called "killed virus" vaccine. Albert Sabin (as well as Enders and others) believed that it was necessary to use a live vaccine.

Treatment of polio patients was also a part of the foundation's mission. It is credited with setting up "respiratory" centers that housed iron lungs, the instruments of both torment and survival that maintained the lives of severely affected polio victims. The foundation also endorsed the controversial methods of Australian nurse Sister Elizabeth Kenny. Kenny's system of rehabilitating polio victims went against the received wisdom that it was best to immobilize the limbs of polio patients.

The foundation changed both its mission and its name as progress was made against polio. The development of vaccines greatly reduced (but did not eliminate) the incidence of the disease, and the foundation turned its attention to other physical disabilities of infants and children. In 1978, the name was changed to the March of Dimes Birth Defects Foundation, and in 1998 it became simply the March of Dimes.

Beyond the effects of its efforts to raise both funds and public awareness, the foundation pioneered a kind of

Primary Source

March of Dimes Poster

SYNOPSIS: The child pictured on this billboard was one of many who both symbolized and brought success to the work of the National Foundation for Infantile Paralysis. The organization received many contributions for victims of polio despite the general lack of money during the Depression. COURTESY OF THE FDR LIBRARY.

biomedical public relations that went beyond that of its predecessors (such as the National Tuberculosis Association). The image of the brave crippled child struggling to walk again was in itself a powerful instrument in both efforts. At the same time, however, the foundation operated at a local level that invoked grass-roots support. Each state had a "poster child" each year; the term is now used to describe a person who serves as a highly publicized example (positive or negative) of a particular problem or situation.

Further Resources

BOOKS

Gould, Tony. *A Summer Plague: Polio and Its Survivors.* New Haven, Conn.: Yale University Press, 1995.

Rogers, Naomi. *Dirt and Disease: Polio Before FDR.* New Brunswick, N.J.: Rutgers University Press, 1992.

WEBSITES

March of Dimes Home Page. Available online at http://www.modimes.org (accessed March 3, 2003).

Shadow on the Land

Nonfiction work

By: Thomas Parran, M.D.

Date: 1937

Source: Parran, Thomas. *Shadow on the Land: Syphilis, the White Man's Burden.* New York: Waverly, 1937, 59–69.

About the Author: Thomas Parran, M.D. (1892–1968) was the director of the U.S. Public Health Service's Division of Venereal Disease in 1932, when the Tuskegee Experiment began. He was serving as U.S. surgeon general at the time he wrote this book. ■

Introduction

No one knows the origin of syphilis. What is clear is that Africans brought to the United States as slaves did not suffer from the disease before they encountered white men. Because far more African Americans than whites were poor and uneducated, they were less likely to receive treatment when they did contract syphilis. The treatment did not cure the disease, but studies had by 1932 proved that it reduced death rates.

The 1930s were a time when paternalistic racism was the best treatment that many African Americans could expect. This view held that blacks were an inferior race and that it was the duty of whites to look after them. The living conditions of many poor blacks in the American rural South made it clear that no one did care.

Poor rural blacks were viewed as cheap labor. In most cases, their employers were interested in their workers' health only because a worker afflicted with syphilis could not do nearly as much work, and thus the worker constituted an economic loss to the owner. Medical care for blacks was limited; few had access to clinics and hospitals or money to pay private physicians.

The surgeon general's book marked the start of a major public health campaign against syphilis. Dr. Parran wrote his book to educate the American public on the problem of syphilis and encourage afflicted people to seek treatment.

Thomas Parran, Jr., in 1936, shortly after being appointed U.S. Surgeon General. Parran's *Shadow on the Land* helped start a national health campaign against syphilis. In it he argued that whites were responsible for spreading the disease to blacks. AP/WIDE WORLD PHOTOS. REPRODUCED BY PERMISSION.

Significance

Shadow on the Land was an important book for several reasons, but modern readers must think of it in the context of the time. In an era in which many whites would not employ blacks because they feared syphilis, Parran made what was then a relatively enlightened argument that having spread syphilis to blacks in the first place, whites had some responsibility for helping them receive treatment. He was, so to speak, talking out of both sides of his mouth; the Tuskegee Experiment was never intended to provide treatment.

Although the methods that Parran and his colleagues devised for recruiting subjects, initially for treatment and later for the study, were indeed racist, they also showed cultural awareness. The investigators studied the cultural beliefs of the people and tailored their methods of recruitment to fit those beliefs. They noted that the black community was more likely to become involved if the study was promoted by its most respected members, the well educated and the clergy. They recognized that the people involved would respond better to black health care professionals and recruited as many as they could, including Nurse Eunice Rivers, who became a major figure in the study. These methods anticipated those that became common in later years.

Parran made another argument that was unusual for the time: that poverty, not race, accounted for the high rates of syphilis among some groups of blacks. The standard explanation for these high rates was that blacks, in general, contracted syphilis because they were more sexually active than whites. Parran used statistics to show that rates of syphilis were the same in both races when groups lived under the same conditions of poverty and hopelessness. His unspoken argument was that people of both races were sexually active because they had nothing significant to do, no education, and no hope of improving their situation.

The surgeon general's criticism of American churches also differed markedly from the prevailing attitudes. He made the cynical point that the "great churches" pay far more attention to saving souls in Africa and other lands than they do working for a better earthly life for their own fellow citizens.

A third significant aspect of Parran's book was less noble. He used it to justify the failure to treat the subjects in the Tuskegee Experiment. That experiment lasted forty years and was designed to follow the natural history of the disease if left untreated. Parran's arguments, coming from the nation's highest-ranking medical official, placed a stamp of approval on the Tuskegee Experiment that medical researchers did not question until they were forced to do so.

Primary Source

Shadow on the Land [excerpt]

SYNOPSIS: In *Shadow on the Land,* Surgeon General Thomas Parran argues that contrary to the popular belief, syphilis among blacks was spread by whites, who then failed to help improve the lives of poor black Americans. At the same time, he used the book as a platform for justifying the ongoing Tuskegee Experiment, which withheld treatment for syphilis from a group of black men and continued to do so for forty years.

Syphilis is the white man's disease. He may, as medical historians tell us, have contracted it from the American Indian following Columbus' discovery. But the brown, the yellow, and the black races seem to have been infected with it only after the visits of the white explorers to their native lands, and it has continued to decimate the white populations of the earth.

It has been said that the negro slave brought to America malaria and hookworm disease. If he did, the white man paid him back with usury by giving him tuberculosis and syphilis. The fact that he is at the bottom of the economic ladder contributes to his abnormally high death rate. For among the third of our population which is ill fed, ill clothed, and ill housed, as a race, north and south, and especially in the rural south, his house is the most miserable, his clothing the scantiest, and his food ration the most poorly balanced.

Scattered evidence accumulated over a period of years had indicated a high prevalence of venereal disease, and especially syphilis, among the Negroes. Wenger had shown this in several Mississippi counties. He had shown also that the Negroes welcomed these blood tests. "Holding high Wassermann in the market place," Keyes called it after seeing Wenger at work on Saturday afternoon in a crossroads store. Until 1929, however, when the Rosenwald Fund of Chicago began a study of syphilis and a demonstration of treatment among the Negroes of six counties in five southern states, exact knowledge on the subject justified only generalizations concerning it.

For many years the late Julius Rosenwald was interested in giving the Negro a better chance for an education. Having been interested in the problem by their director of medical service, Dr. Michael M. Davis, the philanthropic corporation bearing Rosenwald's name expanded its activities in 1928 to include the improvement of health status for the race. Joining with the U.S. Public Health Service and the state and local departments of health, the studies supported by the Fund attempted to find the answer to eight questions:

1. What is the incidence of syphilis as shown by the Wassermann tests among the rural negro population of all ages?
2. Can rural Negroes be induced to accept Wassermann tests and those with syphilis induced to take an amount of treatment sufficient to render them noninfectious?
3. Can satisfactory treatment of syphilis be given under field conditions?
4. Can these special activities for syphilis control be integrated with the general health program of the community?
5. At what cost can the case-finding and treatment methods be carried out?
6. To what extent can funds be secured from state and local tax sources to bear the cost of this project?
7. What are the direct and indirect effects of syphilis upon these negro populations in terms of sickness and death? And finally, the most important question,
8. Can syphilis be controlled by these intensive medical methods; and if so, how soon and at what rate can its prevalence be reduced?

At the time these studies were begun, I was an assistant surgeon general of the U.S. Public Health Service in charge of the Division of Venereal Diseases. During the discussion of practical methods to be used in conducting the studies, we were guided largely by Wenger's successful study of prevalence. Also, I recalled reports of intensive syphilis control a few years earlier in areas of Eastern Europe overrun by armies during the World War and where, in many of the villages, syphilis was almost pandemic—practically everybody had it. The method followed here was to make routine Wassermann tests on whole population groups in one community after another. A similar Wassermann dragnet was determined upon as a starting point among the southern Negroes.

But the practical problem was how to do it. We realized that many of these people had never in their lives been treated by a doctor. Few of them had even seen a hypodermic needle. How, then, without the exercise of brute force could we get blood specimens for diagnosis? For the group with latent syphilis, who felt well, who had no "misery" to bring them to the doctor, how persuade them to take the long-continued, somewhat uncomfortable treatments which would protect them against late, serious symptoms? How start the job among folk who did not even know the word syphilis?

From the beginning it was decided to use as many Negroes as possible in the professional personnel. Although methods in each of the counties differed somewhat in detail, the general plan was to provide a syphilis control unit consisting of a physician, a nurse, and a clerk in each area, working with the local health departments under state supervision, the Public Health Service acting as a co-ordinator.

In selecting the counties in which studies were to be made, two factors were taken into consideration: First, their unlikeness; for little would be learned concerning syphilis among Negroes unless as many different types as possible were brought into the demonstration and from communities varying as widely as possible as to industry, literacy, and economic status. The second and very important factor, however, was one of similarity; for, unless both the state and local health departments were interested in carrying out the study and concerned about the basic problem of syphilis control, failure was inevitable.

On these bases, the following locations for the studies were agreed upon:

1. Scott, Mississippi, on the plantation of the Delta & Pine Land Company.
2. Albemarle County, Virginia, a community above the average in literacy and where good medical care has been available.
3. Macon County, Alabama, the most primitive of the communities studied and the most poverty ridden.
4. Brunswick, Georgia, and the turpentine forests back of it in Glynn County.
5. Tipton County, Tennessee, a cotton-growing section normally above the average in economic status.
6. Pitt County, North Carolina, a tobacco-growing section in the eastern part of the state.

Not only was it necessary in beginning this work to get the co-operation of state and local health officers, but it was vitally necessary to sell the idea of testing and treatment to the Negro concerned.

In the first place, it is true in the South, by and large, that the Negro instinctively trusts the white man, except where he has suffered from sharp dealing and has good reason to be suspicious. He trusts the doctor—thanks to the fine character of many of our rural southern physicians. He trusts the Government, because in spite of clumsy dealing and mistakes since the post-civil war period, he has believed that the Government is a friend of his and tries to help him. The "government health doctor" therefore has an entreé. If he deals fairly and is considerate, it is not too difficult to get co-operation.

The Negro trusts the elders of his own race. Their older generation has an influence with the young that is far greater than among us. He trusts the educated man and woman of his race; except, again, when he has suffered from some attempt of theirs to take advantage of his lack of education. The negro preacher, the school-teacher, the occasional doctor are the acknowledged leaders of their race. Arrangements were made through them for talks in the schools and churches.

Though most of the audience did not know the word syphilis, many of them were familiar with what they called "bad-blood" disease and the miseries it brought. After the talk came the call for testing. Sometimes it was done on the spot, blood specimens taken from everybody in the place, and a date set for a second clinic to which each person present was asked to bring all members of his own family and his friends. Usually it was not difficult to get blood specimens from the whole crowd, once a leader among them had been persuaded to submit to the first test. When testing was done at a school session, a lollypop apiece helped to motivate the timid small fry.

We had some good arguments to use in conferences with the plantation owners and white leaders of the community. Public health in the South has done some impressive things in the reduction of typhoid fever, malaria, and pellagra. Some of the old-timers could remember the terror of yellow fever and how it had vanished. In asking help for syphilis control, I am not ashamed of the fact that we made a great point of the improved labor efficiency that would result from healthy Negroes, though I am glad to say that every doctor and nurse who worked on the project was thinking in the more human terms of relief from suffering, prevention of needless deaths, and the addition to human happiness.

After all, however, whether it is public health or sewing machines you have to sell, you must talk to your customer in his own language. I knew that the majority of these plantation owners, fine fellows that they were, would give us their sympathetic good wishes in whatever we ourselves chose to do to improve the welfare and promote the happiness of the Negroes on their plantations. But if we expected them to do anything about it, I knew we had to use the argument that it would be more profitable to work a healthy field hand than a sick one.

Usually we got a prompt response. "Tell those niggers the health doctor will be at the Possom Hollow school tonight. He's got some government medicine to cure the blood disease. A lot of these niggers have got blood trouble, sickly, no 'count, lazy; but maybe it's not their fault. This doctor will find out." Or again, "Yes, Doctor, go ahead, I've got about forty of them here pickin' cotton. Can you test them here? How long does it take?"

Man, woman, or child, as one after another reached the end of the cotton row there was the doctor to take the blood test and a brief history. Some would hold back, only to be joshed by the more courageous fellows who had found the test not to be much of an ordeal.

We debated at length one question: Should we disregard the cases of late syphilis, concentrating on the early infectious case? Public health theory said, "Yes. The old syphilitic can't hurt anyone but himself. Concentrate on the infectious case and try to slow up the spread." The practical psychology of Wenger said, "No. Treat the old syphilitic with 'rheumatism,' give him the painless mercury rubs. He will feel better and will bring in the whole family for the treatment they need. Don't forget, they listen to their granddaddies."

It was decided not to give intravenous (arsphenamine) treatment to those over 50, or whose history of syphilis antedated 20 years. It was early decided, too that intramuscular injections of bismuth or mercury in the buttocks could not be used. Except with very careful management, they may cause painful lumps which, it had been observed in clinics, the Negro particularly dislikes. How, then, could the heavy metals be given effectively?

Mercury ointment is effective if rubbed in properly. The rural Negroes wear no shoes, so ointment in the sock was out of the question. On ships in the early days it was traditional for the syphilitic sailors to sit on stools in a circle, backs bare, and rub each other with mercury ointment.

Could the same plan be used here? Get them together in the church, sitting in a circle, have the pastor lead them in a spiritual, keeping time to the up-and-down and round-and-round rubbing of mercury ointment into the backs. This was tried, but with indifferent success; partly, someone said, because the pastor thought he didn't get rubbed hard enough.

The best method proved to be the use of a mercury ointment on a rubber and canvas belt—endowed by the doctor, it is true, with all the white magic of health and strength-giving qualities his tongue could contrive.

"Take this package of salve, cut it into six pieces. Every morning, smear one piece on the belt; like this. Tie the belt tightly around your waist; on the seventh day, wash yourself thoroughly and meet me here. Don't forget, one week from today, and you'll feel strong as a mule."

At first, we cast about for a place where we could get such belts, cheaply, because the budget was small. There were no W.P.A. sewing rooms then. But then, as now, there was the Red Cross. In half a dozen county seats, the local chapters made the canvas and rubber belts in their sewing rooms by the hundreds, at a cost of only a few cents for the materials.

How much syphilis was found in these rural negro groups? In Albemarle County, Virginia (Charlottesville), the ratio was less than among many white groups—8.9 per cent. Here for a hundred years, the University of Virginia Hospital has furnished good medical care to the Negroes. Through rendering domestic and other services, they have been in close contact with the whites. They have better than the average schools; their general economic conditions were much better than in the deep South. The result was little syphilis.

At the other extreme was Macon County, Alabama, where in spite of the wholesome influence of Tuskegee Institute, very primitive conditions exist. Even in prosperous times, the poverty exceeded anything most of us have seen. The houses were tumble-down shacks, many without floors, with no furniture, and only a few rags for bedding; there were no screens, a privy only when underbrush was not conveniently close.

One reaction to their dreary surroundings was their constant wandering about in search of something better, with respect both to housing and labor terms.

They ate a pellagrous diet—salt pork, hominy grits, and molasses. They had no green vegetables, no fruit, no milk, no red meat. What they had was usually insufficient in amount. The only well-fed Negroes I saw in Macon County were the students in Tuskegee Institute and the patients in the nearby Veterans Hospital, many paretics among these last.

Southern counties in those days had little idea of public relief for the destitute. When I was there in 1932 a devoted social worker who combined the positions of county truant officer, welfare commissioner, and children's aid official in this county of 30,000 said: "I think they have done very well in this county in taking care of the poor. The county appropriated $300 for me to use this year. Then, too, I can get some clothes and things from the church groups, which helps out."

Destitution, ignorance, lack of medical care—the Wassermann dragnet showed a different record from that in Albemarle County, Virginia, where the Negroes' environment more nearly approached the white man's. In all age groups 39.8 per cent were positive. That represents almost the saturation point when one considers that in older age groups, the blood of some syphilis patients spontaneously became negative, even though symptoms of late syphilis may persist; that the congenital syphilitics presumably are immune to acquired infection, and some of them show negative tests in early adult life; and that in the age group under puberty, infection usually has not yet been acquired.

With so many of the population infected, only a limited section of Macon County could be included in the demonstration. Even in this limited area, the prevalence of syphilis was not uniform. There was one plantation where most of the tests were negative. The medical officer thought something had gone wrong in the laboratory with this batch of specimens, but a re-check confirmed the results. There were about 30 families here, nearly all of whose ancestors had been slaves on the same place. Very few had moved away. The owner and his father both had been doctors. The sick Negroes had been treated by the best of the existing medical knowledge. Lack of migration and good treatment were the only observable factors differentiating this group from the rest of Macon County. Is it not likely that here as in Charlottesville if the white man gives the Negro a chance the result is less syphilis?

In general, it was found that work was being done with syphilis in its native state, without the modifications that arise from treatment in any quantity, no matter how inadequate.

Of the 1,400 cases admitted to treatment in Macon County, only 33 had ever taken any previous treatment and these had had an average of 4.3 doses of neoarsphenamine.

The Wassermann dragnet method of case finding showed that from a total 33,234 persons who were tested in the six counties, 6,800 or 20.5 per cent were found to be positive. Of the total patients for whom the time of infection was ascertained, 14.4 per cent were congenital. This means that today, syphilis is a more important factor in the southern states than malaria, pellagra, or hookworm.

The average cost in all six demonstrations of case finding, plus treatment of positives, was $8.60 per case on an annual basis, or $2.30 per capita of the population tested.

Studies show that syphilis cuts in half the ability to do a full day's work, doubles the load of the unemployables. Yet the cost of finding and treating a case of syphilis among rural Negroes is less than one week's relief wages. If the Government were to take one fifty-second of the annual average wage, one week's pay, and spend it in finding and treating syphilis, the results would more than pay for the cost in better labor efficiency. The delayed deaths and lessened disability would be a net gain.

Started under good auspices, using methods soundly conceived and well executed, these demonstrations gave promise of excellent and lasting results. But when the depression came the Rosenwald Fund was unable to carry on. At the same time the communities themselves were faced with the acute depression problem of six-cent cotton and could not possibly take up the added load.

The spirochetes, however, were only temporarily depressed. They have continued to thrive since the demonstrations closed. Syphilitic Negroes continue to drag their diseased bodies across the cotton fields. The relief rolls are swelled by the disabling effects of late syphilis.

The Negro is not to blame because his syphilis rate is six times that of the white. He was free of it when our ancestors brought him from Africa. It is not his fault that the disease is biologically different in him than in the white; that his blood vessels are particularly susceptible so that late syphilis brings with it crippling circulatory diseases, cuts his working usefulness in half, and makes him an unemployable burden upon the community in the last years of his shortened life. It is through no fault of hers that the colored woman remains infectious two and one-half times as long as the white woman. In the white man, diseases of the central nervous system are more likely to occur; but though there are some racial differences in the type of disablement suffered by white and black in late syphilis, both pay the extreme penalty.

It has been argued that greater sexual promiscuity accounts for the increased prevalence of syphilis among the Negro. Even if this were true, and it is certainly not the whole truth, whose fault is it? Promiscuity occurs among the black race as it does among the white in groups and communities of the under privileged. It is the smug citizen, satisfied with the *status quo,* who is to blame for the children, black or white, without moral standards, brought up in the slums, without decent education, wholesome play, or useful work, without ambition because without hope.

We are apt to think of slums as belonging to the congested districts of the great cities. The rural slums where many Negroes live in this country are far more miserable. They are tucked away where complacent white folks are not reminded of them. They are teeming with disease. There are no school doctors to find sick children; no clinics where the sick and the handicapped receive help; no visiting nurses to look after the sick in their homes. There is no control over polluted milk or water and there is very little milk. There is no money to buy medical service, and only a little offered through charity.

In many sections of the deep South, until some very recent efforts to improve his economic status without doing much to improve the Negro to take advantage of it, the only wholesome influence the Negro has enjoyed has been the influence of his religion. And simple-minded folk, no matter what their color, would be apt to find religion more convincing if they saw more of it practiced by the white people they know who seem to have enough to eat. As it stands, the restrictions of a good life are preached to the Negro, while the rewards of a good life invariably seem to go to someone else. Even the exhortation is likely to be sporadic, for most of the great churches apparently take more real interest in saving the souls of the brown or yellow heathen in far countries than in services to the souls within our immediate boundaries.

Wherever education and living conditions among the negro race approximate that of the white race, the syphilis rate approximates that of the white. The most recent evidence comes from physicians at the Meharry Medical College in Nashville, who find that among the professional students, there was a blood-positive rate of 5.9. They found that in one college, the negro girls showed a rate of less than 2 per cent.

Promiscuity, with its admitted impetus to the spread of syphilis, occurs among both white and black where we permit children to grow up ignorant among depraved surroundings. I cannot see how the white man may divest himself of his burden of responsibility for syphilis among the Negro by being sanctimonious about it.

Ignoring the psychological advantage of facing our problems squarely, however, there may be those who are comforted by feeling superior to the poor, ignorant, unmoral creatures, who fall sick and die so readily from the disease we gave them. Such superior beings need to be frightened within an inch of their lives, however, about their own lack of safety from infection if this is allowed to continue. For it is my firm belief that no man or woman, no family, can be so highly placed, so surrounded by privilege, as to be safe from syphilis if we permit it to saturate the deep strata of the less privileged, white and black, in our civilization.

That is a hypothetical situation, however. From the end of the fifteenth century when syphilis was called the "court disease" in Spain, the rich and the powerful have suffered from it. It is true that they have suffered less, for the best medical service of the day always has been ready to their call.

There are those who are afraid to employ Negroes because of the syphilis from which so many of them suffer. In the first place, without examination, one cannot be sure that the white employee is not suffering from the same condition; and further, a syphilitic under treatment is completely safe to have about one's business or household in any ordinary capacity. The risks are much less than in employing an unexamined person in any walk of life. The thing for an employer to do is to set a good example by taking a blood test himself and require it of every person employed, making clear—and sticking to it—that the results will be without prejudice if proper medical treatment is taken. . . .

The white man, let me reiterate it, gave syphilis to the Negro. He controls the purse strings and dominates the medical services which can eradicate it as a public health menace to white and colored alike. Aside from the elemental justice involved, it will be cheaper, easier, safer for the individual and the nation, white citizen and colored citizen together, to institute practical measures for the control of the disease, than for us all to muddle along, as we have in the past, with the dead weight of it upon public tax rolls and constituting an unnecessary stumbling block to our movements for social betterment.

The whole nation owes the negro doctors a debt of gratitude for the enthusiasm and courage with which they take up their share of the load. I hope that the rest of us may measure up as well to our share of the responsibility.

Further Resources

BOOKS

Jones, James H. *Bad Blood: The Tuskegee Syphilis Experiment.* New York: Free Press, 1981.

Reverby, Susan M., ed. *Tuskegee's Truth's: Rethinking the Tuskegee Syphilis Study.* Chapel Hill, N.C.: The University of North Carolina Press, 2000.

PERIODICALS

Heller, Jean. "Syphilis Victims in U.S. Study Went Untreated for 40 Years." *The New York Times,* July 26, 1972.

"Dust"

Essay

By: Hilda Polacheck

Date: 1938

Source: Polacheck, Hilda. "Dust." *American Life Histories: Manuscripts from the Federal Writers' Project, 1936–1940.* American Memory digital primary source collection, Library of Congress. Available online at http://memory.loc.gov /ammem/wpaintro/wpahome.html; website home page: http://memory.loc.gov (accessed March 18, 2003).

About the Author: Born in Poland in 1882, Hilda Polacheck moved to Chicago in 1892 in the neighborhood surrounding the Jane Addams Hull House. There she learned how to write. The author was one of many writers who would probably have been unemployed if President Franklin Roosevelt's New Deal had not included the Works Progress Administration Federal Writers' Project. ■

Introduction

The telltale hacking cough that produced bloody sputum, the gradual waning of physical strength, the pallor—all were signs of tuberculosis, one of the leading causes of death until the discovery of an antibiotic that killed the bacteria that caused it.

Until 1883, when bacteriologist Robert Koch identified the tubercle bacillus that caused the disease, many people believed that it was due to either poverty and dirt or to a generally dissolute way of living. Known as "consumption" for its most visible symptom, wasting, tuberculosis had among writers and artists of the nineteenth century a faintly romantic reputation, as though genius, suffering, and early death were somehow linked. The image was perpetuated in plays such as *The Lady of the Camellias,* filmed as *Camille* and starring Greta Garbo, who remains stunningly beautiful until her final delicate cough carries her off.

There was, in fact, nothing even slightly romantic about tuberculosis; it was a lingering, painful way to die. After Koch discovered the bacillus, it became evident that tuberculosis was another infectious disease that was spread through poor sanitation. It was also an airborne disease, one transmitted when a tubercular person sprayed out bacilli with each cough or expectoration.

In the popular view, tuberculosis was a problem of immigrants and poor people, a notion that contained some truth. Because people who lived in poverty had a much harder time maintaining a clean environment, they were more susceptible to the disease. Poor families very often lived in crowded quarters, with large families in one or two rooms and no running water, which made it less likely that the family could keep the house sanitary and more likely that members would be exposed to and catch the disease. At the same time, those who did not live in poverty imposed a moral judgment on the tubercular poor. The belief was that the United States was the land of opportunity, and those who were poor probably had not worked hard enough to escape their status.

For more well-to-do people, a diagnosis of tuberculosis might well be the result more of extremely bad luck than bad hygiene, although the practice of spitting and using spittoons was common and surely a source of contagion among the well-heeled. At the same time, the middle and upper classes might easily catch the disease from a servant, a waiter in a fancy restaurant, or an encounter with a shopkeeper or barber.

The middle- or upper-class "lunger," as they were known in the slang of the early twentieth century, often took great pains to hide the diagnosis. After the discovery of the tuberculin bacilli, tuberculosis patients became pariahs. Sheila M. Rothman, writing in *Living in the Shadow of Death,* describes people who told their friends and family that they needed to rest from "stomach trouble" or nervous exhaustion. Tuberculosis patients were advised to seek the warmer, dryer climates of the West, but communities in Arizona, New Mexico, Colorado, and elsewhere were often hostile to these would-be visitors. Boardinghouses and hotels turned them away; in some communities, tent towns sprang up, populated by the tubercular.

Tuberculosis sanatoriums came into being in Europe in the late 1800s and spread to the United States soon thereafter. Edward Livingston Trudeau, a physician who was himself tubercular, started the first free, private sanatorium for the poor at Saranac Lake in the Adirondack Mountains of New York (an area to which tuberculosis patients had been coming for years). Trudeau's institution became a model for many others in both its physical plant and its emphasis on a fixed regime. The treatment of tuberculosis, like the perceived causes of filth and poverty, had a certain moral quality to it; patients would submit to the discipline of the hospitals, and that strict regime would effect a cure. It was believed that those who left before they were cured or who deviated from the discipline lessened their chances of recovery.

Significance

"Dust," one of many narratives that preserved American life in the 1930s, is significant for several reasons. First, it contradicts the image of the lazy poor as victims of tuberculosis. The family described is in fact one of hardworking immigrants in which the father contracts the disease from contaminated dust while sorting rags. During the Depression, this is the only work he has been able to find.

Second, again running against popular images of the chronically poor, the family is very much interested in education and in having the children make use of their talents and improve their lot in life. The son who studied music with Jane Addams of Hull House is an example of the poor people she wanted to help and how they profited from her efforts. In the end, however, these efforts could not protect the son from death by tuberculosis.

In a broader sense, this narrative and others like it helped to raise awareness of the conditions that caused tuberculosis, often in the workplace. Addams and her co-workers did identify the dust in the rag shop as the source of the tuberculosis, although it was too late for this family. Nevertheless, these early efforts at promoting a disease-free workplace eventually had results. They planted the seeds that would grow into such institutions as the federal Occupational Safety and Health Administration.

Primary Source

"Dust"

SYNOPSIS: "Dust" is a narrative that describes the hard work, disease, glimmers of hope, and eventual death that were often the lot of immigrant families. The disease that kills two family members, tuberculosis, was commonly spread in the workplace.

Jacob Saranoff worked in a rag-shop near Hull-House. He had come to Chicago from Russia in 1902, bringing his wife and two children with him. The family was met at the train by a relative who helped to find a home for them. They rented four rooms in a rear tenement on Halsted Street. After visiting several second hand furniture stores, the Saranoffs bought two second hand beds, a kitchen stove, a kitchen table and four chairs. They unpacked the bedding that they had brought with them from Russia and spent their first night in their first American home.

The next morning the children were enrolled in the public school. The first great ambition of Jacob and Sarah Saranoff had been realized. Their children were in school.

After paying a month's rent and the price of the furniture and the most necessary household utensils, Jacob had two dollars left. It was necessary for Jacob to take the first job that he could find. The job was sorting rags. His wages were eight dollars a week. The rent was six dollars a month. Jacob and Sarah decided that they could get along.

The rag-shop was located in an abandoned barn. There was a small window in the rear of this barn which had been opened when the horses were housed in it. But since it had become a rag-shop, the window had been nailed up to keep out any possible thieves. Ventilation was not considered.

The floor of the rag-shop was never swept. The dust was allowed to gather day after day, week after week. But Jacob paid no attention to the dust. His children were in school. They could not have gone to school in Russia. There were no schools for Jewish children in the village where he had lived. So why pay attention to dust?

Solomon, or Solly, as he was called, the older of the two children, wanted to learn to play the piano. But how does one get piano lessons and buy a piano on which to practice on eight dollars a week?

"Some day I will learn to play," Solly said. "All sorts of miracles happen in America. Maybe something will happen so that I can learn."

Solly was eight years old. His sister, Rosie, was six. They were learning American games. They now played hide and seek, run-sheep-run and peg, with the American born children. These American born children took Solly and Rosie to Hull-House.

The children ran up the stairs to a play-room in which there was a piano. It was the first time that Solly had been near a piano. He struck a note and was thrilled with the sound. He looked around, and no one seemed to mind his touching the piano. So he struck a few more notes. This was indeed a

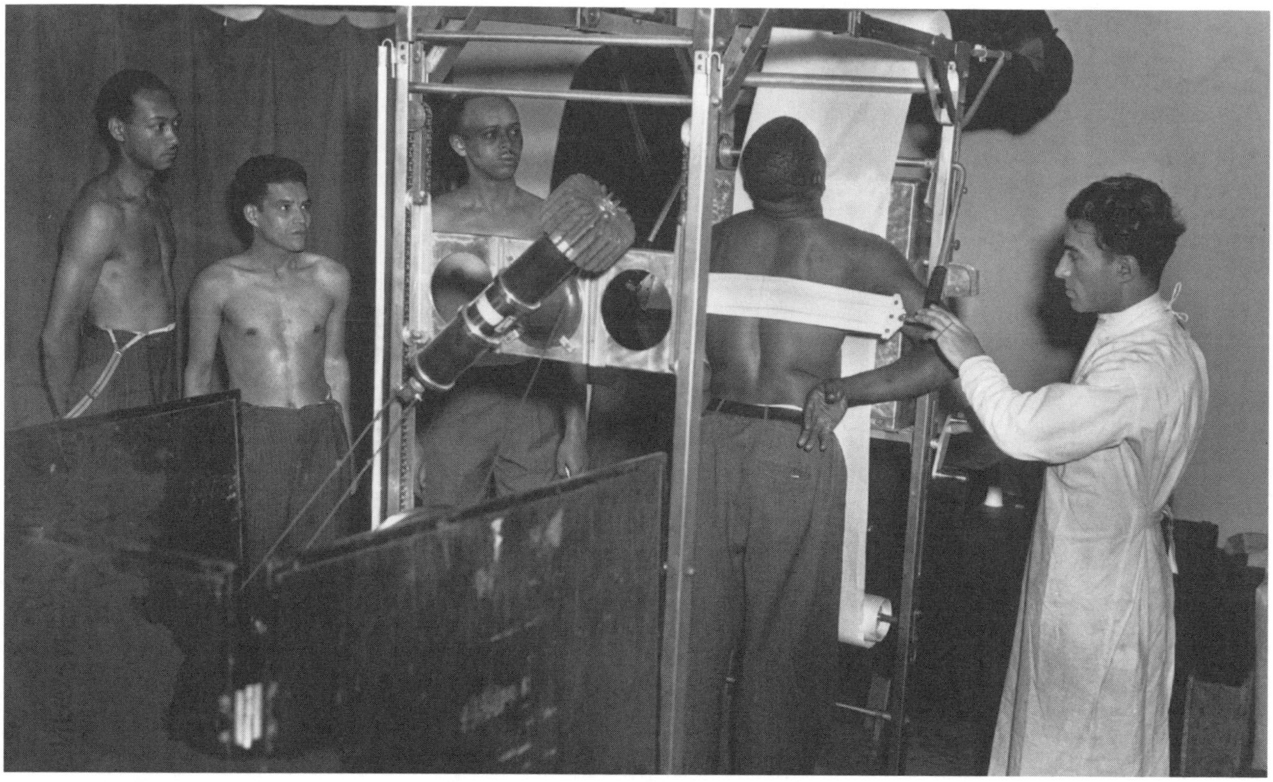

A doctor performs chest x-rays to screen for tuberculosis. The WPA narrative "Dust" helped dispel the popular belief that tuberculosis only affected the lazy poor. CORBIS-BETTMANN. REPRODUCED BY PERMISSION.

miracle! Such miracles could only happen in America, thought Solly. When the play director entered to organize some games for the children. Patrick Ryan, who lived across the hall from the Saranoff family, took Solly to her.

"This is Solly," said Patrick "He's daffy about piano."

"Would you like to learn to play?" asked the director.

"Oh, yes! Could I?" Solly asked eagerly.

So Solly started to take piano lessons and he was allowed to come to Hull-House to practice.

Jacob had now been sorting rags for three years. He had been inhaling the dust for the same length of time. He would have liked to find other work. Something more interesting—something that would pay a little more money. He began to dream of the possibility of buying a piano for Solly. But he was afraid to take a day off to look for a better job. He was afraid he might lose the one he had. He could not risk having the family go without food. And there were shoes to buy. And the rent had to be paid. So he continued to sort rags, paying no attention to the dust on the floor. It was bad when the bales of rags were dumped on the floor and the dust rose and filled the room. The men who were sorting rags would get coughing spells when that happened. But the dust was soon settled, and the men went on sorting rags.

The Saranoff children were bringing good reports from school. Solly could now play the piano well. He was told at school that he would be allowed to play a solo when he graduated.

Solly found out that fathers and mothers could go to lectures and concerts at Hull-House. So on Sunday afternoon or evening, the Saranoffs listened to lectures they did not understand and to concerts that they did understand and loved. They found out that they could learn English, so they hurried through with the supper dishes and became members of the English class. One evening, Mrs. Ryan, their neighbor, took Jacob and Sarah to a Hull-House party. At this party they met Jane Addams.

"Miss Addams," said Jacob one night while he was at Hull-House, "do you know that I have never heard Solly play the piano."

"Well, that is too bad," said Jane Addams. "I must see that you hear him soon."

A Disease Without Boundaries

Poor families lost many members to tuberculosis, but the disease did not discriminate by race, class, or income. Tuberculosis's victims included:

- Mabal Normand, Film Star, 33. Mabel Normand had a promising career as a comedy actress in the early 1920s. She appeared in one of the major comedy series of the time, the Mack Sennett troup, which did the Keystone Cops movies. Miss Normand's career essentially ended, however, with a scandal from which she herself was exonerated: the murder of movie director William Desmond Taylor. She was the last person to see Taylor, a well-known ladies' man, alive, but although she was never a suspect in his murder, many theater owners considered her morally suspect and refused to show her pictures. Even as she was dying, her publicists were issuing news about her miraculous recovery.
- Colonel W. H. Lanhorne, Virginia politician, age 55. Colonel Langhorne came from a wealthy and prominent Virginia family and was himself active in politics. He was best known, however, because of his sisters' marriages, one of whom became Mrs. Charles Dana Gibson, creator of fashion's "Gibson Girl"; the other was the Viscountess Astor, whose marriage to a British aristocrat brought her prominence, if not popularity, in England as Lady Astor. The colonel's obituary, published in the *New York Times* highlighted the social distinctions that were important at the time. His wife, the former Miss Edna Forsythe, was born on Long Island but raised in New Orleans, a place of greater social stature than Long Island.
- Vincent Youmans, composer, 47. Mr. Youmans had already made his mark on popular culture with his songs, which included "Tea for Two," and "No, No, Nanette." and was considered the equal of the songwriters Irving Berlin and Jerome Kern. His personal history was common for the time; during World War I, he was assigned to the "entertainment unit," where he composed various songs. After the war, he worked promoting the songs of Victor Herbert, whose influence helped to get Youmans's songs into musicals. Today, fans of 1930s and 1940s popular song remember the work of Mr. Kern, Mr. Berlin, and Mr. Herbert. Vincent Youmans might have been as well known today.
- Senator Bernard Downing, member of the New York State Senate, 62. Mr. Downing was a classic rags-to riches story. The son of Irish immigrants, his childhood friends included boys who later occupied influential positions in the New York City government. With the help of these friends, Mr. Downing was employed by the city; through his own talents, he succeeded and was eventually appointed a state senator to fill a vacancy. He backed many social welfare causes. His obituary suggests that his work was his life; he did not marry, but left many friends who paid tribute to his talents.
- Corporal James E. Newman, 25. Corporal Newman served in the United States Army during World War II. He survived the Bataan Death March. He endured three years in a Japanese prisoner-of-war camp. By the time he was released from the camps, he was gravely ill with tuberculosis. Corporal Newman held on, though, because he wanted to die "at home." Home was Ft. Worth, Texas. "It's so good to be home, it's so good to be home," he said repeatedly. A week after he arrived in Ft. Worth, he died.

A week later Solly brought home a card announcing a piano recital to be given by Solomon Saranoff, at the Hull-House Music School.

There were about fifty people present at Solly's first recital. The Ryans were there. Sarah Saranoff had invited Mrs. Schultz, her German neighbor who lived on the floor above. The Molinari family, whose son was learning to play the violin at Hull-House, were there. Just before the recital started, Jane Addams came into the room and sat down next to Jacob Saranoff.

Solly played with a delicacy and warmth that made him a part of the piano. When the first piece was finished, the tears were rolling down Jacob's cheeks. Solly played and Jacob's heartbeats accompanied him. He was thanking God for America—for Hull-House—for Jane Addams.

"For the last number," the piano teacher announced, "Solly will play a piece that he wrote. I am very proud of Solly, for it is not often that a child of his age can compose music. I think Solly will be a great musician."

Solly played his composition. It was a haunting little melody. There was a little of the Russian persecution in it. There was a little of the joy of Hull-House. There was a little of the dust of the rag-shop.

The concert was over. The entire audience surrounded the Saranoff family. Janc Addams invited everybody into the coffee-house for refreshments.

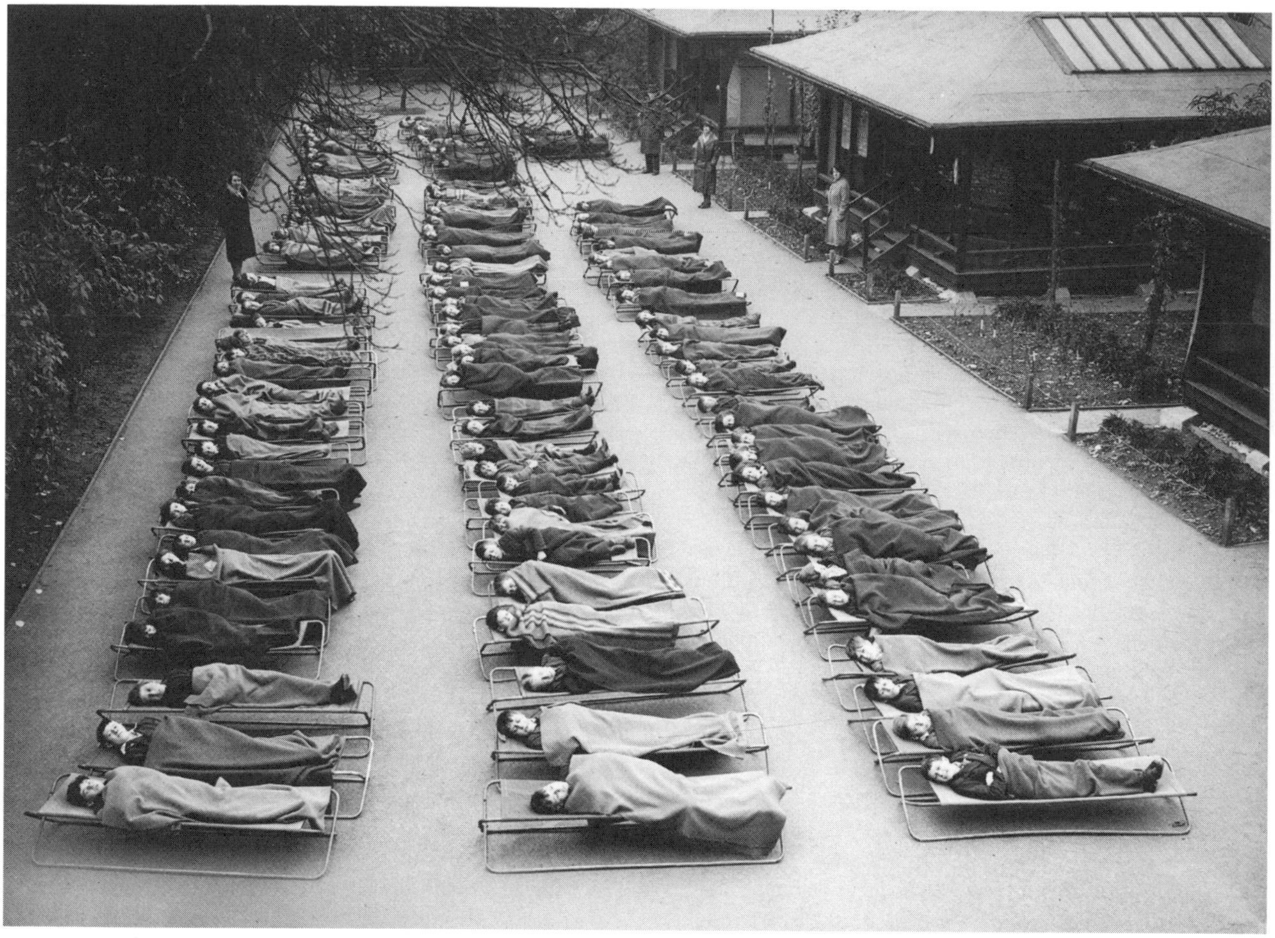

Children suffering from tuberculosis sleep outside as part of their treatment, November 8, 1932. Sunbathing had curative effects on tuberculosis, as extended exposure to heat and the sun's UV rays helped kill TB bacteria. GETTY IMAGES. REPRODUCED BY PERMISSION.

The dream of buying a piano now became an obsession with Jacob. He had heard one of the men who worked in the rag-shop, say that his two brothers were coming from Russia and that they would be looking for a place to live. The idea came to Jacob that he could rent one of the bedrooms to these two men. He broached the subject to Sarah. She thought it would be a good idea. Sarah had heard that pianos could be bought on easy payments. Perhaps she could get enough from the man to make the payments on a piano.

The boarders moved into one of the two bedrooms. A shiny new piano was moved into the bare parlor. A relative gave the family a discarded cot which was put into the parlor. On this Solly slept. Rosie was moved into the bedroom where her parents slept. Her bed was made up of the four chairs.

Solly practiced every minute that he could spare from his school work. He had graduated from grammar school and had entered high school.

Jacob went on sorting rags. But the sorting was now accompanied by the tunes that Solly played. Jacob noticed that he would get very tired, long before the day was over. He coughed a good deal when the bales of rags were dumped on the floor. He would sweat during the night, even when the bedroom was very cold. But he said nothing to his wife.

Solly was ready to graduate from high school. He was to play one of his own compositions at the graduation exercises. This graduation was another event in the life of the Saranoff family. Jacob was proud of his tall, dark haired son, who was loudly applauded by the audience. Solly bowed again and again. Jacob thought: if only the cough did not bother him; he would be the happiest man in the world. But the cough did bother him.

Jacob would have liked to stay in bed the morning after the graduation. But a man had been fired the week before for staying home one day. So he dragged himself out of the bed and went to the rag-shop. Several hours later he was brought home by two men. They said that Jacob had started to cough and had spit large chunks of blood.

"Yes, the dust in the rag-shop is bad," said one of the men.

Sarah was panic stricken. The neighbors called a doctor from the health department. A week later, Jacob was dead.

The relatives and neighbors collected money for the funeral. Solly did not quite realize what had happened. He sat between his mother and Jane Addams. He heard the Rabbi say:

"Then shall the dust return to the earth as it was."

But the day after the funeral, Solly knew that he was now the head of the family. The owner of the rag-shop offered him a job as bookkeeper and Solly took it. He earned more money than his father had earned. But the dust was on the floor of the office.

Solly continued to take lessons at Hull-House in the evening, when he was not too tired. He had very little time to practice, now. After nine hours in the dirty office, weighing bales of rags, keeping books, haggling with the people who were selling the rags, he was too tired to practice.

Sarah was sorry that he could not go on with his music, but the rent had to be paid, food had to be bought, shoes did wear out.

One morning Solly noticed several people from Hull-House walk into the rag-shop. They spoke to one of the men in the shop; they gathered some of the dust from the floor into small white papers, and left.

That night Solly went to Hull-House. He found Jane Addams and asked about the dust that had been gathered.

"We are trying to find out whether the dust contains any tuberculosis germs," Jane Addams told him.

"Dust—tuberculosis," said Solly in a bewildered tone. "Every other house on the block has some one sick with tuberculosis. I heard an old woman say that a dybbuk has attacked the neighborhood. Perhaps it is a dybbuk! Perhaps there is a dybbuk in the dust that my father breathed into his lungs. I have been breathing into my lungs. The dybbuk always kills the person it attacks!"

Solly was hysterical! He was taken to a room and a doctor was called. The doctor looked very grave. Solly['s] temperature was quite high. The doctor was sure he had tuberculosis. He had been working too hard. He had been inhaling the dust from the rag-shop.

Sarah was like a stone image when she was told.

"Thank God you will take care of him," she said to Jane Addams. "Rosie will now have to go to work. I wanted her to finish high school."

Solly was well cared for in a sanitarium which Jane Addams had helped to create. As he lay on his cot on the sun-porch, he was putting notes together that he would fashion into songs, when he got well.

At Hull-House a fight was going on to bring air into dark homes. Shorter working hours—less fatigue—less tuberculosis. Court proceedings were started to have the barn that housed the rag-shop, condemned. It took months to accomplish this. But the rag-shop was condemned.

Jane Addams travelled all the way to the sanitarium to tell Solly the news. But he was too ill to be told that the dust had at last been removed. He had become a part of the dust.

Further Resources

BOOKS

Bates, Barbara. *Bargaining for Life: A Social History of Tuberculosis, 1876–1938.* Philadelphia: University of Pennsylvania Press, 1992.

Dormandy, Thomas. *The White Death: A History of Tuberculosis.* New York: New York University Press, 1999.

Rothman, Sheila M. *Living in the Shadow of Death.* New York: Basic Books, 1994.

Alcoholics Anonymous

Handbook

By: Anonymous

Date: 1939

Source: *Alcoholics Anonymous.* New York: Works Publishing Company, 1939. Reprinted Malo, Wash.: Anonymous Press, n.d., 70–72.

About the Author: Although the book *Alcoholics Anonymous* is traditionally attributed to no single author, the organization acknowledges that it was written by one of the founding members of AA, William Griffith Wilson (1895–1971). Details of Wilson's early life are extremely sketchy. He attended Norwich University in Vermont and served in the U.S. Army in World War I. He worked as a stockbroker. Most important, he was an alcoholic, and he discovered a way to transform his life and help others as well. ■

Introduction

The idea behind Alcoholics Anonymous (AA) was conceived when Bill W. and Dr. Bob S. met in Akron,

Ohio, in 1934. Bill W. recognized what was to become one of the fundamental principles of the organization: an alcoholic can best be helped by someone who has been there and come back, a sober alcoholic.

The organization itself, however, has its roots in an evangelical movement. Bill W. had achieved sobriety through his work with an organization known as the Oxford Groups. The Oxford Groups were started by an American, Frank Buchman, as an evangelical movement. The movement espoused surrendering one's will to God's guidance and various other principles that were also to guide AA. Bill W. became involved with the group through a friend who was a recovering alcoholic, and while working with alcoholics himself, he became and stayed sober. Bill espoused the notion of alcoholism as a disease. Dr. Bob S. had also been involved in the Oxford Group in Akron, but his participation had not curbed his drinking. His meeting with Bill did.

The first groups were not called Alcoholics Anonymous. After the Akron group formed, another began in Cleveland, and in 1935, a group was started in New York. Beginning in 1938, Bill W. began writing *Alcoholics Anonymous,* often referred to as the "bible" of AA and the many twelve-step groups that followed. The jacket blurb on the original edition reads: "Many could recover if they had the opportunity we have enjoyed. How then shall we present that which has been so freely given us? We have concluded to publish an anonymous volume. . . ."

The book contained Bill's own story of how he "hit bottom" (another phrase that was to become vital to the AA vocabulary), as well as those of many other recovering alcoholics. The core of the book, though, and of the organization, was the Twelve Steps, known also as the Twelve Traditions. Neither Bill W. nor anyone else involved claimed that it was easy to follow these steps. They did contend, however, that individuals who genuinely desired to become sober could become sober if they followed the steps.

The group did not have money to publicize the book, but gradually, newspapers and magazines began writing about the book and the group itself. By the end of 1939, the group had about two thousand members. In 1941, the *Saturday Evening Post,* one of the largest general-circulation magazines in the United States, published an article on AA that brought a huge response. Membership tripled that year, and by 1950, AA claimed at least a hundred thousand recovered alcoholics worldwide.

Statistics on alcoholism and AA participation at the time are hard to find, but they do not really matter. As the organization became better known, more and more alcoholics who wanted to stop drinking sought help, which was evidence enough of a real problem for some people.

Significance

The book *Alcoholics Anonymous* was relevant to many health problems, not only those related to alcohol. Its immediate focus, though, was alcoholism. AA brought to public attention a problem that touched many lives, yet for which few could receive treatment. Treatment at the time consisted mostly of hospitalization while the alcoholic "dried out," after which many returned to drinking. This treatment was available only to those with enough money to pay for it. The poor were left to fend for themselves.

What AA gave to alcoholics, rich and poor, was a safe place in which to seek help among people who understood their situations. The stigma of being a "drunk" deterred people from turning to physicians, who could not have done much anyway. People who had lost their jobs and their families had a supportive environment in which they could try to put their lives together again. It also raised the public consciousness about alcoholism and its effects.

AA was also important in recognizing the problems of the families of alcoholics. The organization generated several associated groups, like Alateen and Al-Anon. These groups not only provide support for spouses and children but also emphasize that no one can change an alcoholic's behavior except the alcoholic.

The organization has been the subject of controversy and has generated competition from other groups. Some have challenged AA's contention that absolute abstinence is the only way an alcoholic can remain sober. Studies of controlled drinking, or drinking moderately, have yielded mixed results. Courts and law enforcement agencies that order convicted people to attend AA meetings have been challenged for forcing attendance at what is a faith-based, essentially Christian, organization. AA's emphasis on a Higher Power (which need not be but generally is God) has led to new approaches, such as Secular Sobriety.

Beyond treatment for alcoholism, though, AA and its Twelve Steps (or traditions) spawned countless similar organizations dedicated to helping people with various forms of addictions and compulsive behaviors. Some, such as Narcotics Anonymous, do treat actual physical addictions. More, however, deal with out-of-control behavior: Shoppers Anonymous, Overeaters Anonymous, Gamblers Anonymous, Kleptomaniacs and Shoplifters Anonymous, Workaholics Anonymous, and what is presumably the opposite problem, Fear of Success Anonymous.

Primary Source

Alcoholics Anonymous [excerpt]

SYNOPSIS: In this excerpt from the original edition of *Alcoholics Anonymous,* the writer lists the Twelve

Steps, or Twelve Traditions, that are the heart of this organization and many others.

How It Works

Rarely have we seen a person fail who has thoroughly followed our path. Those who do not recover are people who cannot or will not completely give themselves to this simple program, usually men and women who are constitutionally incapable of being honest with themselves. There are such unfortunates. They are not at fault; they seem to have been born that way. They are naturally incapable of grasping and developing a manner of living which demands rigorous honesty. Their chances are less than average. There are those, too, who suffer from grave emotional and mental disorders, but many of them do recover if they have the capacity to be honest.

Our stories disclose in a general way what we used to be like, what happened, and what we are like now. If you have decided you want what we have and are willing to go to any length to get it—then you are ready to take certain steps.

At some of these we balked. We thought we could find an easier, softer way. But we could not. With all the earnestness at ou r command, we beg of you to be fearless and thorough from the very start. Some of us have tried to hold on to our old ideas and the result was nil until we let go absolutely.

Remember that we deal with alcohol—cunning, baffling, powerful! Without help it is too much for us. But there is One who has all power—That One is God. May you find Him now!

Half measures availed us nothing. We stood at the turning point. We asked His protection and care with complete abandon.

Here are the steps we took, which are suggested as a Program of Recovery:

1. We admitted we were powerless over alcohol—that our lives had become unmanageable.
2. Came to believe that a Power greater than ourselves could restore us to sanity.
3. Made a decision to turn our will and our lives over to the care of God *as we understood Him.*
4. Made a searching and fearless moral inventory of ourselves.
5. Admitted to God, to ourselves, and to another human being the exact nature of our wrongs.
6. Were entirely ready to have God remove all these defects of character.
7. Humbly asked Him to remove our shortcomings.
8. Made a list of all persons we had harmed, and became willing to make amends to them all.
9. Made direct amends to such people wherever possible, except when to do so would injure them or others.
10. Continued to take personal inventory and when we were wrong promptly admitted it.
11. Sought through prayer and meditation to improve our conscious contact with God *as we understood Him* praying only for knowledge of His will for us and the power to carry that out.
12. Having had a spiritual experience as the result of these steps, we tried to carry this message to alcoholics, and to practice these principles in all our affairs.

Many of us exclaimed, "What an order! I can't go through with it." Do not be discouraged. No one among us has been able to maintain anything like perfect adherence to these principles. We are not saints. The point is, that we are willing to grow along spiritual lines. The principles we have set down are guides to progress. We claim spiritual progress rather than spiritual perfection.

Who Was Bill W.?

William Griffith Wilson was a man who defined his life by alcohol—first drinking it, then ceasing to drink it, then working to help others stop drinking it. Other aspects of his life are peripheral to his addiction to alcohol. He took pains to avoid leaving any record of his childhood and youth. He began his college education, but quickly changed to Norwich College in Vermont, noted in his biography primarily because it was the place he first consumed alcohol. During World War I, he served in the Army, but never saw combat. He met his wife, Lois, during his college years. His self-description focuses almost exclusively on his insecurities and how they were relieved when he consumed alcohol.

After he left college and the military, he floated from job to job until he enrolled in Brooklyn Law School, where he finally completed the coursework after, according to his account, he missed a final exam because he was too drunk to take it. He made up the exam, but never collected the diploma and never practiced law. He later worked as a stockbroker, but again, his drunkenness prevented him from succeeding.

Further Resources

BOOKS

Alcoholics Anonymous Comes of Age: A Brief History. New York: Alcoholics Anonymous Publishing, 1957.

Fletcher, Anne M. *Sober for Good.* Boston: Houghton Mifflin, 2001.

Plant, Martin, and Douglas Cameron, eds. *The Alcohol Report.* London: Free Association Press, 2000.

Raphael, Matthew J. *Bill W. and Mr. Wilson: The Legend and Life of AA's Cofounder.* Amherst, Mass.: University of Massachusetts Press, 1999.

Rudy, David R. *Becoming Alcoholic: Alcoholics Anonymous and the Reality of Alcoholism.* Carbondale, Ill.: Southern Illinois University Press, 1986.

PERIODICALS

Carr, Neil J. "Liberation Spirituality: 60 years of A.A." *America,* June 17, 1995.

Cheever, Susan. "The Healer: Bill W." *Time,* June 14, 1999.

Gleick, Elizabeth. "Sobering Times for A.A." *Time,* July 10, 1995.

WEBSITES

Alcoholics Anonymous home page. Available online at www.alcoholics-anonymous.org (accessed March 4, 2003).

"Bill Wilson." Biography.com. Available online at http://search.biography.com/print_record.pl?id=20862; website home page: http://www.biography.com (accessed August 29, 2002).

Online Intergroup of Alcoholics Anonymous home page. Available online at http://www.aa-intergroup.org (accessed August 29, 2002).

Online Recovery Resources. Available online at http://www.recovery.org (accessed March 4, 2003).

"Hot Lunches for a Million School Children"

Speech

By: Ellen S. Woodward

Date: c. 1939

Source: Woodward, Ellen S. "Hot Lunches for a Million School Children." Available at the New Deal Network online at http://newdeal.feri.org/texts/500.htm; website homepage: http://newdeal.feri.org (accessed March 17, 2003).

About the Author: Ellen S. Woodward (1887–1971) was born in Oxford, Mississippi. The daughter of a Congressman, young Ellen lived in Washington and developed an interest in politics and public affairs. In the 1930s she became an assistant administrator of the Works Progress Administration and later director of work relief programs for women. As a leader among women's clubs and political groups in the United States, she was an effective advocate for economic security for women and children. ■

Introduction

The Great Depression encompassed more than ten years of hunger. When the family breadwinner, usually the man of the house, lost his job, the family often had no way to buy food. Sometimes another family member, a wife or child, would be able to find lower-paying work, but those few dollars a week were not enough to feed a family.

In the early years of the Depression, the inability to feed a family was a mark of shame, viewed by many as a sign of personal failure. Families were reluctant to apply for "the relief," as government assistance was called. They had been taught that they should be self-sufficient and neither need nor accept charity. Parents interviewed by Works Progress Administration (WPA) writers reported feelings of desperation at watching their children grow hungry, of being willing to do any work to keep food on the table. Some declared themselves willing to steal to support their families, if they had the nerve.

By the mid-1930s, people were more willing to accept relief as they recognized that their plight was not their fault. They received grocery coupons and food deliveries from relief workers, who also gave them a lot of generally unwanted advice about how they should be spending their food money.

Inadequate nutrition was particularly damaging to children, whose growth and development could be permanently stunted and otherwise damaged. At the same time, children who attended school on empty stomachs could not concentrate and learn properly.

Significance

The school lunch program that began as a way to help a modest number of undernourished children increased, in subsequent decades, to include millions of children who receive breakfast and lunch at their schools, as well as after-school snacks. In its early years, the program quickly expanded to include all children who wanted to take part, not only those who had been identified as needy. This inclusive policy allowed children who might not be officially classed as "undernourished" to have a solid meal without any loss of pride. It also preserved the dignity of children and families who really needed the meal; if anyone could take advantage of the program, then they were not singled out as being especially needy. By using this approach, the school lunch program helped to reduce the stigma of accepting government help in feeding families during hard times.

The results of the school lunch program were tangible. Children gained weight. Their classroom work improved. Some who had been described by teachers as "sullen and inattentive" became better students when they began receiving at least one complete meal daily. The prospect of a meal also increased attendance, suggesting that lunch lured children who otherwise might not have come to school.

The WPA school lunch program became law in 1946, when the Congress passed the National School Lunch Act, administered by the Food and Nutrition Service of the U.S. Department of Agriculture (USDA). The law institutionalized the provision of lunch to schoolchildren. It did more than that, however. By linking nutrition, learning, and development in a concrete way, the School Lunch program set the stage for the many government food programs. The WIC program—women, infants, and children—recognizes that early nutritional intervention can stave off problems of learning and development. The school lunch program also used agricultural surpluses that the government bought from farmers.

The effort that began as a means to help hungry children during the Great Depression has expanded in other ways. In 1997, the federal government established the "farms-to-schools" program, a venture that improved school meals while giving small farmers a market for their goods. The program has helped schools to offer salad bars, a popular alternative for many students. In 1998, the USDA expanded to include after-school snacks for schoolchildren. The program also now operates year round, with the addition of the Summer Food Service Program. The summer program reimburses community and other nonprofit camps and programs for meals and snacks.

The school lunch program, although still committed to serving nutritious foods and excluding those of minimal nutritional value, has also come a long way in creating child-pleasing menus. Children today may choose among pizza, subs, fresh fruit, and salads instead of the one-menu option offered to their parents and grandparents (meatloaf, mashed potatoes, canned vegetables, and the ever-present "beanie weenies," hot dogs and canned baked beans, among other offerings). To a hungry child, though, it did and does still look good.

Primary Source

"Hot Lunches for a Million School Children"

SYNOPSIS: In this speech, Ellen S. Woodward describes the problems caused by undernutrition in children and the positive effects that the school lunch program had on the health and well-being of children.

One million undernourished children have benefited by the Works Progress Administration's school lunch program. In the past year and a half 80,000,000 hot well-balanced meals have been served at the rate of 500,000 daily in 10,000 schools throughout the country.

This work of rehabilitating underprivileged children is supervised in all instances by competent WPA workers, who while earning money with which to clothe and feed their own families, are given an opportunity for wider training to equip them to take their places in private employment when the opportunity arises. On March 31, 1937, the projects employed nearly 12,000 needy economic heads of families.

The School Lunch Program, like all other WPA projects, must be sponsored by tax-supported public bodies. Boards of Education usually are the official sponsors of the school lunch programs. Many civic organizations and individual patrons, however, may, and often do, render very valuable assistance by cooperating unofficially with the legitimate sponsors. The active interest of Parent-Teacher Associations all over the country, has been an important factor in the universal success with which these projects have met.

School lunch projects have aroused such community interest that in some instances, South Carolina, for example, members of various civic organizations and other responsible citizens have formed Advisory Councils, which actively support this work by contributions of food, equipment, and sometimes money.

The school lunch projects were originally intended to serve only children from relief families, but experience taught that growing children need a hot mid-day meal irrespective of their financial condition. It was found also that many children from homes where there was an adequate supply of certain kinds of food, were not receiving the proper kind of diet. It has become the policy in many communities, therefore, to serve a hot lunch to all the school children who care to partake. Parent-Teacher Associations have been largely responsible for making arrangements in many instances, whereby parents of children, who can afford it, contribute food supplies. This, however, is generally voluntary, and in no case is any distinction made in the lunch rooms between those who do and those who do not make a contribution.

Many of the children, who are fed on WPA projects, come from homes where milk is a luxury. In some instances, teachers have reported that nearly all their pupils who partake of the school lunch, have no meal during the 24 hours of the day other than that furnished on the project. For many children, who

New York City elementary school students wait in the cafeteria lunch line for hot stew. During the Depression, the Work's Progress Administration helped combat undernourished children by implementing school lunch programs. **AP/WIDE WORLD PHOTOS. REPRODUCED BY PERMISSION.**

are required to leave home early in the morning and travel long distances after school hours to reach their homes, the WPA lunch constitutes the only hot meal of the day. In an even greater number of cases, children come to school with either no breakfast at all or a meager one at best.

Only those who have had occasion to witness the type of lunch that many of the children were bringing to school before the inauguration of the WPA, can fully understand or appreciate the value of those projects.

Insufficient or improper food takes not only a physical toll, but a mental toll as well. Children after all are sensitive beings. In some instances, children, from underprivileged families have been known to slip away alone to eat their lunches in some secluded spot—ashamed to have the other school children witness their meager fare.

In some of the poorer communities of Georgia, for example, many of the children brought only cold bread or baked sweet potatoes. Sometimes a child's lunch consisted of a biscuit and a piece of fried fish. If any meat at all was included, it was usually fat white meat. Prior to the inauguration of the WPA school lunch projects, a cold sweet potato or a poorly cooked biscuit spread with fat constituted the usual lunch of many children in the rural communities of South Carolina.

Before the institution of the WPA projects, many children, in certain sections of Colorado, were reported to be bringing for lunch a piece of corn bread with molasses or a cold pancake. The common kind of meat found in the children's lunches—when there was meat—was salt pork. In many of the rural districts the lunches which were brought, were frozen or half-frozen by noon.

Even after the establishment of the WPA project, an effort was made to have each child in certain Colorado communities bring his or her own bread from home to supplement the hot dishes. This had to be discontinued because the bread that the children brought was not fit to eat. It was dirty, dry and even moldy.

South Carolina, which feeds more than 77,000 children daily in over 2300 public schools, has the largest WPA school lunch program of all the states, except New York State, in which New York City alone feeds a daily average of 37,230 children.

All school children, who desire the hot lunch in South Carolina, are permitted to partake. Sponsors and co-sponsors make contributions of everything from money to beef on the hoof, and the parents of children, who can afford to do so, also contribute small amounts of food or money. Parents' weekly contribution for a child may be a box of cocoa, a can of tomatoes, a quart of milk—or if they contribute money, it is usually 10 cents—2 cents a day.

School attendance has increased and classroom work has improved in every school in South Carolina where the school lunch project operates. Satisfactory gains in weight have been noted in previously undernourished school children. In Greenville County, for example, children, who were weighed at the beginning of the project, have been weighed again at the end of each five-week period. The records showed an average gain in weight of from three to eight pounds per child for the first five-week period.

Teachers in Decatur County, Georgia, declare that the school attendance for children, who are fed on free WPA school lunch projects, has increased 80 percent as a result of the wholesome, well-balanced, nourishing noonday meals which are served daily in the schools.

Through the cooperation of the Decatur County Health Commissioners, a weight chart was made for each child, and records have been taken at regular intervals. The average increase in weight has been shown to be from two to five pounds per month. Higher marks also have been made, some children being promoted to A—or high section of their classes—for the first time since they entered school. Greater general alertness, better deportment, and an improved attitude toward teachers and classmates are among the many manifested gains.

A school lunch project in Bryan County, Georgia, employed three WPA workers to prepare and serve hot mid-day meals to 200 children. The food was furnished by the local community through donations, supplemented by supplies from the Surplus Commodities Division.

Henry Ford, who has displayed an active interest in the health and welfare of his neighbors in Bryan County where he has an estate, has taken over on his own payrolls the three workers formerly paid by the WPA. He also has supplied the school lunch project with seventeen dozen each of certain dishes, spoons, and other tableware and has furnished tables and chairs, so that all the children may sit down together for their noonday meal.

In many Vermont towns, responsible groups of people, including the Parent-Teacher Associations and service and civic clubs, have cooperated with the WPA to provide a valuable hot lunch project and have been rewarded by watching the steady mental and physical development of the children fed.

Weight records on Vermont projects taken at the beginning of the school lunch project and again at the close, show an average gain of from two to four pounds per child. Teachers also report an increase in energy, greater accomplishment in school work, and a marked improvement in the general appearance of the pupils.

Educators, health officers and state officials in Minnesota agree that increased weight, great concentration in the classroom and fewer absences from school are some of the immediate gains resulting to children who are being fed on the WPA school lunch projects. They state that the hot lunch is of particular value to the children of unemployed parents whose food budget has been reduced to a minimum, or below the amount required for proper growth and health protection. For many of the children in Minnesota and elsewhere, the school lunch is not only the best, but sometimes the only adequate meal of the day.

To further this work of overcoming malnutrition and preventing its further progress, certain public tax-supported bodies in Minnesota have sponsored allied projects for which the WPA has supplied the labor. In some instances, milk stations provide mid-morning lunches for the needy; and in several poor districts, where children are known to leave home on almost empty stomachs milk and graham crackers are served at school before the beginning of classes.

In New York City alone, one WPA project employs 2,346 persons who serve free lunches to thousands of pupils in over 1,000 schools. Health records show uniformly marked improvement in the children's physical condition, and scholastic records show a parallel upward trend. Teachers state that pupils, who once exhibited sullen unresponsiveness, have become alert, interested, and in many cases, above the average in intelligence.

Dr. Louise Stanley, Chief of the Bureau of Home Economics, U. S. Department of Agriculture, expressing, in a recent letter to the Director of the Division of Women's and Professional Projects, her appreciation of the work performed under the school lunch program, declared:

> I have been very much impressed with what this has meant in making available to school children much-needed food. . . . The meals, where I have seen them, have been attractive, well-served, and palatable, and have contributed much in setting food standards and good food habits for the children.

Through the daily service of warm, nourishing food, prepared by qualifi ed, needy women workers, the WPA is making it possible for many underprivileged children of the present to grow into useful, healthy citizens of the future.

Further Resources

BOOKS

McElvaine, Robert S. *The Great Depression: America, 1929–1941.* New York: Times Books, 1984.

Terkel, Studs. *Hard Times: An Oral History of the Great Depression.* New York: Random House, 1970.

Watkins, T. H. *The Hungry Years: A Narrative History of the Great Depression.* New York: Henry Holt, 1999.

WEBSITES

Overview of the School Lunch Program. Pennsylvania Department of Education homepage. Available online at http://www.pde.psu.edu/nutrition/lunch.html; website homepage: http://www.pde.psu.edu (accessed March 4, 2003).

10

RELIGION

PETER J. CAPRIOGLIO

Entries are arranged in chronological order by date of primary source. For entries with one primary source, the entry title is the same as the primary source title. Entries with more than one primary source have an overall entry title, followed by the titles of the primary sources.

CHRONOLOGY

PRIMARY SOURCES

Important Events in Religion, 1930–1939

1930

- Charles E. Fuller, perhaps the most popular evangelist to appear on the scene between Billy Sunday and Billy Graham, begins his long-lived radio program *The Radio Revival Hour,* later called *The Old Fashioned Revival Hour.* On October 3, 1937, he moves to the Mutual Broadcasting Network, where he developed one of the largest audiences ever for religious programs.
- On February 26, *The Green Pastures,* a controversial depiction of African American religiosity by white playwright Marc Connelly, opens in New York. The play, written in 1929 and based on Roark Bradford's sketches *Ol' Man Adam an' His Chillun* (1928), wins the Pulitzer Prize for drama.
- On July 4, in a speech to supporters in Detroit, W.D. Fard (later known as Wallace Fard Muhammad) announces that he is the Mahdi, the chosen messenger to Muslims, and institutes the Nation of Islam. During his short ministry, Fard would teach that African Americans are members of a Muslim "Lost-Found Tribe of Shabazz" and that separation from whites, self-knowledge, and self-help will restore them to their proper place in the world. He founds a Temple of Islam, a University of Islam, and the Fruit of Islam (a self-defense organization) before his mysterious disappearance in 1934. His follower, Elijah Muhammad, continues the development of the Nation of Islam.
- On October 2, Dr. Walter A. Maier presents the first broadcast of *The Lutheran Hour* on the CBS radio network. In 1935 the program begins airing nationwide. Maier continues to host until his death in 1950.
- On December 31, Pope Pius XI issues the encyclical *Casti Connubii,* in which he prohibits Catholics from using artificial birth control under penalty of grave sin, claiming that it is against the laws of God and nature. The rhythm method, in which couples refrain from intercourse during ovulation, is permitted.

1931

- The American Lutheran Church is formed from a merger of the Joint Synod of Ohio, the Buffalo Synod, the Texas Synod, and the Iowa Synod.
- The General Council of Congregational Christian Churches is formed by the union of the National Council of Congregational Churches and the General Convention of Christian Churches. In 1955, the General Council merges with other churches to form the National Association of Congregational Christian Churches.
- The International Bible Students Association changes its name to Jehovah's Witnesses. In 1939, the organization is incorporated as the Watch Tower Bible and Tract Society of Pennsylvania.
- In March, the use of artificial contraceptives is defended before the Federal Council of Churches.

1932

- Lloyd C. Douglas publishes his religious bestseller *Forgive Us Our Trespasses.*
- Xavier University in New Orleans is dedicated. Founded in 1915 by the Sisters of the Blessed Sacrament for Indians and Colored People, Xavier is the first Roman Catholic university in the United States created specifically for African American students.
- On January 7, John Voris and other activists meet in New York and form Save the Children, a charity designed to relieve the plight of Depression-era Appalachian children. In 1938, Save the Children institutes its "Hot School Lunch" program, which will become the model for the national program instituted in 1941.

1933

- Bob Jones moves his Bob Jones College from College Point, Florida, to Cleveland, Tennessee. The college, founded in 1927, offers a fundamentalist view of Christianity and education.
- Congress modifies the Volstead Act, which established Prohibition, to allow the sale of beer and wine with a 3.2 percent alcohol content. The Twenty-first Amendment, repealing the Prohibition amendment, is adopted, ending an experiment in social control passed largely with the support of Protestant churches.
- On May 1, "The Humanist Manifesto I" appears in the May-June issue of *The New Humanist.*
- On May 1, the *Catholic Worker,* founded by Dorothy Day, distributes its first issue, priced at a penny a copy. Within three years more than 150,000 copies per issue are printed, and the Catholic Worker movement spreads across the nation's cities.
- On November 3, Theologian Paul Tillich—whose first book, *The Religious Situation* (1925), was translated by Richard Niebuhr in 1932—arrives in the United States as a refugee from Nazi Germany after being dismissed from the University of Frankfurt. He is hired as a visiting professor at Union Theological Seminary in New York when the faculty at that institution pools 5 percent of their salaries for his pay. His position later becomes permanent.

1934

- Professor Mordecai M. Kaplan publishes his influential book *Judaism as a Civilization,* which insists that Judaism is not only a religion but an entire way of life. His book inspires the beginning of Reconstructionist Judaism.

- Rev. George W. Truett of Dallas is elected president of the Baptist World Alliance at its meeting in Berlin.
- The Evangelical and Reform Church is organized from the union of the Reformed Church in the United States and the Evangelical Synod of North America.
- On January 7, Herbert W. Armstrong begins broadcasting his "Radio Church of God," from Pasadena, California. His ministry grows into what is now called the Worldwide Church of God.
- On January 7, Rev. Billy Sunday begins a two-week revival in New York City, his first series of services in that city since his great meetings in 1917.
- On February 15, the first Muslim mosque in North America, the Mother Mosque of America, opens in Cedar Rapids, Iowa.

1935

- Rev. Norman Vincent Peale, recently named pastor of the Marble Collegiate Church (Reform) in New York City, begins his radio broadcast for the Federal Council of Churches of Christ, *The Art of Living.* The Saturday program becomes one of the most successful religious programs of the decade.
- On June 10, Bill Wilson (as Bill W.) and Robert E. Smith ("Dr. Bob") hold the first meeting of Alcoholics Anonymous (AA) at Dr. Bob's home in Akron, Ohio. AA expands through word of mouth and with support from churches and synagogues. Bill W.'s name is revealed after his death in 1971.

1936

- The Union Party, organized by the forces of Senator Huey Long, Francis Townsend, and Father Charles E. Coughlin, nominates William Lemke for the presidency. Long, the logical nominee, had been assassinated the previous year. His following supposedly is led by Rev. Gerald L.K. Smith, who later establishes a career as an anti-Semite.
- Eugenio Cardinal Pacelli, papal secretary of state, visits the United States, the first man holding that office to do so. In 1939, he is elected Pope, taking the name Pius XII.

1937

- The Central Conference of American Rabbis, meeting in Columbus, Ohio, adopts the Columbus Platform, which reflects a growing interest in reviving traditional Jewish religious practices. The platform supports the Saturday, rather than the Sunday, Sabbath and historic Jewish festivals and holy days and replaces "confirmation" with the bar mitzvah. The platform also encourages the use of Hebrew and cantorial music and the optional use of prayer shawls and yarmulkes. The platform commits Reform Jews to Zionism, saying, "We affirm the obligation of all Jewry to aid in [Palestine's] upbuilding as a Jewish homeland by endeavoring to make it not only a haven of refuge for the oppressed but also a center of Jewish cultural and spiritual thought."

1938

- Louis Finkelstein of the Jewish Theological Seminary of America invites prominent Christians, such as Henry P. Van Dusen and Henry Sloane Coffin of Union Theological Seminary, the prominent Protestant pastor Harry Emerson Fosdick, and John Courtney Murray, S.J., to help him organize the Institute for Religious and Social Studies. This ecumenical group begins a process of dialogue across religious lines that continues throughout the twentieth century.

1939

- Edgar J. Goodspeed and J.M. Powis Smith complete a translation of the Old and New Testaments into the contemporary American vernacular. This "American Bible" begins a series of such translations in the following decades.
- On November 23, President Franklin D. Roosevelt delivers his radio Thanksgiving address to the nation. Earlier that year he had moved the holiday from the last Thursday to the second-to-last Thursday in November at the request of several large merchants still suffering from the Depression economy who wanted an extended Christmas shopping season. On December 26, 1941, Congress establishes the current pattern: Thanksgiving now falls on the fourth Thursday in November.
- In April, the Northern and Southern Methodist Churches unite after 105 years of separation; they had split in 1844 over slavery. They are joined in the union by the Methodist Protestant Church, which had become separate in 1830. The new denomination, the Methodist Church, becomes the largest Protestant church in the United States, with more than seven million members.
- On November 8, Rev. Martin Luther King Sr. leads a march of several thousand African Americans from his Ebenezer Baptist Church to Atlanta's city hall to protest the denial of African American voting rights.
- On December 24, President Franklin D. Roosevelt appoints Myron C. Taylor as his special envoy to the Vatican, arousing a chorus of opposition from Protestants who opposed direct ties between the United States government and a religious institution.

Court used what is now called the child benefit theory in justifying its decision. The justices reasoned that the true recipients of the state aid were the children, not the schools themselves, and determined that students as well as the state benefited from the funding.

Significance

Americans have debated the issue of separation of church and state ever since the founding fathers created the Constitution. Some people believe in a strict separation with no government aid ever going to any type of religious school. They fear that such actions would eventually blur church/state separation, allowing the state to support one religious group over another. Other people agree with the Supreme Court that in certain cases limited aid can be directed to religious schools. They believe that the benefits to children of providing state aid outweigh the possible negative impact of blurring the separation between church and state.

Although the United States was founded as a secular country, religion has always played a uniquely important role in the formation of American culture and everyday life. Some observers have called the United States one of the most religiously oriented societies in the world, even though the separation of church and state has existed since its birth as a nation.

Because of the country's religious orientation, the temptation to violate this separation can be very strong at times. The Supreme Court must examine possible violations and keep them in check within the framework of the Constitution. Importantly, the court has stated that government should not be hostile to religion but rather very careful not to support or favor one religion or set of religious beliefs over another.

The issue of government aid to religious schools proved divisive during much of the twentieth century. At times the debate became bitter. In the late 1940s, for example, Eleanor Roosevelt supported federal aid to education that would exclude church-run schools. Cardinal Francis Spellman, the archbishop of the Roman Catholic Church in New York, so strongly disagreed with her position that he vowed to never publicly acknowledge her again. The dispute between Mrs. Roosevelt and Cardinal Spellman triggered the revitalization of a group called Protestants and Others Organized for the Separation of Church and State.

Those who argue for rigid separation point out that denying the state any authority in religious questions creates freedom for people to follow their own consciences. The Supreme Court has consistently tried to maintain this separation by balancing the needs of the state with the needs of the individual. In the case of *Cochran v. Louisiana State Board of Education,* the court decided that the needs of the students came first.

Cochran v. Louisiana State Board of Education

Supreme Court decision

By: Charles Evans Hughes

Date: April 28, 1930

Source: *Cochran v. Louisiana State Board of Education.* 281 U.S. 370 (1930). Available online at http://caselaw.lp.findlaw.com/scripts/getcase.pl?navby=case&court=us&vol=281&page=370; website home page: http://www.findlaw.com (accessed February 14, 2003).

About the Author: Charles Evans Hughes (1862–1948), born in Glens Falls, N.Y., was governor of New York from 1906 to 1910. During the presidencies of Warren G. Harding (served 1921–1923) and Calvin Coolidge (served 1923–1929), Hughes was secretary of state. As chief justice of the United States Supreme Court from 1930 to 1941, his positions on issues of civil liberties and civil rights anticipated the Court's future actions. Noteworthy is his strong stance in favor of free speech, free press, and equal protection of the laws. ■

Introduction

In 1928 Louisiana passed legislation that permitted the use of state funds to purchase secular, or nonreligious, textbooks for all schoolchildren. This legislation, which applied to both public and private schools, prohibited the purchase of religious textbooks with state funds.

A group of Louisiana taxpayers objected to this law, claiming state funds should not be used to buy any kind of books for children in religious schools. They sued the Louisiana State Board of Education, the state agency responsible for purchasing schoolbooks, on the grounds that the law violated the due process clause of the Fourteenth Amendment. The due process clause states that laws may not include any measure that would cause an individual to be treated unfairly or unreasonably. After losing their case in the state courts, Cochran and the others appealed to the U.S. Supreme Court.

The Supreme Court's decision in *Cochran v. Louisiana State Board of Education* established for the first time that indirect aid to religious schools was allowable under the Constitution of the United States. The

Children sit in class in an elementary school in Tuscumbria, Alabama, 1932. In *Cochran v. Louisiana State Board of Education* (1930), the Court decided that state money could be used to pay for non-religious books in parochial schools. Opponents argued that this practice violated the separation of church and state. © SCHENECTADY MUSEUM; HALL OF ELECTRICAL HISTORY FOUNDATION/CORBIS. REPRODUCED BY PERMISSION.

Primary Source

Cochran v. Louisiana State Board of Education [excerpt]

SYNOPSIS: In this landmark decision the United States Supreme Court ruled for the first time that indirect aid to religious schools, under certain conditions, was permissible under the Constitution of the United States. A state could provide funding for children's nonreligious textbooks in private schools, religious or not. This case was argued on April 15, 1930, and decided on April 28, 1930.

Mr. Chief Justice Hughes delivered the opinion of the Court.

The appellants, as citizens and taxpayers of the state of Louisiana, brought this suit to restrain the State Board of Education and other state officials from expending any part of the severance tax fund in purchasing school books and in supplying them free of cost to the school children of the state, under Acts No. 100 and No. 143 of 1928, upon the ground that the legislation violated specified provisions of the Constitution of the state and also section 4 of article 4 and the Fourteenth Amendment of the Federal Constitution. . . .

The Supreme Court of the state, following its decision in *Borden v. Louisiana State Board of Education* . . . , held that these acts were not repugnant to either the state or the Federal Constitution.

No substantial Federal question is presented under section 4 of article 4 of the Federal Constitution guaranteeing to every state a republican form of government, as questions arising under this provision are political, not judicial, in character. . . .

The contention of the appellant under the Fourteenth Amendment is that taxation for the purchase of school books constituted a taking of private property for a private purpose. . . . The purpose is said to be to aid private, religious, sectarian, and other schools not embraced in the public educational system of the state by furnishing text-books free to the children attending such private schools. The operation and effect of the legislation in question were described by the Supreme Court of the state as follows . . . : "One may scan the acts in vain to ascertain where any money is appropriated for the purchase of school books for the use of any church, private, sectarian, or even public school. The appropriations were made for the specific purpose of purchasing school books for the use of the school children of the state, free of cost to them. It was . . . for their benefit and the resulting benefit to the state that the appropriations were made. True, these children attend some school, public or private, the latter, sectarian or nonsectarian, and that the books are to be furnished them for their use, free of cost, whichever they attend. The schools, however, are not the beneficiaries of these appropriations. They obtain nothing from them, nor are they relieved of a single obligation, because of them. The school children and the state alone are the beneficiaries. It is also true that the sectarian schools, which some of the children attend, instruct their pupils in religion, and books are used for that purpose, but one may search diligently the acts, though without result, in an effort to find anything to the effect that it is the purpose of the state to furnish religious books for the use of such children. . . ."

Viewing the statute as having the effect thus attributed to it, we cannot doubt that the taxing power of the state is exerted for a public purpose. The legislation does not segregate private schools, or their pupils, as its beneficiaries or attempt to interfere with any matters of exclusively private concern. Its interest is education, broadly; its method, comprehensive. Individual interests are aided only as the common interest is safeguarded.

Judgment affirmed.

Further Resources

BOOKS

Blandford, Linda A. *Supreme Court of the United States, 1789–1980: An Index to Opinions Arranged by Justice.* Millwood, N.Y.: Kraus International Publications, 1983.

Harrell, Mary Ann. *Equal Justice Under Law: The Supreme Court in American Life.* Washington, D.C.: Supreme Court Historical Society, 1982.

The Supreme Court Justices: Illustrated Biographies, 1789–1995. Washington, D.C.: Congressional Quarterly, 1995.

PERIODICALS

"High Court Shifts Church-State Stance." *U.S. News & World Report,* March 19, 1984, 10.

McGreevy, John T. "Paying the Words Extra: Religious Discourse in the Supreme Court of the United States." *Commonweal,* June 16, 1995, 24.

"New Legislation on Religious Liberty." *The Christian Century,* August 2, 2000, 786.

WEBSITES

Batte, Susan M. "A Table of Important Establishment Clause Cases Dealing with Religion and Education: 1899 to 1970." The Constitutional Principle: Separation of Church and State. Available online at http://members.tripod.com/~candst/table1.htm; website home page: http://members.tripod.com (accessed August 29, 2002).

"Charles Evans Hughes." Biography.com. Available online at http://search.biography.com/print_record.pl?id=16050; website home page: http://search.biography.com (accessed August 29, 2002).

Walsh, Mark. "Public vs. Private." *Education Week.* Available online at http://www.edweek.org/ew/vol-19/08privats1.h19; website home page: http://www.edweek.org (accessed August 29, 2002).

Casti Connubii

Papal encyclical

By: Pope Pius XI

Date: December 31, 1930

Source: Pope Pius XI. *Casti Connubii.* Rome, December 31, 1930. Available online at http://www.vatican.va/holy_father/pius_xi/encyclicals/documents/hf_p-xi_enc_31121930_casti-connubii_en.html; website home page: http://www.vatican.va (accessed February 9, 2003).

About the Author: Pope Pius XI (1857–1939) was born Ambrogio Damiano Achille Ratti in Desio, Italy, and ordained a priest in 1879. A superb scholar, he committed most of the next 43 years to work as a church librarian. In 1918 Pope Benedict selected him for diplomatic service and dispatched him to Poland as an apostolic visitor. Three years later Ratti returned to Italy and was appointed the cardinal archbishop of Milan. He was elected pope by the College of Cardinals in 1922 and served until his death in 1939. ■

Introduction

Pope Pius XI addressed three major issues facing Roman Catholics in his encyclical *Casti Connubii* (On Christian Marriage): birth control, abortion, and eugenics (the scientific and social control of human reproduction). Since the opening of the first birth-control clinic in the United States in 1916, the Catholic Church had identified birth control, abortion, and eugenics as major moral and social problems. The church had opposed these practices before this time but strengthened its position after World War I (1914–1918) as birth control became more widely used in the United States and elsewhere. Pope Pius XI saw a need to formally warn Catholics by issuing a papal encyclical, which is a letter to the church's leadership and one of the most powerful documents that the church can present.

The 1930 encyclical stated that married Catholics may use natural birth control, or natural family planning, but not artificial birth control. Natural birth control involves preventing pregnancy by abstaining from sexual intercourse during the most fertile times of the woman's cycle. The church did not disapprove of this method because by preventing conception, it does not interfere with the "order of nature"—the natural outcome of sexual intercourse. Artificial birth control, according to the church, includes any action that deliberately interferes with sexual intercourse's "natural power and purpose" to "generate new life."

The pope's encyclical also discussed abortion any procedure used to intentionally end a pregnancy. During the depression some women chose to have abortions to avoid bearing children they couldn't afford to raise. The church considered abortion morally wrong because only God has absolute dominion, or authority, over human life.

Eugenics—the controlled, selective mating of people intended to improve the human species genetically—is the third major issue discussed in the encyclical. Advocates of eugenics wished to discourage the mentally and physically below-average from having children or at least many children. The Catholic Church disapproved of eugenics because some of its supporters advocated the use of sterilization. Sterilization is any surgical procedure that makes people incapable of reproduction, which the church opposed as immoral. The church also opposed eugenics on the grounds that it involves dehumanization or the limiting of human freedom.

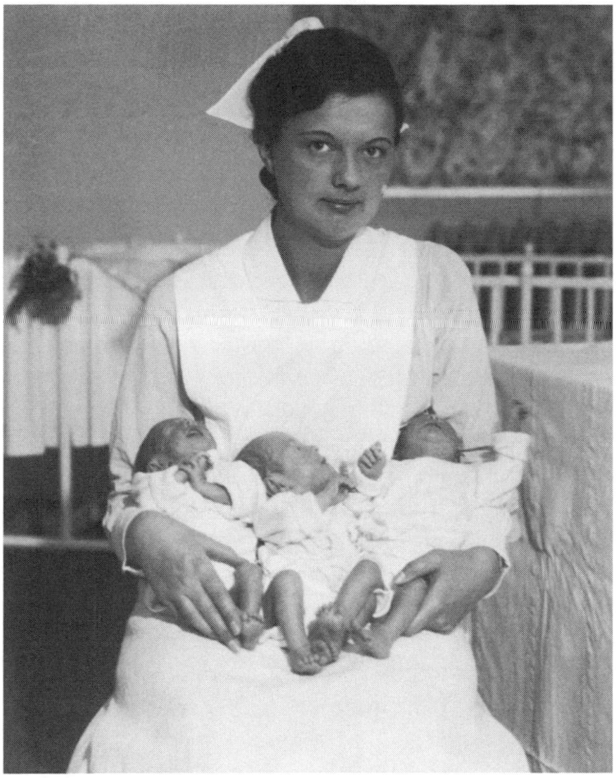

A nurse holds triplets in a Philadelphia hospital, 1933. In 1930 Pope Pius XI issued an encyclical asserting the Catholic Church's opposition to abortion, artificial birth control, and eugenics. The Church's position led to mixed reactions by Catholics who held various positions of their own on the issues. © **BETTMANN/CORBIS. REPRODUCED BY PERMISSION.**

Significance

American Catholics reacted to Pope Pius XI's encyclical in different ways: some chose to follow all the church's teachings, others adhered to most of them, and still others accepted only some of them. Many Catholics decided to use artificial birth control methods but followed the church's teachings against abortion and eugenics.

This mixed reaction produced a dilemma for Catholics. If they accepted some or even most but not all of the teachings on Christian marriage, were they still faithful to the church? Could Catholics pick and choose which teachings to follow and still remain in the church? These difficult questions divided many Catholics. Some chose to follow their own consciences and made their own decisions about the morality of these issues. If their beliefs differed somewhat from those of the church, they still considered themselves good practicing Catholics. Others believed that they must adhere completely to the teachings of the church to be "good" rather than "fallen" or "lapsed" Catholics.

All the popes since Pius XI have upheld the principles he set on birth control, abortion, and eugenics. The Catholic Church has not changed its official position much since the 1930 encyclical, even though many American Catholics have stated that they do not follow the church's prohibition on birth control and abortion.

Primary Source

Casti Connubii [excerpt]

SYNOPSIS: This encyclical by Pope Pius XI deals with the general nature of a Christian marriage, including the church's teachings on birth control, abortion, and eugenics. The church's objections to artificial birth control begin in paragraph 53 of the encyclical. Its objections to abortion and eugenics are addressed starting in paragraph 63 and paragraph 68, respectively.

How great is the dignity of chaste wedlock, Venerable Brethren, may be judged best from this that Christ Our Lord, Son of the Eternal Father, having assumed the nature of fallen man, not only, with His loving desire of compassing the redemption of our race, ordained it in an especial manner as the principle and foundation of domestic society and therefore of all human intercourse, but also raised it to the rank of a truly and great sacrament of the New Law, restored it to the original purity of its divine institution, and accordingly entrusted all its discipline and care to His spouse the Church. . . .

53. And now, Venerable Brethren, we shall explain in detail the evils opposed to each of the benefits of matrimony. First consideration is due to the offspring, which many have the boldness to call the disagreeable burden of matrimony and which they say is to be carefully avoided by married people not through virtuous continence (which Christian law permits in matrimony when both parties consent) but by frustrating the marriage act. Some justify this criminal abuse on the ground that they are weary of children and wish to gratify their desires without their consequent burden. Others say that they cannot on the one hand remain continent nor on the other can they have children because of the difficulties whether on the part of the mother or on the part of family circumstances.

54. But no reason, however grave, may be put forward by which anything intrinsically against nature may become conformable to nature and morally good. Since, therefore, the conjugal act is destined primarily by nature for the begetting of children, those who in exercising it deliberately frustrate its natural power and purpose sin against nature and commit a deed which is shameful and intrinsically vicious.

55. Small wonder, therefore, if Holy Writ bears witness that the Divine Majesty regards with greatest detestation this horrible crime and at times has punished it with death. As St. Augustine notes, "Intercourse even with one's legitimate wife is unlawful and wicked where the conception of the offspring is prevented. Onan, the son of Juda, did this and the Lord killed him for it."

56. Since, therefore, openly departing from the uninterrupted Christian tradition some recently have judged it possible solemnly to declare another doctrine regarding this question, the Catholic Church, to whom God has entrusted the defense of the integrity and purity of morals, standing erect in the midst of the moral ruin which surrounds her, in order that she may preserve the chastity of the nuptial union from being defiled by this foul stain, raises her voice in token of her divine ambassadorship and through Our mouth proclaims anew: any use whatsoever of matrimony exercised in such a way that the act is deliberately frustrated in its natural power to generate life is an offense against the law of God and of nature, and those who indulge in such are branded with the guilt of a grave sin. . . .

63. But another very grave crime is to be noted, Venerable Brethren, which regards the taking of the life of the offspring hidden in the mother's womb. Some wish it to be allowed and left to the will of the father or the mother; others say it is unlawful unless there are weighty reasons which they call by the name of medical, social, or eugenic "indication." Because this matter falls under the penal laws of the state by which the destruction of the offspring begotten but unborn is forbidden, these people demand that the "indication," which in one form or another they defend, be recognized as such by the public law and in no way penalized. There are those, moreover, who ask that the public authorities provide aid for these death-dealing operations, a thing, which, sad to say, everyone knows is of very frequent occurrence in some places.

64. As to the "medical and therapeutic indication" to which, using their own words, we have made reference, Venerable Brethren, however much we may pity the mother whose health and even life is gravely imperiled in the performance of the duty allotted to her by nature, nevertheless what could ever be a sufficient reason for excusing in any way the direct murder of the innocent? This is precisely what we are dealing with here. Whether inflicted upon the mother or upon the child, it is against the precept of God and the law of nature: "Thou shalt not kill." The life of each is equally sacred, and no one has the power, not even the public authority, to destroy it. It is of no use to appeal to the right of taking away life for here it is a question of the innocent, whereas that right has regard only to the guilty; nor is there here question of defense by bloodshed against an unjust aggressor (for who would call an innocent child an unjust aggressor?); again there is not question here of what is called the "law of extreme necessity" which could even extend to the direct killing of the innocent. Upright and skillful doctors strive most praiseworthily to guard and preserve the lives of both mother and child; on the contrary, those show themselves most unworthy of the noble medical profession who encompass the death of one or the other, through a pretense at practicing medicine or through motives of misguided pity.

65. All of which agrees with the stern words of the Bishop of Hippo in denouncing those wicked parents who seek to remain childless, and failing in

this, are not ashamed to put their offspring to death: "Sometimes this lustful cruelty or cruel lust goes so far as to seek to procure a baneful sterility, and if this fails the fetus conceived in the womb is in one way or another smothered or evacuated, in the desire to destroy the offspring before it has life, or if it already lives in the womb, to kill it before it is born. If both man and woman are party to such practices they are not spouses at all; and if from the first they have carried on thus they have come together not for honest wedlock, but for impure gratification; if both are not party to these deeds, I make bold to say that either the one makes herself a mistress of the husband, or the other simply the paramour of his wife."

66. What is asserted in favor of the social and eugenic "indication" may and must be accepted, provided lawful and upright methods are employed within the proper limits; but to wish to put forward reasons based upon them for the killing of the innocent is unthinkable and contrary to the divine precept promulgated in the words of the Apostle: Evil is not to be done that good may come of it.

67. Those who hold the reins of government should not forget that it is the duty of public authority by appropriate laws and sanctions to defend the lives of the innocent, and this all the more so since those whose lives are endangered and assailed cannot defend themselves. Among whom we must mention in the first place infants hidden in the mother's womb. And if the public magistrates not only do not defend them, but by their laws and ordinances betray them to death at the hands of doctors or of others, let them remember that God is the Judge and Avenger of innocent blood which cried from earth to Heaven.

68. Finally, that pernicious practice must be condemned which closely touches upon the natural right of man to enter matrimony but affects also in a real way the welfare of the offspring. For there are some who over solicitous for the cause of eugenics, not only give salutary counsel for more certainly procuring the strength and health of the future child—which, indeed, is not contrary to right reason—but put eugenics before aims of a higher order, and by public authority wish to prevent from marrying all those whom, even though naturally fit for marriage, they consider, according to the norms and conjectures of their investigations, would, through hereditary transmission, bring forth defective offspring. And more, they wish to legislate to deprive these of that natural faculty by medical action despite their unwillingness; and this they do not propose as an infliction of grave punishment under the authority of the state for a crime committed, not to prevent future crimes by guilty persons, but against every right and good they wish the civil authority to arrogate to itself a power over a faculty which it never had and can never legitimately possess.

69. Those who act in this way are at fault in losing sight of the fact that the family is more sacred than the State and that men are begotten not for the earth and for time, but for Heaven and eternity. Although often these individuals are to be dissuaded from entering into matrimony, certainly it is wrong to brand men with the stigma of crime because they contract marriage, on the ground that, despite the fact that they are in every respect capable of matrimony, they will give birth only to defective children, even though they use all care and diligence.

70. Public magistrates have no direct power over the bodies of their subjects; therefore, where no crime has taken place and there is no cause present for grave punishment, they can never directly harm, or tamper with the integrity of the body, either for the reasons of eugenics or for any other reason. St. Thomas teaches this when inquiring whether human judges for the sake of preventing future evils can inflict punishment, he admits that the power indeed exists as regards certain other forms of evil, but justly and properly denies it as regards the maiming of the body. "No one who is guiltless may be punished by a human tribunal either by flogging to death, or mutilation, or by beating."

71. Furthermore, Christian doctrine establishes, and the light of human reason makes it most clear, that private individuals have no other power over the members of their bodies than that which pertains to their natural ends; and they are not free to destroy or mutilate their members, or in any other way render themselves unfit for their natural functions, except when no other provision can be made for the good of the whole body.

Further Resources

BOOKS

Abortion: Opposing Viewpoints. San Diego, Calif.: Greenhaven Press, 2002.

Kevles, Daniel J. *In the Name of Eugenics: Genetics and the Uses of Human Heredity.* New York: Knopf, 1985.

Newman, Lucile F. *Birth Control: An Anthropological View.* Reading, Mass.: Addison-Wesley, 1972.

WEBSITES

"Birth Control." Catholic Answers. Available online at http://www.catholic.com/library/Birth_Control.asp; website home page: http://www.catholic.com (accessed August 29, 2002).

"Birth Control." A Catholic Response. Available online at http://users.binary.net/polycarp/nobirth.html; website home page: http://www.users.binary.net (accessed August 29, 2002).

"The Church and Eugenics." New Advent. Available online at http://www.newadvent.org/cathen/16038b.htm; website home page: http://www.newadvent.org (accessed August 29, 2002).

Roosevelt and/or Ruin?

"Roosevelt or Ruin"

Speech

By: Father Charles E. Coughlin

Date: November 27, 1933

Source: Coughlin, Charles E. "Roosevelt or Ruin." National newsreel broadcast, November 27, 1933. Available online at http://www.pbs.org/greatspeeches/timeline/index.html#1930; website home page: http://www.pbs.org/greatspeeches (accessed February 10, 2002).

"Roosevelt and Ruin"

Radio address

By: Father Charles E. Coughlin

Date: June 19, 1936

Source: Coughlin, Charles E. "Roosevelt and Ruin." National radio address, June 19, 1936. Available online at http://www.pbs.org/greatspeeches/timeline/index.html#1930; website home page: http://www.pbs.org/greatspeeches (accessed February 10, 2002).

About the Author: Charles Edward Coughlin (1891–1979), born in Ontario, was ordained a Roman Catholic priest in 1916. From 1926 to 1966 he served as pastor of the Shrine of the Little Flower in Royal Oak, Michigan. He became a political organizer and popular radio personality during the 1930s. Because of his anti-Semitic, or anti-Jewish, statements on the radio in the mid- and late 1930s, the Catholic Church ordered Coughlin to cease broadcasting in 1942. He spent the rest of his career as pastor of the Shrine of the Little Flower until his death. ■

Introduction

Charles Coughlin's radio career began in 1926 with a local weekly program in Detroit, Michigan. His radio sermons and talks to children proved popular, and within a year he was receiving thousands of letters from listeners every week. His show did so well locally that four years later it became a nationally broadcast program.

Critics at the time noted that Coughlin had a charismatic voice well suited to radio. In a series of broadcasts in early 1930, he delivered strongly worded attacks against communism. Later that year, as the economic depression began to spread and many people lost their jobs, he began calling for major changes to the American capitalist system. He also spoke against birth control and Prohibition, the18th Amendment to the Constitution that prohibited the production, sale, transportation, import, and export of alcohol. These topics attracted hundreds of thousands of radio listeners.

Coughlin's consistent attacks on the administration of President Herbert Hoover (served 1929–1933) prompted the radio network that carried his program to cancel it. Determined not to be silenced he organized his own radio network with the help of contributions from his audience. He soon broadcast his show to 26 radio stations. In the early 1930s his mail averaged about 80,000 letters a week and his listeners contributed about five million dollars a year.

During the 1932 presidential campaign Coughlin strongly endorsed Franklin D. Roosevelt (served 1933–1945). The radio priest appealed to his listeners to vote for Roosevelt with slogans such as "Roosevelt or ruin." During the first year of Roosevelt's administration, Coughlin supported the New Deal, the president's economic and social relief program, and offered his own plans for fighting the Depression.

In 1934 Coughlin founded the National Union for Social Justice, a nationwide organization dedicated to fighting communism and advocating government control of big business. The same year, a falling-out occurred between the president and the priest because Roosevelt would not fully accept Coughlin's ideas about reforming the country's financial system.

In 1936, when the president ran for reelection, Coughlin made a complete turnaround and became a vigorous critic of Roosevelt's administration. His slogan became "Roosevelt *and* ruin" instead of "Roosevelt *or* ruin." He raged against the president, calling him a liar and accusing him of being anti-God, while also attacking communism and Judaism. At times his attacks seemed to get out of control and some of his critics began calling him the "Father of Hate."

Coughlin's National Union for Social Justice supported the Union Party, a small political party that ran a candidate against Roosevelt and received very few votes. Roosevelt's huge popular vote won him a second term in office and Coughlin's influence on the radio began to lessen.

Significance

The popularity of Father Coughlin's show grew enormously during the early days of the depression. In

Reverend Charles E. Coughlin delivers a fiery speech in Detroit, 1936. Father Coughlin was a popular radio personality during the 1930s. Initially a vocal supporter of Franklin D. Roosevelt, he became one of the president's harshest critics. AP/WIDE WORLD PHOTOS. REPRODUCED BY PERMISSION.

1934 he received more mail than any other American radio personality and an estimated 30 to 45 million Americans listened to his show each week.

In the second half of the 1930s Coughlin's popularity began to decline. His attacks on the immensely popular Roosevelt caused some people to stop listening to him. By 1937 Coughlin increasingly made anti-Semitic statements on his weekly broadcasts and in his newspaper *Social Justice.* He repeatedly linked Jews with communists and blamed them for the Depression. The Roman Catholic Church did not want to be associated with Coughlin's viewpoints and issued statements asserting that he did not speak for the church. Because of all the controversy surrounding his broadcasts, they were taken off the air in 1942. He lost the nation's attention and never regained it.

Primary Source

"Roosevelt or Ruin"

SYNOPSIS: Coughlin delivered his decidedly pro-Roosevelt speech "Roosevelt or Ruin" in a national newsreel broadcast in 1933.

Ladies and gentlemen:

It is almost preposterous on my part to advocate your loyalty to Franklin D. Roosevelt. The events of the past three weeks are eloquent in themselves: Our laborers are being restored to remunerative operation; our factories are being opened; the prices of our commodities are being raised, and why may I ask you?

Simply because the money-changers are being driven from the temple. Simply because the outworn gold standard which held you and myself in bondage for generations has evaporated into the mists of the past. The great advantages obtained through the National Recovery Act are more or less insignificant compared to the greater advantages which the future holds for us, once the fulfillment of Franklin Roosevelt's monetary policy will become history.

Ladies and Gentlemen, this is the day, despite all opposition to the contrary, that you remain steadfast behind the one man who can save this civilization of ours.

It is either Roosevelt or ruin! I thank you.

Primary Source

"Roosevelt and Ruin" [excerpt]

SYNOPSIS: In 1936, three years after Coughlin delivered his pro-Roosevelt speech, he presented "Roosevelt and Ruin," a notably anti-Roosevelt address, to a national radio audience.

Ladies and gentlemen:

In the autumn of 1932, it was my privilege to address the American people on the causes of the so-called depression and upon the obvious remedies required to bring about a permanent recovery.

Those were days which witnessed a complete breakdown of the financial system under which our Western civilization had been developed. It was also evident that under this financial system there resulted a concentration of wealth and a multiplication of impoverished families. Unjust wages and unreasonable idleness were universally recognized as contradictions in an age of plenty.

To my mind it was inconceivable that irrational and needless want should exist in an age of plenty. Were there not plenty of raw materials in America? Were not our citizens and our countryside inhabited by plenty of skilled inventors, engineers, executives, workmen and farmers? At no time in the history of civilization was it possible for man to produce such an abundant supply, thanks to the benedictions of mass production machinery. At no time within the last two centuries was there such a demand on the part of our population for the thousands of good things capable of being produced in our fields and in our factories.

What was the basic cause which closed factories, which created idleness, which permitted weeds to overrun our golden fields and plowshares to rust? There was and is but one answer. Some call it lack of purchasing power. Others, viewing the problem in a more philosophic light, recognize that the financial system which was able to function in an age of scarcity was totally inadequate to operate successfully in an age of plenty.

Let me explain this statement briefly: Before the nineteenth century, the ox-cart, the spade and the crude instruments of production were handicaps to the rapid creation of real wealth.

By 1932, a new era of production had come into full bloom. It was represented by the motor car, the tractor and the power lathe, which enabled the laborer to produce wealth ten times more rapidly than was possible for his ancestors. Within the short expanse of 150 years, the problem of production had been solved, due to the ingenuity of men like Arkwright and his loom, Fulton and his steam engine, and Edison and his dynamo. These and a thousand other benefactors of mankind made it possible for the teeming millions of people throughout the world to transfer speedily the raw materials into the thousand necessities and conveniences which fall under the common name of wealth.

Thus, with the advent of our scientific era, with its far-flung fields, its spacious factories, its humming motors, its thundering locomotives, its highly trained mechanics, it is inconceivable how such a thing as a so-called depression should blight the lives of an entire nation when there was a plenitude of everything surrounding us, only to be withheld from us because the so-called leaders of high finance persisted in clinging to an outworn theory of privately issued money, the medium through which wealth is distributed.

Before the year 1932, very few persons fully realized the existence of this financial bondage. Millions of citizens began asking the obvious questions: "Why should the farmer be forced to follow his plow at a loss?" "Why should the citizens—at least 90 per cent of them—be imprisoned behind the cruel bars of want when, within their grasp, there are plenty of shoes, of clothing, of motor cars, of refrigerators, to which they are entitled?" At last, when the most brilliant minds amongst the industrialists, bankers and their kept politicians had failed to solve the cause of the needless depression, there appeared upon the scene of our national life a new champion of the people, Franklin Delano Roosevelt! He spoke golden words of hope. He intimated to the American people that the system of permitting a group of private citizens to create money, then to issue it to the government as if it were real money, then to exact payment from the entire nation through a system of taxation earned by real labor and service, was immoral.

With the whip of his scorn he castigated these usurers who exploited the poor. With his eloquent tongue he lashed their financial system which devoured the homes of widows and orphans. No man in modern times received such plaudits from the poor as did Franklin Roosevelt when he promised to drive the money-changers from the temple—the money-changers who had clipped the coins of wages, who had manufactured spurious money, and who had brought proud America to her knees.

March 4, 1933! I shall never forget the inaugural address, which seemed to re-echo the very words employed by Christ Himself as He actually drove the money-changers from the temple. The thrill that was mine was yours. Through dim clouds of the depression, this man Roosevelt was, as it were, a new savior of his people! Oh, just a little longer shall there be needless poverty! Just another year shall there be naked backs! Just another moment shall there be dark thoughts of revolution! Never again will the chains of economic poverty bite into the hearts of simple folks, as they did in the past days of the Old Deal! Such were our hopes in the springtime of 1933. It is not pleasant for me who coined the phrase "Roosevelt or ruin"—a phrase fashioned upon promises—to voice such passionate words. But I am constrained to admit that "Roosevelt and ruin" is the order of the day, because the money-changers have not been driven from the temple.

My friends, I come before you tonight not to ask you to return to . . . the Hoovers, to the Old Deal exploiters, who honestly defended the dishonest system of gold standardism and rugged individualism. Their sun has set never to rise again. America has turned its back definitely upon the platitudinous platforms of "rugged individualism." These Punch and Judy Republicans, whose actions and words were dominated by the ventriloquists of Wall Street, are so blind that they do not recognize, even in this perilous hour, that their gold basis and their private coinage of money have bred more radicals than did Karl Marx or Lenin. To their system or ox-cart financialism we must never return!

On the other hand, the Democratic platform is discredited before it is published. Was there not a 1932 platform? By Mr. Roosevelt and its colleagues, was it not regarded as a solemn pledge to the people? Certainly! [But] it was plowed under like the cotton, slaughtered like the pigs. . . . Therefore, the veracity of the future upstage pledges must be judged by the echoings of the golden voice of a lost leader.

Said he, when the flag of hope was proudly unfurled on March 4, 1933: "Plenty is at our doorsteps, but the generous use of it languished in the very sight of the supply. . . . Primarily, this is because the rulers of the exchange of mankind's goods have failed through their own stubbornness and their own incompetence—have admitted their failure and abdicated. Practices of the unscrupulous money-changers stand indicted in the court of public opinion, rejected by the hearts and minds of men. . . ."

These words, my friends, are not mine. These are the caustic, devastating words uttered by Franklin Delano Roosevelt on March 4, 1933, condemning Franklin Delano Roosevelt in November of 1936.

Alas! The temple still remains the private property of the money-changers. The golden key has been handed over to them for safekeeping—the key which now is fashioned in the shape of a double cross!

Further Resources

BOOKS

Bennett, David Harry. *Demagogues in the Depression: American Radicals and the Union Party, 1932–1936.* New Brunswick, N.J.: Rutgers University Press, 1969.

Tull, Charles J. *Father Coughlin and the New Deal.* Syracuse, N.Y.: Syracuse University Press, 1965.

Wolfskill, George. *All but the People: Franklin D. Roosevelt and his Critics.* New York: Macmillan, 1969.

WEBSITES

"Father Charles E. Coughlin: National Union for Social Justice." The Religious Movements Homepage at the University of Virginia. Available online at http://religiousmovements.lib.virginia.edu/nrms/coughlin.html; website home page: http://religiousmovements.lib.virginia.edu (accessed August 29, 2002).

Father Charles E. Coughlin radio broadcast. Social Security Online History Page. Available online at http://www.ssa.gov/history/coughlinradio.html; website home page: http://www.ssa.gov (accessed August 29, 2002).

"Father Coughlin." Biography.com. Available online at http://search.biography.com/print_record.pl?id=13867; website home page: http://www.search.biography.com (accessed August 29, 2002).

Letter to the Nation's Clergy and Their Responses

Franklin D. Roosevelt to the Nation's Clergy, September 24, 1935

Letter

By: Franklin D. Roosevelt

Date: September 24, 1935

Source: Roosevelt, Franklin D. Letter to the Nation's Clergy, Washington, D.C. September 24, 1935. FDR Library. President's Personal File. Entry 21. Box 1. Reproduced as "Letter to the Nation's Clergy, Franklin D. Roosevelt" in the New Deal Document Library. Available online at http://newdeal.feri.org/texts/394.htm; website home page: http://newdeal.feri.org (accessed February 11, 2003).

About the Author: Franklin Delano Roosevelt (1882–1945) was born in Hyde Park, N.Y. He became assistant secretary of the Navy in 1913 and governor of New York in 1928. He is the only U.S. president to have been elected four times (in 1932, 1936, 1940, and 1944). He died during his fourth term on April 12, 1945. Many historians consider him one of the most successful American presidents. He is noted especially for his leadership during the Great Depression, World War II, and for the establishment of the United Nations.

President Franklin D. Roosevelt (center), with son John (right) and Reverend E. Jerome Pipes (left) in front of Emmanuel Episcopal Church, August 31, 1936. During the Depression, Roosevelt wrote to clergy members throughout the nation asking them to inform him about the feelings and needs of their congregations. The responses helped shape his New Deal policies. AP/WIDE WORLD PHOTOS. REPRODUCED BY PERMISSION.

Clergy Response to FDR

Letters

By: Rev. James J. O'Reilly; Rabbi Simon Cohen; Rev. H. B. Hawkins; Rev. Walter G. Procter

Date: October 1935

Source: O'Reilly, James J.; Simon Cohen; H. B. Hawkins; Walter G. Procter. Letters to Franklin D. Roosevelt. October 3, 1935; October 27, 1935; October 19, 1935; October 10, 1935. FDR Library. President's Personal File. Entry 21. Box 22; Box 22; Box 8; Box 10. Reproduced as "Clergy Letter, Church of St. John the Baptist, Brooklyn, NY"; "Clergy Letter, Temple Emanuel, Brooklyn, NY"; "Clergy Letter, Chicago, IL"; "Clergy Letter, Mayer Chapel, Indianapolis, IN" in the New Deal Document Library. Available online at http://newdeal.feri.org/texts/index.htm; website home page: http://newdeal.feri.org (accessed February 7, 2003). ■

Introduction

The most serious challenge Roosevelt faced in the early years of his administration was reducing the tremendous negative impact the Depression was having on the American people. Along with Congress he started a number of government-sponsored national programs to create jobs and revive the economy. Roosevelt realized he also had to address problems troubling Americans on the local level. Instead of relying only on the reports from politicians and local government agencies, he wanted to obtain information about such problems directly from community resources.

Roosevelt decided to tap churches, synagogues, and other religious organizations for information. During the Depression, many Americans turned to the religious organizations in their communities for material help and spiritual guidance. Priests, rabbis, and ministers were often the first to extend assistance to needy families. Until Roosevelt's administration, very few government programs existed to help families stricken by unemployment, hunger, and homelessness. Often the generosity of the local churches, synagogues, and other religious groups kept people alive.

Most major religious groups saw a slight rise in their membership during the Depression. Fundamentalist religions, which interpret the Bible literally, attracted the greatest numbers of new followers. The lower socio-economic classes were more likely than the higher classes to turn to religion during the 1930s, seeking comfort and refuge from poverty and unemployment. Roosevelt and his advisers, therefore, decided to write to clergy members throughout the nation, asking them to inform the president about the feelings and needs of their congregations.

Significance

Roosevelt's letter generated a huge response, of which several thousand letters totaling about 28,600 pages have been preserved. Most of the clergy's responses helped the Roosevelt administration identify the problem areas that most needed to be addressed. Besides providing concrete information, these letters allowed the president and his advisers to gain a better understanding of what people thought and experienced in their daily lives.

These direct, individualized responses enabled the government to tailor its programs for economic and personal recovery (known collectively as the "New Deal") to the needs of specific localities. The administration passed the information received from these letters to federal, state, and local governments and agencies so they could take appropriate action as well.

Primary Source

Franklin D. Roosevelt to the Nation's Clergy, September 24, 1935

SYNOPSIS: The president's letter, sent to Protestant, Catholic, and Jewish clergy and other religious leaders all over the country, requests advice and suggestions.

Reverend and Dear Sir:

Your high calling brings you into intimate daily contact not only with your own parishioners, but with people generally in your community. I am sure you see the problems of your people with wise and sympathetic understanding.

Because of the grave responsibilities of my office, I am turning to representative Clergymen for counsel and advice—feeling confident that no group can give more accurate or unbiased views.

I am particularly anxious that the new Social Security Legislation just enacted, for which we have worked so long, providing for old age pensions, aid for crippled children and unemployment insurance, shall be carried out in keeping with the high purposes with which this law was enacted. It is also vitally important that the Works Program shall be administered to provide employment at useful work, and that our unemployed as well as the nation may derive the greatest possible benefits.

I shall deem it a favor if you will write to me about conditions in your community. Tell me where you feel our government can better serve our people.

We can solve our many problems, but no one man or single group can do it—we shall have to work together for the common end of better spiritual and material conditions for the American people.

May I have your counsel and your help? I am leaving on a short vacation but will be back in Washington in a few weeks, and I will deeply appreciate your writing to me.

Very sincerely yours,
Franklin D. Roosevelt
The White House
Washington
September 24, 1935

Primary Source

Clergy Response to FDR [excerpt]

SYNOPSIS: These responses by various clergymen illustrate the severity, complexity, and diversity of the problems that afflicted Americans during the Depression.

James J. O'Reilly to Franklin D. Roosevelt, Brooklyn, New York, October 3, 1935

Dear Mr. President:

I was more than pleased to receive your letter a few days ago asking for my suggestions wherein the Government can best serve the people. Well, my dear President, this would be a big undertaking as I know not all the minds look at the same subject in the same manner. . . .

I think your idea of getting the suggestions from the Clergymen of the different denominations will greatly help you in the solution of your problems, if all the Clergy will give their honest opinions and not take this opportunity to criticize and find fault with the government, forgetting even the dignity of your own person and the virtue of charity toward all men.

The conditions in this parish are very poor. Heads of families not working and not getting relief because they own their homes or are insured and trying to keep their families together. Many come to the Rectory day after day begging for food or clothing. When they apply for a job to the welfare office they get very curt answers and are told there is not a job for them, and they see young men and women sitting around in offices doing nothing but drawing big salaries while they and the members of their families are starving. In some places they are asked their religious belief, and are told they cannot help them. Around New York and Brooklyn the Jews and Italians are well taken care of. There are others that have to live and eat but are starving because they cannot get work, especially those who were at one time prosperous but through depression lost their all and are too proud to beg for help. . . .

This is my council and advice sincerely given, as you asked.

I am,
Sincerely yours,
Rev. James J. O'Reilly
Church of St. John the Baptist
75 Lewis Ave
Brooklyn, New York
October 3, 1935

Simon Cohen to Franklin D. Roosevelt, Brooklyn, New York, October 27, 1935

Dear Mr. Roosevelt:

I have hesitated all this time to answer your letter of September 24, feeling that I probably did not come within the class of representative clergymen to whom it was addressed. I feel, however, that as one who has met all classes of the community, and one, who, from a long time back has been one of your sincerest supporters and well-wishers, I cannot deny the appeal so graciously expressed in your letter.

For about two years now I have been the supervisor of a project first in Work Relief and then under the Works Progress Administration. In addition during the last month I have acted as secretary for a bureau conducted by Temple Emanuel and other congregations to furnish free seats for the Jewish holidays for those who could not afford to pay. This has brought me into direct contact with the very people for whom the Social Security Legislation and Works Program has been intended. . . .

It goes then without question that I heartily applaud the work that the government has done in this direction and that I feel that it must continue as long as the necessity exists. . . .

As for the Works Program itself, I find that while it has been nobly conceived, it is often ineptly administered. Despite the fact that we have been called upon to make plans for a long time back and to elaborate on specifications, there is still great difficulty in fitting the right man to the job. I have sat for days at the central clearing offices, and know what I am talking about. Time after time I have been sent people who are absolutely disqualified for my work, just because no one else knows what to do with them; while on the other hand, those for whom I asked and whom I knew would be both serviceable to me and happy in the work are the very ones that I have been unable to obtain. . . .

With all good wishes, I remain,
Yours sincerely,
Rabbi Simon Cohen
587 East 8th Street
Brooklyn, NY
October 27, 1935

H. B. Hawkins to Franklin D. Roosevelt, Chicago, Illinois, October 19, 1935

My Dear Mr. Roosevelt:

In reply to your letter of September 24th, I wish to say that it was quite an agreeable surprise for me to hear from you.

Your Social Security Legislation recently enacted, making provisions for the indigent is an ethical advancement towards ideal civic righteousness.

It appears to me, your program not withstanding many encumbrances has been a "square deal" for every individual, most especially for the man that is farther down.

And, now, Mr. Roosevelt! I wish to stress the most important needs of our group (Negroes) in this locality. We need a large religious, social, industrial and cultural center for Negroes on the south side.

Our people need practical training in the most vital things that enter into their every day life which could be had through the establishment of such an institution.

Many persons could be given useful employment in serving the community in this capacity.

There are two available locations adequately suited for this purpose. They may be held for a reasonable appropriation.

Trusting that this tentative suggestion will meet your approval and that I hear from you at your earliest convenience in regard to this matter, I am,

Very respectfully yours,
H. B. Hawkins, Reverend
3541 S. Michigan Ave.
Chicago, IL
October 19, 1935

Walter G. Procter to Franklin D. Roosevelt, Indianapolis, Indiana, October 10, 1935

Dear Mr. President:

Received your communication of September 23rd. requesting my views of conditions in my community.

Permit me at the outset to say that I am complying with your request for information and our reaction to the "new Social Legislation just enacted" with the same honesty and good faith as I feel sure your letter was sent to me and other ministers. The following expressions of my views are based not only on my own observation and conclusions, but on conversations with representative people of my Church and neighborhood.

In my capacity as pastor and superintendent of Mayer Chapel and Neighborhood House (Presbyterian) I come in daily contact with the under-privileged victims of this depression, administering relief and endeavoring in many ways to ameliorate their condition and to keep up their morale. . . .

We are noting more pronounced effects of malnutrition among our clinic babies as a result of the mothers' pre-natal insufficiency of nourishment, as well as the unpalatable monotony and inadaptability of the food during this period. . . .

Things cannot go on indefinitely as they have been. They are bound to reach a breaking point. Human nature can endure much, but it ultimately reaches its limits, and that means revolution. Free men will finally revolt. The American worker—manual or brain—is not a dumb, brutalized serf. He is a man. He is emerging from the stage of dumb acquiescence in things as they have been. He is asking why should they continue? How come these conditions? Why should "opportunity" mean only opportunity for the privileged few to exploit the helpless many? What is the way out? . . .

Please accept my highest regard.

Yours Most sincerely,
Walter G. Procter
Mayer Chapel
448 W. Norwood Street
Indianapolis, IN
October 10, 1935

Further Resources

BOOKS

Garraty, John Arthur. *The Great Depression: An Inquiry into the Causes, Course, and Consequences of the Worldwide Depression of the Nineteen-thirties, as Seen by Contemporaries and in the Light of History.* San Diego: Harcourt Brace Jovanovich, 1986.

McElvaine, Robert S. *The Great Depression: America, 1929–1941.* New York: Times Books, 1984.

Watkins, T.H. *The Great Depression: America in the 1930s.* Boston: Little, Brown, 1993.

PERIODICALS

Church, George J. "Taking Care of Our Own: The New Deal Probed the Limits of Government." *Time,* March 9, 1998.

"FDR and the New Deal." *The Economist* (US), December 25, 1999, 49.

Lewis, James W. "A Catholic New Deal: Religion and Reform in Depression Pittsburgh." *The Journal of Religion* 80, July 2000, 518.

WEBSITES

"The Depression News: The 1930s." Michigan Historical Museum. Available online at http://www.michiganhistory.org/museum/explore/museums/hismus/1900-75/depressn/index.html; website home page: http://www.michiganhistory.org (accessed August 29, 2002).

"The Great Depression and The New Deal." Bergen County Technical Schools. Available online at http://www.bergen.org/AAST/Projects/depression; website home page: http://www.bergen.org (accessed August 29, 2002).

"Religion During the Depression." Urban and Urbane: The *New Yorker* Magazine in the 1930s. University of Virginia American Studies home page. Available online at http://xroads.virginia.edu/%7EUG02/NewYorker/religion.html; website home page: http://www./xroads.virginia.edu (accessed August 29, 2002).

"Pacifism"

Newspaper article

By: Dorothy Day
Date: May 1936

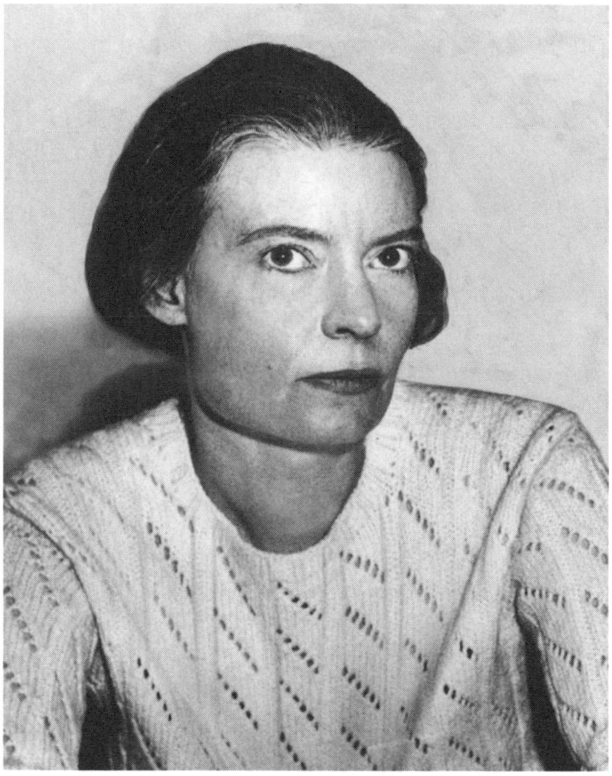

Dorothy Day, 1934. Dorothy Day was a prominent social activist for nonviolence and pacifism. She founded and published many articles in the *Catholic Worker,* including her famous one entitled "Pacifism," which criticized the United States for preparing for war instead of peace leading into WWII. THE LIBRARY OF CONGRESS.

Source: Day, Dorothy. "Pacifism." *The Catholic Worker,* May 1936, 8. Available online at http://www.catholicworker.org/dorothyday/daytext.cfm?TextID=215; website home page: http://www.catholicworker.org (accessed February 11, 2002).

About the Author: Dorothy Day (1897–1980), born in Brooklyn, New York, was a noted social reformer and activist. A dedicated Marxist in her youth, she later experienced a change of heart and converted to Roman Catholicism in 1927. Five years later she cofounded the Catholic Worker Movement. For more than four decades she guided this Catholic social activism movement in the areas of peace advocacy, labor union justice, and civil rights. ■

Introduction

Dorothy Day cofounded the Catholic Worker Movement and *The Catholic Worker,* the newspaper that represented it, in New York City in May 1933. The movement and the newspaper both acted directly on behalf of workers and the poor. Day's strong belief in pacifism, the philosophy that violence should never be used as a means of solving disputes, inspired many Catholics and non-Catholics who believed in social justice. Her commitment to pacifism led many to label her as the radical conscience of American Catholicism.

Catholic Worker activists were usually pacifists dedicated to helping establish a nonviolent culture. They used nonviolent protests and demonstrations to get their message across. During times of the military draft, they would register as conscientious objectors, people who refuse to fight because of their moral or religious beliefs. In conjunction with this pacifist position, Dorothy Day stressed the importance of faith and prayer. She said if one doesn't pray, then one misses the whole point of the movement.

In addition to promoting pacifism, members of the Catholic Worker movement established centers that provided shelter, food, and clothing for needy people in the poor sections of many cities. Members also tried to meet the spiritual needs of people. These centers succeeded so well in the cities that the Catholic Worker also set up some rural centers.

There were some other Catholic peace groups at the time but none received the same public awareness as Day's organization. Her combination of concern for the poor, social justice, and pacifism attracted the attention and the imagination of people who wanted to bring about social change.

Significance

Day's article on pacifism in *The Catholic Worker* appeared in 1936, the year the Spanish Civil War (1936–1939) began. Day believed that the Roman Catholic Church, which had considerable influence in Spain, should have done more to avoid bloodshed there. The members of her movement could not do much to stop the conflict in Spain, but they were determined to stop American involvement in future wars.

Although most American Catholics did not agree with The Catholic Worker's position of pacifism, especially during World War II, Day would not be moved from the unshakable conviction that Christians should not kill their brothers and sisters. Her belief in absolute nonviolence and pacifism was grounded in her personal relationship with Jesus and his espousal of nonviolence as a way of life. Day quoted St. Peter (Acts 5:29) when she said that it was better to obey God than obey men.

Even those who differed with Day's position on pacifism and nonviolence tended to respect her deep religious feelings and the motivations of the members of the Catholic Worker Movement. The social part of the movement, helping the poor and the ill-disposed, earned admiration from many because it helped meet the needs of the time.

During the antiwar protests of the 1960s, Dorothy Day's movement was in the forefront of demonstrating for peace. Along with other antiwar groups, her followers, many of whom were young, rallied against the war in

Vietnam (1964–1975). The Catholic Worker movement has continued into the twenty-first century. There are approximately 150 Catholic Worker communities across the United States. They still are committed to pacifism, prayer, and help for the needy; and continue Day's dedication to protesting war, injustice, and violence of any kind.

In 1972 the magazine *America* devoted an entire issue to Dorothy Day in celebration of her seventy-fifth birthday. This special recognition honored the 40 years she had devoted to the Catholic Worker Movement and her singular contribution to church and society. The editors stated that if one had to choose a single individual to symbolize the best in the aspiration and action of the American Catholic community during the last forty years, that one person would certainly be Dorothy Day.

Primary Source

"Pacifism"

SYNOPSIS: Dorothy Day, an outspoken advocate for nonviolence and pacifism, published many articles in *The Catholic Worker*. One of her most famous articles deals with the subject of pacifism and expresses her fear that America was misguided in preparing for war instead of peace in the years prior to World War II (1939–1945). She asks her readers to pray for peace and to actively work toward convincing the government to disarm. Day believed all wars were morally wrong, and peace activists should be so committed to their cause that they would be willing to die for it.

The Catholic Worker is sincerely a pacifist paper.

We oppose class war and class hatred, even while we stand opposed to injustice and greed. Our fight is not "with flesh and blood but principalities and powers."

We oppose also imperialist war.

We oppose, moreover, preparedness for war, a preparedness which is going on now on an unprecedented scale and which will undoubtedly lead to war. The Holy Father Pope Pius XI said, in a pastoral letter in 1929:

> And since the unbridled race for armaments is on the one hand the effect of the rivalry among nations and on the other cause of the withdrawal of enormous sums from the public wealth and hence not the smallest of contributors to the current extraordinary crisis. We cannot refrain from renewing on this subject the wise admonitions of our predecessors which thus far have not been heard.
>
> We exhort you all, Venerable Brethren, that by all the means at your disposal, both by preaching and by the press, you seek to illumine minds and open hearts on this matter, according to the solid dictates of right reason and of the Christian law.

Why not prepare for peace?

Let us think now what it means to be neutral in fact as well as in name.

American bankers must not lend money to nations at war.

We must renounce neutral rights at sea.

These three points are made by Herbert Agar in "Land of the Free." Neutrality "in fact," he says, could be practiced on[ly] by either saint or cynic.

In fact, it would mean that either we must not pass judgments (upholding a positive stand for peace instead) or else in condemning Italy, also to condemn Ethiopia for resisting. To do this one would indeed have to be either saint or cynic.

The cynic would say, "It is none of my business."

The Saint would say, and perhaps he would be a very wise man in saying it, "The conquered conquers in the end. Christ was overcome and He overcame. There was His ostensible failure on the Cross, yet He rose triumphant and Christianity spread over the world. The Christian thing to do would be not to resist, but when anyone asked for one's coat, to give up one's cloak besides. As Peter Maurin pointed out in the last instance, Australia could be given up to Japanese expansion for instance, if England objected on "noble" grounds for Japan's aggression in Manchuria. But recognizing that the majority of people are not Saints; that they are swift to wrath, to resist aggression (when they are not the aggressors), then we can only insist ceaselessly that even when the people are taking sides mentally they must keep out, they must not participate in "a War to end War."

In the last war we helped to impose an unjust peace, even if we grant that we sincerely thought we were engaged in a noble crusade and were throwing our support on the right side in the conflict. We were influenced to this way of thinking not only by deliberate propaganda, but also by the muddle-headedness of pacifists who were not truly "peace-lovers."

If we are calling upon nations to disarm, we must be brave enough and courageous enough to set the example.

Nations can live at home. That is the title of a recent book, and many surveys are being made at present to find out how many nations can do without trade and "live at home."

If we abandoned our neutral rights at sea, we would still have a surplus of food and material goods with which to help feed nations which had been made gaunt by war. We are not suggesting this as a business note but as a reminder of Christian Charity.

Do we believe we help any country by participating in an evil in which they are engaged? We rather help them by maintaining our own peace. It takes a man of heroic stature to be a pacifist and we urge our readers to consider and study pacifism and disarmament in this light. A pacifist who is willing to endure the scorn of the unthinking mob, the ignominy of jail, the pain of stripes and the threat of death, cannot be lightly dismissed as a coward afraid of physical pain.

A pacifist even now must be prepared for the opposition of the next mob who thinks violence is bravery. The pacifist in the next war must be ready for martyrdom.

We call upon youth to prepare!

Further Resources

BOOKS

Kent, Deborah. *Dorothy Day: Friend to the Forgotten.* Grand Rapids, Mich.: W.B. Eerdmans, 1996.

O'Connor, June. *The Moral Vision of Dorothy Day: A Feminist Perspective.* New York: Crossroad, 1991.

Roberts, Nancy L. *Dorothy Day and the Catholic Worker.* Albany, N.Y.: State University of New York Press, 1984.

PERIODICALS

Anderson, George M. "Dorothy Day Centenary." *America,* November 29, 1997.

Gneuhs, Geoffrey B. "Revolutionary of the Heart." *First Things: A Monthly Journal of Religion and Public Life,* May 1, 1998.

Krupa, Stephen J. "Celebrating Dorothy Day: Dorothy Day Continues to Represent the Radical Conscience of American Catholicism." *America,* August 27, 2001.

WEBSITES

"Dorothy Day." Biography.com. Available online at http://search.biography.com/print_record.pl?id=14114; website home page: http://www.search.biography.com (accessed August 29, 2002).

"Dorothy Day." The Catholic Worker Movement. Available online at http://www.catholicworker.org/dorothyday/index.cfm; website home page: http://www.catholicworker.org (accessed August 29, 2002).

"Dorothy Day." Resources for Catholic Educators. Available online at http://www.silk.net/RelEd/day.htm; website home page: http://www.silk.net (accessed August 29, 2002).

Divini Redemptoris

Papal encyclical

By: Pope Pius XI

Date: March 19, 1937

Source: Pope Pius XI. *Divini Redemptoris.* Rome, March 19, 1937. Available online at http://www.vatican.va/holy_father/pius_xi/encyclicals/documents/hf_p-xi_enc_19031937_divini-redemptoris_en.html; website home page: http://www.vatican.va (accessed February 9, 2003).

About the Author: Pope Pius XI (1857–1939) was born Ambrogio Damiano Achille Ratti in Italy. Ordained a priest in 1879 and known as a brilliant scholar, he devoted most of the subsequent 43 years to work as a church librarian. He was selected by Pope Benedict for diplomatic service and sent as an apostolic visitor to Poland in 1918. He returned to Italy in 1921 and became cardinal archbishop of Milan. He was elected pope in 1922 and served until his death in 1939. ■

Introduction

Pope Pius XI wrote an encyclical, or letter to leaders of the Roman Catholic Church, on Atheistic Communism in 1937 to warn the world that Bolshevik and atheistic communism threatened the basic social structure of Christian civilization. Pope Pius accused communist authorities in the Soviet Union of directing this struggle against God, Christianity, and the existing social order.

Communism is based on doctrines established by Karl Marx in his book *The Communist Manifesto* (1848). Marx predicted that capitalism in Europe and North America would eventually collapse and be replaced by communism, an economic and political system that includes communal ownership of all property, classless society, and the eventual abolishment of the state. One of the enemies of the communist revolution, according to Marx, was religion, which he referred to as the opium or tranquilizer of the masses. He believed that churches and other religious institutions supported capitalism and blocked the advancement of communism. Likewise he thought that people's belief in God stood in the way of social advancement. Therefore, Marx asserted, people must embrace atheism, the disbelief or denial of the existence of God, in order for the communist revolution to succeed.

Marx's theories took a particularly strong hold in Russia. By 1903 two main branches of Russian communism had emerged: Bolshevism and Menshevism. In 1917 the Bolsheviks staged a revolt and seized control of the government. By 1921 they had suppressed the Mensheviks and sought to spread their way of life and type of government to other nations, beginning with eastern Europe. The communist regimes set up there vigorously promoted atheism and systematically attacked the Roman

Catholic Church, arresting high church officials and priests, suppressing religious orders, and abolishing religious education.

Pope Pius XI feared that if the communists succeeded, Christianity (as well as the other major religions of the world) would be crushed along with the institutionalized church. He intended his warning to rally Catholics and other Christians around the world to do all they could to keep the faith in the face of communist advancements.

Pius XI was not the first pope to sound the alert against atheistic communism. As early as 1846 Pius IX had issued a solemn condemnation, stating that communism went against the natural law and that its establishment would result in the destruction of the rights, property, and possessions of all people. Pius IX also feared that the adoption of communism would destroy the very fabric of society.

Significance

Catholics in America, like others in the nation, were trying to survive the severe economic depression of the 1930s. Some Catholics began to wonder if communism would solve the terrible problems they faced: lack of jobs, difficulty providing for one's family, and general despair. The pope warned Catholics against communism, not because he was necessarily in favor of capitalism, but because it promoted atheism, the antithesis of Christianity and most other religions.

As a result of the encyclical, Roman Catholic priests delivered sermons to their parishioners in many Catholic churches in America and around the world. They told the Catholic faithful to be wary of the promises of communism because acceptance of it might mean the denial of their faith in God and in the church. Catholic church lay organizations like the Knights of Columbus actively took part in the effort to inform people about the growing threat of atheistic communism.

All the popes since Pius XI have continued the warning against atheistic communism. John Paul II (served 1978–present) personally experienced the threats of communism when he worked as a priest in Poland, a formerly communist-controlled nation.

Primary Source

Divini Redemptoris [excerpt]

SYNOPSIS: When deemed necessary and prudent, the papacy of the Roman Catholic Church issues an encyclical, a letter addressed to the leaders of the church. In this encyclical on atheistic communism, Pope Pius XI delivers a strong statement attacking the growing influence and control by the forces of communist-controlled governments.

Pope Pius XI. In response to the rise of communism in the Soviet Union, Pope Pius XI issued a papal encyclical warning Catholics of communism's atheism and threat to Christianity. ARCHIVE PHOTOS, INC. REPRODUCED BY PERMISSION.

The promise of a Redeemer brightens the first page of the history of mankind, and the confident hope aroused by this promise softened the keen regret for a paradise which had been lost. It was this hope that accompanied the human race on its weary journey, until in the fullness of time the expected Savior came to begin a new universal civilization, the Christian civilization, far superior even to that which up to this time had been laboriously achieved by certain more privileged nations.

2. Nevertheless, the struggle between good and evil remained in the world as a sad legacy of the original fall. Nor has the ancient tempter ever ceased to deceive mankind with false promises. It is on this account that one convulsion following upon another has marked the passage of the centuries, down to the revolution of our own days. This modern revolution, it may be said, has actually broken out or threatens everywhere, and it exceeds in amplitude and violence anything yet experienced in the preceding persecutions launched against the Church. Entire peoples find themselves in danger of falling back into a barbarism worse than that which oppressed the greater part of the world at the coming of the Redeemer.

3. This all too imminent danger, Venerable Brethren, as you have already surmised, is bolshevistic and atheistic Communism, which aims at upsetting the social order and at undermining the very foundations of Christian civilization.

4. In the face of such a threat, the Catholic Church could not and does not remain silent. This Apostolic See, above all, has not refrained from raising its voice, for it knows that its proper and social mission is to defend truth, justice and all those eternal values which Communism ignores or attacks. Ever since the days when groups of "intellectuals" were formed in an arrogant attempt to free civilization from the bonds of morality and religion, Our Predecessors overtly and explicitly drew the attention of the world to the consequences of the dechristianization of human society. With reference to Communism, Our Venerable Predecessor, Pius IX, of holy memory, as early as 1846 pronounced a solemn condemnation, which he confirmed in the words of the Syllabus directed against "that infamous doctrine of so-called Communism which is absolutely contrary to the natural law itself, and if once adopted would utterly destroy the rights, property and possessions of all men, and even society itself." Later on, another of Our predecessors, the immortal Leo XIII, in his Encyclical *Quod Apostolici Muneris,* defined Communism as "the fatal plague which insinuates itself into the very marrow of human society only to bring about its ruin." With clear intuition he pointed out that the atheistic movements existing among the masses of the Machine Age had their origin in that school of philosophy which for centuries had sought to divorce science from the life of the Faith and of the Church.

5. During Our Pontificate We too have frequently and with urgent insistence denounced the current trend to atheism which is alarmingly on the increase. In 1924 when Our relief-mission returned from the Soviet Union We condemned Communism in a special Allocution which We addressed to the whole world. In our Encyclicals *Miserentissimus Redemptor, Quadragesimo Anno, Caritate Christi, Acerba Animi, Dilectissima Nobis,* We raised a solemn protest against the persecutions unleashed in Russia, in Mexico and now in Spain. Our two Allocutions of last year, the first on the occasion of the opening of the International Catholic Press Exposition, and the second during Our audience to the Spanish refugees, along with Our message of last Christmas, have evoked a world-wide echo which is not yet spent. In fact, the most persistent enemies of the Church, who from Moscow are directing the struggle against Christian civilization, themselves bear witness, by their unceasing attacks in word and act, that even to this hour the Papacy has continued faithfully to protect the sanctuary of the Christian religion, and that it has called public attention to the perils of Communism more frequently and more effectively than any other public authority on earth.

6. To Our great satisfaction, Venerable Brethren, you have, by means of individual and even joint pastoral Letters, accurately transmitted and explained to the Faithful these admonitions. Yet despite Our frequent and paternal warning the peril only grows greater from day to day because of the pressure exerted by clever agitators. Therefore We believe it to be Our duty to raise Our voice once more, in a still more solemn missive, in accord with the tradition of this Apostolic See, the Teacher of Truth, and in accord with the desire of the whole Catholic world, which makes the appearance of such a document but natural. We trust that the echo of Our voice will reach every mind free from prejudice and every heart sincerely desirous of the good of mankind. We wish this the more because Our words are now receiving sorry confirmation from the spectacle of the bitter fruits of subversive ideas, which We foresaw and foretold, and which are in fact multiplying fearfully in the countries already stricken, or threatening every other country of the world.

7. Hence We wish to expose once more in a brief synthesis the principles of atheistic Communism as they are manifested chiefly in bolshevism. We wish also to indicate its method of action and to contrast with its false principles the clear doctrine of the Church, in order to inculcate anew and with greater insistence the means by which the Christian civilization, the true *civitas humana,* can be saved from the satanic scourge, and not merely saved, but better developed for the well-being of human society.

8. The Communism of today, more emphatically than similar movements in the past, conceals in itself a false messianic idea. A pseudo-ideal of justice, of equality and fraternity in labor impregnates all its doctrine and activity with a deceptive mysticism, which communicates a zealous and contagious enthusiasm to the multitudes entrapped by delusive promises. This is especially true in an age like ours, when unusual misery has resulted from the unequal distribution of the goods of this world. This pseudo-ideal is even boastfully advanced as if it were responsible for a certain economic progress. As a matter of fact, when such progress is at all real, its true causes are quite different, as for in-

stance the intensification of industrialism in countries which were formerly almost without it, the exploitation of immense natural resources, and the use of the most brutal methods to insure the achievement of gigantic projects with a minimum of expense.

9. The doctrine of modern Communism, which is often concealed under the most seductive trappings, is in substance based on the principles of dialectical and historical materialism previously advocated by Marx, of which the theoricians of bolshevism claim to possess the only genuine interpretation. According to this doctrine there is in the world only one reality, matter, the blind forces of which evolve into plant, animal and man. Even human society is nothing but a phenomenon and form of matter, evolving in the same way. By a law of inexorable necessity and through a perpetual conflict of forces, matter moves towards the final synthesis of a classless society. In such a doctrine, as is evident, there is no room for the idea of God; there is no difference between matter and spirit, between soul and body; there is neither survival of the soul after death nor any hope in a future life. Insisting on the dialectical aspect of their materialism, the Communists claim that the conflict which carries the world towards its final synthesis can be accelerated by man. Hence they endeavor to sharpen the antagonisms which arise between the various classes of society. Thus the class struggle with its consequent violent hate and destruction takes on the aspects of a crusade for the progress of humanity. On the other hand, all other forces whatever, as long as they resist such systematic violence, must be annihilated as hostile to the human race.

10. Communism, moreover, strips man of his liberty, robs human personality of all its dignity, and removes all the moral restraints that check the eruptions of blind impulse. There is no recognition of any right of the individual in his relations to the collectivity; no natural right is accorded to human personality, which is a mere cog-wheel in the Communist system. In man's relations with other individuals, besides, Communists hold the principle of absolute equality, rejecting all hierarchy and divinely-constituted authority, including the authority of parents. What men call authority and subordination is derived from the community as its first and only font. Nor is the individual granted any property rights over material goods or the means of production, for inasmuch as these are the source of further wealth, their possession would give one man power over another. Precisely on this score, all forms of private property must be eradicated, for they are at the origin of all economic enslavement.

Further Resources

BOOKS

Hibbert, Christopher. *The Popes.* Chicago: Stonehenge, 1982.

Holmes, J. Derek. *The Papacy in the Modern World, 1914–1978.* New York: Crossroad, 1981.

McBrien, Richard P. *Lives of the Popes: The Pontiffs from St. Peter to John Paul II.* San Francisco: HarperSanFrancisco, 1997.

WEBSITES

Divini Redemptoris [Pope Pius XI's encyclical on atheistic communism]. Vatican home page. Available online at http://www.vatican.va/holy_father/pius_xi/encyclicals/documents/hf_p-xi_enc_19031937_divini-redemptoris_en.html; website home page: http://www.vatican.va (accessed August 29, 2002).

"The Guiding Principles of Reform Judaism"

Declaration

By: Central Conference of American Rabbis

Date: 1937

Source: Central Conference of American Rabbis. "The Guiding Principles of Reform Judaism." Columbus, 1937. Available online at http://uahc.org/ccar/platforms/columbus.html; website home page: http://www.ccarnet.org (accessed February 10, 2003).

About the Organization: The Central Conference of American Rabbis, established in 1889, assists rabbis and their congregations in the practice of Reform Judaism. At a major meeting in Columbus, Ohio, in 1937, the Conference produced "The Guiding Principles of Reform Judaism." Also known as "The Columbus Platform," this document served as a guide to progressive Jewish beliefs and practices. ■

Introduction

The history of Reform Judaism begins with the experiences of Jewish German immigrants who started coming to America in the mid-1840s. These new arrivals clung to the traditional Judaism of their European background. Life in America, however, presented significant cultural, social, and economic differences. These differences, coupled with the scarcity of trained Jewish religious leaders in the United States and the lack of contact with European Jews, led to demands for reform. There was a call for new synagogues and new ways wherever Jews settled across the country.

Jewish people attend Yom Kippur services. In 1937 the Central Conference of American Rabbis issued "The Guiding Principles of Reform Judaism," a document that was meant to update and restate the principles of Reform Judaism in the light of changes taking place in the world since the movement's inception. AP/WIDE WORLD PHOTOS. REPRODUCED BY PERMISSION.

The Reform movement emphasized rationality, the moral aspects of religion, and the supernatural. Two major figures appeared to lead the Reform movement, Rabbi Isaac Mayer Wise and Rabbi David Einhorn. Wise, the main organizer of the movement, developed reforms that reevaluated Jewish practices that visibly set Jews apart from their neighbors. Considered a moderate reformer, Wise judged each practice in the light of Jewish history and emphasized living in fear of the Lord and loving many in harmony with the dictates of reason. His prayer book, *Minhag America* (translated as *American Ritual*), published in 1857, abbreviated many of the prayers for daily and Sabbath services and eliminated others entirely. In 1885 Wise presided over the Pittsburgh Conference of Reform rabbis, which approved a "Declaration of Principles of Reform Judaism."

The second major figure in the Reform movement, Rabbi Einhorn, was largely responsible for formulating the distinctive central currents in Reform Judaism. Einhorn called for a radical restructuring of Jewish life and thought. He wanted to locate and preserve the eternal essence of Judaism and to purge all that was temporary. Einhorn dispensed with many Jewish customs. Not only were they inconvenient and out of step with the nineteenth century, he argued; they also were unnecessary if the real purpose of Judaism was to bring monotheism and a right understanding of the importance of an ethical life to the world.

The Conference stated that Reform rabbis differed from the more ritually observant rabbis mainly because they viewed their Jewish heritage as evolving over the many centuries of its existence. Judaism had gone through changes as a way of adapting to new conditions and times and Reform rabbis professed that it must continue to do so to survive.

Significance

The Columbus Platform further explained and developed the system of belief outlined in the 1885 Pittsburgh Conference and set basic guidelines rather than rigid rules for Reform beliefs and practices. With the adoption of the Columbus Platform, Reform Jews across the United States found common religious themes that united them in the process of adjusting to their new country. Reform Judaism came to meet the needs of newly arrived immigrants as well as those already settled in America.

The Columbus Platform helped Reform Jews in America attain a better understanding of that branch of Judaism and served as a linkage to the overall Jewish experience and previous meetings. The Columbus Conference thus was perceived as a continuance of the Pittsburgh Conference, which was considered a continuation of the Philadelphia Conference held in 1869. The Philadelphia Conference, in turn, was viewed as a continuance of the German Conference of 1841 to 1846.

Currently the Central Conference of American Rabbis recognizes that Judaism not only accepts pluralism but also encourages it. Because of this characteristic, the Conference maintains that the worldwide community of Jews includes all the branches of this religion: Orthodox, Conservative, Reconstructionist, and Reform. The 1990 National Jewish Population Survey undertaken by the Council of Jewish Federations estimated that about 42 percent of the almost six million American Jews belonged to the Reform movement.

Primary Source

"The Guiding Principles of Reform Judaism"

SYNOPSIS: "The Guiding Principles of Reform Judaism" addresses three broad topics: the foundation of Judaism (the nature of Judaism, God, man, the Torah (Jewish scripture), and Israel; ethics (ethics and religion, social justice, and peace); and religious practice (the religious life). The document's appearance in 1937 coincided with the Central Conference's perception of a need to update the growing Reform Judaism movement in the United States. In view of the changes that had been taking place in the world and the consequent need to state anew the teachings of Reform Judaism, the Central Conference of American Rabbis made the following declaration of principles.

A. Judaism and its Foundations

Nature of Judaism

Judaism is the historical religious experience of the Jewish people. Though growing out of Jewish life, its message is universal, aiming at the union and perfection of mankind under the sovereignty of God. Reform Judaism recognizes the principle of progressive development in religion and consciously applies this principle to spiritual as well as to cultural and social life. Judaism welcomes all truth, whether written in the pages of scripture or deciphered from the records of nature. The new discoveries of science, while replacing the older scientific views underlying our sacred literature, do not conflict with the essential spirit of religion as manifested in the consecration of man's will, heart and mind to the service of God and of humanity.

God

The heart of Judaism and its chief contribution to religion is the doctrine of the One, living God, who rules the world through law and love. In Him all existence has its creative source and mankind its ideal of conduct. Though transcending time and space, He is the indwelling Presence of the world. We worship Him as the Lord of the universe and as our merciful Father.

Man

Judaism affirms that man is created in the Divine image. His spirit is immortal. He is an active coworker with God. As a child of God, he is endowed with moral freedom and is charged with the responsibility of overcoming evil and striving after ideal ends.

Torah

God reveals Himself not only in the majesty, beauty and orderliness of nature, but also in the vision and moral striving of the human spirit. Revelation is a continuous process, confined to no one group and to no one age. Yet the people of Israel, through its prophets and sages, achieved unique insight in the realm of religious truth. The Torah, both written and oral, enshrines Israel's ever-growing consciousness of God and of the moral law. It preserves the historical precedents, sanctions and norms of Jewish life, and seeks to mould it in the patterns of goodness and of holiness. Being products of historical processes, certain of its laws have lost their binding force with the passing of the conditions that called them forth. But as a depository of permanent spiritual ideals, the Torah remains the dynamic source of the life of Israel. Each age has the obligation to adapt the teachings of the Torah to its basic needs in consonance with the genius of Judaism.

Israel

Judaism is the soul of which Israel is the body. Living in all parts of the world, Israel has been held together by the ties of a common history, and above all, by the heritage of faith. Though we recognize in the group loyalty of Jews who have become estranged from our religious tradition, a bond which still unites them with us, we maintain that it is by its religion and for its religion that the Jewish people has lived. The non-Jew who accepts our faith is welcomed as a full member of the Jewish community. In all lands where our people live, they assume and seek to share loyally the full duties and responsibilities of citizenship and to create seats of Jewish knowledge and religion. In the rehabilitation of Palestine, the land hallowed by memories and hopes, we behold the promise of renewed life for many of our brethren. We affirm the obligation of all Jewry to aid in its upbuilding as a Jewish homeland by endeavoring to make it not only a haven of refuge for the oppressed but also a center of Jewish culture and spiritual life. Throughout the ages it has been Israel's mission to witness to the Divine in the face of every form of paganism and materialism. We regard it as our historic task to cooperate with all men in the establishment of the kingdom of God, of universal brotherhood, Justice, truth and peace on earth. This is our Messianic goal.

B. Ethics

Ethics and Religion

In Judaism religion and morality blend into an indissoluble unity. Seeking God means to strive after holiness, righteousness and goodness. The love of God is incomplete without the love of one's fellow men. Judaism emphasizes the kinship of the human race, the sanctity and worth of human life and personality and the right of the individual to freedom and to the pursuit of his chosen vocation. Justice to all, irrespective of race, sect or class, is the inalienable right and the inescapable obligation of all. The state and organized government exist in order to further these ends.

Social justice

Judaism seeks the attainment of a just society by the application of its teachings to the economic order, to industry and commerce, and to national and international affairs. It aims at the elimination of man-made misery and suffering, of poverty and degradation, of tyranny and slavery, of social inequality and prejudice, of ill-will and strife. It advocates the promotion of harmonious relations between warring classes on the basis of equity and justice, and the creation of conditions under which human personality may flourish. It pleads for the safeguarding of childhood against exploitation. It champions the cause of all who work and of their right to an adequate standard of living, as prior to the rights of property. Judaism emphasizes the duty of charity, and strives for a social order which will protect men against the material disabilities of old age, sickness and unemployment.

Peace

Judaism, from the days of the prophets, has proclaimed to mankind the ideal of universal peace. The spiritual and physical disarmament of all nations has been one of its essential teachings. It abhors all violence and relies upon moral education, love and sympathy to secure human progress. It regards justice as the foundation of the well-being of nations and the condition of enduring peace. It urges organized international action for disarmament, collective security and world peace.

C. Religious Practice

The Religious Life

Jewish life is marked by consecration to these ideals of Judaism. It calls for faithful participation in the life of the Jewish community as it finds expression in home, synagogue and school and in all other agencies that enrich Jewish life and promote its welfare. The Home has been and must continue to be a stronghold of Jewish life, hallowed by the spirit of love and reverence, by moral discipline and religious observance and worship. The Synagogue is the oldest and most democratic institution in Jewish life. It is the prime communal agency by which Judaism is fostered and preserved. It links the Jews of each community and unites them with all Israel. The perpetuation of Judaism as a living force depends upon religious knowledge and upon the Education of each new generation in our rich cultural and spiritual heritage.

Prayer is the voice of religion, the language of faith and aspiration. It directs man's heart and mind Godward, voices the needs and hopes of the community and reaches out after goals which invest life with supreme value. To deepen the spiritual life of our people, we must cultivate the traditional habit of communion with God through prayer in both home and synagogue.

Judaism as a way of life requires in addition to its moral and spiritual demands, the preservation of the Sabbath, festivals and Holy Days, the retention and development of such customs, symbols and ceremonies as possess inspirational value, the cultivation of distinctive forms of religious art and music and the use of Hebrew, together with the vernacular, in our worship and instruction.

These timeless aims and ideals of our faith we present anew to a confused and troubled world. We call upon our fellow Jews to rededicate themselves to them, and, in harmony with all men, hopefully and courageously to continue Israel's eternal quest after God and His kingdom.

Further Resources

BOOKS

American Rabbinate: A Century of Continuity and Change, 1883–1983. Hoboken, N.J.: Ktav, 1985.

Blau, Joseph L. *Reform Judaism: A Historical Perspective: Essays from the Yearbook of the Central Conference of American Rabbis.* New York: Ktav, 1973.

Gurock, Jeffrey S., ed. *History of Judaism in America: Transplantations, Transformations, and Reconciliations.* New York: Routledge, 1998.

PERIODICALS

Leff, Laurel. "A Tragic 'Fight in the Family': *The New York Times,* Reform Judaism and the Holocaust." *American Jewish History,* March 1, 2000.

Van Biema, David. "Back to the Yarmulke . . . In a 'Radical' Decision, Reform Jews Embrace Some Religious Rituals that Were Once Shunned as Archaic." *Time,* June 7, 1999.

Wolf, Arnold Jacob. "Reforming Reform Judaism." *Judaism: A Quarterly Journal of Jewish Life and Thought,* June 22, 1999.

WEBSITES

"The Battle over Reform Judaism." Salon.com. Available online at http://www.salon.com/news/feature/1999/05/01/jews; website home page: http://www.salon.com (accessed August 30, 2002).

"Declaration of Principles: 1885 Pittsburgh Conference." The Internet Sacred Text Archive. Available online at http://www.sacred-texts.com/jud/1885.htm; website home page: http://www.sacred-texts.com (accessed August 30, 2002).

Central Conference of American Rabbis home page. Available online at http://www.ccarnet.org (accessed August 30, 2002).

Reform Judaism home page. Available online at http://www.rj.org (accessed August 30, 2002).

"Civilizations Have Perished"

Sermon

By: Father Divine

Date: June 1, 1938

Source: Baker, George. "Civilizations Have Perished." Speech delivered at Father and Mother Divine's International Peace Mission Movement. New York, June 1, 1938. Transcript available online at http://www.libertynet.org/fdipmm/word1/38060113.html; website home page: http://www.libertynet.org (accessed February 9, 2002).

About the Author: Father Divine (c. 1880–1965) was born George Baker in rural Georgia and became a noted African-American evangelist. He organized a religious movement called the Peace Mission and served as its director from 1915 to 1965. He built a large following among African Americans, especially in New York and Philadelphia. In addition to his spiritual mission, he was also a strong advocate for racial equality. ■

Introduction

Baker's ministry began in 1899 in Baltimore, Maryland, where he taught Sunday school and preached in storefront churches. Around 1912 he went back to Georgia to establish a new ministry. A few years later he returned to New York City and assumed the name Major J. Divine. He established a communal home in Brooklyn, New York, in 1915 and then moved to Sayville, Long Island, in 1919. He later relocated his headquarters to Harlem and eventually to Philadelphia. In both cities he established centers, referring to them as heavens and to his followers as angels. He named his religious movement the "Peace Mission" and consistently spoke about the need for peace, harmony, democracy, and brotherhood. He openly opposed the racial segregation that was so prevalent during most of his life.

By 1931, calling himself "Father Divine," the minister had attracted thousands of worshippers to services in his home. This angered his white neighbors, who summoned police in November 1931. The police arrested Father Divine for disturbing the peace and producing a public nuisance. Found guilty, he received the maximum fine and a sentence of one year in jail. Four days later the sentencing judge suddenly died, launching Father Divine into the limelight. Some saw it as evidence of his great powers; others viewed it as sinister retribution. Father Divine denied any responsibility for the judge's death but the incident captured the public's imagination. Throughout the 1930s the news media, capitalizing on the widespread interest in Father Divine, continued to report on his activities.

The Peace Mission movement grew throughout the United States and to major cities abroad. From his headquarters in Harlem, Father Divine guided the movement, conducted worship services, and ran an employment agency. The Peace Mission opened businesses, sponsored relief shelters, and provided thousands of poor people with food, clothes, and jobs.

Father Divine's extraordinary appeal during the 1930s began to falter when the U.S. economy improved in the 1940s. Membership began to fall off and some Peace Missions were forced to close. In 1946, he reappeared in news headlines when he married one of his followers, Sweet Angel, whom he had chosen to succeed him.

Father Divine died in 1965. Shortly afterward the *Los Angeles Herald-Examiner* quoted a follower as saying that he had not left them. Another of the faithful explained that God can't die and he is still present despite his apparent personal absence. Father Divine's Peace Mission movement would continue without his bodily presence.

Significance

During the 1930s Father Divine earned intense devotion from his disciples. Some of his followers became worshippers, claiming he healed them of diseases and personal problems. According to sociologist Sara Harris, his

Father Divine (George Baker). Father Divine attracted many followers to his "Peace Mission" movement. He preached the need for brotherhood, democracy, and harmony in the troubled times of the Great Depression. THE LIBRARY OF CONGRESS.

black followers accepted him as God because they needed him to be God. Father Divine provided a loving, protective atmosphere and hope for people who found themselves in desperately impoverished conditions. Father Divine's special appeal derived from a mixture of African-American folk religion, Methodism, Catholicism, and Pentecostalism. His mind-power theology, based on the power of positive thinking, attracted many people because it gave them a sense of control over their destinies.

After his death, his wife, Sweet Angel, became the leader of the movement. She explained that Father Divine had given up his body so he could continue to exist as a spirit. She would be his living physical representative. However, only a small number of followers and businesses remained faithful to the movement.

Primary Source

"Civilizations Have Perished" [excerpt]

SYNOPSIS: Father Divine issues a dire warning in this speech, "Civilizations Have Perished." A typical example of his messages, it cautions his followers and the rest of the world that if they do not turn to moral righteousness, American society will ultimately crumble into ruins. He urges people to stop acting selfishly if they want to avoid this downfall. This somber warning came while the United States still suffered from the consequences of the Great Depression.

This astounding and significant information which came to us through the courtesy, through the Love and through the lips of Our LORD, FATHER DIVINE, is a rare and priceless legacy bequeathed to us as heirs and joint heirs with CHRIST. Even ancient history could not supply us with this information which we have hereby become the possessors of on this day of Our LORD, FATHER DIVINE. Even science, a most efficient agency of the Infinite One, has not produced and could not produce such knowledge. Even discoveries and inventions, great as they have been, have not revealed the Truths that are now coming to light so freely from the Infinite Mind of GOD.

Before science and invention were, GOD IS; therefore, where human traces and historical records have been lost to civilizations in the passing of time, these facts, which are mysteries to the nations, were known by GOD, as HE permitted them to be destroyed, as it were, lost to a civilization which had forgotten GOD. Through His Mercies, Love and Compassion, GOD is restoring man to his former estate, that he may no longer be as the "prodigal son," denied the abundant blessings of his FATHER; but through this process of restoration, he is permitted to become the Son of GOD, through the sacrifice of the Life of One Whose Love was so great that HE gave up His Life freely for the redemption and the return of man to the Garden of Eden, which is the Unity of Spirit, of Mind, of Aim and of Purpose.

For thy great Love, FATHER DIVINE, Our LORD and Our Redeemer, for forgiving us our trespasses of generations upon generations, and receiving us unto THYSELF, we thank THEE, we love THEE and adore THEE. Blessed be the Name of the LORD! FATHER speaks as follows: PEACE EVERYONE! ("Peace, FATHER Dear"! responded the happy assembly.) Good Health! Good Will! A good Appetite, with all Wisdom, Knowledge and all Understanding, especially for the re-establishment of a Righteous Government.

This Message just read shall go forth into all the land. It is not obliged to go forth from a literary point of view especially, but it shall go forth conquering and to conquer, for it is the foundation of all government. In the future, all government shall be founded upon this of which I have spoken in this especial message. Mankind in the commercial world will learn to be governed by this system as outlined in this message just read. When they learn to be economical and yet learn to sell the best and the most for the least, the volume of business will increase ten thousand per cent and they will have success and all prosperity.

As a Sample and as an Example I stand. You can see the abstract expression of it. You can see all success and all prosperity in all of My Actions, Words and Endeavors, whatsoever I may endeavor. Why? I AM even successful in My Endeavors as a Sample and the Example for others. Copy after the Fashion I have shown you, for what said the Epistle concerning the mystery? Jesus was a Sample and an Example for others. In other words, Copy after the Fashion CHRIST in Jesus has shown you. You will not have an occasion to fret nor worry, neither will you have an occasion to be a failure.

Righteousness Will Exalt All Creation

. . . In other words:

> Righteousness will exalt a nation, but sin is a reproach to any people.

The outstanding expression for consideration is:

> Righteous[ness] will exalt all creation, but sin is a reproach to every living creature.

Take these thoughts to consideration. Tell all of the inhabitants of the earth wherever you go, I have solved the problem for all living creatures. Even the animal kingdom must recognize the blessings they are receiving by the recognition of GOD'S actual Presence when they reckon GOD among them.

Forget About Yourself

Oh, it is a privilege to observe the mystery! Then I say, "Let this Mind be in you that was in CHRIST JESUS." Do not feel exalted and stop and consider you can and will exalt yourselves personally and be abundantly blessed by being one with, or equal with GOD. This should not be in your consideration. Forget about yourself! If you forget about yourself as a person and recognize GOD'S actual Presence and live in the recognition of it, lo, I will be with you.

If you forget about yourself, GOD will think about you; but so long as you remember yourself, you are not mindful of the things that pertain to GOD and the Kingdom, the Works of GOD, whichever. With or without a person, your minds are deteriorating. You are detracting from that of which you should be attached to, and from the way you should go mentally and Spiritually; therefore, your ambition and energy will be directed in a different direction. You cannot love GOD whole-heartedly, according to the first and the great Commandment.

Oh, it is a privilege to observe it! Aren't you glad? Forget about yourself! Leave yourself completely out of the picture and others will think about you while you are not thinking of yourself, but thinking for the good of others. If you build upon this foundation and recognize GOD'S actual Presence at all times, how marvelous it will be to dwell in such a recognition and to build upon a foundation that cannot be shaken! . . .

Cause of the Fall of Civilization

For the disrecognition of GOD'S actual Presence; or because of the disrecognition of GOD'S actual Presence; because of selfishness, sin and sinning and civilization returning back to the earth from whence it came. All science, yea, all discoveries and all inventions went back into delusion and back into the earth from whence they came, losing all recognition by the children of men who dwelt upon the earth plane. That was the cause of the fall of civilization. That is the reason that men could not have a record and could not bear record of a civilization before four thousand and four years B.J. [Before Jesus]. That is the reason why men did not have history that could bear record of it, because of sin.

Such a civilization had been forgotten until I came in this dispensation by inspiration to inspire science to go into the mysteries of GOD'S Hidden Treasures and bring out the things that were hidden for ages. Such a civilization perished from the earth because of sin and the continuance of sin, of vice and of crime and of selfishness. Such a civilization perished according to science. It went down, not only going down mentally and Spiritually and from a scientific point of view, from an intellectual point of view, from the light of a civilizational point of view, but it went down physically, to let you see and know that which goes down mentally or Spiritually will go down physically, if it continues to go down.

Then I say, except this civilization, not only this government of this country, of these United States of America, but except this civilization universally accept of My Message and refuse to neglect such a great Salvation, this civilization in which we are now living would perish from the earth. I AM not merely speaking of, nor concerning the countries, at this instance. I AM speaking concerning the Light of civilization.

"I came to convert systems," I said the other day; but I have come into consideration for the purpose of converting this international civilization. Oh, it is a privilege to observe the mystery! The Spirit of GOD'S actual Presence will perform it and bring it into observation, that you might observe it.

Righteousness will exalt the nation, but sin is a reproach to any people.

Righteousness will exalt all creation,

I quote MYSELF,

. . . . but sin is a reproach to any living creature.

Further Resources

BOOKS

Braden, Charles Samuel. *These Also Believe: A Study of Modern American Cults & Minority Religious Movements.* New York: Macmillan Company, 1949.

Harris, Sara. *Father Divine, Holy Husband.* Garden City, N.Y.: Doubleday, 1953.

Weisbrot, Robert. *Father Divine and the Struggle for Racial Equality.* Urbana, Ill.: University of Illinois Press, 1983

PERIODICALS

"God, Harlem U.S.A.: The Father Divine Story." *Publishers Weekly,* December 13, 1991, 41.

WEBSITES

"Father Divine." Biography.com. Available online at http://search.biography.com/print_record.pl?id=12494; website home page: http://www.search.biography.com (accessed August 30, 2002).

"Father Divine: International Peace Mission Movement." The Religious Movements Homepage at the University of Virginia. Available online at http://cti.itc.virginia.edu/~jkh8x/soc257/nrms/Fatherd.html; website home page: http://www.cti.itc.virginia.edu (accessed August 30, 2002).

Miller, Timothy. "Father Divine: A General Overview." CENSUR (Center for Studies on New Religions). Available online at http://www.cesnur.org/testi/bryn/br_miller.ht; website home page: http://www.cesnur.org (accessed August 30, 2002).

"The Universal Peace Mission Movement of Father Divine." Institute for the Study of American Religion. Available online at http://www.americanreligion.org/cultwtch/frdivine.html; website home page: http://www.americanreligion.org (accessed August 30, 2002).

"Coughlin, the Jews, and Communism"

Magazine article

By: William C. Kernan

Date: December 17, 1938

Source: Kernan, William C. "Coughlin, the Jews, and Communism." *The Nation,* December 17, 1938. Reproduced in American Journey. Available online at http://www.americanjourney.psmedia (accessed February 10, 2002).

About the Author: William Charles Kernan (1900–??) was ordained a deacon in the Episcopal Church in 1926. After several years of ministerial work, he became pastor of St. James the Lesser in Scarsdale, N.Y. In 1938, he grew so upset with Father Charles Coughlin's radio sermons criticizing Jews that he decided to write a response to them. In 1952 Kernan renounced his Episcopalian ministry of 26 years and sought admission to the Roman Catholic Church, believing it to be the one true Christian church. ■

Introduction

Kernan's article, "Coughlin, the Jews, and Communism," published in *The Nation* in 1938, focused on a criticism of Father Charles E. Coughlin's position concerning Jews and communism. Father Coughlin, called "the radio priest" because of the weekly sermons he broadcast during the 1930s, had made some extreme statements about alleged connections between Jews and Communists.

Since *The Nation,* founded in 1865 as an independent magazine, was dedicated to promoting neutral yet critical discussion of political and social issues and to discourage extremist political writing, the editors decided that Kernan's challenge to Father Coughlin's views would uphold the magazine's mission and make a noteworthy article.

Kernan and *The Nation* were not the only ones critical of the priest. The *Detroit News* observed that Coughlin displayed a strange blend of compassion and venom. He showed compassion when he demanded social justice for the poor, the paper noted, but displayed venom in his attacks on Jews and in his sudden turning against President Roosevelt, labeling him "the great liar and betrayer." Coughlin accused Jews of introducing Communist international banking and repeatedly blamed them for the worldwide economic crisis. Jews, he alleged, had drawn America into World War I (1914–1918) and would lead the United States into another world war.

Significance

By 1942 the controversy over Coughlin reached a climax and the authorities of the Roman Catholic Church ordered him to end his radio program. Coughlin's viewpoints, however, have continued to have an effect. Scholars have noted his enduring reputation as a venomous anti-Semitist who engineered the most dangerous anti-Jewish movement in American history and a pro-Nazi sympathizer. The Ku Klux Klan, a white supremacist group, has issued statements similar to Coughlin's to justify their anti-Semitic views. Racist leaflets distributed by the Klan from the late 1940s through the 1990s denounced Jews as communists and international bankers who wished to take control of the American economic system. These statements, never proven, nonetheless bolstered anti-Semitic attitudes in the United States.

Primary Source

"Coughlin, the Jews, and Communism" [excerpt]

SYNOPSIS: Kernan's criticism of Coughlin represents the opposition to the priest's anti-Semitic statements on his weekly radio sermons during the 1930s. Kernan systematically addresses Coughlin's accusations about Jews, presenting counterarguments and evidence that demonstrate Coughlin's mistakes.

On the past few Sundays the Reverend Charles E. Coughlin of Detroit has made radio addresses which are of grave concern to America. Their purpose has apparently been to stir up racial hatred against the Jewish people in a country whose traditions, laws, and institutions are the expression of racial and religious equality. Primarily Father Coughlin has attempted to link the Jewish people with an unpopular social and economic movement known as communism, and by this and similar devices to place the race in a most unfavorable light. His line of reasoning is clever but nonetheless distasteful and full of error.

His contention is that Nazism is the effect of communism, that it is a defense mechanism against communism, and that there will always exist some defense against communism "as long as misguided Jews and Gentiles in such great numbers continue to propagate the doctrines of anti-God, anti-Christ, anti-patriotism, and anti-property." It will be noted that here Father Coughlin names Gentiles with Jews as the agents responsible for communism. The speech is interlarded with references to atheistic Jews and Gentiles in order to make us think that the speaker is harmlessly impartial.

But as he proceeds, the Gentile agents who are responsible for communism gradually cease to be of importance. The weight of his argument is gradually but certainly thrown against the Jews. "It is the belief, be it well or ill founded, of the present German government," he tells us, "that Jews . . . were responsible for the economic and social ills suffered by the Fatherland since the signing of the Treaty of Versailles." Our attention is drawn here only to Jews. Nothing is said about the German dislike for the Treaty of Versailles itself, which was drawn up by Gentiles and to the destruction of which the Hitler

A Jewish family flees Nazi Germany. April 1, 1933. Anti-Semitism was not uncommon in the United States during the 1930s, and there were those, like Father Coughlin, who publicly applauded the Nazi persecution of the Jews. © BETTMANN/CORBIS. REPRODUCED BY PERMISSION.

government is committed in the belief that Germany's economic and social ills were due to its provisions as well as to Jewish influence.

Continuing, he says that the Nazi movement was formed "to rid the Fatherland of Communists whose leaders, unfortunately, they identified with the Jewish race." At this point he identifies the Jews not only with the ills suffered by the Fatherland but also with communism. It is not even mentioned, it is not granted, that in all Germany there were any Gentile Communists. Again—and more strongly now—the weight of the argument is thrown against the Jews, who are painted as at once destroyers of Germany and one with the Communist movement.

From this point on the argument against the Jews moves more rapidly and with less discretion. It is charged that in 1917 "of the twenty-five quasi-Cabinet members" of the Soviet Republic "twenty-four were atheistic Jews," whose names Father Coughlin said he had before him; that in 1935 "the Central Committee of the Communist Party operating in Russia consisted of fifty-nine members," of whom fifty-six were Jews and the three remaining non-Jews were married to Jewesses. Then comes a revealing quotation from a Jewish magazine, the *American Hebrew,* for September 10, 1920: "The achievement, the Russian Jewish revolution, destined to figure in history as the overshadowing result of the World War, was largely the outcome of Jewish thinking, of Jewish discontent, of Jewish effort to reconstruct." The Jews and communism again, linked this time by one of their own publications. What could be clearer?

To clinch his argument of Jewish responsibility for communism, only one more indictment need be added. And Father Coughlin adds it. It is that not only were Jews in Russia responsible for communism, but American Jewish financiers aided the revolution by supplying the money. To prove this most telling point Father Coughlin goes to a book by Professor Denis Fahey. He unearths a secret document of the American Secret Service and tells us that he regrets being forced to reveal the contents of such a "closely guarded and certified document." He dips into an official British document which he calls the British "White Paper," and which he says is in his possession. He assures us that this official "White Paper" contains damning evidence against the Jewish financiers. And he concludes that now all the world may know "what was restricted only to the few some years ago"—namely, that the Russian Revolution "was launched and fomented by distinctively Jewish influence." The Jews and communism again—this time with their money-bags!

And then Father Coughlin uncovers the last, terrible, shocking result of the Jewish-Communist link. "Between the years 1917 and 1938 more than 20 million Christians were murdered by the Communist government in Russia. . . . Between these same years not 400 million dollars but 40 billion dollars of Christian property was appropriated" in Russia. We see at last where the argument takes us. Great care has been exercised to make it clear that communism and the Jewish race are one and the same thing. Look for a Communist and find a Jew! And then the murder of 20 million Christians, the appropriation of 40 billion dollars worth of Christian property. Who did that? The Communists! And who are the Communists? They are Jews!

The answer to these charges is not difficult to give because, fortunately, we have access to the sources from which Father Coughlin claims that he got his information. And when we examine these sources we are compelled, in all fairness, to come to conclusions which are far different from those drawn by Father Coughlin.

To begin with, the definition of Nazism as a defense mechanism against communism and the statement that "there will always exist some defense mechanism against communism" which will always be "characterized by persecution" are oversimplifications of fact. There are many of us, including the President of the United States, who believe that the best defense against communism is not Nazism but democracy—a way not "characterized by persecution." There is the answer to communism of Pope Pius XI—a way not "characterized by persecution." There are the pronouncements of the bishops of the Episcopal church which point to a way not "characterized by persecution." It gives us pause to wonder why Father Coughlin cannot see, as the answer to communism, any other way but that of Nazism or some other defense mechanism "characterized by persecution." Are these words of his an invitation to the Nazi forces in America to set up their defenses here against communism—defenses "characterized by persecution"?

As to Father Coughlin's inferences of Jewish responsibility for communism, many facts about the Jews in Germany before the rise of Hitler indicate that such a link cannot be forged. We might cite the fact that some of the leading newspapers in Germany at that time were Jewish-owned and were opposed to communism, or the fact that the economic interests of the Jewish people in Germany at that time made them, of necessity, the opponents of communism, or the fact that in pre-Nazi Germany the Jews who voted were for the most part members of the liberal democratic parties. But we do not have to mention these things. We have only to recall that before the Nazis came into power, the Communist voting strength in Germany was 6,000,000. And in all of Germany there were only some 300,000 Jews who had the right to vote. Even if these 300,000 Jews had all voted Communist, a completely untenable assumption in itself, what would they have amounted to among 6,000,000? . . .

In the light of these facts can we Christians have any part in the persecution of a defenseless people? Shall we, reared in the American tradition of tolerance and goodwill, join forces with those who, like Father Coughlin, would mock our tradition[s?] and with their mockery destroy our civilization?

Further Resources

BOOKS

Kernan, William C. *My Road to Certainty.* New York: David McKay Company, 1953.

Tull, Charles J. *Father Coughlin and the New Deal.* Syracuse, N.Y.: Syracuse University Press, 1965.

Wolfskill, George. *All But the People: Franklin D. Roosevelt and His Critics.* New York: Macmillan, 1969.

WEBSITES

"Father Charles E. Coughlin: National Union for Social Justice." The Religious Movements Homepage at the University of Virginia. Available online at http://religiousmovements.lib.virginia.edu/nrms/coughlin.html; website home page: http://www.religiousmovements.lib.virginia.edu (accessed August 30, 2002).

Father Charles E. Coughlin radio broadcast. Social Security Online History Page. Available online at http://www.ssa.gov/history/coughlinradio.html; website home page: http://www.ssa.gov (accessed August 30, 2002).

"Father Charles E. Coughlin, the Radio Priest." *The Detroit News.* Available online at http://detnews.com/history/coughlin/coughlin.htm; website home page: http://www.detnews.com (accessed August 30, 2002).

Federal Writers' Project Interviews on Religion

Interviews

By: Wayne Walden; J.F. Ariza; Ruth D. Bolton; Robert V. Williams

Date: 1938–1939

Source: Walden, Wayne. "Big Fred Tells a Tale: A Baptism that Didn't Take." Interview with Fred Roys, New York, October 30, 1938. Ariza, J.F. "Jesus Will Save an Irishman." Interview with Colonel John W. Foulkes, Seattle, December 19, 1938. Bolton, Ruth D. "Life History of Rev. Harden W. Stuckey." Interview with Rev. Harden W. Stuckey, South Carolina, June 23, 1939. Williams, Robert V. "Shouting for Heaven." Interview with Brother Fisher (Rev. W. M. Stallings), Charlotte, North Carolina, January 20, 1939. Reproduced in "American Life Histories: Manuscripts From the Federal Writers' Project, 1936–1940." American Memory digital primary source collection, Library of Congress. Available online at http://memory.loc.gov/ammem/wpaintro/wpahome.html; website home page: http://www.memory.loc.gov (accessed February 12, 2003).

About the Organization: The Federal Writers' Project was funded by the Works Progress Administration, part of Franklin Delano Roosevelt's (served 1933–1945) economic and social recovery program known as the "New Deal." The project provided jobs for an assortment of unemployed writers, who interviewed ordinary citizens across the country and wrote about their lives and experiences. ■

Introduction

The Great Depression caused the unemployment rate to rise to about 25 percent during the 1930s. In response the federal government organized the Works Progress Administration (WPA), which made jobs available for roughly 8,500,000 people. While the WPA created mostly manual jobs in fields such as construction, it also provided work for unemployed artists and writers through the Federal Arts Project. This program employed about 6,500 men and women around the country, paying them small salaries of approximately $20 a week. The Federal Writers' Project (FWP) was designed to use the interview process to discover the stories of diverse individuals, what their lives were like, and how they were influenced by the bad times.

Americans' anxiety during the Depression worsened by the end of the 1930s, when increasing tensions in Europe and Asia threatened to draw the United States into another world war. Some people turned to religion for guidance and support. The religious community responded in a variety of ways. In 1932 the General Assembly of the Northern Presbyterian Church resolved that the present economic order was now on probation and its continued existence must be found in its contribution to social service and social justice, not in the wealth produced or the power gained. These were strong words coming from a mainstream Protestant church in America. A Roman Catholic priest, Rev. Charles E. Coughlin, used his weekly radio programs to call for the nationalization of banks, utilities, and natural resources. Even though he was speaking for himself and not for the church, his words reached millions of Americans. The Southern Baptist Convention drew up a resolution in 1938 stating that radical socialism and atheistic communism were not acceptable answers to America's problems. Popular evangelist Billy Sunday preached that religion did not promise its rewards in this world but in the next. Another evangelist, Charles Fuller, on his radio program, Old Fashioned Revival Hour, preached about traditional religion and how it could meet the needs of the people during difficult times. The Roman Catholic Church reminded its parishioners that the church would always be there and assured the faithful that their reward would come in heaven. African American churches, like the African Methodist Episcopal Church and the Colored Methodist Episcopal Church, promised hope in this world and salvation in the next.

Despite the responsiveness of traditional mainline religions, attendance at those churches did not increase substantially during the Depression. Fundamentalist groups, like the Pentecostals, showed significant increases in attendance while the more traditional denominations either suffered a decrease in attendance or saw only small increases.

A number of Christian groups experienced not only attendance problems but also financial problems. People who couldn't feed their own families could not afford to give money to their churches. Judaism was going through a similar experience. Traditionally Jews helped the needy through their own charities. The Depression became too

A crowd listens to an itinerant preacher in a courtyard in Campton, Kentucky. The Federal Writer's Project, created by the New Deal, helped to develop a portrait of the religious influence on the lives of ordinary people during and after the Depression by interviewing them and publishing the accounts. **THE LIBRARY OF CONGRESS.**

much of a burden for Jewish organizations and they, like the Christian groups, faced financial difficulties.

Significance

The Federal Writers' Project helped to develop a portrait of religious influences on the lives of ordinary people for the historical record. The bad economic times were found to have influenced people's religious lives. These oral reports helped the writers compile a picture of what it was like to live during the Depression—noting that religion was an important part of many people's lives.

The four interviews presented below, samples from the more than 10,000 interviews with men and women conducted by the FWP, showed that the religious experiences of individuals, even though affected by their religious affiliations, were still quite personal and unique.

Primary Source

Federal Writers' Project Interviews on Religion [excerpt]

SYNOPSIS: These excerpts of interviews from the Federal Writers' Project deal with a variety of religious topics. The first two were compiled in 1938; the next two were written in 1939. These documents provide insight into the meaning of religion to ordinary people during the Depression.

"Big Fred Tells a Tale: A Baptism that Didn't Take" [excerpt]

Them religious revivals they used to have, you don't see much of that sort of goings-on nowadays; but in them days they was great doin's. When I was a kid we used to look forward to 'em like we did the circus. Sometimes they was as good as a circus. It was a case of come to Jesus everybody. You had to come in or they'd hound the hell out of you if you didn't. The woods was full of Billy Sundays, and if you could stand out against their persuadin' you, you was a good one. You had to have what they call stamina. Generally when some of those old hens got a hold of a guy, he was a goner, 'cause the women then went into the revival business with both feet. When they took out after you, there wasn't much use a [runnin'?].

But there was one old codger they had a devil of a time a snarin! He wouldn't fall for their bait at all. They tried every which way to get him, but old Rufe—Rufus Gray his name was—was one guy they couldn't bring into the fold. He had read Bob Ingersoll, I guess, and didn't seem to give a damn if his soul was saved or not. Pie in the sky couldn't move him. The chase went on for years, revival after revival, and still old Rufe couldn't be swayed from the paths of wickedness he preferred to travel. His soul was getting blacker and blacker with accumulatin' sins, but still the old cuss hung back. The stubborn old geeser seemed sure as hell-bound-for-hell, and the bettin' was odds against his ever being corraled.

Well, it finally happened that a revival came on and, whether the Bible-pounder was more convincin', or whether the sistern put on greater pressure in their persuadin' whatever it was, old Rufe—maybe he thought it was better to get it over with, but anyhow the old guy shows signs of weakening. He give up arguin' and told 'em O-Kay, that he was ready to submit at last.

Well, of course, landin' a hardshell old sinner, the likes of him, caused a lot of rejoicing among the sistern and the brethren. It was a great triumph, something to holler about. All that was lacking now was the baptism. And for old Rufus it'd need more'n a little sprinkling. It'd need a whole damned puddle of water for him to be made pure and radiant!

The baptisings was most of the time done in a lake, about a mile and a half from town. The preacher, and whoever would be his helpers, would lead the converts out to where the water was about arm-pit deep, and then dip 'em under. That's what they done to old Rufe too—they leads him out to where the water was up to his whiskers and then topples him under. But he wasn't countin' on being ducked.

So he comes up sputtering, and pawing, and madder'n hell. Soon as he untangles himself from their hanging on to him, he starts out swimmin' to beat the devil himself, and when he gets out in about the middle of the lake he turns his head and hollers out—"Yeah, you would, would you? You'd try to drown somebody, would you? You gawd-damned fools."

"Jesus Will Save an Irishman" [excerpt]

People are getting more Godless and cynical. Atheism is openly discussed and has many adherents. Forty years ago when I first came to Seattle our Volunteers of America hall was across the street from Billy the Mugg's saloon, one of the toughest places in the entire country. It was tough, no mistake. But, despite the supposedly rough element we had to deal with, there was more religion in people's hearts than there is today. . . .

About 1903, occasionally we had an Indian couple, fiery Baptist missionaries who had worked among tribesmen in the North, hold service for us. They were good talkers. One evening when we were holding a street meeting the Indian woman was preaching, telling the big gathering of Jesus' love for man. "Come to Jesus!" she importuned. "Jesus will save you! Jesus will save the blackest sinner—the drunkard, the thief, the home wrecker, the profligate, the murderer. He will save anyone—anyone—even an Irishman!" she shouted in a final burst of [fervor?].

She was unable to resume for five minutes. The crowd howled, numbers among them singling out big men with unmistakably Irish features, in an effort to taunt them. But it failed. They laughed as uproariously as their would-be tormentors.

"Life History of Rev. Harden W. Stuckey" [excerpt]

Rev. Harden W. Stuckey, was born in Bishopville, S.C. 43 years ago, one of a family of thirteen. Although this family was large, it had no effect upon the financial status, as his parents were prosperous farmers. However, Rev. Stuckey, would not like to have a large family, because he feels that it requires more to rear children now. He is rather proud of his ancestry, as his mother was of Indian descent, and a look at him, makes this statement obvious.

At the age of four years he was struck in the eye with a sling-shot stick, the right eye affected the left, and in a month or two he was totally blind. This did not prove a hinderance to his education, however. For ten years he went to school, stopping only when a nervous breakdown make it imperative. Rev. Stuckey stated that had it not been for his little education he would be among the beggars and recipients of charity. His greatest ambition is to be called to a church of sufficient size to pay him a living wage. . . .

Rev. Stuckey votes and votes a ticket as he chooses.

Rev. Stuckey quite naturally feels that religion influences the morale greatly in the right direction, as he is a minister, this is to be expected.

When it comes to amusements, his attitude is rather broad. Although he is unable to do the things we do like dancing and the like, he feels that a person is entitled to what he likes and the matter is to be settle[d] between him and his God.

He attends church regularly and does not ask aid from the church ever. His health is very good, so good that luckily, diet plays no part, as being unable to do for himself, he eats what is put before him, balanced diet or not.

The one room that Rev. Stuckey rents was very clean. He had cleaned it himself, he said.

Time on his hands is a luxury, when he finishes his work, if he does not go to church to a program or just regular services, he has quite a few friends that he visits. They are not all blind, either. Some of the outstanding ministers are quite fond of him.

"Shouting for Heaven" [excerpt]

We had always gone to a Baptist church back up in the mountains and though I had never been saved I did consider myself a Baptist. Oh yes, I can remember some grand times we use-ta have there at that country church back home. Mother was a member and a very active one, too, but Dad, as I said before, didn't take much hand in church affairs. He'd go with Mother all the time, but that was about the extent of it.

When we moved to Gastonia all of us thought of it as a big city. The people dressed differently than we had up in the mountains. Why, when we went to church up there all we needed was a clean pair of overalls and that was good enough, but we sorta felt out of place in a city church with everybody dressed up in store-bought clothes. That in itself was one reason we started goin' to a tent revival that The Church of God was holdin'. We felt more at home and wasn't ashamed of our clothes. The services that they held were something like ours had been up home but somehow there seemed to be more power in their meetin's than we'd ever had. Of course we had seen shoutin' before, but not the kind that they were doin' there.

I never will forget the night I was saved. We'd been attendin' the revival for several nights and had witnessed a number of souls saved. After about four nights I felt the pull of the altar. Well, I didn't go up right away. I never will forget when Mother came from her seat up near the front back to where I was sittin' with some of the neighbor boys. I made a step toward the aisle, and, with her arm around me, mother and son walked down the sawdust trail to lay my sins and burdens at the feet of Jesus.

He was there that night as surely as there is a God. There on that crudely built altar I poured out my soul to Him. I had been under conviction for two or three nights, and my built-up emotions and feelings came surgin' out as I sobbed and cried for the blood of Jesus and its cleansing power. It wasn't long before I felt that He was there, extendin' His holy hand and biddin' me to follow Him. Then I knew that the debt had been paid and my slate was as clean as snow. Oh, my, was I happy! It's good to think of that hour even today, and to know that it was from that moment that life started all anew!

Further Resources

BOOKS

O'Gara, Geoffrey. *A Long Road Home: In the Footsteps of the WPA Writers.* Boston: Houghton-Mifflin, 1990.

———. *A Long Road Home: Journeys through America's Present in Search of America's Past.* New York: Norton, 1989.

Remembering America: A Sampler of the WPA American Guide Series. New York: Columbia University Press, 1985.

WEBSITES

"Authors and the Federal Writers' Project." Library of Congress. Available online at http://www.loc.gov/exhibits/african/afam014.html; website home page: http://www.loc.gov (accessed August 30, 2002).

"American Life Histories: Manuscripts from the Federal Writers' Project, 1936–1940." Library of Congress. Available online at http://www.bigchalk.com/cgi-bin/WebObjects/WOPortal.woa/wa/HWCDA/file?fileid=239107&flt=CAB&tg=; website home page: http://www.bigchalk.com (accessed August 30, 2002).

"The Federal Writers' Project and the History of Everyday Life." University of Iowa Social Studies home page. Available online at http://www.uiowa.edu/~socialed/lessons/wpa.htm; website home page: http://www.uiowa.edu (accessed August 30, 2002).

A Guide to Understanding the Bible

Guidebook

By: Harry Emerson Fosdick

Date: 1938

Source: Fosdick, Harry Emerson. *A Guide to Understanding the Bible.* New York, London: Harper & Brothers, 1938. Available online at http://www.religion-online.org/cgi-bin/relsearchd.dll/showbook?item_id=545; website home page: http://www.religion-online.org (accessed February 10, 2003).

About the Author: Harry Emerson Fosdick (1878–1969), was born in Buffalo, New York, and became a Baptist minister in 1903. After a professorship at Union Theological Seminary, he served as pastor of Riverside Church in New York City from 1925 to 1946. During his tenure at the church he influenced the development of Christian theology and became a well-known author, lecturer, and religious radio broadcaster. His liberal theology at times brought him into conflict with more orthodox Christians. ■

Introduction

The "Idea of God" is the title of the first chapter in Fosdick's book *A Guide to Understanding the Bible.* In this chapter he carefully examines the Jewish conception of God as presented in the Old Testament of the Bible. He then leads the reader to a new conception of God, based on the early Christians' understanding of Jesus Christ, as found in the New Testament.

Fosdick wrote *A Guide to Understanding the Bible* to help ordinary people understand the development of the most important ideas in both the Old Testament and the New Testament. With little formal training in reading and understanding the Bible, many Christians became frustrated in their attempts to grasp the development of religious ideas. He found that many Christians who read the Bible needed a framework to understand it and so he aimed to produce a practical and user-friendly publication. He did not write for casual Bible readers but for motivated seekers of biblical understanding.

Fosdick's love of the Bible provided a driving force in his ministry; although he did not believe in the inerrancy of the Bible or in some of the doctrines it teaches, he felt committed to showing how the Gospels met the real challenges of everyday personal, national, and international concerns. Whether he spoke from the pulpit at the Riverside Church or from the radio broadcasting studio, he consistently emphasized the role of the Bible and the careful reading of it.

Fosdick believed that for Christianity to prosper and be relevant, it must concentrate on basic issues: the love of God, spiritual growth through Jesus, ethical help in everyday life, and the possibilities of personal and social renewal. He emphasized that everyone can receive these benefits by reading the Bible, especially the teachings of Jesus.

In other chapters of his book Fosdick outlined the changing views of humanity found in the Old and New Testaments; traced the differences between the two testaments in defining what was good human behavior and what was not acceptable, and discussed the idea of suffering, fellowship with God, and immortality. Approximate chronologies of Old Testament and New Testament writings served as additional aides for the Bible reader.

Significance

A Guide to Understanding the Bible came at a time when American Christians were trying to make some sense of the Great Depression and the conflicts occurring in Europe that would eventually lead to World War II (1939–1945). During this period of great anxiety, a number of people turned to their own reading of the Bible to seek hope and perspective.

Fosdick's books and his biblical teachings on the radio were well received by most Christians in mainline

Harry Emerson Fosdick. Fosdick's *Guide to Understanding the Bible* (1938) was written to help ordinary people—with little formal training in reading and understanding the Bible—understand the development of its major religious ideas. **THE LIBRARY OF CONGRESS.**

Protestant churches in the 1930s and the following decades. *A Guide to Understanding the Bible* is still used today by Christian laypersons and others who desire a guide to prepare them for a better comprehension of the Bible.

Primary Source

A Guide to Understanding the Bible [excerpt]

SYNOPSIS: In these excerpts from "The Idea of God," the first chapter of his *Guide to Understanding the Bible,* Fosdick presents historical evidence concerning how the human conceptualization of God evolved in several stages from the Old Testament to the New Testament. He meant this chapter and the entire book to guide readers to a better understanding and appreciation of the Bible.

Nowhere do the early documents of the Bible more obviously carry us back to the ideas of primitive religion than in dealing with the concept of God. The first chapter of Genesis reveals a confident monotheism, but that represents centuries of developing life and thought from the time the Hebrews were introduced at Sinai to their god, Yahweh.

At the beginning, the distinctive deity of the Hebrews was a tribal divinity to whom the clans of Joseph first gave their allegiance at the time of the Exodus from Egypt. That previously the Israelites had not known their god, Yahweh, by his name is explicitly stated in the Bible: "God spake unto Moses, and said unto him, I am Yahweh: and I appeared unto Abraham, unto Isaac, and unto Jacob, as El Shaddai; but by my name Yahweh I was not known to them." (Exodus 6:2-3). . . .

According to the available evidence, Moses first came upon Yahweh at "the mountain of God," (Exodus 3:1 ff.) called both Sinai and Horeb. (Horeb and Sinai are presumably different names for the same mountain variously located. Horeb may be the more primitive. See W. J. Phythian-Adams: *The Call of Israel,* pp. 131-133.) Like Zeus upon Olympus and many another primitive deity, Yahweh, at the first, was a mountain god. Indeed, he was so confined to his habitat that, when the tribesmen under Moses left Sinai the problem of believing in Yahweh's continuing presence with them was serious. According to the oldest traditions they did not suppose Yahweh himself would go with them—he was attached to his mountain home. Three times it is explicitly stated that not he but his angel was to accompany them on the journey to Canaan. (Exodus 23:20-23; 32:34; 33:1-3.)

As for the train of events which led to the momentous introduction of Israel to Yahweh at the "mountain of God," the probabilities are strong. Moses, fleeing from Egypt to the wilderness, joined himself to the Kenites, a Midianite tribe of nomads living in the desert about Sinai. Into this tribe Moses married. His father-in-law was its religious head, "the priest of Midian," (Exodus 3:1) and Moses, associating himself with his wife's clan, became a devotee of Yahweh, the Kenite god. In such an incident as is presented in Exodus 18:1-12, revealing the pride of Jethro, priest of Yahweh, in the conquests of his tribal deity, this "Kenite hypothesis" seems to fit the facts.

To emphasize the fresh start initiated by the creative influence of Moses need not involve forgetfulness of the ancestral background. Religion among the Semites had had a rich history before Moses, and he and his people were the inheritors of a long and significant tradition. Doubt of Abraham's personal existence, for example, once prevalent, is surrendering to an increasing confidence in the Biblical accounts of his migration. . . . New in name, therefore, Yahweh may have been old in meaning, and into Moses' creative faith doubtless went long accumulating ideas and attitudes from his ancestral heritage. Substantial truth may lie in the Scripture's verbal anachronism which represents Yahweh as saying: "I am the God of thy father, the God of Abraham, the God of Isaac, and the God of Jacob." (Exodus 3:6, 15, 16; 4:5.)

Passing from the Old Testament into the New

When one passes from the Old Testament into the New, one does move into the presence of fresh ideas about God and experiences with him. A major factor in producing this change in spiritual climate and scenery was the expulsion of the Christian movement from the synagogue.

Just as Wesleyanism started as a phase of Anglicanism and remained so until it was coerced into separatism by the Church of England itself, so the first Christians were simply Jews who had found the Messiah and who intended remaining as the true Judaism within the larger matrix of the national faith. When they were driven out from synagogue and temple, they faced a disruption in their religious thought and practise comparable with the shock of the Exile to the Jews over six centuries before. That is, they lost the old trellis on which their faith had twined. The temple was no longer theirs; they were denied the sacrifices; they were outlawed from both cult and legal system; they were expelled from the synagogue and regarded as aliens by the Jewish community.

The theological effect of all this was immense. What had happened partially when the physical temple had been destroyed and the nation exiled in Babylon now happened thoroughly. Yahweh lost his coercive entanglements with national loyalty and racial cult, and in a new liberation, unimaginable had not the expulsion of Christianity from Judaism taken place, he became a universal God, with no local temple or chosen people to limit him, and with worshipers of all tongues and nations on equal terms—neither Jew nor Greek, neither Scythian, barbarian, bond nor free, but one man in Christ.

The New Testament as a whole comes to us out of this completed separation of church from synagogue, with Christianity rapidly becoming more Gentile than Jewish. Paul had done his work and the church was an inter-racial, international brotherhood. The God of the New Testament, therefore, is universal, not only in the sense of being cosmic, but in the deeper and more difficult sense of being God of all mankind alike and "no respecter of persons." (Acts 10:34.)

The direct effect of this in freeing monotheism from the Old Testament's constricting particularisms was great, but perhaps even more important was its indirect effect: it opened the idea of God in Christian minds to the influence of all the theologies of the Greco-Roman world. Long before Christ, the Jews in Alexandria had felt the nobility of Plato's theistic philosophy and had labored to blend their religious traditions with the best thought of Greece.

The thought of the New Testament, however, had no such protection against the influential philosophies of the Greco-Roman world. To be sure, the Old Testament was at first the only Christian Bible, and Christian doctrine was validated by appeal to the sacred Book. Alexandrian Judaism, however, long since had shown that the Old Testament could be interpreted by allegory so as to abstract from it any philosophy one pleased. In the Christian thinking of the first century, therefore, the liberation of church from synagogue inaugurated a new era; the apologetic necessity of being persuasive to Gentiles overbore the tendency to be content with Hebraisms; and even in the New Testament, predominantly Jewish though it is in its backgrounds, one sees the beginning of that larger mental hospitality which led at last to the overwhelming influence of Greek thought on Christian theology.

When it is said, therefore, as it commonly is said, that the New Testament simply takes over the Old Testament's theocratic idea of God, wide areas of fact are forgotten. The God of the New Testament is the eternal Spirit, God of no special nation and of no chosen race, accessible everywhere to every soul without requirement of special ritual or legalistic act, who, being spirit, can be worshiped only in spirit, who, being love, dwells wherever love dwells, and who supremely has shined in the face of Jesus Christ. . . .

The common statement, therefore, that Jesus took over unchanged the Jewish idea of God needs at least an initial qualification. Which Jewish idea of God did he take over? His ministry was a concentrate[d] protest against ideas and practises that had sprung from the lower levels of Hebrew tradition. His God was the God of the supreme prophetic passages—spiritual and universal, caring for all mankind across all boundaries of race and nation, near at hand to the humble and the contrite, a God of grace and forgiveness as well as of justice and retribution, redemptively merciful to sinners, demanding not ritualistic conformity but moral genuineness within and brotherly conduct without.

To say, therefore, that Jesus took the Jewish idea of God at its best but had no new idea of his own presents a false antithesis. The truth is that by taking the Jewish idea of God at its best and by treating this idea with thoroughgoing moral seriousness, sloughing off hostile adhesions and limitations, Jesus achieved a consequence so new as to be revolutionary.

Further Resources

BOOKS

Fosdick, Harry Emerson. *Adventurous Religion and Other Essays.* New York and London: Harper & Brothers, 1926.

———. *The Living of These Days: An Autobiography.* New York: Harper, 1956.

Miller, Robert M. *Harry Emerson Fosdick: Preacher, Pastor, Prophet.* New York: Oxford University Press, 1976.

WEBSITES

Ferm, Deane W. "The Living of These Days: A Tribute to Harry Emerson Fosdick." Religion-Online.org. Available online at http://www.religion-online.org/cgi-bin/relsearchd.dll/showarticle?item_id=1788; website home page: http://www.religion-online.org (accessed August 30, 2002).

Fosdick, Harry Emerson. "Twelve Tests of Character." Religion-Online.org. Available online at http://www.religion-online.org/cgi-bin/relsearchd.dll/showbook?item_id=690; website home page: http://www.religion-online.org (accessed August 30, 2002).

"Harry Emerson Fosdick." Biography.com. Available online at http://search.biography.com/print_record.pl?id=14865; website home page: http://www.search.biography.com (accessed August 30, 2002).

"The Rising Tide of Anti-Semitism"

Magazine article

By: Alvin Johnson

Date: February 1939

Source: Johnson, Alvin. "The Rising Tide of Anti-Semitism." *Survey Graphic,* February 1939. Available online at http://newdeal.feri.org/survey/39a01.htm; website home page: http://newdeal.feri.org (accessed February 11, 2002).

About the Author: Alvin Saunders Johnson (1874–1971) was born in Homer, Nebraska. He earned a Ph.D. in economics in 1902 and then taught at several universities. In 1917 Johnson was appointed editor of the magazine *The New Republic.* He remained editor until 1923, when he assumed the directorship of the New School for Social Research in New York City. There, during the 1930s, he provided a home for refugee scholars from Nazi Germany. ■

Introduction

Very much concerned about the presence of anti-Semitism, or prejudice against Jews, in America during

Adolf Hitler, 1939. Hitler's anti-Semitic Nazi regime in Germany encouraged a rise in anti-Semitism around the world, including the United States. This prompted others, including Alvin Johnson, to speak out against it. **CORBIS-BETTMANN. REPRODUCED BY PERMISSION.**

the 1930s, Alvin Saunders Johnson wrote "The Rising Tide of Anti-Semitism." He cautioned all Americans to help in the fight against this kind of prejudice before it increased even further.

Before anti-Semitism emerged in the United States, it had a long history in Europe. For many centuries European Jews faced conditions of prejudice, discrimination, and segregation by predominantly Christian societies. Jews lived in minority groups in many places and had often became scapegoats, taking the blame for the ills or problems of a country. In many cases they did not have the same rights as others and became isolated from the larger society. In some cities they were forced to live in separate sections called ghettos, intentionally alienated from the mainstream population.

In the late 1800s and early 1900s, many Jews in Russia and Poland were killed in organized massacres called pogroms. In 1933 Adolf Hitler, the Nazi leader, came to power in Germany and made anti-Semitism an official government policy. The German government deprived Jews of their citizenship, seized their property, and later sent thousands to concentration camps. By the end of World War II (1939–1945) the Nazis had killed about six million Jews in a campaign of mass murder known as the Holocaust.

Anti-Semitism during the first hundred years in American history was somewhat contained. After 1880 it increased greatly due to developments in Europe as well as America. The rapid rise of anti-Semitic movements, political parties with anti-Jewish agendas, and hateful propaganda against Jews in Europe affected American attitudes. Immigration trends in America also led to anti-Jewish feelings. The economic success of German Jews who had arrived in the mid-1880s produced jealousy in other Americans. After 1885, hundreds of thousands of culturally distinctive eastern European Jews immigrated to the United States. Their obvious differences made them open to stereotyping and scapegoating.

From the 1920s through the 1940s anti-Semitism developed even further. Non-Jews became resentful over the growing presence of American Jews. Some people blamed the Jews for political, economic, and social problems in the United States and abroad. Organizations around the nation displayed anti-Semitic tendencies. One group in particular, the Ku Klux Klan, an extremist white secret society, was the most dangerous and widespread.

From 1915 to 1944 the Klan actively opposed and often used violence against American Jews as well as African Americans, Catholics, and members of other minority groups. Klansmen, known for wearing robes and hoods and burning crosses, made up a relatively small proportion of the total white Protestant population but often gained sympathizers who already had anti-Semitic feelings. By the mid-1920s there were more than two million Klan members across the United States. By the 1930s only local Klan groups in the South remained strong. Nevertheless the seeds of anti-Semitism had been planted by the Klan and other anti-Semitic organizations throughout the country.

Significance

Most non-Jewish Americans in the 1930s knew about negative attitudes and discrimination toward Jews and Judaism but did little about it. They did not consider the problems endured by Jewish people as important as the economic problems facing the nation. Many Americans of good will ignored anti-Semitism.

Alvin Johnson's article in the *Survey Graphic* focused attention on how widespread anti-Semitism had become and how many organized groups actively promoted it. This wake-up call to Americans did increase awareness of this important issue and some people made a greater effort to denounce extremist anti-Semitic groups. When the United States entered World War II in 1941 and joined in the fight against the Nazis, anti-Semitism in the United States did lessen somewhat.

Primary Source

"The Rising Tide of Anti-Semitism" [excerpt]

SYNOPSIS: Alvin Johnson's article in the *Survey Graphic* expresses concern about the spread of anti-Semitism, not only in Europe but also in the United States. Johnson warns that prejudice against Jewish Americans could increase to dangerous proportions.

Anti-Semitism is on the increase in America. This is to be sure just an opinion, for there are no reliable quantitative estimates available to the public. Private polls may even [have] been held; there are not uncertain rumors afloat of such polls, and they are alleged to exhibit a marked increase in antagonism to the Jews. But polls of public opinion record only the view of an instant, and offer a very inadequate basis for conclusions on lasting realities. The Gallup poll of early December indicated that 94 per cent disapproved of Hitler's treatment of the Jews. But we cannot draw too heavily upon this particular fact. One may be anti-Semitic without approving of the pillage and murder of Jews.

What no one doubts may commonly be taken for pragmatically true, and no one, Gentile or Jew, doubts that there is more active anti-Semitism in present day America than there was, say, in 1930. No one believes that anti-Semitism has passed its peak, although there is much fragmentary evidence that it suffered a setback after the recent German pogrom. A considerable number of conservative Americans, who had viewed with complacency the [ou]sting of Jews from public offices, universities and the practice of law, have been deeply shocked by the brutal [at]tacks on Jewish property. Property is property, and if it not sacred, what security is there in the world? But not too much dependence may be placed upon property owners' solidarity. The strength of the feudal aristocracy lay in the fact that the whole class was disposed to stand any members who fell into hard luck. The same thing is true, within limits, of the modern proletariat. But the strength of the propertied middle class lies in the promptness with which it turns a cold shoulder on the dispropertied. . . .

We have before us the example of Germany. Hitler could have talked himself black in the face on parliamentary shortcomings and the iniquity of the Treaty of Versailles. He had the genius to blow up into a flame the endemically smoldering embers of anti-Semitism. Every vulgar and designing scoundrel in America who schemes to substitute dictatorship for democracy casts a greedy eye upon the potentialities of an anti-Semitic campaign. We who love liberal democracy, who have faith in its unlimited possibilities for humanity and civilization, are dunces if we refuse to face the menace of anti-Semitism, and weaklings if we fail to apply our resources to combating it.

What Anti-Semitism Is Made Of

Let us try to break down the general phenomenon of anti-Semitism into its main constituent elements.

There is instinctive anti-alienism, which has always set us against unassimilated and partly assimilated members of our society. Four fifths of the Jews have been with us only since Kishineff; too many of them are only partly assimilated to the commanding externals of American life, language, dress and manners.

There is the age-old antipathy on the part of the farmer and manual worker to the "middleman," and the Jews still group themselves heavily in that class.

There is the fundamentalist hatred of the Jews on the basis of the over simplified view that the Jews crucified the Christ, never amplified to a recognition that Jesus, the Christ, was a Jew.

The business and professional hatred of the Jew as a redoubtable competitor.

What one may call parlor anti-Semitism, boldly paraded by well groomed young men of social status, who need to appear strong men to their women folk and know the passionate virtue of blood curdling sentiments.

The unhappy denizens of overtame environments, who were happy in spy hunting during the war and desire nothing so much as conspiracies to track down now, "Great Jewish conspiracies."

Who Promotes Anti-Semitism?

That, in brief, is the endemiology of American anti-Semitism. These are the embers the present day propaganda is blowing upon, in the hope of consuming, not the Jew in particular, but democracy and liberalism also. It is an extensive propaganda. There are about 800 organizations in the United States carrying on a definite anti-Semitic propaganda. Some are nation-wide in their operations, some regional; but most of them are one man shows, with a few dues paying members and small sales of anti-Semitic literature, meagerly maintaining a bony, neurotic "president," mixed dunce and knave. The most important organizations are:

The Silver Shirts

The Defenders of the Christian Faith

The Industrial Defense Association

The American Nationalist Confederation

The James True Associates

The Knights of the White Camellia

Also, there is the notorious "Bund," a monstrous and impudent intrusion into our American life, far more worthy of expulsion than the half-witted bevies of "spies," but which blunders so egregiously that it ought to be subsidized by the Jews.

To this list we should add the most reckless one man show of the entire unsavory lot, Father Coughlin.

It is a motley array that has been waiting for years for a Hitler to come and organize them into a unified power.

Collectively they claim six million followers, and allege that they reach one third of the population of the United States by literature of personal agitation. There is no possibility of checking their claims; we may prudently assume that they do not understate them. Cut the claims in two: we still have to do with a stupendous anti-democratic activity. It is an activity that could not be carried on without considerable financial resources. It is not credible that these resources could be made up from the modest and occasional dues of the members and from sales of horrendous slanders at 3 or 4 cents a copy. Perhaps some part of Goebbels' $20 million for foreign propaganda reaches us here. This is, however, not a necessary conclusion. We have our fair share of rich men who would be glad to help us to a safe and sane dictatorship, and who have never stopped to consider that their privileges rest on the Bill of Rights. . . .

It Behooves Us to Do More Than Wring Our Hands

Far more important is the general disposition to view alienism and a permanent minority position with distrust. Toleration in the form in which it has been taught for the last two hundred years is essentially a liberal doctrine. It derived its force from antagonism to the absolute monarchy. Our present conflict is between democracy and dictatorship, and while democracy generates its own type of tolerance in contrast to dictatorial intolerance, the type is not necessarily the same as that of liberalism. The democracy has always exhibited certain reservations about persistent minority groupings. One may recall the universal response, at the time of the World War, to Theodore Roosevelt's attacks on the "hyphenated-Americans."

Is there any reason why democracy should not accept the Jew as unqualifiedly sound material for a democratic polity? Fundamentally, none. Most Jews of old American stock are so accepted. Differences in religion have never counted importantly with the democracy. Nevertheless, there is at present a disposition to impute permanent minority characteristics to the mass of the Jews. And this is a danger for the future. We shall see the current anti-Semitic wave subsiding, no doubt. But who shall say that in a future decade we may not be overwhelmed by a greater economic depression than the last, with a government less energetic in combating the general distress? In such event any weakness in our system may be disastrous, and latent anti-Semitism is one of the most dangerous.

It behooves us, as good American citizens, to set about building a bridge of understanding between the two groups, Jewish and Christian. By good modern practice, a bridge is always begun from both sides of the river simultaneously. Most of the building must be done from the side of the Christians, who have the most to lose from anti-Semitism, being the more numerous group. But the Jews have to do some building, too. There was never a persecuted race that did not develop some characteristics that seemed to give color of justification to persecution. Abolish persecution and such characteristics disappear. In time, but in how much time? And does fate give us sufficient time?

It is wise not to presume on fate, at least so long as there is something we can do ourselves. It is still open to us to form an engineering organization representing both groups, to discuss frankly, without reservations or taboos, ways and means for softening the edges of inter-group conflict, of clearing away inter-group misunderstanding. At least we owe it to our democratic civilization to do something more than denounce and wring our hands. We can try.

Further Resources

BOOKS

Abel, Ernest L. *The Roots of Anti-Semitism.* Rutherford, N.J.: Fairleigh Dickinson University Press, 1975.

Belth, Nathan C. *A Promise to Keep: A Narrative of the American Encounter with Anti-Semitism.* New York: Times Books, 1979.

Dobkowski, Michael N. *The Tarnished Dream: The Basis of American Anti-Semitism.* Westport, Conn.: Greenwood Press, 1979.

PERIODICALS

Beyer, Lisa. "Issues of Color and Creed." *Time,* May 28, 1990.

Talbott, Strobe. "Freedom's Ugly Underside." *Time,* November 27, 1989.

WEBSITES

Anti-Defamation League home page. Available online at http://www.adl.org/adl.asp; website home page: http://www.adl.org (accessed August 30, 2002).

"Antisemitism." David Dickerson home page. Available online at http://www.igc.org/ddickerson/antisemitism.html; website home page: http://www.igc.org (accessed August 30, 2002).

"Holocaust and Anti Semitism." Jewish Community Online. Available online at http://www.jewish.com/search/Holocaust_and_Anti_Semitism; website home page: http://www.jewish.com (accessed August 30, 2002).

"This Is My Task"

Sermon

By: Aimee Semple McPherson

Date: March 12, 1939

Source: McPherson, Aimee Semple. "This Is My Task." Sermon delivered at Angelus Temple, Los Angeles, March 12, 1939. Transcript available online at http://www.libertyharbor.org/sermon.htm; website home page: http://www.libertyharbor.org (accessed February 12, 2003).

About the Author: American evangelist Aimee Semple McPherson (1890–1944), a popular preacher in the 1920s and 1930s, was a nonbeliever until the age of 17 when she met a Scottish evangelist, Robert Semple, who helped to convert her. They married in 1908 and he died shortly after. In 1913 she married Harold S. McPherson. Five years later that marriage ended in divorce and McPherson began her life as a lay—untrained and unordained—evangelist and conducted many revivals. ■

Introduction

McPherson, one of the most famous and celebrated Pentecostal preachers in America, turned to the ministry after a near-death experience in a hospital. In the spring of 1913, the 23-year-old was rushed to the hospital suffering from appendicitis and nearly died. In later sermons she emphasized the importance of that sickroom incident to her ministry. She preached that she heard a voice asking her if she were willing to go. The mysterious voice, perhaps that of God, was asking her to choose between going into eternity or going into the ministry. She chose the latter and instantly the pain disappeared. Her breathing eased and she soon regained her strength. From that time on she was determined to make good her commitment to God and began the first steps toward creating her ministry.

McPherson chose to became a Pentecostal preacher. Pentecostals are Christians who emphasize individual experiences of grace, faith healing, expressive worship, and evangelism. In her sermon, "This Is My Task," McPherson explained to her congregation that her task in life was to get the gospel spread to every person all around the world. She never managed to travel the world as much as she desired but she did go across the United States

Aimee Semple McPherson, c. 1930. Called to the ministry by a near-death experience, "Sister Aimee" became a popular Pentecostal preacher, one of the first to achieve national prominence. AMERICAN STOCK/GETTY IMAGES. REPRODUCED BY PERMISSION.

with her message of hope and love and preached about the Bible to hundreds of thousands of people.

Her first contact with the Pentecostals occurred at a local meeting. She was deeply moved by the evening's speaker, Robert Semple, who encouraged his audience to experience "the baptism of the Holy Spirit" and to repent of worldly pleasures. She became convinced that the Pentecostal way was the path she would take and converted.

After her recovery from the near-fatal illness of 1913, she became an itinerant preacher and found herself in an ongoing impoverished condition. Her life changed in 1923 when she established the Angelus Temple in Los Angeles, California. Throughout the 1930s she impressed her congregation at the grand Angelus Temple with her distinctively life-lifting messages of happiness, healing, holiness, and Heaven. Wherever she traveled around the country people received her message enthusiastically.

Much of McPherson's energy was devoted to the recovery of Bible Christianity. Her favorite quote came from Hebrews 13:8, which states that Jesus Christ is the same yesterday, and today, and forever. She explained to her listeners that the Bible was open to everyone, making Christ available for all. She would speak often about the lavish feast Christ offered the faithful and would summon people with the words of a familiar gospel song: "Come and dine, the Master calleth, come and dine!"

Significance

Known as "Sister," McPherson became one of the most famous residents of Los Angeles and one of the first Pentecostals to achieve national fame. Her comings and goings from the city's train station drew more people than the visits of presidents and other dignitaries. Angelus Temple floats won prizes in Rose Bowl parades and the Temple itself became a tourist attraction.

Well-advertised, illustrated sermons drew large numbers of the curious as well as the faithful. Catchy music, award-winning bands, parades, uniforms, and programs for all ages drew the attention of many. People would stand in line for hours for seats to the Angelus Temple. Daytime services accommodated those who wanted to remain for baptism in the Holy Spirit. A prayer room was open around the clock and was used by throngs of people.

One of Sister's most notable public achievements in the 1930s was a social program under which the Angelus Temple's Commissary provided food, clothing, and other necessities to needy families. When the Depression began she opened a Free Dining Hall, which supplied over 80,000 meals in its first two months of operation.

McPherson died in 1944 but the Angelus Temple continued. The church is still going strong, providing food, clothing, education, housing, job training, and Biblical training for thousands of needy children and adults.

Primary Source

"This Is My Task" [excerpt]

SYNOPSIS: Aimee Semple McPherson is considered to be one of the first Pentecostals to become famous at the national level. In this sermon, delivered at the Angelus Temple in Los Angeles, California, she promises her congregation that she will try to spread the good news of the Bible to everyone around the world. Acknowledging the vast scope of her Christian campaign, she states that with the help of God and the members of the temple she could accomplish her objective.

What is my task? To get the gospel around the world in the shortest possible time to every man and woman and boy and girl!

You say, "Well, Sister, you won't make much headway in Tibet, I'm afraid—that's kind of a closed country yet." Well, I don't know . . . by God's grace we're gonna back a short-wave radio station right up against their border and shoot her over—and get the men there to pick it up and to amplify it. I never saw any one of those people in those countries who didn't like to hear a phonograph, to play over and over and over and over and over, or like to hear a radio. You say, "Well, maybe the government won't let you!" Well, how 'bout letting the government broadcast the weather report and the things they want to do certain hours and then we have certain hours. I think there's a way that anything can be done. Oh—I just feel my task this morning! . . .

I feel that way this morning! With God, I can do all things! But with God and you, and the people who you can interest, by the grace of God, we're gonna cover the world!

You say, "Well, Sister dear, we're looking for Jesus to come." I know we are. "But how long is this going to take?" It shouldn't take long. These are days when you can go around the world in less than a week in an aeroplane. These are days when we listen by radio. . . .

I thought, "My, won't it be wonderful when our High Priest, Jesus Christ, comes back again." Oh, if we do our task! I'll tell you, even you stiff-folks might bend and wave our handkerchiefs that day, when the Lord comes back. Amen?! Glory be to God! . . .

What is my task? First of all, my task is to be pleasing to Christ. To be empty of self and be filled with Himself. To be filled with the Holy Spirit; to be led by the Holy Spirit. Perhaps, students, you could put into words for me, could you, "I'll be somewhere working, for my Lord." Will you do it? Will you sing it right now? For the radio audience and the recording. . . .

Oh, to be filled with the Spirit means to be filled with a burning desire to see other men and women saved, and to carry the gospel around the whole world. There are so many people who could—but they won't. . . .

You all remember, perhaps, the story of a little girl who some time ago discovered a broken rail on a certain railroad track. She had wits enough about her to run to a telephone and call the superintendent, or rather I should say, the man at the depot. And he said, "Little girl, the train's already passed the station . . . stop it some way!" She never thought to argue. She said, "I'm little, but I'll do my best." She ran so fast and she waved her apron so hard, that the train stopped, and every life was saved.

This is my task.

It isn't how important you are and what great knowledge you have—it's a willingness to do it. To let God fill your life. Amen!

In the old-fashioned day of the stagecoach, over the Blue Ridge Mountains, a man was very much amused when the cabby asked him whether he wished to ride 1st class, 2nd class, or 3rd class. And he said, "Well, I'll ride 1st class." He paid the money. And when he got in, he was rather interested. He looked around and he discovered that they all sat in the same place. He wondered, "Why the difference of a few pennies?" But he noticed when they came to the stiff climb that the cabby put on the brakes. He said: "All 1st class passengers, keep your seats. Second class passengers, get out and walk! Third class passengers, get out and push!"

Praise the Lord! We may not be all 1st class bankers and lawyers and millionaires; but we certainly can get out and push! Amen! Let's encourage each one that is here for the Lord Jesus Christ.

This is my task. Let us be workers, not shirkers. I must finish my task. . . .

Show me your hands. My brother, my sister, we sing: "If you live right, heaven belongs to you." But, I believe that if we're living right; that entails working for Jesus Christ. Either going with the gospel, or paying the way for someone else to go! Either preaching, or making it possible for someone else to preach! But we mustn't muzzle the ox, you know, that treadeth out the corn.

Jesus is coming soon! Jesus is so exquisitely glorious! Salvation is so real and so to be desired. It must be had. The whole success or failure of these last few days depends on you, and God help me, upon me.

Adam had a task; to dress a garden and keep it. I'm sorry to tell you, he failed. And the whole world has always heard a man who failed. It doesn't matter very much how rich one dies, or how poor. The big thing is what you did when you were here. Did you do your task?

Noah had a job. His task, do you remember? (It) was to build the ark. He built it. Men bless him to this day.

Moses had a task. Go now to Exodus 3:9 and 10. "Go therefore." He was going to bring out all these multitudes of the children of Israel. And he did it.

Nehemiah had a task. The second chapter (of the book of Nehemiah), 5th to the 18th verse. He was sent to rebuild the walls. He was just a little man. He had just a little donkey to ride on. And no one even believed him at first. But he was so in earnest about the whole business, he kept shouting, "This is my task!" People began to believe him. They pitched in and helped him. . . .

I notice those who don't believe in uniting with a church or organization. I notice y'all use electric lights—that's organized! If it wasn't, you'd be electrocuted. I know Dr. Knight's always warning me, "Don't put your hands on the microphone!" It does something or other to the people listening in, it spoils the reception. Now, just a few minutes ago I was reminded of it. I don't know whether he realized it. I took a hold of the microphone and of my electric light here at the same time. I felt a little shock! Not very strong, but a little one. And I haven't put my hands on it since. I think it's a good way to break me of it. My Lord, put our task on us so that we'll feel a shock of the Spirit of God going through us! I know God has called me to send His gospel out and He wants you to help me. And we're going to do it. Why, this world's a little bit of a place.

Nehemiah finished his task; they went all the way around that wall. Why can't I go all the way around the world? With your help, and the Foursquare Gospel?!

A very famous Salvation Army lady went to India when a loved one died. "I must go on with my task. . . ." Mrs. Booth Tucker, who when death had come in the family and they said, "Oh, but you must take your time of mourning!" She said, "I am mourning. We all do when loved ones die, but I must go out and go on with my task."

Friends, this thing's bigger than I am! It's bigger than my family! It's bigger than you are. It's the world for God! I don't belong to anybody. I belong to Him. And because I belong to Him, I belong to everybody. You belong to me because you belong to Him, and if we Christians would ever get organized and join hands here, and stop punching each other, saying "Well, I don't like the way so-and-so does their hair, or I don't like the way they tie their shoelaces," we'd begin to preach Jesus Christ and Him crucified, and get out and go on with the work, Glory to God! We can win the world for the Lord Jesus!

Martin Luther and Gutenberg, the printer, had a task. To print the Bible. Hid it away in bales of tea and cotton and smuggled it into England. They did it. True, people were burned at the stake for it—that was their task. It was brought to the attention of the king—you don't matter! Foxe's Book of Martyrs is well worth reading. Oh, it always gives me the shivers though when I read it. How those men stood there and were burned at the stake. But that's why we have the Bible I'm using today, to the King James Version; this was their task. . . .

This is my task! And by His grace, we'll get the gospel clear around the world!

You say, "Sister, it seems to me that you've bitten off a pretty big task there. You and who else can do all this?" God and you and I.

Further Resources

BOOKS

Epstein, Daniel Mark. *Sister Aimee: The Life of Aimee Semple McPherson.* New York: Harcourt Brace Jovanovich, 1993.

McPherson, Aimee Semple. *The Story of My Life.* Waco, Tex.: Word Books, 1973.

Thomas, Lately. *Storming Heaven: The Lives and Turmoils of Minnie Kennedy and Aimee Semple McPherson.* New York: Morrow, 1970.

PERIODICALS

Blumhofer, Edith L. "Sister." *Christian History,* May 1, 1998.

Pierce, J. Kingston. "The Abduction of Aimee." *American History,* February 1, 2000.

Schwarz, Frederic D. "Aimee and Coue Improve Your Life." *American Heritage,* December 1, 1997.

WEBSITES

"Aimee: A Short Biography." Liberty Harbor Foursquare Church. Available online at http://www.libertyharbor.org/aimee.htm; website home page: http://www.libertyharbor.org (accessed August 30, 2002).

Aimee Semple McPherson Resource Center. Available online at http://members.aol.com/xbcampbell/asm/indexasm.htm; website home page: http://www.members.aol.com (accessed August 30, 2002).

11

Science and Technology

CHRISTOPHER CUMO

Entries are arranged in chronological order by date of primary source. For entries with one primary source, the entry title is the same as the primary source title. Entries with more than one primary source have an overall entry title, followed by the titles of the primary sources.

Important Events in Science and Technology, 1930–1939

1930

- On January 25, a new amendment to the Air Commerce Regulations sets five hundred feet as a minimum altitude at which aircraft may fly except during landing and takeoff.
- On February 17, Louis Bamberger and his sister, Mrs. Felix Fuld, the widow of his late partner, found the Princeton Institute for Advanced Study.
- On February 18, Clyde William Tombaugh confirms the existence of Pluto, the ninth and last planet in Earth's solar system, which had been calculated by Percival Lowell in 1906.
- In March, Harlow Shapley calculates the Milky Way galaxy to be 250,000 light years in diameter.
- In March, chemist Thomas Midgley Jr. develops the manufacturing process for Freon, a gas used in refrigerators and air conditioners.
- On March 10, Eleanor Smith establishes a women's flight altitude record of 27,418 feet.
- On April 4, the American Interplanetary Society (later the American Rocket Society) is founded for the "promotion of interest in and experimentation toward interplanetary expeditions and travels."
- On April 22, W.A. Mudge at International Nickel produces the first age-hardening wrought-nickel alloy, K-monel.
- In May, Transcontinental and West Airlines establish the first transcontinental New York-Los Angeles air link.
- In June, Cadillac offers V-16 and V-12 models for sale, while Studebaker introduces the freewheel transmission.
- On July 15, the first institute for training psychoanalysts in the United States opens in Boston.
- In August, Andrew Ellicott Douglass, an anthropologist, develops the science of dendrochronology when, while working at a Native American site, he uses tree rings to determine the age of the site.
- On October 4, chemist W.L. Semon of B.F. Goodrich invents polyvinyl chloride (PVC), used in electrical insulation and pipes.
- In November, Charles Scribner's Sons publishes *Science and the New Civilization* in which Nobel laureate Robert A. Millikan praised American science and technology for their practical achievements. The idea that American science and technology should be practical traces its roots to the ideas of Thomas Jefferson and Benjamin Franklin.

1931

- On January 2, Ernest O. Lawrence invents the cyclotron, the first operational particle accelerator, thus inaugurating the modern era of high-energy physics.
- In March, Louis S.B. Leakey makes his first trip to Africa, where he and his wife Mary began their search for the remains of early man. In 1959 and throughout the 1960s, they would make stunning finds of Australopithecines and Homo habilis, the founder of our genus.
- On March 4, Congress appropriates more than one hundred million dollars for military, naval, and commercial aviation for the coming year.
- On March 18, Margaret Mead arrives in New Guinea, where she discovered that male and female roles were different from those in the West. She concluded that no universal norms guided the behavior of males and females. Rather, each society constructed its own norms. The claim that norms are not universal but vary from society to society is cultural relativism.
- On April 11, the Empire State Building, begun in 1930, is completed in New York City. The tallest building in the world for forty years, it represents a marvel of engineering and architectural science.
- On April 22, Harold Urey, a professor at Columbia University, discovers heavy water, thus named because it contains deuterium, a rare hydrogen isotope that has an extra neutron.
- In May, Sewall Wright announced that biologists could build statistical models of the rate of evolution for a species.
- On May 27, the first full-scale wind tunnel for testing airplanes is dedicated at the Langley Memorial Aeronautical Laboratory in Hampton, Virginia.
- In October, Pontiac offers its V-6 and V-8 models. Oldsmobile introduces a downdraft carburetor and synchromesh transmission.
- On October 24, the George Washington Bridge, built under the direction of O.H. Ammann, chief engineer of the New York Port Authority, is dedicated. The new crossing is 3,500 feet long between the two suspension towers.
- In November, Vannevar Bush announces in the *Journal of the Franklin Institute* his invention of the first analog computer, which he calls a differential analyzer. An analog computer uses mechanical or electrical devices to represent the manipulation of numbers.
- On December 28, the George Westinghouse Bridge on the Philadelphia-Pittsburgh pike, begun in May 1930, is completed at a cost of $1.6 million. It has the longest central concrete arch in the United States at the time.

1932

- The Ford V-8 is introduced in the Model A. The Pierce-Arrow company introduces hydraulic valve lifters in its new models, while Buick, Lasalle, and Cadillac all offer vacuum-operated clutches.

- In June, W.W. Norton published *The Scientific Basis of Evolution* in which Nobel laureate Thomas Hunt Morgan united the study of genetics and evolution by demonstrating that genetic variation among organisms gave them differential rates of survival. That is, nature selected those individuals for survival whose variations best matched them to the environment. Charles Darwin had called this winnowing process natural selection, the mechanism of evolution.
- On August 25, Amelia Earhart, who recently received the Gold Medal of the National Geographic Society and the Distinguished Flying Cross from Congress, completes the first nonstop transcontinental flight, from Los Angeles to Newark, New Jersey, in nineteen hours, five minutes. The following year she breaks her time by almost two hours.
- On September 21, Robert A. Millikan, head of the California Institute of Technology, completes measurements on the intensity of cosmic rays at various altitudes.
- On November 26, Carl David Anderson discovers the positron, a positively charged electron, the first identified antiparticle, when examining cosmic-ray tracks, thus confirming physicist Paul A. M. Dirac's hypothesis of its existence.
- On December 1, the U.S. Department of Commerce introduces the first teletypewriter weather map service.
- On December 22, RCA gives the first demonstration of television with a cathode-ray screen.

1933

- The use of the accelerator pedal to start the car is generalized in the United States. Independent wheel suspension is also introduced.
- In January, William J. Eckert, an astronomy assistant at Columbia University who had been the first to use an electric Munroe calculator in a science class, obtains from IBM a series of computing machines that formed the basis for the Astronomical Computing Bureau.
- In February, the determination of the speed of light, begun by Albert Michelson in 1887, is completed. It travels at 300,000 kilometers per second, or 186,000 miles per second.
- On March 24, Albert Einstein immigrates to the United States and becomes professor emeritus at the Institute for Advanced Study at Princeton University.
- On April 4, the U.S. Navy dirigible *Akron* crashes at sea, killing seventy-three.
- On April 17, biochemist Roger J. Williams isolates the B vitamin pantothenic acid, a substance useful in fighting beriberi.
- On August 7, the Du Pont Company acquires the Remington Arms Company to secure a market for its smokeless powder, to be used by hunters.
- On December 11, Werner Heisenberg delivers his Nobel lecture. The Royal Academy had voted him the Nobel Prize in physics in 1932 for his discovery of the Uncertainty Principle, which claims that one cannot understand the fundamental units of reality with precision. That is, only an approximate knowledge of reality is possible. Heisenberg's principle implied that no stable entity called reality existed, a position that went too far for Albert Einstein and most American physicists.
- On December 12, Erwin Schrodinger received the Nobel Prize in physics for his mathematical models that described atoms as the interaction of waves rather than particles, a model that went beyond French physicist Louis De Broglie's idea that electrons were waves. The idea that the atom is an aggregate of waves and that all matter is made of atoms leads to the conclusion that all matter is an aggregate of waves. Humans for example are nothing more than a complex of waves. Albert Einstein and most American physicists did not believe Schrodinger's mathematics had any correlation with reality.

1934

- In February, American biochemist J.P. Lent discovers an anticoagulant now known as coumarin.
- On February 27, Lincoln Ellsworth and Baard Holth attempt to fly from the Antarctic Peninsula to the Ross Sea, but their efforts are hampered by poor weather. A short flight along the east coast of Trinity Peninsula is nevertheless carried out in 1935.
- In June, Houghton Mifflin publishes *Patterns of Culture* in which Ruth Benedict argued that the Western prohibition against murder and suicide has not held for all societies at all times. Western norms are thus relative. Along with Franz Boas, Ruth Benedict and Margaret Mead founded the study of cultural anthropology, whose cardinal belief is that all norms vary from society to society.
- On June 4, Thomas Hunt Morgan delivers his Nobel lecture. The Swedish Royal Academy had voted him the Nobel Prize in physiology and medicine in 1933 for establishing that chromosomes contain the genes, in linear fashion, that code for traits in all organisms including humans. A chromosome then is analogous to a package of Certs with each mint analogous to a gene.
- On June 27, Congress passes the Communications Act of 1934 creating the Federal Communications Commission, which replaces the Interstate Commerce Commission as the agency overseeing phone service.
- On July 12, Charles William Beebe and Otis Barton set a depth record by diving in a tethered bathysphere to a depth of 1,001 meters.
- In July and August, both Chrysler and De Soto introduce streamlined Airflow models that include automatic transmission overdrives. Knee-action (front wheel independent suspension) is introduced in the United States.
- On November 29, the American Polar Society is founded in New York.

1935

- On July 29, Congress passes the Bankhead-Jones Act, funding the study of agricultural economics and rural sociology at agricultural experiment stations.
- In November, George Horace Gallup founds the American Institute of Public Opinion. Using statistical methods to poll

small yet representative sections of the American population, he predicts electoral returns the following year more closely than any other statistical group.

- In November, Lincoln Ellsworth, along with Canadian pilot Herbert Hollick-Kenyon and Hartreg Olsen, makes the first transantarctic flight, from Dundee Island to the Bay of Whales.
- On November 11, in a flight sponsored jointly by the National Geographic Society and the U.S. Army Air Corps, Capt. O. A. Anderson and A. W. Stevens rise to an altitude of 13.71 miles (72,395 feet) aboard the balloon *Explorer II,* thereby exceeding all previous attempts to reach the stratosphere.
- On December 12, James Chadwick receives the Nobel Prize in physics for his discovery of the neutron, a subatomic particle equal in mass to the proton but of neutral charge.

1936

- In February, Robert Broom stuns the anthropological community by discovering the first of a number of skeletal remains of early man in South Africa, confirming Louis S.B. Leakey's belief that the lineage leading to Homo sapiens arose in Africa and contradicting the widespread belief that Asia was the cradle of humanity. Geologists would later date Broom's discoveries at some two million years old.
- On March 1, the Hoover Dam, in the Black Canyon on the Colorado River, is completed, making Lake Mead the world's largest reservoir.
- In May, the Reo Company stops producing cars and concentrates on trucks. Its Diamond-T company builds a diesel-powered truck.
- Between June and November, Franz Weidenrich discovers the fragments of three skulls of Homo erectus in China. Homo erectus was an early man that may have given rise to the first species of Homo sapiens, called archaic sapiens.
- In July, Theodosius Dobzhansky announces that the position of a gene on a chromosome affected the behavior of that gene.
- On November 23, the fluorescent lamp is first introduced during the centennial celebration of the U.S. Patent Office.

1937

- In January, IBM develops the model 077 collator to help the federal government maintain employment records on some twenty-six million Americans. The collator, which uses punched cards, allows the government to track people in other programs.
- In January, Theodosius Dobzhansky defines a species as a group of organisms that cannot interbreed with other organisms to produce fertile offspring, a definition close to the modern concept: a species is all organisms that can interbreed to produce fertile offspring.
- In March, Ford offers customers a choice of sixty- or eighty-five-horsepower engines on its models. The steering column gearshifts are reintroduced on some automobiles, while Buick and Oldsmobile offer automatic transmissions.
- On May 6, the German airship *Hindenburg* bursts into flames upon landing in Lakehurst, New Jersey.
- In August, physicist Max Delbruck announces that scientists could achieve a complete understanding of life by reducing it to the sum of the actions of molecules. The attempt to reduce life to the simplest physical and chemical processes has been a hallmark of modern science. Reductionism may be the feature of science that Americans most dislike, for it implies that all life is simply matter and has no spiritual dimension.
- In September, Grote Reber completes the first radio telescope in Wheaton, Illinois.
- In December, John Atanasoff begins work on what will in 1942 be the first digital computer.
- On December 13, Clinton Davisson receives the Nobel Prize in physics for experiments that confirmed French physicist Louis De Broglie's counterintuitive idea that electrons were waves rather than particles. We now think of electrons as both wave and particle, an idea that is a contradiction but that physics forces upon us. These are the ideas that strengthened Werner Heisenberg's belief that no objective reality exists, an idea that overthrew all philosophy since Plato.

1938

- In February, Perlon, a synthetic fiber, is developed.
- On March 24, J. Robert Oppenheimer and George Michael Volkoff predict the existence of pulsars, which is confirmed three decades later.
- In June, Chrysler introduces fluid coupling for transmissions.
- On October 22, American physicist Chester F. Carlson, assisted by German engineer Otto Kornei, succeeds in making the first copy by an electrostatic process called xerography.
- On December 12, Enrico Fermi received the Nobel Prize in physics for being the first to split atoms by shooting neutrons at them. This would lead to the development of the atomic bomb, an achievement in which Fermi played a leading role, in July 1945.

1939

- On February 15, Physicist J. Robert Oppenheimer, with the assistance of George Michael Volkoff, presents his calculations on the nature of black holes, stars that had collapsed under intense gravitation.
- On April 4, following the introduction by Western Union of a cable system that allows transmission of six-by-seven-inch photographs, the first such picture, of a hydroplane, is sent from London to New York and published in American newspapers.
- In June, Oldsmobile offers a "hydramatic" drive, an automatic drive that uses hydraulic pressure to shift gears, while automatic overdrive becomes more widely available.
- On August 2, at the suggestion of fellow physicist Leo Szilard, Albert Einstein writes President Franklin D. Roosevelt to recommend development of an atomic bomb.
- On September 14, Igor Sikorsky flies the first helicopter designed for mass production.
- On October 31, the New York World's Fair ends its first of two seasons, totaling about 25.8 million visitors.

"The Relation of Science to Industry"

Speech

By: Robert A. Millikan

Date: November 1928

Source: Millikan, Robert A. "The Relation of Science to Industry." Address delivered at the annual dinner of the New York Chamber of Commerce, November 1928. Published in Millikan, Robert A. *Science and the New Civilization.* New York: Charles Scribner's Sons, 1930, 36–39.

About the Author: Robert Andrews Millikan (1868–1953), a native of Morrison, Illinois, received his Ph.D. in physics in 1895 from Columbia University. He then studied at Göttingen and Berlin in Germany, returning the following year to take a position at the Ryerson Laboratory of the University of Chicago. While there, he conducted an "oil-drop" experiment that measured the charge of an electron, which won him the Nobel Prize for physics in 1923. From 1921 to 1945 Millikan worked at the California Institute of Technology, contributing to the knowledge of cosmic rays and vacuum ultraviolet spectroscopy. ■

Introduction

The idea that science yields practical results has a long history in America. Thomas Jefferson and Benjamin Franklin, two leading American statesmen and scientists of the eighteenth century, distinguished between European and American science. They believed that European science sought knowledge without regard to practical benefit and was thus old-fashioned. America was a new land that needed a new science, one focused on practical benefit to the nation. They envisioned scientists working alongside farmers, teaching them the science of producing more food. This concept inspired President George Washington (served 1789–1797) to ask Congress to create a national institute to teach farmers the latest science of food production.

In 1862 Congress created the U.S. Department of Agriculture and the agricultural and mechanical colleges and in 1887 funded the agricultural experiment stations. Agricultural science responded by eliminating Texas cattle fever in the 1890s, discovering the first vitamin in 1914 (with the discovery of other vitamins to follow), producing vitamin-fortified milk and food, pioneering crop dusting, and breeding varieties of hybrid corn in the 1920s.

Other scientists and inventors ushered in the era of electricity. Engineers built a network of telegraph lines. Alexander Graham Bell invented the telephone in 1876 and had produced 300,000 of them by 1895. Thomas Edison patented the light bulb in 1879 and was manufacturing more than 1 million bulbs per year by 1890. In 1882 engineers built the first hydroelectric power plant in Wisconsin and by 1930 these plants dotted the nation's rivers. By the 1930s American science had justified Jefferson and Franklin's faith in its practicality.

Significance

A typical American, Robert Millikan championed the practical benefits of science, rooting the development of radio and the airplane in science. The case for radio was straightforward, acknowledged Millikan. Since Guglielmo Marconi sent the Morse code by radio waves in 1899, physicists and engineers learned to transmit information by varying, or modulating, the amplitude or height of radio waves. The first radio station in 1920 used this type of transmission, known as AM (amplitude modulation). In 1929 an American engineer transmitted information by varying the frequency, the number of waves that pass a point per second, of radio waves. This method of transmission became known as FM (frequency modulation).

Millikan was more speculative in making the case for the airplane, rooting its development not in American science but in the Copernican Revolution of the sixteenth century. Millikan believed that scientists had to understand the behavior of the planets before they could master the mechanics of flight, and that they had to understand Isaac Newton's laws of motion and the idea of force before they could design the gasoline engine to power the first airplanes. Millikan summarized his argument in the conviction that "Pure science begat modern industry."

Millikan was right in asserting the practical achievements of science, which were numerous during the 1930s. In 1933 Congress created the Tennessee Valley Authority to generate hydroelectric power for the valley's homes and businesses. In 1934 the American physician Thomas Francis developed a vaccine for a strain of influenza. Wernher von Braun built on the work of the American physicist Robert Goddard in designing the V-2 rocket in 1938. The next year President Franklin D. Roosevelt (served 1933–1945) created the committee that would grow into the Manhattan Project, the program to build an atomic bomb during World War II. Also that year computer scientists John Atanasoff and Clifford Berry began

Guglielmo Marconi sits near his invention, the electric wireless. Robert Millikan championed the practical benefits of science, noting that the radio industry was born of research done in the late 1800s and early 1900s. © HULTON-DEUTSCH COLLECTION/CORBIS. REPRODUCED BY PERMISSION.

work on a digital computer, and inventor Igor Sikorsky built a helicopter that he would fly in 1941. By the 1930s science had become the engine of technology.

Primary Source

"The Relation of Science to Industry" [excerpt]

SYNOPSIS: In this excerpt, Robert Millikan roots the development of radio and the airplane in science. The practicality of science led Millikan to assert that "Pure science begat modern industry." His faith in the practical benefits of science was typical of an American scientist.

Look for a moment at the historic background out of which these modern marvels, as you call them, the airplane and the radio, have sprung. Neither of them would have been at all possible without 200 years of work in pure science before any bread and butter applications were dreamed of—work beginning in the sixteenth century with Copernicus and Kepler and Galileo, whose discoveries for the first time began to cause mankind to glimpse a nature, or a God, whichever term you prefer, not of caprice and whim as had been all the Gods of the ancient world, but instead a God who rules through law, a nature which can be counted upon and hence is worth knowing and worth carefully studying. This discovery which began to be made about 1600 A.D. I call the supreme discovery of all the ages, for before any application was ever dreamed of, it began to change the whole philosophical and religious outlook of the race, it began to effect a spiritual and an intellectual, not a material revolution—the material revolution came later. It was this new knowledge that began at that time to banish the monastic ideal which had led thousands, perhaps millions of men, to withdraw themselves from useful lives. It was this new knowledge that began to inspire man to know his universe so as to be able to live in it more rationally.

As a result of that inspiration there followed 200 years of the pure science involved in the development of the mathematics and of the celestial mechanics necessary merely to understand the movements of the heavenly bodies—useless knowledge to the unthinking, but all constituting an indispensable foundation for the development of the terrestrial mechanics and the industrial civilization which actually followed in the nineteenth century; for the very laws of force and motion essential to the design of all power machines of every sort were completely unknown to the ancient world, completely unknown up to Galileo's time.

Do you practical men fully realize that the airplane was only made possible by the development of the internal combustion engine, and that this in its turn was only made possible by the development of the laws governing all heat engines, the laws of thermodynamics, through the use for the hundred preceding years of the steam engine, and that this was only made possible by the preceding 200 years of work in celestial mechanics, that this was only made possible by the discovery by Galileo and by Newton of the laws of force and motion which had to be utilized in every one of the subsequent developments. That states the relationship of pure science to industry. The one is the child of the other. You may apply any blood test you wish and you will at once establish the relationship. *Pure science begat modern industry.*

In the case of the radio art, the commercial values of which now mount up to the billions of dollars, the parentage is still easier to trace. For if one's vision does not enable him to look back 300 years, even the shortest-sighted of men can scarcely fail to see back as much as eighteen years. For the whole structure of the radio art has been built since 1910 definitely and unquestionably upon researches carried on in the pure science laboratories for 20 years before any one dreamed that there were immediate commercial applications of these electronic discharges in high vacuum.

Further Resources

BOOKS

Ben-David, Joseph. *The Scientist's Role in Society: A Comparative Study.* Chicago: University of Chicago Press, 1984.

Brush, Stephen G. *The History of Modern Science: A Guide to the Second Scientific Revolution, 1800–1950.* Ames: Iowa State University Press, 1988.

Daniels, George H. *Science in American Society: A Social History.* New York: Knopf, 1971.

Durbin, Paul, ed. *A Guide to the Culture of Science, Technology, and Medicine.* New York: Free Press, 1984.

Oleson, Alexandra, and Sanborn C. Brown, eds. *The Pursuit of Knowledge in the Early American Republic: American Scientific and Learned Societies from Colonial Times to the Civil War.* Baltimore: Johns Hopkins University Press, 1976.

PERIODICALS

Shryock, Richard. "American Indifference to Basic Science During the Nineteenth Century." *Archives Internationales d'Histoire des Sciences* 1, 1948, 50–65.

WEBSITES

University of Delaware. "Applied Science and Engineering Laboratories." Available online at http://www.asel.udel.edu; website home page: http://www.udel.edu/ (accessed October 16, 2002).

Yale University. "Engineering and Applied Science Resources." Available online at http://www.library.yale.edu/eas; website home page: http://www.yale.edu/ (accessed October 16, 2002).

The Physical Principles of the Quantum Theory

Monograph

By: Werner Heisenberg

Date: July 1930

Source: Heisenberg, Werner. *The Physical Principles of The Quantum Theory.* Carl Eckart and Frank C. Hoyt, trans. Chicago: Dover Publications, 1930, 1–4.

About the Author: Werner Heisenberg (1901–1976) was born in Wurzburg, Germany. He received a Ph.D. in physics from the University of Munich in 1923, then assisted physicist Max Born at the University of Göttingen, and in 1924 worked with Niels Bohr at the University of Copenhagen. Heisenberg's publication of his theory of quantum mechanics in 1925 at the age of 23 won him the Nobel Prize in 1932. In 1941 he became Director of the Kaiser Wilhelm Institute for Physics, as well as Professor of Physics at the University of Berlin. He was taken prisoner at the end of World War II and removed to England, but later returned as head of the Max Planck Institute for Physics. The extent of his involvement with Nazi nuclear weapons research has been a subject of controversy. ■

Introduction

The principal tenet of physics is that a distinction exists between an observer and the object being observed. An observer, being distinct from an object, can measure and manipulate it. Because an object is distinct from whoever observes it, several observers can each measure it and agree that their measurement is valid, each having arrived at the same measurement.

A person takes for granted, for example, that he or she is distinct from their car. Suppose their car is in their garage. They can observe it there, along with a friend, both of whom agree that the car is in the garage. In addition, both can drive the car north on a road at 50 miles per hour, agreeing on the car's direction and speed.

An observer's separateness from the objects of the world provides confidence that the observer can manipulate them with predictable results. In other words, the law of causation holds for observer and object. The driver in a car, for example, can slam on the brakes, knowing that this action will cause the car to stop. Were the car to continue in motion, it would be obvious that the brakes had failed, for no other rationale could explain why effect did not follow cause. We take these facts so much for granted that we consider them common sense.

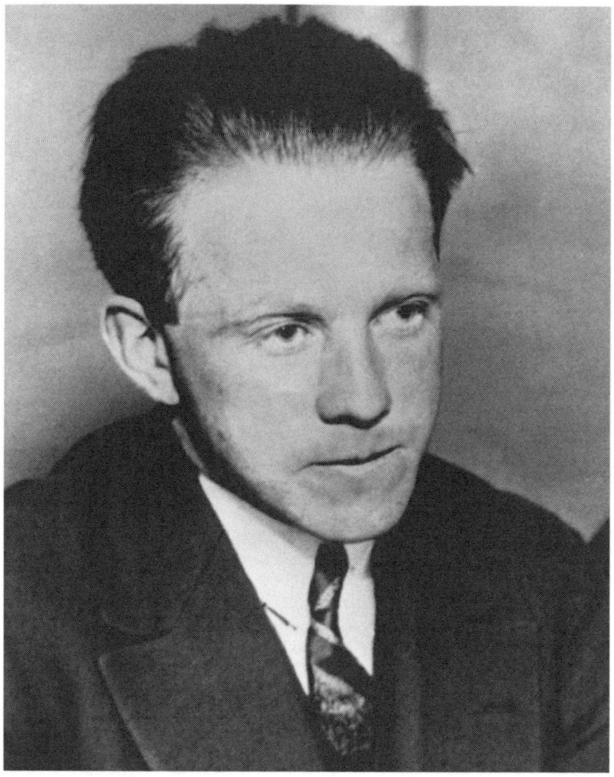

Dr. Werner Karl Heisenberg is a theoretical physicist and one of the principal developers of quantum theory. © HULTON-DEUTSCH/CORBIS. REPRODUCED BY PERMISSION.

Significance

German physicist Werner Heisenberg discovered that the commonsense distinction between observer and object breaks down at the atomic level. He wrote that in the act of observing a subatomic particle, an observer changes the properties of that particle and cannot claim to have observed it, but rather to have observed the interaction between the observer and the particle.

Put simply, Heisenberg's discovery was this: Suppose a physicist wishes to observe an electron (an incredibly small subatomic particle) and determine its position and speed. Since the electron is much too small to see, the physicist can only measure its position and speed by using special instruments to aim a wave of light at the electron and waiting for it to rebound from the electron and return to the physicist, not unlike radar. However, the electron is so small that the beam of light can actually push it, changing the electron's position and speed as it collides with it. This makes a precise, objective, measurement of the electron's position or speed impossible. Moreover, electrons and other subatomic particles are constantly moving in wave patterns themselves, so the light will collide with the electron at its crest, its trough, or somewhere between the two, and the observer has no way of knowing where on the wave this collision will occur. The physicist can only hope to measure the interaction between the wave and electron, not the electron itself, within the margin of error of the wavelength of light that was used. This degree of error represents the uncertainty of that measurement, and every measurement will have some degree of error and thus of uncertainty. Hence Heisenberg's rationale is known as the Uncertainty Principle.

The significance of Heisenberg's Uncertainty Principle is that, at least at a subatomic level, some things simply cannot be precisely measured and determined. This was a radical idea, with enormous implications for traditional physics and for science in general, which rests upon the ability to make objective and precise measurements. For this reason, some American physicists were initially skeptical of Heisenberg's claims. The American physicist and Nobel laureate Robert Millikan maintained that he could objectively measure the charge on an electron and that observer and object were distinct entities. Indeed, the trend in American physics during the 1930s favored the traditional distinction between observer and object. Only by clinging to this premise could physicists rationalize the building of cyclotrons at American universities, for these machines could, American physicists maintained, objectively quantify the behavior of atoms and subatomic particles. Not until after the 1930s did the Uncertainty Principle become widely accepted by American physicists.

The Uncertainty Principle had an immediate impact well beyond the field of particle physics. In blurring the distinction between observer and object, the Uncertainty Principle implied that scientists could not claim a statement as absolute truth, that is, as truth that is independent of all circumstances. The statement that a triangle is a three-sided figure, the sum of whose angles equals 180 degrees is such a truth. But it is the truth of the mathematician, not the scientist. The truths of science are relative to the observer. The idea of relative truth resonated with anthropologists. American anthropologists Franz Boas, Margaret Mead and Ruth Benedict argued in the 1920s and 1930s that norms and ethics are relative to the culture that creates them, just as the behavior of an object is relative to the observer measuring it. Heisenberg's Uncertainty Principle thus aligned the method and results of science with those of the social sciences in America. In doing so, Heisenberg, if unsettling to American physicists, was in the mainstream of American thought during the 1930s.

Primary Source

The Physical Principles of the Quantum Theory [excerpt]

SYNOPSIS: In this excerpt, Werner Heisenberg describes some of the basic principles of quantum physics, including the Uncertainty Principle that he discovered.

Theory and Experiment

The experiments of physics and their results can be described in the language of daily life. Thus if the physicist did not demand a theory to explain his results and could be content, say, with a description of the lines appearing on photographic plates, everything would be simple and there would be no need of an epistemological discussion. Difficulties arise only in the attempt to classify and synthesize the results, to establish the relation of cause and effect between them—in short, to construct a theory. This synthetic process has been applied not only to the results of scientific experiment, but, in the course of ages, also to the simplest experiences of daily life, and in this way all concepts have been formed. In the process, the solid ground of experimental proof has often been forsaken, and generalizations have been accepted uncritically, until finally contradictions between theory and experiment have become apparent. In order to avoid these contradictions, it seems necessary to demand that no concept enter a theory which has not been experimentally verified at least to the same degree of accuracy as the experiments to be explained by the theory. Unfortunately it is quite impossible to fulfil this requirement, since the commonest ideas and words would often be excluded. To avoid these insurmountable difficulties it is found advisable to introduce a great wealth of concepts into a physical theory, without attempting to justify them rigorously, and then to allow experiment to decide at what points a revision is necessary.

Thus it was characteristic of the special theory of relativity that the concepts "measuring rod" and "clock" were subject to searching criticism in the light of experiment; it appeared that these ordinary concepts involved the tacit assumption that there exist (in principle, at least) signals that are propagated with an infinite velocity. When it became evident that such signals were not to be found in nature, the task of eliminating this tacit assumption from all logical deductions was undertaken, with the result that a consistent interpretation was found for facts which had seemed irreconcilable. A much more radical departure from the classical conception of the world was brought about by the general theory of relativity, in which only the concept of coincidence in space-time was accepted uncritically. According to this theory, ordinary language (i.e., classical concepts) is applicable only to the description of experiments in which both the gravitational constant and the reciprocal of the velocity of light may be regarded as negligibly small.

Although the theory of relativity makes the greatest of demands on the ability for abstract thought, still it fulfils the traditional requirements of science in so far as it permits a division of the world into subject and object (observer and observed) and hence a clear formulation of the law of causality. This is the very point at which the difficulties of the quantum theory begin. In atomic physics, the concepts "clock" and "measuring rod" need no immediate consideration, for there is a large field of phenomena in which $1/c$ is negligible. The concepts "space-time coincidence" and "observation," on the other hand, do require a thorough revision. Particularly characteristic of the discussions to follow is the interaction between observer and object; in classical physical theories it has always been assumed either that this interaction is negligibly small, or else that its effect can be eliminated from the result by calculations based on "control" experiments. This assumption is not permissible in atomic physics; the interaction between observer and object causes uncontrollable and large changes in the system being observed, because of the discontinuous changes characteristic of atomic processes. The immediate consequence of this circumstance is that in general every experiment performed to determine some numerical quantity renders the knowledge of others illusory, since the uncontrollable perturbation of the observed system alters the values of previously determined quantities. If this perturbation be followed in its quantitative details, it appears that in many cases it is impossible to obtain an exact determination of the simultaneous values of two variables, but rather that there is a lower limit to the accuracy with which they can be known.

The starting-point of the critique of the relativity theory was the postulate that there is no signal velocity greater than that of light. In a similar manner, this lower limit to the accuracy with which certain variables can be known simultaneously may be postulated as a law of nature (in the form of the so-called uncertainty relations) and made the starting-point of the critique which forms the subject matter of the following pages. These uncertainty relations give us that measure of freedom from the limitations of classical concepts which is necessary for a consistent description of atomic processes. The program of the following considerations will therefore be: first, to obtain a general survey of all concepts whose introduction is suggested by the atomic experiments; second, to limit the range of application of these concepts; and third, to show that the concepts thus limited, together with the mathematical formulation of quantum theory, form a self-consistent scheme.

Further Resources

BOOKS

Cassidy, David Charles. *Uncertainty: The Life and Science of Werner Heisenberg.* New York: W.H. Freeman, 1992.

Heisenberg, Werner. *"The Development of Quantum Mechanics."* Nobel Prize in Physics Award Address, December 11, 1933. Reprinted in Weaver, Jefferson H., ed. *The World of Physics,* vol. 2. New York: Simon & Schuster, 1987, 356–367.

———. *Introduction to the Unified Field Theory of Elementary Particles.* London and New York: InterScience, 1966.

———. *Philosophical Problems of Quantum Physics.* Woodbridge, Conn: Ox Bow Press, 1979.

Price, William C., and Seymour S. Chissick. *The Uncertainty Principle and Foundations of Quantum Mechanics: A Fifty Year Survey.* New York: Wiley, 1977.

WEBSITES

American Institute of Physics, Center for History of Physics. "Werner Heisenberg and the Uncertainty Principle." Available online at http://www.aip.org/history/heisenberg; website home page: http://www.aip.org/history/ (accessed October 15, 2002).

"Beginner's Guide to Research in the History of Science: Werner Heisenberg." Available online at http://www.horuspublications.com/guide/ph116.html; website home page: http://www.horuspublications.com/guide/tp1.html (accessed October 15, 2002).

"Shade Tree Physics." Available online at http://www.ebicom.net/~rsf1 (accessed October 15, 2002).

"Werner Karl Heinsenberg." Available online at http://www-groups.dcs.st-and.ac.uk/~history/Mathematicians/Heisenberg.html; website home page: http://www-maths.mcs.st-andrews.ac.uk/ (accessed October 15, 2002).

The World as I See It

Nonfiction Work

By: Albert Einstein

Date: 1933

Source: Einstein, Albert. *The World as I See It.* Alan Harris, trans. New York: Covici-Friede, 1934, xv–xvi, 278–284. Originally published as *Mein Weltbild.* Amsterdam: Querido Verlag, 1933.

About the Author: Albert Einstein (1879–1955) was born in Ulm, Germany. Although interested in mathematics, Einstein did not do well in Germany's rigid school system. His family moved to Berne, Switzerland, where he found employment as an assistant patents clerk. It was during his spare time at this job that he jotted down the ideas that would become the basis for his revolutionary theories, most notably his general and special theories of relativity. In 1921, Einstein won the Nobel Prize in Physics for his work on the photoelectric effect. In 1933, the Nazi persecutions of Jewish scientists caused Einstein to flee to the United States, where he became professor of theoretical physics at Princeton University in New Jersey. He held that position until 1945, spending his last years in semiretirement in Princeton. ■

Introduction

By the 1930s, Albert Einstein was perhaps the world's most famous person. His fame rested on his scientific work, especially his theories of relativity. Although nonscientists seldom drew the distinction, relativity was not a single idea, but rather two separate theories: the special theory of relativity (1905) and the general theory of relativity (1916).

The special theory of relativity states that space and time are not constant, but depend on an observer's position and speed. Two observers traveling at different speeds will measure different lengths of the same object, and their watches will tick at different rates. These differences are only appreciable near light speed. People moving at 90 percent of light speed will find that they are only half as wide as they had been when traveling at, say, 5 miles per hour, and their watches will take twice as long to tick a second as at 5 miles per hour.

The general theory of relativity replaced Isaac Newton's law of gravity with the notion that objects distort the space around them. The Earth travels around the sun not because the sun's gravity tugs it, but because the sun distorts or curves the space around it, forcing the Earth to travel in a curve, namely an ellipse, around the sun. The notion that space is curved rather than linear seems counter to one's intuition, but the crucial test came in 1919 during an eclipse of the sun. The eclipse allowed astronomers to see light from a star passing near the sun. This would not have been possible without the eclipse, because the sun's light is too bright to permit astronomers to detect the faint light from a star passing near the sun. Newton and Einstein both predicted that the sun should bend the star's light—Newton because gravity would pull the light from its linear path, and Einstein because space near the sun is curved. The measurement of the degree to which light bent as it traveled near the sun agreed with Einstein's prediction, not Newton's. The announcement that Einstein was right made headlines around the world and catapulted him to worldwide fame.

Significance

Einstein came to the United States in 1933 an international celebrity. But the world-famous scientist had as much admiration for his new home as it did for him. He was greatly impressed that Americans could admire a scientist whose ideas had nothing to do with the world of

Renowned scientist Albert Einstein stands at a blackboard. AP/WIDE WORLD PHOTOS. REPRODUCED BY PERMISSION.

commerce and finance. He also praised the achievements of American science, which he felt had made tremendous strides in a very short period of time.

Einstein's remarks were significant because they validated America's scientific pursuits. The most important physicist in Europe had just acknowledged the vigor of American science. Thomas Jefferson and Benjamin Franklin, America's leading scientists and statesmen of the eighteenth century, had labored to create an American science that would enjoy as much prestige as European science. Their vision had become reality by the 1930s: Thomas Hunt Morgan and his team of researchers at Columbia University had founded modern genetics; American astronomers Vesto Slipher and Edwin Hubble had demonstrated that the universe was expanding; and Clyde Tombaugh had discovered Pluto. In addition, American physicists Albert Michelson, Robert Millikan, and Arthur Compton had each won a Nobel Prize. Taken together, these achievements justified Einstein's admiration of American science.

Primary Source

The World as I See It [excerpt]

SYNOPSIS: In these excerpts, Einstein begins by acknowledging the numerous contributions of German Jews, many of whom were being severely persecuted by Hitler's Nazi regime. Later, Einstein admits that he feels unworthy of his celebrity and would have trouble enduring it, were it not for the fact that it demonstrates that Americans truly recognize and appreciate scientific achievement. Einstein realizes that Americans value science because they link it to technology and that technology is more abundant in the United States than in Europe or Asia. Einstein also praises the achievements of American science.

A Foreword

The following pages are dedicated to the appreciation of the achievements of German Jews. It must be remembered that we are concerned here with a body of people amounting, in numbers, to no more than the population of a moderate-sized town, who have held their own against a hundred times as many Germans, in spite of handicaps and prejudices, through the superiority of their ancient cultural traditions. Whatever attitude people may take up towards this little people, nobody who retains a shred of sound judgment in these times of confusion can deny them respect. In these days of persecution of the German Jews especially, it is time to remind the western world that it owes to the Jewish people (a) its religion and therewith its most valuable moral ideals, and (b), to a large extent, the resurrection of the world of Greek thought. Nor should it be forgotten that it was a translation of the Bible, that is to say, a translation from the Hebrew, which brought about the refinement and perfection of the German language. Today the Jews of Germany find their fairest consolation in the thought of all they have produced and achieved for humanity by their efforts in modern times as well; and no oppression however brutal, no campaign of calumny however subtle will blind those who have eyes to see the intellectual and moral qualities inherent in this people. . . .

Some Notes on My American Impressions

I must redeem my promise to say something about my impressions of this country. That is not altogether easy for me. For it is not easy to take up the attitude of impartial observer when one is received with such kindness and undeserved respect as I have been in America. First of all let me say something on this score.

The cult of individual personalities is always, in my view, unjustified. To be sure, Nature distributes her gifts variously among her children. But there are plenty of the well endowed, thank God, and I am firmly convinced that most of them live quiet, unregarded lives. It strikes me as unfair, and even in bad taste, to select a few of them for boundless admiration, attributing superhuman powers of mind and character to them. This has been my fate, and the contrast between the popular estimate of my powers and achievements and the reality is simply grotesque. The consciousness of this extraordinary state of affairs would be unbearable but for one great consoling thought: it is a welcome symptom in an age which is commonly denounced as materialistic, that it makes heroes of men whose ambitions lie wholly in the intellectual and moral sphere. This proves that knowledge and justice are ranked above wealth and power by a large section of the human race. My experience teaches me that this idealistic outlook is particularly prevalent in America, which is usually decried as a particularly materialistic country. After this digression I come to my proper theme, in the hope that no more weight will be attached to my modest remarks than they deserve.

What first strikes the visitor with amazement is the superiority of this country in matters of technics and organisation. Objects of every-day use are more solid than in Europe, houses infinitely more convenient in arrangement. Everything is designed to save human labour. Labour is expensive, because the country is sparsely inhabited in comparison with its natural resources. The high price of labour was the stimulus which evoked the marvellous development of technical devices and methods of work. The opposite extreme is illustrated by over-populated China or India, where the low price of labour has stood in the way of the development of machinery. Europe is half way between the two. Once the machine is sufficiently highly developed it becomes cheaper in the end than the cheapest labour. Let the Fascists in Europe, who desire on narrow-minded political grounds to see their own particular countries more densely populated, take heed of this. The anxious care with which the United States keep out foreign goods by means of prohibitive tariffs certainly contrasts oddly with this notion. . . . But an innocent visitor must not be expected to rack his brains too much, and when all is said and done, it is not absolutely certain that every question admits of a rational answer.

The second thing that strikes a visitor is the joyous, positive attitude to life. The smile on the faces of the people in photographs is symbolical of one of the greatest assets of the American. He is friendly, confident, optimistic, and without envy. The European finds intercourse with Americans easy and agreeable.

Compared with the American the European is more critical, more self-conscious, less good hearted and helpful, more isolated, more fastidious in his amusements and his reading, generally more or less of a pessimist.

Great importance attaches to the material comforts of life, and peace, freedom from care, security are all sacrificed to them. The American lives for ambition, the future, more than the European. Life for him is always becoming, never being. In this respect he is even further removed from the Russian and the Asiatic than the European is. But there is one respect in which he resembles the Asiatic more than the European does: he is less of an individualist than the European—that is, from the psychological, not the economic, point of view.

More emphasis is laid on the 'we' than the 'I'. As a natural corollary of this, custom and convention are extremely strong, and there is much more uniformity both in outlook on life and in moral and aesthetic ideas among Americans than among Europeans. This fact is chiefly responsible for America's economic superiority over Europe. Co-operation and the division of labour are carried through more easily and with less friction than in Europe, whether in the factory or the university or in private good works. This social sense may be partly due to the English tradition.

In apparent contradiction to this stands the fact that the activities of the state are comparatively restricted as compared with those in Europe. The European is surprised to find the telegraph, the telephone, the railways, and the schools predominantly in private hands. The more social attitude of the individual, which I mentioned just now, makes this possible here. Another consequence of this attitude is that the extremely unequal distribution of property leads to no intolerable hardships. The social conscience of the rich man is much more highly developed than in Europe. He considers himself obliged as a matter of course to place a large portion of his wealth, and often of his own energies too, at the disposal of the community; public opinion, that all-powerful force, imperiously demands it of him. Hence the most important cultural functions can be left to private enterprise and the part played by the state in this country is, comparatively, a very restricted one.

The prestige of government has undoubtedly been lowered considerably by the Prohibition law. For nothing is more destructive of respect for the government and the law of the land than passing laws which cannot be enforced. It is an open secret that the dangerous increase of crime in this country is closely connected with this.

There is also another way in which Prohibition, in my opinion, has led to the enfeeblement of the state. The public house is a place which gives people the opportunity to exchange views and ideas on public affairs. As far as I can see, people here have no chance of doing this, the result being that the Press, which is mostly controlled by definite interests, has an excessive influence over public opinion.

The over-estimation of money is still greater in this country than in Europe, but appears to me to be on the decrease. It is at last beginning to be realised that great wealth is not necessary for a happy and satisfactory life.

In regard to artistic matters, I have been genuinely impressed by the good taste displayed in the modern buildings and in articles of common use; on the other hand the visual arts and music have little place in the life of the nation as compared with Europe.

I have a warm admiration for the achievements of American institutes of scientific research. We are unjust in attempting to ascribe the increasing superiority of American research work exclusively to superior wealth; zeal, patience, a spirit of comradeship and a talent for co-operation play an important part in its successes. One more observation, to finish up. The United States is the most powerful and technically advanced country in the world today. Its influence on the shaping of international relations is absolutely incalculable. But America is a large country and its people have so far not shown much interest in great international problems, among which the problem of disarmament occupies first place today. This must be changed, if only in the essential interests of the Americans. The last war has shown that there are no longer any barriers between the continents and that the destinies of all countries are closely interwoven. The people of this country must realise that they have a great responsibility in the sphere of international politics. The part of passive spectator is unworthy of this country and is bound in the end to lead to disaster all round.

Further Resources

BOOKS

Clark, Ronald W. *Einstein: The Life and Times.* New York: HarperCollins, 1971. Reprint, New York: Avon, 1999.

Einstein, Albert. "The Fundamental Ideas and Problems of the Theory of Relativity." Nobel Prize Award Address, 1921. In *The World of Physics,* vol. 2. Jefferson H. Weaver, ed. New York: Simon & Schuster, 1987, 213–222.

———. *Ideas and Opinions.* New York: Bonanza, 1954. Reprint, New York: Crown, 1995.

———. *Relativity: The Special and General Theory.* London: Methuen, 1920. Reprint, New York: Crown, 1961.

———. *Sidelights on Relativity.* New York: Dover, 1983.

Einstein, Albert, and Leopold Infeld. *The Evolution of Physics.* New York: Simon & Schuster, 1961.

PERIODICALS

Einstein, Albert. "Atomic War or Peace." *Atlantic Monthly* 180, no. 5, November 1945, 29–32.

———. "How I Created the Theory of Relativity." *Physics Today* 35, no.8, August 1982, 45–47.

WEBSITES

"A. Einstein: Image and Impact." American Institute of Physics. Available online at http://www.aip.org/history/einstein; website home page: http://www.aip.org (accessed October 15, 2002).

Patterns of Culture

Nonfiction work

By: Ruth Benedict

Date: 1934

Source: Benedict, Ruth. *Patterns of Culture.* Boston: Houghton Mifflin, 1934. Reprint, with a new preface by Margaret Mead, 1959, 45–47.

About the Author: Ruth Fulton Benedict (1887–1948), born in New York, received a Ph.D. in anthropology from Columbia University in 1923. She began teaching at that institution the following year, and was appointed its Director of Anthropology in 1936. In 1941, Benedict became a founding member of the Institute for Intercultural Studies. At the time of her death she was in the midst of a four-year Contemporary Cultures Project for Columbia, which involved more than 120 participants studying seven divergent cultures. ■

Introduction

Anthropology developed in nineteenth-century Europe and the United States. Its practitioners were men of European ancestry who regarded Western culture as the pinnacle of human achievement. They regarded non-Western cultures as inferior to the West. A corollary of this belief was the insistence that non-Europeans—Africans, Asians, Native Americans, aboriginal Australians, Polynesians—were inferior to Europeans and Americans of European descent.

This racism and sense of cultural supremacy comforted many anthropologists but not the German-American

Native American boys dressed in required school uniforms illustrate early attempts at forced cultural assimilation. NATIONAL ARCHIVES AND RECORDS ADMINISTRATION

Franz Boas. From his professorship at Columbia University he shaped American anthropology during the early twentieth century. He put all cultures on an equal footing. None was superior to another. The behaviors and norms of culture *A* were neither more nor less legitimate than those of culture *B.* Boas substituted cultural relativism for cultural supremacy.

His pupil Margaret Mead advanced cultural relativism in her work. In *Coming of Age in Samoa* (1928) she argued that Polynesian culture was as legitimate as Western culture. In fact she found the sexual norms of Polynesian culture more liberating than those of the West. In 1931 she studied the natives of New Guinea, concluding that no universal masculine and feminine roles exist. Each culture constructs its own definition of masculinity and femininity.

Significance

Boas and Mead influenced Ruth Benedict. In *Patterns of Culture* (1934) she rejects the widespread belief that a universal standard condemns murder and suicide. Rather, she argued, some non-Western cultures permit murder and suicide and others even encourage them under certain circumstances. Suicide, she wrote, "may be the highest and noblest act a wise man can perform." Behaviors derive their acceptance from and within the culture that generates them. As such, behaviors are as variable as the diversity of the world's cultures, and none can claim absolute truth. All truths are cultural constructs and, as such, are bounded by time and circumstance.

Benedict was influential not only for advancing the notion of cultural relativism but, like Mead, for her status as a woman who derived prestige from her profession, instead of from the traditional status of woman as homemaker. Benedict and Mead demonstrated that women could excel as social scientists at a time when men dominated the natural sciences. The roster of names in the biological and physical sciences in the 1930s were men: Arthur Compton, Robert Millikan, Thomas Hunt Morgan, and Hermann J. Muller.

This polarization, with women as social scientists and men as natural scientists, fed the belief that women could excel in the soft sciences (such as psychology or sociology) but not in the hard sciences where mathematics and experimental rigor characterized research. Women were descriptive rather than analytical, attuned to emotions rather than ideas. The result of this stereotype is evident in the fact that today female sociologists outnumber female physicists, and women are more numerous in psychology than in mathematics.

Primary Source

Patterns of Culture [excerpt]

SYNOPSIS: In this excerpt, Ruth Benedict denies that absolute standards of behavior exist. All behaviors and norms are rooted in the time and circumstances of a culture and are therefore relative. Truth is a cultural construct, not a timeless universal.

The Integration of Culture

The diversity of cultures can be endlessly documented. A field of human behaviour may be ignored in some societies until it barely exists; it may even be in some cases unimagined. Or it may almost monopolize the whole organized behaviour of the society, and the most alien situations be manipulated only in its terms. Traits having no intrinsic relation one with the other, and historically independent, merge and become inextricable, providing the occasion for behaviour that has no counterpart in regions that do not make these identifications. It is a corollary of this that standards, no matter in what aspect of behaviour, range in different cultures from the positive to the negative pole. We might suppose that in the matter of taking life all peoples would agree in condemnation. On the contrary, in a matter of homicide, it may be held that one is blameless if diplomatic relations have been severed between neighbouring countries, or that one kills by custom his first two children, or that a husband has right of life and death over his wife, or that it is the duty of the child to kill his parents before they are old. It may be that those are killed who steal a fowl, or who cut their upper teeth first, or who are born on a Wednesday. Among some peoples a person suffers torments at having caused an accidental death; among others it is a matter of no consequence. Suicide also may be a light matter, the recourse of anyone who has suffered some slight rebuff, an act that occurs constantly in a tribe. It may be the highest and noblest act a wise man can perform. The very tale of it, on the other hand, may be a matter for incredulous mirth, and the act itself impossible to conceive as a human possibility. Or it may be a crime punishable by law, or regarded as a sin against the gods.

The diversity of custom in the world is not, however, a matter which we can only helplessly chronicle. Self-torture here, head-hunting there, prenuptial chastity in one tribe and adolescent licence in another, are not a list of unrelated facts, each of them to be greeted with surprise wherever it is found or wherever it is absent. The taboos on killing oneself or another, similarly, though they relate to no absolute standard, are not therefore fortuitous. The significance of cultural behaviour is not exhausted when we have clearly understood that it is local and man-made and hugely variable. It tends also to be integrated. A culture, like an individual, is a more or less consistent pattern of thought and action. Within each culture there come into being characteristic purposes not necessarily shared by other types of society. In obedience to these purposes, each people further and further consolidates its experience, and in proportion to the urgency of these drives the heterogeneous items of behaviour take more and more congruous shape. Taken up by a well-integrated culture, the most ill-assorted acts become characteristic of its peculiar goals, often by the most unlikely metamorphoses. The form that these acts take we can understand only by understanding first the emotional and intellectual mainsprings of that society.

Such patterning of culture cannot be ignored as if it were an unimportant detail. The whole, as modern science is insisting in many fields, is not merely the sum of all its parts, but the result of a unique arrangement and interrelation of the parts that has brought about a new entity. Gunpowder is not merely the sum of sulphur and charcoal and saltpeter, and no amount of knowledge even of all three of its elements in all the forms they take in the natural world will demonstrate the nature of gunpowder. New potentialities have come into being in the resulting compound that were not present in its elements, and its mode of behaviour is indefinitely changed from that of any of its elements in other combinations.

Cultures, likewise, are more than the sum of their traits. We may know all about the distribution of a tribe's form of marriage, ritual dances, and puberty initiations, and yet understand nothing of the culture as a whole which has used these elements to its own purpose. This purpose selects from among the possible traits in the surrounding regions those which it can use, and discards those which it cannot. Other traits it recasts into conformity with its demands. The process of course need never be conscious during its whole course, but to overlook it in the study of the patternings of human behaviour is to renounce the possibility of intelligent interpretation.

Further Resources

BOOKS

Boas, Franz. *Race, Language, and Culture.* Chicago: University of Chicago Press, 1982.

Golde, Peggy, ed. *Women in the Field: Anthropological Experiences.* Berkeley: University of California Press, 1986.

Malefijt, Annemarie de Wall. *Images of Man: A History of Anthropological Thought.* New York: Knopf, 1974.

Mead, Margaret. *Coming of Age in Somoa: A Psychological Study of Primitive Youth for Western Civilization.* New York: Perennial Classics, 2001.

Modell, Judith. *Ruth Benedict: Patterns of a Life.* Philadelphia: University of Pennsylvania Press, 1983.

Silverman, Sydel, ed. *Totems and Teachers: Perspectives on the History of Anthropology.* New York: Columbia University Press, 1981.

PERIODICALS

Ardener, Shirley. "The Social Anthropology of Women and Feminist Anthropology." *Anthropology Today* 1, 1985, 24–26.

Speth, William W. "The Anthropogeographic Theory of Franz Boas." *Anthropos* 1978, 1–31.

Tiffany, Sharon. "Anthropology and the Study of Women." *American Anthropologist* 82, 1980, 374–380.

WEBSITES

Celebrating Women Anthropologists. *Ruth Fulton Benedict 1887–1948.* Available online at http://www.cas.usf.edu/anthropology/women/ruthb/ruthbenedict.htm; website home page: http://www.cas.usf.edu/anthropology/women/index.html (accessed October 16, 2002).

Bankhead-Jones Act of 1935

Law

By: U.S. Congress

Date: June 29, 1935

Source: U.S. Congress. *Bankhead-Jones Act of 1935.* 49 Stat. 436. June 29, 1935. Reprinted in Knoblauch, Harold C., Ernest M. Law, and W.P. Meyer. *State Agricultural Experiment Stations: A History of Research Policy and Procedure.* Washington, D.C.: U.S. Government Printing Office, 1962, 223–225.

About the Author: John Hollis Bankhead Jr. (1872–1946) was born in Jasper, Alabama. He received his law degree from Georgetown University in 1893 and was admitted to the bar that same year. Elected to the U.S. Senate as a Democrat in 1930, he was reelected in 1936 and 1942, while at the same time serving as trustee of the University of Alabama. He was also chairman of the Congressional Committee on Irrigation and Reclamation. He died while serving in office. ■

Introduction

American farmers prospered during World War I (1914–1918) as they fed not only Americans but their British and French allies. The war's end in 1919 allowed British and French farmers to resume production, leaving American farmers with a surplus they couldn't sell overseas. This surplus drove down food prices, which had not regained their World War I levels when the Great Depression struck. Between 1929 and 1933 U.S. farm prices fell 60 percent as farmers tried to produce more food to compensate for low prices. But this approach only worsened matters by enlarging the surplus, further lowering prices. Farmers on the plains suffered acutely from drought and grasshoppers in addition to low prices. Thousands lost their farms and migrated to California in search of work.

Amid this crisis, Congress called on science to help farmers survive the depression. That Congress would turn to science was no surprise, for scientists had proven they could help farmers. They had eliminated the Texas cattle fever, pioneered crop dusting, and bred high-yielding, drought-tolerant varieties of hybrid corn. By 1930 agricultural science had fulfilled the expectations of Congress and the state legislatures.

Significance

In 1935 Congress passed the Bankhead-Jones Act, named after its author, Alabama Senator John Hollis Bankhead Jr., and its Congressional sponsor, Minnesota Congressman John D. Jones. It granted $5,000 per year to each agricultural experiment station to help farmers find markets for their surplus food. A key provision called on the stations to discover the "laws and principles underlying basic problems of agriculture." This was tantamount to asking scientists to transform agriculture into a branch of physics. Physics had its laws in the law of gravity and the laws of thermodynamics, for example. Agriculture, if it was to be on a par with physics, had to discover its own laws.

The Bankhead-Jones Act demanded much from agricultural science, which was to help farmers produce and distribute food more efficiently, to discover new markets for food, and to conserve soil and water. The Act expected the experiment stations to cooperate with the U.S. Department of Agriculture and the land-grant colleges in achieving these goals.

The Bankhead-Jones Act thus reinforced a strength of American science: the cooperation between federal and state scientific agencies. This model worked not only in agriculture but in all fields of science where the federal government funded research at the state universities. In the United States, science was the preserve of neither Congress nor the states. Rather it was a cooperative venture between both. This cooperation made American science the world's envy. It also made possible the development of the atomic bomb in 1945 and is today at the heart of medical research.

Primary Source

Bankhead-Jones Act of 1935 [excerpt]

SYNOPSIS: The Bankhead-Jones Act of 1935 granted each agricultural experiment station $5,000 a year to help farmers produce food more efficiently, to distribute it more efficiently, to discover new markets for food, and to conserve soil and water. The Act called on the experiment stations to cooperate with the U.S. Department of Agriculture and the land-grant colleges in achieving these goals.

Act of 1935 Providing for Agricultural Research and More Complete Endowment and Support of Land-Grant Colleges

An act to provide for research into basic laws and principles relating to agriculture and to provide for the further development of cooperative agricultural extension work and the more complete endowment and support of land-grant colleges.

Be it enacted by the Senate and House of Representatives of the United States of America in Congress assembled,

Title I

Section 1. [Amended by Act of August 14, 1946] The Secretary of Agriculture is authorized and directed to conduct research into laws and principles

A state agricultural experiment station resides near Black Mountain, North Carolina. THE LIBRARY OF CONGRESS.

underlying basic problems of agriculture in its broadest aspects; research relating to the improvement of the quality of, and the development of new and improved methods of production of, distribution of, and new and extended uses and markets for, agricultural commodities and byproducts and manufactures thereof; and research relating to the conservation, development, and use of land and water resources for agricultural purposes. Research authorized under this section shall be in addition to research provided for under the existing law (but both activities shall be coordinated so far as practicable) and shall be conducted by such agencies of the Department of Agriculture as the Secretary may designate or establish.

Sec. 2. The Secretary is also authorized and directed to encourage research similar to that authorized under section 1 to be conducted by agricultural experiment stations established or which may hereafter be established in pursuance of the act of March 2, 1887, providing for experiment stations, as amended and supplemented, by the allotment and payment as provided in section 5 to Puerto Rico and the States and Territories for the use of such experiment stations of sums appropriated therefor pursuant to this title.

Sec. 3. For the purposes of this title there is authorized to be appropriated, out of any money in the Treasury not otherwise appropriated, the sum of $1,000,000 for the fiscal year beginning after the date of the enactment of this title, and for each of the four fiscal years thereafter $1,000,000 more than the amount authorized for the preceding fiscal year, and $5,000,000 for each fiscal year thereafter. Moneys appropriated in pursuance of this title shall also be available for the purchase and rental of land and the construction of buildings necessary for conducting research provided for in this title, for the equipment and maintenance of such buildings, and for printing and disseminating the results of research. Sums appropriated in pursuance of this title shall be in addition to, and not in substitution for, appropriations for research or other activities of the Department of Agriculture and sums appropriated or otherwise made available for agricultural experiment stations.

Sec. 4. Forty per centum of the sums appropriated for any fiscal year under section 3 shall be available for the purposes of section 1: *Provided,* That not to exceed 2 per centum of the sums appropriated may be used for the administration of section 5 of this title. The sums available for the purposes of section 1 shall be designated as the "Special research fund, Department of Agriculture," and no part of such special fund shall be used for the prosecution of research heretofore instituted or for the prosecution of any new research project except upon approval in writing by the Secretary. One-half of such special research fund shall be used by the Secretary for the establishment and maintenance of research laboratories and facilities in the major agricultural regions at places selected by him and for the prosecution, in accordance with section 1, of research at such laboratories.

Sec. 5. [Amended by Act of September 21, 1944] *(a)* Sixty per centum of the sums appropriated for any fiscal year under section 3 shall be available for the purposes of section 2. The Secretary shall allot, for each fiscal year for which an appropriation is made, to Puerto Rico and each State and Territory an amount which bears the same ratio to the total amount to be allotted as the rural population of Puerto Rico or the State or Territory bears to the rural population of Puerto Rico and all the States and Territories as determined by the last preceding decennial census. No allotment and no payment under any allotment shall be made for any fiscal year in excess of the amount which Puerto Rico or the State or Territory makes available for such fiscal year out of its own funds for research and for the establishment and maintenance of necessary facilities for the prosecution of such research. If Puerto Rico or any State or Territory fails to make available for such purposes for any fiscal year a sum equal to the total amount to which it may be entitled for such year, the remainder of such amount shall be withheld by the Secretary. The total amount so withheld may be allotted by the Secretary of Agriculture to Puerto Rico and the States and Territories which make available for such year an amount equal to that part of the total amount withheld which may be allotted to them by the Secretary of Agriculture, but no such additional allotment to Puerto Rico or any State or Territory shall exceed the original allotment to Puerto Rico or such State or Territory for that year by more than 20 per centum thereof.

(b) The sums authorized to be allotted to Puerto Rico and the States and Territories shall be paid annually in quarterly payments on July 1, October 1, January 1, and April 1. Such sums shall be paid by the Secretary of the Treasury upon warrant of the Secretary of Agriculture in the same manner and subject to the same administrative procedure set forth in the act of March 2, 1887, as amended June 7, 1887.

Sec. 6. As used in this title the term "Territory" means Alaska and Hawaii.

Sec. 7. The Secretary of Agriculture is authorized and directed to prescribe such rules and regulations as may be necessary to carry out this act.

Sec. 8. The right to alter, amend, or repeal this act is hereby expressly reserved. . . .

Sec. 22. [Amended by Act of June 12, 1952] In order to provide for the more complete endowment and support of the colleges in the several States and the Territory of Hawaii entitled to the benefits of the act entitled "An act donating public lands to the several States and Territories which may provide colleges for the benefit of agriculture and the mechanic arts," approved July 2, 1862, as amended and supplemented (U.S.C., title 7, secs. 301–328; Supp. VII, sec. 304), there are hereby authorized to be appropriated annually, out of any money in the Treasury not otherwise appropriated, the following amounts:

(a) For the fiscal year beginning after the date of the enactment of this act and for each fiscal year thereafter, $980,000; and,

(b) For the fiscal year following the first fiscal year for which an appropriation is made in pursuance of paragraph *(a)* $500,000, and for each of the two fiscal years thereafter $500,000 more than the amount authorized to be appropriated for the preceding fiscal year, and for each fiscal year thereafter $1,500,000. The sums appropriated in pursuance of paragraph *(a)* shall be paid annually to the several States and Territory of Hawaii in equal shares. The sums appropriated in pursuance of paragraph *(b)* shall be in addition to sums appropriated in pursuance of paragraph *(a)* and shall be allotted and paid annually to each of the several States and the Territory of Hawaii in the proportion which the total population of each such State and the Territory of Hawaii bears to the total population of all the States and the Territory of Hawaii, as determined by the last preceding decennial census. Sums appropriated in pursuance of this section shall be in addition to sums appropriated or authorized under such act of July 2, 1862, as amended and supplemented, and shall be applied only for the purposes of the colleges defined in such act, as amended and supplemented. The provisions

of law applicable to the use and payment of such sums under the act entitled "An act to apply a portion of the proceeds of the public lands to the more complete endowment and support of the colleges for the benefit of agriculture and the mechanic arts established under the provisions of an act of Congress approved July second, eighteen hundred and sixty-two," approved August 30, 1890, as amended and supplemented, shall apply to the use and payment of sums appropriated in pursuance of this section.

Approved June 29, 1935 (49 Stat. 436).

Further Resources

BOOKS

Bunker, Nancy J., and Tom Dupree. *100 Years: A Century of Growth through Agricultural Research.* Atlanta: University of Georgia Press, 1975.

Busch, Lawrence, ed. *Science and Agricultural Development.* Totowa, N.J.: Allanheld, Osmun, 1981.

Busch, Lawrence, and William B. Lacy. *Science, Agriculture, and the Politics of Research.* Boulder, Colo.: Westview Press, 1983.

Dallavalle, Rita S. *Agricultural Research in the United States.* Washington, D.C.: Library of Congress, 1981.

Dupree, A. Hunter. *Science in the Federal Government: A History of Policies and Activities.* Cambridge, Mass.: Harvard University Press, 1957.

Hadwiger, Donald F. *The Politics of Agricultural Research.* Lincoln: University of Nebraska Press, 1982.

Harding, Thomas Swann. *Two Blades of Grass: A History of Scientific Development in the U.S. Department of Agriculture.* Norman: University of Oklahoma Press, 1947.

PERIODICALS

Blasé, Melvin G., and Paulsen, Arnold. "The Agricultural Experiment Station: An Institutional Development Perspective." *Agricultural Science Review,* 10, no. 2, Second Quarter 1972, 11–16.

Bonnen, James T. "The First 100 Years of the Department of Agriculture–Land-Grant College System." *Journal of Farm Economics,* 44, 1962, 1279–1294.

"Riddle of Life"

Memo

By: Max Delbrück

Date: August 1937

Source: Delbrück, Max. "Riddle of Life." Memorandum to Niels Bohr, Berlin, August 1937. Published as an Appendix to "A Physicist's Renewed Look at Biology—Twenty Years Later." Nobel lecture, December 10, 1969. Reprinted in Fischer, Ernst Peter, and Carol Lipson. *Thinking About Science: Max Delbrück and the Origins of Molecular Biology.* New York: W.W. Norton, 1988, 99–101. Available online at http://www.nobel.se/medicine/laureates/1969/Delbruck-lecture.html; website home page: http://www.nobel.se (accessed March 17, 2003).

About the Author: Max Delbrück (1906–1981) obtained a Ph.D. in Theoretical Physics at Göttingen University in 1930. Over the next several years, he worked with Niels Bohr in Copenhagen and Otto Hahn and Lise Meitner at the Kaiser Wilhelm Institute in his native Berlin. The Nazi persecution of Jewish scientists caused Delbrück to leave for the United States in 1937, where he spent two years at Cal Tech on a Rockefeller fellowship. Delbrück served as Professor of Physics at Vanderbilt University from 1939 to 1947, then returned to Cal Tech as a biology professor. His contributions to the emerging field of molecular biology were numerous, and earned him a Nobel Prize in Physiology and Medicine in 1969. ■

Introduction

In the early twentieth century, biologists had a great deal of knowledge about living things in their entirety, or with the larger structures, like organs and bones, that are found within them. However, their understanding of the molecules that living things are made up of was limited. Questions about the nature of viruses were one example of this. All life shares three characteristics: the metabolism of nutrients, the excretion of waste, and the ability to reproduce. The simplest example is a bacterium, a single cell with no nucleus in its center. One thinks of the bacteria that cause strep throat or pneumonia, but most bacteria are harmless to humans. A type of bacterium lives in the nodules of pea roots. It eats the gases in the soil and excretes as waste chemicals that the pea roots absorb as nutrients. These bacteria, as do all bacteria, reproduce by cell division. Each divides into two, producing a carbon copy of the original. One bacterium divides into two, two into four, four into eight, and so forth.

One should note that every organism need not exhibit the three characteristics of life in the same degree. A man with low sperm count, for example, may have trouble reproducing, but no one would doubt he is alive. The same applies to a Catholic priest. No one doubts he is alive because his vow of chastity prevents him from having children.

In contrast to these examples, a virus seems to inhabit a netherworld between life and nonlife. Outside a cell, a virus is inert. It does nothing and seems no more alive than a rock.

Inside a cell, the story is quite different. Suppose a virus enters a human through a cut. It will float through the blood until it latches onto the surface of a cell, riding piggyback. The cell will detect something foreign on it

Max Delbrück, a noted physicist and molecular biologist, receives the Nobel Prize in Physiology and Medicine in December 1969. **AP/WIDE WORLD PHOTOS. REPRODUCED BY PERMISSION.**

and bring it inside, apparently to learn what it is. Once inside, the virus "hijacks" the machinery of the cell, forcing it to make copies of the virus. Whether a virus takes in nutrients and excretes waste is open to question, but no one can doubt its ability to reproduce once inside a cell. There, a virus can make millions of copies of itself in hours.

Significance

Trained as a subatomic physicist, in the 1930s Max Delbrück became fascinated with the study of the physical and chemical processes underlying life. Viruses were one of the topics that interested him most. Delbrück knew that a virus inside a cell could reproduce. For him, the question was whether to credit the cell or the virus with this reproduction. If the cell guided the reproduction of a virus, Delbrück would conclude that it was not alive. If, on the other hand, a virus guided its reproduction within a cell, Delbrück would believe it to be alive.

Delbrück concluded that the steps leading to the manufacture of a virus were sufficient in number and complexity that a cell did not, and could not, manufacture a virus on its own. That is, a cell did not guide the reproduction of a virus. This conclusion left only a virus as the agent of its reproduction. Delbrück thus concluded that a virus is alive. He went beyond this conclusion to compare the reproduction of viruses to the reproduction of genes (long chains of large molecules that code for traits). Delbrück was right in this comparison, although it was not until the 1950s and 1960s that it was proved that viruses and genes have similar structures and copy themselves in much the same manner.

While Delbrück was specifically interested in viruses in this early inquiry, this and his other work had much broader implications. In his 1969 Nobel acceptance speech, Delbrück said, "Discussions of [new findings] . . . strengthened the notion that genes had a kind of stability similar to that of the molecules of chemistry. From the hindsight of our present knowledge one might consider this a trivial statement: what else could genes be but molecules? However, in the mid-1930s, this was not a trivial statement." By looking at life as a physical and chemical process, Delbrück helped to create the field that we now call molecular biology. Delbrück is sometimes referred to as the "Father of Molecular Biology." Since the 1930s, molecular biology has proved to be one of the great scientific breakthroughs of the twentieth century, responsible for enormous advances in our understanding of how living things function and in the creation of many new medical techniques and drugs.

Primary Source

"Riddle of Life"

SYNOPSIS: This memo gives an insight into some of Max Delbrück's earliest ideas about what would become molecular biology. In his 1969 Nobel lecture, he describes where and how he wrote the following memo: "To illustrate our state of mind at that time [mid-1930s] I will append to this lecture a memorandum on the "Riddle of Life," written to clarify my own thinking in the fall of 1937, just before leaving Germany to go to the United States. I found this note a few years ago among my papers. This memorandum would appear to be a summary of discussions at a little meeting in Copenhagen, arranged by Niels Bohr, to which Timofeeff-Ressovsky, H.J. Muller and I had travelled from Berlin. These discussions occurred very much under the impact of the W.M. Stanley findings reporting the crystallization of tobacco mosaic virus."

We inquire into the relevance of the recent results of virus research for a general assessment of the phenomena peculiar to life.

These recent results all agree in showing a remarkable uniformity in the behavior of individuals belonging to one species of virus in preparations employing physical or chemical treatments mild enough not to impair infective specificity. Such a collection of individuals migrates with uniform velocity in the electrophoresis apparatus. It crystallizes uniformly from solutions such that the specific infectivity is not altered by recrystallization, not even under conditions of extremely fractionated recrystallization. Elementary analysis gives reproducible results, such as might be expected for proteins, with perhaps the peculiarity that the phosphorus and sulfur contents appear to be abnormally small.

These results force us to the view that the viruses are things whose atomic constitution is as well defined as that of the large molecules of organic chemistry. True, with these latter we also cannot speak of unique spatial configurations, since most of the chemical bonds involve free rotation around the bond. We cannot even decide unambiguously which atoms do or do not belong to the molecule, since the degree of hydration and of dissociation depends not only on external conditions, but even when these are fixed, fluctuates statistically from molecule to molecule. Nevertheless, there can be no doubt that such large molecules constitute a legitimate generalization of the standard concept of the chemical molecule. The similarity between virus and molecule is particularly apparent from the fact that virus crystals can be stored indefinitely without losing either their physico-chemical or infectious properties.

Therefore we will view viruses as molecules.

If we now turn to that property of a virus which defines it as a living organism, namely, its ability to multiply within living plants, then we will ask ourselves first whether this accomplishment is that of the host, as a living organism, or whether the host is merely the provider and protector of the virus, offering it suitable nutrients under suitable physical and chemical conditions. In other words, we are asking whether we should view the injection of a virus as a stimulus which modifies the metabolism of the host in such a way as to produce the foreign virus protein instead of its own normal protein, or whether we should view the replication as an essentially autonomous accomplishment of the virus and the host as a nutrient medium which might be replaced by a suitably offered synthetic medium.

Now it appears to me, that upon close analysis the first view can be completely excluded. If we consider that the replication of the virus requires the accurate synthesis of an enormously complicated molecule which is unknown to the host, yet though not as to general type, in all the details of its pattern and therefore of the synthetic steps involved, and if we consider further what extraordinary production an organism puts on to perform in an orderly way the most minute oxidation or synthesis in all those cases that do not involve the copying of a particular pattern—setting aside serology, which is a thing by itself—then it seems impossible to assume that the enzyme system for the host could be modified in such a far-reaching way by the injection of a virus. There can be no doubt that the replication of a virus must take place with the most direct participation of the original pattern and even without the participation of any enzymes specifically produced for this purpose.

Therefore we will look on virus replication as an autonomous accomplishment of the virus, for the general discussion of which we can ignore the host.

We next ask whether we should view virus replication as a particularly pure case of replication or whether it is, from the point of view of genetics, a complex phenomenon. Here we must first point out that with higher animals and plants which reproduce bisexually replication is certainly a very complex phenomenon. This has been shown in a thousand details by genetics, based on Mendel's laws and on modern cytology, and must be so, in order to arrive at any kind of order for the infinitely varied details of inheritance. Specifically, the close cytological analysis of the details of meiosis (reduction division) has shown that it is a specialization of the simpler mitotic division. It can easily be shown that the teleological point of this specialization lies in the possibility of trying out new hereditary factors in ever-new combinations with genes already present, and thus to increase enormously the diversity of the genotypes present at any one time, in spite of low mutation rates.

However, even the simpler mitotic cell division cannot be viewed as a pure case. If we look first at somatic divisions of high animals and plants, then we find here that an originally simple process has been modified in the most various ways to adapt it to diverse purposes of form and function, such that one cannot speak of an undifferentiated replication. The ability to differentiate is certainly a highly important step in the transition from the protists to the multicellular organisms, but it can probably be related in a natural way to the general property of protists that they can adapt themselves to their environment and change phenotypically without changing genotypically. This phenotypic variability implies that with simple algae like Chlorella we can speak of simple replication only so long as the physical conditions are kept constant. If they are not kept constant, then, strictly speaking, we can only talk of a replication of the genomes which are embedded in a more or less well-nourished, more or less mistreated, specific protoplasma, and which, in extreme cases, may even replicate without cell division.

There can be no doubt, further, that the replication of the genome in its turn is a highly complex affair, susceptible to perturbation in its details without impairing the replication of pieces of chromosomes or of genes. Certainly the crucial element in cell replication lies in the coordination of the replication of a whole set of genes with the division of the cell. With equal certainty this coordination is not a primitive phenomenon. Rather it requires that particular modification of a simple replication system which accomplishes constancy of supply of its own nutrient. By this modification it initiates the chain of development which until now has been subsumed under the title "life."

In view of what has been said, we want to look upon the replication of viruses as a particular form of a primitive replication of genes, the segregation of which from the nourishment supplied by the host should in principle be possible. In this sense, one should view replication not as complementary to atomic physics but as a particular trick of organic chemistry.

Such a view would mean a great simplification of the question of the origin of the many highly complicated and specific molecules found in every organism in varying quantities and indispensable for carrying out its most elementary metabolism. One would assume that these, too, can replicate autonomously and that their replication is tied only loosely to the replication of the cell. It is clear that such a view in connection with the usual arguments of the theory of natural selection would let us understand the enormous variety and complexity of these molecules, which from a purely chemical point of view appears so exaggerated.

Further Resources

BOOKS

Cairns, John, et al., eds. *Phage and the Origins of Molecular Biology.* Cold Spring Harbor, N.Y.: Cold Spring Harbor Laboratory Press, 1992.

Delbrück, Max. *Mind From Matter? An Essay on Evolutionary Epistemology.* Gunther Stent et al., eds. Palo Alto, Calif.: Blackwell Scientific, 1986.

Fisher, Ernest Peter, and Carol Lipson. *Thinking About Science: Max Delbrück and the Origins of Molecular Biology.* New York: Norton, 1988.

PERIODICALS

Delbrück, Max. "A Physicist Looks at Biology." *Transactions of the Connecticut Academy of Science,* 38, 1949, 173–190.

Stanley, W.M. "Isolation of a Crystalline Protein Possessing the Properties of Tobacco Mosaic Virus." *Science,* 81, no. 2113, 1935.

WEBSITES

Cal Tech Archives: Max Delbrück (1906–1981). Available online at http://www.cshl.org/public/History/scientists/Delbruck.html (accessed October 15, 2002).

Carmosino, Penni. "From Darwin to the Human Genome Project: Delbrück's Contributions in Context." Available online at http://www.csuchico.edu/anth/CASP/Carmosino_P.html (accessed October 15, 2002).

Table of Historical Events in Genetics and Molecular Biology. Available online at http://www.cs.stedwards.edu/~kswank/HistoryTable.html; website home page: http://www.cs.stedwards.edu/~kswank/cancerpage1.html (accessed October 15, 2002).

Winfree, A.T. "Book Review: 'Mind From Matter? Essay on Evolutionary Epistemology,' by Max Delbrück." *Bulletin of Mathematical Biology* 50, no. 2, 1988, 193–207. Available online at http://cochise.biosci.arizona.edu/~art/Delbruck.pdf (accessed October 15, 2002).

The Story of the Winged-S

Autobiography

By: Igor Sikorsky

Date: October 1938

Source: Sikorsky, Igor. *The Story of the Winged-S: With New Material on the Latest Development of the Helicopter.* 5th ed. New York: Dodd, Mead and Company, 1938, 24–26.

About the Author: Igor Sikorsky (1889–1972) was born in Kiev, Russia. He attended the Naval War College in St. Petersburg, but his interested turned to aviation. Sikorsky designed aircraft in Russia, including the first-ever four-engine plane, until the Bolshevik Revolution of 1917. He then emigrated to the United States. In 1923, he and other Russian emigrants formed the Sikorsky Aero Engineering Company. This firm designed a number of fixed-wing aircraft, but it was not until Sikorsky developed the first practical helicopter in 1939 that it enjoyed real success. ■

Introduction

As early as 400 C.E. the Chinese developed a prototype of the helicopter by designing a kite with a rotary blade for vertical lift. Medieval Europeans developed toy helicopters in which one pulled a string to spin the blade. In the fifteenth century Leonardo da Vinci drew diagrams of a helicopter with a spiral airscrew for lift.

The twentieth century witnessed the transition from toy to real helicopters. In September 1907 the French inventors Louis and Jacques Breguet built a helicopter with a 45-horsepower engine that reached an altitude of two

Igor Sikorsky handles the controls of one of his helicopters. **AP/WIDE WORLD PHOTOS. REPRODUCED BY PERMISSION.**

feet. Two months later French inventor and bicycle maker Paul Cornu built a helicopter with a 24-horsepower engine that reached an altitude of one foot, remaining aloft for 20 seconds.

Less successful was the Russian inventor Igor Sikorsky who designed a helicopter in 1909 and a second in 1910, but failed to get either aloft. He concluded that he did not have the technical knowledge to build a working helicopter and shelved the idea until the 1930s.

In 1912 the Danish inventor Jacob Ellehammer made a series of short helicopter flights, and in 1922 the U.S. Army Air Corp tested a helicopter that remained aloft for two minutes. That year the American inventors Emile and Henry Berliner built a helicopter that rose vertically and flew horizontally once aloft. This was an important achievement because many helicopters could only rise and descend vertically without the ability to fly horizontally. In 1924 the French inventor Etienne Oehmichen set a distance record by flying a kilometer. In 1936 German engineers built the most advanced helicopter of the day. This machine reached an altitude of 11,243 feet and flew 143 miles in 1938.

Significance

Sikorsky, who had come to the United States in 1919, learned from these successes and determined to surpass them. In 1939 he built his first successful helicopter and flew a modification of it in 1941 for a record one hour and 32 minutes. In this excerpt Sikorsky compared the designing of a helicopter to the creative inspiration of art and poetry. Both require the free play of the imagination and an innovative spirit. But Sikorsky did not equate designing a helicopter with writing a poem. A poem may have aesthetic appeal, but it will have no practical application. The inventor, however, concerns himself solely with practical matters. Because this is so, he must stick close to facts and "calculated figures."

Helicopters are useful because unlike fixed-wing aircraft they do not have to keep moving forward in order to stay aloft. Since a helicopter can stop in mid-air, and move up, down, or sideways without turning, it can interact more easily with people and things on the ground than fixed-wing aircraft. Sikorsky predicted that the helicopter's principal value would be in the rescue of people caught in fires and floods and estimated that the helicopter saved more than 50,000 lives during the 1940s. The helicopter had broader use than Sikorsky had forseen. After World War II (1939–45), helicopters were used to fight fires and crime, spray crops with insecticides and herbicides, airlift patients to hospitals, report on news and traffic, and to carry mail. In addition to these civilian uses, helicopters are used in the military to transport soldiers into battle, to scout the forces of an enemy, and to attack from the air.

Sikorsky typified the success of immigrants to the U.S. in science and technology. Albert Michelson, America's first Nobel laureate in physics, was an immigrant as were Nicola Tesla and the Nobel laureates Enrico Fermi and Albert Einstein. Sikorsky and these others demonstrated that the United States was a land of opportunity for immigrants talented in science and technology.

Primary Source

The Story of the Winged-S [excerpt]

SYNOPSIS: In this excerpt Sikorsky describes his early work on helicopters in 1909 while still a student. He was one of many people interested in flight at that time who tried and failed to build useful, working helicopters. Unlike these others, however, Sikorsky persisted in his interest and experimentation until he developed the first workable helicopter in 1939.

The First Helicopter

The four months spent in Paris in the cradle of European aviation proved to be very helpful. In addition to the engine, materials, books and magazines, I brought back a good store of information. I had obtained valuable experience from the few successful attempts and the numerous failures that I had seen. However, I learned very little about the flying machine itself. I saw airplanes and I, myself, was working on a helicopter, and I got hold of some fundamental ideas on methods of creative development work in a new branch of engineering, where reliable information was scarce. This being the case, it was necessary to rely on intuition, which at an early period is often the major source of information in inventive engineering work. Intuition or inspiration, which guides an inventor toward achieving technical possibilities that are not yet known, are liable to evolve into day-dreaming, in which case the work has a good chance of becoming a failure. Therefore, while some part of inventive activities may well be compared to the work of an artist or even a poet, yet to achieve his purpose, the pioneer designer must keep all his ideas under strict control and must reduce them as much as possible to proven facts and measured or calculated figures, so that every idea will be verified no matter how excellent and correct it may appear. Another important fact learned was the necessity to design the new flying machine flexibly, so as to make corrections and changes easily, since difficulties and troubles in a new machine may develop where they are least expected.

At the beginning of May, 1909, not yet twenty years old, with a few ideas, no experience, some caution and, of course, with plenty of enthusiasm, I started the construction of my first flying machine. At that time, I had no mechanics or workmen to assist me. I had brought back from Paris the transmission and shafts which were built there in accordance with my drawings. I ordered other parts and materials from Kiev and did all the assembly work myself. It was really a wonderful feeling to see how the strange looking machine which I had been dreaming and thinking about was gradually taking shape in one of the rooms in our house which had been transformed into a shop.

The helicopter had a wooden frame similar to a large rectangular box, with a 25 horsepower Anzani engine on one side and the proposed seat or platform for the operator on the other. In the center of the frame was the transmission box. A large wooden pulley was connected by a four-inch-wide belt to a smaller pulley on the motor. Two concentric vertical tubular shafts were connected with the transmission box and were guided by an upper bearing at the top of the frame. On each of the shafts there was mounted a two-bladed lifting propeller, the upper one having a diameter of about fifteen feet, and the lower one sixteen and a half feet. They rotated in opposite directions at the rate of 160 r.p.m. The blades were supported by piano wires which were connected to two rings fixed to each shaft above and below each propeller. By changing the length of the wires by the use of turnbuckles, it was possible to adjust the pitch of the lifting propellers. On the basis of results obtained with small models, I intended to produce a forward motion and to regulate the speed by inclining the machine forward. This I expected to obtain by the use of control surfaces that were to be placed below the outer part of the lifting propellers. I intended to adjust them so as to obtain the desired results from the air pressure created by the combined action of the slipstream and of the forward motion. Control surfaces were not built for this machine because it appeared desirable first to make a test of the proper operation of all mechanisms and to check the lifting capacity.

During the month of July, the helicopter was completed and the tests were started. Various minor troubles developed which required some adjustments and changes. At first, it became necessary to fix the transmission because the belt kept slipping. When this was adjusted and I could increase somewhat the power transmitted to the propellers, the main shafts started to shake so badly that it was immediately necessary to slow down the engine. The propeller blades were then dismounted and carefully adjusted for weight, and reassembled. The machine was again tested and still proved to be unsatisfactory.

Further Resources

BOOKS

Delear, Frank J. *Igor Sikorsky: His Three Careers in Aviation.* New York: Dodd, Mead, 1976.

WEBSITES

American Institute of Aeronautics and Astronautics, Inc. "History of Flight: Pioneer Profiles: Igor Sikorsky." Available online at http://www.flight100.org/history/sikorsky.html; website home page: http://www.flight100.org/index.cfm (accessed Octobe 16, 2002).

The Helicopter and Igor Sikorsky. Available online at http://inventors.about.com/library/inventors/blhelicoptor.htm (accessed October 16, 2002).

Russian Aviation Page. "Early Sikorsky Aircraft Built in Russia." Available online at http://aeroweb.lucia.it/~agretch/Features/EarlySikorsky.html; website home page: http://aeroweb.lucia.it/~agretch/RAP.html (accessed October 16, 2002).

Sikorsky Archives. Available online at http://www.sikorskyarchives.com/ (accessed October 16, 2002).

Sikorsky's Helicopters: http://www.loc.gov/exhibits/treasures/trr081.html; website home page: http://www.loc.gov/exhibits/treasures/ (accessed October 16, 2002)

Letter to President Franklin Delano Roosevelt

Letter

By: Albert Einstein

Date: August 2, 1939

Source: Einstein, Albert. Letter to President Franklin Delano Roosevelt, August 2, 1939. Albert Einstein Archives. The Jewish National and University Library. Hebrew University, Jerusalem, Israel. Available online at http://www.aip.org/history/einstein/nuclear1.htm; website home page: http://www.aip.org (accessed October 16, 2002).

About the Author: Albert Einstein (1879–1955) was born in Ulm, Germany. Although interested in mathematics, Einstein did not do well in the rigid German school system. His family moved to Berne, Switzerland, where he found employment as an assistant patents clerk. It was during his spare time at this job that he jotted down the ideas that would be the basis for his revolutionary theories, including his theories of relativity, which led to his winning the Nobel Prize in 1921. The Nazi persecutions of Jewish scientists caused Einstein to flee to the United States in 1933, where he became Professor of Theoretical Physics at Princeton University. He held that position until 1945, and spent his last years in semi-retirement at Princeton. ■

Introduction

In 1905, Albert Einstein announced that mass and energy are not separate quantities as physicists had thought. Instead, they could be converted from one to the other according to the famous equation: energy equals mass times the speed of light squared. Because the speed of light squared equals 90 million billion meters per second squared, a tiny mass would generate enormous energy. The mass of an atom is in the nucleus, and physicists could convert it into energy either by splitting a nucleus (fission) or by causing nuclei to bond together (fusion). This nuclear energy could be used to generate electricity (as it does today in nuclear power plants). It could also generate an explosion more powerful than thousands of tons of TNT.

In 1939, the German physicist Otto Hahn and his Austrian colleague Lise Meitner bombarded uranium atoms with neutrons (particles in the nucleus of an atom equal in mass to a proton but neutral in charge), splitting their nuclei to release energy as Einstein's equation predicted. Hahn and Meitner's work could hardly have come at a more ominous moment. Since assuming power in 1933, Adolf Hitler had withdrawn Germany from the League of Nations, rearmed at breakneck speed, and occupied the Rhineland, Austria, and Czechoslovakia. That Hitler would attempt to build an atomic bomb became clear when, after occupying Czechoslovakia in 1939, he stopped selling uranium from its mines.

American physicists, many of them refugees from Europe, were quick to recognize the danger of a nuclear-armed Germany. Nobel laureate Enrico Fermi, who had fled fascist Italy, was among the first to sense danger. By the summer of 1939 he persuaded the Hungarian physicist and refugee Leo Szilard that the United States needed to build an atomic bomb before Germany did. But how would they convince the federal government to mount an immediate and massive effort to build an atomic bomb?

The site of the first atomic bomb testing is near Alamogordo, New Mexico. © CORBIS. REPRODUCED BY PERMISSION.

Significance

Fermi and Szilard turned to Einstein, sure that his prestige would get the attention of President Franklin D. Roosevelt (served 1933–1945). Einstein was a pacifist by nature, but he was also deeply disturbed by the thought of Adolf Hitler having unchallenged might in the form of atomic weapons. He agreed to help, and sent a letter (that many historians believe Szilard actually wrote) to Roosevelt alerting him to the possible military uses of atomic energy, and to the frightening possibility of a Nazi Germany armed with such weapons. He urged Roosevelt to establish and fund a program in hopes of beating Germany to a uranium bomb.

Roosevelt's response was hardly vigorous. He formed a committee to study the matter and secured for it a Congressional appropriation of $6,000. In this small act lay the beginning of the American effort to build an atomic bomb. This effort grew enormously in size and cost in the years that followed, and became known as the Manhattan Project. The Project succeeded: by July 1945 U.S. physicists had built three bombs, one out of uranium and two from the element plutonium, synthesized for the first time as part of the project. One plutonium bomb was successfully tested in the New Mexico desert. The other two bombs were dropped on Hiroshima and Nagasaki, Japan, prompting Japan to surrender and end World War II.

The Manhattan Project, born of Einstein's 1939 letter to Roosevelt, demonstrated the close relationship between the federal government and American science, a relationship that sank roots in the eighteenth century. Both George Washington and Thomas Jefferson urged Congress to fund science, and Congress responded in the nineteenth century by funding the U.S. Geological Survey and the U.S. Department of Agriculture. Einstein's letter thus lies within a long tradition of cooperation between the federal government and science. Its significance lies less in establishing a new program, which the Manhattan Project was, than in affirming a long partnership between government and science, a partnership that has given Americans antibiotics, vitamins, vaccines, and high-yielding crops.

Primary Source

Letter to President Franklin Delano Roosevelt

SYNOPSIS: On August 2, 1939, Einstein sent this letter to President Roosevelt, alerting him to the fact that physicists had recently discovered that it was possible to create weapons of enormous power out of uranium. Einstein cited the fact that Germany had stopped selling uranium from Czechoslovakian mines as evidence that Hitler was intent upon building these weapons. He urged Roosevelt to establish and fund a program in hopes of beating Nazi Germany to a uranium bomb.

Albert Einstein
Old Grove Rd.
Nassau Point
Peconic, Long Island

August 2nd, 1939

F.D. Roosevelt
President of the United States,
White House
Washington, D.C.

Sir:

Some recent work by E. Fermi and L. Szilard, which has been communicated to me in manuscript, leads me to expect that the element uranium may be turned into a new and important source of energy in the immediate future. Certain aspects of the situation which has arisen seem to call for watchfulness and, if necessary, quick action on the part of the Administration. I believe therefore that it is my duty to bring to your attention the following facts and recommendations:

An atomic bomb blast, as viewed from ground level. **NATIONAL ARCHIVES AND RECORDS ADMINISTRATION.**

In the course of the last four months it has been made probable—through the work of Joliot in France as well as Fermi and Szilard in America—that it may become possible to set up a nuclear chain reaction in a large mass of uranium, by which vast amounts of power and large quantities of new radium-like elements would be generated. Now it appears almost certain that this could be achieved in the immediate future.

This new phenomenon would also lead to the construction of bombs, and it is conceivable—though much less certain—that extremely powerful bombs of a new type may thus be constructed. A single bomb of this type, carried by boat and exploded in a port, might very well destroy the whole port together with some of the surrounding territory. However, such bombs might very well prove to be too heavy for transportation by air.

The United States has only very poor ores of uranium in moderate quantities. There is some good ore in Canada and the former Czechoslovakia while the most important source of uranium is Belgian Congo.

In view of the situation you may think it desirable to have more permanent contact maintained between the Administration and the group of physicists working on chain reactions in America. One possible way of achieving this might be for you to entrust with this task a person who has your confidence and who could perhaps serve in an inofficial capacity. His task might comprise the following:

a. to approach Government Departments, keep them informed of the further development, and put forward recommendations for Government action, giving particular attention to the problem of securing a supply of uranium ore for the United States;

b. to speed up the experimental work, which is at present being carried on within the limits of the budgets of University laboratories, by providing funds, if such funds be required, through his contacts with private persons who are willing to make contributions for this cause, and perhaps also by obtaining the cooperation of industrial laboratories which have the necessary equipment.

I understand that Germany has actually stopped the sale of uranium from the Czechoslovakian mines which she has taken over. That she should have taken such early action might perhaps be understood on the ground that the son of the German Under-Secretary of State, von Weizsäcker, is attached to the Kaiser-Wilhelm-Institut in Berlin where some of the American work on uranium is now being repeated.

Yours very truly,
(Albert Einstein)

Further Resources

BOOKS

Clark, Ronald W. *Einstein: The Life and Times.* New York: Wings Books, 1995.

Einstein, Albert. "The Fundamental Ideas and Problems of the Theory of Relativity." Nobel Award Address, 1921. In *The World of Physics,* vol.2, ed. Jefferson H. Weaver. New York: Simon and Schuster, 1987, 213–222.

———. *Ideas and Opinions,* 3rd ed. New York: Crown, 1995.

———. *Relativity: The Special and General Theory.* New York: Routledge, 1961.

———. *Sidelights on Relativity.* New York: Dover, 1983.

———. *The World As I See It.* New York: Covici-Friede Publishers, 1934.

Einstein, Albert, and Leopold Infeld. *The Evolution of Physics.* New York: Simon & Schuster, 1961.

PERIODICALS

Einstein, Albert. "Atomic War or Peace." *Atlantic Monthly,* 180, no. 5, November 1945, 29–32.

———. " How I Created the Theory of Relativity." *Physics Today,* 35, no. 8, August 1982, 45–47.

WEBSITES

American Institute of Physics, Center for the History of Physics. Einstein—Image and Impact. Available online at http://www.aip.org/history/einstein/ (accessed October 16, 2002).

Atomic Bomb: Decision. Documents on the Decision to Use Atomic Bombs on the Cities of Hiroshima and Nagasaki. Available online at http://www.dannen.com/decision/index.html (accessed October 16, 2002).

"History of the Atomic Bomb." Available online at http://inventors.about.com/library/weekly/aa050300ahtm (accessed October 16, 2002).

Leo Szilard Online. Available online at http://www.dannen.com/szilard.html (accessed October 16, 2002).

"The Struggles to Find the Ninth Planet"

Memoir

By: Clyde W. Tombaugh

Date: Unknown

Source: Tombaugh, Clyde W. "The Struggles to Find the Ninth Planet." NASA Jet Propulsion Laboratory (JPL) Outer Planets Solar Probe Project. Available online at http://www.jpl.nasa.gov/ice_fire/9thplant.htm; website home page: http://www.jpl.nasa.gov (accessed October 15, 2002).

About the Author: Clyde Tombaugh (1906–1997) attended high school in his native Streator, Illinois. His amateur astronomy work won him a place at the Lowell Observatory in Flagstaff, Arizona, where he discovered Pluto in 1930. He received his M.S. in physics in 1938 from the University of Kansas, while continuing to work full-time at the Lowell Observatory. During World War II (1939–1945), he was a navigation instructor for the U.S. Navy at Arizona State University. From 1955 until 1973, Tombaugh taught at New Mexico State University, where he founded that school's astronomy program. ■

Introduction

In the sixteenth century, Nicholas Copernicus announced that Earth was a planet, bringing the number of planets to six. (In sequence from the sun, they are Mercury, Venus, Earth, Mars, Jupiter, and Saturn.) Until the eighteenth century, astronomers believed these six planets were the only ones in our solar system.

In the 1770s, astronomers Johann Bode and Johann Daniel Titius independently derived what came to be known as the Titius-Bode Law. They tripled each number in the series of integers 0, 1, 2, 4, 8, 16, 32, and so on, added 4 to the product, and divided the sum by 10. The calculations gave the average distance of each planet from the sun in astronomical units. An astronomical unit represents the average distance between the earth and sun: approximately 93 million miles.

The crucial point is that one could expand the series of integers beyond six numbers, implying that the solar system contained more than six planets. The integer 64, which would follow 32 in the above series, yields 19.6 astronomical units. That is, if a planet existed beyond Saturn, it should be 19.6 times more distant from the sun than is the earth.

In 1781, British astronomer William Herschel discovered Uranus at 19.3 astronomical units, very close to the Titius-Bode prediction. This discovery led astronomers to seek planets beyond Uranus at the distance predicted by the Titius-Bode Law. The search was intense, because Uranus's orbit deviated from what astronomers expected, suggesting that the gravitational attraction from an unknown planet must pull Uranus from its path. In 1846, French astronomer U.J.J. LeVerrier discovered Neptune, though it was at 30.2 astronomical units rather than the 38.8 predicted by the Titius-Bode Law.

Significance

Like Uranus, Neptune's orbit was imperfect, and if a ninth planet existed, the Titius-Bode Law would put it

Clyde Tombaugh, the discoverer of Pluto, stands in 1930 with a telescope he built. © BETTMANN/CORBIS. REPRODUCED BY PERMISSION.

at either 38.8 astronomical units, assuming that Neptune was out of place, or at 77.2 astronomical units. The American astronomer Percival Lowell led the search for the ninth planet from the Lowell Observatory at Flagstaff, Arizona, but he died in 1916 without finding it. Instead, Clyde Tombaugh discovered Pluto, the first two letters of which commemorate Percival Lowell, in 1930.

Tombaugh's discovery demonstrated America's rise to prominence in astronomy. By 1930, the United States had well-funded observatories with huge telescopes, and American astronomers had proved that they could excel at basic research (research that generated knowledge for its own sake rather than for a practical purpose). America's success in astronomy was a surprising and important development in a nation that had prized applied research (research that leads to practical knowledge) above basic research since its founding in the eighteenth century.

Primary Source

"The Struggles to Find the Ninth Planet" [excerpt]

SYNOPSIS: Tombaugh makes clear in this excerpt that much of science is long, tedious work. He describes the hours he spent sweeping the heavens with his telescope and the additional hours of scrutinizing the photographs he took with his telescope. Only this perseverance, he says, allowed him to discover Pluto.

Many papers have been written and published on the triumphal detection and discovery of Pluto. As the sole survivor of the Lowell Observatory staff in that frustrating year of 1929, I thought that it might be of some interest to relate the "down mood" and emotions experienced by those persons involved. I shall give a little history to illustrate the setting and circumstances. . . .

I had just come upstairs from the darkroom, when I saw V. M. Slipher removing the last pair from the Blink-Comparator. "Did you find Planet X?" I asked. In a resigned voice, he said, "No, we didn't find anything." He appeared to be very sad—as if all hope had fled. Naturally, he wanted to be the one to find Planet X. He had met defeat, and he knew it. Perhaps, Planet X was in some other region of the Zodiac. Because of their other work, no one of the senior staff could devote much time to the laborious task of blinking. I have often wondered what they expected to see on plates taken so far from 'opposition'. By this time, all the asteroids in Gemini would be moving eastward again after a brief temporary stationary, even Pluto just a little past its western stationary point.

I began to realize that Slipher was under pressure. Now they had the super-camera, they had better find Planet X.

By the middle of June, one hundred big plates had accumulated, but only a few pairs had been blinked. I was exhausted from a heavy 2-week run at the 13-inch telescope, when V. M. Slipher came to my office and said they wanted me to 'blink' the plates. I shuddered at the prospect of this grim assignment. After blinking two pairs, I realized that I had a dilemma. How was I to distinguish an asteroid near its stationary point from Planet X?

During the Flagstaff rainy season, I studied the changing positions of Uranus and Neptune from the 1928 and 1929 American Ephemeris. The advantage of taking the plates at opposition became obvious. Also, that for a given region in the Zodiac, there was only a one month observing window.

In September 1929, I started taking plates in Pisces, and blinked them in the following full moon period. I encountered a few false planet suspects of the 16th and 17th magnitude on almost every pair of plates. These were beyond the reach of the 5-inch companion camera. These had to be checked with a third plate taken on a third date. Taking three plates had the additional advantage in that one could select the best matched pair for blinking. Each succeeding month, I marched 30 degrees eastward to keep up with the opposition region. Several times during the Fall of 1929, V. M. Slipher would come to the Blinker-room to inquire if I was finding anything, (namely Planet X). As the Milky Way was approached in Taurus, the great number of star-images slowed down the blinking.

In January 1930, I re-photographed Gemini. On the crystal clear night of 21 January, I took the first plate of the Delta Geminorum region. Soon after I started the exposure, a strong Northeast wind came up, and the 3rd magnitude guide star was darting about wildly, and swelled up to over 2 times the angular diameter of Jupiter—completely fading away at times. I never saw worst seeing in my life before or since. I continued the exposure until the end of the hour and quit for the night. The images were badly swollen, but showed Pluto's image in the right place—consistent with the shift on the 23 and 29 January plates, which I detected at about 4:00 P.M. Mountain Time on 18 February 1930.

The following years, 1931–1932, I photographed two strips around the sky, one on each side of the Zodiac. After learning of Pluto's 17 degree inclination, it seemed best to search thru a wider area. I always calculated the necessary overlap when there was a gap in time between adjacent plate regions. I continued the search at greater distances from the Zodiac until 1943 when World War II engaged my teaching Navigation in a Navy V-12 school, set up on the Arizona State College at Flagstaff.

1929 was a very hectic year compared to the triumphant year of the discovery of Pluto in 1930.

■ ■ ■

One last shadow: After the discovery, Mrs. Lowell wanted to name the new planet "Lowell". She soon changed her mind and wanted the planet named "Constance". This went over like a lead balloon at the observatory, and V. M. Slipher chose to ignore this delicate matter. Instead of Plutonium, you all might have known it as "Constancium"!

Further Resources

BOOKS

Hoyt, William Graves. *Planets X and Pluto.* Tucson: University of Arizona Press, 1981.

Levy, David H. *Clyde Tombaugh: Discoverer of Planet Pluto.* Tucson: University of Arizona Press, 1991.

Tombaugh, Clyde. "The Discovery of Pluto." In *Source Book in Astronomy, 1900–1950.* Harlow Shapley, ed. Cambridge, Mass: Harvard University Press, 1960.

Tombaugh, Clyde, and Patrick Moore. *Out of the Darkness: The Planet Pluto.* Harrisburg, Pa.: Stackpole, 1980.

PERIODICALS

Tombaugh, Clyde. "Reminiscences on the Discovery of Pluto." *Sky & Telescope* 19, no. 5, March 1960, 264–270.

WEBSITES

"Clyde Tombaugh, Ph.D.: Interview, October 26, 1991." Academy of Achievement. Available online at http://www.achievement.org/autodoc/page/tom0int-1; website home page: http://www.achievement.org (accessed October 15, 2002).

NASA-JPL Outer Planets/Solar Probe Project. Available online at http://www.jpl.nasa.gov/ice_fire; website home page: http://www.jpl.nasa.gov (accessed October 15, 2002).

Whittle's Turbojet Engine

Photographs

By: Frank Whittle

Date: 1941

Source: Midland Air Museum. "The Jet Engine." Available online at http://www.midlandairmuseum.org.uk/thejet.html (accessed October 15, 2002).

About the Inventor: Frank Whittle (1907–1996) was born in Earlsdon, England. The son of a mechanic, he was inspired to join the Royal Air Force (RAF) because of a toy airplane his father made for him. In 1928 Whittle joined a fighter squadron, and remained with the RAF until 1948. Afterward, he continued devising improvements to gas turbines and served as adviser to the aviation industry. He moved to the United States in 1976, and became a research professor at the U.S. Naval Academy. ■

Introduction

Early aircraft were much slower than those used today. At first, this was due to the relatively weak engines

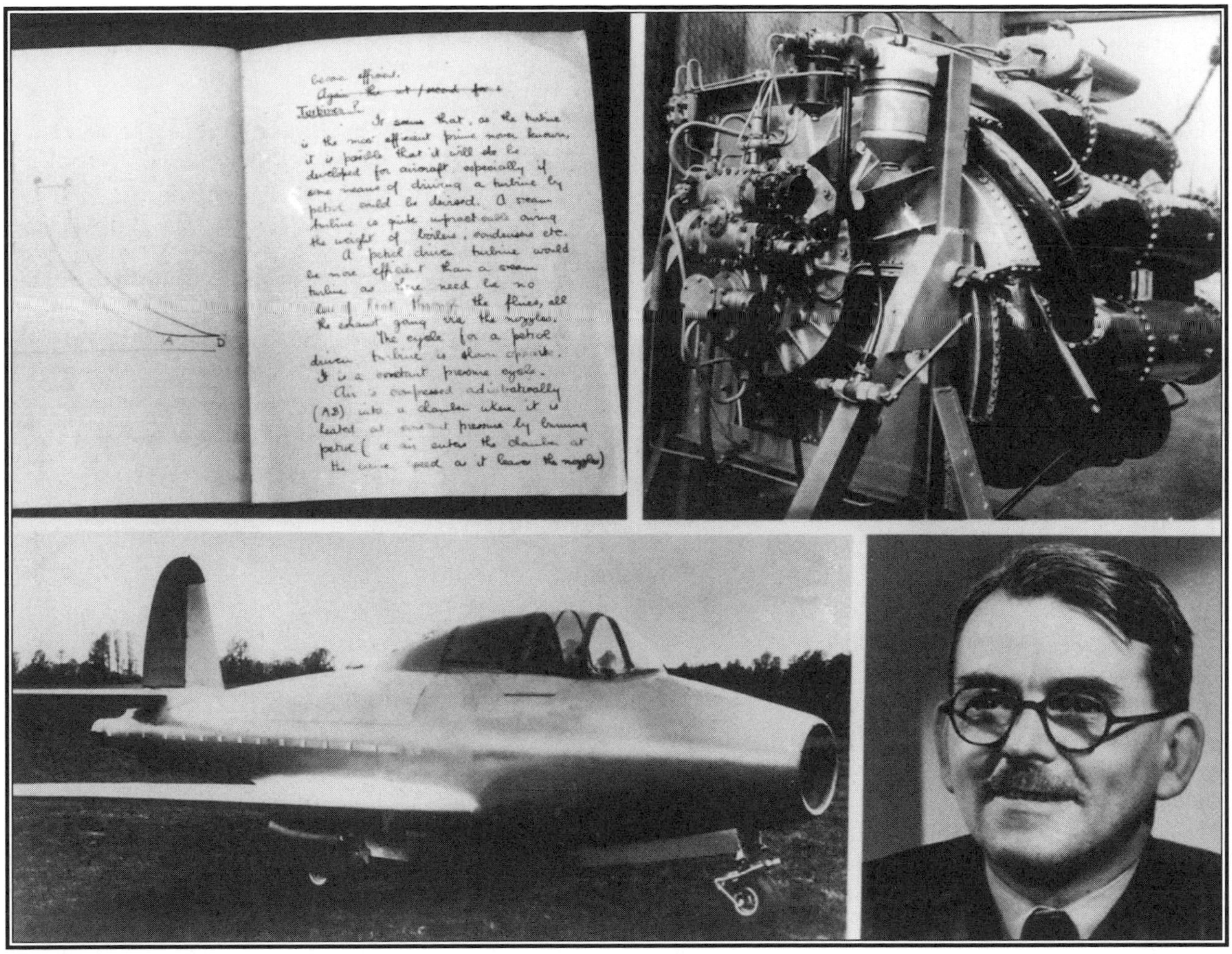

Primary Source

Sir Frank Whittle's First Jet Aircraft

SYNOPSIS: These four photos show the progressive development of Sir Frank Whittle's turbojet engine. On the top left is Whittle's 1928 notebook, where he laid out the concepts of his engine. An engine built to Whittle's design in the 1930s, a WIX engine, is shown on the top right. The Gloster E28/39 on the bottom left was the first airplane to fly with the WIX jet engine, in 1941. The last photo is of Sir Frank Whittle in 1949. AP/WIDE WORLD PHOTOS. REPRODUCED BY PERMISSION.

driving their propellers and their boxy shapes. During the 1920s more powerful engines and a more streamlined fuselage and wings increased the top speed of aircraft, but exposed a new problem. As an airplane approaches the speed of sound (also called Mach 1, 745 miles per hour at sea level and decreasing to 660 miles per hour at 36,000 feet) drag increases and air stops behaving like a fluid through which a plane travels and becomes instead a shock wave, destabilizing the plane. The spin of propellers gives them greater velocity than the rest of the plane, subjecting them to particularly strong shock waves and making the plane even more unstable. Propeller-driven planes therefore had an upper limit on their speed that was well below Mach 1.

The limit on speed of a propeller-driven plane might not have been troublesome had planes filled only a civilian role, but their military use made speed much more important. The emphasis on mobility and quick-strike capability led military leaders to demand the construction of the fastest possible aircraft.

Significance

The answer to the problem of higher speeds was to come up with a method of flying that did not rely on propellers. In 1928 Frank Whittle, a Royal Air Force (RAF) College cadet in Cranwell, England, designed a gas turbine to replace the propeller-driven engine, and the next year he designed a turbojet. A turbojet is shaped like a tube that is wider in its middle than at its front and back. Air is sucked in through the front of the engine and compressed to a high pressure, then released into a combustion chamber in the middle of the engine. Fuel is mixed with the air here and ignited. This causes the compressed air, already trying to expand, to blast out of the rear of the engine with great force, pushing the aircraft forward while also turning a small turbine that generates power for the compressor to continue the process of pulling in air.

Whittle patented his turbojet in 1930, but in the difficult economic times of the Great Depression he was unable to find a manufacturer. The RAF saw promise in Whittle's work, however, and sent him to Cambridge where he continued his education and refined his designs. Finally, in 1936, Whittle secured financial backing and was able to produce a working engine, which he tested on the ground in 1937. Work then proceeded on an actual jet-powered aircraft. The Gloster E 28/39 became the first plane to fly using Whittle's engine on May 15, 1941.

Although Whittle was the first man to design a workable turbojet engine, his design was not the first to actually fly. Independently of Whittle, three German engineers designed jet engines between 1933 and 1937. Hans-Joachim Pabst von Ohain's engine, very similar in design to Whittle's, was the first ever used in flight in 1939, two years before Whittle.

It took several years for jet aircraft to make the transition from experimental test aircraft to active use, but by the end of World War II in 1945 both sides were using small numbers of jet-powered aircraft, with the Americans and British using Whittle's designs. By 1949 they had been introduced for commercial service as well. The Korean War (1950-1953) saw widespread use of jet aircraft in combat. In the 20 years that followed, the turbojet engine, first designed by Frank Whittle, came to dominate military and civilian air travel.

Further Resources

BOOKS

Golley, John & Bill Gunston. *Genesis of the Jet: Frank Whittle and the Invention of the Jet Engine.* Shrewsbury, England: Airlife Publishing, 1996.

Golley, John (in association with Sir Frank Whittle). *Whittle: The True Story.* (Technical Editor Bill Gunston). Shrewsbury, England: Airlife Publishing, 1987.

Jones, Glyn. *The Jet Pioneers: The Birth of Jet-Powered Flight.* London: Methuen, 1989.

Rowland, John. *The Jet Man: The Story of Sir Frank Whittle.* London: Lutterworth Press, 1967.

Whittle, Sir Frank. *Gas Turbine Aero-Thermodynamics: With Special Reference to Aircraft Propulsion.* New York: Pergamon Press, 1981.

———. *Jet: The Story of a Pioneer.* London: Muller, 1953.

WEBSITES

BBC Horizon. "Genius of the Jet." Available online at http://www.bbc.co.uk/horizon/jetgenie.shtml; website home page: http://www.bbc.co.uk/ (accessed October 15, 2002).

CWN. "Sir Frank Whittle: Jet Engine Inventor." http://www.cwn.org.uk/heritage/people/whittle/; website home page: http://www.cwn.org.uk/index.html (accessed October 15, 2002).

Mattingly, Jack. "Jet Engine History." Available online at http://www.aircraftenginedesign.com/history.html (accessed October 15, 2002).

Smithsonian National Air and Space Museum. "Jet Aviation." http://www.nasm.si.edu/galleries/gal106/gal106.htm; website home page: http://www.nasm.si.edu/NASMhome.html (accessed October 15, 2002).

"The Evolution of the Cyclotron"

Lecture

By: Ernest O. Lawrence

Date: December 11, 1951

Source: Lawrence, Ernest O. "The Evolution of the Cyclotron." Nobel lecture, December 11, 1951. Available online at http://www.nobel.se/physics/laureates/1939/lawrence-lecture.html; website home page: http://www.nobel.se (accessed October 16, 2002).

About the Author: Ernest O. Lawrence (1901–1958) was born in Canton, South Dakota. He earned a Ph.D. in physics from the University of Minnesota in 1925. Three years later he obtained a position of Associate Professor of Physics at the University of Berkeley. Lawrence was appointed the university's youngest professor in 1930, and in 1936 he also became Director of the university's Radiation Lab. Lawrence made many contributions to nuclear physics, including the invention of the cyclotron in 1929. He won the Nobel Prize in 1939. ■

Introduction

In 1802 the British chemist John Dalton resurrected the ancient Greek idea that atoms compose all matter. Atoms were the fundamental building blocks of matter and could not be divided, thought Dalton.

Physicists retained Dalton's belief that atoms compose all matter, but by the 1930s they understood that atoms could be divided into smaller units: the positively-charged proton, the negatively-charged electron, and the uncharged neutron. Physicists were eager to learn how atoms and their subatomic particles behaved at high speeds, a curiosity that French astronomer George Lemaitre had fueled in 1927.

That year Lemaitre proposed the Big Bang theory. The universe had begun as a massive, dense point of matter that expanded at light speed, the maximum speed anything could achieve according to Albert Einstein, in an initial explosion of great energy and heat. That galaxies

Ernest O. Lawrence leans on the Cyclotron. © CORBIS. REPRODUCED BY PERMISSION.

were receding from one another, as the American astronomers Vesto Slipher and Edwin Hubble demonstrated in the 1920s, was the residual effect of the Big Bang.

Physicists wanted to know how matter behaved in the initial moments of the Big Bang, as they felt it would give them great insight into the nature of matter and the universe in general. Although they could not duplicate the Big Bang in the laboratory, they could approximate it if they could accelerate atoms and subatomic particles to speeds near light speed.

Significance

As early as 1919 British physicist Ernest Rutherford accelerated helium nuclei to speeds great enough that they could cause nitrogen atoms to break down into oxygen and hydrogen atoms on impact. As intriguing as this result was, it did not solve the problem of accelerating atoms and subatomic particles to speeds near light speed. In 1929, Ernest Lawrence devised a machine that could accomplish this feat. This device, which he called a cyclotron, could move subatomic particles in a circle within the machine at ever increasing speed by using a rapidly alternating magnetic field. Over the next several years, Lawrence and his collaborators built and tested the first cyclotrons.

The cyclotron proved to be everything Lawrence and other physicists had hoped for, opening a new era in subatomic physics by making it possible for physicists to approximate the conditions of the initial moments of the Big Bang. The cyclotron quickly became one of the basic tools for studying the nature of atoms and subatomic particles, with models of ever increasing size and sophistication continuing to be built up to the present day. Lawrence received the 1939 Nobel Prize in Physics for the invention and development of the cyclotron. At the high speeds in the modern cyclotron (known as a synchrotron), not only do atoms of an element break down into subatomic particles on collision, but indirect evidence points to the existence of even smaller particles called quarks. Physicists today believe that quarks are themselves composed of a vibrating wave or string. Hence physicists use the name Superstring Theory for the idea that nothing more substantial than waves are the building blocks of quarks and thus of all matter.

Primary Source

"The Evolution of the Cyclotron" [excerpt]

SYNOPSIS: Lawrence's Nobel lecture was delayed by World War II and other considerations until 1951. In this excerpt, he discusses how he developed the idea for a cyclotron. He was inspired by the discovery of a 1929 article in a German electrical engineering journal. The author had accelerated positively charged ions in steps by jolting them with electricity each time they passed the source of electricity in their movement around a cylinder. The limitation of this method was that to achieve the near-light speeds physicists sought would require nearly infinte power. Lawrence sidestepped this problem by substituting a magnetic field for the surges of electricity.

The development of the cyclotron was begun more than twenty years ago and perhaps it is appropriate on this occasion to give something of an historical account. The story goes back to 1928 when I had the good fortune of becoming a member of the Faculty of the University of California. At that time it seemed opportune to review my plans for research, for the pioneer work of Rutherford and his school had clearly indicated that the next great frontier for the experimental physicist was surely the atomic nucleus.

It seemed equally obvious also at that time that a prerequisite to a successful experimental attack on the nucleus was the development of means of accelerating charged particles to high velocities—to energies measured in millions of electron volts, a task which appeared formidable indeed! Accordingly, I devoted considerable time and thought to the technical problem of ways and means of reaching millions of electron volts in the laboratory. The problem seemed to reduce itself to two parts, *(a)* the production of high voltages, and *(b)* the development of accelerating tubes capable of withstanding such high voltages.

Since transformers and rectifiers for such high voltages seemed rather out of the question for various reasons, not the least of which were connected with financial limitations, I naturally looked for alternative means of producing high voltages: the surge generator which was used by Brasch and Lange; the electrostatic generator which Professor W. F. G. Swarm was working on when I was a student under him at the University of Minnesota in 1924 and which was later brought to practical development by Van de Graaff; and the Tesla coil source of high voltage which Tuve, Breit, and Hafstad brought to a fruitful stage of development.

One evening early in 1929 as I was glancing over current periodicals in the University library, I came across an article in a German electrical engineering journal by Wideröe on the multiple acceleration of positive ions. Not being able to read German easily, I merely looked at the diagrams and photographs of Wideröe's apparatus and from the various figures in the article was able to determine his general approach to the problem—i.e. the multiple acceleration of the positive ions by appropriate application of radio frequency oscillating voltages to a series of cylindrical electrodes in line. This new idea immediately impressed me as the real answer which I had been looking for to the technical problem of accelerating positive ions, and without looking at the article further I then and there made estimates of the general features of a linear accelerator for protons in the energy range above one million volt electrons. Simple calculations showed that the accelerator tube would be some meters in length which at the time seemed rather awkwardly long for laboratory purposes. And accordingly, I asked myself the question, instead of using a large number of cylindrical electrodes in line, might it not be possible to use two electrodes over and over again by sending the positive ions back and forth through the electrodes by some sort of appropriate magnetic field arrangement. Again a little analysis of the problem showed that a uniform magnetic field had just the right properties—that the angular velocity of the ions circulating in the field would be independent of their energy so that they would circulate back and forth between suitable hollow electrodes in resonance with an oscillating electrical field of a certain frequency which now has come to be known as the "cyclotron frequency".

Further Resources

BOOKS

Davis, Nuel Pharr. *Lawrence and Oppenheimer.* New York: Da Capo Press, 1986.

Edwards, Donald A., and Syphers, M. J. *Introduction to the Physics of High Energy Accelerators.* New York: Wiley, 1993.

Heilbron, John L., and Robert W. Seidel. *Lawrence and His Laboratory: A History of the Lawrence Berkeley Laboratory.* Berkeley: University of California Press, 1989.

Livingston, M. Stanley, ed. *The Development of High-Energy Accelerators.* New York: Dover, 1966.

Mann, Wilfrid B. *The Cyclotron.* 4th ed. New York: Wiley, 1953.

Solomon, Arthur. *Why Smash Atoms?* Baltimore: Penguin, 1960.

WEBSITES

Nobel e-Museum. "Ernest Lawrence—Biography." Available online at http://www.nobel.se/physics/laureates/1939/lawrence-bio.html; website home page: http://www.nobel.se/index.html (accessed October 16, 2002).

Weisstein, Eric W. "Cyclotrons." Available online at http://www.ericweisstein.com/encyclopedias/books/Cyclotrons.html; website home page: http://www.ericweisstein.com (accessed October 16, 2002).

12

SPORTS

STEPHEN BRAUER

Entries are arranged in chronological order by date of primary source. For entries with one primary source, the entry title is the same as the primary source title. Entries with more than one primary source have an overall entry title, followed by the titles of the primary sources.

Important Events in Sports, 1930–1939

1930

- The first James E. Sullivan Memorial Trophy, awarded to the country's top amateur athlete, goes to golfer Bobby Jones. Jim Bausch, Glenn Cunningham, Lawson Little, and Don Budge are other winners during the decade.
- On March 18, Montreal Canadian center Howie Morenz, called the "Babe Ruth of Hockey," scores five goals in one game against the New York Americans.
- On May 17, Gallant Fox, ridden by jockey Earl Sande, wins the Kentucky Derby. The three-year-old completes the Triple Crown with wins at the Preakness and the Belmont Stakes.
- On May 31, Bobby Jones wins the British Amateur, the only title he had never won.
- On June 20, Jones wins the British Open, shooting 291 for seventy-two holes, ten strokes lower than Walter Hagen's record-breaking score in 1924.
- On July 12, Jones wins the U.S. Open, his fourth Open victory and twelfth golf title.
- In September, Hack Wilson of the Chicago Cubs ends the season with 190 runs batted in (RBIs), and Bill Terry of the New York Giants hits for a .401 average. Baseball is America's national pastime, as attendance climbs to more than ten million, a figure that will not be reached again until after World War II.
- On September 18, the racing yacht *Enterprise* defeats Sir Thomas Lipton's *Shamrock V* to win the United States's seventy-ninth consecutive America's Cup. It is Lipton's fifth loss to the Americans in thirty-two years of competing.
- On September 27, Bobby Jones completes his grand slam victory at the Merion Cricket Club in Ardmore, Pennsylvania. He is the first man to win the Amateur and Open titles of Great Britain and the United States. Jones promptly retires from the sport.
- On November 8, in Knute Rockne's last great game as Notre Dame coach, the Fighting Irish crush the University of Pennsylvania, 60-20.

1931

- Frankie Frisch of the St. Louis Cardinals is the first player to win the Most Valuable Player (MVP) honor, awarded by the Baseball Writers' Association of America.
- Knute Rockne, the legendary coach of Notre Dame, dies in a plane crash. In thirteen years as coach, he led Notre Dame to 105 wins, twelve losses, and five ties.
- On May 13, in the first international Golden Gloves boxing tournament, the United States defeats France, five bouts to three.
- On November 12, Conn Smythe's Maple Leaf Gardens opens in Toronto.
- On November 21, Notre Dame, leading 14-0 and unbeaten in three years, loses to Southern California, 16-14, in the final quarter of play.

1932

- On February 4, the Winter Olympic Games open for the first time in the United States, at Lake Placid, New York.
- On June 2, in Montgomery Lake, Georgia, George W. Perry catches a 22-pound, 4-ounce, largemouth bass, still an IGFA Freshwater All-Tackle world record.
- On June 21, Jack Sharkey defeats world champion Max Schmeling in fifteen rounds in what sportswriter Paul Gallico calls "one of the dullest heavyweight fights in the history of the ring."
- On July 30, after twelve years of planning and nine years of labor, the Summer Olympics open in Los Angeles, California. It is the first summer Olympics in America since 1904.
- On July 31, U.S. athletes set five Olympic track-and-field records, including Babe Didrikson's javelin throw of 143 feet, 4 inches, and Eddie Tolan's 10.4-second 100-meter run.
- On August 6, former University of Kansas football fullback Jim Bausch wins the pole vault and javelin throw, and sets new world and Olympic records in the decathlon.
- On September 30, in the third game of the Yankees-Cubs World Series, Lou Gehrig and thirty-eight-year-old Babe Ruth hit two home runs apiece. In a dramatic moment, Ruth, being heckled by Cubs players from the dugout, points to a spot in the upper deck and promptly hits a home run.

1933

- The NFL makes the forward pass (previously permitted only five yards behind the line) legal anywhere behind the line of scrimmage. Further, the league moves the goalposts to the goal line.
- On April 3, in the last game of the Stanley Cup semifinals, the Boston Bruins and the Toronto Maple Leafs play 164 minutes and 45 seconds of scoreless hockey. At 4 minutes and 46 seconds into the sixth overtime, Toronto's Ken Doraty beats Tiny Thompson, the league's best goalie, for the winning score.
- On May 6, Broker's Tip wins the fifty-ninth Kentucky Derby, and jockeys Donald Meade and Herbert Fisher come to blows after Fisher charges Meade with a foul, which officials disallow.
- On June 25, the Chicago White Sox's Al Simmons tops all major-league players in nationwide voting for the first baseball All-Star Game (the brainchild of sportswriter Arch Ward of the *Chicago Tribune*), to be played in July at Chicago's Comiskey Park.

- On June 29, Primo Carnera knocks out Jack Sharkey in the sixth round of the heavyweight title bout in Madison Square Garden.
- On July 6, the American League team, managed by Connie Mack, defeats the National League team, managed by John McGraw, 4-2, in the first baseball All-Star Game.
- In August, the Negro League plays its annual East-West All-Star Game at Comiskey Park. Fifty thousand fans attend the game.
- On August 27, Helen Jacobs wins her second straight national women's singles tennis championship at Forest Hills. Her rival, Helen Wills Moody, defaults because of back and hip pain in the third set.
- On October 7, the Washington Senators lose the last World Series game they will ever play, to the New York Giants. The Giants win the series four games to one.
- On December 12, Ace Bailey of the Toronto Maple Leafs is nearly killed by an unprovoked blind-side check from Boston's Eddie Shore, who is later suspended. Bailey suffers a fractured skull and never plays hockey again.

1934

- Yachting reporter William H. Taylor of the *New York Herald Tribune* becomes the first sportswriter to win a Pulitzer Prize, for his coverage of the America's Cup races.
- The Augusta National, a golf course inspired by Bobby Jones, becomes the site of the Masters Tournament. Horton Smith wins the first tournament.
- On January 1, in its first-ever appearance in a Rose Bowl, Columbia upsets Stanford, 7-0.
- On February 14, as a benefit for the injured Ace Bailey, the NHL holds its first All-Star Game. Toronto defeats the best players from around the league, 7-0. Two other fund-raising all-star games will be held: on November 2, 1937, and October 29, 1939.
- On May 8, Mack Garner, a veteran jockey, rides Cavalcade to a Kentucky Derby victory at Churchill Downs, Garner's first Derby win in a twenty-year career.
- On June 14, Max Baer becomes heavyweight champion of the world on a TKO of Primo Carnera, who drops to the canvas eleven times during the bout.
- On June 30, after defeating Bill Bonthron and George Venzke at the Princeton University invitation games two weeks earlier, Glenn Cunningham loses to Bonthron in the fifth and deciding 1,500-meter race at the National Amateur Athletic Union (AAU) championship meet in Milwaukee, Wisconsin.
- On August 31, nearly eighty thousand fans pack Soldiers Field in Chicago to watch the collegiate All Americans play the professional champion Chicago Bears to a scoreless tie.
- On September 20, Jim Londos becomes the undisputed heavyweight wrestling champion of the world by pinning Ed "Strangler" Lewis, who had defeated Londos fourteen times before.
- On October 9, the St. Louis Cardinals win a bitterly fought World Series against the Detroit Tigers, 11-0, behind a six-hitter by Dizzy Dean. During the seventh game, a riot almost breaks out after Cardinal player Joe Medwick spikes Marvin Owen.
- On November 17, playing flawless defense, Yale upsets Princeton, 7-0, on a sensational first-quarter touchdown catch by Larry Kelley.

1935

- On January 1, as the era of the forward pass dawns, Alabama, led by future NFL Hall of Famer receiver Don Hutson, defeats Stanford, 29-13, in the Rose Bowl.
- On May 24, Cincinnati hosts Philadelphia in the first major league night game. President Franklin D. Roosevelt illuminates Crosley Field by pressing a button from the White House.
- On May 25, Ohio State University's Jesse Owens, "The Ebony Antelope," breaks five world records and ties another in one afternoon at the AAU Nationals outdoor track-and-field meet in Ann Arbor, Michigan.
- On May 28, Barney Ross regains the welterweight title with a unanimous decision against Jimmy McLarnin at the New York Polo Grounds.
- On May 30, Amelia Earhart is honorary judge at the Indianapolis 500. Thirty-one-year-old California fruit merchant Kelly Petillo wins the race in record time.
- On June 13, James J. Braddock defeats Max Baer to become the heavyweight boxing champion of the world.
- On July 6, an aging Helen Wills Moody wins her seventh Wimbledon title by defeating Helen Jacobs, 6-3, 3-6, 7-5.
- On August 14, Greyhound, a three-year-old gray gelding, clocks in a record time in two heats, to win the Hambletonian Stakes at Goshen, New York.
- On August 31, Glenna Collett (Mrs. Edwin H. Vare Jr.) wins the women's national golf championship for the sixth straight year, at the Interlachen Country Club in Hopkins, Minnesota.
- On September 3, at Bonneville Salt Flats, Utah, race car driver Sir Malcolm Campbell becomes the first person to exceed 300 mph.
- On September 14, British Amateur champion Lawson Little Jr. of California wins the U.S. Amateur Open at the Country Club of Cleveland.
- On October 7, Mickey Cochrane and the Detroit Tigers win their first world championship, beating the Chicago Cubs four games to two.
- On November 2, losing 13-0 going into the fourth quarter, Notre Dame scores three touchdowns to defeat Ohio State, 18-13.

1936

- The Associated Press selects the University of Minnesota as its first National Collegiate Athletic Association (NCAA) football champion.
- On February 8, the NFL holds its first college draft. University of Chicago halfback and Heisman Trophy winner Jay Berwanger is selected first by Philadelphia. However, Berwanger decides not to turn professional.

- On March 24, in the first game of the best-of-five playoff series, the Detroit Red Wings and the Montreal Maroons play the longest game in NHL history. At 16:30 of the sixth overtime, Detroit wins, 1-0.
- On June 19, Max Schmeling knocks out undefeated Joe Louis in the twelfth round of their first fight.
- On August 1, ten African American athletes, labeled "American auxiliaries" by Adolf Hitler, participate in the Eleventh Olympiad in Berlin. All but one of the Americans win gold medals.
- From August 2 to August 9, Jesse Owens wins four gold medals, in the 100-meter and 200-meter races, the long jump, and the 4x400-meter sprint relay.
- On August 6, in the Olympic 1,500-meter race, Jack Lovelock of New Zealand defeats old foe Glenn Cunningham in world-record time.
- On August 8, backstroke champion Eleanor Holm, recently dropped from the U.S. swim team for drinking, shooting craps, and violating curfew while on board a ship carrying U.S. athletes to Germany, is barred from further amateur competition for writing daily stories for an American news syndicate.
- On October 2, in game two of the World Series, the Yankees crush the New York Giants, 18-4, on their way to the first of four consecutive world championships.

1937

- George Preston Marshall moves his NFL Eastern Division champion Boston Redskins to Washington, D.C.
- College basketball eliminates the center jump after every basket; games become faster and more wide open.
- On June 22, Joe Louis knocks out Jim Braddock in the eighth round at Comiskey Park, to begin his long reign as heavyweight champion of the world.
- On July 20, after defeating Baron Gottfried Von Cramm, Wimbledon champion Don Budge is on a pace to lead the United States to its first Davis Cup victory since 1926.
- On August 5, the New York Yacht Club again wins the America's Cup, as Harold S. Vanderbilt's *Ranger* defeats *Endeavour II* of the Royal Yacht Squadron of Cowes, England.
- On October 17, for the third straight year, Fordham University and Rose Bowl champion University of Pittsburgh play to a scoreless tie.

1938

- In the first National Invitational Tournament (NIT) in basketball, Temple defeats Colorado, 60-36.
- On January 1, Stanford's Hank Luisetti, master of the running one-handed jump shot, scores fifty points in a game against Duquesne.
- On March 25, Man o' War wins the 100th Grand National Steeplechase in Aintree, England. It is the first American-owned horse to win the event.
- On April 12, the Chicago Blackhawks, winners of only fourteen of forty-eight regular season games, defeat the reigning champion Toronto Maple Leafs, 4-1, to capture their second Stanley Cup.
- From June 11 to June 15, Cincinnati's Johnny Vander Meer throws back-to-back no-hitters: 3-0 against the Boston Braves and 6-0 against the Brooklyn Dodgers. The latter victory is the first night game in New York.
- On June 23, heavyweight champion Joe Louis evens the score by knocking out Max Schmeling in the first round of a title fight at Yankee Stadium.
- On August 17, lightweight Henry Armstrong defeats Lou Ambers at Madison Square Garden to become the first man to hold three boxing titles at one time. Armstrong won the welterweight title on May 31 and the featherweight championship on October 29, 1937.
- On September 24, Don Budge becomes the first player to win all four of the major world tennis titles in the same year, by beating Gene Mako at Forest Hills, 6-3, 6-8, 6-2, 6-1.
- On November 1, Seabiscuit (grandson of Man o' War) beats War Admiral (son of Man o' War) at Pimlico by three lengths and in record time, returning better than two-to-one odds.
- On December 12, the New York Giants win the NFL championship, defeating the Green Bay Packers, 23-17, before 48,120 people.

1939

- The Montreal Maroons withdraw from the NHL, which ends the league's old divisional format. Six of the seven teams can now qualify for the 1938–1939 Stanley Cup playoffs.
- The NCAA holds its first Final Four championship at Northwestern University in Evanston, Illinois. In the finals, Oregon beats Ohio State, 46-33.
- Little League baseball is born in Williamsport, Pennsylvania.
- On May 2, Lou Gehrig takes himself out of the starting lineup, ending his consecutive game streak at 2,130. The "Iron Man" streak spans fifteen years.
- On May 12, with war perilously close at hand, the European Golden Gloves team defeats the Chicago team, five bouts to three.
- On June 11, after winning the first match, 11-7, on June 4, the U.S. polo team wins the International Cup series against Great Britain, 9-4, at the Meadow Brook Club in Westbury, Long Island. The English have not beaten the Americans since 1914.
- On October 8, the Yankees win their fourth straight World Series, sweeping the Cincinnati Reds in four games.

A Dizzy Dean baseball card from 1934. **CORBIS/LAKE COUNTY MUSEUM. REPRODUCED BY PERMISSION.**

"Dizzy Dean's Day"

Newspaper article

By: Red Smith

Date: September 30, 1934

Source: Smith, Red. "Dizzy Dean's Day." The *St. Louis Star,* September 30, 1934. Reprinted in Smith, Red. *The Red Smith Reader.* Dave Anderson, ed. New York: Random House, 1982, 137–140.

About the Author: Walter "Red" Smith (1905–1982) began his sportswriting career in St. Louis. He eventually moved to the *Philadelphia Record, New York Herald Tribune,* and, finally, to *The New York Times.* There he wrote a column four times a week, winning a Pulitzer Prize for his work in 1976. He was a lifetime newspaperman, who covered a wide range of sports, from baseball to boxing to horse racing to fishing. By the time he died, he was widely considered America's preeminent sportswriter. ■

Introduction

On September 5, 1934, the St. Louis Cardinals were seven games behind the New York Giants in the National League pennant race. By the end of the month, however, they had overtaken the Giants for the right to meet the Detroit Tigers in the World Series. Their ace pitcher, Jay "Dizzy" Dean—who compiled a masterful 30-7 record that season, with an earned run average of 2.66—led their stunning comeback. Dean pitched seven shutouts in 1934 and held opposing hitters to a .241 batting average. This accomplishment is even more impressive considering that Dean won three games for the Cardinals in the last week of the season, as the team surged from behind to beat the Giants for the pennant.

Dizzy Dean was the leader of the Cardinals—known in that era as the Gashouse Gang—but he was not alone in his exemplary achievements. Dizzy's brother Paul, for instance, also pitched for the Cardinals and had a 19-11 record that year. Frankie Frisch was the player-manager of the team. He put together eleven straight .300 seasons at the plate and personified the style of hard-nosed play that earned the team its nickname. He was matched by fellow infielder Leo Durocher, who, likewise, had a combative, fiery style of play. Another standout was future Hall of Famer Joe Medwick. In his seventeen years in the major leagues, Medwick batted over .300 thirteen times. He would win the Triple Crown in batting in 1937, on his way to earning that year's National League Most Valuable Player award.

The Cardinals gained widespread attention and respect for their refusal to give in or quit in the face of adversity. They were a team with plenty of fight, which served them well against the Tigers in the World Series. Although the Cardinals were down three games to two, the Dean brothers combined to give up just thirteen hits and three runs over the last two games to give St. Louis the championship.

Significance

The Cardinals also won the World Series in 1931, but the 1934 team possessed a different charisma that led them to wider renown. Certainly, part of the allure were the Dean brothers, both of whom suffered abbreviated careers. Paul Dean went 19-12 the next year but never again performed at the same high level. Dizzy, meanwhile, averaged twenty-four wins in his first five full seasons, winning four National League strikeout crowns. In 1937, however, a broken toe led to an arm injury that brought his pitching days to an early end. The 1934 season marked his apex and was the last time a pitcher won thirty games in the National League.

Dizzy Dean winds up for a pitch against the Cincinnati Reds—on his way to helping the St. Louis Cardinals clinch the National League pennant in 1934. © BETTMANN/CORBIS. REPRODUCED BY PERMISSION.

Even beyond the charisma of Dizzy Dean, the Cardinals possessed a grit that appealed to Middle America. In their refusal to quit under trying circumstances, in their ability to claw back into the pennant race and then to overtake the Giants, the Gashouse Gang symbolized hard work and determination, values that were fundamentally important to many Americans during the Depression era. The Cardinals were a team that everyone could embrace because they embodied an approach to adversity from which nearly every American could draw inspiration. They were a team that fit squarely within the culture of their times.

Primary Source

"Dizzy Dean's Day"

SYNOPSIS: Red Smith's article on the Cardinals' pennant-clinching victory offers his trademark personal and personable perspective. He begins with the celebration after the game and then focuses on Dean's dominance during the game itself. He imparts a sense of drama to a lopsided, undramatic 9-0 win, noting that the great filmmaker Cecil B. DeMille "would have ordered things better" to add some dramatic tension. Smith portrays Dean as a quiet and unassuming leader on this day, possessed of a dignity he had never shown before.

Through the murk of cigarette smoke and liniment fumes in the Cardinals' clubhouse a radio announcer babbled into a microphone.

"And now," he read with fine spontaneity from a typewritten sheet prepared hours in advance, "and now let's have a word from the Man of the Hour, Manager Frank Frisch."

The Man of the Hour shuffled forward. He had started changing clothes. His shirttail hung limply over bare thighs. The Man of the Hour's pants had slipped down and they dragged about his ankles. You could have planted petunias in the loam on his face. The Man of the Hour looked as though he had spent his hour in somebody's coal mine.

Beside him, already scrubbed and combed and natty in civilian clothes, awaiting his turn to confide to a nationwide audience that "the Cardinals are the greatest team I ever played with and I sure am glad we won the champeenship today and I sure hope we can win the World Series from Detroit," stood Dizzy Dean, destiny's child.

There was a conscious air of grandeur about the man. He seemed perfectly aware of and not at all surprised at the fact that just outside the clubhouse five thousand persons were pressing against police lines, waiting to catch a glimpse of him, perhaps even to touch the hem of his garment.

He couldn't have known that in that crowd one woman was weeping into the silver fox fur collar of her black cloth coat, sobbing, "I'm so happy! I can't stand it!" She was Mrs. Dizzy Dean.

All afternoon Dizzy Dean had seemed surrounded by an aura of greatness. A crowd of 37,402 persons jammed Sportsman's Park to see the game that would decide the National League pennant race. To this reporter it did not appear that they had come to see the Cardinals win the championship. Rather, they were there to see Dizzy come to glory.

It was Dean's ball game. He, more than anyone else, had kept the Cardinals in the pennant race throughout the summer. He had won two games in the last five days to help bring the Red Birds to the top of the league. Here, with the championship apparently hinging upon the outcome of this game, was his chance to add the brightest jewel to his crown, and at the same time to achieve the personal triumph of becoming the first National League pitcher since 1917 to win 30 games in a season.

And it was Dizzy's crowd. Although the game was a box office "natural," it is doubtful that, had it not been announced that Dean would pitch, fans would have been thronged before the Dodier street gate when the doors were opened at 9:30 A.M. They were, and from then until game time they came in increasing numbers. Eventually, some had to be turned away from lack of space.

Packed in the aisles, standing on the ramps and clinging to the grandstand girders, the fans followed Dizzy with their eyes, cheered his every move.

They whooped when he rubbed resin on his hands. They yowled when he fired a strike past a batter. They stood and yelled when he lounged to the plate, trailing his bat in the dust. And when, in the seventh inning, with the game already won by eight runs, he hit a meaningless single, the roar that thundered from the stands was as though he had accomplished the twelve labors of Hercules.

The fact was, the fans were hungry for drama, and that was the one ingredient lacking. With such a stage setting as that crowd provided, with such a buildup as the National League race, with such a hero as Dizzy, Mr. Cecil B. DeMille would have ordered things better.

He would have had the New York Giants beat Brooklyn and thus make a victory essential to the Cards' pennant prospects. He would have had Cincinnati leading St. Louis until the eighth inning, when a rally would have put the Red Birds one run ahead. Then Mr. DeMille would have sent ex-St. Louis Hero Jim Bottomley, now one of the enemy, to bat against Hero Dean, with Cincinnati runners on every base. And he would have had Dizzy pour across three blinding strikes to win the ball game.

In the real game there was no suspense. Cincinnati tried, but the Cards couldn't be stopped. They just up and won the game, 9-0, and the pennant, and to blazes with drama.

Still, drama is where you find it. The crowd seemed to find it in the gawky frame of Mr. Dean, and in the figures on the scoreboard which showed Brooklyn slowly overhauling the Giants in their game in the east.

Dean was warming up in front of the Cardinal dugout when the first-inning score of the New York–Brooklyn game was posted, showing four runs for the Giants and none for the Dodgers. As an apprehensive "Oooooh!" from the fans greeted the score, Dizzy glanced toward the scoreboard. Watching through field glasses, this reporter saw his eyes narrow slightly. That was all. A moment later he strolled to the plate, entirely at ease, to accept a diamond ring donated by his admirers.

Then the game started, and for a few minutes the customers' attention was diverted from their hero by the exploits of some of his mates.

In the first inning Ernie Orsatti, chasing a low drive to right center by Mark Koenig, raced far to his left, dived forward, somersaulted, and came up with the ball. To everyone except the fans in the right field seats it seemed a miraculous catch. The spectators closest to the play were sure they saw Orsatti drop the ball and recover it while his back was toward the plate. But everyone screamed approbation.

Magnificent plays, one after another, whipped the stands into a turmoil of pleasure. In Cincinnati's second inning, after Bottomley had singled, Leo Durocher scooted far to his right to nail a grounder by Pool and, in one astonishingly swift motion, he pivoted and whipped the ball to Frisch for a force-out of Bottomley.

Again in the fourth inning, there was a play that brought the fans whooping to their feet. This time Frisch scooped up a bounder from Pool's bat and beat Koenig to second base, Durocher hurdling Frisch's prostrate body in order to avoid ruining the play. A few minutes earlier Frisch had brought gasps and cheers from the stands by stretching an ordinary single into a two-base hit, reaching second only by the grace of a breakneck headfirst slide.

Play by play, inning by inning, the crowd was growing noisier, more jubilant. Cheer followed exultant cheer on almost every play.

Meanwhile the Cards were piling up a lead. Meanwhile, too, Brooklyn was chiseling runs off New York's lead, and the scoreboard became a magnet for all eyes. When Brooklyn scored two runs in the eighth inning to tie the Giants, Announcer Kelly didn't wait for the scoreboard to flash the news. He shouted it through his megaphone, and as fans in each succeeding section of seats heard his words, waves of applause echoed through the stands.

Shadows were stretching across the field when Cincinnati came to bat in the ninth inning. The National League season was within minutes of its end. The scoreboard long since had registered the final tallies for all other games. Only the tied battle in New York and the contest on this field remained unfinished.

Dean lounged to the pitching mound. The man was completing his third game in six days. He was within three putouts of his second shutout in those six days. He didn't seem tired. He hardly seemed interested. He was magnificently in his element, completely at ease in the knowledge that every eye was on him.

The first two Cincinnati batters made hits. Dizzy was pitching to Adam Comorosky when a wild yell from the stands caused him to glance at the scoreboard. The Dodgers had scored three runs in the tenth. New York's score for the inning had not been posted.

Seen through field glasses, Dean's face was expressionless. He walked Comorosky. The bases were filled with no one out. Was Dizzy tiring, or was he deliberately setting the stage for the perfect melodramatic finish?

The scoreboard boy hung up a zero for the Giants. The pennant belonged to the Cardinals. Most pitchers would have said, "the hell with it," and taken the course of least resistance, leaving it to the fielders to make the putouts.

But this was Dean's ball game. Seen through a haze of fluttering paper, cushions and torn scorecards, he seemed to grow taller. He fanned Clyde Manion. A low roar rumbled through the stands. The fans saw what was coming. Dizzy was going to handle the last three batters himself.

Methodically, unhurriedly, he rifled three blinding strikes past Pinch-Hitter Petoskey. Was that a faint grin on Dizzy's face? The roar from the stands had become rolling thunder. The outfielders foresaw what was coming. They started in from their positions as Dizzy began pitching to Sparky Adams.

They were almost on the field when Adams, in hopeless desperation, swung at a pitch too fast for him to judge. His bat just tipped the ball, sending it straight upward in a wobbly, puny foul fly to DeLancey.

Dean didn't laugh. He didn't shout or caper. The man who has been at times a gross clown was in this greatest moment a figure of quiet dignity. Surrounded by his players he walked slowly to the dugout, a mad, exultant thunder drumming in his ears.

Further Resources

BOOKS

Berkow, Ira. *Red: A Biography of Red Smith.* New York: Times Books, 1986.

Feldmann, Doug. *Dizzy and the Gas House Gang: The 1934 Cardinals and Depression-Era Baseball.* Jefferson, N.C.: McFarland, 2000.

Fleming, G.H. *The Dizziest Season: The Gashouse Gang Chases the Pennant.* New York: William Morrow, 1984.

Frisch, Frank. *Frank Frisch: The Fordham Flash.* Garden City, N.Y.: Doubleday, 1962.

Gregory, Robert. *Diz: Dizzy Dean and Baseball During the Great Depression.* New York: Viking, 1992.

Smith, Curt. *America's Dizzy Dean.* St. Louis: Bethany, 1978.

Staten, Vince. *Ol' Diz: A Biography of Dizzy Dean.* New York: HarperCollins, 1992.

Fifteen-Thirty: The Story of a Tennis Player

Autobiography

By: Helen Wills Moody

Date: 1937

Source: Wills, Helen. *Fifteen-Thirty: The Story of a Tennis Player.* New York: Charles Scribner's Sons, 1937, 287–291.

About the Author: Helen Wills Moody (1905–1998) was one of the best women's tennis players in history. She reached the finals of the U.S. Open at age 16. Although she lost that year, she went on to nineteen singles titles at the French Open, Wimbledon, and U.S. Open. She was inducted into the Tennis Hall of Fame in 1969 and died in 1998 at the age of 92. ■

Introduction

Between 1919 and 1938, Helen Wills Moody won fifty-two of the ninety-two tournaments she entered, boasting a 398-35 match record and a .919 winning percentage. From 1927 to 1932, she did not lose a set in *any* of her singles matches. Wills, who wed in 1930 and adopted the married name Moody, set a standard for excellence that is still the measuring stick for female tennis players everywhere.

The numbers bear out Moody's lofty stature. She won the Wimbledon title eight times—a record that stood until Martina Navratilova broke it in 1990—losing only in her first appearance in 1924. She won the French Open four times and the U.S. Open seven times. She won nineteen of the twenty-two major singles competitions she entered, posting a 126-3 record. She was never eliminated before the finals. Moody was an accomplished doubles player as well, winning the French title in 1930 and 1932; Wimbledon in 1924, 1927, and 1930; and the U.S. title in 1922, 1924–1925, and 1928. In 1924, she won the Olympic gold medal in both singles and doubles.

Moody was quiet and reserved when playing, earning the nickname Little Miss Poker Face. Her play was steady and unruffled, perhaps lacking the style for which her rival Suzanne Lenglen was known. She tended to wear a white sailor suit, white eyeshadow, and white shoes and stockings when competing. What Moody may have lacked in flair, however, she more than made up for in sheer power. The speed, pace, and depth of her shots tended to overwhelm her opponents. She went to the net only occasionally, though she was skilled in volleying and overhead smashes. She relied on her power game from the baseline, using a keen sense of anticipation to be in the right position to return any shot.

In 1933, Moody had to default in the third set of the finals of the U.S. Open against Helen Jacobs because of back pain. Her victory over Jacobs in the 1935 Wimbledon finals—a match she won after trailing 5-2 in the third and final set—capped her return from injury and recovery.

Helen Wills Moody prepares for a match at Wimbledon in July 1931. AP/WIDE WORLD PHOTOS. REPRODUCED BY PERMISSION.

Significance

Moody was a captivating public figure not merely because of her success as a tennis player. Off the court, she held a variety of interests that made her an intriguing and compelling figure. She was educated at the University of California, where she was a member of Phi Beta Kappa. She was also an accomplished painter, who exhibited her work in galleries and museums. During her career, she engaged in discussions and correspondence with artists and intellectual figures, including historian Will Durant, painter Augustus John, and playwright George Bernard Shaw.

Certainly, on the tennis court, Moody dominated her era, with only Suzanne Lenglen and Helen Jacobs offering her much competition. She held and broke all manner of records in the game's history. Moreover, she displayed many of the characteristics of women's tennis in the late twentieth century, as the power game that she relied upon has taken a greater role in high-level play. Perhaps most notable of all was the intense concentration she brought to her game. During play, she was fully immersed in the moment. She described this immersion as a sharp feeling of pleasure, "almost as if you were a tree with the bark stripped off, feeling the air about you for the first time." Complementing this focus was a powerful sense of willpower that helped Moody overcome her rivals, even when she seemed most in danger on the court. This was highlighted by her stunning Wimbledon comeback against Jacobs.

Primary Source

Fifteen-Thirty: The Story of a Tennis Player [excerpt]

SYNOPSIS: Moody's account of the 1935 Wimbledon finals offers a compelling portrait of her emotions as she played that day against Helen Jacobs, one of her main rivals. She speaks of focusing so clearly in the moment that she was virtually unaware of anything else around her. As she speaks of the dramatic third set, which she came back to win 7-5, she never mentions the change in score as she rebounded from well down and shocked Jacobs and the spectators. For Moody, the pleasure came in the playing, not in the keeping of score. She claims that, afterward, she wasn't even fully aware that she had won.

It was time to go over to the courts. I went to my room to gather my tennis things together, for while I left my tennis dresses and shoes in the locker room at the club, I kept my racquets and my other things at the hotel. Then I went over to the club by myself. It was only the second time I had played in the finals at Wimbledon without any one in my family on hand. It was a reassuring thing, in a way, to have some one on the side lines who you were certain wanted you to win. However, it was not as if I had not been many times on the center court. I had had as much experience on it as possibly any other player. Always there is the thought when you step upon the center court for a singles finals match—at least there was for me—"This is the final!" It was familiar, and yet it had all the newness, surprise, and urgency in it that was a part of the moment. It belonged so emphatically to the present, that a clarity, unusual to your eye and mind, seemed to take possession of you. And when the preliminary rally was over which made you impatient, you began play with a sharp feeling of pleasure, almost as if you were a tree with the bark stripped off, feeling the air about you for the first time.

The sunshine seemed bright, the mass of press cameras black and rather insectlike with their round lenses touched with reflected highlight. The formality of a spun racquet. "Rough or smooth?" The umpire noted down who was to serve. I chose to serve, having won the toss. Another final match on the center court! I had the curious feeling that time had been turned back, and that it was the first year.

But my opponent was not Kathleen McKane, it was Helen Jacobs, and I was not nervous as I had been the first time at Wimbledon. I was happy that it was the final match because, like the last day of school, it had seemed so far away, if, indeed, ever possible.

So I hit the ball in the preliminary rally with real pleasure. What a lovely court! How white the balls were! They were cold in my hand because they had been in the icebox at the side of the court.

After the preliminary rally we started playing, with hardly any tentative shots such as are usually hit during the first few games of a match until the players get into the swing of it. It was a very hot afternoon, which might have been partly responsible, as it is easier to start quickly on a warm day because your muscles are limbered up. I won the first three games, losing three points. Then the score drew even in games, but I fell behind 40-love in the point score on the following game. I managed to make this up and drew even. After several advantage points this game went to me. With this gain, the score mounted to 6-3 for the set in my favor. There had been no specially outstanding points in this set. It was mainly one in which the tempo was steady, with the ball going back and forth regularly.

Miss Jacobs made few errors at this stage of the match and went ahead to lead 4-2, and finally took the set at 6-3. It was at the beginning of the third set that I felt as if the strain of the long rallies was too much both for my muscles and for my breathing, which was very short. It seemed as if my endurance, upon which I had always counted in other years had deserted me. This, however, may have been a momentary thing, due to the fact that I had had no competitive tennis for such a long time. Nevertheless, it seemed then to my friends looking on that I was going to lose the set and the match. This idea did not occupy my thoughts, probably because I had not been in the habit of thinking in this way during all the many years that I had played in tournaments.

Habits of the past are more likely to return to one at a moment which appears to be critical, than to desert one, I imagine, even in a game. Miss Jacobs then stepped one more game ahead to lead at 5 to 3, and reached what could have been the very last point of the match, point set! Here she missed a fairly easy shot, a lob of mine which she volleyed outside. I knew naturally, that the point set had been saved, but there was no way of telling that the match itself had been rescued. During the last couple of games, my "wind" had returned—why, I don't know. It may have been "second wind," or it may have been a quieting down of the breathing process induced because of the demands of what seemed to me to be an emergency.

There is no actual proof that people do not become more calm at a difficult moment than more nervous. Sometimes you see in sport a participant who is less controlled during the easier part of an event than when the situation reaches a crisis. But this is inexplicable, and I do not claim that it is the reason why I happened to win the match. So much depends upon chance, when the score reaches the last stage. After the recovery of the set point, however, I have never felt as confident in any match within my memory. I was not sure that the set was mine, by any means, because looking ahead to the conclusion of a match is beyond the demand of the moment. The immediate thing was the returning of the ball, and this was the only thought that was in my mind. It may have been that Miss Jacobs had looked ahead to the end, which was not illogical, seeing that she was so near to it, and that during the following points she did not regain the perspective of regarding the urgency of the immediate point. I can remember that this was the case in my match against Kathleen McKane, in my first final at Wimbledon. I saw the end before I arrived.

It is always difficult to explain the why of a match. I am sure of one thing, though, and that is, that a final match usually represents the summing up of all the knowledge gained in past matches—knowledge that reappears almost as an instinct, and often without the player being wholly aware of why he plays as he does. He reacts to certain situations with a kind of unconscious intuition, which is the result of much repetition. When there are evidently so many elements to be considered, it may be easier to say "So and so won the championship" and let it go at that. My feelings at the moment did not require analysis. I was very happy, and on my way through the door met Sir Herbert Wilberforce, about whom I threw my arms, giving him a good kiss. I had always wanted to, because he was so sweet. Then several of my friends began to complain, because of the suspense of the match, during which they said they had suffered.

As we left the court, in order to make sure, I asked the first person I met in the hall of the clubhouse if it were true that I had won. It happened to be a friend, who was very excited. "What!" he roared crossly. "You don't know whether you've won or not—and I have just died six times in the last set!"

Further Resources

BOOKS

Englelmann, Larry. *The Goddess and the American Girl.* New York: Oxford University Press, 1988.

Wade, Virginia. *Ladies of the Court: A Century of Women at Wimbledon.* New York: Atheneum, 1984.

Wimmer, Dick, ed. *The Women's Game.* Short Hills, N.J.: Burford, 2000.

Cincinnati Reds v. Brooklyn Dodgers, June 15, 1938, Box Score

Box score

By: *The New York Times*

Date: June 16, 1938

Source: Cincinnati Reds v. Brooklyn Dodgers, June 15, 1938, Box score, *The New York Times,* June 16, 1938.

About the Author: Sportswriter Roscoe McGowen wrote the article from which this box score was taken. Beginning in 1929, he worked for thirty years as a correspondent for *The New York Times.* He also served as a longtime contributor to *The Sporting News.* ■

Introduction

Box scores tell stories, allowing fans to know the performances of individual batters and pitchers, and to recognize a team's ability to turn a series of consecutive hits into a string of runs or its failure to knock home a runner.

The box score of the baseball game between the Cincinnati Reds and Brooklyn Dodgers on June 15, 1938, tells the reader that Johnny Vander Meer, pitcher for the Reds, threw a no-hitter. Not one single Dodger managed to get a hit off of Vander Meer, though he walked eight batters. Cincinnati scored four runs in the third inning and then added one run each in the seventh and eighth innings to make the final score 6-0.

Johnny Vander Meer of the Cincinatti Reds pitches to Buddy Hassett of the Brooklyn Dodgers at Brooklyn's Ebbets Field. AP/WIDE WORLD PHOTOS. REPRODUCED BY PERMISSION.

No-hitters are a rare feat in baseball. The box score for this game tells a marvelous story of a pitcher mastering his opponents, in this case even while struggling to contain his own wildness—as evidenced by Vander Meer's eight walks. Even so, the box score does not tell the whole story. With this game Johnny Vander Meer accomplished what no pitcher in major league baseball history had ever done—pitch a second consecutive no-hitter. He had also recorded a no-hitter against Boston four days earlier, on June 11.

At the start of the game, Vander Meer wasn't even the main topic of conversation. The game was the first major league baseball game played at night in New York. Cincinnati had hosted the first major league night game in 1935. Now it was New York's turn. Historic Ebbets Field was the site for the game, and chief executive for the Dodgers Larry MacPhail made sure to offer a spectacle for the inaugural night game.

Significance

No other pitcher in major league history has pitched two consecutive no-hitters. Vander Meer was only twenty-three years old at the time and would never again achieve the same level of fame or accomplishment. Nevertheless,

The box score:

CINCINNATI (N.)

	ab.	r.	h.	po.	a.	e.
Frey, 2b	5	0	1	2	2	0
Berger, lf	5	1	3	1	0	0
Goodman, rf.	3	2	1	3	0	0
McC'mick, 1b	5	1	1	9	1	0
Lombardi, c.	3	1	0	9	0	0
Craft, cf	5	0	3	1	0	0
Riggs, 3b	4	0	1	0	3	0
Myers, ss	4	0	0	0	1	0
V. Meer, p.	4	1	1	2	4	0
Total	38	6	11	27	11	0

BROOKLYN (N.)

	ab.	r.	h.	po.	a.	e.
Cuyler, rf	2	0	0	1	0	0
Coscarart, 2b	2	0	0	1	2	0
aBrack	1	0	0	0	0	0
Hudson, 2b.	1	0	0	1	0	0
Hassett, lf	4	0	0	3	0	0
Phelps, c.	3	0	0	9	0	0
bRosen	0	0	0	0	0	0
Lavagetto, 3b	2	0	0	0	2	2
Camilli, 1b.	1	0	0	7	0	0
Koy, cf	4	0	0	4	0	0
Durocher, ss.	4	0	0	1	2	0
Butcher, p.	0	0	0	0	1	0
Pressnell, p.	2	0	0	0	0	0
Hamlin, p.	0	0	0	0	1	0
cEnglish	1	0	0	0	0	0
Tamulis, p.	0	0	0	0	0	0
Total	27	0	0	27	8	2

aBatted for Coscarat in sixth.
bRan for Phelps in ninth.
cBatted for Hamlin in eighth.

Cincinnati	0 0 4	0 0 0	1 1 0	—6
Brooklyn	0 0 0	0 0 0	0 0 0	—0

Runs batted in—McCormick 3, Riggs, Craft, Berger.

Two-base hit—Berger. Three-base hit—Berger. Home run—McCormick. Stolen base—Goodman. Left on bases—Cincinnati 9, Brooklyn 8. Bases on balls—Off Butcher 3, Vander Meer 8, Hamlin 1. Struck out—By Butcher 1, Pressnell 3, Vander Meer 7, Hamlin 3. Hits—Off Butcher 5 in 2 2-3, Hamlin 2 in 1 2-3, Pressnell 4 in 3 2-3, Tamulis 0 in 1. Losing pitcher—Butcher. Umpires—Stewart, Stark and Barr. Time of game—2:22.

Primary Source

Cincinnati Reds v. Brooklyn Dodgers, June 15, 1938, Box Score

SYNOPSIS: The box score for the June 15, 1938, game between the Cincinnati Reds and Brooklyn Dodgers offers a summary of each player's performance in terms of at bats, runs scored, hits, putouts, assists, and errors, and offers totals for the teams. At the bottom of the box score, there is more detailed information, such as substitutions, extra-base hits, and hit-batsmen. THE NEW YORK TIMES.

his place in the storybooks was secured by his success that night at Ebbets Field, especially considering the spectacle of the evening as a whole.

This kind of entertainment would become more and more central to the major league baseball experience, as well as big business for teams. Baseball, of course, is very much a business-oriented enterprise. The spectacle of the games often overwhelms the play on the field. The revenue from television coverage, which in 1938 was soon to come for baseball fans, has changed the dynamics of the staging of the game. Television networks now dictate the starting times for games. Almost all games are held at night, when the networks can get better advertising revenue because of the larger nighttime television audience. Night baseball, once an innovation, is now the expectation for baseball fans. Like the story of Vander Meer's consecutive no-hitters, the story of night baseball in New York is not part of the story of the box score. But it is part of the story of what was to come for the game of baseball.

Further Resources

BOOKS

Dickey, Glenn. *The Great No-Hitters.* Radnor, Pa.: Chilton, 1976.

Graham, Frank. *Great No Hit Games of the Major Leagues.* New York: Random Library, 1968.

Lichtman, Paul. *The Dutch Master: The Life and Times of Johnny Vander Meer.* New York: Vantage, 2001.

Pietrusza, David. *Lights On! The Wild Century-Long Saga of Night Baseball.* Lanham, Md.: Scarecrow, 1997.

PERIODICALS

Berkow, Ira. "A Feat That May Never Be Bettered." *The New York Times,* October 8, 1997, C28.

Fiffer, Steve. "A Few Enlightening Facts." *Sport* 75, October 1984, 44.

"Seabiscuit vs. War Admiral"

Newspaper article

By: Bryan Field

Date: November 1, 1938

Source: Field, Bryan. "Seabiscuit vs. War Admiral." *The New York Times,* November 1, 1938. Reprinted in *The Greatest Sport Stories From "The New York Times": Sport Classics of a Century.* Allison Danzig and Peter Brandwein, eds. New York: A.S. Barnes, 1951, 496–499.

About the Author: Bryan Field was a correspondent for *The New York Times* from the 1920s to the 1940s, serving as turf editor in charge of all horseracing coverage. He later held the position of president and general manager of Delaware Park, a renowned racing facility outside of Wilmington, Delaware. ■

Introduction

The story of Seabiscuit and War Admiral begins with Man o' War, the legendary thoroughbred. Man o' War lost only one race during his life, as a two-year-old, when a botched start left him caught in the gate while his competitors gained a large lead. He never lost again and was so dominant that he once beat another horse by one hundred lengths. He was voted the greatest horse of the first half of the twentieth century.

Man o' War sired War Admiral, who won the Triple Crown in 1937 and was undefeated in eight starts. Man o' War was also the grandfather of Seabiscuit, who, after a faulty start to his racing career, became one of the finest horses of his generation, under the steady hand of his trainer, Tom Smith. These two horses came together in the fall of 1938 to race a challenge match, because horseracing fans had come to demand it—a race between the two top horses of the time. Their shared connection to Man o' War made the match all the more compelling.

The story of Seabiscuit captured the public imagination as a prototypical rags-to-riches story. Just three years earlier, in 1936, he was struggling badly from weariness, having had over three times the typical race workload for a three-year-old. He was often foul-tempered and belligerent and did not have a remarkable record to show for all his work. Nonetheless, trainer Tom Smith saw something worthwhile in him, and after Chester Howard bought Seabiscuit for a mere $7,500, Smith nursed his horse back to health.

Under Smith's care, Seabiscuit soon had a new and thriving career as a racehorse. Howard put together coast-to-coast racing campaigns and Seabiscuit traveled over fifty thousand railroad miles to get to eighteen tracks in seven states and Mexico. The itinerary made the horse into a popular success, and his speed brought him 1937's highest earnings. He had more newspaper column inches written about him than internationally renown political leaders such as Roosevelt, Hitler, and Mussolini. But he lost the award for Horse of the Year to War Admiral, who, that year, became just the fourth horse to win the Triple Crown.

By the time they raced a year later, War Admiral was a prohibitive favorite because of his remarkable speed and history. Seabiscuit still struggled with an iffy left foreleg, but he challenged War Admiral's speed from the beginning of the race and eventually held off War Admiral's furious late charge for the victory. He was duly voted Horse of the Year for 1938 and ended his racing career two years later, in 1940, having earned a world record $437,730—nearly sixty times his purchase price.

Significance

The match between these two horses, which the famed sportswriter Grantland Rice called the greatest race he had ever witnessed, was the highlight of horse racing's rise in the popular imagination in the 1930s. A record crowd of forty thousand spectators mobbed the track and millions more listened to it on the radio, including President Franklin D. Roosevelt (served 1933–1945). It fully lived up to its billing, as each horse performed magnificently and came close to running in world record time.

Along with Gallant Fox's charismatic capturing of the Triple Crown in 1930, the success of each of these two horses brought newfound attention and money to the sport during a time when the nation was trying to recover from the Depression. The California legislature legalized pari-mutuel racing, and it became a boost to state revenues. Across the country, payouts for victories and for bettors grew along with the increased crowds.

Perhaps what was most remarkable about the events of November 1, 1938, however, was the symbolism of Seabiscuit's win. He signified the underdog making good, succeeding because of grit and determination. When Seabiscuit—with damaged leg, odd gait, quirky behavior, and all—bore down and beat what seemed to be the best horse of his generation, it suggested that anyone could do it, that even the little guy could sometimes overcome all odds to win out in the end. His was a fairy tale that all underdog athletes can look to for inspiration.

Primary Source

"Seabiscuit vs. War Admiral"

SYNOPSIS: Bryan Field's report captures the breathtaking energy of an event that truly lived up to its billing. He underscores the nature of the upset, with Seabiscuit taking a surprising early lead and then, even with a weakened foreleg, holding off the charging War Admiral.

Seabiscuit defeated War Admiral today, amid scenes of frantic enthusiasm, created by a record crowd of 40,000 persons, that simple fact stood high and alone and it will leave its impression on the American turf. Historic Pimlico never had seen anything like it.

Smashing the track record, beating War Admiral at his own game, the phlegmatic ugly duckling with the lame leg from the Pacific Coast did all, and more, than the son of Man o' War. There was glory enough for the two, but to Charles S. Howard's champion son of Hard Tack and the grandson of Man o' War went the distinction and an honor that probably no other thoroughbred in this equine generation will earn.

Thousands rushed the unsaddling enclosure after the finish and all but upset Matchmaker Alfred Gwynne Vanderbilt, Owner Howard and the veteran trainer, Tom Smith. Answering the pleas of hundreds, Smith grasped a single chrysanthemum for himself and then thrust the enormous bow of flowers into the reaching hands. In a twinkling ferns, leaves, flowers and even petals were wrenched apart as cheers still rolled forth from the souvenir hunters.

Virtually unnoticed, blanketed and hooded, out on the middle of the track, War Admiral walked alone toward his stall. But he was not quite alone. The hot

Jockey George Woolf and Seabiscuit lead War Admiral and jockey Charles Kurtsinger around the first turn at the Pimilco Race Course in Baltimore, Maryland. AP/WIDE WORLD PHOTOS. REPRODUCED BY PERMISSION.

favorite of a few minutes before, who had been made a 1-4 shot with the thousands in the stands, still had his faithful trainer, George Conway, watching his stride. Scanning his charge's every step for any sign of ailment, Conway then went his way alone.

It was a hard, bitter and punishing race. Until the last furlong it had the thousands on their feet. The time of 01:56 3-5, lowering Pompoon's record by a fifth of a second, surprised few. Both horses were going all out from the fall of the starting flag to the finish and it was Seabiscuit who led, for all except a brief span, when War Admiral tried and failed.

At the end of the mile and three-sixteenths the margin was three lengths, and if they had gone farther the margin would have been greater. The $15,000 which went to the winner brought Seabiscuit's total to $340,480, moving him from fifth to second place among the world's money-winners and placing him within striking distance of Sun Beau's record of $376,744. And this sort of horse was neglected in the betting, returning $6.40 for $2, or 11 to 5.

Although both horses appeared to come out of the race in excellent condition, future plans for War Admiral were thrown into confusion. It is possible that he may race again instead of being retired to stud immediately. Seabiscuit will continue racing, with the Riggs Handicap here Saturday his next start.

Mr. and Mrs. Howard were overwhelmed with congratulations as cameras clicked. Police, friends, hostlers [horse caretakers] and society well-wishers joined in a frenzied outburst produced perhaps by racing only. The Howards hardly had a chance to do more than bow and smile, but the San Franciscans at last got free and paid tribute to Samuel D. Riddle, owner of War Admiral, and Conway.

Smith, asked for a statement, declared, "I said mine on the track!" George Woolf, shouted at and queried before he could even dismount, had his first thought for Red Pollard, Seabiscuit's injured and regular jockey, who heard the race from a hospital bed by radio.

Charlie Kurtsinger, who handled War Admiral, congratulated Woolf, and was able to muster a grin after a finish that must have been as much of a shock to him as to most others. He offered no alibi, nor did any one else. It was the kind of race in which there could be no alibi.

While all the uproar was going on about him, Seabiscuit stood stolidly. A few minutes before his legs had flown, doubtless as they never had flown before, but now he was at ease. Even flashlight bulbs exploding right under his muzzle caused only a slight toss of his head. And the knee that had forced Smith to scratch him from the $100,000 special at Belmont Park last spring looked as good after as it had in the race.

While the plaudits of the great crowd were for Owner Howard, he was the first to acknowledge his debt to Smith and Woolf. Smith, an old cowhand from the Northwest, who learned the horse business the hard way, bought Seabiscuit as a three-year-old for $8,500, when the handicap champion virtually was a discard from the Wheatley Stable.

Most of the horse's earnings have been garnered since because Smith has been able to keep in training, and at his fittest, a thoroughbred campaigned up and down the country, from coast to coast, at strange as well as familiar race tracks. Always Seabiscuit has run gamely under heavy weight.

The impost today was 120 pounds for each, and it must have seemed light to the horse who now at five is the outstanding thoroughbred in America. As for Woolf, he won the race by taking the track from War Admiral. The wiseacres had said this could not be done.

Woolf accomplished it by whipping Seabiscuit away from the starting post. Turning on a tremendous burst of speed that must have caught Kurtsinger by surprise, Seabiscuit jumped a length in front under the sting of the lash.

Passing the stands for the first time, Seabiscuit was well enough in front to be able to cross over from the No. 2 post position and take the rail from War Admiral. Then Woolf put in a shrewd touch. Coming to the first turn he deliberately slowed Seabiscuit, so that his mount's churning quarters were right in front of War Admiral's nose. This served the double purpose of giving Seabiscuit a bit of a breather and forcing Kurtsinger to check somewhat to prevent War Admiral from running on the heels of the horse in front.

Around that first turn and into the backstretch Woolf eased his mount a trifle wide, forcing War Admiral wider. These were the same tactics Kurtsinger had worked with War Admiral against Pompoon when those two clashed in the memorable Preakness of 1937 that War Admiral won.

Coming into the backstretch Kurtsinger, always cool and collected, knew that he was getting the worst of things and decided to ask War Admiral for his best in the long, straight run that stretched away to the far turn. He turned loose his hold and slashed with the whip. The Man o' War colt went forward with a bound. Within thirty yards the two were head and head as the deafening roar billowed from the crowd, "There he goes!"

For another furlong the two were head and head. Then War Admiral's nose showed in front. Now Woolf slashed with the whip, and the nose of War Admiral showed no more.

But neither could Seabiscuit draw away. The two went to the far turn as one horse, went around that bend as one horse and headed for the top of the homestretch still with nothing between them.

Kurtsinger, who stated before the race that he never had had to ask War Admiral for his best, asked now. With all the power that has made him one of the country's first-flight riders, he drove forward with War Admiral. Again and again the black-clad arm with the yellow bars rose and fell, but War Admiral could do no more. He had met a better horse.

Woolf, too, was driving. He knew that final turn into the stretch was the last try of the horse justly called Man o' War's greatest son. He, too, flung everything into the drive.

Smith, grizzled and tight-lipped, must have wondered how Seabiscuit's knee was standing the twisting, as well as the pounding, that a turn produces. It is on turns that thoroughbreds' knees give way, when hearts do not.

But Seabiscuit's knee did not give and his courage had been proved in many a racing war. Through the last furlong it was a procession, with the horses speeding like vivid but silent phantoms as the waves of cheering from the stands submerged and overwhelmed the pounding thud of the hoofs.

Further Resources

BOOKS

Bowen, Edward L. *War Admiral: Thoroughbred Legends.* Lexington, Ky.: Eclipse, 2002.

Hillenbrand, Laura. *Seabiscuit: An American Legend.* Waterville, Maine: G.K. Hall, 2001.

PERIODICALS

Barich, Bill. "Why Horse Racing Keeps Falling Short of Its Ideals." *The New York Times,* July 24, 1983, 22.

Nack, William. "A Match Made in Heaven: November 1, 1938. Seabiscuit Races War Admiral." *Sports Illustrated* 91, no. 21, 128.

"61,808 in Gehrig Tribute"

Magazine article

By: *The Sporting News*

Date: July 12, 1939

Source: "61,808 in Gehrig Tribute." *The Sporting News,* July 12, 1939. ■

Introduction

Lou Gehrig (1903–1941) was born in New York and died there of amyotrophic lateral sclerosis, a hardening of the spinal cord that is now more commonly known as Lou Gehrig's disease. Gehrig played first base for the New York Yankees from 1923 to 1939, ending his career only when physically unable to perform because of his increasing disability. He was a special player who enjoyed great success on the baseball diamond. But more importantly he was a special man who articulated the best of the human spirit. His speech on July 4, 1939, when the New York Yankees retired his uniform and so many of his old teammates came out to honor him, may stand as baseball's most sentimental moment. However, the power of the moment should not be dismissed, for Gehrig displayed great courage on that day and throughout his last few years.

His achievements on the field were of the very highest caliber. Gehrig was a lifetime .340 hitter and hit 493 home runs in his career. He ranks fourth among all players, with 1,995 runs batted in. He had a daunting .632 slugging percentage and an impressive .447 on-base percentage. He batted at least .300 for the first twelve years of his career and knocked home over one hundred runs thirteen years in a row. His twenty-three grand slams are still a major league record. He was elected to the Baseball Hall of Fame by special vote the same year he retired.

He was known as the Iron Horse for his incredible consistency and durability. He played in 2,130 consecutive games between 1925 and 1939, when he pulled himself from the lineup, aware that he was physically unable to perform well enough to help his team. He did not yet know of the disease that would end his career and take his life in a few short years.

Gehrig rarely wanted to be in the spotlight. For much of his career he had the benefit of Babe Ruth's presence on the Yankees to divert attention away from himself. While Ruth loved the attention, Gehrig preferred the more quiet camaraderie of his teammates. After Ruth's career ended in New York, the Yankees' fortunes shot up even higher than when he played, and Gehrig became the heart of the team, a quiet and steady leader. The Yankees won the championship in 1936, 1937, and 1938.

Gehrig, though, started to struggle physically in 1938 and, at the beginning of the 1939 season, was playing poorly in the field and at the plate. His performance was out of character. After voluntarily ending his consecutive playing streak on May 2, he went to the Mayo Clinic for medical treatment, where he was diagnosed with his terminal illness. He was forced to retire immediately. Two months later, he was honored on Independence Day at Yankee Stadium.

Significance

What happened to Lou Gehrig shocked the nation. It seemed painfully ironic that this physically strong and vibrant athlete, who had consistently displayed endurance beyond that of his fellow athletes, could be the victim of such a physically debilitating disease. Gehrig distinguished himself by refusing to give in to self-pity and instead offering a stoic face to the public that suggested they should not feel sorry for him. His farewell speech summarizes his outlook. He was a man who had been blessed and was grateful for the opportunities he had received.

Gehrig's attitude elevated the moment beyond sentimentality. Much as he had throughout his career, he refused to put himself first or to bemoan his fate. His selflessness in the face of the greatest adversity became

Lou Gehrig gives his farewell speech in Yankee Stadium on July 4, 1939. © BETTMANN/CORBIS. REPRODUCED BY PERMISSION.

the measuring stick against which other athletes were considered. Lou Gehrig was an exceptional baseball player, one of the best of his generation. It was his approach to his disease, even as he understood that it would soon take his life, that marked Lou Gehrig as a hero.

Nobody really knows exactly what he said on July 4, 1939, the day the Yankees retired his uniform number, four, the first time that honor had been bestowed on a ballplayer. His speech has become part of our national mythology; however, as the Baseball Hall of Fame has made clear, no official audio recording of the entire speech is known to actually exist. While the now-famous passages at the beginning and end of the speech survive, all the other accounts of the speech, transcribed by those in attendance, are imprecise and often erroneous. We simply do not know exactly what Lou Gehrig said. What follows is the account we find most authoritative.

Primary Source

"61,808 in Gehrig Tribute"

SYNOPSIS: Nervous and visibly moved, Lou Gehrig addressed over 60,000 fans during a specially arranged ceremony in which the Yankees retired his uniform number. Gehrig's powerful address speaks simply and eloquently to his courageous and thoughtful character. The following article contains quotes from the beginning and end of Gehrig's famous speech, in which he refuses pity and instead suggests that he has been rewarded with great blessings.

In a 40-minute ceremony between games of the July 4 double-header at Yankee Stadium, witnessed by 61,808 fans, Lou Gehrig, ailing captain of the world champions, received a tribute unprecedented in the annals of the game.

The ceremonies, held at home plate, included speeches by Postmaster General James A. Farley, Mayor F. H. LaGuardia, Manager Joe McCarthy and others. Lou received gifts from the club, teammates, baseball writers, Stadium employes, the Giants, the concessionaires and others, while being given a thunderous ovation by the crowd.

Former teammates on the 1927 Yankees, present for the occasion, included: Babe Ruth, Tony Lazzeri, Joe Dugan, Bob Meusel, Earle Combs, Mark Koenig, Herb Pennock, Waite Hoyt, Bob Shawkey, George Pipgras, Wally Schang and Benny Bengough. Others on hand were Wally Pipp, whose first base job Gehrig took in 1925, and Everett Scott, whose old consecutive-game record of 1,307 was far eclipsed by Lou, with 2,130 games.

Gehrig, affected to the point of tears by the stirring tributes paid to him, was unable at first to respond. However, after President Ed Barrow of the Yankees whispered a few words to buck him up, Lou took the microphone and said:

"Fans, for the past two weeks you have been reading about a bad break I got. Yet, today, I consider myself the luckiest man on the face of the earth. I have been in ball parks 16 years, and have never received anything but kindness and encouragement from you fans.

"Wouldn't you consider it an honor just to be with such great men even for one day?" he continued, motioning to present-day and past Yankees lined up at the plate.

"Sure, I'm lucky! Who wouldn't consider it an honor to have known Jake Ruppert, builder of baseball's greatest empire; to have spent six years with such a grand little fellow as Miller Huggins; to have spent nine years with that smart student of psychology—the best manager in baseball today—Joe McCarthy?

"Who wouldn't feel honored to room with such a grand guy as Bill Dickey?

"When the New York Giants, a team you would give your right arm to beat, and vice versa, send a gift—that's something. When the ground keepers and office staff and writers and old-timers and players and concessionaires all remember you with trophies—that's something.

"When you have a wonderful mother-in-law, who takes sides with you in squabbles against her own daughter—that's something; when you have a father and mother who work all their lives so that you can have an education and build your body—it's a blessing. When you have a wife who has been a tower of strength, and shown more courage than you dreamed existed—that's the finest I know.

"So I close in saying that I might have had a tough break; but I have an awful lot to live for."

Further Resources

BOOKS

Gallico, Paul. *Lou Gehrig, Pride of the Yankees.* New York: Grosset and Dunlap, 1942.

Graham, Frank. *Lou Gehrig, A Quiet Hero.* New York: Putnam, 1942.

Robinson, Ray. *Iron Horse: Lou Gehrig in His Time.* New York: W.W. Norton, 1990.

Rubin, Robert. *Lou Gehrig, Courageous Star.* New York: Putnam, 1979.

PERIODICALS

Robinson, Ray. "Gehrig's Streak Ended When Gehrig Said So." *The New York Times,* September 24, 1997, C5.

"Sepia Stars Only Lukewarm Toward Campaign to Break Down Baseball Barriers"

Newspaper article

By: Sam Lacy

Date: August 12, 1939

Source: Lacy, Sam. "Sepia Stars Only Lukewarm Toward Campaign to Break Down Baseball Barriers." *The Washington Tribune,* August 12, 1939. Reprinted in Reisler, Jim. *Black Writers/Black Baseball: An Anthology of Articles From Black Sportwriters Who Covered the Negro Leagues.* Jefferson, N.C.: McFarland, 1994, 15–17.

About the Author: Sam Lacy (1903–2003) was the first black member of the Baseball Writers Association of America. He was a longtime contributor to *The Baltimore Afro-American* and also wrote for *The Washington Tribune* and *The Chicago Defender.* He was one of the first black sportswriters to push actively for the integration of major league baseball. For his work he won numerous awards, including four National Newspaper Writing Awards. ■

Introduction

Since the mid-1880s, black players had been banned from participating in major league baseball. Integration would come only when Jackie Robinson joined the Brooklyn Dodgers in 1947. In order to compete, black players had to join teams that eventually combined into what were known as the Negro Leagues. Often these teams would barnstorm across the country, picking up games wherever and whenever they could, setting their schedule according to the availability of suitable stadiums in which they could play.

While play was disrupted by the Depression in the early 1930s, a new Negro National League formed in 1933, and a Negro American League took shape in 1937. The play in this league was at an exceptionally high level, led by such players as Josh Gibson, James "Cool Papa" Bell, Buck Leonard, and Satchel Paige.

Two teams especially, the Pittsburgh Crawfords and the Homestead Grays, competed heatedly against each other for the championship during the decade. In 1931, the Grays had a record of 136-10 and were led by Gibson and the renowned Smokey Joe Williams. The next year, though, the Crawfords convinced Gibson to play for them, and they soon became the dominant team in the

(Left to right) Oscar Charleston, Josh Gibson, Ted Page, and Judy Johnson helped lead the Pittsburgh Crawfords to the 1932 Negro League championship. **AP/WIDE WORLD PHOTOS. REPRODUCED BY PERMISSION.**

league, with Paige, Bell, Oscar Charleston, and Judy Johnson joining Gibson to comprise a group of five future Hall of Famers on the same squad.

However, the Negro Leagues struggled to attain consistent financial success, due partly to mismanagement and partly to the fact that owners had to pay not only player salaries but for the stadiums in which the games took place. While teams were often covered in black newspapers, getting crossover coverage from white newspapers was a much greater challenge. The creation of the East-West Game in 1933—modeled after the All-Star Game of the major leagues—was an attempt to gain national attention and to showcase the finest black players. It proved a resounding success and, along with the stirring exploits of the black stars of the league, encouraged further discussion of ending the color ban.

Significance

During the off-season, many black players competed and held their own against white players on the barnstorming circuit in such warm-weather sites as California. But the Negro Leagues were a source of pride for many blacks around the country and were valued as a means of showcasing black athletes. Such opportunities were often rare in the 1930s.

Following the population shifts of the Great Migration of the early twentieth century, in which millions of blacks left the agricultural South for northern urban industrial centers, the new Negro Leagues of the 1930s were part of a cultural shift that saw a rise in the visibility and presence of blacks in the national spotlight. The Harlem Renaissance of the 1920s was an artistic flowering of deeply talented black writers and artists, such as Langston Hughes, Zora Neale Hurston, and Aaron Douglas, who had never before had the opportunity for a broad audience. Likewise, jazz was quickly gaining a greater toehold in dance halls and on the radio. The Negro Leagues were part of this cultural evolution, as well.

Discussion of integration, therefore, was seen as an exciting sign of the advancement that blacks had made in America. It signaled a growing acceptance of them as equal citizens. However, as some blacks noted, integration of the major leagues might jeopardize the viability of the Negro Leagues, where blacks had been showcased. Moreover, integration might mean the end of the Negro Leagues, as players and audiences would go to places where more economically viable ball clubs could sustain an engaging game. In fact, as the events of the late 1940s and early 1950s showed, this is exactly what happened, as integration did eventually cause the end of the Negro Leagues.

Primary Source

"Sepia Stars Only Lukewarm Toward Campaign to Break Down Baseball Barriers"

SYNOPSIS: Here Sam Lacy articulates his objective of giving black players a chance to voice their thoughts about an end to the color ban. In quoting four different players, Lacy demonstrates some of the problems resulting from integration, including questions about how many players were good enough to make it in the major leagues, what kind of racism they would experience, and whether it would have damaging consequences for the Negro Leagues.

Although there has been much agitation for the inclusion of colored players in major league baseball, it occurred to me recently that few people, if any, seemed to care a rap about what the players themselves think of the idea.

Newspapermen all over the country have at some time or other in the past two years, spoken out in favor of admitting qualified colored performers into the organized diamond sport. And liberal fans of both groups have raised a howl at the bars that are maintained against the potential big leaguers of the darker race.

In fact, every corner has been surveyed, every stop-gap plugged by people who sought to lend a hand in the campaign. Even major league club owners have been quoted and league presidents solicited. The leagues, from the commission on down to the players, have been canvassed for their views on the matter.

What about the Players?

But no one seems to have given a tinker's damn about the ideas of the guys they're trying to boot into the organized game.

The colored player, evidently, is big enough in the mind of the public to make top-line baseball, but too small to have any worth toward opinions on the matter.

But I remembered what a kick I got when, as a kid, I was asked how I'd like to get a bike for Christmas. And I recalled the thrill that even now never completely spends itself while I am waiting for my nightly ice cream.

Since man first became endowed with conscience and a sense of appreciation, he has felt keenly elated at the prospect of getting something. Why then, shouldn't the colored player be interrogated on the proposal to open big league ball to him, something we *think* he wants, but never bothered to *ask him* whether he does?

Vic Harris

Vic Harris, captain of the colored world champions, the Homestead Grays, was questioned on the proposition.

"It might be a good thing and then again, it might not be," the easy-going, soft-spoken Smoky City leader said.

"It's like this," he said. "We do have some good ballplayers among us, but not nearly as many fit for the majors as seems to be the belief. But, if they start picking them up, what are the remaining players going to do to make a living?

"Our crowds are not what they should be now. And suppose our stars—the fellows who do draw well—are gobbled up by the big clubs. How could the other 75 or 80% survive?"

Jud Wilson

A somewhat different slant was given by Jud Wilson, veteran third baseman of the Philadelphia Stars.

"Something may come from this thing in time," he said, "But I seriously doubt it. In the first place, it's too big a job for the people who are now trying to put it over. It will have to be a universal movement, and that will never be.

"It will never be, because the big league game, as it is now, is over-run with Southern blood. Fellows from the South are in the majority on almost every team in the major leagues. The New York Yankees, I believe, is about the only club made up almost entirely of players from the North, East and West.

"The training camps are in the South, the majority of minor leagues are in the South and there's a strong Southern sentiment in the stands. When the teams are on the road, these fellows would have to stop at the same hotels, eat in the same dining rooms and sleep in the same train compartments with the colored players.

"There'd be trouble for sure. And, if we were sent to other hotels or otherwise separated, the colored fans and the colored players would get hotter than they are over the present arrangement."

Names 13

"There are some fellows who could probably make it," Jud went on, "but at least half of them wouldn't because they are too old.

"Dick Seay, Willie Wells, Mule Suttles [Newark]; Jim West, Pat Patterson [Philadelphia Stars]; Sammy Bankhead, Josh Gibson, Buck Leonard [Homestead Grays]; Bill Wright and Sam Hughes [Elites] would have a good chance. So would Johnny Taylor, Barney Brown and Bill Perkins, now playing in Mexico.

"But you can't tell about them," Wilson concluded. "These fellows in our leagues lie too much about their ages."

Felton Snow

Catching a word from him between innings as he found time to sit down on the bench beside me, I got the following version from Felton Snow, manager of the Baltimore Elite Giants:

"I don't know if it would be a good thing, because we've got so many guys who just wouldn't act right. Some of these fellows who are pretty good out there on the diamond would give you a heartache elsewhere.

"You see, there are so many men who get $3 or $4 in their pockets, and right away, they want to tell 'the man' where he can go.

"We have some good players, yes. And, some of them would certainly qualify, but it is quite a task finding the right combination. Many of the good players are bad actors and many of the ordinary players are fine characters."

Dick Lundy

Dick Lundy, regarded by many as the greatest shortstop that colored baseball has ever seen, laid the blame for lack of progress at the feet of the colored leaders themselves.

"For 25 years," Lundy said, "I have listened to them get in their meetings and lament the fact that 'colored baseball is still in its infancy, so we can't do this and we can't do that.' The result is that we're no further now than we were when the thought of organizing first came up.

"In order to get anywhere in this movement, we've got to perfect our own organization. We've got to get some men in the game with some money and who don't have to pull a lot of funny moves to cover up every little loss. It's foolish to expect to make any headway when the money is being put up by people who don't stand to lose a penny.

"With one or two of these kinds of people in colored baseball, we could adopt some hard and fast rules that would protect the organization. Then, there wouldn't be all of this jumping from one team to another and the reins could be drawn tighter all around.

"Another thing is that we haven't yet seen the advantage of keeping those of our men who know baseball in the game. Colored baseball wants to have nothing to do with a fellow after he has passed his usefulness as a player, no matter how much he knows about the game.

"If these faults are corrected and a definite publicity program arranged and followed, then perhaps colored baseball would make some headway. A strong organization of our own thus formed, it would naturally follow that we would *demand* rather than *solicit* recognition."

Colored baseball, itself, has now spoken.

Further Resources

BOOKS

Craft, David. *The Negro Leagues: 40 Years of Black Professional Baseball in Words and Pictures.* New York: Crescent, 1993.

Dixon, Phil. *The Negro Baseball Leagues, 1867–1955: A Photographic History.* Mattituck, N.Y.: Amereon House, 1992.

Holway, John. *Black Diamonds: Life in the Negro Leagues From the Men Who Lived It.* Westport, Conn.: Meckler, 1989.

McNeil, William. *Cool Papas and Double Duties: The All-Time Greats of the Negro Leagues.* Jefferson, N.C.: McFarland, 2001.

Ribowsky, Mark. *A Complete History of the Negro Leagues: 1884 to 1955.* New York: Birch Lane, 1995.

Rogosin, Donn. *Invisible Men: Life in Baseball's Negro Leagues.* New York: Atheneum, 1983.

AUDIO AND VISUAL MEDIA

"Only the Ball Was White." WTTW Chicago. Produced and directed by Ken Solarz. MPI Home Video, 1992, VHS.

Wings on My Feet

Autobiography

By: Sonja Henie

Date: 1940

Source: Henie, Sonja. *Wings on My Feet.* New York: Prentice-Hall, 1940, 70–76.

About the Author: Sonja Henie (1912–1969) was born in Oslo, Norway. She first laced up a pair of skates at age eight and, at ten, won the first of six straight Norwegian figure-skating championships. She had stunning success as a figure skater, winning the European title for eight consecutive years and winning the world championship ten years in a row. She won Olympic gold in 1928, 1932, and 1936, after which she turned professional and began a career in Hollywood as a movie star. ■

Introduction

Sonja Henie dominated amateur women's figure skating from the late 1920s into the 1930s. Her record of success and longevity at the top of her sport, by today's standards, is breathtaking. She first competed at the Winter Olympics at the age of twelve and won her first gold medal at age sixteen. Eight years later, she was still at the peak of her skating powers, having won all the major figure-skating titles for years on end. With nothing more to prove in her sport, and still only in her mid-twenties, it was time to look elsewhere.

Henie moved permanently to the United States in 1936, turned professional, and became the star of a touring ice show. She performed in these popularly and critically acclaimed shows into the 1950s. Her ice carnivals attracted millions of adoring fans. At the same time, she sought to break into Hollywood films, hoping to capitalize on her popularity as an internationally known athlete. She succeeded in this arena as well, appearing in a number of films in the 1930s and 1940s, performing with such respected actors as Tyrone Power, Ethel Merman, Milton Berle, and Don Ameche.

Significance

Henie's enormous success as a figure skater and film actress helped increase the popularity of competitive figure skating in America and worldwide. Indeed, she was one of the first international superstars, recognized not only in her native Norway but also throughout Europe and in the United States. Up to that point, few non-American athletes had ever achieved Henie's level of acceptance in this country. By breaking through in the United States, she helped open the door for future athletes to crack the barrier of foreign nationality.

Henie pioneered the use of modern costumes and choreography in figure skating. Her skills did not merely derive from her athletic ability but also from her artistic inclinations. Her innovations have had a tremendous impact on the sport, as artistry has taken on increasing importance in competition figure skating.

Clearly, part of Henie's success was due to her recognition that she was perceived not only as an athlete but as an entertainer. Her emphasis on artistry, on the "performance" in competition, is evident in her autobiography, *Wings on My Feet,* in which she includes photographs of some of her signature jumps and turns. These were not always the most difficult moves athletically, but they added to the overall effect of the artistic interpretation that she hoped to offer an audience.

Her understanding of her role as an entertainer led her naturally to films. In Hollywood, she joined other Olympic athletes such as Johnny Weismuller, who played Tarzan in a number of films, and Buster Crabbe, who held the roles of Flash Gordon and Buck Rogers. These athletes-turned-actors helped lay the groundwork for today's athletes to perform in other media and also to demand that they be paid not only as athletes but as entertainers, as well.

Primary Source

Wings on My Feet [excerpt]

SYNOPSIS: In this excerpt from her autobiography, Henie recalls the enormous popularity of her ice carnivals in America following her triumph in the 1936 Olympics. Henie capitalized on her success by aiming for a film career in Hollywood. Her arrival there at the end of the tour capped the success of her ice performances, and the huge popularity of the tour culminated in a contract with Darryl Zanuck, head of the Twentieth Century Fox movie studio.

So I pinned my hope of Hollywood on the contacts that might be made during the tour. Plenty of motion picture people did come to the performances in Madison Square Garden. All my numbers were in dance form, and nicely costumed. I had a white satin dress, designed by Patou, that I wore with a Juliet cap, for my fox-trot-tempo solo; a gay peasant bodice dress for a Mazurka, and my classic ballet dress with the wings for the Swan. Jack did a rhumba, and it all went off quite brilliantly. But there was not the response we had expected from the cinema forces.

Hope finally got a substantial toe-hold when we were in Chicago, and then through our own enterprise rather than anyone's else foresight. We learned, in Chicago, that Hollywood had an ice rink, the "Polar Ice Palace." This made a radical difference. Perhaps it is reasonable for the average movie-struck girl who "wants to get into Hollywood" to go out there quite simply and hound the producers' offices until she lands a job as an extra, and then try to work up from there. In my case, it would have been senseless. I had something new to offer that could be made tremendously valuable or of complete inconsequence. I was certain that the method of knocking on doors and presenting myself with nothing but words and theories to show for what I believed could be accomplished, would get nowhere. We were all certain that it would be useless to go to Hollywood unless we either went on a likely sounding call from the fortress or at least were sure there was some ice in Hollywood to prove our theories on, to an audience.

The Polar Palace opened the door. Father got in touch with Los Angeles, and discovered it would be possible for us to rent the rink for a period of days. Immediately we turned a remote notion into a plan. At the end of the tour, we would go to Hollywood and I would give an exhibition on my own that would show Hollywood, or show us it couldn't be done. Father wired, clinching our rental of the Palace.

The tour was a great success in itself. We played to packed houses everywhere, and from the warmth of the audiences and the reviews we received came overwhelming proof that the American public would be glad to have more. On April 15, when the tour closed in Detroit, I had exactly three weeks in which to go on to the coast and prepare myself and all my arrangements for the crucial exhibition. We had named May 7 and May 9 as the dates of the two performances.

I had a dreadful moment the first day out there. I told the taxi driver I wanted to go to the skating rink.

"Here y'are, lady," he said, as we pulled up to the curb. My eager eyes fell upon bright signs urging me to come roller skating. Then with relief like food to the starving, I found this was not the Polar Palace. My driver had never heard of the Polar Palace, nor of skating on ice, but we got there via a consultation with the telephone book.

Sonja Henie executes one of her routines on the ice. AP/WIDE WORLD PHOTOS. REPRODUCED BY PERMISSION.

Four people were on the ice when I took my first look at it, and I learned from the manager that this was practically rush hour. Gradually I was becoming aware that Hollywood was not ice-conscious.

Under the circumstances, we saw that it was going to be a job to get an audience of any sort, let alone the influential type that was essential to the plan. We sent out invitations and we advertised. The newspapers were helpful. Reporters with the big news services knew of my work abroad and in the East. There were many stories, all of them friendly.

I packed all the dance and sparkle I could into the program. I had six pairs to open it with a tango, then an Apache pair, then a bit of comedy, next Jack's rhumba, and then me. During the course of the evening I would give all my three tour solos, ending with the Mazurka from Coppelia. Having the rink to ourselves several days in advance, we succeeded in teaching the workmen how to put a perfect surface on the ice. We hired a good orchestra, and good lighting staff. The rink was smaller than the arena ice we had been accustomed to, so it took constant rehearsing to whip our numbers into shape, all apart from the other elements of the production. The three weeks evaporated. Before they were quite gone, we had the satisfaction of knowing that both performances were sellouts in advance. We had our audience all right. The remaining question was, would people of that sun-blessed, iceless, skateless area have any idea what our performance was about?

The night of May seventh they came, in quantity and quality—Mary Pickford, Douglas Fairbanks, John Barrymore, Spencer Tracy, Clark Gable, Myrna Loy, Robert Taylor, and a glittering host of others. The scene outside the entrance was evidently unusual. Jeannette Meehan, Hollywood correspondent of the *New York World-Telegram,* saw it, as I didn't, and wrote a description I have kept:

"People shoved—cars jammed—parking prices had been put up another twenty-five cents. Limousines were parked in the tumble weeds in a vacant lot across the street, and stars got their hose ruined treking through to the side-walk. The whole thing had the standing, staring, curbstone-sitting look of an old-fashioned Hollywood première.

"Inside there was bedlam. The bleachers were packed. There were chairs in the aisles, people standing behind the orchestra, others seated in chairs on the floor boarding. A squad of hefty cops kept people from crowding on the rink itself.

"Everybody was there—society, Main Street, Hollywood's great and near-great. Carole Lombard, Jeanette MacDonald and Gene Raymond, Ginger Rogers, James Stewart, Jean Arthur, Bette Davis, Gary and Mrs. Cooper, Norma Shearer. . . . Every production boss in the business. But the people weren't there to see Hollywood.

"One could sense [as the program got under way] a current of tense anticipation. Thousands of eyes kept glancing up to the grey curtain at the far side where the name of the evening's star performer was spelled in glittering letters four feet high. Again the lights went out. Excited voices hushed. Suddenly a single spotlight broke through the smoky atmosphere and flattened out on the ice. Into its gleam floated a small white figure—Sonja Henie."

At this point, Miss Meehan gave a complimentary account of my three appearances, including a statement that I "had the audience in the palm of my hand." Then, to quote a little more, since this night was the foundation of everything that has come since:

"They wouldn't let her go. 'Encore! Encore!' People jumped up and down. Stars forgot themselves in her performance and yelled themselves hoarse. Producers eyed one another and fervently prayed that the other fellow wasn't thinking in terms of a contract. Pandemonium continued. When Miss Henie finally withdrew, the rafters complained of the applause.

"The next morning, Hollywood had elbow bruises on its ribs, and Sonja Henie was the talk of the town. Studios were cooing at her. Universal, Paramount, M-G-M wanted her. It has been a long time since Hollywood's producer contingent has devised as many attractive contracts for one person."

What Miss Meehan didn't know was that the one producer we most wanted to reach wasn't there the first night. Darryl F. Zanuck's reputation for recognizing the possibilities in new things, ideas, and personalities and for initiative and courage in putting them forward, had made us feel he was our best hope. I had people keep watch to see if he came that night, and they all made the same disappointing report. The genius of Twentieth Century-Fox had not come with the rest.

We couldn't find him the second night, either. Apart from that, the evening went very well, but his absence almost overshadowed the success. Mary Pickford gave me flowers. I greeted a long procession of stars who had come back a second time. They all assured me that skating would be Hollywood's next craze.

In those three days Hollywood became ice-minded. Offers fell into our lap like ripe fruit. Darryl Zanuck appeared. He had escaped our vigil at the second performance. He had seen it after all.

I remember our momentous conversation very well. We were sitting together, mother and I on a settee, Mr. Zanuck across from us. He asked me, in just so many words, what I wanted. I said, "The title role," and he let go a good cross between a snort and a laugh and said, "Miss Henie, not that!"

The moves were rapid from there on. I told him, in that case I wasn't interested. That I had no desire to play supporting roles in films that would be carried by my skating. That I was looking beyond tomorrow. That my first film would be decisive both for the company and for me.

He was listening with interest. Mother nudged me. She saw a change of tone coming, and in a moment it came. Mr. Zanuck proceeded more softly. He said the exhibition had convinced him that skating was a thing of importance, but that he didn't believe that skating scenes should dominate the picture.

"Someone else must have the lead. But don't worry," he added kindly, "you'll show them."

So I went about making it clear that I wasn't interested in putting myself before the public. It was my skating I wanted to have given place and scope, and I felt if I didn't have the leading role this couldn't be done.

"I want to have a real chance at it," I said, mustering all the bravery I had. "I'll sink or swim, and if you don't want to take the chance with me, I'll go elsewhere."

The contract was signed. We had carried the hill. There followed talk about the first film, and about when I'd go to work. The contract was a long one, for five years, but that was usual. From the day I put my name on that hard-earned line, I found in Mr. Zanuck one of the best of advisers, a man with a fantastically sharp grasp of details and a surpassing instinct for knowing what the public wants.

Further Resources

BOOKS

Copley-Graves, Lynn. *Figure Skating History: The Evolution of Dance on Ice.* Columbus, Ohio: Platoro, 1992.

Milton, Steve. *Skate: 100 Years of Figure Skating.* North Pomfret, Vt.: Trafalgar Square, 1996.

Strait, Raymond. *Queen of Ice, Queen of Shadow: The Unsuspected Life of Sonja Henie.* New York: Stein and Day, 1985.

Whedon, Julia. *The Fine Art of Figure Skating: An Illustrated History and Portfolio of Stars.* New York: H.N. Abrams, 1988.

AUDIO AND VISUAL MEDIA

Happy Landing. Original release, 1938, Twentieth Century Fox. Directed by Roy Del Ruth. The Sonja Henie Collection, VHS, 1994.

One in a Million. Original release, 1936, Twentieth Century Fox. Directed by Sidney Lanfield. The Sonja Henie Collection, VHS, 1994.

Second Fiddle. Original release, 1939, Twentieth Century Fox. Directed by Sidney Lanfield. VHS, 1994.

Sun Valley Serenade. Original release, 1941, Twentieth Century Fox. Directed by H. Bruce Humberstone. VHS, 1991.

The Babe Ruth Story

Autobiography

By: Babe Ruth, as told to Bob Considine

Date: 1948

Source: Ruth, Babe, as told to Bob Considine. *The Babe Ruth Story.* New York: E.P. Dutton, 1948, 192–194.

About the Author: George Herman "Babe" Ruth (1885–1948), born in Baltimore, was the most celebrated athlete of his time and is widely considered the best player in baseball history. After a tumultuous childhood, he started his career in 1914 as a pitcher with the Boston Red Sox, winning three World Series. In 1920, Ruth was sold to the New York Yankees, where he transformed himself into baseball's most prolific slugger and won four more World Series. After his retirement in 1935, Ruth became much sought after as a television personality. He died in 1948 in New York City at the age of 53. ■

Introduction

Babe Ruth's lifetime statistics speak for themselves: a .342 batting average, 714 home runs, 2,210 runs batted in, 2,056 walks, a .690 slugging percentage, and a .474 on-base percentage. And that's just as a hitter. As a pitcher, he was 94-46, with an earned run average of just 2.28. He was one of the best pitchers of his era before he turned full-time to hitting, at which point he dominated the game far and above his peers.

The fans loved Babe Ruth for his play but also for his acceptance of the spotlight. He was the most prominent celebrity athlete in an age of increased attention to athletes. A rich lore came to be associated with his name, such as his promising a child confined to a hospital that he would hit two home runs for him in the game that day. It is diffcult to determine whether such stories are true. Part of the lore surrounding Ruth came about because of his close relationship with sportswriters, such as Grantland Rice, who helped create the legend of the Babe. Ruth was embraced by the media of the day; they rarely reported his more problematic off-the-field activities, such as drinking and womanizing.

"The Called Shot" may be Ruth's most famous moment. In the third game of the World Series against the Chicago Cubs in 1932, facing pitcher Charley Root, Ruth reportedly pointed toward center field and predicted that he would hit a home run in his current at bat. He did, in fact, hit a home run, breaking a 4-4 tie and propelling the Yankees to victory. New York went on to sweep the series, further cementing the legend of the Babe. But whether he actually pointed to the outfield is very much in question. Some historians have argued that he did not point toward center field, but that he did challenge the Cubs and predict that he would hit a home run.

Babe Ruth gets a hit in the 1932 World Series against the Chicago Cubs. AP/WIDE WORLD PHOTOS. REPRODUCED BY PERMISSION.

Significance

Even in the 1930s, when he was starting to age, Ruth was still a dominant hitter, bashing 172 home runs from 1930 to 1934. By 1934, however, his years of fast and hard living—especially during the 1920s, when he was one of the biggest celebrities in the country and enjoying the spoils of his notoriety—were beginning to catch up to him. He had fought for years with Yankees manager Joe McCarthy and president Ed Barrow for increased control of the team, but was repeatedly rebuffed. In 1935, he was forced to sign with the Boston Braves, who gave him a chance to apprentice for a position as manager while finishing out his playing career. In the end, Ruth played only twenty-eight games for the Braves before he retired from baseball, never getting the chance to manage.

In some ways, the "Called Shot" in 1932 stands as Ruth's last great moment. He had success on the field in the next two years, but not quite as much as he had previously enjoyed. The team was changing, with McCarthy establishing firm control and other players and other teams—such as the Gashouse Gang in St. Louis—grabbing more headlines. The "Called Shot" seemed of heroic proportions, and the culture treated Ruth as a hero. The lore surrounding him speaks to this very concept: Babe Ruth provided the country with someone it could always believe in, someone who would always deliver. Whether it was all exactly "true" or not is not as important as our wish to believe it was true.

Primary Source

The Babe Ruth Story [excerpt]

SYNOPSIS: In this excerpt from his life story, written with the assistance of well-known syndicated columnist Bob Considine, Ruth recalls the famous moment when he predicted a home run against the Chicago Cubs. There was no love lost between the Yankees and the Cubs, for they had a long-running feud. Ruth, for instance, alludes to the way Chicago fans had treated his wife Claire by berating and spitting on her. His desire to not only beat, but also to embarrass, the Cubs was obvious.

The Yanks and Cubs were two of the sorest ball clubs ever seen when they took the field for the third game, with George Pipgras pitching for us and Charley Root throwing for them.

But no member of either team was sorer than I was. I had seen nothing my first time at bat that came close to looking good to me, and that only made me more determined to do something about taking the wind out of the sails of the Chicago players and their fans. I mean the fans who had spit on Claire.

I came up in the fourth inning with Earle Combs on base ahead of me. My ears had been blistered so much before in my baseball career that I thought they had lost all feeling. But the blast that was turned on me by Cub players and some of the fans penetrated and cut deep. Some of the fans started throwing vegetables and fruit at me.

I stepped back out of the box, then stepped in. And while Root was getting ready to throw his first pitch, I pointed to the bleachers which rise out of deep center field.

Root threw one right across the gut of the plate and I let it go. But before the umpire could call it a strike—which it was—I raised my right hand, stuck out one finger and yelled, "Strike one!"

The razzing was stepped up a notch.

Root got set and threw again—another hard one through the middle. And once again I stepped back and held up my right hand and bawled, "Strike two!" It was.

You should have heard those fans then. As for the Cub players they came out on the steps of their dugout and really let me have it.

I guess the smart thing for Charley to have done on his third pitch would have been to waste one.

But he didn't, and for that I've sometimes thanked God.

While he was making up his mind to pitch to me I stepped back again and pointed my finger at those bleachers, which only caused the mob to howl that much more at me.

Root threw me a fast ball. If I had let it go, it would have been called a strike. But this was *it.* I swung from the ground with everything I had and as I hit the ball every muscle in my system, every sense I had, told me that I had never hit a better one, that as long as I lived nothing would ever feel as good as this.

I didn't have to look. But I did. That ball just went on and on and hit far up in the center-field bleachers in exactly the spot I had pointed to.

To me, it was the funniest, proudest moment I had ever had in baseball. I jogged down toward first base, rounded it, looked back at the Cub bench and suddenly got convulsed with laughter.

You should have seen those Cubs. As Combs said later, "There they were—all out on the top step and yelling their brains out—and then you connected and they watched it and then fell back as if they were being machine-gunned."

That home run—the most famous one I ever hit—did us some good. It was worth two runs, and we won that ball game, 7 to 5.

Further Resources

BOOKS

Creamer, Robert W. *Babe: The Legend Comes to Life.* New York: Simon & Schuster, 1974.

Ritter, Lawrence S., and Mark Rucker. *The Babe: A Life in Pictures.* New York: Ticknor & Fields, 1988.

Smesler, Marshall. *The Life That Ruth Built.* New York: Quadrangle, 1975.

Sobol, Ken. *Babe Ruth and the American Dream.* New York: Random House, 1974.

PERIODICALS

Creamer, Robert W. "Ruth? He Is Still in the Spotlight, Still Going Strong." *Smithsonian* 25, no. 11, 68–78.

Nack, William. "The Colossus." *Sports Illustrated* 89, no. 8, 58–69.

This Life I've Led: My Autobiography

Autobiography

By: Babe Didrikson Zaharias, as told to Harry Paxton

Date: 1955

Source: Zaharias, Babe Didrikson, as told to Harry Paxton. *This Life I've Led: My Autobiography.* New York: A.S. Barnes, 1955, 47–50.

About the Author: Mildred Ella "Babe" Didrikson (1914–1956), born in Port Arthur, Texas, was by many accounts the greatest female athlete of the twentieth century. Borrowing her nickname from baseball hero Babe Ruth, Didrikson distinguished herself in any number of sports. She set numerous records in track and field, was a three time All-American in basketball, and won every major women's golf championship, including amateur and professional titles. She died of cancer in 1956, at the age of forty-one. ■

Introduction

Babe Didrikson was a precocious teenage athlete in the small town of Beaumont, Texas, when she was discovered by Colonel M.J. McCombs. He brought her to Dallas to play basketball for the Amateur Athletic Union (AAU), the women's team he sponsored through Employers Casualty Insurance. Didrikson starred for the team, earning All-American honors three times. She also excelled in track and field, representing the United States in the 1932 Olympics. Her performance there, in which she set records for the javelin throw and the 80-meter hurdles, put her prominently in the national spotlight.

Mildred "Babe" Didrikson poses for a 1932 photo. AP/WIDE WORLD PHOTOS. REPRODUCED BY PERMISSION.

Following the Olympics, Didrikson set off on a barnstorming exhibition designed to promote her as a marketable public figure. She often encouraged legends and lore about her exploits, such as striking out major league baseball players as a pitcher or excelling at golf the very first time she picked up a set of clubs. Didrikson understood the value of a good and memorable story and how it could affix an athlete in the public imagination.

Unfortunately, Didrikson's attempts to make a living off her athletic success eventually caused problems with her status. Because she appeared in an automobile advertisement, the American Athletic Union (AAU) declared that she could no longer compete as an amateur. When she switched to golf as her main sport, she was likewise barred from participating as an amateur. She later turned professional and won all of the major titles in the newly formed Ladies Professional Golf Association (LPGA), which she helped establish.

Significance

Versatility was Didrikson's calling card—she loved to compete and was willing to do so in any sport. Because she was a highly skilled natural athlete, she often won, no matter the sport. However, her competitive drive sometimes caused her problems, for many at the time did not believe she was feminine enough. She did not always exhibit the most "ladylike" behavior, boasting and cursing and getting angry when she lost. She believed that women could improve their skills if they played with and against men, and as a result she sometimes defeated male competitors. As a result of her success and outspokenness, she drew fire from some sectors of the public.

Didrikson was forced to face what many other successful female athletes have had to endure: questions about their sexual orientation and about their sense of decorum. Especially in the 1930s—but still common even today—assertions of "manliness" often accompanied female athletes who were not notably feminine in appearance or behavior. By marrying professional wrestler George Zaharias in 1938, Didrikson hoped to put an end to the rumors and name-calling, though they persisted until the end of her life. She served as an emblem of how the public sometimes responded to women who did not act as expected.

Part of this response, however, was based on class. Didrikson grew up without much money and had a strong sense of its value and importance as a means to a better life. She used athletics as a way to climb the social and economic ladder, but, in so doing, often angered and embittered those in the upper classes—especially in the country clubs at which she sometimes played golf. Accusations of masculinity, therefore, served in part as a way to erect a social barrier against Didrikson's ascent to a higher economic sphere.

Primary Source

This Life I've Led: My Autobiography [excerpt]

SYNOPSIS: Babe Didrikson attended the 1932 national track and field championships and Olympic tryouts as a one-woman team, sponsored by the Employers Casualty Insurance Company of Dallas. Not yet of adult age, she was accompanied by a chaperone, Mrs. Henry Wood, who became her main cheering section during what many have called the greatest performance ever by an athlete.

One time I really needed my confidence was when Employers Casualty sent me up to Chicago as a one-girl track team for those combined 1932 national championships and Olympic tryouts. The meet was being held at Dyche Stadium, the Northwestern University field, which is in Evanston, just outside Chicago.

I never can recite all the details of my performance that afternoon without checking the record book, but I can tell you everything that happened the night before in my hotel room in Chicago. I couldn't sleep. I kept having severe pains in my stomach. When I put my hand on it, the hand would just bounce up and down.

Mrs. Henry Wood was chaperoning me. She was our "team mother" at Employers Casualty. Naturally she wasn't doing any sleeping either, the way I was tossing around. She got worried and called the hotel doctor. She was afraid I might be coming down with an appendicitis attack or something.

The doctor came and examined me. He said, "There's nothing wrong with her. She's just all excited. The excitement is affecting the nerve center in her diaphragm." And that's what it was. I've found out since that whenever I get all keyed up like that before an event, it means I'm really ready.

We finally did fall asleep around dawn. And then we overslept. When we woke up, there was barely time for us to get ourselves ready and make it out to Evanston for the start of the meet.

We got down to the front of the hotel as quick as we could, and jumped into a taxicab. But when we told the driver we wanted to go to Dyche Stadium, he wouldn't take us. He said he just operated in Chicago.

So we got out of that cab and tried another one. This driver agreed to go to Evanston. What with the traffic and everything, though, it began to look like there wouldn't be time for me to dress out at the field. There was only one way we could make sure. Mrs. Wood held up a blanket around me and I changed into my track suit while we were riding along in the cab.

In spite of all those difficulties, it was one of those days in an athlete's life when you know you're just right. You feel you could fly. You're like a feather floating in air. I wasn't worried about the fact that of the ten individual events on the program I was entered in eight, including a couple I'd hardly ever done before, the shot put and the discus throw. I was going to be in everything but the fifty-yard and 220-yard dashes.

Mrs. Wood and I just did get there in time for the opening ceremonies. They announced each team over the loud-speaker, and then the girls on that team would run out on the track and get a hand. There were over 200 girls there. Some of those squads had fifteen or more girls. The Illinois Women's Athletic Club had twenty-two.

It came time to announce my "team." I spurted out there all alone, waving my arms, and you never heard such a roar.

It brought out goose bumps all over me. I can feel them now, just thinking about it.

Babe Didrikson throws a discus. © **CORBIS. REPRODUCED BY PERMISSION.**

Some of the events that afternoon were Olympic trials. Others were just National A.A.U. events. But they all counted in the team point scoring. So they were all important to me if I was going to bring back the national championship for Employers Casualty.

For two-and-a-half hours I was flying all over the place. I'd run a heat in the eighty-meter hurdles, and then I'd take one of my high jumps. Then I'd go over to the broad jump and take a turn at that. Then they'd be calling for me to throw the javelin or put the eight-pound shot.

Well, there were several events I didn't figure to do too much in. One was the 100-meter dash, and

I drew a blank there, although I just missed qualifying for the finals. I was edged out for third place in my semifinal heat.

But that was the only thing I got shut out in. Even in the discus, which wasn't a specialty of mine at all, I placed fourth to pick up an extra point. And I actually won the shot put, which was a big surprise. A girl named Rena MacDonald was supposed to be the best woman shot putter, but I beat her out with a throw of thirty-nine feet, six and a quarter inches

I won the championship in the baseball throw for the third straight year. My distance was 272 feet, two inches. Then in three Olympic trial events I broke the world's record. In two of them it was a case of beating a record that I already held myself. I threw the javelin 139 feet, three inches, which was nearly six feet better than my old mark of 133 feet, five and-a-half inches. I won an eighty-meter hurdle heat in 11.9 seconds, a tenth of a second faster than my previous mark. In the finals of the eighty-meter hurdles I didn't do quite that well, but my time of 12.1 seconds was good enough to win.

In the high jump I was competing against a very fine specialist, Jean Shiley. When everybody had been eliminated except us two, they moved the bar up just a fraction above the world's record, held by a Dutch girl, Fraulein M. Gisolf. She'd cleared five feet, three-and-one-eighth inches. Now they had Jean Shiley and me try it at five feet, three-and-three-sixteenths inches. Jean and I both got over. Neither of us could make it any higher that day, so we wound up in a first-place tie.

When I came off the field at the end of the afternoon, all puffing and sweating, Mrs. Wood was so happy and excited she was crying. She said, "You did it! You did it! You won the meet all by yourself!"

Further Resources

BOOKS

Cayleff, Susan E. *Babe: The Life and Legend of Babe Didrikson Zaharias.* Urbana, Ill.: University of Illinois Press, 1995.

Freedman, Russell. *Babe Didrikson Zaharias: The Making of a Champion.* New York: Clarion, 1999.

Schoor, Gene. *Babe Didrikson, The World's Greatest Athlete.* New York: Doubleday, 1978.

PERIODICALS

Berg, Patty. "Babe Graced Sports With Her Skill and Courage." *The New York Times,* July 15, 1984, S2.

McGrath, Charles. "Babe Zaharias: Most Valuable Player." *The New York Times Magazine,* November 24, 1996, 62.

Postman, Andrew. "Athlete of the Century: Babe Didrikson." *Women's Sport and Fitness* 3, no. 2, 110.

Golf Is My Game

Autobiography

By: Robert Tyre Jones Jr.

Date: 1959

Source: Jones, Robert Tyre Jr. *Golf Is My Game.* Garden City, N.Y.: Doubleday, 1959, 163–164.

About the Author: Robert Tyre Jones Jr. (1902–1971), better known as "Bobby," was the most accomplished American amateur golfer of his day or since. He was the only golfer to ever win the Grand Slam of golf, which he did in 1930. However, he never turned pro, choosing instead to work as a lawyer after graduating from Harvard. However, he did go on to help design and found the Masters Tournament in 1934. He died at his home in Atlanta in 1971. ■

Introduction

Born in Atlanta in 1902, Bobby Jones began competing in national amateur tournaments at age fourteen and retired from active competition just fourteen years later, at age twenty-eight. He won thirteen of the twenty-one major championships that he entered between 1923 and 1930. His record of success was striking for a golfer who only entered six or seven tournaments annually.

Jones maintained a number of interests, many of which were inspired by his success on the links, including writing a series of syndicated newspaper columns. However, he never played a tournament as a professional athlete, maintaining his amateur status throughout his short career. A lawyer by profession—he studied law at Harvard University—Jones always intended to devote himself full-time to law. He never desired to pursue a golf career for a living.

At the beginning of his career, Jones struggled to maintain an even-keeled demeanor while playing, so strong was his zeal to win. By the end of his career, he was renowned as a gentleman who was charming and courteous on the course. He had learned to tame and channel that competitive spirit into an iron will to overcome his opponents, even when he was not playing well.

He won the U.S. Open four times, the U.S. Amateur five times, and the British Open three times. In 1926, he became the first player to win the U.S. Open and British Open in the same year. In 1930, he became the only player to ever win the Grand Slam of golf, when he won the U.S. Open, the U.S. Amateur, the British Open, and the British Amateur—the four major tournaments of his day—in the same year.

Significance

Jones influenced thousands of middle-class Americans to take up what had been previously a country club sport. In so doing, he introduced golf to a whole new audience, prefiguring the effect that Tiger Woods would have on minority involvement in golf in the late 1990s. At the same time, Jones' retirement at such an early age signaled that he believed the sport to be a recreation, not an occupation. His grace on and off the golf course set the standard for sportsmanship, influencing generations of golfers in the process.

Jones is widely remembered for his role in designing the Augusta National course in Augusta, Georgia, and for founding the Masters Tournament, which is now one of the preeminent golf tournaments in the world. However, he is perhaps most renowned for capturing the Grand Slam in 1930, a feat that has yet to be duplicated—though some have come close. Tiger Woods, for instance, won each of the four major golf tournaments in a row in 2000 and 2001, but did not do so in the same calendar year, as Jones had. Note that the four major tournaments that are now considered to comprise the Grand Slam—the U.S. Open, the British Open, the Masters, and the PGA Championship—have changed since Jones' day.

Jones' achievement in 1930 was especially remarkable for the strategy he set out with and the way in which he was able to maintain his objectives, even when he did not play as well as he could. His decision to plan for the Grand Slam—training the previous winter and entering two specific tournaments in the spring to get himself into playing form—has served as a blueprint for other ambitious athletes. While he did not always play to the best of his abilities between May and September, he played well enough to win those four tournaments. The lesson he derived from those victories—that his success resulted from his ability to keep control of himself and to try as hard as he could, even when there was no apparent hope for victory—offered a valuable moral for all athletes: focus on how you are playing, rather than on the results you are achieving.

Bobby Jones drives a ball at the 1934 Masters Invitation Golf Tournament at the Augusta Golf Club in Augusta, Georgia. © BETTMANN/CORBIS. REPRODUCED BY PERMISSION.

Primary Source

Golf Is My Game [excerpt]

SYNOPSIS: In thinking back to his achievements of 1930, Jones understands that, more than any natural athletic ability, it was his will and determination that allowed him to win the Grand Slam. He writes that he was not clear what lay on the horizon after capturing the fourth tournament, but that it had been a physically and mentally exhausting journey for him and he wanted time off to pursue his other interests and to focus less intensely on golf for a while.

Reflections and an Appraisal

Immediately after this final trick of the Grand Slam, of course, came the question, "What would I do now? Would I continue to play in tournaments, or would I retire?"

I answered, as truthfully as I could, that I did not know. At this point, I truly did not know. I had started in the first place to play in golf tournaments for fun, and I had continued to play because I enjoyed doing so. But when I began to win, I also began to feel a certain responsibility in connection with competitive golf. Each year had ended with speculation upon the future. It had seemed to be expected by others, as well as myself, that this thing would go on indefinitely, and that I would always be beating my brains out trying to win either the Open or Amateur Championship.

At the conclusion of the Merion tournament, in response to these queries, I said what was on my mind and in my heart, namely, that I intended to settle down to the practice of law, and that I could henceforward recognize no obligation to play in any golf tournaments. I thought it would be nice to feel free to play in a tournament now and then if I felt like doing so at the time, but I thought it would also be nice if I could merely neglect to send in my entry for a championship and let it go at that. I had never played golf with any idea of making a career of the game. Above all things, I wanted to avoid ever getting myself into such a position that I would have to keep on playing. Now seemed a good time to make this position clear. So, still at Merion, I allowed myself to be quoted as follows:

> I expect to continue to play golf, but just when and where I cannot say now. I have no definite plans either to retire or as to when and where I may continue in competition. I might play next year and lay off in 1932. I might stay out next season and feel like another tournament the following year. What I want most right now is to be free of any obligation, express or implied, to continue playing each year in both major championships.

In my mind today the accomplishment of the Grand Slam assumes more importance as an example of the value of perseverance in the abstract than as a monument to skill in the playing of a game. I am certain that in those moments when the success of the project was most in doubt, the decisive factor in each case had been my ability, summoned from somewhere, to keep control of myself and to keep trying as hard as I could, even when there was no clear indication of the direction in which hope of victory might lie.

In at least two matches, those with Tolley and Voigt at St. Andrews, I had been outplayed throughout; and in the final round of each of the two Open Championships I had made mistakes of grievous proportions. On several occasions I had lost control of my game. But having once found myself in these dire predicaments, I had managed, from the point of realization, to drive myself to the end, when it would have been easy, even pleasant, to play the "give-up" shot.

Further Resources

BOOKS

Keeler, O.B. *The Bobby Jones Story.* Atlanta: Tupper and Love, 1953.

Matthew, Sidney L. *Bobby Jones: Extra!* Atlanta: Longstreet, 2001.

Miller, Dick. *Triumphant Journey: The Saga of Bobby Jones and the Grand Slam of Golf.* Dallas: Taylor, 1994.

PERIODICALS

Anderson, Dave. "How Bobby Jones Planned the First Grand Slam." *The New York Times,* April 8, 2001, 30.

Fimrite, Ron. "The Emperor Jones." *Sports Illustrated* 80, no. 14, 104.

Goodwin, Stephen. "Heroes for the Ages: Through the 20th Century, America's Golf Heroes Have Reflected the Times They Lived In." *Golf Magazine* 39, no. 12, 48.

Maybe I'll Pitch Forever

Autobiography

By: Leroy Paige, as told to David Lipman

Date: 1962

Source: Paige, Leroy, as told to David Lipman. *Maybe I'll Pitch Forever: A Great Baseball Player Tells the Hilarious Story Behind the Legend.* Garden City, N.Y.: Doubleday, 1962. Reprint, Lincoln, Nebr.: University of Nebraska Press, 1993, 75–76.

About the Author: Leroy "Satchel" Paige (1906–1982) was born in Mobile, Alabama. A talented ballplayer, he barnstormed across the country, pitching for any team that offered him secure payment. In 1948, he was sold to Cleveland and became the oldest rookie in major league history, helping the Indians win the World Series that year. In 1965, Paige pitched three scoreless innings for the Kansas City Athletics, becoming the oldest player to ever play in the big leagues. He died in Kansas City, Missouri, in 1982. ■

Introduction

Leroy Paige—nicknamed "Satchel" because of his prowess as a childhood baggage handler—was the Negro Leagues' biggest gate attraction in the 1930s, pitching for the Pittsburgh Crawfords and, later, for the Kansas City Monarchs. With a wide array of pitches complementing an overwhelming fastball, Paige was a difficult assignment for hitters. He struck out eighteen batters in one game in 1934. That same year, on July 4, he threw a no-hitter against the powerful Homestead Grays, the first time in their history that the Grays had failed to get a hit in a game.

Paige's lifetime statistics are hard to ascertain, because he pitched in so many different leagues and for so many different teams. His record in the Negro Leagues was 123-79 and he had almost twice as many career strikeouts than anyone else. But he also played in many other places, including North Dakota, the Dominican Republic, Puerto Rico, Mexico, and California. He pitched for any team that offered him the best terms. Paige understood the power of his stardom; he recognized that he

Satchel Paige practices at New York's Yankee Stadium before a Negro League game between his Kansas City Monarchs and the New York Cuban Stars. AP/WIDE WORLD PHOTOS. REPRODUCED BY PERMISSION.

was a major attraction and, as such, had a tremendous negotiating advantage. He always tried to work this advantage to his full benefit.

The public embraced Paige in part because of his personality. He entertained the crowd on the mound with flamboyant gestures and chatter that often goaded opposing teams. Off the field, he garnered attention with his legendary wit and willingness to speak his mind. At the same time, Paige was prone to telling somewhat tall tales. For instance, in his autobiography, Paige claims that he had a 31-4 record in 1933 while pitching for the Crawfords. In the introduction to the 1993 printing of that autobiography, however, John Holway indicates that Paige was only 5-7 before leaving the Crawfords to play the rest of the season in North Dakota. That and other discrepancies aside, Paige's accomplishments as a pitcher are unquestionable: he was one of the finest pitchers of his day, white or black. But it is nonetheless important to note that he was often the author of his own legend.

Significance

Paige's success against white players from the major leagues while on the barnstorming circuit offered important evidence that black players were the equal of whites. Dizzy Dean called him the best pitcher he'd ever seen. Players like Ted Williams and Joe DiMaggio marveled at him. His performances in the 1930s in the off-season against such players helped pave the way for integration of the major leagues in the 1940s. Paige himself was vocal in his advocacy that blacks should get the opportunity to compete against major leaguers. However, he believed that integrating blacks into white teams would prove overly problematic because of the racism that would be prevalent. Instead, he thought that all-black teams should be allowed into the major leagues to play against white teams.

He was also a pioneer in salary negotiations, because of his ability to get paid as much as he could for his services. He understood his value as a marquee player and believed that he should be duly compensated for what he brought in at the gate. His efforts at myth-making and self-promotion can be seen as part of a larger marketing strategy to entice people to the ball park. It didn't matter if they cheered for or against him, as long as they showed up at the game as paying customers. His battles over money serve as an interesting precursor to later free-agency fights in professional sports, and his use of the media to further establish his legend serves as an antecedent to the public-relations campaigns of present-day athletes.

Satchel Paige was a born showman who loved to entertain. He had the ability to back up what he said, and felt he should be paid for attracting customers. Moreover, he was a proud man. When the Baseball Hall of Fame announced in 1971 the creation of a separate wing for Negro League players, Paige refused to participate, insisting that blacks should be inducted as full members alongside whites. Later that year, the Hall of Fame did just that and Paige was among the first so inducted.

Primary Source

Maybe I'll Pitch Forever [excerpt]

SYNOPSIS: In this excerpt, Paige asserts that the black players of the 1930s were at least the equal of white players of the same era. He offers as evidence his performances against prominent white players in the winter barnstorming league on the West Coast, a league that brought together white and black players in competition.

By 1933 I'd hit my full stride, which is a pretty long step when you figure the size of my legs.

For the Crawfords that season I pitched in forty-one games, winning thirty-one and losing only four. I had sixteen shutouts in those games, so there wasn't too many guys scoring off me. With me going strong like that, people began saying we could hold our own against the New York Yankees or Chicago Cubs or St. Louis Cardinals or New York Giants or Washington Senators or any of the top major league clubs.

I figured we could too.

"You write that I'll take a team from the Negro leagues and we'll play the all-stars from the major leagues," I told some baseball writers in Pittsburgh. "We'll play 'em right across the country, anywhere and anytime. You write that, hear, and you write we'll beat 'em so bad they won't ever play anymore."

Everybody made a big thing out of what I said, but no major league all-star club was got up to play any Negro team. Those club owners didn't want the people all over the country to know there were Negro players better than a lot of the white boys.

That might mean they'd have to take us into the majors.

But even the major league players themselves wouldn't say anything about taking us on. I guess I can't blame them. Who wants to play against guys like Josh Gibson, George Perkins, Cool Papa Bell, Judy Johnson, Poindexter Williams, or a couple of dozen others I could name?

I'd given up on that all-star game by the time the regular 1933 season ended. The only plans I had were to take a couple of weeks off and squire Janet around, then get me some work for the rest of the winter. But I never got those two weeks off. Before I even got started on a vacation, I got me an offer to go out to the West Coast and do some throwing there.

I didn't lose a game that season on the Coast. In fact, I went from 1933 to 1937 without hardly losing there. And my ball clubs won something like a hundred and fifty games and lost maybe twenty-five in that same time. A third of those games was against major leaguers, too—pitchers like Dizzy and Paul Dean, and hitters like Rogers Hornsby and Jimmy Foxx and Charlie Gehringer and Pepper Martin. And I struck out those guys.

Further Resources

BOOKS

Holway, John. *Josh and Satch: The Life and Times of Josh Gibson and Satchel Paige.* Westport, Conn.: Meckler, 1991.

Ribowsky, Mark. *Don't Look Back: Satchel Paige in the Shadows of Baseball.* New York: Simon & Schuster, 1994.

Sterry, David, and Arielle Eckstut, eds. *Satchel Sez: The Wit, Wisdom, and World of Leroy "Satchel" Paige.* New York: Three Rivers, 2001.

PERIODICALS

Anderson, Dave. "Looking Back at Satchel." *The New York Times,* June 10, 1982, 29.

Jesse: The Man Who Outran Hitler

Autobiography

By: Jesse Owens, with Paul Neimark

Date: 1978

Source: Owens, Jesse, with Paul Neimark. *Jesse: The Man Who Outran Hitler.* New York: Fawcett, 1978, 86–90.

About the Author: James Cleveland "Jesse" Owens (1913–1980) was born in Alabama and later moved with his family to Cleveland, Ohio, where he blossomed as a high school track star. He continued his success while attending Ohio State University, breaking a number of world records in competition. At the infamous 1936 Olympic Games in Berlin, he won four gold medals in track and field, becoming a symbol of American patriotism in the process. Owens died in Tucson, Arizona, in 1980. ■

Introduction

The athletic achievements of the 1936 Olympics were largely overshadowed by politics, as Germany's chancellor, Adolf Hitler, used the Games to showcase his ideology of Aryan superiority. Leni Riefenstahl, who had directed *Triumph of the Will*, a propaganda film about the Nazi party rally in Nuremberg in 1934, filmed the games and edited the footage. Despite this and other pro-Nazi tactics, Jesse Owens' extraordinary performance during the Olympics exploded any notions about the superiority of the Aryan race. A year earlier, Owens had demonstrated remarkable skill in breaking three world records and tying a fourth in a mere forty-five minutes at the Big Ten Championships while he was a collegian at Ohio State University. Many wondered if he could repeat the feat in Berlin.

He did not disappoint. By the time of his performance in the broad jump, Owens had already won gold medals and broken world records in the 100- and 200-meter dashes and 400-meter relay. He should not have had much difficulty in the broad jump, since it was perhaps his strongest event and the one in which he held the world record. But he did, in fact, struggle during the competition.

Owens was in danger of missing the finals in the competition, because he was consistently fouling on his jumps by stepping over the line. In a show of inspiring sportsmanship, Luz Long—a German competitor in the same event, whom Hitler had designated an Aryan superman—advised Owens to start his leap six inches earlier than what he was used to, in order to ensure that he did not foul. Long even placed his own towel on the spot where he advised Owens to jump, and the subsequent attempt was enough to propel Owens into the finals. After Owens beat Long in the competition, Hitler allegedly snubbed him, refusing to acknowledge his victory.

Significance

Owens returned home to America unable to compete further as an amateur athlete, because the Amateur Athletic Union (AAU) had stripped him of his amateur status after he refused to stay in Europe following the Olympic games for an exhibition tour. He resorted to running exhibitions at events across the country against other athletes—and even horses and dogs—before later participating in the administration of youth athletic programs. While he was a powerful illustration of the heights to which an African American could rise, he was still subject to prejudice and discrimination in the decades before the changes in civil rights legislation. Once, he was even barred from using the front door of the Waldorf-Astoria Hotel in New York City as he sought entrance to a reception in his own honor.

The spirit of fellowship that is captured in Owens' story of the broad jump at the 1936 Olympics is a powerful evocation of how sports can often speak to a higher ideal. The sportsmanship that Long showed Owens culminated in a fierce battle in the finals between the two competitors, in which each pushed the other further and further, ultimately to the Olympic record and gold medal for Owens. These two athletes embodied the Olympic ideal in disregarding nationality in the name of fair and equal competition. While Owens' deeds created the lasting legend of the courageous African American who performed so admirably in front of the racist and anti-Semitic Hitler, in his recollection of the broad jump Owens does not take sole credit for his victory. He not only thanks Long for his assistance and hails his fellowship, but he also demonstrates a deep and abiding faith in God as his ultimate motivation. Long, Owens claims, served as God's messenger in helping show the world that Hitler's politics of hate were not a truth to be believed in. The power of sports as a medium for a spiritual message is prevalent in his words, which foreshadow the actions and words of later athletes who likewise approached sports as a means to a higher purpose.

Primary Source

Jesse: The Man Who Outran Hitler [excerpt]

SYNOPSIS: In this excerpt, Owens captures the sense of camaraderie of two athletes performing at their very peak, each propelling the other to a higher level of achievement. Owens' spiritual belief is especially evident, not only in how he thinks of his success in the event but also in how he understands the importance of Long's support and the overwhelming applause he received from the German audience.

The day of the broad jump arrived. One by one, the other finalists fell by the wayside. Then, it was only Luz Long and Jesse Owens.

Jesse Owens is presented with his gold medal for the long jump after defeating Lutz Long (right) during the 1936 Summer Olympics in Berlin. AP/WIDE WORLD PHOTOS. REPRODUCED BY PERMISSION.

His first leap took the lead.

I beat it.

His second of three was even better.

I beat it by half an inch.

I watched him take a deep breath before his final leap. I watched his blue eyes look up into the sky, then down, fixing on a point which he knew—and I knew—would be well over an Olympic record. I could see him transforming the same beautiful energy which had enabled him to come to me and change the course of my life when I needed it most into the determination to do what had never been done before—to do what most men would call a miracle.

He stood perfectly still, as still as a statue, for an instant, and only his eyes moved as they looked skyward once more, and then he began his run. Fast from the beginning, not gradual like most, but then faster. His perfectly proportioned legs working like pistons now, his finely honed physique working like one total machine, all for one purpose, for one split second—

"Berlin Opening" [excerpt]

[In his account of the opening ceremony of the 1936 Olympics, *New York Times* reporter Frederick Birchall records the pageantry and the implied politics of the events with a reporter's eye, but with little skepticism. While he notes Hitler's inclusion of racist rhetoric in his opening address, Birchall has come under attack for failing to regard the glitter of the ceremony as hiding a fascist regime.]

They [Olympic athletes] marched in a procession once around the arena, saluting the dais, each nation according to its custom, as they passed; then, turning across the field, they took their stand in columns great and small in front of the Führer and the guests of honor, their flags at their head.

Quite naturally, in this long march the interest was centered in the applause given respectively to each and the type of salute each nation gave the dais. The last item wasn't always easily determined because the Olympic and Nazi salutes are very similar, the former being with the right arm stretched out sidewise or nearly so from the shoulder, and the latter being with the arm stretched out in front.

Nevertheless, the crowd carefully noted each salute as indicating the degree of sympathy for the Nazi regime betokened by it. In turn also the mode of saluting had a manifest influence upon the volume of applause received.

In general the salutes stood about equally divided between the Olympic and Nazi, but "eyes-right," with some individual modifications, was common to all. The Americans provided their own special salute by giving eyes right and placing their straw hats over their hearts.

The Turks were the only team to give a military salute throughout. The Bulgarians drew down handsome applause by flattering German sympathies in a double way. They goose-stepped past Hitler and gave the Nazi salute to boot. The Nazi salute was also given by Afghanistan, Bermuda, Bolivia and Iceland, besides, of course, Italy, which originated it, and the Germans.

But all the flags of the nations were lowered while passing Hitler with one exception; that of the United States went by proudly borne aloft. An official statement published in all newspapers, however, explained this was due to army regulations and asked for public understanding in the matter.

The biggest applause was given the French, who marched by most smartly giving the Olympic salute. The crowd rose and cheered them to the echo and it was obviously a genuine tribute. Next to the biggest applause went to the Austrians. Third in the respect of volume of applause were the Hungarians and Japanese. The Czechoslovaks and Rumanians got little, if any. The Americans received a cordial if not an overwhelming welcome when their massive column appeared, but just as its head approached the dais the first of the succeeding German contingent came into sight at the Marathon Gate. Immediately the band forgot the march it was playing and broke into "Deutschland über alles" and the "Horst Wessel" song in turn. The audience, rising promptly, froze in silent attention, so that the Americans marched not to applause but to the tune of these two German national anthems.

SOURCE: Birchall, Frederick T. "Berlin Opening." *The New York Times,* August 1, 1936. Reprinted in *The Greatest Sport Stories From "The New York Times": Sport Classics of a Century.* Allison Danzig and Peter Brandwein, eds. New York: A.S. Barnes, 1951, 449–455.

And then it happened. High. Higher than I'd ever seen anyone leap. But with so much power that it was not merely high, it was far. Incredibly far.

It seemed for a split second that he would never come down. But then he did, straining his body more than I'd ever seen any man strain, as if he were an eagle attempting at the last minute to rise above an infinite mountain . . . straining . . . moving forward as he fell downward . . . forward farther . . . forward . . .

He landed!

Exactly in the spot on which his eyes had fixed.

Luz Long had set a new Olympic record.

I rushed over to him. Hugged him. I was glad. So glad.

But now it was my turn.

I took my time, measured my steps once, then again. I was tense, but that good kind of tense that you feel when you have to be tense to do your best. Deep, deep inside, under all the layers, there was a clear, placid pool of peace.

Now I, too, stood perfectly still.

I, too, looked up at the sky.

Then, I looked into Luz's blue eyes, as he stood off to the side, his face wordlessly urging me to do my best, to do better than I'd ever done. Looking into his eyes was no different than looking into the blue, cloudless sky.

I didn't look at the end of the pit. I decided I wasn't going to come down. I was going to fly. I was going to stay up in the air forever.

I began my run, also fast from the beginning, not gradual like most, but then faster.

I went faster, precariously fast, using all my speed to its advantage. And then!

The *Hindenberg* passes over the Olympic Stadium during the opening ceremonies of the 1936 Olympics in Berlin. **AP/WIDE WORLD PHOTOS. REPRODUCED BY PERMISSION.**

I hit the take-off board. Leaped up, up, up—

. . . My body was weightless . . . I surged with all I had but at the same time merely let it float . . . higher . . . higher . . . into the clouds . . . I was reaching for the clouds . . . the clouds . . . the heavens—

I was coming down! Back to earth.

I fought against it.

I kicked my legs.

I churned my arms.

I reached to the sky as I leaped, for the farthest part of the ground.

The farthest—

I was on the earth once again. I felt the dirt and the sand of the pit in my shoes and on my legs. Instinctively, I fell forward, my elbows digging in, the tremendous velocity of my jump forcing sand into my mouth.

It tasted good. Because, almost instinctively, I sensed it was the sand from a part of the pit which no one had ever reached before.

Luz was the first to reach me. "You did it! I know you did it," he whispered.

They measured.

I had done it.

I had gone farther than Luz. I had set a new Olympic record. I had jumped farther than any man on earth.

Luz didn't let go of my arm. He lifted it up—as he had lifted me up in a different way a few days before—and led me away from the pit and toward the crowd. "Jazze Owenz!" he shouted. "Jazze Owenz!"

Some people in the crowd responded, "Jazze Owenz!"

Luz shouted it louder. "Jazze Owenz!"

Now a majority of the crowd picked it up. "Jazze Owenz! Jazze Owenz! Jazze Owenz!" they yelled.

Luz yelled it again. The crowd yelled it again. Luz again. And now the whole crowd, more than a hundred thousand Germans, were yelling, "Jazze Owenz! Jazze Owenz! Jazze Owenz!"

They were cheering me. But only I knew who they were really cheering.

I lifted Luz Long's arm.

"Luz Long!" I yelled at the top of my lungs. "Luz Long! Luz Long! Luz Long! Luz Long!"

Yet it wasn't Luz who had lifted me into the heavens today.

I knew who had brought me from the precipice of hell to be able to ascend into the heavens today.

It wasn't Jesse Owens. It wasn't anyone who ever ran, or jumped, or balanced on the precipice of hell.

Luz Long may not have believed in God.

But God had believed in Luz Long.

He had made Luz His sacred messenger.

Further Resources

BOOKS

Bachrach, Susan D. *The Nazi Olympics: Berlin 1936.* Boston: Little, Brown, 2001.

Baker, William Joseph. *Jesse Owens: An American Life.* New York: Free Press, 1998.

Barry, James P. *The Berlin Olympics, 1936: Black American Athletes Counter Nazi Propaganda.* Danbury, Conn.: Franklin Watts, 1975.

Hart-Davis, Duff. *Hitler's Games: The 1936 Olympics.* New York: Harper & Row, 1986.

Mandell, Richard D. *The Nazi Olympics.* Champaign, Ill.: University of Illinois Press, 1987.

Nuwer, Hank. *The Legend of Jesse Owens.* Danbury, Conn.: Franklin Watts, 1998.

Owens, Jesse. *Blackthink: My Life as a Black Man.* New York: William Morrow, 1970.

———. *The Jesse Owens Story.* New York: Putnam, 1970.

PERIODICALS

Bennett, Lerone, Jr. "Jesse Owens' Olympic Triumph Over Time and Hitlerism." *Ebony* 51 no. 6, 68.

Berkow, Ira. "Anti-Semitism by Americans in Berlin Rejects a Sprinter: The Snub, the Voice, the Heart." *The New York Times,* January 7, 2001, 25.

Eskenazi, Gerald. "Glickman, Kept From Shot at Gold in 1936 Games, Is Honored at Last." *The New York Times,* March 30, 1998, C16.

Taylor, Phil. "Flying in the Face of the Fuhrer: August 3–9, 1936: Jesse Owens Dominates the Berlin Olympics." *Sports Illustrated* 91 no. 21, 136.

AUDIO AND VISUAL MEDIA

Olympia. Original release, 1938. Directed by Leni Riefenstahl. Home Vision Entertainment, 1997, VHS.

General Resources

General

Aaron, Daniel, and Robert Bendiner. *The Strenuous Decade: A Social and Intellectual Record of the 1930's.* Garden City, N.Y.: Anchor Books, 1970.

Allen, Frederick Lewis. *Since Yesterday: The 1930's in America, September 3, 1929–Semptember 3, 1939.* New York: Perennial Library, 1986.

Clark, Linda Darus. *Interwar America 1920–1940.* Rocky River, Ohio: Center for Learning, 2001.

Craats, Rennay. *History of the 1930s.* Mankato, Minn.: Weigl Publishers, 2002.

Crowley, Malcolm, and Henry Dan Piper. *Think Back On Us: A Contemporary Chronicle of the 1930s.* Carbondale: Southern Illinois University, 1967.

Cummings, D. Duane, and William Gee White. *Contrasting Decades, the 1920's and 1930's.* Encino, Calif.: Glencoe Publishing, 1980.

Feinstein, Stephen. *The 1930s: From the Great Depression to the Wizard of Oz.* Berkeley Heights, N.J.: Enslow Publishers, 2001.

Gloversmith, Frank. *Class, Culture, and Social Change: A New View of the 1930's.* Atlantic Highlands, N.J.: Humanities Press, 1980.

Hall, Carolyn. *The Thirties in Vogue.* New York: Harmony Books, 1985.

Kyvig, David E. *Daily Life in the United States, 1920–1939: Decades of Promise and Pain.* Westport, Conn.: Greenwood Press, 2002.

Pierson, Frank. *A Nation Lost and Found: 1936 America Remembered by Ordinary and Extraordinary People.* Los Angeles: Tallfellow Press, 2002.

Prescott, Jerome. *America at the Crossroads: Great Photographs From the Thirties.* New York: Smithmark, 1995.

Wilson, Edmund. *The American Earthquake: A Documentary of the Twenties and Thirties.* New York: Octagon Books, 1971.

The Arts

Alexander, Charles C. *Here the Country Lies.* Bloomington: Indiana University Press, 1980.

Arnason, H. Harvard. *History of Modern Art: Painting, Sculpture, Photography.* 3rd ed. Englewood Cliffs, N.J.: Prentice-Hall, 1986.

Balio, Tino. *Grand Design: Hollywood as a Modern Business Enterprise 1930–1939.* vol. 5. of *History of the American Cinema,* Charles Harpole, ed. New York: Scribners, 1993.

Balliett, Whitney. *American Musicians: Fifty Portraits in Jazz.* New York: Oxford University Press, 1986.

Baxter, John. *Hollywood in the Thirties.* London: Tantivy Press, 1968.

Becker, Stephen. *Comic Art in America.* New York: Simon & Schuster, 1959.

Bell, Bernard. *The Afro-American Novel and Its Tradition.* Amherst: University of Massachusetts Press, 1987.

Benton, Thomas Hart. *An American in Art.* Lawrence: University Press of Kansas, 1969.

Bergman, Andrew. *We're in the Money: Depression America and Its Films.* New York: New York University Press, 1971.

Berkow, Ita G.. *Edward Hopper: An American Master.* New York: Smithmark, 1996.

Bloom, Harold, ed. *Twentieth-Century American Literature.* New York: Chelsea House, 1987.

Bradbury, Malcolm *The Modern American Novel.* rev. ed. New York: Viking, 1992.

Brockett, Oscar G., and Robert Findlay. *Century of Innovation: A History of European and American Drama Since the Late Nineteenth Century.* New York: Simon & Schuster, 1991.

Brown, Lorraine, and John O'Connor. *Free, Adult, Uncensored: The Living History of the Federal Theatre Project.* Washington, D.C.: New Republic Books, 1978.

Carr, Patrick, ed. *The Illustrated History of Country Music.* Garden City, N.Y.: Doubleday, 1980.

Charters, Samuel B., and Leonard Kunstadt. *Jazz: A History of the New York Scene.* Garden City, N.Y.: Doubleday, 1962.

Chase, Gilbert. *America's Music: From the Pilgrims to the Present.* revised third edition. Urbana & Chicago: University of Illinois Press, 1987.

Clurman, Harold. *The Fervent Years: The Story of the Group Theatre and the Thirties.* New York: Harcourt Brace Jovanovich, 1975.

Cowart, Jack and Juan Hamilton. *Georgis O'Keefe: Art and Letters.* Washington, D.C.: National Gallery of Art, 1987.

Cowley, Malcolm. *The Dream of the Golden Mountain.* New York: Viking, 1964.

———. *A Second Flowering.* New York: Viking, 1973.

Craven, Wayne. *American Art: History and Culture.* New York: Harry N. Abrams, Inc., 1994.

Cripps, Thomas. *Slow Fade to Black: The Negro in American Film, 1900–1942.* New York: Oxford University Press, 1977.

Curley, Dorothy Nyren, Maurice Kramer, and Elaine Fialka Kramer, eds. *Modern American Literature: A Library of Literary Criticism.* New York: Ungar, 1969.

Davis, Francis. *The History of the Blues: The Roots, the Music, the People from Charley Patton to Robert Cray.* New York: Hyperion, 1995.

de Mille, Agnes. *America Dances.* New York: Macmillan, 1980.

Dizikes, John. *Opera in America: A Cultural History.* New Haven, Conn.: Yale University Press, 1993.

Ewen, David. *New Complete Book of the American Musical Theater.* New York: Holt Rinehart and Winston, 1970.

Feather, Leonard. *The Book of Jazz.* New York: Bonanza Books, 1965.

Flanagan, Hallie. *Arena: The Story of the Federal Theatre.* New York: Duell, Sloan & Pearce, 1940.

Frank, Rusty E. *Tap! The Greatest Tap Dance Stars and Their Stories, 1900–1955.* New York: Morris, 1990.

Freeman, Joseph. *An American Testament.* New York: Farrar, Straus & Giroux, 1973.

Fuchs, Wolfgang and Reinhold Reitberger. *Comics: Anatomy of a Mass Medium.* Boston: Little, Brown, 1970.

Gordon, Lois G., and Alan Gordon. *American Chronicle: Six Decades in American Life.* New York: Atheneum, 1987.

Halliwell, Leslie. *Halliwell's Film Guide.* New York: Harper & Row, 1990.

Howard, John Tasker, and George Kent Bellows. *A Short History of Music in America.* New York: Crowell, 1957.

Hughes, Robert. *American Visions: The Epic History of Art in America.* New York: Alfred A. Knopf, 1997.

Janson, H.W. *History of Art.* 5th ed.. New York: Abrams, 1995.

Katz, Ephraim. *The Film Encyclopedia.* revised edition. New York: HarperPerennial, 1994.

Kernfield, Barry Dean. *The Blackwell Guide to Recorded Jazz.* Oxford, U.K., & Cambridge, Mass.: Blackwell, 1991.

Madden, David, ed. *Tough Guy Writers of the Thirties.* Carbondale: Southern Illinois University Press, 1968.

Malone, Bill C. *Country Music U.S.A.: A Fifty Year History.* Austin: University of Texas Press, 1968.

Mazo, Joseph H. *Prime Movers: The Makers of Modern Dance in America.* New York: Morrow, 1977.

McCarty, John. *Hollywood Gangland.* New York: St. Martin's Press, 1993.

McDonagh, Don. *The Complete Guide to Modern Dance.* Garden City, N.Y.: Doubleday, 1976.

McKinzie, Richard D. *The New Deal for Artists.* Princeton: Princeton University Press, 1973.

Melosh, Barbara. *Engendering Culture: Manhood and Womanhood in New Deal Public Art and Theatre.* Washington, D.C.: Smithsonian Institution Press, 1991.

Newhall, Beaumont. *The History of Photography.* Boston: Little, Brown, 1982.

Oliver, Paul, Max Harrison, and William Bolcom. *The New Grove Gospel, Blues and Jazz.* New York: Norton, 1986.

Pells, Richard H. *Radical Visions and American Dreams: Culture and Social Thought in the Depression Years.* Middletown, Conn.: Wesleyan University Press, 1973.

Ramsey, Frederic, Jr., and Charles Edward Smith, eds. *Jazzmen.* New York: Harcourt, Brace, 1939.

Sangos, Nikos. *Concepts of Modern Art.* New York: Thames & Hudson, 1994.

Sanjek, Russell. *American Popular Music and Its Business, Vol. III: From 1900 to 1984.* New York: Oxford University Press, 1988.

Schatz, Thomas. *The Genius of the System.* New York: Pantheon, 1988.

Sennett, Ted. *Hollywood's Golden Year, 1939.* New York: St. Martin's Press, 1989.

———. *This Fabulous Century: The Thirties.* New York: Time-Life Books, 1969.

Smith, Wendy. *Real Life: The Group Theatre and America, 1931–1940.* New York: Knopf, 1990.

Southern, Eileen. *The Music of Black Americans: A History.* New York: Norton, 1983.

Stearns, Marshall W. *The Story of Jazz.* New York: Oxford University Press, 1956.

Stott, William. *Documentary Expression and Thirties America.* Chicago: University of Chicago Press, 1973.

Stowe, David W. *Saving Changes.* Cambridge, Mass.: Harvard University Press, 1994.

Struble, John Warthen. *The History of American Classical Music.* New York: Facts On File, 1995.

Tawa, Nicholas E. *Serenading the Reluctant Eagle: American Musical Life, 1925–1945.* New York: Schirmer, 1984.

Tosches, Nick. *Country: Living Legends and Dying Metaphors in America's Biggest Music.* London: Secker & Warburg, 1985.

vanden Heuvel, Katrina, ed. *The Nation, 1865–1990.* New York: Thunder's Mouth Press, 1990.

Williams, Martin. *The Jazz Tradition.* New York: Oxford University Press, 1993.

Business and the Economy

Attack, Jeremy, and Peter Passell. *A New Economic View of American History: from Colonial Times to 1940.* New York: W. W. Norton, 1994.

Bernstein, Irving. *A Caring Society: The New Deal, the Worker, and the Great Depression: A History of the American Worker, 1933–1941.* Boston: Houghton Mifflin, 1985.

———. *Turbulent Years: A History of the American Worker, 1933–1941.* Boston: Houghton Mifflin, 1971.

Bernstein, Michael A. *The Great Depression: Delayed Recovery and Economic Change in America, 1929–1939.* New York: Cambridge University Press, 1987.

Brody, David. *Workers in Industrial America: Essays in the Twentieth-Century Struggle.* New York: Oxford University Press, 1993.

Brunner, Karl, ed. *The Great Depression Revisited.* Boston: Martinus Nijhoff, 1981.

Friedman, Milton, and Anna Schwartz. *A Monetary History of the United States, 1867–1960.* Princeton, N.J.: Princeton University Press, 1963.

Garraty, John A. *The Great Depression.* New York: Harcourt Brace Jovanovich, 1986.

Green, James R. *The World of the Worker: Labor in Twentieth-Century America.* New York: Hill and Wang, 1980.

Hawley, Ellis W. *The New Deal and the Problem of Monopoly: A Study in Economic Ambivalence.* New York: Fordham University Press, 1995.

Himmelberg, Robert F. *The Great Depression and the New Deal.* Westport, Conn.: Greenwood Press, 2001.

Kindleberger, Charles. *The World in Depression, 1929–1939.* Berkeley: University of California Press, 1986.

Lens, Sidney. *The Labor Wars: From the Molly Maguires to the Sitdowns.* Garden City, New York: Doubleday, 1974.

McElvaine, Robert S. *The Great Depression: America, 1929–1941.* New York: Times Books, 1993.

———, ed. *Down and Out in the Great Depression.* Chapel Hill: University of North Carolina Press, 1983.

Milton, David. *The Politics of U.S. Labor: From the Great Depression to the New Deal.* New York: Monthly Review Press, 1982.

Phillips, Cabell. *From the Crash to the Blitz, 1929–1939.* New York: Macmillan, 1969.

Simon, Rita James, ed. *As We Saw the Thirties: Essays on Social and Political Movements of a Decade.* Urbana: University of Illinois Press, 1986.

Temin, Peter. *Did Monetary Forces Cause the Great Depression?* New York: W. W. Norton, 1976.

———. *Lessons from the Great Depression.* Cambridge: MIT Press, 1989.

Turkel, Studs. *Hard Times: An Oral History of the Great Depression.* New York: Pantheon Books, 1986.

Wilson, Edmund. *The Thirties: From Notebooks and Diaries of the Period.* New York: Farrar, Straus, and Giroux, 1980.

Worster, Donald. *Dust Bowl: The Southern Plains in the 1930s.* New York: Oxford University Press, 1982.

Websites

"1930s Great Depression Gallery: Michigan Historical Museum." Available online at http://www.sos.state.mi.us/history/museum/explore/museums/hismus/1900-75/depressn/index.html (accessed March 24, 2003).

"Documenting America: America from the Great Depression to World War II." Prints and Photographs Division, Library of Congress. Available online at http://memory.loc.gov/ammem/fsowhome.html (accessed March 24, 2003).

"The Great Depression." Point Grey Mini School. Available online at http://trinculo.educ.sfu.ca/pgm/depress/greatdepress.html (accessed March 24, 2003).

"The Great Depression and the New Deal." Available online at http://www.bergen.org/AAST/Projects/depression (accessed March 17, 2003).

"H102 Lecture 18: The Crash and the Great Depression." Available online at http://us.history.wisc.edu/hist102/lectures/lecture18.html (accessed March 24, 2003).

"New Deal Network: The Great Depression, the 1930s, and the Roosevelt Administration." Available online at http://newdeal.feri.org (accessed March 17, 2003).

"Photographs of the Great Depression." Available online at http://history1900s.about.com/library/photos/blyindexdepression.htm (accessed March 17, 2003).

"Recalling the Great Depression." Available online at http://www.mcsc.k12.in.us/mhs/social/madedo (accessed March 17, 2003).

"Sliding into the Great Depression." Available online at http://econ161.berkeley.edu/TCEH/Slouch_Crash14.html (accessed March 17, 2003).

"Songs of the Great Depression." Available online at http://www.library.csi.cuny.edu/dept/history/lavender/cherries.html (accessed March 17, 2003).

Education

Altenbaugh, Richard J. *The American People and Their Education: A Social History.* Upper Saddles River, N.J.: Prentice Hall, 2003.

———. *Education for Struggle: The American Labor Colleges of the 1920s and 1930s.* Philadelphia: Temple University Press, 1990.

Anderson, James D. *The Education of Blacks in the South, 1860–1935.* Chapel Hill: University of North Carolina Press, 1988.

Cremin, Lawrence A. *Popular Education and Its Discontents.* New York: Harper & Row, 1990.

Cuban, Larry. *How Teachers Taught: Constancy and Change in American Classrooms, 1890–1980.* New York: Longman, 1984.

Eaton, William E. *The AFT, 1916–1961: A History of the Movement.* Carbondale: Southern Illinois University Press, 1975.

Gaither, Milton. *American Educational History Revisited: A Critique of Progress.* New York: Teachers College Press, 2003.

Good, Thomas L. *American Education: Yesterday, Today and Tomorrow.* Chicago: National Society for the Study of Education, 2000.

Hawes, Joseph M. *Children between the Wars: American Childhood, 1920–1940.* New York: Twayne Publishers, 1997.

Krug, Edward A. *The Shaping of the American High School, vol. 2, 1920–1941.* Madison: University of Wisconsin Press, 1972.

Lazerson, Marvin, ed. *American Education in the Twentieth Century: A Documentary History.* New York: Teachers College Press, 1987.

Moreo, Dominic W. *Schools in the Great Depression.* New York: Garland Publishers, 1996.

Murphy, Marjorie. *Blackboard Unions: The AFT and the NEA, 1900–1980.* Ithaca, New York: Cornell University Press, 1990.

Ravitch, Diane. *Left Back: A Century of Failed School Reform.* New York: Simon & Schuster, 2001.

Seller, Maxine S., ed. *Women Educators in the United States, 1820–1993.* Westport, Conn.: Greenwood Press, 1994.

Spring, Joel H. *The American School, 1642–2000.* Boston: McGraw-Hill, 2001.

Tyack, David, Robert Lowe, and Elisabeth Hansot. *Public Schools in Hard Times: The Great Depression and Recent Years.* Cambridge: Harvard University Press, 1984.

Urban, Wayne J. *American Education: A History.* Boston: McGraw-Hill, 2000.

Wallace, James M. *Liberal Journalism and American Education, 1914–1941.* New Brunswick, N.J.: Rutgers University Press, 1991.

Wrigley, Julia. *Class Politics and Public Schools: Chicago, 1900–1950.* New Brunswick, N.J.: Rutgers University Press, 1982.

Websites

"American Elementary Schools in the 1930s." Available online at http://library.thinkquest.org/J002606/1930s.html?tqskip1=1&tqtime=0508 (accessed March 17, 2003).

"The American Federation of Teachers." Available online at http://www.aft.org (accessed March 17, 2003).

"American History—1930–1939: Education." Available online at http://www.nhmccd.edu/contracts/lrc/kc/decade30.html#education (accessed March 17, 2003).

"History of American Education." Available online at http://www.edst.purdue.edu/georgeoff/hist_am_ed/welcome.html (accessed March 17, 2003).

"History of American Education." Available online at http://www.nd.edu/rbarger/www7 (accessed March 17, 2003).

"History of the Civilian Conservation Corps." Available online at http://www.cccalumni.org/history1.html (accessed March 17, 2003).

"National Youth Administration." Available online at http://www.nps.gov/elro/glossary/nya.htm (accessed March 17, 2003).

"School: The Story of American Public Education. Available online at http://www.pbs.org/kcet/publicschool (accessed March 17, 2003).

"Schools in the 1930s." Teaneck Public Library Online. Available online at http://www.teaneck.org/virtualvillage/PublicSchools/1930/1930sfront.html (accessed March 17, 2003).

"U.S. Department of Education." Available online at http://www.ed.gov (accessed March 17, 2003).

Fashion and Design

Batterberry, Michael, and Ariane Batterberry. *Mirror, Mirror: A Social History of Fashion.* New York: Holt, Rinehart & Winston, 1977.

Blackman, Cally. *20th Century Fashion: The 20s & 30s: Flappers and Vamps.* Milwaukee: Gareth Stevens Publishing, 2000.

Brockman, Helen L. *The Theory of Fashion Design.* New York: Wiley, 1965.

The Changing American Woman: Two Hundred Years of American Fashion. New York: Fairchild, 1976.

Contini, Mila. *Fashion: From Ancient Egypt to the Present Day.* New York: Odyssey, 1965.

Constantino, Maria. *Fashions of a Decade: The 1930s.* New York and Oxford: Facts On File, 1991.

Dolan, Maryanne. *Vintage Clothing, 1880–1960: Identification and Value Guide.* Florence, Ala.: Books Americana, 1984.

Ewing, Elizabeth. *History of Twentieth Century Fashion.* rev. and updated ed.. London: Batsford, 1992; Lanham, Md.: Barnes & Noble, 1992.

Flink, James J. *The Automobile Age.* Cambridge, Mass. & London: MIT Press, 1988.

Gaines, Jane and Herzog, Charlotte, eds. *Fabrications: Costume and the Female Body.* New York: Routledge, 1990.

Ley, Sandra. *Fashion for Everyone: The Story of Ready-to-Wear, 1870–1970s.* New York: Scribners, 1975.

Liebs, Chester H. *Main Street to Miracle Mile: American Roadside Architecture.* Boston: Little, Brown, 1985.

Lloyd, Valerie. *The Art of Vogue Photographic Covers: Fifty Years of Fashion and Design.* New York: Harmony, 1986.

McAlester, Virginia, and McAlester, Lee. *A Field Guide to American Houses.* New York: Knopf, 1992.

McDowell, Colin. *McDowell's Directory of Twentieth Century Fashion.* Englewood Cliffs, N.J.: Prentice-Hall, 1985.

Melosh, Barbara. *Engendering Culture: Manhood and Womanhood in New Deal Public Art and Theater.* Washington, D.C. & London: Smithsonian Institution Press, 1991.

Milbank, Caroline Rennolds. *New York Fashion: The Evolution of American Style.* New York: Abrams, 1989.

Nash, Eric Peter. *Frank Lloyd Wright: Force of Nature.* New York: Smithmark Pulishers, 1996.

Rogers, Meyric R. *American Interior Design: The Traditions and Development of Domestic Design from Colonial Times to the Present.* New York: Norton, 1947.

Ryan, Mary Shaw. *Clothing: A Study in Human Behavior.* New York: Holt, Rinehart & Winston, 1966.

Sears, Stephen W. *The Automobile in America.* New York: American Heritage Publishing, 1977.

Stowell, Donald, and Erin Wertenberger. *A Century of Fashion 1865–1965.* Chicago: Encyclopaedia Britannica, 1987.

Trahey, Jane. *The Mode in Costume.* New York: Scribners, 1958.

———. *Harper's Bazaar: One Hundred Years of the American Female.* New York: Random House, 1967.

Tyrrell, Anne V. *Changing Trends in Fashion: Patterns of the Twentieth Century, 1900–1970.* London: Batsford, 1986.

Whiffen, Marcus, and Frederick Koeper. *American Architecture 1607–1976.* Cambridge, Mass.: MIT Press, 1981.

Wood, Barry James. *Show Windows: Seventy-five Years of the Art of Display.* New York: Congdon & Weed, 1982.

Government and Politics

Andersen, Kristi. *The Creation of a Democratic Majority, 1928–1936.* Chicago: University of Chicago Press, 1979.

Baldwin, Neil. *Henry Ford and the Jews: The Mass Production of Hate.* New York: Public Affairs, 2001.

Brinkley, Alan. *The End of Reform: New Deal Liberalism in Recession and War.* New York: Alfred A. Knopf, 1995.

———. *Voices of Protest: Huey Long, Father Coughlin, and the Great Depression.* New York: Knopf, 1982.

Brock, William R. *Welfare, Democracy, and the New Deal.* New York: Cambridge University Press, 1988.

Cohen, Lizabeth. *Making a New Deal: Industrial Workers in Chicago, 1919–1939.* New York: Cambridge University Press, 1990.

Cohen, Robert. *Dear Mrs. Roosevelt: Letters from Children of the Great Depression.* Chapel Hill: University of North Carolina Press, 2002.

Cole, Wayne S. *Roosevelt and the Isolationists, 1932–1945.* Lincoln: University of Nebraska Press, 1983.

Cook, Blanche Wiesen. *Eleanor Roosevelt.* New York: Viking, 1992.

Dallek, Robert A. *Franklin D. Roosevelt and American Foreign Policy, 1932–1945.* New York: Oxford University Press, 1981.

Feingold, Henry L. *The Politics of Rescue: The Roosevelt Administration and the Holocaust, 1938–1945.* Expanded and updated ed. New York: Holocaust Library, 1980.

Fine, Sidney. *Sit-Down: The General Motors Strike of 1936–37.* Ann Arbor: University of Michigan Press, 1969.

Fraser, Steve, and Gary Gerstle, eds. *The Rise and Fall of the New Deal Order, 1930–1980.* Princeton: Princeton University Press, 1989.

Freidel, Frank. *Franklin D. Roosevelt: A Rendezvous with Destiny.* Boston: Little, Brown. 1990.

Graham, Otis L., Jr. *An Encore for Reform: The Old Progressives and the New Deal.* New York: Oxford University Press, 1967.

Gustin, Lawrence. *Billy Durant: Creator of General Motors.* Grand Rapids, Mich.: Eerdmans, 1973.

Hamilton, David E. *From New Day to New Deal: American Farm Policy from Hoover to Roosevelt, 1928–1933.* Chapel Hill: University of North Carolina Press, 1991.

Hawley, Ellis W. *The New Deal and the Problem of Monopoly.* Princeton: Princeton University Press, 1966.

Hoffman, Abraham. *Unwanted Mexican Americans in the Great Depression; Repatriation Pressures, 1929–1939.* Tucson: University of Arizona Press, 1974.

Hoff-Wilson, Joan. *Herbert Hoover, Forgotten Progressive.* Boston: Little, Brown, 1975.

Hofstadter, Richard. *The American Political Tradition and the Men Who Made It.* New York: Knopf, 1948.

Jonas, Manfred. *Isolationism in America, 1935–1941.* Ithaca, N.Y.: Cornell University Press, 1966.

Kennedy, David M. *Freedom From Fear: The American People in Depression and War, 1929–1945.* New York: Oxford Press, 1999.

Kennedy, Joseph P., and Amanda Smith, ed. *Hostage to Fortune: The Letters of Joseph P. Kennedy.* New York: Viking, 2001.

Lester, Robert. *Native Americans and the New Deal: The Office Files of John Collier, 1933–1945* Bethesda, Md.: University Publications of America, 1993.

Leuchtenburg, William E. *Franklin D. Roosevelt and the New Deal, 1932–1940.* New York: Harper & Row, 1963.

———. *New Deal and Global War.* New York: Time-Life Books, 1964.

Levine, Lawrence W. *The People and the President: America's Conversation with FDR.* Boston: Beacon Press, 2002.

Lookstein, Haskell. *Were We Our Brothers' Keepers?: The Public Response of American Jews to the Holocaust, 1938–1944.* New York: Hartmore House, 1985.

Lowitt, Richard. *The New Deal and the West.* Norman: University of Oklahoma Press, 1993.

Mangione, Jerre Gerlando. *The Dream and the Deal: The Federal Writers' Project.* Boston: Little, Brown, 1972.

McElvaine, Robert S. *The Depression and New Deal: A History in Documents.* New York: Oxford Press, 2000.

McLoughlin, Thomas. *Lost Illusions: Soft Hearts & Hard Times in the Great Depression, 1921–1941.* Chicago: T. McLoughlin, 1997.

Moley, Raymond. *The First New Deal.* New York: Harcourt, Brace & World, 1966.

Mullins, William H. *The Depression and the Urban West Coast, 1929–1933: Los Angeles, San Francisco, Seattle, and Portland.* Bloomington: Indiana University Press, 1991.

Offner, Arnold A. *American Appeasement: United States Foreign Policy and Germany, 1933–1938.* New York: Norton, 1976.

Patterson, James T. *Congressional Conservatism and the New Deal.* Lexington: Organization of American Historians/University of Kentucky Press, 1967.

Phillips, Cabell. *From Crash to the Blitz, 1929–1939.* New York: Macmillan, 1969.

Rosen, Elliot A. *Hoover, Roosevelt, and the Brains Trust: From Depression to New Deal.* New York: Columbia University Press, 1977.

Schlesinger, Arthur M., Jr. *The Age of Roosevelt.* 3 vols. Boston: Houghton Mifflin, 1956–1960.

Terkel, Studs. *Hard Times: An Oral History of the Great Depression.* New York: Pantheon Books, 1970.

Tugwell, Rexford G. *The Brains Trust.* New York: Viking, 1968.

Ward, Geoffrey. *A First-Class Temperment: The Emergence of Franklin Roosevelt.* New York: Harper & Row, 1989.

Ware, Susan. *Holding Their Own: American Women in the 1930s.* Boston: Twayne, 1982.

Warren, Donald. *Radio Priest: Charles Coughlin, The Father of Hate Radio.* New York: Free Press, 1996.

Watkins, Lucy Rodgers. *A Generation Speaks: Voices of the Great Depression.* Chapel Hill: University of North Carolina Press, 2000.

Watkins, T.H. *The Hungry Years: A Narrative History of the Great Depression in America.* New York: Henry Holt & Co., 1999.

Weinstein, Allen. *The Haunted Wood: Soviet Espionage in America—The Stalin Era.* New York: Random House, 1999.

Worster, Donald. *Dust Bowl: The Southern Plains in the 1930s.* New York: Oxford University Press, 1979.

Law and Justice

Abraham, Henry J. *Justices and Presidents.* New York: Oxford University Press, 1991.

Burg, David F. *The Great Depression: An Eyewitness History.* New York: Facts on File, Inc., 1996.

Carter, Dan T. *Scottsboro: A Tragedy of the American South.* Baton Rouge: Louisiana State University Press, 1979.

Hall, Kermit L., ed. *The Oxford Companion to the Supreme Court.* New York: Oxford University Press, 1992.

Harrison, Maureen, and Steve Gilbert, eds. *Landmark Decisions of the United States Supreme Court II.* Beverly Hills: Excellent Books, 1992.

Himmelberg, Robert F. *The Great Depression and the New Deal.* Westport, Conn.: Greenwood Press, 2000.

Kelly, Alfred H., Winfred A. Harbison, and Herman Belz. *The American Constitution: Its Origins and Development—Vol. II.* 7th ed. New York: Norton, 1991.

Kelly, Robert J. *Encyclopedia of Organized Crime in the United States: From Capone's Chicago to the New Urban Underworld.* Westport, Conn.: Greenwood Press, 2000.

Leuchtenburg, William E. *The Supreme Court Reborn: The Constitutional Revolution in the Age of Roosevelt.* New York: Oxford University Press, 1995.

McElvaine, Robert S. *The Depression and the New Deal: A History in Documents.* New York: Oxford University Press Children's Books, 2000.

Mikula, Mark F., and L. Mpho Mabunda, eds. *Great American Court Cases.* Farmington Hills, Mich.: Gale Group, 2000.

Palmer, Kris E., ed. *Constitutional Amendments: 1789 to the Present.* Farmington Hills, Mich.: Gale Group, 2000.

Schwarz, Jordan A. *The New Dealers.* New York: Random House, 1994.

Smith, Page. *Redeeming the Time: A People's History of the 1920s and the New Deal.* New York: Penguin, 1991.

Toland, John. *The Dillinger Days.* Cambridge, Mass.: Da Capo Press, 1995.

Watkins, T.H. *The Great Depression: America in the 1930s.* New York: Little, Brown, & Co., 1995.

West's Encyclopedia of American Law, 2nd ed. 12 vols. St. Paul, Minn.: West Publishing Co.

Websites

"The American Experience: Public Enemy Number 1, The Legendary Outlaw John Dillinger." Available online at http://www.pbs.org/wgbh/amex/dillinger/index.html; website home page: http://www.pbs.org (accessed March 16, 2003).

"The Franklin D. Roosevelt Presidential Library and Museum Website." Available online at http://www.fdrlibrary.marist.edu (accessed March 16, 2003).

"The New Deal (1933–late 1930s)." *History of the FBI.* Federal Bureau of Investigation. Available online at http://www.fbi.gov/libref/historic/history/newdeal.htm; website home page: http://www.fbi.gov/homepage.htm (accessed March 2, 2003).

"The New Deal Network Website." Available online at http://www.newdeal.feri.org (accessed March 16, 2003).

"U.S. Supreme Court Opinions." Available online at http://www.findlaw.com/casecode/supreme.html; website home page: http://www.findlaw.com (accessed March 16, 2003).

Lifestyles and Social Trends

Balderrama, Francisco, and Raymond Rodriguez. *Decade of Betrayal: Mexican Repatriation in the 1930s.* Albuquerque: University of New Mexico Press, 1995.

Brinkley, Alan. *Culture and Politics in the Great Depression.* Waco, Tex.: Markham Press Fund, 1999.

Franklin, John Hope, and Isidore Starr. *The Negro in Twentieth Century America.* New York: Random House, 1967.

Furnas, J.C. *Stormy Weather: Crosslights on the Nineteen Thirties: An Informal Social History of the United States, 1929–1941.* New York: Putnam, 1977.

Gregory, James N. *American Exodus: The Dust Bowl Migration and Okie Culture in California.* New York: Oxford University Press, 1989.

Hawes, Joseph. *Children Between the Wars: American Childhood, 1920–1940.* New York: Twayne Publishers, 1997.

Hearn, Charles. *The American Dream in the Great Depression.* Westport, Conn.: Greenwood Press, 1977.

Hurt, R. Douglas. *The Dust Bowl: An Agricultural and Social History.* Chicago: Nelson-Hall, 1981.

Kirby, John. *Black Americans in the Roosevelt Era.* Knoxville: University of Tennessee Press, 1992.

Kyvig, David. *Daily Life in the United States, 1920–1939: Decades of Promise and Pain.* Westport, Conn.: Greenwood Press, 2002.

Low, Ann Marie. *Dust Bowl Diary.* Lincoln: University of Nebraska Press, 1984.

McGovern, James. *And a Time for Hope: Americans in the Great Depression.* Westport, Conn.: Praeger, 2000.

Sternsher, Bernard, ed. *Hitting Home: The Great Depression in Town and Country.* Chicago: I. R. Dee, 1989.

Stimson, Eddie, Jr. *My Remembers: A Black Sharecropper's Recollection of the Depression.* Denton: University of North Texas Press, 1996.

Terkel, Studs. *Hard Times: An Oral History of the Great Depression.* New York: Random House, 1970.

Ware, Susan. *Holding Their Own: American Women in the 1930s.* Boston: Twayne, 1982.

Watkins, T.H. *The Hungry Years: A Narrative History of the Great Depression in America.* New York: Henry Holt & Co., 1999.

Westin, Jeane. *Making Do: How Women Survived the '30s.* Chicago: Follett, 1976.

Websites

Bonnifield, Paul. "1930s Dust Bowl." Available online at http://www/ptsi.net/user/museum/dustbowl.html (accessed March 15, 2003).

"Century of Progress." Available online at http://www.chicagohs.org/history/century.html; website home page: http://www.chicagohs.org/history/index.html (accessed March 15, 2003).

"The Great Depression: An African American Perspective." Available online at http://mtungsten.freeservers.com (accessed March 15, 2003).

"'I Remember . . .'—Reminiscences of the Great Depression." Available online at http://www.michigan.gov/hal/0,1607,7-160-17451_18670_18793-53511—,00.html; website home page: http://www.michigan.gov/hal (accessed March 15, 2003).

"Riding the Rails: Teenagers on the Move During the Great Depression." Available online at http://www.erroluys.com/RidingtheRails.htm (accessed March 15, 2003).

"Surviving the Dust Bowl." Available online at http://www.pbs.org/wgbh/amex/dustbowl (accessed March 15, 2003).

"Welcome to Tomorrow" [The 1939 New York World's Fair]. Available online at http://xroads.virginia.edu/1930s/DISPLAY/39wf/frame.htm; website home page: http://xroads.virginia.edu/1930s/front.html (accessed March 15, 2003).

Media

Barfield, Ray. *Listening to Radio, 1920–1950.* Westport, Conn.: Praeger, 1996.

Barnouw, Erik. *The Golden Web: A History of Broadcasting in the United States, Vol. II, 1933 to 1953.* New York: Oxford University Press, 1968.

Bauman, John, and Thomas Coode. *In the Eye of the Great Depression: New Deal Reporters and the Agony of the American People.* DeKalb: Northern Illinois University Press, 1988.

Benton, Mike. *The Comic Book in America: An Illustrated History.* rev. ed. Dallas: Taylor, 1993.

Bonn, Thomas L. *Under Cover: An Illustrated History of American Mass Market Paperbacks.* New York: Penguin, 1982.

Browder, Laura. *Rousing the Nation: Radical Culture in Depression America.* Amherst: University of Massachusetts Press, 1998.

Brown, Robert J. *Manipulating the Ether: The Power of Broadcast Radio in Thirties America.* Jefferson, N.C.: McFarland & Co., 1998.

Craig, Douglas. *Fireside Politics: Radio and Political Culture in the United States, 1920–1940.* Baltimore: Johns Hopkins University Press, 2000.

Emery, Michael, and Edwin Emery. *The Press and America: An Interpretive History of the Mass Media,* 8th ed. Boston: Allyn & Bacon, 1996.

Goodstone, Tony, ed. *The Pulps: Fifty Years of American Popular Culture.* New York: Chelsea House, 1970.

Goulart, Ron. *Cheap Thrills: An Informal History of the Pulp Magazines.* New Rochelle, N.Y.: Arlington House, 1972.

———. *The Dime Detectives.* New York: Mysterious Press, 1988.

———, ed. *The Encyclopedia of American Comics.* New York & Oxford: Facts On File, 1990.

Hilmes, Michele. *Radio Voices: American Broadcasting, 1922–1952.* Minneapolis: University of Minnesota Press, 1997.

Janello, Amy, and Brennon Jones. *The American Magazine.* New York: Abrams, 1991.

Klein, Norman M. *Seven Minutes: The Life and Death of the American Animated Cartoon.* London and New York: Verso, 1993.

Leab, Daniel J. *A Union of Individuals: The Formation of the American Newspaper Guild, 1933–1936.* New York: Columbia University Press, 1970.

MacDonald, J. Fred. *Don't Touch That Dial: Radio Programming in American Life from 1920 to 1960.* Chicago: G. K. Hall, 1979.

Maltin, Leonard. *The Great American Broadcast: A Celebration of Radio's Golden Age.* New York: Dutton, 1997.

———. *Of Mice and Magic: A History of American Animated Cartoons.* rev. ed. New York: New American Library, 1987.

Miller, Edward. *Emergency Broadcasting and 1930s American Radio.* Philadelphia: Temple University Press, 2003.

Mott, Robert. *Radio Sound Effects: Who Did It, and How, in the Era of Live Broadcasting.* Jefferson, N.C.: McFarland, 1993.

Natanson, Nicholas. *The Black Image in the New Deal: The Politics of FSA Photography.* Knoxville: University of Tennessee Press, 1992.

Paglin, Max D., ed. *A Legislative History of the Communications Act of 1934.* New York: Oxford University Press, 1989.

Peeler, David. *Hope Among Us Yet: Social Criticism and Social Solace in Depression America.* Athens: University of Georgia Press, 1987.

Pells, Richard. *Radical Visions and American Dreams: Culture and Social Thought in the Depression Years.* Middletown, Conn.: Wesleyan University Press, 1973.

Schneider, Steve. *That's All Folks!: The Art of Warner Bros. Animation.* New York: Holt, 1988.

Server, Lee. *Danger Is My Business: An Illustrated History of the Fabulous Pulp Magazines.* San Francisco: Chronicle, 1993.

Websites

"America from the Great Depression to World War II: Photographs from the FSA-OWI, 1935–1945." Available online at http://memory.loc.gov/ammem/fsowhome.html (accessed March 15, 2003).

"The Depression News: The 1930s." Available online at http://www.sos.state.mi.us/history/museum/explore/museums/hismus/1900-75/depressn/index.html; website home page: http://www.michigan.gov/hal (accessed March 15, 2003).

"1930s On the Air." Available online at http://xroads.virginia.edu/1930s/DISPLAY/39wf/frame.htm; website home page: http://xroads.virginia.edu/1930s/front.html (accessed March 15, 2003).

"1930s in Print." Available online at http://xroads.virginia.edu/1930s/PRINT/printframe.html; website home page: http://xroads.virginia.edu/1930s/front.html (accessed March 15, 2003).

Medicine and Health

The Cambridge World History of Human Disease. New York: Cambridge University Press, 1993.

Cartwright, Frederic Fox. *Disease and History.* New York: Crowell, 1972.

Cassady, James M. *Medicine in America: A Short History.* Baltimore: Johns Hopkins University Press, 1991.

Chase, Allan. *Magic Shots: A Human and Scientific Account of the Long and Continuing Struggle to Eradicate Infectious Diseases by Vaccination.* New York: Morrow, 1982.

Companion Encyclopedia of the History of Medicine. London: Routledge, 1993.

Cooter, Roger, and John Pickstone. *Medicine in the Twentieth Century.* New York: Harwood Academic, 2000.

Corsi, Pietro, ed. *Information Sources in the History of Science and Medicine.* Boston: Butterworth Scientific, 1983.

Egendorf, Laura K. *Medicine.* San Diego: Greenhaven Press, 2003.

Freymann, John G. *The American Health Care System: Its Genesis and Trajectory.* Huntington, New York: R.E. Krieger, 1980.

Karlen, Arno. *Man and Microbes.* New York: Putnam, 1995.

Lyons, Albert S. *Medicine: An Illustrated History.* New York: Abrams, 1978.

Marks, Geoffrey, and William K. Beatty. *The Story of Medicine in America.* New York: Scribners, 1973.

Milestones of Medicine. Pleasantville, New York: Reader's Digest, 2000.

Professional Guide to Diseases. 6th ed. Springhouse, Pa.: Springhouse Corporation, 1998.

Reynolds, Moira D. *The Outstretched Hand: Modern Medical Discoveries.* New York: R. Rosen Press, 1980.

Sheehan, John C. *The Enchanted Ring: The Untold Story of Penicillin.* Cambridge: MIT Press, 1982.

Shorter, Edward. *The Health Century.* New York: Doubleday, 1987.

Stanton, Jennifer. *Innovations in Health and Medicine: Diffusion and Resistance in the Twentieth Century.* New York: Routledge, 2002.

Stevens, Rosemary. *American Medicine and the Public Interest.* Berkeley: University of California Press, 1998.

Turney, Jon. *Medicine and Health Science.* Chicago: Fitzroy Dearborn, 2001.

Websites

"American Association of the History of Medicine." Available online at http://www.histmed.org (accessed March 17, 2003).

"Golden Age of Medicine." Available online at http://ccat.sas.upenn.edu/goldenage/exp/exp.htm (accessed March 17, 2003).

"Medicine and Madison Avenue—Student Guide." Available online at http://scriptorium.lib.duke.edu/mma/section2.html (accessed March 17, 2003).

"National Institutes of Health (NIH)." Available online at http://www.nih.gov (accessed March 17, 2003).

"National Library of Medicine." Available online at http://www.nlm.nih.gov (accessed March 17, 2003).

"Nobel e-Museum." Available online at http://www.nobel.se (accessed March 17, 2003).

"Nuclear Medicine History." Available online at http://www.nucmednet.com/history.htm (accessed March 17, 2003).

"OHSU Library—History of Medicine Collection." Available online at http://www.ohsu.edu/library/hom/homindex.shtml (accessed March 17, 2003).

"Penicillin: The First Miracle Drug." Available online at http://www.herb.lsa.umich.edu/kidpage/penicillin.htm (accessed March 17, 2003).

"Timeline of Microbiology 1930s–1940s." Available online at http://www.microbeworld.org/htm/aboutmicro/timeline/tmln_3.htm (accessed March 17, 2003).

Religion

Ahlstrom, Sydney E. *A Religious History of the American People.* 2 vols. Garden City, N.Y.: Doubleday, 1975.

Albanese, Catherine. *America, Religions and Religion.* Belmont, Calif.: Wadsworth, 1981.

Ammerman, Nancy T. *Bible Believers: Fundamentalists in the Modern World.* New Brunswick, N.J.: Rutgers University Press, 1987.

Bauer, Yehuda. *American Jewry and the Holocaust: The American Joint Distribution Committee, 1939–1945.* Detroit: Wayne State University Press, 1981.

Bellah, Robert N., and Frederick E. Greenspahn, eds. *Uncivil Religion: Irreligious Hostility in America.* New York: Crossroads, 1987

Bennett, David H. *Demagogues in the Depression: American Radicals and the Union Party, 1932–1936.* New Brunswick, N.J.: Rutgers University Press, 1969.

Black, Gregory D. *Hollywood Censored: Morality Codes, Catholics, and the Movies.* New York: Cambridge University Press, 1994.

Braden, Charles Samuel. *These Also Believe: A Study of Modern American Cults and Minority Religious Movements.* New York: Macmillan, 1949.

Brauer, Jerald C. *Protestantism in America: A Narrative History.* Philadelphia: Westminster, 1953.

Brinkley, Alan. *Voices of Protest: Huey Long, Father Coughlin and the Great Depression.* New York: Knopf, 1982.

Burnham, Kenneth E. *God Comes to America: Father Divine and the Peace Mission Movement.* Philadelphia: Imperial Press, 1982.

Carpenter, Joel A. *Revive Us Again: The Reawakening of American Fundamentalism.* New York: Oxford, 1997

Carroll, Jackson W. *Beyond Establishment: Protestant Identity in a Post-Protestant Age.* Louisville, Ky.: Westminster/John Knox, 1993.

Cavert, Samuel McCrea. *The American Churches in the Ecumenical Movement, 1900–1968.* New York: Association Press, 1968.

Crews, Mickey. *The Church of God: A Social History.* Knoxville: University of Tennessee Press, 1990.

Dolan, Jay P. *The American Catholic Experience: A History from Colonial Times to the Present.* Garden City, N.Y.: Doubleday, 1985.

Drinan, Robert F. *Religion, the Courts, and Public Policy.* New York: McGraw-Hill, 1963.

Eighmy, John L. *Churches in Cultural Captivity: A History of the Social Attitudes of Southern Baptists.* Knoxville: University of Tennessee Press, 1987 [1972].

Feingold, Henry L. *A Time for Searching: Entering the Mainstream, 1920–1945.* Baltimore: Johns Hopkins University Press, 1992.

Finke, Roger, and Rodney Strunk. *The Churching of America, 1779–1990: Winners and Losers in Our Religious Economy.* New Brunswick, N.J.: Rutgers University Press, 1992.

Flynn, George Q. *American Catholics and the Roosevelt Presidency, 1932–1936.* Lexington: University Press of Kentucky, 1968.

———. *Roosevelt and Romanism: Catholics and American Diplomacy, 1937–1945.* Westport, Conn.: Greenwood Press, 1976.

Friedman, Saul S. *No Haven for the Oppressed: United States Policy toward Jewish Refugees, 1938–1945.* Detroit: Wayne State University Press, 1973.

Hennesey, James J. *American Catholics: A History of the Roman Catholic Community in the United States.* New York: Oxford University Press, 1981.

Hertzberg, Arthur. *The Jews in America: Four Centuries of an Uneasy Encounter—A History.* New York: Simon & Schuster, 1989.

Hudson, Winthrop S. *Religion in America: An Historical Account of the Development of American Religious Life.* New York: Scribners, 1981.

Hutchinson, William R. *The Modernist Impulse in American Protestantism.* Cambridge: Harvard University Press, 1976.

Kincheloe, Samuel C. *Research Memorandum on Religion in the Depression.* Westport, Conn.: Greenwood Press, 1970.

Lippy, Charles H. *Being Religious, American Style: A History of Popular Religiosity in the United States.* Westport, Conn.: Greenwood Press, 1994.

Lotz, David W., ed. *Altered Landscapes: Christianity in America, 1935–1985.* Grand Rapids, Mich.: Eerdmans, 1989.

Marty, Martin E. *Pilgrims in Their Own Land: Five Hundred Years of Religion in America.* Boston: Little, Brown, 1984.

Meyer, Donald B. *The Protestant Search for Political Realism, 1919–1941.* Berkeley & Los Angeles: University of California Press, 1960.

Myers, Constance Ashton. *The Prophet's Army: Trotskyists in America, 1928–1941.* Westport, Conn.: Greenwood Press, 1977.

Nelson, John K. *Peace Prophets: American Pacifist Thought, 1919–1945.* Chapel Hill: University of North Carolina Press, 1967.

Noll, Mark A. *A History of Christianity in the United States and Canada.* Grand Rapids, Mich.: Eerdmans, 1992

Norwood, Frederick A. *The Story of American Methodism: A History of the United Methodists and Their Relations.* Nashville: Abingdon, 1974.

Piehl, Mel. *Breaking Bread: The Catholic Worker and the Origin of Catholic Radicalism in America.* Philadelphia: Temple University Press, 1982.

Reichley, A. James. *Religion in American Public Life.* Washington, D.C.: Brookings Institution, 1985.

Richey, Russell E., and Donald G. Jones, eds., *American Civil Religion.* San Francisco: Mellen Research University Press, 1990.

Ross, Robert W. *So It Was True: The American Protestant Press and the Nazi Persecution of the Jews.* Minneapolis: University of Minnesota Press, 1980.

Roy, Ralph Lord. *Apostles of Discord: A Study of Organized Bigotry and Disruption on the Fringes of Protestantism.* Boston: Beacon, 1953.

Sachar, Howard M. *A History of the Jews in America.* New York: Knopf, 1992.

Skinner, James M. *The Cross and the Cinema: The Legion of Decency and the National Catholic Office for Motion Pictures, 1933–1970.* Westport, Conn.: Praeger, 1993.

Weisbrot, Robert. *Father Divine and the Struggle for Racial Equality.* Urbana: University of Illinois Press, 1983.

Science and Technology

Allen, Garland. *Life Science in the Twentieth Century.* Cambridge: Cambridge University Press, 1978.

Brush, Stephen G. *The History of Modern Science: A Guide to the Second Scientific Revolution, 1800–1950.* Ames, Iowa: Iowa State University Press, 1988.

Carnegie Library of Pittsburgh, Science and Technology Department. *Science and Technology Desk Reference.* Detroit: Gale Research, 1993.

Cline, Barbara L. *Men Who Made a New Physics: Physicists and the Quantum Theory.* Chicago: University of Chicago Press, 1987.

Corsi, Pietro, ed. *Information Sources in the History of Science and Medicine.* Boston: Butterworth Scientific, 1983.

Cravens, Hamilton. *The Triumph of Evolution: American Scientists and the Heredity-Environment Controversy, 1900–1941.* Philadelphia: University of Pennsylvania Press, 1978.

Gillespie, Charles Coulston, ed. *Dictionary of Scientific Biography.* 18 vols. New York: Scribners, 1970–1990.

Golde, Peggy, ed. *Women in the Field: Anthropological Experiences.* Chicago: Aldine, 1970.

Kevles, Daniel J. *In the Name of Eugenics: Genetics and the Uses of Human Heredity.* New York: Knopf, 1985.

———. *The Physicists: The History of a Scientific Community in Modern America.* New York: Knopf, 1978.

Kuznick, Peter J. *Beyond the Laboratory: Scientists as Political Activists in 1930s America.* Chicago: University of Chicago Press, 1987.

Lang, Kenneth R., and Owen Gingerich, eds. *Sourcebook in Astronomy and Astrophysics, 1900–1975.* Cambridge, Mass: Harvard University Press, 1979.

Leakey, Louis S.B. *Adam's Ancestors: The Evolution of Man and His Culture.* New York: Harper, 1960.

Mayr, Ernst. *The Growth of Biological Thought: Diversity, Evolution, and Inheritance.* Cambridge, Mass.: Harvard University Press, 1982.

Mayr, Ernst, and William B. Provine. *The Evolutionary Synthesis: Perspectives on the Unification of Biology.* Cambridge, Mass.: Harvard University Press, 1980.

McGraw-Hill Encyclopedia of Science and Technology. 9th ed. 14 vols. New York: McGraw-Hill, 2002.

Modell, Judith. *Ruth Benedict: Patterns of a Life.* Philadelphia: University of Pennsylvania Press, 1983.

Provine, William B. *Sewall Wright and Evolutionary Biology.* Chicago: University of Chicago Press, 1986.

Pursell, Carroll W., ed. *Technology in America.* Washington, D.C.: USIA Forum Series, 1979.

Rossiter, Margaret W. *Women Scientists in America: Struggles and Strategies to 1940.* Baltimore: Johns Hopkins University Press, 1982.

Websites

"1930s Aviation History." Available online at http://www.start-flying.com/Aviation%20history/coming%20of%20/age/introduction.htm (accessed March 17, 2003).

"GM Corporate History—1930s." Available online at http://www.gm.com/company/corp_info/history/gmhis1930.html (accessed March 17, 2003).

"History of Science Society." Available online at http://www.hssonline.org (accessed March 17, 2003).

"Human Evolution: The Fossil Evidence in 3D." Available online at http://anth.ucsb.edu/projects/human (accessed March 17, 2003).

"Institute for Advanced Study." Available online at http://www.ias.edu (accessed March 17, 2003).

"Nobel e-Museum." Available online at http://www.nobel.se (accessed March 17, 2003).

"Nuclear Physics in the 1930s—Ernest Lawrence and the Cyclotron." Available online at http://www.aip.org/history/lawrence/physicsinthe1930s.htm (accessed March 17, 2003).

"Robert Broom, 1866–1951." Available online at http://emuseum.mnsu.edu/information/biography/abcde/broom_robert.html (accessed March 17, 2003).

"Ruth Fulton Benedict, 1887–1948." Available online at http://www.cas.usf.edu/anthropology/women/ruthb/ruthbenedict.htm (accessed March 17, 2003).

"Sewall Wright Institute." Available online at http://www.stat.wisc.edu/wright (accessed March 17, 2003).

Sports

Adler, David A., and Terry Widener. *Lou Gehrig: The Luckiest Man Alive.* San Diego: Harcourt Brace, 1997.

Alexander, Charles C. *Breaking the Slump: Baseball in the Depression Era.* New York: Columbia University Press, 2002.

———. *John McGraw.* New York: Viking, 1988.

———. *Ty Cobb.* New York: Oxford Press, 1984.

Bachrach, Susan D. *The Nazi Olympics: Berlin 1936.* Boston: Little, Brown, 2000.

Barrow, Joe Louis. *Joe Louis: 50 Years an American Hero.* New York: McGraw-Hill, 1988.

Bernstein, Mark F. *Football: The Ivy League Origins of an American Obsession.* Philadelphia: University of Pennsylvania Press, 2001.

Bevis, Charlie. *Mickey Cochrane: The Life of a Baseball Hall of Fame Catcher.* Jefferson, N.C.: McFarland, 1998.

Brandt, Nat. *When Oberlin was King of the Gridiron: the Heisman Years.* Oberlin, Ohio: Kent State University Press, 2001.

Budge, John Donald. *Don Budge: A Tennis Memoir.* New York: Viking, 1969.

Carroll, John M. *Red Grange and the Rise of Modern Football.* Urbana: University of Illinois Press, 1999.

Clark, Dick, and Larry Lester, eds. *The Negro Leagues Book.* Cleveland: Society for American Baseball Research, 1994.

Cline-Ransome, Lesa, and James Ransome. *Satchel Paige.* New York: Simon & Schuster, 2000.

Cohane, Tim. *Great College Football Coaches of the Twenties and Thirties.* New Rochelle, N.Y.: Arlington House, 1973.

Creamer, Robert W. *Babe: The Legend Comes to Life.* New York: Simon & Schuster, 1974.

———. *Stengel: His Life and Times.* New York: Simon & Schuster, 1984.

Danzig, Allison. *Oh, How They Played the Game: The Early Days of Football and the Heroes Who Made It Great.* New York: MacMillan, 1971.

Falls, Joe, et al. *The Legacy of Champions: The Story of the Men Who Built University of Michigan Football.* Farmington Hills, Mich.: CTC Productions & Sports, 1996.

Fine, Gary Alan. *With the Boys: Little League Baseball and Preadolescent Culture.* Chicago: University Chicago Press, 1987.

Freedman, Russell. *Babe Didrikson Zaharias: The Making of a Champion.* New York: Clarion Books, 1999.

Gems, Gerald R. *For Pride, Profit, and Patriarchy: Football and the Incorporation of American Cultural Values.* Lanham, Md.: Scarecrow Press, 2000.

Gentry, Tony. *Jesse Owens.* New York: Chelsea House, 1990.

Gorn, Elliott J. *The Manly Art.* Ithaca, N.Y.: Cornell University Press, 1986.

Greenberg, Hank, and Ira Berkow. *Hank Greenberg, The Story of My Life.* New York: Times Books, 1989.

Gregory, Robert. *Diz: The Story of Dizzy Dean and Baseball During the Great Depression.* New York: Viking, 1992.

Halas, George Stanley, et al. *Halas.* New York: McGraw-Hill, 1979.

Hietala, Thomas R. *The Fight of the Century: Jack Johnson, Joe Louis, and the Struggle for Racial Equality.* Armonk, N.Y.: M. E. Sharp, 2002.

Higbe, Kirby, and Martin Quigley. *The High Hard One.* Lincoln: University of Nebraska Press, 1998.

Hillenbrand, Laura. *Seabiscuit: An American Legend.* New York: Random House, 2001.

Hunter, Doug. *War Games: Conn Smythe and Hockey's Fighting Men.* Toronto: Viking, 1996.

Jones, Bobby. *Golf is My Game.* Garden City, N.J.: Doubleday, 1960.

Kaye, Ivan N. *Good Clean Violence: A History of College Football.* Philadelphia: Lippincott, 1973.

Kelley, Brent P. *The Early All-Stars: Conversations with Standout Baseball Players of the 1930s and 1940s.* Jefferson, N.C.: McFarland, 1997.

———. *In the Shadow of the Babe: Interviews with Baseball Players Who Played with or Against Babe Ruth.* Jefferson, N.C.: McFarland, 1995.

Maltby, Marc S. *The Origins and Early Development of Professional Football.* New York: Garland Publishing, 1997.

Mandel, Richard D. *The Nazi Olympics.* New York: Macmillan, 1971.

Nolan, William F. *Barney Oldfield: The Life and Times of America's Legendary Speed King.* New York: Putnam, 1961.

Olsen, Jack. *The Black Athlete: A Shameful Story.* New York: Time-Life Books, 1968.

Parker, Clifton, Blue. *Fouled Away: The Baseball Tragedy of Hack Wilson.* Jefferson, N.C.: McFarland, 2000.

Peterson, Robert. *Pigskin: The Early Years of Pro Football.* New York: Oxford University Press, 1997.

Pietrusza, David. *Judge and Jury: The Life and Times of Judge Kenesaw Mountain Landis.* South Bend, Ind.: Diamond Communications, 1998.

Pont, Sally. *Fields of Honor: The Golden Age of College Football and the Men Who Created It.* New York: Harcourt, 2001.

Rader, Benjamin G. *American Sports: From the Age of Folk Games to the Age of Spectators.* Englewood Cliffs, N.J.: Prentice-Hall, 1983.

Ribowsky, Mark. *The Power and the Darkness: The Life of Josh Gibson in the Shadows of the Game.* New York: Simon & Schuster, 1996.

Robinson, Ray. *Iron Horse: Lou Gehrig in His Time.* New York: W.W. Norton, 1990.

———. *Rockne of Notre Dame: The Making of a Football Legend.* New York: Oxford Press, 1999.

Sperber, Murray. *Shake Down the Thunder: The Creation of Notre Dame Football.* New York: Holt, 1993.

Stump, Al. *Cobb: A Biography.* Chapel Hill, N.C.: Algonquin Books, 1994.

Tofel, Richard J. *A Legend in the Making: The New York Yankees in 1939.* Chicago: Dee, Ivan R., 2002.

Umphlett, Wiley Lee. *Creating the Big Game: John Heisman and the Invention of American Football.* Westport, Conn.: Greenwood Press, 1992.

Watterson, John Sayle. *College Football: History, Spectacle, Controversy.* Baltimore: Johns Hopkins Press, 2000.

Whitehead, Eric. *The Patricks, Hockey's Royal Family.* Toronto: Doubleday, 1980.

Whittingham, Richard. *Rites of Autumn: The Story of College Football.* New York: Free Press, 2001.

Primary Source Type Index

Primary source authors appear in parentheses. Page numbers in italics indicate images, and those followed by the letter t *indicate tables.*

Primary source authors appear in parentheses. Page numbers in italics indicate images, and those followed by the letter *t* indicate tables.

Primary source authors appear in parentheses. Page numbers in italics indicate images, and those followed by the letter *t* indicate tables.

Sermons

Songs

Speeches

Statements

Studies

Supreme Court decisions

Surveys

Syllabuses

Tables

Testimonies

Primary source authors appear in parentheses. Page numbers in italics indicate images, and those followed by the letter *t* indicate tables.

General Index

Page numbers in bold indicate primary sources; page numbers in italic indicate images; page numbers in bold italic indicate primary source images; page numbers followed by the letter t *indicate tables. Primary sources are indexed under the entry name with the author's name in parentheses. Primary sources are also indexed by title. All primary sources can be identified by bold page locators.*

Page numbers in bold indicate primary sources; page numbers in italic indicate images; page numbers in bold italic indicate primary source images; page numbers followed by the letter *t* indicate tables.

Page numbers in bold indicate primary sources; page numbers in italic indicate images; page numbers in bold italic indicate primary source images; page numbers followed by the letter *t* indicate tables.

Page numbers in bold indicate primary sources; page numbers in italic indicate images; page numbers in bold italic indicate primary source images; page numbers followed by the letter *t* indicate tables.

Page numbers in bold indicate primary sources; page numbers in italic indicate images; page numbers in bold italic indicate primary source images; page numbers followed by the letter *t* indicate tables.

Page numbers in bold indicate primary sources; page numbers in italic indicate images; page numbers in bold italic indicate primary source images; page numbers followed by the letter *t* indicate tables.

Page numbers in bold indicate primary sources; page numbers in italic indicate images; page numbers in bold italic indicate primary source images; page numbers followed by the letter *t* indicate tables.

Page numbers in bold indicate primary sources; page numbers in italic indicate images; page numbers in bold italic indicate primary source images; page numbers followed by the letter *t* indicate tables.

Page numbers in bold indicate primary sources; page numbers in italic indicate images; page numbers in bold italic indicate primary source images; page numbers followed by the letter *t* indicate tables.

Page numbers in bold indicate primary sources; page numbers in italic indicate images; page numbers in bold italic indicate primary source images; page numbers followed by the letter *t* indicate tables.

Page numbers in bold indicate primary sources; page numbers in italic indicate images; page numbers in bold italic indicate primary source images; page numbers followed by the letter *t* indicate tables.

O

Page numbers in bold indicate primary sources; page numbers in italic indicate images; page numbers in bold italic indicate primary source images; page numbers followed by the letter *t* indicate tables.

Page numbers in bold indicate primary sources; page numbers in italic indicate images; page numbers in bold italic indicate primary source images; page numbers followed by the letter *t* indicate tables.

Page numbers in bold indicate primary sources; page numbers in italic indicate images; page numbers in bold italic indicate primary source images; page numbers followed by the letter *t* indicate tables.

Page numbers in bold indicate primary sources; page numbers in italic indicate images; page numbers in bold italic indicate primary source images; page numbers followed by the letter *t* indicate tables.

Page numbers in bold indicate primary sources; page numbers in italic indicate images; page numbers in bold italic indicate primary source images; page numbers followed by the letter *t* indicate tables.

Page numbers in bold indicate primary sources; page numbers in italic indicate images; page numbers in bold italic indicate primary source images; page numbers followed by the letter *t* indicate tables.

Page numbers in bold indicate primary sources; page numbers in italic indicate images; page numbers in bold italic indicate primary source images; page numbers followed by the letter *t* indicate tables.